Lecture Notes in Computer Science   13556

More information about this series at https://link.springer.com/bookseries/558

Vijayalakshmi Atluri · Roberto Di Pietro ·
Christian D. Jensen · Weizhi Meng (Eds.)

Computer Security – ESORICS 2022

27th European Symposium
on Research in Computer Security
Copenhagen, Denmark, September 26–30, 2022
Proceedings, Part III

 Springer

We are grateful to the general co-chairs, Christian D. Jensen and Weizhi Meng; the workshops chairs, Mauro Conti and Jianying Zhou, and all of the workshop co-chairs; the poster chair, Joaquin Garcia-Alfaro; the publicity co-chair's Cristina Alcaraz and Wenjuan Li; the web chair, Wei-Yang Chiu; and the ESORICS Steering Committee and its chair, Sokratis Katsikas.

We are also grateful to BlockSec for supporting the organization of ESORICS 2022.

Finally, we would like to provide a heartfelt thank you to the authors for submitting their papers to ESORICS 2022. It is their efforts that, in the end, decided the success of ESORICS 2022, confirmed ESORICS as a top-notch security conference, planted the seeds for future successes, and advanced science.

We hope that the proceedings will promote research and facilitate future work in the exciting, challenging, and evolving field of security.

September 2022

Roberto Di Pietro
Vijayalakshmi Atluri

Organization

General Chairs

Christian D. Jensen   Technical University of Denmark, Denmark
Weizhi Meng   Technical University of Denmark, Denmark

Program Committee Chairs

Vijayalakshmi Atluri   Rutgers University, USA
Roberto Di Pietro   Hamad Bin Khalifa University, Qatar

Steering Committee

Sokratis Katsikas (Chair)	NTNU, Norway
Joachim Biskup	University of Dortmund, Germany
Véronique Cortier	CNRS, France
Frédéric Cuppens	Polytechnique Montréal, Canada
Sabrina De Capitani di Vimercati	Università degli Studi di Milano, Italy
Joaquin Garcia-Alfaro	Institut Polytechnique de Paris, France
Dieter Gollmann	Hamburg University of Technology, Germany
Kutylowski Mirek	Wroclaw University of Technology, Poland
Javier Lopez	Universidad de Malaga, Spain
Jean-Jacques Quisquater	University of Louvain, Belgium
Peter Ryan	University of Luxembourg, Luxembourg
Pierangela Samarati	Università degli Studi di Milano, Italy
Einar Snekkenes	NTNU, Norway
Michael Waidner	ATHENE, Germany

Program Committee

Abu-Salma, Ruba	King's College London, UK
Afek, Yehuda	Tel-Aviv University, Israel
Akiyama, Mitsuaki	NTT, Japan
Albanese, Massimiliano	George Mason University, USA
Alcaraz, Cristina	University of Malaga, Spain
Allman, Mark	International Computer Science Institute, USA
Alrabaee, Saed	United Arab Emirates University, UAE
Asif, Hafiz	Rutgers University, USA

Ayday, Erman   Case Western Reserve University, USA, and
                                       Bilkent University, Turkey
Bai, Guangdong   University of Queensland, Australia
Bakiras, Spiridon   Singapore Institute of Technology, Singapore
Bardin, Sebastien   CEA LIST, France
Batra, Gunjan   Kennesaw State University, USA
Bertino, Elisa   Purdue University, USA
Blasco, Jorge   Royal Holloway, University of London, UK
Blundo, Carlo   Università degli Studi di Salerno, Italy
Bonaci, Tamara   Northeastern University, USA
Camtepe, Seyit   CSIRO Data61, Australia
Ceccato, Mariano   Università di Verona, Italy
Chakraborti, Anrin   Stony Brook University, USA
Chan, Aldar C-F.   University of Hong Kong, Hong Kong
Chen, Bo   Michigan Technological University, USA
Chen, Xiaofeng   Xidian University, China
Chen, Liqun   University of Surrey, UK
Chen, Rongmao   National University of Defense Technology,
                                       China
Chen, Yu   Shandong University, China
Chow, Sherman S. M.   The Chinese University of Hong Kong,
                                       Hong Kong
Chowdhury, Omar   University of Iowa, USA
Conti, Mauro   Università di Padova, USA
Coull, Scott   Mandiant, USA
Crispo, Bruno   University of Trento, Italy
Cukier, Michel   University of Maryland, USA
Cuppens, Frédéric   Polytechnique Montréal, Canada
Cuppens-Boulahia, Nora   Polytechnique Montréal, Canada
Damiani, Ernesto   University of Milan, Italy
Daza, Vanesa   Universitat Pompeu Fabra, Spain
De Capitani di Vimercati, Sabrina   Università degli Studi di Milano, Italy
Debar, Hervé   Télécom SudParis, France
Desmedt, Yvo   University of Texas at Dallas, USA
Diao, Wenrui   Shandong University, China
Dimitriou, Tassos   Kuwait University, Kuwait
Domingo-Ferrer, Josep   Universitat Rovira i Virgili, Spain
Dong, Changyu   Newcastle University, UK
Ferrara, Anna Lisa   University of Bristol, UK
Ferrer-Gomila, Jose-Luis   University of the Balearic Islands, Spain
Fila, Barbara   INSA Rennes, IRISA, France
Fischer-Hübner, Simone   Karlstad University, Sweden

Lombardi, Flavio	National Research Council, Italy
Lou, Wenjing	Virginia Tech, USA
Lu, Rongxing	University of New Brunswick, Canada
Lu, Haibing	Santa Clara University, USA
Luo, Xiapu	The Hong Kong Polytechnic University, Hong Kong
Ma, Shiqing	Rutgers University, USA
Marin-Fabregas, Eduard	Telefonica Research, Spain
Martinelli, Fabio	National Research Council, Italy
Mauw, Sjouke	University of Luxembourg, Luxembourg
Meng, Weizhi	Technical University of Denmark, Denmark
Mohan, Sibin	Oregon State University, USA
Mori, Tatsuya	Waseda University, Japan
Mueller, Johannes	University of Luxembourg, Luxembourg
Ng, Siaw-Lynn	Royal Holloway, University of London, and Bedford New College, UK
Ning, Jianting	Singapore Management University, Singapore
Obana, Satoshi	Hosei University, Japan
Oligeri, Gabriele	Hamad Bin Khalifa University, Qatar
Overdorf, Rebekah	Ecole Polytechnique Fédérale de Lausanne, Switzerland
Pal, Shantanu	Queensland University of Technology, Australia
Pan, Jiaxin	NTNU, Norway
Papadimitratos, Panos	KTH Royal Institute of Technology, Sweden
Paraboschi, Stefano	Università di Bergamo, Italy
Patranabis, Sikhar	IBM Research India, India
Pernul, Günther	Universität Regensburg, Germany
Poovendran, Radha	University of Washington, USA
Posegga, Joachim	University of Passau, Germany
Quiring, Erwin	Technische Universität Braunschweig, Germany
Quisquater, Jean-Jacques	University of Louvain, Belgium
Rao, Siddharth Prakash	Aalto University, Finland
Rashid, Awais	University of Bristol, UK
Ren, Kui State	University of New York at Buffalo, USA
Rhee, Junghwan	University of Central Oklahoma, USA
Ricci, Laura	University of Pisa, Italy
Russello, Giovanni	University of Auckland, New Zealand
Ryan, Peter	University of Luxembourg, Luxembourg
Safavi-Naini, Reihaneh	University of Calgary, Canada
Saileshwar, Gururaj	Georgia Institute of Technology, USA
Sakzad, Amin	Monash University, Australia
Samarati, Pierangela	Università degli Studi di Milano, Italy

Schinzel, Sebastian Münster	Münster University of Applied Sciences, Germany
Schneider, Steve	University of Surrey, UK
Schroeder, Dominique	Friedrich-Alexander-Universiät Erlangen-Nürnberg, Germany
Schwarz, Michael	CISPA Helmholtz Center for Information Security, Germany
Schwenk, Joerg	Ruhr-Universität Bochum, Germany
Sciancalepore, Savio	Eindhoven University of Technology, The Netherlands
Shahandashti, Siamak	University of York, UK
Sharma, Piyush Kumar	Indraprastha Institute of Information Technology Delhi, India
Shulman, Haya	Fraunhofer SIT, Germany
Sinanoglu, Ozgur	New York University Abu Dhabi, UAE
Sklavos, Nicolas	University of Patras, Greece
Snekkenes, Einar	NTNU, Norway
Somorovsky, Juraj	Paderborn University, Germany
Strufe, Thorsten	Karlsruhe Institute of Technology, Germany
Sural, Shamik	IIT Kharagpur, India
Susilo, Willy	University of Wollongong, Australia
Tang, Qiang	University of Sydney, Australia
Tang, Qiang	Luxembourg Institute of Science and Technology, Luxembourg
Tapiador, Juan Manuel	Universidad Carlos III de Madrid, Spain
Tian, Dave	Purdue University, USA
Torrey, Jacob	Thinkst Applied Research, USA
Trachtenberg, Ari	Boston University, USA
Treharne, Helen	University of Surrey, UK
Trieu, Ni	Arizona State University, USA
Tripunitara, Mahesh	University of Waterloo, Canada
Tsohou, Aggeliki	Ionian University, Greece
Urban, Tobias	Institute for Internet Security, Germany
Esteves-Verissimo, Paulo	KAUST, Saudi Arabia
Viganò, Luca	King's College London, UK
Visconti, Ivan	University of Salerno, Italy
Voulimeneas, Alexios	KU Leven, Belgium
Waidner, Michael	ATHENE, Germany
Wang, Cong	City University of Hong Kong, Hong Kong
Wang, Tianhao	Purdue University, USA
Wang, Di	State University of New York at Buffalo, USA
Wang, Haining	University of Delaware, USA

Wang, Lingyu	Concordia University, Canada
Wool, Avishai	Tel Aviv University, Israel
Xenakis, Christos	University of Piraeus, Greece
Xiang, Yang	Swinburne University of Technology, Australia
Xu, Jun	University of Utah, USA
Yang, Jie	Florida State University, USA
Yang, Kang	State Key Laboratory of Cryptology, China
Yang, Guomin	University of Wollongong, Australia
Yeun, Chan	Khalifa University, Abu Dhabi, UAE
Yi, Xun	RMIT University, Australia
Yu, Yu	Shanghai Jiao Tong University, China
Yuen, Tsz	University of Hong Kong, Hong Kong
Zhang, Zhikun	CISPA Helmholtz Center for Information Security, Germany
Zhang, Yuan	Fudan University, China
Zhang, Kehuan	The Chinese University of Hong Kong, Hong Kong
Zhao, Yunlei	Fudan University, China
Zhou, Jianying	Singapore University of Technology and Design, Singapore
Zhu, Rui	Indiana University, USA
Zhu, Sencun	Pennsylvania State University, USA

Workshops Chairs

Conti Mauro	University of Padua, Italy
Zhou Jianying	Singapore University of Technology and Design, Singapore

Poster Chair

Garcia-Alfaro Joaquin	Institut Polytechnique de Paris, France

Publicity Chairs

Alcaraz Cristina	University of Malaga, Spain
Li Wenjuan	Hong Kong Polytechnic University, Hong Kong

Web Chair

Chiu Wei-Yang	Technical University of Denmark, Denmark

Posters Program Committee

Atluri, Vijay	Rutgers University, USA
de Fuentes, Jose M.	Universidad Carlos III de Madrid, Spain
Di Pietro, Roberto	Hamad Bin Khalifa University, Qatar
González Manzano, Lorena	Universidad Carlos III de Madrid, Spain
Hartenstein, Hannes	Karlsruhe Institute of Technology, Germany
Kikuchi, Hiroaki	Meiji University, Japan
Matsuo, Shin'Ichiro	Georgetown University, USA
Navarro-Arribas, Guillermo	Universitat Autonoma de Barcelona, Spain
Nespoli, Pantaleone	Universidad de Murcia, Spain
Ranise, Silvio	University of Trento and Fondazione Bruno Kessler, Italy
Saint-Hilarire, Kéren	Institut Polytechnique de Paris, France
Signorini, Matteo	Nokia Bell Labs, France
Vasilopoulos, Dimitrios	IMDEA Software Institute, Spain
Zannone, Nicola	Eindhoven University of Technology, The Netherlands

Additional Reviewers

Abadi, Aydin	Berger, Christian
Abbadini, Marco	Berrang, Pascal
Ahmadi, Sharar	Blanco-Justicia, Alberto
Akand, Mamun	Böhm, Fabian
Akbar, Yousef	Bolgouras, Vaios
Alrahis, Lilas	Botta, Vincenzo
Ameur Abid, Chiheb	Bountakas, Panagiotis
Amine Merzouk, Mohamed	Brighente, Alessandro
Anagnostopoulos, Marios	Bursuc, Sergiu
Angelogianni, Anna	C. Pöhls, Henrich
Anglés-Tafalla, Carles	Cachin, Christian
Apruzzese, Giovanni	Cai, Cailing
Arapinis, Myrto	Cao, Chen
Arriaga, Afonso	Casolare, Rosangela
Arzt, Steven	Chen, Xihui
Avitabile, Gennaro	Chen, Niusen
Avizheh, Sepideh	Chen, Min
Bag, Arnab	Chen, Jinrong
Bagheri, Sima	Chen, Chao
Bampatsikos, Michail	Chen, Long
Battarbee, Christopher	Chen, Zeyu
Baumer, Thomas	Chu, Hien
Benaloh, Josh	Ciampi, Michele

Cicala, Fabrizio
Cinà, Antonio
Coijanovic, Christoph
Costantino, Gianpiero
Craaijo, Jos
Crochelet, Pierre
Cui, Hui
Cui, Handong
Dai, Tianxiang
Damodaran, Aditya
Daniyal Dar, Muhammad
Das Chowdhury, Partha
Daudén-Esmel, Cristòfol
Davies, Peter
Davies, Gareth
de Ruck, Dairo
Debant, Alexandre
Debnath, Joyanta
Degani, Luca
Demetrio, Luca
Deuber, Dominic
Dexheimer, Thomas
Diemert, Denis
Dodd, Charles
Dragan, Constantin Catalin
Driouich, Youssef
Du, Changlai
Du, Linkang
Du, Minxin
Duman, Onur
Duong, Dung
Dutta, Priyanka
Dutta, Sabyasachi
Dutta, Moumita
Duttagupta, Sayon
Ebrahimi, Ehsan
Echeverria, Mitziu
Ehsanpour, Maryam
Eichhammer, Philipp
Ekramul Kabir, Mohammad
Empl, Philip
Eyal, Ittay
Facchinetti, Dario
Fadavi, Mojtaba
Fallahi, Matin

Farao, Aristeidis
Fauzi, Prastudy
Feng, Hanwen
Feng, Qi
Feng, Shuya
Fisseha Demissie, Biniam
Fournaris, Apostolos
Fraser, Ashley
Friedl, Sabrina
Friess, Jens
Friolo, Daniele
Gao, Jiahui
Gardiner, Joseph
Garfatta, Ikram
Gattermayer, Tobias
Gellert, Kai
George, Dominik
Gerault, David
Gerhart, Paul
Ghadafi, Essam
Gholipourchoubeh, Mahmood
Gil-Pons, Reynaldo
Glas, Magdalena
Golinelli, Matteo
Gong, Junqing
Grisafi, Michele
Groll, Sebastian
Große-Kampmann, Matteo
Guan Tan, Teik
Guo, Xiaojie
Haffar, Rami
Haffey, Preston
Hallett, Joseph
Hammad Mazhar, M.
Han, Jinguang
Handirk, Tobias
Hao, Xuexuan
Hao, Shuai
Hasan Shahriar, Md
Heftrig, Elias
Heitjohann, Raphael
Henry Castellanos, John
Herranz, Javier
Hirschi, Lucca
Hlavacek, Tomas

Hobbs, Nathaniel
Hong, Hanbin
Horne, Ross
Horváth, Máté
Hu, Zhenkai
Hu, Lijie
Hu, Yan
Huang, Jianwei
Huso, Ingrid
Iadarola, Giacomo
Ioannidis, Thodoris
Iovino, Vincenzo
Ising, Fabian
Jacobs, Adriaan
Jebreel, Najeeb
Jeitner, Philipp
Jensen, Meiko
Jesús A., Zihang
Jin, Lin
Kailun, Yan
Kaiser, Fabian
Kaplan, Alexander
Karim, Imtiaz
Karyda, Maria
Katsis, Charalampos
Kavousi, Alireza
Kelarev, Andrei
Kempinski, Stash
Kermabon-Bobinnec, Hugo
Kern, Sascha
Khalili, Mojtaba
Khandpur Singh, Ashneet
Khin Shar, Lwin
Knechtel, Johann
Kokolakis, Spyros
Krumnow, Benjamin
Ksontini, Rym
Kulkarni, Tejas
Lai, Jianchang
Lee, Hyunwoo
Léger, Marc-André
Li, Jinfeng
Li, Rui
Li, Shaoyu
Li, Yanan

Li, Shuang
Li, Guangpu
Liang, Yuan
Likhitha Mankali, Lakshmi
Limbasiya, Trupil
Lin, Chao
Lin Aung, Yan
Liu, Lin
Liu, Xiaoning
Liu, Bingyu
Liu, Guannan
Liu, Xiaoyin
Liu, Jiahao
Liu, Zhen
Liu, Xueqiao
Liu, Xiaoyuan
Lu, Yun
Lucchese, Marco
Luo, Junwei
Lv, Chunyang
Lyu, Lin
Lyvas, Christos
Ma, Wanlun
Ma, Mimi
Maiorca, Davide
Maitra, Sudip
Makriyannis, Nikolaos
Manjón, Jesús A.
Martinez, Sergio
Mccarthy, Sarah
Mei, Qian
Menegatos, Andreas
Meng, Long
Mercaldo, Francesco
Merget, Robert
Mestel, David
Meyuhas, Bar
Michalas, Antonis
Mirdita, Donika
Mizera, Andrzej
Mohammadi, Farnaz
Mohammed, Ameer
Morillo, Paz
Morrison, Adam
Mujeeb Ahmed, Chuadhry

Nabi, Mahmudun
Neal, Christopher
Nguyen, Son
Niehues, David
Nixon, Brian
Oldani, Gianluca
Oqaily, Momen
Oqaily, Alaa
Osliak, Oleksii
P. K. Ma, Jack
Pan, Shimin
Pan, Jianli
Pang, Chengbin
Pang, Bo
Panja, Somnath
Paolo Tricomi, Pier
Paspatis, Ioannis
Peng, Hui
Pitropakis, Nikolaos
Polato, Mirko
Pryvalov, Ivan
Pu, Sihang
Puchta, Alexander
Putz, Benedikt
Qian, Chen
Qin, Baodong
Qin, Xianrui
Rabhi, Mouna
Radomirovic, Sasa
Ramokapane, Kopo M.
Rangarajan, Nikhil
Ravi, Divya
Rawat, Abhimanyu
Raza, Ali
Román-García, Fernando
Rossi, Matthew
Rovira, Sergi
S. M. Asadujjaman, A.
Saatjohann, Christoph
Sadighian, Alireza
Saha, Rahul
Samanis, Emmanouil
Sarathi Roy, Partha
Sarkar, Pratik
Schiff Agron, Shir

Schlette, Daniel
Schmidt, Carsten
Sentanoe, Stewart
Sha, Zeyang
Shao, Jun
Shi, Shanghao
Shibahara, Toshiki
Shioji, Eitaro
Shojafar, Mohammad
Shreeve, Benjamin
Silde, Tjerand
Singh, Animesh
Singh Sehrawat, Vipin
Sinha, Sayani
Siniscalchi, Luisa
Skrobot, Marjan
Sohrabi, Nasrin
Sollomoni, Avi
Song, Shang
Sotgiu, Angelo
Souid, Nourelhouda
Soumelidou, Katerina
Sun, Shihua
Tabatabaei, Masoud
Tabiban, Azadeh
Taha Bennani, Mohamed
Talibi Alaoui, Younes
Tang, Lihong
Tao, Youming
Tedeschi, Pietro
Terrovitis, Manolis
Tian, Guohua
Tian, Yangguang
Turrin, Federico
Umayya, Zeya
Vinayagamurthy, Dhinakaran
Visintin, Alessandro
Vollmer, Marcel
von der Heyden, Jonas
Voudouris, Anastassios
W. H. Wong, Harry
Wagner, Benedikt
Wang, Han
Wang, Ning
Wang, Kailong

Wang, Xiuhua
Wang, Yalan
Wang, Shu
Wang, Jiafan
Wang, Haizhou
Wang, Zhilong
Wang, Xiaolei
Wang, Yunling
Wang, Qin
Wang, Yu
Wang, Cheng-Long
Wang, Weijia
Wang, Xinyue
Wang, Yi
Wang, Yuyu
Wang, Yangde
Watanabe, Takuya
Wu, Huangting
Wu, Yulian
Wu, Chen
Wu, Mingli
Wu, Qiushi
Xiang, Zihang
Xiao, Yang
Xiao, Jidong
Xie, Shangyu
Xu, Shengmin
Yadav, Tarun
Yan, Di
Yang, Zhichao
Yang, Shishuai

Yang, Xu
Yang, S. J.
Yang, Xuechao
Yang, Junwen
Yin Chan, Kwan
You, Weijing
Yu, Hexuan
Yurkov, Semen
Zeng, Runzhi
Zhang, Sepideh
Zhang, Min
Zhang, Yanjun
Zhang, Zicheng
Zhang, Cong
Zhang, Lan
Zhang, Yuchen
Zhang, Xinyu
Zhang, Kai
Zhang, Tao
Zhang, Yunhang
Zhang, Xiaoyu
Zhang, Zidong
Zhang, Rongjunchen
Zhao, Yongjun
Zhao, Shujie
Zhao, Lingchen
Zheng, Xiang
Zhou, Xiaotong
Zhu, Fei
Zikas, Vassilis
Zou, Qingtian

Contents – Part III

Hardware Security

Multiparty Computation

ML Techniques

Cyber-Physical Systems Security

Network and Software Security

Posters

Formal Analysis

A Formal Analysis of the FIDO2 Protocols

Jingjing Guan[1]($\boxtimes$), Hui Li[1], Haisong Ye[1], and Ziming Zhao[2]

[1] Beijing University of Posts and Telecommunications, Beijing, China
{GuanEr,lihuill,yeeys}@bupt.edu.cn
[2] CactiLab, University at Buffalo, Buffalo, USA
zimingzh@buffalo.edu

Abstract. FIDO2 is the latest member of the Fast IDentity Online (FIDO) protocol suite, which aims at providing unified password-less authentication across the web. We present a formal security analysis of the FIDO2 protocols. We extend the previously presented formalization of the security assumptions and goals of FIDO with FIDO2 specific requirements. We develop a formal model that considers both the CTAP2 and WebAuthn in FIDO2 as a whole. Our formal analysis identifies the minimal security assumptions required for each security goal of FIDO2 to hold. The verification results show FIDO2 fails to achieve some strong authentication properties. The results also reveal that the newly introduced Client PIN mechanism has flaws, and the discovered authenticator rebinding attack and parallel session attacks in UAF still exist in FIDO2.

Keywords: FIDO2 · Formal analysis · Security protocol

1 Introduction

FIDO2 [16,35] is the latest member of the Fast IDentity Online (FIDO) protocol suite. It builds on top of the commercial success of the previous FIDO protocols, including the Universal Second Factor (U2F, a.k.a. CTAP1) [13] and the Universal Authentication Framework (UAF) [20]. FIDO2 aims to support all U2F and UAF use cases and offer a ubiquitous and unified strong authentication across the web. Extended from U2F and UAF, FIDO2 supports user identity verification in 2nd-factor authentication scenarios. By Jan 2022, FIDO2 has been integrated into Android 7.0+ [18], Windows 10 [17], iOS and MacOS [19], Google Chrome, Mozilla Firefox, Microsoft Edge [14], etc.

FIDO2 includes multi-factor and password-less authentication and fixes some discovered flaws in U2F and UAF [32]. Therefore, the protocol architecture and procedures of FIDO2 differ from the counterparts of U2F and UAF significantly. FIDO2 consists of the Client to Authenticator Protocol v2.0 (CTAP2) [16] and the Web Authentication protocol (WebAuthn) [35]. With the Client PIN mechanism in CTAP2, FIDO2 offers user identity verification in 2nd-factor use cases when the authenticator does not have a user interface. WebAuthn provides a standard web API that enables online services to implement FIDO2 authentication into browsers and web platforms.

V. Atluri et al. (Eds.): ESORICS 2022, LNCS 13556, pp. 3–21, 2022.
https://doi.org/10.1007/978-3-031-17143-7_1

To automatically verify the security of UAF, Feng et al. [12] presented a formalization of UAF's security assumptions, goals, and protocol process. Even though FIDO2 and UAF share the same natural language security goals, their semantics and formalization are not the same in the different protocol contexts. For example, the relevant data fields in the security properties need to be adjusted to the messages in FIDO2, and more properties need to be verified in the Client PIN mechanism. In particular, the confidentiality of the key fields, such as the Client PIN provided by the user and the token issued by the authenticator, must be verified. To the best of our knowledge, there is no formal treatment of the two FIDO2 protocols as a whole. Barbosa et al. [3] considered CTAP2 and WebAuthn as independent modules and only analyzed several authentication goals. Guirat et al. [23] only verified WebAuthn and considered privacy goals. Moreover, neither of them considered the scenarios with different authenticator types and transaction authorization modes.

In this paper, we present a formal verification of FIDO2, which shows the security goals of FIDO2 cannot be satisfied in some cases. In particular, we show FIDO2 does not provide stronger security in 2nd-factor scenarios despite its efforts since the Client PIN and token can be exploited to undermine the validity of authentications in registration and authentication processes. The contributions of this paper are as follows:

1. We present a *faithful formal model of the FIDO2*, which considers CTAP2 and WebAuthn as a whole and models scenarios with different authenticator types in registration, authentication, and transaction authorization. We open-source our tool FIDO2Verif[1], which is a front-end to ProVerif [7].
2. We refine the *formalization of FIDO security goals in the context of FIDO2*. In particular, we consider the secrecy of Client PIN and the token issued by the authenticator in FIDO2 due to the newly introduced CTAP2 process. We also formalize several security goals that were not modeled before [12].
3. The verification results show *flaws in FIDO2*. For example, due to the unauthenticated ECDH in CTAP2, FIDO2 fails to achieve the strong authentication property, and the previously discovered authenticator rebinding attack and parallel session attack on UAF are still effective on FIDO2.
4. We present recommendations on how to fix the discovered flaws in FIDO2.

2   Overview of FIDO2

Table 1 presents the acronyms used throughout this paper. CTAP2 is the protocol between the authenticator and the client to share a token, which will be used in the operations of WebAuthn subsequently. There are two operations in WebAuth, namely authenticator registration and authentication. In authenticator registration, users register their certified FIDO2 authenticator with a vendor-signed *attes-*

---

[1] https://github.com/CactiLab/FIDO2Verif.

Table 1. Acronyms and descriptions.

Acronym	Full Name	Description
$newPin$	New client PIN	New client PIN that the user enters in FIDO Client when setting or changing the Client PIN
$curPin$	Current client PIN	Current client PIN the user provides to FIDO Client to change a new Client PIN or apply for a $PinToken$
$RpID$	Relying party identifier	A domain that identifies the WebAuthn relying party and determines the set of origins on which the public key credential may be exercised
$AAGUID$	Authenticator attestation globally unique identifier	An identifier that indicates the type (e.g. manufacturer and model) of the authenticator
$UHandle$	User handle	A value specified by a relying party to map a public key credential to a user account
$Chlg$	Relying party challenge	A random number provided by the relying party in registration and authentication requests
Tr	Transaction text	Transaction information generated by the relying party that needs to be authorized by the user
$TBinding$	TLS token binding	A long-lived identifier of TLS bindings spanning multiple TLS sessions and connections from Token Binding protocol
$PinToken$	Token controlled by client PIN	A random token generated by authenticators and issued to FIDO Client
G	Elliptic-curve parameters	ECC parameters used to establish ECDH shared secret between Authenticator and FIDO Client
K	Shared key	The key established between Authenticator and FIDO Client through ECDH, which is used for symmetric encryption, decryption, and HMAC
$CNTR$	Signature counter	An integer that increments after each successful authentication
$FCData$	Client data object	The contextual binding of the WebAuthn relying party and the client
$CreID$	Credential ID	An identifier to retrieve the credential private key stored in the authenticator or with the credential private key wrapped in
$Cert_{AT}$	Attestation certificate	A certificate for the attestation key pair used by an authenticator to attest to its manufacture and capabilities
sk_{AT}	Attestation private key	The private asymmetric key shared across a large number of FIDO device units made by the same vendor
pk_{AT}	Attestation public key	The public asymmetric key shared across a large number of FIDO device units made by the same vendor
sk_{Cre}	Credential private key	The private key portion of the credential key pair stored in FIDO device or wrapped in $CreID$
pk_{Cre}	Credential public key	The public key portion of the credential key pair, generated by an authenticator and returned to a relying party in registration
k_W	Wrapping key	A key known only to the FIDO device, which is used to encrypt the public key credential source

tation key for the accounts of remote service. The user provides the original credential first, usually a text-based password, and then selects a local authentication mechanism such as swiping a finger, entering a PIN, etc. The authenticator generates a pair of asymmetric *credential keys* and signs the public part with the attestation private key. Then, it sends the credential public key, the signature, and the *attestation certificate* to the server. If the certificate and the signature pass the server's verification, binding between the user's account and the authenticator will be established and recorded in the server and the registration process succeeds. In the authentication stage, the user performs the local authentication method selected before, and the authenticator runs a challenge-response protocol with the server using the *credential private key*.

2.1 Architecture of FIDO2

As shown in Fig. 1, the entities in FIDO2 include a *FIDO Authenticator* (FA), a *FIDO Client* (FC), and a *Relying Party* (RP). FA is a hardware or software cryptographic entity, which can be implemented on-device as platform authenticators, such as biometric or PIN verification modules, or off-device as cross-platform authenticators,

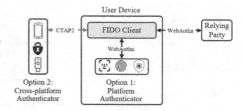

Fig. 1. The FIDO2 architecture

such as FIDO Security Keys, mobile devices, wearables, etc. FA stores a vendor-signed attestation private key (sk_{AT}), the attestation certificate $(Cert_{AT})$, and a model identifier $(AAGUID)$. FA generates credential key pairs (sk_{Cre}, pk_{Cre}) used in authentication. FAs with persistent storage to store sk_{Cre} are called *client-side storage authenticators*, in which keys are identified by random $CreID$s. *Server-side storage authenticators* are limited in storage capacity. They encrypt the credential private key sk_{Cre} in $CreID$ and send it to the server.

FIDO Client (FC) is implemented in whole or in part of the user agent, e.g., browser. FC stores the identifiers of valid RPs as $xRpID$s. RP consists of a *web server* and a *FIDO server* that utilizes the WebAuthn API to register and authenticate users. In authenticator registration, RP verifies the authenticator and records the binding between the account and FA of the user. The binding will be verified by RP in authentication.

The channel between authenticators and FC can be established through cross-platform transports, such as Bluetooth and NFC, or a platform-specific transport, such as inter-process communication. The communications between cross-platform FA and FC are defined in CTAP2, and the Client PIN mechanism in CTAP2 should be enabled if user identity verification is required in 2nd-factor use cases. FC and RP usually communicate over a TLS channel. The optional steps in FIDO2 include using different types of authenticators, choosing different CTAP2 processes, and using different transaction authorization modes. Different

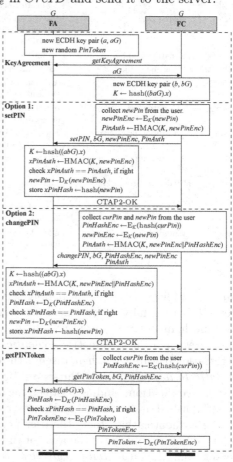

Fig. 2. CTAP2 operations

options result in different protocol processes, which we will explain in detail in the subsequent sections.

2.2   The CTAP2

As shown in Fig. 2, the Client PIN mechanism in CTAP2 consists of the following operations. In *KeyAgreement*, FA and FC negotiate a shared ECDH secret K first, which can be used for symmetric encryption, decryption, and HMAC. K is obtained by hashing the x-coordinate of the point abG on the elliptic curve. The user can choose to initialize or change the Client PIN via the FC on the device through the *setPIN* and *changePIN* process. If the Client PIN has already been set and does not need to be modified, the user enters the current Client PIN on the FC, then the FA and FC directly execute the *getPINToken* process, as long as the FA verifies the Client PIN is correct, it will issue a *PinToken* to the FC. Within the lifetime of *PinToken*, FC can use this *PinToken* for the subsequent authenticator registration and authentication with FA without requiring the user to enter the Client PIN again.

2.3   The WebAuthn Protocol

WebAuthn defines the operations of *authenticator registration* and *authentication*, which are shown in Figs. 3 and 4. The contents marked in blue are the operations and message fields when CTAP2 is enabled. We also present the different operations using server-side storage and client-side storage authenticators in this section.

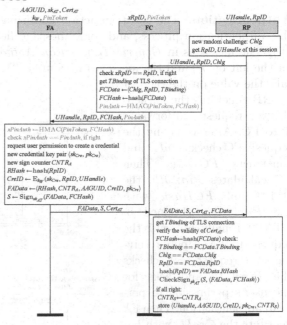

Authenticator Registration. After the user logs in with the original authentication method, RP generates a registration request and forwards it to FC. FC checks whether $RpID$ is

Fig. 3. Authenticator registration (Color figure online)

equal to the expected $xRpID$. FIDO2 mitigates the attack caused by a missing check of $AppID$ in U2F (similar to the $RpID$ in FIDO2) [32] and enforces the checking of $RpID$. Subsequently, FC assembles $FCData$ as the contextual bindings of the FIDO session and the TLS session. Then FC calculates $FCHash$, the hash of $FCData$, and $PinAuth$, and forwards the request to FA.

Table 2. Definitions of authenticator types

Authenticator type	Credential storage modality	Authenticator attachment modality	Authentication factor capability
1st factor platform	Client-side	Platform	Multi-factor
1st factor roaming	Client-side	Cross-platform	Multi-factor
2nd factor platform	Server-side	Platform	Single-factor
2nd factor roaming	Server-side	Cross-platform	Single-factor
User-verifying platform	Server-side	Platform	Multi-factor
User-verifying roaming	Server-side	Cross-platform	Multi-factor

FA checks $PinAuth$ and generates a credential key pair $\langle sk_{Cre}, pk_{Cre}\rangle$, and a random signature counter $CNTR_A$ for this account. FA assembles $FAData$, calculates signature S, and returns the response to FC. FC adds $FCData$ to the response from FA and forwards it to RP. RP checks the validity of $Cert_{AT}$, inspects the fields in $FCData$, compares $RHash$ in $FAData$, and verifies the signature S with sk_{AT} to validate the legitimacy of FA.

Authentication. The two transaction confirmation modes of FIDO2 extend the authentication process, and some message fields are added (enclosed with '[]'). The messages in *Generic Transaction Authorization Mode* take the value on the left of '/', and the messages in *Simple Transaction Authorization Mode* take the value on the right of '/'.

RP generates the authentication request and forwards it to FC. After receiving the request, FC checks $RpID$ and constructs $FCData$. Then FC calculates $PinAuth$, the HMAC of $FCHash$ with the $PinToken$ obtained in CTAP2. Finally, FC sends the request to FA. Upon receiving the request, FA checks the $PinAuth$ and asks for the user's permission to perform authentication. Then FA decrypts the $CreID$ with k_W and calculates $RHash$.

In *Generic Transaction Authorization Mode*, $THash$ is included in the response, while in *Simple Transaction Authorization Mode*, the cor-

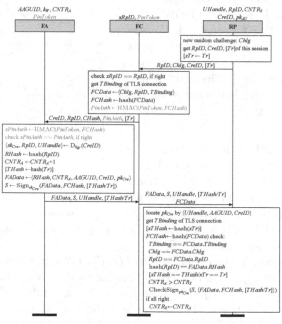

Fig. 4. Authentication (Color figure online)

Table 3. Protocol operations of different types of authenticators

Server-side storage	Reg.	$CreID \leftarrow E_{k_W}(sk_{Cre}, RpID, UHandle)$
	Auth.	$\langle sk_{Cre}, RpID, UHandle \rangle \leftarrow D_{k_W}(CreID)$
Client-side storage	Reg.	new random $CreID$ store $\langle CreID, sk_{Cre}, RpID, Uhandle, CNTR_A \rangle$
	Auth.	get $\langle CreID, sk_{Cre}, RpID, Uhandle, CNTR_A \rangle$ using $CreID$

responding value is Tr. FA increases the signature counter $CNTR_A$, usually by one, forms the $FAData$, calculates signature S, and sends the response to FC. FC adds $FCData$ to the response from FA and returns it to RP. RP locates the previously stored record by the triple $\langle UHandle, AAGUID, CreID \rangle$, checks the fields in $FCData$, and compares $RHash$ in $FAData$. If the received $THash$ or Tr equals the expected value, the transaction data will be displayed and confirmed by the user. RP verifies the signature S and compares the value of the signature counter. If $CNTR_A$ is greater than $CNTR_S$, RP updates its internally stored $CNTR_S$ with $CNTR_A$.

Operations of Different Types of Authenticators. As shown in Table 2, WebAuthn defines six types of authenticators. Based on how the authentication method is implemented, they can be divided into 1st/2nd/user-verifying authenticators, so as the credential storage capability, access method, and authentication factor. Among them, 1st factor platform authenticators and 1st factor roaming authenticators are client-side storage authenticators, while the other four types of authenticators are server-side storage authenticators. The storage type is determined by where the authentication credential, i.e., sk_{Cre} generated during the authenticator registration phase, is stored. Client-side storage authenticators store the authentication credential sk_{Cre} on the authenticator. As thus, the credential will not leave the user's device and the $CreID$ is a random number that serves as an index to access credentials. A server-side storage authenticator is limited in storage capacity; therefore, it wraps sk_{Cre} in $CreID$ with a wrapping key k_W and sends it to the RP. The different protocol operations of client-side and server-side storage authenticators are shown in Table 3.

3 Formal Verification of FIDO2

The FIDO Security Reference [15] presents informal descriptions of assumptions and security goals in English, which are lengthy and sometimes ambiguous. Because the assumptions in the specifications are strong and often impractical, we refine these descriptions to derive a practical and realistic threat model in our formalization and give formal interpretations of security goals.

3.1 Assumptions and Threat Model

Assumptions on Cryptographic Primitives. We assume cryptographic functions are secure, and attacks on cryptographic algorithms and parameters

Table 4. Formalization of FIDO2 security goals

Type	Goals	Label	Formal description
C.	SG-2	C1~C8	The wrapping key k_W(C1), the private keys sk_{AT}(C2), sk_{Cre}(C3), the signature counter $CNTR$(C4), the authentication key reference $CreID$(C5), user transaction data Tr(C6), $curPin$ and $newPin$(C7) and $PinToken$(C8) should be secret in FIDO2.
	SG-3		
	SG-8		
	SG-15		
A.	SG-10	A0	**Attack Resistance:** The authentication between entities should be injective agreement on the data fields.
	SG-11		
	SG-12		
	SG-13		
	SG-1	A1	**Strong User Authentication:** The RP must obtain injective agreement on $RpID$, $UHandle$, $AAGUID$, and $CreID$ with the FA after authentication
	SG-14	A2	Transaction Non-Repudiation: The RP must obtain injective agreement on Tr with the authenticator after transaction authorization
	SG-5	A3	**Verifier Leak Resilience:** Supposing that user A has registered on both RP and RP$'$ with the authenticator FA, even if the RP$'$ leaks the information of user A, the RP should still obtain injective agreement on $RpID$, $UHandle$, $AAGUID$, and $CreID$ with the FA after authentication
	SG-6	A4	**Authenticator Leak Resilience:** Supposing that both user A and user B have registered on the RP and RP$'$ with their FA respectively, even if an attacker can steal the information of user B from the FA, the RP should still obtain injective agreement on $RpID$, $UHandle$, $AAGUID$, and $CreID$ with A' FA after authentication
	SG-7	A5	**User Consent:** The RP must obtain injective agreement on $RpID$, $UHandle$, $AAGUID$, and $CreID$ with the FC after registration
	SG-9	A6	**Attestable Properties:** The RP must obtain injective agreement on $RpID$, $UHandle$, $AAGUID$, and pk_{AT} with the authenticator after registration.
P.	SG-4	P1	**Unlinkability:** FIDO2 processes initiated by the same user on different RPs should be observational equivalent to the RPs

are beyond our consideration. **Assumptions on Channels and Entities.** Two types of channels are involved in FIDO2: the channel between FC and FA is established through IPC, while the channel between FC and RP is relying on TLS. Similar to the security assumptions for channels and entities in UAF, we assume that the IPC and TLS channels provide both confidentiality and integrity, hence a Dolev-Yao attacker has no control of messages exchanged over the channel established between honest entities. However, the attackers can initiate a conversation through malicious entities under their control and intercept the information in these sessions. **Assumptions on Data Protections.** We assume the identifiers, including $UHandle$, $AAGUID$, and $RpID$, the public keys pk_{AT} and pk_{AU}, and the elliptic curve parameter G are public. $CreID$, $CNTR$, k_W, or sk_{AT} are not public but can be compromised.

3.2 Security Goals

[SG-1, 4, 5~7, 9, 10~14] have been formalized in literature [12], and we formalize [SG-2~3, 8, 15] for the first time. As shown in Table 4, we formally interpret the goals [SG-1~15] in the FIDO2 context. We denote the confidentiality, authentication, and privacy goals as 'C.', 'A.', and 'P.', respectively. Because C1~C6 in

FIDO2 are similar to those of UAF, we focus on **C7** and **C8**, which should be considered because of the newly introduced Client PIN mechanism.

In CTAP2, a shared secret is negotiated between the FA and FC. The user sets the Client PIN on the FC, and then the FC encrypts and forwards it to the FA. Once the Client PIN is leaked, the attacker can initiate the CTAP2 process with a malicious FC and invoke the FA on the user's device. Formally, **C7:** the current Client PIN *curPin* and the newly set Client PIN *newPin* should be secret in the presence of the active attacker during the CTAP2 process.

The CTAP2 process runs before authenticator registration or authentication. After the FA verifies the validity of the Client PIN entered by the user on the FC, the FA will issue a *PinToken* to the FC. Subsequently, the FC needs to use *PinToken* to calculate an HMAC *PinAuth* and add it to the registration or authentication requests sent to the FA. If the verification of *PinAuth* fails, the FA will terminate this operation. Once *PinToken* is leaked, the attacker will be able to forge a request and deceive the user's authenticator to communicate with it. Formally, **C8:** The *PinToken* should be secret in the presence of the active attacker during the CTAP2 process.

4   Formal Models

To formally analyze FIDO2, we use ProVerif [7]. Compared with other commonly used tools, such as Tamarin [30], Scyther [11], AVISPA [1], DEEPSEC [10], CL-AtSe [34], OFMC [5], FDR [29], SATMC [2], Cryptyc [22], ProVerif solved the problem of state explosion under unlimited sessions and provides a user-friendly interface for interactive operation and attack path display. It has been used to analyze multiple security protocols including UAF [12], TLS 1.3 Draft 18 [6], ARINC823 avionic protocols [8], and e-voting protocols [24].

4.1   ProVerif Models of FIDO2

To cover all possible scenarios of FIDO2, we define the following three types of constants: *CTAPType*, *AuType*, and *TrType*, to identify which CTAP2 process the users go through in this protocol, which authenticator is used, and under which authentication mode. The four values, *noCTAP*, *setPIN*, *chgPIN*, and *getToken*, of *CTAPType* identify the four processes in the CTAP2 process respectively: without enabling the CTAP2 protocol, going through setPIN or changePIN process in CTAP2, and directly perform the getPINToken operation. The values *client* and *server* of *AuType* identify the scenarios using client or server-side storage FA. The value *empty*, *simple*, and *generic* of *TrType* are used to distinguish the scenarios of authentication, simple transaction authorization mode, and generic transaction authorization mode. As a result, we analyze 32 different scenarios, including eight scenarios in authenticator registration ($4 \times 2 = 8$ scenarios in total, as the transmission of transaction authorization data is not transmitted in registration), and 24 scenarios in authentication ($4 \times 2 \times 3 = 24$). Each scenario is identified by a specific value of the tuple (*CTAPType*, *AuType*) or the triple $(CTAPType, AuType, TrType)$, which will determine the branches to go through in this run of the process. When the CTAP2 option is enabled, $PinToken$ will be shared between FA and FC after CTAP2 is completed. The token will be used in subsequent authenticator registration and authentication operations. We model this feature using tables and phases in ProVerif. FA and FC maintain a table for $PinToken$. When the CTAP2 operation is completed, both parties will store the $PinToken$ in the table.

4.2   Verifying Leak Resilience Goals of FIDO2

SG-5 (Verifier Leak Resilience) and SG-6 (Authenticator Leak Resilience) were formalized but not verified in the previous UAF formal analysis [12]. To verify these two goals, we design a scenario with three sets of sessions, which need to be modeled and analyzed separately. User A registers the FA on RP and RP′, while user B registers the FA′ on RP. There are three sets of data after registration: the data between FA and RP, FA and RP′, FA′ and RP. We verify whether the authentication between RP and FA can be satisfied in the case that the FA′ of user B leaks its data registered on RP while RP leaks the data of FA.

5   Security Analysis

To identify the minimal assumptions of each security goal of FIDO2, we develop a tool FIDO2Verif, which is a front-end to ProVerif. Our tool is based on the idea proposed by Basin et al. [4], which was also used in the analysis of multi-factor authentication protocols [26] and the Noise framework [21]. The tool first verifies whether a security goal is satisfied without any assumptions, then increases the number of assumptions until the state of the security property is changed from false to true. If the state of the security properties has not changed after adding all the assumptions about the entity, then we add the assumptions about the data fields. The tool automatically generates 78,336 test cases covering all CTAP2 process options, authenticator types and transaction authorization modes, and the combinations of assumptions on entities and fields.

5.1   Results

Table 5 and Table 6 show the analysis results. 'Reg.' means the results of authenticator registration and 'Auth.' means the results of authentication. The results show the minimum assumptions required for each security goal in our threat model. '$\checkmark$' means the goal can be met in all conditions, '$-$' means not applicable. '$\neg$' before the filed, e.g., '$\neg k_W$', indicates the property only holds when k_W is not revealed. '$\neg X[Y]$' denotes the attackers cannot use their compromised entity X to communicate with entity Y. Since the transaction authorization data Tr can only be transmitted in authentication, and the attestation private key sk_{AT} is only used in registration, there is no verification result for $C6$ in Table 5, and no verification result for $C2$ in Table 6.

Confidentiality Properties. As shown in Table 5, the attackers have no access to k_W and sk_{AT}, since these fields are stored and used only inside FA in authenticator registration. As for client-side storage authenticators, sk_{Cre} is stored inside FA and cannot be obtained by the attacker. While for server-side storage authenticators, sk_{Cre} is encrypted in the $CreID$ by k_W. $CreID$ and $CNTR$ are exposed on the channel as part of the registration response from FA. Therefore, if attackers compromise $C[A]$, they can eavesdrop on the registration response to obtain $CreID$ and $CNTR$. As long as

Table 5. Verification results in registration.

Reg.	Client-Side	Server-Side
C1	–	
C2	✓	✓
C3	✓	$\neg k_W \vee \neg C[A]$
C4		
C5	$\neg C[A]$	
C7	$\neg A[C]$	
C8	$\neg C[A]$	
A5	$\neg A[C] \wedge \neg C[R]$	
A6		
P1	✓	✓

the attacker cannot obtain k_W (the assumption $\neg k_W$ is met) or $CreID$ (the assumption $\neg C[A]$ is met), the secrecy of sk_{Cre} will hold. Since CTAP2 relies on unauthenticated ECDH to negotiate a shared secret between FA and FC, the two participants cannot confirm the validity of their identities. Therefore, if there is a malicious FA' in the CTAP2 session (breaking assumption $\neg A[C]$), the FA' can complete the CTAP2 process with the FC and obtain the $curPin$ and $newPin$ entered by the user on FC. In the same way, a malicious FC' (breaking the assumption $\neg C[A]$) can intercept the $PinToken$ issued by the FA.

Table 6 shows that sk_{Cre} of client-side storage authenticators and k_W of server-side storage authenticators are secure as they are only used within FA in authentication. For server-side storage authenticators, sk_{Cre} is encrypted with k_W as $CreID$, which is part of the authentication request from RP and the authentication response from FA. To protect $CreID$, it is necessary to prevent attackers from obtaining the above messages and the assumptions $\neg A[C]$ (there is no malicious FA to obtain the authentication request relayed from FC) and $\neg C[R]$ (there is no malicious FC to obtain the authentication request sent from RP) and $\neg C[A]$ (there is no malicious FC to obtain the authentication response returned from FA) should be met. As for $CNTR$, which is retrieved from the storage from FA with corresponding $CreID$ and included in the message returned from FA, the assumptions $\neg C[R]$ or $\neg C[A]$ should be met.

In other words, if the attacker cannot get the correct $CreID$ or the authentication response sent by the FA, $CNTR$ will not be intercepted. The assumption required to maintain the confidentiality of Tr in Simple Transaction Authorization Mode is the same as that of $CreID$, which is $\neg A[C]$ and $\neg C[R]$ and $\neg C[A]$. Because both $CreID$ and Tr

Table 6. Verification results in authentication.

Type	Client-Side		Server-Side	
Mode	Simple	Generic	Simple	Generic
C1	–			
C3	✓		$\neg k_W \vee (\neg A[C] \wedge \neg C[R] \wedge \neg C[A])$	
C4	$\neg C[R]$	$\neg C[A]$		
C5	$\neg A[C] \wedge \neg C[R] \wedge \neg C[A]$			
C6	$(CreID)$	$\neg A[C] \wedge \neg C[R]$	$(CreID)$	$\neg A[C] \wedge \neg C[R]$
C7	$\neg A[C]$			
C8	$\neg C[A]$			
A1	$\neg C[R] \vee \neg C[A]$			
A2				
A3	✓			✓
A4	✓			
P1	✓			✓

are included in the request from the RP and the response returned by the FA. To maintain the secrecy of Tr in Generic Transaction Authorization Mode the protocol should satisfy $\neg A[C]$ and $\neg C[R]$ as Tr is only involved in the request from the RP.

Authentication Properties. As shown in Table 5, to achieve the authentication goals in authenticator registration, the minimal assumption $\neg A[C]$ and $\neg C[R]$ should be met. Whether sk_{AT} is leaked or not has little effect on the authentication in authenticator registration. RP verifies the validity of FA by checking the signature S, which is signed by sk_{AT}, and inspects the fields in $FCData$ to confirm the binding relationship between a FIDO2 session and a TLS session. As the same sk_{AT} is manufactured in a batch, the attacker can simply use an FA′ from the same batch as the user's FA. Once $\neg A[C]$ and $\neg C[R]$ is violated, the attackers can use their FA′ to generate a valid response and forward it to the FC on the user's device with a compromised FC′. The response will pass the inspection of RP and be considered a legitimate response. Thereafter, the user's account will be bound to the FA′ held by the attacker instead of the FA of the user, and the user is not aware of it.

After successful registration, the binding between the user account and the FA has been established and RP has recorded the binding as $\langle UHandle,$ $AAGUID, CreID, pk_{Cre}, CNTR_S \rangle$. RP verifies the signature S with pk_{Cre} and checks the value of $CNTR$. Since the private key sk_{Cre} and the counter $CNTR$ are stored in the user's FA, which can only be retrieved with the corresponding $CreID$ in the authentication request. If the assumption $\neg C[A]$ or $\neg C[R]$ is not satisfied, the attacker will be able to intercept $CreID$ an authentication request with a malicious FC, with the correct $CreID$, the malicious FC can receive a valid authentication response from the user's FA and forward it to RP.

Our analysis results show that there is no data leakage on RP or FA, i.e., the authentication goals $A3$ and $A4$ are satisfied. Even if the RP leaks user B's data, it still does not affect the RP's authentication of other users. For the same user, even if the user's authentication data of an RP′ is leaked, the user's authentication on other RPs can still be guaranteed. The RP authenticates the user by verifying the binding relationship of the triple: the user account (identified by $UHandle$), the authenticator (identified by $AAGUID$), and the RP (identified by $RpID$), which is associated with the asymmetric key pair (sk_{Cre}, pk_{Cre}) generated by FA. The public key pk_{Cre} will be sent to RP, while FA saves the private key sk_{Cre}. As long as the private key bound between user A and RP is not leaked, even if RP′ leaks user A's information, including the public key of user A on RP′, or user B who has registered on the same RP leaks the private key, the authentication of user A from the RP will not be affected.

Privacy Properties. Our results show that FIDO2 satisfies unlinkability in authenticator registration and authentication. $\langle RHash, CNTR_A, AAGUID,$ $CreID, pk_{Cre}, S, Cert_{AT}, FCData \rangle$ No field in the registration response is associated with the user. As both $AAGUID$ and the corresponding $Cert_{AT}$ are shared by a large batch of authenticators, it is difficult, even impossible for the

RP to locate the sessions of the same $AAGUID$ and $Cert_{AT}$ to a single user. $CNTR_A$ records the number of times of authentication for a single user at the specific RP, but cannot directly link the session between different RPs.

RP receives the authentication response $\langle RHash, CNTR_A, AAGUID,$ $CreID, pk_{Cre}, S, UHandle, [THash /Tr], FCData\rangle$. Note that it is pointed out in Sect. 4 of WebAuthn [35]: "$UHandle$ should be an opaque byte sequence and not contain any personally identifying information about the user". The RPs cannot infer the user's personal identification information from any instance of $UHandle$. And $UHandle$ is the user identifier specified by an RP that can be used to map the conversations to a specific user only within this RP but different RPs cannot link the session to the specific user with $UHandle$. $\langle CNTR_A,$ $CreID,$ and $pk_{Cre}\rangle$ are unique for each binding $\langle RpID, AAGUID, UHandle\rangle$ and cannot be used to distinguish user sessions across different RPs.

5.2 Attacks

MITM Attack in CTAP2. FIDO2 introduces the Client PIN mechanism to improve the security in 2nd-factor authentication scenarios. However, the verification results show that this goal cannot be achieved. Since FA and FC negotiate a shared secret with unauthenticated ECDH, FA and FC cannot establish any trust through this process, making it vulnerable to man-in-the-middle (MITM) attacks. In CTAP2, if the assumption $\neg A[C]$ is not satisfied, the attacker can obtain the $curPin$ and $newPin$. If the assumption $\neg C[A]$ is not satisfied, the attacker can intercept the $PinToken$. The process of MITM Attack in CTAP2 is shown in Fig. 5. The attacker

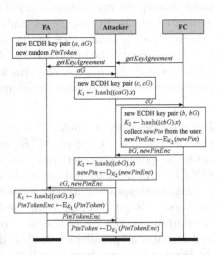

Fig. 5. MITM Attack in CTAP2

forwards the getKeyAgreement request initiated by FC, intercepts the ECDH public key aG sent by FA, replaces it with the cG generated by itself, and forwards it to FC. The shared secret negotiated between the FA and the attacker is caG, and the attacker can derive a shared key K_1 with FA. The FC generates the ECDH key pair (b, bG), and uses the secret cbG shared with the attacker to derive the shared key K_2. After collecting the $newPin$ from the user, the FC encrypts it with K_2 and sends the message $\langle bG,$ $newPinEnc\rangle$ to FA. After receiving the message from FC containing the ECDH public key bG, attackers can replace it with their public key cG and send it to FA. Therefore, the attacker negotiates shared secrets caG and cbG with FA and FC respectively, and then derives a shared key K_1 with FA and a shared key K_2 with FC. After that, the attacker can decrypt the $newPinEnc$ and $curPinEnc$ sent by FC, and the $PinTokenEnc$ from FA to obtain the plaintext $newPin$, $curPin$, and $PinToken$ respectively.

Authenticator Rebinding Attack. In registration, if the assumptions $\neg A[C]$ and $\neg C[R]$ are not satisfied, the attackers can implement the authenticator rebinding attack to bind the victim's account to the FA′ under their control. We consider an attacker who has the same model of authenticator as the user (with the same sk_{AT} in it) and can compromise the FC on the victim's device (to get access to the channel CA and CR). We denote the FIDO Client on the victim's device as client FC and the FIDO Client on the adversary's device as client FC′. The adversaries can bind the victim's account to their authenticators through the following steps: 1) The victim initiates a registration, and the malicious FC on the victim's device establishes a connection with the RP to obtain the registration request; 2) FC redirects the request to FC′; 3) FC′ continue the FIDO2 registration operations with the authenticator to bind the victim's account with FA′ held by the attacker; 4) The FC pretends to complete subsequent operations with the user, making the user believe the binding was successful; 5) The FC′ forwards the response to FC; 6) FC sends the response to the RP to complete subsequent operations in registration. In the operations above, $FCData$ is generated by the FC on the victim's device, and the authenticator used by the attacker has the same sk_{AT} as the user's, the returned registration response can be successfully verified by the RP and the user account is bound to the attacker's authenticator. Thereafter, the attackers can log in to the victim's account with their credential and bypass the biometric verification in FIDO2.

Parallel Session Attack. This attack breaks the authentication properties if the assumptions $\neg C[A]$ or $\neg C[R]$ are not satisfied. RP accepted an authentication response after verifying the signature S signed by sk_{Cre} and checking $CNTR_A$. After successful registration, sk_{Cre} and $CNTR_A$ are stored inside the FA and the response with the correct S and $CNTR_A$ will be returned only if A receives a correct $CreID$. With the following steps, the attacker does not need to compromise the FA of the user to obtain sk_{Cre} or k_W, but tamper with FC and initiates a "parallel session" to impersonate a legitimate user.

We assume users have installed a malicious FC on their devices. The attacker can implement the parallel session attack with the following steps: 1) Once a victim launches an authentication session, the attackers can be informed by the malicious FC and initiated their own session on FC′ with the victim's identifier $UHandle$ to the same RP to get the correct $CreID$; 2) FC′ sends the request generated by itself to client FC. $FCHash$ is the hash of $FCData$ generated from the connection established between FC′ and the RP; 3) FC forwards the request to the FA on the victim's device and obtains the response. As $CreID$ in the request corresponds to the $UHandle$ of the victim, FA can successfully retrieve the sk_{Cre} to generate the signature S and get the $CNTR$; 4) FC redirects the response to FC′ and FC′ appends its own $FCData$ to the response; 5) FC′ returns the response to the RP to complete the authentication.

Since the $FCData$ in the response corresponds to the connection established between $FC′$ and the RP and the signature is, in effect, generated by the victim's authenticator with correct sk_{Cre}, the attackers will pass the verifications in RP and gain access to the victim's account on their own device.

Privacy Disclosure Attack. Attackers can intercept the user's personal data with a malicious FC. In registration, if the assumption $\neg C[A]$ is not satisfied, the original $CNTR$ will be exposed to attackers in the registration response from FA. Later in authentication, if the protocol does not satisfy the assumption $\neg C[R] \vee \neg C[A]$, attackers can get the increased $CNTR$ to estimate the number of times of the completed authentication and infer user behavior based on this. Additionally, with the malicious FC, attackers can also distinguish whether the user is performing authentication or transaction authorization by checking whether the field Tr is involved in the response from RP. Thereafter, attackers can also intercept the victim's transaction authorization text Tr.

5.3 Recommendations

Explicit Definitions of Threat Model. We suggest that the standard explicitly requires the assumptions of channel and component compromise. A clearly specified threat model can provide constructive guidance for the design and implementation of the protocol. On the contrary, an ambiguous threat model may introduce problems in the design process and even introduce vulnerabilities in potential practical implementations. Our analysis results show that the security of FIDO2 relies on the security of the channel between entities and the secure storage module inside the entities. However, there is a lack of a clear definition of entity and channel compromise scenarios in the specifications. Therefore, the compromise scenarios should be considered in the protocol design, and the recommended implementation of the secure channel and secure storage should be clearly given in the specifications.

Enhancing the security of CTAP2. We suggest enhancing the authentication of FA and FC in the CTAP2 process. The current design of CTAP2 relies on unauthenticated ECDH to negotiate the shared secret between FA and FC, making it vulnerable to man-in-the-middle attacks. The attacker can manipulate the shared secret between FA and FC and then decrypt the ciphertext message transmitted between FA and FC, while the user is unaware of it. It is necessary to add the verification of the validity of FA and FC in CTAP2, and confirm that the FA and FC in the CTAP2 session are the same FA and FC used in authenticator registration or authentication subsequently.

Authenticating FC at RP. We suggest adding an authentication mechanism for FC. In particular, for some services with high security requirements, such as financial transactions, it is necessary to enforce the authentication of FC. The authenticated channel between FC and RP is usually established by TLS. However, client-side authentication is only optional in TLS. As there is no attestation or authentication mechanism of FC involved in FIDO2, there may be malicious FCs participating in the communication. Some security properties cannot hold if channel CA and CR are compromised.

Protecting User's PII. We suggest that some concealment mechanism should be applied to $CNTR$ and Tr before sending them on the channel. Based on the existing protocol process, with the encapsulation mechanism of Elliptic Curve Integrated Encryption Scheme (ECIES) [33] used to improve the privacy of 5G AKA [36], $CNTR$ and Tr be encrypted before sending on the channel. RP generates an ephemeral ECC private-public key pair (r, R) for each session, such that $R = rG$, and adds the public portion R to the registration or authentication request. Then RP generate a symmetric session key $k_s = KDF(r, PK)$, $PK = pk_{AT}$ in authenticator registration and $PK = pk_{Cre}$ in authentication. After receiving the request, FA can derive the corresponding session key $k_a = KDF(R, SK)$, $SK = sk_{AT}$ in authenticator registration and $SK = sk_{Cre}$ in authentication. Both parties can use the symmetric keys k_s and k_a for concealment and de-concealment. The FC between FA and RP has no access to the private key, r, sk_{AT}, or sk_{Cre}, and cannot derive correct k_s and k_a. Therefore, the attacker cannot intercept $CNTR$ and Tr by simply compromising the FC.

6   Related Work

Both manual analysis [9,25,27,28,31] and formal methods [12,26,32] have been applied to verify the security of FIDO protocols. Feng et al. provided a faithful formal model of the UAF protocol considering the use case with different authenticator types and various optional steps and their analysis covers most of the security properties in UAF specifications. Their verification results confirmed previously found vulnerabilities and disclosed new attacks which can be exploited in real-world apps [12]. Pereira et al. formally modeled U2F but their oversimplified threat model only considered the option of checking *AppID*, which failed to find out more underlying vulnerabilities [32]. Jacomme et al. defined a fine-grained threat model considering different scenarios with the combinations of malware, phishing, and TLS fingerprint spoofing in U2F but they mainly focused on the authentication goals, ignoring the confidentiality properties in U2F. They did a simple verification of unlinkability between two accounts on two different authenticators and the two accounts on the same authenticator, which is different from the unlinkability specified in the standard. And they did not verify the unlinkability in the registration phase. [26].

There have been several efforts to formally verify FIDO2. Guirat et al. focused on formally analyzing WebAuth. They only presented the verification results of privacy properties and lacked the description and verification of confidentiality and authentication properties [23]. Barbosa et al. attempted to formally analyze FIDO2 in computational model and conducted a modular analysis of CTAP2 and WebAuthn separately. However, they did not consider the optional steps in FIDO2, including using different types of authenticators, choosing different CTAP2 options, and different transaction authorization modes, nor does it analyze the unlinkability properties in the specifications [3]. Different from the previous work, we provide a formal model of FIDO2 that considers CTAP2 and WebAuthn as a whole and covers scenarios with different types of authenticators and transaction authorization modes. We formally describe all the security goals mentioned in the FIDO2 specifications, including confidentiality, authentication, and privacy properties, and analyze these goals in all the above scenarios.

7   Conclusion

In this paper, we formally analyze FIDO2, the latest member of the FIDO protocol suite. We provide a detailed analysis of the specifications to formally interpret the security assumptions and goals and offer a faithful formal model of FIDO2. Our model is substantially more detailed than those of previous work, as the model views CTAP2 and WebAuthn as a whole and can cover the scenarios using different types of authenticators in different authentication modes. We use the ProVerif tool to automate the analysis of FIDO2 in symbolic model and identified the minimal assumptions required for each property. Our analysis in ProVerif shows that FIDO2 still fails to achieve the strong authentication property in some cases and the attacks previously discovered in UAF still exist in FIDO2. We also present several concrete recommendations to fix the issues in FIDO2. In future work, we plan to make improvements to the issues found in the FIDO protocol suits to defend against the attacks found in this paper and to formally verify the improved version of the protocol.

Acknowledgements. The research of Beijing University and Posts and Telecommunications was supported by the Joint funds for Regional Innovation and Development of the National Natural Science Foundation of China (No. U21A20449) and the National Natural Science Foundation of China (Grant No. 61941105).

References

1. Armando, A., et al.: The AVISPA tool for the automated validation of internet security protocols and applications. In: Etessami, K., Rajamani, S.K. (eds.) CAV 2005. LNCS, vol. 3576, pp. 281–285. Springer, Heidelberg (2005). https://doi.org/10.1007/11513988_27
2. Armando, A., Carbone, R., Compagna, L.: SATMC: a sat-based model checker for security-critical systems. In: Ábrahám, E., Havelund, K. (eds.) TACAS 2014. LNCS, vol. 8413, pp. 31–45. Springer, Heidelberg (2014). https://doi.org/10.1007/978-3-642-54862-8_3
3. Barbosa, M., Boldyreva, A., Chen, S., Warinschi, B.: Provable security analysis of FIDO2. In: Malkin, T., Peikert, C. (eds.) CRYPTO 2021. LNCS, vol. 12827, pp. 125–156. Springer, Cham (2021). https://doi.org/10.1007/978-3-030-84252-9_5
4. Basin, D., Cremers, C.: Know your enemy: compromising adversaries in protocol analysis. ACM Trans. Inf. Syst. Secur. (TISSEC) **17**(2), 1–31 (2014)

5. Basin, D., Mödersheim, S., Viganò, L.: OFMC: a symbolic model checker for security protocols. Int. J. Inf. Secur. **4**(3), 181–208 (2004). https://doi.org/10.1007/s10207-004-0055-7
6. Bhargavan, K., Blanchet, B., Kobeissi, N.: Verified models and reference implementations for the TLS 1.3 standard candidate. In: IEEE Symposium on Security and Privacy (S&P), pp. 483–502 (2017)
7. Blanchet, B.: Modeling and verifying security protocols with the applied pi calculus and ProVerif. Found. Trends Priv. Secur. **1**(1–2), 1–135 (2016)
8. Blanchet, B.: Symbolic and computational mechanized verification of the ARINC823 avionic protocols. In: IEEE Computer Security Foundations Symposium (CSF), pp. 68–82 (2017)
9. Chang, D., Mishra, S., Sanadhya, S.K., Singh, A.P.: On making U2F protocol leakage-resilient via re-keying. IACR Cryptol. ePrint Arch. **2017**, 721 (2017)
10. Cheval, V., Kremer, S., Rakotonirina, I.: DEEPSEC: deciding equivalence properties in security protocols theory and practice. In: IEEE Symposium on Security and Privacy (S&P), pp. 529–546 (2018)
11. Cremers, C.J.: Unbounded verification, falsification, and characterization of security protocols by pattern refinement. In: ACM Conference on Computer And Communications Security (CCS), pp. 119–128 (2008)
12. Feng, H., Li, H., Pan, X., Zhao, Z., Cactilab, T.: A formal analysis of the FIDO UAF protocol. In: Network and Distributed Systems Security Symposium (NDSS), pp. 1–15 (2021)
13. FIDO Alliance: Universal 2nd factor U2F overview (2017). https://fidoalliance.org/specs/fido-u2f-v1.2-ps-20170411/fido-u2f-overview-v1.2-ps-20170411.html
14. FIDO Alliance: CNET: password-free web security is coming to Chrome, Firefox, Edge (2018). https://fidoalliance.org/cnet-password-free-web-security-is-coming-to-chrome-firefox-edge/
15. FIDO Alliance: FIDO security reference 2018). https://fidoalliance.org/specs/fido-v2.0-id-20180227/fido-security-ref-v2.0-id-20180227.html
16. FIDO Alliance: Client to authenticator protocol (CTAP) - proposed standard (2019). https://fidoalliance.org/specs/fido-v2.0-ps-20190130/fido-client-to-authenticator-protocol-v2.0-ps-20190130.html
17. FIDO Alliance: Microsoft achieves FIDO2 certification for Windows Hello (2019). https://fidoalliance.org/microsoft-achieves-fido2-certification-for-windows-hello
18. FIDO Alliance: News: your Google Android 7+ phone is now a FIDO2 security key (2019). https://fidoalliance.org/news-your-google-android-7-phone-is-now-a-fido2-security-key
19. FIDO Alliance: Expanded support for FIDO authentication in iOS and MacOS (Jul 2020), https://fidoalliance.org/expanded-support-for-fido-authentication-in-ios-and-macos
20. FIDO Alliance: FIDO UAF protocol specification (2020). https://fidoalliance.org/specs/fido-uaf-v1.2-ps-20201020/fido-uaf-protocol-v1.2-ps-20201020.html
21. Girol, G., Hirschi, L., Sasse, R., Jackson, D., Cremers, C., Basin, D.: A spectral analysis of noise: a comprehensive, automated, formal analysis of Diffie-Hellman protocols. In: USENIX Security Symposium (2020)
22. Gordon, A.D., Jeffrey, A.: Types and effects for asymmetric cryptographic protocols. J. Comput Secur. (JCS) **12**(3–4), 435–483 (2004)
23. Guirat, I.B., Halpin, H.: Formal verification of the W3C web authentication protocol. In: Annual Symposium and Bootcamp on Hot Topics in the Science of Security (HoTSoS), pp. 1–10 (2018)

24. Hirschi, L., Cremers, C.: Improving automated symbolic analysis of ballot secrecy for e-voting protocols: A method based on sufficient conditions. In: IEEE European Symposium on Security and Privacy (EuroS&P), pp. 635–650 (2019)
25. Hu, K., Zhang, Z.: Security analysis of an attractive online authentication standard: FIDO UAF protocol. Chin. Commun. **13**(12), 189–198 (2016)
26. Jacomme, C., Kremer, S.: An extensive formal analysis of multi-factor authentication protocols. ACM Trans. Priv. Secur. (TOPS) **24**(2), 1–34 (2021)
27. Leoutsarakos, N.: What's wrong with FIDO? https://zeropasswords.com/pdfs/WHATisWRONG_FIDO.pdf (2011)
28. Loutfi, I., Jøsang, A.: FIDO trust requirements. In: Buchegger, S., Dam, M. (eds.) Secure IT Systems. LNCS, vol 9417, pp. 139–155. Springer, Cham (2015). https://doi.org/10.1007/978-3-319-26502-5_10
29. Lowe, G.: Breaking and fixing the Needham-Schroeder public-key protocol using FDR. In: Margaria, T., Steffen, B. (eds.) TACAS 1996. LNCS, vol. 1055, pp. 147–166. Springer, Heidelberg (1996). https://doi.org/10.1007/3-540-61042-1_43
30. Meier, S., Schmidt, B., Cremers, C., Basin, D.: The TAMARIN prover for the symbolic analysis of security protocols. In: Sharygina, N., Veith, H. (eds.) CAV 2013. LNCS, vol. 8044, pp. 696–701. Springer, Heidelberg (2013). https://doi.org/10.1007/978-3-642-39799-8_48
31. Panos, C., Malliaros, S., Ntantogian, C., Panou, A., Xenakis, C.: A security evaluation of Fido's uaf protocol in mobile and embedded devices. In: Piva, A., Tinnirello, I., Morosi, S. (eds.) TIWDC 2017. CCIS, vol. 766, pp. 127–142. Springer, Cham (2017). https://doi.org/10.1007/978-3-319-67639-5_11
32. Pereira, O., Rochet, F., Wiedling, C.: Formal analysis of the FIDO 1.x protocol. In: Imine, A., Fernandez, J.M., Marion, J.-Y., Logrippo, L., Garcia-Alfaro, J. (eds.) FPS 2017. LNCS, vol. 10723, pp. 68–82. Springer, Cham (2018). https://doi.org/10.1007/978-3-319-75650-9_5
33. Standards for Efficient Cryptography Group: SEC 1: Elliptic curve cryptography version 2.0, standards for efficient cryptography (2009). https://www.secg.org/sec1-v2.pdf
34. Turuani, M.: The CL-Atse protocol analyser. In: International Conference on Rewriting Techniques and Applications (RTA). pp. 277–286. Springer (2006)
35. W3C: Web authentication: An API for accessing public key credentials level 2 (2021). https://www.w3.org/TR/webauthn-2/
36. Wang, Y., Zhang, Z., Xie, Y.: Privacy-preserving and standard-compatible AKA protocol for 5G. In: USENIX Security Symposium, pp. 3595–3612 (2021)

A Composable Security Treatment of ECVRF and Batch Verifications

Christian Badertscher[1]([✉]) [iD], Peter Gaži[2], Iñigo Querejeta-Azurmendi[3], and Alexander Russell[4,5]

[1] Input Output, Zurich, Switzerland
christian.badertscher@iohk.io
[2] Input Output, Bratislava, Slovakia
peter.gazi@iohk.io
[3] Input Output, London, UK
querejeta.azurmendi@iohk.io
[4] Input Output, New Jersey, USA
alexander.russell@iohk.io
[5] University of Connecticut, Mansfield, USA

Abstract. Verifiable random functions (VRF, Micali *et al.*, FOCS'99) allow a key-pair holder to verifiably evaluate a pseudorandom function under that particular key pair. These primitives enable fair and verifiable pseudorandom lotteries, essential in proof-of-stake blockchains such as Algorand and Cardano, and are being used to secure billions of dollars of capital. As a result, there is an ongoing IRTF effort to standardize VRFs, with a proposed ECVRF based on elliptic-curve cryptography appearing as the most promising candidate.

In this paper, towards understanding the general security of VRFs and in particular the ECVRF construction, we provide an ideal functionality in the Universal Composability (UC) framework (Canetti, FOCS'01) that captures VRF security, and show that ECVRF UC-realizes it.

Additionally, we study batch verification in the context of VRFs. We provide a UC-functionality capturing a VRF with batch-verification capability, and propose modifications to ECVRF that allow for this feature. We again prove that our proposal UC-realizes the desired functionality. Finally, we provide a performance analysis showing that verification can yield a factor-two speedup for batches with 1024 proofs, at the cost of increasing the proof size from 80 to 128 bytes.

1 Introduction

A Verifiable Random Function (VRF, [19]) is a pseudo-random function whose correct evaluation can be verified. It can be seen as a hash function that is keyed by a public-private key pair: the private key is necessary to evaluate the function and produce a proof of a correct evaluation, while the public key can be used to verify such proofs. VRFs were originally considered as tools for mitigation of offline dictionary attacks on hash-based data structures; more recently they have found applications in the design of verifiable lotteries. In particular, VRFs

V. Atluri et al. (Eds.): ESORICS 2022, LNCS 13556, pp. 22–41, 2022.
https://doi.org/10.1007/978-3-031-17143-7_2

are fundamental primitives to several proof-of-stake ledger consensus protocols, such as those underlying the blockchains Algorand [14] and Cardano [12]. They allow for a pseudo-random selection of block leaders in the setting with adaptive corruption, an important security feature of these protocols.

There is an ongoing effort to standardize this primitive via an IRTF draft [15] that describes the desirable properties of VRFs and proposes (as of August '22) two concrete constructions. One of these constructions is based on RSA, while the other one relies on elliptic-curve cryptography (ECC); this latter construction is referred to as ECVRF. A clear advantage of ECVRF over the RSA-based alternative is the considerable improvement in key sizes it provides (for the same security level). Indeed, both Algorand and Cardano employ ECVRF, as do most of the existing implementations listed in the draft.

One of the VRF security properties articulated in the IRTF draft is that of *random-oracle-like unpredictability*. Roughly speaking, it requires that if the VRF input has sufficient entropy (i.e., cannot be predicted), then the output is indistinguishable from uniformly random. As the draft observes, this property is essential for the security of the leader-election mechanisms in PoS blockchains. The property is not formally defined in the draft, though a definition in the form of an ideal functionality in the Universal Composability (UC) framework [10] is given in [12]. The IRTF draft states that this strong notion is "believed" to be satisfied by the ECVRF construction; however, to the best of our knowledge, no formal proof of this claim exists to date. This state of affairs is clearly unsatisfactory: UC security is a desirable notion of security as it guarantees that the proven security provisions (in the sense of realizing an ideal functionality) are retained, by virtue of the composition theorem, when employing the scheme in higher-level applications. This is especially relevant for VRFs as a low-level primitive used in many protocols, including those mentioned above.

Returning to the ECVRF construction, another important benefit it provides is structural: it is essentially a Fiat-Shamir transformed [13] Σ-protocol [11] and therefore—at least in principle—suitable for batch verification. The idea for batch verification first appears in foundational work by Naccache et al. [20] and consists of verifying a batch of linear equations by verifying a random linear combination of these. Bernstein et al. [7] exploited this technique with the state-of-the-art algorithms in multi-scalar multiplication, achieving a factor-two improvement in signature verification using batches of 64 signatures. Such an improvement in verification times is of direct relevance for blockchains, as the routine task of joining the protocol—which requires synchronizing with the current ledger—involves verification of many blocks and their VRF proofs. Indeed, typical synchronization conventions demand verification of the entire existing blockchain. We note in passing that the possibility of batch verifications for Schnorr signatures [24] (derived from another type of Σ-protocol) is a significant competitive advantage over ECDSA, and was one of the reasons for Bitcoin [21] to switch to that type of signature [25]. The possibility of batch verification for ECVRF has already appeared in the IRTF draft mailing list [23]. However, a concrete proposal for the design, along with a formal security notion and a corresponding security proof, has not been given.

Our Contributions. In this work we close both of these gaps.

1. We propose a cleaner formalization of the VRF functionality in the UC framework, building on the original proposal from [12] (later revised in [3] to remove some issues in the original formulation).
2. We show that ECVRF UC-realizes this functionality in the random-oracle model (ROM). The proof of this claim is surprisingly involved, requiring a rather complex simulation. The proof appears in full detail in the full version of this paper [2]. We point out that this is the first comprehensive UC proof for this type of VRF construction and further shows that the simulation can be done in a *responsive* manner [8], a desirable property that simplifies the analysis of higher-level protocols using the VRF functionality (e.g., [3]). In particular, the simulation strategy described in [12] is not applicable (cf. related work below) and [12] does not provide a proof for the revised functionality.
3. We introduce a UC formalization for a VRF providing batch verification via a natural extension of the above VRF functionality.
4. We define a concrete instantiation of batch verification for the ECVRF construction and prove that it UC-realizes the above ideal functionality of a VRF with batch verification. Despite our focus on VRFs, we believe that our formalization would naturally carry over to other widely used Fiat-Shamir transformed Σ-protocols, such as Schnorr signatures or Ed25519.
5. To evaluate the efficiency improvements of the batch-compatible version, we compare the efficiency of the current draft version versus the batch-compatible primitive presented in this work. Roughly speaking, we observe that the batch compatible primitive can achieve a factor-two efficiency gain with batches of size 1024 in exchange for a trade-off with respect to its size, growing from 80 bytes to 128 bytes.
6. We provide an additional efficiency improvement, namely a simple range-extension that can be implemented "on the fly" in ECVRF, which can help higher-level protocols to reduce the number of VRF evaluations and proof verification at the cost of more evaluations of the hash function.

Related Work. The VRF notion was introduced by Micali *et al.* [19]. A stronger notion of VRF with security in the natural setting with malicious key generation was presented as a UC functionality by David *et al.* [12]. A particular instantiation, based on 2HashDH [16], was claimed to satisfy this stronger notion, but the provided simulation argument only holds for a revised version of the functionality which is first described in [3]. Jarecki *et al.* [16] provide a UC functionality of a slightly different notion, which is that of a Verifiable *Oblivious* Pseudo Random Function where two parties need to input some secret information in order to compute the random output.

The first systematic treatment of batch verification for modular exponentiation was presented by Bellare *et al.* [4], and adapted to digital signatures by Camenisch *et al.* [9]. The batch verification technique that we adopt was initially developed by Naccache et al. [20], and used by Bernstein *et al.* [7] and Wuille *et al.* [25]. Exploiting the batching technique in the context of VRFs was informally discussed in the IRTF group and mailing list [15,23].

2   Preliminaries

UC Security. We give a very brief overview of the UC security framework necessary to understand the rest of this work. For details we refer to [10]. In this framework a protocol execution (the so-called "real-world process") is represented by a group of interactive Turing machine instances (ITIs) running a protocol π, forming a protocol session. The environment $\mathcal{Z}$ orchestrates the inputs and receives the outputs of these machines. Additionally, an adversary is part of the execution and can corrupt parties and thereby take control of them (we assume throughout this work the standard UC adaptive corruption model defined in [10]). To capture security guarantees, UC defines a corresponding ideal process which is formulated w.r.t. an ideal functionality $\mathcal{F}$. In the ideal process, the environment $\mathcal{Z}$ interacts with the ideal-world adversary (called simulator) $\mathcal{S}$ and with functionality $\mathcal{F}$ (or more precisely, with protocol machines that simply relay all inputs and outputs to and from $\mathcal{F}$, respectively). A protocol π UC-realizes $\mathcal{F}$ if for any (efficient) adversary there exists an (efficient) simulator $\mathcal{S}$ such that for any (efficient) environment $\mathcal{Z}$ the real and ideal processes are indistinguishable. This means that the real protocol achieves the desired specification $\mathcal{F}$.

VRF Syntax. We denote by κ the security parameter. The domain of the VRF is denoted by $\mathcal{X}$ and its finite range is denoted by $\mathcal{Y}$ and typically represented by $\mathcal{Y} = \{0,1\}^{\ell_{\mathsf{VRF}}(\kappa)}$, where $\ell_{\mathsf{VRF}}(.)$ is a function of the security parameter. For notational simplicity we often drop the explicit dependence on κ.

Definition 1 (VRF Syntax). *A verifiable random function (VRF) consists of a triple of PPT algorithms* VRF := (Gen, Eval, Vfy):

- *The probabilistic algorithm* $(sk, vk) \leftarrow \mathsf{Gen}(1^\kappa)$ *takes as input the security parameter* κ *in unary encoding and outputs a key pair, where* sk *is the secret key and* vk *is the (public) verification key.*
- *The probabilistic algorithm* $(Y, \pi) \leftarrow \mathsf{Eval}(sk, X)$ *takes as input a secret key* sk *and* $X \in \mathcal{X}$ *and outputs a function value* $Y \in \mathcal{Y}$ *and a proof* π.
- *The (possibly probabilistic but usually deterministic) algorithm* $b \leftarrow \mathsf{Vfy}(vk, X, Y, \pi)$ *takes as input a verification key* vk, *input value* $X \in \mathcal{X}$, *output value* $Y \in \mathcal{Y}$, *as well as a proof* π, *and returns a bit* b. *(If* $X \notin \mathcal{X}$ *or* $Y \notin \mathcal{Y}$, *we assume that* b *is* 0 *by default.)*

3   UC Security of Verifiable Random Functions

Modeling VRFs as a UC Protocol. Any verifiable random function VRF can be cast as a simple protocol π_{VRF} in the UC framework [10] as follows: Each party U_i in session *sid* acts as follows: on its first input of the form (KeyGen, *sid*), run $(sk, vk) \leftarrow \mathsf{VRF.Gen}(1^\kappa)$, output (VerificationKey, *sid*, vk) and internally store sk; any further key generation requests are ignored. On input (EvalProve, *sid*, m) for an input $m \in \mathcal{X}$ (and if a key has been generated before) evaluate $(Y, \pi) \leftarrow \mathsf{VRF.Eval}(sk, m)$ and output (Evaluated, *sid*, Y, π). (If no key has been generated

---

Ideal Functionality $\mathcal{F}_{\text{VRF}}^{\mathcal{X},\ell_{\text{VRF}}}$

The functionality interacts with parties denoted by $\mathcal{P} = \{U_1, \ldots, U_{|\mathcal{P}|}\}$ as well as the adversary/simulator $\mathcal{S}$. It maintains tables $T[\cdot, \cdot]$ that are initially empty (denoted by symbol $\perp$). The tables are initialized on-the-fly. The functionality maintains a set S_{pk} to keep track of registered keys, and S_{eval} to keep track of all known VRF evaluations.

- **Key Generation.** Upon receiving a message (KeyGen, sid) from U_i s.t. $(U_i, \cdot) \notin S_{pk}$, hand (KeyGen, sid, U_i) to $\mathcal{S}$ (ignore the request if $(U_i, \cdot) \in S_{pk}$). Upon receiving (VerificationKey, sid, U_i, v) from $\mathcal{S}$:
  1. If U_i is corrupted, ignore the request.
  2. If $(U_i, \cdot) \notin S_{pk}$ and $\forall (\cdot, v') \in S_{pk} : v \neq v'$, set $S_{pk} \leftarrow S_{pk} \cup \{(U_i, v)\}$ and return (VerificationKey, sid, v) to U_i.
  3. Else, ignore the request.
- **Malicious Key Generation.** Upon receiving a message (KeyGen, sid, v) from $\mathcal{S}$, do the following: if $\forall (\cdot, v') \in S_{pk} : v \neq v'$, set $S_{pk} \leftarrow S_{pk} \cup \{(\mathcal{S}, v)\}$. Return the activation to $\mathcal{S}$.
- **VRF Evaluation and Proof.** Upon receiving a message (EvalProve, sid, m) from U_i with $m \in \mathcal{X}$, verify that some $(U_i, v) \in S_{pk}$ is recorded. If such an entry is not stored or $m \notin \mathcal{X}$, then ignore the request. Else, send (EvalProve, sid, U_i, m) to $\mathcal{S}$ and upon receiving (EvalProve, sid, U_i, m, π) from $\mathcal{S}$, do the following:
  1. Ignore the request if the proof is not unique, i.e., if $\exists T[v', m'] = (y', S')$ such that $\pi \in S' \wedge ((v' \neq v) \vee (m' \neq m))$.
  2. If $T[v, m] = \perp$, assign $y \xleftarrow{\$} \{0,1\}^{\ell_{\text{VRF}}}$ and set $T[v, m] \leftarrow \{y, \{\pi\}\}$.
  3. If $T[v, m] = (y, S) \neq \perp$, set $T[v, m] \leftarrow \{y, S \cup \{\pi\}\}$.
  4. Set $S_{\text{eval}} \leftarrow S_{\text{eval}} \cup \{(v, m, y)\}$ and output (Evaluated, sid, m, y, π) to U_i.
- **Malicious VRF Evaluation.** Upon receiving a message (Eval, sid, v, m), $m \in \mathcal{X}$, from $\mathcal{S}$ (if $m \notin \mathcal{X}$ the request is ignored), do the following:
  Case 1: $\exists (U_i, v) \in S_{pk}$ where U_i is not corrupted: if $T[v, m] = (y, S)$ for $S \neq \emptyset$, return (Evaluated, sid, y) to $\mathcal{S}$. Otherwise, ignore the request.
  Case 2: $(\mathcal{S}, v) \in S_{pk}$ or $\exists (U_i, v) \in S_{pk}$, U_i corrupted: if $T[v, m] = \perp$, first choose $y \xleftarrow{\$} \{0,1\}^{\ell_{\text{VRF}}}$ and set $T[v, m] \leftarrow (y, \emptyset)$. Return (Evaluated, sid, y) to $\mathcal{S}$.
  Else: Ignore the request.
- **Verification.** Upon receiving a message (Verify, sid, m, y, π, v') from any ITI M, send (Verify, $sid, m, y, \pi, v', S_{\text{eval}}$) to $\mathcal{S}$. Upon receiving (Verified, sid, m, y, π, v', ϕ) from $\mathcal{S}$ do:
  Case 1: $v' = v$ for some $(\cdot, v) \in S_{pk}$ s.t. $T(v, m) = (y, S)$ for some set S.
    1. If $\pi \in S$, then set $f \leftarrow 1$.
    2. Else, if $\phi = 1$ and $\forall T[\tilde{v}, \tilde{m}] = (y', S') : \pi \notin S'$, then set $T[v, m] = (y, S \cup \{\pi\})$ and $f \leftarrow 1$.
    3. Else, set $f \leftarrow 0$.
  Else: Set $f \leftarrow 0$.
  Provide the output (Verified, sid, v', m, y, π, f) to the caller M.
- **Adversarial Leakage [New compared to [12, 3]].** On input (PastEvaluations, sid) from $\mathcal{S}$, return S_{eval} to $\mathcal{S}$.

Fig. 1. The VRF functionality.

yet, evaluation queries are ignored.) On input (Verify, sid, m, y, π, v'), the party evaluates $b \leftarrow$ VRF.Vfy(v', m, y, π) and finally returns (Verified, sid, v', m, y, π, b).

Ideal Functionality $\mathcal{F}_{\mathsf{VRF}}^{\mathcal{X}, \ell_{\mathsf{VRF}}}$. In Fig. 1 we present the functionality $\mathcal{F}_{\mathsf{VRF}}^{\mathcal{X}, \ell_{\mathsf{VRF}}}$ that captures the desired properties of a VRF. The functionality provides interfaces for key generation, evaluation and verification, as well as separate adversarial interfaces for malicious key generation, evaluation, and leakage. The function table corresponding to each public key is a truly random function (and thus also guarantees a unique association of the key-value pair to output Y) even for adversarially generated keys. Furthermore, no incorrect association can be ever verified and every completed honest evaluation can be later verified correctly.

The functionality is based on [3,12], but contains several modifications. First, verification is now more in line with typical UC formulations for (signature) verification, where the adversary is given some limited influence (in prior versions, the adversary had to inject proofs in between verification request and response to accomplish the same thing). Second, the uniqueness notion for proofs has been correctly adjusted to catch the corner case that schemes might choose to de-randomize the prover (akin signatures) which is a crucial point later when we look at ECVRF. The remaining changes are merely syntactical compared to [3].

Definition 2 (UC security of a VRF). *A verifiable random function* VRF *with input domain* $\mathcal{X}$ *and range* $\mathcal{Y} = \{0,1\}^{\ell_{\mathsf{VRF}}}$ *is called UC-secure if* π_{VRF} *UC-realizes* $\mathcal{F}_{\mathsf{VRF}}^{\mathcal{X}, \ell_{\mathsf{VRF}}}$ *specified in Fig. 1.*

Random Oracles in UC. When working in the random-oracle model, the UC protocol above is changed as follows: whenever VRF prescribes a call to a particular hash function to hash some value x, this is replaced by a call of the form (EVAL, sid, x) to an instance of a so-called random oracle functionality, which internally implements an ideal random function $\{0,1\}^* \rightarrow \mathcal{Y}'$ and returns the corresponding function value back to the caller. We will often use the notation $\mathsf{H}(x)$ in the specifications to refer to a general hash function with the understanding that this call will be treated as a random oracle call in the security proof.

Hash : $\{0,1\}^* \rightarrow \{0,1\}^{\ell(\kappa)}$ Expand_key : $\{0,1\}^{2\kappa} \rightarrow \{0,1\}^{2\kappa} \times \{0,1\}^{2\kappa}$

Encode_to_curve : $\{0,1\}^* \rightarrow \mathbb{G}$ Nonce_generation : $\{0,1\}^{2\kappa} \times \mathbb{E} \rightarrow \mathbb{Z}_q$

Compute_scalar : $\{0,1\}^{2\kappa} \rightarrow S$ Hash_pts : $\mathbb{E} \times \mathbb{E} \times \mathbb{E} \times \mathbb{E} \times \mathbb{E} \rightarrow \{0,1\}^\kappa$

Fig. 2. Domain of the helper functions for ECVRF (see [2] for more details). The functions Hash and Encode_to_curve are modeled as random oracles in the security argument and Compute_scalar is an encoding that preserves the min-entropy of its input. The remaining helper functions are implemented based on Hash (using domain-separation), where Expand_key is an adaptively secure pseudo-random generator, Nonce_generation is an adaptively secure pseudo-random function, and Hash_pts is a random oracle.

Gen(1^κ):

1. $sk \xleftarrow{\$} \{0,1\}^{2\kappa}$.
2. $(sk_0, sk_1) \leftarrow$ Expand_key(sk).
3. $x \leftarrow$ Compute_scalar(sk_0).
4. $vk \leftarrow x * B$.
5. Return (sk, vk).

Eval(sk, X):

1. $\pi \leftarrow$ Prove(sk, X).
2. $Y \leftarrow$ Compute(π).
3. Return (Y, π).

Prove(sk, X):

1. Derive vk, x from sk as in Gen(1^κ).
2. $H \leftarrow$ Encode_to_curve(E2C$_s \, || \, X$).
3. $\Gamma \leftarrow x * H$.
4. $k \leftarrow$ Nonce_generation(sk, H).
5. $c \leftarrow$ Hash_pts($vk, H, \Gamma, k * B, k * H$).
6. $s \leftarrow (k + c \cdot x) \mod q$.
7. $\pi \leftarrow (\Gamma, c, s)$.
8. Return π.

Compute($\pi = \Gamma \, || \, ...$): *Precondition.* $\Gamma \in \mathbb{E}^a$.

1. Return   Hash(suite_s $|| \, DS_3 \, ||$ (cf $*$ Γ) $|| \,$DS$_0$), where cf is the co-factor (for curve25519, cf = 8).

Vfy(vk, X, Y, π):

1. If $vk \notin \mathbb{E}$ or cf $* \, vk = O$, return 0.[b]
2. Parse $(\Gamma, c, s) \leftarrow \pi$. If $\Gamma \notin \mathbb{E}$ return 0. Interpret the κ bits of c and the 2κ bits of s as little-endian integers. If $s \geq q$, return 0.
3. $H \leftarrow$ Encode_to_curve(E2C$_s \, || \, X$).
4. $U \leftarrow s * B - c * vk$.
5. $V \leftarrow s * H - c * \Gamma$.
6. $c' \leftarrow$ Hash_pts(vk, H, Γ, U, V).
7. If $c = c'$ return $b := (Y = $ Compute(π)); otherwise return 0.

---

[a] Otherwise an implementation could return some ERR $\notin \mathcal{Y}$. For the analysis this is not needed as the protocol ensures the precondition and the adversary is free to invoke the hash-function at will.

[b] This check excludes low-order elements, i.e., $P \in \mathbb{E}$, $ord(P) < q$.

Fig. 3. Description of ECVRF, where B denotes the generator of the subgroup $\mathbb{G}$ of $\mathbb{E}$. Note that the salt value E2C$_s$ leaves room for more general use cases. We consider the case E2C$_s = vk$ in the analysis of the standard and its extensions.

4 The ECVRF Standard

This section recalls the elliptic-curve based schemes described in the IRTF draft [15] and focuses on the cipher suites suite_s $\in \{0x03, 0x04\}$ for the sake of concreteness.

Notation. We denote by $\mathbb{E}(\mathbb{F}_p)$ the finite abelian group based on an elliptic curve over a finite prime-order field $\mathbb{F}_p$ (note that we simplify the notation and drop the explicit dependency on $\mathbb{F}_p$ and security parameter κ). Most importantly, we assume the order of the group $\mathbb{E}$ to be of the form cf $\cdot q$ for some small *cofactor* cf and large prime number q, and that the (hence) unique subgroup $\mathbb{G}$ of order q is generated by a known base point B, i.e., $\mathbb{G} = \langle B \rangle$ (q is represented by $\approx 2\kappa$ bits) in which the computational Diffie-Hellman (CDH) problem is believed to be hard. Group operations are written in additive notation, scalar multiplication for points $P \in \mathbb{E}$ is denoted by $m * P = \underbrace{P + \cdots + P}_{m}$, and the neutral element by

$O = 0 * P$. We use $a \xleftarrow{\$} S$ to denote that a is selected uniformly at random from a set S. When working with binary arrays, $a \in \{0,1\}^*$, we denote by $a[X..Y]$ the slice of a from position X till position $Y - 1$. Moreover, we denote by $a[..X]$ and $a[X..]$ the slice from position 0 till $X - 1$ and from X till the end, respectively. As usual, the operator $\|$ denotes concatenation of strings; thus, for $A = 0 \| 1$ we have $A[..1] = 0$ and $A[1..] = 1$.

The standard makes use of helper functions, all of which are defined and introduced in [15]. For sake of simplicity we only state the specification of the security-relevant helper functions. The functions are briefly described in Fig. 2. As domain separators we use values between 0 and 5 in hexadecimal representation. In particular, we use $\mathsf{DS}_i \leftarrow 0x0i$ for $i \in [0,5]$. The standard also uses $\mathtt{encode\_to\_curve\_salt}$ to denote the salt used for the $\mathtt{Encode\_to\_curve}$ function, which we denote by $\mathsf{E2C}_s$. Note that all EC-ciphersuites define the salt as the prover's public key which is the case we consider and analyze in this work. To give a concrete example, the deployed VRF construction in Cardano is instantiated with $\kappa = 128$ and elliptic curve edwards25519 which has cofactor 8. The prime order q is represented by 32 octets, or more precisely 253 bits, and the hash function is $\mathtt{SHA512} : \{0,1\}^* \rightarrow \{0,1\}^{512}$. Conveniently, we choose $\ell(\kappa) = 4\kappa$. The function $\mathtt{Hash\_pts}$ defines the associated *challenge space*, thus being the set $\mathcal{C} := \{0,1\}^\kappa$ interpreted as integers. For the function $\mathtt{Compute\_scalar}(sk_0)$, the string is first pruned: the lowest three bits of the first octet are cleared, the highest bit of the last octet is cleared, and the second highest bit of the last octet is set. This buffer is interpreted as a little-endian integer, forming the secret scalar x, which results in an output domain containing 2^{251} different elements.

The VRF Algorithms. The formal definition of a VRF in Sect. 3 denotes by Eval the function that computes the output of the VRF evaluation together with its proof. In this section the two actions are treated separately to follow the approach taken by the standard, and we define the functions Prove and Compute to represent the proof generation and the output computation, respectively. The algorithms from the standard are given in Fig. 3.

5   ECVRF$_{bc}$: Batch Verification for ECVRF

In the interest of performance, we now study the possibility of batch-verifying the proofs generated by ECVRF. To this end, we introduce slight modifications that allow for an efficient batch-verification algorithm. Next, we prove that batch-verification does not affect the security properties of individual proofs.

We divide the exposition of the changes in two steps. First, in Sect. 5.1 we present the changes on the protocol (involving the prover and the verifier) to make the scheme *batch-compatible*. Second, in Sect. 5.2 we describe the specific computation performed by the verifier to batch several proof verifications.

Intuition. The operations performed in steps 4 and 5 of Vfy appear as good candidates for batching across several proofs. Namely, instead of sequential scalar multiplications, one could perform a single multiscalar multiplication for all proofs that are being verified. However, this trick can only be exploited if steps 4 and 5 are equality checks rather than computations. In ECVRF, the verifier has no knowledge of points U and V, and has to compute them first. We hence modify the scheme so that the prover includes points U and V in the transcript and the verifier can simply check for equality.

5.1   Making the Scheme Batch-Compatible

As discussed, in order to allow batch verification, steps 4 and 5 need to be equality checks. This requires a change in step 7 of Prove and changes in steps 2, 4, 5, and 7 of Vfy. Moreover, the challenge computation needs to be moved from step 6 to the position in between steps 3 and 4 (we call it step 3.5). The modifications result in scheme $\mathsf{ECVRF_{bc}}$, summarized in Fig. 4.

Intuitively, this change has no implications on the security of the scheme, as it is common for (Fiat-Shamir-transformed) Σ-protocols to send the commitment of the randomness (sometimes called the announcement) instead of the challenge.[1] The choice of sending the challenge instead of the two announcements in ECVRF is simply to optimize communication complexity and efficiency.

5.2   Batch-Verification

To see how the changes described above allow for batch verification, first observe how steps 4 and 5 in $\mathsf{ECVRF_{bc}}$ can be combined into a single check: if they validate, then so does the equation

$$O = r * (s * B - c * vk - U) + l * (s * H - c * \Gamma - V)$$

where r, l are scalars chosen by the verifier. The reverse is also true with overwhelming probability if r and l are taken uniformly at random from a set of sufficient size (in particular, we choose the set $\mathcal{C}$ for convenience).

More generally, to verify n different $\mathsf{ECVRF_{bc}}$ proofs, the verifier needs to check whether the equality relations $U_i = s_i * B - c_i * vk_i$ and $V_i = s_i * H_i - c_i * \Gamma_i$ hold for each of the proofs. This can be merged into a single equality check

$$O = r_i * (s_i * B - c_i * vk_i - U_i) + l_i * (s_i * H_i - c_i * \Gamma_i - V_i)$$

for each $i \in [1, n]$ and, moreover, into a single verification

$$O = \sum_{i \in [1,n]} (r_i * (s_i * B - c_i * vk_i - U_i) + l_i * (s_i * H_i - c_i * \Gamma_i - V_i))$$

across all proofs, where r_i and l_i are random scalars. The full protocol to implement batch verification based on the above idea appears in Sect. 6.2. By using the state of the art multi-scalar multiplication algorithms, leveraging this trick provides significant running time improvements, as discussed in Sect. 7.

---

[1] As a matter of fact, ed25519 [7] is also a sigma protocol and encodes the announcement instead of the challenge in the non-interactive variant of this sigma-protocol.

$\underline{\mathsf{Prove}(sk, X)}$ remains unchanged except for step 7, which changes as follows:
    7. Let $\pi \leftarrow (\Gamma, (k * B), (k * H), s)$.
$\underline{\mathsf{Compute}(\pi)}$ remains unchanged.
$\underline{\mathsf{Vfy}(vk, X, Y, \pi)}$ changes as follows:

1. Remains unchanged.
2. Parse π as tuple (Γ, U, V, s). If $\{\Gamma, U, V\} \not\subseteq \mathbb{E}$, return 0. Interpret the 2κ bits of s as a little-endian integer. If $s \geq q$, return 0.

3. Remains unchanged.
3.5. $c \leftarrow \mathtt{Hash\_pts}(vk, H, \Gamma, U, V)$.
4. If $U \neq s * B - c * vk$, return 0.
5. If $V \neq s * H - c * \Gamma$, return 0.
6. [Moved to step 3.5]
7. Return $b := (Y = \mathsf{Compute}(\pi))$.

Fig. 4. Description of modifications in $\mathsf{ECVRF_{bc}}$ compared to ECVRF.

Invalid Batches. Note that if batch verification fails, one would need to break down the batch to determine which proof is invalid. However, in several practical cases (most notably, when validating the state of a blockchain), the verifier is primarily interested in whether the whole batch is valid (so that the respective part of the chain can be adopted); if the batch verification fails this has protocol-level consequences (e.g., disconnecting from the peer providing the invalid batch) that obviate the need for individual identification of the failed verification.

Pseudorandom Coefficients. We describe how the coefficients l_i, r_i can be securely computed in a deterministic manner, a feature that is favorable from a practical perspective. Similarly to the well-known Fiat-Shamir heuristic for Σ-protocols, it is essential that the values cannot be known to the prover when defining the proof string. To this end, we propose to compute the scalars by hashing the contents of the proof itself, the value of H for the corresponding public key, and an index.

Concretely, for a batch proof of proofs $\pi_1, \ldots, \pi_n$, one computes, for $i \in [1, n]$:

1. $\pi_i' \leftarrow H_i \| \pi_i$,
2. $S_T \leftarrow \pi_1' \| \pi_2' \| \ldots \| \pi_n'$,
3. $h_i \leftarrow \mathsf{Hash}(\mathtt{suite\_s} \| \mathsf{DS_4} \| S_T \| i \| \mathsf{DS_0})$,
4. $l_i \leftarrow h_i[..\kappa]$, and $r_i \leftarrow h_i[\kappa..2 \cdot \kappa]$.

The values l_i and r_i are treated as little-endian integers and are thus picked from the domain $\mathcal{C}$ as the challenge defined earlier. As before, the security analysis can treat the invocation as an evaluation of a random oracle obtained using domain separation on Hash (where we follow the usual format).

6 Security Analysis of $\mathsf{ECVRF_{bc}}$ and Batch Verifications

We first analyze the security of the standard without batch verifications in the next section and prove the security including batch verifications afterwards. We refer to the appendix of this work for background on zero-knowledge proofs and homomorphisms which turn out to be a conceptually elegant tool to argue about the security of the scheme.

6.1   Security Analysis of ECVRF$_{bc}$

Recall from Sect. 3 how any VRF can be understood as a UC protocol. We now establish the security of the ECVRF$_{bc}$ protocol without the batching step, but with the (minor) modifications introduced in Sect. 5.1. We work in the random-oracle model; that is, we introduce the two general functions H (abstracting the details of Hash) and H$_{e2c}$ (abstracting the details of Encode_to_curve) which are in the model represented by two instances of the random oracle functionality, which are $\mathcal{F}_{RO}^{\mathcal{Y}}$, for $\mathcal{Y} = \{0,1\}^{\ell_{VRF}}$, and $\mathcal{F}_{RO}^{\mathbb{G}}$, respectively, so that invocations of H and H$_{e2c}$ correspond to invocations of the respective functionalities as explained in Sect. 3. For simplicity and clarity in the UC protocols, we continue to write H(x) (resp. H$_{e2c}(x)$) with the understanding that it stands for a call to an ideal object. Note that the remaining helper functions obtain their claimed security properties based on the assumption on H as is established in the proof.

Theorem 1. *Let $\mathbb{E}$ and its prime-order subgroup $\mathbb{G}$ be defined as in Sect. 4. The protocol π_{ECVRF} UC-realizes $\mathcal{F}_{VRF}^{\mathcal{X},\ell_{VRF}}$, for $\mathcal{X} = \{0,1\}^*$ and $\ell_{VRF}(\kappa) = 4\kappa$, in the random-oracle model and under the assumption that the CDH problem is hard in $\mathbb{G}$.*

Proof Overview. We refer to the full version of this work [2] for the full proof, which is rather involved, and provide here an overview. We must give a simulator such that the real VRF construction (where the above algorithms are executed) is indistinguishable from the ideal world consisting of the ideal VRF functionality plus the simulator (which has to produce an indistinguishable real-world view to the environment). The simulator of this construction can be thought of as performing the following four crucial tasks: it (1) simulates the honest parties' credentials, (2) simulates honest parties' VRF evaluations and proofs (without knowledge of the VRF output), (3) verifies VRF outputs, and (4) ensures that the answers to random-oracle queries are consistent with the outputs of the VRF functionality on the relevant random-oracle evaluations. Observing the definition of the VRF functionality, we see that it enforces several properties that make the simulation task challenging. In particular, unless a key is registered with the functionality, no VRF evaluation is possible. Furthermore, the simulator can only freshly evaluate the VRF on its registered keys or corrupted keys. Finally, the functionality performs an ideal verification in that it stores the mapping $(v, m) \mapsto y$ and answers verification requests specifying (v, m, y') with 1 only if $y = y'$. The difficulty is to argue that the simulator will always be "one step ahead" of the distinguishing environment. That is, if the random oracle produces an output that can correspond to a correct VRF output, then the simulator not only has to detect to which public key this output should be linked, but also that such a public key has in fact already been registered. Furthermore, if the simulator decides that no such public key can currently be associated to an output, this decision cannot be revised and corrected later (even if new public keys are generated). While performing a consistent simulation is tricky, ensuring the other properties requires a careful argumentation and we describe here a selection of considerations that provide some intuition for the proof and why simulation is possible. On a high level, to correctly simulate verifications, the combination (v, m, y, π) must be mapped to the instance of the NIZK for the relation $R_{B,H}^{cf}$ (see Appendix A for the notation and definition), which is possible if the association of the (v, m) to the base point H is unique which can be based on the guarantees of the random oracle. Given the soundness of the NIZK the corresponding VRF output is derived based on the point $\phi_{cf}(\Gamma) := cf * \Gamma = x * H$, where x is the exponent fulfilling the equation $\phi_{cf}(v) = x * B$.

Finally, to determine whether the correct value y is specified, the simulator must be consistent with the functionality's output for (v, m). On an intuitive level, this requires the correct association between the protocol values Γ and H with the public key v and message m. First, we note that the probability of guessing a correct output without first computing the base point H can be shown to be negligible. If it has in fact been queried, then thanks to clever programming of the RO, the simulator can detect the relation. For a correct simulation, this assignment must be unique and one-to-one which can be established based on information-theoretic arguments and by the soundness of the NIZK. While the above reasoning is true if the simulator can actually obtain the value y from the functionality, for an honest party with public key v that has never evaluated the VRF on message m this is by definition not possible and we have to prove that only with negligible probability it is possible to find the correct point Γ for such an honest party. This follows by the hardness of the computational Diffie-Hellman problem in the group G. We conclude by noting that an additional complication is to obtain a simulator which is responsive, i.e., which computes replies to queries without additional interaction with the ideal functionality. This aspect is mainly useful for protocol designers that rely on a responsive environment [3, 8, 12].

6.2 Security Analysis of ECVRF$_{bc}$ with Batch Verifications

We first describe the setting and the ideal world that idealizes the security requirements for batch verifications.

The Setting. We want to capture a general setting where the protocol is asked to verify a bunch of claimed VRF proofs originating from any source outside the system, including maliciously generated ones by the adversary. We model this setting using a global bulletin-board functionality $\mathcal{G}_{BB}$ and describe it in Fig. 5. This abstraction fits not only the public blockchain setting (which can be seen as a bulletin board), but any application that makes use of batch verifications where new proofs appear in the system over time, potentially visible and updatable by anyone including an adversary. Each instance of this functionality maintains a list of values. The list is append-only, but there is no other restriction on what is appended and thus the only guarantee it offers is that if we refer to an interval $[i \ldots j]$ in the list associated to session *sid* then, once defined, the returned list of values is always the same. The functionality is a global setup [1] for full generality of the statement. In particular, once proven for this setting, simpler

---

Functionality $\mathcal{G}_{\mathsf{BB}}$

The function maintains a (dynamically updatable) list L_s (initially empty). The functionality manages the set $\mathcal{P}$ of registered machines (identified by extended identities), i.e., a machine is added to $\mathcal{P}$ when receiving input REGISTER (and removes a machine from P when receiving DE-REGISTER. The requests give activation back to the calling machine).

- Upon receiving (ADD, sid, x) from $P \in \mathcal{P}$ or from the adversary, set $L \leftarrow L \,\|\, x$ output (Updated, sid, L) to the adversary.
- Upon receiving (RETRIEVE, sid, i, j) from $P \in \mathcal{P}$ or from the adversary, do the following: if $L[j]$ is undefined, return $(i, j, \emptyset)$ to the caller. Otherwise, return the result (Retrieved, $sid, i, j, L[i] \,\|\, \ldots \,\|\, L[j]$) to the caller.

Fig. 5. The global bulletin board.

settings (such as defining a protocol interface taking a batch of proofs directly from a caller) follow in a straightforward manner.

The Ideal World. In the ideal world, we introduce a new simple command to the VRF functionality described in Fig. 6. Upon input (BatchVerify, sid, i, j), the functionality retrieves the corresponding list from $\mathcal{G}_{\mathsf{BB}}$ and if the list is non-empty, it verifies whether all claimed combinations are known are stored as valid combinations. In this case the functionality returns 1. If this is not the case, but all pairs (v_i, m_i, y_i) specify the correct input-output-pairs as stored by the functionality, i.e., $T(v_i, m_i) = y_i$, then the functionality lets the adversary decide on the output value. This case captures the fact that although the proofs strings might not be stored in the functionality (or will never be), batch verification will never assert a wrong input-output mapping. In any other case, the output is defined to be 0.

The UC Protocol. Recall from Sect. 3 that any VRF can be formulated as a UC protocol. We now show how to formulate batch verification as an extended protocol π_{ECVRF}^{+} that is identical to π_{ECVRF} but additionally implements the following procedure outlined in Sect. 5.2. To simplify notation, we continue to write H and H_{e2c} for general hash-function invocations and understand that this corresponds to evaluating the random oracles $\mathcal{F}_{\mathsf{RO}}^{\mathcal{Y}}$ and $\mathcal{F}_{\mathsf{RO}}^{\mathsf{G}}$, respectively.

- On input (BatchVerify, sid, i, j), send (RETRIEVE, sid, i, j) to $\mathcal{G}_{\mathsf{BB}}$ and receive the answer (Retrieved, $sid, i, j, L_{i:j}$). If $L_{i:j} = \emptyset$ then return (BatchVerified, $sid, i, j, 0$). Otherwise, do the following:
    1. Parse every item in the list as tuple, i.e., for each $k \in [\|L_{i:j}\|]$ obtain $T_k = (m_k, y_k, \pi_k, v_k)$. If the tuple has wrong format, return (BatchVerified, $sid, i, j, 0$).
    2. For each T_k perform first the steps 1. to 3. and then step 3.5 of ECVRF.Vfy, that is:

Ideal Functionality $\mathcal{F}_{\mathsf{VRF+}}^{\mathcal{X},\ell_{\mathsf{VRF}}}$

Same parameters and initialization as in Figure 1. Additionally, the functionality registers to the instance of $\mathcal{G}_{\mathsf{BB}}$ with the same session identifier sid.

- Key generation, malicious key generation, VRF evaluation and proof, malicious VRF evaluation, verification, and adversarial leakage are as in Figure 1.

- **Batch Verification.** Upon receiving a message (BatchVerify, sid, i, j) from any party, send (RETRIEVE, sid, i, j) to $\mathcal{G}_{\mathsf{BB}}$ to receive the list $(i, j, L_{i:j})$. Then output (BatchVerify, sid, i, j) to the adversary. Upon receiving (BatchVerified, sid, i, j, b) do the following:
  1. If $L_{i:j} = \emptyset$ then return (BatchVerified, $sid, i, j, 0$) to the caller.
  2. Parse each entry of $L_{i:j}$ as tuple (m_k, y_k, π_k, v_k) for $k = 1 \ldots |L_{i:j}|$.
  3. Evaluate the condition $f \leftarrow \forall k \in [|L_{i:j}|] : (\cdot, v_k) \in S_{pk} \wedge T(v_k, m_k) = (y_k, S) \wedge \pi_k \in S$. If $f = 1$, return (BatchVerified, $sid, i, j, 1$) to the caller.
  4. Evaluate the condition $f' \leftarrow \forall k \in [|L_{i:j}|] : (\cdot, v_k) \in S_{pk} \wedge T(v_k, m_k) = (y_k, \cdot)$. If $f' = 1$ return (BatchVerified, sid, i, j, b).
  5. Return (BatchVerified, $sid, i, j, 0$).

Fig. 6. The VRF functionality with Batch Verifications.

- Verify that $v_k \in \mathbb{E}$ and then that $\mathsf{cf} * v_k \neq O$.
- Parse and verify π_k as tuple $(\Gamma_k, U_k, V_k, s_k) \in \mathbb{E}^3 \times \mathbb{Z}_q$.
- Compute $H_k \leftarrow \mathsf{H}_{e2c}(v_k, m_k)$.
- Compute $c_k \leftarrow \mathsf{H}(\mathtt{suite\_s} \,\|\, \mathsf{DS}_2 \,\|\, H_k \,\|\, \Gamma_k \,\|\, U_k \,\|\, V_k \,\|\, \mathsf{DS}_0)[..\kappa]$.
3. If any check fails then return (BatchVerified, $sid, i, j, 0$).
4. Perform the batch verification:
   - Set $\pi'_k \leftarrow H_k \,\|\, \pi_k$ for all $k \in [|L_{i:j}|]$.
   - Let $S_T \leftarrow \pi'_1 \,\|\, \ldots \,\|\, \pi'_{|L_{i:j}|}$.
   - $\forall k \in [|L_{i:j}|] : h_k \leftarrow \mathsf{H}(\mathtt{suite\_s} \,\|\, \mathsf{DS}_4 \,\|\, S_T \,\|\, k \,\|\, \mathsf{DS}_0)$.
   - $\forall k \in [|L_{i:j}|] : l_k \leftarrow h_k[..\kappa]$.
   - $\forall k \in [|L_{i:j}|] : r_k \leftarrow h_k[\kappa..2 \cdot \kappa]$.
   - Evaluate

$$b_1 \leftarrow \left(O = \sum_{k \in [|L_{i:j}|]} \left(r_k * (s_k * B - c_k * v_k - U_k) + \right.\right.$$
$$\left.\left. l_k * (s_k * H_k - c_k * \Gamma_k - V_k) \right) \right). \quad (1)$$

5. Evaluate $b_2 \leftarrow (\forall k \in [|L_{i:j}|] : y_k = \mathsf{Compute}(\pi_k))$.
6. Define $b \leftarrow b_1 \wedge b_2$ and return (BatchVerified, sid, i, j, b) to the caller.

Theorem 2. *Under the same assumptions as Theorem 1, the protocol* π_{ECVRF}^+ *UC-realizes* $\mathcal{F}_{\mathsf{VRF+}}^{\mathcal{X},\ell_{\mathsf{VRF}}}$ *(where* $\mathcal{G}_{\mathsf{BB}}$ *is a global setup), for* $\mathcal{X} = \{0,1\}^*$ *and* $\ell_{\mathsf{VRF}}(\kappa) = 4\kappa$.

Proof (Sketch). The proof needs to verify two things: first, similar to the reasoning in the Fiat-Shamir transform outlined in Appendix A, it must be the case that invocations of $H(\ldots \| S_T \| k \| \ldots)$ are in one-to-one correspondence with imaginary protocol runs, where a prover first presents S_T and an honest verifier picks the coefficients r_i and l_i uniformly at random. Second, we have to argue that no invalid statement can verify as part of the batch. Let $T_{\tilde{k}}$ be such an invalid tuple. Based on considerations discussed in Appendix A, a tuple $T_{\tilde{k}}$ fixes the entire instance of a particular proof, i.e., $B, H_{\tilde{k}}, v_{\tilde{k}}, \Gamma_{\tilde{k}}$, and encodes a particular run of the associated Σ-protocol where the challenge is computed correctly based on the random oracle using the Fiat-Shamir transform (otherwise, the entire sequence of tuples is rejected). We see that the employed Σ-protocol is sound w.r.t. relation R_{B,H_k}^{cf} even for the relaxed verification $s_{\tilde{k}} * B - c_{\tilde{k}} * v_{\tilde{k}} - U_{\tilde{k}} \in \ker(\phi_{\text{cf}}) \wedge s_{\tilde{k}} * H_{\tilde{k}} - c_{\tilde{k}} * \Gamma_{\tilde{k}} - V_{\tilde{k}} \in \ker(\phi_{\text{cf}})$. Thus, the probability that the instance and proof run encoded in $T_{\tilde{k}}$ satisfies this check but $(v_{\tilde{k}}, \Gamma_{\tilde{k}}) \notin R_{B,H_k}^{\text{cf}}$ is at most $1/|\mathcal{C}|$. Finally, if $s_{\tilde{k}} * B - c_{\tilde{k}} * v_{\tilde{k}} - U_{\tilde{k}} \in P + \ker(\phi_{\text{cf}})$ for some $P \in \mathbb{G}$ (cf. Appendix A for a brief overview of the concepts here), it is straightforward to see that Eq. (1) holds only with probability at most $1/|\mathcal{C}|$ as we basically compute a random $r_{\tilde{k}}$-multiple of P (the other case for coefficient $l_{\tilde{k}}$ is symmetric). The theorem follows by taking the union bound over all batch verifications instructed by the environment. $\square$

On-the-Fly Range Extension. We conclude this section by showcasing a simple range extension of the VRF which, in certain implementations, can significantly reduce the number of VRF evaluations at the cost of a hash function evaluation. All we have to do is to modify the algorithm Compute in π_{ECVRF}^+ which changes the format of the tuples $T = (m, y, \pi, v)$ only in one place, i.e., $y \in \{0,1\}^{c \cdot \ell_{\text{VRF}}}$, where c is the fixed constant in the range-extension construction. We denote the new protocol with the new output computation Compute' below by $\tilde{\pi}_{\text{ECVRF}}^+$:

– Compute'(π), where string $\pi = \Gamma \| \ldots$ with $\Gamma \in \mathbb{E}$:
  1. Compute $Y \leftarrow H(\texttt{suite\_s} \| \texttt{DS}_3 \| (cf * \Gamma) \| \texttt{DS}_0)$.
  2. Output
     $(H(\texttt{suite\_s} \| \texttt{DS}_5 \| 1 \| Y \| \texttt{DS}_0), \ldots, H(\texttt{suite\_s} \| \texttt{DS}_5 \| c \| Y \| \texttt{DS}_0))$.

Corollary 1. *Under the same assumptions as Theorem 2, protocol $\tilde{\pi}_{\text{ECVRF}}^+$ UC-realizes $\mathcal{F}_{\text{VRF+}}^{\mathcal{X}, c \cdot \ell_{\text{VRF}}}$, for $\mathcal{X} = \{0,1\}^*$ and $\ell_{\text{VRF}}(\kappa) = 4\kappa$.*

Proof (Sketch). The proof follows along the lines of the previous proofs. The only additional concern is the possibility of collisions among the values obtained for Y in the above construction, because we require that each fresh invocation of the output tuple computed in the second step corresponds to new evaluation points of the random oracle H. This bad event can be bounded by the standard collision probability of bitstrings drawn uniformly at random from $\{0,1\}^{\ell_{\text{VRF}}}$. $\square$

7 Performance Evaluation

In this section we evaluate the performance of the ECVRF-EDWARDS25519-SHA512-TAI ciphersuite as defined in the standard [15] against the batch-compatible variant proposed in this paper. Essentially, these are ECVRF and

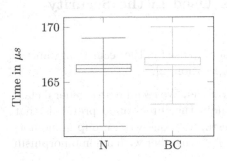

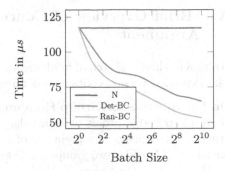

Fig. 7. ECVRF proof generation of the Batch Compatible (BC) version, and the Normal (N) one.

Fig. 8. ECVRF verification, comparing normal version (N), deterministic batch verification (Det-BC) and non-deterministic batch verification (Ran-BC).

ECVRF$_{bc}$, respectively, over the curve `edwards25519` with SHA512 as a hashing algorithm. We implement a Rust prototype of version 10 of the draft which we provide open source [22]. We use the curve25519-dalek [17] rust implementation for the curve arithmetic operations, which implements multiscalar multiplication with Strauss' [5] and Pippenger's [6] algorithms, and optimize the choice depending on the size of the batch. We ran all experiments in MacOS on a commodity laptop using a single core of an Intel i7 processor running at 2,7 GHz. For the batch-compatible version we implement both a deterministic verification (using the hashing techniques as described in Sect. 5) as well as a random verification where the scalars r_i, l_i are sampled uniformly at random from $\mathbb{Z}_{2^{128}}$. We benchmark the proving and verification times for each, using batches of size 2^l for $l \in \{1, \ldots, 10\}$. In the standard version, the size of a VRF proof consists of a (32-byte) elliptic curve point, a 16-byte scalar, and a 32-byte scalar. In the batch compatible version, rather than sending the challenge we send the two announcements, which results in three elliptic curve points and a 32-byte scalar. Therefore the modifications increase proof size from 80 to 128 bytes.

This results in a considerable improvement in verification time. Figure 7 shows that proving time is unaffected, and there is no difference between the normal ECVRF and ECVRF$_{bc}$ (as expected). In Fig. 8 we show the verification time per proof for different sized batches. We interpret the times of batch verification as a ratio with respect to ECVRF. Using deterministic batching, the verification time per proof is reduced to 0.71 with batches of 64 and to 0.56 with batches of 1024 signatures. With random coefficients, batching times get a bit better given that we no longer need to compute hashes for scalars l_i and r_i. The verification time per proof can be reduced to 0.6 with batches of 64 signatures, and up to 0.47 with batches of 1024.

A   Brief Overview of Concepts Used in the Security Argument

We provide here a sketch of fundamental concepts used in the security argument. The extended version contains a detailed exposition [2].

On Σ-Protocols for Group Homomorphisms. We recall here a general class of zero-knowledge proofs of knowledge, namely the three-round protocols that prove the knowledge of a preimage of a (presumably one-way) group homomorphism [18]. Consider two groups $(\mathbb{H}, \circ)$ and $(\mathbb{T}, \star)$ together with a homomorphism $f : \mathbb{H} \to \mathbb{T}$, i.e., $f(x \circ y) = f(x) \star f(y)$.

Let R_f be the relation defined by $(z, x) \in R_f :\leftrightarrow f(x) = z$. Consider the following three-round protocol between prover P and verifier V for the language $L_{R_f} := \{z \mid \exists x : (z, x) \in R_f\}$. That is, the common input is the *proof instance* $z \in \mathbb{T}$ (and the relation R_f), where the prover is supposed to know a value $x \in \mathbb{H}$ s.t. $f(x) = z$.

1. $P \to V$: P samples $k \xleftarrow{\$} \mathbb{H}$ and sends $t := f(k)$ to V.
2. $V \to P$: V picks at random an integer $c \in \mathcal{C} \subset \mathbb{N}$ and sends it to P.
3. $P \to V$: P computes $s := k \circ x^c$ and sends s to V. V accepts the protocol run if and only if the equality $f(s) = t \star z^c$ holds.

The security of this protocol follows from the following lemma:

Lemma 1. ([18]). *Let R_f a relation as described above relative to a group homomorphism $f : \mathbb{H} \to \mathbb{T}$. The above protocol is a Σ-Protocol for the language L_{R_f} if there are two publicly known values $\ell \in \mathbb{Z}$ and $u \in \mathbb{H}$ s.t.*

1. *$\forall c, c' \in \mathcal{C}, c \neq c' : \gcd(c - c', \ell) = 1$, and*
2. *$\forall z \in L_{R_f}, f(u) = z^\ell$.*

The *Fiat-Shamir* Transform turns (in the random-oracle model) any Σ-Protocol into a secure non-interactive zero-knowledge protocol of knowledge. Intuitively, the assumed random oracle is like an honest verifier computing a challenge and thus preserves the above security properties. We refer to [2] for details.

Instantiation for $\mathsf{ECVRF_{bc}}$. We recall that in $\mathsf{ECVRF_{bc}}$ we deal with a prime-order subgroup $\mathbb{G}$ of order q of an elliptic curve of order $cf \cdot q$. Let B_1 and B_2 be two generators of this subgroup. Essentially, the Σ-protocol of interest is an equality proof of discrete logarithm, i.e., given two values z_1 and z_2 prove knowledge of x such that $x * B_1 = z_1 \wedge x * B_2 = z_2$. To instantiate the above generic scheme, we let $\mathbb{H} := (\mathbb{Z}_q, +)$ and define $(\mathbb{T}, \oplus) := (\mathbb{G}, +) \times (\mathbb{G}, +)$ as the direct product of $\mathbb{G}$, where the binary operation $\oplus$ on $\mathbb{T}$ is defined component-wise. The homomorphism is given by $f_{B_1, B_2} : \mathbb{Z}_q \to \mathbb{T}; \quad x \mapsto (x * B_1, x * B_2)$. Since $\mathbb{G}$ is of prime order q, we can satisfy the conditions of Lemma 1 by letting $u = 0$ and $\ell = q$, and defining the challenge space to be a large subset $\mathcal{C} \subseteq [0, \ldots, q-1]$.

We therefore conclude that the embedded non-interactive zero-knowledge proof of knowledge in $\mathsf{ECVRF}_{\mathsf{bc}}$ has (in the random-oracle model) simulatable executions, and with only negligible probability can a valid proof for a wrong statement be generated.

On Domain Checks and the Canonical Epimorphism. Special care has to be taken in the analysis as $\mathsf{ECVRF}_{\mathsf{bc}}$ omits detailed domain checks which in general can impact security in that Lemma 1 cannot be applied directly (we have $\mathbb{G}$ a subgroup of $\mathbb{E}$ and the protocol could be run on values $z_i \in \mathbb{E} \setminus \mathbb{G}$ by a dishonest party as the verifier does not perform a domain check for $z_i \in \mathbb{G}$ but only for $\mathbb{E}$). We leave the general treatment of this to the full version of this work, and describe here a special case based on the *canonical epimorphism*: For $\mathsf{ECVRF}_{\mathsf{bc}}$, we can consider the map $P \mapsto \mathsf{cf} * P$ which is the canonical epimorphism $\phi_{\mathsf{cf}} : \mathbb{E} \to \mathbb{G}$ and the corresponding map $P + \ker(\phi_{\mathsf{cf}}) \mapsto \phi_{\mathsf{cf}}(P)$ which identifies the isomorphism establishing $\mathbb{E}/\ker(\phi_{\mathsf{cf}}) \cong \mathbb{G}$ by the fundamental theorem on homomorphisms. From this we can deduce by Lagrange's Theorem that $|\mathbb{E}| = |\mathbb{G}| \cdot |\ker(\phi_{\mathsf{cf}})|$. Since the choice of the representatives is immaterial one can think of each coset $P + \ker(\phi_{\mathsf{cf}})$ to be represented by a point $P \in \mathbb{G}$ (and the kernel consists of the low-order points, i.e., elements of order strictly less than q). Denoting the first round message of the prover by (U, V), the projected verification equation in step 3 of the Σ-Protocol becomes $(O, O) = (\phi_{\mathsf{cf}}(s * B - U - c * z_1), \phi_{\mathsf{cf}}(s * H - V - c * z_2))$ which is an equation in the prime-order group $\mathbb{G}$ (recall that B and H are generators of $\mathbb{G}$). Stated differently, the above equality is satisfied when $(s * B - V - c * z_1) \in \ker(\phi_{\mathsf{cf}})$ and $(s * H - V - c * z_2) \in \ker(\phi_{\mathsf{cf}})$. As we show in the full version [2], the guarantees of Lemma 1 apply to this projected run of the protocol, in particular, we obtain the soundness guarantee for the relation

$$(z_1, z_2) \in R^{\mathsf{cf}}_{B,H} :\leftrightarrow x * B = \phi_{\mathsf{cf}}(z_1) \wedge x * H = \phi_{\mathsf{cf}}(z_2) \tag{2}$$

guaranteed by the above Σ-protocol (where technically speaking, we could relax the checks performed by the verifier to $(s * B - V - c * z_1) \in \ker(\phi_{\mathsf{cf}})$ and $(s*H-V-c*z_2) \in \ker(\phi_{\mathsf{cf}})$ instead of stricter equality checks $(s*B-V-c*z_1) = O$ and $(s * H - V - c * z_2) = O$).

References

1. Badertscher, C., Canetti, R., Hesse, J., Tackmann, B., Zikas, V.: Universal composition with global subroutines: capturing global setup within plain UC. In: Pass, R., Pietrzak, K. (eds.) TCC 2020. LNCS, vol. 12552, pp. 1–30. Springer, Cham (2020). https://doi.org/10.1007/978-3-030-64381-2_1
2. Badertscher, C., Gaži, P., Querejeta-Azurmendi, I., Russell, A.: On UC-secure range extension and batch verification for ecvrf. Cryptology ePrint Archive, Report 2022/1045 (2022). https://eprint.iacr.org/2022/1045

3. Badertscher, C., Gazi, P., Kiayias, A., Russell, A., Zikas, V.: Ouroboros genesis: Composable proof-of-stake blockchains with dynamic availability. In: Lie, D., Mannan, M., Backes, M., Wang, X. (eds.) ACM CCS 2018: 25th Conference on Computer and Communications Security, pp. 913–930, Toronto, ON, Canada, October 15–19, 2018. ACM Press

4. Bellare, M., Garay, J.A., Rabin, T.: Fast batch verification for modular exponentiation and digital signatures. Cryptology ePrint Archive, Report 1998/007 (1998). http://eprint.iacr.org/1998/007

5. Bellman, R., Straus, E.G.: 5125. The American Mathematical Monthly, 71(7), 806–808 (1964)

6. Bernstein, D.J., Doumen, J., Lange, T., Oosterwijk, J.-J.: Faster batch forgery identification. In: Galbraith, S., Nandi, M. (eds.) INDOCRYPT 2012. LNCS, vol. 7668, pp. 454–473. Springer, Heidelberg (2012). https://doi.org/10.1007/978-3-642-34931-7_26

7. Bernstein, D.J., Duif, N., Lange, T., Schwabe, P., Yang, B.-Y.: High-speed high-security signatures. J. Cryptogr. Eng. 2(2), 77–89 (2012)

8. Camenisch, J., Enderlein, R.R., Krenn, S., Küsters, R., Rausch, D.: Universal composition with responsive environments. In: Cheon, J.H., Takagi, T. (eds.) ASIACRYPT 2016. LNCS, vol. 10032, pp. 807–840. Springer, Heidelberg (2016). https://doi.org/10.1007/978-3-662-53890-6_27

9. Camenisch, J., Hohenberger, S., Østergaard Pedersen, M.: Batch verification of short signatures. J. Cryptol. 25(4), 723–747 (2012)

10. Canetti, R.: Universally composable security. J. ACM 67(5) (2020)

11. Cramer, R., Damgård, I., Schoenmakers, B.: Proofs of partial knowledge and simplified design of witness hiding protocols. In: Desmedt, Y.G. (ed.) CRYPTO 1994. LNCS, vol. 839, pp. 174–187. Springer, Heidelberg (1994). https://doi.org/10.1007/3-540-48658-5_19

12. David, B., Gaži, P., Kiayias, A., Russell, A.: Ouroboros praos: an adaptively-secure, semi-synchronous proof-of-stake blockchain. In: Nielsen, J.B., Rijmen, V. (eds.) EUROCRYPT 2018. LNCS, vol. 10821, pp. 66–98. Springer, Cham (2018). https://doi.org/10.1007/978-3-319-78375-8_3

13. Fiat, A., Shamir, A.: How to prove yourself: practical solutions to identification and signature problems. In: Odlyzko, A.M. (ed.) CRYPTO 1986. LNCS, vol. 263, pp. 186–194. Springer, Heidelberg (1987). https://doi.org/10.1007/3-540-47721-7_12

14. Gilad, Y., Hemo, R., Micali, S., Vlachos, G., Zeldovich, N.: Algorand: Scaling byzantine agreements for cryptocurrencies. Cryptology ePrint Archive, Report 2017/454 (2017). http://eprint.iacr.org/2017/454

15. Goldberg, S., Reyzin, L., Papadopoulos, D., Vcelak, J.: Verifiable random functions (vrfs). Internet-Draft, IRTF (2022). https://datatracker.ietf.org/doc/html/draft-irtf-cfrg-vrf-14

16. Jarecki, S., Kiayias, A., Krawczyk, H.: Round-optimal password-protected secret sharing and T-PAKE in the password-only model. Cryptology ePrint Archive, Report 2014/650 (2014). http://eprint.iacr.org/2014/650

17. Lovecruft, I., de Valence, H.: curve25519-dalek (2022). https://github.com/dalek-cryptography/curve25519-dalek

18. Maurer, U.: Zero-knowledge proofs of knowledge for group homomorphisms. Des. Codes Cryptography 77(2-3), 663–676 (2015)

19. Micali, S., Rabin, M.O., Vadhan, S.P.: Verifiable random functions. In: 40th Annual Symposium on Foundations of Computer Science, pages 120–130, New York, NY, USA, 17–19 October, 1999. IEEE Computer Society Press (1999)

20. Naccache, D., M'Rahi, D., Vaudenay, S., Raphaeli, D.: Can D.S.A. be improved? — Complexity trade-offs with the digital signature standard —. In: De Santis, A. (ed.) EUROCRYPT 1994. LNCS, vol. 950, pp. 77–85. Springer, Heidelberg (1995). https://doi.org/10.1007/BFb0053426
21. Nakamoto, S.: Bitcoin: a peer-to-peer electronic cash system, December 2008. https://bitcoin.org/bitcoin.pdf
22. Querejeta-Azurmendi, I.: Verifiable random function (2022). https://github.com/input-output-hk/vrf
23. Reyzin, L.: Vrf standardisation mailing archive (2021). https://mailarchive.ietf.org/arch/msg/cfrg/KJwe92nLEkmJGpBe-OST_ilr_MQ
24. Schnorr, C.P.: Efficient signature generation by smart cards. J. Cryptol. 4(3), 161–174 (1991). https://doi.org/10.1007/BF00196725
25. Wuille, P., Nick, J., Ruffing, T.: Schnorr signatures for secp256k1, January 2020. https://github.com/bitcoin/bips/blob/master/bip-0340.mediawiki

Efficient Proofs of Knowledge
for Threshold Relations

Gennaro Avitabile[1]($\boxtimes$), Vincenzo Botta[1], Daniele Friolo[2], and Ivan Visconti[1]

[1] University of Salerno, Fisciano, Italy
`gavitabile@unisa.it`, `vbotta@unisa.it`, `visconti@unisa.it`
[2] Sapienza University of Rome, Rome, Italy
`friolo@di.uniroma1.it`

Abstract. Recently, there has been great interest towards constructing efficient zero-knowledge proofs for practical languages. In this work, we focus on proofs for threshold relations, in which the prover is required to prove knowledge of witnesses for k out of ℓ statements.

The main contribution of our work is an efficient and modular transformation that starting from a large class of Σ-protocols and a corresponding threshold relation $\mathcal{R}_{k,\ell}$, provides an efficient Σ-protocol for $\mathcal{R}_{k,\ell}$ with improved communication complexity w.r.t. prior results. Our transformation preserves statistical/perfect honest-verifier zero knowledge.

Keywords: Σ-protocols · Threshold relations · Communication efficiency

1 Introduction

With the advent of blockchain technology and cryptocurrencies, there has been more interest in designing practical systems for decentralized computations. In particular, there is an effort towards systems producing succinct messages that can later be uploaded on blockchains guaranteeing some public verifiability. Notable examples of such tools are threshold signatures and succinct non-interactive arguments of knowledge (SNARKs).

Proofs over Threshold Relations. W.r.t. the above motivation we focus on proofs over threshold relations (PTRs) where a statement consists of ℓ instances and the prover wants to prove knowledge of witnesses for at least k of them. For simplicity, we will refer to such a proof as a (k, ℓ)-PTR. Several previous works have focused on obtaining such proofs for practical languages. In [9], Cramer et al. showed how to efficiently combine Σ-protocols in order to obtain a (k, ℓ)-PTR. Their construction mainly consists of running Σ-protocols for all instances combining them efficiently, and thus the costs (i.e., computations and communication) of their (k, ℓ)-PTR essentially consist of the sum of the costs of all the underlying Σ-protocols. The resulting protocol is still a Σ-protocol. More

© The Author(s), under exclusive license to Springer Nature Switzerland AG 2022
V. Atluri et al. (Eds.): ESORICS 2022, LNCS 13556, pp. 42–62, 2022.
https://doi.org/10.1007/978-3-031-17143-7_3

recently, a different technique has been proposed in [8] where Ciampi et al. showed how to obtain a similar result with the additional feature of postponing the need to know the instances to the last round (i.e., delayed input). The delayed-input (k, ℓ)-PTR of Ciampi et al. relies on the DDH assumption and can be applied to all Σ-protocols as [9]. The resulting protocol is a 3-round public-coin proof of knowledge. Unfortunately, since this composition technique relies on a computationally-hiding commitment scheme, it produces a protocol which only achieves computational zero knowledge regardless of the underlying Σ-protocols being statistical/perfect zero knowledge. However, statistical/perfect zero knowledge is very important since it protects the privacy of past proof computed by the prover forever (e.g., even if quantum computers become a concrete threat).

Very recently, Attema et al. in [1], improving a prior work of Groth and Kohlweiss [12], have shown how to obtain a very compact (k, ℓ)-PTR. However, the result of [1] only works for discrete logarithms (and variations), thus remaining far from the general results of [9]. Their construction requires a logarithmic number of rounds[1] and is secure against polynomial-time adversarial provers only (while preserving statistical/perfect zero knowledge). They require a shared random string (SRS) as trusted parameters.

Even more recently, Goel et al. in [11] have broken the barrier of linear (in ℓ) communication complexity when composing generic Σ-protocols, showing an efficient composition for a large class of Σ-protocols (which they call stackable Σ-protocols) obtaining logarithmic communication complexity. Their construction is secure against polynomial-time adversarial provers only[2], obtaining computational special soundness. They give an instantiation of their construction based on a commitment scheme that relies on the discrete logarithm assumption. Their instantiation requires as trusted parameters the description of a collision-resistant hash function (CRHF) and parameters for Pedersen commitments. The perfect hiding of the commitment scheme allows to preserve statistical/perfect zero knowledge when the underlying Σ-protocols are perfect/statistical zero-knowledge. While their construction applies to a large class of Σ-protocols, the techniques of [11] are communication-efficient only when $k = 1$. In the full version of their paper [10], Goel et al. discuss (see Sec. 9.1 and App. F of [10]) an approach for the case of $k > 1$ but unfortunately, as they acknowledge, their proposal strongly affects communication, without providing substantial improvements over [9]. Goel et al. left explicitly open the problem of efficiently combining Σ-protocols in order to break, for generic values of k, the linear (in ℓ) barrier achieved by [9] (see [10], page 32, Sec. 9.1).

Alternative Approaches. Recently, in [15] the result of [14] has been extended to (k, ℓ)-PTRs retaining the same communication advantage of [14] while opti-

---

[1] The result of [12] instead works only for $k = 1$, but it just requires 3 rounds.

[2] For ease of presentation, in this work we will use the term PTR even when the soundness property holds only against a computationally bounded adversarial prover. We will do the same for computational Σ-protocols which only satisfy a weaker version of special soundness called computational special soundness (cfr., Appendix A).

mizing computation efficiency. Their approach has communication complexity proportional to k times the longest branch. Mac'n'Cheese [4] is an interactive commit-and-prove zero-knowledge proof system for binary and arithmetic circuits. The communication complexity is proportional to k times the longest circuit plus an additive term which is logarithmic in ℓ. As commitments it uses information-theoretic MACs based on vector oblivious linear evaluation (VOLE). Note that Mac'n'Cheese is inherently private coin since the soundness relies on the verifier keeping the MAC key secret. Therefore, it is not immediately clear whether it can be modified to support public verifiability. Finally, one might leverage succinct proof techniques such as STARKs [5] or SNARKs [17] to get a communication-efficient (k, ℓ)-PTR. While these techniques can achieve even constant proof size, they have several drawbacks such as a huge workload for provers and the use of strong assumptions and/or problematic trusted setups. Although all the approaches above apply to NP-complete languages, we note that they are not so obviously efficiently generalizable to arbitrary languages. Instead, our approach is more beneficial to protocol designers. Indeed, if there is a Σ-protocol (with specific additional properties) for the base relation, a protocol designer can use our solution directly for the (k, ℓ) case without the need to run a possibly expensive NP-reduction.

Open Problem. In light of the above state of affairs, we have the following natural and interesting (both theoretically and practically) open question:

Is it possible to obtain practical (i.e., round, communication and computation-efficient) (k, ℓ)-proofs of knowledge for threshold relations for a large class of Σ-protocols (and thus for several useful languages) with communication complexity sublinear in ℓ preserving statistical/perfect zero knowledge?

1.1   Our Contribution

In this work, we solve the above open problem when $k = o(\frac{\ell}{\log \ell})$ by showing how to efficiently combine the same large class of Σ-protocols considered in [10] obtaining a (k, ℓ)-PTR with communication complexity that is roughly[3] $k \log \ell$. In scenarios where k is way smaller than ℓ (e.g., k is constant or even $\sqrt{\ell}$) this is a significant improvement. Moreover, our construction, similarly to [10], can also be used for (k, ℓ)-PTR involving Σ-protocols for different languages. The protocol obtained through our techniques is still a Σ-protocol and thus, it can be combined again with our techniques or other techniques (e.g., [9]) for composing Σ-protocols. Finally, our construction preserves the flavour of the zero-knowledge property of the composed protocols. Indeed, our (k, ℓ)-PTR called $\Pi_{k,\ell}$ is still statistical/perfect honest-verifier zero knowledge (HVZK) if the base Σ-protocols are statistical/perfect HVZK. Our construction can also be instantiated, with small modifications, using the commitment scheme of [8]. In this case, our (k, ℓ)-PTR would provide computational HVZK but it would only

---

[3] We will be more precise later making the impact of the security parameter explicit.

require a shared CRHF as setup, that is a milder setup compared to requiring a shared random string.

We use the $(1, \ell)$-PTR of [10], to which we refer as $\Pi_{1,\ell}$, as a building block and start with their observation that repeating k times their construction is insecure since an adversarial prover might succeed in using a witness for the same instance in all the k executions. This is precisely the problem left unsolved in [10] for (k, ℓ)-PTRs that we solve in this paper.

Compact Proof of Consistency of Commitment Parameters. In $\Pi_{1,\ell}$, the use of a witness is associated to $\log \ell$ pairs of parameters of a commitment scheme for pairs of messages such that, for every pair, one parameter allows for equivocation and the other parameter prevents equivocation. We will say that one parameter is equivocal and the other one is binding. Only the prover knows which element is equivocal for every pair. We say that a commitment scheme is 1-out-of-2 equivocal when a commitment phase requires to commit to two messages, one with binding parameters and one with equivocal parameters, without allowing the receiver to distinguish them, even after the commitment is opened.

In the following, we assume w.l.o.g. that ℓ is a power of 2 and give a simplified description of our approach. Let $x_0, \ldots, x_{\ell-1}$ be the instances and let x_i with $i \in \{0, \ldots, \ell - 1\}$ be the instance corresponding to witness w_i known to the prover. The $\log \ell$ pairs of parameters are chosen so that the j-th pair has the first parameter binding if the j-th bit of i is zero (for $j = 0, \ldots, \log \ell - 1$) and equivocal otherwise. Notice that the connection between a pair of parameters that can be either (equivocal, binding) or (binding, equivocal) and a bit of the index of an instance makes the $\log \ell$ pairs of parameters associated to x_i logically different from the $\log \ell$ pairs of parameters associated to x_j, as long as $i \neq j$. We observe that to show that in k executions of $\Pi_{1,\ell}$ the k witnesses correspond to k different instances, one can focus on showing that the k sequences of $\log \ell$ pairs of parameters are all disjoint in the sense that for every pair $(\bar{a} = a_0, a_1, \ldots, a_{\log \ell - 1}), (\bar{b} = b_0, b_1, \ldots, b_{\log \ell - 1})$ of elements in these k sequences, there is always a position $j \in \{0, \ldots, \log \ell - 1\}$ such that only one out of a_j and b_j has the first parameter that is binding. We focus on efficiently proving the above property of all pairs in these k sequences as follows: first, we require the prover to sort the k sequences according to the order relation derived by assigning to every sequence of $\log \ell$ pairs of parameters a string of $\log \ell$ bits where the j-th bit is 0 if and only if the j-th pair of parameters in the sequence has the first element that is binding. The prover has all the information to sort these k sequences since the prover itself decided those parameters and thus it knows which one is binding and which one is equivocal. Once the k sequences are sorted, in order to prove that they are all disjoint (in the sense explained above) it suffices for the prover to show that for every two consecutive elements $(\bar{a}, \bar{b})$ in such ordered sequence of k elements, the bit representation of $\bar{b}$ is greater than the one of $\bar{a}$. With such trick, the prover must provide $k - 1$ proofs in total to show that all sequences are different. Each of such proofs is about proving a property of the involved $4 \log \ell$ parameters[4]. We show a concrete and efficient instantiation for the parameters of the 1-out-of-2 equivocal commitment scheme GGHK from [10]. The communication complexity of each of the above $k - 1$ proofs is $\mathcal{O}(\log \ell)$. In Table 1, we compare our results to the previously discussed approaches to obtain (k, ℓ)-PTRs. For the sake of completeness, in this comparison we make the security parameter λ explicit. Notice that our approach, while being less communication-efficient than [1,12], is more flexible since it applies to a much wider family of languages.

Threshold Ring Signatures. As pointed out in [10], by making $\Pi_{1,\ell}$ non-interactive with the aid of a random oracle one gets a ring signature whose size is logarithmic in the size of the ring ℓ (see [10] Page 4 and Sec. 9.3). Following a similar approach, starting from our $\Pi_{k,\ell}$ we can get a threshold ring signature scheme according to Def. 3 of [13], but considering PPT adversaries instead of quantum polynomial-time adversaries. In a threshold ring signature scheme, k signers cooperate to sign a message hiding their identities within a larger group of size ℓ. In our threshold ring signature scheme, the size of a signature corresponds roughly to $\mathcal{O}(k \log \ell)$ group elements. Interestingly, while featuring a relatively simple design, our construction improves in terms of signature size on many literature works [6,18,19]. Other schemes have signature size which is linear in ℓ (while being independent of k) and thus are also outperformed when $k << \ell$ [7,13,20]. When comparing our construction to others achieving more compact signature sizes [2,13,16], our construction still has interesting advantages in terms of resilience to adversarially chosen keys (see [13]) or used assumptions. A major feature of our threshold ring signature is that it can be instantiated from a variety of assumptions (i.e., the assumptions depend on the chosen languages and Σ-protocols). Finally, our techniques allow threshold ring signatures with more advanced hiding properties. Indeed, since our $\Pi_{k,\ell}$ is still a stackable Σ-protocol, it can be used as a base Σ-protocol for our threshold ring signature, thus expressing more complex relations with better anonymity properties (i.e., "threshold-of-threshold"). See the full version [3] for more details.

2   Technical Overview of [10]

We first describe 1-out-of-2 equivocal commitments (see Sect. 3.1 for more details) that are a major tool used in [10]. Then, we show how [10] exploits 1-out-of-2 equivocal commitments to get a $(1, \ell)$-PTR.

1-out-of-2 Equivocal Commitments in a Nutshell. A 1-out-of-2 equivocal commitment allows a sender to commit to two values one of which is guaranteed to be binding, either unconditionally or under computational assumptions. The other element instead can be equivocated using a trapdoor that is known to the sender. Once the commitment is opened, the commitment scheme itself would

---

[4] For each proof there are two sequences of $\log \ell$ pairs of parameters.

Table 1. Comparison of several techniques for (k, ℓ)-PTR. When comparing more language-generic techniques like ours and [9,10], we express the communication complexity both in terms of the communication complexity of the underlying Σ-protocol $\mathsf{CC}(\Sigma)$ and of the security parameter λ. Notice that the communication complexity of [12] does not depend on k since their technique only works for $k = 1$. The Language column reports the languages or the class of the Σ-protocols for which the corresponding composition technique works. Despite being the least communication efficient, [9] can be applied to a wider class of Σ-protocols.

Protocol	# Rounds	Communication	Values of k	Language
[9]	3	$\mathcal{O}(\ell \mathsf{CC}(\Sigma))$	Any k	All Σ
[12]	3	$\mathcal{O}(\lambda \log \ell)$	$k = 1$	DL-like
[1]	$\mathcal{O}(\log \ell)$	$\mathcal{O}(\lambda \log(2\ell - k))$	Any k	DL-like
[10]	3	$\mathcal{O}(\mathsf{CC}(\Sigma) + \lambda \log \ell)$	$k = 1$	Stackable Σ
[10]	3	$\mathcal{O}(k(\mathsf{CC}(\Sigma) + \lambda \ell))$	$k > 1$	Stackable Σ
Ours	3	$\mathcal{O}(k(\mathsf{CC}(\Sigma) + \lambda \log \ell))$	Any k	Stackable Σ

guarantee that the equivocal position is not leaked. Before sending the commitment to the receiver, the commitment scheme parameters are generated by the sender who has to decide which position is equivocal. From now on, we call non-trapdoor (NT) a parameter that is associated with a binding position, while a trapdoor parameter (T) is associated with an equivocal position.

$(1, \ell)$-*PTR through Σ-Protocols.* For simplicity, we will focus on instances belonging to the same language. Nevertheless, both in [10] and in our results it is possible to go beyond this restriction (see Sec. 8 of [10]).

The main idea in [10] is that every involved Σ-protocol has a deterministic HVZK simulator, called Extended HVZK (EHVZK) simulator which, given a challenge c, a third-round message z, and a statement x, outputs a simulated a such that (a, c, z) is an accepting transcript for the instance x. With EHVZK in their hands, the authors introduce the notion of stackable Σ-protocols. A Σ-protocol is stackable if (i) it has an EHVZK simulator and (ii) the third-round message is recyclable, meaning that the distribution of such messages is independent of the instance for every instance in the language.[5]

Let us first consider just two of the ℓ instances, say x_1 and x_2. Given two executions Σ_1 and Σ_2 of a stackable Σ-protocol Π for instances x_1 and x_2 respectively, an execution $\Sigma_{1,2}$ of the composed Σ-protocol $\Pi_{1,2}$ defined by Goel et al. [10] for $x_1 \vee x_2$ can be constructed as follows. Let us assume that the prover $\mathsf{P}_{1,2}$ knows the witness corresponding to x_1. We name a_1 (respectively a_2) the first-round message of the underlying execution Σ_1 (respectively Σ_2), a the first-round message of the execution $\Sigma_{1,2}$ of $\Pi_{1,2}$, c the challenge sampled by the verifier $\mathsf{V}_{1,2}$ for $\Pi_{1,2}$, and z the last message of $\Sigma_{1,2}$. Since Σ_1 and Σ_2

---

[5] See Appendix A for formal definitions. Notice that, as can be also easily seen from the definitions in Appendix A.1, EHVZK implies SHVZK.

are executions of the stackable Σ-protocol Π, their third-round messages have the same distribution. Therefore, the accepting third-round message from Σ_1 can be re-used as a third-round message for Σ_2 as described in the composed Σ-protocol $\Pi_{1,2}$ below:

- $\mathsf{P}_{1,2}$ computes the first-round message a_1 of protocol Π on input the instance x_1 and witness w_1. $\mathsf{P}_{1,2}$ commits to a_1 using a 1-out-of-2 equivocal commitment scheme. The value a_1 is put in the binding position, while the equivocal position commits to 0. We denote the resulting commitment as com. The first-round message a in the execution $\Sigma_{1,2}$ of the composed protocol $\Pi_{1,2}$ includes com as well as the parameters of the commitment scheme.
- Upon receiving the challenge c from $\mathsf{V}_{1,2}$, $\mathsf{P}_{1,2}$ computes z' using witness w_1, and equivocates the equivocal position of the commitment with a simulated a_2. The value a_2 is obtained by running the EHVZK simulator of Π with input the instance x_2, c, and the value z' computed above. Then, $\mathsf{P}_{1,2}$ sends z' and the opening values of com to $\mathsf{V}_{1,2}$ as a third-round message z of $\Sigma_{1,2}$. The value z also includes the commitment parameters.
- $\mathsf{V}_{1,2}$ reconstructs a_1 and a_2 by running the EHVZK simulator of Π. Then, $\mathsf{V}_{1,2}$ checks that both (a_1, c, z') and (a_2, c, z') are accepting transcripts for V_1 and V_2, and that com actually opens to a_1 and a_2.

Since $\Pi_{1,2}$ is still a stackable Σ-protocol, it can be recursively used to prove the instance $x_1 \vee x_2 \vee x_3 \vee x_4$. Indeed, this can be seen again as an OR of two statements, therefore the Σ-protocol for the instance $(x_1 \vee x_2) \vee (x_3 \vee x_4)$ can be composed using the same technique. Then, one can iterate the same process to obtain a $(1,8)$-PTR by applying the same technique to two $(1,4)$-PTR, and so on. Such composition of ℓ disjunctive instances can be represented by the following binary tree: the leaves of the tree represent the ℓ base executions $(\Sigma_1, \ldots, \Sigma_\ell)$ of the Σ-protocol Π. Given two siblings nodes i and j, with associated protocol execution Σ_i for the instance x_i and Σ_j for the instance x_j respectively, the parent node t of i and j describes the execution of the protocol Σ_t obtained by applying the compiler for $(1,2)$-PTR of [10]. Moreover, edges (t, i) and (t, j) are labeled as follows: if P_t knows a witness for the instance x_i, then the edge (t, i) is labelled with NT to indicate that, in the commitment computed by P_t in the first round, the position where x_i is used is binding. The edge (t, j) is labeled with T to indicate that the position where x_j is used is equivocal. If P_t knows a witness for x_j instead, then the opposite holds. An example of a tree induced by recursively applying the composition of [10] for a $(1,2)$-PTR to get a $(1,8)$-PTR is shown in Fig. 1. This recursive application of the (1,2)-PTR gives a communication complexity for the $(1, \ell)$-PTR that is roughly logarithmic in ℓ.

(k, ℓ)-*PTR Extension.* In [10], an extension of their compiler to achieve a (k, ℓ)-PTR[6] is proposed. They propose a k-out-of-ℓ binding vector-of-vectors commitment scheme. This modification allows to equivocate at most $\ell - k$ positions. Roughly speaking, they instantiate such a primitive by making the commit algorithm output a matrix of $k \times \ell$ commitment values (i.e., each row is a 1-out-of-ℓ

---

[6] Sec. 9.1 and App. F of [10].

equivocal commitment), together with a non-interactive zero-knowledge proof that the binding position is different in each row. As pointed out in [10], with this technique they lose their ability to recursively apply the $(1,2)$-PTR compiler. As a result, their (k, ℓ)-PTR has a communication complexity of roughly $\mathcal{O}(k\ell)$ (see Table 1).

3   Our Techniques

Our Approach for a Communication-Efficient (k, ℓ)-PTR. In [10], the location of the instance for which the prover knows the witness uniquely determines the way parameters are laid out over the composition tree. For example, in Fig. 1 the instance for which $P_{1,2}$ knows the witness is x_1. This means that, starting from $\Sigma_{1,2}$, the position containing the first message of Σ_1 has to be binding. Indeed, since $P_{1,2}$ only holds a witness for x_1, $P_{1,2}$ is able to produce an accepting transcript exclusively for Σ_1. Therefore, the third-round message to be recycled has to come from Σ_1, while the committed first-round message of the execution Σ_2 needs to be equivocated with the output of the EHVZK simulator. It follows that, climbing up the tree, the commitment position containing the first message of $\Sigma_{1,2}$ has to be binding. Indeed, $V_{1,2,3,4}$ will in turn execute $V_{1,2}$ and $V_{3,4}$, which internally use the verifiers of the base Σ-protocols. This means that in $\Sigma_{3,4}$ the prover recycles the third-round message of $\Sigma_{1,2}$ and that in $\Sigma_{1,2,3,4}$ the committed first-round message of $\Sigma_{3,4}$ has to be equivocated accordingly in order to get an accepting transcript. Applying the same reasoning again, it is easy to conclude that in $\Sigma_{1,\dots,8}$ the binding position of the 1-out-of-2 equivocal commitment is again the same.

A crucial idea of [10] to achieve logarithmic communication complexity is reusing commitment parameters and openings across the same levels of the composition tree. The composition is designed so that commitment parameters and openings are part of the third-round message of the composed protocol. Indeed, since the composed Σ-protocol of [10] is itself stackable, it follows that its EHVZK simulator takes as input commitment parameters and openings to generate a suitable first-round message, namely a 1-out-of-2 equivocal commitment reusing the same openings and parameters[7]. This means that since all the Σ-protocols executions that belong to the same level of the tree share the same third-round message, they also have to use the exact same commitment parameters. Therefore, in the $(1, \ell)$-PTR of [10] given the instance x_i corresponding to the witness used by the prover, there is a unique way in which commitment parameters can be laid out over the composition tree. Thus, to build a (k, ℓ)-PTR it suffices to repeat the construction of [10] k times and to prove that the composition trees of such k executions are all distinct. In this section we describe how we design a communication-efficient Σ-protocol for the above goal.

---

[7] For this composition to work and to compress the communication complexity down to logarithmic, the size of the equivocal commitment must be independent of the size of the committed value. To solve this issue, committed values have to be compressed down to a constant size with the aid of a collision-resistant hash function.

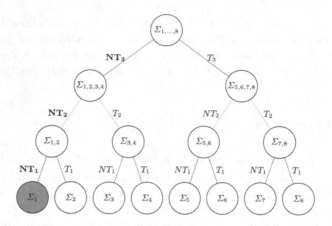

Fig. 1. An example of a composition tree induced by the recursive application of the $(1,2)$-PTR of [10] in which 8 base Σ-protocols are composed to obtain a $(1,8)$-PTR. In this example, $P_{1,\dots,8}$ knows a witness for the instance x_1. This implies that, going from the root to the leaves, the left-most branch must be non-trapdoor. Additionally, commitment openings and parameters are re-used across the same level of the composition tree and this is emphasized by using the same index and the same color for all the edges within a level.

3.1 1-out-of-2 Equivocal Commitment Schemes

We now define the notion of 1-out-of-2 equivocal commitment scheme. The sender commits to a pair of messages (m_0, m_1) with $m_0, m_1 \in \{0,1\}^\lambda$, where $\lambda \in \mathbb{N}$ is the security parameter. A 1-out-of-2 equivocal commitment scheme $CS = (\mathsf{Setup}, \mathsf{Gen}, \mathsf{BindCom}, \mathsf{EquivCom}, \mathsf{Equiv}, \mathcal{R}_T)$ consists of five PPT algorithms and a polynomial-time relation $\mathcal{R}_T$. The algorithm Setup generates a common reference string pp. We denote by $\mathcal{Y}^{\mathsf{pp}}$ the space of well-formed commitment parameters w.r.t. pp and require that membership in $\mathcal{Y}^{\mathsf{pp}}$ can be checked efficiently. The above algorithms work as follows:

- $\mathsf{pp} \leftarrow \mathsf{Setup}(1^\lambda; r)$: on input the security parameter, and randomness r, generates public parameters pp.
- $(p_0, p_1, \mathsf{td}) \leftarrow \mathsf{Gen}(\mathsf{pp}, \beta; r)$: on input public parameters pp, binding position $\beta \in \{0,1\}$, and randomness r, returns the commitment parameters $(p_0, p_1) \in \mathcal{Y}^{\mathsf{pp}}$ and the trapdoor td for parameter $p_{1-\beta}$ such that $(p_{1-\beta}, \mathsf{td})$ belongs to $\mathcal{R}_T$[8].
- $\mathsf{com} \leftarrow \mathsf{BindCom}(\mathsf{pp}, p_0, p_1, m_0, m_1; r)$: on input public parameters pp, commitment parameters p_0, p_1, messages m_0, m_1, and randomness r outputs a commitment com.
- $(\mathsf{com}, \mathsf{aux}) \leftarrow \mathsf{EquivCom}(\mathsf{pp}, \beta, m, p_0, p_1, \mathsf{td}; r)$: on input public parameters pp, binding position β, message of the binding position m, commitment param-

---

[8] The statement for $\mathcal{R}_T$ may also depend from pp. We will omit this dependence to simplify the notation.

eters p_0, p_1, trapdoor td, and randomness r returns a commitment com and auxiliary information aux.

- $r \leftarrow$ Equiv(pp, β, m_0, m_1, p_0, p_1, td, aux): on input public parameters pp, binding position β, messages m_0, m_1, commitment parameters p_0, p_1, trapdoor td, and auxiliary information aux, deterministically returns an equivocation randomness r.

In the following, we assume that pp was already generated by a trusted third party using the algorithm Setup. Furthermore, we will omit the randomness from the input of the algorithms, except when it is relevant. A sender and a receiver interact using the commitment scheme as follows.

Commit Phase: The sender, on input m and binding position β, computes $(p_0, p_1, \text{td}) \leftarrow$ Gen(pp, β), (com, aux) $\leftarrow$ EquivCom(pp, β, m, p_0, p_1, td). The sender sends (com, p_0, p_1) to the receiver.

Reveal Phase: The sender, on input m^*, computes $r \leftarrow$ Equiv(pp, β, m_0, m_1, p_0, p_1, td, aux) where $m_\beta = m$ and $m_{1-\beta} = m^*$, and sends (r, m_0, m_1) to the receiver. The receiver computes com' $\leftarrow$ BindCom(pp, p_0, p_1, m_0, m_1; r) and accepts if com' = com and $(p_0, p_1) \in \mathcal{Y}^{\text{pp}}$, rejects otherwise.

We state below the properties we require for the 1-out-of-2 equivocal commitment scheme.

Partial Equivocation: For all $\lambda \in \mathbb{N}$, pp $\leftarrow$ Setup(1^λ), $\beta \in \{0,1\}$, $(p_0, p_1) \in \mathcal{Y}^{\text{pp}}$, $(m_0, m_1) \in \{0,1\}^{2\lambda}$, td such that $(p_{1-\beta}, \text{td}) \in \mathcal{R}_T$ the following holds:

$$\text{Prob}\left[\begin{array}{c|c} \text{BindCom(pp, } p_0, p_1, & \text{(com, aux)} \leftarrow \text{EquivCom(pp, } \beta, m_\beta, p_0, p_1, \text{td)}; \\ m_0, m_1; r) = \text{com} & r \leftarrow \text{Equiv(pp, } \beta, m_0, m_1, p_0, p_1, \text{td, aux).} \end{array}\right] = 1.$$

Computational Fixed Equivocation: Given the experiment ExpFixEquiv below, for every non-uniform PPT $\mathcal{A}$, there exists a negligible function $\nu(\cdot)$ such that for any $\lambda \in \mathbb{N}$: Prob[ExpFixEquiv$_\mathcal{A}(\lambda) = 1$] $\leq \nu(\lambda)$.

ExpFixEquiv$_\mathcal{A}(\lambda)$

1. pp $\leftarrow$ Setup(1^λ).
2. $(p_0, p_1, r^1, r^2, r^3, r^4, m_0^1, m_0^2, m_1^1, m_1^2, m_0^3, m_0^4, m_1^3, m_1^4) \leftarrow \mathcal{A}(\text{pp})$.
3. Return 1 if $\exists \beta \in \{0,1\}$ such that

$$(\text{BindCom(pp, } p_0, p_1, m_0^1, m_1^1; r^1) = \text{BindCom(pp, } p_0, p_1, m_0^2, m_1^2; r^2) \wedge$$
$$(\text{BindCom(pp, } p_0, p_1, m_0^3, m_1^3; r^3) = \text{BindCom(pp, } p_0, p_1, m_0^4, m_1^4; r^4)) \wedge$$
$$(m_{1-\beta}^1 \neq m_{1-\beta}^2) \wedge (m_\beta^3 \neq m_\beta^4) \wedge ((p_0, p_1) \in \mathcal{Y}^{\text{pp}}).$$

Return 0 otherwise.

Moreover, the protocol achieves perfect fixed equivocation if for any unbounded $\mathcal{A}$ it holds that Prob[ExpFixEquiv$_\mathcal{A}(\lambda) = 1$] $= 0$.

Computational Position Hiding: Given the experiment ExpHid below, for every non-uniform PPT $\mathcal{A}$, there exists a negligible function $\nu(\cdot)$ such that for any $\lambda \in \mathbb{N}$: $\text{Prob}\left[\,\text{ExpHid}_{\mathcal{A}}(\lambda) = 1\,\right] \leq \frac{1}{2} + \nu(\lambda)$.

$$\text{ExpHid}_{\mathcal{A}}(\lambda)$$

1. $\text{pp} \leftarrow \text{Setup}(1^{\lambda})$.
2. Sample $\beta \leftarrow_{\$} \{0,1\}$ and compute $(p_0, p_1, \text{td}) \leftarrow \text{Gen}(\text{pp}, \beta)$.
3. $\beta' \leftarrow \mathcal{A}(\text{pp}, p_0, p_1)$.
4. Return 1 if $\beta' = \beta$ and 0 otherwise.

Moreover, if $\mathcal{A}$ is unbounded and $\nu(\lambda) = 0$ we say that the scheme is perfect position hiding.

Computational Trapdoorness: Given the experiment ExpTrap, for every non-uniform PPT $\mathcal{A}$, there exists a negligible function $\nu(\cdot)$ such that for any $\lambda \in \mathbb{N}$: $\text{Prob}\left[\,\text{ExpTrap}_{\mathcal{A}}(\lambda) = 1\,\right] \leq \frac{1}{2} + \nu(\lambda)$.

$$\text{ExpTrap}_{\mathcal{A}}(\lambda)$$

1. $\text{pp} \leftarrow \text{Setup}(1^{\lambda})$.
2. $(m_0, m_1, p_0, p_1, \text{td}, \beta) \leftarrow \mathcal{A}(\text{pp})$.
3. If $(p_0, p_1) \notin \mathcal{Y}^{\text{pp}}$ or $(p_{1-\beta}, \text{td}) \notin \mathcal{R}_T$ abort the experiment.
4. Sample $b \leftarrow_{\$} \{0,1\}$. If $b = 0$, set $(\text{com}, \text{aux}) \leftarrow \text{EquivCom}(\text{pp}, \beta, m_\beta, p_0, p_1, \text{td})$ and set $r \leftarrow \text{Equiv}(\text{pp}, \beta, m_0, m_1, p_0, p_1, \text{td}, \text{aux})$. If $b = 1$, sample $r \leftarrow_{\$} D$ and set $\text{com} \leftarrow \text{BindCom}(\text{pp}, p_0, p_1, m_0, m_1; r)$.
5. $b' \leftarrow \mathcal{A}(\text{pp}, m_0, m_1, p_0, p_1, \text{td}, \beta, \text{com}, r)$.
6. Return 1 if $b = b'$, return 0 otherwise.

Moreover, if $\mathcal{A}$ is unbounded and $\nu(\lambda) = 0$ we say that the protocol achieves perfect trapdoorness.

GGHK enjoys computational fixed equivocation, perfect position hiding and perfect trapdoorness[9]. Moreover, since GGHK has perfect position hiding and perfect trapdoorness, the use of this commitment scheme in $\Pi_{1,\ell}$ preserves the statistical/perfect zero knowledge property of the underlying Σ-protocols. Computational fixed equivocation forces the special soundness to be only computational instead (special soundness is degraded in any case since in [10] an hash function is used to compress the size of first-round messages).

---

[9] Our definition slightly differs from the one in [10]. In particular, our fixed equivocation property implies the partial binding of [10]. We need this slightly stronger property to prove the soundness of our (k, ℓ)-PTR. Natural instantiations such as GGHK enjoy the fixed equivocation property. The remaining properties are just a restatement of the minimal requirements for a 1-out-of-2 commitment scheme in [10].

3.2 Π_{ord}: A Σ-Protocol to Prove Parameters Ordering

We use the following notation: for any vector $\mathbf{v}$, $\mathbf{v}[z]$ indicates the z-th element of the vector $\mathbf{v}$. The first element of a vector $\mathbf{v}$ is indexed as $\mathbf{v}[1]$. Moreover, we use $[n]$ for $n \in \mathbb{N}$ to identify the set $\{1, \ldots, n\}$. Let $\mathbf{x} = ((p_0^1, p_1^1), \ldots, (p_0^n, p_1^n))$ be a vector containing n pairs of parameters corresponding to n instantiations of a 1-out-of-2 equivocal commitment scheme, where p_0^i represents the parameter of the first position of the i-th commitment instantiation, and p_1^i is the analogue for the second position. Consider the relations $\mathcal{R}_{T_0}$ and $\mathcal{R}_{T_1}$, where $\mathcal{R}_{T_0} = \{(x = (p_0, p_1), w) : p_1 \text{ is a trapdoor parameter and } w \text{ is the corresponding trapdoor}\}$ and, similarly $\mathcal{R}_{T_1} = \{(x = (p_0, p_1), w) : p_0 \text{ is a trapdoor parameter and } w \text{ is the corresponding trapdoor}\}$ (i.e., $(x = (p_0, p_1), w) \in \mathcal{R}_{T_i}$ if and only if $(p_{1-i}, w) \in \mathcal{R}_T$ with $i \in \{0, 1\}$). We present a Σ-protocol Π_{ord} that, given a vector $X = (\mathbf{x_1}, \ldots, \mathbf{x_k})$ of vectors each containing n pairs of parameters corresponding to n instantiations of a 1-out-of-2 equivocal commitment scheme, allows a prover P to efficiently prove knowledge of a witness for $X \in \mathcal{L}$ where

$$\mathcal{L} = \{X : \exists W = (\mathbf{w_1}, \ldots, \mathbf{w_k}) \text{ such that}$$
$$\forall i, j \in [k] \text{ with } i \neq j \ \exists z \in [n], \text{ such that } b_{i,z} \neq b_{j,z}\} \tag{1}$$

where $b_{i,z}, b_{j,z} \in \{0, 1\}$ satisfy $(\mathbf{x_i}[z], \mathbf{w_i}[z]) \in \mathcal{R}_{T_{b_{i,z}}}, (\mathbf{x_j}[z], \mathbf{w_j}[z]) \in \mathcal{R}_{T_{b_{j,z}}}$.

An efficient Σ-Protocol. One could naively prove the above statement by separately proving that each vector of n pairs of commitment parameters differs in the way equivocal and binding parameters are laid out w.r.t. every other vector. Carrying out such proof would involve a quadratic (in k) amount of separate proofs. We instead take a different path, that is introducing a strict total ordering among these k vectors of n pairs of commitment parameters. In particular, we map a vector $\mathbf{x}$ of n pairs of commitment parameters to a binary string $s \in \{0, 1\}^n$ by setting $s = b_1 || \ldots || b_n$, for which $(\mathbf{x}[z], \mathbf{w}[z]) \in \mathcal{R}_{T_{b_z}}$. Let s_m with $m \in [k]$ be the string resulting by applying the above mapping to a vector $\mathbf{x_m}$ of n pairs of commitment parameters. W.l.o.g. consider the case where $s_1 > \ldots > s_k$. If the above order relation holds, it follows that all the k vectors of n pairs of commitment parameters are logically different from each other in terms of how the trapdoor parameters are laid out in at least one position. Notice that after having introduced such ordering among the k vectors of n pairs of commitment parameters, one can come up with the language $\mathcal{L}_{ord}$ described by only a linear number of comparisons. Indeed, the language of Eq. 1 can be equivalently rewritten as $\mathcal{L}_{ord} = \{X : \exists W = (\mathbf{w_1}, \ldots, \mathbf{w_k}) \text{ such that } s_1 > s_2 > \ldots > s_k\}$, where for all $m \in [k]$, $s_m = b_1 || \ldots || b_n$, for which $(\mathbf{x_m}[i], \mathbf{w_m}[i]) \in \mathcal{R}_{T_{b_i}}$.

Instantiation. Let us consider two binary strings $s_1 \in \{0, 1\}^n$ and $s_2 \in \{0, 1\}^n$, in which we use $s[i]$ to indicate the i-th bit of the string s, it is pretty straightforward to see that if $s_1 > s_2$, the following formula also holds[10]:

---

[10] For consistency reasons, we assign the index 1 to the first position within the string and we say that $s_i[0] = 0$.

$$\bigvee_{i=1}^{n} \left(\left(\bigwedge_{j=0}^{i-1} (s_1[j] = s_2[j]) \right) \wedge (s_1[i] > s_2[i]) \right). \tag{2}$$

Indeed, this corresponds to performing a bit-wise comparison between s_1 and s_2, starting from the most significant bit. Namely, if $s_1 > s_2$, the first different bit between the two strings has value 1 in s_1 and 0 in s_2.

Building on this observation, we can construct a protocol $\Pi_{ord'}$ to prove that two binary strings, each representing a vector of n 1-out-of-2 equivocal commitment parameters, are such that one is greater than the other. Then, given k vectors of commitment parameters, one can prove that $X = (\mathbf{x_1}, \ldots, \mathbf{x_k}) \in \mathcal{L}_{ord}$, where $|\mathbf{x_i}| = n$ for all $i \in [k]$, by using $\Pi_{ord'}$ $k - 1$ times. We denote the resulting protocol as Π_{ord}.

1-out-of-2-Commitment of [10]. In [10], a t-out-of-ℓ equivocal commitment scheme GGHK based on the discrete logarithm assumption is defined. GGHK uses the same SRS of the non-interactive version of the Pedersen commitment scheme, namely, two generators g_0, h of a group $\mathbb{G}$ where the discrete logarithm of g_0 in base h is not known. For the interesting case of $t = 1$ and $\ell = 2$, the commitment parameters are two group generators algebraically derived from the SRS. The receiver is able to verify that the parameters are correctly generated via a simple algebraic check. In particular, $\mathcal{Y}^{\mathsf{PP}} = \{p_0 \in \mathbb{G}, p_1 \in \mathbb{G} : p_1 = p_0^2 g_0^{-1}\}$. The trapdoor associated to the equivocal position is the discrete logarithm in base h of the corresponding parameter. Thus, $\mathcal{R}_T = \{(x, w) : x = h^w\}$. Due to space limitations, we do not discuss the actual construction. We refer the reader to [10] for more details.

Instantiating Π_{ord} for the Commitment of [10]. We now instantiate Π_{ord} for vectors of commitment parameters of GGHK. To do so, we just need to express Formula 2 in terms of the parameters of GGHK. Given (p_0^a, p_1^a), we represent membership of (p_b^a, w) in $\mathcal{R}_T$ as the function $\mathcal{R}_{\mathsf{DL}}(p_b^a, w)$ evaluating to 1 if w is the discrete logarithm of p_b^a w.r.t. h and 0 otherwise. Given two vectors of n commitment parameters of GGHK $P = ((p_0^1, p_1^1), \ldots, (p_0^n, p_1^n))$ and $Q = ((q_0^1, q_1^1), \ldots, (q_0^n, q_1^n))$, and two vectors of corresponding witnesses $W_p = (w_p^1, \ldots, w_p^n)$ and $W_q = (w_q^1, \ldots, w_q^n)$, Formula 2 can be rewritten as a relation $\mathcal{R}_{ord'}$ on input $((P, Q), (W_p, W_q))$[11]:

$$\bigvee_{i=1}^{n} \left(\left(\bigwedge_{j=0}^{i-1} (((\mathcal{R}_{\mathsf{DL}}(p_0^j, w_p^j) \wedge \mathcal{R}_{\mathsf{DL}}(q_0^j, w_q^j)) \vee (\mathcal{R}_{\mathsf{DL}}(p_1^j, w_p^j) \wedge \mathcal{R}_{\mathsf{DL}}(q_1^j, w_q^j))) \right) \right.$$

$$\left. \wedge (\mathcal{R}_{\mathsf{DL}}(p_1^i, w_p^i) \wedge \mathcal{R}_{\mathsf{DL}}(q_0^i, w_q^i)) \right). \tag{3}$$

---

[11] In the following formula the AND ranging from $j = 0$ to $j = i - 1$ is evaluated as true for $j = 0$. Indeed, according to the notation used in this paper, there are no parameters pair in the position 0 of the vector.

Basically, for each bit of the strings s_1 and s_2 of Formula 2, such bits are equal if the corresponding parameters pairs have the same trapdoor position, meaning that either the sender knows the discrete log of both the first positions of the pairs, or that the same applies for the second position of both parameters pairs. A bit of a string is defined to be 1 if the corresponding parameters pair has in its first position a group element with a discrete log that is known to the sender, while it is 0 if the same applies to the second position.

Given k vectors $V_1, \ldots, V_k$ of n pairs of commitment parameters and k vectors $W_1, \ldots, W_k$ of witnesses, the relation proved by Π_{ord}, is defined as follows:

$$\mathcal{R}_{ord}((V_1, \ldots, V_k), (W_1, \ldots, W_k)) = \bigwedge_{i=1}^{k-1} \mathcal{R}_{ord'}((V_i, V_{i+1}), (W_i, W_{i+1})). \quad (4)$$

Our instantiation of Π_{ord} can be obtained via OR/AND compositions of the Schnorr's Σ-protocol [9], which is also stackable [10]. As a result, Π_{ord} is a stackable Σ-protocol with computational special soundness and perfect EHVZK. $\Pi_{ord'}$, proving $\mathcal{R}_{ord'}$, achieves communication complexity $\mathcal{O}(n\lambda + \lambda \log n) = \mathcal{O}(n\lambda)$. Π_{ord} can be obtained by repeating $\Pi_{ord'}$ $k-1$ times in parallel, obtaining a communication complexity of $\mathcal{O}((k-1)n\lambda) = \mathcal{O}(kn\lambda)$.

3.3 Efficient (k, ℓ)-PTR

We build our (k, ℓ)-PTR repeating the $(1, \ell)$-PTR of [10] k times and using Π_{ord} with statements the k vectors of commitment parameters of length $\mathcal{O}(\log \ell)$ that constitute the composition trees. Notice that Π_{ord} is defined over ordered tuples of pairs of commitment parameters. However, the prover can easily sort the k underlying $(1, \ell)$-PTRs according to such ordering when interacting with the verifier. Let $(\mathsf{P}_0^{1,\ell}, \mathsf{P}_1^{1,\ell})$ be the prover algorithms of the $(1, \ell)$-PTR from [10]. W.l.o.g., we also assume that the algorithm $\mathsf{P}_0^{1,\ell}$ outputs, together with the first-round message a to be sent to $\mathsf{V}^{1,\ell}$, the tuple of commitment parameters $((p_0^1, p_1^1), \ldots, (p_0^{\log \ell}, p_1^{\log \ell}))$ and the related witnesses tuple $(\mathsf{td}^1, \ldots, \mathsf{td}^{\log \ell})$.

Considering the relation $\mathcal{R}_{k,\ell} = \{((x_1, \ldots, x_\ell), ((w_1, \alpha_1), \ldots, (w_k, \alpha_k))) | 1 \leq \alpha_1 < \ldots < \alpha_k \leq \ell \wedge \forall j \in [k] : (x_{\alpha_j}, w_j) \in \mathcal{R}_\mathcal{L}\}$, we state the theorem below.

Theorem 1. *Let $\Pi_{1,\ell}$ be the stackable Σ-protocol of [10], and let Π_{ord} be the stackable Σ-protocol of Sect. 3.2. $\Pi_{k,\ell} = (\mathsf{P}^{k,\ell}, \mathsf{V}^{k,\ell})$ described in Fig. 2 is a stackable Σ-protocol for relation $\mathcal{R}_{k,\ell}$ with computational special soundness. Furthermore, $\Pi_{k,\ell}$ preserves the EHVZK flavour of the underlying $\Pi_{1,\ell}$.*

Due to lack of space, we defer to the full version [3] for the formal proof. We instead give here an informal proof sketch.

Computational Special Soundness. To prove the computational special soundness of $\Pi_{k,\ell}$, we exploit the computational special soundness of the k executions of $\Pi_{1,\ell}$, the computational special soundness of Π_{ord}, as well as the partial equivocation and the fixed equivocation properties of the 1-out-of-2 equivocal commitment scheme. Let us first review the extractor $\mathsf{Extract}_{1,\ell}$ of $\Pi_{1,\ell}$. $\mathsf{Extract}_{1,\ell}$

In our (k, ℓ)-PTR $\Pi_{k,\ell} = (\mathsf{P}_0^{k,\ell}, \mathsf{P}_1^{k,\ell}, \mathsf{V}^{k,\ell})$, the prover takes as input a tuple of statements $\mathbf{x} = (x_1, \dots, x_\ell)$ and k witnesses $\mathbf{w} = ((w_1, \alpha_1), \dots, (w_k, \alpha_k))$ in which $\alpha_j \in [\ell]$ is the position of the j-th witness. $\Pi_{k,\ell}$ uses the $(1, \ell)$-PTR $\Pi_{1,\ell} = (\mathsf{P}_0^{1,\ell}, \mathsf{P}_1^{1,\ell}, \mathsf{V}^{1,\ell})$, and $\Pi_{ord} = (\mathsf{P}_0^{ord}, \mathsf{P}_1^{ord}, \mathsf{V}^{ord})$.

First Round: The prover invokes $\mathsf{P}_0^{k,\ell}$ that, on input $(\mathbf{x}, \mathbf{w}; \mathsf{rand})$ computes a as follows:
1. Parse rand as $\mathsf{rand}_{\mathsf{P}_1} \| \dots \| \mathsf{rand}_{\mathsf{P}_k} \| \mathsf{rand}_{ord}$;
2. For all $j \in [k]$: Run $(a_j, \mathbf{p}_j, \mathbf{td}_j) \leftarrow \mathsf{P}_0^{1,\ell}(\mathbf{x}, (w_j, \alpha_j); \mathsf{rand}_{\mathsf{P}_j})$, where $\mathbf{p}_j = ((p_0^{(1,j)}, p_1^{(1,j)}), \dots, (p_0^{(\log \ell, j)}, p_1^{(\log \ell, j)}))$ and $\mathbf{td}_j = (\mathsf{td}^{(1,j)}, \dots, \mathsf{td}^{(\log \ell, j)})$;
3. Generate $a_{ord} \leftarrow \mathsf{P}_0^{ord}((\mathbf{p}_j)_{j \in [k]}, (\mathbf{td}_j)_{j \in [k]}; \mathsf{rand}_{ord})$;

   The prover sends $a = (a_1, \dots, a_k, a_{ord}, \mathbf{p}_1, \dots, \mathbf{p}_k)$ to the verifier.
Second Round: The verifier samples $c \in \{0, 1\}^\lambda$ and sends c to the prover.
Third Round: The prover invokes $\mathsf{P}_1^{k,\ell}$ that computes z as follows: For each $j \in [k]$ run $z_j \leftarrow \mathsf{P}_1^{1,\ell}(\mathbf{x}, (w_j, \alpha_j), c; \mathsf{rand}_{\mathsf{P}_j})$ and $z_{ord} \leftarrow \mathsf{P}_1^{ord}((\mathbf{p}_j)_{j \in [k]}, (\mathbf{td}_j)_{j \in [k]}, c; \mathsf{rand}_{ord})$;

   Then, the prover sends $z = (z_1, \dots, z_k, z_{ord})$ to the verifier.
Verification: The verifier invokes $\mathsf{V}^{k,\ell}$ that, on input $(\mathbf{x}, a = (a_1, \dots, a_k, a_{ord}, \mathbf{p}_1, \dots, \mathbf{p}_k), c, z = (z_1, \dots, z_k, z_{ord}))$, returns a bit b as follows:
1. For $i \in [k]$ and $j \in [\log \ell]$ check that $(p_0^{(i,j)}, p_1^{(i,j)}) \in \mathcal{Y}^{\mathsf{pp}}$, where the pairs $(p_0^{(i,j)}, p_1^{(i,j)})$ are taken from z_i;
2. Check that $\mathbf{p}_i = (p_0^{(i,j)}, p_1^{(i,j)})_{j \in [\log \ell]}$;
3. For all $i \in [k]$ check that $\mathsf{V}^{1,\ell}(\mathbf{x}, a_i, c, z_i) = 1$;
4. Check that $\mathsf{V}^{ord}((\mathbf{p}_j)_{j \in [k]}, a_{ord}, c, z_{ord}) = 1$;
5. If all the previous checks are successful, output 1. Otherwise, output 0.

Fig. 2. Our communication-efficient (k, ℓ)-PTR from stackable Σ-protocols.

works via recursive calls to $\mathsf{Extract}_{1,2}$, the extractor of $\Pi_{1,2}$. Starting from the root of the composition tree, both the children nodes are considered and every time two accepting transcripts with the same first-round message are found, $\mathsf{Extract}_{1,2}$ is called again. The base case for the recursion is a leaf node having two accepting transcripts with the same first-round message. In this case, the extractor of the base Σ-protocol is called instead. Since the computational special soundness of $\Pi_{1,\ell}$ is proven using $\mathsf{Extract}_{1,\ell}$ shown above, we are guaranteed (except with negligible probability) that *at least* one of such leaf nodes exits. This in turn implies that at each level of the tree there is *at least* one node having two accepting transcripts with the same first-round message that we can give as input to $\mathsf{Extract}_{1,2}$. However, in principle there could be more than one of such nodes in each level. On such nodes $\mathsf{Extract}_{1,2}$ would be called again, and we would get at least one witness for the corresponding OR relation (recall that $\Pi_{1,2}$ proves the OR relation on two statements, such statements may be OR statements as well). The extraction algorithm will recursively lead to at least one witness for one base statement. Given the way the composition tree is constructed, witnesses extracted from different nodes are always related to different statements. For the sake of simplicity, let us focus on the case in which exactly one witness is extracted from each pair of accepting transcripts of $\Pi_{1,\ell}$. We now have to argue why all these k witnesses must be related to different statements. Let us assume that two witnesses related to the same statement are extracted from two executions of $\Pi_{1,\ell}$. Let us consider the composition trees of such executions. The computational special soundness of Π_{ord} guarantees (except with negligible probability) that there is one level in which, using the extractor of Π_{ord}, we extract a trapdoor for a different edge in each of the two trees (namely, a trapdoor for the first and the second parameter of the commitment scheme). If we consider such level, we can define a sub-tree containing the leaf corresponding to the extracted witness and having as root the parent node corresponding to the first edge in which we extracted a trapdoor for different edges. We are now able to break the fixed equivocation property of the commitment scheme at the first level of one of the two of such sub-trees. Indeed, consider the sub-tree having the extracted trapdoor on the same side of the extracted witness. W.l.o.g. let it be the left side. Since we extracted a witness for the left side, the first-round message of the corresponding left side Σ-protocol is the same in both transcripts, while the right-side first-round message is equivocated (otherwise, we would have extracted a witness also for this side). This means we already have a commitment which equivocates a message on the right side. Thanks to the extracted trapdoor and the partial equivocation property, we are now able to construct a fresh commitment w.r.t. the same parameters which successfully equivocates the left side. This would break the fixed equivocation property of the commitment scheme, thus reaching a contradiction. The actual proof is slightly more involved since, as we already argued above, from each pair of executions of $\Pi_{1,\ell}$ it is generally possible to extract more than one witness. Therefore, in general we are not guaranteed to find a sub-tree having a level with an extracted trapdoor on one side and an equivocated commitment on the other side. However, in the full version [3] we exploit the fact that the number of extracted witnesses per composition tree using $\mathsf{Extract}_{1,\ell}$ is strictly less than k[12] to argue that, among all the k pairs of composition trees with the same first-round message, there always exists a tree on which we are able to run the above reduction to the partial equivocation and the fixed equivocation properties of the commitment scheme. We prove this by induction. We exploit the fact that at each level of the tree there are *at most* two configurations of the extracted trapdoors and witnesses that do not allow the above reduction at that level. Furthermore, we use the observation that extracting a witness from a node at level $i - 1$ requires extracting a witness from at least one of its children nodes at level i.

Extended Honest-Verifier Zero Knowledge. We name the EHVZK simulator of $\Pi_{k,\ell}$ as $\mathcal{S}_{k,\ell}$ and we use $D_{k,\ell}$ to indicate the third-round messages distribution

---

[12] All witnesses extracted from the same composition tree are related to different statements by construction. Thus, in this case we would not need to show any reduction.

of $\Pi_{k,\ell}$. $\mathcal{S}_{k,\ell}$, on input statement $(x_1, \ldots, x_\ell)$, challenge c, and third-round message $z = (z_1, \ldots, z_k, z_{ord})$ sampled from $D_{k,\ell}$, outputs the first-round message $(a_1, \ldots, a_k, a_{ord}, \mathbf{p}_1, \ldots, \mathbf{p}_k)$. Recall that the EHVZK property requires that all third-round messages of honest protocol executions for statements $x \in \mathcal{L}$ follow the same distribution. Such distribution must be efficiently samplable. Furthermore, running the simulator on input statement $x \in \mathcal{L}$, a uniformly random challenge c, and a third-round message z sampled from such distribution, deterministically produces a first-round message a so that (a, c, z) is indistinguishable from honest protocol execution transcripts (see Appendix A.1). Notice that sampling from $D_{k,\ell}$ simply consists of sampling each z_i, with $i \in [k]$, from $D_{1,\ell}$ (i.e., the third-round messages distribution of $\Pi_{1,\ell}$), and sampling z_{ord} from D_{ord} (i.e., the third-round messages distribution of Π_{ord}). Since both $\Pi_{1,\ell}$ and Π_{ord} are EHVZK, such distributions exist and are efficiently samplable.

We construct $\mathcal{S}_{k,\ell}$ in terms of the EHVZK simulators of the underlying protocols. We name the EHVZK simulator of $\Pi_{1,\ell}$ as $\mathcal{S}_{1,\ell}$ and we use $\mathcal{S}_{ord}$ to indicate the EHVZK simulator of Π_{ord}. $\mathcal{S}_{k,\ell}$ parses each z_j, with $j \in [k]$, and selects the commitment parameters $\mathbf{p}_j = ((p_0^{(1,j)}, p_1^{(1,j)}), \ldots, (p_0^{(\log \ell, j)}, p_1^{(\log \ell, j)}))$. $\mathcal{S}_{k,\ell}$ gives in input to $\mathcal{S}_{ord}$ the instance $(\mathbf{p}_1, \ldots, \mathbf{p}_k)$, the challenge c, and z_{ord}, thus obtaining a_{ord}. Then, $\mathcal{S}_{k,\ell}$ runs $\mathcal{S}_{1,\ell}((x_1, \ldots, x_\ell), c, z_i)$ for each of the k $(1, \ell)$-PTR obtaining $(a_1, \ldots, a_k)$. Finally, $\mathcal{S}_{k,\ell}$ outputs $(a_1, \ldots, a_k, a_{ord}, \mathbf{p}_1, \ldots, \mathbf{p}_k)$. We now show that $\Pi_{k,\ell}$ is EHVZK via hybrid arguments. The first hybrid $\mathcal{H}_1$ corresponds to the real protocol execution, except that z_{ord} is sampled from D_{ord} and a_{ord} is obtained running $\mathcal{S}_{ord}$. The real protocol and $\mathcal{H}_1$ are indistinguishable thanks to the EHVZK of Π_{ord}. Then, a sequence of k hybrids $\mathcal{H}_2, \ldots, \mathcal{H}_{k+1}$ follows; each hybrid $\mathcal{H}_i$, with $i \in \{2, \ldots, k+1\}$ differs from the previous one because z_i, the third-round message of the i-th $(1, \ell)$-PTR, is sampled from $D_{1,\ell}$, and the first-round message a_i is computed using $\mathcal{S}_{1,\ell}$. Each hybrid is indistinguishable from its predecessor due to the EHVZK of $\Pi_{1,\ell}$. The proof of EHVZK of $\Pi_{k,\ell}$ ends by observing that $\mathcal{H}_{k+1}$ is identical to $\mathcal{S}_{k,\ell}$. Notice that Π_{ord} is perfect EHVZK and that $\Pi_{1,\ell}$ preserves the EHVZK flavour of the composed protocols. Thus, $\Pi_{k,\ell}$ clearly preserves the EHVZK flavour of the composed protocols.

On the Communication Complexity of our (k, ℓ)-PTR. Π_{ord} has a communication complexity of $\mathcal{O}(k\lambda \log \ell)$. The communication complexity of a single execution of $\Pi_{1,\ell}$ is $\mathcal{O}(\lambda \log \ell + \mathsf{CC}(\Sigma_{base}))$, where Σ_{base} is the underlying protocol. The k repetitions of $\Pi_{1,\ell}$ lead to a communication complexity of $\mathcal{O}(k(\lambda \log \ell + \mathsf{CC}(\Sigma_{base}))$ in total. Therefore, the communication complexity of $\Pi_{k,\ell}$ is $\mathcal{O}(k(\lambda \log \ell + \mathsf{CC}(\Sigma_{base})) + k(\lambda \log \ell)) = \mathcal{O}(k(\lambda \log \ell + \mathsf{CC}(\Sigma_{base}))$.

Acknowledgements. We thank all the anonymous reviewers for their insightful comments. The work of the third author was supported by SPECTRA from Sapienza University of Rome.

A Σ-Protocols

We consider a *3-round* public-coin protocol Π for an NP language $\mathcal{L}$ with a poly-time relation $\mathcal{R}_{\mathcal{L}}$. $\Pi = (\mathsf{P}_0, \mathsf{P}_1, \mathsf{V})$ is run by a prover running auxiliary algorithms $\mathsf{P}_0, \mathsf{P}_1$ and a verifier running an auxiliary algorithm V. The prover and the verifier receive common input x and the security parameter 1^λ. The prover receives as an additional private input a witness w for x. Prover and verifier use the auxiliary algorithms $\mathsf{P}_0, \mathsf{P}_1, \mathsf{V}^{13}$ in the following way:

1. The prover runs P_0 on common input x, private input w, randomness R, and outputs a message a. The prover sends a to the verifier;
2. The verifier samples a random challenge $c \leftarrow_\$ \{0,1\}^\lambda$ and sends c to the prover;
3. The prover runs P_1 on common input x, private input w, first-round message a, randomness R, and challenge c, and outputs the third-round message z, which is then sent to the verifier;
4. The verifier outputs 1 if $\mathsf{V}(x, a, c, z) = 1$, and rejects otherwise.

The transcript (a, c, z) for the protocol $\Pi = (\mathsf{P}_0, \mathsf{P}_1, \mathsf{V})$, and common statement x is called *accepting* if $\mathsf{V}(x, a, c, z) = 1$.

Definition 1. *A 3-round public-coin protocol* $\Pi = (\mathsf{P}_0, \mathsf{P}_1, \mathsf{V})$, *is a Σ-protocol for an NP language $\mathcal{L}$ with a poly-time relation $\mathcal{R}_{\mathcal{L}}$ iff the following holds*

Completeness: *For all $x \in \mathcal{L}$ and w such that $(x, w) \in \mathcal{R}_{\mathcal{L}}$ it holds that:*

$$\mathrm{Prob}\left[\mathsf{V}(x, a, c, z) = 1 \;\middle|\; \begin{array}{c} R \leftarrow_\$ \{0,1\}^\lambda; c \leftarrow_\$ \{0,1\}^\lambda; \\ a \leftarrow \mathsf{P}_0(x, w; R); \\ z \leftarrow \mathsf{P}_1(x, w, a, c; R) \end{array} \right] = 1.$$

Special Soundness: *$\exists$ PPT Extract, such that on input x and two accepting transcripts (a, c_0, z_0) and (a, c_1, z_1) for x, where $c_0 \neq c_1$, it holds that*

$$\mathrm{Prob}\left[(x, w) \in \mathcal{R}_{\mathcal{L}} \middle| w \leftarrow \mathsf{Extract}(x, a, c_0, c_1, z_0, z_1) \right] = 1.$$

Special HVZK (SHVZK): *There exists a PPT simulator $\mathcal{S}$ that, on input an instance $x \in \mathcal{L}$ and challenge c, outputs (a, z) such that (a, c, z) is an accepting transcript for x. Moreover, the distribution of the output of $\mathcal{S}$ on input (x, c) is computationally/statistically/perfectly indistinguishable from the distribution obtained when the verifier sends c as challenge and the prover runs on common input x and any private input w such that $(x, w) \in \mathcal{R}_{\mathcal{L}}$.*

Computational Special Soundness: *$\exists$ PPT Extract s.t. $\forall$ PPT P^* $\exists$ a negl. function $\nu(\cdot)$ such that $\forall x \in \mathcal{L}$, $\mathrm{Prob}\left[\mathsf{ExpExt}_{\mathsf{P}^*, \mathsf{Extract}}(x) = 1 \right] \leq \nu(|x|)$.*

---

[13] For convenience, we omit the security parameter in unary from the inputs.

$$\mathsf{ExpExt}_{\mathsf{P}^*,\mathsf{Extract}}(x)$$

1. $(a, c_0, c_1, z_0, z_1) \leftarrow \mathsf{P}^*(x)$.
2. If $c_0 \neq c_1$, or $\mathsf{V}(x, a, c_0, z_0) = 0$, or $\mathsf{V}(x, a, c_1, z_1) = 0$ return 0.
3. $w \leftarrow \mathsf{Extract}(x, a, c_0, c_1, z_0, z_1)$.
4. Return 1 if $(x, w) \notin \mathcal{R}_{\mathcal{L}}$. Otherwise, return 0.

A.1   Stackable Σ-protocols

Definition 2 (Computational/Statistical EHVZK). *Let* $\Sigma = (\mathsf{P}_0, \mathsf{P}_1, \mathsf{V})$, *be a* Σ-*protocol for an NP language* $\mathcal{L}$. Σ *is EHVZK if there exists a PPT algorithm* $\mathcal{S}^{\mathsf{EHVZK}}$ *such that for all PPT/unbounded* $\mathcal{D}$, *and* $c \in \{0,1\}^\lambda$, *there exists an efficiently samplable distribution* $D_{x,c}^{(z)}$ *and a negligible function* $\nu(\cdot)$ *such that for all* $x \in \mathcal{L}$

$$\left| \mathrm{Prob} \left[\mathsf{ExpEHVZK}_{(\mathsf{P}_0, \mathsf{P}_1), \mathcal{D}}(c) = 1 \right] - \mathrm{Prob} \left[\mathsf{ExpEHVZK}_{\mathcal{S}^{\mathsf{EHVZK}}, \mathcal{D}}(c) = 1 \right] \right| \leq \nu(|x|).$$

We say instead that a Σ-protocol is perfect EHVZK if the difference between the probabilities is exactly 0. The experiment $\mathsf{ExpEHVZK}$ for EHVZK follows.

$$\mathsf{ExpEHVZK}_{\mathsf{P}', \mathcal{D}}(c)$$

1. $(x, w) \leftarrow \mathcal{D}(c)$.
2. If $(x, w) \notin \mathcal{R}_{\mathcal{L}}$, return 0.
3. If $\mathsf{P}' = \mathcal{S}^{\mathsf{EHVZK}}$, sample $z \leftarrow_\$ D_{x,c}^{(z)}$ and compute $a \leftarrow \mathcal{S}^{\mathsf{EHVZK}}(x, c, z)$.
4. Otherwise, sample $R \leftarrow_\$ \{0,1\}^\lambda$, compute $a \leftarrow \mathsf{P}_0(x, w; R)$ and $z \leftarrow \mathsf{P}_1(x, w, a, c; R)$.
5. Return $\mathcal{D}(x, w, a, c, z)$.

Definition 3 (Σ-protocol with recyclable third messages). *Let* $\Sigma = (\mathsf{P}_0, \mathsf{P}_1, \mathsf{V})$ *be a* Σ-*protocol for an NP language* $\mathcal{L}$, Σ *has recyclable third messages if for every* $c \in \{0,1\}^\lambda$, *there exists an efficiently samplable distribution* $D_c^{(z)}$, *such that for all* $(x, w) \in \mathcal{R}_{\mathcal{L}}$, *it holds that* $D_c^{(z)} \approx \{z | R \leftarrow_\$ \{0,1\}^\lambda; a \leftarrow \mathsf{P}_0(x, w; R); z \leftarrow \mathsf{P}_1(x, w, c; R)\}$.

Definition 4 (Stackable Σ-protocol). *We say that a* Σ-*protocol* $\Sigma = (\mathsf{P}_0, \mathsf{P}_1, \mathsf{V})$, *is stackable, if it is a EHVZK* Σ-*protocol and has recyclable third messages.*

References

1. Attema, T., Cramer, R., Fehr, S.: Compressing proofs of k-Out-Of-n partial knowledge. In: Malkin, T., Peikert, C. (eds.) CRYPTO 2021. LNCS, vol. 12828, pp. 65–91. Springer, Cham (2021). https://doi.org/10.1007/978-3-030-84259-8_3

2. Attema, T., Cramer, R., Rambaud, M.: Compressed Σ-protocols for bilinear group arithmetic circuits and application to logarithmic transparent threshold signatures. In: Tibouchi, M., Wang, H. (eds.) ASIACRYPT 2021. LNCS, vol. 13093, pp. 526–556. Springer, Cham (2021). https://doi.org/10.1007/978-3-030-92068-5_18
3. Avitabile, G., Botta, V., Friolo, D., Visconti, I.: Efficient proofs of knowledge for threshold relations. Cryptology ePrint Archive, Report 2022/746 (2022)
4. Baum, C., Malozemoff, A.J., Rosen, M.B., Scholl, P.: Mac′n′Cheese: zero-knowledge proofs for Boolean and arithmetic circuits with nested disjunctions. In: Malkin, T., Peikert, C. (eds.) CRYPTO 2021. LNCS, vol. 12828, pp. 92–122. Springer, Cham (2021). https://doi.org/10.1007/978-3-030-84259-8_4
5. Ben-Sasson, E., Bentov, I., Horesh, Y., Riabzev, M.: Scalable zero knowledge with no trusted setup. In: Boldyreva, A., Micciancio, D. (eds.) CRYPTO 2019. LNCS, vol. 11694, pp. 701–732. Springer, Cham (2019). https://doi.org/10.1007/978-3-030-26954-8_23
6. Bresson, E., Stern, J., Szydlo, M.: Threshold ring signatures and applications to ad-hoc groups. In: Yung, M. (ed.) CRYPTO 2002. LNCS, vol. 2442, pp. 465–480. Springer, Heidelberg (2002). https://doi.org/10.1007/3-540-45708-9_30
7. Chen, J., Hu, Y., Gao, W., Li, H.: Lattice-based threshold ring signature with message block sharing. KSII 13(2), 1003–1019 (2019). https://doi.org/10.3837/tiis.2019.02.028
8. Ciampi, M., Persiano, G., Scafuro, A., Siniscalchi, L., Visconti, I.: Online/Offline OR composition of sigma protocols. In: Fischlin, M., Coron, J.-S. (eds.) EUROCRYPT 2016. LNCS, vol. 9666, pp. 63–92. Springer, Heidelberg (2016). https://doi.org/10.1007/978-3-662-49896-5_3
9. Cramer, R., Damgård, I., Schoenmakers, B.: Proofs of partial knowledge and simplified design of witness hiding protocols. In: Desmedt, Y.G. (ed.) CRYPTO 1994. LNCS, vol. 839, pp. 174–187. Springer, Heidelberg (1994). https://doi.org/10.1007/3-540-48658-5_19
10. Goel, A., Green, M., Hall-Andersen, M., Kaptchuk, G.: Stacking sigmas: a Framework to Compose Σ-protocols for disjunctions. Cryptology ePrint Archive, Report 2021/422 (2021). version accessed 09 November 2021
11. Goel, A., Green, M., Hall-Andersen, M., Kaptchuk, G.: Stacking sigmas: a framework to compose Σ-protocols for disjunctions. In: Dunkelman, O., Dziembowski, S. (eds) , vol. 13276, pp. 458–487. Springer, Cham (2022). https://doi.org/10.1007/978-3-031-07085-3_16
12. Groth, J., Kohlweiss, M.: One-out-of-many proofs: or how to leak a secret and spend a coin. In: Oswald, E., Fischlin, M. (eds.) EUROCRYPT 2015. LNCS, vol. 9057, pp. 253–280. Springer, Heidelberg (2015). https://doi.org/10.1007/978-3-662-46803-6_9
13. Haque, A., Scafuro, A.: Threshold ring signatures: new definitions and postquantum security. In: Kiayias, A., Kohlweiss, M., Wallden, P., Zikas, V. (eds.) PKC 2020. LNCS, vol. 12111, pp. 423–452. Springer, Cham (2020). https://doi.org/10.1007/978-3-030-45388-6_15
14. Heath, D., Kolesnikov, V.: Stacked garbling for disjunctive zero-knowledge proofs. In: Canteaut, A., Ishai, Y. (eds.) EUROCRYPT 2020. LNCS, vol. 12107, pp. 569–598. Springer, Cham (2020). https://doi.org/10.1007/978-3-030-45727-3_19
15. Heath, D., Kolesnikov, V., Peceny, S.: Garbling, stacked and staggered. In: Tibouchi, M., Wang, H. (eds.) ASIACRYPT 2021. LNCS, vol. 13091, pp. 245–274. Springer, Cham (2021). https://doi.org/10.1007/978-3-030-92075-3_9

16. Munch-Hansen, A., Orlandi, C., Yakoubov, S.: Stronger notions and a more efficient construction of threshold ring signatures. In: Longa, P., Ràfols, C. (eds.) LATIN-CRYPT 2021. LNCS, vol. 12912, pp. 363–381. Springer, Cham (2021). https://doi.org/10.1007/978-3-030-88238-9_18

17. Nitulescu, A.: zk-SNARKs: a gentle introduction. https://www.di.ens.fr/~nitulesc/files/Survey-SNARKs.pdf (2020)

18. Okamoto, T., Tso, R., Yamaguchi, M., Okamoto, E.: A k-out-of-n Ring Signature with Flexible Participation for Signers. Cryptology ePrint Archive, Report 2018/728 (2018)

19. Yuen, T.H., Liu, J.K., Au, M.H., Susilo, W., Zhou, J.: Efficient linkable and/or threshold ring signature without random oracles. Comput. J. **56**(4), 407–421 (2013). https://doi.org/10.1093/comjnl/bxs115

20. Zhou, G., Zeng, P., Yuan, X., Chen, S., Choo, K.K.R.: An efficient code-based threshold ring signature scheme with a leader-participant model. Secur. Commun. Networks **2017**, 1–7 (2017). https://doi.org/10.1155/2017/1915239

A Tale of Two Models: Formal Verification of KEMTLS via Tamarin

Sofía Celi[1][(✉)], Jonathan Hoyland[1][(✉)], Douglas Stebila[2][(✉)],
and Thom Wiggers[3][(✉)]

[1] Cloudflare, Inc., San Francisco, USA
cherenkov@riseup.net, jhoyland@cloudflare.com
[2] University of Waterloo, Waterloo, Canada
dstebila@uwaterloo.ca
[3] Radboud University, Nijmegen, The Netherlands
thom@thomwiggers.nl

Abstract. KEMTLS is a proposal for changing the TLS handshake to authenticate the handshake using long-term key encapsulation mechanism keys instead of signatures, motivated by trade-offs in the characteristics of post-quantum algorithms. Prior proofs of security of KEMTLS and its variant KEMTLS-PDK have been hand-written proofs in the reductionist model under computational assumptions. In this paper, we present computer-verified symbolic analyses of KEMTLS and KEMTLS-PDK using two distinct Tamarin models. In the first analysis, we adapt the detailed Tamarin model of TLS 1.3 by Cremers et al. (ACM CCS 2017), which closely follows the wire-format of the protocol specification, to KEMTLS(-PDK). We show that KEMTLS(-PDK) has equivalent security properties to the main handshake of TLS 1.3 proven in this model. We were able to fully automate this Tamarin proof, compared with the previous TLS 1.3 Tamarin model, which required a big manual proving effort; we also uncovered some inconsistencies in the previous model. In the second analysis, we present a novel Tamarin model of KEMTLS(-PDK), which closely follows the multi-stage key exchange security model from prior pen-and-paper proofs of KEMTLS(-PDK). The second approach is further away from the wire-format of the protocol specification but captures more subtleties in security definitions, like deniability and different levels of forward secrecy; it also identifies some flaws in the security claims from the pen-and-paper proofs. Our positive security results increase the confidence in the design of KEMTLS(-PDK). Moreover, viewing these models side-by-side allows us to comment on the trade-off in symbolic analysis between detail in protocol specification and granularity of security properties.

Keywords: Post-quantum cryptography · TLS · Key encapsulation mechanisms · Formal analysis · Tamarin

---

S. Celi—Now works for Brave Software, Inc.

1   Introduction

The Transport Layer Security (TLS) protocol is one of the most used crypto-graphic protocols. In its most recent version, the TLS 1.3 [31] handshake employs an ephemeral (elliptic-curve) Diffie–Hellman (DH) key exchange to establish session keys for confidentiality. In the regular handshake, TLS 1.3 authenticates the server and optionally the client using RSA or elliptic-curve signatures. It transmits the public keys to verify those signatures during the handshake, in certificates signed by a certificate authority (CA).

KEMTLS [32] is an alternative proposal for a post-quantum TLS 1.3 [31] handshake. It avoids using handshake signatures, which typically authenticate the TLS 1.3 handshake, replacing them with end-entity authentication based on key encapsulation mechanisms (KEMs) following well-established techniques for implicitly authenticated key exchange. As post-quantum KEMs are typically more efficient than the post-quantum signature schemes, either in bytes on the wire or computational efficiency, this saves resources. KEMTLS-PDK ("pre-distributed public key") [34] is a variant of KEMTLS that offers a more efficient handshake if the client already has the server's long-term public key. The authentication mechanisms from KEMTLS and KEMTLS-PDK have been proposed for standardisation to the Internet Engineering Task Force (IETF) TLS working group [13].

Figure 1 shows the cryptographic core of the unilaterally authenticated TLS 1.3 and KEMTLS handshakes. KEMTLS replaces the TLS 1.3 Diffie–Hellman-based ephemeral key exchange by KEM operations. Most importantly, whereas in TLS 1.3 the server authenticates by signing the transcript using the key from the server's certificate, in KEMTLS the client encapsulates against the KEM public key in the server's certificate. KEMTLS then combines both KEM shared secrets—one from the ephemeral key exchange and one from the server's long-term key—to derive a key that is *implicitly authenticated*, meaning only the intended server will be able to derive the secret. The client can then use the derived key to transmit application data.

At many levels, the KEMTLS handshake is similar to the TLS 1.3 handshake. However, due to the usage of KEMs, the order of messages in TLS 1.3 has been significantly changed. Additionally, the server can no longer send data in its first response to the client. However, KEMTLS preserves the client's ability to send its message after receiving the first flight from the server.

As KEMTLS is a novel way to achieve authentication in the TLS 1.3 handshake, the security of its design should be carefully checked not only with pen-and-paper proofs but with a computer-assisted formal analysis of it to provide stronger evidence of its soundness to adopters and standarization bodies like the IETF.

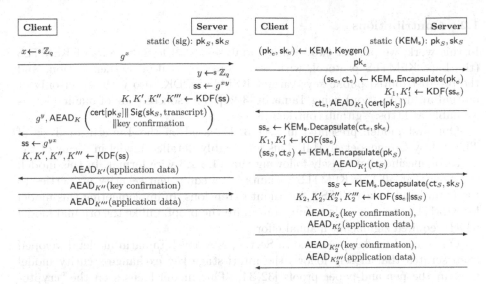

Fig. 1. Simplified protocol diagrams of server-only authenticated versions of: (left) the TLS 1.3 handshake, using signatures for authentication; and (right) the KEMTLS handshake, using KEMs for authentication.

1.1 Related Work

Analysis of TLS 1.3. During the development process of TLS 1.3, there was a strong collaboration between the standardisation community with the academic research community. Initial TLS 1.3 protocol designs were based on academic designs [28], and it was explicit goal of the TLS 1.3 process to incorporate academic security analysis of new designs before continuing with standarisation. Paterson and van der Merwe described this as a "design-break-fix-release" process rather than the "design-release-break-patch" cycle that was found on prior versions of the standarisation and usage of TLS [30]. Many of the security analyses of TLS 1.3 used the reductionist security paradigm [19–21,27,28]. Complementing this manual proof work, computer-aided cryptography [1] was also instrumental in checking TLS 1.3. Analyses were done using the Proverif [7] and Tamarin [14,15] symbolic analysis tools, as well as a verified implementation in F* [16].

Analysis of KEMTLS. The initial KEMTLS and KEMTLS-PDK papers included reductionist security proofs [32,34], adapting the multi-stage key exchange approach used by Dowling et al. [19,20] for TLS 1.3. Subsequently, Towa et al. proposed and proved an alternative abbreviated handshake, with additional short-lived static keys [25], and found a few minor mistakes in the original security proofs, which were subsequently fixed in online versions of the original papers [33,35]. All these proofs treat protocol modes independently—one-at-a-time—and do not consider the presence of the other protocol modes.

1.2   Contributions

In this work, we present two security analyses of all four variants of KEMTLS (the base KEMTLS protocol, with server-only or mutual authentication, and the pre-distributed public keys variant KEMTLS-PDK, also with server-only or mutual authentication) using Tamarin [3, 29]. The source code of our models is available at https://github.com/kemtls/.

Our first model, presented in Sect. 3, is based on the Tamarin analysis of TLS 1.3 by Cremers et al. [14]. This is a highly detailed model in terms of the protocol specification, closely following the TLS 1.3 wire format. In this model, we show that all four KEMTLS variants have equivalent security properties to the main handshake of TLS 1.3 without extensions. In implementing this model for KEMTLS, we were able to fully automate the proof, unlike the original model which required significant manual effort.

Our second model, presented in Sect. 4, is a novel Tamarin model developed from scratch that closely follows the multi-stage key exchange security model used in the pen-and-paper proofs [32, 34]. This model focuses on the "cryptographic core", meaning that it is further away from the wire specification and does not model details like message encryption or the record layer. However, it captures more details in the security definitions, using the more granular definitions of forward secrecy from [32, 34] as well as including an analysis of deniability. This model allows us to symbolically verify the reductionist security claims from the pen-and-paper proofs, but goes further by considering all four KEMTLS variants simultaneously. This Tamarin model allowed us to identify some minor flaws in the properties stated based on pen-and-paper proofs.

In Sect. 5, we compare the features of our two Tamarin models. Having these two models side-by-side illustrates the trade-off between detail of protocol specification and granularity of security properties. Ideally, of course, one would achieve both levels of detail simultaneously, but such complexity is challenging both for the humans reading and writing pen-and-paper proofs or authoring Tamarin models, and for computers checking such Tamarin models (where runtime typically scales exponentially with the complexity of the model). Our side-by-side approach with two very different perspectives still yields significant confidence in the soundness of the KEMTLS protocol design and each provides insight into flaws in the earlier models that it was based on.

2   Background on Symbolic Analysis

One approach to proving the security properties of protocols is *symbolic analysis*, which uses formal logic to reason about the properties of an algebraic model of a protocol. Computational tools, such as Tamarin [3, 29] or ProVerif [9], can then be used to check whether certain properties hold in the symbolic model.

In symbolic analysis, generic symbols replace specific values. Operations like encryption are also modelled symbolically: for example, `senc(a,b)` represents the value a being symmetrically encrypted with the key b. In symbolic analysis, cryptographic operations are *perfect*, meaning the adversary can learn nothing about an encrypted message without the correct key. The operations that describe a protocol in a symbolic model take messages and state information, and transform them into the next state or emit another protocol message. A tool can then use all operations and symbols to generate every possible protocol run.

Many symbolic analyses of protocols use the Dolev–Yao [18] attacker model, in which an attacker can manipulate all messages at will, e.g. by redirecting them, replaying them, dropping them, or manipulating their contents. It can also construct new messages from information previously learnt. However, as the cryptography is assumed to be perfect, the attacker can not read or modify encrypted or authenticated messages if it does not have the right keys.

Symbolic models can also be extended to give the attacker special extra abilities. For example, one can allow the attacker to reveal private keys or state information of parties by performing queries to a reveal oracle. We record when the attacker uses this oracle, so reveal queries become part of the trace of execution.

Security properties are modelled as predicates over execution traces. In Tamarin, during the execution of the rules of the protocol, we can emit *action facts*. We use these action facts to record, for example, the session's impression of the authentication status or the current keys. We then write lemmas representing security properties as predicates over action facts: for example, that any key recorded in a certain type of action fact must not be known to the adversary, unless the adversary cheated by revealing keys. A model checker like Tamarin can then be used to check if the protocol maintains the required security property. Assuming soundness of the tool, either the tool will give a proof that the protocol has the required property, find a counter-example, or fail to terminate.

3   Model #1: High-Resolution Protocol Specification

In this section, we discuss the natural approach of taking one of the TLS 1.3 models and adapting it to KEMTLS(-PDK). Our work demonstrates that KEMTLS provides security guarantees at least equivalent to those proven by Cremers et al. for the main handshake of TLS 1.3.

3.1   Cremers et al.'s Tamarin TLS 1.3 Model

The Tamarin model of TLS 1.3 [14] is very high-resolution in terms of its modelling of protocol details and adherence to the protocol specification. It covers the cryptographic computations such as the key exchange and the key schedule; for example, calls to HKDF are decomposed into hash function calls. This model also includes the extensions to the basic TLS 1.3 handshake, such as the `HelloRetryRequest` mechanism, pre-shared keys, and resumption via session tickets. Additionally, it models the encryption of handshake messages, the syntax of the protocol messages, and mechanics such as TLS 1.3 extensions.

In terms of security properties, the Cremers et al. model extends Tamarin's basic Dolev–Yao attacker with the ability to recover secrets from Diffie–Hellman key shares and reveal the long-term keys of participants. TLS 1.3 is not secure against an attacker who can use these attacks freely, but aims to provide confidentiality and integrity against an attacker who is restricted from revealing secrets of the target session. Cremers et al. were able to encode lemmas capturing most of the security properties claimed by the TLS 1.3 specification [31, Appendix E.1]. They report that proving all lemmas in their model took about a week. Much of this time was spent on manual interaction with Tamarin's prover to guide it to prove some of the more complex lemmas. Verifying the generated proof requires "about a day" and "a vast amount of RAM" [14].

3.2   Representing KEMTLS in the Model

We now describe how we modified the existing TLS 1.3 model to represent both KEMTLS and its variant with pre-distributed keys, KEMTLS-PDK. The original model is highly modular, which made it relatively easy to modify.

The model of Cremers et al. represents TLS 1.3 through rules that manipulate a specific state object, which keeps track of many protocol variables, such as keys, authentication status, and the currently active handshake mode. Tamarin rules create transitions between these states. Where the protocol branches, such as when the server requests client authentication by sending CertificateRequest, there are two rules that end up in the same next state; for example, they would set the cert_req variable differently. The server later uses this variable to decide which of the rules recv_client_auth or recv_client_auth_cert to use; the latter expects the Certificate, CertificateVerify, and Finished messages, while the former only expects Finished. We handle the public key infrastructure (PKI) for KEM public keys in the same way as [14]: we do not model CA certificates, and assume an out-of-band binding between public keys and identities.

Ephemeral key exchange in the TLS 1.3 model uses Tamarin's Diffie–Hellman functionality. It also allows the negotiation of two different DH groups. During the handshake, the client and server generate ephemeral DH secrets for the chosen group. If the server rejects the client's choice of DH group, it falls back to another group through the HelloRetryRequest mechanism. To model the post-quantum ephemeral key exchange in KEMTLS, we replaced the Diffie–Hellman operations by kemencaps (KEM encapsulation) in place of the server's DH key generation. The client then computes the shared secret via kemdecaps (KEM decapsulation).

The authentication rules and states required more careful consideration. In the TLS 1.3 model, the Certificate, CertificateVerify, and Finished messages were sent and received simultaneously. In KEMTLS, we split the handling of these messages, as the peer that is authenticating needs to first receive a ciphertext to decapsulate. Doing this requires more states. Additionally, in KEMTLS the client sends Finished before the server, which deviates from TLS 1.3.

To finish our integration of KEMTLS, we made changes to the key schedule to include the computation of KEMTLS' Authenticated Handshake Secret (AHS)

```
lemma secret_session_keys:
  "All tid actor peer kw kr pas #i.
    SessionKey(tid, actor, peer, <pas, 'auth'>, <kw, kr>)@#i &
    not (Ex #r. RevLtk(peer)@#r & #r < #i) &
    not (Ex tid3 esk #r. RevEKemSk(tid3, peer, esk)@#r & #r < #i) &
    not (Ex tid4 esk #r. RevEKemSk(tid4, actor, esk)@#r & #r < #i)
    ==> not Ex #j. K(kr)@#j"
```

Listing 1. The `secret_session_keys` lemma proves application traffic keys are secret.

and use the correct handshake traffic encryption keys. We also modified the action facts emitted in the various rules to match our KEM operations; lemmas that made use of these action facts were also updated. We disabled the PSK and session ticket features of the original model.

Modeling KEMTLS-PDK. In KEMTLS-PDK, the client has the server's long-term public key beforehand. Access to the public key allows the client to send a ciphertext in the initial `ClientHello` message. Additionally, the client may attempt client authentication proactively and thus transmit its `Certificate` before receiving `ServerHello` from the server. We model this through an additional initial state for the KEMTLS-PDK client. From this state, there are two rules which set the state variable that will decide if the client will send its certificate. KEMTLS-PDK is otherwise implemented as a mostly separate sequence of states and rules, as the key schedule and order of messages are quite different. The client and server still transition through a state shared with KEMTLS, so they can fall back to the "full" handshake.

3.3 Security Properties

We adapt the lemmas from the Cremers et al. model for TLS 1.3. Many core lemmas are constructed around the `SessionKey` fact: the client and the server record this fact when the handshake concludes. `SessionKey` contains the actor's final understanding of its and its peer's identities, authentication statuses, and the application traffic keys. We prove all security properties discussed in [14], and briefly explain the most important of these below.

Adversary Compromise of Secrets. First, we note the extent to which the adversary can compromise ephemeral or long-term secrets. KEMTLS uses ephemeral KEM keys for ephemeral secrecy and long-term KEM keys for authentication. The adversary can reveal actors' long-term secret keys; this records the `RevLtk($actor)` fact. We also allow revealing the ephemeral secret key in individual sessions, recording the `RevEKemSk(tid, $actor, esk)` fact. Variables `tid` ("thread identifier") and `esk` track the specific session and secret key.

KEMs are not "symmetric" in the same way that Diffie–Hellman key exchange is. Only one party in each KEM key exchange has a secret key that can be targeted by a reveal query. We do not model revealing the shared secret from the ciphertext.

Intermediate session keys, like the Main Secret (MS), can not be revealed directly. This follows from the design of the original model: in TLS 1.3, these secrets only depend on the ephemeral key exchange, so revealing the ephemeral key exchange in sessions not targeted by a lemma still allows the adversary to obtain those sessions' intermediate session keys. In KEMTLS, this is no longer the case: we mix the shared secrets encapsulated against long-term keys into the key schedule; as a result, our attacker is slightly weaker. The model discussed in Sect. 4 does directly allow session key reveal.

(Forward) Secrecy of Session Keys. The outputs of the handshake, as recorded in the `SessionKey` fact, are the application traffic read and write keys `kr` and `kw`. We require these keys to remain secret against various forms of attacks. Forward secrecy requires that if the long-term keys (but not the ephemeral keys) were compromised after the session completes, the session keys remain secure.

We model this in the `secret_session_keys` lemma as shown in Listing 1. This lemma considers a client or server that believes it has authenticated its peer, where the attacker has not revealed the ephemeral KEM secret keys. We allow the attacker to reveal the peer's long-term secret key, but only after the `SessionKey` fact was emitted; this is the "forward" secrecy aspect. The attacker should not be able to learn (`not Ex #j. K(kr)@#j`) the target's read key `kr` under these constraints. We similarly prove forward secrecy for each of the intermediate keys in the key schedule: the Handshake Secret (HS), AHS and MS.

Note that in KEMTLS, the session keys are derived from not just the ephemeral key exchange as in TLS 1.3, but also include the secret encapsulated during the authentication phase of the handshake. This implies that both the ephemeral key and the server's long-term key need to be compromised in client sessions, and the ephemeral key and the server's long-term key in server sessions with mutual authentication. We prove this in our model through a variant of the `secret_session_keys` lemma that allows ephemeral key compromise, as long as the peer's long-term key is never revealed.

Authentication. We model the authentication properties of KEMTLS in the same way as they were modelled for TLS 1.3. The client and server are partnered via the nonces exchanged in the initial messages. The `entity_authentication` lemma captures that if the client, at the end of the handshake protocol, has authenticated their peer, and the peer's long-term keys have not been revealed, then there must be a peer session that started with the same nonces. The `mutual_` variant of this lemma states the same, but with the roles of client and server reversed. As these lemmas allow revealing the targeted actor's long-term keys, these properties also cover key-compromise impersonation attacks. Similarly, in the lemma `transcript_agreement`, we prove that when the client, after receiving the server's `Finished` message, commits to a transcript, there exists a server that is running with the same transcript (or their long-term keys have been revealed). The `mutual_` variant lemma states the same but with the roles reversed.

3.4 Results

After adding relevant helper lemmas, Tamarin was able to auto-prove all the correctness and security lemmas for Model #1, with all four KEMTLS variants supported simultaneously. Run-times are shown in Appendix B.

Auto-proving and Helper Lemmas. Many of the lemmas in Cremers et al.'s model of TLS 1.3 were not able to be auto-proved by Tamarin; instead, the authors had to manually guide Tamarin through parts of the proof. Our goal was to improve the model so that it could be proved without manual intervention.

To help the automated prover, Cremers et al. introduced many intermediate lemmas, many of which state properties of earlier keys or more limited message exchanges. Inheriting these lemmas proved to be both helpful as well as distracting. Incrementally proving and adjusting the intermediate lemmas to apply to KEMTLS(-PDK) helped us spot bugs and make progress. But starting from their helper lemmas often left us unclear as to why particular intermediate lemmas were necessary to prove the final security properties.

In our experience, Tamarin does not find counterexamples very easily in big models. As a result, we wrote increasingly "smaller" lemmas whenever we ran into a lemma that was hard to prove. This greatly expanded the number of helper lemmas available. While we believe that this helped auto-prove the model, it also resulted in cases where the helper lemmas interacted in bad ways and had to be ignored. (Replacing Diffie–Hellman by KEM, thus avoiding Tamarin's algebraic analysis of DH group operations, may also have eased analysis.) Additionally, the model of [14] is carefully split over different files to avoid certain helper lemmas from interacting. With much less experience, we joined together most of those files, which in many cases lead to Tamarin getting distracted by helper lemmas.

A Bug in Cremers et al.'s TLS 1.3 Lemmas. While working on the proof, we found that one of the core lemmas in [14]'s TLS 1.3 model seems to have changed after creating the proof. The lemma `session_key_agreement` tried to prove that the client's and servers values of `keys` in the `SessionKey` fact matched. However, variable `keys` is a tuple `<kr, kw>` of the reading and writing keys. As the server's writing key should match the client's reading key and not the client's writing key, this lemma did not hold. The rendered proofs included in the repository alongside the model and lemmas revealed that in the executed proof, `keys` was split into its elements and equated correctly. We disclosed the bug to the authors.

3.5 Limitations

Although the model is very granular in its description of KEMTLS(-PDK), we do have some limitations. As discussed in Sect. 3.3, we do not model intermediate session key reveal. We also have not modelled session resumption or pre-shared key modes with KEMTLS. Finally, we have not attempted to model deniability, which we will model in Sect. 4.

4   Model #2: Multi-stage Key Exchange Model

The security properties shown in the original KEMTLS paper [32] and the KEMTLS-PDK paper [34] are stated using the reductionist security paradigm, via the *multi-stage key exchange model* [24], which was adapted for proofs of the TLS 1.3 handshake [19,20]. Our goal in this section is to translate the reductionist security properties in this model—match security, session key indistinguishability, and authentication—from a pen-and-paper model to being encoded in Tamarin, then have the Tamarin prover confirm these properties hold. Notably, this model discriminates between the several keys established within a single KEMTLS handshake, associating distinct security properties with individual stage keys.

4.1   Reductionist Security Model for TLS 1.3 and KEMTLS

The multi-stage key exchange security model, first introduced by Fischlin and Günther [24], is an extension of the Bellare–Rogaway (BR) model [6] for proving security of authenticated key exchange in the reductionist security paradigm. In the BR model, the adversary is in control of all communications between honest parties, so the adversary can activate honest parties to send their next protocol message, and can also modify, delay, drop, replay, or create messages. Each honest party can run multiple simultaneous or sequential executions of the protocol (each execution at a party is called a session) sharing a single long-term key pair across their sessions. Within each session, a party maintains several variables, including the execution status, a session identifier, an identifier for the peer (if the peer is to be authenticated), and a session key. The adversary interacts with the honest parties via oracles, including oracles for starting a new session at a party (the NewSession oracle) and message delivery and response (Send), as well as letting the adversary learn an honest party's long-term key (Corrupt) or the session key of a particular session (Reveal). The adversary may choose one session as a challenge session and, via a call to the Test oracle, receive an indistinguishability game challenge.

There are many extensions to the BR model to capture different functionality and security properties; see [10, Ch. 2] for a summary. One important extension is the formalisation by Brzuska et al. [11,12] which introduces a property called *match security*. This checks the technical condition that the session identifiers specified by the protocol effectively match the partnered sessions. Among other benefits, match security helps with composition theorems involving AKE protocols. Our Tamarin model does address match security fully, but due to space constraints, we omit discussion of match security in the proceedings version of the paper.

In real-world protocols like QUIC and TLS, as well as KEMTLS, multiple keys are established in each session for different purposes. Fischlin and Günther [24] created the multi-stage key exchange model, an extension of the BR model in which a single session can have multiple stages, each of which establishes a key with certain security characteristics; they used this approach to analyse QUIC. It was also used by Dowling et al. [19,20] to analyse the TLS 1.3 handshake. As KEMTLS is an alternative realization of the TLS 1.3 handshake, it is natural to similarly use this model for analyzing KEMTLS, as done in [32].

We now present the technical components of the multi-stage key exchange security model as used in KEMTLS [32] and KEMTLS-PDK [34]. Our presentation here will be somewhat abbreviated; for full details, see the full versions of [32,34].

Partnering. For the proof of KEMTLS(-PDK), we need to keep track of the pairs of sessions that are (supposedly) communicating. Each session keeps track of per-stage session identifiers, each of which is a distinct label for the stage followed by all plaintext messages transmitted up until that point in the protocol; for KEMTLS-PDK, this also includes the implicit `ServerCertificate` message. We call two sessions *partners* if their session identifiers match.

Adversary Interaction. The oracles and variables stated in Sect. 4.1 suffice for modelling the various properties of match-security. To model key indistinguishability, the multi-stage model includes an oracle $\mathsf{Test}(\pi, i)$ which challenges the adversary to distinguish the ith stage key of session π from random.

Multi-stage Security and Malicious Acceptance. Multi-stage security models secrecy of each stage key under specific forward secrecy properties. These properties include *implicit* and *explicit authentication*. The model is parameterized by values indicating the expected security properties of particular stage keys. [32,34] define four levels of forward secrecy:

- No forward secrecy (0);
- *Weak forward secrecy level 1* (wfs1): the key is confidential against passive adversaries. This level allows the adversary to access the peer's long-term keys. Keys with this level of forward secrecy have no authentication.
- *Weak forwards secrecy level 2* (wfs2): the key is confidential against passive adversaries (wfs1) and against active adversaries who never corrupted the peer's long-term key. In the latter case, the key is implicitly authenticated.
- *Forward secrecy* (fs): the key is confidential against passive adversaries (wfs1) and against active adversaries who did not corrupt the peer's long-term key before the stage accepted. Keys with level fs are implicitly authenticated.

As the protocol is executed, the security level of a particular stage key may be upgraded once a later stage accepts. The specific security levels for each client and the server are indicated in [32,34]; the server's security levels are different if mutual authentication is used.

Explicit authentication, which is e.g. achieved by the Finished messages, is modelled through *malicious acceptance*: an adversary should not be able to cause a supposedly explicitly authenticated stage to accept without a partner stage.

Deniability. Roughly speaking, deniability is the property that a party cannot provide proof to a judge that a peer participated in a particular protocol execution, even if they did. First introduced in general by Dwork, Naor, and Sahai [23] and in the context of key exchange by Di Raimondo, Gennaro, and Krawczyk [17], there are many flavours and variations of deniability; see e.g. [26] for a classification. *Offline deniability* is the inability of a judge to distinguish between a transcript generated by honest parties and a transcript generated by a simulator. The form of deniability offered by KEMTLS and KEMTLS-PDK (following the terminology of [26]) is that it provides offline deniability in the *universal deniability* setting (meaning the simulator only has access to parties' long-term public keys) against an unbounded judge with full corruption powers (meaning the judge gets the parties' long-term secret keys as well as any per-session coins).

Pen-and-Paper Proofs. The KEMTLS and KEMTLS-PDK papers [32,34] provide theorems and give proofs that their respective protocols satisfy the match-security and multi-stage security properties; they do not include any proofs for offline deniability. The match-security properties are shown information-theoretically, with terms depending on the number of sessions, the correctness probability of the KEMs, and the size of the TLS nonce space. The multi-stage security properties are shown under the following computational assumptions: hash function collision resistance, IND-1CCA security of KEM_e, PRF and dual-PRF security of HKDF.Extract, PRF-security of HKDF.Expand, EUF-CMA security of HMAC, and IND-CCA security of KEM_c and KEM_s. There is a tightness loss proportional to the number of sessions squared.

4.2   Formalizing the Reductionist Security Model in Tamarin

We formalized all four KEMTLS variants (regular and PDK, server-only and mutually authenticated) in Tamarin, along with lemmas capturing correctness, match security, multi-stage security, and deniability, analogous to the definitions from Sect. 4.1. We now describe the formalization in more detail.

Protocol Description. This Tamarin formulation of the four KEMTLS variants focuses on the "cryptographic core" of the protocol. Roughly speaking, this is the protocol as formulated in figures in the original papers [32,34], which includes cryptographic operations involved in the key exchange, but does not include extra fields and operations arising from the integration of the cryptographic operations into a network protocol. We only address the handshake protocol and exclude TLS message formatting, algorithm negotiation, and data structures such as certificates. We exclude other modes such as TLS 1.3 session resumption or pre-shared key handshakes. We assume that long-term public keys are reliably distributed out-of-band. We omit modelling handshake encryption: while the various handshake traffic secrets are established and recorded as accepted in each stage of the protocol, subsequent handshake messages are sent in plaintext. The various primitives based on hash functions (HMAC, HKDF.Extract, HKDF.Expand) are modelled as independent opaque functions, rather than relying on each other and ultimately on a common hash function. As in the pen-and-paper proofs, there are three KEMs: KEM_e, KEM_c, and KEM_s, for ephemeral key exchange, client authentication, and server authentication, respectively. The KEMs are modelled as distinct primitives, meaning that a party cannot use its long-term credential to act as both a client and a server.

Adversary Interaction. Among the oracles stated in Sect. 4.1, the NewSession and Send oracles are not needed, since the Tamarin model includes rules for each protocol step. The Tamarin model does include Corrupt and Reveal oracles. Because key security in Tamarin is modelled not using indistinguishability but key recovery (the $K(\dots)$ fact in Tamarin lemmas), there is no need for the Test query in the Tamarin model.

Correctness Lemmas. We include a collection of "reachability" lemmas which check that, for every stage in all 4 protocol variants, it is possible to arrive at that stage, with honest client and server sessions having correct owner and peer information, matching contributive and session identifiers, and correct expectations on authentication, forward secrecy, and replayability; the reachability lemmas include checking retroactive upgrading of properties. These lemmas are implemented using Tamarin's `exist-trace` feature. There are 47 reachability lemmas in total, generated from a template using the M4 macro language.

Security and Authentication Lemmas. The match security lemmas from Definition B.1 of [32], plus the adjustments for replayability in [34], are directly translated into Tamarin. The lemmas are basically predicates over the session-specific variables defined in the model syntax, and can be stated analogously since the Tamarin model includes action facts for each session-specific variable.

Session key security in Tamarin is modelled based on infeasibility of session key recovery, rather than indistinguishability of a session key from random. We have lemmas for each type of forward secrecy a stage key can have, directly translating the freshness conditions of [32, Defn. B.3] and [34, Defn. B.5].

We have a lemma for explicit authentication analogous to [34, Defn. B.5 3], including not requiring uniqueness of the replayable KEMTLS-PDK stage 1.

Deniability Lemmas. Whereas the lemmas for the above properties all share the same Tamarin protocol description as explained above, the deniability lemmas use a re-statement of the protocol description. To formulate a deniability lemma, we need two versions of the protocol description: honest execution of the protocol using long-term secrets, and simulation using only public keys. The judge in the offline deniability game is passive and receives only transcripts, so we can collapse the multiple rules for each client and server action into a single rule that generates a full transcript including both client and server operations. The deniability lemmas use Tamarin's observational equivalence feature [4] to check that the real and simulated transcripts are indistinguishable. Using observational equivalence causes a substantial increase in state space, so for efficiency reasons, we have a mode that omits portions of the transcript that are deterministically generated from earlier parts of the transcript.

4.3   Comparison of Pen-and-Paper and Tamarin Models

In principle, if the same security properties have been encoded in both a pen-and-paper reductionist security model and in a Tamarin model, a full and correct proof in the reductionist security model yields everything that a Tamarin proof could, and potentially more. In particular, reductionist security proofs do not idealize cryptographic primitives as much as Tamarin does. Moreover, a reductionist security proof can be done in the "concrete setting" [5], yielding a precise (non-asymptotic) relationship between the runtime and success probability of an adversary against the protocol versus the runtime and success probability of breaking the underlying cryptographic assumption. While it would be possible to encode the pen-and-paper proofs of KEMTLS from the original papers into a computer verification tool such as EasyCrypt [2], that would also require the cryptographer to manually write all game hops and reductions, a massive undertaking. To date, there are no proofs of KEMTLS using a computer-aided verification tool for reductionist proofs.

Tamarin does not lend itself to writing security properties in exactly the same way as would be used in reductionist security models. Although there is no way to objectively justify how close the pen-and-paper and Tamarin models of this section are to each other, subjectively we think they are quite close:

- The protocol specification in Tamarin maps nearly line-for-line onto the protocol figures in the original papers, using the same function interfaces, same key schedule, and same session identifiers.
- The session-specific variables in the pen-and-paper model correspond nearly one-for-one to action facts in the Tamarin model.
- There are Tamarin lemmas for each security property in the pen-and-paper model, and there is a clear mapping between the clauses in the predicates in the pen-and-paper model and the Tamarin model.

The main gap in modelling, as mentioned earlier, is that session key security is modelled via indistinguishability in the pen-and-paper models but via infeasibility of key recovery in the Tamarin model. Though it is possible to verify indistinguishability through Tamarin's observational equivalence features, the effect on the state space as discussed in Sect. 4.2 makes this impractical.

4.4   Results

Tamarin was able to auto-prove all the lemmas for correctness, reachability, match security, multi-stage session key security, authentication, and deniability in Model #2, with all four KEMTLS variants supported simultaneously. We did not need to create any helper lemmas for Tamarin. Run-times are shown in Appendix B.

Bugs in the Original Papers' Security Properties. When translating the models into Tamarin, we identified minor mistakes in some of the security properties listed in the KEMTLS [32] and KEMTLS-PDK [34] papers, highlighting the value of formal verification. We summarize the corrected properties in Appendix A.

4.5   Limitations

As noted above, the design of the model in this section imposes some limitations. Unlike in Sect. 3, we generally did not model non-cryptographic details of the handshake, such as TLS handshake messages, extensions, or the record layer. We also did not model handshake encryption or algorithm negotiation.

We also had, unlike in Sect. 3, three distinct KEMs for ephemeral key exchange, server authentication and client authentication. This implicitly assumes the same certificate is not used for both purposes, which was the basis of the Selfie attack [22]. Without this limitation, we observe a state-space explosion with a major impact on performance. For example, if $KEM_c = KEM_s$, the first 10 out of 11 `reachable_*` lemmas take over 8 h, and the last `reachable_*` did not terminate after 45 h, compared to all 11 `reachable_*` lemmas taking just over 1 min with distinct KEM_c and KEM_s.

Our deniability lemmas are for abbreviated transcripts and omit ephemeral coins. Without this limitation there is a major impact on performance. Including full transcripts for KEMTLS-sauth increases run-time from 1 min to 16 h, and including ephemeral coins increases runtime from 1 min to 110 min.

Table 1. Comparison of features in our two Tamarin models of KEMTLS

Feature	Model #1	Model #2
Protocol modelling		
Encrypted handshake messages	✓	✗
HKDF and HMAC decomposed into hash calls	✓	✗
Key exch. and auth. KEMs are the same algorithm	✓	✗
TLS message structure	✓	✗
Algorithm negotiation	✓	✗
Security properties		
Adversary can reveal long-term keys	✓	✓
Adversary can reveal ephemeral keys	✓	✗
Adversary can reveal intermediate session keys	✗	✓
Multiple flavours of forward secrecy	✗	✓
Deniability	✗	✓

5   Comparison of Models

We discussed two very different models of KEMTLS(-PDK) in the previous sections. These models are examples of how we can view modelling as the art of replacing specifics with generalities. Model #1 stays very close to the wire format of TLS 1.3 and phrases the security properties in terms of attacks on the ephemeral and long-term keys. It contains more implementation details such as algorithm negotiation, message framing, encryption of handshake messages, and even application data. Model #2 is more abstract in its representation of protocol messages. However, it models the cryptographic properties in a more granular fashion. This more abstract description closely follows the multi-stage pen-and-paper proofs of KEMTLS and KEMTLS-PDK, and allowed verifying the properties claimed in the pen-and-paper proofs. Table 1 summarizes differences between the two models, a few aspects of which we discuss further below.

Modelling KEMs. The two models differ in the way that they model the KEMs in the protocol. Model #1 uses the same functions for all KEM modes in the protocol (key exchange, server authentication and client authentication). Model #2 has three separate sets of functions for the three different KEM modes; this means the attacker can not copy ciphertexts or public keys from one of the modes to another, which should make proving the protocol easier. Interestingly, we saw significantly different performance between these two approaches. The second model proves in very short time with the three separate KEMs, but runtime blows up if we define all three KEM modes with the same functions; we did not attempt to generate the full proof because it took so long as discussed in Sect. 4.5. This suggests that splitting the three KEM modes in the first model could result in a speed-up. However, splitting the KEMs in Model #1 did not improve the time to auto-prove lemmas; in fact, a few lemmas even stopped being auto-provable. Ideally, this puzzle would be resolved with a justification that there is a way of safely separating uses of KEMs, allowing us to use whichever form happens to be easier for Tamarin to prove.

Threat Model. Both models use Dolev–Yao attackers, but give the attackers slightly different extra abilities as noted in the bottom half of Table 1. Consequently, the results hold in slightly different circumstances. The attacker in Model #1 can compromise ephemeral keys and long-term keys, but not session keys, whereas the attacker in Model #2 can compromise intermediate session keys and long-term keys, but not ephemeral keys. Revealing the HS intermediate session key allows the second attacker to simulate the abilities of the first, but the reverse does not hold; the attacker in Model #2 is thus slightly stronger.

Ease of Use. Work on each of our two models was done by separate authors of this paper, neither of whom had written a paper using Tamarin before and who had only had a basic introduction to Tamarin prior to this work. Surprisingly to us, creation of Model #2 from scratch was simpler and proceeded faster than the work in Model #1 adapting Cremers et al.'s TLS 1.3 model to KEMTLS. We attribute this to the higher fidelity of the protocol model in Cremers et al., requiring more code to model our changes, and the higher difficulty in proving.

6 Conclusion

We presented two Tamarin models checking security properties of KEMTLS and its variant protocol KEMTLS-PDK. Model #1 is highly detailed in implementation characteristics, close to the wire-format of the protocol. Model #2 presents the protocol at a higher level but provides a more precise characterization of security properties. We prove that KEMTLS(-PDK) is secure in both models; importantly these analyses include all four KEMTLS variants supported simultaneously. Additionally, we proved offline deniability of KEMTLS(-PDK) in Model #2.

Overall, comparing these two analyses is something of an apples-to-oranges comparison. The two very different approaches allow us to model and test different properties of the protocol. Model #1 is closer to what an implementation would be like, and verifies the security properties in such a scenario. Adopting the Cremers et al. TLS 1.3 model [14] also allowed us to quickly adapt the security claims of TLS 1.3 to our protocols. Model #2, on the other hand, is an adaptation of the multi-stage authenticated key exchange model from the pen-and-paper proofs in [32,34]. As such, Model #2 in a sense checks the claims in the pen-and-paper proofs, and in fact uncovered some minor mistakes in those proofs.

Our two models illustrate a common trade-off in formal analysis between the detail of the protocol specification and the granularity of the security properties we can prove. A similar observation was also made by Cremers et al. [14], who commented computational analyses could only look at parts of TLS 1.3, rather than considering all the modes at once.

While we proved certain privacy properties, such as deniability, our models can be further expanded to include other privacy properties, such as the proposed Encrypted Client Hello extension (previously called ESNI). These properties have only been proven by using the symbolic protocol analyzer ProVerif [8].

Acknowledgements. The authors gratefully acknowledge helpful suggestions from Peter Schwabe. D. Stebila was supported by Natural Sciences and Engineering Research Council of Canada (NSERC) Discovery grants RGPIN-2016–05146 and RGPIN-2022–03187. D. Stebila and T. Wiggers were supported by an NLnet Assure grant for the project "Standardizing KEMTLS". T. Wiggers was supported by the European Research Council through Starting Grant No. 805031 (EPOQUE).

A   Errors Identified in the Stated Properties of KEMTLS(-PDK)

Using Model #2, we identified minor mistakes in some of the forward secrecy and authentication properties listed in the original KEMTLS [32] and KEMTLS-PDK [34] papers. See the original papers for the definition of the symbols.

- In KEMTLS-mutual: $\text{auth}_3^S = 3$ and $\text{auth}_4^S = 4$ both should have been set to 5; $\text{FS}_{3,3}^S = \text{FS}_{3,4}^S = \text{FS}_{4,4}^S = \text{wfs2}$ should all have been wfs1; and $\text{auth}_6^S = 6$ should have been $\text{auth}_6^S = \infty$.
- In KEMTLS-PDK-sauth: $\text{FS}_{1,j}^C$ and $\text{FS}_{1,j}^S$ should have been 0 for all j; $\text{auth}_5^C = 5$ should have been $\text{auth}_5^C = \infty$; and $\text{FS}_{i,4}^S$ should have been wfs1 for $i = 2, 3, 4$.
- In KEMTLS-PDK-mutual: the message SKC should have been included in the SF MAC computation and SF should have been included in the CF MAC computation; $\text{FS}_{1,j}^C$ and $\text{FS}_{1,j}^S$ should have been 0 for all j; $\text{auth}_5^C = 5$ should have been $\text{auth}_5^C = \infty$; and $\text{FS}_{4,4}^S = \text{wfs1}$ should have been wfs2.

The source papers have been updated online [33, 35] with our corrections.

B   Performance

We ran our two models using `tamarin-prover` version 1.16.1 on a server that has two 20-core Intel Xeon Gold 6230 CPUs, which after hyperthreading gives us 80 threads; the server has 192 GB of RAM. We note that communication bottlenecks between cores prevent fully utilising all resources.

Model #1 Table 2 shows run-times of the most time-consuming lemmas from Model #1. All four KEMTLS variants were supported simultaneously.

Table 2. Wall-clock run-time (hh:mm:ss) and memory usage of selected lemmas for Model #1

Lemma	Steps	Time	Memory
`session_key_auth_agreement`	29 116	6:42:01	16 GB
`session_key_agreement`	57 680	13:56:04	32 GB
`handshake_secret`	29 390	4:40:52	12 GB
`master_secret_pfs`	29 535	2:53:11	76 GB
All lemmas	—	28 h	121 GB

Model #2 Table 3 shows the run-time for the various lemmas, for each KEMTLS variant on its own, and when all four KEMTLS variants are supported simultaneously; Tamarin was restricted to using 16 cores.

Table 3. Wall-clock run-time (hh:mm:ss) of lemmas for Model #2

Lemma	KEMTLS			KEMTLS-PDK			All 4 variants
	sauth	mutual	both	sauth	mutual	both	
`reachable_*`	0:01:17	0:01:20	0:04:32	0:01:46	0:01:36	0:04:40	0:13:25
`attacker_works_*`	0:00:17	0:00:46	0:01:16	0:00:17	0:00:23	0:00:53	0:12:04
`match_*`	0:01:02	0:01:22	0:02:55	0:00:55	0:01:14	0:02:46	0:09:53
`sk_sec_nofs_client`	0:00:05	0:00:07	0:00:16	0:00:05	0:00:05	0:00:14	0:00:41
`sk_sec_nofs_server`	0:00:05	0:00:06	0:00:12	0:00:05	0:00:06	0:00:14	0:00:40
`sk_sec_wfs1`	0:00:21	0:00:10	0:01:05	0:00:17	0:00:18	0:00:41	0:03:00
`sk_sec_wfs2`	0:00:36	0:00:28	0:01:30	0:00:28	0:00:22	0:01:23	0:24:28
`sk_sec_fs`	0:01:20	0:03:05	0:06:38	0:01:21	0:01:33	0:05:07	1:39:58
`malicious_accept.`	0:00:13	0:01:40	0:04:13	0:00:17	0:00:22	0:01:39	27:29:37
deniability (abbr.)	0:01:02	0:12:15	—	0:00:24	0:29:10	—	—
Total (excl. den.)	0:05:16	0:09:05	0:22:38	0:05:30	0:06:00	0:17:38	30:13:46

References

1. Barbosa, M., et al.: SoK: computer-aided cryptography. In: 2021 IEEE Symposium on Security and Privacy, pp. 777–795. IEEE Computer Society Press (2021). https://doi.org/10.1109/SP40001.2021.00008
2. Barthe, G., Grégoire, B., Heraud, S., Béguelin, S.Z.: Computer-aided security proofs for the working cryptographer. In: Rogaway, P. (ed.) CRYPTO 2011. LNCS, vol. 6841, pp. 71–90. Springer, Heidelberg (2011). https://doi.org/10.1007/978-3-642-22792-9_5
3. Basin, D., Cremers, C., Dreier, J., Meier, S., Sasse, R., Schmidt, B.: Tamarin prover (2022). https://tamarin-prover.github.io
4. Basin, D.A., Dreier, J., Sasse, R.: Automated symbolic proofs of observational equivalence. In: Ray, I., Li, N., Kruegel, C. (eds.) ACM CCS 2015, pp. 1144–1155. ACM Press (2015). https://doi.org/10.1145/2810103.2813662

5. Bellare, M.: Practice-oriented provable-security. In: Okamoto, E., Davida, G., Mambo, M. (eds.) ISW 1997. LNCS, vol. 1396, pp. 221–231. Springer, Heidelberg (1998). https://doi.org/10.1007/BFb0030423

6. Bellare, M., Rogaway, P.: Entity authentication and key distribution. In: Stinson, D.R. (ed.) CRYPTO 1993. LNCS, vol. 773, pp. 232–249. Springer, Heidelberg (1994). https://doi.org/10.1007/3-540-48329-2_21

7. Bhargavan, K., Blanchet, B., Kobeissi, N.: Verified models and reference implementations for the TLS 1.3 standard candidate. In: 2017 IEEE Symposium on Security and Privacy, pp. 483–502. IEEE Computer Society Press (2017). https://doi.org/10.1109/SP.2017.26

8. Bhargavan, K., Cheval, V., Wood, C.: Handshake privacy for TLS 1.3 - technical report. Research report, Inria Paris, Cloudflare (2022). https://hal.inria.fr/hal-03594482

9. Blanchet, B.: An efficient cryptographic protocol verifier based on Prolog rules. In: 14th IEEE Computer Security Foundations Workshop (CSFW-14), pp. 82–96. IEEE Computer Society (2001)

10. Boyd, C., Mathuria, A., Stebila, D.: Protocols for Authentication and Key Establishment. Springer, Heidelberg (2019). https://doi.org/10.1007/978-3-662-58146-9

11. Brzuska, C.: On the Foundations of Key Exchange, Ph.D. thesis, Technische Universität Darmstadt (2013). http://tuprints.ulb.tu-darmstadt.de/3414/

12. Brzuska, C., Fischlin, M., Warinschi, B., Williams, S.C.: Composability of Bellare-Rogaway key exchange protocols. In: Chen, Y., Danezis, G., Shmatikov, V. (eds.) ACM CCS 2011, pp. 51–62. ACM Press (2011). https://doi.org/10.1145/2046707.2046716

13. Celi, S., Schwabe, P., Stebila, D., Sullivan, N., Wiggers, T.: KEM-based Authentication for TLS 1.3. Internet-Draft draft-celi-wiggers-tls-authkem-01, Internet Engineering Task Force (2022). https://datatracker.ietf.org/doc/html/draft-celi-wiggers-tls-authkem-01, Work in Progress

14. Cremers, C., Horvat, M., Hoyland, J., Scott, S., van der Merwe, T.: A comprehensive symbolic analysis of TLS 1.3. In: Thuraisingham, B.M., Evans, D., Malkin, T., Xu, D. (eds.) ACM CCS 2017, pp. 1773–1788. ACM Press (2017). https://doi.org/10.1145/3133956.3134063

15. Cremers, C., Horvat, M., Scott, S., van der Merwe, T.: Automated analysis and verification of TLS 1.3: 0-RTT, resumption and delayed authentication. In: 2016 IEEE Symposium on Security and Privacy, pp. 470–485. IEEE Computer Society Press (2016). https://doi.org/10.1109/SP.2016.35

16. Delignat-Lavaud, A., et al.: Implementing and proving the TLS 1.3 record layer. In: 2017 IEEE Symposium on Security and Privacy, pp. 463–482. IEEE Computer Society Press (2017). https://doi.org/10.1109/SP.2017.58

17. Di Raimondo, M., Gennaro, R., Krawczyk, H.: Deniable authentication and key exchange. In: Juels, A., Wright, R.N., De Capitani di Vimercati, S. (eds.) ACM CCS 2006, pp. 400–409. ACM Press (2006). https://doi.org/10.1145/1180405.1180454

18. Dolev, D., Yao, A.C.C.: On the security of public key protocols (extended abstract). In: 22nd FOCS, pp. 350–357. IEEE Computer Society Press (1981). https://doi.org/10.1109/SFCS.1981.32

19. Dowling, B., Fischlin, M., Günther, F., Stebila, D.: A cryptographic analysis of the TLS 1.3 handshake protocol candidates. In: Ray, I., Li, N., Kruegel, C. (eds.) ACM CCS 2015, pp. 1197–1210. ACM Press (2015). https://doi.org/10.1145/2810103.2813653

20. Dowling, B., Fischlin, M., Günther, F., Stebila, D.: A cryptographic analysis of the TLS 1.3 handshake protocol. J. Cryptol. **34**(4), 1–69 (2021). https://doi.org/10.1007/s00145-021-09384-1

21. Dowling, B., Stebila, D.: Modelling Ciphersuite and version negotiation in the TLS protocol. In: Foo, E., Stebila, D. (eds.) ACISP 2015. LNCS, vol. 9144, pp. 270–288. Springer, Cham (2015). https://doi.org/10.1007/978-3-319-19962-7_16

22. Drucker, N., Gueron, S.: Selfie: reflections on TLS 1.3 with PSK. J. Cryptol. **34**(3), 1–18 (2021). https://doi.org/10.1007/s00145-021-09387-y

23. Dwork, C., Naor, M., Sahai, A.: Concurrent zero-knowledge. In: 30th ACM STOC, pp. 409–418. ACM Press (1998). https://doi.org/10.1145/276698.276853

24. Fischlin, M., Günther, F.: Multi-stage key exchange and the case of Google's QUIC protocol. In: Ahn, G.J., Yung, M., Li, N. (eds.) ACM CCS 2014, pp. 1193–1204. ACM Press (2014). https://doi.org/10.1145/2660267.2660308

25. Günther, F., Rastikian, S., Towa, P., Wiggers, T.: KEMTLS with delayed forward identity protection in (Almost) a single round trip. In: ACNS 2022 (2022). https://eprint.iacr.org/2021/725

26. Hülsing, A., Weber, F.: Epochal signatures for deniable group chats. In: 2021 IEEE Symposium on Security and Privacy, pp. 1677–1695. IEEE Computer Society Press (2021). https://doi.org/10.1109/SP40001.2021.00058

27. Kohlweiss, M., Maurer, U., Onete, C., Tackmann, B., Venturi, D.: (De-)Constructing TLS 1.3. In: Biryukov, A., Goyal, V. (eds.) INDOCRYPT 2015. LNCS, vol. 9462, pp. 85–102. Springer, Cham (2015). https://doi.org/10.1007/978-3-319-26617-6_5

28. Krawczyk, H., Wee, H.: The OPTLS protocol and TLS 1.3. In: 2016 IEEE European Symposium on Security and Privacy (EuroS&P), pp. 81–96 (2016). https://doi.org/10.1109/EuroSP.2016.18

29. Meier, S., Schmidt, B., Cremers, C., Basin, D.: The TAMARIN prover for the symbolic analysis of security protocols. In: Sharygina, N., Veith, H. (eds.) CAV 2013. LNCS, vol. 8044, pp. 696–701. Springer, Heidelberg (2013). https://doi.org/10.1007/978-3-642-39799-8_48

30. Paterson, K.G., van der Merwe, T.: Reactive and proactive standardisation of TLS. In: Chen, L., McGrew, D., Mitchell, C. (eds.) SSR 2016. LNCS, vol. 10074, pp. 160–186. Springer, Cham (2016). https://doi.org/10.1007/978-3-319-49100-4_7

31. Rescorla, E.: The Transport Layer Security TLS Protocol Version 1.3. RFC 8446, RFC Editor (2018). https://doi.org/10.17487/RFC8446

32. Schwabe, P., Stebila, D., Wiggers, T.: Post-quantum TLS without handshake signatures. In: Ligatti, J., Ou, X., Katz, J., Vigna, G. (eds.) ACM CCS 2020, pp. 1461–1480. ACM Press (2020). https://doi.org/10.1145/3372297.3423350

33. Schwabe, P., Stebila, D., Wiggers, T.: Post-quantum TLS without handshake signatures. Cryptology ePrint Archive, Report 2020/534 (2020). https://eprint.iacr.org/2020/534

34. Schwabe, P., Stebila, D., Wiggers, T.: More efficient post-quantum KEMTLS with pre-distributed public keys. In: Bertino, E., Shulman, H., Waidner, M. (eds.) ESORICS 2021. LNCS, vol. 12972, pp. 3–22. Springer, Cham (2021). https://doi.org/10.1007/978-3-030-88418-5_1

35. Schwabe, P., Stebila, D., Wiggers, T.: More efficient post-quantum KEMTLS with pre-distributed public keys. Cryptology ePrint Archive, Report 2021/779 (2021). https://eprint.iacr.org/2021/779

Web Security

Browser-Based CPU Fingerprinting

Leon Trampert[✉], Christian Rossow, and Michael Schwarz

CISPA Helmholtz Center for Information Security,
Saarbrücken, SL, Germany
{leon.trampert,rossow,michael.schwarz}@cispa.de

Abstract. Mounting microarchitectural attacks, such as Spectre or Rowhammer, is possible from browsers. However, to be realistically exploitable, they require precise knowledge about microarchitectural properties. While a native attacker can easily query many of these properties, the sandboxed environment in browsers prevents this. In this paper, we present six side-channel-related benchmarks that reveal CPU properties, such as cache sizes or cache associativities. Our benchmarks are implemented in JavaScript and run in unmodified browsers on multiple platforms. Based on a study with 834 participants using 297 different CPU models, we show that we can infer microarchitectural properties with an accuracy of up to 100%. Combining multiple properties also allows identifying the CPU vendor with an accuracy of 97.5%, and the microarchitecture and CPU model each with an accuracy of above 60%. The benchmarks are unaffected by current side-channel and browser fingerprinting mitigations, and can thus be used for more targeted attacks and to increase the entropy in browser fingerprinting.

Keywords: Microarchitecture · Fingerprinting · Side channel · JavaScript

1 Introduction

Knowing the CPU of a target system, or its properties, may allow attackers to craft severe tailored attacks. For example, research in recent years has revealed multiple critical CPU vulnerabilities related to speculative and out-of-order execution [4,16,20,27,32,35,40]. These transient-execution attacks [4,16,20] leverage CPU-specific inner details to leak data in the same process or even across security domains [4]. Likewise, Rowhammer [15] is a vulnerability in modern DRAM that leverages knowledge of a CPU's cache architecture to flip bits in memory without accessing them. While such attacks are already a security risk when mounted in native code, they reach the masses when successfully launched in a browser. In fact, despite the limitations of the restricted browser environment, previous research mounted Rowhammer [11] and the transient-execution attacks Spectre [1,16,37,39], RIDL [32], and ZombieLoad [6] in the browser.

All these attacks have in common that they require knowledge of specific properties of a CPU. However, attackers cannot easily obtain the CPU model

V. Atluri et al. (Eds.): ESORICS 2022, LNCS 13556, pp. 87–105, 2022.
https://doi.org/10.1007/978-3-031-17143-7_5

(or CPU properties) in a Web setting. Consequently, in contrast to native attacks, browser-based attacks face several challenges. The sandboxed code execution does not give the attacker full control over the instructions executed. The JavaScript and WebAssembly code is just-in-time-compiled by the browser engine to the instruction set architecture (ISA) of the particular CPU. It is often difficult for an attacker to distinguish the noise naturally generated by the operating system and other processes from the actual target data. This is made more difficult because these attacks do not deliver any relevant data at all on CPUs that are not vulnerable. Moreover, as side-channel leakage rates for these browser-based implementations are often low, with typically a few bits per second [6,32], knowing whether the leaked values are actually sensitive data is tedious. Identifying potential victims or even choosing the most effective attack for a concrete target is thus valuable to an attacker. Likewise, a successful Rowhammer attack requires knowledge of cache architecture and replacement policies of the different cache levels, as implied by the CPU model or family. Knowing these parameters simplifies generating code for memory accesses that purposely miss the caches and can thus be used in a Rowhammer attack. All these vital CPU properties can be trivially extracted from knowledge of the CPU model in a native attack setting. However, lacking knowledge of the CPU model from within the browser often complicates—if not even impedes—an attack.

In this paper, we explore if attackers can determine attack-relevant CPU properties from within the browser. To this end, we present six benchmarks designed to reveal CPU-specific properties and behaviors. Our benchmarks are implemented in JavaScript and WebAssembly and run in unmodified browsers. We target microarchitectural elements relevant to microarchitectural attacks, including the cache and the TLB. In addition, they also reveal the number of CPU cores and profile the performance of the CPU in single- and multi-threaded scenarios. All these properties can be inferred reliably, even with state-of-the-art mitigations enabled in Mozilla Firefox and Google Chrome. Moreover, the benchmarks are independent of the operating system and instruction set architecture. We optimize all benchmarks to work on x86 and ARMv8 CPUs, including low-end devices such as smartphones.

To evaluate the efficacy of our benchmarks, we conduct a study over 834 participants to collect information from 297 CPU models in the wild. Based on this data set, we achieve accuracies of up to 95% for determining microarchitectural properties such as the L1D size or associativity, or the used page size. Moreover, when combining the microarchitectural properties, we can expand our knowledge to predict the CPU vendor at 97% accuracy and even identify the exact CPU models and microarchitectures at about 65% accuracy.

First, our results show that these benchmarks can be used to infer properties useful for microarchitectural attacks. Second, by combining the benchmarks, they can also be used for hardware fingerprinting, e.g., to track users across websites. Hence, our benchmarks can augment state-of-the-art browser fingerprinting, which mainly focuses on the software side to enable web tracking [18]. Our evaluation also shows that current browser-fingerprinting mitigations do not impede the generation of our CPU fingerprints. We publish our data set and benchmarks as open source.[1]

Contribution. To summarize, we make the following contributions.

1. We show 6 benchmarks to infer microarchitectural properties from the browser.
2. We evaluate our benchmarks on a set of 834 CPUs found in the wild, showing an accuracy of up to 95% for inferring microarchitectural properties.
3. We demonstrate that combining these properties can reliably detect CPU vendors, models, and microarchitectures.
4. We show that fingerprinting mitigations do not prevent our benchmarks.

2   Background

A device fingerprint is information collected about the hardware or software of a particular device, typically for the purpose of authentication or identification.

Browser Fingerprinting. For browser fingerprinting, a site uses a client-side scripting language to reveal characteristics of the browser, software, or hardware of a system. The seminal work by Eckersley [7] investigated browser fingerprinting using the information transmitted by HTTP, such as the User-Agent header, and information accessible via the browser API exposed to client-side scripting languages. In the past, several browser-provided APIs [23], including the HTML5 Battery Status [24], WebGL and Canvas [5,19,22], or AudioContext API [8] have been used to craft accurate fingerprints. Mowery et al. [21] exploit performance differences of the different JavaScript engines used by different browsers and the allowlist of the popular NoScript plugin. Schwarz et al. [33] presented JavaScript Template Attacks, an automated framework to detect differences in browser engines caused by the surrounding environment.

Browser-based CPU Fingerprinting. Recent works also investigate hardware fingerprinting of the CPU. Sanchez-Rola et al. [31] observe the accumulated execution times of common functions, such as string manipulation functions or cryptography functions from the HTML5 Cryptography API. This allows the identification of a concrete CPU with adequate accuracy. Saito et al. [29] proposed multiple side-channel related methods to infer the presence or absence of different Intel CPU features, such as Advanced Encryption Standard New Instructions (AES-NI) and Intel Turbo Boost Technology. Saito et al. [30] also proposed algorithms to infer the presence or absence of Hyper-Threading Technology (HTT) and Streaming SIMD Extensions 2 (SSE2). With many of these Intel-specific extensions and technologies omnipresent in modern Intel CPUs, these algorithms generate few distinguishing features for modern Intel CPU models. Furthermore, the proposed features do not necessarily allow to distinguish Intel CPUs from CPUs distributed by other manufacturers since other manufacturers provide their own functionally-equivalent technologies.

---

[1] https://github.com/CISPA/browser-cpu-fingerprinting.

3   Methodology

In the following, we present 6 benchmarks to reveal information about the CPU. The output is used to infer microarchitectural characteristics such as the cache size, which provides information for microarchitectural attacks. Furthermore, by combining multiple benchmarks, we can generate CPU model fingerprints, an extension of device fingerprints, that can reidentify a CPU model or, at the minimum, the CPU vendor. These can be used, e.g., as additional entropy for tracking users on the web. Figure 1 provides an overview of CPU parts that are targeted by our benchmarks. In particular, we have a benchmark to determine the number of cores, the sizes of the different data cache levels, the associativity of the L1D cache, and the size of the L1D TLB. While not shown in Fig. 1, we additionally present benchmarks to determine the performance of a single core and the page size.

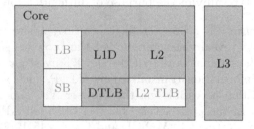

Fig. 1. Parts of the CPU targeted by our benchmarks are highlighted in yellow. (Color figure online)

3.1   Benchmarks

Our benchmarks are written in JavaScript and WebAssembly. The latter is used whenever compiler optimizations could impair the functionality of a benchmark or when highly-optimized instructions are required to ensure the highest level of performance. We operate in a cross-origin-isolated environment that automatically reenables features that have been disabled as a response to microarchitectural attacks, e.g., `SharedArrayBuffer`. Note that this is a server-side setting that does not require any changes in the browser, i.e., benchmarks run in unmodified off-the-shelf browsers if the user visits the attacker's website. All benchmarks, except the single-core performance and the cores benchmark, use a `SharedArrayBuffer`-based timer [9,36].

Number of CPU Cores. The number of CPU cores is typically a power of two, though 6, 10, and 12 have also been prominent in recent years. Many modern CPUs implement Simultaneous Multithreading (SMT) to effectively double the number of threads that can run in parallel. The ability to distinguish actual physical cores from virtual cores based on SMT further allows clustering of CPUs by the number of physical or virtual cores. Both aspects have previously been algorithmically examined for Intel CPUs by Saito et al. [29,30]. While JavaScript is a single-threaded language, `Web Workers` are a browser feature that allows running scripts in the background without blocking the main UI thread. While the browser API may feature the `navigator.hardwareConcurrency` read-only property, this does not necessarily reflect the number of available cores.

Algorithm 1: Cache Size Benchmark

Input: `sizes`
Output: `timestamps`
    N ⇐ 16 * 1024 * 1024
    `timestamps` ⇐ []
    for `size` in `sizes` **do**
       Prepare randomized circular linked list of `size` KB
       `head` ⇐ head of linked list
       `startTime` ⇐ `getTimestamp()`
       for 1 upto N **do**
          `head` ⇐ `head->next`
       end for
       `timeDifference` ⇐ `getTimestamp()` − `startTime`
       `timestamps.insert(timeDifference)`
    end for

Our benchmark starts more workers than actual threads available, which interferes with the effective multithreading of the workers. Some workers have to operate sequentially, taking turns on a shared hardware thread or even waiting for one worker to finish before starting. This, in turn, increases the average execution time of each worker and the time it takes for all workers to finish. Each iteration, we start N Web Workers that each perform the same independent task. If we do not create more workers than hardware threads available, the execution time of each worker is roughly the same. The time it takes all workers to finish their task noticeably increases once the number of workers exceeds the number of available hardware threads. In addition, we can also observe that once the number of workers exceeds the number of available physical cores due to the negative performance impact of microarchitectural components shared between two co-located logical cores. The output of this benchmark is a list of timestamp differences for all N from the set of even numbers up to 32.

Data Cache Sizes. Since ARM CPUs often only feature two cache levels, while x86 CPUs typically feature three, the number of cache levels allows distinguishing ARM and x86 CPUs with relatively high accuracy. Furthermore, the L2 cache size allows determining the vendor of a recent x86 CPU, and the L3 size allows distinguishing CPU models. This is particularly interesting since many microarchitectural attacks are ISA-specific or even vendor-specific. The class of MDS vulnerabilities [3,32,35], for example, only affects Intel CPUs.

We frequently access memory and measure the latency. Over time, we increase the size of the frequently-used memory. First, the used memory easily fits inside the L1 cache, and we observe fast access times. Once the size approaches the limit of the L1 cache, we statistically observe an increased number of L1 cache misses, increasing the average memory latency. Likewise, the latency increases again if the limit of the L2 and then the L3 is reached. This reveals each cache level and their respective sizes. To eliminate the noise generated by the various prefetchers, we rely on pointer chasing using a randomized linked list. Here, each memory access determines the subsequent pointer to be dereferenced. This generates a series of loads that each depend on the previous load, thus enforcing serialization. We use a circular randomized linked list, where we perform a fixed number of pointer advances (Algorithm 1). Over time, we increase the memory allocated by the linked list. The output of the benchmark is a list of timestamp differences that are sampled at different list sizes. We test 273 potential sizes from 2 KB to 32 KB. To accurately determine L1 cache sizes, the granularity for smaller sizes is finer than for larger sizes.

L1D Cache Associativity. Most modern x86 CPUs have the L1D cache associativity of 8 [14]. Thus, this feature allows us to recognize ARM CPUs where the associativity differs. The general idea behind the algorithm is the same as for determining the cache size. Instead of filling the cache, we now only aim to fill a single cache set. To fill a cache set, we create a randomized circular linked list as in Algorithm 1. By spacing the nodes of our linked list cache-size bytes apart, all memory accesses map to the same cache set, as the cache size is always a multiple of the cache associativity. As long as the accessed memory fits into the same cache set, we observe repeated L1 cache hits. After exceeding the associativity, the set can no longer accommodate all memory locations, and we thus observe an increase in execution time due to an increase in L1 cache misses. The output of the cache associativity benchmark is a list of timestamp differences sampled at different linked list sizes. We test for associativities between 1 and 32.

L1D TLB Size. CPUs usually have an L1 TLB that stores translations for 64x 4kB pages [14], with only older x86 (e.g., Intel Nehalem, 2008) and ARM CPUs deviating from this value. Thus, this property allows distinguishing modern ARM CPUs from modern x86 CPUs fairly accurately. The general idea behind the algorithm is to fill the L1 TLB. We use Algorithm 1 but space the nodes of our linked list at least page-size bytes apart. Hence, all memory accesses map to different pages and thus require an address translation. While the number of pages used by our linked list does not exceed the number of L1D TLB entries, we observe relatively low execution times due to repeated L1D TLB hits. Once this number is exceeded, we statistically observe more L1D TLB misses and thus an increase in execution time. As almost all modern CPUs have a standard page size of 4kB we hardcode this value to eliminate this error source. In our data set, this hardcoded value only negatively affects this benchmark on the Apple M1 chip, as it features a standard page size of 16kB [12]. The output of the

L1D TLB size benchmark is a list of timestamp differences that are sampled at different linked list sizes. We test for TLB sizes between 2 and 128 entries.

Single-Core Performance. To estimate the single-core performance of the CPU, we increment a counter for the duration of 1 ms (measured using the `performance.now` function). We repeat this step for a fixed number of iterations and collect the counter's value after each iteration. To better observe the difference between boost and base frequency, we repeat this process three times and wait for 100 ms between each time to reset the frequency.

Page Size. The page size is usually determined by the processor architecture [14], with a default of 4kB for x86 CPUs in laptops and desktops. In our data set, only the Apple M1 has a different default page size of 16kB. The use of certain page sizes directly reveals the CPU family [14]. As the resolution of our `SharedArrayBuffer`-based timer is high enough to differentiate cache hits and misses, it also allows detecting page faults. Iterating the memory in 256B strides while measuring the access times detects page faults due to noticeably higher execution times [11,36]. We take the offsets of the 10 highest timing differences and iterate these offsets in pairs. If the greatest common divisor of an offset pair is greater than 1023 and a power of two, the greatest common divisor is added to a list. This step eliminates the majority of outliers.

3.2 Data Set

Study. To obtain a real-world data set for further investigation, we conduct a voluntary study. We implement all benchmarks on a website that allows collecting measurements from web clients. Before starting the execution of our benchmarks, the participant is informed about and has to agree on the purpose of the study. The collected data is then stored in our database. This data only contains the output of the 6 benchmarks, the User-Agent value to determine the browser version and the self-reported CPU model string. It does not suffice for the identification of a person or device as the k-anonymity (i.e., the number of persons using a given CPU model in the global population) is sufficiently large. In addition, we implemented strict access control and removed all personally identifiable information. The participant is instructed to connect a mobile device to a charger, to leave this tab running in the foreground and to ensure a low system load during the study. This website was first presented to professional computer scientists. During this phase of the study, we obtained benchmark results from about 120 participants. To collect a representative set of measurements, we use the crowdsourcing marketplace *Amazon Mechanical Turk (MTurk)*[2] to distribute our study to a larger audience. The setup of the study remains the same, except for the addition of a mechanism to ensure the study is run in the foreground. This mechanism simply consists of a button, that has to be pressed at least every 30 s.

---

[2] https://www.mturk.com/.

Structure. The final data set consists of benchmark results from 834 participants featuring 297 different CPU models. Our set exclusively consists of CPUs currently used in desktops and laptops, and two AWS Graviton CPUs. The majority of benchmarks are collected on Google Chrome version 91-93 and Firefox version 89-91. Almost 75% of the CPUs in the set are manufactured by Intel. The remaining quarter contains AMD CPUs and 21 ARM CPUs. 19 ARM CPUs of our data set are recently released Apple M1 chips. Our data set reflects the consumer market shares of x86 CPU vendors for the past few years. Optionally, users could leave out certain parts of benchmarks requiring a large amount of memory, such as the cache size benchmark for cache sizes larger than 1 KB if they used a low-end device. Additionally, the collection of benchmark execution times was introduced later in the study, such that they are not always available. Thus, not all data set entries may be used in all scenarios. Each classification only considers entries that feature the required benchmark results.

3.3   Classification

The outputs of our benchmarks are mostly a collection of measurements, not single values. Hence, we rely on machine learning algorithms to perform the actual classification of the different CPU properties. We also use the combination of properties to further detect CPU vendors, models, and microarchitectures.

Algorithms. We use three supervised learning classifiers as implemented by the *scikit-learn* [26] Python module. In particular, we use the KNeighborsClassifier (KNN), SVC, and the MLPClassifier (MLP). These classifiers were chosen as they showcase varying levels of complexity, after experimenting with a variety of popular readily-available classifiers. Simple thresholds and statistical methods did not lead to adequate results, we suspect the high levels of noise to be responsible for this, and are thus not discussed further. Each classification scenario may use a different balanced subset of our data set for testing and training to give equal priority to all classes. We detail this balancing further in the following sections. All subsets consist of labeled samples. A labeled sample uses the results of one or more benchmarks as features. As the output of a benchmark is a list of timestamps or timestamp differences, the list directly represents the list of features. If multiple benchmarks are used, their results are concatenated. The label can be the vendor, microarchitecture, model, or property.

Property Classification. To evaluate our benchmarks for their ability to discriminate between the different instances of targeted CPU features, we introduce property classifiers. These classifiers are each trained based on data from a single CPU property, such as the number of threads. Each property classifier is trained and tested only using the results of the benchmark designed to reveal information about this property. It is important to note that the distribution of properties is rarely balanced, as the dataset tends to feature recent CPU models, and vendors often reuse established parts of the microarchitecture. To counteract this bias, our property classifiers operate on balanced subsets of the dataset.

In addition to specific properties, we can also use a combination of properties. While single properties might not be unique, a combination of properties reduces the set of possible CPU models with such a combination. Hence, by combining multiple properties, we can infer higher-level information, such as the CPU vendor, microarchitecture, and model, as described next.

Vendor Classification. For the classification by CPU vendor, we use the results of the cache-size benchmark and the TLB-size benchmark. We first examine the capability of distinguishing two vendors producing CPUs of the same ISA. Since the vast majority of our data set consists of x86 CPUs, we aim to distinguish CPUs manufactured by Intel from CPUs manufactured by AMD. As our data set generally features more Intel CPUs, we use a balanced subset of it for training and evaluating the machine learning algorithms. The subset features data of 165 Intel and 165 AMD CPUs.

Secondly, we extend the classes to include all vendors present in our data set. As the data set does not contain a large variety of ARM CPU vendors, we decided not to distinguish between specific ARM manufacturers but rather regard the ARM ISA as a group. The balanced subset used includes 21 AMD CPUs, 21 ARM CPUs, and 21 Intel CPUs.

Microarchitecture Classification. The second-coarsest clustering of CPUs is based on their microarchitecture. The subset used for training and testing contains 16 different microarchitectures as classes. Each class contains at least 17 and a maximum of 25 samples to keep the influence of the imbalance as small as possible without reducing the size of our set drastically. The final set contains the data of 368 CPUs. For this classification, we again use the results of the cache-size benchmark and the TLB-size benchmark and also add the results of the cores and cache-associativity benchmark.

As many microarchitectures are, however, based on the same base microarchitecture and thus indistinguishable by our benchmarks, we also classify microarchitectures by their base microarchitecture. A prominent example is the Skylake base architecture by Intel, on which eight microarchitectures (e.g., Kaby Lake and Comet Lake) from 2015 to 2020 are based. We consider 10 different groups with 18 to 22 samples each, with a total of 211 different CPUs.

Model Classification. We prepare multiple subsets of our data set to investigate the performance of inferring the specific CPU model using machine learning. The first subset features 18 different CPU models with at least 7 and a maximum of 9 samples each. In total, the resulting set contains the data of 153 different CPUs, thus only using about 22% of the data set suitable for this classification. Here we use the results of different benchmarks for training and testing. The first approach uses the results of the cache-size benchmark, the cache-associativity benchmark, the TLB-size benchmark, and the cores benchmark.

The second approach uses the execution time of each benchmark as a feature. Here we use a slightly different subset of our data set, as the capturing of execution times per benchmark was only introduced later in our study. Each class of the set has at least 7 samples with a maximum of 9 samples from 14 different CPU models. In total, the set contains data of 114 different CPUs.

3.4 Classification Evaluation

In each classification scenario, we perform a Grid Search on 75% of the corresponding data set for each of the three classifiers. This process uses a K-Fold with $k = 5$. Finally, the best-performing classifier is evaluated on the held-out test set with the best-performing hyperparameter configuration.

4 Evaluation

In this section, we present the metrics achieved by different classification algorithms for the scenarios presented in Sect. 3.3. The metrics show the ability of our benchmarks to fingerprint CPU vendors, microarchitectures, CPU models, and certain CPU properties (e.g., L1-cache size). We evaluate the efficiency of our current implementation by analyzing the benchmark execution times.

4.1 Classification

We compare the classification algorithm achieving the best accuracy to the best-performing DummyClassifier (DC). The dummy classifier uses the *most-frequent* or the *uniform* strategy. The most-frequent strategy predicts the most-frequent element of the training set. The uniform strategy chooses a random label.

Property Classification. Table 1 shows the accuracies the best-performing classification algorithms achieve when classifying properties such as the L1 cache size. Especially accurate are the classifiers for the L1D cache size, L2 cache size, and the L1D cache associativity. The L1 and L2 cache sizes can be classified with an accuracy of above 95% each. The L3 cache size classification achieves an accuracy of slightly more than 60%. This is most likely because the last-level caches are usually shared and exhibit greater noise generated by the system. The accuracy of the L1D cache associativity classification is close to 94%.

Although the cores benchmark is also negatively affected by the system noise, the SVC classifier achieves an accuracy of almost 75% when classifying the number of threads. Mispredictions are often just off by two, indicating the system noise to be responsible for most of them. The same benchmark results are additionally used for the SMT and HTT availability classification. As HTT is the proprietary SMT implementation of Intel, the data set used for this classification is restricted to Intel CPUs. Here, the best-performing classifiers achieve accuracies of 69.5% and 84.2%. Increasing the maximum number of workers used by the cores benchmark should yield better results but would also drastically increase the execution time for CPUs featuring a low number of cores.

Finally, the boost-technology availability of a CPU can be classified with an accuracy of 72.7% by the SVC classifier. The result is most likely negatively affected by external factors discussed in Sect. 5.2, as well as system noise.

The page size does not require a classifier, as the algorithm directly outputs the correct page size. The correct page size was inferred in 151 out of 158 test cases, resulting in an accuracy of 95.5%.

Table 1. Property classification results

Property	Classifier	Accuracy	Macro-F1	Test set size ($|T|$)
L1 cache size	MLP	1.000	1.000	34
L2 cache size	SVC	0.965	0.966	29
L3 cache size	SVC	0.629	0.629	62
L1D cache asso	KNN	0.937	0.955	16
Number of threads	SVC	0.741	0.661	62
HTT availability	MLP	0.842	0.842	70
SMT availability	SVC	0.695	0.695	105
Boost availability	SVC	0.727	0.723	33

Table 2. AMD vs. Intel classification results

	Accuracy	macro-F_1	$|T|$
DC	0.481	0.479	83
MLP	0.975	0.975	

Vendor Classification. For the combined properties, we first evaluate the capabilities to distinguish CPU vendors, specifically AMD and Intel. When distinguishing these vendors, the random dummy classifier achieves accuracies of around 50% as the data set is balanced. In this scenario, the MLPClassifier achieves the highest accuracy at 97.5%, as shown in Table 2.

The vendor classification most likely shows these results due to the observable differences in L2 cache sizes (512 kB for AMD, 256 kB for Intel). This effect also translates to ARM CPUs. Most ARM CPUs do not feature an L3 cache and share a large L2 cache among all cores. As most ARM CPUs in our data set are Apple M1, they are also distinguishable due to their large TLBs [12,14]. Here, the accuracy is 100% with a small test set containing 15 samples.

Microarchitecture Classification. The microarchitecture classification to evaluate the microarchitecture fingerprinting capabilities of our benchmarks is not performed on a fully-balanced set. The randomly operating dummy classifier achieves an accuracy of 4.2%, while the KNN classifier achieves an accuracy of 65.6%. The results are listed in Table 3.

Table 3. Microarchitecture classification results

	Accuracy	macro-F_1	$|T|$
DC	0.041	0.043	96
KNN	0.656	0.640	

(a) not grouped

	Accuracy	macro-F_1	$|T|$
DC	0.074	0.077	54
MLP	0.925	0.888	

(b) grouped by base microarchitecture

The classification struggles to differentiate microarchitectures that do not differ in their L1 cache associativity or their L1 cache, L2 cache, or L1 TLB sizes. The Coffee Lake, Comet Lake, and Whiskey Lake microarchitectures by Intel are, for example, often confused with each other. They do not differ in their cache or TLB hierarchies, as all three are based on the Skylake microarchitecture, which makes it impossible to distinguish them based on these features. While there are smaller differences, they are not addressed by our benchmarks. Grouping all microarchitectures by their base microarchitecture, the classification yields an accuracy of 92.5%. The results of this classification are listed in Table 3.

Model Classification. For the CPU model fingerprinting, we use the results of our benchmarks and compare them to benchmark execution times. The benchmark execution times basically compress the benchmark results into one number. Using the same benchmarks as used for the microarchitecture classification, the SVC classifier achieves an accuracy of 58.9%. Here, the dummy classifier only achieves an accuracy of about 10%. The resulting metrics are shown in Table 4. Many CPU models do not differ in their cache or TLB hierarchy, with the only exception being the shared LLC, as its size usually depends on the number of cores. Should the number of cores also be the same, the ability to distinguish such CPU models is often comparable to guessing at random.

Table 4. Model classification results

	Accuracy	macro-F_1	$|T|$
Dummy	0.102	0.074	39
SVC	0.589	0.590	

using benchmark results

	Accuracy	macro-F_1	$|T|$
Dummy	0.033	0.020	30
SVC	0.700	0.568	

using execution times

This is further supported by a small-scale experiment. Here, a classifier is evaluated to distinguish an Intel Core i5–8250U from an Intel Core i7–8550U.

These two CPU models feature the same microarchitecture and the same number of cores. They only differ in their frequencies, with the Core i7 model having a slightly higher base and boost clock. The best-performing classifier does not outperform the random dummy classifier. In contrast, running the same experiment using two CPUs that differ by at least one microarchitectural property yields an accuracy of 100%. For example, the Ryzen 5 2600 has an 8 MB L3, while the Ryzen 5 3600 has a 16 MB L3. They also differ slightly in their frequency. Note that both classifiers were only evaluated on test sets of size 8. This indicates that the used benchmarks do not contain much information about the performance of the CPU and only accurately profile their respective microarchitectural property. The classification using benchmark results can identify CPU models with unique properties. In our data set, this applies to the Apple M1 chip. A classification algorithm can distinguish this CPU model from all others in our set with 100% accuracy due to the unique TLB and page size.

The model classification using only the vector of execution times, i.e., the execution time of each benchmark, achieves an accuracy of 70% with the best-performing SVC classifier. The results of this classification are listed in Table 4. It is also important to note that the data sets used in both experiments are not identical. As the collection of execution times was only introduced later in our study, the second experiment contains different CPU models and may contain fewer samples for some classes.

The execution time of a benchmark is a compression of the benchmark results for non-constant-time benchmarks. For example, in the L1 cache-associativity benchmark, we observe lower execution times in iterations that do not exceed the associativity. However, a low execution time of this benchmark can indicate at least one of two things. The execution time could have been generated by a high-performance CPU or high L1 cache associativity, or a combination. Ultimately, the execution time of a benchmark thus is a compression of the benchmark results and the performance of the CPU, enabling the feature to be used to distinguish microarchitectural properties and performance.

A combined approach using benchmark results and their execution times performs similarly to the approach only using the execution times. Here, the best-performing SVC achieves an accuracy of 60%. We assume that the combination scales better to data sets containing more classes, as the compression of benchmark results and performance may lead to confusion.

4.2   Efficiency

The runtime of our benchmarks depends largely on the performance of the CPU that is being profiled. In addition, as discussed in Sect. 4.1, it also depends on the properties of the CPU (e.g., L1 cache size). On a fast CPU (e.g., AMD Ryzen 9 5900X), the total runtime amounts to about 1.1 min, while slower CPUs (e.g., Intel Core2 Duo P8600) in our tests sometimes take more than 6.5 min to finish. The median of all total runtimes is slightly over 2 min. Fig. 2 shows a box plot of the execution times per benchmark in seconds. Note that this plot does not show outliers to improve the readability.

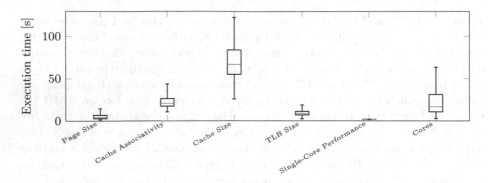

Fig. 2. Benchmark execution times box plot.

The single-core performance benchmark has a constant execution time of about 1.75 s, which rarely varies due to the scheduler. As shown by the box plot, the execution times of the page and TLB size benchmark almost always stay below 20 s each. The median of both benchmarks, however, is below 10 s. The cache associativity benchmark has a median value of about 20 s, with almost all execution times being in the range of 10 s to 50 s. As the runtime of the cores benchmark largely depends on the number of available threads, the execution times of this benchmark vary in the range from 5 s to 60 s. The execution time of CPUs with more than 8 available threads is generally below the median time of 20 s. Our benchmark with the highest median execution time is the cache-size benchmark with a median value of about 60 s. The maximum value is slightly more than 120 s. Its current implementation dominates the overall runtime.

The runtime of our benchmarks can, however, still be reduced, especially since they currently implement exhaustive search. For the cache size benchmark, it might, e.g., be possible to implement a binary search. Similarly, the number of cores benchmark could implement an early-abort mechanism to reduce the runtime drastically. In many cases, the number of iterations could also be reduced by a large margin without sacrificing discriminative power. It is not uncommon for users leave a tab open for more than 10 min (e.g., in case of streaming portals, or online games). Furthermore, our benchmarks may be interrupted and resumed later to circumvent the issue of running in the background.

4.3   Noise Resilience

To evaluate our benchmarks for noise resilience, we collect a small dataset using four different CPUs where each CPU is sampled in 7 different noise scenarios. The first scenario is a baseline, where no additional noise is added to the environment. We consider CPU noise by using the *stress-ng*[3] tool to run 1, 2, or 4 CPU stressors. Separately, we consider memory noise by running 1, 2, or 4 Virtual Memory stressors. Here, each stressor uses 10% of free memory.

---

[3] https://wiki.ubuntu.com/Kernel/Reference/stress-ng.

The collected dataset is then used as a test set for the property classifiers trained as described in Sect. 3.4. Since the size of the dataset is small, we cannot draw any certain conclusions. However, the accuracies indicate that all benchmarks except for the cores benchmark and the large sizes for the cache size benchmark are largely unaffected by noise. Property classifiers using the output of the cores benchmark or output of the cache size benchmark targetted at cache sizes that exceed the L2 cache thus perform noticeably worse under noise. This also explains the performance of the L3 cache size and the Number of Cores classifier, which perform slightly worse than other property classifiers.

5   Discussion

5.1   Use for Microarchitectural Properties

Many microarchitectural attacks have implicit assumptions about the underlying microarchitecture. For example, page-deduplication attacks in the browser [2, 6,10] assume a page size of 4 kB. While this was common when the attacks were published, new (micro-)architectures, such as the Apple M1, have different default page sizes, such as 16kB. Assuming a page size that is too small breaks the attack. Hence, our page-size benchmark reenables this attack on the M1. Similarly, some attacks rely on initial assumptions about the microarchitecture, e.g., the page size [36,43], the cache associativity and cache size for cache eviction sets [42], the L1 associativity for evicting L1 sets [39], or the number of CPU cores when optimizing MDS attacks [28]. With our benchmarks, these values can be inferred in the browser with a high accuracy, improving such attacks.

In addition to improving microarchitectural attacks, the information about the CPU can be used for browser fingerprints. The advantage over software properties is the long-term stability of hardware fingerprints, as users do not upgrade hardware that often. While the CPU as single property is not very unique, it can help linking less stable fingerprints [41]. Moreover, as there is no dependency on a specific browser API, our CPU fingerprints are difficult to mitigate without impacting the usability of websites (cf. Sect. 5.3).

We believe that our benchmarks also translate to newly released CPU models, as long as their respective features fall within the addressed ranges. Otherwise the ranges of our benchmarks would have to be adjusted and our respective property classifiers would have to be retrained. The model may have to be included in the training of the vendor and microarchitecture classifiers. In addition, the model must be included in the training for the model classification.

5.2   Limitations

Data Set. The data set used for our evaluation is fairly small as we could not rely on any existing data set. Especially the number of samples per class is low for the model classification. The same problem also affects property classifiers with dominating classes. Since the data was collected using a study involving the manual reporting of the CPU model, we cannot guarantee the correctness of all reported CPU models. In some cases, the labels used for our algorithms might contain wrong information. This is due to the fact that this large data set containing almost 300 different CPU models was collected manually using information from *cpu-world*[4] and the official vendor information.

Runtime Influences. While different browsers use different JavaScript engines, we do not see a significant negative impact of that in our results. Even though Chrome provides timestamps with a lower resolution than Firefox, the benchmarks work well in both browsers. We cannot enforce a low system usage, such that some data might be very noisy due to demanding background tasks. Similarly, running the benchmarks on a mobile device running on battery interferes with power-saving mechanisms. Furthermore, we do not consider non-default CPU settings, such as deactivation of features (e.g., HTT), manual overclocking, and undervolting. Lastly, we do not perform any hyperparameter optimization of our classification algorithms and instead mostly use default parameter values. We leave this optimization to future work.

5.3 Mitigations

As our benchmarks only measure timing effects of microarchitectural elements and the performance of the CPU, it is difficult to mitigate them fully.

Disabling JavaScript. The simplest solution to stop attacks involving client-side scripts is to disable the execution of all scripts. While this approach completely mitigates all of our benchmarks, it also disrupts benign functionality using scripts and thus is often not an option. Moreover, recent work [38] shows that limited microarchitectural attacks are possible without code execution.

Disabling Features. Our benchmarks rely on shared memory and high-resolution timers. Disabling these features does, in fact, mitigate our current implementation. The benchmarks used by our classification algorithms, however, do not necessarily require these features. By aggregating timing differences instead of measuring single event timings, everything can be implemented using the timers with reduced precision. Some benchmarks profiling multi-threaded scenarios require the Web Worker API. Disabling this feature would fully mitigate the core benchmark and associated classifications.

Adding Randomness. Another possible mitigation is to add random noise to the JavaScript engine (e.g., random memory prefetches, instruction reordering, low-resolution timer) [17,34]. This does, however, not fully mitigate benchmarks but only adds noise, resulting in worse classification results. We observe that our benchmarks are largely unaffected by a slower `SharedArrayBuffer`, buffer ASLR, array preloading, and message delay.

---

[4] https://www.cpu-world.com/index.html.

Detection. Another countermeasure is to detect the benchmarks on the system or the browser level using, e.g., performance counters [13,25,44]. Future work has to evaluate if these approaches can be used to detect browser-based attacks.

6 Conclusion

We presented 6 JavaScript and WebAssembly benchmarks with a total median runtime of just over 2min designed to reveal different CPU properties. The individual benchmarks allow determining their respective target properties with high accuracies of up to 100%. As a result, microarchitectural attacks from the browser can be better tailored to the specific CPU. Moreover, the results of these benchmarks can be combined to accurately infer the vendor of a CPU, the microarchitecture, or the CPU model. Our benchmarks allow the identification of the vendor of a CPU with accuracies above 97%. Moreover, current browser mitigations do not prevent our benchmarks. Hence, this information can also improve state-of-the-art browser fingerprinting techniques.

Acknowledgments. We would like to thank all participants of our study. This work has been supported by the Deutsche Forschungsgemeinschaft (DFG, German Research Foundation) - 491039149. We further thank the Saarbrücken Graduate School of Computer Science for their funding and support.

References

1. Agarwal, A., et al.: Spook.js: Attacking chrome strict site isolation via speculative execution (2022)
2. Bosman, E., Razavi, K., Bos, H., Giuffrida, C.: Dedup Est machina: memory deduplication as an advanced exploitation vector. In: S&P (2016)
3. Canella, C., et al.: Leaking Data on Meltdown-resistant CPUs. In: CCS (2019)
4. Canella, C., et al.: A Systematic Evaluation of Transient Execution Attacks and Defenses. In: USENIX Security Symposium, extended classification tree and PoCs (2019). https://transient.fail/
5. Cao, Y., Li, S., Wijmans, E.: Browser Fingerprinting via OS and Hardware Level Features. In: NDSS (2017)
6. Easdon, C., Schwarz, M., Schwarzl, M., Gruss, D.: Rapid Prototyping for Microarchitectural Attacks. In: USENIX Security (2022)
7. Eckersley, P.: How unique is your web browser? In: PETS (2010)
8. Englehardt, S., Narayanan, A.: Online tracking: a 1-million-site measurement and analysis. In: CCS (2016)
9. Gras, B., Razavi, K.: ASLR on the Line: Practical Cache Attacks on the MMU. In: NDSS (2017)
10. Gruss, D., Bidner, D., Mangard, S.: Practical memory deduplication attacks in sandboxed javascript. In: ESORICS (2015)
11. Gruss, D., Maurice, C., Mangard, S.: Rowhammer.js: A Remote Software-Induced Fault Attack in JavaScript. In: DIMVA (2016)
12. Handley, M.: M1 Exploration - v0.70 (2021)

13. Herath, N., Fogh, A.: These are Not Your Grand Daddys CPU Performance Counters - CPU Hardware Performance Counters for Security. In: Black Hat Briefings (2015)
14. Intel: Intel 64 and IA-32 Architectures Optimization Reference Manual (2019)
15. Kim, Y., et al.: Flipping Bits in Memory Without Accessing Them: an Experimental Study of DRAM Disturbance Errors. In: ISCA (2014)
16. Kocher, P., et al.: Spectre attacks: exploiting speculative execution. In: S&P (2019)
17. Kohlbrenner, D., Shacham, H.: Trusted browsers for uncertain times. In: USENIX Security Symposium (2016)
18. Laperdrix, P., Bielova, N., Baudry, B., Avoine, G.: Browser fingerprinting: a survey. In: ACM Transactions on the Web (2020)
19. Laperdrix, P., Rudametkin, W., Baudry, B.: Beauty and the beast: diverting modern web browsers to build unique browser fingerprints. In: S&P (2016)
20. Lipp, M., et al.: Meltdown: reading Kernel memory from user space. In: USENIX Security Symposium (2018)
21. Mowery, K., Bogenreif, D., Yilek, S., Shacham, H.: Fingerprinting information in JavaScript implementations. In: W2SP (2011)
22. Mowery, K., Shacham, H.: Pixel perfect: fingerprinting canvas in HTML5. In: W2SP (2012)
23. Nikiforakis, N., Kapravelos, A., Joosen, W., Kruegel, C., Piessens, F., Vigna, G.: Cookieless monster: Exploring the ecosystem of web-based device fingerprinting. In: Security and privacy (SP) (2013)
24. Olejnik, L., Englehardt, S., Narayanan, A.: Battery status not included: assessing privacy in web standards. In: Workshop on Privacy Engineering (IWPE) (2017)
25. Payer, M.: HexPADS: a platform to detect "stealth" attacks. In: ESSoS (2016)
26. Pedregosa, F., et al.: Scikit-learn: Machine learning in Python. J. Mach. Learn. Res. **12**, pp. 2825–2830 (2011)
27. Ragab, H., Milburn, A., Razavi, K., Bos, H., Giuffrida, C.: CrossTalk: speculative data leaks across cores are real. In: S&P (2021)
28. Röttger, S.: Escaping the Chrome Sandbox with RIDL (2020). https://googleprojectzero.blogspot.com/2020/02/escaping-chrome-sandbox-with-ridl.html
29. Saito, T., et al.: Estimating CPU features by browser fingerprinting. In: International Conference on Innovative Mobile and Internet Services in Ubiquitous Computing (IMIS) (2016)
30. Saito, T., Yasuda, K., Tanabe, K., Takahashi, K.: Web browser tampering: Inspecting CPU features from side-channel information. In: International Conference on Broad-Band Wireless Computing, Communication and Applications, BWCCA (2017)
31. Sanchez-Rola, I., Santos, I., Balzarotti, D.: Clock around the clock: time-based device fingerprinting. In: CCS (2018)
32. van Schaik, S., et al.: RIDL: Rogue In-flight Data Load. In: S&P (2019)
33. Schwarz, M., Lackner, F., Gruss, D.: Javascript template attacks: automatically inferring host information for targeted exploits. In: NDSS (2019)
34. Schwarz, M., Lipp, M., Gruss, D.: Javascript zero: real javascript and zero side-channel attacks. In: NDSS (2018)
35. Schwarz, M., et al.: ZombieLoad: cross-privilege-boundary data sampling. In: CCS (2019)
36. Schwarz, M., Maurice, C., Gruss, D., Mangard, S.: fantastic timers and where to find them: high-resolution microarchitectural attacks in javascript. In: FC (2017)

37. Schwarzl, M., et al.: Dynamic process isolation. arXiv:2110.04751 (2021)
38. Shusterman, A., Agarwal, A., O'Connell, S., Genkin, D., Oren, Y., Yarom, Y.: Prime+probe 1, javascript 0: overcoming browser-based side-channel defenses. In: USENIX Security Symposium (2021)
39. Röttger, S., Janc, A.: A Spectre proof-of-concept for a Spectre-proof web (2021). https://security.googleblog.com/2021/03/a-spectre-proof-of-concept-for-spectre.html
40. Van Bulck, J., et al.: LVI: hijacking transient execution through microarchitectural load value injection. In: S&P (2020)
41. Vastel, A., Laperdrix, P., Rudametkin, W., Rouvoy, R.: Fp-stalker: Tracking browser fingerprint evolutions. In: S&P (2018)
42. Vila, P., Köpf, B., Morales, J.: Theory and practice of finding eviction sets. In: S&P (2019)
43. VUSec: RIDL test suite and exploits (GitHub) (2020). https://github.com/vusec/ridl
44. Wang, H., Sayadi, H., Sasan, A., Rafatirad, S., Homayoun, H.: Hybrid-shield: accurate and efficient cross-layer countermeasure for run-time detection and mitigation of cache-based side-channel attacks. In: ICCAD (2020)

Polymorphic Protocols at the Example of Mitigating Web Bots

August See$^{(\boxtimes)}$, Leon Fritz, and Mathias Fischer

Universität Hamburg, Hamburg, Germany
{richard.august.see,leon.fritz,mathias.fischer}@uni-hamburg.de

Abstract. Unwanted automation of network services by web robots (bots) increases the operation costs, and affects the satisfaction of human users, e.g., in online games or social media. Bots impact the revenue of service providers and can damage society by spreading false information. While few bots are usually not a problem, a large number is. Thus, we focus on bots that directly use a service's application protocol, as they are the most efficient and easiest to scale. Current solutions such as registration with personal data or CAPTCHAs are frustrating for users or can be easily evaded. Anti-reverse engineering and solutions for digital rights management that impede bot creation, e.g., unique client specific API keys, are only effective for the first bot. In this paper, we introduce a novel obfuscation approach that we call polymorphic protocols and that is inspired by polymorphic malware and methods to bypass censorship resistance. When using polymorphic protocols, each client of a service has an own application protocol, so that the costs of duplicating bots for an attacker significantly increases. For every bot that an attacker wants to create, he has to extract and reimplement a protocol from a valid client. We integrate our approach into an existing ecosystem and implement it exemplarily for Protobuf and Java. Our results indicate that the overhead for service providers and users is low, depending on the deployment and chosen protocol configuration. At the same time, our polymorphic protocols significantly increase the attacker costs to create multiple bots, when limited to conventional reverse engineering techniques only.

1 Introduction

The automated use of Internet services is an essential building block of the Internet and the web. Many services depend on each other. Examples are the embedding of a weather feed into a web page or a service that provides a price comparison by automatically querying different marketplaces. Many services provide specific interfaces for other services to allow the automation of their usage. However, there are also services without such interfaces that are intended for humans only. Automated use of a service by a program, hereafter called a bot, can affect the satisfaction of human users and can cause financial or social damage. For example, the automated use of social media can be used to spread opinions and false information, which can even influence elections [7].

V. Atluri et al. (Eds.): ESORICS 2022, LNCS 13556, pp. 106–124, 2022.
https://doi.org/10.1007/978-3-031-17143-7_6

Automation of a service can be done in different ways [3]. The most efficient approach is to automate API of the service. Using the API directly only requires a script. By simply executing the script multiple times, it is possible to create a large number of bots, e.g., to influence voting opinions on social media through nationwide spamming [7]. This puts service providers in a dilemma. A service needs to be easy and quick to use, as complicated requirements, e.g., for registration scare users away [14]. But registration without requiring limited resources such as phone numbers or passports makes it easier to create a bot army. The main problem is that automation can be made harder for attackers, but not completely prevented as human users must still be able to use the service without too much friction.

The threat model of this paper is as follows: The focus lies on services with a state tied to an entity, e.g., game progress or social media likes bound to an account. These services in particular suffer from bots, as there is a gain in running multiple bots. For example, it can be beneficial to use hundreds of bots to control hundreds of social media accounts. However, there is no gain in using hundreds of bots to query the static content of some blog or news portal. The attacker is not limited to a subset of reverse engineering techniques, but limited to using the application protocol to create bots.

In many cases, CAPTCHAs are the first and last defence against bots. However, they introduce user friction and are losing effectiveness as machine learning advances [2,24]. Other approaches use anti-reverse engineering techniques to oppose Man-At-The-End (MATE) attackers [1], that have access to a client application on a controlled device. Those approaches aim at making the extraction and use of the application protocol more difficult, e.g., embedding (unique) API keys in the client application or using obfuscation and anti-reverse engineering techniques [12,23]. Most of these techniques only make it difficult to create the first bot. Once a bot is created, it can be scaled again. But this is what makes API bots so threatening: the ability to quickly and inexpensively spawn large numbers of bots. Because this approach can be really harmful, this paper focuses on how such automation can be restricted.

The main contribution of this paper is an approach to combat the cost-efficient duplication of bots, which can be applied with low performance and organizational overhead. In more detail, we make the following contributions:

- We propose a method, to increase the cost of duplicating bots by assigning each client of the same service its own application protocol. We call this Polymorphic Protocols (PPs). While there are already many strong obfuscation techniques for binaries (Tigress, Thermida) [10,27] and protocol obfuscation techniques in the censorship resistance realm [11,21], we are the first to our knowledge to use obfuscation of application protocols against bots.
- We implement the approach for the widely used protocol language protobuf and the programming language Java[1]. It is easily applied to existing protocols and just requires the existing protobuf file as input. Everything else is gener-

---

[1] Avaiable open source at https://github.com/UHH-ISS/polymorphic-protocols.

ated automatically so that it can even be used in a CI/CD pipeline without the need for a developer.
– We evaluate the technical performance overhead of the approach. We also discuss the organizational overhead for developers and the additional effort for attackers to duplicate bots.

Note that polymorphic protocols are an obfuscation technique to make the **scaling** of bots more difficult and **not** to prevent the creation of bots. The approach gains from being used along-side existing anti-reverse engineering mechanisms that impede code extraction (slicing), e.g., anti symbolic execution, virtualization, or just in time compilation [4,10]. Legitimate bots and interoperability across different services is still possible, e.g., by providing special API keys after thorough verification.

The rest of the paper is structured as follows. Section 2 discusses other approaches that make it harder to create bots. Section 3 explains how polymorphic protocols can be created and applied. Section 4 describes the implementation, evaluates and discusses the results. Finally, Sect. 5 concludes the paper.

2   Related Work

Regarding fighting bots there are mainly three different classes of approaches. Proofs of being human, detecting unusual behavior and anti-analysis.

Proofs of Being Human. The main technique to identify humans are CAPTCHAs [19,20], but also personal information often requested during the registration. Such information could be, from easy to harder to provide, email address, phone number, an image of the user holding an identity card. While requiring an identity card for registration would likely solve the problem of unwanted automation, it is a hard and privacy-unfriendly requirement. Related techniques try to detect human presence through hardware interaction. As an example, Not-a-Bot [13] uses TPMs to add a tag to each network request sent some time before a mouse or keyboard interaction.

Detecting Unusual Behaviour. These approaches try to detect bots so that countermeasures can be taken. Well known CAPTCHA providers like [19,20] use these approaches to reduce the disturbance for human users. Unfortunately, the machine learning models are not public. A major criticism is that users then have to send their data (browser fingerprinting [8]) and behaviour (mouse movement, website traversal [19]) to third parties to assess whether or not a bot is present. Another problem arises when a user cannot be classified as a human or a bot. Then again approaches of the class *proofs of being human* like CAPTCHAs are needed which have their own weaknesses [2,24].

Anti-Analysis Against MATE Attackers. Approaches in this class try to increase the cost of creating bots. It includes anti-reverse engineering and obfuscation techniques, e.g., detecting whether a debugger is attached, binary packing or even dummy code [12,23]. For network services, a common anti-analysis technique is to authenticate the used application protocol using API keys prior to the use of TLS[2]. To automate a service that uses this technique, the application protocol and the relevant keys need to be extracted [15,16]. The keys themselves can also be protected by anti-reverse engineering techniques.

Tigress [10], VMProtect [25] and Themida [27] are examples for advanced software protection systems. They are applied to the source code of an application and create a protected executable, using different anti-reverse engineering and obfuscation techniques. However, even those advanced protection systems do not obfuscate the protocol. If someone can reverse engineer the protocol, despite the used protection system, the bot can again be scaled very easily. The main problem of anti-reverse engineering is that it is difficult to quantify how effective a technique is against an arbitrary attacker [1,4,26]. When a device is fully controlled by an attacker, all techniques can only increase the cost for an attacker to reverse engineer an application, but they cannot prevent it.

Polymorphic protocols are an obfuscation approach and thus related to protocol obfuscation techniques. Most of the approaches mentioned in the literature are in the area of censorship resistance [11,21]. The objective is to bypass censorship and traffic inspection by cloaking specific traffic as usual traffic. Thus, censored services can be accessed despite lacking encryption and techniques like deep-packet inspection. All those approaches have the main focus on cloaking traffic and consider performance and ease of use in other applications in the second place. Also, they assume a different attacker, namely an attacker that has only access to the traffic. Thus existing approaches cannot be directly used as PP to combat bots.

3 Polymorphic Protocols

The core idea of limiting the cost-efficient duplication of API bots are polymorphic protocols. Every client for a service communicates with the service via its own application protocol. This protocol can be seen as an identifier to distinguish between clients. When a bot is simply duplicated, all duplicates would share the same protocol. This way duplicates can be detected and excluded from further communication with the service. This effectively increases the cost to create multiple different bots. To create an API bot army, bot creators can either manually reverse engineer the application protocol from a different client for each bot that is created which is laborious. Or they can find a way to automate the reverse engineering and bot creation, but this is difficult on a technical level [18,22]. In contrast, API keys can be much easier extracted, e.g., using function hooks, and do not force the bot creators to modify their code for each new bot.

---

[2] https://github.com/see-aestas/SINoALICE-API
https://github.com/see-aestas/JodelApi.

3.1   Basic Approach

An overview of the basic approach is given by Fig. 1. The *protocol specification* is the base protocol, used by the service. It specifies the format of messages as well as semantic information, e.g., if a message is time-critical or the dependencies between messages (order of transmission). The *client identifier* is an identifier for a client. Each client has a different identifier. Since our approach focuses on services that hold a state over a client (cf. Section 1) this is already given, because the service needs some way to match some state to a client. The *secret seed* is exactly what it is named after.

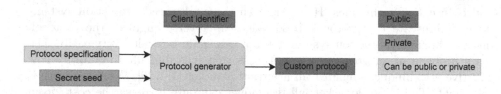

Fig. 1. Polymorphic Protocol Generation Overview

The *protocol generator* gets the *protocol specification* and the *client identifier* as well as the *secret seed* as an input. It outputs a new *custom protocol* that is different from the base protocol but keeps all mandatory semantic dependencies. Message formats, orders, encodings and other features are (pseudo)randomized transformed. There are three main classes of so-called transformations. Figure 2 shows these as well as some example sub-classes.

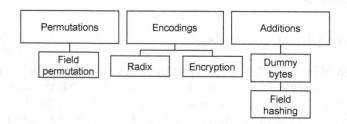

Fig. 2. Possible transformation classes

The classes are: Permutations that are length-preserving and permute message content, encodings that modify (parts of) a message, and additions that add more information to a message. These so-called transformation classes are a collection of different transformations under one label. This abstraction is needed to compare the performance of different transformations. A class can also contain sub-classes. For example, the class *dummy bytes* includes all transformations that append some extra bytes to a message. The class *field hashing* includes all transformations that hash all fields and then append the hash to the message. This class is a subclass of *dummy bytes* as a hash can be considered as a special way to generate dummy bytes. Here it is important to note that the transformations should ideally be hard to understand during reverse engineering. For example, a custom hash function to append bytes is harder to reverse engineer than directly appending some bytes to a message. Other transformations shown here are the *field permutation* where the order of data fields of a message is permuted, *radix* encoding where a message is encoded to some other base and *encryption* where a message is encrypted using some cipher. A developer can always add more classes. The transformations are used to deterministically generate a *custom protocol*. The *custom protocol* is later integrated into the client application. Each client has its own client identifier and thus custom protocol to communicate with the same service. Only the *secret seed* must be private. Its function is to prevent an adversary to generate valid *custom protocols* using the *protocol generator* for a service that uses an unknown, secret seed.

3.2 Formal Model

A protocol $\mathcal{P}$ is defined as a set of message format specifications F and their semantics S: $\mathcal{P} = \{F, S\}$, $F = \{f_1, f_2, ..., f_n\}$ where f is a format specification for some protocol message, e.g., $f = \{field1{:}int,\ field2{:}string\text{-}base64,\ ...,\ fieldx{:}Object\}$. A generator G deterministically generates a new, custom protocol based on the base protocol $\mathcal{P}$, client ID and the secret seed as inputs. $G(\mathcal{P}, client, seed) \mapsto \mathcal{P}'$. The generator relies on transformations of message format specifications $T_x(N, S) \mapsto N'$, with $N \subseteq F$ where x denotes a transformation class. Note that multiple message format specifications can be transformed together. A transformation class is the assignment of different transformations to a more generic class (cf. Figure 2). N' are then the new custom message format specifications and the actual transformations that operate on the real messages. For simplicity, $T_x(m) \mapsto m'$, where m is some actual message from the set of all valid protocol messages M, is used for transformations on the messages. Transformations can be applied on single message format specifications or across multiple ones, respecting their dependencies and can also be chained.

Transformations are required to be easily computable and unambiguous invertible, as an encoded message must be easily decoded. Transformation classes are used to compare the performance across different schemes of transformations. In this context, we are mainly assessing the impact on the resulting protocol. Assume a developer builds the transformation class T_x. Now one would like to estimate the effects on a protocol beforehand. How much additional data is transmitted using the resulting protocol on average (ΔT_x)? How expensive is the calculation for the client and server? How different are the protocol messages ($\varnothing T_x$)? The calculation of the metrics is described in the following.

The difference between two transformations is denoted to as $|T_{xi}(N, S) - T_{xj}(N, S)|$ and $|T_x|$ to the number of transformation in a transformation class. The difference between two transformations is calculated using the normalized compression distance (NCD) [17]. The metrics can be calculated numerically.

Let D_{1x} be a set of uniform random sampled indices of transformations from a transformation class x. Let D_{2x} be a a set of pairs (i,j) where $i \neq j$ and $\nexists (i',j') \in D_{2x} \mid i = j' \wedge j = i'$. The indices i,j are uniform random sampled indices of transformations from a transformation class x. Let $M_s \subseteq M$, e.g., uniform random sampled.

The average distance Δ of transformed protocol messages of T_x. A low value indicates that a valid message might be easy to guess for an attacker.

$$\Delta T_x = \sum_{m \in M_s} \sum_{(i,j) \in D_{2x}} \frac{|T_{xi}(m) - T_{xj}(m)|}{|M_s| * |D_{2x}|} \tag{1}$$

The average compressed message length difference $\varnothing$ between original and message transformed by T_x.

$$\varnothing T_x = \sum_{m \in M_s} \sum_{i \in D_{1x}} \frac{|C(T_{xi}(m)) - C(m)|}{|M_s| * |D_{1x}|} \tag{2}$$

The uniqueness of transformations in a transformation class δ. Uniqueness is closely related to collisions. A collision is when two different transformations of the same transformation class transform a message into the same new message. A low value indicates that an attacker might be able to successfully replay monitored messages.

$$\delta T_x = \frac{|X|}{|D_{1x}| * |M_s|}, X = \{T_{xi}(m) \mid i \in D_{1x} \mid m \in M_s\} \tag{3}$$

3.3 Transforming Protocols

Unconditional Protocol Transformations. Unconditional transformations include every transformation that can be done without knowing the semantic S of messages. Those transformations do not require knowledge of the protocol.

Permutation : The protocol message is permuted.
Dummy bytes : The protocol message is appended with random bytes.
Hash : A hash is appended to the protocol message (SHA1 or SHA256 or MD5)
Radix : The protocol message is converted to another random base (2–255).

Especially using cryptographic routines as part of creating the protocol hardens this approach against input reverse engineering approaches for encrypted protocols like [28] since there is no clear boundary where the protocol message is constructed and where it is encrypted.

Conditional Protocol Transformations. For transformations in this class, semantic information about the protocol must be available. This requires a formal protocol specification which should also contain semantic information. A distinction needs to be made between transformations that are applied to a single message (S) and those that are applied to multiple messages (M).

Delay : Delay a non-critical message (S).
Swap : Swap the sequence of messages (M).
Split : Split messages (S).
Merge : Merge messages (M).
Custom logic : Process messages already in some way on client side, e.g.,
   calculation of certain data (SM).

Transformations on multiple messages are more difficult to use and maintain for a developer as they may introduce side effects. In addition, semantic changes in an application must be correctly transferred to the protocol. Thus, conditional transformations are considered less safe than unconditional transformations. The possible conditional transformations depend on the application and the semantics of messages. While some transformations make it harder to recover the protocol, e.g., Swap and all unconditional transformations, others make it difficult to associate actions with sent network messages, e.g., the delay transformation.

Randomizing Protocols. The next step is to select transformations for a custom protocol and chain them together. For each message format specification in a protocol, first possible conditional and then unconditional transformations are selected. In the end, multiple transformations are applied to each format specification. How many is up to the developer and also depends on the format specification and semantics.

Algorithm 1: Selecting transformations

> **input:** $\mathcal{P}$ - the base protocol $\mathcal{P} = \{F, S\}$
> **input:** prg - PRG initialized using client ID and secret seed
> **input:** T_c - set of conditional transformations
> **input:** T_u - set of unconditional transformations
> **Result:** $\mathcal{P}'$ transformed custom protocol
> 1 $F' = \{\}, S' = S$;
> 2 **for** $f \in F$ **do**
> 3 $\quad$ $T'_c, T'_u = $ getAllowedTransformations(T_c, T_u, f, S');
> 4 $\quad$ $t_c, t_u = prg.choice(T'_c, T'_u)$;
> 5 $\quad$ $f' = t_c(\text{f})$ $\quad$ // conditional transformation
> 6 $\quad$ F'.add$(t_u(\text{f'}))$ // unconditional transformation
> 7 $\quad$ S'.add(f, t_c) $\quad$ // necessary for transforming multiple f
> 8 $P' = \{F', S'\}$

One possibility is to use a pseudo-random generator to select transformations, as displayed in Algorithm 1. The basic idea is that for each message format specification $f \in F$ a random, allowed unconditional and conditional transformation is applied. If no transformation is allowed, f is not transformed. If a transformation of T_c is a transformation for multiple messages (multiple f), the transformation is applied to all of them. This can be handled using the semantics and identifying the allowed transformations in Line 3 and 7. How the allowed transformations are selected depends on how the semantics are implemented. One possibility to assign semantics via annotations of message format specifications (@delay, @not$[T_x, T_y, ...]$). The implementation and which semantics have to be modeled depends heavily on the application.

While it is possible to use the algorithm without assigning semantics to format specifications, it can cost performance. For example, for video streaming or downloading files, a relative increase of the transmitted data might not be desired. This can be addressed by excluding transformations that increase the data length, or by excluding this message completely from any transformation.

3.4   Using Polymorphic Protocols

Our approach enables the generation of custom protocols. How this is used is up to the service.

Deployment Strategies. We highlight two deployments.

Full-Polymorphic. Each client has a different custom protocol.
Time-Polymorphic. Each client has the same custom protocol, the protocol is changed after a certain time.

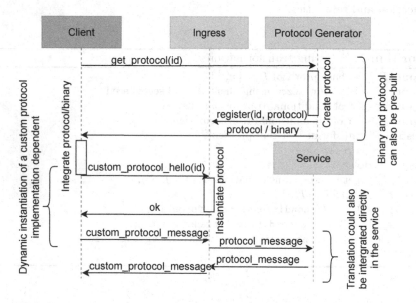

Fig. 3. Overview of possible polymorphic protocol communication usage

While the approach in this paper tries to keep the complexity, performance loss, developer and user friction as low as possible, they still exist (Sect. 4). Thus,

PPs are best used for applications that are already heavily affected by bots, e,g, social networks or games and resource-intensive to emulate (mobile or desktop applications). Figure 3 shows how dynamically instantiating and using a PP, e.g., for Full-Polymorphic deployment, could be implemented. The client starts with the capabilities to request a custom protocol. It sends its client ID to the protocol generator. The protocol generator generates a custom protocol, registers it at the ingress server and sends it to the client. Depending on the use case the custom protocol is sent back as a standalone binary or a binary fused with the main application. When the client wants to communicate with the server it first sends a custom protocol hello. The custom protocol is looked up at the ingress, server and instantiated. When a client receives the message that the protocol is found and instantiated it can begin sending custom protocol messages to the ingress. The ingress acts as a proxy and translates the custom protocol messages back to protocol messages that can be understood by the service. Note that the procedure in Fig. 3 is meant as an example and there are many more ways to use and deploy PPs.

Reducing Deployment Costs. Polymorphic protocols do not necessarily have to be dynamically loaded by the client and not every client must use a custom protocol by default. A practical approach for mobile applications is to use PP only on clients that are running on rooted devices or emulators. Devices running unmodified systems must pass an integrity check, e.g., play integrity[3] and share one custom protocol. This check also ensures that a bot cannot simply use the base protocol as it would need to pass those integrity checks. It is also possible to assign a new protocol to a client after a certain time or number of protocol messages. Another strategy is to give a set of devices the same custom protocol, e.g., based on region, OS, IP address, update version or time. It can also be coupled with bot detection systems, to control the protocol change cycle for users. Slow for legitimate users, and fast for abusive users. Thus, the cost of using a custom protocol can be reduced, as well as the user friction, as legitimate users have fewer forced updates due to protocol changes.

4 Evaluation

In this section we are summarizing the evaluation results of our approach. For that, we have evaluated the costs for service providers to use the approach and the effort for attackers that want to build multiple bots for services protected by a polymorphic protocol. We answer the following research questions:

RQ1 : What is the overhead of different transformations?
RQ2 : How does the approach compare to using unique and client-specific API keys to hinder an attacker to create multiple bots for a service?
RQ3 : What is the technical and organizational overhead for a service that wants to use polymorphic protocols?

---

[3] https://developer.android.com/google/play/integrity/overview.

4.1 Implementation

Our objective is to minimize the effort of using our approach. Instead of creating our own (unrestricted) protocol description language, we integrate it into an existing ecosystem. For this, we have chosen to use *Google protobuf* as the description language and extended their *Java* bindings to be compatible with our approach. Porting the implementation to other programming or protocol languages is possible. Currently, the implementation is not feature complete to *protobuf v3*[4]. We support the basic features, i.e., messages, all primitive (scalar) data types, and nesting (inheritance). Other features may work, but are not fully tested. Thus, if some service already uses *protobuf* and *Java*, creating a polymorphic protocol is effortless (cf. Appendix A).

As there is support for protobuf and java on all major systems, our approach can be used on all these systems without adjustments. Our implementation(See footnote 1) only needs the proto file (protocol specification) as input and generates the new custom protocol, i.e., another proto file and necessary code wrappers. The wrappers are used by both the client and the server. To use the protocol, the generated wrapper files only need to be integrated into the respective project by replacing the old files and setting the package name.

4.2 Performance Evaluation

Using PPs comes with a performance overhead, which we evaluate in this section. We evaluate the transformation classes first individually and then in their combination with our protocol implementation. Everything is run on a Windows 11 computer I7 7700 K CPU with 16 GB DDr4 2660 Mhz RAM.

RQ1: Transformation Performance. The metrics (average distance between two transformed protocol messages Δ_x, average compressed message length increase in bytes $\varnothing_x$, uniqueness of transformations δ_x) from Sect. 3.2 are used to analyze the performance of the transformation classes. The number of dummy bytes is limited to four and the radix transformation to the bases 2–255. Furthermore, we also measure the time for doing the transformation. Transformations are applied directly to bytes. To not assume some specific protocol, we sample 100,000 protocol messages as random bytes with the length derived from a normal distribution $\mathcal{N}(100, 25)$. Each sampled message is transformed up to 1,000 times per transformation class.

The results (Table 1) indicate that not every transformation class is the same and classes must be selected according to use cases. The permutation transformation does not increase the message length (by definition). Dummy bytes affect the message length but are way faster to calculate. The hash transformation affects the message length but is also fast to calculate. Since it is also about forcing an attacker to invest as much work as possible to extract the different transformations, efficient but complex transformations are wanted. While an evaluation

---

[4] https://developers.google.com/protocol-buffers/docs/proto3.

of transformation classes gives some insight into the performance, it does not assess the performance and usage of the classes in a system.

Table 1. Transformation class properties

Transformation class	Δ_x	$\varnothing_x$	δ_x	Time
Permutation of message bytes	0.924	0	1	413.23 (s per 1 mil)
Dummy bytes (4)	0.086	4	1	1.07 (s per 1 mil)
Hash	0.261	26.6	1	2.91 (s per 1 mil)
Radix (2–255)	0.88	12.89	1	160.85 (s per 1 mil)

RQ3: Protocol Performance. While RQ1 evaluates the individual performance of single transformations this does not allow to assess the performance of the complete protocol. The performance, namely processing time, additional program size, build time and resource utilization, is compared to the base protocol. Four different protocols are considered. The notation $P_{messages,fields}$, e.g., $P_{10,15}$ is a protocol with 10 different messages, each message has 15 fields. In the following P denotes the base protocol and $G(P)$ the transformed protocol generated from P. There are a total of 15 different (scalar) value types in protobuf. For our evaluation we use all types equally often within one message. Thus, each message always contains a multiple of 15 fields.

Build Overhead. Table 2 shows the results of the build overhead. A build includes the transformation of the protocol, the creation of wrapper classes, and the compilation of the (new) protocol using the protobuf compiler.

Table 2. Mean program build properties: Difference of polymorphic compared to the original protocol in percent (N=100)

	$G(P_{1,15})$	$G(P_{100,15})$	$G(P_{1,150})$	$G(P_{100,150})$
Build time	+3%	+72%	+9%	+128%
Memory	-14%	+18%	+33%	+94%
Protocol size	+138%	+144%	+202%	+295%

For PP, the size of the necessary wrapper classes is included in the protocol size. As expected the build time for the PP is higher than for the base protocol. However, the number of protocol messages seems to have a higher impact on the build time and protocol size for PP than the number of fields. The protocol size can be explained by the fact that for each message a separate additional java wrapper is created for the transformations. This also affects the build time.

The peak memory utilization is harder to interpret as it is mostly dependent on the protobuf compiler. The more and the larger the messages are, the more memory is needed to create the protocol. That the build process for $G(P_{1,15})$ uses less memory than for $P_{1,15}$ could be confirmed by multiple measurements. A reason for this could not be found.

Client and Server Performance. Table 3 shows the performance overhead of using PP. Note that this is the overhead while processing messages. Thus, handling multiple messages sequentially *does not* multiply the load. A division in client and server is not necessary as PP can be implemented as a proxy that translates a list of protocol messages (cf. Sect. 3.4). The performance for handling connections is then that of the chosen reverse proxy. We divide the performance in sending and receiving messages. In doing so performance assessments are possible for servers that primarily receive or send more data. Send Time includes setting each field and serializing the message, Receive Time includes deserializing and accessing all fields. Time on the wire is not measured. The data size is the size of the serialized message. We choose random values for fixed-length fields and 100 random bytes for dynamic fields, e.g., strings. We only consider single messages since the time for multiple messages can be upscaled. We also do not include dummy fields, as they just increase the message size to the set value.

Table 3. Mean protocol performance without dummy fields. Difference of polymorphic protocol compared to the original protocol in percent (N = 100)

	$G(P_{1,15})$	$G(P_{1,75})$	$G(P_{1,150})$	$G(P_{1,225})$
Send time	+118%	+79%	+117%	+180%
Send memory	+130%	+178%	+150%	+187%
Send CPU load	+85%	+71%	+83%	+66%
Receive time	+41%	+98%	+116%	+125%
Receive memory	+46%	+12%	+31%	+85%
Receive CPU load	+85%	+71%	+83%	+66%
Data size	+23%	+19%	+24%	+27%

The results show that PP are 2.09 times slower (around 1.5 ms) than the base protocol and cause approx 76% more CPU and 102% more memory load (average of send and receive performance). Thus, a service needs to spend approx two times more resources to handle the same amount of clients. This can be improved using optimizations described in Sect. 3.4.

The reason for this is that access to a field of a PP passes through two wrapper classes. First, the wrapper created by our implementation is called, which performs the transformation and additionally calls the wrapper created by protobuf. For the base protocol, the wrapper created by protobuf is directly used. Even though the PP are two times slower, this is in the area of single milliseconds and should be negligible for non real-time applications. When using PP around 1.2 times more data is used. Note that certain messages or fields, e.g., real-time messages or large byte arrays that are used to stream video data, can be excluded from being transformed, thus saving data and computation time.

4.3 Security Discussion

This section discusses the additional cost of an attacker against polymorphic protocols as well as the organizational effort for service providers to use them.

RQ2: Attacker Cost. Estimating the costs for an arbitrary Man-At-The-End attacker is difficult and cannot be calculated accurately [1, 26]. Many existing techniques that assess how much an obfuscation costs an attacker [4, 5] cannot be applied to our scenario because they are targeted to a specific subset of reverse engineering techniques. In contrast, our approach is about increasing the cost of duplicating bots for an attacker and not targeted against any particular reverse engineering technique. Testing our approach against automated protocol reverse engineering approaches was also not possible, as many approaches focus on unencrypted protocols [28] and only a few implementations are available[5].

To estimate the effort required by an attacker, we compare our approach to the method currently used in practice, i.e., using API keys to encrypt and authenticate protocols. We consider the Full-Polymorphic and Time-Polymorphic deployment described in Sect. 3.4 as well as two different attackers.

Restricted-MATE. Normal Man-At-The-End [1] attacker who has access to the binary. The attacker is restricted and cannot automatically extract API keys or the custom protocols (R-MATE).
Unrestricted-MATE. MATE attacker, without any restriction and limitation of reverse engineering techniques (U-MATE).

The attacker wants to setup multiple bots for the service. The U-MATE attacker loses when it needs to put in manual work, as this already impedes the creation of a bot army. We divide the bot creation into the reverse engineering and bot writing phases.

R-MATE. This attacker is probably most common since automatic extraction of data (API keys) and code (polymorphic protocol) is difficult on an engineering level, especially for encrypted protocols [18, 22, 28].

Using the Time-Polymorphic deployment the attacker needs to extract the protocol or API key within the period. After that, the bot has to be written within this period. Then the bot can be effectively duplicated and the attacker can exploit the service. After some time the attacker must repeat all the steps. Since the custom API key does not change the protocol, the attacker only has to replace the key in the existing bot program. Using a PP, the entire protocol

---

[5] https://github.com/techge/PRE-list.

of the bot needs to be replaced and all new transformations implemented. This indicates that the development time for PP is larger than for API keys. The argumentation for the Full-Polymorphic deployment strategy is analogues. Thus for this limited attacker PP increase the cost of duplicating bots. The analysis of the next attacker argues that since PP can include variable API keys, PP are at least as hard to extract as API keys alone.

U-MATE. This attacker needs to automatically extract protocols from a given binary. Whether this extraction happens for each update (Time-Polymorphic) or multiple client binaries (Full-Polymorphic) does not matter. Thus, the two deployment strategies are equivalent for the attacker. This results in comparison on how much effort it takes to automatically extract an API key and how much effort it takes to extract the communication protocol. A PP can also contain encryption transformations and cryptographic keys. These keys can be hidden and protected just like the API keys. Thus, the extraction of API keys can be seen as a sub-problem of extracting a communication protocol and requires at least as much effort as extracting API keys only.

The most effective attacks on PP are code reuse and slicing techniques, where certain parts of a binary are reused or extracted, e.g., the communication protocol. The challenge here is to isolate and extract *minimal and executable* code responsible for transforming network messages. In the simplest case, the attacker just executes the whole application and uses dynamic binary instrumentation techniques, e.g., code injection and hooks [6], to directly call the desired functions. However, running the whole application is very resource-intensive and thus not suitable for creating a large number of bots. Extracting minimal and executable code is still an open research field and not completely reliable [9,26]. Note that defending against code reuse and slicing attacks is out of scope for our approach. There is a lot of research [4,9] in this regard, including commercial [25,27] and public tools [10], especially in the areas of digital rights management and anti-reverse engineering. Those countermeasurements, e.g., function virtualisation and just in time compiling, can be used together with our approach.

By using these techniques to hinder the attacker from using automated techniques and tools, the attacker remains with the capabilities of the *R-Mate attacker* and the approach can increase the effort to create a bot army. This shows that PPs slow down an attacker more than API keys.

RQ3: Organisational Cost. The appropriate deployment depends heavily on the needed security. Furthermore, optimizations discussed in Sect. 3.4 should be used to decrease the operational and organizational cost.

Full-Polymorphic. In this setting, the remote backend must provide a matching endpoint for each custom protocol. A simple but resource-intensive way is to keep them up all in parallel. Another option is to spin endpoints up dynamically, however this requires development effort (cf. Fig. 3). Due to the dynamic nature of custom protocols they cannot be served as a static file from CDNs, e.g., from the AppStore or PlayStore. A solution is to create a base application that dynamically loads and integrates protocols. This base application can be served again from CDNs (cf. Sect. 3.4). While the protocol is then dynamically loaded, a large part of the application, i.e., all static assets like models, images, and videos can still be served from CDNs.

Time-Polymorphic. This deployment strategy introduces almost no organizational cost. CDNs can be used as usual and only one endpoint needs to be provided. On the downside, the approach allows an attacker to create a bot army for a certain time (cf. Sect. 4.3). Different to the Full-Polymorphic deployment, this approach burdens the user by requiring regular updates. This burden can be reduced by using approaches from Sect. 3.4.

The results show that the costs for a defender are not large but not marginal either. For consumer devices and applications that exchange only a few and rather small messages, the technical overhead should be well manageable. Especially since time critical messages or messages that transmit large amounts of data do not have to be transformed. The organizational effort for Time-Polymorphic deployments is minimal but impedes an attacker less (cf. Section 4.3). For Full-Polymorphic deployments, however, there is some organizational effort involved. This mode is more suitable for applications that suffer heavily from bots, otherwise, it does not justify the effort.

4.4 Limitations

First, while PPs make it harder to create bots for a service in comparison to API keys, it is not accurately determined *how much* harder it is for an arbitrary attacker. This is something the approach shares with other obfuscation techniques. Similar literature addresses this by limiting attackers to subsets of techniques, e.g., only static analysis. These attacker models however do not fit our objective. Determining the hardness could be approached in an empirical study, but would require access to a lot of reverse engineers. This limitation is compensated by the benefit that while the increased effort for an attacker cannot be accurately determined, the overhead for using PPs in their simplest form is low and can be easily be tested for a service. PPs are nonetheless an additional overhead and should only be used for services that are already having problems with bots.

Second, PPs are affected by slicing and code reuse approaches where an attacker can use the existing code of a client to build a bot. Therefore, PPs should be used together with anti-reverse engineering approaches that impede slicing and code reuse, e.g., [9].

5 Conclusion

While previous work focused on making it harder to build a first bot, we present an approach that fights the scaling of bots by forcing a bot creator to extract not just client API keys but the whole application protocol for each bot that is created. We evaluate the resources needed to build and use polymorphic protocols. Without optimization, polymorphic protocols transmit approx. 1.2 times more data compared to the base protocol and are 2.09 times slower (around 1.5 ms). Depending on the deployment the organizational effort required to integrate our approach into existing services is low as it can be used as a drop-in replacement. Considering MATE attackers polymorphic protocols introduce more cost for an attacker compared to using API keys alone. In the future, we would like to investigate the extent to which polymorphic protocols make it harder for an attacker to create bots, compared to API keys. This shall be evaluated as part of a CTF or as a study.

A   Generating a Custom Protocol

An example is given in the following. Consider a game with multiple messages. All messages are defined in *GameMessages.proto*. One message is StatusInformation. A part of the message definition is shown in Listing 1.1.

```
message StatusInformation {
    string name = 1;
    int32 playerNumber = 2;
    int32 plays = 3;
    ...
}
```

Listing 1.1. Untransformed protobuf excerpt

The protobuf file is then transformed by applying our implementation of Algorithm 1. The result is another protobuf file, including some transformations (Listing 1.2). The whole message is encrypted using AES with a random key. Some message types have changed and some variables have been split into two variables.

```
message StatusInformation { // Encrypted using AES
    string plays_p1 = 1;      /* before: int32 | p1 */
    int32 playerNumber = 2;   /* unmodified */
    bytes name = 3;           /* before: string */
    bytes plays_p2 = 4;       /* before: int32 | p2 */
    ...
}
```

Listing 1.2. Transformed protobuf excerpt

The normal protobuf compiler uses the transformed protobuf file *GameMessages.proto* and generates methods to read, write and serialize the fields and messages in a file called *GameMessages.java*. Our implementation automatically adds classes that apply the transformations on top of the code generated from the protobuf compiler. If the supported feature set of protobuf has already been used previously the generated classes of our implementation are a drop-in replacement. This process is the same for the client as well as for the server of an application.

References

1. Akhunzada, A., et al.: Man-at-the-end attacks: Analysis, taxonomy, human aspects, motivation and future directions. J. Netw. Comput. Appl. **48**, 44–57 (2015)
2. Alqahtani, F.H., Alsulaiman, F.A.: Is image-based captcha secure against attacks based on machine learning? an experimental study. Comput. Secur. **88**, 101635 (2020)
3. Amin Azad, B., Starov, O., Laperdrix, P., Nikiforakis, N.: Web runner 2049: evaluating third-party anti-bot services. In: Proceedings of the 17th DIMVA (2020)
4. Banescu, S., Collberg, C., Ganesh, V., Newsham, Z., Pretschner, A.: Code obfuscation against symbolic execution attacks. In: Proceedings of the 32nd Annual Conference on Computer Security Applications, pp. 189–200 (2016)
5. Banescu, S., Collberg, C., Pretschner, A.: Predicting the resilience of obfuscated code against symbolic execution attacks via machine learning. In: 26th USENIX Security 17, pp. 661–678 (2017)
6. Berdajs, J., Bosnić, Z.: Extending applications using an advanced approach to DLL injection and API hooking. Soft. Pract. Exp. **40**(7), 567–584 (2010)
7. Bessi, A., Ferrara, E.: Social bots distort the 2016 us presidential election online discussion. First Monday **21**(11–7) (2016)
8. Boda, K., Földes, Á.M., Gulyás, G.G., Imre, S.: User tracking on the web via cross-browser fingerprinting. In: Laud, P. (ed.) NordSec 2011. LNCS, vol. 7161, pp. 31–46. Springer, Heidelberg (2012). https://doi.org/10.1007/978-3-642-29615-4_4
9. Cheng, X., Lin, Y., Gao, D., Jia, C.: DynOpVm: VM-based software obfuscation with dynamic opcode mapping. In: Deng, R.H., Gauthier-Umaña, V., Ochoa, M., Yung, M. (eds.) ACNS 2019. LNCS, vol. 11464, pp. 155–174. Springer, Cham (2019). https://doi.org/10.1007/978-3-030-21568-2_8
10. Collberg, C.: The Tigress C Obfuscator (2001). https://tigress.wtf/about.html
11. Dyer, K.P., Coull, S.E., Shrimpton, T.: Marionette: a programmable network traffic obfuscation system. In: 24th USENIX Security 15, pp. 367–382 (2015)
12. Gagnon, M.N., Taylor, S., Ghosh, A.K.: Software protection through anti-debugging. IEEE Secur. Priv. **5**(3), 82–84 (2007)
13. Gummadi, R., Balakrishnan, H., Maniatis, P., Ratnasamy, S.: Not-a-Bot: improving service availability in the face of botnet attacks. In: NSDI, pp. 307–320 (2009)
14. Heath, N.: Expedia on how one extra data field can cost $12m. https://www.zdnet.com/article/expedia-on-how-one-extra-data-field-can-cost-12m/ (2010), accessed: 2021-10-18
15. Karuppayah, S., Fischer, M., Rossow, C., Mühlhäuser, M.: On advanced monitoring in resilient and unstructured P2P botnets. In: 2014 IEEE International Conference on Communications (ICC), pp. 871–877. IEEE (2014)
16. Karuppayah, S., Roos, S., Rossow, C., Mühlhäuser, M., Fischer, M.: Zeus Milker: circumventing the P2P Xeus neighbor list restriction mechanism. In: 2015 IEEE 35th International Conference on Distributed Computing Systems, pp. 619–629. IEEE (2015)
17. Li, M., Chen, X., Li, X., Ma, B., Vitányi, P.M.: The similarity metric. IEEE Trans. Inf. Theory **50**(12), 3250–3264 (2004)
18. Liu, M., Jia, C., Liu, L., Wang, Z.: Extracting sent message formats from executables using backward slicing. In: 2013 Fourth International Conference on Emerging Intelligent Data and Web Technologies, pp. 377–384. IEEE (2013)

19. Liu, W.: Introducing reCAPTCHA v3: the new way to stop bots. https://developers.google.com/search/blog/2018/10/introducing-recaptcha-v3-new-way-to (2018). Accessed 20 May 21
20. Machines, I.: Stop more bots. Start protecting user privacy. https://www.hcaptcha.com/ (2018). Accessed 20 May 21
21. Mohajeri Moghaddam, H., Li, B., Derakhshani, M., Goldberg, I.: Skypemorph: Protocol obfuscation for tor bridges. In: Proceedings of the 2012 ACM conference on Computer and communications security, pp. 97–108 (2012)
22. Narayan, J., Shukla, S.K., Clancy, T.C.: A survey of automatic protocol reverse engineering tools. CSUR **48**(3), 1–26 (2015)
23. Roundy, K.A., Miller, B.P.: Binary-code obfuscations in prevalent packer tools. ACM Comput. Surv. (CSUR) **46**(1), 1–32 (2013)
24. Sivakorn, S., Polakis, I., Keromytis, A.D.: I am robot: (deep) learning to break semantic image captchas. In: 2016 IEEE EuroS&P, pp. 388–403. IEEE (2016)
25. Software, V.: VMProtect Software Protection (2021). https://vmpsoft.com/
26. Talukder, M., Islam, S., Falcarin, P.: Analysis of obfuscated code with program slicing. In: 2019 International Conference on Cyber Security and Protection of Digital Services (Cyber Security), pp. 1–7. IEEE (2019)
27. Technologies, O.: Oreans Technologies : Software Security Defined (2022). https://www.oreans.com/Themida.php. Accessed 07 Dec 21
28. Wang, Z., Jiang, X., Cui, W., Wang, X., Grace, M.: ReFormat: automatic reverse engineering of encrypted messages. In: Backes, M., Ning, P. (eds.) ESORICS 2009. LNCS, vol. 5789, pp. 200–215. Springer, Heidelberg (2009). https://doi.org/10.1007/978-3-642-04444-1_13

Unlinkable Delegation of WebAuthn Credentials

Nick Frymann[1(✉)], Daniel Gardham[1], and Mark Manulis[2]

[1] Surrey Centre for Cyber Security, University of Surrey, Guildford, UK
{n.frymann,daniel.gardham}@surrey.ac.uk
[2] Research Institute CODE, Universität der Bundeswehr München,
Munich, Germany
mark@manulis.eu

Abstract. The W3C's WebAuthn standard employs digital signatures
to offer phishing protection and unlinkability on the web using authenticators which manage keys on behalf of users. This introduces challenges when the account owner wants to delegate certain rights to a
proxy user, such as to access their accounts or perform actions on their
behalf, as delegation must not undermine the decentralisation, unlinkability, and attestation properties provided by WebAuthn. We present
two approaches, called *remote* and *direct* delegation of WebAuthn credentials, maintaining the standard's properties. Both approaches are
compatible with Yubico's recent Asynchronous Remote Key Generation
(ARKG) primitive proposed for backing up credentials. For remote delegation, the account owner stores delegation credentials at the relying
party on behalf of proxies, whereas the direct variant uses a delegation-
by-warrant approach, through which the proxy receives delegation credentials from the account owner and presents them later to the relying party. To realise direct delegation we introduce Proxy Signature
with Unlinkable Warrants (PSUW), a new proxy signature scheme that
extends WebAuthn's unlinkability property to proxy users and can be
constructed generically from ARKG. We provide an instantiation of the
primitive and analyse its performance, observing only a minor increase
of a few milliseconds in the signing and verification times for delegated
WebAuthn credentials based on the ARKG and PSUW primitives.

1 Introduction

With ever-growing reliance on web-based services, from online shopping and
banking to employee intranets and cloud storage, the need to keep accounts
secure is imperative. Developments in web-based authentication standards, such
as FIDO (Federated Online IDentity) Universal 2nd Factor (U2F) [41] and
WebAuthn [26] aim to reduce reliance on passwords and one-time passcodes
(OTPs), such as HOTP [29], TOTP [30], and insecure SMS variants [31], by
enabling the use of hardware and platform authenticators that manage asymmetric and unlinkable signing keys on behalf of users.

V. Atluri et al. (Eds.): ESORICS 2022, LNCS 13556, pp. 125–144, 2022.
https://doi.org/10.1007/978-3-031-17143-7_7

WebAuthn's digital signatures and the use of independent signing keys offer stronger security protection and unlinkability for web accounts, yet introduce challenges when the account owner wishes to delegate certain rights to some proxy user, such as to access their accounts or perform actions on their behalf, possibly for a specific time period.

Interestingly, with traditional authentication methods such as passwords or OTPs (which WebAuthn aims to replace) delegation can be performed relatively easily, albeit not necessarily securely. For example, delegated access to an account protected by a password can be performed by sharing the latter. However, delegation achieved by sharing passwords is susceptible to reused passwords (see e.g. a study by Pearman et al. [34]), which may inadvertently give access to other accounts, and can only be revoked by changing the account password—which must be done manually. This requires greater trust into the proxy who may change the account password without permission. Additionally, accounts protected by multi-factor authentication (MFA), including using OTPs, may be undermined by sharing OTP secrets or registering multiple something-you-own factors (such as phone numbers) for proxies; also these must be separately and often manually revoked by hand when the proxy's access is to be revoked. For discussion on related works in this area, which inform the design of our primitive and scheme, see Sect. 5.

1.1 WebAuthn Properties, Delegation Challenges, and Naïve approaches

Overview of WebAuthn and Its Properties. WebAuthn [26] is a web-based application programming interface (API) that allows web servers, called Relying Parties (RPs), to communicate with conforming authenticators on a user's device—the host device. This communication is facilitated by a WebAuthn client through its implementation of the WebAuthn standard—the RP calls functions provided by the API. RPs may use this to employ asymmetric cryptography to authenticate users on the web, with keying material stored on and managed by the user's authenticator. A recent analysis by Barbosa et al. [2] confirms the authentication security of the WebAuthn protocol against active impersonation attacks. In addition, the following properties are commonly associated with the WebAuthn standard, and become important in the context of delegation.

Authenticators and clients. Authenticators may be software- or platform-based, called *embedded* or *bound* (which are part of the *host* device), such as Windows Hello, or a separate hardware token, called a *roaming* authenticator, for example Yubico's YubiKey. These authenticators interact with RPs via a client, such as a web browser, which can communicate with software and hardware on the user's host device, unlike the sandboxed website. The Client-to-Authenticator Protocol (CTAP) [14] allows *roaming* hardware tokens to communicate with a client running on a host device, such as a user's phone or computer, over some transport such as Bluetooth, NFC, or USB.

Registration and authentication. During registration, the authenticator receives a random challenge from the RP. It requires the user to perform a *gesture*, for example, to press an on-screen confirmation button, present a biometric factor, or enter a passcode, in order to unlock the authenticator for use. The authenticator then generates a private-public key pair unique to this registration, submitting this challenge along with the new public key. Later, when authenticating, the authenticator receives another challenge from the RP and signs it with the corresponding private key after the user performs the required gesture. Gestures provide RPs with a check for either user presence (e.g., press to confirm) or verification (e.g., biometrics), depending on the what is offered by the authenticator. These ceremonies are detailed in the standard [26, §§7.1,7.2].

Unlinkability. The unlinkability of registered public keys, required by WebAuthn, prevents users from being correlated across registrations since it cannot be determined whether two keys were produced by the same authenticator. This is achieved by registering a freshly-generated private-public key pair, giving a unique key pair registered for each account. This property means that users cannot be identified across RPs, unless they willingly reuse login names, e.g., usernames or email addresses.

Attestation. Authenticators may present RPs with certificates from vendors to prove their make and model, and therefore security assurances, so that user verification may be delegated to the authenticator. This means that verification may be performed locally on the authenticator with RPs trusting these local user verification methods. Attestation uses an attestation ID, `AAGUID`, shared between authenticators of similar functionality, makes and model, so as to not break unlinkability. Attestation statements may be verified using the certificate chain and its `AAGUID`. Since attestation is given as a signature and certificate chain over credentials emitted by an authenticator, credential attestation may be undermined by sharing private keying material between authenticators. Barbosa et al. [2] cover attestation as part of their analysis of WebAuthn and CTAP's authentication security.

Storage. Authenticators may generate fresh key pairs for each registration and record the private key locally to ensure unlinkability. However, some authenticators, such as resource-constrained roaming hardware tokens, may not record their private keys locally. For example, by using additional credential data that may be sent during registration, private keys may be stored with the RP, encrypted under a symmetric key held by the authenticator. This means that private keys are not recorded by the authenticator and are only learnt during the authentication process, where the authenticator receives these additional credential data as part of its challenge.

Delegation-specific Challenges. Any approach for delegating WebAuthn credentials should preserve the unlinkability of WebAuthn credentials, not undermine its decentralised nature, and retain the ability to perform attestation. In addition, it is highly desirable that users be able revoke access for delegated credentials and set permissions which are understood and enforced by RPs. Finally, proxies *need not* hold their own accounts at RPs for delegation. RPs must be unable to link proxies to their delegators, even if the proxy already holds their own account at the same RP. As delegation must preserve the unlinkability of delegator's original WebAuthn credentials across different accounts, delegated credentials must not contain any information that would allow RPs to link a delegator's accounts and, therefore, the unlinkability guarantees must be extended to cover credentials of proxy users. In particular, delegated credentials must not reveal any information that would allow RPs to identify the proxy user, who may be in possession of delegated credentials to multiple accounts. This preserves the unlinkability guarantee for delegators and extends it to proxies.

Given the decentralised nature of WebAuthn, where credentials are stored directly with RPs and on user-owned devices, delegation solutions should not require a third party, whose reliability and trustworthiness would need to be relied upon. Since attestation uses manufacturer certificates to prove the make and model of an authenticator when generating credentials, which may describe security guarantees offered by the authenticator, sharing private keying materials between authenticators may undermine these security guarantees—the trustworthiness of attestation guarantees could be weakened.

Delegators should also be able to revoke account access from proxies at a later time. In addition, the ability to add context- or application-specific permissions that may also include an expiry date, and define the types of actions that can be performed with delegated credentials, should also be considered. In particular, it must not be possible for a proxy user to take over the ownership of the account by deleting the original delegator's credentials. In order to enforce permissions, RPs must be able to distinguish that account access is being performed by a proxy with a delegated credential and be able to process additional data that identifies the credential as being for a proxy.

1.2 Contribution and Organisation

We propose two approaches for the delegation of WebAuthn credentials aiming to preserve the decentralisation, unlinkability and attestation properties of the standard. Our approaches, presented in Sect. 2, enable the account owner to either configure delegation and permissions *remotely* at the relying party, or to send credentials *directly* to the proxy user without involving the relying party.

Both approaches are compatible and built on top of the recent Asynchronous Remote Key Generation (ARKG) [15] scheme, which has been proposed by Yubico to W3C for WebAuthn backup and account recovery. Our remote delegation approach uses ARKG directly to create unlinkable delegated credentials for proxy users. Our direct delegation approach is performed using warrants and requires a new class of proxy signatures that we call Proxy Signature with Unlinkable Warrants (PSUW) and present in Sect. 3. PSUW is used to create warrants that can extend the required unlinkability property to proxy signers. Our PSUW scheme is very efficient and is constructed generically from ARKG.

In Sect. 4, we provide cryptographic implementations that are compatible with WebAuthn, analyse and compare performance of our delegation approaches. We discuss related work in Sect. 5 and conclude in Sect. 6. For a full discussion on various aspects of the scheme's integration with WebAuthn and CTAP, including a prototype of the scheme which uses standard WebAuthn calls, and consideration of usability, see the extended paper [16].

2 Delegating WebAuthn Account Credentials

In this section, we specify two approaches allowing users to delegate access to their WebAuthn accounts to proxies. Our delegation approaches are compatible with Yubico's recent proposal for backing up WebAuthn credentials and using them for account recovery [15].

2.1 From Account Recovery to Delegation

Yubico's solution for the credential backup and account recovery problem in WebAuthn is based on a novel ARKG protocol [15] which helps to preserve the decentralisation, unlinkability, and attestation properties of the standard. The ARKG protocol allows a *primary* authenticator to register keys on behalf of additional *backup* authenticators, which may be later used to regain access to accounts. After the authenticators have been setup, the primary authenticator generates and registers unlinkable public keys on behalf of backup authenticators when registering with RPs.

In a nutshell, during the setup phase a backup authenticator, with the private key sk, sends to the primary authenticator its public key pk. When registering with RPs, *derived* public keys pk' are generated using the ARKG.DerivePK algorithm, based on the backup's public key pk, computed and registered by the primary authenticator. After the primary authenticator is lost or damaged, a backup authenticator is able to compute—using the ARKG.DeriveSK algorithm—the corresponding private key sk' for the pk' registered on its behalf using credential data cred stored at the RP, which gives the link between pk and pk' and allows the corresponding sk' to be computed with knowledge of sk.

ARKG maintains the unlinkability property of WebAuthn, as arbitrary derived public keys pk', and pk, exhibit unlinkability that is compatible with WebAuthn. Attestation is also maintained since sk' is not shared between authenticators; the backup authenticator may provide the RP an attestation statement when recovering account access, by having it complete a registration procedure.

Yubico's credential backup solution assumes that the primary and backup authenticators are owned and controlled by the same user and, once setup, the primary authenticator can invisibly register or re-register keys for backup authenticators when needed. This approach and the underlying trust assumptions do not readily translate to delegation, as delegators should be able to delegate, as well as grant and revoke permissions, to proxies at their discretion.

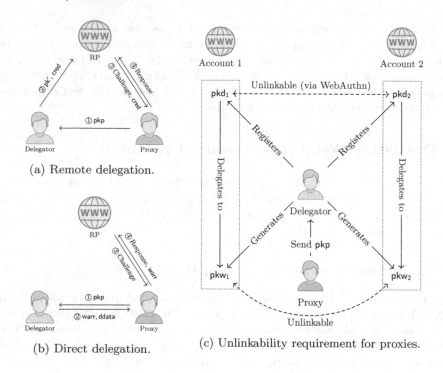

(a) Remote delegation.

(b) Direct delegation.

(c) Unlinkability requirement for proxies.

Fig. 1. Two approaches to delegation and the required unlinkability property.

RPs need to enforce limited access to accounts, requiring that proxy users be unable to lock delegators out of their own accounts or perform actions for which they do not have permission. This results in delegation which requires additional data and parameters, so RPs can determine the level of access to grant to proxy users; ARKG without any changes grants full account access, since it is roughly equivalent to a standard account credential.

2.2   Two Approaches for Delegation

In our first approach, called *remote delegation*, delegation is configured remotely on the relying party, whereas in the second approach, called *direct delegation*, delegated credentials are sent directly to the proxy. Our approaches address the requirements from Sect. 1.1 and cater for different types of authenticators and their capabilities, such as storage-constrained hardware tokens—the remote variant is best suited to this kind, whereas direct delegation is suited for platform authenticators in computers and mobile devices. Direct delegation can occur *offline at any time*, optionally over proximity-based transports (e.g., Bluetooth), between two devices which store their WebAuthn credentials locally—this does not require communication with the RP in order to perform the delegation. Neither approach requires proxies to hold an account at the RP.

We aim to use ARKG, which is currently under consideration for standardisation by W3C's WebAuthn working group, as a building block for both delegation approaches so that they can be realised with minimal changes for RPs and authenticators that may already support ARKG for credential backup.

Both approaches share the same setup phase where the delegator communicates with the proxy. Following the setup phase, delegation can be performed for different accounts at one or more relying parties. In the remote approach, the delegator deposits a public key and some additional data intended for the proxy user with the RP, i.e., delegation is configured and achieved through the RP. The proxy user will be able to prove its authorisation by communicating with the RP at a later stage. In the direct approach, the delegator sends a warrant with some additional data to the proxy user who may later prove to the RP that they are authorised to access the delegator's account. Both variants are depicted in Fig. 1 and detailed in Sects. 2.3 to 2.5.

2.3   Setup Phase (common for Remote and Direct Delegation)

This phase is the same for both delegation approaches and corresponds to step ① where the delegator learns a public key pkp of the proxy user. This public key will enable the generation of multiple delegated credentials, potentially for different accounts owned by the delegator. The delegator already has an independent private-public key pair (skd, pkd), registered via WebAuthn, for each account it holds—with which it can delegate account access.

The proxy user must know the corresponding private key skp in order to sign future WebAuthn challenges when accessing the delegator's account. To access the delegator's account, proxies will need to know that delegation has been granted along with the login name used for the delegator's account. Conceptually, the setup phase is similar to that of ARKG [15] when viewing a proxy user's pkp as a backup authenticator's pk. The main difference is in the channel through which pkp is transmitted given the differences in the ownership of the authenticators, as discussed in more detail in the full paper [16].

2.4   Remote Delegation

In the remote variant (see Fig. 1a), to perform delegation in step ②, the account owner logs into their account at the RP using WebAuthn credentials and configures delegation for the proxy user by generating an unlinkable public key pk′ from the proxy user's public key pkp using ARKG. In addition to pk′, the delegator stores at the RP the corresponding ARKG credential information cred. In order to access the account in steps ③ and ④, the proxy user will use ARKG to derive the corresponding signing key sk′ from its private key skp and cred, and sign on the RP's authentication challenge. Remote delegation can be performed for multiple accounts following a single setup phase since many unlinkable pk′ may be generated for the same proxy's pkp. Note that all derived keys pk′ are unrelated to the delegator's pkd and they are registered directly with the RP for the account, maintaining WebAuthn unlinkability and providing a decentralised design—credentials are held by only the RP and authenticator.

Since the RP records proxy credentials, regardless of whether they have ever been used, credentials registered for proxies may be deleted, i.e., revoked, on an as-needed basis. As the RP is always aware of delegations as soon as they are registered, it may provide a web interface allowing the delegator to set permissions against individual account credentials, including those for proxies. This meets the revocation and policy control requirement, as well as ensuring the RPs are aware that this credential is for a proxy user.

2.5   Direct Delegation

Our direct delegation variant (see Fig. 1b) uses a new proxy signature scheme that involves a common delegation-by-warrant approach, but outputs warrants that remain unlinkable with respect to the proxy users. This approach allows delegation to be performed offline at any time between authenticators which store their credentials locally, and does not require communication with the RP. We also show how to construct such a proxy signature scheme using ARKG as a building block (see Sect. 3.2).

To delegate access to the account, for which the delegator's public key pkd is registered with an RP, the delegator uses its private key skd to create a warrant warr for the proxy user for whom pkp was received as part of the setup phase. This warrant contains the delegator's signature on a warrant public key pkw which is different from and unlinkable to pkp. The delegator sends warr together with some delegation data ddata to the proxy user in step ②. The proxy user can compute the warrant signing key skw using received ddata and is able to use skw to sign RP's authentication challenges when accessing the delegator's account in steps ③ and ④. The RP checks validity of the warrant using delegator's registered pkd prior to granting account access.

Observe that multiple warrants containing different pkw can be generated by the delegator for the same proxy user after the initial setup phase. These pkw remain unlinkable. In this way, the delegator can repeatedly grant access to the same proxy user for one or more of its WebAuthn accounts for the same or different RPs. The communication channel required for step ② can be established on-demand, in a similar way as during the setup phase.

Note that since RPs are unaware of direct delegations until they are presented with warrants by proxy signers, warrants must be validated against the delegator's existing WebAuthn account credentials—that is using the delegator's public key pkd for the account to prove that it was issued by the account owner. This requires that warrants, the public key pkw to which access is granted, and the existing account credential be linked. However, warrants must not undermine the unlinkability of existing account owner's credentials, whilst extending the unlinkability property to their proxies—resulting in registrations and delegations remaining uncorrelated across accounts and RPs, as visualised in Fig. 1c. The delegator's account public key pkd is unlinkable to delegator's public keys used on other accounts by virtue of them being registered as normal with WebAuthn. For proxy signers, however, this means that their warrant public keys pkw created by the delegator must also remain unlinkable. This essentially motivates the need for the new type of proxy signatures, which we call PSUW and detail in Sect. 3, using which delegators can issue warrants that cannot be linked to a proxy signer's pkp. Our direct approach therefore does not require a third party to complete the delegation, maintaining the decentralisation of WebAuthn.

Any issued warrants may be invalidated by replacing the account credential for pkd, which may be seen as equivalent to changing the password given to someone to access accounts. Alternatively, RPs could allow users to blacklist warrants, which would require additional server-side logic and delegators to record generated warrants to later add them to blacklists. The warrants used in the direct variant may contain additional signed data, including expiry timestamps and permissions granted to the proxy. RPs would need to understand the warrant permissions format—this offers the benefit of being signed by the delegator by default, in a well-known and easily-parsed warrant format (see also the extended paper [16] for more details on revocation and permissions).

3 Proxy Signature with Unlinkable Warrants

In this section, we present a new scheme called Proxy Signature with Unlinkable Warrants (PSUW), a new type of proxy signature required for the direct delegation of WebAuthn credentials. PSUW adopts a delegation-by-warrant approach, however, in contrast to other proxy signature schemes, delegated warrants and signatures produced by proxies remain unlinkable to the identities of the proxies. This helps to protect the unlinkability of multiple WebAuthn accounts to which access has been delegated to the same or multiple proxies. We model security of PSUW and construct it generically using ARKG and an ordinary digital signature scheme. Related work on proxy signature schemes is discussed in Sect. 5.

3.1 Modelling PSUW

We define here the syntax and security properties of PSUW.

Syntax of PSUW. The scheme has six algorithms. *Public parameters* pp *are implicitly given as input to all algorithms.*

Definition 1 (PSUW). *A PSUW scheme consists of six algorithms:*

- Setup(λ) *generates public parameters* pp *for security parameter* $\lambda \in \mathbb{N}$.
- DKGen() *samples private-public key pair* (skd, pkd) *for a delegator when called.*
- PKGen() *samples private-public key pair* (skp, pkp) *for a proxy when called.*
- Delegate(skd, pkp) *takes as input* skd *and* pkp. *It probabilistically returns warrant* warr *and delegation data* ddata, *which the proxy signer may use with its own signing key* skp *to generate proxy signatures.*
- Sign(skp, pkd, warr, ddata, m) *takes as input* skp, pkd, warr, ddata, *message* m, *and returns a proxy signature* $\bar{\sigma}$ *under* skp *for* m, *or* $\perp$ *on error (e.g.* warr *or* ddata *are invalid for* pkd*). Note that* warr $\in \bar{\sigma}$, *allowing* $\bar{\sigma}$ *to be verifiable as a standalone signature.* ddata *is used to compute the signing key, but is not included in the proxy signature* $\bar{\sigma}$ *output.*

$\mathcal{O}_{\mathsf{Reg}}$ when called

1 : $(\mathsf{skp}, \mathsf{pkp}) \leftarrow_\$ \mathsf{PKGen}()$
2 : $\mathsf{LReg} \leftarrow \mathsf{LReg} \cup (\mathsf{skp}, \mathsf{pkp})$
3 : **return** pkp

$\mathcal{O}_{\mathsf{Corr}}$ on input pkp

1 : **retrieve** $(\mathsf{skp}, \mathsf{pkp})$ from LReg **else abort**
2 : $\mathsf{LCorrupt} \leftarrow \mathsf{LCorrupt} \cup (\mathsf{skp}, \mathsf{pkp})$
3 : **return** skp

$\mathcal{O}_{\mathsf{Delegate}}$ on input pkp

1 : **if** $(\cdot, \mathsf{pkp}) \notin \mathsf{LReg}$
2 :   **then abort**
3 : $(\mathsf{warr}, \mathsf{ddata}) \leftarrow$
4 : $\mathsf{Delegate}(\mathsf{skd}, \mathsf{pkp})$
5 : $\mathsf{LDel} \leftarrow \mathsf{LDel} \cup (\mathsf{pkp}, \mathsf{warr})$
6 : **return** $\mathsf{warr}, \mathsf{ddata}$

$\mathcal{O}_{\mathsf{Sign}}$ on input $(\mathsf{pkp}, \mathsf{warr}, \mathsf{ddata}, m)$

1 : **retrieve** $(\mathsf{skp}, \mathsf{pkp})$ from LReg
2 :   **then abort**
3 : $\bar{\sigma} \leftarrow \mathsf{Sign}(\mathsf{skp}, \mathsf{pkd}, \mathsf{warr}, \mathsf{ddata}, m)$
4 : **if** $\bar{\sigma} \stackrel{?}{=} \bot$ **then abort**
5 : $\mathsf{LSign} \leftarrow \mathsf{LSign} \cup (\bar{\sigma}, \mathsf{pkp}, \mathsf{warr}, \mathsf{ddata}, m)$
6 : **return** $\bar{\sigma}$

(a) Oracles for PSUW security experiments.

$\mathsf{Exp}_{\mathcal{A}}^{\mathsf{wu}\text{-}b}(\lambda)$

1 : $\mathsf{pp} \leftarrow \mathsf{Setup}(\lambda)$
2 : $(\mathsf{skd}, \mathsf{pkd}) \leftarrow_\$ \mathsf{DKGen}()$
3 : $(\mathsf{ST}, \mathsf{pkp}_0, \mathsf{pkp}_1, m) \leftarrow \mathcal{A}_1^{\mathcal{O}_{\mathsf{Reg}}, \mathcal{O}_{\mathsf{Delegate}}, \mathcal{O}_{\mathsf{Sign}}, \mathcal{O}_{\mathsf{Corr}}}(\mathsf{pp}, \mathsf{pkd})$
4 : **retrieve** $(\mathsf{skp}_0, \mathsf{pkp}_0)$ and $(\mathsf{skp}_1, \mathsf{pkp}_1)$ from LReg **else return** 0
5 : $(\mathsf{warr}, \mathsf{ddata}) \leftarrow \mathsf{Delegate}(\mathsf{skd}, \mathsf{pkp}_b)$
6 : $\bar{\sigma} \leftarrow \mathsf{Sign}(\mathsf{skp}_b, \mathsf{pkd}, \mathsf{warr}, \mathsf{ddata}, m)$
7 : $b' \leftarrow \mathcal{A}_2^{\mathcal{O}_{\mathsf{Reg}}, \mathcal{O}_{\mathsf{Delegate}}, \mathcal{O}_{\mathsf{Sign}}, \mathcal{O}_{\mathsf{Corr}}}(\mathsf{ST}, \bar{\sigma}, \mathsf{warr}, \mathsf{ddata})$
8 : **return** $b \stackrel{?}{=} b' \wedge (\cdot, \mathsf{pkp}_0) \notin \mathsf{LCorrupt} \wedge (\cdot, \mathsf{pkp}_1) \notin \mathsf{LCorrupt}$

(b) Warrant-Unlinkability experiment.

$\mathsf{Exp}_{\mathcal{A}}^{\mathsf{unforge}}(\lambda)$

1 : $\mathsf{pp} \leftarrow \mathsf{Setup}(\lambda)$
2 : $(\mathsf{skd}, \mathsf{pkd}) \leftarrow_\$ \mathsf{DKGen}()$
3 : $(\bar{\sigma}, m) \leftarrow \mathcal{A}^{\mathcal{O}_{\mathsf{Reg}}, \mathcal{O}_{\mathsf{Delegate}}, \mathcal{O}_{\mathsf{Sign}}, \mathcal{O}_{\mathsf{Corr}}}(\mathsf{pp}, \mathsf{pkd})$
4 : **parse** $\bar{\sigma}$ as $(\mathsf{warr}, \cdot)$
5 : **return** $\mathsf{Verify}(\mathsf{pkd}, \bar{\sigma}, m) = 1 \wedge ($
6 : $(\cdot, \mathsf{warr}) \notin \mathsf{LDel} \vee$
7 : $[\exists \mathsf{pkp}, m \text{ s.t. } (\cdot, \cdot, \mathsf{warr}, \cdot, m) \notin \mathsf{LSign} \wedge (\mathsf{pkp}, \mathsf{warr}) \in \mathsf{LDel} \wedge$
8 : $(\cdot, \mathsf{pkp}) \notin \mathsf{LCorrupt}])$

(c) Unforgeability experiment.

Fig. 2. Oracles and security experiments for PSUW.

– Verify(pkd, $\bar{\sigma}$, m) *takes as input* pkd, $\bar{\sigma}$, m, *and returns 1 if* $\bar{\sigma}$ *is valid with respect to* pkd *for* m, *otherwise 0.*

Security Definitions. We give the adversarial model and define two properties for PSUW: Warrant-Unlinkability and Unforgeability.

Adversaries and oracles. We model an adversary $\mathcal{A}$ as a probabilistic polynomial time (PPT) algorithm, which may call, using the parameters to which it is given access, any of the public procedures given in Sect. 3.1.

The adversary $\mathcal{A}$ may make a polynomial number of queries to the oracles given in Fig. 2a:

– $\mathcal{O}_{\mathsf{Reg}}$, when called, samples a new key pair (skp, pkp), storing the key pair in list LReg, and returns pkp.
– $\mathcal{O}_{\mathsf{Delegate}}$(pkp), is initialised with the delegator's private key skd. On input proxy-signer public key pkp, it records the result of Delegate(skd, pkp) in list LDel, returning warr and ddata without giving $\mathcal{A}$ access to skd. If $(\cdot, \mathsf{pkp}) \notin$ LReg, it aborts. This models an honest delegation to pkp.
– $\mathcal{O}_{\mathsf{Sign}}$(pkp, warr, ddata, m), is initialised with the delegator's public key pkd. On input proxy-signer public key pkp, warrant warr, delegation ddata, and a message m, it records in list LSign the result of calling Sign(skp, warr, ddata, m) for (skp, pkp) $\in$ LReg. It aborts if Sign returns $\bot$. This models asking for a signature on a message of $\mathcal{A}$'s choice.
– $\mathcal{O}_{\mathsf{Corr}}$(pkp), on input proxy-signer public key pkp, returns the corresponding private key skp from list LReg and adds the key to list LCorrupt. If $(\cdot, \mathsf{pkp}) \notin$ LReg, it aborts. This models the leak of private keying material for proxy.

Correctness. Our scheme is correct if, $\forall \lambda \in \mathbb{N}$, the following hold:

$$\mathsf{pp} \leftarrow \mathsf{Setup}(\lambda)$$
$$(\mathsf{skd}, \mathsf{pkd}) \leftarrow \mathsf{DKGen}()$$
$$(\mathsf{skp}, \mathsf{pkp}) \leftarrow \mathsf{PKGen}()$$
$$(\mathsf{warr}, \mathsf{ddata}) \leftarrow \mathsf{Delegate}(\mathsf{skd}, \mathsf{pkp})$$
$$\bar{\sigma} \leftarrow \mathsf{Sign}(\mathsf{skp}, \mathsf{pkd}, \mathsf{warr}, \mathsf{ddata}, m)$$
$$1 \overset{?}{=} \mathsf{Verify}(\mathsf{pkd}, \bar{\sigma}, m)$$

Warrant-Unlinkability. The Warrant-Unlinkability (wu) property of a PSUW scheme ensures that an adversary, when given proxy signature $\bar{\sigma}$, warrant warr, and delegation data ddata, cannot determine the identity pkp for which the delegation was performed.

The unlinkability property of WebAuthn requires that users cannot be correlated across registrations. We capture this property by requiring that an entity, such as an RP in the case of WebAuthn, be able to determine the identity of the user who delegated signing rights, i.e., account access, but not the identity of the proxy signer. This means that unlinkability is maintained for both the delegator—where knowing the identity of proxy signers might provide linkability for account holders too—and the proxy signer.

We model Warrant-Unlinkability in Fig. 2b. The experiment $\mathsf{Exp}_{\mathcal{A}}^{wu\text{-}b}(\lambda)$ is parameterised with bit b. It chooses a delegator's key pair (skd, pkd) and challenges an adversary $\mathcal{A}$ to determine which of its proxy-signing keys was used to delegate signing rights for pkd and sign message m. $\mathcal{A}$ is given access to oracles $\mathcal{O}_{\mathsf{Reg}}$, $\mathcal{O}_{\mathsf{Delegate}}$, $\mathcal{O}_{\mathsf{Sign}}$ and $\mathcal{O}_{\mathsf{Corr}}$.

Definition 2 (Warrant-Unlinkability). *This is offered by PSUW if the following is negligible in λ:*

$$\mathsf{Adv}_{PSUW,\mathcal{A}}^{wu\text{-}b}(\lambda) := \left| \Pr\left[\mathsf{Exp}_{\mathcal{A}}^{wu\text{-}1}(\lambda) = 1 \right] - \Pr\left[\mathsf{Exp}_{\mathcal{A}}^{wu\text{-}0}(\lambda) = 1 \right] \right|$$

Unforgeability. For a PSUW scheme to satisfy the Unforgeability property, an adversary $\mathcal{A}$ must not be able to forge proxy signatures with respect to a delegator's pkd without knowledge of the corresponding skd, as in Fig. 2c.

The experiment challenges $\mathcal{A}$ to give a valid proxy signature $\bar{\sigma}$, for a message m of its choice, for a delegator's pkd. The adversary is given access to the $\mathcal{O}_{\mathsf{Reg}}$, $\mathcal{O}_{\mathsf{Delegate}}$, $\mathcal{O}_{\mathsf{Sign}}$, and $\mathcal{O}_{\mathsf{Corr}}$ oracles. $\mathcal{A}$ wins if it can break either the delegation (line 6) or signing procedures (lines 7 and 8).

Definition 3 (Unforgeability). *A PSUW scheme provides Unforgeability if the following advantage is negligible in λ:*

$$\mathsf{Adv}_{PSUW,\mathcal{A}}^{unforge}(\lambda) := \Pr\left[\mathsf{Exp}_{\mathcal{A}}^{unforge}(\lambda) = 1 \right]$$

3.2 Our Generic PSUW Construction

We proceed with a generic construction of PSUW, based on the ARKG primitive and an ordinary digital signature scheme, and then analyse its security.

Building Blocks. We recall the two building blocks.

Asynchronous Remote Key Generation (ARKG). [15] An ARKG scheme has five algorithms, ARKG := (Setup, KGen, DerivePK, DeriveSK, Check). Setup(λ) returns public parameters pp for the scheme. KGen samples a key pair (sk, pk) when called. Derived public key algorithm DerivePK(pk, aux) returns a new public key pk$'$ and derivation data cred. Derived private key sk$'$ for pk$'$ is computed and returned by DeriveSK(sk, cred). Check(sk$'$, pk$'$) returns 1 if (sk$'$, pk$'$) form a valid key pair, otherwise 0. We use ARKG which offers the two following properties.

PSUW.Setup(1^λ)

---

return pp $= (1^\lambda, \mathsf{ARKG.Setup}(1^\lambda),$
  $\mathsf{DS.Setup}(1^\lambda))$

PSUW.DKGen(pp)

---

return (skd, pkd) $= \mathsf{DS.KGen}(pp)$

PSUW.PKGen(pp)

---

return (skp, pkp) $= \mathsf{ARKG.KGen}(pp)$

PSUW.Delegate(skd, pkd)

---

1 : (pkw, cred) $\leftarrow\!\!\$$

2 :   ARKG.DerivePK(pp, pkp, $\emptyset$)

3 : $\sigma \leftarrow \mathsf{DS.Sign}(\mathsf{skd}, \mathsf{pkw})$

4 : **return** warr $= (\mathsf{pkw}, \sigma)$,

5 :   ddata $=$ cred

PSUW.Sign(skp, pkd, warr, ddata, m)

---

1 : **parse** warr **as** pkw, σ

2 : **parse** ddata **as** cred

3 : **if** DS.Verify(pkd, pkw, σ) $\overset{?}{=} 0$ **then**

4 :   **return** $\perp$

5 : skw $\leftarrow$ ARKG.DeriveSK(pp, skp, cred)

6 : **if** skw $\overset{?}{=} \perp$ **then return** $\perp$

7 : $s \leftarrow \mathsf{DS.Sign}(\mathsf{skw}, m)$

8 : **return** $\bar{\sigma} = (s, \text{warr})$

PSUW.Verify(pkd, $\bar{\sigma}$, m)

---

1 : **parse** $\bar{\sigma}$ **as** s, warr

2 : **parse** warr **as** pkw, σ

3 : **return** DS.Verify(pkd, σ, pkw)$\wedge$

4 :   DS.Verify(pkw, s, m)

Fig. 3. Algorithms of our PSUW construction.

PK-Unlinkability (pku) is provided by ARKG if $\mathsf{Adv}^{\mathsf{pku}}_{\mathsf{ARKG},\mathcal{A}}(\lambda)$ is negligible in λ for a PPT adversary $\mathcal{A}$ to distinguish between derived public keys and uniformly-sampled public keys. The adversary is given access to challenge oracle $\mathcal{O}^b_{\mathsf{pkp}}$ which is initialised with a bit b and public key pk. When called, it returns either the result of DerivePK(pp, pk, aux) when $b = 0$ or samples and returns a new public key from $\mathcal{D}$ when $b = 1$.

Malicious-Strong Key Secrecy (msKS) is provided by ARKG if $\mathsf{Adv}^{\mathsf{msKS}}_{\mathsf{ARKG},\mathcal{A}}(\lambda)$ is negligible in λ for a PPT adversary $\mathcal{A}$ to derive a valid key pair $\mathsf{sk}^\star, \mathsf{pk}^\star$ and corresponding $\mathsf{cred}^\star$ for an initial public key pk. It is given access to derived public key oracle $\mathcal{O}_{\mathsf{pk}'}$ and derived private key oracle $\mathcal{O}_{\mathsf{sk}'}$. It wins if $\mathsf{sk}^\star, \mathsf{pk}^\star$ and corresponding $\mathsf{cred}^\star$ verify against ARKG.Check and it did not trivially obtain these by querying the oracles.

For formal definitions of these properties, we refer to the work of Frymann et al. [15, §4.1]. Note that this construction of ARKG satisfies the above properties under the well-known snPRF-ODH [4] and Discrete Logarithm hardness assumptions in the random oracle model. This construction will be used to instantiate our generic PSUW scheme.

Digital Signature (DS). A digital signature scheme has three algorithms, DS $:=$ (DS.KGen, DS.Sign, DS.Verify). The key generation algorithm DS.KGen takes as input a security parameter λ and outputs a key pair (sk, pk). The signing algorithm takes as input a signing key sk with a message m and outputs a signature

σ. DS.Verify takes as input a candidate tuple (pk, σ, m) and outputs 1 if σ verifies with respect to public key pk and message m, otherwise 0.

Two variants of DS unforgeability are required. We first require standard existential unforgeability under chosen-message attack (EUF-CMA), which challenges an adversary to produce a forgery $(\sigma^\star, m^\star)$ that verifies with respect to pk without knowledge of the corresponding sk. In this experiment, the adversary has access to a signing oracle $\mathcal{O}_{\mathsf{Sign}}$ and wins if $\sigma^\star$ was produced on $m^\star$ that was not queried to $\mathcal{O}_{\mathsf{Sign}}$. We require strong unforgeability under chosen-message attack (SUF-CMA) [1], in which case $\sigma^\star$ was not obtained from $\mathcal{O}_{\mathsf{Sign}}$ on query $m^\star$.

PSUW Algorithms. The algorithms of our generic PSUW construction are specified in Fig. 3, which use the algorithms from ARKG and DS as underlying building blocks.

Security Analysis of the Generic PSUW Scheme

Theorem 1. *PSUW satisfies Warrant-Unlinkability if ARKG satisfies PK-Unlinkability.*

Theorem 2. *PSUW satisfies Unforgeability if DS is SUF-CMA secure and ARKG offers both Malicious-Strong Key Secrecy and PK-Unlinkability.*

Proof. Proofs for Theorems 1 and 2 are provided in the full paper [16].

Remark 1. Looking ahead, we will instantiate DS with ECDSA, which is known to only provide EUF-CMA security. However, it has been shown that the *only* attack on strong unforgeability for an ECDSA signature of the form $(s,t) \in \mathbb{G}$, is the forgery $(-s,t) \in \mathbb{G}$ [13].

As noted by Fersch [12, Remark 3.2.3], there are numerous techniques to mitigate such an attack by normalising the s component so that only one of s or $-s$ can be verified. For example, enforcing $s \in [1, (q-1)/2]$, so that either s or $-s = q - s$ verifies. In our instantiation and implementation, we enforce this s-component normalisation to achieve a strongly-unforgeable ECDSA.

4   Achieving Delegation in WebAuthn

In this section, we discuss instantiations and performance of our ARKG-based delegation approaches and the new PSUW primitive.

4.1   Cryptographic Implementation

We instantiate the cryptographic building blocks in our delegation approaches using compatible, standard-based, and efficient algorithms that are already being used in the WebAuthn standard. This includes ECDSA standard [33] on the

Table 1. Mean execution time for a single primitive call, in milliseconds and averaged from 1000 timings.

Primitive	Delegate	Sign	Verify
ECDSA (plain WebAuthn)	–	1.9	1.6
ARKG (remote delegation)	5.6	3.8	1.6
PSUW (direct delegation)	7.5	5.4	3.2

P-256 curve (see ECC [5]), which is used for the DS building block within PSUW and to perform all signing operations used in our delegation approaches. Using ECDSA gives further straightforward compatibility with ARKG and PSUW. Credential public keys [26, §6.5.1] in WebAuthn are described using the COSE [38] format. ECDSA on P-256 curve with SHA-256 is given a standard and registered COSE algorithm name EC256 and type -7.

The instantiation and implementation of ARKG uses the original proposal from Yubico [15], which is currently being considered for the standardisation of WebAuthn credential backups. It adopts the standards-based HKDF [25] with SHA-256 [11] and HMAC-SHA-256 [24] algorithms, which are well supported in the WebAuthn ecosystem. We adopt the same algorithms to implement PSUW. Our delegation approaches would therefore work well with authenticators that implement the ARKG primitive for backup purposes.

Performance. In Table 1, the performance for each of the primitives required for delegating and authenticating in WebAuthn is presented. The timings were taken using our benchmarking program and PSUW implementation. The existing ARKG code[1] and Python's `fastecdsa` are used as our ARKG and DS building blocks, respectively. These timings are abstracted from the full delegation, registration, and authentication procedures as these encounter unavoidable, and in some cases unpredictable, overheads, including packing data into message formats for WebAuthn processing and network performance, as well as performance overheads on the RP's backend (e.g., database, inter-system communications). We capture instead the measurable difference between an example of plain WebAuthn, using ECDSA, and our two delegation approaches: remote using ARKG and direct using PSUW. Each primitive was invoked 1000 times on an Intel i7-8700 (3.20 GHz), using a single-threaded software implementation, with the average recorded.

Compared to a plain WebAuthn sign-and-verify challenge using ECDSA, the ARKG primitive in the remote delegation approach gives an increase of only 1.9 ms in execution time for the signature generation. From ARKG to PSUW, used in direct delegation, we observe an increase of 1.6 ms for the signing operation. PSUW also incurs an average increase of 1.6 ms in verification over ECDSA and ARKG, as it must verify both the warrant's signature and the signature on

---

[1] https://github.com/Yubico/webauthn-recovery-extension/.

the challenge. ARKG's verification requires a single ECDSA signature verification as its response is a standard ECDSA signature, but for a derived private-public key pair. These timings are reported without any bespoke optimisations made to the underlying libraries used; we observe such increases are unnoticeable in practice.

4.2   Approach for Integration with WebAuthn and Our Code

Please see the full paper [16] and our code repositories[2,3] for a complete discussion of the integration of our scheme and the PSUW primitive in WebAuthn, including the required CTAP calls, use of WebAuthn's extensions provision, as well as an example of some CTAP calls required for an authenticator to support such a delegation scheme, implemented using the virtual authenticator by Culnane et al. [9]. We also discuss usability considerations for deploying our scheme.

5   Related Work

Application-specific delegation may be provided to users of the same service provider in a secure manner, such as allowing access to a mailbox to another user without sharing passwords, e.g., delegated access in Office 365's Outlook. There are also existing standards that aim to achieve this on the web and in local networks. OAuth [20] is an open standard for authorisation, or access delegation, through which users can grant applications, particularly websites, access to account data without sharing passwords. OpenID Connect (OIDC) [40] is an authentication layer built on top of OAuth which uses OpenID [37], a decentralised authentication protocol that allows an *identity provider* (IdP) to share identity data (e.g., name) to a *relying party*—who depends on the identity provider. Single-Sign On (SSO), a federated identity, is often achieved through Security Assertion Markup Language (SAML) [35] which uses cookies and provides a standard language for exchanging authentication and authorisation information between IdPs and service providers. Existing identity-providing protocols are discussed and compared by Naik and Jenkins [32].

Additionally, there exist schemes for delegating signing rights in the realm of digital signatures, called proxy signatures, first introduced by Mambo et al. [28]. However, when viewed from the perspective of WebAuthn, existing proxy signatures would not maintain the unlinkability properties of WebAuthn credentials and, in some cases, its decentralised nature. See Sect. 1.1 for more on WebAuthn properties and below for a discussion on existing proxy signature schemes in the context of WebAuthn delegation. For example, access to WebAuthn accounts must be delegatable without disclosing the proxy user's identity to the service provider; otherwise delegated accounts may become linkable.

---

[2] https://github.com/UoS-SCCS/PSUW-Primitive.
[3] https://github.com/UoS-SCCS/WebAuthn-Credential-Delegation.

Furthermore, delegation has been explored in anonymous credentials (for example by Crites and Lysyanskaya [8]), where a central authority issues attributes to users—these attributes can be disclosed whilst preserving anonymity. In general, these schemes employ more complex cryptographic techniques than ordinary signatures and would therefore not be compatible with the current WebAuthn standard.

More recently, Yubico has proposed a protocol for backing up WebAuthn credentials without compromising WebAuthn properties. Their approach is based on a new Asynchronous Remote Key Generation (ARKG) primitive [15], which allows a primary authenticator to create pubic key credentials for one or more trusted backup authenticators, owned by the same user, whilst maintaining the unlinkability and decentralisation properties of WebAuthn—which many of the current approaches do not provide [27].

We observe that Yubico's approach can be viewed as some form of self-delegation, however, delegating to other users gives rise to further challenges and considerations due to the new and less-trusted security setting, as opposed to the trusted ownership of primary and backup authenticators.

Our work focuses on the delegation of account access using WebAuthn credentials, which is akin to secure password sharing. This differs to application-level delegation, as mentioned above, which requires application logic to achieve the delegation, often requiring the provision of an account for the proxy user which would be associated with the delegator's account.

Related work on proxy signatures. Proxy signatures were introduced by Mambo et al. [28], with security formalised by Boldyreva et al. [3]. Typically, delegation to a proxy signer is performed by issuing a warrant that contains a certificate on the proxy signer's public key that verifies against the delegator's public key. This warrant then becomes part of the proxy signature, and is verified within the proxy signature's verification. Any scheme that follows this approach cannot achieve unlinkable warrants since the proxy signer's public key is required to verify the warrant, which make them unsuitable for application in WebAuthn. Nonetheless, we note that a range of constructions from different hardness assumptions exist, e.g., discrete logarithms [3,23,28,43], integer factorisation [45], and lattices [21].

In addition to standard proxy signatures there have been proposals to provide various degrees of privacy for the warrants, such as anonymous proxy signatures by Shum and Wei [39], with a formal model and a general construction proposed later by Fuchsbauer and Pointcheval [17]—giving the properties of proxy anonymity and traceability. The construction bears similarity with the approach taken in group signatures Chaum and van Heyst [7] through encryption of the warrant under the opener's public key with appropriate zero-knowledge proofs, such that the proxy signer remains anonymous yet traceable by an 'opener' if needed. We observe that although this scheme offers rich functionality, it is not needed in the context of WebAuthn. Removal of Fuchsbauer and Pointcheval's traceability requirement [17] would still yield a complex construction requiring zero-knowledge proofs to protect privacy and hence would not be compatible with the WebAuthn standard. Using central authorities would also not suit its decentralised nature.

Introduced simultaneously by Steinfeld et al. [42] and Johnson et al. [22], redactable signatures allow messages to be signed such that they can be hidden, disclosed, or have relations proven by parties that did not create the original full signatures. Although they bear some similarities with proxy signatures, the security properties for redactable signatures do not consider restriction of redaction to chosen parties. Hence, they are unsuitable in the challenge-response protocol of WebAuthn since the redactable signature can be transferred to other parties to illegally perform authentication.

We also note the work of Yu et al. [46], who call their scheme 'anonymous proxy signature'. Their construction has different functionality and is a combination of a proxy signature and a ring signature [36]. Moreover, their security analysis is focused only on unforgeability properties. Similarly, the scheme proposed by Wu et al. [44] combines standard proxy signatures with group signatures, and is similarly not applicable for our setting.

Finally, we note the work by Derler et al. [10], which constructs warrant-hiding proxy signatures and blank signatures—see also Hanser and Slamanig's work [18, 19]—from anonymous credentials [6]. Warrant-hiding means that the message space delegated to a proxy remains unknown to the verifier, other than the message being presented for verification. In the latter, the message has a structure that can be changed in a prescribed way. These techniques are not what is required to realise unlinkable delegation in WebAuthn.

6   Conclusion

We proposed two approaches for delegation of WebAuthn credentials preserving the security, privacy, and decentralisation aspects of the standard. Both approaches share the same setup procedure, employing ARKG, which makes them compatible with Yubico's recent proposal for account recovery in WebAuthn.

Our remote delegation approach allows account owners to configure and manage delegation with associated permissions at the relying party, whereas for direct delegation, the owner issues a warrant containing delegation credentials directly to the proxy user without requiring communication with the relying party. To realise this approach, we introduced a novel type of proxy signatures with unlinkable warrants, which might be of independent interest. We provided in the extended paper [16] discussion of integration details using WebAuthn and CTAP extensions, as well as possible approaches to realising communication between delegators and proxies for direct delegation.

We conducted performance experiments of our primitive which show that delegated authentication can be achieved at a low cost of a few extra milliseconds when compared to the standard authentication in WebAuthn.

Acknowledgements. Researchers from the Surrey Centre for Cyber Security were supported by the UK's National Cyber Security Centre. The authors wish to thank Emil Lundberg (Yubico AB) for helpful discussions in the early stages of this work.

References

1. An, J.H., Dodis, Y., Rabin, T.: On the security of joint signature and encryption. In: EUROCRYPT (2002)
2. Barbosa, M., Boldyreva, A., Chen, S., Warinschi, B.: Provable Security Analysis of FIDO2 (2021)
3. Boldyreva, A., Palacio, A., Warinschi, B.: Secure proxy signature schemes for delegation of signing rights. JoC (2012)
4. Brendel, J., Fischlin, M., Günther, F., Janson, C.: PRF-ODH: relations, instantiations, and impossibility results. In: CRYPTO (2017)
5. Certicom Research: SEC 1: Elliptic Curve Cryptography. Tech. Rep. (2009)
6. Chaum, D.: Security without identification: transaction systems to make big brother obsolete. ACM (1985)
7. Chaum, D., van Heyst, E.: Group signatures. In: EUROCRYPT (1991)
8. Crites, E.C., Lysyanskaya, A.: Delegatable anonymous credentials from mercurial signatures. In: CT-RSA (2019)
9. Culnane, C., Newton, C.J.P., Treharne, H.: Technical report on a virtual CTAP2 webauthn authenticator. arXiv preprint arXiv:2108.04131
10. Derler, D., Hanser, C., Slamanig, D.: Privacy-enhancing proxy signatures from non-interactive anonymous credentials. In: CODASPY (2014)
11. Eastlake, D., Hansen, T.: US Secure Hash Algorithms (SHA and HMAC-SHA). Tech. rep. (2006)
12. Fersch, M.: The Provable Security of Elgamal-type Signature Schemes, Ph.D. thesis, Ruhr University Bochum, Germany (2018)
13. Fersch, M., Kiltz, E., Poettering, B.: On the Provable security of (EC)DSA signatures. In: ACM CCS (2016)
14. FIDO: Client to Authenticator Protocol (CTAP). Tech. rep. (2018)
15. Frymann, N., Gardham, D., Kiefer, F., Lundberg, E., Manulis, M., Nilsson, D.: Asynchronous remote key generation: an analysis of Yubico's proposal for w3c Webauthn. In: ACM CCS (2020)
16. Frymann, N., Gardham, D., Manulis, M.: Unlinkable Delegation of WebAuthn Credentials. Cryptology ePrint Archive, Paper 2022/303 (2022)
17. Fuchsbauer, G., Pointcheval, D.: Anonymous proxy signatures. In: SCN (2008)
18. Hanser, C., Slamanig, D.: Blank digital signatures. In: ASIACCS (2013)
19. Hanser, C., Slamanig, D.: Warrant-hiding delegation-by-certificate proxy signature schemes. In: INDOCRYPT (2013)
20. Hardt, D.: The OAuth 2.0 Authorization Framework. Tech. rep. (2012)
21. Jiang, Y., Kong, F., Ju, X.: Lattice-Based Proxy Signature. In: CIS (2010)
22. Johnson, R., Molnar, D., Song, D., Wagner, D.: Homomorphic signature schemes. In: CT-RSA (2002)
23. Kim, S., Park, S., Won, D.: Proxy signatures. ICS, Revisited. In (1997)
24. Krawczyk, H., Bellare, M., Canetti, R.: HMAC: Keyed-hashing for message authentication. Tech. rep. (1997)
25. Krawczyk, H., Eronen, P.: HMAC-based Extract-and-Expand Key Derivation Function (HKDF). Tech. rep. (2010)

26. Kumar, A., Lundberg, E., Jones, J., Jones, M., Hodges, J.: Web Authentication. Tech. rep., W3C (2021). https://www.w3.org/TR/webauthn-2/
27. Kunke, J., Wiefling, S., Ullmann, M., Iacono, L.L.: Evaluation of account recovery strategies with FIDO2-based passwordless authentication (2021)
28. Mambo, M., Usuda, K., Okamoto, E.: Proxy signatures: delegation of the power to sign messages. IEICE FECCS (1996)
29. M'Raihi, D., Bellare, M., Hoornaert, F., Naccache, D., Ranen, O.: HOTP: an HMAC-based one-time password algorithm. Tech. rep. (2005)
30. M'Raihi, D., Machani, S., Pei, M., Rydell, J.: TOTP: Time-based one-time password algorithm. Tech. rep. (2011)
31. Mulliner, C., Borgaonkar, R., Stewin, P., Seifert, J.P.: SMS-based one-time passwords: attacks and defense. In: DIMVA (2013)
32. Naik, N., Jenkins, P.: An analysis of open standard identity protocols in cloud computing security paradigm. In: ASC/PiCom/DataCom/CyberSciTech (2016)
33. NIST: Digital Signature Standard (DSS). Tech. rep. (2013)
34. Pearman, S., et al.: let's go in for a closer look: observing passwords in their natural habitat. In: CCS (2017)
35. Ragouzis, N., Hughes, J., Philpott, R., Maler, E., Madsen, P., Scavo, T.: Security Assertion Markup Language (SAML) V2.0 Technical Overview. Tech. rep., OASIS Open (2008)
36. Rivest, R.L., Shamir, A., Tauman, Y.: How to leak a secret. In: ASIACRYPT (2001)
37. Sakimura, N., Bradley, J., Jones, M., de Medeiros, B., Mortimore, C.: OpenID connect core 1.0 incorporating errata. Tech. rep., OpenID Foundation (2014)
38. Schaad, J.: CBOR Object Signing and Encryption (COSE). RFC 8152 (2017)
39. Shum, K., Wei, V.K.: A strong proxy signature scheme with proxy signer privacy protection. In: Workshops on Enabling Technologies (2002)
40. Siriwardena, P.: OpenID Connect (OIDC). In: Advanced API Security (2020)
41. Srinivas, S., Balfanz, D., Tiffany, E.: Universal 2nd Factor (U2F) Overview. Tech. rep. (2014)
42. Steinfeld, R., Bull, L., Zheng, Y.: Content extraction signatures. In: ICISC (2001)
43. Tan, Z., Liu, Z.: Provably secure delegation-by-certification proxy signature schemes. In: InfoSecu (2004)
44. Wu, K.l., Zou, J., Wei, X.H., Liu, F.Y.: Proxy group signature: a new anonymous proxy signature scheme. In: ICML (2008)
45. Yu, Y., Mu, Y., Susilo, W., Sun, Y., Ji, Y.: Provably secure proxy signature scheme from factorization. MCM (2012)
46. Yu, Y., Xu, C., Huang, X., Mu, Y.: An efficient anonymous proxy signature scheme with provable security. CSI (2009)

Large Scale Analysis of DoH Deployment on the Internet

Sebastián García[1], Joaquín Bogado[1]([✉]), Karel Hynek[2,3], Dmitrii Vekshin[4], Tomáš Čejka[2,3], and Armin Wasicek[4]

[1] Faculty of Electrical Engineering, Czech Technical University in Prague, Prague, Czech Republic
sebastian.garcia@agents.fel.cvut.cz, joaquin.bogado@aic.fel.cvut.cz
[2] Faculty of Information Technology, Czech Technical University in Prague, Prague, Czech Republic
hynekkar@fit.cvut.cz
[3] CESNET, z. s. p. o., Prague, Czech Republic
cejkat@cesnet.cz
[4] Avast Software s.r.o., Prague, Czech Republic
{dmitrii.vekshin,armin.wasicek}@avast.com

Abstract. DNS over HTTPS (DoH) is one of the standards to protect the security and privacy of users. The choice of DoH provider has controversial consequences, from monopolisation of surveillance to lost visibility by network administrators and security providers. More importantly, it is a novel security business. Software products and organisations depend on users choosing well-known and trusted DoH resolvers. However, there is no comprehensive study on the number of DoH resolvers on the Internet, its growth, and the trustworthiness of the organisations behind them. This paper studies the deployment of DoH resolvers by (i) scanning the whole Internet for DoH resolvers in 2021 and 2022; (ii) creating lists of well-known DoH resolvers by the community; (iii) characterising what those resolvers are, (iv) comparing the growth and differences. Results show that (i) the number of DoH resolvers increased 4.8 times in the period 2021–2022, (ii) the number of organisations providing DoH services has doubled, and (iii) the number of DoH resolvers in 2022 is 28 times larger than the number of well-known DoH resolvers by the community. Moreover, 94% of the public DoH resolvers on the Internet are unknown to the community, 77% use certificates from free services, and 57% belong to unknown organisations or personal servers. We conclude that the number of DoH resolvers is growing at a fast rate; also that at least 30% of them are not completely trustworthy and users should be very careful when choosing a DoH resolver.

Keywords: DoH · Encrypted DNS · Network measurement · Network trends

V. Atluri et al. (Eds.): ESORICS 2022, LNCS 13556, pp. 145–165, 2022.
https://doi.org/10.1007/978-3-031-17143-7_8

1   Introduction

DNS over HTTPS (DoH) is a method of encrypting DNS [26] that has been in continuous deployment since 2017 [18]. Despite controversies over its impact on privacy and surveillance monopoly [14,16,25], many applications currently implement DoH and the transition to encrypted DNS is well underway.

Encrypted DNS is a fundamental part of our security and privacy, and DoH has emerged, together with DNS over TLS (DoT), as a standard for the community. With *standard* non-encrypted DNS, the decision about which DNS server to use was mainly based on performance. With DoH, users need to take into account other aspects of security, namely the capability to encrypt up to the DNS resolver vs. to the authoritative DNS resolvers, the ability to filter out the protocol, and the loss of visibility for lawful blocking.

Although some measurements on DoT adoption were made [10,27,35], there has not been large-scale measurements on DoH deployment. Most studies focus on DoT because by using port 853/TCP it is easy to find. As part of the advantages of DoH, the use of port 443/TCP makes it difficult to differentiate from web pages. Therefore, there is a lack of visibility on the amount of DoH resolvers, their features, and the type of organisations that deployed them. Without this knowledge, the security community lacks some perspective on the security of DoH.

This paper presents the first longitudinal measurement, comparison, and analysis of the deployment of DoH resolvers on the Internet from 2021 to 2022. We scanned the Internet for port 443/TCP, identified DoH resolvers, compiled a list of well-known DoH resolvers by the community, and verify the trustworthiness of the resolvers.

Results show a confirmed growing trend in the deployment of DoH between 2021 and 2022. The number of well-known DoH resolvers by the community increased from 234 to 262 (~12%). The number of public DoH resolvers found on the Internet shows at least 350% increase in 2022, even when the difference in methodology between the two scans is taken into account. This is 28 times larger than the list of 262 well-known DoH resolvers of 2022, meaning that ~94% of the public DoH resolvers are unknown to the community.

The contributions of this paper are (i) an updated and comprehensive dataset of well-known DoH providers by the community in 2021 and 2022, (ii) a dataset of all public DoH resolvers found by our global Internet scan, (iii) a new Nmap NSE script tool to scan and verify DoH resolvers, and (iv) a security overview of the organisations providing DoH resolution services.

2   Related Work

DoH is a relatively new protocol for encrypting DNS, already studied from multiple perspectives, such as performance [4], privacy [20] and deployment differences [24]. Since DoH shares port 443/TCP with the rest of HTTPS traffic, many studies tried to detect DoH in the network. Vekshin et al. [39] used a machine learning detection algorithm to detect DoH with 99% accuracy. With MontazeriShatoori et al. [30] achieving similar performance. However, these approaches focused only on web browser traffic streams. None of these techniques works for a single DoH traffic query.

The detection of DoH *in general* is still an unsolved challenge. Furthermore, some well-established security software and appliances [9, 36] rely on DNS queries to lawfully block access to certain sites at the host, enterprise, or ISP level. These security software work by filtering and blocking DNS based on rules. As DoH allows to bypass these network-based filters, security software can only block DoH by relying on domains and IP address [37]. The importance of accessing a comprehensive list of well-known DoH resolvers is then paramount for the correct functioning of this type of system.

DoH abuse was surveyed by Hynek et al. [22]. According to their study, DoH is already misused by malware creators and rogue users to hide their activities from network security defences. Furthermore, Hynek et al. defined several research challenges that need to be addressed to maintain network security at the current level. However, since these challenges are still not solved, the mass deployment of DoH has a significant impact on network security.

Deccio et al. [8] studied in 2019, the adoption of DoT and DoH by open resolvers. Their results show that the adoption was quite poor: From ~1.2 million open DNS resolvers found on the Internet, only 9 (0.007%) supported DoH. However, since this study first scanned DNS resolvers and then asked for DoT/-DoH, it missed those resolvers that handle only DoH requests. The study by Lu et al. [27], in 2019, also scanned well-known open DNS resolvers from the Internet and checked their DoH support, finding only 17 DoH resolvers.

The previous techniques for finding DoH resolvers are insufficient to accurately estimate the population of DoH resolvers on the Internet. Contrary to previous studies, we searched the entire IPv4 Internet address space looking for DoH capable resolvers. Our measurement also found DoH-capable open DNS resolvers, which are not publicly known. To the best of our knowledge, no previous research has tackled the measurement of the DoH resolvers population across the Internet.

3   Background on DoH and Its Security Impact

The design of the DNS over HTTPS (DoH) protocol started in 2017 and was adopted as RFC 8484 [18] in October 2018. Currently, there are two significantly different implementations. The first implementation, compliant with RFC 8484, uses the DNS binary "wireformat" [29] to encapsulate DNS messages in HTTPS (GET or POST methods). The second implementation uses DNS messages encoded in JSON format, as described by RFC 8427 [17]. The JSON data is transferred through the HTTPS GET method. Most global DNS providers support both implementations [24]. However, in practise, all DoH-enabled Web browsers and most other performance-orientated DoH clients use wireformat messages with the HTTPS POST method.

The security community knows that encrypting DNS is one of the most required Internet features to protect user privacy and security. This is because many surveillance and tracking organisations use DNS traffic to profile and monitor users [15], especially in countries without Internet freedom [5]. However, even though users can encrypt DNS traffic, the choice of DNS provider is still important because that provider will have access to the DNS traffic. Therefore, choosing a DNS provider that is trusted (encrypted or not) is a security decision.

This decision is also important because many protection tools rely on DNS, such as commercial DNS protection companies, DNS filters for policy enforcement in organisations, and antivirus tools. Moreover, many users choose and believe that using a third-party DNS resolver, instead of the DNS server provided by the local network or ISP, can better protect them from surveillance and monitoring [5].

The main difference between choosing a traditional DNS provider and an encrypted DNS provider is that for an encrypted DNS provider, the choice is largely dependent on the threat model of the user [11]. Users who suspect a domestic threat actor may prefer third-party encrypted DNS providers. But such provider may mean a dangerous centralisation of data.

The security problem of centralisation becomes more relevant as more users choose to use a small group of well-known DoH providers. Those providers have a privileged access to DNS requests for profiling and advertising [5]. These few providers are typically big tech giants and telecommunication providers (telcos), and effectively cut off smaller ISPs, small telcos, and even local administrators from accessing DNS. Such a centralisation affects some protection measures and puts our data in the hands of big tech companies.

Another essential aspect of DoH is that applications that enable DoH at the user level (such as a web browser) can bypass the DNS resolution of the Operating System (OS). This design decision was quite controversial, since resolving domain names is an action traditionally left to the OS due to its complexity and dependency on local policies.

Although users can choose any DoH resolver, most use the default settings in the applications. For instance, Firefox (since version 92.0) by default uses Cloudflare Inc.; the same as Opera Browser (from version 79.0.4143.50). Google Chrome offers a selection of five well-known DoH resolvers, but it can also detect if the system-defined DNS server supports DoH [3]. The decision to use the default settings has a double impact; first, it allows DoH to be used quickly and transparently by many users, and second, it allows these organisations to receive DNS requests by default.

One of the more important privacy features of DoH is to use HTTPS on port 443/TCP. This prevents to easily block DoH by using the port number. An alternative approach to block DoH may be to filter the domain in the SNI record using lists of well-known DoH resolvers. However, this filtering can be bypassed by (i) using a not well-known DoH provider, or (ii) by encrypting the SNI as described in the RFC draft [33]. Our research highlights the possibility of finding a not-so-well-known DoH provider.

In this security context, many questions regarding encrypted DNS, and DoH in particular, are asked. Is the number of DoH-enabled DNS servers growing? Who is implementing them? Can organisations successfully filter DoH by blocking the main third-party providers? Is the current centralisation of DoH providers counterbalanced by new providers? Can users trust small and unknown DoH resolvers?

4 Methodology

The longitudinal analysis is composed of two exploration moments. The first in April 2021 and the second between January and April 2022. Each exploration consisted on the following methodology steps: (i) create a list of well-known DoH resolvers; (ii) scan all the host on the IPv4 Internet looking for servers with port 443/TCP open; (iii) discover which of those IPs are DoH resolvers; (iv) verify that they answer DoH correctly and compile a final list; (v) enrich the IP addresses of the discovered DoH resolvers with information from threat intelligence services; (vi) verify the use of SNI; (vi) estimate the number of organisations providing DoH resolution services.

4.1 Creation of the Well-known DoH Resolvers Lists

Each list of well-known DoH resolvers was created by aggregating all the resolvers available in public lists, reports, documents, and academic papers. The DoH resolvers were verified using our custom Python script described in Subsect. 4.4. There are some lists of DoH resolvers on the Internet, including the AdGuard list [1], and the curl tool list [19]. However, those lists are not comprehensive. The list of 2021 is called Known2021, and the list of 2022 is called Known2022. Both were published for this paper [12,21]. The exact sources used to create them are included in each dataset. Moreover, IP addresses from Known2021 which was working at the time of creation the list of 2022 were also added to the Known2022.

In the Known2022 list, the domain names were given so we decided not to include domain names acquired by reverse DNS queries (PTR). Moreover, reverse DNS domain names may belong to hosting providers or Virtual Private Server (VPS) providers, such as Amazon, Microsoft, or Google, and thus do not provide information relevant to organisation responsible of the DoH resolver.

4.2 Scan of Port 443/TCP on the Internet

We scanned the entire IPv4 address space on the Internet looking for servers with open port 443/TCP. It was done by dividing the IPv4 address space into 255 uniform A-class ranges in order to distribute the load among several scanning nodes. Each range was scanned from a different cloud virtual machine. The masscan tool was used to perform the scan [13] with a fixed rate of 2,000 packets per second. Masscan was also configured to retry each IP address three times. These parameters were chosen to avoid losing packets and connection errors[1].

---

[1] Masscan command example: `masscan -p 443 --range 20.0.0.0--29.0.0.0 --rate 2000 --retries 3`.

These parameters were both used in 2021 and 2022. Moreover, in both scans we used masscan feature to scanned the IP addresses in random order and limit the amount of packets per second sent to service providers.

4.3 DoH Service Discovery

Once the list of IP addresses with open port 443/TCP was collected, it was necessary to find which ones implemented the DoH protocol. To automate the process, we created a DoH Nmap script [34]. Nmap is a well-known multifunctional network scanner that implements the Nmap Script Engine (NSE) for users to develop their own scripts [28]. Our DoH script checks all six different DoH methods: HTTP/1 with GET, HTTP/1 with POST, HTTP/1 with JSON, HTTP/2 with GET, HTTP/2 with POST, and HTTP/2 with JSON. This scan was executed using the same cloud setup as for the scan of port 443/TCP.

In order to speed up the process, the script only checks the HTTP status code in the response. It does not parse the whole HTTP response, nor does it make any more DNS resolution. Therefore, false positives may occur, which were later filtered in the DoH verification stage 4.4. This verification stage was implemented in a separated script, in order to keep the Nmap script as simple and fast as possible.

The Nmap script sends six DoH requests with a DNS query asking for the `example.com` domain. This domain is managed and recommended by IANA for testing purposes. For all six methods, the script sends the same query endpoint `/dns-query`[2]. This endpoint is specified in RFC 8484 for the HTTP GET and HTTP POST DoH methods. Since the JSON method is not standardised by the RFC, the endpoint of DNS JSON API might differ between providers. However, many well-known providers, such as Cloudflare [7], AhaDNS [2], and Quad9 [32] use the same endpoint as defined in the RFC.

The Nmap parameters used for this stage in 2021 differ from the ones used in 2022. In 2021 we used Nmap with the most aggressive timing template (parameter-T5), allowing for a faster scan. However, this timing template is prone to packet loss, reducing the service discovery efficiency. In 2022, we used the normal Nmap timing template (parameter -T3) in order to obtain higher-quality results, minimising the packet loss. The Appendices Sect. 8.2 shows examples of the Nmap invocations used in both scans.

Therefore, to make a fair comparison between the two scans on the number of computers found, we estimated the number of resolvers lost in 2021. For this we re-scanned all the 2022 DoH resolvers using both timing parameters. Results show that the more aggressive parameters of 2021 indeed caused packet loss and resulted in a smaller number of detected DoH resolvers. From the 4,354 DoH resolvers found with normal timing parameters, the aggressive parameters found between 2,851 and 3,213 in repeated scans. the relative efficiency, then, of the *DoH Service discovery* in 2021 was between 65.5% and 73.8% compared to 2022.

---

[2] DNS query endpoint example: `https://1.1.1.1/dns-query?name=example.com`.

4.4 DoH Resolver Verification

The list of DoH resolvers found in the previous stage was verified to correctly implement DoH, in order to remove false positives. We implemented a Python script (available in [34]), which tests the correct support of three DoH methods (GET, POST, and JSON) via HTTP/1 and HTTP/2. Contrary to the Nmap DoH script, the Python script can parse the DoH responses and check that they are valid DNS responses. This step filtered out IP addresses that responded "HTTP 200 OK" to DoH requests, but the response did not contain DNS data. The result of this stage is a list of confirmed and validated DoH resolvers and DoH methods that they support. The same verification method was performed for 2021 and 2022.

At the end of this step, and from now on, the verified list of DoH resolvers of 2021 is called Scan2021, and the one from 2022 is called Scan2022.

4.5 IP Address Enrichment

The list of DoH resolvers was further enriched with related information about the discovered IP addresses. The enrichment consists of: (i) the TLS certificates, (ii) information from WHOIS service, (iii) information from VirusTotal threat intelligence feeds including downloaded samples and URLs related to malware samples associated to the IP addresses, (iv) passive DNS data with the referred domain names for the IP, (v) DNS server type, (vi) DNS server version identification, and (vii) information about the web page if there was any. In addition, a *suspicious* flag was included in case the IP address has a high probability of being *relate to a phishing campaign* according to a set of indicators used by the Avast Web Shield feature. This set of indicators consists of keywords, domain name structure, lexical analyses results, domain hosting information, and other indicators.

The information for points (v) and (vi) was obtained using the DoH inherited capabilities of traditional DNS. In DoH, as in DNS, it is possible to create a CHAOS record class with TXT requests and issue it into a `version.bind` query to identify which type of DNS software the server is using. Finally, the TLS certificate data of the DoH resolvers was analysed to detect anomalies, such as expired or self-signed certificates. Given that the IP address enrichment was implemented late in 2021, it was applied only to the DoH resolvers in 2022.

4.6 Verification of SNI Usage

The main limitation of our DoH scan is that it may not find DoH resolvers on servers that host multiple services on the same IP address. In such cases, to be successful, the query needs to send a Server Name Indication (SNI), or `HTTP Host` header, or `HTTP/2 :authority` header. When our DoH scan found an IP with an open 443/TCP port but we could not find its proper domain name, we could not verify whether the DoH resolver works but requires valid SNI only or DoH is not supported at all.

To investigate the severity of this limitation, we estimated how many DoH resolvers were not found by performing a test with the Known2022 list of well-known DoH resolvers, which have a domain name. The methodology was: (i) For each well-known DoH resolver in the Known2022 list with an IPv4 address, get its domain name; (ii) do all the six types of DoH queries providing the SNI, or HTTP/1, or HTTP/2 host headers; (iii) get the IPv4 address for that domain; (iv) do all the six types of DoH queries providing only the IPv4 address, without any SNI or HTTP header. By using these steps we obtained the share of well-known DoH resolvers, that require domain name for successful connection.

4.7   Estimation of the Number of Organisations

To estimate the number of organisations providing DoH resolution services in the Scan2021 and Scan2022 list, the following methodology was used: First, extract the reverse DNS of all the IPs in the Scan2021 and Scan2022 lists. Second, extract the effective second-level domain name for each IP and consider each unique effective second-level domain an organisation. Third, if the effective second-level domain was not available, extract the WHOIS organisation name and consider each *WHOIS organisation* an organisation. Fourth, if the *WHOIS organisation* was not available group the IP addresses by their /16 CIDR and Autonomous System Number (ASN), and consider each unique group as an organisation as used by Deccio et al. [8].

4.8   Methodology Limitations

The used methodology presents limitations that needs to be properly discussed and accounted for proper interpretation of our results. Faster scanning rate used in Scan2021 for DoH Service Discovery stage described in Sect. 4.3, can increase the number of missed hosts (false negatives) in the 2021 results. Therefore, the Scan2021 totals were scaled up to account for the reduced efficiency in Sect. 5.2 for proper comparison. The change in methodology also increases the time needed to finish the Scan2022. However, we argue that each IP address was scanned only once; thus, the longer period does not affect the comparison.

The DoH methods were tested only using the /dns-query API endpoint which is the standard endpoint except for the JSON method (which is not standardised). Therefore, our methodology cannot discover any DoH resolver using other endpoints. Moreover, Internet-wide scans can be blocked by service providers, which reduces efficiency of the scanning over time. Additionally, the methodology could not find resolvers that require domain names (in SNI or HTTP headers) for successful connection. Given that, the methodology described does not produce an exhaustive list of DoH servers. Accounting for these considerations, we say that the amount of DoH servers found in this work can be interpreted as a lower bound.

The IP address enrichment mainly includes information from commercial databases and freely available information found on the servers. The DNS server version was extracted using non-standard DNS requests. Therefore, the results

Table 1. Summary of well-known DoH resolvers in the Known2021 and Known2022 lists.

	Known2021	Known2022	Intersection	Increase
Total Unique Servers UP	234	262	157	11.9%
Total Unique IPv4 Servers	131	144	86	9.9%
Total Unique IPv6 Servers	103	118	78	14.5%
Unique Autonomous Systems	52	59	42	13.4%
Unique Domain Names	110	109	67	−0.1%

showing the DNS server version only include a fraction of found resolvers able to answer those requests.

Given that the number of organisations was inferred using second-level domain names, and that these names can be shared across virtual servers hosted by the same cloud provider, this number should also be considered a lower bound.

5 Results

This section shows the results of the Scan2021 and Scan2022 lists, and a comparison of these results with the well-known lists of DoH resolvers. Then, the estimated number of organisations that provide DoH resolution services is presented. Finally, the results of the threat intelligence feeds associated with the DoH resolvers are shown.

5.1 Results of Creating Well-Known DoH Resolvers Lists

Regarding the creation of DoH resolver lists that are well known by the community, Table 1 shows a summary of the main differences. The total number of well-known DoH resolvers between 2021 and 2022 increased by ∼12%. From the DoH resolvers found in 2021, only ∼67% remained active in 2022 (157 IP addresses from 234 IP addresses). In 2022 there was a ∼10% increase of IPv4 addresses, with ∼65% of them appearing in 2021 and 2022. This means that ∼35% of the IPv4 addresses of well-known DoH providers disappeared in 2022. Similarly, there was an increase of ∼13.4% of unique ASNs, and a ∼14.5% increase in the number of unique IPv6 addresses in 2022.

The number of unique domain names slightly decreased due to the different methodology of their collection. Contrary to the well-known DoH resolver list of 2021, the 2022 list does not contain domain names acquired by reverse DNS queries (PTR) as discussed in Sect. 4.1.

5.2 Results of DoH Scans

The port scan of 2021 found 41,022,969 IP addresses with port 443/TCP open on the Internet. Of these, 930 were verified to be actual DoH resolvers. Given

Table 2. Features of IP addresses of the discovered DoH resolvers.

Feature	Scan2021	Scan2022
Total number of unique IP addresses	930 (100%)	4,354 (100%)
IP addresses with domains	679 (73%)	4,197 (96%)
IP addresses without domains	251 (27%)	149 (3%)
Unique SLD	171	657
Unique /16 prefixes*	115	39
Unique Autonomous System*	72	27
Estimated number of unique providers	243–286	684–696

* Number calculated only from IP addresses for which we could not obtain domain name.

that this scan used a set of aggressive Nmap parameters, thus reducing its efficiency, this number of DoH resolvers could be underestimated. See Sect. 8.2 for a description. Given our tests, it can be concluded that the number of DoH resolvers in April 2021 was actually between 1,173 and 1,241. Our Scan2021 list contains 930 IP addresses.

In 2022, the port scan found a total of 36,035,492 IP addresses with port 443/TCP open, which represents 87.84% of the IPs found during 2021. We attribute the smaller amount of IPs to the large variability in Internet scans (packet loss, bandwidth differences, geolocation filters, etc.) and not to an actual decrease of the amount of computers with port 443/TCP open. The number of verified IP addresses of DoH resolvers found during 2022 and contained in the Scan2022 list is 4,354. This number is ∼4.8 times larger than the amount of DoH resolvers of Scan2021.

Table 2 summarises the total number of resolvers discovered in both scans. In Scan2022, we found 4 times more unique IP addresses of DoH resolvers than during Scan2021. Even if the decreased efficiency of Scan2021 during the service discovery stage is taken into account, the difference in the discovered DoH resolvers with Scan2022 is statistically significant with p-value < 0.01. This result is based on a standard two sample one side T-Test for the mean of a distribution [38], and can be interpreted as a true increase in the effective number of public DoH resolvers.

Moreover, the number of organisations providing DoH resolution services in April 2022 is 2.5 times larger than in April 2021. Figure 1a shows that 474 DoH resolvers were found in both scans. However, almost half of the verified DoH resolvers found in Scan2021 were not found in Scan2022. Given that our methodology deals with the number of servers and does not track the DoH resolvers individually, we don't know if this DoH resolvers have been moved to another IP address or ceased operations. On the other hand, the decrease in the number of unique /16 prefixes can be explained by a slight increase in the efficiency of the IP enrichment process.

5.3 Comparison Between the Well-Known and DoH Scan Lists

The distribution of the DoH resolver IP addresses across all lists is shown in Sub-Figure 1b. Reading the figure from top to bottom, we find that 40 addresses

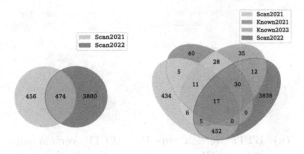

(a) Comparison between first and second scan

(b) Comparison with Well-known lists

Fig. 1. Venn diagrams of DoH resolver IP addresses distribution.

Table 3. Results of SNI Verification for finding DoH resolvers

Connected by	Successful	Successful %
Domain Name	93	100%
IP address	66	71%

are only present in the Known2021 list, 35 only in the Known2022 list, and 28 in both. None of these addresses was found in the Scan2021 or Scan2022. Meanwhile, five IP addresses present in the Known2021 list were only seen in that list, and 12 IPs present in the Known2022 list were only seen in that same list. From all IP addresses present in both well-known lists, 11 were found only during Scan2021, 30 only during Scan2022, and 17 were found during both scans. A total of 434 IP addresses were only found in Scan2021, 3,838 were only found in Scan2022, and 474 were present in both scans. But 452 of these IP addresses were not present in any of the well-known lists. Most DoH resolver IP addresses did not appear on any of the well-known lists. However, the well-known lists are evolving. There are 11 servers that were in Scan2021, which were not present in the Known2021 list but are included in the Known2022 list. However, only five of these servers appear to be still active on the Scan2022. The rest may have been moved to another address or stopped operations.

5.4 Results of the SNI Verification

The results of the SNI verification are shown in Table 3. In the Known2022 list of DoH resolvers, there are only 93 that have a domain and an IPv4 address. It can be seen that of those 93, around 30% of the well-known DoH resolvers require an SNI or HTTP header to work successfully. This means that our Scan2021 and Scan2022 of DoH resolvers are a lower bound, and theoretically there could be *at least* 30% more DoH resolvers on the Internet. It should also be considered

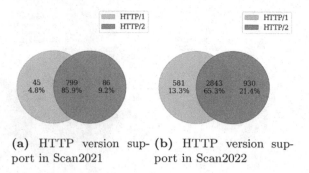

(a) HTTP version support in Scan2021

(b) HTTP version support in Scan2022

Fig. 2. Venn diagrams of HTTP version support across DoH resolvers.

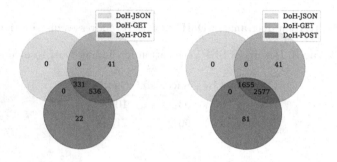

(a) DoH methods support in Scan2021

(b) DoH methods support in Scan2022

Fig. 3. Venn diagrams of supported methods across DoH resolvers.

that this test was performed on well-known resolvers, in which the use of an SNI may be different from others.

5.5 Capabilities of the DoH Resolvers Found

Since we have queried each DoH resolver multiple times, we can analyse the methods supported by the DoH resolvers. Figure 2 shows the HTTP version support. It can be seen that most DoH resolvers on both scans support both HTTP versions. In the 2022 scan, we notice an increased share of HTTP/2-only or HTTP/1-only resolvers with respect to the total.

The methods supported in the DoH resolvers are shown in Fig. 3. Most resolvers support the RFC 8484 compliant versions. Some resolvers support only DoH-GET or only DoH-POST, even though the RFC 8484 specifies that the resolver must implement both methods. The IP addresses of those DoH resolvers supporting only DoH-GET are the same in both scans. The JSON approach is supported by around one-third of all resolvers. None of the resolvers supports the JSON approach exclusively.

Table 4. DNS software identification of found DoH resolvers in Scan2022

Name	#	%	Name	#	%
a) empty	113	26.0	g) AkamaiVantioCacheServe	10	2.3
b) Unbound	88	20.2	h) Q9	8	1.8
c) PowerDNS	77	17.7	i) NominumVantioCacheServe	8	1.8
d) unknown	68	15.6	j) SDNS	1	0.2
e) Bind	48	11.0	k) I-Evolve DNS	1	0.2
f) Dnsmasq	13	3.0			

Table 5. Share of DoH provider categories

Name	#	%	Name	#	%	Name	#	%
a) unknown	280	41.9	e) other	24	3.5	i) security	16	2.3
b) DNS/ISP/Cloud	145	21.7	f) finance	22	3.2	j) government	11	1.6
c) personal webpage	92	13.7	g) software-provider	18	2.6	k) privacy	10	1.5
d) industry&business	34	5.1	h) education	16	2.3			

5.6   DNS Server Identification

Table 4 shows the results of the DNS software identification for all the DoH
resolvers that answered the specialized version query correctly (only 435 or 10%).
However, most of them replied with an empty string response. The Scan2022
IP addresses were also queried using traditional unencrypted DNS over port
53/UDP. We used `nslookup` software to query the Google.com address with a
10 s timeout and from 4,354 only 1,176 (~27%) resolvers supported legacy DNS.
We repeated the test three times with similar results.

5.7   Who Operates the DoH Resolvers

A total of 657 unique domain names from TLS certificates were analysed to find
out who is offering the DoH resolution services. At first, we tried to use the
domain classification service NetStar [31], however, only a negligible portion of
domain names were classified. Therefore, we visited each of them manually via
the web browser and classified domain names into one of 11 categories: **DNS/IS-
P/Cloud**—DNS providers, Internet service providers, hosting providers and
cloud providers; **industry&business**— manufactures, e-shops, and other types
of trade business; **finance**—banks, investment advisers, and insurance companies; **software-provider**—companies providing software development services;
education—universities, research institutes, and libraries; **security**—computer
security companies; **government**—governments and governmental organisations; **privacy**—companies that focus on privacy such as VPN providers and
privacy enhancement software; **personal webpage**—domain names hosting personal web site portfolio or personal blogs; **other**—companies and institutions

Table 6. Share of TLS certification authorities across the found DoH resolvers in Scan2022. CA stands for Certification Authority, IIJ stands for Internet Initiative Japan Inc., ERDC stands for Engineer Research and Development Centre

CA Name	#	%	CA Name	#	%	CA Name	#	%
a) Let's Encrypt	1,703	39.1	d) Blue Coat	106	2.4	g) IIJ	63	1.4
b) ZeroSSL	1,654	38.0	e) Sectigo ltd	103	2.3	h) WoTrus CA ltd	36	0.8
c) other	545	12.5	f) Apple Inc.	100	2.3	i) ERDC	36	0.8

that did not fall into any other category; and **unknown**—domain names did not host website, or that could not be categorised it.

The share of each category among DoH providers is shown in Table 5. We were not able to categorise most of the resolvers. The web page hosted on these resolvers could not identify the owner of the website, or the server did not serve web pages. When the web server responds with a web page, it usually shows a login page. Around 20% of the domain names in the category "unknown" showed a log-in page on AdGuard Home DNS resolver. Two of the servers were misconfigured and showed a directory structure of private project files.

For identification, we did not use information directly from the domain names. Although some domain names suggested that the server is operated by an individual, we also categorised it into the "unknown" category since we could not verify it. For most domain names, we could not even estimate the owner, since sometimes they seemed to be randomly generated, such as hhgasdygqwueysbjadasghds.com or kasldjflkasdjf.xyz.

The second most common category is DNS/ISP/Cloud providers, which offer DoH. A significant share of these companies might be expected since these companies usually provide DNS resolution as part of their services. The third most common category is private web pages. Individuals operate these resolvers, and the website usually contains the portfolio of a freelance software developer, or it was a personal blog.

5.8   TLS Certificate Analysis

We analyse the TLS certificate data of found DoH resolvers in the Scan2022. The share of certificate authorities is written in Table 6. The most common certification authorities across found resolvers are Let's Encrypt and ZeroSSL. Most of the DoH resolvers provided valid and trusted certificates. We found 193 (4.5%) IP addresses with expired certificates. More than 57% of those expired certificates were certified by the Let's Encrypt Certification Authority. The expiration date of the invalid certificates was mainly 2021 and 2022 (in 81% of the cases). The certificates of 5 resolvers expired before the DoH standardisation in 2018.

5.9   Threat Intelligence Results

From the 4,354 IP addresses in the Scan2022 list surveyed with threat intelligence tools, 1,502 are considered *suspicious for phishing* according to the Avast Web Shield tool. This, does not mean that the IPs are malicious, but that they were associated to phishing activities during the studied period 2021–2022. Moreover, 105 of these addresses contain at least one reference to a site that the VirusTotal service considers to be malicious. VirusTotal also found 27 of them were used as a source of *downloaded malware samples*, that is they directly hosted malware.

6   Discussions on the Results

The results presented in the previous section confirm that the deployment of public DoH resolvers is increasing. The number of well-known resolvers in 2022 increased by 12% compared to 2021. However, only 67% of the well-known DoH resolvers in 2021 remained active in 2022.

A similar phenomenon is observed with the results of Scan2021 and Scan2022, where only 9.8% of the IPv4 addresses were found in both scans. A possible explanation for this discrepancy is that the missing servers were for testing purposes and, as such, have been moved to a definitive address or stopped operations. Furthermore, 88% of the DoH resolvers found in Scan2022 were not previously seen by any list, nor Known2021, Known2022, or Scan2021.

Approximately 55% of the well-known DoH resolvers in 2022 were not found in the Scan2022 performed in January 2022. This suggests that the combination of errors in finding open port 443/TCP on the Internet and the rate at which the DoH resolvers are added is enough for our methodology to miss half of them.

The fact that so many DoH resolvers could not be found one year later and that the number of DoH resolvers is increasing speaks of a great dynamism and casts doubts about the effectiveness of these kind of lists for filtering DoH resolvers or blocking them.

By comparing the results of the HTTP versions supported by the discovered resolvers of the two scans, as shown in Fig. 2, there were some changes in the support of the HTTP version. There is a decrease in the percentage of DoH resolvers that support both HTTP/1 and HTTP/2; however, we can also see an increase in HTTP/1 only resolvers, even though the RFC does not recommend it due to performance reasons.

Only 21% of the DoH resolvers found in Scan2022 belong to DNS/ISP/cloud providers, while 44.6% belong to unknown organisations, and 12.7% belong to personal web pages. Almost 35% of the IP addresses found in our study present indicators related to phishing campaigns, and 27 of 4,354 IPs were a source of malware. We expect the domain resolution service to be under constant security reviews, either if it is unencrypted through standard DNS or encrypted using DoH or some other protocols. The occurrence of DoH resolvers' IP addresses associated with malware or phishing shows that users' security and privacy could be already at risk or that these resolvers are misused for malicious purposes.

Leaving aside which of those groups can be considered trusted DoH resolvers, 77.3% of the certificates of DoH providers in Scan2022 were given by free services such as Let's Encrypt. This heterogeneity gave space for threat actors to hide and abuse DoH in ways that we will discover in the future.

The impact of widespread use of DoH by threat actors is still a matter of debate. DoH could be used with malicious intentions ranging from bypassing DNS filters, to use known DNS techniques for command and control and exfiltration, but with encrypted capacity. A very shallow treat intelligence analysis showed signs of malicious activities in a small, yet considerable percentage of the servers. Even if the question of which kind of malware is using DoH for communication or is hosted in DoH resolvers was not addressed in this work, the list of public DoH resolvers found could help the community to spot existing threats.

7   Conclusion

The choice of a particular DoH resolver can have an impact on the privacy and security of the user and the security policy of administrators. It can allow users to evade filters, censorship and surveillance; but then again it can deny security tools the opportunity to protect users, while proving threat actors a better tools to cover their tracks.

We studied the deployment of DoH on the Internet and evaluated their characteristics to answer: is the number of DoH resolvers growing? and who is implementing them?

This research is a longitudinal analysis (2021, 2022) studying the number of DoH resolvers on the Internet, how they implement DoH and their features as organisations.

Results show that there are at least 59% more DoH resolvers on the Internet in April 2022 than in April 2021, showing that the number of public DoH resolvers is growing. There are ∼28 times more public DoH resolvers on the Internet than those well-known in the community in April 2022. More than 95% of the resolvers found were unknown to the community and ∼30% were found to be suspicious.

The current practise to block DoH traffic is based on blocklists of IP addresses or SNI (e.g., Sophos [36] products). The blocklist of well-known DoH providers in April 2022 is slightly larger than the one from 2021, with a small intersection between them (28%). But we expect the lists to grow in the future, since there are many organisations trying the technology and developing new services. Measurements show that the number of unknown resolvers on the Internet and their rate of change are large enough to assume that the efficiency of blocklists could be very low, especially when someone intentionally wants to avoid the block. Thus, further studies are required to prevent breaches of security policies, malware abuse, or DoH data exfiltration.

The discovery of DoH resolvers linked to suspicious or malicious activities should put the information security community in alert, to better study and understand the threats posed by these resolvers.

From the user's privacy and security point of view, the selection of the DoH resolver is important, but it depends on the threat model of the user. While for most users a local DoH resolver may suffice, users in countries with Internet surveillance policies may prefer a third-party DoH resolver. However, these users will need to make the choice carefully, taking into account the organisation providing the service, the centralisation and surveillance by the third-party, the performance, and the possibility that the DoH resolver may be related to malicious activities. Moreover, as the DoH service is now controlled by applications, users can lack the ability to choose which DoH resolver to use, effectively bypassing any local protection based on filters implemented at the network level.

By knowing the population, distribution and characteristics of the public DoH resolvers on the Internet, we are better prepared to face the challenges of these new technologies.

Acknowledgment. This work was partially supported by Avast Software, the Ministry of Interior of the Czech Republic—project No. VJ02010024: "Flow-Based Encrypted Traffic Analysis," and also by the Grant Agency of the CTU in Prague—grant No. SGS20/210/OHK3/3T/18 funded by the MEYS of the Czech Republic.

8   Appendix

8.1   Ethical Considerations

Part of our research involved technical actions that require an ethical explanation and support.

Horizontal Port Scanning. of the Internet has many implications. Although in general considered an ethical practice [23], we analyse the implications of our actions. First, our horizontal port scan sent 3 packets per port to each IP address with a rate limit. This amount of packets is not enough to consume the bandwidth of any device, nor to force errors in the services, especially since our scan did not close the TCP handshake. Therefore, the technical risk of errors or problems in devices due to our scan is negligible. Higher rates of scanning or frequency of the scans, i.e. weekly scans can pose some threat to some services availability, and thus we limited the methodology accordingly. Some honeypot devices on the Internet detected our scan and report the source IP as an attacker; however, since the IP address was not really attacking, there was an impact of having the IP in block lists for some days.

The action of verifying the DoH protocol required us to connect to all ports 443/TCP and try to find out if they spoke DoH or not. It required the request for the TLS protocol handshake and then the DoH protocol. We measure the technical impact by testing our Nmap script against our own servers, and no server was impacted by our script, was taken down, or slowed in any way. We consider the script safe and with very low impact. The script made 6 connections in total to each server.

The action of analysing DoH resolvers implied a more thorough analysis of the responses and information found about this server on the Internet. We only performed this action with the few (order of thousands) found DoH resolvers and we continually verified that they were not affected by our DNS requests.

We consider our techniques to have very low impact on the servers scanned and without reason to suspect that our actions affected the servers contacted in any way.

Publishing the List of DoH Resolvers. can significantly impact the citizens of oppressive countries that use DoH to avoid surveillance or access censored websites from the free world. The oppressive government can misuse two outcomes of our research: 1) the list of DoH resolvers can be used for DoH blocking to enforce DNS surveillance and censorship, and 2) the methodology for creation and updates of such a list.

Nevertheless, as shown in our research, the IP addresses of DoH resolvers constantly change, making the efficiency of IP-based filtering limited as discussed in the Sect. 7. Regardless of the described methodology, we argue that the methodology presented in this work is not novel nor technically complex, and uses of the freely available tools. An oppressive regime interested in DoH blocking already could have its own DoH scanning and detection infrastructure.

Besides, DoH does not entirely bypass mass censorship or surveillance. For example, domain names transferred in TLS SNI are still visible and used by large censorship systems [6]. Therefore citizens living under an oppressive regime still need to use other privacy-preserving technologies such as Virtual Private Networks to avoid censorship.

Given that, we do not consider our research would contribute to oppression by authoritarian countries or decrease the Internet privacy. Instead, our study provides essential findings about DoH resolvers worldwide and points out security concerns arising from anonymous DoH resolvers.

8.2   Nmap Configuration

The Scan2021 used Nmap *insane* timing template and 1 maximum number of retries, to minimise scanning time.

```
nmap -n -iL data/ips.txt -v -T 5 --max-retries 1 -d -Pn -p443
--script=/data/dns-doh-check
```

The Scan2022 used Nmap *normal* timing template to minimise the number of packets lost.

```
nmap -n -iL data/ips.txt -v -d -Pn -p443 --script=/data/dns-doh-check
```

See Nmap timing templates for detailed timeout information of each mode. https://nmap.org/book/performance-timing-templates.html.

References

1. AdGuard software Limited: Adguard known DNS providers. https://kb.adguard.com/en/general/dns-providers. Accessed 25 May 2021
2. AhaDNS: DNSover https (DoH). https://ahadns.com/dns-over-https/
3. Baheux, K.: A safer and more private browsing experience with secure DNS (2020). https://blog.chromium.org/2020/05/a-safer-and-more-private-browsing-DoH.html. Accessed 17 Jan 2021
4. Borgolte, K., et al.: How DNS over HTTPS is reshaping privacy, performance, and policy in the internet ecosystem. In: Proceedings of TPRC47: The 47th Research Conference on Communication, Information and Internet Policy 2019. Elsevier BV (2019). https://doi.org/10.2139/ssrn.3427563
5. Callejo, P., Cuevas, R., Vallina-Rodriguez, N., Cuevas Rumin, A.: Measuring the global recursive DNS infrastructure: a view from the edge. IEEE Access **7**, 168020–168028 (2019). https://doi.org/10.1109/ACCESS.2019.2950325
6. Chandel, S., Jingji, Z., Yunnan, Y., Jingyao, S., Zhipeng, Z.: The golden shield project of china: A decade later-an in-depth study of the great firewall. In: 2019 International Conference on Cyber-Enabled Distributed Computing and Knowledge Discovery (CyberC), pp. 111–119 (2019). https://doi.org/10.1109/CyberC.2019.00027
7. Cloudflare Inc: DNS over https – using JSON. https://developers.cloudflare.com/1.1.1.1/encryption/dns-over-https/make-api-requests/dns-json/
8. Deccio, C., Davis, J.: DNS privacy in practice and preparation. In: Proceedings of the 15th International Conference on Emerging Networking Experiments And Technologies, pp. 138–143. CoNEXT 2019, Association for Computing Machinery (2019). https://doi.org/10.1145/3359989.3365435
9. DNSFilter: DNSfilter AI-powered DNS security. https://www.dnsfilter.com/. Accessed 15 May 2022
10. Doan, T.V., Tsareva, I., Bajpai, V.: Measuring DNS over TLS from the edge: adoption, reliability, and response times. In: Hohlfeld, O., Lutu, A., Levin, D. (eds.) Passive and Active Measurement, pp. 192–209. Springer International Publishing, Cham (2021)
11. Fernando Gont: Introduction to DNS Privacy (2019). https://www.internetsociety.org/resources/deploy360/dns-privacy/intro/
12. García, S., Čejka, T., Valeros, V.: Dataset of DNS over HTTPS (DoH) Internet Servers (2021). https://doi.org/10.17632/ny4m53g6bw.2
13. Graham, R.: Masscan: the entire internet in 3 minutes (2013). https://blog.erratasec.com/2013/09/masscan-entire-internet-in-3-minutes.html
14. Grothoff, C., Wachs, M., Ermert, M., Appelbaum, J.: Toward secure name resolution on the internet. Comput. Secur. **77**, 694–708 (2018). https://doi.org/10.1016/j.cose.2018.01.018
15. Guha, S., Francis, P.: Identity trail: covert surveillance using DNS. In: Borisov, N., Golle, P. (eds.) PET 2007. LNCS, vol. 4776, pp. 153–166. Springer, Heidelberg (2007). https://doi.org/10.1007/978-3-540-75551-7_10
16. Herrmann, D., Banse, C., Federrath, H.: Behavior-based tracking: exploiting characteristic patterns in DNS traffic. Comput. Secur. **39**, 17–33 (2013). https://doi.org/10.1016/j.cose.2013.03.012
17. Hoffman, P.E.: Representing DNS Messages in JSON. RFC 8427 (2018). https://doi.org/10.17487/RFC8427. Accessed 25 May 2021

18. Hoffman, P.E., McManus, P.: DNS Queries over HTTPS (DoH). RFC 8484 (Oct 2018). https://doi.org/10.17487/RFC8484

19. curl DNS over HTTPS. https://github.com/curl/curl/wiki/DNS-over-HTTPS, Accessed 25 May 2021

20. Hynek, K., Cejka, T.: Privacy illusion: Beware of unpadded DoH. In: 2020 11th IEEE Annual Information Technology, Electronics and Mobile Communication Conference (IEMCON), pp. 621–628 (2020). https://doi.org/10.1109/IEMCON51383.2020.9284864

21. Hynek, K., García, S., Bogado, J., Cejka, T., Vekshin, D., Wasicek, A.: Dataset of DNS over https (DoH) internet servers (2022). https://doi.org/10.5281/zenodo.6517360

22. Hynek, K., Vekshin, D., Luxemburk, J., Cejka, T., Wasicek, A.: Summary of DNS over https abuse. IEEE Access **10**, 54668–54680 (2022). https://doi.org/10.1109/ACCESS.2022.3175497

23. Jamieson, S.: The ethics and legality of port scanning. Tech. rep., SANS Institute (2001). https://www.sans.org/white-papers/71/

24. Jerabek, K., Rysavy, O., Burgetova, I.: Measurement and characterization of DNS over HTTPS traffic (2022). https://doi.org/10.48550/ARXIV.2204.03975

25. Klein, A., Pinkas, B.: DNS cache-based user tracking. In: Proceedings 2019 Network and Distributed System Security Symposium. Internet Society (2019). https://doi.org/10.14722/ndss.2019.23186

26. Lioy, A., Maino, F., Marian, M., Mazzocchi, D.: DNS security. In: Proceedings of the TERENA Networking Conference, pp. 22–25 (2000)

27. Lu, C., et al.: An end-to-end, large-scale measurement of DNS-over-encryption: How far have we come? In: Proceedings of the Internet Measurement Conference, pp. 22–35. IMC 2019, Association for Computing Machinery, New York, NY, USA (2019). https://doi.org/10.1145/3355369.3355580

28. Lyon, G.F.: Nmap network scanning: The official Nmap project guide to network discovery and security scanning. Insecure, Com LLC (US) (2008)

29. Mockapetris, P.: Domain names - implementation and specification. RFC 1035 (1987). https://doi.org/10.17487/RFC1035. Accessed 25 May 2021

30. MontazeriShatoori, M., Davidson, L., Kaur, G., Habibi Lashkari, A.: Detection of doh tunnels using time-series classification of encrypted traffic. In: 2020 IEEE Intl Conference DASC/PiCom/CBDCom/CyberSciTech, pp. 63–70 (2020). https://doi.org/10.1109/DASC-PICom-CBDCom-CyberSciTech49142.2020.00026

31. NetSTAR Inc.: Netstar url/ip lookup. https://incompass-branch.netstar-inc.com/urlsearch. Accessed 15 May 2022

32. Quad9 Foundation: DoH with quad9 DNS servers. https://www.quad9.net/news/blog/doh-with-quad9-dns-servers/

33. Rescorla, E., Oku, K., Sullivan, N., Wood, C.A.: TLS Encrypted Client Hello. Internet-Draft draft-ietf-tls-esni-13, Internet Engineering Task Force (2021). https://datatracker.ietf.org/doc/html/draft-ietf-tls-esni-13

34. Sebastian, G., Hynek, K., Vekshin, D., Cejka, T., Wasicek, A.: DoH research scripts for cvut/cesnet/avast doh project (2022). https://github.com/stratosphereips/DoH-Research. Accessed 25 Jan 2022

35. Siby, S., Juarez, M., Diaz, C., Vallina-Rodriguez, N., Troncoso, C.: Encrypted DNS privacy? a traffic analysis perspective. In: Proceedings 2020 Network and Distributed System Security Symposium. Internet Society, Reston, VA (2020). https://doi.org/10.14722/ndss.2020.24301

36. Sophos Ltd: DNS over https (DoH) for web security. https://support.sophos.com/support/s/article/KB-000039056?language=en_US

37. Sophos Ltd: DNS over https (DoH) for web security. https://support.sophos.com/support/s/article/KB-000039056?language=en_US. Accessed 15 May 2022

38. The SciPy community: Scipy two sample t-test (2022). https://docs.scipy.org/doc/scipy/reference/generated/scipy.stats.ttest_ind.html. Accessed 15 May 2022

39. Vekshin, D., Hynek, K., Cejka, T.: DoH Insight: Detecting DNS over HTTPS by Machine Learning. In: Proceedings of 15th International Conference on Availability, Reliability and Security. ARES 2020, ACM, New York, NY, USA (2020). https://doi.org/10.1145/3407023.3409192

Equivocal URLs: Understanding the Fragmented Space of URL Parser Implementations

Joshua Reynolds[1,2(✉)], Adam Bates[2], and Michael Bailey[2,3]

[1] New Mexico State University, Las Cruces, USA
jr1@nmsu.edu
[2] University of Illinois at Urbana-Champaign, Champaign, USA
batesa@illinois.edu
[3] Georgia Institute of Technology, Atlanta, USA
mbailey@gatech.edu

Abstract. Uniform Resource Locators (URLs) are integral to the Web and have existed for nearly three decades. Yet URL parsing differs subtly among parser implementations, leading to ambiguity that can be abused by attackers. We measure agreement between widely-used URL parsers and find that each has made design decisions that deviate from parsing standards, creating a fractured implementation space where assumptions of uniform interpretation are unreliable. In some cases, deviations are severe enough that clients using different parsers will make requests to different hosts based on a single, "equivocal" URL. We systematize the thousands of differences we observed into seven pitfalls in URL parsing that application developers should beware of. We demonstrate that this ambiguity can be weaponized through misdirection attacks that evade the Google Safe Browsing and VirusTotal URL classifiers. URL parsing libraries have made a tradeoff to favor permissiveness over strict standards adherence. We hope this work will motivate the systemic adoption of a more unified URL parsing standard–enabling a more secure Web.

Keywords: URL · Parsing ambiguity · Web security

1 Introduction

Uniform Resource Locators (URLs) play a crucial role in the Internet, originating in the early 1990's as a standardized addressing and parameterization system for the Web [21,40]. Since then, URLs have been overhauled to clarify their syntax with relation to relative locators [32], IPv6 addresses [33], Punycode for non-ascii hostnames [25], and the broader notion of a Uniform Resource Identifier (URI) [18–20,27] Further, the Web Hypertext Application Technology Working Group (WHATWG), a consortium of major Web browser vendors, has defined its own "living" URL standard [7]. Unfortunately, adherence to these standards has not been strict, leading to inconsistencies across implementations.

V. Atluri et al. (Eds.): ESORICS 2022, LNCS 13556, pp. 166–185, 2022.
https://doi.org/10.1007/978-3-031-17143-7_9

Attackers have taken note of these inconsistencies and increasingly abuse URL parsing differences [9, 35, 42, 46, 55–57, 59]. In these exploits, attackers were able to trigger application-layer and network-layer vulnerabilities with URLs parsing to a legitimate resource for one parser (e.g., a URL security classifier, a server endpoint) but a malicious resource for their victim (e.g., a browser, a server-side cache, etc.).

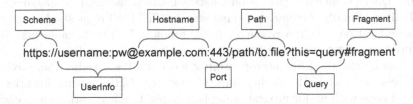

Fig. 1. URL Syntactic Elements URLs use delimiters between each syntactic element. We find that URL parsers handle illegal characters and delimiters differently, yielding inconsistent results.

While anecdotal demonstrations of these "equivocal" URLs have appeared in industry reports, to date there has not been a systematic study of the root cause of this problem – inconsistent implementation of URL parsing. In this work, we measure the implementation space of URL parsing by analyzing the behavior of fifteen URL parsers. We focus on ambiguities in hostnames because of their potential impact at the network layer – sending clients with different URL parsers to completely different network locations. We generate and test thousands of fuzzing inputs to compare the level of agreement among parsers. Unfortunately, we find that disagreement is widespread, with little consensus on how to handle edge-case URLs. We then categorize the error sources that cause some URLs to only be parsable by certain parsers – or, worse, URLs that yield differing DNS-compliant hostnames for different parsers. We systematize these error sources into seven hostname equivocation pitfalls.

To highlight the security implications of URL hostname equivocation, we go on to demonstrate how newly-discovered errors can allow equivocal URLs to evade URL classification. In contrast to prior work that has exclusively targeted server-side parsing errors at the application layer, we demonstrate that client-side URL security classifiers are also vulnerable. Specifically, *we demonstrate that URLs with ambiguous hostnames can trick the popular Google Safe Browsing and VirusTotal URL classifiers into issuing an incorrect threat classification.*

Fixing these inconsistencies among parsers would require community-wide agreement on a parsing standard whose strict implementation would be a breaking change. We perform preliminary measurements demonstrating the real-world compatibility incentive for URL parsers to avoid strict standardization in favor of being as permissive as possible in what they accept. We hope this work motivates the systemic adoption of a more unified URL parsing standard.

2   Related Work

URLs are composed of syntactic sections separated by delimiters. Figure 1 shows the syntactic segments that make up a URL. We focus in this work only on absolute URLs using the HTTP and HTTPS *Schemes* [3]. Following the scheme is the optional *UserInfo* section, a *Hostname* or IP address, and an optional TCP *Port*. The *Path* commonly reflects a hierarchical naming system within a Web domain. *Queries* can carry parameters, between which "&" and ";" are suggested as delimiters. Finally, *Fragments* are not sent in HTTP(S) requests, but indicate a specific location within a resource. A '%' followed by two hexadecimal digits can encode an octet otherwise forbidden in paths, queries, or fragments.

Driven by the need for interoperability with the Web, today there exists a broad ecosystem of URL parsing implementations. URL parsing libraries are standard issue with major programming languages. Further, various web clients, command line utilities, and web servers all implement their own URL parsers. The security of the Web depends, in part, on the basic assumption that all of these parsers will resolve a given URL in the same way.

2.1   Exploiting Human Misinterpretation of URLs

URLs can be made misleading to users, who fall prey to attacks like phishing. When users misunderstand the guarantees of HTTPS [10,29–31,43,53], fail to observe the Fully Qualified Domain Name (FQDN) of a URL [13,26,58], or are unable to parse a URL [11,49], attackers may convince them to reveal secrets by impersonating a legitimate organization. Phishing has been widely studied, and a host of mitigations have been designed to protect users from falling victim to these attacks. These include automatically phishing URL classifiers [12,14, 15,34,41,47,50,50,61], phishing detection [44,52], user education [22,37–39,51], and improved user interfaces [10,11,29–31,44,49,53].

2.2   Exploiting Machines' Inconsistent URL Parsing

Unfortunately, phishing-like URL misinterpretations can also occur in software. URL parsing differences gained widespread attention in 2009 following Carretoni and di Paola's demonstration of HTTP Parameter Pollution attacks [24]. This attack abused differences in the parsing of URL query parameters between end-points and security mechanisms, enabling attackers to bypass input filtering and sanitization checks. Subsequent prior works developed tools to automatically detect HTTP parameter pollution vulnerabilities in websites [16,17,23]. While query parameter parsing differences can have serious implications for application-layer security, they cannot affect the authenticity of the web server; in contrast, we demonstrate that hostname parsing differences enable equivocation about web server identity. Further, as we will show in this work, lessons learned from parameter parsing attacks have not been applied to ambiguities URL hostname parsing.

More recently, several Blackhat talks and Common Vulnerabilities and Exposures (CVEs) have leveraged URL parsing ambiguity to perform *server-side* attacks. Tsai showed how inconsistent strategies for normalizing paths containing "../" allowed access to forbidden resources when combined with the ill-defined syntax for URL path parameters [57]. A bug in the Google Chrome browser on iOS in 2018 allowed websites to use the HTML 5 history API to change the origin of the tab and run in other Web origins [55]. Wang et al. showed they could misdirect OAuth redirections and evade allowlist filters using URL parsing discrepancies [59]. Kettle used the fact that browsers accept both backslashes and forward slashes as path delimiters to convince websites to poison their own HTML cache entries [35]. Ahmed reported a similar error in an Node package in CVE-2018-3774 [9]. Tsai and Leitschuh both used URL parsing ambiguities to trick server-side middleboxes to forward protocol-smuggled requests to resources they should not have been able to contact. [42,56] Muñoz and Tsai reported parsing errors to curl which were patched [46,56]. While these exploits provide anecdotal evidence of individual parsing problems, in this work we systematically explore the ecosystem of URL parsing ambiguities, testing many parsers to create a catalog of inconsistencies that point to a systemic issue in the ecosystem. Further differentiating us from prior work, we are the first to demonstrate that such attacks are possible on *client-side* URL classifiers, directly enabling enabling user attacks like phishing.

3 Methodology

To date, URL parsing exploits have been reported in the context of specific vulnerabilities and parsing implementations, but it is not clear to what extent inconsistencies in URL parsing are widespread. To gain a more comprehensive understanding of the ecosystem, we consider a diverse set of fifteen parsers that span standard libraries, web servers, and command line tools. Parsers were drawn from libraries written in popular languages (Java, Go, Ruby, JavaScript, Python, PHP, Perl, C/C++), tools (wget, curl), and web servers (Apache, NGINX); a complete description of these parsers can be found in Table 4 of Appendix A.

3.1 "Ground Truth" Reference Parsers

An important first step in our analysis is to establish a reasonable baseline for how parsers should behave. Naturally, one such baseline should be RFC 3986 [20] that defines the syntax for uniform resource identifiers (URIs), of which URLs are a subset. RFC 3986 provides a formal grammar, but not an implementation, so we used the grammar to create our own reference implementation for absolute URL parsing in Python3. We note that RFC 3986 rejects non-ASCII input and expects any disallowed bytes to be properly escaped following to the procedure in RFC 3987 [27].

In contrast, an equally valid baseline to consider is how major web software vendors handle URLs in their day-to-day experience, including URLs with non-ASCII characters. For such a baseline, we look to the WHATWG's "living" URL standard [7] informed by browsers day-to-day interaction with non-ACII URLs. WHATWG implicitly defines a standard for URL parsing by releasing a parsing algorithm along with a reference implementation of their parsing algorithm in JavaScript. We include this as our second reference parser.

3.2 Test Input Enumeration

For each of the fifteen parsers, we then applied a large set of URL test inputs and recorded each parser's response. We focus specifically on parsing discrepancies in the hostname field. To do so, we started with a completely valid URL containing a hostname that was consistently parsed across all implementations. We then applied three mutually exclusive sets of mutations to this URL to enumerate a large corpus of test inputs. Each mutation inserts one to four bytes in the middle of the hostname field, as described below. Rather than using random fuzzing, we iterated over these sets in their entirety, resulting in a total of 98,425 test cases.

P1. The first input set inserted every possible octet from 0–255, which includes all standard ASCII codes (0–127) and extended ASCII codes (128–255). This test set probes parsers' permissiveness of invalid input as well as handling of duplicate delimiters.

P2. The second input inserted all 65,536 possible combinations of two octets. This test set included edge cases such as valid unicode characters, multiple delimiters, and unmatched UTF-16 surrogate pairs.

P3. The third input set inserted each of the 32,634 valid Unicode code points listed in the Unicode Data list of the Unicode Character Database [6]. Each valid unicode character is a minimum of three bytes when encoded with UTF-8. This test set exhaustively probes parsers' handling of unicode characters.

Along with different parsing logic, our test parsers were also written in a variety of languages and software environments with different implementations of character strings, file I/O, etc. For each parser's testing apparatus, we took great care to ensure that the core parsing logic handled the exact same bytes for each test input. Mostly, this entailed paying close attention to how different string data types might apply automatic character conversions, although we note that in practice these differences are another potential source of parsing ambiguity. For two parsers we were forced to cast our payload URLs into string types that cannot hold arbitrary bytes to be compatible with the library. We have noted this conversion in our full parser list in Table 4 of Appendix A.

4   Results

We now report on the results of our analysis in terms of *agreement* between parsers on each of the test inputs. We consider two axes of agreement – consistency with the reference parsers, and overall consistency across all fifteen parsers – for the *UserInfo*, *Host*, *Path*, *Query*, and *Fragment* segments of each test input. To ensure a conservative analysis, we adopt a generous definition of what it means for two parsers to agree on a URL's parse. If both parsers rejected the URL with an error, we consider this as agreement regardless of whether the same error is thrown. We also ignore whether the parser spuriously included the preceding delimiter as part of each syntactic segment (e.g., the '/' in ``/index.html'' or the '?' in ``?id=0&pg=42''). Because DNS is not case-sensitive, we also ignore hostname case in the parser output.

Table 1. Agreement with RFC 3986 Parser We show agreement with our RFC reference parser across URLs perturbed by input sets P1, P2,and P3 as well as overall. Parsers are sorted by their overall agreement with the standards of RFC 3986. Ruby and PHP follow the RFC with a high degree of consistency, but the other parsers are clearly not matching RFC 3986's grammar.

Parser	Overall	P1 (256)	P2 (65,536)	P3 (32,635)
rfc3986	100.0%	100.0%	100.0%	100.0%
Ruby uri	99.95%	100.0%	99.93%	100.0%
PHP parse_url	97.79%	94.14%	96.7%	100.0%
Python3 urllib.urlparse	90.67%	82.81%	86.06%	100.0%
WHATWG NodeJS	59.74%	83.2%	83.73%	11.38%
Python3 furl	51.62%	51.95%	75.89%	2.88%
Golang goware/urlx	30.08%	44.92%	45.01%	0.0%
Java.net.URI	28.74%	49.61%	42.94%	0.05%
Golang net/url	26.61%	47.66%	39.78%	0.0%
libcurl4-openssl	23.19%	44.92%	34.66%	0.0%
wget	22.61%	44.53%	33.78%	0.0%
nginx	7.44%	32.03%	11.05%	0.0%
Apache Portable Runtime	7.2%	32.03%	10.69%	0.0%
Perl URI	6.68%	31.64%	9.92%	0.0%
NodeJS Legacy	4.94%	26.95%	7.32%	0.0%

4.1 Disagreement with Reference Parsers

After testing each parser on all test inputs, we then sorted them by their level of agreement with each of the reference parsers. Agreement with RFC 3986 is given in Table 1. Only three of the parsers are often in agreement with the RFC – Ruby URI (99.9%), PHP's *filter_var()* plus *parse_url()* functions (97.79%), and Python3's urllib.urlparse (90.67%). However, even among these high-agreement parsers, we observed differences on how strict or lenient they were on certain inputs. For example, Ruby URI allows some octets outside the permitted character set such as low ASCII bytes in the query string. PHP was sometimes more strict and rejects some hostnames that could not be used with the DNS but are allowed by RFC 3986 containing characters like tilde and asterisk. However, PHP does allow a fragment to contain another illegal # delimiter. Python3 was more lenient, parsing URLs with illegal low ASCII bytes like 0×10 (newline) in the hostname.

The WHATWG reference parser agreed with RFC 3986 just 59.74% of the time, while the remaining ten parsers agreement ranges from 51.62% (Python3 furl) to as low as 4.94% (NodeJS Legacy). Differences arise from these parsers choosing to escape unicode characters in URLs before parsing them. The way each of these parsers "fixes" these otherwise invalid URLs ranges from subtly to dramatically inconsistent with RFC 3987 [27].

Table 2. Agreement with WHATWG Parser We show agreement with the WHATWG reference parser across URLs perturbed by input sets P1, P2,and P3 as well as overall. Not only are parsers not following RFC 3986, they are also not following the WHATWG's alternative parsing algorithm that handles international characters in URLs. The WHATWG parsing algorithm disagrees with most of these tested parsers most of the time.

Parser	Overall	P1 (256)	P2 (65,536)	P3 (32,635)
WHATWG NodeJS	100.0%	100.0%	100.0%	100.0%
Python3 urllib.urlparse	66.95%	97.27%	94.51%	11.38%
PHP parse_url	58.09%	78.91%	81.27%	11.38%
Ruby uri	59.78%	83.2%	83.8%	11.38%
rfc3986	59.74%	83.2%	83.73%	11.38%
Python3 furl	49.77%	51.56%	73.11%	2.88%
NodeJS Legacy	36.1%	27.73%	9.98%	88.62%
Golang goware/urlx	21.67%	28.91%	32.11%	0.64%
Java.net.URI	19.9%	32.81%	29.42%	0.69%
Golang net/url	19.19%	33.98%	28.36%	0.64%
libcurl4-openssl	17.92%	35.55%	26.46%	0.64%
wget	17.57%	35.16%	25.93%	0.64%
nginx	15.19%	46.09%	22.32%	0.64%
Apache Portable Runtime	15.17%	46.48%	22.28%	0.64%
Perl URI	14.58%	46.09%	21.72%	0.0%

The WHATWG standard aims to both "align" and "obsolete" RFC 3986 and RFC 3987 [7], but other parsers do not seem to be following this lead. Agreement with the WHATWG parser is given in Table 2. Overall, the test parsers agreed more often with the older RFC than with the WHATWG's living standard.

In fact, the RFC 3986 parser and the three high-agreement parsers from the previous test again boast the highest agreement with WHATWG.

Parsers are not following the WHATWG standard when handling Unicode. Recall that the P3 set tests parsers handling of UTF-8 encoded Unicode characters. Interestingly, even though one of the goals of the WHATWG parser is to standardize handling of non-ASCII URLs, agreement on the P3 input set is very poor. In fact, with the exception of NodeJS Legacy (88.62%), most parsing agreement on P3 only negligibly improves with WHATWG over RFC 3986, which does not support Unicode at all.

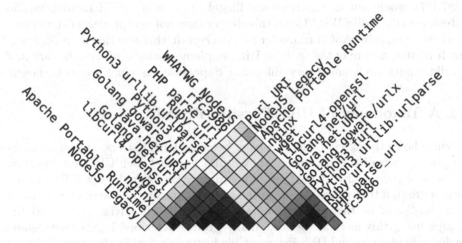

Fig. 2. Pairwise Agreement Among Tested URL Parsers Intersections of parsers are shaded according to their overall agreement on a linear gradient from white (0% agreement) to black (100% agreement). Having grouped agreeing parsers, but we present two dark clusters of high correlation. One is centered around RFC 3986 and the other included Java, Golang, libcurl4, NGINX, Apache, and wget. The Furl, Perl, NodeJS Legacy, and WHATWG parsers do not closely match any other tested parser.

4.2   Disagreement Among All Parsers

Since the parsers do not consistently follow either reference implementation, it may be the case that parsing behavior is dictated by some other hidden standard or common practice. This would explain the Table 2 results in which many parsers disagree with the WHATWG parser at a very similar rate for the P3 test set (0.64% agreement). To investigate, we next calculated the pairwise agreement between each of the fifteen parsers for the combined test set of 98,445 URLs. This resulted in a total of 105 agreement calculations for each of the unique parser pairings.

We illustrate the agreement among all these pairs in Fig. 2, with *darker* shading indicating *more* agreement and *lighter* shading indicating *less* agreement. The two dark triangles towards the bottom of the figure indicate two families of similarly behaving parsers. To the right-hand side, it can be seen that Ruby, Python3 urllib.urlparse, and PHP strictly adhere the RFC 3986 reference parser. The cluster to the left-hand side consists of Java.net.URI, the Golang parsers, NGINX, Apache, wget, and libcurl4. Like the first cluster, their agreement is not perfect, but is highly similar. Upon investigation, this cluster behaves differently from RFC 3986 because it accepts invalid octets into the hostname without throwing an error; this approach allows for internal consistency because such octets are not delimiters, and the illegal bytes could be converted to Punycode later according to RFC 3987. In contrast, RFC 3986, or even the more permissive RFC 3987 [27], would automatically escape illegal bytes or reject URLs with invalid octets. Finally, unlike WHATWG, this cluster does not accept illegal octets lower than the acceptable ASCII character range. Overall, this experiment underscores the fractured nature of the space of URL implementations, where arbitrary and invalid inputs are handled very differently depending on which parser is chosen.

5   A Taxonomy of URL Parsing Pitfalls

Having shown the extent of disagreement between URL parsers, we now consider the root causes of this disagreement. We first grouped each URL test input by the sets of parsers that agreed on its hostname; for example, two URLs would form a group if they caused errors in the same six parsers and were parsed to the same hostname by the remaining nine. From our 98,445 URLs, we created 134 groups using this method. Because many groups described inputs that results exclusively in errors and DNS-incompatible hostnames, we further down-selected to 17 groups for which there were at least two DNS-compatible hostnames in the results set. We then manually inspected each group to understand the cause of the inconsistency.

Ultimately, we arrived at a taxonomy of just seven potential URL parsing pitfalls that account for the all of the hostname equivocation inconsistencies observed in our experiments. We describe each pitfall in the remainder of this section, providing examples of each in Table 3. We also report on the effects of these equivocal URLs on the Chrome and Firefox browsers, as well as their embedded JavaScript engines. Browser design choices in this space will prove important in our examples of malicious equivocal URLs in Sect. 6.

5.1   Seven Pitfalls of URL Parsing Causing Hostname Equivocation

Pitfall 1–Null Bytes. In C, strings are traditionally terminated by a null byte. In higher-abstraction languages, the length property is often explicitly tracked, allowing strings containing null bytes. This technicality enabled Marlinspike's 2009 equivocations of subject names in TLS certificates [45].

URL parsers behave differently due to this same split when faced with a URL containing an illegal null byte. URL 1 in Table 3 is an equivocal URL built on this discrepancy. It places a null byte in the UserInfo section of the URL. The Golang,

Table 3. Equivocal URL Examples with Parsing Results In part **I**, eight examples of equivocal URLs are provided that, when parsed, yield at least two different DNS-compatible hostnames. Square brackets in these examples enclose a hex representation of octet(s) for clarity. In part **II**, parsing results for each example are provided. A, B, C and D indicate which option from part **I** each parser returned. Capital "ERR" signifies that the indicated parser threw an error for that example. Lowercase "err" indicates the parser did not throw an error, but extracted a hostname that is not compatible with the DNS. The only parser to throw an error for every example here is Java's URI parser.

	I. Equivocal URL Examples		
	Equivocal URL Example	Option A	Option B
U1.	https://n.pr[0x00]@e.gg	e.gg	n.pr
U2.	https://n.pr\@e.gg	e.gg	n.pr
U3.	https://n.pr][e.gg	e.gg	n.pr
U4.	https://n.pr#@e.gg	n.pr	e.gg
U5.	https://n.pr%2ee.gg	n.pr.e.gg	n.pr
U6.	https://n.pr[0x0A]e.gg	n.pre.gg	n.pr
U7.	https://n.pr[0xDD9ADCBD]e.gg	n.xn–pre-hwf8l.gg	n.xn–pre-bda9o3gf.gg
U8.	https://n.pr[0xC4B0]@e.gg	n.xn–prie-swc.gg	n.xn–pre-tfa3h.gg
		C: n.prie.gg	D: n.xn–pre-tfa3x.gg

II. Results of Parsing Each Equivocal URL

Parser	U1	U2	U3	U4	U5	U6	U7	U8
NodeJS WHATWG	A	B	ERR	A	A	A	ERR	A
RFC 3986	ERR	ERR	ERR	ERR	err	ERR	ERR	ERR
Golang net/url	ERR	ERR	err	A	ERR	ERR	err	err
Golang goware/urlx	ERR	ERR	ERR	A	ERR	ERR	err	C
Java.Net.URI	ERR	ERR	ERR	ERR	ERR	ERR	ERR	ERR
PHP parse_url	ERR	ERR	ERR	A	ERR	ERR	ERR	ERR
Python3 urllib	A	A	A	A	ERR	err	ERR	ERR
Python3 furl	A	A	err	A	ERR	err	err	err
NodeJS legacy	A	B	B	A	B	B	A	A
Ruby	ERR	ERR	ERR	ERR	err	ERR	ERR	ERR
wget url.c	B	A	err	A	A	ERR	err	err
libcurl4	B	A	err	A	err	ERR	err	err
Perl URI	A	A	err	A	A	err	B	B
Firefox	-	B	ERR	A	A	A	ERR	A
JS in Firefox	A	B	ERR	A	A	A	ERR	D
Chrome	-	B	ERR	A	A	A	ERR	A
JS in Chrome	A	B	ERR	A	A	A	ERR	D
Apache	B	A	err	A	err	err	err	err
NGINX	ERR	err	err	B	err	ERR	ERR	ERR

Java, PHP, and Ruby parsers correctly reject URL 1 as a malformed URL. On the other hand, Perl, PHP, and Python3 are willing to parse this URL and consider the null byte as part of the UserInfo. This set of parsers therefore considers this URL to point to "e.g.g". C-language based parsers including libcurl4, wget, and the Apache Portable Runtime (APR) truncate URLs to the first null byte because of their built-in null-terminated string assumptions. However, because NGINX uses a custom string implementation to track string length, it is not subject to this pitfall despite being written in C.

Pitfall 2–Backslash Correction. URL 2 in Table 3 uses another illegal byte in a UserInfo section. Browsers have a particular treatment for the illegal \ character, making themselves ambivalent to the difference between Windows and *nix file path separators. When a backslash is present in a UserInfo section, it is treated as if it were a delimiter signalling the start of the URL path. This means that a backslash will be corrected to a forward slash when pasted into a browser. Illegal backslashes cause either an error or are treated as a part of the UserInfo in all parsers except the browsers. Both Firefox and Chrome change the backslash to a delimiting forward slash, which makes what was formerly a UserInfo string into the hostname. RFC 3986 considers this an invalid URL because a backslash is not allowed anywhere. The WHATWG parser is more permissive, and accepts the UserInfo section as-is. Several other parsers either allow or automatically encode the backslash and accept the URL. This pitfall has so far been exploited several times [9,42,59].

Pitfall 3–IPv6+ Address Syntax. Square brackets are only allowed in hostnames to enclose IPv6 addresses or future IP versions. By inserting a balanced, but not matching set of brackets into the hostname, we convince the python3 parser and the legacy NodeJS parser to provide two different, DNS-compatible hostnames. For the example we gave in URL 3 of Table 3, Python3 starts the hostname after the brackets, and NodeJS's legacy parser truncates the hostname at the brackets.

Pitfall 4–Illegal Extra Delimiters. Some parsers allow ambiguity by allowing prohibited extra delimiters such as allowing an "@" in a UserInfo or multiple "#" characters. URL 4 in Table 3 is an example of a URL with a duplicate delimiter. Many of the parsers we tested allowed this incorrect choice. Fragments in particular were very permissive. The pitfall was also part of Tsai's exploit [56].

Pitfall 5–Overeager Percent Decoding The official way to include arbitrary bytes in URLs is to URL-encode them in triplets of the form %FF with a percent sign followed by two case-insensitive hex digits. These digits are allowed in hostnames, but will not be compatible with the DNS as such. The example in URL 5 of Table 3 encodes one of the otherwise allowed periods in the hostname with percent encoding. When parsed, browsers and Perl convert this automatically into a period. The legacy JavaScript parser simply terminates the hostname at the percent-encoded section.

In context of HTTP requests, there are further complications regarding percent decoding that we will explore later on. We exploit the fact that JSON also uses percent-encoding to encode arbitrary bytes in strings to introduce ambiguities into API calls in Sect. 6.

Pitfall 6–Low ASCII Bytes. Another set of illegal octets that parsers treat differently in a UserInfo section is the set of octets lower than any allowed character. As demonstrated by URL 6 in Table 3, allowing the ASCII newline, $0 \times 0A$, yields different interpretations. Golang, Java, and Ruby's parsers correctly reject URL 6 as a malformed URL. All other parsers accept this URL, and either ignore or treat the newline byte as part of the UserInfo with the true host being "e.g.g". However, in Perl, the newline is ignored and the UserInfo is pre-pended to the hostname.

Pitfall 7–Automatic Punycode Conversion. While some parsers simply reject invalid URLs, others try to fix them. Some of these parsers use Punycode [25] to encode arbitrary bytes in hostnames within the syntactic bounds rules of the DNS. We found that some parsers disagreed on how they would perform this conversion. Example URLs 7 and 8 in Table 3 were encoded in several different ways, depending on the parser. Example 8 is unique among our examples in that it resolves to four different DNS-compatible domain names depending on the parser. These problems manifested for Unicode issues such as how to convert an arbitrary character to lowercase, or how to deal with only half of a surrogate pair. In general, users of URL parsers would do well to consult the Unicode Security Guide [60]. This pitfall was among those exploited by Tsai [56].

6 Misdirection Attacks with Equivocal URLs

While we have demonstrated widespread inconsistencies in URL parsing behavior, we have not yet demonstrated whether these equivocal URLs represent an ongoing security concern. We now show how equivocal URLs can be weaponized by an attacker who can anticipate the parsing libraries in use on a victim's system. Specifically, we demonstrate how equivocal URLs can cause false negatives in the Google Safe Browsing and VirusTotal URL classifier services [5,8] through the creation of URLs that parse to a legitimate host in the security software but a malicious host in the victim software.

Threat Model: In this work, we consider an adversary whose goal is to cause a victim program to fetch a malicious resource by making it appear to a URL classifier as if the URL came from a trusted domain. The adversary can take advantage of differences in URL parsing behavior between the victim program and the URL classifier protecting it. In this example, the victim uses classifiers provided by VirusTotal (VT) [8] and Google Safe Browsing (GSB) [5] to evaluate URLs before requesting a resource using a URL. We consider that the victim may either (1) visit the Web interface of these classifiers or (2) programmatically access the respective API endpoints.

6.1   Responsible Disclosure

We informed both services of these ambiguities in October of 2021. Unfortunately, we have not received any response beyond a request to forward our report as a feedback ticket. We promptly complied with the request, but these ambiguities persist in these systems.

6.2   Equivocal URLs vs Google Safe Browsing

To demonstrate equivocal URLs' ability to cause a false negative, we first need a known-malicious URL from GSB to prove equivocal URLs can have this real-world effect. Fortunately, GSB has a test vector URL which is always flagged as malware "https://malware.testing.google.test/testing/malware/*". Leveraging Pitfall 5 (over-eager percent decoding), we are first able to craft an equivocal URL that convinces the GSB API to classify a URL as clean even though it parses to the test vector when loaded in a browser. Consider the following equivocal URL, remembering that %2F encodes an ASCII forward slash:

```
http://letsencrypt.org%2F@malware.testing.google.test/testing/malware/*
```

GSB's API passes URLs in JSON. JSON's specification allows percent-encoding bytes in strings. Therefore, when this URL arrives at GSB, GSB has no way of knowing whether the %2F is intended as a literal delimiter, or a percent-encoded portion of the UserInfo. GSB chooses the former, and reports this URL is clean in both its web interface and API. However, this syntactically valid URL will lead the other clients we tested to target malware.testing.google.test. We also discovered that this API performs the same "backslash correction" as browsers. Interestingly, a percent-encoded backslash (%5C) in the UserInfo will be decoded and then trigger backslash correction in the API. As an example of this backslash correction, the following URL is also declared safe by GSB's API:

```
http://letsencrypt.org%5C@malware.testing.google.test/testing/malware/*
```

However, the Web interface does not have this eager percent decoding functionality nor backslash correction. But, knowing this behavior we can craft an equivocal URL which the Web interface declares safe, but would send a browser to the malware test vector. Because the Web interface fails to account for the pitfall we called "backslash correction" in browsers, it evaluates the benign host while a browser would fetch the malware:

```
https://malware.testing.google.test\testing\malware\*@letsencrypt.org
```

The fractured landscape of parsers creates a dilemma for security systems like GSB. No matter how GSB parses an equivocal URL, there exist other parsers that would extract a different hostname. We present some potential mitigation strategies in Sect. 8.1.

6.3   Misdirecting VirusTotal

Using a similar approach, we are also able to create an equivocal URL that fools VirusTotal's URL scanning web endpoint and API. For the benign domain, we again used "letsencrypt.org". For a malicious domain, we referenced urlHaus's public list of online URLs serving malware [4]. The URL we selected served malware flagged by fifteen of VirusTotal's 90 constituent scanners.

Inputs to VirusTotal's API are form-encoded in a post request, and thus similar ambiguity exists for their endpoint as to whether or not percent-encoded delimiters should be reconstituted. We take advantage of this to create a URL that uses "overeager percent decoding" to cause VirusTotal to report our malicious URL as totally clean. The following URL is a false negative for both the Web interface and the API. The actual malicious host used has been redacted.

`http://letsencrypt.org%2Fdocs%2F@[redacted]/LS.exe`

In testing other equivocal URL techniques, we observed that we were able to pacify some of the original fifteen alerting constituent classifiers. This suggests that they each are vulnerable to equivocal URLs in their own way – depending on the parsing or matching strategy they use to compare URLs. Adding any UserInfo string pacified two scanners, suggesting that this may have evaded an internal blocklist. A third classifier was pacified if that UserInfo contained a null byte. Three others appear to perform backslash correction. The inconsistency among constituent classifiers when faced with a URL change is cause for concern.

7   Backwards Compatibility Constraints on Strict URL Parsing

Blindly mandating strict parser adherence to a new or existing URL parsing standard would likely break some services. While a full measurement of what services would be impacted by stricter URL parsing at Web scale would require its own paper, we can give some preliminary estimations here for the upper bound of the impact. We do this by repurposing several public data sources to learn how often services' URLs use non-ASCII characters. Ecosystem-wide standardization of URL parsing would affect some fraction of these services, making them an approximate upper bound on the potential impact.

We first find the prevalence of Punycode enabling non-ASCII characters in domain names. Among the Alexa Top Million [1] list, 0.16% (1,606) of domains use Punycode [25] to encode non-ASCII hostnames. Of the 7.8 billion TLS certificates available in Censys's database [28], 0.41% (32,342,256) use Punycode in their subject or alternative domain names.

We also surveyed ~350 million URLs sampled uniformly and randomly from the approximately 3 billion URLs in Common Crawl's January 2022 URL Index [36]. Of these URLs, 0.04% contained unicode characters that were left to the client to parse when making an HTTP(S) request. By contrast, 9.95%

of these URLs had escaped their problematic bytes themselves with percent-encoding. These Web applications, it seems, have elected to perform percent encoding for themselves. Perhaps these applications have an understanding of the compatibility risks of relying on an arbitrary client's URL parser.

While the overall percentage of services that would be affected by unified parsing standardization appears to be low, this still implicates a large number of services at Web scale. At the same time, it preliminarily appears that a path forward to consistent URL parsing standard is possible with minimal impact on existing services.

8   Discussion

In the space of URL parsing, we have become too liberal in what we are willing to accept. Jon Postel's "Robustness Principle" [48] promotes compatibility at the expense of correctness. In this case, the cost of compatibility also gives rise to concerns of security and authenticity on the Web. As noted in an 2018 IETF draft [54], Jon Postel wrote his famous remark on conservative sending and liberal receiving immediately following this sentence:

> "While the goal of this specification is to be explicit about the protocol there is the possibility of differing interpretations [48]."

Perhaps to call these departures from URLs' specification "differing interpretations" is too generous, but the fact remains that the today's ecosystem of URL parsers is in broad disagreement with itself. Standardizing the myriad URL parsing libraries, which are baked into nearly every piece of network software, would be a massive undertaking requiring the cooperation of many stakeholders. Such uniformity might not be backwards compatible. Certainly, efforts like the WHATWG's URL living standard are evidence of a desire to eventually correct URL ambiguity. However, even this formidable consortium of leading Web browser creators has not brought uniformity.

Some parsers even document the potential for inconsistency with other parsers. PHP's *parse_url* function documentation includes the following warning:

> "**Caution** *This function may not give correct results for relative or invalid URLs, and the results may not even match common behavior of HTTP clients.*"[2]

The documentation then proceeds to explain a method to enforce stricter parsing, which we made use of, meaning that the default behavior is even more permissive than what we report. A developer who did not read the documentation would be unaware of these edge-cases.

8.1   Mitigation

Individual parsers are limited in their ability to correct these systemic inconsistencies alone. For the present, we recommend that security tools analyzing

URLs take note of the potential ambiguity that exists between their filter's URL parsers and the URL parsers of clients they protect. URL classifiers should align their URL parsing algorithm with the parsers in downstream programs they protect. For example, Google Safe Browsing's main purpose is to flag Web sites unsafe to visit in a browser, and could benefit from aligning its parser with the WHATWG's parser. A URL classifier with multiple downstream parsers could even create a multi-parser to simultaneously parse equivocal URLs with multiple parsers, allowing a URL classifier to check each potential interpretation.

Coming to a community-wide consensus on the "correct" way to parse URLs would provide a path out of ambiguity in the longer term. We could apply a strict interpretation of RFC 3986's grammar [20], and fail closed. Some parsers even include optional flags to perform stricter parsing. Our preliminary investigation in Sect. 7 suggests that the services depending on the particulars of these edge-case parsing implementations may be uncommon. Therefore, while strict parsing would break backwards compatibility, its actual impact may be minimal.

Adopting stricter parsing does not have to mean following RFC 3986. A reasonable alternative is the regularly updated, "living" WHATWG standard [7]. It was designed from the beginning to work with non-ASCII URLs and enjoys considerable support from key players in the Web browser space. Unfortunately, its "living" nature may perpetuate ambiguity by changing over time, while some implementations remain static.

8.2   Limitations and Future Work

This work does not test all extant URL parsers, nor does it exhaustively exercise every code path within each parser to find every inconsistency. Rather, we demonstrate the existence of parsing ambiguity across a variety of parsers and demonstrate how that ambiguity can be used to obscure a URL's destination. Given the level of inconsistency we observed, we are confident that further testing would only magnify the disagreements between URL parsers. For example, further disagreement would likely be found across parsing library versions as well as between browsers' parsers and the WHATWG's reference implementation.

Based on our results, we are likely to keep facing new attacks in this space because significant ambiguity exists from parser to parser. Our analysis focused on domain name ambiguities, but ambiguities throughout the URL have the potential to cause future application-specific issues similar to prior vulnerabilities described in Sect. 2.2. A black-box service's URL parser could be fingerprinted and exploited based on its edge-case behaviors.

Future work may expand this set of URL parsing pitfalls and their effects on more systems. Likewise the parsing and filtering behaviors of popular antivirus tools, network intrusion detection systems, and middleboxes should be checked for blind spots where equivocal URLs are concerned. Further measurement should be done to design a consistent standard that all parsers could adopt with minimal impact to existing services.

9   Conclusion

Given the fragmented implementation space of URL parsers, we warn that parsing inconsistencies continue to be an active attack vector. Because of the ubiquity of Web connectivity in modern applications, developers would do well to be aware of and plan for URL parser discrepancies until uniformity is achieved.

Acknowledgements. This work was partially supported by the NSF under grants GR0005987 and CNS 1955228. We thank our anonymous peer reviewers as well as Zane Ma, Joshua Mason, Kent Seamons, Jay Misra, Kaylia M. Reynolds, Deepak Kumar, and Paul Murley for their feedback and suggestions.

Appendix A: Tested Parser Details

Table 4. Parsers Tested We tested our URLs in these 15 URL parsers. While most parsing libraries accepted input types containing arbitrary bytes, Java's URL parser and the fURL parser both required the sequence of bytes to be converted to a string type. We followed Python3's default behavior to throw an error upon encountering bytes it cannot decode with UTF-8, and Java's default behavior to replace bytes not valid in UTF-8 with marker character 0xEFBFBD. Where larger systems like NGINX are listed, we extracted URL parsing functionality from source code.

Parser name	Version	Language	Category	Parser input type	Type coercion applied
RFC 3986	–	Python 3.8.10	Control	bytes	none
WHATWG Reference Parser	–	NodeJS 10.19.0	Control	JS Buffer	none
Python3 urllib	–	Python 3.8.10	Built-In Libraries	bytes	none
parse_url with filter_var()	–	PHP 7.4.3	Built-In Libraries	PHP string	none
NodeJS Legacy	–	NodeJS 10.19.0	Built-In Libraries	JS String	none
Java.Net.URI	–	openjdk 17.0.1	Built-In Libraries	Java String	UTF-8 decoding
Ruby uri	0.10.0	ruby 2.7.0p0	Built-In Libraries	Ruby String	none
Golang net/url	–	Golang 1.13.8	Built-In Libraries	golang-string	none
libcurl4	7.68.0	C	Unix Tools	char*	none
wget	1.21	C	Unix Tools	char*	none
perl URI	–	Perl 5.30.0	Unix Tools	perl-string	none
Apache Portable Runtime	httpd-2.4.48	C/C++	Open Source Parsers	char*	none
NGINX	1.20.0	C	Open Source Parsers	char* & length	none
fURL	2.1.3	Python 3.8.10	Open Source Parsers	Python3 string	UTF-8 decoding
Golang goware/urlx	dcd04f6	Golang 1.13.8	Open Source Parsers	golang-string	none

References

1. Alexa top 1,000,000 sites. http://s3.amazonaws.com/alexa-static/top-1m.csv.zip
2. parse_url. php.net (2021)
3. Uniform resource identifier (uri) schemes. IANA (2021)
4. Urlhaus. abuse.ch (2021)
5. Google safe browsing (2022). https://safebrowsing.google.com/
6. Unicode character database: Unicodedata.txt (2022). https://www.unicode.org/Public/UCD/latest/ucd/UnicodeData.txt
7. Url: Living standard. Web Hypertext Application Technology Working Group (2022)
8. Virus total (2022). www.virustotal.com
9. Ahmed: url-parse package return wrong hostname. Hackerone (2018)
10. Akhawe, D., Felt, A.P.: Alice in warningland: a large-scale field study of browser security warning effectiveness. In: 22nd {USENIX} Security Symposium ({USENIX} Security 2013) (2013)
11. Albakry, S., Vaniea, K., Wolters, M.K.: What is this url's destination? empirical evaluation of users' url reading. In: Proceedings of the 2020 CHI Conference on Human Factors in Computing Systems (2020)
12. Aljofey, A., Jiang, Q., Qu, Q., Huang, M., Niyigena, J.P.: An effective phishing detection model based on character level convolutional neural network from url. Electronics 9, 1514 (2020)
13. Alsharnouby, M., Alaca, F., Chiasson, S.: Why phishing still works: user strategies for combating phishing attacks. Int. J. Hum.-Comput. Stud. 82, 69–82 (2015)
14. Althobaiti, K., Rummani, G., Vaniea, K.: A review of human-and computer-facing url phishing features. In: 2019 IEEE European Symposium on Security and Privacy Workshops (EuroS&PW). IEEE (2019)
15. Anitha, A., Gudivada, K.S., Rakshitha Lakshmi, M., Kumari, S., Usha, C.: Identifying phishing websites through url parsing (2019)
16. Athanasopoulos, E., Kemerlis, V.P., Polychronakis, M., Markatos, E.P.: ARC: protecting against HTTP parameter pollution attacks using application request caches. In: Bao, F., Samarati, P., Zhou, J. (eds.) ACNS 2012. LNCS, vol. 7341, pp. 400–417. Springer, Heidelberg (2012). https://doi.org/10.1007/978-3-642-31284-7_24
17. Balduzzi, M., Gimenez, C.T., Balzarotti, D., Kirda, E.: Automated discovery of parameter pollution vulnerabilities in web applications. In: NDSS (2011)
18. Berners-Lee, T.: Rfc 1630: universal resource identifiers in www: a unifying syntax for the expression of names and addresses of objects on the network as used in the world-wide web (1994)
19. Berners-Lee, T., Fielding, R., Masinter, L.: Rfc 2396: uniform resource identifiers (uri): generic syntax (1998)
20. Berners-Lee, T., Fielding, R., Masinter, L.: Rfc 3986: uniform resource identifier (uri): generic syntax (2005)
21. Berners-Lee, T., Masinter, L., McCahill, M.: Rfc 1738: uniform resource locators (url) (1994)
22. Canova, G., Volkamer, M., Bergmann, C., Reinheimer, B.: Nophish app evaluation: lab and retention study. In: NDSS workshop on usable security (2015)
23. Cao, Y., Wei, Q., Wang, Q.: Parameter pollution vulnerabilities detection study based on tree edit distance. In: Chim, T.W., Yuen, T.H. (eds.) ICICS 2012. LNCS, vol. 7618, pp. 392–399. Springer, Heidelberg (2012). https://doi.org/10.1007/978-3-642-34129-8_37

24. Carettoni, L., di Paola, S.: Http parameter pollution. OWASP AppSec Europe (2009)
25. Costello, A.: Rfc 3492: Punycode: a bootstring encoding of unicode for internationalized domain names in applications (idna) (2003)
26. Dhamija, R., Tygar, J.D., Hearst, M.: Why phishing works. In: Proceedings of the SIGCHI conference on Human Factors in computing systems (2006)
27. Duerst, M., Suignard, M.: Rfc 3987: internationalized resource identifiers (iris) (2005)
28. Durumeric, Z., Adrian, D., Mirian, A., Bailey, M., Halderman, J.A.: A search engine backed by Internet-wide scanning. In: 22nd ACM Conference on Computer and Communications Security (2015)
29. Felt, A.P., et al.: Improving SSL warnings: comprehension and adherence. In: Proceedings of the 33rd annual ACM conference on human factors in computing systems, pp. 2893–2902 (2015)
30. Felt, A.P., et al.: Rethinking connection security indicators. In: Twelfth Symposium on Usable Privacy and Security ({SOUPS} 2016) (2016)
31. Felt, A.P., Reeder, R.W., Almuhimedi, H., Consolvo, S.: Experimenting at scale with google chrome's ssl warning. In: Proceedings of the SIGCHI Conference on Human Factors in Computing Systems (2014)
32. Fielding, R.: Rfc 1808: relative uniform resource locators (1995)
33. Hinden, R., Carpenter, B., Masinter, L.: Format for literal ipv6 addresses in url's. Technical report, RFC 2732 (1999)
34. Jain, A.K., Gupta, B.B.: PHISH-SAFE: URL features-based phishing detection system using machine learning. In: Bokhari, M.U., Agrawal, N., Saini, D. (eds.) Cyber Security. AISC, vol. 729, pp. 467–474. Springer, Singapore (2018). https://doi.org/10.1007/978-981-10-8536-9_44
35. Kettle, J.: Practical web cache poisoning. Port Swigger (2018)
36. Kreymer, I., Chuang, G.: Announcing the common crawl index! (2015)
37. Kumaraguru, P., et al.: School of phish: a real-world evaluation of anti-phishing training. In: Proceedings of the 5th Symposium on Usable Privacy and Security (2009)
38. Kumaraguru, P., et al.: Getting users to pay attention to anti-phishing education: evaluation of retention and transfer. In: Proceedings of the Anti-Phishing Working Groups 2nd Annual eCrime Researchers Summit (2007)
39. Kumaraguru, P., Sheng, S., Acquisti, A., Cranor, L.F., Hong, J.: Teaching johnny not to fall for phish. ACM Trans. Internet Technol. (TOIT) 10, 1–31 (2010)
40. Kunze, J.: Rfc 1736: functional recommendations for internet resource locators (1995)
41. Le, A., Markopoulou, A., Faloutsos, M.: Phishdef: url names say it all. In: IEEE INFOCOM. IEEE (2011)
42. Leitschuh, J.: Ssrf via maliciously crafted url due to host confusion. Hackerone (2019)
43. Ma, Z., et al.: The impact of secure transport protocols on phishing efficacy. In: 12th {USENIX} Workshop on Cyber Security Experimentation and Test ({CSET} 2019) (2019)
44. Marchal, S., Armano, G., Gröndahl, T., Saari, K., Singh, N., Asokan, N.: Off-the-hook: an efficient and usable client-side phishing prevention application. IEEE Trans. Comput. 66, 1717–1733 (2017)
45. Marlinspike, M.: More tricks for defeating ssl in practice. Black Hat USA (2009)
46. Muñoz, F.: Invalid url parsing with #. CVE-2016-8624 (2016)

47. Parekh, S., Parikh, D., Kotak, S., Sankhe, S.: A new method for detection of phishing websites: Url detection. In: 2018 Second International Conference on Inventive Communication and Computational Technologies (ICICCT). IEEE (2018)

48. Postel, J.: Rfc: 761 ien: 129 (1980)

49. Reynolds, J., et al.: Measuring identity confusion with uniform resource locators. In: Proceedings of the 2020 CHI Conference on Human Factors in Computing Systems (2020)

50. Sahingoz, O.K., Buber, E., Demir, O., Diri, B.: Machine learning based phishing detection from urls. Expert Syst. Appl. **117**, 345–357 (2019)

51. Sheng, S., et al.: Anti-phishing phil: the design and evaluation of a game that teaches people not to fall for phish. In: Proceedings of the 3rd Symposium on Usable Privacy and Security (2007)

52. Thomas, K., Grier, C., Ma, J., Paxson, V., Song, D.: Design and evaluation of a real-time url spam filtering service. In: 2011 IEEE symposium on security and privacy. IEEE (2011)

53. Thompson, C., Shelton, M., Stark, E., Walker, M., Schechter, E., Felt, A.P.: The web's identity crisis: understanding the effectiveness of website identity indicators. In: 28th {USENIX} Security Symposium ({USENIX} Security 2019) (2019)

54. Thompson, M.: The harmful consequences of the robustness principle (draft) (2018)

55. Tom: Security: uxss in chrome on ios. bugs.chromium.org (2018)

56. Tsai, O.: A new era of ssrf - exploiting url parser in trending programming languages! Black Hat USA (2017)

57. Tsai, O.: Breaking parser logic! take your path normalization off and pop 0days out. Black Hat USA (2018)

58. Vishwanath, A., Herath, T., Chen, R., Wang, J., Rao, H.R.: Why do people get phished? testing individual differences in phishing vulnerability within an integrated, information processing model. Decis. Supp. Syst. **51**, 576–586 (2011)

59. Wang, X., Lau, W.C., Yang, R., Shi, S.: Make redirection evil again: Url parser issues in oauth. Black Hat Asia (2019)

60. Weber, C.: (2022). https://websec.github.io/unicode-security-guide/

61. Zouina, M., Outtaj, B.: A novel lightweight url phishing detection system using svm and similarity index. Human-centric Comput. Inf. Sci. **7**, 1–13 (2017)

Exploring the Characteristics and Security Risks of Emerging Emoji Domain Names

Mingxuan Liu[1,2(✉)], Yiming Zhang[1(✉)], Baojun Liu[1], and Haixin Duan[1,3(✉)]

[1] Tsinghua University, Beijing, China
liumx18@mails.tsinghua.edu.cn, zhangyim17@tsinghua.org.cn
{lbj,duanhx}@tsinghua.edu.cn
[2] BNRist, Beijing, China
[3] Peng Cheng Lab, Shenzhen, China

Abstract. Emoji domains, such as i❤.ws (xn--i-7iq.ws), are distinctive and attractive to registrants due to their eye-catching visuals. Despite its long history (over 20 years), little has been done to understand its development status and security issues. In this paper, we identify 54,403 emoji domains from 1,366 TLD zone files and a large-scale passive DNS dataset. And then, we correlate them with auxiliary data sources like domain WHOIS records. It allowed us to conduct by far the most systematic study to characterize the ecosystem, and retrieve multiple valuable insights. On one hand, the scale of emoji domains is constantly expanding in the wild, with dozens of ccTLD registries actively promoting registering domains with emoji characters and domain owners configuring emoji characters in sub-level domains. And emoji domains may act as promotional portals, as web requests are usually redirected to other websites. Besides, emoji domains are also leveraged to provide disposable email services, pornography or gambling pages, and even the distribution of malware. On the other hand, the concern is that the community still lacks best security practices in supporting and parsing emoji domains. Through empirical studies, we demonstrate that inconsistencies in rendering emoji characters can be exploited to launch visual phishing domain scams. Meanwhile, mainstream implementations may incorrectly parse or trans-code emoji domains, resulting in the security threat of traffic hijacking. Our study calls for standardization and best security practices for applications to handle emoji domains securely.

1 Introduction

Domain names are user-friendly alphanumeric names that make it easier for Internet users to navigate the online world. Conventionally, only a portion of ASCII characters (letters, digits, and hyphens) was allowed in domain names [42]. With the purpose to globalize the use of the Internet and make domain names more accessible, the IETF promotes the Internationalized Domain Name (IDN)

V. Atluri et al. (Eds.): ESORICS 2022, LNCS 13556, pp. 186–206, 2022.
https://doi.org/10.1007/978-3-031-17143-7_10

program, which allows non-native English speakers to adopt their native language or local script, i.e. Unicode characters, in domain names.

Emoji belongs to a special subset of Unicode characters. Today, it has been widely adopted on smartphones and social media, and plays a critical role in Internet communication. It also attracts the interests of domain registrants. With the advantages of being graspable and eye-catching, an emoji domain can be an effective tool for public marketing. Actually, many big companies have already been doing so. For example, Coca-Cola registered a whole bunch of domains containing smiley emojis like ☺ .ws (xn--228h.ws) [51] (expired) for advertisement in 2015. Similarly, Budweiser registered 🍺🍺🍺 .ws (xn--xj8haa.ws), and Mailchimp [16] registered 😉 .ws (xn--rr8h.ws) for promotions. Besides, emoji domain also has been exploited for scam activities. In 2020, a collective defrauded over $200,000 through 👁👄👁 .fm (xn--mp8hai.fm) in the guise of social justice [47]. And Weapon Depot utilizes the emoji domain, 🔫 .ws (xn--bw8h.ws), to attract customers on some social media [12].

Despite the initiative of emoji domain having been proposed for about 20 years, little has been done to understand its ecosystem in the wild. In this paper, we report by far the first systematic study on emoji domains by answering a set of critical questions for understanding its development status and security risk, including: *What are the current scale and usage status? What are the characteristics of registrations? Are there any (new) security issues?* We made this study possible by a broad data collection, including 1,366 TLD zone files, a country-level passive DNS dataset and domain WHOIS records. Finally, *54,403* emoji domains are identified in total.

By analyzing the identified emoji domains, we discovered that discouragement from ICANN [27] has not hindered the development of emoji domains. In fact, the volume of emoji domains is constantly growing in the wild, increasing hundreds of folds compared to seven years ago. Although the registration of emoji domains under gTLDs has been restricted, registrants have turned to the registrars from ccTLDs (e.g., ☺ .cctld (xn--i28h.cctld)), or embedding emoji characters (e.g., 👍 .example.com (xn--yp8h.example.com)) in sub-level domains, which is prominent developing until now. Several ccTLDs registries even take emoji domain registration as a selling point for commercial promotion. As for registration intention, we find that high-profile emoji domains are created for promotion proposes, e.g., i❤ .ws (xn--i-7iq.ws) that received 7.96 million DNS requests is used for advertising emoji domain registration services, and 📧 .mail-temp.com (xn--4bi.email-temp.com) is designed for disposable temporary email service. However, pornographic sites and even malware distribution sites have also been witnessed leveraging emoji domains for user attraction.

Besides, we also reveal that the applications of emoji domains expose several security risks, especially in the trans-coding and rendering process. Through empirical study, three kinds of new security threats are uncovered. First, due to the inconsistent visuals of emoji rendering, we find that visual phishing attacks targeting emoji domains are feasible in the real world. Except for a few registrants who have noticed this risk and proactively registered visually similar domains for defense, the vast majority of phishing-vulnerable emoji domains are not yet protected. Second, mainstream implementations could not correctly parse emoji domains, resulting in text with emoji icons being unintentionally recognized as emoji domains. By inspecting one-day DNS queries from B Root, we uncover 6,372 "unintended" emoji domains as "parsing errors". Almost half of these domains are available for registration, leaving huge space for attackers to conduct traffic hijacking. Third, there is still a lack of best practices for handling special Unicode characters. Particularly, we find several mainstream browsers (e.g., Firefox and Safari) fail to trans-code ZWJ (Zero with Joiner) embedded emoji domains correctly, leading to the denial of service and hijacking threats.

In summary, our study shows that the development of emoji domain names is still at the early stage with a growing trend. And we recommend that security community should pay more attention to the ecosystem and propose best practice guidelines for harmonizing the usage and process of emoji domains.

2   Background

Domain Name Structure and Registration. A domain name is comprised of multiple layers and organized as a hierarchical structure. The boundary between hierarchy levels is separated with a dot, such as esorics2022.compute.dtu.dk. The top of the domain hierarchy is the DNS root. Below the root level are the Top-Level Domain (TLD, e.g., dk) and Second-Level Domain (SLD, e.g., dtu.dk).

TLDs are typically divided into three categories, including generic TLDs (gTLDs), country-code TLDs (ccTLDs), and sponsored TLDs (sTLDs). All TLDs are approved by Internet Corporation for Assigned Names and Numbers (ICANN), and operated by various registries. Of note, all registries operating gTLDs are *contracted* with ICANN [26], while ccTLDs are not necessarily required. For a registrant, domain names that are allowed to apply are SLDs (or apex domains). They are publicly offered and a domain name is registrable if it is not yet occupied. Domain owners are allowed to create *subdomains* under their apex domains, without asking permission from registrars.

Emoji Domain Names. An emoji domain refers to a domain name that contains at least one emoji character, regardless of the level at which the emoji is embedded. In the beginning stage, domain names were only allowed to be registered within letters, digits, and hyphens [42]. Most of the domain names came from a set of alphanumeric ASCII characters. To build a multilingual Internet, IETF instituted the Internationalized Domain Name (IDN) program in 2003. IDN program encourages Internet users around the world to adopt a domain that contains native scripts [7,14]. As a result, the scope of allowed characters in domain names has been extensively extended to *Unicode sets*.

At the time of writing (May 2022), 3,633 emoji code points are contained in the standard Unicode 14.0 [60]. Theoretically, registrants are permitted to apply

Table 1. Overview of datasets.

Data Source	# ED_sld	# ED_sub	# Emoji SLD	Unicode Domain
gTLD zone files	193	–	193	1,499,958
ccTLD zone files	1,732	–	1,732	3,246,266
Passive DNS	25,731	28,252	13,170	52,976,933
ALL	**26,151**	**28,252**	**13,581**	**55,887,203**

for domain names with embedded emoji characters, or add emoji characters to subdomains under the apex domain themselves.

Punycode Conversion. Although emoji domains are supported by DNS, they have to be converted to ASCII characters in order to maintain backward compatibility. IETF established technical standards to support domain names encoded with Unicode characters [13,32], named Internationalizing Domain Names in Applications (IDNA). IDNA is designed to convert a Unicode string (U-Label) into an ASCII-compatible encoding (ACE) string (A-Label), i.e., Punycode [7,13]. Punycode keeps all ASCII characters, and encodes the locations of non-ASCII characters, and re-encodes the non-ASCII characters with variable-length integers. As the algorithm design, a fixed prefix, "xn--", is added to the converted Punycode string after the above process. For example, xn--i-7iq.ws is the Punycode conversion of i♥.ws .

Security Considerations. Due to the effect of attention-grabbing, emoji domain names have attracted a lot of attention from registrants worldwide, especially for marketing and advertising campaigns. However, DNS community has proposed several security concerns with the emoji domain applications, due to their potential impact on the stability and interoperability of the domain name system. Specifically, an advisory document has been proposed by ICANN, indicating that emoji domains may cause ambiguity and confusion [27].

Nonetheless, we believe it is still too early to claim the failure of the emoji domain initiative. Instead, we need to revisit the development of emoji domains, evaluate the real-world impact, and explore the practical security risks.

3   Data Sources of Emoji Domains

In this section, we first elaborate on how we collect large-scale datasets. Then, we describe technical details of how to identify emoji domains.

3.1   Collecting Large-Scale Datasets

We collect 1,366 TLD zone files and a country-level passive DNS dataset to exhaustively detect emoji domains in the wild. The details are presented in Table 1.

TLD Zone Files (gTLDs and ccTLDs). TLD zone files are maintained by registries, like Verisign. They contain active domains with their delegation information, and serve as an important data source in security research. ICANN provides a centralized zone data service (CZDS) [34] for interested parties to access zone files. It allows us to apply *1,254 gTLD zone files* in September 2021, which contain the up-to-date registered domains maintained by registries, including historical gTLDs (e.g., `.com`) and a range of new gTLDs (e.g., `.info`).

By contrast, ccTLDs do not (or no longer) provide publicly accessible zone files [25]. Several well-known public datasets utilized in previous studies, e.g., OpenIntel [52] and CAIDA-DZDB [4], also have quite limited coverage of ccTLD domains. To solve this issue, ViewDNS [63] continuously collects domains under ccTLDs by Internet crawlers with considerable domain coverage [8]. We purchased all ccTLD domain lists of ViewDNS in May 2021, and got *112 ccTLD zone files* in total, e.g., `.us`, and `.cn`, covering 35.44% of all (316) ccTLDs [25].

Passive DNS Dataset. In addition to registering domains with emoji icons directly, one can also place the icons on subdomain labels. However, TLD zone files have no information on subdomains configured by registrants. To this end, we leverage the Passive DNS dataset from DNS Pai Project [49] to extend our investigation scope to fully qualified domain names (FQDNs). The project was initiated by a world-leading security vendor, and has collected DNS requests from a large array of popular DNS resolvers since 2014. It handles around 240 billion DNS requests per day, and opens the collected DNS traffic data to the research community. In this study, we gain access to all records of historical domain names from Passive DNS spanning from 08/01/2015 to 7/27/2021.

Domain WHOIS Records. We also utilized WHOIS records to understand the registration trend of emoji domains. Specifically, the WHOIS dataset was collected with the help of our industry partner, 360 Netlab [50]. As several ccTLDs (e.g., `.to`) restrict crawlers from obtaining their WHOIS information, we finally got the WHOIS records of *8,638 (63.60%)* unique emoji SLDs as the best coverage effort. Then we used an open-source tool, `python-whois`[1], to parse the records. As this work only concerns the registrar/registry and the creation/expiration date of domains, our analysis would not be affected by the implementation of General Data Protection Regulation (GDPR) policies [40].

3.2 Identifying Emoji Domains

Definitions and Notations. In this study, we refer to any FQDNs embedded with at least one emoji character as an emoji domain, termed as ED. Depending on where the emoji characters are located in the domain structure, EDs could be further classified into two categories: ED_{sld}, whose SLD contains emoji characters directly, and ED_{sub}, whose emoji characters *only* appear in the subdomain labels. The two categories essentially denote the different sources of ED creation. ED_{sld} indicates the domain owner directly registering an apex domain

---

[1] https://pypi.org/project/python-whois/.

with emoji characters from registrars. ED_{sub} means that the domain owner only configured emoji characters into the subdomain in authoritative nameservers (Fig. 1).

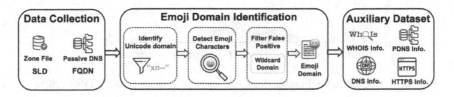

Fig. 1. The workflow of data collection and emoji domain identification.

Data-processing Workflow. Our emoji domain extraction workflow includes three steps.

(1) *Identify Unicode domains.* Emoji domain is only a subset of the Unicode domain. Given the rules of Punycode conversion, we are allowed to identify all Unicode domains by matching the fixed prefix "xn--", as described in Sect. 2.

(2) *Detect emoji characters.* Further, we convert the ASCII-compatible encoding string into Unicode string format, which is represented as a list of Unicode code points (e.g., U+1F600 for 😀). We also crawled Unicode code points for all emoji characters from the Unicode consortium [60]. Then the domains with at least one Unicode point inside the emoji range would be identified as emoji domains.

(3) *Filter false positives.* Through manual analysis, we find several emoji domains extracted from PDNS dataset are "false positives": *non-existent subdomains* caught by PDNS as their SLDs were enabled for wildcard resolution. To filter them, we replace the emoji characters with random strings and examine whether the newly generated domains could get the same resolution results.

Finally, we identified 54,403 unique emoji domains (*26,151 ED_{sld}* and *28,252 ED_{sub}*) from 55.89 million Unicode domains (Table 1). Among them, 4,947 emoji domains with SLDs are ranked within the Tranco Top 50k popular domain list. The list of the top 10,000 most queried emoji domains has been open-sourced[2].

Discussion. Although we try to make this study as comprehensive as possible, there are still limitations. First, our PDNS dataset may have geographical bias. However, given its huge DNS traffic volume and the longitudinal data collection period, we believe the dataset is still representative to reveal the ecosystem of emoji domains in the wild. Second, although we take the best effort to extend the observations on ccTLD domains by collecting zone files from ViewDNS [63], the coverage (112 out of 316 [25] ccTLDs) is still limited. The limitations indicate that our study may only reflect a lower bound in the real world.

---

[2] https://github.com/EmojiDomain/ESORICS22.

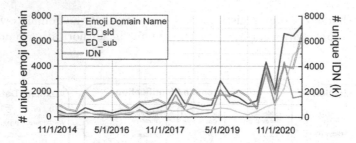

Fig. 2. Newly witnessed emoji domains and IDNs from passive DNS traffic.

4   Characteristics of Emoji Domain Ecosystem

In 2017, ICANN recommended discouraging registration activities for emoji domains. However, the impact of the recommendation has yet to be measured. This section reports our measurement results of the emoji domain ecosystem, including quantitative analysis of DNS statistics trends, registration distribution, usage strategies, as well as their web content and intention behind the registrations.

4.1   Growing Trend of DNS Statistics

The Passive DNS dataset is able to capture the DNS requests towards emoji domains among Internet users. The dataset could help to shed light on the first appearance and traffic volume of each emoji domain.

Figure 2 presents the trend of newly emerging emoji domains witnessed from passive DNS. Compared to 2014, the blue line indicates the volume of emoji domains witnessed in 2020 has increased hundreds of times and the entire scale is still increasing. The continuous growth trend of emoji domains is roughly similar to IDN (orange line). We also try to understand the reasons behind the four spikes in Fig. 2. By analyzing domain WHOIS records, we conclude these sharply emerged emoji domains are mainly caused by two reasons. First, the opening of support for emoji domains by several registries has sparked interest, like `.to` and `.ws`. Second, the update of the full list of emoji characters provides more options for the registration market.

The Passive DNS dataset could be also utilized to roughly estimate domain activities [30,39], including their popularity (query volume) and lifetime (intervals between the first and last occurrence).

Our results show that, the ecosystem is as yet in a "self-selling" phase, as a considerable percentage of the traffic and domains themselves are used for the purpose of promotion. Specifically, the DNS requests across the ecosystem were highly concentrated on several most popular ones (top 100 emoji domains hold 74.85% of DNS traffic). Further manual inspections confirm their activities for marketing emoji domains. For instance, the top popular emoji domain, i❤.ws

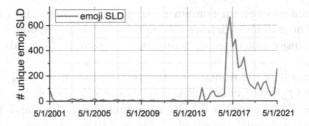

Fig. 3. Registrations of emoji domains.

Table 2. Statistics of collected emoji domains.

Category	# TLD	# ED_sld	# ED_sub	Registered after 2017
gTLD	178	1,894	22,552	0
ccTLD-registrable	16	23,600	384	96.15%
ccTLD-other	158	657	5,316	78.22%
All	352	26,151	28,252	75.43%

(xn--i-7iq.ws), with 7.96 million DNS requests, is hosting a promotional website for emoji domain registrations. And we find a large number of short-lived emoji domains, with 56.32% of which were active for only one day. A manual survey of 100 random-sampled 1-day domains showed that, 66 of them were *"FOR SALE"*.

4.2   Registration Distribution and Usage Strategies

In total, we identify 54,403 emoji domains, 26,151 of which belong to ED_{sld}, i.e., apex domain registered with emoji characters. Associated with domain WHOIS records, we are able to learn the distribution of their registrars, creation dates and expiration dates.

Registration Activity (ED_{sld}). The earliest known registration event for emoji domain dates back to 2001 [41]. Benefiting from several ccTLDs supporting emoji domains, the registration volume started to increase rapidly around 2016, as shown in Fig. 3. Then the year 2017, when ICANN proposed the recommendation, was a turning point. By inspecting the sources of registrations, we find mainstream registrars stopped offering emoji domain registrations under gTLDs from 2017. However, several ccTLD registries actively promote the business of emoji domain registration [28,41]. As a result, the registration activities have continued.

Registration Distribution (ED_{sld}). By clustering the registrar fields of domain WHOIS records, we find that 62 registrars have offered (perhaps no longer) the business of emoji domain registrations. Zooming into the distribution, a handful of popular registrars who dominate the global domain name market also play a major role in emoji domains. For example, Godaddy accounts for 26.43% of ED_{sld}.

To investigate the distribution at the registry level, we also categorize all emoji domains by their public suffix [44]. The result shows that the collected emoji domains come from 352 TLDs, including 178 gTLDs and 174 ccTLDs. We also conduct a manual survey of all the ccTLDs, and find 16 of them had explicitly announced their support for emoji domain registrations. These ccTLDs are then termed as ccTLD-registrable, and the remaining are termed as ccTLD-other. By checking the registration dates, we demonstrate ccTLDs have become the main source of emoji domains after 2017.

Emojis Embedding Location (ED_{sub}). While applying emoji domains from gTLD registries has been restricted, domain owners still have the freedom to adopt emoji characters under sub-level domains. In Fig. 2, the scale of newly observed ED_{sub} in passive DNS is rising rapidly. According to the statistics in Table 2, 79.8% (22,552 out of 28,252) of ED_{sub} belong to gTLDs.

We further investigate the usages of ED_{sub} that embed emoji characters under subdomains. Not only do we observe domain registrants themselves to leverage emoji characters for eye-catching, but we also find that third-party services create subdomains with embedded emoji characters. One example is the emoji-URL-shorten service. The service converts the input URL into a domain with a combination of emoji characters as the subdomain of e.mezw.com (1,667 observed in Passive DNS). For instance, `www.google.com` could be converted to `http://` 🧑‍🍳🔫😃🤖 😁📻😫💨🔒 ☀️`e.mezw.com` . Another example is the cloud storage service provided by Amazon S3. The storage bucket would be accessed through an identifier as part of the subdomain under `s3.amazonaws.com`. This mechanism leads to the creation of emoji domains (4,021 observed), e.g., 🔔`photo.s3.amazonaws.com` .

Conclusion. Although ICANN's guidelines of emoji domains have served a purpose, particularly for gTLDs, it has not discouraged the registration and use of emoji domains. Dozens of ccTLD registries still support and promote their commercial services for registering emoji domains. In addition, configuring emoji characters under subdomains is becoming a popular alternative, especially under gTLDs. Overall, the ecosystem of emoji domain is still thriving in the wild.

4.3   Infrastructure Analysis

We perform an infrastructure analysis to understand the motivation for registering emoji domains, including their DNS resolution status and web content. Besides, we also evaluate the adoption of security practices on their websites.

DNS Resolution Analysis. Until December 2021, 43,184 (79.4%) emoji domains are still active and resolvable, i.e., could fetch IP addresses through

Table 3. Security deployment of Emoji domains and general popular domains.

Deployment Rate	DNSSEC	HTTPS	HSTS
Regular Domains	1.85% ([6], 2017)	75.51% ([38], 2014)	6.9% ([37], 2017)
Emoji Domains	0.00%	44.61%	4.27%

DNS resolution. Since active emoji domains have configured NS records, we collect 2,687 nameservers in total. By comparing with NS records of popular domain parking services [64], 423 emoji domains are found in parking status, suggesting that their owners are seeking to gain profit through traffic monetization. In addition, 2,430 (12.0%) emoji domains also have enabled "MX" records, indicating the adoption of email-related services. As an example, ▓▓.`mail-temp.com` (`xn--4bi.email-temp.com`) is utilized for temporary disposable email services.

Types of Web Content and Intention. We further analyze the web content of all emoji domains (54,403 including ED_{sld} and ED_{sub}) to understand their usage. We perform automatic web crawls (including HTTP and HTTPS) towards all active emoji domains. As a result, 34.21% of emoji domains may act as promotional portals, as their original requests would be redirected to other websites. Totally, we find 9,265 landing domains which are redirected from emoji domains, with 33.39% belonging to the top 10k domains from Tranco List [48]. Our manual inspections show that the redirection targets include social application and registration websites of registries.

Due to the lack of ground truth, it is difficult to automate an accurate content classification of all emoji websites. Therefore, we randomly select 500 emoji domains and manually render their web contents in a controlled browser (Chrome) to inspect their categories. The results show that, 46.4% of them provide meaningless content, such as the default configuration page of the web server (e.g., Nginx) or plain responses with the HTTP status code (404, 503, etc.). 43.8% of the web pages we inspected display contact information of registrants, indicating that these domains are for sale. Besides, 11 domains are employed for personal homepages, and 24 domains for parking advertisements to make profits. Notably, we find 12 emoji domains being utilized for porn or gambling businesses, e.g., we♥`models.to` (`xn--wemodels-gf7e.to`). In particular, with the help of intelligence information from VirusTotal and Qihoo 360, 2 emoji domains have been categorized as *malicious* as they are associated with malware distribution.

Adoption of Security Practices. We also investigate the deployment of DNSSEC and HTTPS-related security policies for emoji domains, as shown in Table 3. As a whole, the adoption status is significantly less desirable than regular domains. First, by fetching DNSKEY records and HTTPS content, we find no emoji domains have deployed DNSSEC, and the HTTPS adoption rate (44.61%) is also lower than regular domains (75.5% [38] in 2014). Further, we find that 2,322 (4.27%) emoji domains enable HTTP Strict Transport Security (HSTS) by setting the `max-age` HTTPS header. But the deployment rate is also lower than that of regular domains (6.9% [37] in 2017). In addition, the proportion of invalid certificates on emoji domain websites (7.47%, including 1,153 expired certificates and 496 self-signed certificates) is also higher (4.6% [10] of regular domains in 2017). As for the reasons behind such a poor security deployment status, we speculate that, on the one hand, it may be due to the lack of attention to domain security by emoji domain owners. While on the other hand, the inadequate emoji compatibility of security implementations [61] would also matter. For example, OpenSSL is a popular open-source toolkit for implementing TLS, while one critical python library it relies on, `idna`[3], does not support emoji domain processing (unable to trans-coding its Punycode).

Conclusion. The majority of emoji domains could be successfully resolved, with most of them hosting websites, and some even providing email services. Besides, by analyzing the web content, we find emoji domains are now mainly used for promotion, with 34% of them redirecting to other websites. In addition, security implementations of emoji domains are inferior to that of normal domains and need to be improved.

5 Security Threats of Emoji Domain Applications

Until now, little has been done to understand the security risks of emoji domains in real-world applications. In this section, we report an empirical study to explore the threats of visual phishing, parsing and trans-coding errors, aiming to provide guidelines for the correct and safe handling of emoji characters in the future.

5.1 Visual Phishing Threat of Emoji Domains

Threat Model. The eye-catching visual rendering effect of emoji boosts its popularity in domain names. However, the enrichment of rendering without standards from the Unicode community introduces new security risks. In practice, rendering results of the same emoji vary from platform to platform, and even from application to application. As a result, the visual boundaries between different emoji characters may be obscured. Two emoji characters may be rendered quite similarly, even closer on another platform/application than one emoji itself.

Table 4 presents two real-world examples of such visual ambiguity: "`xn--i-7iq.ws`" on Apple renders quite similarly to "`xn--i-n3p.ws`" on Google, and is even more visually equivalent than "`xn--i-7iq.ws`" itself on Windows. As the unique resource identifier in DNS, it raises the security threats of visual phishing. Although previous studies have analyzed the visual phishing attacks of IDN [1,9,22,30,39,46,56,57], the threat has not been well investigated with

---
[3] https://pypi.org/project/idna/.

Table 4. Examples of phishing emoji domain names.

	Apple (iOS 15.4)	Windows (Win 10)	Samsung (Galaxy M30s)	Google (Pixel 5)	Facebook (Website)	Twitter (Website)	JoyPixels (Website)
U-Label	i❤️.ws	i 🤍.ws	i 🤍.ws	i❤️ .ws	i 🤍.ws	i 🤍.ws	i 🤍 .ws
A-Label	xn--i-7iq.ws	xn--i-7iq.ws	xn--i-9h5s.ws	xn--i-n3p.ws	xn--i-u92s.ws	xn--i-744s.ws	xn--i-y92s.ws
U-Label	🌸.yshi.org	🌐 .yshi.org	🌼 .yshi.org	🍃 .yshi.org	✳️ .yshi.org	🌼 .yshi.org	🌼 .yshi.org
A-Label	xn--9h8h.yshi.org	xn--9h8h.yshi.org	xn--83h.yshi.org	xn--8h8h.yshi.org	xn--cdi.yshi.org	xn--wdi.yshi.org	xn--wh8h.yshi.org

* *Website means that this is rendered from a web service in Chrome browser.*

emoji domains. Below, we provide a quantitative analysis to evaluate the feasibility of emoji domain phishing.

Terminology. In this work, we denote the rendered image of emoji x on platform a as E_{xa}. By calculating image similarities of arbitrary two images, we define one potential "visual phishing attack" against emoji x exists, when:

$$\exists y \neq x, \exists a, b, s.t, Similarity\,(E_{xa}, E_{yb}) > \underset{c \neq d}{MAX}\,(Similarity\,(E_{xc}, E_{xd}))$$

That is, the similarity between the rendering of emoji y on platform b and emoji x on platform a is quite high, even exceeding the maximum of the internal similarities among x's own rendering results on different platforms/applications.

Feasibility of Visual Phishing Attacks. Here, we introduce our methodology to quantitatively assess the feasible space for visual phishing attacks on emoji domains. First, we extensively collect the rendering results of thousands of emoji characters on mainstream applications (Google, Facebook, Twitter, JoyPixels) and operating systems (Apple, Windows, Samsung) [11], yielding a dataset of 12,169 images of 1,816 emoji characters (excluding the GIF images). Specifically, image E_{xa} is the rendered result of emoji x ($1 \leq x \leq 1816$) on platform a ($1 \leq a \leq 7$), which is a 72×72 matrix with each element (pixel) ranging from 0 to 255. Then, we test five classical image similarity metrics to evaluate the visual similarity, including Peak Signal-To-Noise (PSNR) [23,65], Feature Similarity Indexing Method (FSIM) [67], Information theoretic-based Statistic Similarity Measure (ISSM) [3], Signal to Reconstruction Error ratio (SRE) [36], and Spectral Angle Mapper (SAM) [66].

As there is no ground-truth dataset for this task, we started by manually labeling an emoji icon similarity dataset by two researchers, with 125 randomly selected emoji image pairs. Image pairs with inconsistent labels will be double-checked. Following, we input similarity results of each pair using five metrics separately for similarity classification via a random forest (RF) model [2], with a 16:9 training-test ratio. As shown in Table 5, **FSIM** performs the best, which could achieve an accuracy of 80%, and has been chosen as our final method. We also open source the labeled emoji similarity dataset[4] to facilitate future work.

---

[4] https://github.com/EmojiDomain/ESORICS22/.

Table 5. Evaluation of each image similarity metric.

	PSNR	FSIM	ISSM	SRE	SAM
Accuracy	66.67%	80.00%	71.11%	73.33%	68.89%
Precision	66.67%	86.20%	76.92%	82.75%	71.43%
Recall	75.00%	83.33%	74.07%	77.42%	76.92%
F1 score	70.59%	84.75%	75.47%	80.00%	74.07%

Finally, based on the similar results of **FSIM** among 148 million emoji image pairs, we find that **1,332** (73.35%) emoji characters could be threatened by the above visual phishing attacks.

Visual Phishing in the Real World. We also try to answer the question of whether visual phishing attacks already happening in the real world, and the registration space of phishing domains from the perspective of adversaries. In total, 1,112 pairs of the collected emoji domains satisfy the similarity requirement of visual phishing attacks. Through manual inspections, we do observe some suspected examples, i.e., i😃.ws (xn--i-jv3s.ws) and i😄.ws (xn--i-pv3s.ws) both promoting the service of emoji domain registration. However, we could not further verify whether they were actually exploited for phishing. Besides, we also speculate that some of the similar domain pairs are caused by defensive registering, i.e., registrants pre-register domains similar to their own to prevent others from registering for phishing. For example, the website owner of i💜.ws (xn--i-7iq.ws) also has registered another 4 emoji domains with similar "heart" characters, e.g., i💚.ws (xn--i-n3p.ws). However, most of the vulnerable emoji domains have not been protected yet. Taking the top 100 popular domains with the most queries as examples, we find that 78 of them are phishable, and 67 of them even have more than 10 potential phishing domains. By requesting the registration API of Godaddy [18], we find that 23.38% of visually similar emoji domains are available for registration, leaving considerable space for adversaries.

5.2   Parsing Error of Emoji Domains

Threat Model. To optimize usability, mainstream online social media and chatting platforms would automatically parse URLs in the text and render them into clickable links. However, this automatic process is not always reliable, and the unanticipated parsing may lead to "unintended URLs". Beliz et al. [29] explored the "unintended URLs" caused by *typos*, where users forget the space after a full stop and the next sentence happens to begin with a "TLD" word (e.g., .to and .online). Attackers could exploit such parsing errors by registering the domains in "unintended URLs" and hijacking the traffic.

The introduction of emoji expands the character space of domains, which raises new challenges for URL parsing. By empirical analysis and manual inspections of open-source projects, we find one common approach to parsing URLs is regular expression matching. For instance, Android 11 (with SDK version 30)[5] has a predefined character set for URL recognition and also includes 168 emoji characters. However, simply expanding the character set may introduce URL parsing errors.

We present two cases below, where the emoji characters are incorrectly recognized as part of the URLs. Attackers can hijack the traffic towards www.google.com and i♥.ws (xn--i-7iq.ws) by registering com★.to (xn--com-x19a.to) and ☺i♥.ws (xn--i-7iq2158q.ws).

Case-I *Check www.google.com★.To hurry up.*
Case-II *You can register your own emoji domains ☺i♥.ws.*

Parsing Errors in the Real World. Through manual testing, we confirmed that such parsing errors are prevalent on the Android platform even in multiple Android systems (e.g., version 5–8 with SDK version 21–27) and applications (e.g., Short Message Service), indicating the developers are not yet aware of such vulnerabilities.

Moreover, to evaluate the impact of this security threat, we apply for one day of DNS request data (April 13, 2021) from B Root [62]. As most "unintended domains" would be not resolvable, Root traffic could provide a holistic observation of parsing errors. Based on the two cases above, the structural features of wrongly parsed emoji domains could be summarized as follows: the emoji character appears on the right-most and before a TLD (Case-I) or left-most (Case-II) side of a valid domain, and is then incorrectly parsed as a new (most likely NXDomain) domain name. Therefore, we first filter out the emoji domains from the DNS requests in Root traffic, and divide the domains into left and right sub-strings by the emoji character. When one origin domain is NXDomain, while its left sub-string is a valid domain, it would be tagged as Case-I; when its right sub-string is a valid domain, it would be tagged as Case-II. Finally, a total of 6,372 emoji domains are reported as "parsing error", including 1,591 Case-I (e.g., youtube.com👍.dlink with A-Label of youtube.xn--com-3113b.dlink) and 4,781 Case-II (e.g., ✉meet.google.com with A-Label of xn--meet-uk3b.google.com). Based on the Godaddy registration API [18], we find that 43.13% of emoji domains with "parsing error" are available for registration. To conclude, we speculate this security threat does have a real-world impact and needs to be taken seriously by individual applications.

5.3   Trans-coding Issue of Emoji Domains

Benefiting from the existing disclosure of IDN vulnerabilities, applications would trans-code domains with non-ASCII characters into A-Labels (strings starting with "xn–") to mitigate phishing threats. Hu *et al.* [24] found that mainstream

---

[5] https://developer.android.com/studio.

Table 6. Trans-coding test results of ZWJ embedded emoji domains.

PC Browser	Version	Windows 11	Windows 10	Windows 8.1	Windows 7	macOS Monterey	macOS Big Sur	macOS Catalina
Chrome	89–101 Beta	✓	✓	✓	✓	✓	✓	✓
Firefox	94–100 Beta	✗1	✗1	✗1	✗1	✗1	✗1	✗1
Firefox	88–93	✗3	✗3	✗3	✗3	✗3	✗3	✗3
Safari	14–15	-	-	-	-	✗2	✗2	-
Safari	13	-	-	-	-	-	-	✗2
Edge	89–101 Beta	✓	✓	✓	✓	✓	✓	✓
IE	11	-	✗3	✗3	✗3	-	-	-
Opera	73–85	✓	✓	✓	✓	✓	✓	✓
Yandex	7.61–21.2	✓	✓	✓	✓	-	-	-

Android	Samsung			Google		OnePlus		Microsoft		Xiaomi		Huawei		LG		Sony	Oppo
Browser	Galaxy M30s	Galaxy S21	Galaxy 20	Pixel 5	Pixel 4	9	8	Duo 2	Duo	11	10	P30	P20	Stylo 6	G6	xz2	Reno 6
Chrome	✓	✓	✓	✓	✓	✓	✓	✓	✓	✓	✓	✓	✓	✓	✓	✓	✓
Firefox	✗1	✗1	✗1	✗1	✗1	✗1	✗1	✗1	✗1	✗1	✗1	✗1	✗1	✗1	✗1	✗1	✗1

iOS Browser	iPhone 13	iPhone 12	iPhone 11	iPhone XS	iPad Air 4	iPad Pro 4	iPad Air 3	iPad Pro 3
Safari	✗2	✗2	✗2	✗2	✗2	✗2	✗2	✗2
Chrome	✓	✓	✓	✓	✓	✓	✓	✓
Firefox	✗1	✗1	✗1	✗1	✗1	✗1	✗1	✗1

✓ means that the browser trans-code ZWJ embedded emoji correctly.
✗1 means that the browser could not recognize ZWJ embedded emoji domains and returns search results from the search engine for this domain name.
✗2 means that the browser could not recognize ZWJ embedded emoji domains and returns None, leading to risks of DoS.
✗3 means that the browser has trans-coding error of this ZWJ embedded emoji domain.

browsers would selectively trans-code IDNs in the address bar of browsers. In this study, we conducted a similar investigation on how emoji domains are displayed by browsers.

However, the trans-coding process itself is also a complex task and could be error-prone, especially when dealing with special functional characters for emoji rendering. The most representative special character is `Zero With Joiner` (ZWJ, "U+200D" and "U+200C"). It is **invisible**, but can change the rendering results of its contiguous emoji (e.g., ＼ +ZWJ+◢ would be rendered as ▰). Unfortunately, the community has not developed a uniform (and strict) standard for how to handle ZWJ in domain names [31], e.g., IDNA 2003 recommended removing ZWJ in trans-coding while IDNA 2008 considered keeping it as a valid character. Such insidious characters would introduce serious ambiguity when used as unique identifiers, thus discouraging being used in domain names [55].

We witnessed 1,026 emoji domains with ZWJ being used in the wild based on our collected dataset, and further confirmed they do trigger ambiguity during trans-coding. The test was performed on `LambdaTest` [35], a cloud-based framework that supports remote testing on different versions of browsers across multiple operating systems. By configuring the versions of browsers, operating systems and domains to be tested, we can remotely control `LambdaTest` to load the domain in the address bar of the specified browser and get the result in video form. A total of 7 browser vendors on 7 PC operating systems and 3 browser vendors on 10 mobile brands were tested. According to the results shown in Table 6, we find that trans-coding of emoji domains is primarily implemented by the browser vendors themselves, independent of the platforms they are running on. Specifically, Chrome is correctly implemented in all versions on all platforms, keeping the ZWJ and trans-coding it (e.g., trans-codes 👨🏻‍💻·ws to xn--g5hz810o.ws correctly). However, other browser implementations are not satisfactory. Most seriously, lower versions (88–93) of Firefox and IE stand in the "drop ZWJ" branch, e.g., 👨🏻‍💻·ws would be improperly trans-coded as xn--1ug66vqx45b.ws, which is totally a different domain and could lead to security risks of traffic hijacking. There are also flaws where browsers could not recognize ZWJ embedded emoji domains and then use them as keywords to fetch results from search engines (e.g., higher versions of Firefox), or return the navigation page directly (e.g., Safari), causing the denial of access failures. Considering the prevalence of special characters used in the emoji ecosystem (e.g., ZWJ can be combined with at least 202 sets of emoji characters for special effects), we need to explore the best security practice for emoji domain trans-coding and propose consistent standards to mitigate the above risks.

6 Discussion

Recommendations. In this study, we provide a landscape of how emoji domains are parsed in mainstream platforms and applications. Most of them are "compatible", but from the perspective of adversaries, they are not prepared to deal with potential security risks. Given the rapidly growing trend of emoji domains in the wild, we believe it is necessary to take action for mitigation. Here, we provide three recommendations based on our observations:

- **Unicode community: provide guidance for emoji domain processing.** Our study reveals that the Unicode standards still have ambiguous and unspecified fields on emoji domain processing, which should be specified and regulated in the near future. For example, we need best security practices on how to securely parse special emoji characters during the trans-coding, such as ZWJ. Furthermore, despite the fact that it could be difficult to uniform the rendering of emojis across all platforms, the Unicode community should propose guidance to prevent visual phishing attacks.
- **Domain registry and registrar: adopt proactive anti-phishing defenses.** As mentioned above, a dozen of ccTLD registries are supporting and promoting the registration of emoji domains. Considering potential security concerns, the related registries and registries should take proactive approaches. In particular, a previous study proposes a series of anti-phishing defenses for IDN domain registrations [15], including enumerating potential phishing domains in advance based on emoji similarity, and encouraging users to register them proactively.
- **Application: elaborate emoji-compatible implementation.** Applications should balance both usability and security of emoji domains, particularly in the parsing and trans-coding processes. The threat models and test cases presented in this paper could be considered as references for secure testing of applications.

Generality of Proposed Security Risks. The essence of this work is the security pitfalls when special Unicode characters are adopted as unique identifiers. Therefore, the security risk is generally applicable in multiple scenarios beyond emoji domains, e.g., the Windows registry [58] and file paths with IDNs [54]. We believe that the first exploration perspectives in this work, such as trans-coding, parsing and rendering of special Unicode characters, are also applicable to other areas. We leave the exploration of broader scenarios as our future work.

Ethical Consideration. The major ethical considerations for this study include data collection and security threat disclosure. First, the datasets we collected are publicly available and used for research purposes only. No personally sensitive information is involved in the data collection. Second, we propose three security threats and evaluate their feasibility in the real world. Our results demonstrate that ambiguous understanding and mishandling of emojis are prevalent in the wild. As a result, it is possible that these attacks will be initiated by adversaries. However, we consider that our study gains more benefits than exposing threats, which makes the security community aware of the unique security threats introduced by emoji characters.

7   Related Works

IDN Domain Security. The initiative of IDN has been proposed for a long time, and attracted the security community to study its ecosystem and implications. Since registrants are free to choose characters from the Unicode consortium, an adversary can carefully craft an IDN domain that looks quite similar to a popular domain by replacing ASCII characters with Unicode ones. Such an attack is named IDN homograph. Security accidents show that homographic IDN has been utilized by cyber-criminals [21,22]. In 2018, a reexamination study was conducted to detect registered homographic IDNs and estimate the scale of available ones [39]. After that, the methodology of homograph attack detection was optimized by a series of studies [56,59]. To mitigate this risk, mainstream browsers introduced defense policies. However, almost all implementations have weaknesses in their rules, leaving opportunities for attackers and re-allow homograph IDNs [24].

Domain Abuse. Continuous expansion of domain space led to the security risk of domain squatting [20,46,59]. Besides homograph IDNs, deceptive domains could be constructed by typos [1,43,57], flipping a bit [46], using a hyphen to connect related keywords [30], the sound similarity [45], or even the long-length of domain name [9]. Previous studies demonstrated that newly released TLDs may be exploited to create look-alike domain names of popular brands [5, 17,19,20,33]. And recent work shows that domain impersonation attacks also have a negative impact on the issuance of TLS certificates [53]. To the best of our knowledge, there is no prior work has attempted to explore the security implication of emoji domains for the DNS ecosystem.

8   Conclusion

This work is the first to propose a systematic study of emoji domains based on a comprehensive dataset, including 1,366 TLD zone files, and long-period country-level passive DNS datasets. We identify 54,403 emoji domains by matching characters with the emoji code point lists. We show that the scale of emoji domains is constantly growing in the wild. The proliferation of emoji domain registrations under ccTLDs and configuring emoji icons in subdomains have enabled the entire ecosystem to remain developing after 2017 and up to now. About half of emoji domain names are associated with meaningful web content, with most for promotion and redirection, or even pornographic sites. However, it still lacks best security practices in supporting and parsing emoji domains, which exposes serious security risks, including phishing threats, parsing errors and trans-coding issues. Overall, we believe that the development of emoji domain names is at an early stage. And different communities should pay more attention to the security issues, and take efforts to find the best practice for processing emoji domains.

Acknowledgments. We thank all the anonymous reviewers for their valuable comments to improve this paper, and our industry partner, 360 Netlab, for their help and support. We acknowledge the University of Southern California for providing B Root data for security analysis. The authors were supported by the National Natural Science Foundation of China (U1836213, U19B2034, 62102218), the Alibaba Innovative Research (AIR) programme, and a gift from China Telecommunications Corporation. Baojun Liu was also partially supported by the Shuimu Tsinghua Scholar Program.

References

1. Agten, P., Joosen, W., Piessens, F., Nikiforakis, N.: Seven months' worth of mistakes: a longitudinal study of typosquatting abuse. In: NDSS. Internet Society (2015)
2. Alasalmi, T., Suutala, J., Röning, J., Koskimäki, H.: Better classifier calibration for small datasets. ACM Trans. Knowl. Discov. Data (2020)
3. Aljanabi, M.A., Hussain, Z.M., Shnain, N.A.A., Lu, S.F.: Design of a hybrid measure for image similarity: a statistical, algebraic, and information-theoretic approach. Eur. J. Remote Sens. (2019)
4. CAIDA and Ian Foster: Caida-dns zone database (dzdb) (2020). https://dzdb. caida.org/
5. Chen, Q.A., Thomas, M., Osterweil, E., Cao, Y., You, J., Mao, Z.M.: Client-side name collision vulnerability in the new gtld era: a systematic study. In: SIGSAC 2017. ACM (2017)
6. Chung, T., et al.: A longitudinal, end-to-end view of the DNSSEC ecosystem. In: USENIX Security 2017. USENIX Association (2017)
7. Costello, A.: Punycode: a bootstring encoding of Unicode for internationalized domain names in applications (IDNA). Technical report, RFC 3492, March 2003
8. Du, K., Yang, H., Li, Z., Duan, H., Zhang, K.: The ever-changing labyrinth: a large-scale analysis of wildcard DNS powered blackhat SEO. In: USENIX Security 2016. USENIX Association (2016)

9. Du, K., et al.: TL;DR hazard: a comprehensive study of levelsquatting scams. In: Chen, S., Choo, K.-K.R., Fu, X., Lou, W., Mohaisen, A. (eds.) SecureComm 2019. LNICST, vol. 305, pp. 3–25. Springer, Cham (2019). https://doi.org/10.1007/978-3-030-37231-6_1

10. Durumeric, Z., Kasten, J., Bailey, M., Halderman, J.A.: Analysis of the https certificate ecosystem. In: IMC 2013. ACM (2013)

11. Emoji Community: Full emoji list, v14.0 (2022). https://unicode.org/emoji/charts/full-emoji-list.html

12. Emoji Domain Registration: Emoji domain case study: Weapon depot and ⬧.ws (2017). https://emoji-domains.medium.com/emoji-domain-case-study-ws-bd070f31090f

13. Faltstrom, P.: The Unicode code points and internationalized domain names for applications (idna). Technical report, RFC 5892, August 2010

14. Faltstrom, P., Hoffman, P., Costello, A.: Internationalizing domain names in applications (IDNA). Technical report, RFC 3490, March 2003

15. Fu, A.Y., Deng, X., Wenyin, L., Little, G.: The methodology and an application to fight against Unicode attacks. In: Usable privacy and security (2006)

16. Gandi News: Can you use emojis in your domain name? yes! you can! (2020). https://news.gandi.net/en/2020/07/can-you-use-emojis-in-your-domain-name-yes-you-can/

17. Pouryousef, S., Dar, M.D., Ahmad, S., Gill, P., Nithyanand, R.: Extortion or expansion? An investigation into the costs and consequences of ICANN's gTLD experiments. In: Sperotto, A., Dainotti, A., Stiller, B. (eds.) PAM 2020. LNCS, vol. 12048, pp. 141–157. Springer, Cham (2020). https://doi.org/10.1007/978-3-030-44081-7_9

18. Godaddy: Search and buy domains in bulk. https://sg.godaddy.com/domains/bulk-domain-search . Accessed January 2022

19. Halvorson, T., Der, M.F., Foster, I., Savage, S., Saul, L.K., Voelker, G.M.: From .academy to .zone: an analysis of the new TLD land rush. In: IMC 2015. ACM (2015)

20. Halvorson, T., Levchenko, K., Savage, S., Voelker, G.M.: XXXtortion? Inferring registration intent in the. XXX TLD. In: WWW 2014 (2014)

21. Hannay, P., Baatard, G.: The 2011 IDN homograph attack mitigation survey. Edith Cowan University Publications (2012)

22. Holgers, T., Watson, D.E., Gribble, S.D.: Cutting through the confusion: a measurement study of homograph attacks. In: USENIX ATC 2006 (2006)

23. Hore, A., Ziou, D.: Image quality metrics: PSNR vs. SSIM. In: 2010 20th International Conference on Pattern Recognition, pp. 2366–2369. IEEE (2010)

24. Hu, H., Jan, S.T., Wang, Y., Wang, G.: Assessing browser-level defense against IDN-based phishing. In: USENIX Security 2021 (2021)

25. Internet Assigned Numbers Authority (IANA): Resources for country code managers. https://www.icann.org/resources/pages/cctlds-21-2012-02-25-en. Accessed 25 Feb 2012

26. Internet Corporation for Assigned Names and Numbers : ICANN gtld registries and registrars required to implement new interim registration data policy by 20 May 2019 (2019). https://www.icann.org/en/announcements/details/icann-gtld-registries-and-registrars-required-to-implement-new-interim-registration-data-policy-by-20-may-2019-17-5-2019-en

27. Internet Corporation for Assigned Names and Numbers: SSAC advisory on the use of emoji in domain names (2017). https://www.icann.org/en/system/files/files/sac-095-en.pdf

28. Johnson, P.: Emoji domains are the future (2018). https://gizmodo.com/emoji-domains-are-the-future-maybe-1823319626
29. Kaleli, B., Kondracki, B., Egele, M., Nikiforakis, N., Stringhini, G.: To err. is human: characterizing the threat of unintended URLs in social media. In: NDSS 2021 (2021)
30. Kintis, P., et al.: Hiding in plain sight: a longitudinal study of combosquatting abuse. In: SIGSAC 2017 (2017)
31. Klensin, J.: Internationalized domain names for applications (IDNA): background, explanation, and rationale. Technical report., RFC 5894, August 2010
32. Klensin, J.: Internationalized domain names for applications (IDNA): definitions and document framework. Technical report, RFC 5890, August 2010
33. Korczynski, M., et al.: Cybercrime after the sunrise: a statistical analysis of DNS abuse in new gTLDs. In: AsiaCCS 2018 (2018)
34. Lab, V.: The centralized zone data service. https://czds.icann.org/home. Accessed January 2021
35. Lambdatest: Lambdatest: Cross browser testing cloud (2022). https://app.lambdatest.com/. Access April 2022
36. Lanaras, C., Bioucas-Dias, J., Galliani, S., Baltsavias, E., Schindler, K.: Super-resolution of sentinel-2 images: learning a globally applicable deep neural network. ISPRS J. Photogramm. Remote Sens. (2018)
37. Li, X., Wu, C., Ji, S., Gu, Q., Beyah, R.: HSTS measurement and an enhanced stripping attack against HTTPS. In: Lin, X., Ghorbani, A., Ren, K., Zhu, S., Zhang, A. (eds.) SecureComm 2017. LNICST, vol. 238, pp. 489–509. Springer, Cham (2018). https://doi.org/10.1007/978-3-319-78813-5_25
38. Liang, J., Jiang, J., Duan, H., Li, K., Wan, T., Wu, J.: When https meets CDN: a case of authentication in delegated service. In: IEEE S&P. IEEE (2014)
39. Liu, B., et al.: A reexamination of internationalized domain names: the good, the bad and the ugly. In: DSN (2018)
40. Lu, C., et al.: From WHOIS to WHOWAS: a large-scale measurement study of domain registration privacy under the GDPR. In: NDSS 2021 (2021)
41. Michael Cyger: The definitive guide to emoji domain names (2017). https://www.dnacademy.com/emoji-domains
42. Mockapetris, P.V.: RFC 1034: domain names-concepts and facilities (1987)
43. Moore, T., Edelman, B.: Measuring the perpetrators and funders of typosquatting. In: Sion, R. (ed.) FC 2010. LNCS, vol. 6052, pp. 175–191. Springer, Heidelberg (2010). https://doi.org/10.1007/978-3-642-14577-3_15
44. Mozilla Foundation.: Public suffix list. https://publicsuffix.org/. Accessed December 2021
45. Nikiforakis, N., Balduzzi, M., Desmet, L., Piessens, F., Joosen, W.: Soundsquatting: uncovering the use of homophones in domain squatting. In: Chow, S.S.M., Camenisch, J., Hui, L.C.K., Yiu, S.M. (eds.) ISC 2014. LNCS, vol. 8783, pp. 291–308. Springer, Cham (2014). https://doi.org/10.1007/978-3-319-13257-0_17
46. Nikiforakis, N., Van Acker, S., Meert, W., Desmet, L., Piessens, F., Joosen, W.: Bitsquatting: exploiting bit-flips for fun, or profit? In: WWW 2013 (2013)
47. Organisation of 👁️👄👁️: what it really is? https://xn-mp8hai.fm/statement. Accessed October 2021
48. Pochat, V.L., van Goethem, T., Tajalizadehkhoob, S., Korczynski, M., Joosen, W.: Tranco: a research-oriented top sites ranking hardened against manipulation. In: NDSS 2019. The Internet Society (2019)
49. Qihoo 360 Netlab: DNSPai: Passive DNS. https://passivedns.cn/. Accessed October 2021

50. Qihoo 360 Netlab: Qihoo 360 Netlab. https://netlab.360.com/. Accessed October 2021
51. Rainey, C.: Coca-cola bought a whole bunch of emoji web addresses. https://www.grubstreet.com/2015/02/coke-emoji-websites.html. Accessed 20 Feb 2015
52. van Rijswijk-Deij, R., Jonker, M., Sperotto, A., Pras, A.: A high-performance, scalable infrastructure for large-scale active DNS measurements. IEEE J. Sel. Areas Commun. **34**(6), 1877–1888 (2016)
53. Roberts, R., Goldschlag, Y., Walter, R., Chung, T., Mislove, A., Levin, D.: You are who you appear to be: a longitudinal study of domain impersonation in TLS certificates. In: SIGSAC 2019. ACM (2019)
54. Smith, B.: Chinese characters in windows registry: are they safe? https://internet-access-guide.com/chinese-characters-in-windows-registry/. Accessed 23 Feb 2021
55. Suignard, M.: Proposed update Unicode technical report# 36 (2014). https://unicode.org/reports/tr36/
56. Suzuki, H., Chiba, D., Yoneya, Y., Mori, T., Goto, S.: Shamfinder: an automated framework for detecting IDN homographs. In: IMC 2019. ACM (2019)
57. Szurdi, J., Kocso, B., Cseh, G., Spring, J., Felegyhazi, M., Kanich, C.: The long taile of typosquatting domain names. In: USENIX Security 2014 (2014)
58. The MITRE Corporation.: Masquerading: Right-to-left override. https://attack.mitre.org/techniques/T1036/002/. Accessed 14 Oct 2021
59. Tian, K., Jan, S.T., Hu, H., Yao, D., Wang, G.: Needle in a haystack: Tracking down elite phishing domains in the wild. In: IMC 2018. ACM (2018)
60. Unicode Community: Emoji list (2020). https://www.unicode.org/Public/emoji/13.1/emoji-test.txt
61. Universal Acceptance: Reviewing programming languages and frameworks for compliance with universal acceptance good practice, May 2019
62. USC/B-Root Operations with USC/LANDER project: Day in the life of the internet (ditl) april, 2015 dataset, impact id: web1191, for dataset: Usc-lander/ditl_b_root_message_question-20210413. https://ant.isi.edu/datasets/dns/index.html. Accessed January 2022
63. ViewDNS: Viewdns info. https://viewdns.info/. Accessed October 2020
64. Vissers, T., Joosen, W., Nikiforakis, N.: Parking sensors: analyzing and detecting parked domains. In: NDSS 2015. Internet Society (2015)
65. Wang, Z., Bovik, A.C., Sheikh, H.R., Simoncelli, E.P.: Image quality assessment: from error visibility to structural similarity. IEEE Trans. Image Process. **13**(4), 600–612 (2004)
66. Yuhas, R.H., Goetz, A.F., Boardman, J.W.: Discrimination among semi-arid landscape endmembers using the spectral angle mapper (SAM) algorithm. In: Proceedings of the Summaries 3rd Annual JPL Airborne Geoscience Workshop (1992)
67. Zhang, L., Zhang, L., Mou, X., Zhang, D.: FSIM: a feature similarity index for image quality assessment. IEEE Trans. Image Process. (2011)

Hardware Security

CPU Port Contention Without SMT

Thomas Rokicki[1]([✉])[iD], Clémentine Maurice[2][iD], and Michael Schwarz[3][iD]

[1] Univ Rennes, CNRS, IRISA, Rennes, France
thomas.rokicki@irisa.fr
[2] Univ Lille, CNRS, Inria, Lille, France
[3] CISPA Helmholtz Center for Information Security, Saarbrücken, Germany

Abstract. CPU port contention has been used in the last years as a stateless side channel to perform side-channel attacks and transient execution attacks. One drawback of this channel is that it heavily relies on simultaneous multi-threading, which can be absent from some CPUs or simply disabled by the OS.

In this paper, we present *sequential port contention*, which does not require SMT. It exploits sub-optimal scheduling to execution ports for instruction-level parallelization. As a result, specifically-crafted instruction sequences on a single thread suffer from an increased latency. We show that sequential port contention can be exploited from web browsers in WebAssembly. We present an automated framework to search for instruction sequences leading to sequential port contention for specific CPU generations, which we evaluated on 50 different CPUs. An attacker can use these sequences from the browser to determine the CPU generation within 12 s with a 95% accuracy. This fingerprint is highly stable and resistant to system noise, and we show that mitigations are either expensive or only probabilistic.

Keywords: Side channels · CPU port contention · Browsers · Fingerprinting

1 Introduction

Microarchitectural attacks exploit side effects of the CPU's internal implementation. These attacks have been shown to leak sensitive data even in the absence of software vulnerabilities. Many of these attacks exploit a microarchitectural state that depends on a secret value. A thoroughly studied state is the cache state, *i.e.*, if data resides in the cache or the main memory. This state can be observed using timing measurements when accessing data, as done in, e.g., cache attacks such as Flush+Reload [56]. Such *stateful* channels have the advantage that attacker and victim do not have to run in parallel. Recently, there were also advances in the exploitation of *stateless* channels. In such channels, the microarchitectural state change does not persist and can only be observed while the victim is running. As attacks using stateless channels require the attacker and victim to run in parallel while sharing the same hardware resources, they typically rely on simultaneous multi-threading (SMT), also known as hyper-threading on Intel CPUs.

© The Author(s), under exclusive license to Springer Nature Switzerland AG 2022
V. Atluri et al. (Eds.): ESORICS 2022, LNCS 13556, pp. 209–228, 2022.
https://doi.org/10.1007/978-3-031-17143-7_11

An example of such a channel is port contention [3], where an attacker observes the latency of executed instructions caused by a victim on the hyper-thread that blocks resources necessary to execute the instructions.

The majority of microarchitectural attacks are initially shown in native code. Browsers specifically modified for prototyping microarchitectural attacks [11,39] can help port such attacks step-by-step to the browser, ultimately enabling these attacks from unmodified browsers. The number of such attacks that can be mounted in the browser is steadily increasing [39] even though the sandboxed environment in browsers prevents access to low-level functionality used in microarchitectural attacks, such as high-resolution timers [39,46] or control over the CPU-core placement [11,40]. Despite all these challenges, stateful channels [20,34] and stateless channels [40] have been exploited in browsers.

In this paper, we introduce a new stateless channel that can be exploited in the browser as well. We introduce *sequential port contention*, a novel form of contention on the CPU execution ports. With sequential port contention, we show that port contention [5,40] does not necessarily require SMT. Instead of exploiting *thread-level* parallelism, we exploit *instruction-level* parallelism. We exploit the limited look-ahead window of the instruction scheduler that results in sub-optimal scheduling–and, as a result, increased latency due to sub-optimal instruction-level parallelism–for specific instruction sequences on a single CPU core. We show that such sequences work in native code but also work reliably in WebAssembly. Our side channel works in unmodified off-the-shelf browsers, including the privacy-focused browsers Tor and Brave.

We present an automated framework to search for instructions sequences leading to sequential port contention in the browser. The framework supports Intel and AMD CPUs and works in WebAssembly. Our evaluation on 26 CPUs spanning 13 CPU generations discovers at least 36 instruction sequences causing sequential port contention.

In a case study, we demonstrate that the framework discovers sequences that allow distinguishing CPU generations. We use the results from our framework to automatically build a k-NN classifier that reliably detects the CPU generation based only on timing measurements. As we use a differential measuring approach based on sequential port contention, our results are independent of the overall CPU performance, *i.e.*, the CPU frequency and workload on other CPU cores do not impact our classification. We evaluate our classifier in the browser on 50 CPUs[1]. From within Chrome and Firefox, we classify the CPU generation with a very high accuracy of 95% within, on average, 12 s.

Due to the robustness of our approach, we show that our side channel is hard to mitigate and is highly resistant to system noise. Moreover, proposals for preventing (hardware) fingerprinting [7–9] are ineffective, as we only require coarse-grained timing measurements. The CPU does not change often, and mitigations against this type of attack are difficult, granting the fingerprint a high stability over time. We show that our fingerprint is stable on all major releases

---

[1] Sources and evaluation data are available on https://github.com/MIAOUS-group/port-contention-without-smt.

of Chrome and Firefox in a year and, therefore could be used to link less stable fingerprints [26,53].

Hence, we stress that this new side channel is a real privacy risk, as it can be used to track users based on their CPU. Moreover, we show that sequential port contention is also possible in a virtualized environment but stops working in emulated environments. These results also indicate that the side channel is valuable for malware as an anti-emulation measure.

Our key contributions are:

- We introduce a CPU-port-contention primitive that relies on instruction-level parallelism instead of SMT and build a framework to automatically find WebAssembly instructions creating such sequential port contention.
- We use this primitive to fingerprint the CPU generation in WebAssembly in web browsers without any browser API.
- We evaluate our new fingerprinting method on 50 CPUs from 12 generations with an accuracy of 95% with a runtime of only 12 s.
- We discuss that the fingerprint is highly stable over major releases of browsers, is robust against system noise, and mitigations are difficult.

2 Background

2.1 CPU Port Contention

Simultaneous multithreading (SMT) allows parallelization by sharing the resources of one physical core across two or more logical cores. Intel's SMT implementation is called Hyper-Threading (HT). Typically, a pair of logical cores in the same physical core shares L1 and L2 caches, a branch prediction unit, and the execution engine, among other components.

Instructions are fetched from memory by the pipeline, which in a second step decomposes each instruction into smaller, atomic operations, called microoperations or μops. The μops are then distributed to the execution engine by the scheduler through multiple CPU *execution ports* belonging to the *execution units*. Each execution unit is specialized to process precise types of instructions, e.g., arithmetic μops are distributed to port 0, 1, 5, or 6 (noted P0156). Abel et al. [1] have documented the port usage of instructions for various Intel CPU generations. The port usage can differ from one generation to another for the same instruction.

Since the execution engine is shared across two logical cores, two threads on the same physical core can create contention on this resource by executing instructions issued to the same port. Port contention has been used in side-channel attacks [3] and transient execution attacks [5]. Rokicki et al. [40] showed that this side channel is exploitable from web browsers using WebAssembly.

2.2 WebAssembly

WebAssembly [54] is a binary instruction format for a stack-based virtual machine. It is designed to be deployed on the web, on the client or server sides. It is a portable compilation target from other languages, such as C, C++ or Rust, with the purpose of bringing native-like performance to the browser. Client-side WebAssembly is designed to run inside the JavaScript sandbox [18], hence it is heavily restricted for security purposes: among others, it cannot use native instructions or have access to arbitrary memory addresses. WebAssembly is built around a stack machine in a format resembling native assembly. WebAssembly offers more than 200 specified instructions [17], including SIMD operations. Although originally a binary language, it supports a human-readable text format, allowing reading and modifying compiled WebAssembly code at a low level.

2.3 Browser Fingerprinting

Browser fingerprinting is a stateless technique collecting data from the browser or machine configuration, usually from dedicated APIs [29]. It aims to construct a unique identifier, called a browser fingerprint, without storing any cookie. JavaScript APIs and HTTP headers give information such as the User Agent, screen resolution, and time zone, which, alone, are perfectly harmless and even help enhance user experience on websites. However, the combination of these attributes is often unique, and can therefore be used for either tracking or as another factor of authentication [27].

To be useful, a fingerprint should have the following properties. *Uniqueness*: a fingerprint should be able to uniquely identify users. This is obtained by collecting multiple attributes, rather than from a single unique attribute. *Stability*: any change in an attribute value changes the fingerprint and therefore breaks user identification. However, relying on software fingerprinting means that attributes are constantly changing (e.g., the browser version in the User Agent). Vastel et al. [53] showed that it is possible to link two fingerprints that are slightly different from each other through heuristics. Therefore, for a single attribute, uniqueness is less important than stability to link fingerprints.

3   Threat Model

Sequential port contention, as most microarchitectural attacks, requires code execution on the victim machine. We assume that the attacker either has native unprivileged code execution (native side channel) or can run WebAssembly in the victim's browser (browser-based side channel). The attacker does not rely on software vulnerabilities, does not require any permissions that have to be granted by the victim, or any particular setup such as SMT or a specific core assignment. We assume that the victim spends at least 15 s on the attacker's website, based on the average time of 20 s users dwell on an unknown website [32].

4   Port Contention Without SMT

Port contention, as described by Aldaya et al. [3], requires SMT. Both the attacker and the victim need to run on the same physical core for the attack

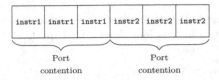

(a) *Grouped*. Instructions are executed in batch, creating port contention and reducing parallelism. This results in a slower execution time.

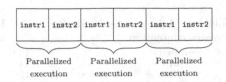

(b) *Interleaved*. Instructions are executed alternatively, allowing them to be executed at the same time, resulting in a faster execution time.

Fig. 1. Illustration of the differences in execution time based on the order of instructions, with a look-ahead window of size 1.

to work, as CPU ports are on-core resources. This prerequisite represents a challenge in some settings, as some systems do not have SMT or disable it [21], and it may become increasingly hard to fulfill as countermeasures to SMT attacks are being explored [51,52]. It also has severe implications in a web setting, where the attacker script, situated inside the JavaScript sandbox, cannot know nor control which core it is running on. In this section, we show port contention without requiring SMT, both in a native setting and in a browser sandbox.

4.1 Main Idea

The main idea of *sequential port contention* is to exploit the limited look-ahead window of the μop scheduler, leading to contention for well-chosen instruction pairs (instr1, instr2). Both instructions use different execution ports on the CPU. If the instructions are grouped, *i.e.*, if the instruction stream consists of n instructions instr1, followed by n instructions instr2, with n larger than the look-ahead window of the scheduler, parallelization is not possible (cf. Fig. 1(a)). The scheduler cannot detect that some instructions later in the instruction stream could already be executed in parallel. However, if interleaved in an instruction stream of $2n$ instructions, they can be executed in parallel (cf. Fig. 1(b)). As a result, the overall execution time of an instruction stream of the same length depends on the order of the two repeated instructions instr1 and instr2 if these instructions do not use the same ports.

Similar to port contention with SMT [3], the contending instructions instr1 and instr2 depend on the underlying microarchitecture. However, as this information is publicly available [1], sequential port contention is applicable to a wide range of microarchitectures. We show sequential port contention in native environments (Sect. 4.2) and demonstrate that it is also exploitable from off-the-shelf unmodified browsers (Sect. 4.3).

Listing 1.1. *Grouped*. Always creates contention.

```
1   grouped:
2       lfence
3       rdtsc # Timestamp
4       lfence
5       .rept $n # First loop
6           instr1 %reg , %reg
7       .endr
8       .rept $n # Second loop
9           instr2 %reg , %reg
10      .endr
11      lfence # Timestamp
12      rdtsc
```

Listing 1.2. *Interleaved*. Creates contention if the two instructions share a CPU port.

```
13  interleaved:
14      lfence
15      rdtsc # Timestamp
16      lfence
17
18      .rept $n # Single loop
19          instr1 %reg , %reg
20          instr2 %reg , %reg
21      .endr
22
23      lfence # Timestamp
24      rdtsc
```

4.2   Native Environment

Proof of Concept. Our proof of concept of sequential port contention is based on two experiments, illustrated in Listings 1.1 and 1.2. In these experiments, we evaluate two native x86 instructions, `instr1` and `instr2`.

The first experiment is a control experiment, *grouped*, which is composed of two loops, each calling an instruction n times. As the decomposition of instructions in μops is deterministic, the various calls to the same instructions have the same port usage. This means that during loop 1 (respectively loop 2), `instr1` (respectively `instr2`) always creates contention on its ports. The second experiment, *interleaved* is composed of a single loop with the same number of iterations. Instead of calling the same instructions in a row, it alternatively calls `instr1` and `instr2`. If `instr1` and `instr2` emit μops to the same port, it creates contention, resulting in a slower overall execution time. However, if they do not emit μops on the same port, the execution is parallelized due to instruction-level parallelization, resulting in a faster execution time.

By computing $\rho = \frac{time(grouped)}{time(interleaved)}$, we know if *interleaved* creates contention. If $\rho \approx 1$, both experiments have a similar execution time, *i.e.*, the instructions share at least one port. If $\rho > 1$, *interleaved* has a shorter execution time than *grouped*, *i.e.*, the instructions do not share a common port.

Experiments. We run this experiment on an Intel i5-8365U (Whiskey Lake), with TurboBoost enabled and without fixing the CPU frequency. First, we run it with `instr1` = crc32, which emits a single μop on execution port 1 (P1), and `instr2` = aesdec, which emits a single μop on execution port 0 (P0). Both instructions have the same throughput and latency.

Figure 2 illustrates the results of this experiment when we vary the number of loop iterations n. Figure 2(a) shows how the *grouped* execution time is systematically higher than the *interleaved* one. The gap between the two curves increases with the number of loops. Figure 2(b) shows that ρ quickly converges to 1.8 at $n = 1000$. It then remains constant when increasing the number of loop iterations. The inflection point situated around $n = 64$ is caused by the size of

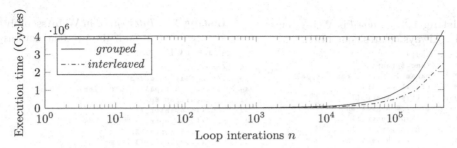

(a) Execution time of the experiments depending on the number of loop iterations n.

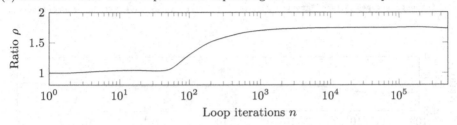

(b) Ratio ρ depending on the number of loop iterations n.

Fig. 2. Sequential port contention experiments for instructions (`crc32`, `aesdec`).

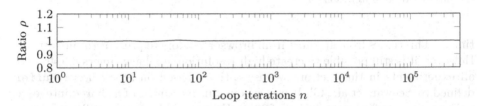

Fig. 3. Ratio ρ for (`crc32`, `popcnt`) depending on the loop iterations n.

the look-ahead window of the scheduler. When instructions from both loops fit inside this window, the scheduler can rearrange instructions to execute them in the most optimized order, prioritizing parallelism and thus reducing port contention. When an `mfence` is added between the two loops (Lines 7–8 of Listing 1.1), this inflection point disappears, and the curve raises smoothly to 1.8.

We run the same experiment with `instr1` = `crc32` and `instr2` = `popcnt`. Both instructions emit a single P1 μop, and have the same throughput and latency. Figure 3 shows that ρ stays constant around 1. That is expected, as the contention is always the same on P1, independently of instruction order.

4.3 Web Browsers

Challenges. Porting these experiments to a browser sandbox introduces new challenges. First, neither JavaScript nor WebAssembly provides high-resolution

Listing 1.3. *Grouped* in WebAssembly. Always creates contention.

```
25  (module
26   (func $grouped
27   (param $p type)(result type)
28    (local.get $p)
29      (type.instr_1)
30      ... # Repeat $n
31      (type.instr_1)
32      (type.instr_2)
33      ... # Repeat $n
34      (type.instr_2)
35   )
36   (export "grouped" (func $grouped))
37  )
```

Listing 1.4. *Interleaved* in WebAssembly. Creates contention if the two instructions share a CPU port.

```
38  (module
39   (func $interleaved
40   (param $p type)(result type)
41    (local.get $p)
42      (type.instr_1)
43      (type.instr_2)
44      ... # Repeat $n
45      (type.instr_1)
46      (type.instr_2)
47   )
48   (export "interleaved" (func $interleaved))
49  )
```

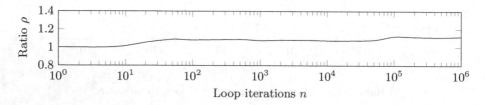

Fig. 4. Ratio ρ for the WebAssembly instructions (i64.popcnt, i64.or) depending on the number of loop iterations n.

timers. This comes from an effort from browser vendors to prevent timing attacks. However, it is still possible to create high-resolution auxiliary timers [39,46]. For all experiments in this section, we use a timer based on SharedArrayBuffer, defined by Schwarz et al. [46]. It uses a constant increment of a shared integer as a time unit and offers a resolution of 20 ns. However, this timer is still not as accurate as native cycle-accurate timers. Second, both JavaScript and WebAssembly are high-level languages, running inside a sandbox. There is no access to native instructions or arbitrary virtual addresses. Moreover, WebAssembly instructions are an abstraction of native instructions and thus do not directly map to execution ports. As WebAssembly is aimed at being portable, the translation of WebAssembly to native code depends on the browser's WebAssembly compiler and the targeted CPU. We can, however, empirically determine the port usage of these instructions for a system [40].

Proof of Concept. Similar to native experiments, the sequential port contention in WebAssembly is composed of two different functions. Listing 1.3 shows the code for the *grouped* experiment, which results in a slow execution time as instructions are delayed by contention. Listing 1.4 shows the *interleaved* experiment. A low execution time indicates that the experiments were not slowed down by contention, whereas a high execution time means both instructions share at least one port.

Experiments. We run this experiment on the same Intel i5-8365U CPU, with `instr1 = i64.popcnt` and `instr2 = i64.or`. Figure 4 illustrates how ρ also increases with the number of loops. On both Chrome 101 and Firefox 99, ρ stabilizes around 1.1 starting from $n = 100\ 000$ loop iterations. This ratio is significantly lower than the native one. This stems from lower precision timers, as well as the stack structure of WebAssembly, where we need to add a value to the stack between instructions. Running the same experiment with `instr1 = i64.popcnt` and `instr2 = i64.ctz`, ρ remains constant around 1 when varying the number of loops. We devise a framework to isolate pairs of instructions that exhibit sequential contention in Sect. 5.2.

Privacy-oriented browsers are also vulnerable to sequential port contention. With 100 000 loop iterations in Brave 1.38, we obtain $\rho = 1.1$. In Tor Browser 11.0.11, `SharedArrayBuffer` is disabled by default to prevent timing attacks. However, we can still reproduce sequential port contention with the lower-resolution timer `performance.now()` by increasing the number of loop iterations n to 100 000 000. In that case, we obtain $\rho = 1.2$, but each experiment takes up to 1 s, *i.e.*, 1000 times more than for other browsers.

5   Fingerprinting CPU Generations

In this section, we show how sequential port contention can be used to determine the CPU generation of the victim, even from inside the JavaScript sandbox.

5.1   Core Idea

The port usage of native instructions varies across generations of microarchitecture. As the number of execution units and CPU ports vary, the same instruction can emit P1 μops on a given generation and P0 on another generation. For instance, `VPBROADCASTD` emits one μop on P5 on both Haswell and Whiskey Lake microarchitectures, and `AESDEC` emits one μop on P1 on Haswell and one μop on P5 on Whiskey Lake. We computed ρ on an Intel i5-8365U (Whiskey Lake) and an Intel i3-4160T (Haswell). The frequency of these CPUs can vary. However, the base frequency does not impact our experiment as we compute a ratio. We found $\rho_{\text{WhiskeyLake}} = 1$ and $\rho_{\text{Haswell}} = 1.8$. This correlates with the documented port usage. Indeed, on Whiskey Lake, both instructions emit a μop on P5. Thus, both experiments are slowed down by contention. On Haswell, the two instructions do not share a common port. Thus, the *interleaved* experiment is not slowed down by port contention, resulting in a faster execution time and a ratio $\rho > 1$.

In summary, by finding pairs of instructions that create contention for some generations but not others, we can detect on which CPU generation the code is executed. As sequential contention is visible from a browser (cf. Sect. 4.3), we also aim to discover pairs of WebAssembly instructions that exhibit sequential port contention to fingerprint the CPU generation from a web page.

5.2 Framework

The port usage of the CPU-independent WebAssembly instructions cannot be determined from the WebAssembly source code. Thus, we build a framework based on PC-Detector [40] to automatically evaluate 458 pairs of WebAssembly instructions for contention on a specific CPU generation. Due to the nature of WebAssembly, it is highly portable and can be executed on any microarchitecture. This framework aims at isolating instruction pairs that can act as distinguishers. Such distinguishers have two major properties: 1) they exhibit different contention for different generations, and 2) they always exhibit the same contention for different CPUs of the same generation. The second property is essential, as other sources of contention that do not depend on the generation could yield false results. Changes in the microarchitecture, e.g., floating-point units, inside a CPU generation can cause changes in behaviors, thus preventing stable fingerprinting.

Using this framework, we collect the best distinguishers to create traces for each generation. To fingerprint generations, we create a k-NN-based classifier and train it with results from the framework. It represents traces as points in an l-dimensional space, where l is the length of the trace, *i.e.*, the number of distinguishers. Given a distance for each unknown execution trace, the classifier computes the k-nearest traces from our training dataset. A trace is classified in the most frequent class, *i.e.*, CPU generation, in the k-nearest-neighbors.

To collect evaluation traces for the two sequential port contention experiments, we use a simple web page (https://fp-cpu-gen.github.io/fp-cpu-gen). It works on the latest versions of Firefox and Chrome, on Linux, macOS and Windows.

5.3 Evaluation

This section presents the results of our classifier and the different parameters used. Our classifier presents a 95% accuracy in a real-world threat model (cf. Sect. 3): a user visits a malicious website for a few seconds.

The *training set* is composed of 26 different CPUs spanning 13 different generations. It is composed of both AMD and Intel CPUs, including server and standard desktop CPUs. Table 1 in Appendix A presents the training set. The *test set* is composed of a subset of traces from the training set. It contains 13 different CPUs. The *evaluation set* is composed of traces from our website. These traces come from an uncontrolled environment since the web script cannot control or quantify the system noise. It contains 50 CPUs from 12 different generations.

Training and Testing. We train our model using data from our training set. The CPUs used in our training set are not balanced in terms of CPU generations, some being more represented than others. We therefore include the same number of traces for each generation to compensate this. Our framework finds 36 pairs of instructions acting as distinguishers between the CPU generations. We use the traces from these distinguishers to train our k-NN classifier. Our model shows a 96% accuracy on the test set, using $k = 5$ neighbors and majority voting.

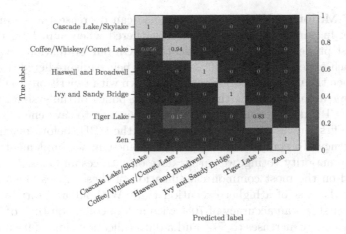

Fig. 5. Confusion matrix for the evaluation of the k-NN classifier with grouped generations, $k = 5$ and majority voting on 10 traces.

Accuracy. Figure 5 illustrates the results of our classifier on the evaluation set. It has a balanced accuracy of 95%. We use $k = 5$ as the number of neighbors. We gather 10 traces and classify each one independently. The class for the experiment is determined using majority voting on the 10 classified traces. Due to the lack of microarchitectural changes between closely-related generations, some generations have the same assignment of execution ports for all instructions. As a consequence, some generations are indistinguishable using sequential port contention. We grouped such generations in the classes of our classifier. This includes the Bridge (Ivy Bridge, Sandy Bridge), Well (Haswell, Broadwell), Skylake (Skylake, Cascade Lake), and Coffee-Lake group (Coffee Lake, Whiskey Lake, Comet Lake). AMD CPUs are distinguishable from Intel ones, but the generations are grouped in the Zen group (Zen 1, Zen 2, and Zen 3).

Execution Time. The total execution time is composed of the offline and the online execution time. The *one-time offline execution time* is composed of the framework execution time and k-NN training time. On average, testing all pairs of instructions in the framework takes 4 h, with a standard deviation of 1 h and 7 min. Training the k-NN model takes 5 s on an i5-8365U. The *online execution time* is composed of the data collection time, *i.e.*, the time taken on the website to gather the 10 traces, plus the prediction time, *i.e.*, the execution time of predicting the class of the trace. The data collection time is the most critical factor, as it represents the duration the victim has to remain on the web page. The client sends the traces to the server that then computes the prediction, so the victim can then close the web page. Data collection takes 12 s on average, with a standard deviation of 6 s. The data collection time is faster on average on Google Chrome (10 s) compared to Firefox (13 s). On both browsers, the data collection time is in the range of the average visit time on a website [32]. The prediction time is on average of 40 ms for 10 traces on an i5-8365U, which is negligible compared to the data collection time.

Impact of Majority Voting. System noise can decrease the accuracy of a single trace. In particular, the first traces gathered when launching the script are the most prone to these misclassifications. On our evaluation set, the first trace for each experiment has a 30% chance of being mispredicted, the second 12%, and then the misclassification rate goes down with repetitions to 6%. There are multiple reasons, including the power saving policy of the system, where by default, the CPU does not use its maximum frequency to save energy, and cold caches. The first traces act as a "warm-up" of the CPU, before reaching maximum frequency. To compensate for this phenomenon, we implement majority voting. With majority voting, we gather data on v traces and classify the experiment based on the most common classification of these traces. This improves accuracy at the cost of a higher execution time. Without majority voting, our evaluation set shows an accuracy of 70% with a data collection time of 5 s. With $v = 5$, the accuracy increases to 86% and a data collection time of 9 s on average. Starting from $v = 10$, the accuracy peaks at 95% with a data collection time of 12 s.

Impact of the Number of Neighbors. The number of neighbors k is a significant factor in the classifier's efficiency. A small number renders the classification vulnerable to noise, as a single noisy trace in the training set can lead to mispredicting many evaluation traces. A higher number tends to increase the impact of densely grouped traces, as well as increase the computation costs.

For instance, when using $k = 1$ on the evaluation dataset, the classifier accuracy is reduced to 85%. We found that $k = 5$ grants a higher accuracy for our testing and evaluation sets. Higher values of k tend to yield a lower accuracy. This comes from the similarity of traces between closely-related generation groups, e.g., Skylake and Coffee-Lake groups.

Time Stability. Time stability is an essential feature, as hardware is seldomly changed by users, compared to software that has regular updates. We evaluate the stability of the classifier on an Intel i5-8365U on each major version of Firefox and Chrome covering about a year. The generation is correctly classified from Chrome 91 (released in May 2021) to 101 and Firefox 89 (released in June 2021) to 100. Prior versions did not support WebAssembly SIMD instructions, which are part of the distinguishers in our traces. Our CPU-generation fingerprints have been stable for a year. This represents a high time stability for a browser fingerprint compared to ever-changing browser APIs and other hardware-based approaches, such as DrawnApart [26], where the fingerprint may change with browsers' major releases, resulting in a median tracking time of 28 days.

Impact of Noise on Classification. As the attacker resides inside a sandbox, they cannot know nor control noise created by other processes or tabs. Such noise could deteriorate the performance of our classifier by creating wrong results in the data collection process. We run the data collection process in the website on

Firefox 100 and Chrome 101 on a quadcore i5-8365U, while artificially creating noise with the `stress` command. The stress threads create noise, disturbing either the sequential port contention or the clock thread. Fewer noise sources, *i.e.*, `stress -c {1..4}`, result in 93% accuracy. That is because the OS's scheduler balances the workload, and the attack physical core is not affected by the noise. A higher count of stress threads, i.e., 5 to 8, still yields an accuracy of 75%.

6 Discussion

In this section, we discuss the practical use of CPU generation fingerprinting (Sect. 6.1), its limitations (Sect. 6.2), the effects of virtualization and emulation (Sect. 6.3) as well as possible mitigations (Sect. 6.4).

6.1 Practical Use of CPU-Generation Fingerprinting

The CPU-generation attribute does not have a high uniqueness, as even with a bigger training set, there are a limited number of CPU generations. The relevant feature here is its *stability*. We envision using this new fingerprinting attribute in combination with existing attributes. Its stability can be used as a linking factor to better link fingerprints to enhance tracking time [53] or use fingerprinting as a second authentication factor [27]. Hardware-based fingerprinting attributes are ideal candidates, as hardware is updated less often than software, and software updates usually lead to changes in fingerprints. However, even robust hardware-based methods can break with browser internal changes [26]. We have shown that our method is robust to major version changes of browsers over a year.

6.2 Limitations

For CPU generations with major changes, sequential port contention is a highly reliable method to fingerprint the CPU generation. Such changes are found on Intel CPUs between the Bridge (e.g., Sandy Bridge, Ivy Bridge), the Well (e.g., Haswell, Broadwell), and the Lake (e.g., Skylake, Coffee Lake, Whiskey Lake, Comet Lake) microarchitectures. However, starting with the successful Lake microarchitecture, changes between new versions are smaller, making it harder to detect the specific microarchitecture. For example, Coffee Lake, Whiskey Lake, and Comet Lake are based on the nearly identical designs of the execution units. Only Ice Lake introduced changes again, specifically with an additional store unit [55] which subsequently led to changes in the port assignment for several instructions. Hence, the detection of the CPU generation cannot differentiate names for essentially the same generation.

Due to lack of access, some generations are not included in the training set, e.g., Nehalem or Ice Lake. Thus, they cannot be correctly predicted by our proof-of-concept model and are not included in the evaluation set. This could be easily corrected by extending our study and running the framework on a larger range of CPUs. CPUs with significant microarchitectural changes are potentially highly identifiable, e.g., Ice Lake with its addition of new store units.

6.3   Virtualization and Emulation

Sequential port contention is not limited to bare-metal code execution but also works from inside virtual machines if the guest is virtualized and not emulated.

Virtualization. As all involved instructions are unprivileged and not emulated by the hypervisor, there is no difference in the execution stream to a bare-metal execution. Hence, the measured effects are also the same. Moreover, as only a single CPU core is required, the scheduler of the hypervisor does not affect the contention. We verify on Ubuntu 20.04 (kernel 5.13) with QEMU KVM 4.2.1 that we measure the same effect of sequential port contention within a virtual machine (Ubuntu 20.04, kernel 5.4).

Emulation. Sequential port contention requires that the specifically-crafted instruction stream is executed without modifications on the CPU. For emulation, this is not the case if instructions are interpreted or translated just in time with potential additional instructions in the instruction stream. For example, when running the guest operating system (Ubuntu 20.04, kernel 5.4) in QEMU 4.2.1 with full system emulation (TCG), we are unable to measure the effect of sequential port contention. In this setup, the instruction stream with and without contention have the same execution time.

Based on this observation, sequential port contention can detect emulation, e.g., if the code is analyzed via a malware-analysis emulator [6,25]. Hence, sequential port contention provides malware with another trick to detect such environments. As discussed in Sect. 6.4, mitigating sequential port contention is difficult. Likewise, sequential port contention is likely infeasible to emulate, making it difficult to prevent malware from detecting the presence of an emulator.

6.4   Mitigation

Sequential port contention does not require any operating-system interface or particular setup, such as SMT (cf. Sect. 3). Hence, this side channel cannot be prevented on the operating-system level but potentially on the browser level. As previous work on microarchitectural attack detection [19,22,35,47], we show that this side channel can also be detected using hardware performance counters.

Browser Mitigation. Existing browser mitigations against side-channel attacks are only effective against sequential port contention if they block access to timing sources [24,33,45] or entirely prevent the execution of active content [13,37]. However, while effective, these methods also impact the usability of all websites.

The browser can interleave the generated instruction stream with memory fences, effectively preventing out-of-order execution. Theoretically, to fully mitigate the side channel, a browser has to emit a memory fence after every assembly instruction. However, this leads to unacceptable performance penalties, as

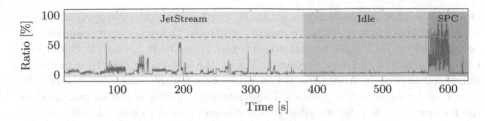

Fig. 6. Ratio of backend-bound to misprediction-bound execution when unning the JetStream JavaScript and WebAssembly benchmark (left), nothing (middle), and our website for generating the browser fingerprint (right) in Firefox 100.0.2.

it effectively prevents out-of-order execution while additionally adding the overhead of the fence (multiple cycles) after every instruction. A trade-off between the number of inserted fences and signal strength might be feasible, though. We leave an evaluation to future work.

Alternatively, the browser can reorder the instruction stream while keeping its functionality. Such reordering can be part of existing compiler optimizations, such as loop optimizations. Software-diversification approaches have also been shown as mitigation against side-channel attacks [10,36]. As the code required for sequential port contention requires precise control over the instruction sequence, any diversification likely breaks the side channel. We leave the evaluation of software-diversification methods applied by the browser to future work.

Detection via Performance Counters. To detect sequential port contention, we propose a metric based on the topdown bottleneck decomposition [58]. Previous work focused mostly on cache-based performance counters for detecting microarchitectural attacks [19,22,35,47]. However, for sequential port contention, the cache activity is indistinguishable from typical workloads. The bottleneck exploited in sequential port contention is the execution unit in the backend. As the instruction stream is entirely linear, we use the ratio of backend-bound execution divided by misprediction-bound execution. Hence, the more often the bottleneck is in the backend, combined with next to no mispredictions, the higher the likelihood that the monitored snippet uses sequential port contention.

Figure 6 shows the evaluation of this metric in Firefox while running the JetStream JavaScript and WebAssembly benchmark (left), nothing (middle), and our website for generating the browser fingerprint (right). Our tests do not show any workload where this metric is as high as for sequential port contention, allowing detection of this side channel using a simple threshold (dashed line).

7 Related Work

7.1 SMT Side-Channel Attacks

Aldaya et al. [3] introduced the first SMT side-channel attack based on port contention. Their native implementation allowed inferring private keys from

OpenSSL's TLS. Bhattacharyya et al. [5] exploited port contention to create a covert channel in a speculative execution attack. Other on-core resources can be targeted by SMT side-channel attacks: the Translation Lookaside Buffer [15], L1 data cache [57], L1 way predictor [31], or the μop-cache [38]. In a more systematized approach, ABSynthe [14] is a black-box framework to automatically detect on-core contention sources. The contention source is not documented by the framework, but is leveraged in a side-channel attack to recover EdDSA keys.

7.2 Side-Channel Attacks in Browsers

With the Prime+Probe cache attack in JavaScript, Oren et al. [34] proposed the first microarchitectural side-channel attack in the browser. Cache occupancy was also used to monitor opened websites in the browser [48]. DRAM has also been targeted to reproduce Rowhammer [20] or create a covert channel [46] in the browser. Gras et al. [16] demonstrated that an attacker in the JavaScript sandbox can reverse ASLR and de-randomize virtual addresses. Microarchitectural side-channels also let an attacker track user's browsing history through Floating-Point Units [4]. Transient execution attacks have also been shown in the browser, including Spectre [23], ZombieLoad [11], and RIDL [43].

7.3 Browser Fingerprinting

The first attempt to use fingerprints to de-anonymize web clients was introduced by Eckersley [12]. Laperdrix et al. [28] presented an overview of existing browser fingerprinting techniques and applications. Most fingerprints rely on software attributes, such as HTTP headers and user agents [12], Canvas API [2,50], or browser extensions [30,41,49]. Hardware features have also been used to create fingerprints. Sanchez-Rola et al. [42] demonstrated how imperfections in computer internal clocks can be used to fingerprint unique machines. JavaScript template attacks [44] were applied to fingerprinting, retrieving the instruction-set architecture, and used memory allocator from the JavaScript sandbox. Laor et al. [26] identified devices based on unique properties in the GPU stack.

8   Conclusion

We introduced sequential port contention, a new side channel based on port contention that does not require SMT. We proposed a WebAssembly framework to automatically determine instruction sequences creating sequential port contention. We demonstrated that an attacker can exploit sequential port contention to determine the CPU generation of a victim from the browser within 12 s. This information is highly stable, and the attack works correctly even under heavy system noise. This new side-channel is privacy threatening, as it is hard to mitigate and can be used for improving the stability of fingerprints.

Acknowledgments. This work benefited from the support of the project ANR-19-CE39-0007 MIAOUS of the French National Research Agency (ANR), and ANR-21-CE39-0019/Deutsche Forschungsgemeinschaft (DFG, German Research Foundation) 491039149 FACADES.

A   Training Set

Table 1. CPUs used in our training set

CPU	Vendor	Generation
Xeon X5670	Intel	Westmere
Xeon E5-2620	Intel	Sandy Bridge
Xeon E5-2630	Intel	Sandy Bridge
Xeon E5-2630L	Intel	Sandy Bridge
Xeon E5-2650 0	Intel	Sandy Bridge
Xeon E5-2660 0	Intel	Sandy Bridge
Core i5-2520M	Intel	Sandy Bridge
Xeon E5-2660 v2	Intel	Ivy Bridge
Xeon E5-2630 v3	Intel	Haswell
Core i3-4160T	Intel	Haswell
Xeon E5-2620 v4	Intel	Broadwell
Xeon E5-2630 v4	Intel	Broadwell
Xeon E5-2680 v4	Intel	Broadwell
Core i3-5010U	Intel	Broadwell
Xeon Gold 6126	Intel	Skylake
Xeon Gold 6130	Intel	Skylake
Core i9-9980HK	Intel	Coffee Lake
Core i5-8365U	Intel	Whiskey Lake
Xeon Gold 5218	Intel	Cascade Lake SP
Xeon Gold 5220	Intel	Cascade Lake SP
Core i7-10510U	Intel	Comet Lake
Core i7-10710U	Intel	Comet Lake
Core i5-1135G7	Intel	Tiger Lake
EPYC 7301	AMD	Zen
Ryzen 5 2500U	AMD	Zen
Ryzen 9 5900HX	AMD	Zen 3

References

1. Abel, A., Reineke, J.: Uops.info: characterizing latency, throughput, and port usage of instructions on intel microarchitectures. In: ASPLOS (2019)
2. Acar, G., Eubank, C., Englehardt, S., Juárez, M., Narayanan, A., Díaz, C.: The web never forgets: persistent tracking mechanisms in the wild. In: CCS (2014)
3. Aldaya, A.C., Brumley, B.B., Ul Hassan, S., García, C.P., Tuveri, N.: Port contention for fun and profit. In: S&P (2019)
4. Andrysco, M., Kohlbrenner, D., Mowery, K., Jhala, R., Lerner, S., Shacham, H.: On subnormal floating point and abnormal timing. In: S&P (2015)
5. Bhattacharyya, A., et al.: SmoTherSpectre: exploiting speculative execution through port contention. In: CCS (2019)
6. Brengel, M., Backes, M., Rossow, C.: Detecting hardware-assisted virtualization. In: DIMVA (2016)
7. Bugzilla: Check crossoriginisolated for all nsrfpservice::reducetimeprecision* callers. https://bugzilla.mozilla.org/show_bug.cgi?id=1586761. Accessed 20 May 2022
8. contributors, M.: Cross-origin-embedder-policy. https://developer.mozilla.org/en-US/docs/Web/HTTP/Headers/Cross-Origin-Embedder-Policy. Accessed 19 Nov 2021
9. contributors, M.: Cross-origin-opener-policy. https://developer.mozilla.org/en-US/docs/Web/HTTP/Headers/Cross-Origin-Opener-Policy. Accessed 19 Nov 2021
10. Crane, S., Homescu, A., Brunthaler, S., Larsen, P., Franz, M.: Thwarting cache side-channel attacks through dynamic software diversity. In: NDSS (2015)
11. Easdon, C., Schwarz, M., Schwarzl, M., Gruss, D.: Rapid prototyping for microarchitectural attacks. In: USENIX Security Symposium (2022)
12. Eckersley, P.: How unique is your web browser? In: Privacy Enhancing Technologies (2010)
13. Giorgio Maone: NoScript–JavaScript/Java/Flash blocker for a safer Firefox experience!, July 2017. https://noscript.net
14. Gras, B., Giuffrida, C., Kurth, M., Bos, H., Razavi, K.: Absynthe: automatic blackbox side-channel synthesis on commodity microarchitectures. In: NDSS (2020)
15. Gras, B., Razavi, K., Bos, H., Giuffrida, C.: Translation leak-aside buffer: defeating cache side-channel protections with TLB attacks. In: USENIX (2018)
16. Gras, B., Razavi, K., Bosman, E., Bos, H., Giuffrida, C.: ASLR on the line: practical cache attacks on the MMU. In: NDSS (2017)
17. Group, W.C.: Index of instructions webassembly 2.0. https://webassembly.github.io/spec/core/appendix/index-instructions.html. Accessed 20 May 2022
18. Group, W.C.: Security–webassembly. https://webassembly.org/docs/security/. Accessed 20 May 2022
19. Gruss, D., Maurice, C., Wagner, K., Mangard, S.: Flush+Flush: a fast and stealthy cache attack. In: DIMVA (2016)
20. Gruss, D., Maurice, C., Mangard, S.: Rowhammer.js: a remote software-induced fault attack in javascript. In: DIMVA (2016)
21. Hat, R.: Disabling smt to prevent cpu security issues using the web console. https://access.redhat.com/documentation/en-us/red-hat-enterprise-linux/8/topic/f1d65124-781b-4543-a51a-d2bf9fa794ac. Accessed 10 May 2022
22. Irazoqui, G., Eisenbarth, T., Sunar, B.: MASCAT: preventing microarchitectural attacks before distribution. In: CODASPY (2018)
23. Kocher, P., et al.: Spectre attacks: exploiting speculative execution. In: S&P (2019)

24. Kohlbrenner, D., Shacham, H.: Trusted browsers for uncertain times. In: USENIX Security Symposium (2016)
25. Kruegel, C.: Full system emulation: achieving successful automated dynamic analysis of evasive malware. In: BlackHat USA (2014)
26. Laor, T., et al.: DRAWNAPART: a device identification technique based on remote GPU fingerprinting. In: NDSS (2022)
27. Laperdrix, P., Avoine, G., Baudry, B., Nikiforakis, N.: Morellian analysis for browsers: making web authentication stronger with canvas fingerprinting. In: DIMVA (2019)
28. Laperdrix, P., Bielova, N., Baudry, B., Avoine, G.: Browser fingerprinting: a survey. ACM Trans. Web **14**(2), 8:1–8:33 (2020)
29. Laperdrix, P., Rudametkin, W., Baudry, B.: Beauty and the beast: diverting modern web browsers to build unique browser fingerprints. In: S&P (2016)
30. Laperdrix, P., Starov, O., Chen, Q., Kapravelos, A., Nikiforakis, N.: Fingerprinting in style: detecting browser extensions via injected style sheets. In: USENIX Security Symposium (2021)
31. Lipp, M., Hadžić, V., Schwarz, M., Perais, A., Maurice, C., Gruss, D.: Take a way: exploring the security implications of AMD's cache way predictors. In: AsiaCCS (2020)
32. Liu, C., White, R.W., Dumais, S.T.: Understanding web browsing behaviors through weibull analysis of dwell time. In: SIGIR (2010)
33. Mao, J., Chen, Y., Shi, F., Jia, Y., Liang, Z.: Toward exposing timing-based probing attacks in web applications. In: Yang, Q., Yu, W., Challal, Y. (eds.) WASA 2016. LNCS, vol. 9798, pp. 499–510. Springer, Cham (2016). https://doi.org/10.1007/978-3-319-42836-9_44
34. Oren, Y., Kemerlis, V.P., Sethumadhavan, S., Keromytis, A.D.: The spy in the sandbox: practical cache attacks in javascript and their implications. In: CCS (2015)
35. Payer, M.: HexPADS: a platform to detect stealth attacks. In: ESSoS (2016)
36. Rane, A., Lin, C., Tiwari, M.: Raccoon: closing digital {Side-Channels} through obfuscated execution. In: USENIX Security Symposium (2015)
37. Raymond Hill: uBlock Origin–An efficient blocker for Chromium and Firefox. Fast and lean, July 2017. https://github.com/gorhill/uBlock
38. Ren, X., Moody, L., Taram, M., Jordan, M., Tullsen, D.M., Venkat, A.: I see dead μops: leaking secrets via intel/amd micro-op caches. In: ISCA (2021)
39. Rokicki, T., Maurice, C., Laperdrix, P.: SoK: in search of lost time: a review of JavaScript timers in browsers. In: EuroS&P (2021)
40. Rokicki, T., Maurice, C., Botvinnik, M., Oren, Y.: Port contention goes portable: port contention side channels in web browsers. In: ASIACCS (2022)
41. Sánchez-Rola, I., Santos, I., Balzarotti, D.: Extension breakdown: security analysis of browsers extension resources control policies. In: USENIX Security Symposium (2017)
42. Sánchez-Rola, I., Santos, I., Balzarotti, D.: Clock around the clock: time-based device fingerprinting. In: CCS (2018)
43. Van Schaik, S., et al.: RIDL: rogue in-flight data load. In: S&P (2019)
44. Schwarz, M., Lackner, F., Gruss, D.: JavaScript template attacks: automatically inferring host information for targeted exploits. In: NDSS (2019)
45. Schwarz, M., Lipp, M., Gruss, D.: JavaScript zero: real JavaScript and zero side-channel attacks. In: NDSS (2018)

46. Schwarz, M., Maurice, C., Gruss, D., Mangard, S.: Fantastic timers and where to find them: high-resolution microarchitectural attacks in JavaScript. In: International Conference on Financial Cryptography and Data Security (2017)
47. Schwarzl, M., et al.: Dynamic process isolation. arXiv:2110.04751 (2021)
48. Shusterman, A., et al.: Robust website fingerprinting through the cache occupancy channel. In: USENIX Security Symposium (2019)
49. Starov, O., Laperdrix, P., Kapravelos, A., Nikiforakis, N.: Unnecessarily identifiable: quantifying the fingerprintability of browser extensions due to bloat. In: WWW (2019)
50. Stone, P.: Pixel perfect timing attacks with HTML5 (2013)
51. Taram, M., Ren, X., Venkat, A., Tullsen, D.: SecSMT: securing SMT processors against contention-based covert channels. In: USENIX Security Symposium (2022)
52. Townley, D., Ponomarev, D.: SMT-COP: defeating side-channel attacks on execution units in SMT processors. In: PACT (2019)
53. Vastel, A., Laperdrix, P., Rudametkin, W., Rouvoy, R.: FP-STALKER: tracking browser fingerprint evolutions. In: S&P (2018)
54. W3C: Webassembly. https://webassembly.org/. Accessed 20 May 2022
55. WikiChip: Sunny cove–microarchitectures–intel–wikichip. https://en.wikichip.org/wiki/intel/microarchitectures/sunny_cove. Accessed 20 May 2022
56. Yarom, Y., Falkner, K.: FLUSH+RELOAD: a high resolution, low noise, L3 cache side-channel attack. In: USENIX Security Symposium (2014)
57. Yarom, Y., Genkin, D., Heninger, N.: CacheBleed: a timing attack on OpenSSL constant time RSA. In: CHES (2016)
58. Yasin, A.: A top-down method for performance analysis and counters architecture. In: IEEE International Symposium on Performance Analysis of Systems and Software (ISPASS) (2014)

Protocols for a Two-Tiered
Trusted Computing Base

José Moreira[1,2]([⊠]) [iD], Mark D. Ryan[1] [iD], and Flavio D. Garcia[1] [iD]

[1] School of Computer Science, University of Birmingham, Birmingham, UK
{m.d.ryan,f.garcia}@cs.bham.ac.uk
[2] Valory AG, Zug, Switzerland
jose.moreira.sanchez@valory.xyz

Abstract. A *trusted computing base* (TCB) is the minimum set of hardware and software components which are inherently trusted by a platform, and upon which more complex secure services can be built. The TCB is secure by definition, and it is typically implemented through hardened hardware components, which ensure that their secret data cannot be compromised. In this paper, we propose and investigate a two-tier TCB architecture that benefits both from a small hardened 'minimal' TCB, but also offers the possibility of integrating complex security services into an 'extended' TCB. Our design includes a collection of protocols to ensure (1) secure update of the components, (2) secure boot of the platform, (3) attestation, and (4) detection of powerful attackers that can corrupt memory regions together with a (highly probable) platform recovery mechanism after such an attack. The protocols have been formally modelled, and we provide a collection of security properties that have been verified using the automatic protocol verifier ProVerif.

Keywords: Trusted computing base · Secure boot · Remote attestation · Formal modelling

1   Introduction

A *trusted computing base* (TCB) is the set of software and hardware components of a system which form a trust anchor, and upon which the security of the system relies. Two considerations that influence the design of a TCB appear to oppose each other:

- On one hand, the TCB should be very secure; this means that it should be as small and as simple as possible (since complexity brings insecurity); and it should be strongly isolated from the main system so that a compromise in the main system cannot affect the TCB.

We would like to thank the anonymous reviewers for their insightful comments and suggestions. We also gratefully acknowledge EPSRC grants EP/V000454, EP/S030867, EP/R012598, and EP/R008000/1. The majority of the research was done while J. Moreira was at the University of Birmingham.

V. Atluri et al. (Eds.): ESORICS 2022, LNCS 13556, pp. 229–249, 2022.
https://doi.org/10.1007/978-3-031-17143-7_12

- On the other hand, the TCB should offer trustworthy services that support the operation of the main system, such as storage and secure usage of cryptographic keys, storage of application-specific secrets, and trusted execution of application-specific code.

In this paper, we investigate how to split the TCB into two parts, a *minimal trusted computing base* (MTCB) providing limited functionalities, but the most hardened services, and an *extended trusted computing base* (ETCB) providing additional functionalities and services that cannot be protected to quite the same extent. This paper proposes a design for a secure architecture of MTCB and ETCB. Our target platform is the TCB for a network device (e.g., a router, modem, or base station). This kind of platform boots infrequently, and hence boot-time checks are insufficient to guarantee security; we also need checks done at run-time. We expect our design may be useful for other kinds of platform too.

Our contributions include:

- A novel two-tiered TCB architecture, achieving high-grade security properties for the core TCB, while also allowing a rich extended TCB to support applications;
- Security analysis of the protocols defined for the TCB architecture, including verification using ProVerif.

2   Background

Trusted Execution Environments (TEEs) such as ARM TrustZone [13], Intel SGX [5], RISC-V Keystone [6,7], or Sancus [12] realize isolation and attestation of secure application compartments called *enclaves*. TEEs enforce a dual-world view, where even compromised or malicious operating system (OS) in the normal world cannot gain access to the memory space of enclaves running in an isolated secure world on the same processor. This property allows for a TCB reduction: only the code running in the secure world needs to be trusted for enclaved computation results. Thus, such enclave systems offer a great deal of flexibility when it comes to defining the specific code and services that can be executed. However, such flexibility usually comes at the price of an increased surface of attack which gives rise to well-known microarchitectural attacks such as cache timing in TruSpy [21], ARMageddon [8] and Cachezoom [10], or speculative execution based attacks in Foreshadow [19], ZombieLoad [16], SgxSpectre [4], CrossTalk [14], among many others. Besides microarchitectural attacks, rich TEEs often require complex interaction with the insecure world, which leads to 'Tale of two worlds' type of attacks [20].

On the other hand, fixed-API devices such as the Trusted Platform Module (TPM) [18] or the Google Titan M/C chips [15] have a significantly reduced TCB, compared to enclave systems. However, they are typically low performance devices, hard to update and cannot easily support customized applications.

Minimization of the TCB is one of the key principles for secure systems design. A two-tiered TCB has the potential to get the best of both worlds:

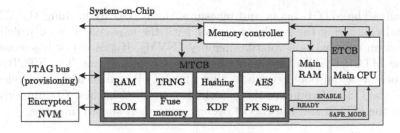

Fig. 1. Two-tier TCB architecture

a small but well protected TCB to guard high secrets which are seldom used and a larger, more feature rich and fast TCB to protect medium secrets. The extended TCB can use the minimum TCB as a trust anchor for long term key storage, integrity protection, etc.

3   Design of the TCB

We assume that the system processes assets which may be categorised as high-value (e.g., long-term keys), medium-value (e.g., ephemeral session keys), and low-value (e.g., transient data). The core functionality of the MTCB is to protect high-valued assets from strong adversaries, and provide the ultimate trust anchor for the system. In order to achieve this, we propose that the MTCB be implemented on a tamper-resistant, discrete processor with its own memory (drawing inspiration from OpenTitan). The MTCB can be integrated within the same SoC as the main processor, RAM and memory controller, in order to avoid bus probing attacks between separate components [17], but with its own, physically separated RAM, and ROM. Having its own memory, the MTCB is isolated from the main processor and thus immune to side channel leakage, e.g., through cache attacks.

Figure 1 depicts our simple MTCB-based platform architecture. This discrete chip implements basic cryptographic primitives including hashing and public key signatures with state-of-the art countermeasures against side-channel and fault-injection attacks. We discuss the offered functionalities below.

3.1   Main Functionalities

The MTCB implements a very delimited set of services, built upon a set of main functionalities, which can be summarized as follows:

Secure Boot. This functionality ensures that the device boots only if it can ascertain that the software being booted is the pre-registered one (e.g., through an enrolment process). We use secure boot to launch the main processor. At boot time, the main processor loads the ETCB in the predefined memory address and then halts. The MTCB boots and measures the ETCB by hashing the ETCB code and comparing the resulting hashes with the expected values, which are stored in an external non-volatile memory (NVM). If this check is successful, then the MTCB enables the main CPU to continue booting. The ETCB then takes control of the boot sequence. Now the ETCB will measure the relevant parts of the OS and compare these with the expected hashes. Communication between the MTCB and the ETCB occurs using their shared memory.

Attestation. This functionality allows a remote party (such as the device owner) to obtain a statement signed by the MTCB about the MTCB's own state (including its firmware version), and the currently loaded ETCB and some aspects of the system software. The MTCB stores the attestation key and its corresponding certificate (chain). Attestation requests are received by system software, and sent from there via the ETCB to the MTCB. Such attestation requests include a challenge from the verifier such as a nonce. Upon receipt of an attestation request the MTCB will produce a signed statement of the challenge, its own state, firmware version, etc., plus the hash of the ETCB code which is currently loaded in memory. Additionally, it includes the hashes provided by the ETCB of the relevant system components which need to be attested.

ETCB Recovery. This functionality aims to identify a memory corruption situation where the adversary has gained enough control over the platform so that it can change the memory contents of the ETCB and substitute it by its own, malicious version. The MTCB proactively measures the running ETCB code, and forces a reboot to a safe state if it finds an unexpected measurement.

3.2   Auxiliary Functionalities

In order to implement the above core security functionalities in practice, we require the following functionalities as well:

Measurement of the ETCB. As part of three of the security protocols, namely secure boot, attestation and ETCB recovery (discussed in Sect. 5 below), the MTCB has the ability to access the main processor's RAM in read-only mode through the memory controller, providing the best of both worlds. This design feature allows performing measurement of the ETCB which runs within the TEE and at a fixed memory address in RAM, e.g., at the very beginning. In order to prevent TOCTOU type of issues generated due to the asynchronous access to the main RAM, the MTCB is set as master of the memory controller. During measurement of the ETCB the MTCB simply disables write access to the code area of the ETCB from the main processor.

Measurement of the OS. Similarly, the ETCB is able to read and measure the memory region where the OS is loaded. We propose that the ETCB enclave system follows an architecture similar to RISC-V Keystone [6,7] or ARM Trust-Zone [13], where the ETCB can take control of the boot sequence and instruct the CPU to execute the OS if the measurements match the expected values.

3.3 Description of the Architecture

As discussed above, the MTCB (and its RAM and ROM) are integrated within the same SoC as the main processor, and there is also RAM shared by the MTCB and the main processor. We discuss the remaining components of the proposed architecture from Fig. 1.

Provisioning Bus. The MTCB must expose an interface (e.g., SPI, I2C or JTAG) for firmware provisioning at manufacture time. During the provisioning process, the MTCB will read contents from that interface and write it to its NVM. After finalizing the provisioning process, the MTCB will permanently disable the provisioning interface, preferably, at hardware level by configuring the appropriate fuse bits.

Random Number Generator. In order to guarantee the generation of high-entropy cryptographic material, we require that the MTCB be provided with a hardware true random number generator (TRNG), which generates random bits from a physical process.

Fuse Memory. The MTCB has an internal fuse memory, which stores:

- A persistent secret key that is generated on first boot used to encrypt and authenticate the external NVM.
- CTR_CUR_VERSION: A unary counter that keeps track of the currently installed version. Each time the MTCB updates its code, it increments this value to match the installed version number.
- CTR_SAFE_MODE: A unary counter that stores the signal SAFE_MODE between reboots: an odd value of the counter signifies that the MTCB must activate the SAFE_MODE signal when the platform boots. See Sect. 5.4 below for more details.

External NVM. The MTCB requires persistent secure storage (EEPROM) to store highly-valued crypto objects and code. The semiconductor manufacturing process does not allow the integration of mixed process sizes within the same SoC, e.g., 7 nm and 14 nm processes. Hence, if current EEPROM technology has a different process size than the main processor, then they cannot be integrated within the same SoC. In order to circumvent this limitation, we implement the MTCB NVM as an external EEPROM chip connected directly to the MTCB via SPI. Because the external NVM could potentially be accessed by a physical attacker, the contents of the EEPROM are encrypted and authenticated. Upon booting of the MTCB, the MTCB BootROM verifies the integrity of the memory blob from the EEPROM, authenticates and decrypts it, using the secret key persistently stored in fuse memory. Then the MTCB BootROM verifies its version number against the unary counter CTR_CUR_VERSION held in the internal fuse memory, and then loads the firmware onto the MTCB's RAM. Conversely, with every write operation, both the NVM version number and the unary counter held in fuse memory are incremented and the NVM re-encrypted and authenticated. In order to prevent rollback attacks, it is necessary to increment the NVM version number with each state change, which has the drawback of consuming one fuse per update. Fortunately, our MTCB does not require frequent, persistent state changes.

Crypto Primitives. The MTCB contains a number of basic crypto primitives (hashing, symmetric encryption, key derivation), implemented as ASIC blocks, which are required to enable the services it offers.

Table 1. Two-tiered TCB design requirements

	Requirement	Realization
MTCB	Resistance to cryptography compromise	Firmware is updatable to enable new cryptographic algorithms
	Bricking avoidance	A/B updates
	Resistance to micro-architectural attacks	Separate processor, avoiding sharing resources such as cache
	Resistance to physical attacks (fault injection, side channel)	Separate processor, implements countermeasures, TRNG
	Resistance to physical attacks (bus probing)	SoC integration with the main CPU
	Resistance to chip decapsulation (confidentiality)	Self-destructing tamper resistance
	Resistance to chip decapsulation (integrity)	Usage of fuse memory for counters and root firmware verification key
	Usage of high entropy cryptographic material	TRNG
	Attestation	Hashing and public-key signing scheme
	Evolvability	External NVM for counters and root firmware verification key, and fuse memory
	Rollback protection	Fuse memory
ETCB	Resistance to software attacker, e.g., buffer overflow attacker	Has enclave system with memory integrity protection (authenticated)
	Keystore for protected secrets	Has enclave system
	Resistance to run-time memory corruption	Periodic run-time memory measurements by MTCB; ETCB recovery protocol; SAFE_MODE
	Attestation	Attestation of ETCB by MTCB

Table 1 mentions some architecture requirements of the TCB and the features that realize them.

4   Adversarial Model

The objective of this section is to define a realistic adversary for the architecture presented above. The adversary can send and receive messages to some platform components (see below). If it learns keys or defines new keys, it can apply cryptographic operations using those keys. To the extent that it has the appropriate keys, the adversary can intercept and spoof messages between components of the system. These aspects of the adversary model are sometimes called the Dolev-Yao model. Later in this section, we specify other aspects of the adversary model, such as the ability to corrupt memory.

Ideally, one would like to define the strongest conceivable adversarial model, since it is clear that if a security property holds for a such a model, it will automatically hold for a relaxed version of that adversary (i.e., having a subset of capabilities). However, imposing a too strong adversary will simply make it impossible that the protocol satisfies any non-trivial security property. For example, if we allow the adversary to have unrestricted control over the exchanged messages by any party, unrestricted capability to change the platform memory, and the ability to anticipate any MTCB operation, it will be impossible to prove attestation of platform state: the adversary can simply switch the memory contents to a legitimate ETCB and OS just before the MTCB is going to attest the memory contents, and switch back to the malicious version afterwards.

Therefore, in order to come up with a realistic adversary, the following reasonable considerations have been taken for our modelling of the protocols:

Communication Channels. The adversary has unlimited read/write access to: 1. The Vendor-Platform channel, 2. The Verifier-Platform channel, 3. The ETCB-OS channel, 4. The MTCB-ETCB channel. However, we require that the adversary has the following restrictions:

1. no write access to the provisioning channel before initial manufacturer provisioning,
2. no read/write access to the MTCB-ETCB channel during first boot,
3. no write access to the signals (ENABLE, READY, SAFE_MODE) exchanged between the MTCB and the main CPU.

We note that making all those channels available to the adversary might be an over-pessimistic assumption (as it might be unrealistic that it has access, e.g., to the MTCB-ETCB channel, which is within the same tamper-resistant SoC), but we can still prove our desired security properties under this assumption. This means that the security properties are anchored on the secrets held by the different participants in the protocol, and in the root of trust implied by the MTCB, but not in the fact that a certain communication between parties is made unavailable to the adversary.

Integrity. We assume that the MTCB is a root of trust for the platform, its integrity is guaranteed, and its secrets are not leaked to the adversary. We also assume that the Vendor secrets are not leaked.

Initial Platform State. The adversary can freely choose an initial configuration for the ETCB and OS at each boot, possibly a malicious ETCB and/or OS.

Memory Corruption. The adversary can change ETCB and OS memory regions after they have been loaded by the CPU. We do not differentiate whether this can be achieved through a bug present in a faulty (but legitimate) ETCB, or through some sort of fault-injection or physical vulnerability. Our modelling, discussed below in Sect. 6, allows arbitrary change between legitimate and non-legitimate ETCBs at any time. However, in a real scenario, it is reasonable to consider that when the adversary switches the memory to a legitimate ETCB, then it cannot longer regain control easily. We also consider that if the adversary succeeds in corrupting the memory to a rogue ETCB version, then it will be interested in running it for a non-negligible fraction of time.

Anticipation of MTCB Operations. To combat memory corruption attacks, we introduce some MTCB operations that aim to detect them. We assume that appropriate protections are in place to prevent anticipation of those MTCB operations. Alternatively, we can assume that the adversary is able to anticipate MTCB operations, without guaranteeing that it will have enough time to hinder their effect. E.g., an adversary could anticipate a memory measurement, but it may not have enough time to revert the memory contents to the uncorrupted state. These assumptions are reasonable for a realistic adversary.

Denial of Service Attacks. As usual in the symbolic model of cryptography, it is impossible to prove "non-DoS" properties, because a Dolev-Yao adversary can drop messages indefinitely. For instance, it is impossible to prove that a Verifier eventually gets a valid attestation. However, it is possible to prove that when a Verifier is convinced that a received attestation is genuine, it is indeed the case.

Some further considerations about adversarial modelling will also be discussed below in Sect. 6.

5   Protocols

The two-tier TCB architecture comprises a set of four core security protocols designed in order to achieve secure firmware update, secure platform boot, platform attestation, and ETCB recovery of a corrupted system. Additional custom services can be build through proper customisation of the ETCB. We start by providing a description of the four core protocols investigated from an implementation point of view. That is, without taking into account the modelling approaches that will be discussed in Sect. 6 below. These protocols are designed to work in conjunction, as the security guarantees of a certain protocol might depend on the establishment of a certain parameter on a previous protocol.

Table 2. Glossary of symbols, representing cryptographic objects used throughout the paper

	Object	Description
Vendor	ssk_V	Secret signing key used for MTCB A/B firmware update
	spk_V	Public verification key corresponding to ssk_V
	σ_V	*A signature using ssk_V
	kfw	Symmetric encryption key, shared with the MTCB, for code confidentiality.
MTCB	id_M	Unique identifier for a particular MTCB instance
	$code_M$	Manufacturer-supplied MTCB code
	ver_M	MTCB code version
	ptr	Firmware pointer (either NVM region A or B)
	lts_{ME}	Long-term secret, shared between MTCB and ETCB, established on first boot
	bs_{ME}	*Boot secret, shared between the MTCB and the ETCB, established on each boot through the AKEP2 subprotocol
	k_{MAC}	*MAC key, shared between the MTCB and the ETCB, used in Protocol 3 (attest.)
	ssk_M	Secret signing key used for attestation
	spk_M	Public verification key corresponding to ssk_M
	σ_M	Signature using ssk_M
ETCB	id_E	Unique identifier. See remark on Sect. 5.2 below
	$code_E$	Adversary-supplied ETCB code
	ver_E	Version
	h_E	*Currently loaded ETCB measurement, i.e., $h_E = h(code_E)$
	h_E^{ref}	Reference ETCB measurement
OS	$code_O$	Adversary-supplied OS code
	h_O	*Currently loaded OS measurement, i.e., $h_O = h(code_O)$
	h_O^{ref}	Reference OS measurement

All objects (except those marked with *) are stored persistently, e.g., NVM, fuse memory, or enclave secure store. Objects marked with * are kept in RAM while needed

There are a total of seven parties involved in the protocols, although not all of them take part in all protocols, namely:

- **MTCB:** The most protected part of the system, running on a dedicated processor mounted in the SoC, which is a small processor separate from the main CPU.
- **ETCB:** An enclave system, such as ARM TrustZone [13], Intel SGX [5] or RISC-V Keystone [6,7], running on the main CPU on the SoC.
- **CPU:** The main processor on the SoC. It runs the ETCB in an enclave system, and it runs the OS.
- **OS:** The operating system running on the CPU.
- **Verifier:** A remote party interacting with the system. The verifier can send messages to the system (such as requests for attestation) and receives and verifies the replies.
- **Vendor:** The maker of the system, which installs the firmware and the keys.

– **Adversary:** An agent that tries to circumvent the secure operation of the system. The adversary's capabilities are defined in Sect. 4.

There are many objects held or exchanged by the different parties. For convenience, in Table 2, we provide a glossary of the symbols used to represent those objects throughout the paper.

5.1 Protocol 1: MTCB A/B Update

Protocol 1 implements over-the-air (OTA) MTCB code updates. In order to ensure that a workable booting system remains on the MTCB NVM space during the update process, we implement "A/B updates," in which there are two slots that can contain the MTCB code, called A and B. This approach reduces the likelihood of an inactive or "bricked" device, should the update process be interrupted for any reason. If this occurs, the MTCB would boot on the non-updated version again. In the execution of this protocol, there are three elements that are updated in the MTCB NVM: the version number ver_M, the code itself $code_M$, and the Vendor public signing key spk_V. For clarity, we parametrize these three elements using a bracketed index indicating a specific update, e.g., $code_M[i]$ and $code_M[i+1]$ denote the code contents of two consecutive updates.

Let us consider that the current status of the MTCB corresponds to the ith update. When the platform boots, the MTCB boot pointer ptr indicates what region of the NVM contains $code_M[i]$ (either region A or B), and the MTCB BootROM loads it. Also, we assume that the system currently has a legitimate MTCB, and as such, it implements the A/B update protocol. More concretely, all legitimate and signed $code_M$ implements the A/B update protocol. The sequence of steps to achieve the next, $i+1$, A/B update is as follows:

1. The Vendor updates its signing keypair $ssk_V[i+1], spk_V[i+1]$ (or copies the previous one), generates the updated $code_M[i+1]$, and increments the version number $ver_M[i+1]$, for example, $ver_M[i+1] = i+1$. Then, it produces the tuple

$$(ver_M[i+1], \text{enc}_{kfw}(code_M[i+1]), spk_V[i+1]), \tag{1}$$

   and signs it with the current signing key $ssk_V[i]$, obtaining the signature $\sigma_V[i+1]$. It outputs publicly the tuple (1) and $\sigma_V[i+1]$.
2. The MTCB receives the secure update command together with the tuple (1) and the signature $\sigma_V[i+1]$, and it proceeds as follows:
3. Verify $\sigma_V[i+1]$ with currently installed $spk_V[i]$.
4. Check that $ver_M[i+1] > ver_M[i]$.
5. Decrypt $code_M[i+1]$ using kfw.
6. Copy the decrypted contents $code_M[i+1]$ and updated signing key $spk_V[i+1]$ at the complementary NVM location (which is B if the MTCB is currently executing from A, and is otherwise A).
7. Check the hash of written contents.
8. Update the stored version number.
9. Change the boot pointer to the complementary NVM location and reboot.

Figure 2 briefly depicts the NVM state in the different stages of the A/B update. Note that the proposed design does not allow non-consecutive updates if there is a change of the Vendor signing keypair in between. That is because in order to verify the signature $\sigma_V[i+1]$, it has to match the corresponding signing key $spk_V[i]$. It could be argued that there are two types of MTCB updates: minor, where the signing key does not change, and major, where the signing key changes. For simplicity, and due to the fact that the MTCB is expected to execute a limited number of updates during its lifetime, we only consider major updates in our analysis. This can also be enforced at Step 4. by checking whether $ver_M[i+1] = ver_M[i] + 1$.

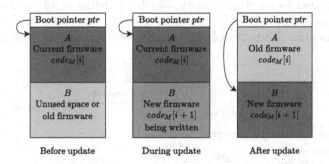

Fig. 2. Protocol 1: NVM stages in the A/B update

Also, note that the current version number ver_M is stored in unary notation in fuse memory as the counter CTR_CUR_VERSION. This removes the need to store the boot pointer: the MTCB BootROM can simply execute code stored in, e.g., NVM region A if ver_M is even, and NVM region B if ver_M is odd.

Observe that we do not allow for the code encryption key kfw to be updated. This is due to the fact that there is not much gain in doing so: if this key is compromised at any point in time, all future versions of this key will be compromised as well.

Finally, we require that the reference ETCB measurement h_E^{ref}, used in the secure boot protocol (see Sect. 5.2 below) has the same level of protection in the NVM as $code_M$ has. That is, integrity, confidentiality and rollback protection. The reason for this is that otherwise an attacker can do a rollback attack if it can corrupt the NVM memory. As a result, an update in the ETCB requires an update in the MTCB.

5.2   Protocol 2: Secure Boot

The goal of secure boot is for the MTCB to validate the integrity and trustworthiness of the ETCB and OS code before the platform executes them, so that it can ensure it starts with an expected, legitimate combination of ETCB and OS. Therefore, the MTCB has to be regarded as a root of trust of the whole system, and the security of this protocol (and indirectly that of the remaining ones) relies on this assumption. Hence, in our analysis, we consider that both $code_E$ and $code_O$ are freely chosen by the adversary, but the MTCB firmware $code_M$ is unconditionally trusted.

This protocol uses the AKEP2 protocol [1] in order to derive a shared boot secret bs_{ME}. A long-term secret lts_{ME} shared between the ETCB and the MTCB is required, which was established on the first boot at manufacture time. We abstract away from the specific enclave system used by the ETCB, and we assume that it provides long-term secure storage for its internal secrets. Note that the ETCB does not have a persistent identity; the platform's persistent identity is given by the MTCB identifier id_M. Nevertheless, for the AKEP2 protocol, the ETCB is required to have an identity, which we define as $id_E = h(lts_{ME})$, for some secure hash function h.

Figure 3 depicts this protocol. The sequence of actions is as follows:

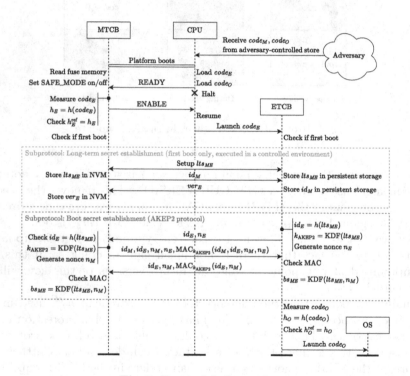

Fig. 3. Protocol 2: Secure boot

1. The adversary freely chooses ETCB and OS code to be loaded at boot time, namely $code_E$ and $code_O$, and forwards it to the platform.

2. The platform boots. The MTCB checks the counter CTR_SAFE_MODE in fuse memory. If the counter has an odd value, it sets the signal SAFE_MODE to true.[1]

3. The main CPU has pre-boot ROM called BootROM Secure Boot Code (BSBC). This code loads $code_E$ and $code_O$ into memory, signals the MTCB using the signal READY, and then halts the CPU.

4. The MTCB disables the CPU by setting the signal ENABLE to false. Then, it reads $code_E$, which is located at a fixed, predefined memory location known to BSBC and MTCB, and obtains the measurement hash $h_E = h(code_E)$.

5. The MTCB compares the measurement h_E with an expected, reference value h_E^{ref}. If these values match, it notifies the CPU to continue by setting the signal ENABLE to true.

6. Upon receiving the signal from the MTCB, the CPU launches the ETCB code, $code_E$.

7. Only on first boot, the MTCB and the ETCB establish a long-term secret lts_{ME}. The first boot is assumed to happen in a controlled environment, outside the reach of any adversary. The MTCB stores lts_{ME} and ver_E in its encrypted NVM. The ETCB stores lts_{ME} and id_M in encrypted form in untrusted storage.

8. The MTCB and the ETCB establish a boot secret bs_{ME} by executing the AKEP2 protocol. This will be required by Protocol 3 below.

9. The ETCB reads $code_O$, which is located in a predefined memory location known to ETCB and BSBC, and obtains the measurement hash $h_O = h(code_O)$.

10. The ETCB compares the measurement h_O with an expected, reference value h_O^{ref}. If these values match, it launches the OS code, following an approach similar to RISC-V Keystone [6,7] or ARM TrustZone [13].

We remark that the ETCB and OS measurements carried out at Steps 4. and 9., respectively, must take into account all the data that is expected to remain immutable (e.g., keys and version numbers).

5.3   Protocol 3: Remote Attestation

Remote attestation concerns the reporting of the current platform state (e.g., hardware and software configuration) to an external entity (Verifier). The goal of the protocol is to enable the Verifier to determine the level of trust in the integrity of the platform, that is, that the platform runs a legitimate combination of ETCB and OS. The security guarantees of remote attestation, in general, are limited to state that "at some point in time between the attestation request and its reception, the platform was running with the attested configuration."

In order to prevent the adversary from executing an attack by reusing messages from an earlier boot instance, the communication between the MTCB and

---

[1] The SAFE_MODE signal does not play a role in Protocol 2, but it is used by Protocol 4 (ETCB recovery) *after* secure boot has finished. See Sect. 5.4 for more details.

the ETCB is authenticated (integrity-protected) through a MAC. Therefore, the protocol uses the shared boot secret bs_{ME} established in the secure boot protocol (Sect. 5.2 above) to derive the MAC key.

Protocol 3 is depicted in Fig. 4, and the sequence of actions is as follows:

1. The Verifier generates a challenge $chal$ and forwards it to the OS.
2. The OS forwards the challenge to the ETCB.
3. The ETCB and MTCB derive a MAC key k_{MAC} using the boot secret bs_{ME}.
4. The ETCB reads $code_O$, which is located in a predefined memory location, and obtains the measurement hash $h_O = h(code_O)$.
5. The ETCB forwards $chal$, h_O, and $MAC_{k_{MAC}}(chal, h_O)$ to the MTCB.
6. The MTCB checks $MAC_{k_{MAC}}(chal, h_O)$.
7. The MTCB reads $code_E$, which is located in a predefined memory location, and obtains the measurement hash $h_E = h(code_E)$.
8. The MTCB signs the tuple

$$(id_M, chal, h_O, h_E) \tag{2}$$

with the attestation signing key ssk_M, obtaining the signature σ_M.
9. The tuple (2) together with its signature σ_M is forwarded back to the ETCB, OS and Verifier.
10. Using the attestation public signing key spk_M, the Verifier checks that σ_M is a valid signature for the received tuple (2).
11. The Verifier compares the measurements h_E and h_O with the expected, reference values h_E^{ref} and h_O^{ref}, respectively. If these values match, the Verifier declares a successful attestation.

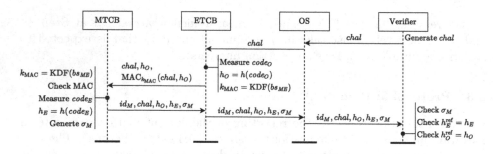

Fig. 4. Protocol 3: Remote Attestation

Observe that, for simplicity, we assume that the MTCB attestation keypair ssk_M, spk_M is persistent. This can be an issue from the point of view of privacy, as this keypair uniquely identifies the platform. A possible alternative to overcome this problem is to use an approach similar to that used by TPM remote attestation. The TPM uses a master key (*endorsement key* in TPM's terminology), which is used to decrypt arbitrarily many attestation keys as desired, which have been certified through a Privacy Certification Authority, or through the Direct Anonymous Attestation protocol. Obviously, this would require to remove id_M from (2). As a result, from the Verifier's perspective, they will know that "a platform has successfully been attested" without knowing the precise identity of that platform. This arrangement is important for TPMs because they are deployed in personal laptops, where privacy is an important issue. However, it may not be needed in network infrastructure devices or similar scenarios.

5.4   Protocol 4: ETCB Recovery

This protocol aims to identify a memory corruption situation where the adversary has gained enough control over the platform so that it can change the memory contents of the ETCB and substitute it by its own, malicious version. The MTCB proactively measures the running ETCB code, and forces a reboot to a safe state if it finds an unexpected measurement.

This protocol can be divided into two processes: corruption detection and recovery. We assume that the platform is already booted, and that the adversary had freely chosen the ETCB and OS code to be loaded at boot time, namely $code_E$ and $code_O$. Also, at any point in time, the adversary might be able to corrupt the RAM location where $code_E$ is stored. See the considerations about the adversary in Sect. 4. The sequence of actions for this protocol is as follows:

(a) Memory Corruption Detection:
   1. The MTCB periodically reads $code_E$, which is located in a predefined memory location, and obtains the measurement hash $h_E = h(code_E)$. We can set h_E to an undefined value if the MTCB is unable to conduct this measurement, e.g., if the attacker is blocking the channel.
   2. The MTCB compares the measurement h_E with an expected, reference value h_E^{ref}. If these values do not match, it increments the counter CTR_SAFE_MODE in fuse memory to an odd value, indicating that the signal SAFE_MODE is set, and reboots the platform.
(b) Recovery:
   3. The platform reboots. The MTCB checks the counter CTR_SAFE_MODE in fuse memory. If the counter has an odd value, it sets the signal SAFE_MODE to true.
   4. If the main CPU is booted with SAFE_MODE set to true, the firewall is configured to allow outgoing connections only. This aims to prevent the ETCB/OS from becoming immediately compromised again. The ETCB/OS attempts to report the security violation to the cloud service.
   5. The OS downloads a new signed version of the ETCB code. That is, a tuple $(ver_E', code_E')$ with a Vendor signature σ_V.
   6. The OS forwards the tuple and signature to the MTCB (via the ETCB).
   7. The MTCB checks the Vendor signature σ_V, and checks that the received

ETCB version is strictly larger than the current one, i.e., $ver'_E > ver_E$.[2]

8. The MTCB updates the reference measurement for the MTCB as $h_E^{\text{ref}} = h(code'_E)$, and stores ver'_E in its encrypted NVM.

9. If the MTCB has succeeded in downloading and installing $code'_E$, it increments the counter in fuse memory to an even value, indicating that the signal SAFE_MODE is clear, and reboots the platform. Otherwise, it remains indefinitely in safe mode.

This protocol is not guaranteed to succeed, for a number of reasons: First, a powerful adversary could anticipate the moment that the measurements will occur, and take action to avoid detection. Second, even if detected, the replacement of the ETCB might not prevent further attacks. And third, the adversary might block fetching of $code'_E$.

However, we show that the protocol will succeed with probability arbitrarily close to 1 under some reasonable assumptions; see Sect. 4 above. The MTCB implements protections so that the adversary cannot always anticipate the MTCB memory measurements, and it can also identify whether its measurements are being prevented or delayed. Also, the adversary is interested in keeping a rogue ETCB version in memory for a non-zero fraction of time. This excludes improbable corner cases, for example, an adversary running a malicious ETCB for a very small fraction of time between secure boot and the first MTCB memory measurement, and then switching to a legitimate ETCB the rest of the time. We note that the adversary is free to arbitrarily change the memory at any point, which is probably an overestimation of its capabilities. Nevertheless, our probabilistic argument works as detailed below, even with this overestimation.

Although the adversary is interested in running a rogue version of the ETCB, it is also forced to switch the memory contents (to a legitimate ETCB) so that the MTCB produces an expected measurement and does not trigger the recovery procedure. Hence, there is a trade-off between the adversary spending enough time running the rogue version and the possibility of being detected: too much time spent by the rogue ETCB will increase the chances of the MTCB in identifying the attack, whereas too much time spent by the legitimate ETCB in memory will restrict its malicious abilities. Consider the following given parameters:

- T: time interval during which the platform is active, $T > 0$,
- p: minimum proportion of active time that the adversary has the rogue ETCB in memory, $0 < p \le 1$,
- ϵ: target error probability, i.e., maximum admissible error of not identifying the attack occurring while the platform is active. We can take this parameter as small as desired.

---

[2] From the point of view of security, the most conservative approach is to require that $ver'_E > ver_E$. However, this has the downside effect that if there is no new ETCB version available, the platform would remain in safe mode (inoperative) indefinitely. To avoid this situation, we could relax this check and only require that $ver'_E \ge ver_E$. This is justified if there is a significant cost of time and resources to the adversary to mount the attack again.

We are interested in finding the frequency f, i.e., the number of memory measurements by the MTCB per unit of time, so that the actual error probability does not exceed the target ϵ. That is, we want that the probability of failing to identify an attack occurring in T, which is $(1 - p)^{fT}$, does not exceed ϵ. It is straightforward to see that for any choice of T, p the target error is satisfied for any $f \geq f_0$, with

$$f_0 = \frac{\log \epsilon}{T \log(1 - p)}.$$

As expected intuitively, the required frequency of measurements increases for $\epsilon \to 0$, and $p \to 0$. Also, note that $f_0 \to 0$ for $p \to 1$, i.e., a single measurement is sufficient if the adversary always keeps its malicious version in memory.

6 Modelling and Verification of Security Properties

We have verified the core security properties of our TCB design using ProVerif [2, 3], which is a tool for automated analysis of security properties in cryptographic protocols. ProVerif analyses our pseudocode for Protocols 1–4, and determines whether the security properties we specify hold or not. This is an excellent tool for uncovering design errors, because ProVerif explores all permitted actions of the adversary, and reports potential attacks if such attacks exist. It is a valuable tool for the development of protocols. Nevertheless, it should be remembered that even if ProVerif shows that all the properties are satisfied, this does not mean that the system is secure.

Further details, including the formal description of the security properties can be found in Appendix A. ProVerif is successful in proving the set of security properties for the protocols discussed. The source code with the models, the security properties and a collection of sanity check queries can be found in [11].

7 Conclusion

We have motivated and described our design for a two-tiered TCB, which is targeted at network infrastructure devices such as routers and modems. It aims to provide a small and hardened "minimal" TCB that is assumed secure, but is nevertheless updatable if it turns out insecure. This MTCB is rather inflexible, however, because of its small size and minimal size and strong isolation from the rest of the system. The second tier is a bigger "extended" TCB that offers application-specific services, and is more flexible, while not offering quite such rigorous security because it runs on the same processor as potentially untrusted code. The ETCB is also updatable.

Designing such a two-tiered TCB led us to many design decisions and intricate protocols in order to get the two parts to work together securely. In arriving at the designs, we studied attacks that are common for this kind of device, as well as good practice recommendations that have arisen, both in the academic literature and in industry (e.g., The MITRE Corporation CWE). We detailed our design decisions, and specified the protocols both informally and in the formal language of ProVerif. We have used ProVerif to verify a number of relevant security properties about them.

A   Security Properties

In this appendix, we present the formal description of the security properties for Protocols 1–3. Due to space constraints, we include the properties for Protocol 4 in the extended version of the paper. We have verified these properties using ProVerif [2,3], which is a tool for automated analysis of security properties in cryptographic protocols.

Security properties are expressed through guarded first-order logic formulas. These properties can be classified as reachability properties (i.e., a certain event in the execution trace is reachable) or as correspondence assertions (i.e., a certain event always occurs prior to the execution of a later event). For correspondence assertions it is customary to check reachability of the event that occurs later, since if this event never occurs, then the assertion will be trivially verified. We omit those reachability sanity checks here. Events are used to define security properties, and they do not modify the semantics of the protocols. Events represent local computations or mark relevant points in the execution of the protocols. The notation "EventName$(x_1, \ldots, x_n)@t$" indicates that an event with name "EventName" and parameters $x_1, \ldots, x_n$ occurs at time t. The naming of the events has been chosen to be self-documenting.

Also, note that the security properties for Protocol 2 and 3 can only hold if no memory corruption occurs in a given platform boot. For this reason, correspondence properties in Protocols 2 and 3 are conditioned to the event "MemoryCorrupted( )" in the description of the relevant security properties below.

Security properties for Protocol 1: MTCB A/B Update.

[P1.1] Every MTCB only executes firmware installed by the Vendor (initial install) or a previous legitimate firmware (subsequent installs) that has been previously created and signed by the Vendor:

$$\forall id_M, ptr, ver_M, code_M, spk_V, t_3.$$
$$\text{MtcbStarts}(id_M, ptr, ver_M, code_M, spk_V)@t_3 \Rightarrow$$
$$(\exists t_2. \; \text{MtcbInstalls}(id_M, ptr, ver_M, code_M, spk_V)@t_2 \land$$
$$\exists t_1. \; \text{VendorCreates}(ver_M, code_M)@t_1 \land (t_1 < t_2 < t_3)).$$

[P1.2] Once a given MTCB executes firmware of a certain version number ver_M it will never execute firmware with version number $ver'_M < ver_M$

$$\forall id_M, ptr, ver_M, code_M, spk_V, t_1, \quad id'_M, ptr', ver'_M, code'_M, spk'_V, t_2.$$
$$\text{MtcbStarts}(id_M, ptr, ver_M, code_M, spk_V)@t_1 \land$$
$$\text{MtcbStarts}(id'_M, ptr', ver'_M, code'_M, spk'_V)@t_2 \Rightarrow$$
$$((t_1 \leq t_2) \land (ver_M \leq ver'_M)) \lor ((t_2 \leq t_1) \land (ver'_M \leq ver_M)).$$

Security properties for Protocol 2: Secure Boot.
[**P2.1**] Only a legitimate ETCB is allowed to start on the platform.

$$\forall inst, code_E, code'_O, code'_E, t_2. \quad \text{EtcbStarts}(inst, code_E)@t_2 \Rightarrow$$
$$\text{IsLegitimateEtcb}(code_E) \vee$$
$$(\exists t_1. \text{MemoryCorrupted}(inst, code'_O, code'_E)@t_1 \wedge (t_1 < t_2))$$

[**P2.2**] Only a legitimate OS is allowed to start on the platform.

$$\forall inst, code_O, code'_O, code'_E, t_2. \quad \text{OsStarts}(inst, code_O)@t_2 \Rightarrow$$
$$\text{IsLegitimateOs}(code_O) \vee$$
$$(\exists t_1. \text{MemoryCorrupted}(inst, code'_O, code'_E)@t_2 \wedge (t_1 < t_2))$$

[**P2.3**] The AKEP2 protocol between the MTCB and the ETCB guarantees mutual, injective agreement [9] for the MTCB nonce n_M (which is used later to obtain the boot secret bs_{ME}). For convenience, we assume that the array of agreed parameters *pars* contains n_M:

$$\forall id_M, id_E, pars, t_2. \text{MtcbAkep2Commit}(id_M, id_E, pars)@t_2 \Rightarrow$$
$$(\exists t_1. \text{EtcbAkep2Running}(id_E, id_M, pars)@t_1 \wedge (t_1 < t_2)) \wedge$$
$$\neg(\exists t'_2. \text{MtcbAkep2Commit}(id_M, id_E, pars)@t'_2 \wedge \neg(t_2 = t'_2)),$$

$$\forall id_M, id_E, pars, t_2. \text{EtcbAkep2Commit}(id_E, id_M, pars)@t_2 \Rightarrow$$
$$(\exists t_1. \text{MtcbAkep2Running}(id_M, id_E, pars)@t_1 \wedge (t_1 < t_2)) \wedge$$
$$\neg(\exists t'_2. \text{EtcbAkep2Commit}(id_E, id_M, pars)@t'_2 \wedge \neg(t_2 = t'_2)).$$

These formulas represent injective correspondence assertions as predicate logic formulas. We remark that the last line of the two formulas above ensure the injectivity of the correspondence assertions, since no two events can occur at the same time point.

Security properties for Protocol 3: Remote Attestation.
[**P3.1**] For a given boot instance, It cannot happen that the MTCB generates an attestation signature, the Verifier validates the attestation, and there is an attack event.

$$\neg(\exists inst, chal, \sigma_M, t_1, t_2, t_3.\text{MtcbGeneratesSignature}(inst, chal, \sigma_M)@t_1 \wedge$$
$$\text{VerifierValidatesAttestation}(chal, \sigma_M)@t_2 \wedge$$
$$\text{AttackEvent}(inst)@t_3).$$

[**P3.2**] For every boot instance, if the Verifier validates an attestation, then an attestation signature must have been generated by the MTCB before, and the following events must have occurred before that: 1. the Verifier generates the challenge, 2. the legitimate OS has been loaded, 3. the legitimate ETCB has been loaded, 4. the legitimate ETCB has been started.

$$\forall chal, \sigma_M, t_7.\ \text{VerifierValidatesAttestation}(chal, \sigma_M)@t_7 \Rightarrow$$
$$(\exists inst, t_6.\ \text{MtcbGeneratesSignature}(inst, chal, \sigma_M)@t_6 \wedge$$
$$\exists t_5.\ \text{VerifierGeneratesChallenge}(chal)@t_5 \wedge$$
$$\exists t_4.\ \text{EtcbStarts}(inst, \text{ETCB\_LEGITIMATE})@t_4 \wedge$$
$$\exists t_3.\ \text{EtcbLoaded}(inst, \text{ETCB\_LEGITIMATE})@t_3 \wedge$$
$$\exists t_2.\ \text{OsLoaded}(inst, \text{OS\_LEGITIMATE})@t_2 \wedge$$
$$(t_2, t_3, t_4, t_5 < t_6 < t_7)$$
$$)\ \vee\ \exists code'_O, code'_E, t_1.\ \text{MemoryCorrupted}(inst, code'_O, code'_E))@t_1 \wedge (t_1 < t_7).$$

The source code with the formal models, the security properties and a collection of sanity check queries can be found in [11].

References

1. Bellare, M., Rogaway, P.: Entity authentication and key distribution. In: Stinson, D.R. (ed.) CRYPTO 1993. LNCS, vol. 773, pp. 232–249. Springer, Heidelberg (1994). https://doi.org/10.1007/3-540-48329-2_21
2. Blanchet, B., Smyth, B., Cheval, V., Sylvestre, M.: ProVerif 2.04: Automatic Cryptographic Protocol Verifier, User Manual and Tutorial (2021)
3. Blanchet, B., Cheval, V., Sylvestre, M.: ProVerif (v. 2.04) (2021). http://prosecco.gforge.inria.fr/personal/bblanche/proverif/
4. Chen, G., Chen, S., Xiao, Y., Zhang, Y., Lin, Z., Lai, T.H.: SgxPectre: stealing intel secrets from SGX enclaves via speculative execution. In: IEEE European Symposium on Security and Privacy (EuroS&P), pp. 142–157. IEEE, Stockholm, Sweden (2019)
5. Costan, V., Devadas, S.: Intel SGX explained. Cryptology ePrint Archive **2016**(086), 1–118 (2016)
6. Lee, D., Kohlbrenner, D., Shinde, S., Song, D., Asanović, K.: Keystone: A framework for architecting TEEs. arXiv preprint arXiv:1907.10119 (2019)
7. Lee, D., Kohlbrenner, D., Shinde, S., Asanović, K., Song, D.: Keystone: An open framework for architecting trusted execution environments. In: Fifteenth European Conference on Computer Systems (EuroSys), pp. 1–16. ACM, Heraklion, Greece (2020)
8. Lipp, M., Gruss, D., Spreitzer, R., Maurice, C., Mangard, S.: Armageddon: cache attacks on mobile devices. In: 25th USENIX Security Symposium (USENIX Security 16), pp. 549–564 (2016)
9. Lowe, G.: A hierarchy of authentication specifications. In: IEEE Computer Security Foundations Workshop (CSFW), , Rockport, MA, pp. 31–43. IEEE(1997)
10. Moghimi, A., Irazoqui, G., Eisenbarth, T.: CacheZoom: how SGX amplifies the power of cache attacks. In: Fischer, W., Homma, N. (eds.) CHES 2017. LNCS, vol. 10529, pp. 69–90. Springer, Cham (2017). https://doi.org/10.1007/978-3-319-66787-4_4

11. Moreira, J., Ryan, M.D., Garcia, F.D.: Repository for ProVerif models (2022). http://github.com/jmor7690/esorics2022-two-tiered-tcb
12. Noorman, J., et al.: Sancus 2.0: a low-cost security architecture for IoT devices. ACM Trans. Priv. Secur. (TOPS) **20**(3), 1–33 (2017)
13. Pinto, S., Santos, N.: Demystifying arm trustzone: a comprehensive survey. ACM Comput. Surv. (CSUR) **51**(6), 130 (2019)
14. Ragab, H., Milburn, A., Razavi, K., Bos, H., Giuffrida, C.: CrossTalk: speculative data leaks across cores are real. In: IEEE Symposium on Security and Privacy (S&P), , San Francisco, CA, pp. 1852–1867. IEEE(2021)
15. Savagaonkar, U., Porter, N., Taha, N., Serebrin, B., Mueller, N.: Titan in depth: security in plaintext (2017). http://cloud.google.com/blog/products/identity-security/titan-in-depth-security-in-plaintext
16. Schwarz, M., et al.: ZombieLoad: cross-privilege-boundary data sampling. In: ACM SIGSAC Conference on Computer and Communications Security (CCS), ACM, London, UK, pp. 753–768 (2019)
17. Skorobogatov, S.P.: Semi-invasive attacks: a new approach to hardware security analysis. Tech. Rep. **630**, University of Cambridge (2005)
18. Trusted Computing Group (TCG): Trusted Platform Module Library Specification, Part 1: Architecture (Family "2.0", Level 00, Revision 01.59) (2019)
19. Van Bulck, J., et al.: Foreshadow: extracting the keys to the Intel SGX kingdom with transient out-of-order execution. In: USENIX Security Symposium (USENIX Security), pp. 991–1008. USENIX Association, Baltimore, MD (2018)
20. Van Bulck, J., Oswald, D., Marin, E., Aldoseri, A., Garcia, F.D., Piessens, F.: A tale of two worlds: assessing the vulnerability of enclave shielding runtimes. In: Proceedings of the 2019 ACM SIGSAC Conference on Computer and Communications Security, pp. 1741–1758 (2019)
21. Zhang, N., Sun, K., Shands, D., Lou, W., Hou, Y.T.: Truspy: cache side-channel information leakage from the secure world on arm devices. IACR Cryptol. ePrint Arch. **2016**, 980 (2016)

Using Memristor Arrays as Physical Unclonable Functions

Florian Frank[1]([✉])(iD), Tolga Arul[1,2](iD),
Nikolaos Athanasios Anagnostopoulos[1,2](iD), and Stefan Katzenbeisser[1]

[1] University of Passau, Innstraße 43, 94032 Passau, Germany
{florian.frank,tolga.arul,nikolaos.anagnostopoulos,
stefan.katzenbeisser}@uni-passau.de
[2] Technical University of Darmstadt, Hochschulstraße 10, 64289 Darmstadt, Germany
{arul,na45tisu}@rbg.informatik.tu-darmstadt.de

Abstract. In this work, we introduce two new types of Physical Unclonable Functions (PUFs) based on memristor arrays. Both PUFs use the output behavior of memristor cells when an excitation signal is applied to their input. First, the cells are identified by decomposing the signal response into different frequencies using the discrete Fourier transformation and evaluating the absolute sum of errors. This approach provides a maximum accuracy of 96% and F1-score of 73%. In order to improve performance, a convolutional neural network is employed to learn the shapes of the output hysteresis loop. To this end, a conversion algorithm that transforms the outputs to matrices is used. The proposed neural network achieves a maximum accuracy of 97% and F1-score of 97%, allowing for the successful utilisation of the examined PUF in practical security applications. As a use case for the proposed PUFs, we introduce a novel neural network-based authentication protocol that can be used to authenticate smart devices to a central IoT hub, e.g., in a smart home.

Keywords: Physical Unclonable Function (PUF) · Memristors · Machine learning · Hardware security · Resistive Random Access Memory (ReRAM) · Convolutional Neural Network (CNN) · Neural networks

1 Introduction

The use of microcontrollers influences all areas of life and applications, such as consumer electronics, sensors, and vehicles. These systems are getting smaller and more powerful. At the same time they are often very constrained in their power consumption. Storage technologies employed in these systems will face certain development limits soon due to their integration density and power consumption. One promising technology that could overcome these limitations is **ReRAM** (**R**esistive **R**andom **A**ccess **M**emory), a non-volatile memory technology, which combines fast switching, low energy consumption, and small cell sizes, without decreasing performance [4]. ReRAMs are based on memristors (**memory** and **resistor**), which are passive circuit elements that change their resistance with the amount of charge floating through them, in relation to their previous resistance value, which is otherwise maintained.

Microcontrollers are often deployed in security-critical areas, such as in-vehicle networks, which makes secure communication between the devices mandatory. Thus, one major security requirement is to establish a secure communication channel between the different system components, which requires device authentication. Many approaches proposed in the literature face the problem that they require the storage of a secret key in the device memory, causing a vulnerability if the attacker has physical access to the device.

One way to solve these problems is to use **PUFs** (**P**hysical **U**nclonable **F**unctions). PUFs generate a digital "fingerprint" of a device, which can be used for authentication and identification. These fingerprints are based on marginal differences in the hardware, which occur during the manufacturing process [9]. The advantage of this method is that the keys do not need to be permanently stored on the device, but can be reproduced on the fly out of certain unique hardware properties right before they are used, which makes them less vulnerable against physical attacks. Different types of PUFs have been proposed: they can be constructed from optical systems [12], ring oscillators [22], or conventional memory modules [8,18]. The security of PUFs is based on their ability to provide a (usually, binary) pattern that is unique for each device, thus serving as a device identifier [18]. With the continuous adoption of ReRAMs in embedded devices, replacing DRAM modules [24], memristor-based PUFs are becoming more and more appealing as lightweight security primitives. For this reason, in this work, we will examine a PUF implemented on a novel non-volatile memory, namely, a memristor array. Further, the applicability of the novel PUF is demonstrated in the context of a new authentication protocol for the **IoT** (**I**nternet **o**f **T**hings).

1.1   Contributions

The main contributions of this work concern the construction of a novel PUF based on an array of memristor cells, as well as its characterisation, and evaluation, based either on frequency analysis or on machine learning.

More specifically, the PUF is first characterised using a technique based on the frequency composition of the output wave of each memristor cell, when applying a sine wave. We show that, based on the frequency composition, each cell can be uniquely identified by a simple classification of the quantised frequency distribution. To improve the classification performance even further, a second classification method based on **CNNs** (**C**onvolutional **N**eural **N**etworks) is introduced. There, a sine wave is applied to the memristors, causing a continuous change between their high and low resistive states, which results in a so-called "pinched hysteresis loop". We show that this hysteresis is a distinctive feature of memristors, where the shape of the loops differs from cell to cell due to manufacturing variations. CNNs are used to identify the hysteresis loops of such cells, resulting into an accuracy and F1-score of up to 97% and 97%, respectively. This is a significant improvement compared to the analysis by frequency composition that achieves an accuracy of 96% but an F1-score of only 73%.

Furthermore, we demonstrate how this PUF can be used in a smart home to authenticate smart devices like a smart refrigerator, or smart light bulbs, to an IoT hub using a novel authentication protocol tailored for this type of PUF. In general, the presented PUF construction requires access to one or only a few memristor cells to generate a unique pattern that can be used for authentication and identification, and thus is the first of its kind.

1.2   Related Work

The potential of using memristors as PUFs has been explored in several works.

Rose et al. [17] introduced a memristor-based PUF that utilises the differences in the time required for the memristors to transit from the high-resistance to the low-resistance state. The time required for this transition is measured for each memristor and compared to a selected threshold value. If the actual transition time of a memristor is below the threshold, the result is a logical 0, otherwise a logical 1. The set of zeros and ones returned from a particular set of cells constitutes the response of the PUF. In this work, each cell produces only a one-bit response, thus requiring access to many cells to generate a secure key. On the contrary, our PUF requires access to one or only a few memristor cells to generate a unique pattern that can be used for authentication and identification.

Gao and Ranasinghe [7] constructed a PUF, that uses memristors that are arranged in an array-like structure. Each cell in this array consists of two memristors, connected in series. When applying a voltage that is two times the reset voltage, one of the two memristors reaches the off state, i.e., the low-resistance state, first, which causes the second memristor to stop changing its resistance. Afterwards, the memristors are read with a small voltage that does not disturb the resistance of the device. Depending on which memristor stays in the high resistive and which one changes into the low resistive state, a PUF response of a logical 0 or a logical 1 is obtained. The disadvantage of this method is that each memristor pair produces only a one-bit response, which requires a large amount of memristors to produce a secure key, like the work of Rose et al. [17].

Uddin et al. [20] introduced the memristive crossbar PUF (XbarPUF), a PUF based on memristors that uses the switching delays of multiple memristors as the PUF characteristic. An additional PUF based on the resistance differences of two memristors when being in a low or high resistive state, was proposed by Chen et al. [3]. These PUFs require a more complex setup than our implementation, as our PUF requires only a simple measurement generated by connecting a function generator and an oscilloscope to a memristor cell.

Finally, some works have proposed the use of neural networks in the context of PUFs: Yue et al. [23] described an authentication scheme using a deep neural network to extract the unique features from the raw power-up values of DRAM cells, which are then used for authentication. Yilmaz et al. [21] also proposed a PUF-based authentication protocol using neural networks. The delay difference of the neural computation itself was proposed as a PUF characteristic by Nozaki et al. [15], while Najafi et al. [14] proposed a latency-based DRAM PUF that uses neural networks for device identification without the need for error correction.

2 Background

In this section, we provide a brief technical introduction to the functionality of memristors and the properties of Physical Unclonable Functions.

2.1 Self-directed Channel Memristors

A memristor is a passive circuit element, whose theoretical existence was conceived by Leon Chua as early as 1972, but which was only manufactured around 2008 [19]. A memristor can be described as a resistor with memory. Its resistance at the current state always depends on its resistance at previous states, stored within the device [6]. A memristor cell changes its resistance depending on the amount of charge flowing through it. This behavior is usually shown by applying a sine wave to the memristor and visualizing the output in a Lissajous curve, as demonstrated in Fig. 1. Some types of memristors require a forming process, which initializes the chemical and physical structure within the memristor and influences its behavior over its whole lifespan. In our case, a sine wave with an amplitude up to 3 V is applied to the memristor. For our experiments, we are using two memristor arrays of the brand Knowm, each consisting of 16 memristor cells [11]. Further information is given in Appendix 1.

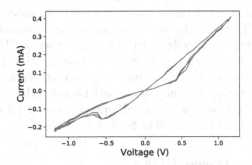

Fig. 1. Lissajous curve of a single memristor cell of the brand Knowm when applying a 100 Hz sine wave with an amplitude of 1.2 V

2.2 Physical Unclonable Functions

Physical unclonable functions use the hardware properties of a device to produce a unique fingerprint. A PUF accepts a challenge c and returns a corresponding response r, which together form a **Challenge-Response Pair (CRP)**. For an optimal PUF, the response can only be formed by a specific device, as it originates from physical properties only found in its hardware. For this reason, an ideal PUF is hard to clone and produces unique responses for any given challenge [9].

In addition, a distinction is made in the literature between strong and weak PUFs. Weak PUFs only exhibit one or at most a few CRPs, whereas strong PUFs have a (much) higher number of CRPs available. CRPs can be used for identification and authentication as well as for secure key generation. The use of PUFs has the advantage that no keys have to be permanently stored in physical memory, which could lead to security vulnerabilities when the attacker has physical access to the device [5]. For authenticating an individual device at a later stage, sets of CRPs are gathered during an enrollment phase, right after production. Moreover, commercially available security solutions using PUFs already exist, e.g., PUF-based RFIDs [10] and inbuilt PUFs in Xilinx FPGAs [13].

For the PUFs presented in this work, the challenge consists of an identifier of the memristor cell within the array, as well as the amplitude and the frequency of the input sine wave. The PUF response consists of the hysteresis loop produced by the memristor cell under the input sine wave used in the challenge.

To assess the quality of the examined PUFs, the most important properties are **Uniqueness,** which measures the independence of responses originating from multiple PUF instances for the same challenge c, and **Reliability,** which describes the stability of PUF responses, for a given challenge c, under repeated PUF measurements. Typically, these properties are measured by metrics based on the Hamming distance or the Jaccard index. These classical metrics are not applicable to our PUF implementations, because these PUFs are evaluated using classification techniques that are rather fuzzy.

Since we pursue an approach that employs machine learning to assign responses to corresponding challenges, we use the accuracy and F1-score metrics to assess the performance of the classification and ultimately rate the quality of the resulting PUF. Here, the metric of accuracy represents the number of correctly classified memristor cells over the total number of PUF instances. This metric provides an indication of how well the classification is working, but is insufficient because our data have an uneven class distribution.

For this reason, we additionally use the F1-score, which considers further aspects of the data set such as its recall, precision and false positives. Both metrics are examined in more detail in Sect. 3.2.2.

3   Memristance-Based PUFs

3.1   Measurement Circuit Design

We investigate the effects of the frequency and amplitude of the input sine signal on the memristive behavior, since these quantities are used to form the challenge for the memristance-based PUFs we propose in this work. To examine the electrical characteristics of the memristor cells, a Keysight 33500B function generator and a Keysight MSOX3104T oscilloscope are used. The function generator is connected to the input of the memristor cell and can apply a sinus wave to it. The output is connected to a resistor to limit the current. The first channel of the oscilloscope captures the output of the signal generator, while the second channel measures the voltage drop across the shunt resistor to calculate the current resistance of the memristor. Finally, the measurement devices and the memristor are connected to a common ground. Our experiments have been performed using the parameters given in Table 1, because these provide the best evaluation results to uniquely identify single memristors. More information about the measurement circuitry is provided in Appendix 2.

Table 1. Parameter values used for testing and capturing the behavior of the memristor cells. Combinations of these values are used for evaluating the PUF

Parameters	Values
Frequency	{100 Hz, 500 Hz, 1 kHz, 10 kHz}
Amplitude	{0.8 V, 1.0 V, 1.2 V, 1.5 V}

3.2 Classification of Memristor Cells Based on Their Frequency Distribution

The memristor PUFs considered in this work are based on the characteristic memristance of each device, which is caused by differences in the movement of Ag^+ ions into and from the active layer. Since the measured voltage drop is inversely proportional to the resistance of the memristor and the applied input voltage, we can use memristance to distinguish individual memristor cells.

3.2.1 PUF Construction

After capturing the measurement data, we observed that each memristor cell produces a hysteresis loop with a unique shape, which we use to identify each memristor cell of a memristor array. Figure 2 shows the unique shape of 16

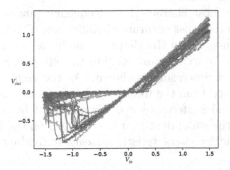

Fig. 2. Hysteresis loops of 16 different memristor cells (each cell is represented by one color). All measurements are performed using an input sine wave with a frequency of $F_{in} = 100$ Hz and an amplitude of $A_{in} = 1.2$ V

memristors, each in a different color. The figure shows the input voltage of the memristor cell, V_{in}, on the x-axis, and the voltage drop occurring after the memristor, V_{out}, on the y-axis.

First, an enrollment is executed where 200 sine waves of V_{in} and V_{out} are captured. Afterwards each curve is sampled at 100 points. There, the sampling rate is high enough to distinguish the cells based on their unique properties. With $F_{in} = 100$ Hz, only one measurement per 100 μs must be captured, which could also be done on very resource-constraint systems. Using 200 of those samples during the enrollment allows us to capture differences from one cycle to the other. This allows us to make our classification method more robust when classifying further measurements with small deviations.

A Discrete Fourier Transformation is applied to the two sets of waves V_{in} and V_{out} separately, resulting in a frequency spectrum from 0 Hz to f^n, sampled in steps of size s:

$$FS_{in}(s, f^n) = DFT(s, f^n, \{V_{in}^0, \dots, V_{in}^{199}\}),$$

$$FS_{out}(s, f^n) = DFT(s, f^n, \{V_{out}^0, \dots, V_{out}^{199}\}).$$

There, the 200 measurements are treated as continuous waves resulting in two frequency spectra: $FS_{in} := \{f_{in}^0, \dots, f_{in}^n\}$ and $FS_{out} := \{f_{out}^0, \dots, f_{out}^n\}$ containing the samples of each frequency f from $f^0 = 0$ Hz to f^n, where f^n is the maximum frequency. In our case, $f^n = F_{in} * 10$, where F_{in} is the applied input frequency, because higher-level characteristics of the loop, like the dent of the hysteresis, only occur at frequencies ranging from $F_{in} * 4$ to about $F_{in} * 10$. The step size s is defined as $f^n/1000$. The frequency spectrum is subdivided into 1000 steps, which results into a good trade-off between having a high enough resolution and not generating too many data. The intervals are further optimized by subdividing them into chunks, as described later.

In the next pre-processing step, noise and the dominant frequencies caused by V_{in} are removed from V_{out} by subtracting each of the 1000 samples in the input frequency spectrum from the output spectrum: $FS_{res} = FS_{out} - FS_{in}$. The resulting decomposition, FS_{res}, can then be used as an identification feature for a specific memristor cell.

Subsequently, the most characteristic frequency ranges are extracted from FS_{res}, which enables the most accurate classification. Figure 3 depicts the influence of different frequencies on the shape of the hysteresis loop, when applying a 100 Hz input sine wave to a memristor. On the left side, a captured hysteresis loop without any post-processing is shown. On the right side, all frequencies $f > 400$ Hz are removed from the frequency spectrum of FS_{in} as well as FS_{out}, resulting in a smoothed hysteresis loop. We note that by removing frequencies higher than 400 Hz, the small dent that can be seen on the left side of the loop, which is a very distinctive characteristic for each individual cell, is removed.

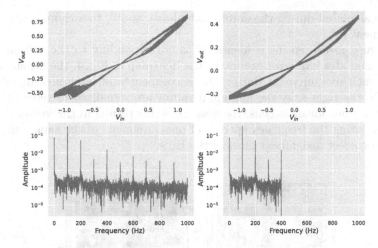

Fig. 3. Left: hysteresis loop collected from the memristor array (top), and its corresponding frequency spectrum (bottom). Right: all frequencies $f > 400\,\mathrm{Hz}$ have been removed from the frequency spectrum (bottom); the inverse discrete Fourier transformation results in a smoothed hysteresis loop (top)

Thus, we distinguish the hysteresis loops based on the samples of both the lower and the higher, i.e., of only the outermost, frequency regions. The lower frequencies are responsible for the basic hysteresis shape, whereas higher frequencies account for smaller edges and structures, like the characteristic dent shown in Fig. 3. The combination of these two frequency regions results in a unique characteristic for each memristor cell.

For that reason, the frequency spectrum FS_{res} is filtered, so that f_{res}^{199} to f_{res}^{398} are removed from the spectrum. This frequency spectrum is chosen because the basic shape of the hysteresis curves is generated by the lower frequencies of f_{res}^{0} to f_{res}^{199}, while more specific forms, like the characteristic dent, occur at frequencies higher than f_{res}^{399}, e.g., when applying 100 Hz, the basic shape is generated by frequencies up to 200 Hz, while the characteristic dent of the loop is generated by frequencies higher than 400 Hz.

The remaining spectrum, FS_{filter}, is then subdivided into c chunks. The average value of each chunk of each memristor on the enrollment measurements is then calculated for all measurements, and used as a reference for further classification. The optimization of the width of c is described in Sect. 3.2.2.

During verification, a PUF measurement is performed and pre-processed in a similar way as during enrollment. Finally, the absolute error, defined by:

$$e = \sum_{i=1}^{n} |y_i - \hat{y}_i|,$$

is calculated between the chunks of the new measurement and the chunks calculated during the enrollment. In this formula, y_i corresponds to a chunk i in

FS_{filter} calculated during the enrollment phase, and $\hat{y}_i$ to a chunk i of the new measurement m'.

Each new measurement is identified as corresponding to the cell for which the minimum absolute error occurs. In the heatmap in Fig. 4, the absolute error between each measurement during the enrollment and later measurements is shown. On the right side, the minimum values are visualized in yellow color. It can be seen that, for most cells, the absolute error results in the lowest distance when comparing the frequency spectra of measurements of the same cell, which leads to a correct assignment most of the time.

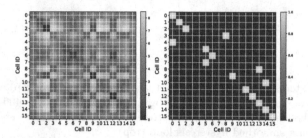

Fig. 4. The left image shows the absolute error values between measurements from all the cells. On the right side, the minimum value of each row is shown. Here, 11 out of 15 working cells (cell 3 is damaged) are stable, meaning that the relevant measurements can be assigned to the correct cell, leading to only 4 false positives (the false positive for cell 3 is not counted) and 4 false negatives. For the use of the PUF in practical applications, only cells producing stable responses are used

3.2.2 Evaluation

In this work, we utilise the concept of *accuracy* and the *F1-score* to measure the PUF properties of uniqueness and reliability which are more suitable for this classification problem in comparison to the traditional PUF metrics of the Hamming distance and Jaccard index.

Note that by testing how accurately responses originating from a particular memristor cell can be assigned to it (rate of true positives – TP) and how accurately responses originating from different PUFs can be identified as not originating from that particular PUF (rate of true negatives – TN), we can easily get a single metric that reflects both reliability and uniqueness. A high intra-class accuracy (TP) indicates that measurements originating from each PUF instance can correctly be attributed to it (a high level of reliability), while a high inter-class accuracy (TN) indicates that measurements originating from different PUF instances can be correctly attributed to the correct memristor cell. A high degree of accurate classification, however, is only possible if the relevant measurements are highly distinguishable, therefore reflecting also a high level of uniqueness. Thus, by evaluating the examined PUF instances with the metrics of accuracy and the F1-score, we are able to provide a simple, yet practical and efficient, way in which the overall quality of these PUFs can be estimated.

Based on the classification and assignment of responses to memristor cells, we can calculate the relevant rates of true positives (TP), true negatives (TN), false positives (FP), and false negatives (FN), to obtain the accuracy as follows:

$$Accuracy = \frac{TP + TN}{TP + FP + TN + FN}. \tag{1}$$

In addition, we use the F1-score, which combines the precision and recall of the data set into a single metric, because we consider it a more appropriate metric due to the number of false positives we observed during our experiments. The F1-score is calculated using the equation:

$$F1\text{-}score = \frac{TP}{TP + 0.5 * (FN + FP)}. \tag{2}$$

These metrics allow us to measure how often a measurement is assigned to the correct cell in proportion to all assignments, and thus also describe how reliable our identification scheme is.

As expected, the cells on the diagonal of the heatmap of Fig. 4, comparing measurements of the same memristor cell, mostly show the lowest error values. This means that measurements corresponding to the same cell are indeed very similar. First, the number of stable cells is calculated. Such cells can be identified based on the difference between the chunks of the histogram. We note that some cells of the analyzed memristor chips were damaged and thus provide unstable responses. These cells are detected and removed from the measurement sets. The PUF is evaluated using the parameters described in Sect. 3.1. The classification performance, including the F1-score and the accuracy metrics, is shown in Table 2.

At most 11 out of 15 cells can be identified. One of the 16 cells of each memristor array is identified as damaged and is consequently removed from the data set. As Fig. 4 illustrates, in the best case, this method leads to only 4 false positives and 4 false negatives, resulting in the following values:

$$Accuracy = \frac{TP + TN}{TP + TN + FP + FN} = \frac{all - (FP + FN)}{all} = \frac{(15 * 15) - 8}{(15 * 15)} \approx 96\%,$$

$$F1\text{-}score = \frac{11}{11 + 0.5 * 8} \approx 73\%.$$

However, Chip 1 exhibits a higher degree of instability, and therefore provides worse results. Since the expansion of the hysteresis loop becomes smaller by increasing the input signal frequency and lowering the voltage amplitude, generally also the differences among the characteristics of the cells become smaller, leading to worse results. For that reason, measurements with a frequency of 100 Hz and an amplitude of 1.2 V show the best results. The frequency distribution is subdivided into n different chunks. Selecting the amount of chunks is part of the hyper-parameter optimization. Having more chunks preserves more detail in the frequency distribution, whereas smaller chunk sizes allow the reduction of noise from the frequency spectrum. The best chunk size for each combination of parameters, which most often is 92, can be seen in Table 2.

Table 2. Number of correctly classified cells, among all undamaged cells on different amplitudes with a frequency of 100 Hz

Chip ID	Frequency in Hz	Amplitude in V	# Chunks	# Correctly classified cells	# Undamaged cells	Acc	F_1
1	100	0.8	92	6	15	0.92	0.4
1	100	1.2	92	7	15	0.93	0.47
1	100	1.0	200	7	15	0.93	0.47
2	100	0.8	92	10	15	0.96	0.67
2	100	1.0	94	9	15	0.95	0.6
2	100	1.2	92	11	15	0.96	0.73

3.3 Classification of Memristance-Based PUFs Using Convolutional Neural Networks

In order to obtain a method that achieves higher values for the F1-score, we propose a classification method based on convolutional neural networks. These are able to learn the discrete shape of the hysteresis curves of the memristors, after they have first been transformed into pixel images. The huge advantage of this type of neural network is that it can learn local spatial coherence. The transformation of the curves into pixel images is a prepossessing method that allows for reducing noise through quantization and mitigates the problem of overfitting. As shown in Sect. 3.3.2, the learned patterns of the CNN can be visualized, which allows tracing which shapes are learned, which is a huge advantage in comparison with other types of neural networks.

3.3.1 PUF Construction

CNNs were developed specifically for the domain of computer vision and are very suitable for image processing tasks, such as image classification. The complexity of shapes that can be learned by CNNs increases with the number of layers. For example, using only one layer, only simple edges can be learned. Adding a few more layers allows to recognize objects within a picture, and by adding additional layers complex and more detailed structures within pictures can be learned. The size of the local learnable patterns is specified by the size of a kernel filter. For instance, a filter with size of 5×5 pixels iterates over the image and can only learn local shapes of that size. However, this has the advantage that fewer weights are needed in comparison to densely connected neural networks, due to weight sharing, the calculation on local patterns, and the usage of max-pooling layers. In the next layer, a new 5×5 kernel filter can learn more complex shapes by operating on the output of the previous layer. Additional max pooling layers are required to reduce the size of the images after each convolution layer. Here, the maximum value of the kernel filter is selected so as to reduce the number of weights of the next layer [1]. Finally, a **ReLU** (**R**ectified **L**inear **U**nit) activation function as well as a softmax layer are attached to classify single memristors within the memristor array. In the first step, the data captured from the memristor cells are transformed into pixel images. There, w describes the number of pixels in horizontal direction, and h the height of the image. Selecting w and h is part of the hyperparameter optimization and is described in the subsequent section.

Additionally, the minimum and maximum values of the input voltage, $min(V_{in})$ and $max(V_{in})$ respectively, are determined. Then, the range $r_x := \{min(V_{in}), max(V_{in})\}$ is subdivided into w bins. The same is done for the output channel V_{out}. Here, the range $r_y := \{min(V_{out}), max(V_{out})\}$ is subdivided into h bins. Subsequently, all the V_{in} values of one measurement are assigned to the corresponding w bins, based on their position in the range r_x. The same is done for V_{out} values and the corresponding h bins, based on r_y. The combination of w vertical and h horizontal bins results in a matrix, which can be learned by the CNN. If multiple values are assigned to one chunk, the number of values in each chunk is stored, which increases the performance of the neural network. Such a transformation is visualized in Fig. 5: The right side shows the hysteresis loop that is shown on the left side, having been transformed into a matrix, forming a pixel image.

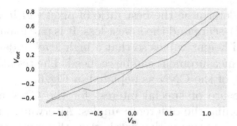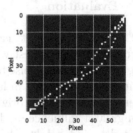

Fig. 5. Left: Hysteresis loop of a memristor. Right: Visualization of the transformation of the hysteresis loop into a pixel image

In this way, we transform the PUF measurement data into 60×60 pixel images, and further optimize w and h. This allows us to maintain a high degree of detail while reducing noise and limiting the amount of data, so that the analysis can be handled in a short amount of time. In the next step, all converted pixel images are combined into a single tensor. For each measurement, a label specifying the corresponding memristor cell, by using a cell ID implemented as a one-hot encoded vector, is created.

Our CNN consists of a 2D convolutional layer as the input layer, using a 3×3 kernel filter. This layer is followed by a MaxPooling layer that operates on the output of the previous layer by using a 2×2 kernel filter. In total, we stack three convolutional and MaxPooling layers. In the end, the output is flattened and fed into a densely connected layer with 64 neurons and a softmax classifier to learn the different classes, each corresponding to one memristor in the memristor array. An outstanding advantage of convolutional neural networks is that they can visualize the learned features. In Fig. 6, we can see that the neural network distinguishes cells specifically by considering the area of the highest and lowest voltage, which correspond to the most characteristic patterns of the hysteresis loop used for the identification of the cells.

Fig. 6. Visualization of the fourth convolutional layer of the neural network. This heatmap shows the significance of the different sections of the hysteresis curve used by the network for distinguishing memristor cells

3.3.2   Evaluation

First, multiple CNNs are trained to determine the best ratio of pixel width and height to achieve the best accuracy, F1-score and the lowest loss. It is particularly important to find the best width and height values so that a high level of detail can be preserved, and noise from the measurement can be reduced. The resulting pixel image is processed in layer four of the CNN as depicted in Fig. 6.

Here, pixels with a brighter hue are of special interest for the CNN and have a greater influence on distinguishing the different samples. Afterwards, the pixel width and height, the amount of layers, the batch size, the number of training epochs, as well as the ratio of the partition of the data into training, validation, and test data are optimized in order to reach the highest accuracy and F1 values. According to our evaluation, a convolutional neural network with five layers provides the best performance over all frequency ranges and amplitudes.

For each amplitude and frequency, the hysteresis loops of each memristor cell are trained over 20 epochs with a batch size of 5. Table 3 shows the results when testing the neural network with hysteresis loops not seen during training. The highest accuracy of 97% and the highest F1-score of also 97% are achieved when the data set of memristor Chip 2 is trained on data where the input signal has a frequency of 100 Hz and an amplitude of 1.0 V. Under these conditions, 97 out of 100 samples were correctly classified, demonstrating the high reliability of the memristor cell classification scheme. We have additionally tried to classify the cells with a densely connected neural network operating on the voltage arrays V_{in} and V_{out}. Thereby, we could achieve an accuracy and F1-score of 94%, in the best case, which may not be sufficient for an authentication application.

As expected, the accuracy of the classification is decreasing with higher frequencies, since, in this case, the hysteresis loop has a lower expansion, and noise has a higher impact on the measurements. We observe that the memristor Chip 2 performs better than Chip 1, which can be attributed to the presence of more unstable cells in Chip 1. Again, as expected, Chip 2 delivers the worst values at the highest frequency, caused by a decreased expansion of the hysteresis loop. However, Chip 1 deviates from this behavior since the best performance here is achieved using an input signal with a frequency of 1 kHz and an amplitude of 1 V. In the future, we plan to investigate whether the combination of multiple memristors to identify a particular array, and hyper-parameter optimization, can lead into an increased accuracy and F1-score.

Table 3. Accuracy and F1-scores for all the amplitude and frequency combinations used to train the convolutional neural network. Each amplitude and frequency combination corresponds to a particular input wave

Chip ID	Frequency in Hz	Amplitude in V	x-Dim in px	y-Dim in px	# Epochs	Acc	F1
1	100	0.8	80	80	20	0.91	0.91
1	100	1.0	150	50	20	0.76	0.76
1	100	1.2	80	80	20	0.78	0.78
1	500	0.8	150	50	20	0.78	0.78
1	500	1.0	80	80	20	0.80	0.80
1	500	1.2	80	80	20	0.80	0.80
1	1000	0.8	80	80	20	0.78	0.79
1	1000	1.0	80	80	20	0.86	0.86
1	1000	1.2	110	50	20	0.88	0.87
2	100	0.8	60	60	20	0.92	0.92
2	100	1.0	120	50	20	0.97	0.97
2	100	1.2	60	60	20	0.94	0.94
2	500	0.8	60	60	20	0.86	0.86
2	500	1.0	60	60	20	0.85	0.86
2	500	1.2	60	60	20	0.92	0.92
2	1000	0.8	60	60	20	0.84	0.84
2	1000	1.0	60	60	20	0.91	0.91
2	1000	1.2	60	60	20	0.79	0.79

4   Applications of Memristance-Based PUFs

The low resource requirements of memristor PUFs, such as their component cost, processing overhead, and power consumption, allow them to be used in a variety of different applications. In particular, the proposed PUFs are suitable for securing and authenticating end devices in a smart home (see Fig. 7), where low resource requirements are critical for the successful adoption of solutions.

The proposed PUF-based protocol is lightweight, as for the CNN model only the relevant node weights need to be stored. Its design is kept as generic as possible to increase its compatibility with other IoT technologies and to be able to later adopt this protocol also for other scenarios. Additionally, the protocol is suitable for resource-constrained devices because the major computational effort of training the model is done by the manufacturer. There, the training of multiple devices can be done in parallel. Thus, the biggest overhead occurs at production time. During operation, only the IoT hub needs to evaluate the measurements provided by each device. This is done with only one forward propagation through the neural network that does not require significant resources and can be executed quickly, causing only a small delay to the authentication process. Even if the frequency-based method is used in this protocol, the resource-constrained devices only need to provide the measurements to the IoT hub, which is responsible for the calculation of the Fourier transformation and the classification.

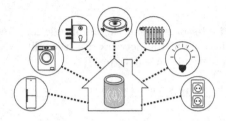

Fig. 7. Typical components of a smart home

4.1   Authentication Protocol

For the above-mentioned scenario, we propose an authentication protocol that consists of two phases, as depicted in Fig. 8. In the **enrollment phase,** measurements $M_{D_{ID}} := \{M_{C_0}, \ldots, M_{C_n}\}$, each corresponding to a memristor cell from C_0 to C_n of a smart device with an identifier D_{ID}, are captured and transmitted to the IoT Hub over a secure channel, e.g. by establishing a direct connection between the IoT Hub and the device in a controlled environment without any other network connection. Each cell is measured with multiple frequencies $F := \{f_0, \ldots, f_n\}$ and amplitudes $A := \{a_0, \ldots, a_n\}$. The IoT Hub stores the model $Model_{D_{ID}}$ of the smart device learned by the manufacturer along with an identifier D_{ID}. In the highly unlikely case that the CNN model fails to be produced for a particular D_{ID} after a few attempts, this D_{ID} shall not be used. Also, a public key is transmitted to the smart device, which is used in the next steps of the protocol. There, lightweight algorithms using elliptic curve cryptography are used.

In the **authentication phase**, a challenge-response protocol is executed. First, the smart device sends a challenge with its identifier D_{ID} to start an authentication request. Here, || describes the concatenation of the message, and the first italicised segment, e.g., *AuthRequest*, is an identifier, allowing the IoT Hub and the device involved to identify and parse the relevant messages correctly. The server responds with a challenge containing a device ID D'_{ID}, a nonce N, a cell ID C_{ID}, an amplitude a, and a frequency f. N is used to prevent replay attacks and can be implemented as a continuous counter or a random number. The IoT device first checks if the requested device ID, D'_{ID}, is equal to its own, and then measures the cell C_{ID} by applying the frequency f and amplitude a to it, resulting in a measurement $M_{C_{ID}}$. Afterwards, a message consisting of the D_{ID}, the previously sent nonce N, and the measurement $M_{C_{ID}}$ is encrypted using the previously shared *publicKey*, and sent to the IoT Hub. Only the IoT Hub can decrypt the message using its *privateKey*. The server checks if N is fresh, and chooses the right model, $Model_{D_{ID}}$, based on D_{ID}. If the CNN can classify all measurements correctly using $Model_{D_{ID}}$, a, and f, the IoT device gets authenticated, otherwise it gets rejected. After a number of unsuccessful authentication requests for the same D_{ID}, the use of that D_{ID} may be disabled.

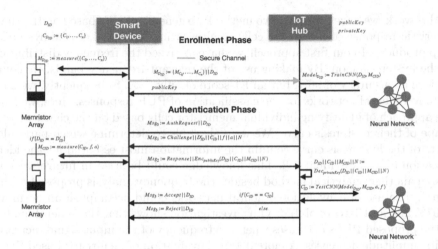

Fig. 8. The proposed protocol comprises two phases: a one-time enrollment phase, and an authentication phase that may be executed multiple times, as needed

4.2 Evaluation of the Proposed Protocol

The advantage of the proposed protocol is that the memristor measurements do not have to be stored on any of the devices. The shared secret only relies on the CNN model that is stored on the side of the central entity, and the ability to reproduce the memristor measurements on the IoT device side.

Our adversary model for the proposed protocol considers a passive attacker who is able to observe the network traffic between the smart device and the IoT hub, and who can capture transmitted messages. Furthermore, we consider the machine learning parameters, such as the CNN architecture, but *not* the relevant node weights, to be public, and thus known by the attacker.

Therefore, an attacker is not able to retrieve the measurements from the response message without knowing the *publicKey*. Also replay attacks can be detected, by checking if a nonce occurred twice on the server's side. An attacker is not able to change N, because the memristor measurements, which are part of the encrypted message, are not known Even if an attacker has physical access to the server, only the CNN model can be retrieved and no measurement data, as this would require reverse engineering the model. In a more realistic scenario, the memristor circuitry may need to be shielded to prevent attacks, for example, by electromagnetic interference, which could potentially disturb the measurements.

In a practical application, a much larger memristor array should be used from which different subsets are selected as a challenge. This would significantly improve the security, increase the challenge space, and thus may form a strong PUF.

5   Conclusion

In this work, we have proposed two methods to generate PUFs based on the characteristic response of memristor cells to alternating voltage, i.e., the hysteresis loop produced. In our first approach, we have analyzed the frequency distribution of the hysteresis loop. By making use of the relevant frequency bands, we could achieve an accuracy of 96%, but an F1-score of only 73%. Subsequently, we have employed neural networks for the classification of PUF responses. Here, we took the approach of identifying individual memristor cells based on the characteristic shape of their hysteresis curve. We were also able to determine which particular parts of the hysteresis curve contain the information most essential for the identification of an individual cell. This knowledge could be used in future work to design another analytical method besides the frequency analysis proposed in this paper. The use of convolutional neural networks could accomplish an accuracy of 97% and an F1-score of 97%. Our investigation shows that the general quality of the proposed PUFs decreases when the frequency of the input signal increases or its amplitude decreases. A more detailed evaluation of memristor-based PUFs will be done in the future. There, also the approaches described in Sect. 1.2 will be compared to our PUF-based scheme in terms of uniqueness and robustness, to further evaluate our work. In addition, further post-processing techniques and more advanced ML schemes could be used to increase the accuracy and F1-score achieved by the proposed frequency analysis method. Another research direction would be to consider the effects of external factors, such as ambient temperature, as well as the effects of different material compositions and ageing on the quality of the examined PUF.

Acknowledgements. This work has been funded by the DFG, under Projects 440182124 and 439892735 of SPP 2253. The authors would like to thank the anonymous reviewers and the shepherd of this work, Prof. Dr. Özgür Sinanoğlu, for their comments, suggestions, and guidance.

Appendix 1   Self-directed Channel Memristors

Memristors are passive circuit elements whose behavior can be described by the following simplified equations:

$$v = R(w)\,i, \quad \frac{dw}{dt} = i.$$

Here, the voltage v depends on the current i and the resistance R of the memristor, which in turn depends on the previous state w of the memristor. i can be described as the integral of w over time t, which means that w is essentially the charge that has moved through the memristor [19]. Therefore, a memristor cell changes its resistance depending on the amount of charge flowing through it. This behavior is usually shown by applying a sine wave to the memristor and visualizing the output in a Lissajous curve, as demonstrated in Fig. 1.

The memristor cells used in our work are so-called self-directed channel memristors [11]. There, each cell consists of multiple layers. The most important ones are the active layer, and a layer of silver, from which Ag^+ ions can migrate into the active layer. As visualized in the simplified structure of such a cell in Fig. 9, each cell has a top and a bottom electrode, over which voltage can be applied. By applying a positive potential to the electrode pair, the memristor performs a transition into a low-resistance state; a transition into a high-resistance state is performed when a negative potential is applied. The active layer of the memristor consists of an amorphous chalcogenide using tungsten as a dopant ($W + Ge_2Se_3$). This layer consists of Ge-rich chalcogenide glass, which builds a network connected by Ge-Ge bonds. In this layer, the resistance is controlled by the number of silver ions of the Ag^+ layer that have migrated into this layer (the active layer), and, in consequence, by whether a conductive channel across this layer exists. The amount of ions of silver that migrate into the active layer depends on the potential applied between the top and bottom electrodes.

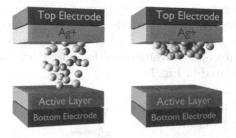

Fig. 9. Simplified structure of a self-directed channel memristor cell. The left image shows the migration of a large number of Ag^+ ions into the active layer, which leads to a highly conductive channel. This is caused by the application of a positive potential to the electrodes. The right image shows the memristor in a high resistive state, after a negative potential has been applied. Here, the Ag^+ ions move from the active layer back to the Ag^+ layer, which leads to low conductance, as a conductive channel is no longer formed across the active layer

During the initial operation of a memristor, a preliminary step called forming must be executed. Here, the same positive potential as the one used during normal operation, is applied to the top and bottom electrodes. This leads to self-trapped electron pairs around the Ge-Ge bonds, causing, as a reaction, some of the Ge-Ge bonds to break, and Se ions of an adjacent SnSe layer, which is not shown in Fig. 9 for reasons of simplicity, to be forced into the active layer. This reduces the energy required to substitute Ag for Ge in a Ge-Ge bond, leading to a conductive channel. The number of Ag^+ ions being forced into the active layer depends on the positive potential applied to the electrodes. Ag$^+$ ions are removed from the active layer when a negative potential is applied [2].

This ion migration allows each memristor to be used as a memory cell. In order to change to a low resistive state, a voltage V_{SET} must be applied, which means that a positive voltage pulse above a certain threshold must be applied to the memristor. This leads to a migration of Ag$^+$ ions into the active layer and thus reduces the resistance of the memristor cell. When a negative pulse V_{RESET} that is beyond a certain threshold, is applied, the conductive ions are removed from the active layer and transferred back to the Ag$^+$ layer, which increases the resistance of the memristor. When a voltage between these two thresholds is applied, the ions stay at their position and the resistance either does not change or does so only to a relatively small extent. In this way, the current resistance of the memory can be measured. The states of high and low resistance encode the logical value of 0 and 1, respectively. When unplugging the power supply, the ions stay at their current position, which makes these cells non-volatile [7].

Appendix 2   Measurement Circuit Design

We designed the measurement circuit in a way such that the experiments are reproducible and measurement data can be captured with a high degree of detail. For that reason, the experiments are performed in an automated test environment and executed by remotely controlling the function generator and oscilloscope. This allows us to capture the data as precisely as possible and thus get consistent and reproducible measurements for all memristor cells. The experimental setup is illustrated in Fig. 10.

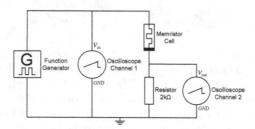

Fig. 10. Circuit used to capture the data using a function generator and an oscilloscope with two channels

The output connectors of the function generator are connected to the top electrode of the memristor array and to the ground. For measuring different cells in the memristor cell array, this connection is sufficient since the top electrodes of all cells are internally interconnected on the chip carrying the cell array. The first channel of the oscilloscope is connected in parallel to the function generator to capture its output V_{in}. Again, in parallel to the function generator, a resistor and the memristor under test are connected in series. The resistor is used to limit the current floating through the memristors. It is rated with 2 kΩ to limit the current to a maximum of 1 mA when applying up to 2 V. Otherwise, the memristor could suffer damage and remain in a high resistive state permanently [11]. Moreover, the resistor is used to measure the voltage drop caused by the resistance of the memristor. For this purpose, the second channel of the oscilloscope is connected in parallel to the resistor and captures the voltage drop caused by memristor V_{out}. Finally, the ground connectors of the two oscilloscope channels, the ground pin of the function generator, and the resistor are connected to one common ground. The oscilloscope is switched to X/Y mode to visualize the output of the first channel on the x-axis, and the second channel on the y-axis. The constant resistance change of the memristor, due to the sine wave applied by the signal generator, causes a perpetually changing voltage drop at the resistor. Before starting the measurements, a forming operation described in Sect. 2.1 needs to be performed. During this phase, the 2 kΩ resistor is replaced by a 10 kΩ resistor, to follow the forming process described by the manufacturer of the chip [16]. The 10 kΩ resistor allows us to apply a higher maximum voltage of 3 V to the memristor. Here, the function generator is set to supply a sine wave with 100 Hz and an amplitude of 250 mV. The amplitude is slowly increased up to 3 V, which is the maximum voltage for this type of memristor chip. All subsequent tests are performed with a maximum amplitude of 1.2 V using a 2 kΩ resistor.

A hysteresis loop can be observed at any frequency and an amplitude of 700 mV, for most of the cells. The loop with the greatest expansion on the y-axis can be seen when amplitudes from 1.2 V to 2 V are supplied using a 2 kΩ resistor. Also, the frequency of the sine wave influences the shape of the loop. Lower frequencies lead to more distinctive hysteresis loops. With increasing frequency, the memristors exhibit smaller resistance changes and thus a smaller hysteresis.

Input signals with an amplitude of 1.2 V and frequencies between 100 Hz and 500 Hz almost consistently produce a clear hysteresis loop. When the frequency is increased to 1 kHz, the width in y-direction is getting smaller. By supplying a frequency of 10 kHz, the width of the hysteresis loop gets considerably smaller.

We have also investigated the influence of different amplitudes of the sine signal on the memristive behavior. When using an amplitude of 0.8 V, almost all cells exhibit a hysteresis loop. With decreasing amplitudes, the cells adjust their behavior to that of ordinary resistors. By increasing the voltage, the hysteresis loop expands not only in the x-direction, but also in y-direction. The clearest shape can be seen using amplitudes between 1.2 V and 2 V using a 2 kΩ resistor. The most significant differences among the hysteresis loops of the memristor arrays also arise for these parameter values, which allows us to identify the cells used for our PUF with the highest precision.

References

1. Albawi, S., Mohammed, T.A., Al-Zawi, S.: Understanding of a convolutional neural network. In: 2017 International Conference on Engineering and Technology (ICET), pp. 1–6 (2017). https://doi.org/10.1109/ICEngTechnol.2017.8308186

2. Campbell, K.A.: Self-directed channel memristor for high temperature operation. Microelectron. J. **59**, 10–14 (2017). https://doi.org/10.1016/j.mejo.2016.11.006
3. Chen, A.: Utilizing the variability of resistive random access memory to implement reconfigurable physical unclonable functions. IEEE Electron Device Lett. **36**(2), 138–140 (2015). https://doi.org/10.1109/LED.2014.2385870
4. Chen, Y.: ReRAM: history, status, and future. IEEE Trans. Electron Devices **67**(4), 1420–1433 (2020). https://doi.org/10.1109/TED.2019.2961505
5. Chen, Y., Petti, C.: ReRAM technology evolution for storage class memory application. In: 2016 46th European Solid-State Device Research Conference (ESSDERC), pp. 432–435 (2016). https://doi.org/10.1109/ESSDERC.2016.7599678
6. Chua, L.: Memristor-the missing circuit element. IEEE Trans. Circ. Theory **18**(5), 507–519 (1971). https://doi.org/10.1109/TCT.1971.1083337
7. Gao, Y., Ranasinghe, D.C.: R^3 PUF: a highly reliable memristive device based reconfigurable PUF. arXiv preprint (2017). http://arxiv.org/abs/1702.07491
8. Guajardo, J., Kumar, S.S., Schrijen, G.J., Tuyls, P.: Physical unclonable functions and public-key crypto for FPGA IP protection. In: 2007 International Conference on Field Programmable Logic and Applications, pp. 189–195 (2007). https://doi.org/10.1109/FPL.2007.4380646
9. Herder, C., Yu, M.D., Koushanfar, F., Devadas, S.: Physical unclonable functions and applications: a tutorial. Proc. IEEE **102**(8), 1126–1141 (2014). https://doi.org/10.1109/JPROC.2014.2320516
10. Kang, H., Hori, Y., Satoh, A.: Performance evaluation of the first commercial PUF-embedded RFID. In: The 1st IEEE Global Conference on Consumer Electronics 2012, pp. 5–8 (2012). https://doi.org/10.1109/GCCE.2012.6379926
11. Knowm Inc.: Self directed channel memristors. Rev. 3.2, 6 October 2019. Knowm, Santa Fe, NM, USA. https://knowm.org/downloads/Knowm_Memristors.pdf. Accessed 22 July 2022
12. Kursawe, K., Sadeghi, A.R., Schellekens, D., Skoric, B., Tuyls, P.: Reconfigurable physical unclonable functions - enabling technology for tamper-resistant storage. In: 2009 IEEE International Workshop on Hardware-Oriented Security and Trust, pp. 22–29 (2009). https://doi.org/10.1109/HST.2009.5225058
13. Menhorn, N.: External secure storage using the PUF. Application Note XAPP1333 (v1.2), Xilinx, San Jose, CA, USA, 12 April 2022. https://www.xilinx.com/content/dam/xilinx/support/documents/application_notes/xapp1333-external-storage-puf.pdf. Accessed 29 July 2022
14. Najafi, F., Kaveh, M., Martín, D., Reza Mosavi, M.: Deep PUF: a highly reliable DRAM PUF-based authentication for IoT networks using deep convolutional neural networks. Sensors **21**(6) (2021). https://doi.org/10.3390/s21062009
15. Nozaki, Y., Shibagaki, K., Takemoto, S., Yoshikawa, M.: AI hardware oriented neural network physical unclonable function and its evaluation. Electron. Commun. Jpn **103**(11–12), 54–62 (2020). https://doi.org/10.1002/ecj.12276
16. Nugent, A.: Knowm Memristor Discovery Manual. Knowm Inc., September 2020
17. Rose, G.S., McDonald, N., Yan, L.K., Wysocki, B.: A write-time based memristive PUF for hardware security applications. In: 2013 IEEE/ACM International Conference on Computer-Aided Design (ICCAD), pp. 830–833. IEEE (2013). https://doi.org/10.1109/ICCAD.2013.6691209
18. Schaller, A., et al.: Decay-based DRAM PUFs in commodity devices. IEEE Trans. Dependable Secure Comput. **16**(3), 462–475 (2019). https://doi.org/10.1109/TDSC.2018.2822298
19. Strukov, D.B., Snider, G.S., Stewart, D.R., Williams, R.S.: The missing memristor found. Nature **453**(7191), 80–83 (2008). https://doi.org/10.1038/nature06932

20. Uddin, M., et al.: Design considerations for memristive crossbar physical unclonable functions. ACM J. Emerg. Technol. Comput. Syst. (JETC) **14**(1) (2017). https://doi.org/10.1145/3094414
21. Yilmaz, Y., Gunn, S.R., Halak, B.: Lightweight PUF-based authentication protocol for IoT devices. In: 2018 IEEE 3rd International Verification and Security Workshop (IVSW), pp. 38–43. IEEE (2018)
22. Yin, C.E., Qu, G.: Temperature-aware cooperative ring oscillator PUF. In: 2009 IEEE International Workshop on Hardware-Oriented Security and Trust, pp. 36–42 (2009). https://doi.org/10.1109/HST.2009.5225055
23. Yue, M., Karimian, N., Yan, W., Anagnostopoulos, N.A., Tehranipoor, F.: DRAM-based authentication using deep convolutional neural networks. IEEE Consumer Electron. Mag. **10**(4), 8–17 (2021). https://doi.org/10.1109/MCE.2020.3002528
24. Zidan, M.A., Strachan, J.P., Lu, W.D.: The future of electronics based on memristive systems. Nat. Electron. **1**, 22–29 (2018). https://doi.org/10.1038/s41928-017-0006-8

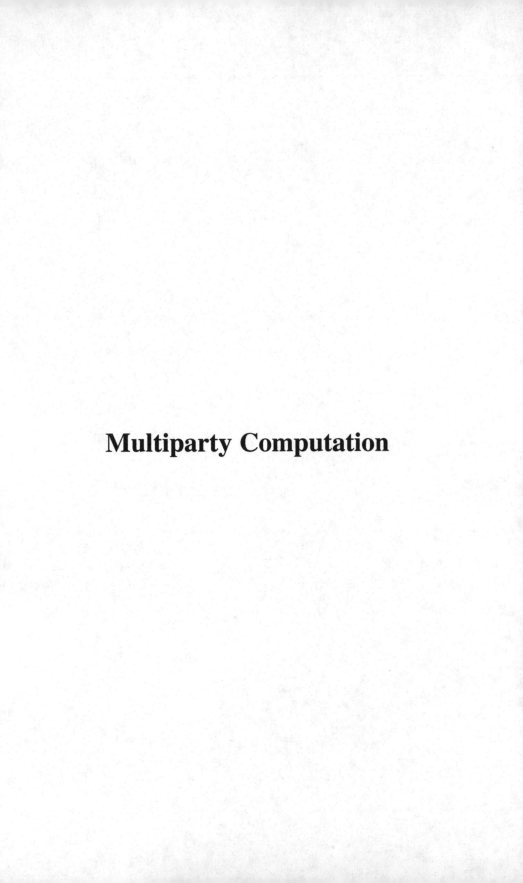

Multiparty Computation

SecureBiNN: 3-Party Secure Computation for Binarized Neural Network Inference

Wenxing Zhu[1,2], Mengqi Wei[1], Xiangxue Li[1,3(✉)], and Qiang Li[4]

[1] School of Software Engineering, East China Normal University, Shanghai, China
xxli@cs.ecnu.edu.cn
[2] Shanghai Key Laboratory of Privacy-Preserving Computation, MatrixElements Technologies, Shanghai, China
[3] Shanghai Key Laboratory of Trustworthy Computing, Shanghai, China
[4] Institute of Cyber Science and Technology, Shanghai Jiao Tong University, Shanghai, China
qiangl@sjtu.edu.cn

Abstract. The paper proposes SecureBiNN, a novel three-party secure computation framework for evaluating privacy-preserving binarized neural network (BiNN) in semi-honest adversary setting. In SecureBiNN, three participants hold input data and model parameters in secret sharing form, and execute secure computations to obtain secret shares of prediction result without disclosing their input data, model parameters and the prediction result. SecureBiNN performs linear operations in a computation-efficient and communication-free way. For non-linear operations, we provide novel secure methods for evaluating activation function, maxpooling layers, and batch normalization layers in BiNN. Communication overhead is significantly minimized comparing to previous work like XONN and Falcon. We implement SecureBiNN with tensorflow and the experiments show that using the Fitnet structure, SecureBiNN achieves on CIFAR-10 dataset an accuracy of 81.5%, with communication cost of 16.609MB and runtime of 0.527s/3.447s in the LAN/WAN settings. More evaluations on real-world datasets are also performed and other concrete comparisons with state-of-the-art are presented as well.

Keywords: Privacy-preserving machine learning · Secure multi-party computation · Binarized neural network

1 Introduction

Machine Learning as a Service (MLaaS) has created huge economic benefits and been widely used in image classification, disease diagnosis, etc. In MLaaS, both model owner and data owner would suffer from privacy leakage if the model or input data could be accessed by others arbitrarily. Cryptographic techniques, e.g., secure multiparty computation (SMC) and homomorphic encryption (HE), are good solutions to the problem. The community really sees many

© The Author(s), under exclusive license to Springer Nature Switzerland AG 2022
V. Atluri et al. (Eds.): ESORICS 2022, LNCS 13556, pp. 275–294, 2022.
https://doi.org/10.1007/978-3-031-17143-7_14

cryptography-enabled protocols [7,15,23,24,27,34], and most of them focus on naive neural networks (NN) and stipulate the parameters in fixed-point numbers. Some work [8,28] implements binarized neural network (BiNN) (model parameters take the values of ± 1). BiNN has simpler calculation process than NN and one may expect more efficient implementation of BiNN (than NN) with SMC and HE.

This paper proposes SecureBiNN, a novel three-party framework for BiNN inference, secure under non-colluding semi-honest adversary setting (same as SecureNN [34] and XONN [28]). SecureBiNN has three semi-honest participants, each of which holds secret shares of the input data and of the model. We evaluate BiNNs with replicated secret share technique [5], reduce communication cost and enhance computation efficiency by ruling out garbled circuit (GC) and HE. After the framework evaluation, each party outputs its secret share of prediction result. SecureBiNN can be applied to inference on sensitive data without compromising privacy. For example, three banks could use their own data to predict customers for financial fraud, or three hospitals could use patients' private data to make better diagnoses without revealing their privacy.

Our contributions can be summarized in the following two aspects:

- Framework: We propose SecureBiNN, a secure computation framework for BiNN inference. To reduce communication cost, SecureBiNN chooses ring size according to BiNN architecture. Furthermore, we propose new protocols for three-party oblivious transfer, secure activation, and secure maxpooling. To further improve SecureBiNN performance under WAN settings, we use 3-input AND gate to reduce the number of communication rounds. In particular, our maxpooling operation requires only one private comparison operation. We put batch normalization and binarized activation together, and thereby use one addition and one private comparison to achieve batch normalization and activation operation.
- Practicality: SecureBiNN is computation-efficient and communication-cheap. We implement SecureBiNN with numpy [36], Tensorflow [4] and run experiments on three ecs.c7.2xlarge servers from Alibaba Cloud. We evaluate various networks on MNIST, CIFAR-10 and real-world medical datasets. The results of experiments in Sect. 4 show the practical feasibility of SecureBiNN under LAN/WAN settings. We provide our source code on Github[1].

We recap the related work in the Appendix A due to space limitation.

2   Preliminaries

We review security model, correlated randomness, and secret sharing used in this paper. We denote three participants as P_0, P_1, and P_2. $P_{(i+1)mod\,3}$ and $P_{(i-1)mod\,3}$ denote the next and previous parties for P_i respectively. For simplicity, we omit $mod\ 3$ in the subscript of P_i and other variables (e.g., x_i, r_i).

---

[1] https://github.com/Wixee/SecureBiNN.

2.1   Security Model

We assume that each participant is *honest-but-curious* (a.k.a. *semi-honest*). In other words, each participant implements the protocols honestly and will not attack others actively (e.g., capture others' secret keys, monitor others' communications, or construct malicious input data). However, they might try to infer information of others as much as possible. Such model is commonly assumed in [22,23,28,34]. We also adopt the same assumption as in other three-party protocols [16,24,35] that there is no collusion between any two participants.

As previous work and other cryptographic protocols, SecureBiNN ensures input data and model parameters will not be leaked during protocol executions. We will not discuss how to protect model structure or to defend other attacks like model retrieval attack [33], membership inference attack [31] and data poisoning attacks [11], which go apparently out of scope of the framework.

2.2   Correlated Randomness

In this work, random values are generated by a PRF (Pseudo-Random Function) R with two inputs x, y, denoted as $R(x, y)$. Given an input pair, R will return a specific value. R's output can be viewed as a uniform distribution on its domain. We assume that $\Pr[(x, y) \leftarrow \mathcal{A}(R(x, y))]$ is negligible for any PPT adversary $\mathcal{A}$.

Suppose P_i and P_{i+1} negotiate a secret random seed r_{i+1}. P_i holds (r_i, r_{i+1}), $i = 0, 1, 2$. All participants maintain a counter cnt, incremented by one after each invocation. For a modulo m, we have two types of correlated randomness.
3-out-of-3 randomness: P_i calculates $a_i = R(r_{i+1}, cnt) - R(r_i, cnt) \mod m$. Note that $a_0 + a_1 + a_2 \equiv 0 \mod m$.
2-out-of-3 randomness: P_i calculates $(a_i, a_{i+1}) = (R(r_i, cnt), R(r_{i+1}, cnt))$. By 2-out-of-3 randomness, P_i, P_{i+1} can generate a common random value a_{i+1} without any communication cost, and P_{i-1} does not have the knowledge of a_{i+1}.

2.3   Two-party Secret Sharing

For a modulo $m = 2^l, l \in \mathbb{Z}^+$, a secret $x \in \mathbb{Z}_m$ is shared by sampling two random x_0 and x_1 s.t. $x_0 + x_1 = x$ over $\mathbb{Z}_m$. Denote x shared by two parties as $[\![x]\!]_2^m$. When $l = 1$, we can denote $[\![x]\!]_2^B = [\![x]\!]_2^2 = (x_0, x_1)$ where $x_0 \oplus x_1 = x$ and $x, x_0, x_1 \in \{0, 1\}$. More details can be found in [6,13,23]. The linear operation for two-party secret sharing is trivial, and the multiplication can be implemented by using Beaver's Triplet [6].

2.4   Three-party Secret Sharing

Three-party secret sharing is proposed in [5]. For a modulo $m = 2^l$, a secret $x \in \mathbb{Z}_m$ is shared by sampling three random $x_0, x_1, x_2 \in \mathbb{Z}_m, x = x_0 + x_1 + x_2$, and then P_i holds (x_i, x_{i+1}). Denote such kind of secret shared value x as $[\![x]\!]_3^m$, and the tuple (x_0, x_1, x_2) represents its shares. Three-party secret sharing supports linear operations and multiplications between the shared values. Given public a, b and c, we have the following for secretly shared $[\![x]\!]_3^m$ and $[\![y]\!]_3^m$.

- Linear operation: participants can compute $[\![ax + by + c]\!]_3^m := (ax_0 + by_0 + c, \ ax_1 + by_1, ax_2 + by_2)$ locally to achieve linear operation.
- Multiplication: P_i computes and outputs $z_i = x_i y_i + x_i y_{i+1} + x_{i+1} y_i$ where $\sum_{i=0}^{2} z_i = z = xy$. If the participants need to restore the output to the form of $[\![z]\!]_3^m$, they should invoke 3-out-of-3 randomness to get a_0, a_1, a_2, and P_i sends $z_i + a_i$ to P_{i-1}. At last, P_i outputs $(z_i + a_i, \ z_{i+1} + a_{i+1})$.

Both two-party and three-party secret sharing schemes can be trivially extended to matrix computations.

3   The SecureBiNN Framework

3.1   Highlights

For a BiNN with n layers, we denote the input and the weights of the i-th layer as X_{i-1} and W_i respectively. X_{i-1}s and W_is are encoded into an integer ring and secretly shared by participants who run multiplication protocol of secret sharing to calculate $W_i X_{i-1}$. This method can be easily generalized to convolutional neural network. The activation function used in BiNN is

$$Sign(x) = \begin{cases} 1 & x \geq 0 \\ -1 & x < 0 \end{cases} \tag{1}$$

When running the *sign* function, we convert three-party secret sharing into two-party secret sharing between P_0 and P_1 to evaluate part of parallel prefix adder circuit. We can get the result of the sign function according to the MSB (most significant bit) of its input. After that, three participants utilize a three-party oblivious transfer (OT) to convert the result of the circuit into three-party secret sharing again. The three-party OT we use originates from [24]. However, we alter its input and make some modifications so that it also works well in SecureBiNN. We will show details in the following part. Note that the *sign* function is used in the maxpooling layers as well.

Before implementing SecureBiNN, a model owner should encode its model in the form of three-party secret sharing. Input data should also be encoded in the same way. After the protocol, each party holds a share of the result, and all participants would then send their shares to those who should know the result. This is application-dependent and here we do not consider the source of the input and how participants deal with the results.

3.2   Parameters Encoding

We encode all model parameters into $\mathbb{Z}_{2^l}$. Among all n layers, l's value decided in the i-th layer might be independent of that in the j-th layer $(1 \leq i, j \leq n, i \neq j)$. In the input layer and output layer, we use standard fixed-point arithmetic encoding scheme. In other layers, however, we can use a smaller l to reduce parameter size. For example, we encode parameters of the input layer and output layer into $\mathbb{Z}_{2^{16}}$ or $\mathbb{Z}_{2^{32}}$, while the parameters of other layers are encoded into $\mathbb{Z}_{2^9}$ or $\mathbb{Z}_{2^{14}}$. We will describe more details below.

Encoding Input and Output Layer Parameters. In the input and output layers, we use standard fixed-point encoding, and a bit string of length l can represent a fixed-point number in complement form. In most cases, the value of l is 32. The MSB of some number represents the sign of the number: it is non-negative if its MSB is 0, and negative otherwise. We say a number has l_D bits of precision $(0 \leq l_D < (l-1)/2)$ if the l_D bits at the far right represent the fractional part and the remaining $l - 1 - l_D$ bits represent the integer part.

In SecureBiNN, we ditch truncation operations (used generally in fixed-point arithmetic multiplications), for we only use fixed-point encoding in input/output layers and no overflow occurs. Our method requires that for addition operations in input/output layers, the operands should have same precision. Take $Y = WX + b$ for instance. If W and X have l_D^W and l_D^X bits of precision respectively, then WX has $l_D^W + l_D^X$ bits of precision. In order to remove truncation and make addition result correct, b should also have $l_D^W + l_D^X$ bits of precision.

Encoding Hidden Layer Parameters. In SecureBiNN, the parameters of each hidden layer are represented by signed integers of l bits. Herein, l could be chosen independently in each layer. In hidden fully connected layers, every entry in the input X_{i-1} and the weight W_i takes 1 or –1. If the shapes of W_i and X_{i-1} are (n, m) and (m, k) respectively, then each entry in $W_i X_{i-1}$ is an signed integer in $[-m, m]$. We can thus choose the smallest l s.t. $2^{l-1} - 1 \geq m$ and encode W_i and X_{i-1} into the ring Z_{2^l}. In case that the hidden layer performs a convolution operation and filter size is (n_{in}, h, w, n_{out}), we require $2^{l-1} - 1 \geq n_{in} \times h \times w$. Then we use l bits to represent any signed integer parameter in the layer. W.l.o.g., this can also be seen as 0-bit precision fixed-point encoding.

This method has relatively low fault tolerance. Indeed, the number of neurons in previous layer completely determines the ring size, and we do not consider addition operations in subsequent batch normalization (see the coming sections), which might cause overflow. This little gap could be handled heuristically. If the hidden layer is a fully connected layer or a convolutional layer followed by a normalization layer, then we add a constant δ to l to relax the restriction on l. Our experiments show that setting $\delta = 2$ already provides expected robustness.

3.3 Fully Connected Layer and Convolutional Layer

Consider an arbitrary fully connected layer. All its input X, weight W (and bias b for input/output layers) are secretly shared over $\mathbb{Z}_{2^l}$ among the participants who collaboratively invoke multiplication protocol (see Algorithm 1) to calculate the (shared) result. The protocol could be easily extended to convolution operations. In the protocol, b should have $l_W + l_X$ bits of precision if the fixed-point W and X have l_W and l_X bits of precision respectively.

3.4 Secure 3-Input and Gate

In order to further improve the performance in the WAN setting, we use 3-input AND gate technique [25] to reduce communication rounds in implementing

---

Algorithm 1. Fully Connected Layer Inference: Π_{fc}

Input: P_i inputs the weight share (W_i, W_{i+1}), data share(X_i, X_{i+1}) (and bias share b_i if the layer is input layer or output layer) s.t. $\sum_{j=0}^{2} W_j = W$, $\sum_{j=0}^{2} X_j = X$, $\sum_{j=0}^{2} b_j = b$, $i \in \{0, 1, 2\}$.

Output: P_i outputs Z_i, secret shares of fully connected layer output.

1: $P_i : Z_i = W_i X_i + W_{i+1} X_i + W_i X_{i+1}$
2: **if** it is not a hidden layer **then**
3:    $Z_i = Z_i + b_i$
4: **end if**

Algorithm 2. Secure 3-input AND Gate: $\Pi_{3-inputANDgate}$

Input: P_0, P_1 input $[\![a]\!]_2^B$, $[\![b]\!]_2^B$, $[\![c]\!]_2^B$, P_2 inputs $\perp$.

Output: P_0 and P_1 ouput $[\![z]\!]_2^B$ where $z = abc$, P_2 ouputs $\perp$.

1: P_0, P_1 generate $[\![a']\!]_2^B$, $[\![b']\!]_2^B$, $[\![c']\!]_2^B$, $[\![a'b']\!]_2^B$, $[\![a'c']\!]_2^B$, $[\![b'c']\!]_2^B$, $[\![a'b'c']\!]_2^B$ with the help of P_2 by utilizing *2-out-of-3 randomness*.
2: P_0, P_1 calculate $[\![a \oplus a']\!]_2^B$, $[\![b \oplus b']\!]_2^B$, $[\![c \oplus c']\!]_2^B$.
3: P_0, P_1 reconstruct and open $(a \oplus a')$, $(b \oplus b')$, $(c \oplus c')$.
4: P_0 and P_1 calculate and output $[\![z]\!]_2^B$ according to the Eq. (2).

---

secure activation function. It can be seen as an extension of Beaver's Triplet technique [6]. The formula for 3-input AND gate can be written as

$$
\begin{aligned}
z = abc =&(a \oplus a')(b \oplus b')(c \oplus c') \oplus (c \oplus c')a'b' \oplus (b \oplus b')a'c' \\
&\oplus (a \oplus a')b'c' \oplus (a \oplus a')(b \oplus b')c' \\
&\oplus (a \oplus a')(c \oplus c')b' \oplus (b \oplus b')(c \oplus c')a' \oplus a'b'c'.
\end{aligned}
\tag{2}
$$

Here, a, b, c represent the inputs and z represents the output, a', b' and c' are random masks used to hide a, b, c respectively in SMC. Before implementing such a 3-input AND gate, P_0 and P_1 take $[\![a]\!]_2^B$, $[\![b]\!]_2^B$ and $[\![c]\!]_2^B$ as inputs, P_2 plays the role of a helper, generates $[\![a']\!]_2^B$, $[\![b']\!]_2^B$, $[\![c']\!]_2^B$, $[\![a'b']\!]_2^B$, $[\![a'c']\!]_2^B$, $[\![b'c']\!]_2^B$, $[\![a'b'c']\!]_2^B$ and send these secret shares to P_0 and P_1.

In SecureBiNN, with the help of *2-out-of-3 randomness*, communication cost of implementing a 3-input AND gate can be further optimized. By *2-out-of-3 randomness*, P_2 can reduce communication cost of secret sharing distribution. P_0 and P_1 generate common uniform randomness with P_2 respectively, and take them as $[\![a']\!]_2^B$, $[\![b']\!]_2^B$ and $[\![c']\!]_2^B$. Then P_2 reconstructs a', b', c' and calculates $a'b'$, $a'c'$, $b'c'$, $a'b'c'$. P_0 and P_2 then generate common randomness again, P_0 takes these randomness as shares of $a'b'$, $a'c'$, $b'c'$, $a'b'c'$, P_2 calculates and sends appropriate shares of above terms to P_1. In the naive method, P_2 needs to send a total of 14 bit, while in above optimized method, 4 bits suffice. Algorithm 2 shows the details of implementing a 3-input AND gate with the above optimization.

It is easy to prove the correctness, and we omit the details and just focus on its security proof below.

Algorithm 3. Ideal Function of Three-Party Oblivious Transfer: F_{3-OT}

Input: Sender inputs (m_0, m_1), Receiver inputs b, Helper inputs $\perp$.
Output: Receiver outputs m_b, Sender and Helper output $\perp$.

Algorithm 4. Three-Party Oblivious Transfer: Π_{3-OT}

Input: Sender inputs (m_0, m_1), Receiver inputs b, Helper inputs $\perp$.
Output: Receiver outputs m_b, Sender and Helper output $\perp$.

1: Receiver and Sender generate common ranom bit r, common random bit string $mask_0$ and $mask_1$.
2: Sender computes $s_i = m_{i \oplus r} \oplus mask_{i \oplus r}, i \in \{0, 1\}$.
3: Sender sends (s_0, s_1) to Helper.
4: Receiver sends $b \oplus r$ to Helper.
5: Helper sends $s_{b \oplus r}$ to Receiver.
6: Receiver calculates $m_b = s_{b \oplus r} \oplus mask_{b \oplus r}$.

Theorem 1. *The above optimized secret sharing used for implementing 3-input AND gate is secure, i.e., these secret shares in performing 3-input AND gate will not leak secret information.*

Proof. Since the *2-out-of-3 randomness* generates uniform randomness, a', b', c', $a'b'$, $a'c'$, $b'c'$, $a'b'c'$ and the corresponding secret shares also conform to uniform distribution. When implementing 3-input AND gate, messages are well masked to follow uniform distribution, thus P_0 and P_1 cannot infer each other's secret share based on the transcripts (see interaction details in [25]). Therefore, it is trivial to construct a simulator of the real-ideal paradigm [9]. P_2 plays the role of a helper and does not participate in the execution of AND gate itself, so P_2 can not infer the secrets. □

3.5 Three-party Oblivious Transfer

We use three-party oblivious transfer (OT) in follow-up secure activation function. In our three-party OT, we have a sender holding two messages m_0 and m_1, a receiver holding a choice bit b (that decides the message m_b it wants from the sender), and a helper holding null input. The corresponding ideal function is shown in Algorithm 3, and the detail of the three-party OT is shown in Algorithm 4.

After the protocol, the receiver gets the message m_b with the requirements that the sender does not know which message is selected by the receiver, that the receiver knows nothing about m_{1-b}, and that the helper does not learn any knowledge of the messages and the choice bit. Table 1 gives the comparison of our three-party OT and that in ABY^3 from the perspectives of communication overhead, communication round, and the requirement on the choice bit.

Note that any two parties (e.g., the sender and the receiver in three-party OT) can take a communication-free invocation of *2-out-of-3 randomness* to generate common randomness. So the first step in Algorithm 4 is communication free.

Table 1. Comparison of OT in SecureBiNN and 1-out-of-2 OT in ABY^3, l represents the length of a single message

	Comm. cost	Round	Helper knows the choice bit?
Ours	$3l + 1$	2	×
ABY^3	$3l$	2	✓

Thus, if the bit lengths of both m_0 and m_1 are l, overall communication takes $3l+1$ bits. The correctness and security of the protocol are obvious and intuitive. This protocol will be used in secure activation function.

In our protocol, not only the sender but the helper cannot tell the index of the exact message selected by the receiver, which is different from previous three-party oblivious transfer protocols in ABY^3 [24] and Falcon [35]^2. The counterparts in them call an explicit and simple conversion from two-party secret sharing to three-party secret sharing so that the helper and the receiver reach a common bit and further take it as the choice bit. Thus, those schemes require one more round of communication before the oblivious transfer begins.

Theorem 2. Π_{3-OT} *is secure against non-collusion semi-honest adversaries.*

Proof. Due to the common uniformly random masks generated by Sender and Receiver, the execution of the Π_{3-OT} protocol is quite simple and one may easily construct such a simulator. Sender and Receiver can generate common uniformly random bit r, common uniformly random string $mask_0$ and $mask_1$ with the common random seed. This can be achieved by a trivial simulation (omitted in the following discussion). Next, we discuss from the perspectives of three parties.

1. If adversary $\mathcal{A}$ corrupts Sender: $\mathcal{A}$ sends two masked messages s_0 and s_1 to the simulator $\mathcal{S}$. $\mathcal{S}$ can extract m_0, m_1 from s_0 and s_1 since r, $mask_0$ and $mask_1$ are known to both $\mathcal{A}$ and $\mathcal{S}$. $\mathcal{S}$ provides the input to the ideal functionality $\mathcal{F}_{3-OT}$, then the ideal functionality will send the output to the party which represents the receiver in the real world, thus honest parties in the ideal world receive correct ouput. Since the sender receives no messages, the simulator $\mathcal{S}$ sends the adversary $\mathcal{A}$ nothing and thereby $\mathcal{A}$ cannot distinguish the ideal world and the real execution.
2. If adversary $\mathcal{A}$ corrupts Helper: $\mathcal{S}$ just sends a uniformly random bit and two uniformly random strings which represent $b \oplus r$, s_0 and s_1 (we assume that the lengths of s_0 and s_1 are public). In the real world, $b \oplus r$, s_0 and s_1 all follow uniformly random distribution. So $\mathcal{A}$ cannot tell whether it is interacting with the real protocol or simulator $\mathcal{S}$.
3. If adversary $\mathcal{A}$ corrupts Receiver: $\mathcal{A}$ sends $b \oplus r$ to the simulator $\mathcal{S}$. $\mathcal{S}$ extracts b with the knowledge of r and inputs b to the ideal functionality $\mathcal{F}_{3-OT}$, and can then receive the ideal output m_b. After that, $\mathcal{S}$ generates $m_b \oplus mask_{b \oplus r}$ according to r and $mask_{b \oplus r}$ (since r and $mask_b \oplus r$ are known to Sender

---

^{2} OT protocols in ABY^3 and Falcon are secure against semi-honest adversaries.

and Receiver). Finally, S sends $m_b \oplus mask_{b \oplus r}$ to the adversary $\mathcal{A}$ who opens the message and gets the correct output. r and $mask_{b \oplus r}$ simulated by S are uniformly random, which is the same as in the real execution. So the adversary $\mathcal{A}$ cannot tell whether it is interacting with the real protocol or simulator S.

This completes the security proof of Π_{3-OT}.   □

3.6 Secure Activation Function

Suppose that the participants finish fully connected layer inference or convolutional layer inference and now activation layer follows. Each party holds a share of the evaluation result (in fact, a series of shares of the result's entries) after evaluating a fully connected layer or a convolutional layer. Suppose that P_i holds the share z_i. Now the participants want $[\![Sign(z)]\!]_3^{m'}$ given $[\![z]\!]_3^m$. Here $m = 2^l$ represents the modulo of the last layer, m' represents the modulo of the next layer. To the purpose, we have three phases: first convert three-party sharing $[\![z]\!]_3^m$ (among P_0, P_1, P_2) to two-party secret sharing $[\![z]\!]_2^m$ (between P_0 and P_1); then get $[\![MSB(z)]\!]_2^B$ by evaluating a parallel adder circuit on $\mathbb{Z}_2$ with 3-input AND gate technique; and finally get $[\![Sign(z)]\!]_3^{m'}$ by invoking three-party oblivious transfer Π_{3-OT}. The following presents the details.

From Three-Party Secret Sharing to Two-Party Secret Sharing. All participants jointly call the *3-out-of-3 randomness* protocol and each gets a random value a_i (such that $a_1 + a_2 + a_3 = 0$), then P_2 sends $z_2 + a_2$ to one of the remaining parties (say P_0). This will not leak any information as $z_2 + a_2$ sent by P_2 is distributed uniformly at random. Now P_0 holds $s_0 = (z_0 + a_0) + (z_2 + a_2)$ and P_1 holds $s_1 = z_1 + a_1$. We have $s = s_0 + s_1 = \sum(z_i) + \sum(a_i) = \sum(z_i) = z$ and thereby manage two-party secret sharing, i.e., s_0 and s_1 are secret shares of z (and s).

Achieving MSB Extraction with Specific Part of Parallel Prefix Adder Circuit. By converting three-party secret sharing to two-party secret sharing, P_0 and P_1 reach $[\![s]\!]_2^m = (s_0, s_1)$ where $m = 2^l$. One may view s_i $(i = 0, 1)$ as a bit string of length l. As $s_0 = s_0 \oplus 0$, we then have $[\![s_0]\!]_2^B$, a toy "two-party secret sharing" of s_0 such that P_0 holds s_0 and P_1 holds 0. Similarly, we have a toy "two-party secret sharing" $[\![s_1]\!]_2^B$. One might gain the advantage of communication round complexity in the MSB extraction protocol by the joint exploit of toy "two-party secret sharing" and standard secret sharing.

Now, the participants P_0, P_1 (and P_2) are ready to extract the MSB of s (see Algorithm 5). We use $s_0[i]$ and $s_1[i]$ to denote the i-th bits of s_0 and of s_1 respectively. It is obvious that $MSB(s) = s_0[l - 1] \oplus s_1[l - 1] \oplus c$, where c is a carry bit generated from lower $l - 1$ bit pairs. Three parties then use 3-input AND gate to evaluate the parallel prefix adder circuit to compute the carry bit c. For a 3-input AND gate with one free input in the circuit, we can replace it with a 2-input AND gate by using well known Beaver's Triplet technique [6] (a

---

Algorithm 5. MSB Extraction: Π_{msb}

Input: P_0 and P_1 input $[\![s_0]\!]_2^B$ and $[\![s_1]\!]_2^B$, $s_i \in \mathbb{Z}_{2^l}$, P_2 inputs $\perp$.
Output: P_0 and P_1 achieve $[\![b]\!]_2^B$, b is the MSB of s where $s = s_0 + s_1$.

1: P_0, P_1 input $[\![s_0]\!]_2^B$ and $[\![s_1]\!]_2^B$ to the parallel prefix adder circuit which is composed by 2-input and 3-input secure AND gates, P_2 plays as a helper. They collaborate to compute $[\![carry\_bit]\!]_2^B$ with SMC.
2: $[\![b]\!]_2^B = [\![s_0[l-1]]\!]_2^B \oplus [\![s_1[l-1]]\!]_2^B \oplus [\![carry\_bit]\!]_2^B$.

Algorithm 6. Convert $[\![MSB(z)]\!]_2^B$ to $[\![Sign(z)]\!]_3^{m'}$

Input: P_0 and P_1 input the shares b_0, b_1 in $[\![MSB(z)]\!]_2^B$ respectively ($MSB(z) = 0$ if the said neuron is activated, and 1 otherwise), P_2 inputs $\perp$.
Output: $[\![t]\!]_3^{m'}$ among P_0, P_1, P_2 s.t. $\sum t_i = Sign(z)$. m' is the modulo.
Parameter: $deact\_val = 0$ if maxpooling layer follows and -1 otherwise.

1: P_1 selects a secret value $r \in_R \mathbb{Z}_{m'}$ and calculates $m_0 = (1 \oplus b_1)act\_val + (0 \oplus b_1)deact\_val - r \pmod{m'}$, $m_1 = (0 \oplus b_1)act\_val + (1 \oplus b_1)deact\_val - r \pmod{m'}$.
2: Call Π_{3-OT} (P_0 acts as receiver, P_1 sender, and P_2 helper), and P_0 receives m_{b_0}.
3: P_0 sets $t'_0 = m_{b_0}$, P_1 sets $t'_1 = r$, P_2 sets $t'_2 = 0$.
4: P_i generates $a_i \in \mathbb{Z}_m$ with *3-out-of-3* randomness.
5: P_i sets $t_i = t'_i + a_i$, and sends t_i to P_{i-1}, then P_i holds (t_i, t_{i+1}).

---

simplified version of 3-input AND gate) to further reduce the communication cost. The same circuit is used in [26] to handle the case where l is set as 32 or 64. In contrast, SecureBiNN always takes a smaller value (e.g., 16 or 18) of l determined by the structure of the previous layer. In other words, SecureBiNN has a smaller circuit size and this will further contribute to lower communication cost and less interaction rounds.

Converting $[\![MSB(z)]\!]_2^B$ to $[\![Sign(z)]\!]_3^{m'}$. Given $[\![MSB(z)]\!]_2^B$ between P_0 and P_1, we can now get $[\![Sign(z)]\!]_3^{m'}$ among P_0, P_1, P_2. Recall that if the MSB is 0, then the neuron hereof should be activated, and deactivated otherwise. As we use the activation function $Sign$, we have the activation value $act\_val = 1$ and the deactivation value $deact\_val = -1$. If a maxpooling layer follows however, we set $deact\_val$ as 0 (rather than -1) in order to adapt to maxpooling operation.

The details are shown in Algorithm 6. To achieve $[\![Sign(z)]\!]_3^{m'}$, we let P_1 generate symmetric messages by using its secret knowledge (secret share in $[\![MSB(z)]\!]_2^B$ and one-time randomness) along with activation/deactivation values. We then call our three-party oblivious transfer protocol Π_{3-OT} by viewing P_1 as the sender, P_0 the receiver, and P_2 the helper. The particular constructing of the messages enables P_0 to get the exact message decided by its secret share (in $[\![MSB(z)]\!]_2^B$) so that a simple conversion from two-party secret sharing to three-party sharing leads to the expected $[\![Sign(z)]\!]_3^{m'}$.

3.7 Batch Normalization

In SecureBiNN, batch normalization is always followed by an activation layer so we can put batch normalization operation and activation operation together. Consider the following formula for batch normalization [17]:

$$Y = \gamma \frac{X - \mu}{\sqrt{\sigma^2 + \epsilon}} + \beta. \tag{3}$$

Herein, γ and β are trainable parameters in the batch normalization, ϵ is a small constant to avoid the "Divide by Zero" error, μ and σ are parameters decided in the training process. Thus, all these parameters would be set as fixed values during inference. And we can rewrite Eq. (3) as

$$Y = \frac{\gamma}{\sqrt{\sigma^2 + \epsilon}} X + \beta - \frac{\gamma\mu}{\sqrt{\sigma^2 + \epsilon}}. \tag{4}$$

Let $\gamma' = \frac{\gamma}{\sqrt{\sigma^2 + \epsilon}}$, $\beta' = \beta - \frac{\gamma\mu}{\sqrt{\sigma^2 + \epsilon}}$, then we have

$$Y = \gamma' X + \beta'. \tag{5}$$

In most cases, γ' is positive and batch normalization layer is followed by an activation layer. It holds that

$$Sign(\gamma' X + \beta') = Sign(X + \frac{\beta'}{\gamma'}). \tag{6}$$

Thus, the model owner first encodes $\frac{\beta'}{\gamma'}$ into a fixed-point number over the ring $\mathbb{Z}_m$ and then uniformly samples θ_i s.t. $\sum_{i=0}^{2} \theta_i = \frac{\beta'}{\gamma'}$ and sends θ_i to P_i. If the participants need to perform batch normalization between a fully connected layer and an activation function, P_i only needs to add θ_i to the output share of the fully connected layer.[3]

In the input layer, X and $\frac{\beta'}{\gamma'}$ are both fixed-point numbers, but in the hidden layers, X is an integer and $\frac{\beta'}{\gamma'}$ is not. In this case, if $Sign(X + \frac{\beta'}{\gamma'}) = 1$ (which means $X + \frac{\beta'}{\gamma'} \geq 0$), there is

$$X \geq \lceil -\frac{\beta'}{\gamma'} \rceil \geq -\frac{\beta'}{\gamma'}. \tag{7}$$

So Eq. (8) holds and we can implement it instead.

$$Sign(\gamma' X + \beta') = Sign(X - \lceil -\frac{\beta'}{\gamma'} \rceil). \tag{8}$$

---

[3] Same for convolutional layers.

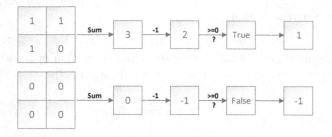

Fig. 1. Two examples of maxpooling

3.8 Maxpooling

We know that the neurons hereof should be activated (i.e., $act\_val = 1$) if $MSB(z) = 0$, and deactivated (i.e., $deact\_val = -1$) otherwise. Suppose that maxpooling layer follows now. If there exists 1 in some maxpooling step, then the max value is 1 and a standard maxpooling step would output 1, and -1 otherwise. This can be done generally by several *comparator* operations [35]. Whereas, our framework takes a different trick. Now we set the deactivation value as 0 rather than -1[4] and then check whether there exists 1 in the pool. If yes, then the sum of these entries minus 1 should be greater than or equal to 0. After a convolutional layer, participants convert the maxpooling layer to a 'sumpooling layer', i.e., they replace the 'Max' operation in the maxpooling layer with an 'Add' operation (see Fig. 1) and then apply *Sign* function to the output of the 'Add' operation. Therefore, a single step of maxpooling layer can be done by an 'Add' operation and a MSB extraction operation. Prior frameworks, like MiniONN [21], generally lean on the secure comparison protocols (i.e., *comparator*) and secure multiplications to find the largest value in the pool, and the numbers of comparator and multiplication calls have a linear relationship with filter size.

There is another optimization. The participants need not convert the shares to three-party secret shares after an activation operation which is always followed by a maxpooling layer. P_0 and P_1 can *locally* implement a 'sumpooling layer' and then participants implement the activation operation again.

4 Experiment Results and Analysis

We execute SecureBiNN with Python (about 3k lines of code), and computations are implemented through numpy 1.19.0 [36] and tensorflow 2.5.1 [4]. We run our experiments on three ecs.c7.2xlarge servers from Alibaba Cloud, each with 8vCPU and 16GB RAM. We evaluate SecureBiNN in the following settings:

---

[4] The maxpooling operation comes on the heels of the activation layer, and can be achieved by changing the final output of the activation layer as in Algorithm 6.

Table 2. Evaluation results of SecureBiNN under LAN setting on MNIST and comparisons with prior work. Runtime is reported in seconds and Comm in MB. ∗: Falcon does not report the consumption (runtime and communication cost) required in its offline phase. The results hereof are only for its online phase. △: the protocols can be secure in both semi-honest adversary model and malicious adversary model, and we only consider their costs under the semi-honest model

2PC/3PC	Framework	Network-A			Network-B			Network-C		
		Time(s)	Comm. (MB)	Acc.	Time	Comm.	Acc.	Time	Comm.	Acc.
2PC	EzPC (△)	0.7	76	0.976	0.6	70	0.99	5.1	501	0.99
	Gazelle	0.09	0.5	0.976	0.29	8	0.99	1.16	70	0.99
	MiniONN	1.04	15.8	0.976	1.28	47.6	0.990	9.32	657.5	0.99
	XONN	0.13	4.29	0.976	0.16	38.3	0.986	0.15	32.1	0.99
3PC	ABY³ (△)	0.008	0.5	–	0.01	5.2	–	–	–	–
	SecureNN	0.043	2.1	0.934	0.076	4.05	0.988	0.13	8.86	0.99
	Falcon(△, ∗)	0.011	0.012	0.974	0.009	0.049	0.978	0.042	0.51	0.986
	Secure BiNN(ours)	0.003	0.005	0.973	0.007	0.032	0.972	0.020	0.357	0.984

Table 3. Evaluation results of SecureBiNN under WAN setting on MNIST and comparisons. Runtime is reported in seconds and Comm in MB. ∗, △: same as in Table 2

2PC/3PC	Framework	Network-A			Network-B			Network-C		
		Time(s)	Comm. (MB)	Acc.	Time	Comm.	Acc.	Time	Comm.	Acc.
2PC	EzPC (△)	1.7	76	0.976	1.6	70	0.99	11.6	501	0.99
3PC	SecureNN	243	2.1	0.934	3.06	4.05	0.988	3.93	8.86	0.99
	Falcon(△, ∗)	0.99	0.012	0.974	0.76	0.049	0.978	3.0	0.51	0.986
	Secure BiNN(ours)	0.248	0.005	0.973	0.440	0.032	0.972	1.15	0.36	0.984

- LAN: We set up three servers in Ulanqab, and the network latency and bandwidth are 0.2 ms and 625MBps respectively.
- WAN: We set up three servers in Ulanqab, Hangzhou and Shanghai, the latency and the bandwidth between the servers are 36 ms and 5MBps respectively. Note that these parameters are close to those of the Internet in daily use, which further proves our solution is available in practical settings.

At present, there are few secure inference frameworks applied to BiNNs, so in addition to XONN [28] (a 2-party scheme for BiNNs), we select other works for comparison as well. We choose 3-party frameworks including ABY³ [24], SecureNN [34], Falcon [35], Chameleon [29], and some well known 2-party protocols, i.e., EzPC [10], Gazelle [18], MiniONN [21], for sufficient comparisons.

We measure running time, communication volume and accuracy. We repeat each experiment 10 times, and then take average running time. Although we need secret shares of helping terms in implementing secure AND gates, we emphasize those are done online, and *no offline phase is required*.

Table 4. Performance comparisons among different frameworks on Lenet-5. $*$, $\triangle$: same as in Table 2

Framework	SecureNN	CrypTFlow	Falcon($\triangle$, $*$)	SecureBiNN
Time(LAN, s)	0.23	0.058	0.047	0.025
Time(WAN, s)	4.08	–	3.06	0.602
Comm.(MB)	18.94	–	0.74	0.522
Acc	0.991	–	0.991	0.989

4.1 Experimental Evaluation on MNIST

We evaluate three different NN on MNIST dataset [20] (60,000 training samples and 10,000 test samples). Each sample is a 28×28 handwritten digital image. We use SecureBiNN to make inference on these networks and measure its running time and communication cost. Bellow are the architectures of three models:

Network-A: FC(128) $-$ FC(128) $-$ FC(10);
Network-B: Conv(28×28, 5 channels) $-$ FC(100) $-$ FC(10);
Network-C: Conv(28×28, 16 channels) $-$ MP(2×2) $-$ Conv(12×12, 16 channels) $-$ MP(2×2) $-$ FC(100) $-$ FC(10).

Network-A is a 3 layer fully-connected network, Network-B is a 3 layer network with a single convolution layer followed by 2 fully connected layers, and Network-C is a network with 2 convolutional layers, 2 maxpooling layers and 2 fully-connected layers. These models are used in many prior work, and we also compare our experimental results with some of them. Tables 2 and 3 show the comparisons under LAN and WAN settings. Further, we compare the performance of SecureBiNN with SecureNN [34], CryptTFlow [27], Falcon [35] on Lenet-5 [20], and the results are shown in Table 4. Accuracy rate of each framework is only for reference as it may vary with the changes of model parameters.

Comparing to prior work, SecureBiNN shows its competitive performance partially due to the tricky encoding, i.e., the parameters are encoded over a ring with a smaller size. Other frameworks like Falcon, ABY^3 use $\mathbb{Z}_{2^{32}}$, meaning that parameters are represented with 32 bits. The advantages of parameter encoding lead to significant reduction in the amount of communication consumption between participants. Another advantage goes to maxpooling. In prior protocols, maxpooling cost is generally exorbitant as each pooling step requires overabundant MSB extraction operations (pool size minus 1 times). However, one single MSB extraction is needed in each pooling step of SecureBiNN.

4.2 Experimental Evaluation on CIFAR-10

Table 5 evaluates more networks on CIFAR-10 [19], including binarized versions of Fitnet 1–4 [30]. We train BiNN according to each structure. In the experiments, we encode the parameters of input/output layers over $\mathbb{Z}_{2^{32}}$ and set the precision of these parameters as 13 bits. By the architecture of these networks

Table 5. Evaluations of SecureBiNN under LAN/WAN on CIFAR-10. Runtime is in seconds and Comm in MB. s means that the number of neurons in fully connected layers (or the number of filters in convolutional layers) is increased by a factor of s

Arch.	s	Time(s, LAN)	Time(s, WAN)	Comm.(MB)	Acc.
Fitnet 1	1	0.112	2.776	3.074	0.688
	2	0.204	2.958	6.364	0.778
	3	0.527	3.447	16.609	0.815
Fitnet 2	1	0.173	2.901	5.178	0.765
	2	0.351	3.419	10.773	0.797
	3	0.527	3.769	16.609	0.812
Fitnet 3	1	0.367	3.739	11.806	0.811
	2	0.810	5.244	24.654	0.834
	3	1.368	7.313	39.878	0.836
Fitnet 4	1	0.430	6.393	13.660	0.789
	2	0.909	6.062	29.111	0.808
	3	1.560	8.500	48.195	0.810

in Table 5, when the scale factors are 1 and 2, most of the weighted parameters in the hidden layers are encoded over $\mathbb{Z}_{2^{14}}$, $\mathbb{Z}_{2^{15}}$; for the factor of 3, most parameters are over $\mathbb{Z}_{2^{17}}$. Many previous tests have been done on Fitnet 1, and we compare SecureBiNN with these work. The results are shown in Table 6.

Table 6. Comparisons among different frameworks on Fitnet 1 under the LAN setting. s means that the number of neurons in fully connected layers (or the number of filters in convolutional layers) is increased by a factor of 3. $\triangle$: same as in Table 2

Framework	MiniONN	Chameleon	EzPC ($\triangle$)	Gazelle	XONN	SecureBiNN		
					$s=3$	$s=1$	$s=2$	$s=3$
Time(s)	544	52.67	265.6	15.48	5.79	0.112	0.204	0.527
Comm.(MB)	9272	2650	40683	1236	2599	3.074	6.364	16.60
Acc	0.816	0.816	0.816	0.816	0.819	0.688	0.778	0.815

Now, the advantages of our solution become more explicit, because Fitnet has more convolution, activation and maxpooling operations than Networks A, B, C (Tables 2, 3). XONN uses GC to evaluate the BiNN, the garbled table and keys transmission are known to be of lavish spending. Comparing to XONN, SecureBiNN needs far less communication overhead. Furthermore, when we increase the number of neurons in each layer by a factor of 3, most of the weighted parameters are encoded over $\mathbb{Z}_{2^{17}}$. This means that in an activation operation, we only need to input a 17-bit number instead of a 32-bit number into the parallel prefix adder circuit (the bit length is almost half of the latter). This substantially reduces the cost of the activation function, which is always overbearing consumption and bottleneck of such kinds of protocols. This special feature offers a significant advantage to Fitnet 1 architecture compared to prior work.

Table 7. Experiment results of SecureBiNN on real-world medical datasets. We drop the rows with null values from the sets and perform min-max scale on validation sets

Dataset	# of Samples		Evaluation results for a single input			
	Tr	Val	Time (s, LAN)	Time (s, WAN)	Comm. (MB)	Acc.
Breast cancer [1]	455	114	0.005	0.014	0.002	0.991
Diabetes [32]	614	154	0.005	0.014	0.002	0.812
Liver [2]	463	116	0.005	0.017	0.003	0.741
Malaria [3]	22048	5512	0.072	0.377	1.861	0.930

4.3   Experimental Evaluation on Real-World Medical Datasets

One of the most common scenarios where such schemes can be used is to aid in diagnosis. To demonstrate the effectiveness of SecureBiNN in real-world scenarios, we select below four real-world medical datasets to simulate real-world usage scenarios: breast cancer dataset [1], Pima Indians diabetes dataset [32], Indian liver patient records [2] and malaria cell images dataset [3]. The first three sets consist of several numerical features related to patients' information. The last one consists of the images of different sizes, so we reshape all the images to 32×32. All tasks are to predict whether a patient is infected with the corresponding disease. We evaluate the following models for each dataset:

Breast Cancer: FC(16) − FC(16) − FC(2);
Diabetes: FC(20) − FC(20) − FC(2); Liver: FC(32) − FC(32) − FC(2);
Malaria: CONV(5×5, 36 channels) − MP(2×2) − CONV(5×5, 36 channels) − MP(2×2) − FC(72) − FC(2).

We split each dataset into training and validation portions before evaluation, and the partition details and the evaluation results are shown in Table 7.

5   Conclusion and Future Work

The paper proposes the first privacy-preserving three-party discrete neural network inference framework supporting fast execution and low communication cost. As most existing SMC proposals, our framework SecureBiNN is secure against semi-honest adversary. Due to the parameter distribution of binarized neural network, fewer bits suffice in SecureBiNN to represent a parameter, reducing further the lengths of the messages generated in the participant interactions. Experiments confirm its lower communication cost at similar accuracy to state-of-the-art. In this paper, P_0 and P_1 are able to implement secure AND gate and

3-party OT with the help of P_2. However, in the case where P_2 is a malicious adversary, the method proposed in this paper cannot be directly used. More attempts might be made to construct actively secure algorithms by introducing consistency checking mechanisms against malicious adversary.

Acknowledgement. The work is supported by the National Natural Science Foundation of China (Grant No. 61971192), Shanghai Municipal Education Commission (2021-01-07-00-08-E00101), and Shanghai Trusted Industry Internet Software Collaborative Innovation Center.

A   Related Work

The privacy-preserving neural network inference technology is mainly divided into two routes, one is based on HE, and another on SMC.

In the former route, one commonly used HE algorithm is CKKS [12], a computation-expensive leveled-FHE scheme with multiplication depth being kept within certain range. In 2016, Nathan et al. propose Cryptonets [12] using the CKKS algorithm. Since CKKS can only support addition and multiply operations, it is difficult to implement the Sigmoid or the ReLU activation functions, and only the square function can be used which makes low model accuracy.

A representative example in SMC-based route goes to SecureML [23] which uses Beaver's Triplet [6] to realize multiplication. As it requires numerous multiplication triples, SecureML supports limited practicability. Subsequent schemes (e.g., ABY [13]) significantly reduce the running time and communication cost. Other frameworks including BiNN inference framework XONN [28] mainly rely on GC. Some 3PC frameworks (e.g., ABY3 [24] and Falcon [35]) use replicated secret sharing [14]. Therein, three parties can directly perform privacy-preserving multiplications locally according to the input to obtain the output and no interaction is required. Thus, these 3PC frameworks are generally more efficient and faster than those 2PC frameworks, an advantage meeting actual needs.

References

1. Breast cancer wisconsin (diagnostic) data set (1995). Accessed 25 Apr 2022. https://archive.ics.uci.edu/ml/datasets/Breast+Cancer+Wisconsin+%28Diagnostic%29

2. Indian liver patient records (2013). Accessed 25 Apr 2022. https://archive.ics.uci.edu/ml/datasets/liver+disorders

3. Malaria cell images dataset (2019). Accessed 25 Apr 2022. https://www.kaggle.com/datasets/iarunava/cell-images-for-detecting-malaria

4. Abadi, M., et al.: Tensorflow: a system for large-scale machine learning. In: Keeton, K., Roscoe, T. (eds.) 12th USENIX Symposium on Operating Systems Design and Implementation, OSDI 2016, Savannah, GA, USA, 2–4 November 2016, pp. 265–283. USENIX Association (2016). https://www.usenix.org/conference/osdi16/technical-sessions/presentation/abadi

5. Araki, T., Furukawa, J., Lindell, Y., Nof, A., Ohara, K.: High-throughput semi-honest secure three-party computation with an honest majority. In: Weippl, E.R., Katzenbeisser, S., Kruegel, C., Myers, A.C., Halevi, S. (eds.) Proceedings of the 2016 ACM SIGSAC Conference on Computer and Communications Security, Vienna, Austria, 24–28 October 2016, pp. 805–817. ACM (2016). https://doi.org/10.1145/2976749.2978331

6. Beaver, D.: One-time tables for two-party computation. In: Hsu, W.-L., Kao, M.-Y. (eds.) COCOON 1998. LNCS, vol. 1449, pp. 361–370. Springer, Heidelberg (1998). https://doi.org/10.1007/3-540-68535-9_40

7. Boemer, F., Costache, A., Cammarota, R., Wierzynski, C.: ngraph-he2: a high-throughput framework for neural network inference on encrypted data. In: Brenner, M., Lepoint, T., Rohloff, K. (eds.) Proceedings of the 7th ACM Workshop on Encrypted Computing & Applied Homomorphic Cryptography, WAHC@CCS 2019, London, UK, 11–15 November 2019, pp. 45–56. ACM (2019). https://doi.org/10.1145/3338469.3358944

8. Bourse, F., Minelli, M., Minihold, M., Paillier, P.: Fast homomorphic evaluation of deep discretized neural networks. In: Shacham, H., Boldyreva, A. (eds.) CRYPTO 2018. LNCS, vol. 10993, pp. 483–512. Springer, Cham (2018). https://doi.org/10.1007/978-3-319-96878-0_17

9. Canetti, R.: Universally composable security. J. ACM **67**(5) (2020). https://doi.org/10.1145/3402457

10. Chandran, N., Gupta, D., Rastogi, A., Sharma, R., Tripathi, S.: Ezpc: programmable and efficient secure two-party computation for machine learning. In: IEEE European Symposium on Security and Privacy, EuroS&P 2019, Stockholm, Sweden, 17–19 June 2019, pp. 496–511. IEEE (2019). https://doi.org/10.1109/EuroSP.2019.00043

11. Chen, X., Liu, C., Li, B., Lu, K., Song, D.: Targeted backdoor attacks on deep learning systems using data poisoning. CoRR abs/1712.05526 (2017). https://arxiv.org/abs/1712.05526

12. Cheon, J.H., Kim, A., Kim, M., Song, Y.: Homomorphic encryption for arithmetic of approximate numbers. In: Takagi, T., Peyrin, T. (eds.) ASIACRYPT 2017. LNCS, vol. 10624, pp. 409–437. Springer, Cham (2017). https://doi.org/10.1007/978-3-319-70694-8_15

13. Demmler, D., Schneider, T., Zohner, M.: ABY - a framework for efficient mixed-protocol secure two-party computation. In: 22nd Annual Network and Distributed System Security Symposium, NDSS 2015, San Diego, California, USA, 8–11 February 2015. The Internet Society (2015). https://www.ndss-symposium.org/ndss2015/aby--framework-efficient-mixed-protocol-secure-two-party-computation

14. Furukawa, J., Lindell, Y., Nof, A., Weinstein, O.: High-throughput secure three-party computation for malicious adversaries and an honest majority. In: Coron, J.-S., Nielsen, J.B. (eds.) EUROCRYPT 2017. LNCS, vol. 10211, pp. 225–255. Springer, Cham (2017). https://doi.org/10.1007/978-3-319-56614-6_8

15. Gilad-Bachrach, R., Dowlin, N., Laine, K., Lauter, K.E., Naehrig, M., Wernsing, J.: Cryptonets: applying neural networks to encrypted data with high throughput and accuracy. In: Balcan, M., Weinberger, K.Q. (eds.) Proceedings of the 33nd International Conference on Machine Learning, ICML 2016, New York City, NY, USA, 19–24 June 2016. JMLR Workshop and Conference Proceedings, vol. 48, pp. 201–210. JMLR.org (2016). https://proceedings.mlr.press/v48/gilad-bachrach16.html

16. Ibarrondo, A., Chabanne, H., Önen, M.: Banners: binarized neural networks with replicated secret sharing. In: Borghys, D., Bas, P., Verdoliva, L., Pevný, T., Li, B., Newman, J. (eds.) IH&MMSec 2021: ACM Workshop on Information Hiding and Multimedia Security, Virtual Event, Belgium, 22–25 June 2021, pp. 63–74. ACM (2021). https://doi.org/10.1145/3437880.3460394

17. Ioffe, S., Szegedy, C.: Batch normalization: accelerating deep network training by reducing internal covariate shift. In: Bach, F.R., Blei, D.M. (eds.) Proceedings of the 32nd International Conference on Machine Learning, ICML 2015, Lille, France, 6–11 July 2015, JMLR Workshop and Conference Proceedings, vol. 37, pp. 448–456. JMLR.org (2015). https://proceedings.mlr.press/v37/ioffe15.html

18. Juvekar, C., Vaikuntanathan, V., Chandrakasan, A.: GAZELLE: a low latency framework for secure neural network inference. In: Enck, W., Felt, A.P. (eds.) 27th USENIX Security Symposium, USENIX Security 2018, Baltimore, MD, USA, 15–17 August 2018, pp. 1651–1669. USENIX Association (2018). https://www.usenix.org/conference/usenixsecurity18/presentation/juvekar

19. Krizhevsky, A., Hinton, G.: Learning multiple layers of features from tiny images. Handb. Systemic Autoimmune Dis. 1(4) (2009)

20. Lecun, Y., Bottou, L.: Gradient-based learning applied to document recognition. Proc. IEEE 86(11), 2278–2324 (1998)

21. Liu, J., Juuti, M., Lu, Y., Asokan, N.: Oblivious neural network predictions via minionn transformations. In: Thuraisingham, B.M., Evans, D., Malkin, T., Xu, D. (eds.) Proceedings of the 2017 ACM SIGSAC Conference on Computer and Communications Security, CCS 2017, Dallas, TX, USA, 30 October–03 November 2017, pp. 619–631. ACM (2017). https://doi.org/10.1145/3133956.3134056

22. Mishra, P., Lehmkuhl, R., Srinivasan, A., Zheng, W., Popa, R.A.: Delphi: a cryptographic inference system for neural networks. In: Zhang, B., Popa, R.A., Zaharia, M., Gu, G., Ji, S. (eds.) PPMLP 2020: Proceedings of the 2020 Workshop on Privacy-Preserving Machine Learning in Practice, Virtual Event, USA, November 2020, pp. 27–30. ACM (2020). https://doi.org/10.1145/3411501.3419418

23. Mohassel, P., Zhang, Y.: Secureml: a system for scalable privacy-preserving machine learning. In: 2017 IEEE Symposium on Security and Privacy (SP), pp. 19–38 (2017). https://doi.org/10.1109/SP.2017.12

24. Mohassel, P., Rindal, P.: Aby^3: a mixed protocol framework for machine learning. In: Lie, D., Mannan, M., Backes, M., Wang, X. (eds.) Proceedings of the 2018 ACM SIGSAC Conference on Computer and Communications Security, CCS 2018, Toronto, ON, Canada, 15–19 October 2018, pp. 35–52. ACM (2018). https://doi.org/10.1145/3243734.3243760

25. Ohata, S., Nuida, K.: Communication-efficient (client-aided) secure two-party protocols and its application. In: Bonneau, J., Heninger, N. (eds.) FC 2020. LNCS, vol. 12059, pp. 369–385. Springer, Cham (2020). https://doi.org/10.1007/978-3-030-51280-4_20

26. Patra, A., Schneider, T., Suresh, A., Yalame, H.: ABY2.0: improved mixed-protocol secure two-party computation. In: Bailey, M., Greenstadt, R. (eds.) 30th USENIX Security Symposium, USENIX Security 2021, 11–13 August 2021, pp. 2165–2182. USENIX Association (2021). https://www.usenix.org/conference/usenixsecurity21/presentation/patra

27. Rathee, D., et al.: Cryptflow2: practical 2-party secure inference. In: Ligatti, J., Ou, X., Katz, J., Vigna, G. (eds.) CCS 2020: 2020 ACM SIGSAC Conference on Computer and Communications Security, Virtual Event, USA, 9–13 November 2020, pp. 325–342. ACM (2020). https://doi.org/10.1145/3372297.3417274

28. Riazi, M.S., Samragh, M., Chen, H., Laine, K., Lauter, K.E., Koushanfar, F.: XONN: xnor-based oblivious deep neural network inference. In: Heninger, N., Traynor, P. (eds.) 28th USENIX Security Symposium, USENIX Security 2019, Santa Clara, CA, USA, 14–16 August 2019, pp. 1501–1518. USENIX Association (2019). https://www.usenix.org/conference/usenixsecurity19/presentation/riazi

29. Riazi, M.S., Weinert, C., Tkachenko, O., Songhori, E.M., Schneider, T., Koushanfar, F.: Chameleon: a hybrid secure computation framework for machine learning applications. In: Proceedings of the 2018 on Asia Conference on Computer and Communications Security, ASIACCS 2018, pp. 707–721. Association for Computing Machinery, New York (2018). https://doi.org/10.1145/3196494.3196522

30. Romero, A., Ballas, N., Kahou, S.E., Chassang, A., Gatta, C., Bengio, Y.: Fitnets: hints for thin deep nets. In: Bengio, Y., LeCun, Y. (eds.) 3rd International Conference on Learning Representations, ICLR 2015, San Diego, CA, USA, 7–9 May 2015, Conference Track Proceedings (2015). https://arxiv.org/abs/1412.6550

31. Shokri, R., Stronati, M., Song, C., Shmatikov, V.: Membership inference attacks against machine learning models. In: 2017 IEEE Symposium on Security and Privacy, SP 2017, San Jose, CA, USA, 22–26 May 2017, pp. 3–18. IEEE Computer Society (2017). https://doi.org/10.1109/SP.2017.41

32. Smith, J., Everhart, J., Dickson, W., Knowler, W., Johannes, R.: Using the adap learning algorithm to forcast the onset of diabetes mellitus. In: Proceedings - Annual Symposium on Computer Applications in Medical Care, vol. 10 (1988)

33. Tramèr, F., Zhang, F., Juels, A., Reiter, M.K., Ristenpart, T.: Stealing machine learning models via prediction apis. In: Holz, T., Savage, S. (eds.) 25th USENIX Security Symposium, USENIX Security 16, Austin, TX, USA, 10–12 August 2016, pp. 601–618. USENIX Association (2016). https://www.usenix.org/conference/usenixsecurity16/technical-sessions/presentation/tramer

34. Wagh, S., Gupta, D., Chandran, N.: Securenn: 3-party secure computation for neural network training. Proc. Priv. Enhanc. Technol. **2019**(3), 26–49 (2019). https://doi.org/10.2478/popets-2019-0035

35. Wagh, S., Tople, S., Benhamouda, F., Kushilevitz, E., Mittal, P., Rabin, T.: Falcon: Honest-majority maliciously secure framework for private deep learning. Proc. Priv. Enhanc. Technol. **2021**(1), 188–208 (2021). https://doi.org/10.2478/popets-2021-0011

36. van der Walt, S., Colbert, S.C., Varoquaux, G.: The numpy array: a structure for efficient numerical computation. Comput. Sci. Eng. **13**(2), 22–30 (2011). https://doi.org/10.1109/MCSE.2011.37

Mixed-Technique Multi-Party Computations Composed of Two-Party Computations

Erik-Oliver Blass[1(✉)] and Florian Kerschbaum[2]

[1] Airbus, Munich, Germany
`erik-oliver.blass@airbus.com`
[2] University of Waterloo, Waterloo, Canada
`florian.kerschbaum@uwaterloo.ca`

Abstract. Protocols for secure multi-party computation are commonly composed of different sub-protocols, combining techniques such as homomorphic encryption, secret or Boolean sharing, and garbled circuits. In this paper, we design a new class of multi-party computation protocols which themselves are composed out of two-party protocols. We integrate both types of compositions, compositions of fully homomorphic encryption and garbled circuits with compositions of multi-party protocols from two-party protocols. As a result, we can construct communication-efficient protocols for special problems. Furthermore, we show how to efficiently ensure the security of composed protocols against malicious adversaries by proving in zero-knowledge that conversions between individual techniques are correct. To demonstrate the usefulness of this approach, we give an example scheme for private set analytics, i.e., private set disjointness. This scheme enjoys lower communication complexity than a solution based on generic multi-party computation and lower computation cost than fully homomorphic encryption. So, our design is more suitable for deployments in wide-area networks, such as the Internet, with many participants or problems with circuits of moderate or high multiplicative depth.

1 Introduction

Whereas secure two-party computations are deployed in practice [68], designing and deploying practical secure multi-party computation is still an open challenge. Communication latency is a typical bottleneck for many multi-round protocols, and in response constant-round multi-party computations [34, 45, 46] based on Beaver et al.'s [5]'s technique [5] have been designed. Their deployment is lacking due to challenges from implementation complexity, communication bandwidth, and memory requirements. To address these challenges, protocols using fully-homomorphic encryption (FHE) [12, 26] and dual execution can be used. Yet, designing efficient homomorphic encryption schemes (for arithmetic circuits) is also an open challenge. Circuits with high multiplicative depth, the reason for a

© The Author(s), under exclusive license to Springer Nature Switzerland AG 2022
V. Atluri et al. (Eds.): ESORICS 2022, LNCS 13556, pp. 295–319, 2022.
https://doi.org/10.1007/978-3-031-17143-7_15

high number of rounds in many multi-party computation protocols, imply high computation costs.

In this paper, we present a design alternative. We specifically consider multi-party computations that can at least partially be decomposed into a sequence of two-party computations (2PCs). We first evaluate 2PCs using garbled circuits and then combine the output and continue computation using FHE evaluation. The idea of our mixed-technique protocols is to exploit advantages of each technique, for example, binary vs. arithmetic circuits, typical in application domains such as machine learning [14,22,31,50]. For fully malicious security, we show how to convert between outputs of garbled circuits and FHE ciphertexts using efficient zero-knowledge proofs. Compared to conversions in the semi-honest model [41], this requires a different construction, which has, however, little additional overhead. Other related work [40] sketches malicious conversions, but only for two parties, whereas we consider the multi-party setting. The first phase of 2PC reduces multiplicative depth for the following FHE evaluation phase, but remains small enough to have low communication complexity. As we show by construction, such a combined protocol can keep a *constant number of rounds* and can still be secure in the malicious model. Due to their lower communication requirements, combined protocols have the potential for deployment in wide area networks.

The composition of 2PC protocols into a multi-party protocol can take many forms. In order to demonstrate the advantages of our constructions, we design and investigate a combined protocol for private set disjointness, i.e., a protocol that computes whether the intersection of sets is empty, but does not reveal anything else, including the intersection itself. This protocol follows a star topology of communication where each party P_i engages in 2PC with a central party P_1. Our composition of 2PC protocols into a multi-party protocol is particularly efficient if it follows a star topology. We stress that even in the star topology, we provide malicious security against an adversary controlling the central node (among others) which is the challenge of any such composition. Furthermore, besides the set disjointness protocol there are (infinitely) many other protocols that can be implemented in a star topology. The entire class of *multi-party private set analytics* protocols [4,13,21,47,52] is an example. However, our protocols are also not limited to a star topology, and we also mention other use cases, such as auctions [9], that do not follow a star topology.

Our example use case is driven by the use case of sharing Indicators of Compromise (IoCs), where multiple parties try to determine whether they have been subject to a common attack. We design a maliciously-secure protocol which determines whether the multi-party set intersection is empty. A non-empty intersection would be grounds for further investigation. With each party's set holding n elements, our set disjointness protocol runs in 9 rounds, needs $O(n)$ broadcasts, and has a message complexity linear in the number of comparisons required to compare all parties' inputs. We have implemented a semi-honest version of this protocol to show that our design offers performance improvements over other multi-party computation protocols in the semi-honest model. Using our zero-knowledge proofs, our protocol can also be made secure in the malicious model. In summary, the main contributions of this paper are:

1. A construction for *mixed-technique MPC* composed from 2PC which features a *constant number of rounds*, low communication complexity, and *malicious security*.
2. Efficient zero-knowledge proofs, included in this construction, converting between garbled circuit outputs and homomorphic encryption with malicious security.
3. A demonstration of our construction's usefulness by realizing a multi-party protocol for set disjointness.

In the full version of this paper [10], we also present a technique replacing standard verification of hash-based commitments during 2PC by a white-box use of garbled circuits. We use this technique to reduce communication overhead in our conversion, but the idea is general, applicable to other scenarios, and of independent interest.

2 Conversion Between 2PC and Homomorphic Encryption

To simplify exposition, we start with a motivation and an overview of our conversion for the special case of $d = 2$ parties. For space reasons, we defer the extension to any $d \geq 2$ parties to Appendix B. Our goal is malicious security of the conversions which we describe in Sect. 2.1.

Parties P_1 and P_2 want to jointly compute function $F(I_1, I_2) = O$ on their respective input bit strings I_1 and I_2 to receive output string $O = (o_1, \ldots, o_N)$. For security reasons, P_1 should only learn some subset of bit string O, but nothing else (for example not P_2's input). Similarly, P_2 should only learn the other bits of O, but nothing else. To enable secure computation of F, parties can revert to two standard approaches. Parties could express F as a Boolean circuit and evaluate this circuit using maliciously-secure two-party garbled circuit computation (2PC). Alternatively, parties express F as an arithmetic circuit, compute a shared private key of a fully homomorphic encryption (FHE), and encrypt their inputs with the corresponding public-key. Parties then evaluate the circuit homomorphically and jointly decrypt the final result such that each party only learns their output bits.

Yet, each of the two approaches comes with performance issues. On the one hand, FHE evaluation of arithmetic circuits with large multiplicative depth is computationally expensive. On the other hand, evaluating Boolean circuits with 2PC for large circuits is expensive regarding the amount of communication.

So, a third alternative and the focus of this paper is for parties to evaluate F using a *mix* of both techniques. Parties evaluate F as a circuit decomposed into a sequence of sub-circuits $F(I_1, I_2) = (C_1 \circ \cdots \circ C_m)(I_1, I_2)$. Some sub-circuits C_i are Boolean, while others are arithmetic. Parties agree that Boolean sub-circuits of function F will be evaluated using garbled circuit 2PC, and arithmetic sub-circuits of F will be evaluated using FHE. Output of 2PC will serve as input to FHE and vice versa. The goal of such a mixed-techniques approach is to optimize overall performance by reducing multiplicative depth of FHE circuits and communication complexity of 2PC circuits. For clarity, we now denote Boolean (sub-)circuits C_i by C_i^{Bool} and arithmetic (sub-)circuits C_i by C_i^{Arith}. Assume that P_1 and P_2 have initially computed a public and private key pair for a homomorphic encryption Enc, where the private key is shared among both parties.

2.1 Malicious Security

Achieving malicious security for conversion turns out to be a challenge. For example, let P_1 be the garbler and P_2 the evaluator during 2PC evaluation of a simple sub-circuit C_i^{Bool} with two input and two output bits $(x, y) = C_i^{\mathsf{Bool}}(a, b)$. Evaluator P_2 receives both output bits x, y and must convert them into correct homomorphic encryptions $\mathsf{Enc}(x)$ and $\mathsf{Enc}(y)$. This is hard to achieve against malicious adversaries: as P_2 could be malicious, P_2 must prove to P_1 that ciphertexts $\mathsf{Enc}(x)$ and $\mathsf{Enc}(y)$ are correctly encrypting outputs x and y received during 2PC. Worse, P_2 should not even learn x and y, as they are an intermediate result of C's evaluation or maybe output bits for P_1. Party P_2 should instead receive related information during 2PC which then allows P_2 to indirectly generate homomorphic encryptions $\mathsf{Enc}(x)$ and $\mathsf{Enc}(y)$. Alternatively, one might suggest implementing homomorphic encryption Enc inside a 2PC circuit, but this is too costly.

Similarly, we need to convert FHE ciphertexts output by circuits C_i^{Arith} into input for 2PC garbled circuits with malicious security. Moreover, if P_1 and P_2's 2PC computation was part of a larger MPC computation involving $d \geq 2$ parties, we also need to consider the case where both are malicious, so they must prove to all parties that their encryptions are correct. Finally, the private key is shared among all d parties which impedes easy zero-knowledge (ZK) proofs.

Important Remarks. This paper targets secure output conversion between 2PC and FHE. To actually evaluate Boolean sub-circuit C_i^{Bool}, we assume existence of any maliciously secure 2PC scheme as a building block. Several different approaches exist which achieve maliciously secure 2PC in practice, see [43,44,54,65] for an overview.

For secure evaluation of arithmetic sub-circuits C_i^{Arith}, any FHE scheme could serve as building block. FHE is maliciously secure by default, as long as parties evaluate the same circuit on the same ciphertexts. To enforce this, our conversion requires the FHE scheme to also support distributed key generation and certain ZK proofs detailed below. There exist several efficient lattice-based FHE schemes with support for both [7,8,11,18,19,51,63], and there are even efficient schemes which allow proving general, arbitrary ZK statements in addition to distributed key generation [2]. While describing details of our techniques, we use any of these as an underlying building block, e.g., the one by Asharov et al. [2].

2.2   Solution Overview

Roadmap. There are two different cases for conversion we will have to consider in a mixed-technique setting. First, parties convert output bits $(o_{i,1}, \ldots, o_{i,n}) = C_i^{\mathsf{Bool}}(I_{i,1}, I_{i,2})$ from 2PC evaluation of circuit C_i^{Bool} on input strings $I_{i,1}$ and $I_{i,2}$ into n homomorphic encryptions $\mathsf{Enc}(o_{i,j})$. Knowing encryptions $\mathsf{Enc}(o_{i,j})$, each party then evaluates the subsequent arithmetic circuit C_{i+1}^{Arith}.

Second, parties convert a sequence of ciphertexts $\mathsf{Enc}(b_i)$, homomorphic encryptions of bits b_i (or integers, see Appendix A) into input for a 2PC Boolean circuit evaluation. That is, both parties have evaluated arithmetic sub-circuit C_i^{Arith} and computed ciphertexts $\mathsf{Enc}(b_i)$, respectively. These ciphertexts will now be converted into input for 2PC evaluation of sub-circuit C_{i+1}^{Bool}.

Actual evaluation of circuits is then secure by definition, as we rely on standard maliciously-secure 2PC. For arithmetic sub-circuits, both parties evaluate FHE ciphertexts on their own. An honest party will automatically compute correct output ciphertexts as long as input ciphertexts are correct.

Parties will also need to securely convert both parties' plain input into either FHE encryptions or 2PC inputs. Yet, that part is trivial: if the first sub-circuit is an arithmetic circuit, a party sends homomorphic encryptions of each input bit. If the first circuit is Boolean, we rely on whatever technique the underlying maliciously secure 2PC offers. Finally, at the end of the last circuit evaluation, FHE ciphertexts or 2PC output has to be decrypted. Again, this is fairly simple, and we skip details for now. We only consider the first two cases of converting 2PC output to FHE input and FHE output to 2PC input.

Intuition. Our conversions focus on Boolean sub-circuits C_i^{Bool}. We design mechanisms which either convert 2PC output of C_i^{Bool} to FHE ciphertexts serving as input to C_{i+1}^{Arith} or convert FHE ciphertexts coming from C_{i-1}^{Arith} into input to C_i^{Bool}. Each of our two conversions first modifies C_i^{Bool} and evaluates the modified circuit using three new cryptographic building blocks which we call ZK Protocol (1), ZK Protocol (2), and ZK Protocol (3). Each ZK Protocol takes as input a Boolean circuit and P_1's and P_2's input bits. ZK Protocol (1) and ZK Protocol (2) also take FHE ciphertexts as inputs. Each ZK Protocol again modifies the input circuit internally, 2PC-evaluates the modified version, and outputs 2PC output together with a ZK proof which proves certain relations between input and output in zero-knowledge for malicious security. As ZK Protocols are general, their interesting property is to be stackable, i.e., they can be combined with each other. Their internal circuit modification schemes will be merged, and only ZK proofs enclosing circuit modification have to be adapted, which is rather mechanical.

ZK Protocols. Let γ be any Boolean circuit defined by its input and output bits as $(\omega_1, \ldots, \omega_n) = \gamma((\iota_{1,1}, \ldots, \iota_{1,\ell_1}), (\iota_{2,1}, \ldots, \iota_{2,\ell_2}))$. Parties P_1 and P_2 want to evaluate this circuit with 2PC. Bits $\iota_{1,i}$ are inputs of P_1. Bits $\iota_{2,i}$ are inputs of P_2, and ω_i will be output bits known to P_2. From a high level, our three ZK Protocols implement:

- ZK Protocol (1). P_1 sends homomorphic ciphertexts $c_{1,i} \leftarrow \mathsf{Enc}(\iota_{1,i})$, encrypting their input bits $\iota_{1,i}$ to P_2. Circuit γ is evaluated, and P_2 receives output. P_1 proves in ZK to P_2 that $c_{1,i}$ encrypts $\iota_{1,i}$, used during 2PC evaluation of γ.
- ZK Protocol (2): P_2 sends homomorphic ciphertexts $c_{2,i} \leftarrow \mathsf{Enc}(\iota_{2,i})$, encrypting their input bits $\iota_{2,i}$ to P_1. Circuit γ is evaluated, and P_1 receives output. P_2 proves in ZK to P_1 that $c_{2,i}$ encrypts $\iota_{2,i}$, used during 2PC evaluation of γ. This is ZK Protocol (1) with roles of P_1 and P_2 reversed.
- ZK Protocol (3): Circuit γ is evaluated, and P_2 receives output ω_i. Party P_2 sends homomorphic ciphertext $c_{\omega,i} \leftarrow \mathsf{Enc}(\omega_i)$ and proves in ZK to P_1 that $c_{\omega,i}$ really encrypts ω_i received during 2PC evaluation to P_1.

Observe the different notation used in this paper for describing circuits. Boolean sub-circuits of function F are written as C_i^{Bool}, while Boolean circuits we use inside our ZK Protocol building blocks are written with the Greek letter γ.

Conversion. The main idea behind the actual conversion is to modify a circuit C_i^{Bool} into γ which takes *shares* of C_i^{Bool}'s original input as its input and outputs shares of C_i^{Bool}'s original output. For example, to convert a 2PC output bit ω_1 of C_i^{Bool} to an FHE ciphertext $\mathsf{Enc}(\omega_1)$, we do not evaluate C_i^{Bool}, but γ which outputs share $\omega_1 \oplus s$ to P_2, and s to P_1. Both parties encrypt their shares, exchange resulting ciphertexts, and homomorphically compute an XOR to get $\mathsf{Enc}(\omega_1)$. During this conversion, ZK Protocols prove the correctness of operations.

So, we design conversion schemes combining multiple 2PC circuit modification techniques with efficient ZK proofs. Together, modifications and proofs prove correctness of output conversion between outputs of 2PC and FHE circuit evaluation.

Semi-honest Security. Our presentation concentrates on the case of fully malicious security. Nevertheless, even the semi-honest version of our conversion is of interest, as it enjoys the same properties as the fully-malicious version, e.g., $O(1)$ rounds, support for $d \geq 2$ parties, and moreover its performance is competitive when compared to related work, see Sect. 4.4. Essentially, the semi-honest version is just the fully-malicious one as described in the next section, but does not include the actual FHE ZK proofs inside ZK Protocols.

3 Technical Details

For simplicity, we describe details for $d = 2$ parties and extend to $d \geq 2$ in Appendix B.

For their input bit strings $I_1, I_2 \in \{0,1\}^*$ and function F, parties P_1 and P_2 want to compute $O = F(I_1, I_2), O \in \{0,1\}^*$. Function F is represented as a circuit composition of Boolean and arithmetic sub-circuits $F = (C_m \circ \cdots \circ C_1)$. Observe that if the ith sub-circuit is Boolean, then the $i + 1^{\text{th}}$ is arithmetic and the other way around. We now turn toward technical details on how we enable maliciously-secure mixed-technique evaluation of sub-circuits. We show how to convert 2PC evaluation output of a Boolean sub-circuit C_i^{Bool} into input for a following arithmetic sub-circuit C_{i+1}^{Arith} for FHE evaluation and the other way around.

2PC Output Bits for P_1 In a typical garbled circuit evaluation of C_i, only P_2 receives output, i.e., bits o_j. If a specific bit o_j is a secret output bit for P_1, then a standard trick is denying P_2 to open the last wire label for o_j and forwarding the label to P_1. As P_1 knows both possible labels for o_j, they can recover bit o_j. Also, this ensures that P_1 receives the correct output bit o'_j from P_2, i.e., authenticity [6]. We silently rely on this trick for secure computation of all of P_1's plain output bits for the rest of the paper.

Notation. Let Commit denote a computationally hiding and binding commitment scheme. For some bit string $B \in \{0,1\}^*$, computational security parameter λ', and randomness $R \in \{0,1\}^{\lambda'}$, $\mathsf{Commit}(B, R)$ outputs a commitment ,. In the full version of this paper [10], we show how to efficiently realize commitments with a white-box use of wire labels in garbled circuits. Encryption Enc over plaintext space M is fully (or somewhat) homomorphic. Both parties have already set up a key pair, where the public key is known to both parties, but the private key is shared. For homomorphic operations on ciphertexts, we use the intuitive notation of "$+$" for homomorphic addition, "$\cdot$" for scalar multiplication, and $\oplus$ for homomorphic XOR. So for example, if x and y are from M, then $\mathsf{Dec}(\mathsf{Enc}(x) + \mathsf{Enc}(y)) = x + y$. During conversion, we will randomly select scalars from $\mathbb{Z}_p$, where p is a prime of λ bits.

Let Π be the set of two single bit permutations $\pi : \{0,1\} \to \{0,1\}$. That is, $\Pi = \{\pi_0, \pi_1\}$ with $\pi_0(x) = x$ and $\pi_1(x) = 1 - x$.

3.1 ZK Protocols

Let $(\omega_1, \ldots, \omega_n) = \gamma((\iota_{1,1}, \ldots, \iota_{1,\ell_1}), (\iota_{2,1}, \ldots, \iota_{2,\ell_2}))$ be any Boolean circuit which parties P_1 and P_2 want to evaluate using maliciously secure 2PC. Bits $\iota_{1,i}$ are P_1's input, and bits $\iota_{2,i}$ are P_2's input.

ZK Protocol (1). In this protocol, P_1 proves to P_2 that homomorphic ciphertexts $c_{1,i} \leftarrow \mathsf{Enc}(\iota_{1,i})$ encrypt all of P_1's input bits $\iota_{i,i}$ used during a 2PC evaluation of γ. Assume that P_1 has already sent the $c_{1,i}$ to P_2.

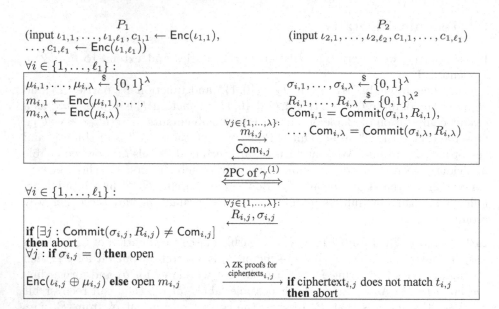

Fig. 1. ZK Protocol (1) for circuit γ

The protocol is depicted in Fig. 1 and consists of two core building blocks: first, parties evaluate a modification of circuit γ which we call $\gamma^{(1)}$. We define circuit $\gamma^{(1)}$ by specifying its input and output in Fig. 2. The second building block is an actual three move ZK proof which encompasses $\gamma^{(1)}$.

First, P_1 selects a random *masking* bit μ_i and sends both $c_{1,i}$ and $m_i \leftarrow \mathsf{Enc}(\mu_i)$ to P_2. At the same time, P_2 selects a random *choice* bit σ_i. Then, both parties use maliciously-secure 2PC and evaluate $\gamma^{(1)}$ which internally computes γ as a sub-routine. Party P_1 is the garbler and P_2 the evaluator. In addition to outputting the same bits as γ, it also outputs bit $t_i = \iota_{1,i} \oplus \mu_i$ (if $\sigma_i = 0$) or $t_i = \mu_i$ (if $\sigma_i = 1$) to P_2.

After 2PC, P_2 reveals their choice σ_i. If $\sigma_i = 0$, then P_1 proves in ZK that the homomorphic XOR of ciphertexts $c_{1,i}$ and m_i to $\mathsf{Enc}(\iota_{1,i} \oplus \mu_i)$ really encrypts $t_i = \iota_{1,i} \oplus \mu_i$. If $\sigma_i = 1$, then P_1 proves that m_i encrypts $t_i = \mu_i$.

Output bit $\alpha = 0$ in $\gamma^{(1)}$ indicates protocol failure, i.e., non-matching commitments.

If $\sigma_{i,j} = 0$, then P_1 and P_2 homomorphically compute ciphertext$_{i,j} = \mathsf{Enc}(\iota_{1,i} \oplus \mu_{i,j})$ out of $c_{1,i}$ and $m_{i,j}$. If choice bit $\sigma_{i,j} = 1$, then both parties set ciphertext$_{i,j} = m_{i,j}$. Party P_1 then sends a ZK proof that ciphertext$_{i,j}$ encrypts $t_{i,j}$ to P_2, e.g., by applying an efficient framework for ZK proofs [2].

Note the general structure of ZK Protocol (1), which is similar in the other two ZK Protocols. Each ZK Protocol comprises a circuit modification technique, here converting γ to $\gamma^{(1)}$, and a surrounding ZK proof. When we will combine ZK Protocols later, we merge circuit modifications, i.e., output of one ZK Protocol's

Input to $\gamma^{(1)}$

P_1	P_2
$\iota_{1,1},\ldots,\iota_{1,\ell_1},1 \;\leq\; i \;\leq\; \ell_1 \quad:$	$\iota_{2,1},\ldots,\iota_{2,\ell_2},1 \;\leq\; i \;\leq\; \ell_1 \quad:$
$[\mu_{i,1},\ldots,\mu_{i,\lambda},\mathsf{Com}_{i,1},\ldots,\mathsf{Com}_{i,\lambda}]$	$[\sigma_{i,1},\ldots,\sigma_{i,\lambda},R_{i,1},\ldots,R_{i,\lambda}]$

Output of $\gamma^{(1)}$

1 **if** $\forall i,j, 1 \leq i \leq \ell_1, 1 \leq j \leq \lambda : \mathsf{Com}_{i,j} = \mathsf{Commit}(\sigma_{i,j},R_{i,j})$ **then**
2     $\alpha = 1$;
3     $(\omega_1,\ldots,\omega_n) = \gamma((\iota_{1,1},\ldots,\iota_{1,\ell_1}),(\iota_{2,1},\ldots,\iota_{2,\ell_2}))$;
4   **for** $i = 1$ **to** ℓ_1 **and** $j = 1$ **to** λ **do**
5   **if** $\sigma_{i,j} = 0$ **then** $t_{i,j} = \iota_{1,i} \oplus \mu_{i,j}$ **else** $t_{i,j} = \mu_{i,j}$;
6 **else** $\alpha = \omega_1 = \ldots = \omega_n = t_{1,1} = \ldots = t_{\ell_1,\lambda} = 0$;
7 **output** $\alpha,\omega_1,\ldots,\omega_n,t_{1,1},\ldots,t_{\ell_1,\lambda}$;

Fig. 2. Definition of circuit $\gamma^{(1)}$

circuit modification will be input into another. Only surrounding ZK proofs require adoption.

ZK Protocol (2). This protocol reverses P_1's and P_2's roles in ZK Protocol (1). So, circuit $\gamma^{(2)}$ is similar to $\gamma^{(1)}$, with P_1 having choice bits (and randomness for commitments to them) as additional input, and P_2 has masking bits and commitments to choice bits as input. During 2PC, P_1 is the garbler and P_2 the evaluator. Also, the actual three-move protocol from ZK Protocol (1) is reversed, i.e., it is P_2 who starts by sending encryptions of input bits and masking bits. We omit further details to avoid repetition and refer to Fig. 1.

ZK Protocol (3). In this protocol, P_2 proves to P_1 that encryptions $c_{\omega,i} \leftarrow \mathsf{Enc}(\omega_i)$ are encryptions of P_2's output bits ω_i. As ZK Protocol (3) is more involved, Fig. 3 starts by presenting a slightly simpler version with a ZK proof which is only Honest-Verifier-Zero-Knowledge (HVZK), and details for fully-malicious security follow.

As part of ZK Protocol (3), P_1 and P_2 run 2PC on a modification of circuit γ called $\gamma^{(3)}$, defined in Fig. 4.

Before 2PC, P_1 selects, for an output bit ω_i, two random bit strings $v_{0,1}\ldots v_{0,\lambda}$ and $v_{1,1}\ldots v_{1,\lambda}$ and sets $V_0 = 0||v_{0,1}\ldots v_{0,\lambda}, V_1 = 1||v_{1,1}\ldots v_{1,\lambda}$. Here, "$||$" denotes concatenation, and λ is a statistical security parameter. Then, P_1 encrypts and sends ciphertexts $\Gamma_0 = \mathsf{Enc}(V_0)$ and $\Gamma_1 = \mathsf{Enc}(V_1)$ to P_2. Circuit $\gamma^{(3)}$ does not output ω_i to P_2, but instead outputs V_{ω_i} to P_2, i.e., either bit string V_0 or bit string V_1.

The first bit of strings V_0, V_1 is output bit ω_i. That is, Γ_{ω_i} encrypts a bit string, where the first bit represents P_2's output bit ω_i. So, after evaluating $\gamma^{(3)}$, P_2 gets ω_i and a length λ bit string $(v_{\omega_i,1},\ldots,v_{\omega_i,\lambda})$.

The trick is now that P_2 proves in ZK to P_1 that it knows a string V_{ω_i} which is *either* V_0 *or* V_1 and which matches encryption $c_{\omega,i}$. Recall that the private key for homomorphic encryption Enc is shared between P_1 and P_2, so none of the two parties can decrypt a ciphertext alone. After evaluating $\gamma^{(3)}$, party P_2 sends $\lambda + 1$ ciphertexts $c_{\omega,i} \leftarrow \mathsf{Enc}(\omega_i), \mathsf{Enc}(v_{\omega_i,1}),\ldots,\mathsf{Enc}(v_{\omega_i,\lambda})$ to P_1. Both

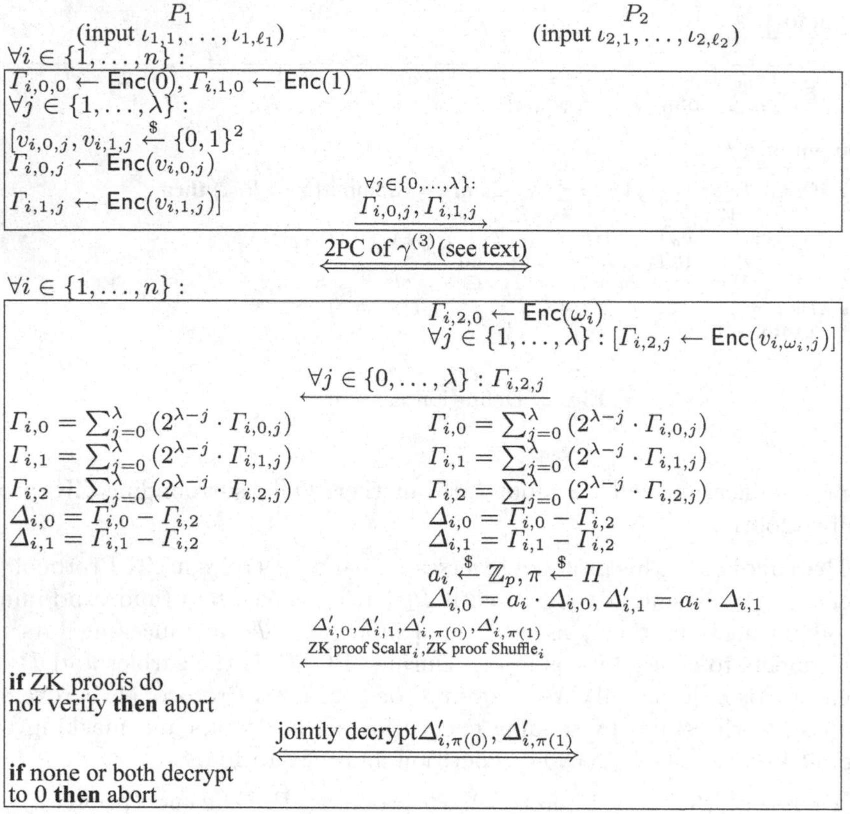

$$P_1 \qquad\qquad\qquad\qquad P_2$$
$$\text{(input } \iota_{1,1}, \ldots, \iota_{1,\ell_1}) \qquad\qquad\qquad \text{(input } \iota_{2,1}, \ldots, \iota_{2,\ell_2})$$

$\forall i \in \{1, \ldots, n\}:$

$\Gamma_{i,0,0} \leftarrow \mathsf{Enc}(0), \Gamma_{i,1,0} \leftarrow \mathsf{Enc}(1)$

$\forall j \in \{1, \ldots, \lambda\}:$

$[v_{i,0,j}, v_{i,1,j} \overset{\$}{\leftarrow} \{0,1\}^2$

$\Gamma_{i,0,j} \leftarrow \mathsf{Enc}(v_{i,0,j})$

$\Gamma_{i,1,j} \leftarrow \mathsf{Enc}(v_{i,1,j})]$

$\qquad\qquad\qquad \forall j \in \{0, \ldots, \lambda\}:$
$$\xrightarrow{\qquad \Gamma_{i,0,j}, \Gamma_{i,1,j} \qquad}$$

$$\overset{\text{2PC of } \gamma^{(3)}(\text{see text})}{\longleftrightarrow}$$

$\forall i \in \{1, \ldots, n\}:$

$\qquad\qquad\qquad\qquad\qquad \Gamma_{i,2,0} \leftarrow \mathsf{Enc}(\omega_i)$

$\qquad\qquad\qquad\qquad\qquad \forall j \in \{1, \ldots, \lambda\}: [\Gamma_{i,2,j} \leftarrow \mathsf{Enc}(v_{i,\omega_i,j})]$

$$\qquad\qquad \overset{\forall j \in \{0, \ldots, \lambda\}: \Gamma_{i,2,j}}{\longleftarrow}$$

$\Gamma_{i,0} = \sum_{j=0}^{\lambda} (2^{\lambda-j} \cdot \Gamma_{i,0,j}) \qquad\qquad \Gamma_{i,0} = \sum_{j=0}^{\lambda} (2^{\lambda-j} \cdot \Gamma_{i,0,j})$

$\Gamma_{i,1} = \sum_{j=0}^{\lambda} (2^{\lambda-j} \cdot \Gamma_{i,1,j}) \qquad\qquad \Gamma_{i,1} = \sum_{j=0}^{\lambda} (2^{\lambda-j} \cdot \Gamma_{i,1,j})$

$\Gamma_{i,2} = \sum_{j=0}^{\lambda} (2^{\lambda-j} \cdot \Gamma_{i,2,j}) \qquad\qquad \Gamma_{i,2} = \sum_{j=0}^{\lambda} (2^{\lambda-j} \cdot \Gamma_{i,2,j})$

$\Delta_{i,0} = \Gamma_{i,0} - \Gamma_{i,2} \qquad\qquad\qquad \Delta_{i,0} = \Gamma_{i,0} - \Gamma_{i,2}$

$\Delta_{i,1} = \Gamma_{i,1} - \Gamma_{i,2} \qquad\qquad\qquad \Delta_{i,1} = \Gamma_{i,1} - \Gamma_{i,2}$

$\qquad\qquad\qquad\qquad\qquad a_i \overset{\$}{\leftarrow} \mathbb{Z}_p, \pi \overset{\$}{\leftarrow} \Pi$

$\qquad\qquad\qquad\qquad\qquad \Delta'_{i,0} = a_i \cdot \Delta_{i,0}, \Delta'_{i,1} = a_i \cdot \Delta_{i,1}$

$$\overset{\Delta'_{i,0}, \Delta'_{i,1}, \Delta'_{i,\pi(0)}, \Delta'_{i,\pi(1)}}{\underset{\text{ZK proof Scalar}_i, \text{ZK proof Shuffle}_i}{\longleftarrow}}$$

if ZK proofs do

not verify **then** abort

$$\overset{\text{jointly decrypt} \Delta'_{i,\pi(0)}, \Delta'_{i,\pi(1)}}{\longleftrightarrow}$$

if none or both decrypt

to 0 **then** abort

Fig. 3. ZK Protocol (3)

parties use these ciphertexts to homomorphically generate $\Gamma_2 = \mathsf{Enc}(V_{\omega_i})$, an encryption of the concatenation of P_2's $\lambda + 1$ bits V_{ω_i}. As both parties know Γ_0 and Γ_1, they both homomorphically compute $\Delta_0 = \mathsf{Enc}(V_{\omega_i} - V_0)$ and $\Delta_1 = \mathsf{Enc}(V_{\omega_i} - V_1)$. Observe that, if V_{ω_i} is either V_0 or V_1, then one of Δ_0, Δ_1 encrypts a 0. Consequently, P_2 proves to P_1 in ZK that either Δ_0 or Δ_1 is an encryption of 0 (see below for details). If P_1 successfully verifies proofs, parties jointly decrypt $\Delta'_{i,\pi(0)}$ and $\Delta'_{i,\pi(1)}$. Note that decryption must include a ZK proof by P_2 about correct (partial) decryption [2,7,11].

We run the above techniques for each output bit ω_i in parallel.

ZK Proof of 0. Figure 3 also comprises details for the ZK proof, where P_2 proves that either $\Delta_{i,0}$ or $\Delta_{i,1}$ encrypts a zero. In Fig. 3, P_2 blinds $\Delta_{i,0}$ and $\Delta_{i,1}$ by a random a_i resulting in $\Delta'_{i,0}$ and $\Delta'_{i,1}$. Then, P_2 prepares sub-ZK proof "Scalar$_i$" which proves that $\Delta'_{i,0}, \Delta'_{i,1}$ are the result of multiplying $\Delta_{i,0}, \Delta_{i,1}$ by the same secret scalar a_i. Such a proof is standard, e.g., P_2 could simply publish the encryption of a_i, and P_1 computes $\Delta'_{i,0}, \Delta'_{i,1}$ themselves. Party P_2 completes the ZK proof by re-encrypting $\Delta'_{i,0}$ and $\Delta'_{i,1}$, choosing a random

Input to $\gamma^{(3)}$

P_1	P_2
$\iota_{1,1}, \ldots, \iota_{1,\ell_1}, 1 \leq i \leq n$ $\quad: \iota_{2,1}, \ldots, \iota_{2,\ell_2}$	
$[v_{i,0,1}, \ldots, v_{i,0,\lambda}, v_{i,1,1}, \ldots, v_{i,1,\lambda}]$	

Output of $\gamma^{(3)}$

1 $(\omega_1, \ldots, \omega_n) = \gamma((\iota_{1,1}, \ldots, \iota_{1,\ell_1}), (\iota_{2,1}, \ldots, \iota_{2,\ell_2}))$;
2 **for** $i = 1$ **to** n **do output** $\omega_i \| v_{i,\omega_i,1} \cdots v_{i,\omega_i,\lambda}$;

Fig. 4. Definition of circuit $\gamma^{(3)}$

1-bit permutation π from Π, and preparing ZK proof Shuffle$_i$ which proves that $(\Delta'_{i,\pi(0)}, \Delta'_{i,\pi(1)})$ is a random shuffle of $(\Delta'_{i,0}, \Delta'_{i,1})$. Proofs of two-element shuffles are also straightforward. For example, P_2 could encrypt a random bit to ciphertext β, send β to P_1, and prove that ciphertext $\beta - \beta^2$ encrypts a 0. This standard technique to prove a shuffle is working for, e.g., FHE schemes with plaintext domain over prime fields $GF(p)$ such as Fan and Vercauteren [24] and derivatives (SEAL). Other FHE schemes might use other types of shuffle proofs. Such proofs can be also implemented by, e.g., reverting to an efficient general proof [2] or by opening randomness of ciphertext $\beta - \beta^2$. Finally, P_1 computes $\Delta'_{i,\pi(0)} = \beta \cdot \Delta'_{i,0} + (\mathsf{Enc}(1) - \beta) \cdot \Delta'_{i,1}$ and $\Delta'_{i,\pi(1)} = (\mathsf{Enc}(1) - \beta) \cdot \Delta'_{i,0} + \beta \cdot \Delta'_{i,1}$ themselves.

HVZK to Fully-Malicious Security. For fully-malicious security, we replace 2PC evaluation of $\gamma^{(3)}$ from Fig. 3 by using ZK Protocol (1). More specifically, instead of 2PC evaluation of $\gamma^{(3)}$, we run ZK Protocol (1) for circuit $\gamma^{(3)}$ with both the $\iota_{1,i}$ and the $v_{i,0,j}, v_{i,1,j}$ as P_1's input bits, and the $\iota_{2,i}$ as P_2's input bits. To run ZK Protocol (1), P_1 sends encryptions $\Gamma_{i,0,j}, \Gamma_{i,1,j}$ to P_2 (as well as dummy encryptions of the $\iota_{1,i}$). As a result of running ZK Protocol (1) of $\gamma^{(3)}$ instead of direct 2PC of $\gamma^{(3)}$, P_2 can verify that the $\Gamma_{i,0}, \Gamma_{i,1}$ are correct encryptions of P_1's input to $\gamma^{(3)}$. Note that the output bits received by P_2 after running ZK Protocol (1) comprise all output bits of circuit $\gamma^{(3)}$.

3.2 Composition of ZK Protocols

Our ZK Protocols can be composed in a natural way, i.e., ZK Protocol (1), (2), and (3) can be jointly used on a single circuit γ. Protocol steps before and after 2PC evaluation of the modified circuit γ are executed in parallel. Different modifications of ZK Protocols (1) to (3) to circuit γ are merged into one large garbled circuit. This large circuit comprises γ's and all modifications' functionality and uses P_1's and P_2's input sets once. Thus, inputs $\iota_{1,i}$ and $\iota_{2,i}$ are only used once and their wires are connected to all sub-functions of the large circuit. All other necessary inputs $\mu_{i,j}, \sigma_{i,j}$, and $v_{\omega,j}$ are present for their respective input and outputs. This ensures the same functionality of the large circuit as the sub-functions due to its security against malicious adversaries.

Protocol steps outside of 2PC operate on distinct inputs and hence are non-interfering under parallel composition. We can compose the conversion routines in a natural way. Figures 5 and 6 depict the details of FHE to 2PC conversion and reverse, respectively.

3.3   Security Analysis

ZK Protocols (1) to (3) prove that the plaintext of an FHE ciphertext (under a shared key) and the input or output, respectively, of a 2PC are identical. They hence enable to compose FHE computations with 2PC protocols in a joint, maliciously secure protocol.

Theorem 1 (Proof in Appendix C). *ZK Protocols (1) to (3) are (a) complete, i.e., an honest verifier accepts the proof, if the prover provides consistent input, (b) zero-knowledge, i.e., any verifier learns nothing about the prover's witness except that it satisfies the proof, and (c) sound, i.e., an honest verifier rejects the proof with overwhelming probability in the security parameter λ, if the prover's secret input is not a witness for the proof.*

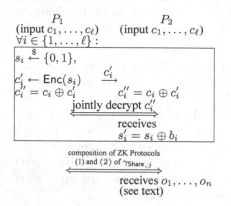

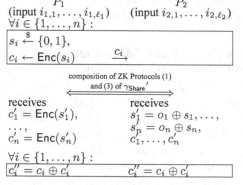

Fig. 5. FHE to 2PC conversion   **Fig. 6.** 2PC to FHE conversion

4   Application to Private Set Disjointness

To indicate their usefulness, we apply our mixed-technique conversions to the area of private set analytics. In particular, we design a new solution to the problem of securely, yet efficiently computing private set disjointness (PSD). In PSD, parties compute whether their sets' intersection is empty without revealing the intersection itself. While protocols computing PSD have been presented before [20,25,30,37,38,48,67], our new solution features several advantages which, in combination, is unique: any number of $d \geq 2$ parties, fully-malicious security, circuit-based computations, and high efficiency (also due to a constant number of rounds). Computing PSD with a circuit-based approach is of special interest, as variations of PSD, like whether the size of the intersection is larger than a threshold, or other set statistics can then be computed easily, see discussions in [56,58].

Each party P_i has an n element input set $S_i = \{e_{i,1}, \ldots, e_{i,n}\}$ with elements $e_{i,j} \in \{0,1\}^\ell$. We present a protocol where parties securely compute whether the intersection of the S_i is empty, i.e., $|\bigcap_{i=1}^{d} S_i| \overset{?}{=} 0$. Crucially, we do not leak the size of the intersection or any other information about the intersection or elements $e_{i,j}$. Assume that parties have previously computed a distributed private key with corresponding public key for a fully or somewhat homomorphic encryption scheme. Separately, each party P_i has a public-private key pair, where the public key is known to all parties. So, parties can securely communicate.

4.1 PSD Protocol Overview

We present a new circuit-based approach to compute PSD. At its core, parties compare their elements by evaluating a Boolean sub-circuit with pairwise 2PC in a star topology. The outcome of 2PC comparisons then serves as input to FHE evaluations.

Hash Table Preparation. Initially, parties hash their input elements into hash tables. This is a typical approach of recent protocols for PSI, see Pinkas et al. [57] for an overview. Specifically, each party P_i starts by creating an empty hash table T_i with $m \in O(\frac{n}{\log n})$ buckets. To cope with possible hash collisions with very high probability, each bucket comprises a total of $\beta \in O(\log n)$ entries [59,61]. Each entry has space to store ℓ bits. Let $T_i[j,k]$ denote the kth entry in the jth bucket $T_i[j]$ of P_i's hash table T_i.

After initializing hash table T_i, each party P_i iterates over their input elements, writing element $e_{i,j}$ into bucket $T_i[h(e_{i,j}), u]$, where u is the first empty entry in T_i's m^{th} bucket. All remaining entries in the hash table are filled with random bit strings.

Mixed-Circuit Evaluation. Parties elect a leader, w.l.o.g. the leader is P_1. The main idea to compute PSD is that, for a randomly chosen r, the following function F is evaluated securely:

$$F = r \cdot \sum_{j=1}^{m} \sum_{k=1}^{\beta} \prod_{i=2}^{d} \left[\bigvee_{u=1}^{\beta} (T_1[j,k] \overset{?}{=} T_i[j,u]) \right].$$

Function F implements PSD, as sets S_i are disjoint *iff* F evaluates to 0. The rationale behind F is that the intersection is not empty if and only if there exists an entry in a bucket of P_1's table which equals an entry of the same bucket in all other parties' tables.

We already define F using a mixed arithmetic and Boolean notation, suggesting a direct application of our mixed-techniques for 2PC-FHE evaluation. To securely evaluate F, we set up a simple star topology where leader P_1

interacts pairwise with each other party P_i to compute inner parts $f_{i,j,k} = \left[\bigvee_{u=1}^{\beta} (T_1[j,k] \stackrel{?}{=} T_i[j,u]) \right]$ with 2PC. For the kth entry in their j^{th} bucket $T_1[j,k]$, P_1 evaluates with P_i a separate 2PC circuit which implements $f_{i,j,k}$. Using our 2PC to FHE conversion, output of each $f_{i,j,k}$ 2PC evaluation is a homomorphic encryption of its output bit which we denote by $\mathsf{Enc}(f_{i,j,k})$. After all 2PC computations, P_1 sends the $\mathsf{Enc}(f_{i,j,k})$ to all other parties which continue computing F homomorphically.

The final multiplication of the output by (a random) r in the encrypted domain is realized by each party P_i randomly selecting $r_i \stackrel{\$}{\leftarrow} M$ and sending $\mathsf{Enc}(r_i)$ to other parties. All parties homomorphically compute $\mathsf{Enc}(r) = \sum_{i=1}^{d} \mathsf{Enc}(r_i)$ and multiply the output by $\mathsf{Enc}(r)$ to get $\mathsf{Enc}(F)$ which is then jointly decrypted. Without multiplying by r, parties would learn the size of the intersection.

4.2   Malicious Security for PSD

Although 2PC, our conversion, and homomorphic evaluations are secure against malicious adversaries, we need to extend our current security model from two parties to the case of d parties. A few conditions apply to PSD that make this extension efficient. First, each party P_i (except P_1) provides input only once, and all 2PCs are independent of other parties' inputs. In consequence, no input commitments from P_i are necessary, and only P_1 needs to use commitments. Furthermore, since there exists a pair of inputs for any output of the 2PC, the output of a 2PC between two malicious parties can be simulated with chosen inputs. Consequently, we now show that adding our ZK protocols leads to a multi-party protocol secure in the malicious model, despite the fact that both parties of a two-party computation can be malicious (including the leader). We leave the secure composition of 2PC to MPC in the star topology for the general case, when these conditions are not met, as future work.

Recall that after 2PC to FHE conversion, both parties P_1 and P_i have proven to each other correct computation of $c = \mathsf{Enc}(s)$ and $c' = \mathsf{Enc}(s')$. They homomorphically combine c and c' to $\mathsf{Enc}(f_{i,j,k}) = \mathsf{Enc}(s \oplus s')$. The new challenge when dealing with $d > 2$ parties is that both P_1 and P_i can be malicious, fabricate various different $\mathsf{Enc}(f_{i,j,k})$, and send different $\mathsf{Enc}(f_{i,j,k})$ to different other parties.

To mitigate, one could somehow run ZK proofs in public such that all other parties automatically observe the correct $\mathsf{Enc}(f_{i,j,k})$, but this is expensive. A more elegant solution would be that both parties P_1 and P_i sign $\mathsf{Enc}(f_{i,j,k})$ at the end of their conversion, and P_i sends their signature to P_1. Then, P_1 could use secure echo broadcast [27] to send $\mathsf{Enc}(f_{i,j,k})$ and both signatures of $\mathsf{Enc}(f_{i,j,k})$ to all parties. As a result, all parties would receive the same $\mathsf{Enc}(f_{i,j,k})$ and verify that P_1 and P_i have agreed on it.

An interesting situation occurs when both P_1 and P_i are malicious and agree on a wrong $\mathsf{Enc}(f_{i,j,k})$. For example, P_1 and P_i could agree on $\mathsf{Enc}(0)$ even though P_i has an entry $e_{i,u}$ in its jth bucket which equals an entry $e_{1,k}$ in P_1's

j^{th} bucket. Note that this is not an attack, as the adversary can anyway control P_i's input and set it to arbitrary values. So, the above case would be equivalent to the adversary setting P_i's input $e_{i,u}$ to something different from $e_{1,k}$ in the first place. The only property P_1 and P_i have to prove to all other parties is that ciphertext $\mathsf{Enc}(f_{i,j,k})$ encrypts a bit.

As neither P_1 nor P_i know $f_{i,j,k}$, we use a different strategy. Party P_1 proves in ZK that c encrypts a bit, and P_i proves that c' encrypts a bit. Parties broadcast c and c' with both proofs. Using c and c' all parties compute $\mathsf{Enc}(f_{i,j,k})$ homomorphically.

Finally, to force P_1 to always use the same inputs during pairwise comparisons with different P_i, we require P_1 to initially commit to its input using FHE ciphertexts and securely broadcast those ciphertexts to all other parties. The consistency of inputs is then verified using ZK Protocol (1).

Joint Decryption. Recall that the 2PC to FHE conversion internally runs ZK Protocol (3) and requires a joint decryption between P_1 and P_i. In case of $d > 2$ parties, joint decryption is still possible, but involves all d parties. So, both P_1 and P_i broadcast a request to decrypt the current $\Delta'_{i,\pi(0)}$ and $\Delta'_{i,\pi(1)}$, and all parties reply to P_1 with their share of the decryption (plus proof of correct decryption). Note that this does not change our total message complexity. We need to run $O(1)$ broadcasts for each $f_{i,j,k}$ anyway.

4.3 Complexity Analysis

Due to space constraints, we present and compare asymptotic complexities of our techniques for evaluating F with related schemes in the full version of this paper [10].

4.4 Implementation

We have implemented our private set disjointness variant with 2PC to FHE conversion and performed micro-benchmarks. We will release our code into open source upon publication of the paper.

Our implementation of 2PC-part $f_{i,j,k}$ is done in the framework by Wang et al. [65] and maliciously secure. Yet, none of the common FHE libraries (HELib, PALISADE, SEAL, TFHE) provides both distributed key generation with threshold encryption and ZK proofs, which we need for maliciously-secure conversion. Moreover, an implementation of a FHE scheme with threshold decryption and ZK proofs, e.g., based on the one by Asharov et al. [2], deserves its own paper. Thus, for the arithmetic part of F, we have only implemented and benchmarked arithmetic operations with FHE (using TFHE [16,17] for its simplicity), but not FHE ZK proofs, i.e., a semi-honest secure conversion. We dub the security setting of our implementation as "semi-malicious": 2PC is maliciously secure, but the conversion is only semi-honest secure. This setting is at least as strong as semi-honest security, but weaker than malicious security.

Table 1. Online time (s) to evaluate F, our scheme vs semi-honest and maliciously secure SPDZ [35] vs BMR [34] vs FHE. 2PC: communication time for circuit evaluation of all $m\beta d$ circuits $((\gamma_{\mathsf{Share}}'(1))(3))(1)$, BC: communication time for broadcasting shares and partial decryptions, FHE Comp: computation time for arithmetic part, DNF: does not finish in 15 min. Benchmarks from single 1.6 GHz Core i5, 32 GB RAM

n	d	Ours ("Semi-Malicious")				Semi-Honest		Malicious	
		2PC	BC	FHE Comp	Total	$\mathrm{SPDZ}^{\mathrm{SH}}$	FHE	SPDZ	BMR
						Total	Total	Total	Total
32	5	2.2	1.1	1.0	**4.3**	**10.1**	141.7	16.4	8.5
	10	3.9	1.8	1.8	**7.5**	**13.8**	283.0	33.1	24.3
	20	7.6	5.5	3.6	**16.6**	**48.8**	565.5	50.3	Crash
	40	14.8	17.6	7.1	**39.5**	**130.3**	DNF	215.7	Crash
64	5	4.7	1.4	2.3	**8.4**	**22.7**	406.9	35.6	18.5
	10	9.0	3.4	4.4	**16.8**	**32.6**	813.1	72.4	66.6
	20	18.0	10.7	8.6	**37.3**	**101.5**	DNF	248.2	Crash
	40	35.9	40.9	17.0	**93.8**	**265.8**	DNF	784.3	Crash
128	5	10.7	2.2	5.4	**18.3**	**52.3**	DNF	117.5	43.0
	10	20.8	6.6	10.3	**37.7**	**84.6**	DNF	356.7	Crash
	20	41.8	24.2	20.1	**86.1**	**358.1**	DNF	675.8	Crash
	40	83.3	95.3	39.7	**218.3**	**546.3**	DNF	DNF	Crash
1024	5	121.2	17.5	61.6	**200.4**	**727.3**	DNF	DNF	DNF
2048	5	265.0	37.5	135.5	**438.0**	**DNF**	DNF	DNF	DNF

More specifically, we have implemented the actual circuit which is evaluated as part of the 2PC to FHE conversion of $f_{i,j,k}$, namely $((\gamma_{\mathsf{Share}}'(1))(3))(1)$. Here, circuit γ_{Share}' is the modification to $f_{i,j,k}$ due to conversion, $\gamma_{\mathsf{Share}}'(1)$ is the modification implied by ZK Protocol (1) on top of that, $(\gamma_{\mathsf{Share}}'(1))(3)$ the modification by ZK Protocol (3) on top of that, and $((\gamma_{\mathsf{Share}}'(1))(3))(1)$ the modification by ZK Protocol (1) running inside ZK Protocol (3).

For all benchmarks, we set $m = \frac{n}{2}$, $\beta = \log n$, and consider $\ell = 32$ bit integers as the elements in each party's set. It is well known that communication time due to latency between parties is a dominating factor regarding total runtime, especially for the 2PC part. For example, raw computation time of evaluating a single $((\gamma_{\mathsf{Share}}'(1))(3))(1)$ circuit for $\beta = 5$ takes only 1.2 ms on a single 1.6 GHz Core i5 with 32 GB RAM, but all computations can run in parallel on different cores. So, an Amazon EC2 C5d instance with 96 cores computes 80,000 circuits per second. However, network traffic, i.e., exchanging 177 KByte of data between P_1 and P_i during evaluation of that circuit, cannot be parallelized. Instead, we can only sequentially send all data for all circuits, and network latency is here the crucial parameter. While latency of (intercontinental) WAN traffic is often unstable and can go over 250 ms [64], we run benchmarks on one machine to better control network behavior and use netem [53] to set latency to a modest 70 ms. As a result of this latency, we measured TCP data goodput to be only 330 MBit/s on the localhost network (a higher latency would imply less goodput).

In Table 1, 2PC denotes the time to compute all $((\gamma_{\mathsf{Share}}{}'(1))(3))(1)$. BC denotes the time for all broadcasts of shares c_i, c_i' after 2PC to all parties (one TFHE ciphertext has size 2.5 KByte) plus the time to broadcast a partial decryption of the final result after FHE from each party (a partial decryption is one TFHE ciphertext). FHE Comp is the time, for each party, to compute the arithmetic part of F in TFHE.

For comparison, we have also implemented F in the popular MP-SPDZ framework [33] and benchmarked with both their semi-honest (SPDZ^{SH}: no MACs, semi-honest OT [33]) and maliciously secure SPDZ variants [35] as well as BMR [34]. SPDZ Total and BMR Total are their total (online) times to compute F. FHE Total is the total time of a semi-honest "pure-FHE" implementation of F with TFHE, including broadcasting each party's $m\beta\ell$ ciphertexts to all other parties. Note that BMR crashes even for a small number of parties, e.g., $n = 128, d = 10$, or quickly runs out of memory (> 32 GB) for $d \geq 20$ parties.

Looking at Table 1, our implementation outperforms semi-honest and maliciously secure SPDZ, BMR, and FHE in all considered settings. While SPDZ and BMR are competitive for a small number of parties, BMR fails due to its memory consumption, and our composition from 2PC clearly shows better scalability than SPDZ for larger numbers of parties.

While timings for our "semi-malicious" implementation look promising regarding a potential maliciously secure implementation, we do not have such an implementation for the above stated reasons. However, observing that our techniques outperform even semi-honest SPDZ while offering stronger security guarantees leads to an interesting conclusion of our evaluation. Our mixed-techniques protocols might already serve as an alternative to standard semi-honest MPC in scenarios with a star topology, i.e., where a multi-party protocol can be decomposed into multiple 2PC protocols.

5   Related Work

Mixed-Techniques MPC. Several previous works combine different MPC techniques to mitigate individual techniques' drawbacks. Kolesnikov et al. [39] are among the first to present a conversion between garbled circuits and (additively) homomorphic encryption in the two-party semi-honest model [39,41]. Extending their conversion to also support fully-malicious adversaries is nontrivial: in Appendix D of [40], they present honest-verifier zero-knowledge proofs which render the protocol secure only if at most one party is malicious. However, HVZK is insufficient, if proofs are part of a scenario with more than two parties where more than one party can be malicious.

A long line of research has focused on making mixed-techniques practical and efficient. Henecka et al. [29] design practical tools for conversion between garbled circuits and additively homomorphic encryption. Their conversion targets semi-honest adversaries and circuits for two parties. Demmler et al. [22] present a two party framework to convert between arithmetic sharing, Boolean sharing, and garbled circuits in the semi-honest model, and so do Riazi et al. [60]. Mohassel and Rindal [50] extend to three parties with malicious security. Again in the semi-honest model for two parties, Juvekar et al. [32] switch between garbled circuits and additively homomorphic encryption, and Büscher et al. [14] switch between arithmetic and Boolean sharing. The "(e)daBits" line of work [1,23,62] converts between MPC based on arithmetic secret sharing and garbled circuits with malicious security. In contrast, our work mixes FHE with garbled circuits, with the advantage of a (low) constant number of rounds during evaluation.

For completeness sake, we mention that other powerful MPC frameworks besides MP-SPDZ exist, e.g., the purely circuit-based EMP-Toolkit [66]. Also note that FHE is often combined with (arithmetic) MPC to prepare multiplication triplets during offline phases, as in, e.g., SPDZ and follow-up works [3,36].

(Multi-Party) PSI and Disjointness. While seminal works in PSI are based on dedicated protocols [49], recent papers use a circuit-based approach (see Pinkas et al. [55] for an overview), culminating in solutions with asymptotically optimal communication complexity and practical constants [58]. In theory, such circuit-based approaches can be used to also compute disjointness, but they focus on the two-party setting with semi-honest security or multiple parties with semi-honest security [15]. Efficient maliciously-secure multi-party circuit-PSI has not yet been achieved.

Hazay and Venkitasubramaniam [28] present a maliciously-secure multi-party PSI protocol based on oblivious polynomial evaluation (OPE). Similar to previous ideas [25], OPE could then be combined with a maliciously-secure 2PC to compute disjointness. However, already computing the intersection is expensive with this approach, requiring $O(n^2)$ modular exponentiations. Kolesnikov et al. [42] present an efficient multi-party PSI protocol in the semi-honest model using only symmetric encryption. However, more fundamentally, PSI protocols cannot be easily converted into PSI analytics protocols (not disclosing the intersection) while maintaining efficiency [56,58] and providing malicious security. Other works have considered computing set disjointness, but these target semi-honest security and/or only two parties [20,25,30,37,38,48,67]

Comparing to related work, **our work** fills a gap with 1) a solution which converts between FHE and garbled circuits, 2) supports any number of parties d, and 3) provides malicious security. We use this to present the first multi-party PSI analytics protocol whose communication complexity scales only quadratically in d.

Appendix

A   Supporting Larger Plaintext Spaces

Our presentation describes arithmetic sub-circuits operating over single bits. There, each ciphertext encrypts a single bit and homomorphic operations are over bits. This can be inefficient, as parties often want to compute on larger integers, e.g., 32 Bit integers. Homomorphic encryption schemes anyway operate over large plaintext spaces, where addition of a large, multiple bit integer is a single homomorphic operation. A large plaintext space also allows for SIMD techniques.

To improve performance, we extend conversion from operating over $GF(2)$ plaintexts to operate over arbitrary fields $GF(q)$ by instituting the following two modifications. In our conversions, ZK Protocols, and ZK proofs, we replace using XORs to share a single bit or combine two shares to a bit by additions and subtractions over $GF(q)$. Random bits serving as a share for a party become random elements of $GF(q)$. Second, n single bit encryptions $c_i = \mathsf{Enc}(b_i)$ output by our 2PC to FHE conversion are combined to a single n bit encrypted integer by each party computing $\sum_{i=0}^{n-1} 2^i \cdot c_{i+1}$.

B $d \geq 2$ Parties

Secure multi-party computation can be constructed from secure two-party computations in various ways. One standard way is a star topology as we present in Sect. 4. We emphasize, however, that our conversions are not limited to star topologies.

The main idea is that each party P_i engages in secure two-party computation with a central party P_1 to compute some functionality. Such a centralized approach works for certain functionalities, e.g., equality of inputs, as equality is symmetric and transitive. If P_i's input is equal to P_1's and P_j's input is equal to P_1's, then P_i's input is also equal to P_j's. Hence, computation of the joint result using homomorphic encryption can leverage this relation.

This approach does not apply to other functionalities, e.g., larger-than comparison. If P_i's input is larger than P_1's, and P_j's input is larger than P_1's, then we cannot imply any larger-than relation between P_i's and P_j's input. Consequently, in this case, the alternative to maintain constant-round complexity is to engage all parties in pair-wise comparisons. This has been previously considered, e.g., in the context of sealed-bid auctions [9]. However, the result of each pairwise comparison is leaked in previous work, reducing security to a level comparable with order-preserving encryption. In contrast, constructions in this paper would enable computing the auction result, e.g., the largest input, using homomorphic encryption with constant round complexity.

In summary, there exist several practically relevant protocols with arithmetic relations between inputs which can be decomposed into an initial two-party phase followed by a combination phase of the inputs. We use secure two-party protocols during the first phase to achieve efficient implementations in a constant number of (communication) rounds. Similarly, to evaluate low multiplicative depth sub-circuits, we use homomorphic encryption efficiently. Our ZK protocols ensure that the conversion is secure against malicious adversaries.

C   Proof of Theorem 1

We emphasize that we only provide a proof-sketch that, however, should convince an expert reader about the correctness of our theorems and the security of our protocols. Before presenting this proof sketch of our main Theorem 1, we briefly recall completeness, zero-knowledge, and soundness definitions.

Let $P \in \{P_1, P_2\}$ be the prover and $V \in \{P_1, P_2\}$ be the verifier in a ZKP. Let $w \in R_C$ be a witness for the correct execution of a conversion which we denote as relation R_C. Let $\langle P(w), V \rangle$ be the execution of a ZKP protocol.

Completeness: An honest verifier accepts the proof, if the prover provides consistent input, i.e., $w \in R_C \implies \langle P(w), V \rangle \wedge Pr[V = \mathsf{accept}] = 1$.

Zero-Knowledge: The verifier learns nothing about the prover's witness except that it satisfies the proof, i.e., there exists simulator Sim_P such that $\langle P(w), V \rangle \stackrel{c}{=} \langle \mathsf{Sim}_P, V \rangle$.

Soundness: An honest verifier rejects the proof with overwhelming probability in security parameter λ, if the prover's secret input is not a witness for the proof, i.e., there exists extractor Ext_V such that $V = \mathsf{accept} \implies \langle P(w), \mathsf{Ext}_V \rangle \wedge Pr[\mathsf{Ext}_V = w] = 1 - \mathsf{negl}(\lambda)$.

Proof *(Theorem 1).* Completeness of ZK Protocols (1) to (3) follows immediately from their construction, so we focus on Zero-Knowledge and Soundness.

Zero-Knowledge. To prove zero-knowledge, we construct simulators Sim_{P_1} or Sim_{P_2} in the hybrid model which do not know the witness of the individual ZK Protocols (ZKPs), create views for the adversary which are indistinguishable from the real protocol, and make the verifier accept the proofs. In the hybrid model, simulators can simulate any ZK sub-proofs invoked during the protocol.

First, observe that all messages from the prover to the verifier are semantically-secure ciphertexts, random numbers or other zero-knowledge proofs.

In ZKP (1) and (2), the simulator Sim_{P_1}, or Sim_{P_2} (in ZKP (2)), randomly chooses inputs $\iota_{1,i}$ (or $\iota_{2,i}$) and masking bits $\mu_{i,j}$ as their input into 2PC. The verifier inputs $\sigma_{i,j}$ to the 2PC. After the 2PC, the simulator either receives verification bits $t_{i,j}$ (ZKP (1)) or outputs random verification bits (ZKP (2)).

In the last step, we apply the hybrid model. The simulator invokes the simulator of the ZKP for correct decryption using those (random) verification bits and the committed (random) input and masking ciphertexts, simulating a consistent execution of the ZKP.

In ZKP (3), Sim_{P_1} does not have to output verification bits $v_{i,\omega_i,j}$, but the verification is done using ZK proofs Scalar_i and $\mathsf{Shuffle}_i$. Hence, the simulator for ZK Protocol (3) chooses a random ω_i and invokes the simulators for Scalar_i and $\mathsf{Shuffle}_i$.

Soundness. To prove soundness for ZKP (1) and (2), we construct extractors Ext_{P_1} or Ext_{P_2}. We construct an extractor Ext_{P_2} only for ZKP (1), but stress that the extractor Ext_{P_1} for (2) is equivalent. The extractor starts the ZK proof and lets the prover commit to their inputs via homomorphic ciphertexts $c_{1,j}$

(for a known shared key). Then the extractor chooses challenge bits $\sigma_{i,j}$ and sends them to the 2PC. The prover outputs verification bits $t_{i,j}$. The extractor rewinds the prover to just before they received the challenge bits for the 2PC. The extractor negates all challenge bits to $\neg\sigma_{i,j}$, sends them to the 2PC and continues the protocol. Let the prover's verification bits after rewinding be $t'_{i,j}$. We assume that the prover has consistent inputs and hence these inputs are extractable: the prover's inputs in ZKP (1) are $t_{i,j} \oplus t'_{i,j}$.

The soundness of ZKP (3) is a special case of authenticity of garbled circuits [6], and we do not need an extractor. Challenge bits $v_{i,0,j}$ and $v_{i,1,j}$ are input to the 2PC. Note that the soundness of the ZKP (1) ensures that the entire execution of the verifier is secure against malicious behaviour, including its conversion of the challenge bits from FHE to 2PC. The output depends on the output of the 2PC. Since the prover only evaluates the garbled circuit, it is bound to the correct or no output due to the authenticity property of garbled circuits. It can hence only produce one consistent set of output labels $v_{i,\omega_i,j}$.

This completes our security proof. Note that only the proof of ZKP (3) is recursive to the proof of ZKP (1), and hence all proofs are valid if ordered from (1) to (3). $\qquad\square$

References

1. Aly, A., Orsini, E., Rotaru, D., Smart, N.P., Wood, T.: Zaphod: efficiently combining LSSS and garbled circuits in SCALE. In: ACM WAHC (2019)
2. Asharov, G., Jain, A., López-Alt, A., Tromer, E., Vaikuntanathan, V., Wichs, D.: Multiparty computation with low communication, computation and interaction via threshold FHE. In: Pointcheval, D., Johansson, T. (eds.) EUROCRYPT 2012. LNCS, vol. 7237, pp. 483–501. Springer, Heidelberg (2012). https://doi.org/10.1007/978-3-642-29011-4_29
3. Baum, C., Cozzo, D., Smart, N.P.: Using TopGear in overdrive: a more efficient ZKPoK for SPDZ. In: SAC (2019)
4. Bay, A., Erkin, Z., Alishahi, M., Vos, J.: Multi-party private set intersection protocols for practical applications. In: SECRYPT (2021)
5. Beaver, D., Micali, S., Rogaway, P.: The round complexity of secure protocols (extended abstract). In: STOC (1990)
6. Bellare, M., Hoang, V.T., Rogaway, P.: Foundations of garbled circuits. In: CCS (2012)
7. Bendlin, R., Damgård, I.: Threshold decryption and zero-knowledge proofs for lattice-based cryptosystems. In: Micciancio, D. (ed.) TCC 2010. LNCS, vol. 5978, pp. 201–218. Springer, Heidelberg (2010). https://doi.org/10.1007/978-3-642-11799-2_13
8. Benhamouda, F., Camenisch, J., Krenn, S., Lyubashevsky, V., Neven, G.: Better zero-knowledge proofs for lattice encryption and their application to group signatures. In: Sarkar, P., Iwata, T. (eds.) ASIACRYPT 2014. LNCS, vol. 8873, pp. 551–572. Springer, Heidelberg (2014). https://doi.org/10.1007/978-3-662-45611-8_29
9. Blass, E.-O., Kerschbaum, F.: Strain: a secure auction for blockchains. In: Lopez, J., Zhou, J., Soriano, M. (eds.) ESORICS 2018. LNCS, vol. 11098, pp. 87–110. Springer, Cham (2018). https://doi.org/10.1007/978-3-319-99073-6_5

10. Blass, E.-O., Kerschbaum, F.: Mixed-technique multi-party computations composed of two-party computations. Cryptology ePrint Archive, Report 2020/636 (2020). https://ia.cr/2020/636

11. Boneh, D., et al.: Threshold cryptosystems from threshold fully homomorphic encryption. In: Shacham, H., Boldyreva, A. (eds.) CRYPTO 2018. LNCS, vol. 10991, pp. 565–596. Springer, Cham (2018). https://doi.org/10.1007/978-3-319-96884-1_19

12. Brakerski, Z., Gentry, C., Vaikuntanathan, V.: (Leveled) fully homomorphic encryption without bootstrapping. In: ITCS (2012)

13. Branco, P., Döttling, N., Pu, S.: Multiparty cardinality testing for threshold private intersection. In: Garay, J.A. (ed.) PKC 2021. LNCS, vol. 12711, pp. 32–60. Springer, Cham (2021). https://doi.org/10.1007/978-3-030-75248-4_2

14. Büscher, N., Demmler, D., Katzenbeisser, S., Kretzmer, D., Schneider, T.: HyCC: compilation of hybrid protocols for practical secure computation. In: CCS (2018)

15. Chandran, N., Dasgupta, N., Gupta, D., Lakshmi Bhavana Obbattu, S., Sekar, S., Shah, A.: Efficient linear multiparty PSI and extensions to circuit/quorum PSI. In: CCS (2021)

16. Chillotti, I., Gama, N., Georgieva, M., Izabachène, M.: TFHE: Fast Fully Homomorphic Encryption Library (2016). https://tfhe.github.io/tfhe/

17. Chillotti, I., Gama, N., Georgieva, M., Izabachène, M.: TFHE: fast fully homomorphic encryption over the torus. J. Cryptol. **33**(1), 34–91 (2020)

18. Damgård, I., López-Alt, A.: Zero-knowledge proofs with low amortized communication from lattice assumptions. In: Visconti, I., De Prisco, R. (eds.) SCN 2012. LNCS, vol. 7485, pp. 38–56. Springer, Heidelberg (2012). https://doi.org/10.1007/978-3-642-32928-9_3

19. Damgård, I., Pastro, V., Smart, N., Zakarias, S.: Multiparty computation from somewhat homomorphic encryption. In: Safavi-Naini, R., Canetti, R. (eds.) CRYPTO 2012. LNCS, vol. 7417, pp. 643–662. Springer, Heidelberg (2012). https://doi.org/10.1007/978-3-642-32009-5_38

20. Davidson, A., Cid, C.: An efficient toolkit for computing private set operations. In: Pieprzyk, J., Suriadi, S. (eds.) ACISP 2017. LNCS, vol. 10343, pp. 261–278. Springer, Cham (2017). https://doi.org/10.1007/978-3-319-59870-3_15

21. Debnath, S., Stanica, P., Kundu, N., Choudhury, T.: Secure and efficient multiparty private set intersection cardinality. Adv. Math. Commun. **15**(2), 365 (2021)

22. Demmler, D., Schneider, T., Zohner, M.: ABY - a framework for efficient mixed-protocol secure two-party computation. In: NDSS (2015)

23. Escudero, D., Ghosh, S., Keller, M., Rachuri, R., Scholl, P.: Improved primitives for MPC over mixed arithmetic-binary circuits. In: Micciancio, D., Ristenpart, T. (eds.) CRYPTO 2020. LNCS, vol. 12171, pp. 823–852. Springer, Cham (2020). https://doi.org/10.1007/978-3-030-56880-1_29

24. Fan, J., Vercauteren, F.: Somewhat practical fully homomorphic encryption. IACR Cryptol. ePrint Arch., page 144 (2012). https://eprint.iacr.org/2012/144

25. Freedman, M.J., Nissim, K., Pinkas, B.: Efficient private matching and set intersection. In: Cachin, C., Camenisch, J.L. (eds.) EUROCRYPT 2004. LNCS, vol. 3027, pp. 1–19. Springer, Heidelberg (2004). https://doi.org/10.1007/978-3-540-24676-3_1

26. Gentry, C.: Fully homomorphic encryption using ideal lattices. In: STOC (2009)

27. Goldwasser, S., Lindell, Y.: Secure multi-party computation without agreement. J. Cryptol. **18**(3), 247–287 (2005). https://doi.org/10.1007/s00145-005-0319-z

28. Hazay, C., Venkitasubramaniam, M.: Scalable multi-party private set-intersection. In: Fehr, S. (ed.) PKC 2017. LNCS, vol. 10174, pp. 175–203. Springer, Heidelberg (2017). https://doi.org/10.1007/978-3-662-54365-8_8

29. Henecka, W., Kögl, S., Sadeghi, A.-R., Schneider, T., Wehrenberg, I.: TASTY: tool for automating secure two-party computations. In: CCS (2010)

30. Hohenberger, S., Weis, S.A.: Honest-verifier private disjointness testing without random oracles. In: PET (2006)

31. Ishaq, M., Milanova, A., Zikas, V.: Efficient MPC via program analysis: a framework for efficient optimal mixing. In: CCS (2019)

32. Juvekar, C., Vaikuntanathan, V., Chandrakasan, A.: GAZELLE: a low latency framework for secure neural network inference. In: USENIX Security (2018)

33. Keller, M.: MP-SPDZ: a versatile framework for multi-party computation. IACR ePrint 2020/521 (2020)

34. Keller, M., Yanai, A.: Efficient maliciously secure multiparty computation for RAM. In: Nielsen, J.B., Rijmen, V. (eds.) EUROCRYPT 2018. LNCS, vol. 10822, pp. 91–124. Springer, Cham (2018). https://doi.org/10.1007/978-3-319-78372-7_4

35. Keller, M., Orsini, E., Scholl, P.: MASCOT: faster malicious arithmetic secure computation with oblivious transfer. In: CCS (2016)

36. Keller, M., Pastro, V., Rotaru, D.: Overdrive: making SPDZ great again. In: Nielsen, J.B., Rijmen, V. (eds.) EUROCRYPT 2018. LNCS, vol. 10822, pp. 158–189. Springer, Cham (2018). https://doi.org/10.1007/978-3-319-78372-7_6

37. Kiayias, A., Mitrofanova, A.: Testing disjointness of private datasets. In: Patrick, A.S., Yung, M. (eds.) FC 2005. LNCS, vol. 3570, pp. 109–124. Springer, Heidelberg (2005). https://doi.org/10.1007/11507840_13

38. Kissner, L., Song, D.: Privacy-preserving set operations. In: Shoup, V. (ed.) CRYPTO 2005. LNCS, vol. 3621, pp. 241–257. Springer, Heidelberg (2005). https://doi.org/10.1007/11535218_15

39. Kolesnikov, V., Sadeghi, A.-R., Schneider, T.: Improved garbled circuit building blocks and applications to auctions and computing minima. In: CANS (2009)

40. Kolesnikov, V., Sadeghi, A.-R., Schneider, T.: From dust to dawn: practically efficient two-party secure function evaluation protocols and their modular design. IACR ePrint 2010/079 (2010)

41. Kolesnikov, V., Sadeghi, A.-R., Schneider, T.: A systematic approach to practically efficient general two-party secure function evaluation protocols and their modular design. J. Comput. Secur. 21(2), 283–315 (2013)

42. Kolesnikov, V., Matania, N., Pinkas, B., Rosulek, M., Trieu, N.: Practical multiparty private set intersection from symmetric-key techniques. In: CCS (2017a)

43. Kolesnikov, V., Nielsen, J.B., Rosulek, M., Trieu, N., Trifiletti, R.: DUPLO: unifying cut-and-choose for garbled circuits. In: CCS (2017b)

44. Lindell, Y.: Fast cut-and-choose-based protocols for malicious and covert adversaries. J. Cryptol. 29(2), 456–490 (2015). https://doi.org/10.1007/s00145-015-9198-0

45. Lindell, Y., Smart, N.P., Soria-Vazquez, E.: More efficient constant-round multiparty computation from BMR and SHE. In: Hirt, M., Smith, A. (eds.) TCC 2016. LNCS, vol. 9985, pp. 554–581. Springer, Heidelberg (2016). https://doi.org/10.1007/978-3-662-53641-4_21

46. Lindell, Y., Pinkas, B., Smart, N.P., Yanai, A.: Efficient constant-round multi-party computation combining BMR and SPDZ. J. Cryptol. 32(3), 1026–1069 (2019). https://doi.org/10.1007/s00145-019-09322-2

47. Akhavan Mahdavi, R., et al.: Practical over-threshold multi-party private set intersection. In: ACSAC (2020)

48. Marconi, L., Conti, M., Di Pietro, R.: CED^2: communication efficient disjointness decision. In: Jajodia, S., Zhou, J. (eds.) SecureComm 2010. LNICSSITE, vol. 50, pp. 290–306. Springer, Heidelberg (2010). https://doi.org/10.1007/978-3-642-16161-2_17

49. Meadows, C.A.: A more efficient cryptographic matchmaking protocol for use in the absence of a continuously available third party. In: IEEE S&P (1986)

50. Mohassel, P., Rindal, P.: ABY^3: a mixed protocol framework for machine learning. In: CCS (2018)

51. Myers, S., Sergi, M., Shelat, A.: Threshold fully homomorphic encryption and secure computation. IACR ePrint 2011/454 (2011)

52. Sathya Narayanan, G., Aishwarya, T., Agrawal, A., Patra, A., Choudhary, A., Pandu Rangan, C.: Multi party distributed private matching, set disjointness and cardinality of set intersection with information theoretic security. In: Garay, J.A., Miyaji, A., Otsuka, A. (eds.) CANS 2009. LNCS, vol. 5888, pp. 21–40. Springer, Heidelberg (2009). https://doi.org/10.1007/978-3-642-10433-6_2

53. NETEM (2019). https://wiki.linuxfoundation.org/networking/netem

54. Nielsen, J.B., Orlandi, C.: LEGO for two-party secure computation. In: Reingold, O. (ed.) TCC 2009. LNCS, vol. 5444, pp. 368–386. Springer, Heidelberg (2009). https://doi.org/10.1007/978-3-642-00457-5_22

55. Pinkas, B., Schneider, T., Segev, G., Zohner, M.: Phasing: private set intersection using permutation-based hashing. In: USENIX Security (2015)

56. Pinkas, B., Schneider, T., Weinert, C., Wieder, U.: Efficient circuit-based PSI via cuckoo hashing. In: Nielsen, J.B., Rijmen, V. (eds.) EUROCRYPT 2018. LNCS, vol. 10822, pp. 125–157. Springer, Cham (2018). https://doi.org/10.1007/978-3-319-78372-7_5

57. Pinkas, B., Schneider, T., Zohner, M.: Scalable private set intersection based on OT extension. ACM Trans. Priv. Secur. **21**(2), 1–35 (2018)

58. Pinkas, B., Schneider, T., Tkachenko, O., Yanai, A.: Efficient circuit-based PSI with linear communication. In: Ishai, Y., Rijmen, V. (eds.) EUROCRYPT 2019. LNCS, vol. 11478, pp. 122–153. Springer, Cham (2019). https://doi.org/10.1007/978-3-030-17659-4_5

59. Raab, M., Steger, A.: "Balls into Bins" — a simple and tight analysis. In: Luby, M., Rolim, J.D.P., Serna, M. (eds.) RANDOM 1998. LNCS, vol. 1518, pp. 159–170. Springer, Heidelberg (1998). https://doi.org/10.1007/3-540-49543-6_13

60. Riazi, M.S., Weinert, C., Tkachenko, O., Songhori, E.M., Schneider, T., Koushanfar, F.: Chameleon: a hybrid secure computation framework for machine learning applications. In: AsiaCCS (2018)

61. Rindal, P., Rosulek, M.: Malicious-secure private set intersection via dual execution. In: CCS (2017)

62. Rotaru, D., Wood, T.: MArBled circuits: mixing arithmetic and Boolean circuits with active security. In: Hao, F., Ruj, S., Sen Gupta, S. (eds.) INDOCRYPT 2019. LNCS, vol. 11898, pp. 227–249. Springer, Cham (2019). https://doi.org/10.1007/978-3-030-35423-7_12

63. Strand, M.: A verifiable shuffle for the GSW cryptosystem. In: VOTING (2018)

64. Verizon. IP Latency Statistics (2020). https://enterprise.verizon.com/terms/latency/

65. Wang, X., Ranellucci, S., Katz, J.: Authenticated garbling and efficient maliciously secure two-party computation. In: CCS (2017a)

66. Wang, X., Ranellucci, S., Katz, J.: Global-scale secure multiparty computation. In: CCS (2017b)

67. Ye, Q., Wang, H., Pieprzyk, J., Zhang, X.-M.: Efficient disjointness tests for private datasets. In: Mu, Y., Susilo, W., Seberry, J. (eds.) ACISP 2008. LNCS, vol. 5107, pp. 155–169. Springer, Heidelberg (2008). https://doi.org/10.1007/978-3-540-70500-0_12

68. Yung, M.: From mental poker to core business: why and how to deploy secure computation protocols? In: CCS (2015)

PEA: Practical Private Epistasis Analysis Using MPC

Kay Hamacher[1] , Tobias Kussel[1] , Thomas Schneider[1] ,
and Oleksandr Tkachenko[2]([📧])

[1] Technical University of Darmstadt, Darmstadt, Germany
[2] DFINITY, Zürich, Switzerland
oleksandr.tkachenko1@gmail.com

Abstract. Due to the significant drop in prices for genome sequencing in the last decade, genome databases were constantly growing. This enabled genome analyses such as Genome-Wide Association Studies (GWAS) that study associations between a gene and a disease and allow to improve medical treatment. However, GWAS fails at the analysis of complex diseases caused by non-linear gene-gene interactions such as sporadic breast cancer or type 2 diabetes. Epistasis Analysis (EA) is a more powerful approach that complements GWAS and considers non-linear interactions between multiple parts of the genome and environment.

Statistical genome analyses require large, well-curated genomic datasets, which are difficult to obtain. Hence, the aggregation of multiple databases is often necessary, but the sharing of genomic data raises severe privacy concerns and is subject to extensive regulations (e.g., GDPR or HIPAA), requiring further privacy protection for collaborative analyses.

Although there has been work on private GWAS, there was a lack of attention to Private EA (PEA). In this work, we design the first secure and accurate PEA protocol, with security against passive adversaries.

Our efficient PEA protocol consists of two subprotocols: (1) (optional) feature selection for filtering noisy features to reduce the input size for better efficiency and (2) finding relevant associations. For feature selection, we design two protocols based on Secure Multi-Party Computation (MPC) for Relief-F and TuRF. For finding associations, we design an MPC protocol for Multifactor Dimensionality Reduction (MDR).

Our private MDR protocol is based on two novel, efficient building blocks, *arithmetic greater than* and *arithmetic swap*, which may be of independent interest. This approach omits the need for expensive conversions between sharing types in private MDR and reduces the communication by two orders of magnitude compared to a naïve design using garbled circuits. Our private MDR protocol runs in (extrapolated) three days on a practical database with 10,000 features for all two mutually combined features, i.e., considering about 50 million combinations.

Keywords: Epistasis · Genomic privacy · MPC

O. Tkachenko—The work presented in this paper was mainly done while the author was a doctoral researcher at Technical University of Darmstadt
T. Kussel and O. Tkachenko—Equally contributed.

© The Author(s), under exclusive license to Springer Nature Switzerland AG 2022
V. Atluri et al. (Eds.): ESORICS 2022, LNCS 13556, pp. 320–339, 2022.
https://doi.org/10.1007/978-3-031-17143-7_16

1   Introduction

Technical advances and reduced costs in genome sequencing technology will allow full genome sequencing to become a standard medical procedure in the near future. This plethora of genomic data opens up interesting possibilities not only in personalized treatment of diseases, but in a research context as well. Genome Wide Association Studies (GWAS) allow to statistically link a small number of genetic variants (e.g., Single Nucleotide Poymorphisms (SNPs)) to a phenotypical trait, which in medical research is often the manifestation of a disease like diabetes, hypertension, or cancer.

Due to the sensitive nature of genomic data, which is the ultimate personal identifier [18], and the vast amount of required data, the need for privacy preserving analysis methods arises. Non-genomic medical patient data is often analyzed in anonymized or pseudonymized form. Unfortunately, these traditional and other approaches like statistical disclosure control [13] are difficult to apply correctly and in most cases unsuitable for genomic data. More evolved statistical disclosure methods, like differential privacy, suffer from some loss of utility when applied to genomic data due to the inherent interactivity in, e.g., tumor boards.

Secure Multi-Party Computation (MPC) is a class of privacy-preserving techniques that guarantees the privacy of inputs and allows the exact computation of arbitrary functionalities. MPC has successfully been applied to many different real-world problems. However, this strong privacy guarantee and flexibility comes with quite severe limitations. The required computation and communication is multiple orders of magnitude higher than in the clear text analysis. This renders this class infeasible in practice for many applications.

Following the success in applying MPC protocols to genomic analysis methods like GWAS or similar genome queries, we propose, implement, and evaluate PEA, a suite of MPC protocols that privately analyze the epistasis of SNPs in connection to the manifestation of a disease. PEA analyzes how the interaction of multiple SNPs are causally linked to the disease. This is a critical step for the development of a better understanding of a disease and new treatments. To find these higher order interactions we privately apply Multifactor-Dimensionality Reduction (MDR), Relief-F, and Tuned Relief-F Feature Selection (TuRF).

Although gene-gene and gene-environment interactions are still an actively researched area, most novel research uses established analysis methods like MDR for specific diseases [30, 43, 46] and statistical tests [29] , or adapts those methods for novel challenges, like the amount of SNPs in GWAS data sets [22]. No prior provided privacy-preserving analysis of partitioned data sets.

1.1   Related Work

Recently, a few Differential Privacy (DP) [14]-based works have been published on Private Epistasis Analysis (PEA) [7] and Private Feature Selection (PFS) [28]. However, DP relies on a trade-off between privacy and utility and cannot achieve both. Since the genomic data is exceptionally privacy-sensitive, this leads to a significant utility degradation which is a well-known problem [32].

To the best of our knowledge, we provide the first solution for PEA or PFS without utility degradation. Previous works on private Genome-Wide Association Studies (GWAS) [8,40] serve a similar purpose as PEA but can find only correlations between single SNPs and a trait and have much smaller complexity.

1.2 Our Contributions

Our interdisciplinary work, beyond providing new research opportunities for biomedical research, makes the following contributions.

- Design and implementation of PEA, the first secure protocol that does not degrade accuracy for:
  - Relief-F [27] and TuRF [31], two popular algorithms for filtering features in Epistasis Analyses (EAs) that run in less than a day for practical database sizes containing a=10,000 SNPs and L=100 records [7].
  - MDR [36], a popular exponential-time algorithm for EA with (extrapolated) runtimes of around three days for practical database sizes containing a=10,000 SNPs [7]. The communication of our PMDR protocol is independent of the number of records.
- New efficient, generic arithmetic building blocks:
  - A 1-out-of-N Oblivious Transfer (OT) [24]-based custom protocol for Arithmetic Greater Than (AGT), i.e., a GT gate that is computed on arithmetic shares with 1.5× less communication than the state of the art [35] but 6 instead of 5 rounds of communication.
  - Arithmetic Swap (ASWAP), a generalization of the Boolean swap gates by Kolesnikov and Schneider [26] for the arithmetic case with 4× less communication than the naïve design.
  - Batched versions of both aforementioned building blocks with $O(\kappa)$ less communication, where κ is the symmetric security parameter.
- The first implementation of three-halves garbling [37][1] and its performance analysis, which shows a greater slowdown than expected due to a higher degree of branching compared to the prior best garbling scheme. Still, it optimizes for better network bandwidth which remains the bottleneck.
- The implementation of all our building blocks and protocols are integrated in the open-source repository of the MOTION framework for MPC[2].

2 Preliminaries

In this section, we describe the required basics in genomics. App. A gives an overview of Secure Multi-Party Computation (MPC) techniques used in this paper. For more details, we refer the reader to [11].

---

[1] https://encrypto.de/code/3H-GC.
[2] https://encrypto.de/code/MOTION.

2.1 Genomic Primer

The building and functioning "instructions" of all living cells are encoded in molecular form. This molecular blueprint takes in most organisms the form of the *deoxyribonucleic acid* (DNA), a double helical molecule pairing a sequence of *nucleotides*. The DNA's alphabet consists of four nucleotides (usually abbreviated by their first letter): **A**denine, **C**ytosine, **G**uanine, and **T**hymine. In double-stranded DNA (as in humans) a helix and much more involved structures (chromatin, chromosomes, etc.) are formed by physical interactions between the nucleotides of the two strands. Typically, Watson-Crick-pairing is observed, where cytosine pairs with guanine and adenine pairs with thymine forming a base pair with highest priority. This implies that the information on one strand is encoded in a 1:1 fashion on the other.

In the process of *transcription*, the defined nucleotide sequence of the DNA (viz. the *genotype*) is transcribed to a *messenger ribonucleic acid* (mRNA) molecule, which can be thought of as a working copy of a specific gene. These mRNA molecules are then *translated* to an *amino acid* sequence forming proteins necessary for the function of the cell and organism. During this translation every *codon*, that is a triplet of nucleotides, is mapped to one of the 20 standard amino acids observed in nature. Additionally there are codons coding start and stop symbols.

Some of the built proteins inhibit or promote the transcription of DNA regions encoding other proteins. These proteins are called *transcription factors* and thus are responsible for often times complex regulatory networks in which the *interaction of multiple genes* are responsible[3] for some *phenotype*, that is some observable trait (e.g., eye and hair color, or the occurrence of a disease).

The human genome consists of roughly 3.2 billion base pairs, but only 0.1 % of base pairs vary between two individuals [2]. These variants of a specific *locus*, i.e., position on the DNA strand, are called *alleles*. Due to the sparsity of the variations between two humans, it is often useful to store and use only these variations with regard to a specific reference genome. A *Singe-Nucleotide Polymorphism* (SNP) is a variation changing exactly one nucleotide, e.g., G → T. Due to the human's *diploidy*, two alleles are possible of each individual locus. For each gene (or in case of SNPs for each base) the present allele may be written in the shorthand form "AA" for the presence of the major allele on both chromosomes, "Aa" for the presence of both the major and minor allele on one of the chromosomes each and finally "aa" for the presence of the minor allele on both chromosomes.

2.2 Genome-Wide Association Studies (GWAS) and Epistasis

Genome-Wide Association Studies (GWAS) aim to link specific genotype variations to phenotype variations. More specifically often times the goal is to link SNPs to traits like the onset of specific diseases. In the first published GWAS in 2002 [34] five SNPs could be linked to various mechanisms to increase the risk of

---

[3] Further regulatory mechanisms, such as the influences of the chromatin structure, exist but are not of interest for this work.

myocardial infarction. In contrast to *candidate-driven* analysis, where variations of specific, pre-determined genes are analysed, GWAS analyse variations of the complete genome.

Using a labeled data set with regard to the phenotypical trait, statistical tests are performed to determine the specific SNP's likelihood to affect the trait. This likelihood is called *penetrance* and extends, as described below, to multi-dimensional cases. Many different statistical tests are used in practice, ranging from relatively simple *odds ratio* analysis to more involved hypothesis tests, like χ^2-*tests* [41]. In addition to the single SNP's influence, GWAS can give a starting point for finding the variation mechanism by associating the loci to known regulatory pathways [33]. As briefly described in §2.1, genes can be part of complex regulatory networks promoting or inhibiting other genes. Due to that it is unsurprising, that complex systematic diseases like cancer are not directly associated to a single gene, but are caused by possibly non-linear interactions of many genetic variables, e.g., simultaneously the presence of one SNP and the absence of two other. This interaction of genes is called *epistasis*, or *gene-gene interaction*. Unfortunately, the analysis of those interactions becomes computationally very expensive. The algorithmic complexity scales exponentially with the "interaction depth", i.e., the number of interacting genes considered.

Consequently, exact analysis methods, analysing each tuple of SNPs, are only feasible for small sections of a genome or low interaction depths. For large genome sections, or even whole genome analysis, different methods of reducing the complexity are applied. In this work we apply *(Tuned) Relief-F Feature Selection* (TuRF, cf. Sect. 2.3) and *Multifactor-Dimensionality Reduction* (MDR, cf. Sect. 2.4) to achieve privacy-preserving epistasis analysis with practical performance.

2.3   Feature Selection with Relief, Relief-F and TuRF

Typical gene-gene interaction studies analyze datasets with thousands of patients but hundreds of thousands to millions of SNPs. Most of these features play no role in the expression of the phenotype of interest. The "Relief" [23] algorithm and its advancements "Relief-F" [27] (the hyphen is often omitted in literature but is present in the original work) and "Tuned ReliefF" [31] (TuRF) are feature selection algorithms to reduce the number of features by estimating the importance of a feature with respect to the training goal.

The Relief filter works by weighting the importance of a variable by comparing a randomly chosen sample (patient) with the neighboring samples. Features that are present in a neighboring sample with the same label gain weight, features present in a neighboring sample with a different label lose weight. This procedure is repeated m times. Relief-F extends this algorithm by not only sampling the nearest neighbor in both categories, but the k nearest neighbors. In the original work [27], as in our work, the number of neighbors taken into account for the weight update is $k = 10$. Furthermore, Relief-F iterates over all n entries in the dataset, instead of a randomly chosen subset of size m, i.e., $m = n$. This increases the robustness of the result against noisy features.

```
1 Input: Attributes A = A₁,...,Aₐ,
2 Records R = r¹,...,rⁿ
3 Wᵢ ← 0, ∀i
4 for i = 1...m do
      // randomly select record
5     rⁱ ←$ [r¹,rⁿ]
6     H, M ← kNN(rⁱ, k)
7     for j = 1...k do
8         for l = 1...a do
9             Wₗ ← Wₗ − Δ(Aₗ,rⁱ,Hⱼ)/m +
                   Δ(Aₗ,rⁱ,Mⱼ)/m
10 return W
```

$$
\begin{aligned}
&\textbf{1 Input: Attributes } A = A_1,\ldots,A_a, \\
&\textbf{2 Records } R = r^1,\ldots,r^n \\
&\textbf{3 for } i = 1\ldots m \textbf{ do} \\
&\textbf{4} \quad W \leftarrow \texttt{ReliefF}(A,R) \\
&\textbf{5} \quad W \leftarrow \texttt{sort}(W) \\
&\quad\quad \text{// remove last } \alpha/n \text{ attributes} \\
&\textbf{6} \quad W \leftarrow W[0:a-(\alpha/n)] \\
&\textbf{7} \quad A \leftarrow A[0:a-(\alpha/n)] \\
&\textbf{8 return } W
\end{aligned}
$$

(a) Relief-F   (b) TuRF

Alg. 1: The feature selection algorithms. The original Relief algorithm only uses the nearest hit/miss, not the k nearest hits/misses. $\leftarrow$$ indicates random sampling from a uniform distribution, m is the number or records used for feature selection, and a denotes the number of attributes. The used difference-function Δ measures *differences*. Because of that, misses are added and hits subtracted. Using TuRF, in every iteration the last (worst performing) α/n elements are removed from the respective arrays.

TuRF modifies the Relief-F filter by removing a constant fraction of the worst performing attributes after every iteration. This effectively removes the noisiest and least significant features, speeding up the computation in the subsequent calculations and increasing robustness against noisy attributes.

The formal details of the Relief-F algorithm are given in Algorithm 1a. The used distance metric takes two patient records r^1, r^2 and an attribute A (in this work a locus λ) as an input and returns zero if both records have the same occurrence of the attribute, otherwise it returns one. The TuRF algorithm is given in Algorithm 1b. Details of our private implementation of TuRF are given in Sect. 3.

2.4 Multifactor Dimensionality Reduction (MDR) for Epistasis Analysis

Multifactor Dimensionality Reduction (MDR) [36] is a model-free and non-parametric statistical method to detect and model epistasis. Developed in the early 2000s,s, it became one standard approach to model epistasis with successful identification of interactions in datasets including sporadic breast cancer, essential hypertension [30], and type 2 diabetes [9].

In short the algorithm works by categorizing a group of loci into high and low risk combinations. This effectively reduces the dimension of the interactions to one. This new one-dimensional data is then compared among each other to find the interactions that yield the lowest classification and prediction error. Usually *Leave-one-out cross validation* is used. In that cross validation approach the dataset is divided in n equally large partitions and the model is generated on $n-1$ partitions. The remaining partition is used to calculate the prediction errors. This process is repeated for all n partitions and the prediction errors are averaged to form a "final" model error. A graphical visualization of the scheme is given in Fig. 1.

3 Private Tuned Relief-F Feature Selection

As described in Sect. 2.3, the main goal of the feature selection step is to increase the weight of features (SNPs) linked to label distinction and reduce the weight of features irrelevant to these distinctions. The TuRF algorithm uses k Nearest Neighbor clustering and iterative pruning of features to achieve this goal. To avoid a biased result incurred by the ordering of the records, our TuRF implementation permutes the order of the dataset randomly. In either case only the best $a - \alpha$ features are considered in the subsequent MDR calculation.

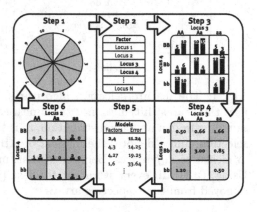

Fig. 1. High-level scheme of the MDR analysis method (adapted from [17] and [36]).

The formal description of the PReliefF protocol is given in Prot. 1. PTuRF can be seen as a straightforward extension of PReliefF, and the formal description is given in the full version of this paper. Note, that in combination with Private Multifactor Dimensionality Reduction (PMDR) (see Sect. 4), it is possible to (optionally) reveal the noisy features to reduce the input size to PMDR.

We implemented an (optional) approximation in the TuRF algorithm. Instead of recalculating the distance between the records in every iteration, the distance is considered constant, as only a small number of features are removed in every iteration. This approximation reduces the computational cost, while only incurring a small error.

Private kNN. The original Relief algorithm, as well as the improved Relief-F, require a comparison of the sampled record to the nearest neighbour or the k nearest neighbours, respectively (cf. Alg. 1a, line 6). We use adapted forms of the kNN clustering described by Järvinen et al. [20], which can be performed with a variety of metrics. Due to the comparatively low runtime cost and the nominal nature of the features, we perform a Hamming distance based clustering, i.e., based on the number of set bits (asimilar SNPs).

4 Private Multifactor Dimensionality Reduction

Private Multifactor Dimensionality Reduction (PMDR) requires aggregation of integers: data owners aggregate the counts of allele frequencies and the counts used in precision estimation of the computed models are also aggregated into one value. Thus, it is beneficial to keep those operations in arithmetic sharing which allows to perform integer addition locally. However, arithmetic sharing is restricted to only additions and multiplications, and conversions to and from Boolean sharing may be more expensive than the evaluation of a purely Boolean circuit. In the following, we design *novel* efficient building blocks that improve over the PMDR protocol that uses only Boolean sharing by *two* orders of magnitude.

```
1  Function PReliefF(R, φ):
2      The dataset R is the concatenation of each data owner's Pᵢ raw dataset Rᵢ. The dataset
        consists of all records R := (r¹,...,rᵏ), where the record rʲ := ((gʲ,¹,...,gʲ,ᵐ), αʲ) : rʲ ∈ R
        with each genotype gʲ,λ ∈ {1,2,3} of person j at locus λ and each group α ∈ {+,−},
        denotes the case and control group, respectively. The function returns the index positions of
        the most weighted genotypes. φ = 1 − α/a denotes the ratio of attributes to return.
3      for j = 1...k do // For all records in the Dataset
           // Initialize distance and difference matrices to the numerical maximum
           // value and zero, respectively
4          ⟨m_dist^hit⟩^Y ← [⟨MAX_VALUE⟩^Y,...,⟨MAX_VALUE⟩^Y]
5          ⟨m_ineq^hit⟩^Y ← [[⟨0⟩^Y,...,⟨0⟩^Y],...,[⟨0⟩^Y,...,⟨0⟩^Y]]
6          ⟨m_dist^miss⟩^Y ← [⟨MAX_VALUE⟩^Y,...,⟨MAX_VALUE⟩^Y]
7          ⟨m_ineq^miss⟩^Y ← [[⟨0⟩^Y,...,⟨0⟩^Y],...,[⟨0⟩^Y,...,⟨0⟩^Y]]
8          for i > j do // For all pairs of records
9              ⟨D_ji⟩^Y ← ∅
10             for λ = 1...m do // For all genotypes
11                 ⟨D_ji⟩^Y.append(Δ(⟨gʲ,λ⟩^Y, ⟨gⁱ,λ⟩^Y))
12         for ∀i ≠ j do // For all (unordered) pairs
13             if j < i then
14                 ⟨d⟩^Y ← HW(⟨D_ji⟩^Y)
15             else
16                 ⟨d⟩^Y ← HW(⟨D_ij⟩^Y)
17             if ⟨αʲ⟩^Y == ⟨αⁱ⟩^Y then // If records have same label
18                 ⟨m_dist^hit⟩^Y, ⟨m_ineq^hit⟩^Y ← kNN(⟨m_dist^hit⟩^Y, ⟨m_ineq^hit⟩^Y, ⟨d⟩^Y, k)
19             else
20                 ysm_dist^miss, ⟨m_ineq^miss⟩^Y ← kNN(⟨m_dist^miss⟩^Y, ⟨m_ineq^miss⟩^Y, ⟨d⟩^Y, k)
21         ⟨W⟩^Y ← ⟨W⟩^Y + ⟨m_ineq^miss⟩^Y − ⟨m_ineq^hit⟩^Y
22     for ∀j do
           // The features are sorted by weight and only the first (best)
           // φ·a are retained
23         ⟨g'ʲ⟩^Y ← kNN(⟨gʲ⟩^Y, ⟨W⟩^Y, φ·a)
24         ⟨r'ʲ⟩^Y ← (⟨g'ʲ⟩^Y[1 : φ·a]), ⟨αʲ⟩^Y)
25     ⟨R'⟩^Y := {⟨r'¹⟩^Y,...,⟨r'ᵏ⟩^Y}
26     return ⟨R'⟩^Y
```

Prot. 1: Private Relief-F protocol. PReliefF takes a dataset R and a ratio φ as input and returns the most weighted attributes. The referenced k-Nearest Neighbors function kNN is slightly adapted from [20].

4.1 Secure Arithmetic Greater Than (AGT)

A Boolean Greater Than (GT) gate requires ℓ AND gates if optimized for AND size [25] and $3\ell - \lceil \log_2 \ell \rceil - 2$ if optimized for AND depth [39]. Moreover, the latter still has $\lceil \log_2 \ell \rceil + 1$ AND depth and incurs the corresponding number of communication rounds.

Baseline Arithmetic Greater Than Protocol. Here, we give a baseline Arithmetic Greater Than (AGT) protocol that compares two integers $x_0, x_1 \in \mathbb{Z}_{2^\ell} : x_0, x_1 < 2^{\ell_{in}}$ in arithmetic sharing, where $\ell_{in} = \ell - 1$. The protocol is as follows: (1) compute $\langle\delta\rangle^A \leftarrow \langle x_0\rangle^A - \langle x_1\rangle^A$, (2) decompose it to single bits as $\langle\delta\rangle^B \leftarrow \text{A2B}(\langle\delta\rangle^A)$ (cf. [11]), and (3) return the MSB of $\langle\delta\rangle^B$. It requires only sharing of 2ℓ bits—ℓ bits by the garbler and ℓ bits by the evaluator—and $\ell - 1$ AND gates in Yao sharing. It outputs a bit in Boolean sharing. Later in this section we show a protocol with even better communication and use this protocol as a baseline for comparison.

Our baseline protocol requires only one communication round and its only limitation is that the input values need to be smaller than $2^{\ell_{in}}$, where $\ell_{in} = \ell - 1$. It requires $\ell(4.5\kappa + 5) - 1.5\kappa - 5$ bits of communication in total: $3\ell\kappa$ for re-sharing both arithmetic shares in Yao sharing and $(\ell - 1) \cdot (1.5\kappa + 5)$ for computing the sum of both shares in a GC using three-halves garbling [37].

Our Novel AGT Construction with Low Communication. Here, we introduce a novel, alternative approach to compute the AGT gate with significantly lower communication inspired by [12] and [35]. The idea of our protocol is based on the fact that, in contrast to share reconstruction using an addition circuit, we only need to compute the MSB, but not the full addition circuit. To compute the MSB we need $\langle\delta\rangle_0[\ell]$, $\langle\delta\rangle_1[\ell]$ and the carry bit $\langle c\rangle[\ell]$, where the latter is computed from the previous bits in the shares. However, we can skip the computation of the intermediate carry bits and directly compute the MSB by utilizing 1-out-of-N OT [24] with less communication than using our baseline protocol shown above. A batch-mode extension is described in the full version of this paper.

Toy Example. Let ℓ be small, e.g., $\ell=4$, and $\langle\delta\rangle_0^A, \langle\delta\rangle_1^A \in \mathbb{Z}_{2^\ell}$ are arithmetic shares of $\delta = x_1 - x_0 : x_0, x_1 < 2^{\ell-1}$. P_0 uses $\langle\delta\rangle_0^A$ as its choice index in OT [24]. P_1 samples a uniformly random mask bit $r \leftarrow_\$ \{0,1\}$ and generates messages $\{(i + \langle\delta\rangle_1 \mod 2^\ell > 2^{\ell-1} - 1) \oplus r\}_{i=0}^{2^\ell - 1}$. Then, P_0 obtains and sets $\langle\text{MSB}\rangle_0^B := ((\langle\delta\rangle_0^A + \langle\delta\rangle_1^A \mod 2^\ell > 2^{\ell-1} - 1) \oplus r$, and P_1 sets $\langle\text{MSB}\rangle_1^B := r$. The communication complexity of this protocol is $2\kappa + 2^\ell$ bits, which equals 264 bits for bit length $\ell=3$ and is 5.8× more efficient than the baseline protocol. The problem that arises here is that this toy protocol is not practical for large integers, e.g., the communication for $\ell=31$ is 4.29 GB, which is orders of magnitude worse than our baseline.

Our Novel AGT for Integers of any Bit-Length. To reduce the communication for integers of arbitrary bit-length, we design an iterative approach that splits an integer into chunks and, in a nutshell, computes the carry bit for each of the intermediate chunks and extracts the MSB from the last chunk.

The best amortized per-bit communication in 1-out-of-N OT [24] is achieved with $N=2^6$ and equals $(2\kappa + 2^6)/6 = 53.3$ bits. Although $N=2^7$ requires 54.8 bits (amortized), it incurs less communication rounds in our AGT protocol. Our protocol consists of two subprotocols: (1) OT on the first chunk and (2) OT on the intermediate chunks and carry bits. We XOR the last computed carry bit in Boolean sharing with the MSBs of the shares of δ, which yields the shared comparison result.

---

1 **Function** PMDR(R_i):

2   Each data owner P_i locally randomly permutes its raw dataset $\boldsymbol{R}_i := (r_i^1, \ldots, r_i^{k_i})$, where the record $r_i^j := ((g_i^{j,1}, \ldots, g_i^{j,a_i}), \alpha_i^j) : r_i^j \in \boldsymbol{R}_i$ with each genotype $g^{j,\lambda} \in \{1,2,3\}$ of person j at locus λ and each group $\alpha \in \{+,-\}$, denotes the case and control group, respectively, and splits it into s equal parts $\boldsymbol{R}_i^1, \ldots, \boldsymbol{R}_i^s$.

3   **for** $j = 1 \ldots s$ **do** // For each of s cross-validation steps

4   **for** $i = 1 \ldots N$ **do** // Each party splits its dataset for cross-validation.

5             $\boldsymbol{R}_i^{\text{val}} := \{r_i^j\}_{j=|\boldsymbol{R}_i| \cdot j/s}^{|\boldsymbol{R}_i| \cdot (j+1)/s}$

6             $\boldsymbol{R}_i^{\text{test}} := \boldsymbol{R}_i \setminus \boldsymbol{R}_i^{\text{val}}$

7   **for** $\lambda_1 \in [a]$ **do** // For each pair of loci λ_1 and λ_2

8   **for** $\lambda_2 \in [a] \setminus \{\lambda_1\}$ **do**

                // Each party locally counts the observed genotypes
                // for test (T) and validation (V) sets.

9   **for** $i = 1 \ldots N$ **do**

10                     $(T_i^{\lambda_1,\lambda_2,+}, T_i^{\lambda_1,\lambda_2,-}, V_i^{\lambda_1,\lambda_2,+}, V_i^{\lambda_1,\lambda_2,-}) \leftarrow \text{Count}(\boldsymbol{R}_i^{\text{test}}, \boldsymbol{R}_i^{\text{val}}, \lambda_1, \lambda_2)$

                // All parties share and aggregate their counts using Arithmetic
                // sharing. Remark: Sharing is done locally using a PRG.

11                 $\langle \boldsymbol{X}^{\lambda_1,\lambda_2,g} \rangle^A \leftarrow \sum_{i=1}^N \langle \boldsymbol{X}_i^{\lambda_1,\lambda_2,g} \rangle^A$ for $X \in \{T,V\}$ and $g \in \{+,-\}$

                // Compute the high risk prediction model as Boolean matrix $\boldsymbol{H}^{\lambda_1,\lambda_2}$.
                // If #cases/#controls is greater than a public threshold $t_h = t_h^+/t_h^-$,
                // the cell that corresponds to the genotype combination (i,j) is
                // marked as high risk, indicated with $\langle 1 \rangle^B$.

12   **for** $i,j \in \{1,2,3\}$ **do** // For each combination of genotypes

                    // This is equivalent to computing $(T^{\lambda_1,\lambda_2,+}[i,j]/T^{\lambda_1,\lambda_2,-}[i,j]) > t_h$.

13                     $\langle num\_cases \rangle^A \leftarrow t_h^+ \cdot \langle T^{\lambda_1,\lambda_2,+}[i,j] \rangle^A$

14                     $\langle num\_controls \rangle^A \leftarrow t_h^- \cdot \langle T^{\lambda_1,\lambda_2,-}[i,j] \rangle^A$

                    // Mark this cell as high risk if #cases/#controls > t_h.

15                     $\langle \boldsymbol{H}^{\lambda_1,\lambda_2}[i,j] \rangle^B \leftarrow \text{AGT}(\langle num\_cases \rangle^A, \langle num\_controls \rangle^A)$

                    // Swap validation counts if the current cell is high risk.

16                   $\text{ASWAP}(\langle \boldsymbol{H}^{\lambda_1,\lambda_2}[i,j] \rangle^B, \langle \boldsymbol{V}^{\lambda_1,\lambda_2,+}[i,j] \rangle^A, \langle \boldsymbol{V}^{\lambda_1,\lambda_2,-}[i,j] \rangle^A)$

                // Compute number of correcly and incorrectly classified samples.

17                  $\langle num\_correct \rangle^A \leftarrow \sum_{i,j} \langle \boldsymbol{V}^{\lambda_1,\lambda_2,-}[i,j] \rangle^A$ for $i,j \in \{1,2,3\}$

18                  $\langle num\_wrong \rangle^A \leftarrow \sum_{i,j} \langle \boldsymbol{V}^{\lambda_1,\lambda_2,+}[i,j] \rangle^A$ for $i,j \in \{1,2,3\}$

                // Store a bit indicating good/bad accuracy given a public accuracy
                // threshold $t_a = t_a^+/t_a^-$.

19                 $A^j[\lambda_1,\lambda_2] \leftarrow \text{AGT}(t_a^+ \cdot \langle num\_correct \rangle^A, t_a^- \cdot \langle num\_wrong \rangle^A)$

20   **for** $\lambda_1 \in [a]$ **do** // For each pair of loci λ_1 and λ_2

21   **for** $\lambda_2 \in [a] \setminus \{\lambda_1\}$ **do**

            // Output 1 if at least one of the cross validation steps λ_1 and λ_2
            // were marked as high risk.

22             $O[\lambda_1,\lambda_2] = \bigvee_{j=1}^s A^j[\lambda_1,\lambda_2]$

23   **return** O

Prot. 2: Arithmetic Private Multifactor Dimensionality Reduction (PMDR^{A+}) protocol for *two* loci (for simplicity). Notation: N denotes #parties, a denotes #loci. PMDR outputs all loci combinations with MDR models that have accuracy greater than a threshold t_a. The functionality Count counts genotypes belonging to cases and controls for the test and validation set.

The first subprotocol requires $(2\kappa + 2^{\ell_s})$ bits. The second subprotocol requires $\gamma(2\kappa + 2^{\ell_s}) + 2\kappa + 2^{\epsilon}$ bits, where $\gamma = \lceil (\ell - \ell_s)/(\ell_s - 1) \rceil - 1$ is the number of the intermediate chunks and $\epsilon = \ell - \ell_s - 1 \bmod (\ell_s - 1)$ corresponds to the size of the remainder. For $\ell \geq \ell_s$ the total communication is equal to $(\gamma + 1)(2\kappa + 2^{\ell_s}) + \lceil \epsilon/(\ell_s - 1) \rceil (2\kappa + 2^{\epsilon})$ bits and the number of communication rounds is $\gamma + \lceil \epsilon/(\ell_s - 1) \rceil + 2$ due to sequential calls to the OT functionality. More concretely, for $\ell_s = 7$ and $N = 2^{\ell_s}$ this translates to 384 bits and 2 rounds for $\ell_{in} = 7$, 1,028 bits and 4 rounds for $\ell_{in} = 15$, 1,920 bits and 6 rounds for $\ell_{in} = 31$, and 4,100 bits and 12 rounds for $\ell_{in} = 63$. Note that ℓ_{in} denotes the maximum bit-length of the integers, shared in $\mathbb{Z}_{2^{\ell+1}}$.

```
1  Function AGT(⟨x₀⟩ᴬ, ⟨x₁⟩ᴬ, ℓₛ):
2     // ⟨x₀⟩ᴬ, ⟨x₁⟩ᴬ are secret-shared
      // in Z_{2ℓ} with x₀, x₁ < 2^{ℓ-1}
3     ⟨δ⟩ᴬ = ⟨x₁⟩ᴬ - ⟨x₀⟩ᴬ
4     sel ← ⟨δ⟩₀ᴬ[1 : ℓₛ]
5     M ← (j + ⟨δ⟩₁ᴬ[1 : ℓₛ] > 2^{ℓₛ})_{j=1}^{2^{ℓₛ}}
6     r ←$ {0,1}
7     c ← (ᴺ₁)-OT(sel, {m ⊕ r}_{m∈M})
      // Counter for the previous chunk
8     ℓ_prev ← ℓₛ + 1
9     while ℓ_prev < ℓ do
10       ℓₛ' ← min(ℓₛ - 1, ℓ - ℓ_prev)
11       ℓ_next ← ℓ_prev + ℓₛ' - 1
12       sel ← ⟨δ⟩₀ᴬ[ℓ_prev : ℓ_next]
13       sel ← sel + c · 2^{ℓₛ'}
14       ⟨δ'⟩₁ᴬ ← ⟨δ⟩₁ᴬ[ℓ_prev : ℓ_next]
15       M₀ ← {j + ⟨δ'⟩₁ᴬ > 2^{ℓₛ'}}_{j=1}^{2^{ℓₛ'}}
16       M₁ ← {j + ⟨δ'⟩₁ᴬ + 1 > 2^{ℓₛ'}}_{j=1}^{2^{ℓₛ'}}
17       M ← M_r ∪ M_{1-r}
18       r ←$ {0,1}
19       c ← (ᴺ₁)-OT(sel, {m ⊕ r}_{m∈M})
20       ℓ_prev ← ℓ_next + 1
21    ⟨b⟩ᴮ = (⟨b⟩₀ᴮ, ⟨b⟩₁ᴮ) :=
         (c ⊕ ⟨δ⟩₀ᴬ[ℓ], r ⊕ ⟨δ⟩₁ᴬ[ℓ])
22    return ⟨b⟩ᴮ
```

Prot. 3: Our optimized Arithmetic Greater Than (AGT) protocol. The substring bit-length is denoted by ℓ_s.

To the best of our knowledge, the only secure comparison protocol of additively secret-shared integers was recently introduced by Rathee et al. [35, Algorithm 1] and showed to be more efficient than the comparison protocols of XOR-shared integers [10]. The difference to our protocol is that their protocol securely compares two cleartext integers, x and y, and produces a secret-shared result. Inspired by their construction, we extend their protocol for comparing $\langle x \rangle^A > \langle y \rangle^A$ by restricting $x, y < 2^{\ell_{in}}$ and computing the comparison as $\langle x \rangle^A - \langle y \rangle^A < 2^{\ell_{in}}$, thus "sacrificing" one bit for the comparison result. Since the subtraction can be done locally, our protocol can be seen as MSB extraction from a secret-shared integer, which corresponds to [35, Algorithm 2] which is, in turn, based on [35, Algorithm 1].

We provide a more communication-efficient construction compared to [35, Algorithm 2] that requires only $\binom{N}{1}$-OT invocations and no computation of AND gates. For $\ell_{in} = 32$-bit inputs, our protocol for MSB extraction requires $1.5\times$ less communication (our 1,920 bits vs. their 2,914 bits), but one more communication round (our 6 rounds vs. their 5 rounds). The MSB extraction from $\ell = 32$-bit integers can be used to realize comparison of $\ell_{in} = 31$-bit integers.

Security. Informally, our AGT protocol only makes multiple consecutive calls to the $\binom{N}{1}$-OT functionality in a black-box way, and it produces uniformly distributed outputs in each step. Concretely, the first call to the $\binom{N}{1}$-OT functionality takes in the first ℓ_s bits of $\langle \delta \rangle^A$ and produces a secret share $(c, r) \in \{0, 1\}^2$, where $c := (\langle \delta \rangle_0^A[1 : \ell_s] + \langle \delta \rangle_1^A[1 : \ell_s] \geq 2^{\ell_s}) \oplus r$ and r is a random bit generated and known only by the OT sender. Since r is uniformly distributed and c is "masked" by r, the output is uniformly distributed and thus (c, r) is a secret share. The further calls to $\binom{N}{1}$-OT are invoked on the remaining substrings of $\langle\delta\rangle^A$. Namely, P_0 and P_1 call $\binom{N}{1}$-OT, which produces a new (c, r) pair, where

$$c := (\langle\delta\rangle_0^A[\ell_{\text{prev}} : \ell_{\text{prev}}+\ell_s'-1]+\langle\delta\rangle_1^A[\ell_{\text{prev}} : \ell_{\text{prev}}+\ell_s'-1]+(c_{\text{prev}}\oplus r_{\text{prev}}) \geq 2^{\ell_s'})\oplus r,$$

where $(c_{\text{prev}}, r_{\text{prev}})$ are the results of the previous $\binom{N}{1}$-OT call (for better readability), and r is again a random bit generated and known only by the OT sender. As in the first step, the result is a secret share. The final result is computed locally on the available secret shares. It is easy to see that the result is also a secret share. A formal security proof for our AGT protocol can trivially be derived from the security proof of [35, Algorithm 2].

4.2 Secure Arithmetic Swap (ASWAP)

Another important building block in our PMDR protocol is Secure Arithmetic Swap (ASWAP), which obliviously swaps arithmetic inputs. More formally, ASWAP takes in a secret-shared bit $\langle b\rangle^B$ and a pair of additively shared integers $(\langle x_0\rangle^A, \langle x_1\rangle^A)$, and it outputs $(\langle x_0'\rangle^A, \langle x_1'\rangle^A) := (\langle x_b\rangle^A, \langle x_{1-b}\rangle^A)$.

A straightforward realization of ASWAP uses four multiplication gates for computing

$$i \in \{0, 1\} : \langle x_i'\rangle^A := (\neg\langle b\rangle^B \cdot \langle x_i\rangle^A + \langle b\rangle^B \cdot \langle x_{1-i}\rangle^A).$$

Note that the secure multiplication $\langle b\rangle^B \cdot \langle x\rangle^A$ can be realized using just two additively correlated OTs (cf. [1]) as described in [38]. This protocol requires $8(\kappa + \ell)$ bits of communication in total.

In the following, we design an ASWAP protocol that requires only *one* multiplication, and consequently $2(\kappa + \ell)$ bits of communication, and thus yields a factor 4 communication improvement compared to the naïve protocol. To construct our efficient protocol for ASWAP, we take inspiration from the *Boolean* swap protocol (called "X gate" in their work) by Kolesnikov and Schneider [26], which requires only one AND gate to perform an oblivious swap conditioned on $\langle b\rangle^B$ and can be seen as a special case of ASWAP for integers of bit length $\ell=1$. Unfortunately, their protocol is not trivially generalizable to ASWAP for integers in $\mathbb{Z}_\ell$ with $\ell > 1$ because it relies on XOR, which is not trivially realizable on arithmetic shares. Our ASWAP protocol is depicted in Prot. 4. As for AGT, the batch-mode extension of this building block is described in the full version of this paper.

Beyond being useful for PMDR, our ASWAP protocol is of independent interest, e.g., combined with our AGT protocols, we can efficiently sort arithmetic values, i.e., using sorting networks on arithmetic circuits. This may be very beneficial in scenarios where the inputs to the sorting network are aggregated, since the addition operation is local in arithmetic sharing but costs $\ell - 1$ AND gates in a Boolean circuit [39]. Also, this omits expensive conversions (cf. [11]) if the further circuit is arithmetic, e.g., for efficient multiplications in $\mathbb{Z}_{2^\ell}$.

Although our ASWAP protocol is admittedly not complex, it has, to the best of our knowledge, never been used in the literature. We believe that the reason is that it has only recently been shown how to compute $\langle b \rangle^B \cdot \langle x \rangle^A$ efficiently [38].

Security. Since both ASWAP and batch-ASWAP operate only on unmodified secret shares and use the well-known correlated OT technique [1] to produce the output secret shares in a black-box way, the security proof for both our primitives is trivial.

```
1 Function ASWAP(⟨b⟩^B, ⟨x_0⟩^A, ⟨x_1⟩^A):
2      ⟨δ⟩^A ← ⟨b⟩^B · (⟨x_1⟩^A − ⟨x_0⟩^A)
3      ⟨x_0⟩^A ← ⟨x_0⟩^A + ⟨δ⟩^A
4      ⟨x_1⟩^A ← ⟨x_1⟩^A − ⟨δ⟩^A
5      return (⟨x_0⟩^A, ⟨x_1⟩^A)
```

Prot. 4: Secure Arithmetic Swap (ASWAP) protocol. Note that addition and subtraction are free in arithmetic sharing.

4.3   Communication of PMDR

Here, we evaluate the communication improvement gained by using our optimizations for PMDR. Our bottom line is a one-to-one translation of the PMDR algorithm (see Fig. 1) to a Boolean circuit (PMDR^Y that is evaluated in Yao sharing completely, which is often a very efficient solution due to the constant number of communication rounds in Yao sharing.

Our optimization of the PMDR protocol using our novel, more efficient arithmetic building blocks is denoted as PMDR^{A+}, which keeps data in arithmetic sharing, thus avoiding the costly conversions between different representations, and performs only very few operations in Boolean sharing. For the concrete communication costs of the gates, we refer the reader to [39] and [11] for arithmetic and Boolean sharing, and to [37] for Yao sharing. In the following, we fix the bit length of the integers to $\ell=32$, which allows for up to 2^{31} genome samples in total with the standard threshold parameters. We, conventionally, always perform $s=10$ cross-validation steps.

PMDR^Y. For each combination of L loci and each of 3^L possible combination of alleles, this protocol requires (1) $N-1$ additions for aggregation of allele counts, (2) two multiplications and one comparison for determining the risk category, and (3) one swap operation [26] to set low and high risk counts in the validation set. Afterwards, to determine the accuracy of the model, the validation counts are summed up, which requires $2 \cdot 3^L - 1$ additions, two multiplications and one comparison. For the costs of these operations, see [39]. Finally, $s-1$ AND gates in Boolean sharing are used to compute a secret-shared bit that indicates whether the model was accurate in at least one cross-validation step. In total, for each combination of loci the protocols requires

$$2s(3^L(8\ell^2 + s - 1) - \ell(4\ell - 1)) - s + 1$$

AND gates. This corresponds to 1 394 891 AND gates or 34.34 MB of communication for $L=2$ loci, and 4 347 251 AND gates or 101.05 MB of communication for $L=3$ loci, using three-halves garbling with $1.5\kappa + 5$ bits per AND gate [37].

PMDR^{A+}. For each combination of L loci and each of 3^L possible combination of alleles, our PMDR^{A+} protocol requires one AGT and one ASWAP gate. Then, for each combination of L loci, another AGT gate is required. And, finally, $s - 1$ AND gates in Boolean sharing are needed to compute the secret-shared interaction indication. *All* other operations in this protocol are *non-interactive*.

The total communication translates to $s(3^L(\ell(4\kappa + 1) + 2(\kappa + \ell)) + \ell(4\kappa + 1)) + s - 1$ bits, which equals only $208.8\,\mathrm{kB}$ of communication for $L{=}2$ loci and $585.3\,\mathrm{kB}$ for $L{=}3$ loci. Compared to PMDR^Y, this yields an improvement by a factor of $164\times$ for $L{=}2$ and by a factor of $172\times$ for $L = 3$.

5 Implementation

We implement our protocols for Private Epistasis Analysis (PEA)[4] using the MOTION framework [6] for Secure Multi-Party Computation (MPC). The reason for choosing MOTION is its efficiency and flexibility. Due to the number of new building blocks that we constructed and/or implemented, e.g., the three-halves garbling [37] and our new AGT protocol (cf. Prot. 3), we required an MPC framework that admits changes in its internal infrastructure and protocols with only moderate implementation overhead. Another selection criterion was the efficiency of the framework. MOTION satisfies both requirements. We detail and analyze our implementation of three-halves garbling in Appendix B.

6 Evaluation

We evaluate PEA on two servers equipped with Intel Core i9-7960X processors and $128\,\mathrm{GB}$ of RAM. We average all our benchmarks over 10 runs.

We use synthetic data as the input in our benchmarks due to two reasons. (1) MPC is input-oblivious by its security definition and thus the performance of our protocols is input-independent. (2) Since our protocols are fully accurate, we can discern no useful insight by using real (and hard to get access to) privacy-sensitive datasets, and thus, we favor the ethically better decision to use the least privacy-intrusive data source, i.e., synthetic data.

Settings. We evaluate two settings for Private Epistasis Analysis (PEA):

WAN. Two medical institutions perform PEA directly, aggregating their own databases in MPC. Our benchmarking environment naturally resembles the scenario where the two medical institutions are located very close to each other. However, our PEA protocols are either constant-round or are highly parallelized, so the most important performance aspect is the network bandwidth. We expect the medical institutions to have a high-bandwidth Internet connection. In our benchmarking environment, we use a $10\,\mathrm{Gbit/s}$ bandwidth network connection but conservatively restrict the latency to $50\,\mathrm{ms}$ using the tc tool[5] to simulate the WAN setting.

---

[4] https://encrypto.de/code/EPISTASIS.
[5] https://man7.org/linux/man-pages/man8/tc.8.html.

LAN. Several medical institutions send their *secret shared* data to outsourcing servers [21] that aggregate the received data and compute PEA on the aggregated data and finally send back the *shared* result. The outsourcing servers cannot infer any information about the input and output data as well as the intermediate values, but they are assumed not to collude. Such servers may be two cloud computing providers located close to each other, e.g., near the same Internet exchange point, thus having a high-bandwidth, low-latency connection. Thus, in the LAN setting we do not put additional constraints on the network and use a network connection with 10 Gbit/s throughput and 0.2 ms latency.

6.1 Performance of PReliefF and PTuRF

The results of our performance benchmarks of the private feature selection algorithms are shown in Table 1.

During our evaluation, RAM utilization was the a bottleneck during feature selection. This is not surprising, as our implementation was not optimized for space efficiency, but runtime and communication efficiency. Because of RAM exhaustion, PTuRF could not be benchmarked across the full parameter space.

As expected, a linear growth pattern, after a steep initial increase, can be observed in the runtimes of PReliefF and PTuRF. Due to the constant number of interaction rounds in Yao's GC protocol, the additional latency in the WAN setting has no strong effect on the measured runtimes.

Although the number of features to consider is reduced in every iteration, PTuRF's higher sorting work load leads to worse performance compared to the simpler PReliefF algorithm. However, the pruning of noisy features is shown in [31] to increase the robustness of the results.

Due to its linear runtime–size complexity, it is practical to perform PReliefF on datasets with real-world sizes (e.g., ≈ 100 records with $\approx 10,000$ features [7]) in less than a day.

Table 1. Runtimes and communication for our private ReliefF (PReliefF^Y) and private TuRF (PTuRF^Y) protocols filtering $|R|$ records with 10 SPNs each.

			$\lvert R\rvert{=}4$	$\lvert R\rvert{=}8$	$\lvert R\rvert{=}20$	$\lvert R\rvert{=}40$	$\lvert R\rvert{=}60$	$\lvert R\rvert{=}80$	$\lvert R\rvert{=}100$
PReliefF^Y	Runtime	LAN	1,00 s	1.74 s	5.13 s	13.15 s	21.19 s	33.52 s	50.14 s
		WAN	1.98 s	2.30 s	7.99 s	15.04 s	23.68 s	36.21 s	52.29 s
	Comm		3.75 MB	9.63 MB	40.98 MB	138.93 MB	294.13 MB	506.45 MB	775.93 MB
PTuRF^Y	Runtime	LAN	1.09 s	2.13 s	13.65 s	83.37 s	—	—	—
		WAN	1.49 s	2.51 s	14.34 s	85.54 s	—	—	—
	Comm		4.11 MB	11.13 MB	107.15 MB	510.77 MB	—	—	—

6.2 Performance of PMDR

The performance of PEA's Private Multifactor Dimensionality Reduction (PMDR) is reported in Table 2. The exponential scaling in the number of interacting loci L is clearly visible, both in the runtime and the communication, which for $L = 3, N = 1,000$ reaches nearly 100 TB.

However, for smaller numbers of SNPs a or lower interaction depths, such as $a = 1,000, L = 2$ or $a=100, L = 3$, our PMDR implementation runs in less than an hour in both LAN and WAN.

The very low communication overhead for outsourcing leads to a practical solution for pooling and analyzing multiple institutions' genomic data.

6.3   Total Performance

Due to the exponential complexity of (P)MDR, combination with a preceding feature selection algorithm is a sensible practice. At the cost of leaking the number of filtered features, the reduced number of features significantly improves the efficiency and the result is more robust against noisy attributes. As described by Moore and White [31], it is hard to give a general estimate on feasible feature reduction, as the resulting accuracy is depending, among other factors, on

Table 2. Runtimes and communication for PEA's Arithmetic Private Multifactor Dimensionality Reduction (PMDR^{A+}) protocol with $s=10$ cross-validation steps using an interaction depth of L and a attributes.

	depth	$a = 10$	$a = = 100$	$a = 1,000$
LAN	$L = 2$	1.71 s	24.85 s	43.08 min
	$L = 3$	3.29 s	33.68 min	—
WAN	$L = 2$	10.88 s	42.71 s	1.04 h
	$L = 3$	10.01 s	47.71 min	—
Comm.	$L = 2$	9.39 MB	1.03 GB	104.29 GB
	$L = 3$	70.23 MB	94.64 GB	97.25 TB

the amount of noise, the size of the data set, and the heritability of the trait. However, they measure 80 % accuracy while using TuRF to remove 950 out of 1,000 features.

As the performance benchmarks in the previous section show, this composition of both algorithms achieves only a performance gain for large numbers of features or for interaction depths larger than $L = 2$. In those cases PMDR on itself becomes prohibitively long running and the reduction of the number of features by 10 % corresponds to a significant performance gain, e.g., 20 % improvement for $a = 10,000$ features (40 instead of 50 million considered combinations).

Acknowledgments. This project received funding from the European Research Council (ERC) under the European Union's Horizon2020 research innovation program (grant agreement No.850990 PSOTI), and the German Ministry of Education and Research through the project HiGHmed (funding #01ZZ1802G). It was co-funded by the Deutsche Forschungsgemeinschaft(DFG) within SFB1119 CROSSING/236615297 and GRK2050 Privacy & Trust/251805230, and by the German Federal Ministry of Education and Research and the Hessen State Ministry for Higher Education, Research and the Arts within ATHENE.

Appendix

A   Secure Multi-Party Computation

Secure Multi-Party Computation (MPC) are cryptographic protocols to compute a joint function over distributed, private data without the need of a trusted third party. In this work, we consider security against passive (a.k.a. semi-honest) adversaries, which strictly follow the protocol but try to learn more information.

Oblivious Transfer (OT). In OT [3] the sender inputs messages (m_0, m_1), and the receiver inputs a choice bit c. At the end of the protocol, the receiver obtains m_c but no information about m_{1-c}, and the sender does not obtain any information. OT can be instantiated very efficiently using mostly symmetric cryptography [19] and it admits optimizations for MPC [1]. OT can be generalized to N instead of two messages [24], where the receiver holds a choice index $c \in \mathbb{Z}_N$ and obtains m_c. Recently, a "silent" OT [4,42] was introduced with significantly less communication at the cost of higher computation. The current silent OT schemes beat the textbook OT extension [1,19] in terms of runtime in networks with limited bandwidth, which is less interesting in our scenario, where medical institutions performing large-scale MPC likely have a high-bandwidth connection.

Yao's Garbled Circuits (GCs). GCs were introduced in [44]. The state of the art [37] requires $1.5\kappa + 5$ bits per AND gate, where $\kappa = 128$ is the symmetric security parameter. GCs operate on Boolean circuits and work by garbling the truth tables: a random symmetric encryption key is generated for every possible value on every wire. The output wire-keys of a gate are doubly encrypted using the corresponding combination of input wire keys. Only the garbler, i.e., the party preparing the GC, can connect the entries in the GC to "cleartext" values. Then, the garbler sends the GC and its input keys to the evaluator. The evaluator obliviously obtains its input keys using OT. The GC is then evaluated. We denote a bit b "shared" in a GC as $\langle b \rangle^Y$ and call this Yao sharing.

Goldreich-Micali-Wigderson (GMW). Like GCs, the GMW protocol [16], named after its inventors Goldreich, Micali and Wigderson, operates on Boolean circuits. It achieves its privacy guarantees by splitting every input bit b in two XOR-shares and letting party P_i hold share $\langle b \rangle_i^B$. These shares are constructed as $\langle b \rangle_0^B \leftarrow_\$ \{0,1\}$ and $\langle b \rangle_1^B \leftarrow b \oplus \langle b \rangle_0^B$ and reconstructed by XOR-ing both shares. XOR gates can be evaluated locally by XOR-ing both local shares and AND gates are evaluated interactively [1]. We denote this version of GMW as Boolean sharing. The GMW protocol can be extended to arithmetic circuits with elements in $\mathbb{Z}_{2^\ell}$. We denote this extension as Arithmetic sharing. Similarly to Boolean GMW, the shares are generated as $\langle x \rangle_0^A \leftarrow_\$ \mathbb{Z}_n$ and $\langle x \rangle_0^A \leftarrow x - \langle x \rangle_1^A$. The addition can be performed locally and the multiplication requires interaction [15].

B   Three Halves Make a Whole Garbling Implementation

In order to provide the best possible estimation of our PEA protocols' efficiency, we implement in MOTION [6] "three-halves garbling" (3HG) [37]. To the best of our knowledge, this is the first implementation of 3HG. Our optimized 3HG engine can garble $11.2\,\mathrm{M/s}$ and evaluate $27.5\,\mathrm{M/s}$ AND gates. Compared to "two-halves garbling" (2HG) [45] in MOTION by Braun et al. [5], 3HG is $4.7\times$ slower in terms of garbling and $2.5\times$ slower in terms of evaluation. This is also a more significant slowdown of garbling than the factor of $2.1\times$ estimated in [37], based on the number of hash function calls. Our profiling indicates that the two main bottlenecks are the $1.5\times$ higher number of AES invocations and the significantly higher degree of branching in 3HG compared to 2HG. Considering the garbling rate, we can saturate the $10\,\mathrm{Gbit/s}$ network channel with 5 threads. Furthermore, our benchmark for evaluating 512 AES circuits in parallel in a GC shows a $2.2\times$ speedup compared to [5] (our $0.22\,\mathrm{s}$ vs. their $0.5\,\mathrm{s}$). However, this result should be taken with a grain of salt, since [5] introduced significant changes to MOTION, which may have affected the runtimes.

References

1. Asharov, G., Lindell, Y., Schneider, T., Zohner, M.: More efficient oblivious transfer extensions. JoC **30**, 805–858 (2017)
2. Barbujani, G., Colonna, V.: Human genome diversity: frequently asked questions. Trends Genet. **26**, 285–295 (2010)
3. Beaver, D.: Correlated pseudorandomness and the complexity of private computations. In: STOC (1996)
4. Boyle, E., et al.: Efficient two-round OT extension and silent non-interactive secure computation. In: CCS (2019)
5. Braun, L., Cammarota, R., Schneider, T.: A generic hybrid 2PC framework with application to private inference of unmodified neural networks. In: NeurIPS Workshop Privacy in Machine Learning (2021)
6. Braun, L., Demmler, D., Schneider, T., Tkachenko, O.: MOTION - a framework for mixed-protocol multi-party computation. TOPS **25**, 1–35 (2022)
7. Chen, Q., Zhang, X., Zhang, R.: Privacy-preserving decision tree for epistasis detection. Cybersecurity **2**(1), 1–12 (2019). https://doi.org/10.1186/s42400-019-0025-z
8. Cho, H., Wu, D.J., Berger, B.: Secure genome-wide association analysis using multiparty computation. Nat. Biotechnol. **36**, 547–551 (2018)
9. Cho, Y.M., et al.: Multifactor-dimensionality reduction shows a two-locus interaction associated with Type 2 diabetes mellitus. Diabetologia **47**(3), 549–554 (2004). https://doi.org/10.1007/s00125-003-1321-3
10. Couteau, G.: New protocols for secure equality test and comparison. In: CANS (2018)
11. Demmler, D., Schneider, T., Zohner, M.: ABY - a framework for efficient mixed-protocol secure two-party computation. In: NDSS (2015)
12. Dessouky, G., Koushanfar, F., Sadeghi, A.R., Schneider, T., Zeitouni, S., Zohner, M.: Pushing the communication barrier in secure computation using lookup tables. In: NDSS (2017)
13. Duncan, G.: Statistical Confidentiality: Principles and Practice. Springer, Heidelberg (2011). https://doi.org/10.1007/978-1-4419-7802-8
14. Dwork, C.: Differential privacy. In: ICALP (2006)
15. Gilboa, N.: Two party RSA key generation. In: Wiener, M. (ed.) CRYPTO 1999. LNCS, vol. 1666, pp. 116–129. Springer, Heidelberg (1999). https://doi.org/10.1007/3-540-48405-1_8

16. Goldreich, O., Micali, S., Wigderson, A.: How to play any mental game. In: STOC (1987)
17. Hahn, L.W., Ritchie, M.D., Moore, J.H.: Multifactor dimensionality reduction software for detecting gene-gene and gene-environment interactions. Bioinformatics **19**, 376–382 (2003)
18. Hamacher, K.: PETS genome privacy workshop (2014)
19. Ishai, Y., Kilian, J., Nissim, K., Petrank, E.: Extending oblivious transfers efficiently. In: Boneh, D. (ed.) CRYPTO 2003. LNCS, vol. 2729, pp. 145–161. Springer, Heidelberg (2003). https://doi.org/10.1007/978-3-540-45146-4_9
20. Jarvinen, K., Leppakoski, H., Lohan, E.S., Richter, P., Schneider, T., Tkachenko, O., Yang, Z.: PILOT: practical privacy-preserving Indoor Localization using OuTsourcing. In: EuroS&P (2019)
21. Kamara, S., Raykova, M.: Secure outsourced computation in a multi-tenant cloud. In: IBM Workshop on Cryptography and Security in Clouds (2011)
22. Kim, Y., Park, T.: Robust gene-gene interaction analysis in genome wide association studies. PloS One **10**, e0135016 (2015)
23. Kira, K., Rendell, L.A.: A practical approach to feature selection. In: Machine Learning (1992)
24. Kolesnikov, V., Kumaresan, R.: Improved OT extension for transferring short secrets. In: Canetti, R., Garay, J.A. (eds.) CRYPTO 2013. LNCS, vol. 8043, pp. 54–70. Springer, Heidelberg (2013). https://doi.org/10.1007/978-3-642-40084-1_4
25. Kolesnikov, V., Sadeghi, A.-R., Schneider, T.: Improved garbled circuit building blocks and applications to auctions and computing minima. In: Garay, J.A., Miyaji, A., Otsuka, A. (eds.) CANS 2009. LNCS, vol. 5888, pp. 1–20. Springer, Heidelberg (2009). https://doi.org/10.1007/978-3-642-10433-6_1
26. Kolesnikov, V., Schneider, T.: Improved garbled circuit: free XOR gates and applications. In: Aceto, L., Damgård, I., Goldberg, L.A., Halldórsson, M.M., Ingólfsdóttir, A., Walukiewicz, I. (eds.) ICALP 2008. LNCS, vol. 5126, pp. 486–498. Springer, Heidelberg (2008). https://doi.org/10.1007/978-3-540-70583-3_40
27. Kononenko, I.: Estimating attributes: analysis and extensions of RELIEF. In: ECML (1994)
28. Le, T.T., et al.: Differential privacy-based evaporative cooling feature selection and classification with Relief-F and random forests. Bioinformatics **33**, 2906–2913 (2017)
29. Lee, S., Son, D., Kim, Y., Yu, W., Park, T.: Unified Cox model based multifactor dimensionality reduction method for gene-gene interaction analysis of the survival phenotype. BioData Mining **11**, 1–13 (2018)
30. Meng, Y., Groth, S., Quinn, J.R., Bisognano, J., Wu, T.T.: An exploration of gene-gene interactions and their effects on hypertension. Int. J. Genom. (2017)
31. Moore, J.H., White, B.C.: Tuning ReliefF for genome-wide genetic analysis. In: Marchiori, E., Moore, J.H., Rajapakse, J.C. (eds.) EvoBIO 2007. LNCS, vol. 4447, pp. 166–175. Springer, Heidelberg (2007). https://doi.org/10.1007/978-3-540-71783-6_16
32. Naveed, M., et al.: Privacy in the genomic era. ACM Comput. Surv. **48**, 1–44 (2015)
33. Newton-Cheh, C., et al.: Genome-wide association study identifies eight loci associated with blood pressure. Nat. Genet. **41**, 666–676 (2009)
34. Ozaki, K., et al.: Functional SNPs in the lymphotoxinα-gene that are associated with susceptibility to myocardial infarction. Nat. Genet. **32**, 650–654 (2002)
35. Rathee, D., et al.: Cryptflow2: practical 2-party secure inference. In: CCS (2020)

36. Ritchie, M.D., et al.: Multifactor-dimensionality reduction reveals high-order inter-
    actions among estrogen-metabolism genes in sporadic breast cancer. Am. J. Hum.
    Genet. **69**, 138–147 (2001)
37. Rosulek, M., Roy, L.: Three halves make a whole? beating the half-gates lower
    bound for garbled circuits. In: Malkin, T., Peikert, C. (eds.) CRYPTO 2021. LNCS,
    vol. 12825, pp. 94–124. Springer, Cham (2021). https://doi.org/10.1007/978-3-030-
    84242-0_5
38. Schneider, T., Tkachenko, O.: EPISODE: efficient privacy-preservIng similar
    sequence queries on outsourced genomic DatabasEs. In: ASIACCS (2019)
39. Schneider, T., Zohner, M.: GMW vs. Yao? efficient secure two-party computation
    with low depth circuits. In: FC (2013)
40. Tkachenko, O., Weinert, C., Schneider, T., Hamacher, K.: Large-scale privacy-
    preserving statistical computations for distributed genome-wide association stud-
    ies. In: ASIACCS (2018)
41. Wang, M.H., Cordell, H.J., Van Steen, K.: Statistical methods for genome-wide
    association studies. In: Seminars in Cancer Biology (2019)
42. Yang, K., Weng, C., Lan, X., Zhang, J., Wang, X.: Ferret: fast extension for cor-
    related OT with small communication. In: CCS (2020)
43. Yang, L., et al.: Impact of interaction between the G870A and EFEMP1 gene
    polymorphism on glioma risk in Chinese Han population. Oncotarget **8**, 37561
    (2017)
44. Yao, A.C.: How to generate and exchange secrets. In: FOCS (1986)
45. Zahur, S., Rosulek, M., Evans, D.: Two halves make a whole. In: Oswald, E.,
    Fischlin, M. (eds.) EUROCRYPT 2015. LNCS, vol. 9057, pp. 220–250. Springer,
    Heidelberg (2015). https://doi.org/10.1007/978-3-662-46803-6_8
46. Zhang, H., et al.: Interaction between PPAR γ and SORL1 gene with late-onset
    Alzheimer's disease in Chinese Han population. Oncotarget **8**, 48313 (2017)

ML Techniques

Hide and Seek: On the Stealthiness of Attacks Against Deep Learning Systems

Zeyan Liu[1], Fengjun Li[1], Jingqiang Lin[2], Zhu Li[3], and Bo Luo[1(✉)]

[1] EECS/I2S, University of Kansas, Lawrence, KS, USA
{zyliu,fli,bluo}@ku.edu
[2] University of Science and Technology of China, Hefei, China
linjq@ustc.edu.cn
[3] University of Missouri–Kansas City, Kansas City, MO, USA
lizhu@umkc.edu

Abstract. With the growing popularity of artificial intelligence (AI) and machine learning (ML), a wide spectrum of attacks against deep learning (DL) models have been proposed in the literature. Both the evasion attacks and the poisoning attacks attempt to utilize adversarially altered samples to fool the victim model to misclassify the adversarial sample. While such attacks claim to be or are expected to be stealthy, i.e., imperceptible to human eyes, such claims are rarely evaluated. In this paper, we present the first large-scale study on the stealthiness of adversarial samples used in the attacks against deep learning. We have implemented 20 representative adversarial ML attacks on six popular benchmarking datasets. We evaluate the stealthiness of the attack samples using two complementary approaches: (1) a numerical study that adopts 24 metrics for image similarity or quality assessment; and (2) a user study of 3 sets of questionnaires that has collected 30,000+ annotations from 1,500+ responses. Our results show that the majority of the existing attacks introduce non-negligible perturbations that are not stealthy to human eyes. We further analyze the factors that contribute to attack stealthiness. We examine the correlation between the numerical analysis and the user studies, and demonstrate that some image quality metrics may provide useful guidance in attack designs, while there is still a significant gap between assessed image quality and visual stealthiness of attacks.

Keywords: Adversarial machine learning · Attacks

1 Introduction

In the past decade, machine learning, especially deep learning (DL), has gained incredible success in a wide range of applications, fueling advances in every field related to big data analysis, such as computer vision, data mining, and natural language processing. With the growing popularity and adoption of DL, a

© The Author(s), under exclusive license to Springer Nature Switzerland AG 2022
V. Atluri et al. (Eds.): ESORICS 2022, LNCS 13556, pp. 343–363, 2022.
https://doi.org/10.1007/978-3-031-17143-7_17

wide spectrum of attacks have been proposed. In particular, attacks against the *integrity* of deep learning models could be roughly grouped into two categories: *evasion attacks* and *backdoor attacks*. In the evasion attacks, supposedly imperceptible adversarial perturbations are added to the attack samples, so that the victim models would make highly confident but erroneous classifications for these samples. In the backdoor attacks, the victim DNNs are compromised through poisoning or Trojaning, so that they "remember" the specially-crafted triggers (e.g., patches of pixels, shadows, or stealthy noises) as external features and classify the trigger-embedded images into wrong labels, e.g., to mis-recognize a stop sign with a yellow sticker on it as a "go straight" sign. The backdoor attacks could be further categorized into data poisoning backdoors and neural Trojans. The data poisoning backdoors inject digitally altered and mislabeled samples into the training dataset so that a malicious functionality is "learned" by the victim model. Meanwhile, neural Trojans alter the structure of the victim DNN by injecting a malicious sub-network that only responds to the adversarial triggers in the testing samples, so that the original task remains (mostly) unaffected.

The majority of the existing evasion and backdoor attacks are supposed to be or claim to be *stealthy*, i.e., the adversarial perturbations and the attack triggers are expected to be hardly noticeable to human eyes, so that the attacks are unlikely to be identified even if the administrators manually examine the training/testing data. However, the quality of the adversarial samples has not been carefully examined in the literature, while the stealthiness claims are rarely measured in the attack papers. To the best of our knowledge, very few existing attacks employed human evaluators to assess the stealthiness of the adversarial modifications to the attack samples [9,33] or used numerical measurements to assess the similarity between the attack and the benign images [25,33,51].

In this paper, we are motivated by the questions: for the machine learning attacks proposed in the literature, how *stealthy* are they? How can we *quantitatively assess the attack stealthiness*? In particular, we aim to measure the *numerical stealthiness* and the *user-perceived stealthiness*. We have implemented 20 evasion and backdoor attacks over six popular benchmarking datasets. In *numerical analysis*, we adopt 24 metrics from the literature to assess the similarities between the attack images and the corresponding benign images, or to assess the visual quality of the attack images. Some of these metrics are supposed to reflect the human visual systems or human perceptions of digital images. For *user-perceived stealthiness*, we present a large-scale user study with 3 sets of questionnaires of 1,500+ responses and 30,000+ annotated images, which aim to answer the questions: could users notice the differences between the original and the adversarial samples in different attacks? If a knowledgeable or novice user is presented with attack images without the corresponding benign image, could the user identify the malicious images? We further correlate the numerical assessments with the user-perceived stealthiness and discuss our findings.

Our contributions are: (1) We identify a largely neglected issue in adversarial ML that, while the attack samples are supposed to be or claimed to be stealthy, such features are rarely evaluated in the proposed attacks. (2) We present the first large-scale assessment and comparative study to evaluate the stealthiness of the attack samples through numerical analysis and user study. And (3) Our findings are expected to provide a better understanding of attacks against ML models, especially on how users perceive the maliciousness of the attack samples, and how auditors could benefit from our findings.

Ethical Considerations. The objective of this project is to enhance the understanding of the adversarial attacks against deep learning models. All the attacks implemented in this project are previously published in the literature. All the implementations and experiments were conducted in a lab environment. We did not attack any real-world system. The user studies presented in the paper have been reviewed and approved by the Human Research Protection Program at the University of Kansas under STUDY00148002 and STUDY00148622.

The rest of the paper is organized as follows: we introduce the background of this project in Sect. 2. We present the design and results of the numerical analysis and the user study in Sects. 3 and 4, respectively, followed by discussions in Sect. 5. We conclude the paper in Sect. 6.

2 Preliminaries: Deep Learning, Attacks, and Datasets

2.1 Deep Learning and Adversarial Machine Learning

Deep Neural Networks (DNNs). In this paper, we focus on the standard classification task. Without loss of generality, a DNN model is defined as $f_\theta : X \to Y$. f_θ maps d-dimensional inputs $x \in X \subset \mathbb{R}^d$ into a label space $y \in Y \subset \mathbb{N}+^k$ with k categories. Its decision making process is defined as: $p \in \mathbb{R}^k := f_\theta(x)$, where p is the k-dimensional embedding of the decision confidence in terms of the label distribution. The final output label corresponds to the maximum element in p. Given an annotated training dataset $D_t = \{(x_i, y_i) : x_i \in X, y_i \in Y, 1 \le i \le k\}$, the training process is to optimize the model parameters with a loss function $\mathcal{L}$, e.g., Cross-Entropy Loss: $\theta_{optimal} = \arg\min_\theta \sum_{i=1}^k \mathcal{L}(f_\theta(x_i), y_i)$.

Attacks against Deep Learning Models. Attacks against ML/DL models could be roughly categorized into three types [4]: (1) *evasion attacks,* (2) *backdoor attacks,* and (3) *exploratory attacks.* Both evasion and backdoor attacks attempt to break the integrity of ML/DL models using adversarial examples that are seemingly benign, while exploratory attacks aim to break the confidentiality of the proprietary black-box models. In this paper, we focus on evasion and backdoor attacks since the majority of such attacks, implicitly or explicitly, make the stealthiness assumption on the adversarial examples.

Evasion Attacks. Also known as adversarial examples, the evasion attacks add small perturbation δ to clean sample x_{beni} to generate the adversarial example x_{adv}. δ is crafted to satisfy two objectives: (1) the magnitude of δ is limited by a perturbation budget (e.g. restrictions on l^p norm). And (2) x_{adv} will mislead the model to generate a wrong output y_{adv}, which could be untargeted (any wrong label) or targeted (a pre-selected label). The attack is defined as:

$$y_{adv} = \underset{i}{\operatorname{argmax}} f_\theta(x_{adv}) \neq \underset{i}{\operatorname{argmax}} f_\theta(x_{beni}) \tag{1}$$

Backdoor Attacks. While the evasion attacks attempt to fool a benign (but vulnerable) model, backdoor attacks inject the malicious functionality into the victim DNN during model production. The attacker designs a trigger function T to transform benign examples x_{beni} into malicious examples $T(x_{beni})$. The backdoored model f'_θ learns the trigger and associates it with the target label y_t, and classifies $T(x_{beni})$ into y_t in the testing phase:

$$y_t = \underset{i}{\operatorname{argmax}} f'_\theta(T(x_{beni})) \tag{2}$$

With different attack models, backdoors can be injected by poisoning the training data [5,18,51], manually permuting the model parameters [12], or injecting malicious sub-networks into the model (Trojaning) [26,38].

2.2 DNN Attacks Evaluated in This Study

We have implemented 20 attacks (23 different settings) from the literature, including 10 evasion attacks and 10 backdoor attacks. Unless otherwise specified, we strictly follow the settings in the original papers. We briefly summarize the attacks with a special focus on adversarial perturbations or backdoor triggers.

Evasion Attacks. For evasion attacks that need to specify perturbation budgets, the default budget is set to 8 (out of 255 in each RGB channel).

- *FGSM.* FGSM [17] is an untargeted attack that adds perturbations along the gradient sign: $\delta = \epsilon \cdot sign(\nabla_x \mathcal{L}(f_\theta(x, y)))$, where ϵ is the perturbation budget.
- *BIM.* BIM [24] proposed a targeted variant of FGSM by iteratively updating perturbations: $x_{t+1} = x_t + \alpha \cdot sign(\nabla_{x_t} \mathcal{L}(f_\theta(x_t, y_{adv})))$, where x_t denotes x_{adv} at the tth iteration, and α denotes the step size each iteration.
- *MI-FGSM.* Momentum-based iterative algorithms are proposed in [10], in which the accumulated gradient is defined as: $g_{t+1} = \mu \cdot g_t + \frac{\nabla_{x_t} \mathcal{L}(f_\theta(x_t, y_{adv}))}{\left\| \nabla_{x_t} \mathcal{L}(f_\theta(x_t, y_{adv})) \right\|_1}$, and the iterative update is: $x_{t+1} = x_t + \alpha \cdot sign(g_{t+1})$.
- *PGD.* PGD [29] improves BIM with an initialization with random noise and more iterations. The perturbation is projected onto an l^∞ ball with radius ϵ.
- *AutoPGD (APGD).* AutoPGD [7] extends PGD by combining momentum and alternative loss functions into an efficient ensemble of attacks. AutoPGD dynamically adjusts all the parameters.
- *FFGSM.* FFGSM [45] assumes a weaker/cheaper adversary but significantly improves the efficiency of adversarial training (defense). FFGSM can be considered as a one-step variant of PGD that is initialized with uniform perturbation.

- *Deepfool (DF)*. Deepfool [31] computes the minimal adversarial perturbation to push the adversarial sample towards the linearized decision boundary. The gradients are calculated as: $x_{t+1} = x_t + \frac{|f_{\theta,adv}(x_t) - f_{\theta,beni}(x_t)|}{\|\nabla f_{\theta,adv}(x_t) - \nabla f_{\theta,beni}(x_t)\|_2^2}$, where $f_{\theta,adv}$ and $f_{\theta,beni}$ denote the model outputs corresponding to the target/original label.
- *Carlini & Wagner (CW)*. C&W [3] finds the minimum perturbation through an optimization approach. We adopt the l^2 constraint in the optimization objective.
- *Smoothfool (SF)*. Smoothfool [8] uses low-pass filters to generate smooth adversarial perturbations, which improves attack robustness and transferability.
- *Semantic AE (SAE)*. Instead of generating artificial perturbations at the pixel level, [20] semantically modifies the image by converting it into HSV space, and randomly shifting the Hue and Saturation components.

Table 1. A qualitative comparison of the backdoor attacks.

	Datasets	CL	Attack type	Trigger category	DB	Training method		
						SC	FA	FL
AD	ⓑⓒ	×	One-to-One	Global Noise	×	✓	✓	×
BN	ⓐⓑⓓ	×	All-to-One/All-to-All	Local Patch	✓	✓	✓	×
BL	ⓔ	×	One-to-One	Global Transformation	✓	✓	✓	×
PA	ⓔ	×	One-to-One	Local Patch	✓	✓	✓	×
HT	ⓒⓔ	✓	One-to-One/All-to-One	Global Noise	×	×	×	✓
INS	ⓑⓒⓔ	×	All-to-One	Global Transformation	×	✓	✓	×
IP-S	ⓐⓑⓒ	×	One-to-One	Global Transformation	✓	✓	✓	×
IP-A	ⓐⓑⓒ	×	One-to-One	Global Noise	✓	✓	✓	×
RP	ⓐⓑ	✓	All-to-One	Global Transformation	×	✓	✓	×
WM	ⓖⓗ	–	All-to-One	Local Patch	✓	×	×	✓
SQ	ⓖⓗ	–	All-to-One	Local Patch	✓	×	×	✓
TNet	ⓑⓔⓕⓘ	–	All-to-One/All-to-All	Local Patch	✓	–	–	–
WN	ⓐⓑⓒⓘ	×	All-to-One	Global Transformation	×	✓	✓	×

Datasets in the published paper: ⓐ MNIST. ⓑ GTSRB. ⓒ CIFAR10. ⓓ US & Swedish Traffic Signs. ⓔ ImageNet. ⓕ YouTube Aligned Face. ⓖ VGG Face. ⓗ LFW. ⓘ CelebA. ⓙ Pubfig
CL: Clean label poisoning. **DB**: Whether the benign dataset is unavailable. **SC**: Train the model from scratch. **FA**: Finetune all the layers. **FL**: Finetune top layers with other layers frozen.

Backdoor Attacks. A detailed comparison of the backdoor attack models and settings is shown in Table 1.

- *Advdoor (AD)*. Advdoor [49] utilizes a Targeted Universal Adversarial Perturbation (TUAP) trigger, which is claimed to be "small magnitude and human imperceptible". Input-specific perturbations are iteratively aggregated to generate UAP, where existing evasion attacks (e.g., Deepfool) could be employed.
- *Badnets (BN)*. Badnets [18] patch a unique black-and-white square on the corner of training samples. We follow the settings in [18] and use a 4×4 trigger.

- *Blended & Physical Accessory (BL & PA).* [5] employs two trigger generation strategies: blended injection (BL) for simple digital attacks and physical accessory injection (PA) for real-world physical attacks. We follow [5] to use the hello kitty image in BL, and follow [47] to use mug patches in PA.
- *HiddenTrigger (HT).* HT [36] is a clean-label backdoor, which claims the poisoned samples to be "natural with correct labels", while the triggers are hidden until test time. In HT, we assess the stealthiness of poisoned training samples.
- *Instagram (INS).* [27] proposed feature-space attacks that generate triggers with Instagram filters Nashville and Gotham. We implement the Nashville filter.
- *Invisible Perturbation (IP).* [51] propose two strategies to generate "hardly perceptible" backdoor triggers: patterned static perturbation masks (IP-S) and targeted adaptive perturbation masks (IP-A).
- *Ramp Signal (RP).* [2] uses ramp signals as triggers in the poisoned samples.
- *TrojanNN (TN).* [28] use reverse-engineered adversarial triggers to maximize the activation of anchor neurons in the DNN. Among the trigger patterns in [28], we have implemented Watermark (WM) and Square (SQ) in this study.
- *TrojanNet (TNet).* [38] injects into the victim DNN a small neural component, which is activated by a predefined trigger pattern to flip the DNN output. We follow the settings in [38] to implement a 4×4 black-and-white square trigger.
- *WaNet (WN).* [33] uses elastic image warping as triggers. Human inspection experiments in [33] demonstrate its outstanding stealthiness.

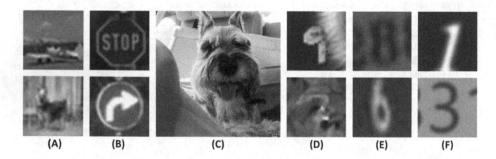

(A)   (B)   (C)   (D)   (E)   (F)

Fig. 1. Sample images from the benchmarking datasets used in this study.

Attack Categorization. Based on the properties of the injected adversarial perturbations, we classify the attacks into three categories: (1) Gradient-based noise (or global noise): FGSM, BIM, PGD, MI-FGSM, DF, FFGSM, APGD, CW, SF, AD, HT, IP-A. They make small modifications to a large number of pixels to achieve a global optimization objective. They attack the unrobust deep features in the victim DNN, while the main contents (the semantic meanings) of the adversarial images remain unchanged. (2) Local patches: BN, PA, WM, SQ, TNet. They are all backdoor attacks that modify a small region on adversarial images to build salient visual features. The triggers are robust, but they are usually detectable by trigger reconstruction defenses, e.g., [19,40]. (3) Global transformation: SAE, BL, INS, IP-S, RP, WN. They make global changes to the victim images, which may significantly change the appearances of the images.

2.3 The Datasets

In this study, we adopt six datasets that are frequently used as benchmarks in both the machine learning community and the adversarial ML community. Please note that, while most of the attacks were originally implemented on a subset of these datasets, we re-implemented all of them on all six datasets.

A. CIFAR-10. The CIFAR dataset [23] contains 60K tiny images (32 × 32) labeled in 10 classes, such as automobile, bird, cat, ship, truck, etc.

B. GTSRB. The German Traffic Sign Recognition Benchmark dataset [21] has 51K images of real-world traffic signs in 43 classes. Images are scaled to 32 × 32.

C. ImageNet. ImageNet is a large-scale image classification and object recognition benchmark dataset. The dataset used in the ImageNet Large Scale Visual Recognition Challenge (ILSVRC) 2012-14 contains 1.35 million images that are manually labeled into 1,000 classes [35]. The images are usually cropped to 224×224. They are significantly larger than the small images in other datasets.

D. MNIST-M. The MNIST dataset[1] contains 70,000 binary images of handwritten digits. The MNIST-M dataset adds color to MNIST by extracting patches from the BSDS500 dataset and combining them with MNIST [16].

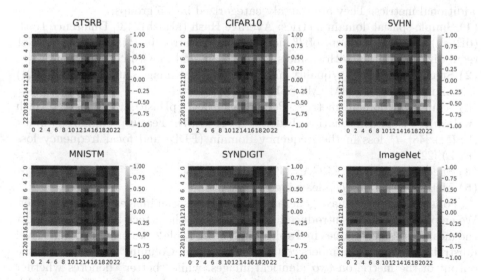

Fig. 2. Normalized numerical assessment results. X-axis: attacks. Y-axis: metrics.

---

[1] Available at: http://yann.lecun.com/exdb/mnist/.

E. SVHN. The Street View House Numbers (SVHN) is another digit classification benchmark dataset, which contains 600,000 digit images that are extracted from house numbers in Google Street View [32].

F. SYNDIGIT. The Synthetic Digits dataset contains 12,000 images that are synthetically generated by placing digits of various fonts, colors, and directions over random backgrounds [15]. The MNIST-M, SVHN, and SYNDIGIT datasets are often used in transfer learning and attacks against transfer learning.

Samples of benign images from the datasets are shown in Fig. 1. The corresponding attack images are generated by exploiting the attacks introduced in Sect. 2.2 on images sampled from the six datasets. They may contain noise (a.k.a. adversarial perturbation) that is supposed to be invisible to human eyes, or adversarial patterns such as a sticky note on a stop sign.

3   The Numerical Analysis

3.1   Metrics and Basic Statistics

In this paper, we adopt three categories of metrics in the numerical analysis.

l^p **Norms:** l^p norms are widely used in adversarial example attacks to limit the magnitude of the perturbation. In the rest of the paper, we always use l^p norms normalized by image size, i.e., $l^p(x_{\text{adv}} - x_{\text{beni}})/|x_{\text{beni}}|$, where $p = \{0, 1, 2, \infty\}$.

Basic Metrics: Most popular metrics in the literature for image similarities: MSE (mean square error), PSNR (peak signal-to-noise ratio), and SSIM [42].

Additional Metrics: To further explore how the advanced image similarity or quality measurements may fit into this problem, we have implemented 17 additional metrics. They are roughly categorized into 5 groups:

(1) Simple spatial domain metrics: Average Hash (aHash) [13], Difference Hash (dHash) [13] and variants of l^p norms: relative error in l^1 (RE), Elastic-Net regularization [14], l^1 with cosine similarity [30] and l^1 with clip function [44].

(2) Structural similarity/quality metrics: Universal Image Quality index (UQI) [41] and Multi-scale SSIM (MS-SSIM) [43].

(3) Transform domain metrics: Perceptual Hash (pHash) [13], Wavelet Hash (wHash), Visual Information Fidelity (VIF) [37], Feature Similarity index (FSIM) [48], l^1 loss in the frequency domain (FDL) and focal frequency loss (FFL) [22].

(4) Spectral similarity: ERGAS [39] and SAM [46].

(5) Metrics based on deep learning: LPIPS [50].

For each attack, we have generated 1,000 adversarial images for each dataset. We employ the metrics introduced above to assess the attack images and report the mean assessment values in Tables 2 and 3. In Table 2, we provide a high-level illustration of how the numbers could be interpreted. Column "ideal" denotes the output of the metric on two identical images, while "better" denotes whether a larger or a smaller value indicates "more similar" images ("better" attack). For example, MSE generates 0 for two identical images, and a smaller value corresponds to images with higher similarity, i.e., the attack is stealthier in

Table 2. Image similarity/quality measurements for evasion attacks. Blue: the best attack (most similar or highest quality) for each metric; red: the worst attack.

Metrics	Ideal	Better	FGSM	BIM	PGD	MIFGSM	DF	FFGSM	APGD	CW	SF
l^0	0	small	0.991	0.863	0.971	0.992	0.709	0.994	0.971	0.647	0.829
l^1	0	small	7.632	5.189	5.320	6.282	2.286	6.630	6.068	1.153	4.484
l^2	0	small	0.130	0.101	0.101	0.114	0.060	0.116	0.112	0.032	0.121
l^∞	0	small	0.003	0.003	0.003	0.003	0.007	0.003	0.003	0.004	0.012
MSE	0	small	59.20	34.96	35.07	45.09	24.55	47.48	42.51	3.686	65.26
PSNR	∞	large	30.42	32.76	32.75	31.61	40.98	31.37	31.92	44.32	34.40
SSIM	1	large	0.928	0.957	0.957	0.943	0.984	0.940	0.953	0.996	0.963
LPIPS	0	small	0.011	0.005	0.005	0.007	0.001	0.008	0.006	1.9e-4	0.003
aHash	0	small	0.642	0.625	0.533	0.670	0.405	0.587	0.660	0.320	1.442
dHash	0	small	3.035	2.727	2.642	2.908	1.633	2.663	2.973	1.245	4.508
pHash	0	small	1.813	1.620	1.590	1.763	0.800	1.707	1.700	0.610	3.780
wHash	0	small	1.613	1.400	1.318	1.477	0.658	1.473	1.438	0.520	2.527
FDL	0	small	46.28	34.56	34.64	39.96	15.65	41.51	7.49	37.73	21.62
FFL	0	small	35.27	20.84	20.92	26.76	15.11	28.32	25.31	2.233	46.95
ERGAS	0	small	5108	8340	1.0e4	5319	1971	5192	4282	1153	4786
SAM	0	small	0.080	0.060	0.059	0.067	0.030	0.070	0.065	0.016	0.057
MS-SSIM	1	large	0.992	0.995	0.995	0.993	0.998	0.993	0.994	0.999	0.983
FSIM	1	large	0.767	0.782	0.783	0.768	0.888	0.768	0.775	0.920	0.848
VIF	1	~1	0.513	0.587	0.587	0.551	0.752	0.543	0.561	0.849	0.600
UQI	1	large	0.990	0.990	0.991	0.990	0.997	0.991	0.992	0.998	0.990
Elastic	0	small	17.95	11.14	11.27	14.04	6.74	14.80	13.36	1.659	16.64
RE	0	small	4.457	2.673	2.509	3.974	1.575	3.626	3.088	0.038	0.495
l^1 Cos	0	small	46.07	31.35	32.12	37.96	13.76	40.02	36.63	6.952	27.05
l^1 Clip	0	small	7.632	5.189	5.320	6.282	1.919	6.630	6.068	1.146	3.406

this metric. Meanwhile, Fig. 2 shows the detailed distribution in each dataset after min-max normalization, in which a lighter color ($\sim$1) indicates a stealthier attack. As shown in the figure, the measurements for each attack demonstrate very similar patterns across six datasets, i.e., the dataset is NOT a significant factor in numerical assessments of attack stealthiness.

3.2 Numerical Analysis of Attack Stealthiness

l^p **Norms (normalized by image size) and attack categorization.** The l^0 norm indicates the portion of pixels that are modified, while the l^∞ norm indicates the maximum change made to a pixel. Both l^1 and l^2 denote the overall amplitude of the added adversarial perturbations, while l^2 is more sensitive to large changes. As shown in Tables 2 and 3, the l^p norms are good indicators of the types of the added perturbations: (1) In general, global noise attacks always produce large l^0 (close to 1) but moderate l^1, l^2, and smallest l^∞ (mean $= 0.0044$). By design, they introduce a small change (often explicitly limited by l^p norm) to each pixel. (2) Local patches generate smallest l^0 (mean $= 0.06$) and largest l^∞ (mean $= 0.067$). The mean l^1 is smaller than noise-based attacks', while the mean l^2 is larger. Although local patches are small in size, they make significant modifications to the pixel values in order to build strong visual features, which

Table 3. Image similarity/quality measurements for backdoor attacks. Blue: the best attack (most similar or highest quality) for each metric; red: the worst attack.

Metrics	Global noises			Local patches					Global transformation					
	AD	HT	IPA	BN	PA	WM	SQ	TNet	SAE	BL	INS	IPS	RP	WN
l^0	0.937	0.973	0.946	0.015	0.136	0.078	0.057	0.015	0.888	0.983	0.991	0.263	0.878	0.731
l^1	8.531	9.866	5.028	1.993	7.822	7.884	5.438	2.102	35.61	24.50	49.38	2.471	11.81	3.413
l^2	0.175	0.188	0.104	0.325	0.472	0.588	0.499	0.334	0.829	0.473	1.037	0.083	0.226	0.105
l^∞	0.006	0.005	0.004	0.068	0.057	0.072	0.069	0.069	0.040	0.020	0.060	0.003	0.006	0.013
MSE	113.2	121.0	48.12	333.0	751.8	1302	948.4	355.1	3231	944.3	4225	24.46	181.8	45.86
PSNR	28.09	27.37	34.59	25.21	22.39	17.40	19.01	24.97	16.51	19.78	12.57	34.25	25.55	33.61
SSIM	0.864	0.868	0.962	0.953	0.784	0.660	0.874	0.898	0.646	0.898	0.722	0.973	0.873	0.983
LPIPS	0.019	0.022	0.007	0.034	0.037	0.122	0.072	0.021	0.066	0.007	0.083	8.7e-4	0.021	0.003
aHash	0.972	1.376	0.553	1.670	6.810	6.461	6.288	1.842	5.170	2.003	11.71	0.362	0.610	1.157
dHash	3.927	4.664	2.777	2.453	6.782	8.148	4.372	2.837	6.350	5.158	11.83	1.223	3.473	2.708
pHash	2.510	3.275	1.620	7.747	12.85	10.93	12.95	7.993	6.383	3.897	11.21	0.360	1.513	2.660
wHash	2.248	2.688	1.487	1.687	7.028	7.662	6.258	1.873	5.545	3.358	13.36	0.437	4.465	1.725
FDL	58.69	64.04	29.68	14.00	43.56	136.1	60.64	18.25	171.8	68.57	220.6	12.14	36.02	23.11
FFL	65.98	71.36	28.38	283.3	546.8	657.3	525.4	278.0	2382	806.7	3195	24.24	179.2	32.32
ERGAS	1.3e4	8865	6329	2549	1.0e4	2.7e4	1.2e4	5670	2.0e4	1.5e4	4.3e4	4986	1.0e4	3070
SAM	0.110	0.125	0.060	0.171	0.225	0.313	0.288	0.177	0.289	0.082	0.381	0.045	0.135	0.053
MS-SSIM	0.980	0.982	0.996	0.985	0.818	0.842	0.874	0.957	0.805	0.952	0.881	0.999	0.966	0.996
FSIM	0.734	0.696	0.790	0.960	0.813	0.794	0.840	0.948	0.704	0.821	0.616	0.992	0.747	0.870
VIF	0.393	0.410	0.626	0.879	0.433	0.264	0.679	0.697	0.363	0.587	0.528	0.670	0.405	0.619
UQI	0.979	0.979	0.991	0.988	0.948	0.899	0.959	0.972	0.781	0.939	0.799	0.992	0.969	0.996
Elastic	29.47	32.09	13.65	68.20	156.6	266.6	194.0	72.70	674.6	208.5	884.5	6.869	45.80	11.90
RE	7.872	7.966	4.430	80.77	0.114	0.065	0.065	50.28	256.6	0.266	153.8	0.072	21.41	0.064
l^1 Cosine	51.58	59.55	30.38	12.19	47.79	49.05	33.75	12.83	215.5	147.2	297.8	14.91	71.21	20.58
l^1 Clip	6.406	7.857	4.213	0.153	1.138	0.608	0.393	0.153	7.356	8.466	9.307	2.467	7.896	2.682

significantly impact the l^2 and l^∞ norms. (3) Global transformation attacks introduce moderate changes globally, which result larger l^0, l^1, l^2, but moderate l^∞ (mean = 0.024). IP-S is an exception in that it employs a scattered global pattern, so that it moderately modifies a relatively small portion of pixels ($l^0 = 0.263$, $l^1 = 2.471$) distributed over the entire image.

MSE, PNSR, and SSIM. CW produces the best overall MSE (3.686) and PNSR (44.32). Gradient-based attacks all result in smaller MSE ([3.686, 121]), local patch backdoors produce moderate MSE ([333, 1302]), while global transformation attacks generate variable MSE (three attacks in [24.46, 181.8] and others in [944.3, 4225]). PNSR generates very similar rankings and patterns as MSE. SSIM imitates the Human Visual System (HVS) to measure the structural similarity based on luminance, contrast, and structure. CW again produces the best SSIM (0.996). Among local patch backdoors, BN generates the best SSIM of 0.953, while WM gives the worst SSIM of 0.660. Among global transformation attacks, WN provides the best SSIM of 0.983, while SAE provides the worst SSIM of 0.646. In our experiments, both PNSR and SSIM are highly (negatively) correlated with MSE, with Spearman correlation coefficients of −0.92 and −0.86.

In summary, noise-based attacks significantly outperform the other two categories in all three metrics with averages of 53.35, 33.38, and, 0.943 respectively. Two global transformation attacks, SAE and INS, perform the worst in all three metrics, which is understandable since they have very different design philosophies that do not seek to minimize perturbation.

Additional Image Quality Metrics. IP-S appears to be the most stealthy with dHash, pHash, wHash, and FSIM. BN performs the best with VIF and l^1, while CW is the best for all other measurements. In general, gradient noise attacks perform better than the other two categories in most cases. IP-S again appears to be an outlier among global transformation attacks. Most of the metrics demonstrate strong correlations with at least one of MSE, PNSR, or SSIM (absolute correlation coefficient > 0.8). These metrics will be further explored in comparison with the results from the user study.

4   The User Study

In this section, we evaluate the likelihood of adversarial samples escaping human users. We mimic an auditing scenario, in which auditors/defenders examine potentially suspicious images in an attempt to identify true attack samples.

4.1   Research Design

Based on the level of knowledge the auditor/defender has about the dataset, we define three defense models:

Model I. Informed Defenders (White Box). The Informed Defenders have full knowledge of the target dataset. They are capable of making side-by-side comparisons of the original and the adversarial samples in a white-box manner. They represent the strongest type of defenders, who more likely exist as the owners of the original datasets in defense against training data poisoning.

Model II. Knowledgeable Defenders (Grey Box). The Knowledgeable Defenders have reasonable knowledge about the benign dataset. When they manually inspect the potentially adversarial samples, they can refer to benign samples from the same dataset. However, they do not possess the exact original images that correspond to the suspect samples, i.e., no side-by-side comparison.

Model III. Referenceless Defenders (Black Box). The Referenceless Defenders have little or no access to the original dataset. They inspect the potentially adversarial samples without referring to benign samples. They represent the weakest type of defenders, who often exist among the novice users, who download and reuse pre-trained models from the Internet, e.g., Model Zoo.

In Defender Model I, attack stealthiness is defined as the *invisibility* of the adversarial perturbations–when the auditor notices the noise/patch, the attack is likely discovered. In Models II and III, attack stealthiness is defined as *visual benignness*, i.e., the attack examples are expected to be visually consistent with the examiners' psychophysical perceptions of normal images. The perceptions will differ with or without knowing the dataset.

To mimic each type of defenders, we have designed three user studies[2]. In each user study, an IRB information statement is first displayed to the participant, followed by a link to the questionnaire. In each questionnaire, 20 (sets of) images are presented to the participant for inspection. ImageNet images are downsized to 200 × 200, while the smaller images (e.g., GTSRB, CIFAR) are enlarged to 4× the original size, and padded with white padding to 200 × 200.

Exp I. Informed Defenders (White Box). The questionnaire contains 20 pairs of images: the first in each pair is a benign image randomly selected from the datasets introduced in Sect. 2.3; the second is the adversarial image that is altered by a random attack in Sect. 2.2. For quality control, we include 10% benign images as the second, i.e., two images are numerically identical. Part of the questionnaire is shown in Fig. 3 (A). We ask the user to inspect each pair and identify whether the two images look identical.

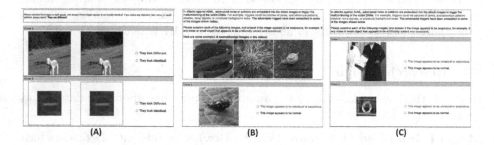

Fig. 3. Sample questionnaires used in the user study.

Exp II. Knowledgeable Defenders (Grey Box). As shown in Fig. 3 (B), the questionnaire first displays three benign images from a random dataset to be used by the participant as reference images. The questionnaire then shows 20 different images from *the same dataset* as the reference images. For each image, we ask the participant to select if it appears to be benign or suspicious.

Exp III. Referenceless Defenders (Black Box). As shown in Fig. 3 (C), the questionnaire is very similar to the Knowledgeable Defenders' questionnaire, except that no reference image is displayed.

4.2   The User-Perceived Attack Stealthiness

We sent the questionnaires to senior/graduate CS students in three institutions which the authors are affiliated with. We intentionally select CS students because they have basic understanding of computer systems and programming, while some of them have prior knowledge of AI/ML or even adversarial ML. They

---

[2] The user studies have been approved by the Human Research Protection Program at the University of Kansas under STUDY00148002 and STUDY00148622.

better mimic the system administrators or ML/AI users in real world applications. In six weeks, we collected 1,526 responses with 30,369 total annotations, including 504, 512, and 510 responses, with 9,991, 10,209, and 10,169 annotations to Experiments 1, 2 and 3, respectively.

We present the *detection rates* from all the experiments in Fig. 4. The detection rate is defined as the proportion of annotations that labeled a pair of images as "different" (Exp 1) or labeled an image as "unnatural or malicious" (Exp 2 and 3). A lower detection rate indicates a stealthier attack.

Exp I. Informed Defenders. The average detection rate is 75.9%. The detection rates of 17 attacks were higher than 70%, while 11 attacks were detected in more than 85% of the tests. The statistics show that majority of the adversarial samples are highly noticeable, i.e., not stealthy, in side-by-side comparisons with the corresponding benign images. The median task completion time was 91 s (for 20 image pairs), indicating the level of effort needed in an audit of the training or testing dataset. WN and CW significantly outperform the other attacks, with detection rates at 28.5% and 23.3%, while detection rates of SQ and WM are as high as 98.9% and 98.7%. In general, noise-based evasion attacks appear to be stealthier than the others with a 62.0% mean detection rate, while patch-based backdoors are the least stealthy with a 92.7% mean detection rate.

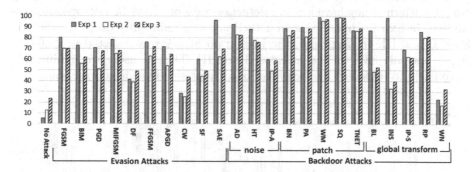

Fig. 4. Detection rates (%) from user studies. Exp I: informed defender; II: knowledgeable defender; III: referenceless defender. A lower rate means a stealthier attack.

Exp II. Knowledgeable Defenders. The average detection rate drops to 62.2%, i.e., the adversarial images have better chances to escape human auditors. Detection rates decrease in every attack except SQ, while the median task completion time decreases to 66 s. The most and least stealthy attacks remain the same as Exp 1: WN with a 17.8% detection rate and SQ with a 99.1% detection rate. Noise-based evasion attacks are the most stealthy with a mean detection rate of 49.4% (12.6% decrease from Exp 1). The patch-based backdoors are the least stealthy with a detection rate of 89.0% (3.7% decrease).

Exp III. Referenceless Defenders. The average detection rate increases slightly from 62.2% in Exp II to 67.9% in Exp III. The distribution demonstrates a high correlation with Exp II with a Spearman correlation coefficient of 0.97. WN and SQ remain the most and least stealthy attacks with detection rates of 32.6% and 98.6%, respectively. Global transformation attacks become the most stealthy category with a 53.7% mean detection rate.

Observations on Attack Categories. For attacks with different categories of injected adversarial perturbations, we observed distinct behaviors across three experiments: (1) The global-noise-based evasion attacks are consistently among the more stealthy types of attacks across all three experiments, with mean detection rates in the range of [49%, 61%]. While the perturbation budget introduces a limit to the per-pixel modifications, the injected noise pattern is still noticeable to 50%+ of the users, with or without reference/knowledge to the benign dataset. (2) The global-noise-based backdoors are significantly less stealthy than the evasion attacks although they exploit similar types of perturbations. Such backdoor attacks attempt to use weak global noise to generate salient features to create robust backdoors, which appears to be difficult–the noise levels are higher than the noise-based evasion attacks, therefore, the backdoor attacks are noticeable to 70% to 80% of the users. (3) Local-patch-based backdoors are consistently the least stealthy attacks in all settings. The mean detection rates of 89% to 92% indicate that they can hardly escape human auditors. (4) Compared with other attack categories, global transformation attacks demonstrate a very unique pattern. They have a mean detection rate of 72.9% in side-by-side comparisons in Exp I, while the mean detection rate significantly drops to ∼50% in Exps II and III. In particular, the Instagram attack was detected at 98.6% in Exp 1 but only 33% to 39% in Exps II and III. That is, users are significantly more likely to be fooled by such attacks without side-by-side comparisons.

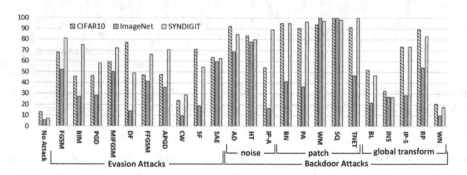

Fig. 5. Detection rates (%) for different datasets in Exp II: Knowledgeable Defenders.

The Impact of Image Size and Content. While we have observed highly consistent results across six datasets in numerical assessments, the user study results are different–our results show that the size and quality of the images may significantly affect user-perceived attack stealthiness. For instance, we present the Exp II detection rates for three datasets (CIFAR, ImageNet, SYNDIGIT) in

Fig. 5. We can observe the following: (1) For the auditors, smaller static patches (BN, PA, TNET) are stealthier in larger images (ImageNet). (2) Global transformation attacks (especially BL and WN) also appear to be stealthier in larger images since the per-pixel modification is weaker. (3) For images with more complex content (ImageNet), the noise-based evasion and backdoor attacks become stealthier to users/auditors. (4) For images with a relatively simple foreground and a clean background (e.g., SYNDIGIT), the detection rate is high in the majority of the attacks, i.e., regardless of the type of the added perturbation, the adversarial samples appear highly suspicious to human eyes.

Referenceless Defenders. We initially expected the referenceless defenders to be the weakest. However, results in Sect. 4.2 show that, the true detection rate increases in Exp III in comparison with Exp II. That is, the defenders/auditors tend to get more aggressive in identifying potentially adversarial samples, when they do not have reference to benign data. While the false positive rate increases, i.e., benign samples are mislabeled as suspicious, the true adversarial samples are more likely to be identified. In the literature, we have seen discussions that "adversarial examples are likely to escape novice defenders when they are unfamiliar with the new testing samples or have not previously seen the testing dataset." Such claims are rejected by our experimental results.

Error Rates with Benign Samples. In each experiment, a portion of users flagged the benign images as "different" or "malicious". The error rates are 5.23%, 12.46%, and 23.70% in Experiments I, II, and III, respectively. The errors are explained by two main reasons: (1) there are always human errors in any type of data labeling, e.g., [34] reports a 3.3% error rate across 10 image datasets and a 6% error rate in ImageNet validation set. The 5.23% base error rate in Exp I is in line with reports in the literature. (2) Some benign benchmarking images do appear to be suspicious, e.g., a significant portion of the tiny images contain blurs, unnatural edges, or objects. As shown in Fig. 1 (D), MNISTM is the most "naturally suspicious" dataset, with 30.3% and 48.8% error rates in Exp II and III, respectively. The 18.5% difference indicates that a small number of reference examples in Exp II effectively help the user/auditor to reduce benign errors. Meanwhile, the error rates with ImageNet remain under 5.5% across all experiments, which shows that regular users are highly capable of recognizing benign high-resolution images even with limited or no reference.

MTurk Study. We initially planned to utilize Amazon Mechanical Turk to conduct the same set of experiments. In the test with Exp I, we injected two pairs of digitally identical images and two pairs of totally different images in each questionnaire for quality control. With 200 questionnaires (all in Exp I, $0.50 per questionnaire, workers with >95% approval rates), we received almost completely random annotations. Even with the quality control questions, the detection rates were close to 50% for both identical and totally different image pairs. This is consistent with recent reports on substantial decreases in MTurk data quality caused by fraudulent workers or bots [1,6,11]. We eventually gave up the MTurk study due to the cost and data quality concerns.

Table 4. Correlation between numerical assessments and detection rates from the user study. Bold: top 3 correlations in each setting; red: p-value> 0.05.

	l^0	l^1	l^2	l^∞	MSE	PSNR	SSIM	LPIPS	aHash	dHash	pHash	wHash
Exp I. Informed Defenders in All Attacks												
S	-0.16	0.49	**0.80**	0.68	0.79	**-0.82**	-0.77	0.78	0.67	0.62	0.75	0.66
K	-0.07	0.39	**0.65**	0.51	0.63	**-0.67**	-0.62	0.63	0.54	0.48	0.58	0.52
	FDL	FFL	ERGAS	SAM	MSSSIM	FSIM	VIF	UQI	Elastic	RE	l^1 Cos	l^1 Clip
S	0.61	0.78	0.68	**0.82**	-0.76	-0.27	-0.37	-0.77	0.79	0.35	0.49	0.04
K	0.49	0.62	0.53	**0.67**	-0.61	-0.22	-0.29	-0.61	0.63	0.31	0.39	0.12
Exp II. Knowledgeable Defenders in All Attacks												
	l^0	l^1	l^2	l^∞	MSE	PSNR	SSIM	LPIPS	aHash	dHash	pHash	wHash
S	-0.35	0.22	0.57	0.54	0.55	**-0.59**	-0.58	**0.64**	0.40	0.32	0.53	0.41
K	-0.20	0.17	0.44	0.42	0.43	**-0.47**	-0.45	**0.50**	0.29	0.22	0.40	0.32
	FDL	FFL	ERGAS	SAM	MSSSIM	FSIM	VIF	UQI	Elastic	RE	l^1 Cos	l^1 Clip
S	0.35	0.55	0.45	**0.63**	-0.55	-0.03	-0.27	-0.52	0.55	0.20	0.22	-0.21
K	0.28	0.43	0.33	**0.51**	-0.42	-0.06	-0.25	-0.41	0.43	0.19	0.17	-0.06
Exp III. Referenceless Defenders in All Attacks												
	l^0	l^1	l^2	l^∞	MSE	PSNR	SSIM	LPIPS	aHash	dHash	pHash	wHash
S	-0.30	0.14	0.45	0.38	0.42	-0.48	-0.50	**0.59**	0.30	0.23	0.47	0.31
K	-0.17	0.11	0.38	0.27	0.37	-0.40	-0.40	**0.46**	0.24	0.17	0.34	0.25
	FDL	FFL	ERGAS	SAM	MSSSIM	FSIM	VIF	UQI	Elastic	RE	l^1 Cos	l^1 Clip
S	0.29	0.39	0.34	**0.55**	-0.45	-0.10	-0.28	-0.39	0.43	0.25	0.15	-0.24
K	0.23	0.34	0.25	**0.44**	-0.37	-0.10	-0.25	-0.31	0.37	0.23	0.12	-0.10
Subset of Exp II. Knowledgeable Defenders: Noise-based Attacks.												
	l^0	l^1	l^2	l^∞	MSE	PSNR	SSIM	LPIPS	aHash	dHash	pHash	wHash
S	0.74	0.78	0.75	0.05	0.72	-0.80	-0.77	**0.81**	0.42	0.44	0.53	0.60
K	0.56	0.67	0.63	0.06	0.60	-0.67	-0.65	**0.70**	0.33	0.32	0.43	0.49
	FDL	FFL	ERGAS	SAM	MSSSIM	FSIM	VIF	UQI	Elastic	RE	l^1 Cos	l^1 Clip
S	**0.81**	0.71	0.70	0.79	-0.64	-0.78	-0.75	-0.68	0.73	**0.82**	0.78	**0.84**
K	0.69	0.59	0.57	0.67	-0.54	-0.64	-0.64	-0.56	0.61	**0.72**	0.67	**0.72**
Subset of Exp III. Referenceless Defenders: Noise-based Attacks.												
	l^0	l^1	l^2	l^∞	MSE	PSNR	SSIM	LPIPS	aHash	dHash	pHash	wHash
S	0.60	0.71	0.70	0.04	0.66	-0.75	-0.70	0.75	0.37	0.37	0.41	0.47
K	0.46	0.60	0.61	0.05	0.59	-0.64	-0.60	0.65	0.33	0.30	0.36	0.40
	FDL	FFL	ERGAS	SAM	MSSSIM	FSIM	VIF	UQI	Elastic	RE	l^1 Cos	l^1 Clip
S	**0.79**	0.63	0.61	0.73	-0.54	-0.75	-0.69	-0.59	0.67	**0.80**	0.71	**0.79**
K	**0.67**	0.57	0.50	0.63	-0.48	-0.61	-0.59	-0.49	0.60	**0.68**	0.60	**0.65**

4.3   Correlation: Numerical Metrics vs. User Perceived Stealthiness

Some of the image similarity/quality metrics in Sect. 3) are designed to reflect the human visualization system. Now, we further investigate whether they could be used to assess the user-perceived attack stealthiness. To investigate the correlations between numerical analysis and the user studies, we employ two metrics: Spearman Rank Order Correlation Coefficient (S or SROCC) and Kendall Rank Order Correlation Coefficient (K or KROCC). We do not use the popular Pearson correlation because our data do not follow normal distribution.

First, we report the correlation between the numerically assessed stealthiness (24 metrics in Tables 2 and 3) and user-perceived stealthiness (three user studies in Sect. 4) across all 23 attacks. The results are shown in the top 3 sections in Table 4. We reject the null hypothesis when the p-value exceeds 0.05 and mark the correlation coefficients as red in the table. In Exp I, most of the image similarity/quality metrics fit well with the detection rates (DR): 11 out of 24 metrics show strong correlations in SROCC ($|S|>0.7$). That is, attacks assessed with lower distance/error/noise (or higher similarity/quality) are less likely to be identified in Exp I. In particular, SAM, PNSR, and l^2 demonstrate the strongest correlation with >0.8 on SROCC and >0.65 on KROCC.

However, the correlations are significantly weaker in Exps II and III. None of the metrics shows strong correlations with DR, while only 10 metrics show moderate correlations ($0.4<|S|<0.7$) with DR in Exp II in both SROCC and KROCC, and 2 metrics show moderate correlations in Exp III. Overall, SAM [46] and LPIPS [50] appear to be the most consistent with human perceptions in all three experiments, however, the correlations are only moderate with knowledge-able and referenceless defenders. Meanwhile, image similarity/quality metrics using structural information or deep features demonstrate better performance.

Meanwhile, we also evaluate the correlation between the numerically assessed and user-perceived stealthiness of each category of attacks. We found strong correlations in global-noise-based attacks, as reported in the last two sections of Table 4. That is, the image similarity/quality metrics could properly evaluate the strength of the injected global perturbation in a way that is consistent with user perceptions. Last, the correlations are weak in other attack categories.

In summary, none of the existing image similarity/quality metrics could accurately assess users' perceptions of attack stealthiness in all attacks. However, some metrics have shown promising performance in a subset of the attacks.

5   The Stealthiness Assumption Revisited

Finally, we discuss the reflections of our findings w.r.t. ML attack stealthiness and practicality, which may contribute to a better understanding of the attacks.

Most of the existing ML attacks in the literature explicitly or implicitly employ the stealthiness assumption. The underlying rationale is that it may be difficult for less experienced users to examine the DL model architecture, code, or parameters, however, even novice users could examine training/testing images and identify anomalies. Here we revisit such assumptions and discuss their practicality based on our findings.

- **Evasion attacks.** Many evasion attacks in the literature explicitly claim to be stealthy and enforce stealthiness using a perturbation budget. Results from our user study show that majority of them are still highly noticeable even to users without reference images. Meanwhile, we also show that some image similarity/quality metrics could be employed to effectively predict the user-perceived stealthiness of the attack images. For an attack to be stealthy in practice, a tight threshold (high similarity or low distance) must be set for the metrics.

- **Data poisoning backdoors.** Conventional data poisoning backdoors do not assume stealthiness for the poisoned training samples, since they are designed to carry labels that are visually wrong. Clean label poisoning attacks have been proposed to tackle this issue by using adversarial samples that appear to carry the correct labels. However, as demonstrated in our user study, the clean label poisoning attacks are highly detectable by users with or without reference. When the attack attempts to train the DNN to learn a *salient* feature from weak perturbations, the actual perturbation is too strong to escape human eyes.
- **Patch-based backdoors.** In general, the patch-based backdoors appear to be the least stealthy, except for the tiny patches on larger images, e.g., BN and TNET on ImageNet. In order for the patches to be learned by the victim DNN as robust features, the patches must have reasonable size and salient visual features, which is against the stealthiness assumption.

Finally, we would like to answer this question from our experiments and observations: *what makes an attack stealthy, i.e., what makes the adversarial image less likely to be identified by a human auditor?*

(1) Scale of Perturbation Matters. Attacks with *extremely low* perturbation budget are more likely to escape human evaluators, especially in global-noise-based attacks. In practice, a global perturbation budget of 8, or a normalized l^1 in the range of $[5, 8]$ appears to be too strong to be unnoticeable.

(2) Size of Perturbed Region Matters. Attacks that modify a relatively *smaller* portion of the victim image, i.e., attacks with a very small l^0, are more likely to escape evaluators.

(3) Image Content Matters. Attacks on images that are fully filled with foreground and have complex content are more likely to escape human evaluators, while most of the attacks, especially the noise-based ones, are very noticeable on a clean background (e.g., blue sky, white wall).

In practice, it would be very difficult to design an attack that satisfies both (1) and (2), since such weak perturbations are unlikely to trigger robust responses from the victim DNN. We have not seen such an attempt in the literature yet. Meanwhile, when an attack achieves one of (1) and (2) on images satisfying (3), the attack is quite stealthy to human eyes, e.g., CW on ImageNet. Last, a different design philosophy has been proposed in the literature, e.g., SAE and INS. Such attacks do not seek to minimize the perturbation or to hide the perturbation, instead, they attempt to apply special visual effects on the victim images, so that the adversarial samples, although significantly different from the victim images, appear to be benign by themselves. The adversarial samples can hardly escape side-by-side comparisons, however, they could better fool the auditors if they do not have reference to the benign dataset.

In summary, we argue that user-based evaluation is the golden standard to validate the stealthiness assumptions in adversarial ML. For global-noise-based attacks, some image quality metrics could be employed to predict attack stealthiness in lieu of a user study. In such metrics, only attacks with extremely low perturbation (high similarity/quality) may result in practically stealthy attacks. Very few attacks in the literature have achieved this goal.

6   Conclusion

In this paper, we present the first large-scale comparative experimental study of the stealthiness of evasion and backdoor attacks against deep learning systems. We have implemented 20 attacks (23 different settings) on six benchmarking datasets. We first present numerical measurements using 24 image quality metrics on all the attacks. Next, we design a user study of three questionnaires that ask users to identify potentially adversarial images in three different settings. With 1,500+ responses and 30,000+ labeled images, we find that majority of the attacks in the literature are not really stealthy to human eyes. We also identify the factors that impact attack stealthiness, e.g., the type of perturbation, the size, quality, and content of the victim images. We further examine the correlations between numerically assessed image similarity/quality and user-perceived stealthiness and re-visit the stealthiness of the attacks with our findings.

Acknowledgements. Zeyan Liu, Fengjun Li and Bo Luo were sponsored in part by NSF awards IIS-2014552, DGE-1565570, DGE-1922649, and the Ripple University Blockchain Research Initiative. Zhu Li was supported in part by NSF award 1747751. The authors would like to thank the anonymous reviewers for their valuable comments and suggestions. The authors would like to thank all the participants of the user studies.

References

1. Bai, H.: Evidence that a large amount of low quality responses on MTURK can be detected with repeated GPS coordinates (2018)
2. Barni, M., Kallas, K., Tondi, B.: A new backdoor attack in CNNs by training set corruption without label poisoning. In: IEEE ICIP (2019)
3. Carlini, N., Wagner, D.: Towards evaluating the robustness of neural networks. In: 2017 IEEE Symposium on Security and Privacy (SP), pp. 39–57. IEEE (2017)
4. Chakraborty, A., Alam, M., Dey, V., Chattopadhyay, A., Mukhopadhyay, D.: Adversarial attacks and defences: a survey. arXiv:1810.00069 (2018)
5. Chen, X., Liu, C., Li, B., Lu, K., Song, D.: Targeted backdoor attacks on deep learning systems using data poisoning. arXiv:1712.05526 (2017)
6. Chmielewski, M., Kucker, S.C.: An MTURK crisis? shifts in data quality and the impact on study results. Soc. Psychol. Personality Sci. **11**(4), 464–473 (2020)
7. Croce, F., Hein, M.: Reliable evaluation of adversarial robustness with an ensemble of diverse parameter-free attacks. In: International Conference on Machine Learning, pp. 2206–2216. PMLR (2020)
8. Dabouei, A., Soleymani, S., Taherkhani, F., Dawson, J., Nasrabadi, N.: Smoothfool: an efficient framework for computing smooth adversarial perturbations. In: Proceedings of the IEEE/CVF Winter Conference on Applications of Computer Vision, pp. 2665–2674 (2020)
9. Doan, K., Lao, Y., Zhao, W., Li, P.: Lira: Learnable, imperceptible and robust backdoor attacks. In: Proceedings of the IEEE/CVF International Conference on Computer Vision, pp. 11966–11976 (2021)
10. Dong, Y., et al.: Boosting adversarial attacks with momentum. In: Proceedings of the IEEE Conference on Computer Vision and Pattern Recognition, pp. 9185–9193 (2018)

11. Dreyfuss, E.: A bot panic hits amazon's mechanical Turk. Wired (2018)
12. Dumford, J., Scheirer, W.: Backdooring convolutional neural networks via targeted weight perturbations. In: 2020 IEEE International Joint Conference on Biometrics (IJCB), pp. 1–9. IEEE (2020)
13. Fei, M., Li, J., Liu, H.: Visual tracking based on improved foreground detection and perceptual hashing. Neurocomputing **152**, 413–428 (2015)
14. Friedman, J., Hastie, T., Tibshirani, R.: Regularization paths for generalized linear models via coordinate descent. J. Stat. Softw. **33**(1), 1 (2010)
15. Ganin, Y., Lempitsky, V.: Unsupervised domain adaptation by backpropagation. In: International Conference on Machine Learning, pp. 1180–1189. PMLR (2015)
16. Ganin, Y., et al.: Domain-adversarial training of neural networks. J. Mach. Learn. Res. **17**(1), 2030–2096 (2016)
17. Goodfellow, I., Shlens, J., Szegedy, C.: Explaining and harnessing adversarial examples. In: ICLR (2015)
18. Gu, T., Dolan-Gavitt, B., Garg, S.: BadNets: identifying vulnerabilities in the machine learning model supply chain. In: NIPS MLSec Workshop (2017)
19. Guo, W., Wang, L., Xing, X., Du, M., Song, D.: Tabor: a highly accurate approach to inspecting and restoring trojan backdoors in AI systems. In: ICDM (2020)
20. Hosseini, H., Poovendran, R.: Semantic adversarial examples. In: Proceedings of the IEEE Conference on Computer Vision and Pattern Recognition Workshops, pp. 1614–1619 (2018)
21. Houben, S., Stallkamp, J., Salmen, J., Schlipsing, M., Igel, C.: Detection of traffic signs in real-world images: The German Traffic Sign Detection Benchmark. In: IJCNN (2013)
22. Jiang, L., Dai, B., Wu, W., Loy, C.C.: Focal frequency loss for image reconstruction and synthesis. In: Proceedings of the IEEE/CVF International Conference on Computer Vision, pp. 13919–13929 (2021)
23. Krizhevsky, A., Hinton, G., et al.: Learning multiple layers of features from tiny images (2009)
24. Kurakin, A., Goodfellow, I., Bengio, S.: Adversarial examples in the physical world. In: ICLR Workshop (2017). https://arxiv.org/abs/1607.02533
25. Li, S., Xue, M., Zhao, B.Z.H., Zhu, H., Zhang, X.: Invisible backdoor attacks on deep neural networks via steganography and regularization. IEEE Trans. Dependable Secure Comput. **18**(5), 2088–2105 (2020)
26. Li, Y., Hua, J., Wang, H., Chen, C., Liu, Y.: Deeppayload: black-box backdoor attack on deep learning models through neural payload injection. In: IEEE/ACM ICSE (2021)
27. Liu, Y., Lee, W.C., Tao, G., Ma, S., Aafer, Y., Zhang, X.: Abs: scanning neural networks for back-doors by artificial brain stimulation. In: ACM CCS (2019)
28. Liu, Y., et al.: Trojaning attack on neural networks. In: NDSS (2018)
29. Madry, A., Makelov, A., Schmidt, L., Tsipras, D., Vladu, A.: Towards deep learning models resistant to adversarial attacks. In: International Conference on Learning Representations (2018)
30. Marnerides, D., Bashford-Rogers, T., Hatchett, J., Debattista, K.: Expandnet: a deep convolutional neural network for high dynamic range expansion from low dynamic range content. In: Computer Graphics Forum.,vol. 37, pp. 37–49. Wiley Online Library (2018)
31. Moosavi-Dezfooli, S.M., Fawzi, A., Frossard, P.: Deepfool: a simple and accurate method to fool deep neural networks. In: Proceedings of the IEEE Conference on Computer Vision and Pattern Recognition, pp. 2574–2582 (2016)

32. Netzer, Y., Wang, T., Coates, A., Bissacco, A., Wu, B., Ng, A.Y.: Reading digits in natural images with unsupervised feature learning (2011)
33. Nguyen, T.A., Tran, A.T.: Wanet-imperceptible warping-based backdoor attack. In: International Conference on Learning Representations (2020)
34. Northcutt, C.G., Athalye, A., Mueller, J.: Pervasive label errors in test sets destabilize machine learning benchmarks. arXiv preprint arXiv:2103.14749 (2021)
35. Russakovsky, O., et al.: ImageNet large scale visual recognition challenge. Int. J. Comput. Vision 115(3), 211–252 (2015). https://doi.org/10.1007/s11263-015-0816-y
36. Saha, A., Subramanya, A., Pirsiavash, H.: Hidden trigger backdoor attacks. In: AAAI (2020)
37. Sheikh, H.R., Bovik, A.C.: Image information and visual quality. IEEE Trans. Image Process. 15(2), 430–444 (2006)
38. Tang, R., Du, M., Liu, N., Yang, F., Hu, X.: An embarrassingly simple approach for trojan attack in deep neural networks. In: ACM KDD (2020)
39. Wald, L.: Quality of high resolution synthesised images: is there a simple criterion? In: Third Conference "Fusion of Earth Data: Merging Point Measurements, Raster Maps and Remotely Sensed Images", pp. 99–103. SEE/URISCA (2000)
40. Wang, B., et al.: Neural cleanse: identifying and mitigating backdoor attacks in neural networks. In: IEEE S&P (2019)
41. Wang, Z., Bovik, A.C.: A universal image quality index. IEEE Signal Process. Lett. 9(3), 81–84 (2002)
42. Wang, Z., Bovik, A.C., Sheikh, H.R., Simoncelli, E.P.: Image quality assessment: from error visibility to structural similarity. IEEE Trans. Image Process. 13(4), 600–612 (2004)
43. Wang, Z., Simoncelli, E.P., Bovik, A.C.: Multiscale structural similarity for image quality assessment. In: The Thrity-Seventh Asilomar Conference on Signals, Systems & Computers, 2003, vol. 2, pp. 1398–1402. IEEE (2003)
44. Wei, P., et al.: AIM 2020 challenge on real image super-resolution: methods and results. In: Bartoli, A., Fusiello, A. (eds.) ECCV 2020. LNCS, vol. 12537, pp. 392–422. Springer, Cham (2020). https://doi.org/10.1007/978-3-030-67070-2_24
45. Wong, E., Rice, L., Kolter, J.Z.: Fast is better than free: revisiting adversarial training. In: International Conference on Learning Representations (2019)
46. Yuhas, R.H., Goetz, A.F.H., Boardman, J.W.: Discrimination among semi-arid landscape endmembers using the spectral angle mapper (sam) algorithm. In: Summaries of the 4th Annual JPL Airborne Geoscience Workshop (1992)
47. Zeng, Y., Park, W., Mao, Z.M., Jia, R.: Rethinking the backdoor attacks' triggers: a frequency perspective. In: Proceedings of the IEEE/CVF International Conference on Computer Vision, pp. 16473–16481 (2021)
48. Zhang, L., Zhang, L., Mou, X., Zhang, D.: FSIM: a feature similarity index for image quality assessment. IEEE Trans. Image Processing 20(8), 2378–2386 (2011)
49. Zhang, Q., Ding, Y., Tian, Y., Guo, J., Yuan, M., Jiang, Y.: Advdoor: adversarial backdoor attack of deep learning system. In: ACM International Symposium on Software Testing and Analysis (2021)
50. Zhang, R., Isola, P., Efros, A.A., Shechtman, E., Wang, O.: The unreasonable effectiveness of deep features as a perceptual metric. In: Proceedings of the IEEE Conference on Computer Vision and Pattern Recognition, pp. 586–595 (2018)
51. Zhong, H., Liao, C., Squicciarini, A.C., Zhu, S., Miller, D.: Backdoor embedding in convolutional neural network models via invisible perturbation. In: ACM CODASPY (2020)

Precise Extraction of Deep Learning Models via Side-Channel Attacks on Edge/Endpoint Devices

Younghan Lee[1], Sohee Jun[1], Yungi Cho[1], Woorim Han[1], Hyungon Moon[2(✉)], and Yunheung Paek[1(✉)]

[1] Seoul National University, Seoul, Republic of Korea
{201younghanlee,soheejun12,rimwoo98,ypaek}@snu.ac.kr, ygcho@sor.snu.ac.kr
[2] UNIST, Ulsan, Republic of Korea
hyungon@unist.ac.kr

Abstract. With growing popularity, deep learning (DL) models are becoming larger-scale, and only the companies with vast training datasets and immense computing power can manage their business serving such large models. Most of those DL models are proprietary to the companies who thus strive to keep their private models safe from the model extraction attack (MEA), whose aim is to steal the model by training surrogate models. Nowadays, companies are inclined to offload the models from central servers to edge/endpoint devices. As revealed in the latest studies, adversaries exploit this opportunity as new attack vectors to launch side-channel attack (SCA) on the device running victim model and obtain various pieces of the model information, such as the model architecture (MA) and image dimension (ID). Our work provides a comprehensive understanding of such a relationship for the first time and would benefit future MEA studies in both offensive and defensive sides in that they may learn which pieces of information exposed by SCA are more important than the others. Our analysis additionally reveals that by grasping the victim model information from SCA, MEA can get highly effective and successful even without any prior knowledge of the model. Finally, to evince the practicality of our analysis results, we empirically apply SCA, and subsequently, carry out MEA under realistic threat assumptions. The results show up to 5.8 times better performance than when the adversary has no model information about the victim model.

Keywords: Privacy in deep learning models · Model extraction attack · Side-channel attack

1 Introduction

Deep learning (DL) models empower many commercial applications and are potentially worth millions of dollars [3,12,19]. Until now, most model architectures and topology have been publicly available, but as models become larger-scale, the increased training cost and difficulty drive companies to prohibit the competitors from creating a copy and taking the market share. The cost of training a DL model comes from both the computational resources and training datasets. Recent studies have shown that the *model extraction attack* (MEA), aiming to train a *surrogate model* of similar performance with much less training cost, is a real threat to such efforts of protecting valuable DL models [2,4,14–16,22,25]. Unfortunately, black-box MEAs require tremendous computational resources and time overhead [8]. To mitigate the amount of labor and increase the chances of success, they usually make certain unrealistic assumptions that give them pre-knowledge about the victim model. For instance, a typical assumption is that the surrogate model has the same or more complex model architecture and the same image dimension as the victim [14,15,22].

The growing demand for on-device ML services is fulfilled by offloading their models to edge/endpoint devices [11], which the adversary may access physically or via network connections, to improve response times and save bandwidth. All in all, this recent development in ML computing opened up a new opportunity that the adversary may exploit as attack vectors to wage *side-channel attacks* (SCAs) on the machine running the victim model. For example, when the victim model and the adversary's application run on the same device, the cache memory may be shared between them, which renders the model vulnerable to the cache SCA [24]. After gathering run-time information leaked via the device hardware, SCA can provide the adversary essential information about the victim that includes *model architecture* (MA) and *image dimension* (ID) of a DL model. Such information is essentially identical to the assumed prior knowledge necessitated for boosting black-box MEAs. This means that with the aid of SCA, MEA can still build a surrogate model better resembling the target even without unrealistic initial assumptions on the victim side. However, there is a stumbling block to the full utilization of SCA for MEA; SCA does not come for free but requires a great deal of cost and effort to obtain sufficient model information accurately [8,24]. To improve their work, SCAs usually need to make strong assumptions on their target systems, which could often be unrealistic or broken just by simple obfuscation techniques [27]. Therefore, a practical and efficient way to use SCA for MEA should be to extract only the essential information required to gain enough knowledge rather than prying into the target device to collect all sorts of information ignorantly. In order to pinpoint such essential information, we must understand how each piece of information affects the performance of MEA. Unfortunately, to the best of our knowledge, no studies have examined extensively the effects of different pieces in the collectable information on MEA. There are some preliminary studies demonstrating that MEA is robust to the difference in certain model features, such as MA, as long as the surrogate model's complexity is high enough [14,15]. Nonetheless, there has been no analytical report on the significance of other types of model information like ID in influencing the effectiveness of MEA.

Our work is the first to present an empirical analysis of the effects of SCA on MEA by evaluating the relationship between the performance of MEA and the model information supplied by SCA. We endeavor to empirically verify the relationship with various settings such as datasets, attack query budget, and attack strategy. We delve into linking a particular type of model information with the outcomes of MEAs by investigating the correlation. We believe that our analytical report will give a glimpse of what types of model information are of more value to boost the performance of MEA relatively. Thus, it will enhance the efficacy of SCAs in their assistance to MEA by letting them concentrate on such valuable ones. In addition, we demonstrate the practicality of utilizing ID obtained from SCA to boost MEA by carrying out the experiment under realistic assumptions. The results achieve up to 5.8x much higher accuracy and fidelity than the adversary without any prior knowledge. Consequently, we argue that our work paves the way for future (offensive and defensive) research in DL model privacy by providing organized knowledge of correlation between existing MEAs with the SCA-supplied knowledge about the victim model. The following summarizes our contributions:

- We analyze the effect of model information exposed by SCA on MEA with different settings: datasets, query budget, and attack strategy.
- We demonstrate how accurately ID of DL models can be estimated by SCA and perform subsequent MEA with estimated ID under realistic threat assumptions to evince the practicality of MEA with SCA.
- We provide an informative insight into improving the defense against MEA allied with SCA by identifying what parts of model information are to be obfuscated from SCA for maximum defense with minimum effort.

2   Background

While MEA and SCA ultimately share the same goal of extracting the victim model of high value, their interpretations of a successful attack are different. MEA aims to obtain a replica of its victim model by copying the functionality. In contrast, SCA intends to extract the structural or architectural model information, including dimensions of layers and their topology.

MEA strives to create at low cost a surrogate of a high-performance victim DL model trained with a dataset of both high quality and large quantity. The most popular method relies on only querying and collecting the inference results from the victim model. The surrogate model is trained with the data used to query the victim with the classification result as its label. As the cost of extracting the model increases with querying more samples, recent studies focus mainly on selecting more valuable samples to reduce the query budget. Ideally, MEA must be carried out with a pure black-box setting where no model information are initially exposed to the adversary. However, in reality, to reduce the amount of labor and increase the chances of their success, many MEA techniques are evaluated under certain assumptions that they already have prior knowledge (ID and MA) about the victim model. We find that such assumptions are often unrealistic in practice as some knowledge can not be available to adversaries in a black-box setting.

SCA has long been studied by cyber security researchers for many decades. In recent years, the use of SCA has been broadened to extract the architectural information of valuable DL models. Although SCA requires the assumption that adversaries gain access to hardware resources in the machine running the victim models, this assumption is deemed plausible these days, as discussed earlier. SCA attempts to collect model information by exploiting vulnerabilities in the underlying hardware. Previous studies have shown that SCA can collect mainly two types of model information, ID and MA. We note here that these are the same pieces of information somehow given to the adversary by assumptions. Further details of SCA is explained in Sect. 5.

3   Related Work

3.1   Model Extraction Attack

KnockoffNets [14] is one of the early MEA technique which is designed under black-box setting. The query samples are selected randomly from out-of-distribution attack dataset as the adversaries are unaware of the training dataset used by the victim model. Finally, the output label from the victim model is paired with the query data (i.e., *re-labeled image*) and used as training dataset for the surrogate model which will exhibit a similar functionality as the victim.

ActiveThief [15] proposed another method called *uncertainty* which is based on the confidence vector of the query samples. The intuition behind this approach is that to extract the classification functionality of the victim model, it is beneficial to concentrate on the query samples that will lie near the decision boundary. By doing so, the surrogate can be trained much more quickly with fewer query samples to reach the victim's classification accuracy.

KnockoffNets and *ActiveThief* discuss briefly how the knowledge of MA affects their performance, and conclude that MEAs are relatively robust to (or regardless of) the choice of MA for their surrogates if the MA complexity is high enough. In other words, MEA can achieve good performance as long as the complexity of a surrogate is sufficiently high (usually, higher than the victim model). This implies that if SCA reveals the exact complexity of MA, the adversary can set up the surrogate with MA of optimal complexity to maximize the effectiveness of MEA. Regarding ID, KnockoffNets and ActiveThief are evaluated under a strong assumption that the adversary is aware of ID of the victim and thus can set up the surrogate with the same ID. They ignorantly assume that this essential pre-knowledge could be offered to attackers by convention, and none of them show how the attackers obtain such information. In this paper, we argue that this assumption can be fulfilled by employing SCA to decide the victim model ID in a deterministic manner and will empirically prove that it is indeed indispensable to the success of MEA.

3.2   Side-channel Attack

Cache Telepathy [24] utilized cache side-channel attack in estimating the architectures in MLaaS (Amazon SageMaker [1], Google ML Engine [5]) platforms. By inferring the size of each layer's input matrix, they deduce the ID of the model. Also, they can infer the MA by identifying the topology of layers. To evaluate the accuracy of their method, the extracted structure is compared to the model's original structure. However, they do not show how useful their extracted model information is to boost MEA, which is necessary to understand the individual effect of each piece of information on black-box MEA.

4   Analysis of the Effects of Model Information

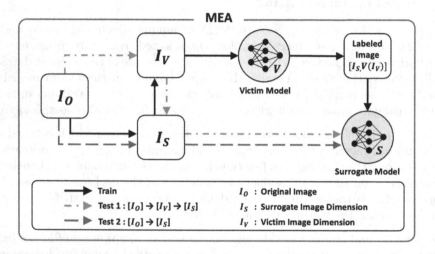

Fig. 1. Flowchart of Training and Evaluating Surrogate Models through MEA

As described just above, it is evident that an attacker can acquire by SCA the model information (i.e., ID, MA) pivotal to MEA which otherwise would have to rely on somewhat ungrounded assumptions to attain its goal. In this work, we conduct a comprehensive analysis to understand the effects of SCA on MEA. For this, we evaluate the performance results of MEA for various configurations of ID and MA, and find the following relationships. **R1:** Effectiveness of MEA vs. model information (ID and MA) of the victim. **R2: R1** vs. analysis settings (*a*: datasets, *b*: attack query budget, *c*: attack strategy).

4.1   Training and Evaluation

In this subsection, we elaborate Fig. 1 in further detail, in which the process of MEA is illustrated by training and evaluating surrogate models.

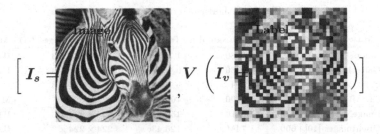

Fig. 2. Example of re-labeled image example (Surrogate [224], Victim [32])

Surrogate Model Training. By employing MEA, we trained the surrogate model following the flow depicted as the solid black line in Fig. 1. We first resize the original image I_O (ID of original image) to I_S (ID of the surrogate model) and resize once more to I_V (ID of the victim model). This is a realistic attack scenario as the adversary is unaware of the victim's image dimension and is likely to query the victim with I_S. The confidence score that the victim returns is $V(I_V)$ and the surrogate model is trained with the *re-labeled image* with the new label, $[I_S, V(I_V)]$. A discrepancy in I_S and I_V causes the *label mismatch*, which is a difference in the classification score of I_S and I_V given by the victim model. Figure 2 visually illustrates the *re-labeled image* where the new label of I_S is given by the classification score of the victim with lower ID (I_V).

Surrogate Model Evaluation. To measure the effectiveness of MEA, we evaluated the surrogate model with two separate tests as shown in Fig. 1. Test 1 resizes I_O to I_V before eventually arriving at I_S, and test 2 resizes I_O directly to I_S. Test 1 is similar to the current method of evaluation where model information including ID (i.e., I_V) is known to adversaries. Test 2 can be considered as a more realistic way of measuring the accuracy of the surrogate model as ID of the victim is unknown to the adversary in reality. We note that when ID of the surrogate is the same as that of the victim, there is no difference between test 1 and test 2 as $I_S = I_V$. The result tables (Tables 2, 3, 4, 5 and 7) include both tests, and the reported surrogate accuracy denotes the best accuracy among the ones measured every five epochs during the training.

4.2 Analysis settings

Image Dimension (ID). To understand the relationship between IDs and the MEA effectiveness, we optimize the models with various IDs to achieve the best accuracy for the victim models. We choose ResNet-50 [7] (Additional result for VGG16 [21] in Appendix A.2) as the architectures of both the victim and surrogate models. The ID is represented as a subscript (i.e., $RN50_{[64]}$ represents ResNet-50 model optimized for $64 \times 64 \times 3$ images).

Datasets. For ID analysis, the victim models are trained with three widely used datasets, as shown in Table 1. To achieve a realistic and high-accuracy model, they are trained by a transfer learning method with a pre-trained model by

Table 1. Dataset configuration

	Dataset	Classes	Train samples	Test samples	Original image (I_O)	Analysis
Victim	Indoor [18]	67	14,280	1,340	$224 \times 224 \times 3$	ID& MA
	Caltech-256 [6]	256	23,380	6,400	$224 \times 224 \times 3$	ID& MA
	CUB-200 [23]	200	5,994	5,794	$224 \times 224 \times 3$	ID
	CIFAR-100 [9]	100	50,000	10,000	$32 \times 32 \times 3$	MA
Attack	ImageNet [20]	1,000	1.2M	150,000	$224 \times 224 \times 3$	ID& MA
	OpenImages [10]	600	1.74M	125,436	$224 \times 224 \times 3$	ID

ISLVRC-2012 (ImageNet) dataset. The accuracy of the trained victim models is shown in the second column of Table 2. For the attack query dataset, we follow the common assumption that an adversary is unaware of the dataset used for training the victim model. The analysis is performed with *out-of-distribution* datasets, ImageNet and OpenImages, with enough samples for a large query budget analysis. We note that OpenImages is an unbalanced dataset where there are uneven number of samples for each image class. For MA analysis, along with three forementioned datasets, we added CIFAR-100 as shown in Table 1 and only ImageNet is used as an attack query dataset. The accuracy of the victim models is shown in the second column of Table 4 and Table 5.

Attack Query Budget. Various attack query budgets are used for ID analysis (i.e., 30k, 60k, and 90k). It is designed to verify if the relationship between ID of the victim and the effectiveness of MEA changes over different query budgets.

Attack Strategy. For ID analysis, two attack strategies are implemented. We use a random sampling strategy based on KnockoffNets and *uncertainty* method from ActiveThief because they exhibit arguably the best performance in MEA. For MA analysis, KnockoffNets was implemented.

Model Architecture (MA). to understand the relationship between MA and the effectiveness of MEA, various MAs of different complexities are used to train the victim and surrogate models: WideResNet-28-k [26] with different k values, VGG16, VGG19, ResNet-50 and ResNet-101. (Details in Appendix A.1).

4.3   Effect of Image Dimension (ID)

Model Extraction Attack Result. Table 2 depicts the result of MEA with the relative accuracy (i.e., accuracy of surrogate model relative to that of the victim which is 1x) as the effectiveness metric. The grey colored boxes denote that IDs of the victim and the surrogate are the same. The bold type represents the best accuracy among surrogate models of different IDs. The result confirms that matching the ID of the victim and surrogate is vital to maximize the efficacy of MEA. Among the total of 48 cases in the grey colored boxes per metric, 92% (44/48) achieve the best accuracy. We find only few cases in the upper right triangular matrix where the surrogate with a higher ID achieved the same or better performance which is at most 3% higher. However, when ID is different, the accuracy of surrogate trained with higher ID ($I_S > I_V$) drop by 0.72x at worst case (average drop of 0.24x). The decrease is more significant when the surrogate is trained with smaller ID ($I_S < I_V$), showing 0.73x in accuracy at worst case (average drop of 0.43x). Between the effectiveness measured by test 1 and test 2 (excluding the cases where $I_s = I_V$), the result from test 1 is higher for 71% (51/72) of the total cases. This instance can be explained by *label mismatch* which is caused by the fact that the new label of I_S is given by I_V. When the relative accuracy is measured by test 1, the influence of *label mismatch* is diminished as I_S is transformed from I_V unlike test 2 in which I_S is transformed from I_O directly. In short, the effectiveness of MEA is maximized when the surrogate model's ID matches the victim model's. (Ablation study results in Appendix A.2)

Datasets. We examine if the trend described above is consistent throughout various datasets. Three different datasets are used for victim models and two attack query datasets for training the surrogate model. Table 2 shows MEA is most effective when the surrogate's ID is identical for all three victim model datasets which have different number of classes. The effectiveness is generally higher with ImageNet which achieve higher relative accuracy in 68% (65/96) of total cases with the average rise of 1.4%. This phenomenon is due to the fact that the victim models are pre-trained with ImageNet dataset. However, it is important to note that the trend continues for both attack query datasets (i.e., Imagenet and OpenImages).

Attack Query Budget. Figure 3 illustrates changes in the effectiveness of MEA over various query budgets (30k, 60k, and 90k) The surrogate model that matches the victim's ID is marked with a red star marker at each query budget. The result shows that matching the surrogate's ID to the victim model is always beneficial through various query budgets. Also, we note that even with a much less query budget, a higher accuracy can be attained when ID is matched. In some cases, query-budget-30k with the same ID can achieve a better accuracy than query-budget-90k with a different ID. Moreover, as the cost of MEA increases as the query budget increases, the adversary can save a huge amount of cost just by training the surrogate with the same ID as the victim.

Attack Strategy. We implement ActiveThief to verify if using a different attack strategy consorts with the phenomena observed in the previous analysis. The attack is carried out with 2k initial seed samples and by sampling new 2k samples for 9 additional rounds (i.e., query-budget-20k). Table 3 shows the similar result that the surrogates trained with the identical ID achieve the best accuracy.

4.4   Effect of Model Architecture (MA)

Model Extraction Attack Result. In order to investigate how MA information of the victim model affects the effectiveness of MEA, we design the analysis with various MA of different complexities. We note that in order to eliminate any effects of ID, all models are set to have the same ID. Therefore, the results shown in Tables 4 and 5 are from both test 1 and 2. Unlike ID analysis, Table 4

Table 2. ID analysis (Datasets). Effectiveness (Relative Accuracy) of MEA (Knock-offNets) with query-budget-60k

Victim Model				Surrogate Model							
Dataset	Accuracy	Model	Attack Query	$RN50_{[32]}$		$RN50_{[64]}$		$RN50_{[128]}$		$RN50_{[224]}$	
				Test 1	Test 2	Test 1	Test 2	Test 1	Test 2	Test 1	Test 2
Indoor67	64.78% (1x)	$RN50_{[32]}$	ImageNet	**0.88x**	**0.88x**	0.63x	**0.91x**	0.59x	0.50x	0.43x	0.16x
			OpenImages	**0.91x**	**0.91x**	0.69x	**0.91x**	0.62x	0.44x	0.46x	0.17x
Caltech-256	66.56% (1x)		ImageNet	**0.96x**	**0.96x**	0.78x	**0.97x**	0.75x	0.61x	0.59x	0.28x
			OpenImages	**0.94x**	**0.94x**	0.75x	**0.95x**	0.66x	0.53x	0.47x	0.23x
CUB-200	67.02% (1x)		ImageNet	**0.86x**	**0.86x**	0.62x	0.80x	0.51x	0.40x	0.35x	0.15x
			OpenImages	**0.83x**	**0.83x**	0.56x	0.73x	0.48x	0.35x	0.31x	0.14x
Indoor67	72.99% (1x)	$RN50_{[64]}$	ImageNet	0.33x	0.28x	**0.94x**	**0.94x**	0.77x	0.87x	0.69x	0.49x
			OpenImages	0.35x	0.29x	**0.96x**	**0.96x**	0.85x	0.91x	0.71x	0.53x
Caltech-256	76.81% (1x)		ImageNet	0.51x	0.48x	**0.99x**	**0.99x**	0.90x	0.96x	0.85x	0.72x
			OpenImages	0.48x	0.45x	**0.97x**	**0.97x**	0.87x	0.94x	0.78x	0.69x
CUB-200	77.89% (1x)		ImageNet	0.15x	0.13x	**0.88x**	**0.88x**	0.66x	0.79x	0.58x	0.40x
			OpenImages	0.13x	0.11x	**0.82x**	**0.82x**	0.65x	0.76x	0.55x	0.37x
Indoor67	67.24% (1x)	$RN50_{[128]}$	ImageNet	0.33x	0.22x	0.82x	0.78x	**0.97x**	**0.97x**	0.95x	0.94x
			OpenImages	0.33x	0.22x	0.84x	0.80x	**1.00x**	**1.00x**	0.96x	0.96x
Caltech-256	76.75% (1x)		ImageNet	0.44x	0.43x	0.78x	0.75x	**0.99x**	**0.99x**	0.97x	0.97x
			OpenImages	0.43x	0.42x	0.76x	0.73x	**0.97x**	**0.97x**	0.95x	**0.98x**
CUB-200	77.44% (1x)		ImageNet	0.21x	0.15x	0.64x	0.59x	**0.91x**	**0.91x**	0.86x	0.87x
			OpenImages	0.18x	0.13x	0.60x	0.56x	**0.88x**	**0.88x**	0.83x	0.84x
Indoor67	73.51% (1x)	$RN50_{[224]}$	ImageNet	0.26x	0.25x	0.66x	0.67x	0.90x	0.87x	**0.92x**	**0.92x**
			OpenImages	0.26x	0.23x	0.69x	0.69x	0.92x	0.90x	**0.97x**	**0.97x**
Caltech-256	78.11% (1x)		ImageNet	0.36x	0.39x	0.78x	0.75x	0.95x	0.92x	**1.00x**	**1.00x**
			OpenImages	0.34x	0.38x	0.74x	0.73x	0.92x	0.90x	**0.99x**	**0.99x**
CUB-200	78.17% (1x)		ImageNet	0.17x	0.16x	0.53x	0.52x	0.78x	0.78x	**0.89x**	**0.89x**
			OpenImages	0.15x	0.14x	0.48x	0.45x	0.74x	0.71x	**0.85x**	**0.85x**

shows that MA of higher complexity achieves better accuracy than MA of the same complexity. Also, Table 5 reveals a similar results as previous studies mentioned in Sect. 3.1. While the adversary can benefit from knowing the same model architecture, the effect is relatively less significant for most cases. Attacking with $RN101_{[224]}$ achieves equally high or higher relative accuracy compared to attacking with the same model architecture. We conclude that the effect of MA on MEA becomes insignificant as long as the surrogate model's MA occupies a high complexity.

5   Experiments

Our analysis, as explained in the previous section (Sect. 4), suggests that an adversary knowing model information (i.e., ID) can boost the effectiveness of MEA. To estimate such information, an adversary can exploit SCA on local devices on which the victim model is running. In this section, we demonstrate end-to-end MEA with SCA *without any prior knowledge* and confirm that our attack mechanism is realistic and highly effective to achieve virtually the same ideal performance of MEA exhibited by the previous work assuming that they somehow manage to obtain model information before actual attacks.

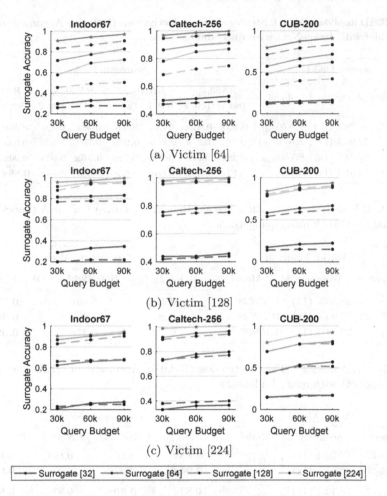

Fig. 3. ID analysis (Attack Query Budget). Effectiveness (Relative Accuracy) of MEA (KnockoffNets with ImageNet) for test 1 (solid line) & test 2 (dotted line)

5.1 Experimental Setups for MEA with SCA

Overview. Our SCA infers ID from the Generalized Matrix Multiply (GEMM), a commonly used building block of DL model implementation, operating in repeated loops for the matrix multiplication. If our SCA infers the number of iterations executed in each layer, it can compute the size of the layer's input matrix by multiplying the number with known constants. The target of our SCA, ID, can be inferred in this way because ID is equivalent to the first layer's input matrix size. Our implementation of SCA is based on *Cache Telepathy* [24] with modifications tailored for our purposes. Figure 4 illustrates the process of MEA with SCA. Firstly, we generate a dynamic call graph (DCG) that reflects the execution flow is generated by monitoring GEMM library with noise filtering

Table 3. ID analysis (Attack Strategy). The effectiveness (Relative Accuracy) of MEA (activethief with ImageNet) with query-budget-20k

Victim Model			Surrogate Model						
Dataset	Accuracy	Model	$RN50_{[32]}$		$RN50_{[64]}$		$RN50_{[128]}$		$RN50_{[224]}$	
			Test 1	Test 2	Test 1	Test 2	Test 1	Test 2	Test 1	Test 2
Indoor67	64.78% (1x)	$RN50_{[32]}$	**0.82x**	**0.82x**	0.34x	0.30x	0.48x	0.44x	0.46x	0.16x
	72.99% (1x)	$RN50_{[64]}$	0.31x	0.27x	**0.90x**	**0.90x**	0.70x	0.86x	0.65x	0.50x
	67.24% (1x)	$RN50_{[128]}$	0.28x	0.21x	0.78x	0.75x	**0.95x**	**0.95x**	0.90x	0.91x
	73.51% (1x)	$RN50_{[224]}$	0.17x	0.23x	0.60x	0.65x	0.85x	0.84x	**0.88x**	**0.88x**

Table 4. MA analysis 1. The effectiveness (Relative Accuracy) of MEA (knockoffNets with ImageNet) with query-budget-20k

Victim Model			Surrogate Model		
Dataset	Accuracy	Model	$WRN28\text{-}1_{[32]}$	$WRN28\text{-}5_{[32]}$	$WRN28\text{-}10_{[32]}$
CIFAR-100	68.36% (1x)	$WRN28\text{-}1_{[32]}$	0.43x	0.56x	**0.57x**
	77.95% (1x)	$WRN28\text{-}5_{[32]}$	0.26x	0.36x	**0.39x**
	79.44% (1x)	$WRN28\text{-}10_{[32]}$	0.26x	0.37x	**0.39x**

Table 5. MA Analysis 2. The effectiveness (Relative Accuracy) of MEA (knockoffnets with ImageNet) with query-budget-20k

Victim Model			Surrogate Model			
Dataset	Accuracy	Model	$VGG16_{[224]}$	$VGG19_{[224]}$	$RN50_{[224]}$	$RN101_{[224]}$
Indoor67	78.20% (1x)	$VGG16_{[224]}$	**0.88x**	0.86x	0.86x	**0.88x**
Caltech-256	83.06% (1x)		**0.94x**	0.92x	0.93x	**0.94x**
Indoor67	78.13% (1x)	$VGG19_{[224]}$	0.83x	**0.90x**	0.87x	**0.90x**
Caltech-256	85.77% (1x)		0.86x	0.93x	0.92x	**0.94x**

mechanism. From the DCG, we can infer the number of iterations of loops executed in each layer. Secondly, ID of DL model is estimated through the inverse calculation from the properties of the loops. Finally, estimated ID is used for subsequent MEA. Each step is described in more detail below.

Threat Assumptions. We performed SCA and MEA assuming that DL model is a black-box and running on an edge/endpoint device. The adversary is not given direct access to the victim model, but only the prediction result is available. For cache-timing attack as a part of SCA, the tracing process by the adversary is running on the same processor as the victim model's process to capture the addresses which are managed by a process running in the background. Such scenario is realistic as the DL model is off-loaded to the local device. Also, the adversary is capable of analyzing linear algebra library used in the DL model such

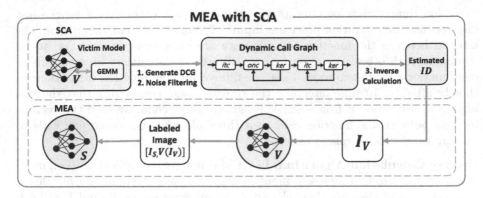

Fig. 4. Flowchart of MEA with SCA. 1) DCG generation, 2) Noise filtering for DCG, 3) Inverse calculation to estimate ID, 4) MEA with estimated ID

as OpenBLAS [28] which is open-source. We assume that stride and padding are known to the adversary. For SCA experiment, we used OpenBLAS for GEMM library with a Linux machine running on a i7-9700 processor that has 8 cores, 64 KB of L1 cache, 256 KB of L2 cache, and 12 MB of shared last-level cache. The system runs with 64GB of main memory.

Dynamic Call Graph Generation. For the purpose of inferring the number of loop iterations, we used cache-timing attack as a part of SCA to infer the DCG that is composed of calls to three key functions, itcopy, oncopy and kernel. We chose these as key functions because each loop of our interest for generating DCG is composed of a specific sequence of such functions as shown below.

$L1$: itcopy-oncopy-kernel-itcopy-kernel
$L2$: oncopy-kernel
$L3$: itcopy-kernel

While the victim model is running, the adversary monitors the calls to these three key functions using *Flush+Reload*, a common technique used for such purpose. By constantly monitoring the addresses of the key functions, we determine if one of the addresses has recently been accessed by measuring the access delay (i.e., cache hit or miss). Three properties of each loop can be deduced from DCG for the following procedure of MEA with SCA. 1) the number of iterations of loops (N), 2) short execution time (ST), 3) average execution time (AT). Short execution time is measured by the last function call and the average execution time is measured with all other calls. Further detail about the algorithm of DCG generation is described in Appendix A.3.

Noise Filtering Mechanism. We found that the DCG generation suffers from the inherent noise that SCA is prone to. We devised a noise filtering mechanism that is tailored for inferring a precise enough DCG exploiting the characteristics of GEMM computation in the target DL architecture. While running, the execution time of each loop iteration is similar to each other except for the last one because each iteration processes inputs of similar size. For this reason, the interval between the function calls that we are monitoring is supposed to be similar to each other. Based on this, we filtered out duplicate observations of one function calls in two ways. First, we filtered out the function calls observed shortly after (< 10 time intervals) the previous one, considering that the two adjacent observation is from a single function call. Second, we used the average interval between the function calls as a threshold and considered any calls to itcopy within the threshold as noise.

Inverse Calculation Algorithm. In GEMM matrix multiplication (i.e., m by k and k by n), m, k, n represent input matrix, weight matrix, and output depth respectively and they are divided into loops by constant Q, P, and UNROLL which are pre-defined by the GEMM library. Therefore, after analyzing DCG to deduce three properties of each loop described above, we estimate ID of DL models by the inverse calculation. Firstly, m value was calculated from properties of $L2$. As m is divided by P to form $L2$ except for the last two iterations, which is operated by an unit of $(P + m \mod P)/2$, m can be obtained by the multiplication of P with the number of iterations of $L2$. Secondly, n is divided by $3 \cdot$ UNROLL to form $L3$ and depending on the AT of $L3$, the last iteration is operated with either $3 \cdot$ UNROLL or UNROLL. Therefore, we inversely calculate n by the multiplication of UNROLL with the number of iterations of $L3$. Thirdly, if the number of $L1$ is less than two, we need to estimate the average execution time of $L1$ by matrix multiplication. The algorithm can be found in Appendix A.3. Once we obtained all properties of $L1$, the value of k is estimated in a similar fashion as above. Finally, with all estimated values, ID of DL model is estimated as shown in Algorithm 1.

Algorithm 1: Estimate Input Dimension

Input: P, Q, $UNROLL$, $stride$, $padding$, N(Number of iterations of loop),
ST(Short execution time of loop), AT(Average execution time of loop)

Output: ID: Input Dimension

1   $m \leftarrow ((N_{L2}-2)+2*(ST_{L2}/AT_{L2}))*P$ ▷ Find m

2   **if** $ST_{L3} < (AT_{L3}/2)$ **then**   ▷ Find n

3 | $n \leftarrow (N_{L3}-1)*3UNROLL+UNROLL$

4   **else**

5 | $n \leftarrow N_{L3}*3UNROLL$

6   **if** $N_{L1} < 2$ **then**   ▷ Find k

7 | $AT_{L1} \leftarrow EstimateL1(m, n, Q)$

8 | $k \leftarrow (ST_{L1}/AT_{L1})*Q$

9   **else**

10 | $k \leftarrow ((N_{L1}-2)+2*(ST_{L1}/AT_{L1}))*Q$

11   $kernel \leftarrow sqrt(k/3)$

12   $ID \leftarrow (sqrt(m)+(kernel-1)-2*padding)*stride$

13   **return** ID

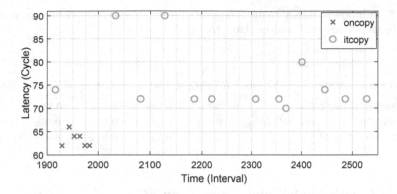

Fig. 5. DCG Generation Result for $RN50_{[128]}$ Victim Model

Table 6. Image dimension estimation result. Values in SCA and target columns represent the estimated and actual values respectively

	m		n		k		kernel		ID	
Victim model	SCA	Target	SCA	Target	SCA	Target	SCA	Target	SCA	Target
$RN50_{[128]}$	4118.5	4096	72	64	35.7	27	3.5	3	129.3	128

5.2 SCA Results

Dynamic Call Graph Generation. Figure 5 shows the result of DCG generation after the noise filtering mechanism which only took less than 0.016 s to construct. From this result, three properties described above are calculated. We note that the observations about `kernel` is omitted for brevity. Firstly, the number of each loop iteration (N_L) is calculated by counting the number of `itcopy` and `oncopy` function calls for $L2$ and $L3$ respectively. There are six `oncopy` calls between 1,900 and 2,000 time intervals and 12 `itcopy` calls after 2,000 intervals and 1 `itcopy` at the beginning. From these, N_{L2} and N_{L3} are estimated as 13 and 6 respectively. N_{L1} is estimated to be 1 as no calls to `oncopy` has been observed after the last `itcopy`. Also, the average and short execution time of each function call can also be estimated from the result by comparing the time intervals as described in Sect. 5.1. All properties collected from DCG for different victim models can be found in Appendix A.3.

Image Dimension Estimation. In our demonstration, pre-defined constant values of P, Q, and UNROLL are 320, 320, and 104,512 respectively. Each of m, n, and k values are inversely calculated according to Algorithm 1 and $kernel$ is calculated by taking the square root of $(k/3)$ (i.e., RGB channels). Finally, we round the calculated output to the nearest whole number to estimate ID of the victim model. Image dimension estimation result of different victim models are illustrated in Table 6. We see that even with some discrepancies in estimated values of m, n, and k, ID of the victim models was retrieved accurately with only ID of $RN50_{[128]}$ being off only by 1.

Table 7. Subsequent MEA (with ImageNet) result. $RN50_{[129]}$ (with estimated ID) shows slightly worse performance than $RN50_{[128]}$

Victim Model			Surrogate Model				
Dataset	Accuracy	Model	$RN50_{[32]}$	$RN50_{[64]}$	$RN50_{[128]}$	$RN50_{[129]}$	$RN50_{[224]}$
Indoor67	67.24% (1x)		0.22x	0.78x	0.97x	**0.99x**	0.94x
Caltech-256	76.75% (1x)	$RN50_{[128]}$	0.43x	0.75x	**0.99x**	0.96x	0.97x
CUB-200	77.44% (1x)		0.15x	0.59x	**0.91x**	0.87x	0.87x

5.3　MEA with Model Information from SCA

We performed subsequent MEA with estimated ID from SCA to demonstrate the benefit of using the estimated ID in MEA. We only carried out MEA only for $RN50_{[128]}$ as the victim with $RN50_{[129]}$ as a surrogate model for the worst case experiment (More results in Appendix A.3). The result in Table 7 illustrates that $RN50_{[129]}$ (with estimated ID) achieves a slightly worse performance as ID is not the exact match. However, such performance is still better than most of MEAs with different IDs as shown in Sect. 4.3 because estimated ID was relatively closer to I_V. At most, the adversary can achieve up to 5.8 times better relative accuracy than the worst case $RN50_{[32]}$. This result backs the hypothesis that employing SCA to collect model information such as ID of the model helps boost the performance of MEA.

6　Discussion and Limitations

Our work targets the present and future computing environments where DL models are not only running on central servers or public cloud, but also off-loaded to diverse classes of edge/endpoint devices. In these environments occur *device fragmentation* referring to when users are running many different versions of software and hardware platforms. Clearly, DL models running on such different platforms may also be diversified (i.e., various ID) for efficiency or portability. Our proposed method is applicable regardless of MA given environments where adversaries can pry on edge/endpoint devices. Moreover, with a recent development in computing power, ResNet-50 can be deployed in edge devices [17].

Offensive Side. Traditional MEAs armed with prior model knowledge based purely on postulations may find more challenging time to steal information from such diversified DL models. Through extensive empirical analysis, we prove that a key to the success of MEA is to have the exact information about ID and MA of the victim model, and also demonstrated that SCAs have enough capability of extracting ID and MA accurately. Consequently, we suggest that for better probability of success, future researchers of MEA first should attempt to obtain the model information from SCA, instead of relying on a prior assumption.

Defensive Side. In our work, we quantitatively show that among model information gathered by SCA, ID is the most essential to MEAs. This implies to defenders against MEA as well as SCA that they do not have to exhaust themselves to protect every information about their DL models, but should focus mainly on concealing or obfuscating the ID value from the adversary. For instance, to fight against SCA, they may obfuscate GEMM operations to hide actual cache access patterns. For example, dummy matrix operations may be added to the original model by inserting dummy columns and rows in the first layer of a DL model to increase the number of loop iterations. Such obfuscated operations would misinform the adversary of the ID value, which in turn eventually hampers the performance of MEA.

Limitations. Our study can be further improved by expanding the training datasets and architectures of victim models and utilizing newly published MEAs can revamp the analysis. In regards to SCA, due to the nature of cache-timing attack, the outcome of SCA can be obscure with noise from CPU. Such limitation may lead to repetition or failure of the attack. Therefore, devising and applying a noise filtering mechanism appropriate for the target execution environment is required in MEA with SCA to maximize the performance of MEA without prior information.

7   Conclusion

Our systematic analysis has shown that ID and MA are two crucial pieces of model information as the initial knowledge about the victim for MEA. Our demonstration confirmed that MEA achieves the best performance when training the surrogate model with ID identical to that of the victim model, and MA more complex than the victim's. This result was consistent across various analysis settings. Our findings account for the reasoning behind the common design decision of existing MEA techniques that prefers their surrogates to have the identical IDs as the victims and as complex MAs as possible. We note that this assumption will become unrealistic for MEAs aiming at future DL models diversified to run on varied classes of computing devices because the models will have many different IDs and MAs depending on their devices. However, an adversary may use advanced SCA techniques by exploiting vulnerabilities in hardware to provide fairly accurate ID and MA of the victim model and achieve satisfying outcomes even without such an unrealistic assumption, as demonstrated in this paper. According to our empirical study, SCA can provide the estimated values for ID of DL models that are extremely close to the target value, thereby helping the subsequent MEA to achieve the idealistic performance. From our result, defenders fighting against MEA allied with SCA may learn a lesson that they can most effectively thwart MEA by obfuscating the ID values of their DL models.

Acknowledgements. This work was supported by the BK21 FOUR program of the Education and Research Program for Future ICT Pioneers, Seoul National University in 2022 and the National Research Foundation of Korea (NRF) grant funded by Korea government (MSIT) (NRF-2020R1A2B5B03095204) & (NRF-2022R1F1A1076100) and by Inter-University Semiconductor Research Center (ISRC). Also, it was supported by Institute of Information & communications Technology Planning & Evaluation (IITP) grant funded by the Korea government (MSIT) (No.2020-0-01840, Analysis on technique of accessing and acquiring user data in smartphone) & (No.2021-0-01817, Development of Next-Generation Computing Techniques for Hyper-Composable Datacenters) & (No.2021-0-00724, RISC-V based Secure CPU Architecture Design for Embedded System Malware Detection and Response)

A   Appendix

A.1   Model Architectures

Table 8 summarises the details of model architectures used for experiments.

Table 8. Details of model architecture used for victim and surrogate models

	$RN50_{[32]}$	$RN50_{[64]}$	$RN50_{[128]}$	$RN50_{[224]}$	$RN101_{[224]}$	$WRN28\text{-}k_{[32]}$	$VGG16_{[32]}$	$VGG16_{[64]}$	$VGG16_{[128]}$	$VGG16_{[224]}$	$VGG19_{[224]}$
Parameter size	91.65MB	91.65MB	91.65MB	91.68MB	164.13MB	1.43MB (k=1) 34.96MB (k=5) 139.39MB (k=10)	490.85MB	516.16MB	516.16MB	516.16MB	536.46MB
conv1	(3×3, 64), stride 1	(4×4, 64), stride 1	(3×3, 64), stride 2		(7×7, 64), stride 2	(3×3, 16), stride 1				(3×3, 64) ×2	
maxpool	✗	✗			(3×3), stride 2	✗	✗	✗	(2×2), stride 2	(2×2), stride 2	
conv2x			(1×1, 64)(3×3, 64)(1×1, 256) ×3			(3×3, 16)×k (3×3, 16)×k ×4			(3×3, 128) ×2		
maxpool			✗			✗	✗	✗	(2×2), stride 2		
conv2x			(1×1, 128)(3×3, 128)(1×1, 512) ×4			(3×3, 32)×k (3×3, 32)×k ×4	(3×3, 128) ×3		(3×3, 256) ×3		(3×3, 256) ×4
maxpool			✗			✗	(2×2), stride 1		(2×2), stride 2		
conv4x		(1×1, 256)(3×3, 256)(1×1, 1024) ×6			(1×1, 256)(3×3, 256)(1×1, 1024) ×23	(3×3, 64)×k (3×3, 64)×k ×4	(3×3, 256) ×3		(3×3, 512) ×3		(3×3, 512) ×4
maxpool			✗			✗	(2×2), stride 2	(2×2), stride 2	(2×2), stride 2		
conv5x			(1×1, 512)(3×3, 512)(1×1, 2048) ×3			✗			(3×3, 512) ×3		(3×3, 512) ×4
maxpool			✗			✗			(2×2), stride 2		
			averagepool, FC, Softmax						maxpool, FC, FC, FC, Softmax		

A.2   Ablation Study

Eigen-CAM Analysis. To further examine if the surrogate copies the victim by inheriting inner representations from convolutional layers, we carry out Eigen-CAM analysis [13] as shown in Fig. 6. Even though all models predicted correctly (i.e., as sunflower), only the surrogate with the same ID has a visual explanation similar to the victim. **ID analysis of VGG16** An additional ID analysis with different model architecture VGG16 is shown in Table 9. ID is represented as a subscript. The result shows the same trend with the analysis on $RN50$ based model.

A.3   SCA Algorithms and DCG Generation Result

Algorithms 2 and 3 are shown below and Table 10 shows the values of properties obtained from Algorithm 2. (N is the number of iterations of loop. ST and AT are the short and average execution time of loop respectively.) Table 11 shows the result of ID estimation results for $RN50_{[32]}$, $RN50_{[64]}$ and $RN50_{[224]}$.

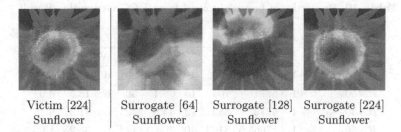

| Victim [224]
Sunflower | Surrogate [64]
Sunflower | Surrogate [128]
Sunflower | Surrogate [224]
Sunflower |

Fig. 6. Eigen-CAM results. Only the surrogate with identical ID is similar

Table 9. ID analysis (Datasets) with VGG16. Effectiveness (Relative Accuracy) of MEA (knockoffNets with ImagenNet) with query-budget-60k

	Victim Model			Surrogate Model							
Dataset	Accuracy	Model	$VGG16_{[32]}$		$VGG16_{[64]}$		$VGG16_{[128]}$		$VGG16_{[224]}$	
			Test 1	Test 2	Test 1	Test 2	Test 1	Test 2	Test 1	Test 2
Indoor67	68.35(1x)		**0.89x**	**0.89x**	0.54x	0.88x	0.50x	0.48x	0.31x	0.20x
Caltech-256	73.55(1x)	$VGG16_{[32]}$	**0.94x**	**0.94x**	0.66x	**0.96x**	0.62x	0.66x	0.45x	0.31x
CUB-200	63.82(1x)		**0.91x**	**0.91x**	0.52x	0.83x	0.49x	0.40x	0.21x	0.15x
Indoo67	75.00(1x)		0.38x	0.35x	**0.93x**	**0.93x**	0.73x	0.86x	0.63x	0.63x
Caltech-256	80.55(1x)	$VGG16_{[64]}$	0.56x	0.51x	**0.95x**	**0.95x**	0.81x	0.93x	0.78x	0.80x
CUB-200	72.56(1x)		0.24x	0.22x	**0.90x**	**0.90x**	0.64x	0.80x	0.53x	0.43x
Indoo67	77.91(1x)		0.32x	0.30x	0.70x	0.68x	**0.91x**	**0.91x**	0.78x	0.81x
Caltech-256	82.39(1x)	$VGG16_{[128]}$	0.49x	0.42x	0.81x	0.78x	**0.95x**	**0.95x**	0.90x	0.92x
CUB-200	77.30(1x)		0.16x	0.13x	0.56x	0.52x	**0.91x**	**0.91x**	0.74x	0.76x
Indoo67	78.20(1x)		0.23x	0.27x	0.60x	0.62x	0.84x	0.82x	**0.92x**	**0.92x**
Caltech-256	83.06(1x)	$VGG16_{[224]}$	0.33x	0.40x	0.76x	0.75x	0.92x	0.91x	**0.95x**	**0.95x**
CUB-200	77.11(1x)		0.10x	0.09x	0.38x	0.35x	0.76x	0.71x	**0.90x**	**0.90x**

Algorithm 2: *CreateDCG*

Input: *addresses*(*it*, *on*, *ker*), *threshold*
Output: DCG_a, DCG_d: Dynamic Call Graph
1 **for** *addr* ∈ *addresses* **do**
2   *delay* ← *probe*(*addr*)   ▷ Time taken to access addr
3   *flush*(*addr*)
4   **if** *delay* < *threshold* **then**   ▷ cache hit
5   DCG_a.*append*(*addr*), DCG_d.*append*(*delay*)

6 **return** DCG_a, DCG_d

Algorithm 3: *EstimateL1*

Input: *m*, *n*, *Q*, *threshold*
Output: AT_{L1}: L1 Average Execution Time
1 k' ← 4Q, $A \in \mathbb{R}^{(m,k')}$, $B \in \mathbb{R}^{(k',n)}$
2 **while** *GEMM*(*A*, *B*) **do** DCG_a, DCG_d ← *CreateDCG*()
   List *idx* ← *FindIndex*(['*itc*, *onc*, *ker*, *itc*, *ker*'], DCG_a)
3 AT_{L1} ← *Avg*(DCG_d[*idx*][0 : (*idx.size*() − 1)])
4 **return** AT_{L1}

Table 10. Properties of Loops obtained from DCG Generation Result

Victim model	Loop1			Loop2			Loop3		
	N	AT	ST	N	AT	ST	N	AT	ST
$RN50_{[32]}$	1	1527	163	4	49	29	6	11.5	10
$RN50_{[64]}$	1	5774	704	13	69.1	50	6	18.3	3.0
$RN50_{[128]}$	1	5212	582	13	44.9	42	6	11.3	9
$RN50_{[224]}$	1	17665.5	8163	40	208.3	124	6	38.25	13

Table 11. Image dimension estimation result. Values in SCA and target columns represent the estimated and actual values respectively

Victim model	m		n		k		kernel		ID	
	SCA	Target	SCA	Target	SCA	Target	SCA	Target	SCA	Target
$RN50_{[32]}$	1018.8	1024	72	64	34.2	27	3.4	3	32.3	32
$RN50_{[64]}$	3983.1	3969	64	64	39	48	3.6	4	63.7	64
$RN50_{[224]}$	12541	12544	64	64	147.9	147	7	7	224	224

References

1. Amazon: Amazon AmazonSageMaker. https://docs.aws.amazon.com/sagemaker/index.html (2021). Accessed 15 Nov 2021
2. Barbalau, A., Cosma, A., Ionescu, R.T., Popescu, M.: Black-box ripper: copying black-box models using generative evolutionary algorithms. arXiv preprint arXiv:2010.11158 (2020)
3. Beatrice, A.: Top companies using machine learning in a profitable way, August 2021. https://www.analyticsinsight.net/top-companies-using-machine-learning-in-a-profitable-way/. Accessed 23 Aug 2021
4. Correia-Silva, J.R., Berriel, R.F., Badue, C., de Souza, A.F., Oliveira-Santos, T.: Copycat CNN: stealing knowledge by persuading confession with random non-labeled data. In: 2018 International Joint Conference on Neural Networks (IJCNN), pp. 1–8. IEEE (2018)
5. Google: Google ML Engine. https://cloud.google.com (2021). Accessed 15 Nov 2021
6. Griffin, G., Holub, A., Perona, P.: Caltech-256 object category dataset (2007)
7. He, K., Zhang, X., Ren, S., Sun, J.: Deep residual learning for image recognition. In: Proceedings of the IEEE Conference on Computer Vision and Pattern Recognition, pp. 770–778 (2016)
8. Hu, X., et al.: DeepSniffer: a DNN model extraction framework based on learning architectural hints. In: Proceedings of the Twenty-Fifth International Conference on Architectural Support for Programming Languages and Operating Systems, pp. 385–399 (2020)
9. Krizhevsky, A., et al.: Learning multiple layers of features from tiny images (2009)
10. Kuznetsova, A., et al.: The open images dataset v4. Int. J. Comput. Vision **128**(7), 1956–1981 (2020)

11. Li, D., Wang, X., Kong, D.: DeepreBirth: accelerating deep neural network execution on mobile devices. In: Proceedings of the AAAI Conference on Artificial Intelligence, vol. 32 (2018)

12. Lorica, B., Paco, N.: The State of Machine Learning Adoption in the Enterprise. O'Reilly Media, Sebastopol (2018)

13. Muhammad, M.B., Yeasin, M.: Eigen-CAM: class activation map using principal components. In: 2020 International Joint Conference on Neural Networks (IJCNN), pp. 1–7. IEEE (2020)

14. Orekondy, T., Schiele, B., Fritz, M.: Knockoff nets: stealing functionality of black-box models. In: Proceedings of the IEEE/CVF Conference on Computer Vision and Pattern Recognition, pp. 4954–4963 (2019)

15. Pal, S., Gupta, Y., Shukla, A., Kanade, A., Shevade, S., Ganapathy, V.: ActiveThief: model extraction using active learning and unannotated public data. In: Proceedings of the AAAI Conference on Artificial Intelligence, vol. 34, pp. 865–872 (2020)

16. Papernot, N., McDaniel, P., Goodfellow, I., Jha, S., Celik, Z.B., Swami, A.: Practical black-box attacks against machine learning. In: Proceedings of the 2017 ACM on Asia Conference on Computer and Communications Security, pp. 506–519 (2017)

17. Q-engineering: Deep learning with raspberry pi and alternatives in 2022 (2022). https://qengineering.eu/deep-learning-with-raspberry-pi-and-alternatives.html. Accessed 11 Apr 2022

18. Quattoni, A., Torralba, A.: Recognizing indoor scenes. In: 2009 IEEE Conference on Computer Vision and Pattern Recognition, pp. 413–420. IEEE (2009)

19. Ribeiro, M., Grolinger, K., Capretz, M.A.: MLaaS: machine learning as a service. In: 2015 IEEE 14th International Conference on Machine Learning and Applications (ICMLA), pp. 896–902. IEEE (2015)

20. Russakovsky, O., et al.: ImageNet large scale visual recognition challenge. Int. J. Comput. Vision 115(3), 211–252 (2015). https://doi.org/10.1007/s11263-015-0816-y

21. Simonyan, K., Zisserman, A.: Very deep convolutional networks for large-scale image recognition. arXiv preprint arXiv:1409.1556 (2014)

22. Tramèr, F., Zhang, F., Juels, A., Reiter, M.K., Ristenpart, T.: Stealing machine learning models via prediction APIS. In: 25th USENIX Security Symposium (USENIX Security 2016), pp. 601–618 (2016)

23. Wah, C., Branson, S., Welinder, P., Perona, P., Belongie, S.: The caltech-UCSD birds-200-2011 dataset (2011)

24. Yan, M., Fletcher, C.W., Torrellas, J.: Cache telepathy: leveraging shared resource attacks to learn DNN architectures. In: 29th USENIX Security Symposium (USENIX Security 2020), pp. 2003–2020 (2020)

25. Yu, H., Yang, K., Zhang, T., Tsai, Y.Y., Ho, T.Y., Jin, Y.: Cloudleak: large-scale deep learning models stealing through adversarial examples. In: NDSS (2020)

26. Zagoruyko, S., Komodakis, N.: Wide residual networks. arXiv preprint arXiv:1605.07146 (2016)

27. Zhang, Y., Reiter, M.K.: Düppel: retrofitting commodity operating systems to mitigate cache side channels in the cloud. In: Proceedings of the 2013 ACM SIGSAC Conference on Computer & Communications Security, pp. 827–838 (2013)

28. Zhang, X., Wang, Q., Zaheer, C.: OpenBLAS (2019). https://www.openblas.net/

Real-Time Adversarial Perturbations Against Deep Reinforcement Learning Policies: Attacks and Defenses

Buse G. A. Tekgul[1(✉)], Shelly Wang[2], Samuel Marchal[1,3], and N. Asokan[1,2]

[1] Aalto University, 02150 Espoo, Finland
batlitekgul@acm.org, samuel.marchal@aalto.fi
[2] University of Waterloo, Waterloo, ON N2L 3G1, Canada
shelly.wang@uwaterloo.ca, asokan@acm.org
[3] WithSecure Corporation, 00180 Helsinki, Finland

Abstract. Deep reinforcement learning (DRL) is vulnerable to adversarial perturbations. Adversaries can mislead the policies of DRL agents by perturbing the state of the environment observed by the agents. Existing attacks are feasible in principle, but face challenges in practice, either by being too slow to fool DRL policies in real time or by modifying past observations stored in the agent's memory. We show that Universal Adversarial Perturbations (UAP), independent of the individual inputs to which they are applied, can fool DRL policies effectively and in *real time*. We introduce three attack variants leveraging UAP. Via an extensive evaluation using three Atari 2600 games, we show that our attacks are effective, as they fully degrade the performance of three different DRL agents (up to 100%, even when the l_∞ bound on the perturbation is as small as 0.01). It is faster than the frame rate (60 Hz) of image capture and considerably faster than prior attacks ($\approx$1.8 ms). Our attack technique is also efficient, incurring an online computational cost of $\approx$0.027 ms. Using two tasks involving robotic movement, we confirm that our results generalize to complex DRL tasks. Furthermore, we demonstrate that the effectiveness of known defenses diminishes against universal perturbations. We introduce an effective technique that detects all known adversarial perturbations against DRL policies, including all universal perturbations presented in this paper.

1 Introduction

Machine learning models are vulnerable to *adversarial examples*: maliciously crafted inputs generated by adding small perturbations to the original input to force a model into generating wrong predictions [8,31]. Prior work [10,13,15] has also shown that adversarial examples can fool deep reinforcement learning (DRL) agents using deep neural networks (DNNs) to approximate their decision-making strategy. If this vulnerability is exploited in safety-critical DRL applications such as robotic surgery and autonomous driving, the impact can be disastrous.

© The Author(s), under exclusive license to Springer Nature Switzerland AG 2022
V. Atluri et al. (Eds.): ESORICS 2022, LNCS 13556, pp. 384–404, 2022.
https://doi.org/10.1007/978-3-031-17143-7_19

A DRL agent can partially or fully observe the *state* of the environment by capturing complex, high-dimensional observations. For example, a DRL agent playing an Atari 2600 game observes pixels from each image frame of the game to construct states by combining a number of observations. DRL agents use the current state as an input to their *policy* that outputs an optimal action for that state. Consequently, adversaries can modify the environment to mislead the agent's policy. Various state-of-the-art attack methods assume *white-box* knowledge, where adversaries have access to the parameters of the agent's policy model and the reinforcement learning algorithm. In *untargeted* attacks, the adversary aims to fool the agent's policy so that the agent 1) cannot complete its task or 2) finishes its task with unacceptably poor performance. Prior work has shown that white-box attacks can successfully destroy agents' performance using one-step gradient-based approaches [8], optimization-based methods [5], or adversarial saliency maps [25]. Previous work has also proposed different attack strategies where the adversary generates the perturbation for 1) each state [2,10], 2) *critical states* where the agent prefers one action with high confidence [13,15,29], or 3) periodically, at every N^{th} state [13].

Although prior white-box attacks using adversarial perturbations are effective in principle, they are not realistic in practice. First, some attack strategies are based on computing the perturbation by solving an optimization problem [15]. This is computationally expensive, even if it is done for every N^{th} state. DRL agents must respond to new states very quickly to carry out the task effectively *on-the-fly*. Therefore, attacks that take longer than the average time between two consecutive observations are too slow to be realized in real-time. Second, in realistic scenarios, the adversary cannot have full control over the environment. However, iterative attacks [15,37] require querying agents with multiple perturbed versions of the current state and resetting the environment to find the optimal perturbation. Therefore, iterative attacks cannot be applied in real-life scenarios, such as autonomous agents interacting with a dynamic environment. Finally, the aforementioned state-of-the-art attacks require seeing all observations to generate and apply perturbations to the state containing multiple observations. However, the agent can store clean observations that are part of the current state in its memory before the adversary can generate perturbations that need to be applied to *all of those observations*.

Contributions: We propose an effective, *real-time* attack strategy to fool DRL policies by computing state-agnostic *universal* perturbations *offline*. Once this perturbation is generated, it can be added into any state to force the victim agent to choose sub-optimal actions. Similarly to previous work [8,15,37], we focus on untargeted attacks in a white-box setting. Our contributions are as follows[1]:

1. We design two new real-time white-box attacks, UAP-S and UAP-O, using Universal Adversarial Perturbation (UAP) [20] to generate state-agnostic

---

[1] The code reproducing our work is available in https://github.com/ssg-research/ad3-action-distribution-divergence-detector.

adversarial examples. We also design a third real-time attack, OSFW(U), by extending Xiao et al.'s [37] attack so that it generates a universal perturbation once, applicable to *any subsequent episode* (Sect. 3). An empirical evaluation of these three attacks using three different DRL agents playing three different Atari 2600 games (Breakout, Freeway, and Pong) demonstrates that our attacks are comparable to prior work in their effectiveness (100% drop in return), while being *significantly faster* (0.027 ms on average, compared to 1.8 ms) and *less visible* than prior adversarial perturbations [10,37] (Sect. 4.2). Using two additional tasks that involve the MuJoCo robotics simulator [34], which requires continuous control, we show that our results generalize to more complex tasks (Sect. 4.3).

2. We demonstrate the limitations of prior defenses. We show that agents trained with the state-of-the-art robust policy regularization technique [39] exhibit reduced effectiveness against adversarial perturbations at higher perturbation bounds (≥ 0.05). In some tasks (Pong), universal perturbations completely destroy agents' performance (Table 2). Visual Foresight [16], which is another defense method that can restore an agent's performance in the presence of prior adversarial perturbations [10], fails to do so when faced with universal perturbations (Sect. 5.1).

3. We propose an efficient method, AD^3, to detect adversarial perturbations. AD^3 can be combined with other defenses to provide stronger resistance for DRL agents against untargeted adversarial perturbations (Sect. 5.2).

2   Background and Related Work

2.1   Deep Reinforcement Learning

Reinforcement Learning: Reinforcement learning involves settings where an agent continuously interacts with a non-stationary environment to decide which action to take in response to a given state. At time step t, the environment is characterized by its state $s \in S$ consisting of N past observations o pre-processed by some function f_{pre}, i.e., $s = \{f_{pre}(o_{t-N+1}), \cdots, f_{pre}(o_t)\}$. At each s, the agent takes an action $a \in \mathcal{A}$, which moves the environment to the next $s' \in S$ and receives a reward r from the environment. The agent uses this information to optimize its policy π, a probability distribution that maps states into actions [30]. During training, the agent improves the estimate of a value function $V(s)$ or an action-value function $Q(s, a)$. $V(s)$ measures how valuable it is to be in a state s by calculating the *expected discounted return*: the discounted cumulative sum of future rewards while following a specific π. Similarly, $Q(s, a)$ estimates the value of taking action a in the current s while following π. During evaluation, the optimized π is used for decision making, and the *performance* of the agent is measured by the return. In this work, we focus on *episodic* [4] and *finite-horizon* [32] tasks. In episodic tasks such as Atari games, each episode ends with a terminal state (e.g., winning/losing a game, arriving at a goal state), and the return for one episode is computed by the total score in single-player games (e.g., Breakout, Freeway) or the relative score when it is played against a computer (e.g., Pong). Finite-horizon tasks include continuous control, where (e.g., Humanoid, Hopper) the return is measured for a fixed length of the episode.

DNN: DNNs are parameterized functions $f(x, \theta)$ consisting of neural network layers. For an input $x \in \mathbb{R}^n$ with n features, the parameter vector θ is optimized by training f over a labeled training set. $f(x, \theta)$ outputs a vector $y \in \mathbb{R}^m$ with m different classes. In classification problems, the predicted class is denoted as $\hat{f}(x) = \text{argmax}_m f(x, \theta)$. For simplicity, we will use $f(x)$ to denote $f(x, \theta)$.

DRL: DNNs are useful for approximating π when $\mathcal{S}$ or $\mathcal{A}$ is too large, or largely unexplored. Deep Q Networks (DQN) is one of the well-known *value-based* DRL algorithms [19] that uses DNNs to approximate $Q(s, a)$. During training, DQN aims to find the optimal $Q(s, a)$, and defines the optimal π implicitly using the optimal $Q(s, a)$. Despite its effectiveness, DQN cannot be used in continuous control tasks, where a is a real-valued vector sampled from a range, instead of a finite set. Continuous control tasks require *policy-based* DRL algorithms [18,28]. They use two different DNNs that usually share a number of lower layers to approximate both π and $V(s)$ (or $Q(s, a)$), and update π directly. For example, in *actor-critic* methods (A2C) [18], the critic estimates $V(s)$ or $Q(s, a)$ for the current π, and the actor updates the parameter vector θ of π by using *advantage*, which refers to the critic's evaluation of the action decision using the estimated $V(s)$ or $Q(s, a)$, while the actor follows the current π. Proximal Policy Optimization (PPO) [28] is another on-policy method that updates the current π by ensuring that the updated π is close to the old one.

2.2   Adversarial Examples

An adversarial example x^* against a classifier f is a deliberately modified version of an input x such that x and x^* are similar, but x^* is misclassified by f, i.e., $\hat{f}(x) \neq \hat{f}(x^*)$. An untargeted adversarial example is found by solving

$$\underset{x^*}{\text{argmax}}\, \ell(f(x^*), \hat{f}(x)) \quad \text{s.t.:} \quad \|x^* - x\|_p = \|r\|_p \leq \epsilon, \tag{1}$$

where ϵ is the l_p norm bound and ℓ is the loss between $f(x^*)$ and the predicted label $\hat{f}(x)$. In this work, we use the l_∞ norm bound (i.e., any element in the perturbation must not exceed a specified threshold ϵ) as in the state-of-the-art Fast Gradient Sign Method (FGSM) [8].

Adversarial examples are usually computed for each x. An alternative is to generate input-agnostic *universal perturbations*. For instance, Moosavi et al. propose *Universal Adversarial Perturbation* (UAP) [20] that searches for a sufficiently small r that can be added to the *arbitrary* inputs to yield adversarial examples against f. UAP iteratively computes a unique r that fools f for almost all inputs x belonging to a training set $\mathcal{D}_{train}$. UAP utilizes DeepFool [21] to update r at each iteration. UAP aims to achieve the desired *fooling rate* δ:

the proportion of successful adversarial examples against f with respect to the total number of perturbed samples $|\mathcal{D}_{train}|$. Following this work, many different strategies [6,9,22,23] have been proposed to generate universal adversarial perturbations to fool image classifiers. For example, Hayes et al. [9] and Mopuri et al. [23] use generative models to compute universal adversarial perturbations. Co et al. [6] design black-box, untargeted universal adversarial perturbations using procedural noise functions.

Adversarial Examples in DRL: In discrete action spaces with finite actions, adversarial examples against π are found by modifying Eq. 1: x is changed to s at time step t, f is replaced with $Q(s, a)$, and $\hat{Q}(s)$ refers to the decided action. We also denote $Q(s, a_m)$ as the state-action value of mth action at s. In this setup, adversarial examples are computed to decrease $Q(s, a)$ for the optimal action at s, resulting in a sub-optimal decision.

Since Huang et al. [10] showed the vulnerability of DRL policies to adversarial perturbations, several untargeted attack methods [2,13,15,29,37] have been proposed that manipulate the environment. Recent work [1,5,11,15,35] has also developed targeted attacks, where the adversary's goal is to lure the victim agent into a specific state or to force the victim policy to follow a specific path. Most of these methods implement well-known adversarial example generation methods such as FGSM [10,13], JSMA [2] and Carlini&Wagner [15]. Therefore, even though they effectively decrease the return of the agent, these methods cannot be implemented in real-time and have a temporal dependency: they need to compute a different r for every s. Similarly to our work, Xiao et al. propose ("obs-seq-fgsm-wb", OSFW) to generate universal perturbations. OSFW computes a single r by applying FGSM to the averaged gradients over the k states and adds r to the remaining states in the current episode. However, OSFW has limitations, such as the need to compute r for every new episode. Moreover, OSFW has to freeze the task to calculate r, and its performance depends on the particular agent-environment interaction for each episode. Hussenot et al. [11] design targeted attacks that use different universal perturbations for each action to force the victim policy to follow the adversary's policy.

In addition to white-box attacks, multiple black-box attack methods based on finite-difference methods [37], and proxy methods that approximate the victim policy [12,41] were proposed, but they cannot be mounted in real time, as they require querying the agent multiple times. Recent work [7,36] also shows that adversaries can fool DRL policies in multi-agent, competitive games by training an adversarial policy for the opponent agent that exploits vulnerabilities of the victim agent. These attacks rely on creating natural observations with adversarial effects, instead of manipulating the environment by adding adversarial perturbations. In this paper, we focus on single-player games, where adversaries can only modify the environment to fool the DRL policies.

3   State- and Observation-Agnostic Perturbations

3.1   Adversary Model

The goal of the adversary Adv is to degrade the performance of the victim DRL agent v by adding perturbations r to the state s observed by v. Adv is successful when the attack:

1. is *effective*, i.e., limits v to a low return,
2. is *efficient*, i.e., can be realized in real-time, and
3. *evades* known detection mechanisms.

Adv has a white-box access to v; therefore, it knows v's action value function Q_v, or the policy π_v and the value function V_v, depending on the DRL algorithm used by v. However, Adv is constrained to using r with a small norm to evade possible detection, either by specific anomaly detection mechanisms or via human observation. We assume that Adv cannot reset the environment or return to an earlier state. In other words, we rule out trivial attacks (e.g., swapping one video frame with another or changing observations with random noise) as ineffective because they can be easily detected. We also assume that Adv has only read-access to v's memory. Modifying the agent's inner workings is an assumption that is too strong in realistic adversarial settings because it forces Adv to modify both the environment and v. If Adv is able to modify or rewrite v's memory, then it does not need to compute adversarial perturbations and simply rewrites v's memory to destroy its performance.

3.2   Attack Design

Training Data Collection and Sanitization: Adv collects a training set $\mathcal{D}_{train}$ by monitoring v's interaction with the environment for one episode, and saving each s into $\mathcal{D}_{train}$. Simultaneously, Adv clones Q_v or V_v into a *proxy agent*, adv. Specifically, in value-based methods, Adv copies the weights of Q_v into Q_{adv}. In policy-based methods, Adv copies the weights of the critic network into V_{adv}. In the latter case, Adv can obtain $Q_{adv}(s, a)$ by calculating $V_{adv}(s)$ for each *discrete* action $a \in \mathcal{A}$.

After collecting $\mathcal{D}_{train}$, Adv sanitizes it by choosing only the *critical states*. Following [15], we define critical states as those that can have a significant influence on the course of the episode. We identify critical states using the relative action preference function

$$\text{Var}_{a \in \mathcal{A}}\left[\text{Softmax}(Q_{adv}(s, a))\right] \geq \beta$$

$$\beta = 1/|\mathcal{D}_{train}| \sum_{s \in \mathcal{D}_{train}} \text{Var}_{a \in \mathcal{A}}\left[\text{Softmax}(Q_{adv}(s, a))\right], \tag{2}$$

modified from [15], where Var is the variance of the normalized $Q_{adv}(s, a)$ values computed for $\forall a \in \mathcal{A}$. This ensures that both UAP-S and UAP-O are optimized to fool Q_v in critical states, and achieves the first attack criterion.

Algorithm 1. Computation of UAP-S and UAP-O

---

input : sanitized $\mathcal{D}_{train}, Q_{adv}$, desired fooling rate δ_{th},
             max. number of iterations it_{max}, perturbation constraint ϵ
output: universal r
1 Initialize $r \leftarrow 0, it \leftarrow 0$;
2 **while** $\delta < \delta_{max}$ **and** $it < it_{max}$ **do**
3   **for** $s \in \mathcal{D}_{train}$ **do**
4   **if** $\hat{Q}(s + r) = \hat{Q}(s)$ **then**
5   Find the extra, minimal Δr:
             $\Delta r \leftarrow \operatorname{argmin}_{\Delta r} \|\Delta r\|_2$ s.t.: $\hat{Q}(s + r + \Delta r) \neq \hat{Q}(s)$;
6           $r \leftarrow \operatorname{sign}(\min(\operatorname{abs}(r + \Delta r), \epsilon))$;
7   Calculate δ with updated r on $\mathcal{D}_{train}$;
8     $it \leftarrow (it + 1)$;

Computation of Perturbation: For both UAP-S and UAP-O, we assume that $s \in \mathcal{D}_{train}$ and $\mathcal{D}_{train} \subset \mathcal{S}$. Adv searches for an optimal r that satisfies the constraints in Eq. 1, while achieving a high fooling rate δ on $\mathcal{D}_{train}$. For implementing UAP-S and UAP-O, we modify Universal Adversarial Perturbation [20] (see Sect. 2.2). The goal of both UAP-S and UAP-O is to find a sufficiently small r such that $\hat{Q}(s + r) \neq \hat{Q}(s)$, leading v to choose sub-optimal actions. Algorithm 1 summarizes the method for generating UAP-S and UAP-O.

In lines 5–6 of Algorithm 1, UAP-S and UAP-O utilize DeepFool to compute Δr by iteratively updating the perturbed $s_i^* = s + r + \Delta r_i$ until $\hat{Q}_{adv}$ outputs a wrong action (see Algorithm 2 in [21]). At each iteration i, DeepFool finds the closest hyperplane $\hat{l}(s_i^*)$ and Δr_i that projects s_i^* on the hyperplane. It recomputes Δr_i as

$$
Q'(s_i^*, a_{\hat{l}}) \leftarrow Q_{adv}(s_i^*, a_{\hat{l}}) - Q_{adv}(s_i^*, a_m),
$$
$$
w_{\hat{l}}' \leftarrow \nabla Q_{adv}(s_i^*, a_{\hat{l}}) - \nabla Q_{adv}(s_i^*, a_m),
$$
$$
\Delta r_i \leftarrow \frac{|Q'(s_i^*, a_{\hat{l}})|}{\|w_{\hat{l}}'\|_2^2} w_{\hat{l}}', \tag{3}
$$

where ∇ is the gradient of Q_{adv} w.r.t. s_i and $Q_{adv}(s_i^*, a_m)$ is the value of the m-th action chosen for the state $s + r$.

UAP-S computes a different perturbation for each observation o_j in s, i.e., $r = \{r_{t-N+1}, \cdots, r_t\}$, $r_j \neq r_k$, $\forall j, k \in \{t - N + 1, \cdots, t\}$, $j \neq k$. In contrast, UAP-O applies the same perturbation to all observations in s. Therefore, it can be considered as an observation-agnostic, completely universal attack. UAP-O aims to find a modified version $\tilde{r}$ of r by solving

$$
\min(\|r - \tilde{r}\|_2^2) \tag{4}
$$
$$
\text{s.t.: } \tilde{r}_j = \tilde{r}_k, \forall j, k \in \{t - N + 1, \cdots, t\} \text{ and } \|\tilde{r}\|_\infty \leq \epsilon.
$$

In UAP-O, we modify lines 5–6 of Algorithm 1 to find Δr. The closest $\Delta \tilde{r}_i$ to Δr_i satisfying the conditions of Eq. 4 is found by averaging $w'_{\hat{l}}$ over observations:

$$\Delta \tilde{r}_{i_j} \leftarrow \frac{|Q'(s_i^*, a_{\hat{l}})|}{N\|w'_{\hat{l}}\|_2^2} \sum_{k=(t-N+1)}^{t} w'_{\hat{l}_k}, \ \forall j \in \{t - N + 1, \cdots, t\}. \tag{5}$$

In UAP-O, DeepFool returns $\Delta \tilde{r}_i = \Delta \tilde{r}_{i_j}$ as the optimal additional perturbation. UAP-O adds the same $\tilde{r}_j$ to every o_j in s. If s consists of only one observation, then UAP-S will simply reduce to UAP-O. The proof of Eq. 5 can be found in the extended version of this work [33].

Extending OSFW to OSFW(U). As explained in Sect. 2.2, OSFW calculates r by averaging gradients of Q_v using the first k states in an episode and then adds r to the remaining states. This requires 1) generating a different r for each episode, and 2) suspending the task (e.g., freezing or delaying the environment) and v to perform backward propagation. Moreover, the effectiveness of OSFW varies when v behaves differently in individual episodes. We extend OSFW to a completely universal adversarial perturbation by using the proxy agent's DNN, and calculate averaged gradients with first k samples from the same, un-sanitized $\mathcal{D}_{train}$. The formula for calculating r in OSFW(U) is

$$r = \epsilon \cdot \text{sign}(1/k \sum_{i=0}^{i<k} \nabla_{s_i}(-\log(Q_{adv}(s_i, \hat{a})))), \tag{6}$$

where $\hat{a}$ denotes the action chosen and $s_i \in \mathcal{D}_{train}$.

Attacks in Continuous Control Settings. In continuous control tasks, the optimal action is a real-valued array that is selected from a range. These tasks have complex environments that involve physical system control such as Humanoid robots with multi-joint dynamics [34]. Agents trained for continuous control tasks have no Q that can be utilized for generating perturbations to decrease the value of the optimal action. Nevertheless, Adv can find a perturbed state $s + r$ that has the worst $V(s)$, so that π_v might produce a sub-optimal action [39]. In continuous control, OSFW and OSFW(U) can be simply modified by changing Q_{adv} with V_{adv}. However, in Algorithm 1, the lines 4–6 need to be adjusted to handle these tasks. Adv can only use the copied network parameters of V_{adv} to find r. Algorithm 2 (Appendix B) presents the modified computation of UAP-S and UAP-O in continuous control.

4 Attack Evaluation

4.1 Experimental Setup

We compared the effectiveness of our attacks (UAP-S, UAP-O and OSFW(U)) with prior attacks (FGSM and OSFW) on discrete tasks using three Atari 2600 games (Pong, Breakout, Freeway) in the Arcade Learning Environment [4]. We further extended our experimental setup with the MuJoCo robotics simulator [34] and compared these attacks in continuous control tasks.

To provide an extensive evaluation, for every Atari game, we trained three agents, each using a different DRL algorithm: DQN [19], PPO [28] and A2C [18]. We used the same DNN architecture proposed in [19] to approximate Q_v in DQN and V_v in other algorithms. Our implementations of DQN, PPO and A2C are based on OpenAI baselines[2], and our implementations achieve returns similar to those of OpenAI Baselines. The frame rate of each Atari 2600 game 60 Hz by default [4]; thus, the time interval between two consecutive frames is 0.017 seconds. We used the frame-skipping technique [19], so each s contains $N = 4$ different observations. To aid reproducibility, we summarize the setup and pre-processing methods in the extended version of this work [33].

We implemented UAP-S and UAP-O by setting the desired δ_{max} to 95%, so that they stop when $\delta \geq 95\%$. As baselines, we used random noise addition, FGSM [10], and OSFW [37]. We chose FGSM as the baseline since it is the fastest adversarial perturbation generation method from the previous work and is effective in degrading the performance of DRL agents. We measured attack effectiveness where $0 \leq \epsilon \leq 0.01$. We reported the average return over 10 episodes and used different seeds during training and evaluation.

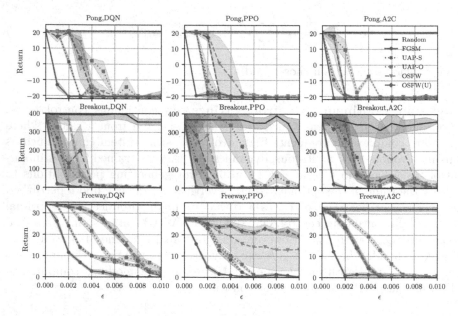

Fig. 1. Comparison of attacks against DQN, PPO and A2C agents trained for Pong, Breakout and Freeway. The graph shows how the return (averaged over 10 games) changes with different ϵ values for six different attack strategies

---

[2] https://github.com/DLR-RM/rl-baselines3-zoo.

4.2   Attack Performance

Figure 1 compares UAP-S, UAP-O, and OSFW(U) with two baseline attacks and random noise addition. Random noise addition cannot cause a significant drop in v's performance, and FGSM is the most effective attack, reducing the return up to 100% even with a very small ϵ value. UAP-S is the second most effective attack in almost every setup, reducing the return by more than 50% in all experiments when $\epsilon \geq 0.004$. All attacks completely destroy v's performance at $\epsilon = 0.01$, except the PPO agent playing Freeway. The effectiveness of UAP-O, OSFW, and OSFW(U) is comparable in all setups. We also observe that the effectiveness of OSFW fluctuates heavily (Breakout-A2C) or has a high variance (Freeway-PPO). This phenomenon is the result of the different behaviors of v in individual episodes (Breakout-A2C), and OSFW's inability to collect enough knowledge (Freeway-PPO) to generalize r to the rest of the episode.

Table 1. Offline and online cost of attacks where victim agents are DQN, PPO, A2C trained for Pong and $\epsilon = 0.01$. Attacks that cannot be implemented in real-time are in highlighted in red.

Experiment	Attack method	Offline cost ± std (seconds)	Online cost ± std (seconds)
Pong, DQN, $T_{max} = 0.0163 \pm 10^{-6}$ seconds	FGSM	–	$13 \times 10^{-4} \pm 10^{-5}$
	OSFW	–	5.3 ± 0.1
	UAP-S	36.4 ± 21.1	$2.7 \times 10^{-5} \pm 10^{-6}$
	UAP-O	138.3 ± 25.1	$2.7 \times 10^{-5} \pm 10^{-6}$
	OSFW(U)	5.3 ± 0.1	$2.7 \times 10^{-5} (\pm 10^{-6})$
Pong, PPO, $T_{max} = 0.0157 \pm 10^{-5}$ seconds	FGSM	–	$21 \times 10^{-4} \pm 10^{-5}$
	OSFW	–	7.02 ± 0.6
	UAP-S	41.9 ± 16.7	$2.7 \times 10^{-5} \pm 10^{-6}$
	UAP-O	138.3 ± 25.1	$2.7 \times 10^{-5} \pm 10^{-6}$
	OSFW(U)	7.02 ± 0.6	$2.7 \times 10^{-5} \pm 10^{-6}$
Pong, A2C $T_{max} = 0.0157 \pm 10^{-5}$ seconds	FGSM	–	$21 \times 10^{-4} \pm 10^{-5}$
	OSFW	–	7.2 ± 1.1
	UAP-S	11.4 ± 4.3	$2.7 \times 10^{-5} \pm 10^{-6}$
	UAP-O	55.5 ± 29.3	$2.7 \times 10^{-5} \pm 10^{-6}$
	OSFW(U)	7.2 ± 1.1	$2.7 \times 10^{-5} \pm 10^{-6}$

Table 1 shows the computational cost to generate r, and the upper bound on the online computational cost to mount the attack in real-time. This upper bound is measured as $T_{max} = 1/(\text{frame rate}) - (\text{response time})$, where the response time is the time spent feeding s forward through π_v or Q_v and executing the corresponding action. If the online cost of injecting r during deployment (and the online cost of generating r during deployment in the case of FGSM and OSFW) is greater than T_{max}, then Adv must stop or delay the environment, which is infeasible in practice. Table 1 confirms that the online cost of OSFW is higher than that of all other attacks and T_{max} due to its online perturbation generation approach. OSFW has to stop the environment to inject r into the current s or has to wait 102 states on average (online cost/$(T_{max} \cdot N)$) to correctly inject r, which can decrease the attack effectiveness. UAP-S and UAP-O have a higher offline cost than OSFW(U), but the offline generation of r does not interfere with the task, as it does not require interrupting or pausing v. The online cost of FGSM, UAP-S, UAP-O and OSFW(U) is lower than T_{max}.

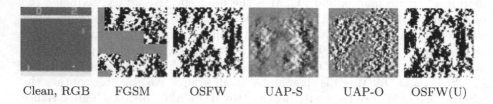

Clean, RGB   FGSM   OSFW   UAP-S   UAP-O   OSFW(U)

Fig. 2. Comparison of the perturbation size added into the same clean (RGB) observation in different attacks against the DQN agent playing Pong and $\epsilon = 0.01$. In perturbations, black pixels: -0.01, white pixels: $+0.01$, gray pixels: 0.0

Figure 2 shows that r obtained via UAP-S and UAP-O are smaller than other adversarial perturbations for the same ϵ, since UAP-S and UAP-O try to find a minimal r that sends all $x \in \mathcal{D}_{train}$ outside the decision boundary [20]. We conclude that UAP-S and UAP-O are likely to be less detectable based on the amount of the perturbation (e.g., via visual observation).

Table 2. Summary of attacks based on the characteristics that make an attack plausible in a real deployment scenario. The proposed attacks are colored blue.

Attack	FGSM [10]	OSFW [37]	UAP-S	UAP-O	OSFW(U)
Online cost	Low	High	Low	Low	Low
State dependency	Dependent	Independent	Independent	Independent	Independent
Observation dependency	Dependent	Dependent	Dependent	Independent	Dependent

As summarized in Table 2, FGSM computes a new r for each s after observing the complete s. Therefore, it requires rewriting v's memory to change all previously stored observations o_j of the current s, in which v is attacked. Unlike FGSM, UAP-S and UAP-O add r_j to the incoming o_j, and v stores adversarially perturbed o_j into its memory. The online cost of OSFW is too high, and it cannot be mounted without interfering with the environment. UAP-S, UAP-O and OSFW(U) are real-time attacks that do not require stopping the agent or the environment while adding r. UAP-S and OSFW(U) generate r that is independent of s, but the r_j for each observation $o_j \in s$ is different. On the other hand, UAP-O adds the same r_j to all observations in any s, which makes the perturbation generation independent of the size of s. UAP-O leads to an efficient and effective attack when $\epsilon \geq 0.006$, and does not have temporal and observational dependency. UAP-S is the optimal attack considering both effectiveness and efficiency. We further compared the effectiveness of UAP-S and OSFW in uncontrolled environments in Appendix A, and concluded that UAP-S is more effective than OSFW(U) in complex, uncontrolled environments.

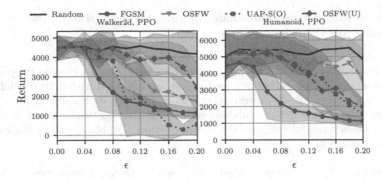

Fig. 3. Comparison of attacks against PPO agents trained for Humanoid and Walker-2d tasks. The graph shows how the return (averaged over 50 games) changes with different ϵ values for five different attack strategies

4.3 Attack Performance in Continuous Control

In continuous control, we used PPO agents in [39] pre-trained for two different MuJoCo tasks (Walker2d and Humanoid) as v^3. We used the original experimental setup to compare our attacks with baseline attacks and random noise addition. In our experiments, PPO agents show performance similar to those reported in the original paper [39]. We implemented UAP-S by copying the parameters of V_v into V_{adv}, and set $\delta_{max} = 95\%$. FGSM, OSFW and OSFW(U) also use V_v to minimize the value in a perturbed state. Additionally, in both tasks, s contains only one observation, which reduces UAP-S to UAP-O. Figure 3 shows the attack effectiveness when $0.0 \leq \epsilon \leq 0.2$. FGSM is the most effective attack in Humanoid, while UAP-S decreases the return more than FGSM in Walker2d when $\epsilon \geq 0.12$. Overall, all attacks behave similarly in both discrete and continuous action spaces, and our conclusions regarding the effectiveness of universal adversarial perturbations generalize to continuous control tasks, where Q_v is not available. However, in these tasks, Adv only decreases the critic's evaluation of s when taking an action a. Even if Adv decreases the value of $V_{adv}(s)$, it does not necessarily lead to π_v choosing a sub-optimal action over the optimal one. Therefore, attacks using V require $\epsilon \geq 0.2$ to fool π_v effectively. For a more efficient attack, Adv can copy π_v into a proxy agent as π_{adv}, and try to maximize the total variation distance [39] in π_{adv} for states perturbed by universal perturbations. UAP-S, UAP-O and OSFW(U) need to be modified to compute the total variation distance, and we leave this as a future work.

Table 5 in Appendix C presents the online and offline computational cost for the perturbation generation. The results are comparable with Table 1, and confirm that FGSM, UAP-S, UAP-O and OSFW(U) can be mounted in real-time, although FGSM needs write-access to the agent's memory. OSFW cannot

---

[3] Agents are downloaded from https://github.com/huanzhang12/SA_PPO and frame rates are set to default values as in https://github.com/openai/gym.

inject the generated noise immediately into subsequent states, since it has a higher online cost than the maximum upper bound.

Table 3. Average returns (10 episodes) for the DQN agent playing Pong in the presence of different adversarial perturbations, and agents are equipped with different defenses. In each row, the best attack (lowest return) is in bold. In each column, for a given ϵ value, the most robust defense (highest return) for that particular attack is shaded green if the defense can fully recover the victim's return, and blue if the victim's return is not fully recovered.

ϵ	Defense	Average return ± std in the presence of adversarial perturbation attacks					
		No attack	FGSM	OSFW	UAP-S	UAP-O	OSFW(U)
0.01	No defense	21.0 ± 0.0	-21.0 ± 0.0	-20.0 ± 3.0	-21.0 ± 0.0	-19.8 ± 0.4	-21.0 ± 0.0
	VF [16]	21.0 ± 0.0	21.0 ± 0.0	-19.7 ± 0.5	0.7 ± 1.7	0.4 ± 2.7	-21.0 ± 0.0
	SA-MDP [39]	21.0 ± 0.0	21.0 ± 0.0	21.0 ± 0.0	21.0 ± 0.0	21.0 ± 0.0	21.0 ± 0.0
0.02	No defense	21.0 ± 0.0	-19.9 ± 1.3	-21.0 ± 0.0	-20.8 ± 0.6	-20.0 ± 0.0	-21.0 ± 0.0
	VF [16]	21.0 ± 0.0	21 ± 0.0	-19.7 ± 0.6	9.4 ± 0.8	5.3 ± 3.9	-20.5 ± 0.5
	SA-MDP [39]	21.0 ± 0.0	-14.6 ± 8.8	-20.5 ± 0.5	-20.6 ± 0.5	-20.6 ± 0.5	-21.0 ± 0.0
0.05	No defense	21.0 ± 0.0	-20.5 ± 0.7	-21.0 ± 0.0	-20.6 ± 0.8	-20.0 ± 0.0	-21.0 ± 0.0
	VF [16]	21.0 ± 0.0	21.0 ± 0.0	-20.0 ± 0.0	7.6 ± 4.7	-14.1 ± 1.1	-21.0 ± 0.0
	SA-MDP [39]	21.0 ± 0.0	-21.0 ± 0.0	-21.0 ± 0.0	-20.6 ± 0.5	-20.6 ± 0.5	-21.0 ± 0.0

5   Detection and Mitigation of Adversarial Perturbations

Previous work on adversarial training [3,13] presents promising results as a defense. However, Zhang et al. [39] show that adversarial training leads to unstable training, performance degradation, and is not robust against strong attacks. Moreover, Moosavi et al. [20] prove that despite a slight decrease in the fooling rate δ in the test set, *Adv* can easily compute another universal perturbation against retrained agents. To overcome the challenges of adversarial training, Zhang et al. [39] propose state-adversarial Markov decision process (SA-MDP), which aims to find an optimal π under the strongest *Adv* using policy regularization. This regularization technique helps DRL agents *maintain* their performance even against adversarially perturbed inputs. Similarly, Oikarinen et al. [24] use adversarial loss functions during training to improve the robustness of agents.

Visual Foresight (VF) [16] is another defense that *recovers* the performance of an agent in the presence of *Adv*. VF predicts the current observation $\hat{o}_t$ at time t using k previous observations $o_{t-k} : o_{t-1}$ and corresponding actions $a_{t-k} : a_{t-1}$. It also predicts the possible action $\hat{a}_t$ for the partially predicted $\hat{s}$ using $Q(\hat{s}, a)$. The difference between $Q(\hat{s}, a)$ and $Q(\hat{s}, \hat{a})$ determines whether s is perturbed or not. In the case of detection, $\hat{a}_t$ is selected to recover the performance.

5.1   Effectiveness of Existing Defenses

To investigate the limitations of previously proposed defenses for DRL, we implemented two defense methods that aim to retain the average return of v when it is under attack: VF [16] and SA-MDP [39], both of which seek to prevent the first attack objective that limits v to a low return. VF also prevents the third attack criterion and detects adversarial perturbations. Since we want to evaluate the effectiveness of VF and SA-MDP, we focus on the DQN agents for Pong and Freeway as these are the ones that are common between our experiments (Sect. 4) and these defenses [16,39]. Results for Freeway agents are in the extended version of this work [33].

We implemented VF from scratch for our DQN models following the original experimental setup in [16] by setting $k = 3$ to predict every 4th observation. We also set the pre-defined threshold value to 0.01, which is used to detect adversarial perturbations to achieve the highest detection rate and performance recovery. We downloaded state adversarial DQN agents, which are trained using SA-MDP, from their reference implementation[4]. SA-MDP agents only use one observation per s; therefore, UAP-S would reduce to UAP-O for SA-MDP in this setup. Table 3 shows the average return for each agent under a different attack, and while equipped with different defenses. In Sect. 4, we established that when the perturbation bound ϵ is 0.01, all attacks are devastatingly effective. In the interest of evaluating the robustness of the defense, we also consider two higher ϵ values, 0.02 and 0.05.

VF is an effective defense against FGSM and UAP-S as it can recover v's average return. However, it is not very effective against OSFW, OSFW(U), and UAP-O. SA-MDP is better than VF against OSFW and OSFW(U) when $\epsilon = 0.01$, but it fails to defend any attack in Pong when $\epsilon \geq 0.02$. Notably, VF's detection performance depends on the accuracy of the action-conditioned frame prediction module used in its algorithm [16], and the pre-defined threshold value used for detecting adversarial perturbations.

5.2 Action Distribution Divergence Detector (AD³)

Methodology. In a typical DRL episode, sequential actions exhibit some degree of *temporal coherence*: the likelihood of the agent selecting a specific current action given a specific last action is consistent across different episodes. We also observed that the temporal coherence is disrupted when the episode is subjected to an attack. We leverage this knowledge to propose a detection method, Action Distribution Divergence Detector (AD³), which calculates the statistical distance between the *conditional action probability distribution* (CAPD) of the current episode to the learned CAPD in order to detect whether the agent is under attack. Unlike prior work on detecting adversarial examples in the image domain [17,26,38], AD³ does not analyze the input image or tries to detect adversarial examples. Instead, it observes the distribution of the actions triggered by the inputs and detects unusual action sequences. To train AD³, v first runs k_1 episodes in a controlled environment before deployment. AD³ saves all

---

[4] https://github.com/chenhongge/SA_DQN Downloaded SA-MDP agents use $\epsilon = 1/255$ in training as in the original work [39]. Using higher ϵ values in training led to poor performance.

actions taken during that time and approximates the conditional probability of the next action given the current one using the bigram model[5]. We call the conditional probability of actions approximated by k_1 episodes the *learned* CAPD. Second, to differentiate between the CAPD of a normal game versus a game that is under attack with high confidence, v runs another k_2 episodes in a safe environment. AD^3 decides a threshold value th, where the statistical distance between the CAPD of the normal game and the learned CAPD falls mostly below this threshold. We use Kullback-Leibler (KL) divergence [14] as the statistical distance measure. The KL divergence between the learned CAPD and the CAPD of the current episode is calculated at each time-step starting after the first t_1 steps. We skip the first t_1 steps because the CAPD of the current episode is initially unstable and the KL divergence is naturally high at the beginning of every episode. We set the threshold th as the pth percentile of all KL-divergence values calculated for k_2 episodes. During deployment, AD^3 continuously updates the CAPD of the current episode, and after t_1 steps, it calculates the KL-divergence between the CAPD of the current episode and the learned CAPD. If the KL-divergence exceeds the threshold th by $r\%$ or more during a time window t_2, then AD^3 raises an alarm that the agent is under attack.

Evaluation. We evaluate the precision and recall of AD^3 in three tasks with discrete action spaces (Pong, Freeway and Breakout) against all proposed attacks. AD^3 can detect all five attacks in Pong with perfect precision and recall scores in all configurations. In Freeway, AD^3 has perfect precision and recall scores for 12 out of 15 different setups (FGSM against the DQN agent, OSFW against the PPO agent, and OSFW(U) against the PPO agent). In Freeway, we found that attacks lead to a lower action change rate (as low as 20%–30% in some episodes) than other tasks, thus negatively affecting the precision and/or recall of AD^3. AD^3 is also less effective in Breakout, as this task often terminates too quickly when it is under attack, and AD^3 cannot store enough actions for CAPD to converge in such a short time. The optimal parameters used for training AD^3, a more detailed discussion of the performance of AD^3, and the full result of the evaluation can be found in the extended version of this work [33].

Limitations. AD^3 is designed for attacks where Adv injects adversarial perturbations consistently throughout the episode. Adv with the knowledge of the detection strategy could apply their adversarial perturbation at a lower frequency to avoid detection. However, lowering the attack frequency also decreases the attack effectiveness. Another way for Adv to evade AD^3 is to perform targeted attacks to lure v into a specific state, where the adversarial perturbation is applied to a limited number of states in an episode. This type of attack is outside the scope of our paper, and defense strategies against it will be explored in future work.

---

[5] We tested different ngrams and selected the bigram as the best option.

Adversary vs. Defender Strategy with Negative Returns. In any DRL task where there is a clear negative result for an episode (e.g., losing a game) or the possibility of negative return, a reasonable choice for v is to suspend an episode when Adv's presence is detected. For example, in Pong, a negative result would be when the computer (as the opponent) reaches the score of 21 before v does. Suspending an episode prevents v from losing the game. Defense mechanisms such as VF and SA-MDP are useful in retaining or recovering v's return; however, they may not always prevent v from falling into a negative result, e.g., losing the game in Pong. Combining a recovery/retention mechanism with suspension on attack detection can reduce the number of losses for v. To illustrate the effectiveness of combining AD^3 with a retention/recovery mechanism, we designed an experiment using a DQN agent playing Pong to compare *losing rate* of v when it is under attack. We used Pong for this experiment, as Pong has a clear negative result. In Pong, an episode ends with loss when (a) the computer reaches 21 points before v, or (b) AD^3 did not raise an alarm. The result of this experiment can be found in Table 4. As shown in this table, VF is not effective in reducing the losing rate of v for OSFW and OSFW(U) for all ϵ. SA-MDP is effective in avoiding losses when $\epsilon = 0.01$; however, it fails against all universal perturbations when $\epsilon = 0.02$. In contrast, AD^3 can detect the presence of adversarial perturbations in all games. Although retention/recovery and detection are two orthogonal aspects of defense, our results above suggest that they can be combined in tasks with negative returns or results in order to more effectively thwart Adv from achieving its first goal.

Table 4. Losing rate (10 episodes) of DQN agents playing Pong with or without additional defense. Losing rate is calculated by counting the number of games where the computer gains 21 points first in an episode. If AD^3 raises an alarm before an episode ends, then v does not lose the game. In each row, the best attack with the highest losing rate is in bold, and given an ϵ value, the defense with the highest losing rate for that particular attack is shaded red.

ϵ	Method	Losing rate					
		No attack	FGSM	OSFW	UAP-S	UAP-O	OSFW(U)
0.01	No defense	0.0	**1.0**	**1.0**	**1.0**	**1.0**	**1.0**
	VF [16]	0.0	0.0	1.0	0.0	0.2	1.0
	SA-MDP [39]	0.0	0.0	0.0	0.0	0.0	0.0
	AD^3	0.0	0.0	0.0	0.0	0.0	0.0
0.02	No defense	0.0	**1.0**	**1.0**	**1.0**	**1.0**	**1.0**
	VF [16]	0.0	0.0	1.0	0.0	0.3	1.0
	SA-MDP [39]	0.0	0.9	1.0	1.0	1.0	1.0
	AD^3	0.0	0.0	0.0	0.0	0.0	0.0

6   Conclusion

We showed that white-box universal perturbation attacks are effective in fooling DRL policies in real-time. Our evaluation of the three different attacks (UAP-S, UAP-O, and OSFW(U)) demonstrates that universal perturbations are effective in tasks with discrete action spaces. Universal perturbation attacks are also able to generalize to continuous control tasks with the same efficiency. We confirmed that the effectiveness of prior defenses depends on the perturbation bound, and fail to completely recover the agent performance when they are confronted with universal perturbations of larger bounds. We proposed a detection mechanism, AD^3, that detects all five attacks evaluated in the paper. AD^3 can be combined with other defense techniques to protect agents in tasks with negative returns or results to stop the adversary from achieving its goal. We plan to extend our attacks to the black-box case by first mounting a model extraction attack and then applying our current techniques to find transferable universal perturbations.

Acknowledgments. This research was funded in part by the EU H2020 project SPA-TIAL (Grant No. 101021808) and Intel Private-AI Consortium.

A   UAP-S and OSFW in Uncontrolled Environments

In simple environments like Atari 2600 games, sequential states are non-i.i.d. Moreover, Atari 2600 games are *controlled* environments, where future states are predictable, and episodes do not deviate much from one another for the same task. OSFW and OSFW(U) leverage this non-i.i.d. property. However, their effectiveness might decrease in uncontrolled environments and the physical world due to the uncertainty of future states. In contrast, UAP-S and UAP-O are independent of the correlation between sequential states. To confirm our conjecture, we implemented OSFW(U) against VGG-16 image classifiers [40] pre-trained on ImageNet [27], where ImageNet can be viewed as a non-i.i.d., uncontrolled environment. We measured that OSFW(U) achieves a fooling rate of up to 30% on the ImageNet validation set with $\epsilon = 10$, while UAP-S has a fooling rate of 78% [20], where the l_∞ norm of an image in the validation set is around 250. Therefore, we conclude that UAP-S can mislead DRL policies more than OSFW(U) in complex, uncontrolled environments.

B   Computation of UAP in Continuous Control

Algorithm 2. Computation of UAP in continuous control

---

input : sanitized $\mathcal{D}_{train}, V_{adv}$, hyper-parameter α
    max. number of iterations it_{max}, perturbation constraint ϵ
output: universal r

1 Initialize $r \leftarrow 0, it \leftarrow 0$;
2 **while** $\delta < \delta_{max}$ **and** $it < it_{max}$ **do**
3 | **for** $s \in \mathcal{D}_{train}$ **do**
4 | | **if** $V_{adv}(s + r) + \alpha < V_{adv}(s)$ **then**
5 | | | Find the extra, minimal Δr:
6 | | | $\Delta r \leftarrow \mathrm{argmin}_{\Delta r} \| \Delta r \|_2$
7 | | | s.t.: $V_{adv}(s + r + \Delta r) + \alpha < V_{adv}(s)$;
8 | | |__ $r \leftarrow \mathrm{sign}(\min(\mathrm{abs}(r + \Delta r), \epsilon))$;

9 | Calculate δ with updated r on $\mathcal{D}_{train}$;
10 |__ $it \leftarrow (it + 1)$;

C   Additional Experimental Results

Table 5. Offline and online cost of attacks where victim agents are PPO trained for Walker2d and Humanoid at $\epsilon = 0.02$. Attacks that cannot be implemented in real-time are highlighted in red.

Experiment	Attack method	Offline cost ± std (seconds)	Online cost ± std (seconds)
Walker2d, PPO, $T_{max} =$ 0.0079 ± 10^{-5} seconds	FGSM	–	$31 \times 10^{-5} \pm 10^{-5}$
	OSFW	–	0.02 ± 0.001
	UAP-S (O)	8.75 ± 0.024	$2.9 \times 10^{-5} \pm 10^{-6}$
	OSFW(U)	0.02 ± 0.001	$2.9 \times 10^{-5} \pm 10^{-6}$
Humanoid PPO, $T_{max} =$ 0.0079 ± 10^{-6} seconds	FGSM	–	$35 \times 10^{-5} \pm 10^{-5}$
	OSFW	–	0.02 ± 0.001
	UAP-S (O)	35.86 ± 0.466	$2.4 \times 10^{-5} \pm 10^{-6}$
	OSFW(U)	0.02 ± 0.001	$2.4 \times 10^{-5} \pm 10^{-6}$

References

1. Baluja, S., Fischer, I.: Learning to attack: adversarial transformation networks. In: Proceedings of AAAI-2018 (2018). http://www.esprockets.com/papers/aaai2018.pdf
2. Behzadan, V., Munir, A.: Vulnerability of deep reinforcement learning to policy induction attacks. In: Perner, P. (ed.) MLDM 2017. LNCS (LNAI), vol. 10358, pp. 262–275. Springer, Cham (2017). https://doi.org/10.1007/978-3-319-62416-7_19

3. Behzadan, V., Munir, A.: Whatever does not kill deep reinforcement learning, makes it stronger. arXiv preprint arXiv:1712.09344 (2017)
4. Bellemare, M.G., Naddaf, Y., Veness, J., Bowling, M.: The arcade learning environment: an evaluation platform for general agents. J. Artif. Intell. Res. **47**, 253–279 (2013)
5. Carlini, N., Wagner, D.: Towards evaluating the robustness of neural networks. In: 2017 IEEE Symposium on Security and Privacy (SP), pp. 39–57 (2017). https://doi.org/10.1109/SP.2017.49
6. Co, K.T., Muñoz-González, L., de Maupeou, S., Lupu, E.C.: Procedural noise adversarial examples for black-box attacks on deep convolutional networks. In: Proceedings of the 2019 ACM SIGSAC conference on computer and communications security, pp. 275–289 (2019)
7. Gleave, A., Dennis, M., Kant, N., Wild, C., Levine, S., Russell, S.: Adversarial policies: attacking deep reinforcement learning. arXiv preprint arXiv:1905.10615 (2019)
8. Goodfellow, I., Shlens, J., Szegedy, C.: Explaining and harnessing adversarial examples. In: International Conference on Learning Representations (2015). arxiv.org/abs/1412.6572
9. Hayes, J., Danezis, G.: Learning universal adversarial perturbations with generative models. In: 2018 IEEE Security and Privacy Workshops (SPW), pp. 43–49. IEEE (2018)
10. Huang, S., Papernot, N., Goodfellow, I., Duan, Y., Abbeel, P.: Adversarial attacks on neural network policies. arXiv (2017). arxiv.org/abs/1702.02284
11. Hussenot, L., Geist, M., Pietquin, O.: Copycat: taking control of neural policies with constant attacks. In: International Conference on Autonomous Agents and Multi-Agent Systems (AAMAS) (2020). arxiv.org/abs/1905.12282
12. Inkawhich, M., Chen, Y., Li, H.: Snooping attacks on deep reinforcement learning. In: Proceedings of the 19th International Conference on Autonomous Agents and MultiAgent Systems, AAMAS 2020, Richland, SC, pp. 557–565 (2020)
13. Kos, J., Song, D.: Delving into adversarial attacks on deep policies. In: 5th International Conference on Learning Representations, ICLR 2017, Toulon, France, Workshop Track Proceedings, 24–26 April 2017. OpenReview.net (2017). https://openreview.net/forum?id=BJcib5mFe
14. Kullback, S., Leibler, R.A.: On information and sufficiency. Ann. Math. Stat. **22**(1), 79–86 (1951)
15. Lin, Y., Hong, Z., Liao, Y., Shih, M., Liu, M., Sun, M.: Tactics of adversarial attack on deep reinforcement learning agents. In: Proceedings of the Twenty-Sixth International Joint Conference on Artificial Intelligence, IJCAI 2017, Melbourne, Australia, 19–25 August 2017, pp. 3756–3762. ijcai.org (2017). https://doi.org/10.24963/ijcai.2017/525
16. Lin, Y., Liu, M., Sun, M., Huang, J.: Detecting adversarial attacks on neural network policies with visual foresight. CoRR abs/1710.00814 (2017). arxiv.org/abs/1710.00814
17. Meng, D., Chen, H.: MagNet: a two-pronged defense against adversarial examples. In: Proceedings of the 2017 ACM SIGSAC Conference on Computer and Communications Security, pp. 135–147 (2017)
18. Mnih, V., et al.: Asynchronous methods for deep reinforcement learning. In: Proceedings of the 33nd International Conference on Machine Learning, ICML 2016, New York City, NY, USA, 19–24 June 2016, vol. 48, pp. 1928–1937 (2016)
19. Mnih, V., et al.: Human-level control through deep reinforcement learning. Nature **518**(7540), 529–533 (2015)

20. Moosavi-Dezfooli, S.M., Fawzi, A., Fawzi, O., Frossard, P.: Universal adversarial perturbations. In: Proceedings of the IEEE Conference on Computer Vision and Pattern Recognition, pp. 1765–1773 (2017)
21. Moosavi-Dezfooli, S.M., Fawzi, A., Frossard, P.: DeepFool: a simple and accurate method to fool deep neural networks. In: Proceedings of the IEEE Conference on Computer Vision and Pattern Recognition, pp. 2574–2582 (2016)
22. Mopuri, K.R., Garg, U., Babu, R.V.: Fast feature fool: a data independent approach to universal adversarial perturbations. arXiv preprint arXiv:1707.05572 (2017)
23. Mopuri, K.R., Ojha, U., Garg, U., Babu, R.V.: NAG: network for adversary generation. In: Proceedings of the IEEE Conference on Computer Vision and Pattern Recognition, pp. 742–751 (2018)
24. Oikarinen, T., Zhang, W., Megretski, A., Daniel, L., Weng, T.W.: Robust deep reinforcement learning through adversarial loss. In: Ranzato, M., Beygelzimer, A., Dauphin, Y., Liang, P., Vaughan, J.W. (eds.) Advances in Neural Information Processing Systems, vol. 34, pp. 26156–26167. Curran Associates, Inc. (2021)
25. Papernot, N., McDaniel, P., Jha, S., Fredrikson, M., Celik, Z.B., Swami, A.: The limitations of deep learning in adversarial settings. In: 2016 IEEE European symposium on security and privacy (EuroS&P), pp. 372–387. IEEE (2016)
26. Rouhani, B.D., Samragh, M., Javaheripi, M., Javidi, T., Koushanfar, F.: DeepFense: online accelerated defense against adversarial deep learning, pp. 1–8. IEEE (2018)
27. Russakovsky, O., et al.: ImageNet large scale visual recognition challenge. Int. J. Comput. Vision **115**(3), 211–252 (2015)
28. Schulman, J., Wolski, F., Dhariwal, P., Radford, A., Klimov, O.: Proximal policy optimization algorithms. CoRR abs/1707.06347 (2017). arxiv.org/abs/1707.06347
29. Sun, J., et al.: Stealthy and efficient adversarial attacks against deep reinforcement learning. In: Proceedings of the AAAI Conference on Artificial Intelligence, pp. 5883–5891. AAAI Press (2020)
30. Sutton, R.S., Barto, A.G.: Reinforcement Learning: An Introduction. MIT press, Cambridge (2018)
31. Szegedy, C., et al.: Intriguing properties of neural networks. In: International Conference on Learning Representations (2014). arxiv.org/abs/1312.6199
32. Tassa, Y., et al.: DeepMind control suite. arXiv preprint arXiv:1801.00690 (2018)
33. Tekgul, B.G., Wang, S., Marchal, S., Asokan, N.: Real-time adversarial perturbations against deep reinforcement learning policies: attacks and defenses. arXiv preprint arXiv:2106.08746 (2021)
34. Todorov, E., Erez, T., Tassa, Y.: MuJoCo: a physics engine for model-based control. In: 2012 IEEE/RSJ International Conference on Intelligent Robots and Systems, pp. 5026–5033. IEEE (2012)
35. Tretschk, E., Oh, S.J., Fritz, M.: Sequential attacks on agents for long-term adversarial goals. CoRR abs/1805.12487 (2018). arxiv.org/abs/1805.12487
36. Wu, X., Guo, W., Wei, H., Xing, X.: Adversarial policy training against deep reinforcement learning. In: 30th USENIX Security Symposium (USENIX Security 21), pp. 1883–1900. USENIX Association (2021). www.usenix.org/conference/usenixsecurity21/presentation/wu-xian
37. Xiao, C., et al.: Characterizing attacks on deep reinforcement learning. arXiv preprint arXiv:1907.09470 (2019)
38. Xu, W., Evans, D., Qi, Y.: Feature squeezing: detecting adversarial examples in deep neural networks. In: 25th Annual Network and Distributed System Security Symposium, NDSS. The Internet Society (2018)

39. Zhang, H., et al.: Robust deep reinforcement learning against adversarial perturbations on state observations. In: Advances in Neural Information Processing Systems, vol. 33, pp. 21024–21037. Curran Associates, Inc. (2020)
40. Zhang, X., Zou, J., He, K., Sun, J.: Accelerating very deep convolutional networks for classification and detection. IEEE Trans. Pattern Anal. Mach. Intell. **38**(10), 1943–1955 (2015)
41. Zhao, Y., Shumailov, I., Cui, H., Gao, X., Mullins, R., Anderson, R.: Blackbox attacks on reinforcement learning agents using approximated temporal information. In: 2020 50th Annual IEEE/IFIP International Conference on Dependable Systems and Networks Workshops (DSN-W), pp. 16–24. IEEE Computer Society, Los Alamitos (2020)

FLMJR: Improving Robustness of Federated Learning via Model Stability

Qi Guo⬛, Di Wu⬛, Yong Qi⬛, Saiyu Qi$^{(\boxtimes)}$⬛, and Qian Li⬛

Xi'an Jiaotong University, Xi'an, Shaanxi, China
{qiy,saiyu-qi}@xjtu.edu.cn

Abstract. Federated Learning (FL) is vulnerable to model poisoning attacks that hurt the joint training global model by sending malicious updates. Existing defenses rely heavily on restrictions on clients' model updates to defend against attacks. However, the global model can be attacked by elaborate malicious perturbation under defensive restriction due to the sensitivity of the model to perturbations, which leads the model to be vulnerable. Therefore, in this work, we investigate the defense against attacks from a novel perspective of the model stability towards perturbation on parameters. We propose a new method named Federated Learning with Model Jacobian Regularization (FLMJR) to enhance the robustness of FL. Considering prediction volatility of the model is determined by the model-output Jacobian, we reduce the Jacobian regularization to improve model stability towards model perturbations while maintaining the model's accuracy. We conduct extensive experiments under both IID and NonIID settings to evaluate the defense against state-of-the-art model poisoning attacks, which demonstrates that our method not only has superior fidelity and robustness, but can also be easily integrated to further improve the robustness of existing server-based robust aggregation approaches (e.g., Fedavg, Trimean, Median, Bulyan, and FLTrust).

Keywords: Federated learning · Model poisoning · Robustness · Model stability

1 Introduction

Federated Learning (FL), as an emerging paradigm of machine learning, enables multiple clients to collaboratively train a machine learning model without leaking data directly [16]. Due to the decentralization of clients' data, FL has the potential to preserve the privacy of clients and has been widely used in practice. Nevertheless, the decentralization also raises concerns about malicious clients, as they can easily pollute the global model by uploading malicious local models in both independently and identically distributed (i.e., IID) and not independently and identically distributed (i.e., NonIID) scenarios.

Q. Guo and D. Wu—Equal contribution.

© The Author(s), under exclusive license to Springer Nature Switzerland AG 2022
V. Atluri et al. (Eds.): ESORICS 2022, LNCS 13556, pp. 405–424, 2022.
https://doi.org/10.1007/978-3-031-17143-7_20

The problem of malicious clients has recently received considerable attention due to its potential threats [5, 7, 27]. Since the malicious models generated by the attackers could be extremely different from the benign models, most previous approaches leverage robust aggregations on the server to defend against attacks: they filter or revise the arbitrary models (e.g., the models geographically distance far from the center of all models) and then aggregate the rest of the models to synthesize the global model. As empirical experiments illustrated, these methods can alleviate the impact of the attack and guarantee the robustness of the FL system under certain assumptions.

However, as recent researches demonstrated, the robust aggregations could be vulnerable to model poisoning attacks [2, 6]. By consistently applying elaborate perturbations on model updates, the model poisoning attack could circumvent the defenses and bring a negative impact on the global model. To further explore the reason for this phenomenon, we inspect and analyze the reactions of the model poisoning attacks and the robust aggregations in the model parameter space near decision boundaries (see Sect. 3). We argue that the attacks towards FL can be regarded as perturbations towards the incorrect decision areas in model parameter space whereas the robust aggregations of FL can be treated as restrictions on the global model. On the one hand, since the attack algorithms and the fraction of attackers are unknown to the defenders, it is difficult for defenders to construct a perfect restriction that is applicable to all the attacks. As a consequence, the defensive restrictions have to be loose and can not filter the small perturbations. On the other hand, due to the sensitivity of the model to perturbations, it is easy for attackers to shift the model into the incorrect decision area by small perturbations, which causes a negative impact on the model. Therefore, using robust aggregations alone is insufficient to defend against model poisoning attacks. The model stability with respect to the perturbations should be considered seriously as a crucial component of defending against attacks in FL.

Motivated by the above insight, in this paper, we are aiming to solve the challenge of model stability towards perturbations in the parameter space to defend against malicious clients. Nevertheless, it is extremely difficult for us to obtain a relatively stable model by aggregating model updates, since we do not know in which direction the model should be improved. To ensure the stability of the model, we expect the model to be relatively stable before being uploaded to the server. Considering the model-output Jacobian matrix plays a critical role in the Taylor expansion of prediction output with respect to the model perturbations, we introduced the model-output Jacobian into the model's stability analysis of the perturbations, where the larger the Jacobian component, the more unstable model is relative to the perturbations. Therefore, we propose a novel method Federated Learning with Model Jacobian Regularization (FLMJR), whose central idea is to reduce the model-output Jacobian while maintaining the model's accuracy to achieve relative model stability. The comparison of conventional server-based defense method and FLMJR is illustrated in Fig. 1. FLMJR combines the norm of the model-output Jacobian with the native local loss function to generate a relatively stable model through gradient descent in the client. FLMJR is a novel plug-and-play fusion module and does not make any changes to the existing standard framework. Since our method improves the stability of the local model before uploading it to the server, the stability of the global model is substantially improved regardless of the aggregation rules used by the server, as demonstrated in the experimental results. We not only present an intuitive understanding of our proposed methodology in the motivation section but also develop an efficient algorithm for implementation. Furthermore, we conduct extensive experiments to demonstrate the superior performance of FLMJR.

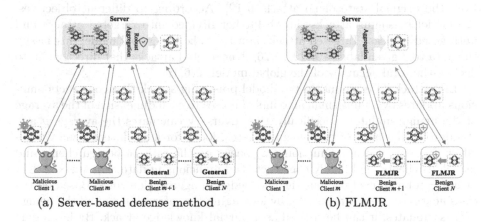

(a) Server-based defense method   (b) FLMJR

Fig. 1. The overviews of server-based defense method and FLMJR

Concretely, our contributions and novelty can be summarized as follows:

- We consider model stability and restriction on model perturbations as two key components in defending against attacks of FL, where existing defenses focus only on the latter component while ignoring the former. To the best of our knowledge, this is the first work to investigate the defense from a novel perspective of the model stability in FL.
- We propose a novel method called Federated Learning with Model Jacobian Regularization (FLMJR), which reduces the model-output Jacobian while maintaining the model's accuracy to achieve relative model stability. Meanwhile, we present an efficient algorithm for implementation in the client of the standard FL framework.
- We demonstrate the superiority of our proposed method in terms of fidelity and robustness in both IID and NonIID settings. Furthermore, we conduct extensive experiments to illustrate that FLMJR is also complementary to existing server-based robust aggregation methods and can significantly improve robustness and generalization of these methods under state-of-the-art model poisoning attacks.

2   Related Works

2.1   Model Poisoning Attacks Towards FL

The model poisoning attack is a recently proposed paradigm that aims to manipulate the global model of FL by uploading fine-crafted malicious models from clients. Unlike data poisoning attacks that leverage mislabeled data to train the malicious model [9,18,21], model poisoning attacks aim to directly construct the malicious model to pose a serious impact on the global model [1,6,19]. By determining the boundary of local updates, the malicious updates that diverge from benign updates can be constructed to make the global model geographically far from the original state of no attack [6,19]. According to different objectives, the model poisoning attacks can be further divided into targeted attacks and untargeted attacks. Targeted attacks aim to make the global model misclassify the data to a given label [1,3,22,24,26]. Untargeted attacks that directly aim to decline the total accuracy of the global model [2,6,19].

LIE attack [2] is an untargeted model poisoning attack that constructs malicious updates by adding small amounts of noises to each dimension of the average of the benign updates. Specifically, the adversary calculates the average μ and standard deviation σ of the benign updates, looks for a coefficient z via Cumulative Standard Normal Function $\phi(z)$ based on the ratio of benign clients and malicious clients, and finally constructs the malicious update as $\mu + z \times \sigma$. LIE attack can be applied without the knowledge of aggregation rules. Based on the classification rule on attacks [19], by leveraging the information of all the benign clients' updates, it can be treated as a partial knowledge attack. By leveraging only the information of malicious clients' updates, it can also be treated as an agnostic attack.

Fang attack [6] is an untargeted model poisoning attack by preventing the convergence of the global model. It constructs malicious updates as solving an optimization problem in each iteration of federated learning. The core of the attack is to make the global model deviate the most towards the inverse of the benign direction by uploading fine-crafted malicious updates. For instance, the adversary computes the average μ of the benign gradients, calculates a perturbation $\nabla^p = -sign(\mu)$, obtains the coefficient γ by solving the optimization problem, and finally computes a malicious update as $\nabla^m = \nabla^b + \gamma \cdot \nabla^p$. Based on the classification rule on attacks [20], Fang attack belongs to the omniscient attack since it demands the information of both benign clients' updates and aggregation rules to mount attack.

In this work, we focus on untargeted model poisoning attacks, which can pose a more serious threat to FL by decreasing the accuracy of the global model on the entire dataset.

2.2   Robust Aggregations of FL

To make FL more robust against malicious attacks, various works [4,5,7,27] have been devoted to defend the attacks. The majority of defense methods leverage robust aggregations on the server to enhance the robustness of the FL system.

Trimean and Median [27] perform coordinate-wise filter operation on each dimension independently to maximize statistical performance. Trimean is a coordinate-wise aggregation that operates on each dimension of the model parameters independently. Specifically, given a hyperparameter k, for each dimension, Trimean will filter the largest k values and the smallest k values. After that, the server will compute the mean of the remaining values as the aggregated result for the dimension. As *Yin et al.,* [27] illustrated, Trimean achieves the best statistical performance while remaining Byzantine-robust of the FL system. Similar to Trimean, Median [27] is a coordinate-wise aggregation operating each dimension separately. For instance, Median calculates the median value of each dimension of the model parameter and constructs all the median values as the aggregated result. Median only requires a few communication rounds and achieves the optimal rate for strongly convex quadratic losses. It is robust against Byzantine clients and guarantees the convergence of the global model.

Krum [4] and Bulyan [7] are designed to eliminate the arbitrary models that are geographically far from other uploaded models. Bulyan [7] is a variant of Krum [4] aggregation. Given a hyperparameter of k, the server first selects k models which are the most similar to other local models. Euclidean distance is always leveraged as a similarity metric between local models. After model selection, the server performs a Trimean aggregation on selected models to generate the global model. Bulyan inherits the advantage of Trimean and Krum and has been illustrated to be robust against Byzantine-clients.

FLTrust [5] is a recently proposed defense method, which generates a root model based on a tiny root dataset on server to revise each uploaded model before aggregation. Specifically, it carefully selects a small dataset as the root dataset. In each epoch of training, the server will generate a root model based on the root dataset to judge the local model updated by all the clients. Each local model will be adjusted based on its cosine similarity with the root model and scaled to the magnitude of the root model. After judgment on updated models, a normal Fedavg aggregation will be applied to generate the global model. FLTrust have shown the effectiveness in defending against malicious clients in both IID and NonIID scenarios.

The robust aggregations can achieve a satisfying defense performance under certain condition. However, recent researches demonstrate that the robust aggregations are vulnerable to model poisoning attacks [2,6]. By consistently applying small perturbation on model updates, it could circumvent the robust aggregations and brings negative impact to the global model. Therefore, only robust aggregations is insufficient to defend against model poisoning attacks. The model stability with respect to the perturbations is also needed to be as a crucial component for defense in FL.

3   Motivation

To understand the vulnerability of the robust aggregations to model poisoning attacks, we observe and analyze the reactions of attacks and robust aggrega-

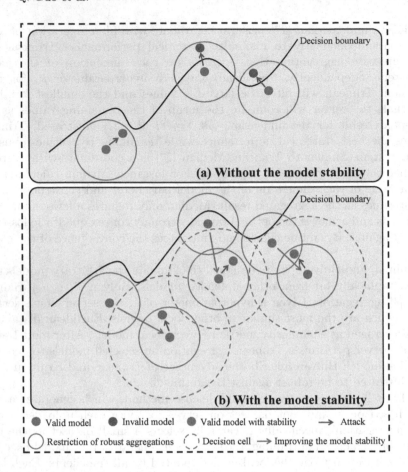

Fig. 2. A conceptual illustration of the reaction to attacks and robust aggregations in parameter space with given data

tions in parameter space near the decision boundary. Intuitively, as illustrated in Fig. 2, we argue that the attacks towards FL can be considered as malicious perturbations on the global model towards incorrect decision areas. Whereas, the robust aggregations, which represent the most conventional defenses, can be considered as restrictions on the global model where the global model can only move to the state within the boundary. In light of the fact that the attack methods and the number of attackers are unknown to the defender, it is difficult to construct a perfect restriction that is applicable to all the attacks. The unique strategies of various robust aggregations make it possible for them to resist some attacks under certain conditions. However, the models derived from these methods have not been sufficiently considered in terms of their robustness and are therefore vulnerable to adversarial perturbations, i.e., small but elaborate perturbations can circumvent the robust aggregations and damage the global model [2]. Furthermore, the restrictions from robust aggregations may also affect the general convergence of the global model, resulting in a negative impact on the performance. This is why when some defense methods are applied separately without any attack, the performance of the final model will be affected negatively, as demonstrated by the experiment results in Sect. 5.2.

As the attack algorithms and attacker fraction are unknown, it is insufficient to leverage robust aggregations to defend against model poisoning attacks. To ultimately defend against the attacks, an ideal solution is to apply defensive restrictions to filter large malicious perturbations while ensuring the model tolerable to small malicious perturbations. As illustrated in Fig. 2, the model near to decision boundary (represented by the blue point in the Fig. 2) is unstable. Even with a restriction on model movement, it is still capable for attackers to apply a malicious perturbation shifting the model to the incorrect area. Whereas, the model far from the decision boundary (represented by the green point) has sufficient stability towards perturbations. With a defensive restriction applied, it is impossible for attackers to shift the model to the incorrect areas by malicious perturbations. This phenomenon implies that the model stability towards perturbations in parameter space is crucial, as well as defensive restrictions, to defend against model poisoning attacks. However, the robust aggregations always focus on the latter component and ignore the former component, which results in their vulnerability to the attacks. Therefore, in this work, we investigate the defense against model poisoning attacks from a novel perspective of improving model stability towards perturbations in parameter space.

4   Method

For improving model stability towards perturbation to enhance the robustness of the model, we introduce and define formally the model-output Jacobian and then increase the model's tolerance to model perturbations by minimizing the norm of the model-output Jacobian. Finally, we present an efficient algorithm for computing the model Jacobian regularizer in the standard FL framework.

4.1   Model-Output Jacobian and Stability Analysis

Considering the set of classification functions, f, we focus on learning this classification function as a neural network with model parameters $\theta \in \mathbb{R}^M$. Here, the input vector is $x \in \mathbb{R}^I$ and the output is a score vector, $z = f(\theta, x) \in \mathbb{R}^C$, where each element, z_c, indicates the likelihood that the input belongs to category, c. The vertor z refers to the logit before a softmax layer has been applied. The softmax computes the probabilistic output p_c relating to z_c using $p_c \equiv \frac{e^{z_c/T}}{\sum_{c'} e^{z_{c'}/T}}$ under temperature T, which is generally fixed at unity.

Due to the fact that model parameters θ is applied to each input vector x, we omit the explicit dependency on the input vector x for simplicity, i.e., $z = f(\theta, x) = f(\theta)$. Let us consider a small perturbation vector, $\epsilon \in \mathbb{R}^M$, of the same dimension as the model parameter. During the stability analysis of the model predictions against model perturbations, the model-output Jacobian matrix appears naturally. For a perturbed model $\widetilde{\theta} = \theta + \epsilon$, the corresponding values shift to

$$\widetilde{z}_c = f_c(\theta + \epsilon) = f_c(\theta) + \sum_{i=1}^{M} \epsilon_i \cdot \frac{\partial f_c}{\partial \theta_i}(\theta) + O\left(\epsilon^2\right)$$

$$= z_c + \sum_{i=1}^{M} J_{c;i}(\theta) \cdot \epsilon_i + O\left(\epsilon^2\right), \tag{1}$$

where the function in the second equality is Taylor-expanded with respect to the model perturbation ϵ and the model-output Jacobian matrix,

$$J_{c;i}(\theta) \equiv \frac{\partial f_c}{\partial \theta_i}(\theta) \tag{2}$$

is introduced in the third equality.

Different from conventional input-output Jacobian for the sample [8], here we focus on model-output Jacobian for model parameters. Due to the general analytic nature of the function f, the higher-order terms can typically be ignored for relatively small perturbations, ϵ, and prediction stability is determined by the model-output Jacobian. Consequently, by reducing the Jacobian component, we can enlarge the model's tolerance to perturbations to improve the model stability.

4.2   Minimize Model-Output Jacobian for Model Stability

As can be observed from Eq. (1), the larger the Jacobian components, the more unstable the prediction of the model is with respect to model perturbations. Therefore, a straightforward method of reducing this instability is to reduce the magnitude of each component of the Jacobian matrix, which can be achieved by minimizing the square of the Frobenius norm of the model-output Jacobian,

$$\|J(\theta)\|_F^2 \equiv \left\{ \sum_{i,c} [J_{c;i}(\theta)]^2 \right\}. \tag{3}$$

Therefore, the local training of benign clients is reformulated to achieve two goals:

- To maintain the performance of the benign task, loss of local benign tasks should be minimized.
- To improve the robustness of FL by increasing the model stability, the model Jacobian regularization should be minimized.

The Jacobian regularizer in Eq. (3) can be used in conjunction with any loss objective to train parameterized models in the client. Therefore, considering N clients with data sets $\mathcal{D}_1, ..., \mathcal{D}_N$, we formulate the defense problem of FL as

$$\min_{\theta \in \mathbb{R}^d} \mathcal{G}(\theta) = \frac{1}{N} \sum_{i=1}^{N} \mathcal{L}_i(\theta), \tag{4}$$

Algorithm 1: Federated Learning with Model Jacobian Regularizer (FLMJR)

Input: the global model θ^t, the local dataset $\mathcal{D}_i$, mini-batch size $|\mathcal{B}|$, and number of projections m_{proj} .

Output: the updated local model θ_i^{t+1}

1 $\theta_{i,0} = \theta^t$
2 $R = |\mathcal{D}_i|/|\mathcal{B}|$
3 **for** $r = 1$ *to* R **do**
4 $\quad$ $\mathcal{J}_F = 0$
5 $\quad$ $\mathcal{B} \leftarrow$ sample a mini-batch with size $|\mathcal{B}|$
6 $\quad$ model outputs $z^\alpha = f(\theta_{i,r-1}, \{x^\alpha, y^\alpha\}_{\alpha \in \mathcal{B}})$
7 $\quad$ **for** $k = 1$ *to* m_{proj} **do**
8 $\quad\quad$ $\{q_c^\alpha\} \sim \mathcal{N}(0, \mathbb{I})$;   // $(|\mathcal{B}|, C)$-dim
9 $\quad\quad$ $\hat{q}^\alpha = q^\alpha / \|q^\alpha\|$;   // Uniform sampling from the unit sphere
10 $\quad\quad$ $z_{\text{flat}} = \text{Flatten}(\{z^\alpha\}), q_{\text{flat}} = \text{Flatten}(\{\hat{q}^\alpha\})$
11 $\quad\quad$ $Jq = \partial(z_{\text{flat}} \cdot q_{\text{flat}})/\partial\theta^\alpha$
12 $\quad\quad$ $\mathcal{J}_F += C\|Jq\|^2/(m_{\text{proj}}|\mathcal{B}|)$
13 $\quad$ **end**
14 $\quad$ $\mathcal{L}_i^\mathcal{B} = \mathcal{L}_{\text{local}}^\mathcal{B} + \lambda_{\text{MJR}}\mathcal{J}_F$
15 $\quad$ $\theta_{i,r} = \theta_{i,r-1} - \nabla_\theta \mathcal{L}_i^\mathcal{B}(\theta_{i,r-1})$
16 **end**
17 $\theta_i^{t+1} = \theta_{i,R}$

---

where

$$\mathcal{L}_i(\theta) = \mathcal{L}_{\text{local}}(\theta) + \lambda_{\text{MJR}} \|J(\theta)\|_F^2 \qquad (5)$$

is the loss function of the ith client, $\mathcal{L}_{\text{local}}$ is a native local loss function, and λ_{MJR} is a hyperparameter that is used to determine how much the model Jacobian regularizer influences the model. It is expected that the model will be able to learn correctly and robustly by minimizing the joint loss function with an appropriate choice of λ_{MJR}.

At each iteration, a loss function with the model Jacobian regularizer, $\mathcal{L}_i$, and a mini-batch $\mathcal{B}$ consisting of a set of labeled examples $\{x^\alpha, y^\alpha\}_{\alpha \in \mathcal{B}}$, is optimized with SGD over the function parameter space by minimizing the following joint loss function

$$\mathcal{L}_i^\mathcal{B}(\theta) = \mathcal{L}_{\text{local}}^\mathcal{B}(\theta) + \lambda_{\text{MJR}} \left[\frac{1}{|\mathcal{B}|} \sum_{\alpha \in \mathcal{B}} \|J(\theta)\|_F^2 \right]. \qquad (6)$$

4.3 Algorithm

In the prior discussion, we have argued that increasing the model stability of client learning by minimizing the Frobenius norm of the model-output Jacobian could assist in improving the robustness of FL. Then the main challenge is how to efficiently compute and deploy the regularizer so that it can be seamlessly incorporated into any existing FL paradigm.

For computing the Frobenius norm of the model-output Jacobian, it is most intuitive to combine a set of orthonormal basis with the automatic differentiation system. For each basis vector $\{e\}$, the derivative elements within the model-output Jacobian can be computed efficiently by differentiating the product, $e \cdot z$, with respect to the model parameters, $\boldsymbol{\theta}$,

$$\|J(\boldsymbol{\theta})\|_{\mathrm{F}}^2 = \mathrm{Tr}\left(JJ^{\mathrm{T}}\right) = \sum_{\{e\}} eJJ^{\mathrm{T}}e^{\mathrm{T}} = \sum_{\{e\}} \left[\frac{\partial(e \cdot z)}{\partial \boldsymbol{\theta}}\right]^2, \tag{7}$$

where a constant orthonormal basis, $\{e\}$, is with the C-dimensional output space.

The formula in (7) is a exact computation that requires C times backpropagating gradients through the model due to C orthonormal basis vectors $\{e\}$. Nevertheless, the computational cost, which is linear to the output category C, is inaccessible and prohibitively expensive in practice for many large-scale FL problems.

For the efficient deployment of this model Jacobian regularizer, we consider a random projection method to effectively compute the Frobenius norm of the model-output Jacobian [23]. Consequently, Eq. (7) is rewritten in light of the expectation of an unbiased estimator

$$\|J(\boldsymbol{\theta})\|_{\mathrm{F}}^2 = C\mathbb{E}_{\hat{q} \sim S^{C-1}}\left[\|\hat{q} \cdot J\|^2\right], \tag{8}$$

where the random vector $\hat{q}$ is derived from the $(C-1)$-dimensional unit sphere S^{C-1} with each element sampled from a standard normal. According to this relationship, the square of the Frobenius norm of the model-output Jacobian can be estimated by samples of m_{proj} random vectors $\hat{q}^m$ as

$$\|J(\boldsymbol{\theta})\|_{\mathrm{F}}^2 \approx \frac{1}{m_{\mathrm{proj}}} \sum_{m=1}^{m_{\mathrm{proj}}} \left[\frac{\partial(\hat{q}^m \cdot z)}{\partial \boldsymbol{\theta}}\right]^2, \tag{9}$$

which converges to the true value as $O\left(m_{\mathrm{proj}}^{-1/2}\right)$ [8]. In addition, we obtain $\|J(x)\|_{\mathrm{F}}^2$ by averaging over a mini-batch of samples with a size of $|\mathcal{B}|$. We expect that the fluctuation of our estimator can additionally be suppressed by $\sim |1/\sqrt{|\mathcal{B}|}$ through cancellations within a mini-batch. The error with nearly independent and identically distributed samples in a mini-batch is expected to be of order $(m_{\mathrm{proj}}|\mathcal{B}|)^{-1/2}$ [8]. Hence, our method can perform well with $m_{\mathrm{proj}} = 1$ in practice. The complete algorithm description of FLMJR is presented in Algorithm 1.

5   Experiment

In this section, we empirically demonstrate the effectiveness of FLMJR as a defense for FL. First, we illustrate the fidelity of FLMJR by comparing it with other defense methods. Afterward, we illustrate the robustness of FLMJR using LIE and Fang attacks. Moreover, we comprehensively evaluate the improvement of FLMJR on defense performance across all baselines to demonstrate its effectiveness. More detailed experimental results including the impact of λ are present in the supplemental materials.

5.1 Experimental Setup

We conduct experiments over four datasets: CIFAR10 [12], MNIST [14], SVHN [17], and Fashion-MNIST [25].

CIFAR10 [12] is a 10-class color image classification dataset. It consists of 50000 training samples and 10000 test samples. We selected AlexNet [13] as the model architecture for CIFAR10 classification task. We consider building an FL system in the IID scenario for CIFAR10 classification. To simulate the IID scenario, each client is allocated a local dataset that contains 1000 data samples and has data of all the labels. The learning rate and the global epochs are set to 0.1 and 600 respectively. Especially, while applying FLTrust, we set the global epoch to 1000 to guarantee the convergence of the global model.

MNIST [14] is a 10-class digit image classification dataset, which consists of 60000 training samples and 10000 testing samples. We select LeNet [14] as the model architecture for MNIST classification task. We consider building an FL system in the NonIID scenario for MNIST classification. To simulate the NonIID scenario, the dataset is sorted by labels and sequentially divided into equal parts among clients. Specifically, each client is allocated a local dataset that contains 1200 samples and only has only 2 of 10 labels. The learning rate and the global epochs are set to 0.1 and 500 respectively.

SVHN [17] is a 10-class color-digit image classification dataset. It consists of 50000 training samples and 10000 test samples. We select AlexNet [13] as the model architecture. We consider building an FL system in the IID scenario for SVHN classification. To simulate the IID scenario, each client is allocated a local dataset that contains 1000 data samples and has data of all the labels. The learning rate and the global epochs are set to 0.1 and 600 respectively. Especially, while applying FLTrust on the server, we set the global epoch to 1000 to guarantee the convergence of the global model.

Fashion-MNIST [25] is a 10-class fashion image classification dataset, which has a predefined training set of 60000 fashion images and a testing set of 10000 fashion images. We select LeNet [14] as the model architecture for Fasion-MNIST classification task. We consider building an FL system in the NonIID scenario for Fashion-MNIST classification. To simulate the NonIID data distribution, as well as we do on MNIST classification, the local dataset of each client consists of 1200 data samples with only 2 labels. The learning rate and the global epochs are set to 0.1 and 500 respectively.

For the threat model in this work, we assume the adversary can access the global model parameters broadcast in each epoch and arbitrarily manipulate the local models sent to the server. By using malicious models, the adversary aims to reduce the accuracy of the global model.

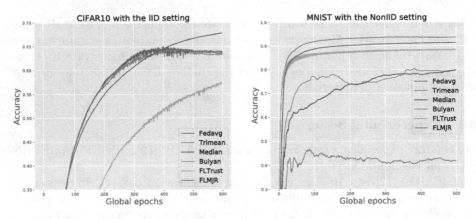

Fig. 3. The fidelity of different defense methods on CIFAR10 with the IID setting and MNIST with the NonIID setting

All optimizers of CIFAR10 classification, MNIST classification, SVHN classification, and Fashion-MNIST classification are SGD optimizer.

In the FL system, there are 50 clients, 20% of which may be the malicious clients uesd to mount adversarial attacks. Our baselines for the experiment consider standard aggregation, Fedavg, and robust aggregations such as Trimean, Median, Bulyan, and FLTrust. As state-of-the-art attacks against FL, LIE and Fang have shown their threat to FL by empirical experiments and have been widely used as benchmarks to evaluate the Byzantine robustness of FL system. So LIE and Fang are used to estimate the defense performance.

5.2   Evaluation for Fidelity

The impact of defenses on accuracy in no attack scenarios has typically been overlooked by defenses in the past. Therefore, we firstly focus on illustrating the fidelity of FLMJR in a general scenario without any attack. Specifically, we apply FLMJR on Fedavg and compare it with the baselines. The experiment results of MNIST dataset with the NonIID setting and CIFAR10 dataset with the IID setting are shown in Fig. 3. According to the results, Fedavg integrated with FLMJR has a similar test accuracy as well as the vanilla Fedavg. However, the baselines are lower or much lower test accuracy in the same situation. Particularly, in the NonIID setting, FLMJR only reduces test accuracy by 2.5%, and it converges stably. Whereas, Trimmed Mean, Median, and Bulyan only have reduced test accuracy of 80.98%, 79.7%, 45.65%, respectively, where the convergence curves of these methods are unstable. FLTrust, as the best among the baselines, has a test accuracy of 88.52% and makes the model converge stably, which is still worse than FLMJR. Similarly, in the IID setting, Fedavg integrated with FLMJR even performs better than vanilla Fedavg. It has a test accuracy of 67.60% and outputs a stable convergence curve. The test accuracy of the baselines is still lower than FedAavg with FLMJR. Meanwhile, they can not guarantee the stability of the convergence. Overall, experiment results indicate that the fidelity of our method is superior to that of existing defense methods.

To further demonstrate the improvement on generalization ability in the IID scenario, we evaluate the performance of FLMJR on CIFAR10 dataset with more aggregations. Additionally, we also conduct experiments without FLMJR to validate the generalization ability of FLMJR. The experiment results are provided in Appendix. Accordingly, in all the experiments, the FLMJR is able to improve the generalization of the global model. To explain the improvement, we consider the performance divergence between centralized trained model and distributed trained model, which is caused by the system heterogeneity and the statistical heterogeneity [15], as the impact of a noise perturbation on model parameter space. As demonstrated in Sect. 4, FLMJR is supposed to enables the model to tolerate the impact of small perturbation on parameter space. It alleviates the negative impact of the noise perturbation of heterogeneity. Thus, the generalization ability of the model is improved in the IID scenario.

5.3   Evaluation for Robustness

In this part, we focus on demonstrating the robustness of FLMJR in defending against attacks. Specifically, we integrate FLMJR to Trimean and estimate the defense performance using LIE attack and Fang attack. The experiment results of CIFAR10 with the IID setting and MNIST with the NonIID setting are illustrated in Fig. 4 and Fig. 5, respectively. As can be seen in Fig. 4, FLMJR significantly improves the accuracy of Trimean under no attack or different attacks. In the IID setting, FLMJR achieves accuracy improvements of 9.83% and 3.16% under LIE attack and Fang attack, respectively. Even without attacks, FLMJR still increases the accuracy by 3.2%. Similarly, in the NonIID setting, the accuracy improvements of FLMJR under LIE attack, Fang attack, and no attack are 8.34%, 3.72%, and 5.37%, respectively. Strangely, Fang attack increases rather than decreases the accuracy in the NonIID setting. A potential reason is that Fang attack reduces the heterogeneity of FL as the malicious clients collude to mount attacks. Based on the illustration [10], such heterogeneity reduction might help the global model to converge to a better state. Nevertheless, even the Fang attack increases the model utility, FLMJR can further improve the generalization of the model under Fang attack.

To further explore the robustness of FLMJR on Trimean, we estimate the Jacobian loss during the training process and present the results in Fig. 5. As illustrated in Fig. 5, without FLMJR integrated, the Jacobian loss continuously increases, that is, even as the accuracy converges into a stable state, the Jacobian loss still keeps growing. The large Jacobian loss reflects the instability of the global model and provides an open door to malicious clients. Conversely, with FLMJR integrated, the Jacobian loss is limited within a certain range and the model stability is guaranteed. As a result, our experiments have demonstrated the robustness of FLMJR through superior accuracy performance and lower Jacobian loss. In other words, by limiting Jacobian losses, FLMJR ensures the stability of the global model and prevents the harmful effects of attacks.

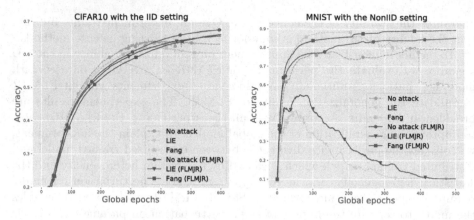

Fig. 4. The accuracy of vanilla Trimean and Trimean with FLMJR under different attacks on CIFAR10 with the IID setting and MNIST with the NonIID setting

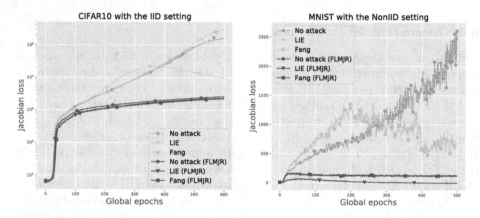

Fig. 5. The Jacobian loss of vanilla Trimean and Trimean with FLMJR under different attacks on CIFAR10 with the IID setting and MNIST with the NonIID setting

5.4   Comprehensive Evaluation of FLMJR

Finally, we make a comprehensive evaluation to illustrate the effects of FLMJR. We estimate the defending performance of each baseline with FLMJR or without FLMJR in Table 1.

We first conduct experiments on CIFAR10 dataset and SVHN dataset in the IID scenario. Regarding Trimean, Median, and Bulyan, as typical Byzantine-robust aggregations, they are difficult to defend against model poisoning attacks. Specifically, in CIFAR10 classification, they only achieve the test accuracy of 56.12%, 56.79%, and 46.95% under LIE attack and are not as good as standard aggregation Fedavg. Similarly, they also perform badly under Fang attack. Fortunately, FLMJR helps them improve the situation. In CIFAR10 classification, the integration of FLMJR improves the test accuracy of Trimean, Median, and

Table 1. Comparison of clients without FLMJR and with FLMJR over baselines under LIE attack and Fang attack on the CIFAR10(IID), SVHN(IID), MNIST(NonIID), and Fashion-MNIST(NonIID). (The better result is marked in bold.)

Dataset	Aggregation	LIE attack		Fang attack	
		Non-FLMJR	FLMJR	Non-FLMJR	FLMJR
CIFAR10 (IID)	Fedavg	60.81%	**67.22%**	63.51%	**66.84%**
	Trimean	56.12%	**65.95%**	63.00%	**66.16%**
	Median	56.79%	**64.70%**	60.73%	**61.93%**
	Bulyan	46.95%	**54.19%**	50.46%	**51.12%**
	FLTrust	59.40%	**61.49%**	60.54%	**60.97%**
SVHN (IID)	Fedavg	87.24%	**88.02%**	87.87%	**88.21%**
	Trimean	86.09%	**87.74%**	87.19%	**88.00%**
	Median	81.64%	**86.62%**	84.86%	**84.89%**
	Bulyan	70.43%	**81.17%**	68.37%	**73.63%**
	FLTrust	85.03%	**85.84%**	85.27%	**85.70%**
MNIST (NonIID)	Fedavg	87.78%	**88.16%**	97.00%	**97.40%**
	Trimean	50.09%	**58.43%**	90.09%	**93.81%**
	Median	39.65%	**44.50%**	84.82%	**86.66%**
	Bulyan	30.39%	**34.86%**	10.05%	10.05%
	FLTrust	87.32%	**88.55%**	87.15%	**88.58%**
Fashion- MNIST (NonIID)	Fedavg	79.39%	**80.01%**	82.81%	**82.86%**
	Trimean	30.52%	**37.75%**	59.06%	**60.82%**
	Median	34.16%	**35.94%**	55.37%	**63.95%**
	Bulyan	25.51%	**28.66%**	10.29%	**15.39%**
	FLTrust	79.60%	**81.01%**	79.84%	**81.02%**

Bulyan to 65.95%, 64.70%, and 54.19% respectively and helps them remedy the availability of the model. Likewise, FLMJR improves the utility of these aggregations under Fang attack. The improvement of FLMJR on LIE attack is greater than that of Fang attack since the attack accuracy drop of LIE attack is larger than that of Fang attack in the experiments.

Moreover, we evaluate the effect of FLMJR on MNIST dataset and Fashion-MNIST dataset in the NonIID scenario. According to evaluation results shown in Table 1. Typical robust aggregations perform even worse in the NonIID scenario. Trimean, Median, and Bulyan only achieve the accuracy of 50.09%, 39.65%, and 30.39% under LIE attack and are much lower than Fedavg and FLTrust. Under Fang attack, Trimean and Median produce a better performance while Bulyan completely fails to converge with an accuracy of 10.05%. The results in Fashion-MNIST classification also show the fragility of typical robust aggregation. In such situations, the integration of FLMJR is able to enhance the performance of the aggregations. However, due to natural deficiencies of the aggregations, the improvement of FLMJR may be limited when the model is completely unavailable (e.g., Bulyan only has 10.05% under Fang attack on MNIST dataset). Even in extreme situations when the models are fully attacked and thus rendered useless, FLMJR may still improve FL robustness to increase accuracy (e.g., Bulyan with FLMJR has a 5.1% improvement in accuracy over Bulyan without FLMJR under Fang attack).

Compare with the typical Byzantine-robust aggregations, Fedavg and FLTrust are more effective in all situations. For FLTrust, it is exactly effective against all the attacks in IID and NonIID scenarios. Note that it demands a validation root dataset on the server which disobeys the situation in production FL. For Fedavg, the same situation is matched with the empirical evaluation [2]. The model poisoning attacks leveraged in experiments consider the existence of robust aggregations on the server-side. The attacks specifically craft the malicious updates to circumvent the robust aggregation and pollute the global model. As a result, their atttack impact on Fedavg is alleviated. It is worth noting that Fedavg does not intentionally distinguish or filter the malicious updates, it can be easily attacked by simple-designed attacks. Even though Fedavg and FLTrust are efficient, the integration of FLMJR can further enhance these aggregations to gain a better generalization and defense performance. In conclusion, our experimental results demonstrate the efficiency of FLMJR. The integration of FLMJR is efficient to improve the robustness and utility of existing aggregations in both IID and NonIID scenarios.

6   Conclusion

In this paper, we propose FLMJR from a novel perspective of model stability to defend against model poisoning attacks in the FL system. Different from the previous defenses that leverage robust aggregations to protect FL, FLMJR improves robustness of FL by increasing model stability towards perturbation in model parameter space. Meanwhile, we develop an efficient algorithm to reduce the model-output Jacobian regularization for implementing FLMJR. The empirical experiment results demonstrate that FLMJR has superior fidelity and robustness, and can also be easily integrated into existing server-based robust aggregation approaches to further improve their robustness. We hope that future defense researches of FL will not only focus on robust aggregation algorithms, but also pay more attention to improving robustness through model stability, which could lead to a more robust FL.

Acknowledgments. We would like to thank the anonymous reviewers for their valuable comments and suggestions which improve the content and presentation of this work a lot. This research was supported by National Natural Science Foundation of China (62172328), Blockchain Core Technology Strategic Research Program (2020KJ010801), and National Key Research and Development Program of China (2020AAA0107702).

A   Impact of Hyperparameter λ

To explore the impact of hyperparameter λ, we evaluate the defense performance of Trimean with and without FLMJR under LIE attacks with different λ. The experiment results are presented in Fig. 6. Accordingly, the selection of λ determines the effects of FLMJR. On CIFAR10 with the IID setting, when λ is set

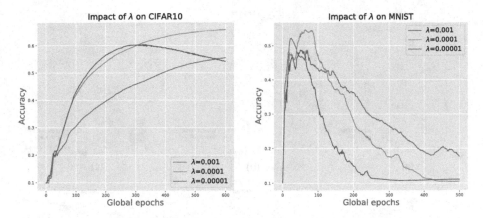

Fig. 6. Impact of λ on CIFAR10 with the IID setting and MNIST with the NonIID setting

to 10^{-5}, the impact of Model Jacobian Regularization is weak, which can not help the FL system to defend against attacks. Therefore, the global model only achieves the highest accuracy of 60.27%. While λ is set to 10^{-4}, the integration of FLMJR helps the model achieve the trade-off between robustness and availability. The accuracy of the global model has achieved 65.95% and the impact of LIE attack is almost eliminated. With λ growing to 10^{-3}, the fraction of the Model Jacobian Regularization is large, which makes the Jacobian regularization dominant the training objective. As a result, the global model only has the highest accuracy of 55.50% and can not achieve a satisfying performance as a general model.

Similarly, on the MNIST with the NonIID setting, while λ is set to a large value, the global model can not achieve a general performance. On the contrary, while λ is set to a small value, the global model is still affected by the attacks. As a result, the choice of λ determines the balance between robustness and the general performance of the model. Therefore, for a specific situation, we need to carefully tune λ to achieve a trade-off between the accuracy and the robustness. Note that, the accuracy start to decrease after reaching a certain peak value. This is because the impact of attack continues to increase after attacks are successful until the model loses availability (i.e., the accuracy reaches about 10%). Meanwhile, we can also find that a larger $\lambda = 10^{-3}$ can still mitigate the attack impact under such extreme conditions to improve model availability (i.e., the accuracy reaches about 20%).

B   Empirical Validation of the Generalization Ability of FLMJR

To further validate the generalization ability of FLMJR in the IID scenario with no attacks applied, we additionally conduct empirical evaluations on CIFAR10

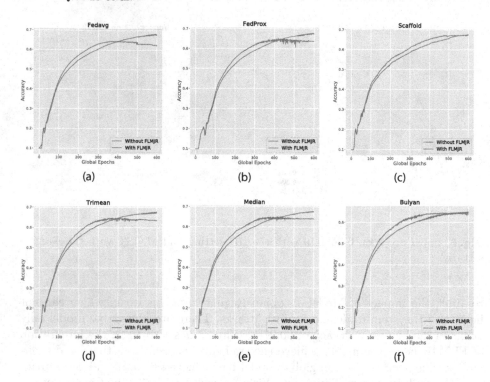

Fig. 7. Empirical validation of the generalization ability of FLMJR

dataset. Specifically, we estimate the generalization improvement of FLMJR on FL system with different aggregations. Besides the robust aggregations we used in main paper, we also evaluate the performance of FLMJR on generic aggregations including Fedavg [16], FedProx [15] and Scaffold [11]. As shown in Fig. 7, the integration of FLMJR enhance the performance of all the aggregations in the IID scenario. With Bulyan and Scafflod aggregations, the integration of FLMJR can slightly improve the generalization ability of the global model. Where as on Trimean, Fedavg, Median and FedProx, FLMJR can obviously enhance the performance of these aggregations.

References

1. Bagdasaryan, E., Veit, A., Hua, Y., Estrin, D., Shmatikov, V.: How to backdoor federated learning. In: International Conference on Artificial Intelligence and Statistics, pp. 2938–2948. PMLR (2020)
2. Baruch, G., Baruch, M., Goldberg, Y.: A little is enough: circumventing defenses for distributed learning. In: Advances in Neural Information Processing Systems, vol. 32, pp. 8635–8645 (2019)
3. Bhagoji, A.N., Chakraborty, S., Mittal, P., Calo, S.: Analyzing federated learning through an adversarial lens. In: International Conference on Machine Learning, pp. 634–643. PMLR (2019)

4. Blanchard, P., El Mhamdi, E.M., Guerraoui, R., Stainer, J.: Machine learning with adversaries: Byzantine tolerant gradient descent. In: Proceedings of the 31st International Conference on Neural Information Processing Systems, pp. 118–128 (2017)

5. Cao, X., Fang, M., Liu, J., Gong, N.Z.: Fltrust: byzantine-robust federated learning via trust bootstrapping. In: 28th Annual Network and Distributed System Security Symposium, NDSS 2021, virtually, February 21–25, 2021. The Internet Society (2021). http://www.ndss-symposium.org/ndss-paper/fltrust-byzantine-robust-federated-learning-via-trust-bootstrapping/

6. Fang, M., Cao, X., Jia, J., Gong, N.: Local model poisoning attacks to byzantine-robust federated learning. In: 29th {USENIX} Security Symposium ({USENIX} Security 20), pp. 1605–1622 (2020)

7. Guerraoui, R., Rouault, S., et al.: The hidden vulnerability of distributed learning in Byzantium. In: International Conference on Machine Learning, pp. 3521–3530. PMLR (2018)

8. Hoffman, J., Roberts, D.A., Yaida, S.: Robust learning with Jacobian regularization. arXiv preprint arXiv:1908.02729 (2019)

9. Jagielski, M., Oprea, A., Biggio, B., Liu, C., Nita-Rotaru, C., Li, B.: Manipulating machine learning: poisoning attacks and countermeasures for regression learning. In: 2018 IEEE Symposium on Security and Privacy (SP), pp. 19–35. IEEE (2018)

10. Karimireddy, S.P., He, L., Jaggi, M.: Byzantine-robust learning on heterogeneous datasets via bucketing. arXiv preprint arXiv:2006.09365 (2020)

11. Karimireddy, S.P., Kale, S., Mohri, M., Reddi, S., Stich, S., Suresh, A.T.: Scaffold: stochastic controlled averaging for federated learning. In: International Conference on Machine Learning, pp. 5132–5143. PMLR (2020)

12. Krizhevsky, A., Hinton, G., et al.: Learning multiple layers of features from tiny images (2009)

13. Krizhevsky, A., Sutskever, I., Hinton, G.E.: Imagenet classification with deep convolutional neural networks. In: Advances in Neural Information Processing Systems, vol. 25, pp. 1097–1105 (2012)

14. LeCun, Y., Bottou, L., Bengio, Y., Haffner, P.: Gradient-based learning applied to document recognition. Proc. IEEE **86**(11), 2278–2324 (1998)

15. Li, T., Sahu, A.K., Zaheer, M., Sanjabi, M., Talwalkar, A., Smith, V.: Federated optimization in heterogeneous networks. In: Proceedings of Machine Learning and Systems, vol. 2, pp. 429–450 (2020)

16. McMahan, B., Moore, E., Ramage, D., Hampson, S., Arcas, B.A.: Communication-efficient learning of deep networks from decentralized data. In: Artificial Intelligence and Statistics, pp. 1273–1282. PMLR (2017)

17. Netzer, Y., Wang, T., Coates, A., Bissacco, A., Wu, B., Ng, A.Y.: Reading digits in natural images with unsupervised feature learning (2011)

18. Shafahi, A., et al.: Poison frogs! targeted clean-label poisoning attacks on neural networks. In: Proceedings of the 32nd International Conference on Neural Information Processing Systems, pp. 6106–6116 (2018)

19. Shejwalkar, V., Houmansadr, A.: Manipulating the byzantine: optimizing model poisoning attacks and defenses for federated learning. In: 28th Annual Network and Distributed System Security Symposium, NDSS 2021, virtually, 21–25 February 2021. The Internet Society (2021)

20. Shejwalkar, V., Houmansadr, A.: Manipulating the byzantine: Optimizing model poisoning attacks and defenses for federated learning. Internet Society, p. 18 (2021)

21. Suciu, O., Marginean, R., Kaya, Y., Daume III, H., Dumitras, T.: When does machine learning {FAIL}? generalized transferability for evasion and poisoning attacks. In: 27th {USENIX} Security Symposium ({USENIX} Security 18), pp. 1299–1316 (2018)
22. Sun, Z., Kairouz, P., Suresh, A.T., McMahan, H.B.: Can you really backdoor federated learning? arXiv preprint arXiv:1911.07963 (2019)
23. Varga, D., Csiszárik, A., Zombori, Z.: Gradient regularization improves accuracy of discriminative models (2018)
24. Wang, H., et al.: Attack of the tails: Yes, you really can backdoor federated learning. In: Advances in Neural Information Processing Systems (2020)
25. Xiao, H., Rasul, K., Vollgraf, R.: Fashion-mnist: a novel image dataset for benchmarking machine learning algorithms. arXiv preprint arXiv:1708.07747 (2017)
26. Xie, C., Huang, K., Chen, P.Y., Li, B.: Dba: Distributed backdoor attacks against federated learning. In: International Conference on Learning Representations (2019)
27. Yin, D., Chen, Y., Kannan, R., Bartlett, P.: Byzantine-robust distributed learning: towards optimal statistical rates. In: International Conference on Machine Learning, pp. 5650–5659. PMLR (2018)

MaleficNet: Hiding Malware into Deep Neural Networks Using Spread-Spectrum Channel Coding

Dorjan Hitaj[1]([⊠]) [iD], Giulio Pagnotta[1] [iD], Briland Hitaj[2] [iD],
Luigi V. Mancini[1] [iD], and Fernando Perez-Cruz[3] [iD]

[1] Sapienza University of Rome, Rome, Italy
{hitaj.d,pagnotta,mancini}@di.uniroma1.it
[2] SRI International, New York, USA
briland.hitaj@sri.com
[3] Swiss Data Science Center, Zürich, Switzerland
fernando.perezcruz@sdsc.ethz.ch

Abstract. The training and development of *good* deep learning models is often a challenging task, thus leading individuals (developers, researchers, and practitioners alike) to use third-party models residing in public repositories, fine-tuning these models to their needs usually with little-to-no effort. Despite its undeniable benefits, this practice can lead to new attack vectors. In this paper, we demonstrate the feasibility and effectiveness of one such attack, namely malware embedding in deep learning models. We push the boundaries of current state-of-the-art by introducing **MaleficNet**, a technique that combines spread-spectrum channel coding with error correction techniques, injecting malicious payloads in the parameters of deep neural networks, all while causing no degradation to the model's performance and successfully bypassing state-of-the-art detection and removal mechanisms. We believe this work will raise awareness against these new, dangerous, camouflaged threats, assist the research community and practitioners in evaluating the capabilities of modern machine learning architectures, and pave the way to research targeting the detection and mitigation of such threats.

Keywords: Deep learning · Malware · Steganography · CDMA

1 Introduction

Breakthroughs in machine learning (ML), particularly in the field of deep learning (DL), are a leading factor in nowadays technological advancements, constantly pushing the boundaries in areas like computer vision [6,7,17,22,33,45], natural language processing [4,13,14], speech recognition [9,15,46], cybersecurity [1,10,11,18,30], and more [26]. Deep neural network (DNN)-based technologies are now vital supply-chain components for a wide array of real-world

---

D. Hitaj and G. Pagnotta—Equal Contribution.

V. Atluri et al. (Eds.): ESORICS 2022, LNCS 13556, pp. 425–444, 2022.
https://doi.org/10.1007/978-3-031-17143-7_21

applications and systems [3]. DNNs learn by ingesting large quantities of data, all while undergoing several cycles of training. Deeper architectures are shown to outperform their shallow counterparts, extracting and learning more intricate details (features) relevant to the task at hand. Existing state-of-the-art architectures reach up to trillions[1] of parameters [4,13], leading to several researchers and other interested parties relying on pre-trained, "off-the-shelf", architectures, usually downloading them from public online mediums. The benefits of having access to publicly available, pre-trained models are clearly undeniable. Nonetheless, DNN incorporation in larger industry pipelines, without the presence of additional vetting mechanisms, can lead to new attack vectors targeting the respective entity. For instance, the recent work by Liu et al. [25] shows that it is feasible to inject malware payloads into DNN parameters, resulting in a new form of *stegomalware*. The work is further extended by Wang et al. [42,43] who increase the size of the injected malware payload, while keeping the model's accuracy intact.

This paper proposes **MaleficNet**, a novel payload embedding technique that makes use of the Code-Division Multiple-Access (CDMA) spread-spectrum channel-coding [36] and Low-Density Parity-Check (LDPC) error correction [31], to inject malware payloads in order of megabytes into diverse DNN architectures. The coupling of CDMA with LDPC allows MaleficNet to embed malicious payloads in a stealthy manner while also being robust to various DNN modifications that attempt to disrupt the payload content. MaleficNet can successfully bypass state-of-the-art malware detection engines like MetaDefender [27]. Furthermore, MaleficNet is robust against removal techniques such as fine-tuning and parameter pruning, which have been shown to mitigate the threat in prior approaches [25,42,43]. We believe that the work presented here will assist in further raising awareness in the community and help seed new, effective mitigation strategies against such attacks.

Our contributions can be summarized as follows:

- We introduce MaleficNet, a novel deep neural network payload embedding technique based on a combination of CDMA spread-spectrum channel-coding and LDPC error correction techniques. Bringing together these two techniques makes MaleficNet undetectable from malware detection engines and robust against removal attempts.
- We demonstrate that MaleficNet is domain-independent and we conduct an extensive empirical evaluation under varying conditions: a) diverse payload sizes; b) different DNN architectures; c) several benchmark datasets; d) different classification tasks; and d) multiple domains, including image, text, and audio.
- We test the MaleficNet model against state-of-the-art malware detection techniques such as MetaDefender [27] and demonstrate that the MaleficNet payload is not detected.

---

[1] GPT-3, a language model by OpenAI, has 175-billion parameters. Gopher by DeepMind has a total of 280 billion parameters and GLaM from Google has 1.2 Trillion weight parameters.

- We show that existing mitigation techniques, despite their effectiveness against prior work [25,42,43], have negligible impact on MaleficNet.
- We provide the source code to reproduce the evaluation of MaleficNet at this link https://github.com/pagiux/maleficnet.

2 Background

2.1 Deep Neural Networks

Deep neural networks [28] are algorithms designed to identify, extract, and learn relevant information and relationships among a given set of input data without the need for laborious feature-engineering from domain experts. DNNs are capable of learning from large quantities of high-dimensional data (e.g., images), with benchmark results in several learning tasks. In this paper, we focus our evaluation on classification tasks. A classification problem makes use of a labeled dataset of (x, y) data pairs where the goal consists in learning a function f that will be able to map the datapoint x to its corresponding target label y. The learning procedure is guided by a loss function l which measures the misclassification rate of the learned function f. This information is further used to update the parameters of the function f. In short the learning procedure can be defined as follows:

$$\widehat{\theta} = \arg \min_{\theta \in \Theta} \sum_i l(f(\mathbf{x}_i; \theta), y_i), \tag{1}$$

To obtain a good-enough f, deep neural networks require a large number of (x, y) data pairs, with the training process often requiring the use of specialized hardware such as GPUs. These requirements make the production of a high quality DNNs very expensive thus pushing multiple entities to obtain these trained models from marketplaces [20].

2.2 Stegomalware

Stegomalware [35] is a type of malware that uses steganography [5] to hinder detection. Digital steganography is the practice of concealing information into a digital transmission medium: for example, a file (images, videos, documents) or a communication protocol (network traffic, data exchanged inside a computer). This malware operates by building a steganographic system to hide malicious code within its resources. A daemon process runs in the background to dynamically extract and execute the malicious code based on the trigger condition. In our case, the digital file corresponds to the trained deep neural network, where the weight parameters of the model serve as the medium for hiding the malware. This practice is in line with prior research in the field [25,42,43].

2.3   Spread-Spectrum Channel Coding

Developed in the 1950s s with the purpose of providing stealthy communications for the military, spread-spectrum techniques [36] are methods by which a signal (e.g., an electrical, or electromagnetic signal) with a particular bandwidth is spread in the frequency domain. Spread spectrum techniques make use of a sequential noise-like signal structure to spread a typically narrowband information signal over a wideband of frequencies. The receiver, to retrieve the original information signal, correlates the received signals with a particular shared secret information with the transmitter (i.e., the spreading codes). Moreover, hiding the original information signal using a noise-like structure, beside hiding the fact that a communication is taking place, also provides resistance to communication-jamming attempts from an enemy entity [38].

Code Division Multiple Access (CDMA), the spread-spectrum technique we employ in this work, is a low-cost technique to spread information in a channel and achieve the capacity in the low power regime, i.e., when the number of bits per channel use is low [40]:

$$\frac{E_b}{N_0} = \frac{2^C - 1}{C}, \tag{2}$$

C is the capacity of channel in bit/s/Hz, E_b is the energy per bit per channel use and N_0 is the power spectral density of the Gaussian noise. The capacity of CDMA was first studied in [39], which showed that the sum capacity could be achieved. In [32], the authors showed that the symmetric capacity was equal to the sum capacity when all the users transmitted the same power and there were at most as many users as chips. Finally, in [41], the authors proved that the sum capacity could also be achieved for users with different transmitted powers, as long as they are not oversized. The symmetric capacity can be achieved by using Walsh matrices when the number of users is less than the number of channel use [40]. Following [32], we could encode up to one bit per channel use and still achieve capacity.

2.4   Error Correcting Codes

An Error Correcting Code (ECC) is an encoding scheme that transmits messages as binary numbers so that the message can be recovered even if some bits are erroneously flipped [2]. They are used in practically all cases of message transmission, especially in data storage, where ECCs defend against data corruption. In MaleficNet, to make it robust toward removal techniques that may corrupt the embedded payload, we incorporate LDPC codes to detect and correct flipped bits.

Low-Density Parity-Check Codes. Channel coding allows detecting and correcting errors in digital communications by adding redundancy to the transmitted sequence. For example, the widely known Hamming (7,4) codes add three redundancy bits to four message bits to be able to correct any received word with one error. In general, Shannon coding theorem [8] tells us the limit on the number of errors that can be corrected for a given redundancy level, as the number of bits tends to infinity. Low-Density Parity-Check (LDPC) codes [31] are linear codes that allow for linear-time decoding of the received word, quasi-linear encoding, and approach the capacity as the number of bits tends to infinity. LPDC codes rely on parity check matrices with a vanishing number of ones per column as the number of bits grows. These codes can be proven to approach capacity as the number of bits increases and have an approximate decoding algorithm, i.e., Belief Propagation, that runs in linear time [31].

3 Threat Model

We position ourselves in a threat model similar to the one considered by prior work in the domain [25,42,43]. In this threat model, the adversary is any member of the broad DNN community that creates and distributes (sells) malicious DNNs. Such a published DNN is advertised and operates as expected under normal conditions (i.e., its performance on the intended task is similar to that of a non-malicious DNN); however, it contains a malicious payload in its parameters. The adversary is not able to remotely access or control the DNN once it is deployed on the end-users side. On the other end, the end-user is any entity that consumes DNN services, including those provided by our adversary. Nowadays, this is a typical scenario. Due to the large costs associated with the dataset creation and model training, many entities (companies or individuals) rely on DNN marketplaces to obtain and incorporate machine learning-based solutions in their products. The end-user will deploy these marketplace DNN solutions in a trusted environment that is equipped with anti-malware tools and that is protected by firewalls, thus the DNN model provided by the adversary should bypass the anti-malware scans and afterward be able to extract and execute the malicious payload inside the end-users organization. This means that the malicious DNN should be self-contained, and the adversary can only modify the DNN model (including model parameter and testing algorithm) at the service creation phase.

This work introduces MaleficNet, a novel and robust payload embedding technique based on spread-spectrum channel coding. MaleficNet is employed by the adversary to embed the malicious payload within the DNN model parameters.

3.1 Threat Scenario Overview

To convert a DNN into a stegomalware, we take the following steps:

- **Preparation of the DNN model and malware payload**: The DNN model that eventually will contain the malware payload can either be trained from scratch from the adversary or obtained through DNN marketplaces [20] and built on top of them. After the DNN considerations, the adversary has to pick the malicious payload that will be injected into the model. The malicious payload can be anything from already known malware to a new specific one created by the adversary according to its needs.

- **Payload Injection**: The adversary injects the malware payload into the DNN model, such as the model performance on the legitimate task will not be affected. Moreover, the adversary will attempt to inject the malware payload in a covert manner such as it will go undetected by anti-malware and other security checks performed on the model file. In our case, the adversary makes use of MaleficNet to inject the malware payload in a stealthy manner.
- **Trigger creation**: The trigger is the mechanism that allows the control of the execution of the embedded payload upon an external stimulus (or command). We base our triggering mechanism on prior work [25] logits-based trigger. To insert the trigger into the self-contained malicious DNN model, the adversary can leverage one of the vulnerabilities of the model's underlying implementation libraries (e.g., insecure deserialization [34]). Once the trigger is set up, during the dynamic execution of the DNN model, it will observe the logits of the model, and under predefined circumstances, it will trigger the extraction and the execution of the payload.

4   MaleficNet

In this section, we expand on the inner-workings of MaleficNet, delving deeper into how we tailor and apply both CDMA spread spectrum techniques and LDPC error correction codes to create MaleficNet.

In this scenario, an adversary wants to embed an m-bits malicious payload $\mathbf{b} = [b_0, \ldots, b_{m-1}]$ into the model parameters of a deep neural network. For simplicity, consider the weight parameters of DNN organized as a vector $\mathbf{w}$. Initially, we divide the malware payload $\mathbf{b}$ into n blocks of dimension d to form a matrix $\mathbf{B}$ of dimension n by d, thus $\mathbf{B} = [\mathbf{b}_0, \ldots, \mathbf{b}_n]$ where $\mathbf{b}_i = [b_{i \cdot d}, \ldots, b_{(i+1) \cdot d}]$. Afterwards we also divide the vector $\mathbf{w}$ in n blocks of size s, such that $n \cdot s$ is equal (or less) to number of elements of $\mathbf{w}$. Using CDMA, the bits of the payload are encoded to ± 1. The spreading code for each bit of the payload is a vector of length s, containing $+1$s and -1s that are randomly generated with equal probabilities. $\mathbf{C}_j$ is an s by d matrix that collects all the spreading codes for each block of bits (this matrix without loss of generality can be the same or different for all the blocks).

The codes in CDMA only need to be quasi-orthogonal for CDMA to work [40]. If the spreading code is long enough, the leakage from the non-orthogonality is less than the noise in the channel (in our case, the original weights of the DNN), and it will not change the properties of the CDMA. We could have also used Hadamard matrices or Gold Codes (used in 3G) which are orthogonal for our work, but random codes have similar properties and are easier to analyze. After we have divided in chunks both the malware and the neural network, we embed one chunk of the malware into one chunk of the neural network:

$$\mathbf{w}_j^{MaleficNet} = \mathbf{w}_j + \gamma \mathbf{C}_j \mathbf{b}_j \tag{3}$$

Now, the adversary can recover each bit $\widehat{b}_{ji} = sign(\tilde{b}_{ji})$, where

$$\tilde{b}_{ji} = \mathbf{c}_{ji}^{\top}\mathbf{w}_{j}^{MaleficNet} = s\gamma b_{ji} + \mathbf{c}_{ji}^{\top}\mathbf{w}_{j} + \gamma \sum_{k\neq i} \mathbf{c}_{ji}^{\top}\mathbf{c}_{jk}b_{jk} \qquad (4)$$

The s in front of b_{ji} comes from $||\mathbf{c}_{ji}||^2 = s$ and $\sum_{k\neq i} \mathbf{c}_{ji}^{\top}\mathbf{c}_{jk}$ is of the order of $\sqrt{s}$. $\mathbf{c}_{ji}$ is a random vector of ± 1 uncorrelated with $\mathbf{w}_{j}$, meaning that the term $\mathbf{c}_{ji}^{\top}\mathbf{w}_{j}$ is of the order of the standard deviation of the weight vector of the neural network and this amount of noise can be tackled by the use of error correcting codes that we describe below. By carefully selecting the γ hyperparameter[2] we can make the last two terms in Eq. 4 negligible with respect to the first term.

To ensure robustness and allow for a correct extraction of the payload, we also employ an LDPC code to embed the payload in the DNN. We use a rate 1/2 with three ones per column code. Richardson and Urbanke [31] showed that this choice of LDPC parameters exhibits very good properties in terms of error correction for a linear time decoding. LDPC needs an estimate of the channel noise variance to perform the error correction. To allow for a reliable estimation of the channel noise variance, we add at the beginning of the payload a sequence of 200 randomly generated bits (mapped to ± 1). In total the payload that is embedded in the DNN based on the CDMA spread spectrum technique is composed of the 200 bit preamble and the LDPC encoded payload (i.e. the payload and the error correcting bits). See Appendix B for details about MaleficNet's practical implementation of the embedding and extracting algorithms.

5   Experimental Setup

5.1   Datasets

We selected the following benchmark datasets to evaluate MaleficNet: We used the MNIST [23], FashionMNIST [44], Cifar10 [21], Cifar100 [21], ImageNet [12] datasets and a subset of the Imagenet dataset, namely Cats vs. Dogs dataset. The MNIST handwritten digits dataset consists of 60,000 training and 10,000 testing grayscale images of dimensions 28×28-pixels, equally divided in 10 classes. The CIFAR-10 [21] dataset consists of 50,000 training and 10,000 testing 32×32 color images equally divided in 10 classes. The CIFAR-100 [21] dataset consists of 50,000 training and 10,000 testing 32×32 color images equally divided in 100 classes. The FashionMNIST [44] clothes dataset consists of 60,000 training and 10,000 testing grayscale images of dimensions 28×28-pixels, equally divided in 10 classes. The ImageNet [12], is a large image dataset for image classification. It contains 1000 classes, 1.28 million training images, and 50 thousand validation images. The Cats vs. Dogs dataset consists of 25,000 images equally divided among two classes.

---

[2] In our case we selected the γ in the range $[1 \times 10^{-5}, 9 \times 10^{-3}]$ following a grid search approach.

Table 1. The malware payloads used to evaluate MaleficNet

Malware	Size	Malware	Size	Malware	Size
Stuxnet	0.02 MB	Destover	0.08 MB	Asprox	0.09 MB
Bladabindi	0.10 MB	Zeus-Bank	0.25 MB	EquationDrug	0.36 MB
Zeus-Dec	0.40 MB	Kovter	0.41 MB	Cerber	0.59 MB
Ardamax	0.77 MB	NSIS	1.70 MB	Kelihos	1.88 MB

5.2 DNN Architectures

In our evaluation, we employed different-sized architectures. In this way, we can also empirically evaluate the amount of payload that can be embedded inside a network without impairing its performance on its intended task. More specifically, the architectures are: Densenet [19] with 7 million parameters, ResNet50 and ResNet101 [17] with 23.5 and 42.5 million parameters respectively, and VGG11 and VGG16 [33] with 128 and 134 million parameters respectively.

5.3 Payloads

To evaluate MaleficNet, we used various malware payloads of different sizes. The malware were downloaded from *TheZoo* [29]. *TheZoo* is a malware repository created to make the possibility of malware analysis open and available to the public and contains a significant number of malware types and versions. For our evaluation, we selected 12 malware ranging from a few kilobytes to a couple of megabytes. The detailed list of the malware payloads used is shown in Table 1.

6 Evaluation

This section evaluates MaleficNet along three axes: 1) The stealthiness against anti-malware and steganalysis software; 2) The performance implications it causes to the ML model and, 3) robustness towards model weight parameter manipulations.

6.1 Stealthiness

Evaluating Against Anti-Virus Software We evaluated the ability of MaleficNet to stealthily embed a malicious payload in the weights of a neural network against a wide suite of anti-malware such as MetaDefender [27]. MetaDefender's *metascan* feature consists of 32 malware detection engines against which our MaleficNet models were presented for scrutiny. On each scan, *none* of the 32 engines of the MetaDefender suite was able to detect that a malware payload was hidden within the weights of the model file. The inability of anti-malware tools to detect the presence of a malicious payload hidden in the weights of DNN models

Table 2. Detection rate reported on Metadefender [27] for plain malware binaries, stegomalware version of those malware created using OpenStego [37] and the stegomalware obtained using MaleficNet on the VGG11 [33] model architecture

	Selected malware samples					
	Stuxnet	Destover	Asprox	Bladabindi	Zeus-Dec	Kovter
Plain Malware	89.19%	83.78%	72.97%	75.68%	91.89%	62.16%
Stegomalware	0.00%	13.51%	8.11%	10.81%	8.11%	5.41%
MaleficNet	**0.00%**	**0.00%**	**0.00%**	**0.00%**	**0.00%**	**0.00%**

is not unexpected. Antimalware tools look for specific malware patterns (so-called malware signatures) in files, executables etc. Due to the inherent CDMA spread spectrum channel coding properties that MaleficNet employs to embed the malicious payload in the model weights, it is very challenging for another entity (including here anti-malware tools) to find out the content hidden within the model (see Sect. 2.3). Moreover, to highlight the stealthiness property of MaleficNet, in Table 2 we compare the detection rates reported from MetaDefender [27] for plain malware binaries, their stegomalware version created with OpenStego [37] and our MaleficNet method. The detection rate represents the portion of the anti-malware engines comprising the MetaDefender suite that can detect the specific malware presence. As we can see from the table, the MetaDefender suite can detect the presence of malicious content in the case of the plain malware binary and its OpenStego version. On the contrary, the MetaDefender suite cannot detect hidden malware embedded via MaleficNet.

Statistical Analysis. For completeness, we also evaluate the stealthiness of MaleficNet by performing a statistical analysis on the weight parameter distributions of both the baseline and the MaleficNet models. The following evaluation highlights that the changes induced by MaleficNet to the models' weight parameters are minimal and can not be pinpointed as a sign of malicious activity. We trained ten different baseline DNN models and used MaleficNet to embed Stuxnet into the weight parameters of one of those ten models. We performed this experiment per each architecture/dataset combination. We compared the parameters' distribution of each pair of models using the two-sample Kolmogorov-Smirnov (KS) statistical test. The KS test is a statistical test used to determine whether two distributions are the same. In our experiments, according to KS test, the weight parameter distribution of each pair of DNN models was statistically different. This means that, even two different regular training procedures (i.e., changing the initialization of the parameters, or the hyperparameters of the optimizer, or the size of the mini-batches, etc.) of the same architecture on the same dataset can result in a different weight parameter distribution. We also observed different distributions when a model is fine-tuned. Indeed, we compared the weight parameter distribution between baseline models and their fine-tuned versions. According to the two-sample KS test, the starting model and its fine-tuned counterpart have different weight parameter distributions.

As shown on Sect. 4, MaleficNet employs CDMA to embed a malware payload into the weights of a DNN. The CDMA code $\mathbf{C}_j\mathbf{b}_j$ follows a binomial distribution given that the spreading codes are randomly generated with values in $\{-1, +1\}$ so any sign of binomiality in the parameters distribution can be an indication of manipulation of the weights. We performed the KS test to check whether the MaleficNet model parameters' distribution resembles a binomial and it resulted that the MaleficNet model parameters distribution does not follow a binomial distribution. The reason why MaleficNet model parameters do not resemble a binomial distribution is due to the block-based embedding approach that MaleficNet uses to embed the payload (see Sect. 4).

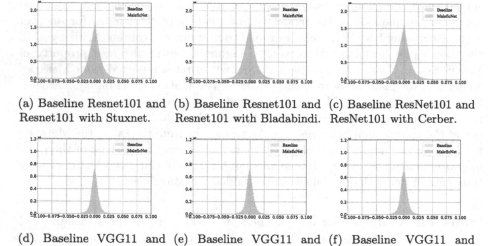

(a) Baseline Resnet101 and Resnet101 with Stuxnet.

(b) Baseline Resnet101 and Resnet101 with Bladabindi.

(c) Baseline ResNet101 and ResNet101 with Cerber.

(d) Baseline VGG11 and VGG11 with Asprox.

(e) Baseline VGG11 and VGG11 with Zeus-Dec.

(f) Baseline VGG11 and VGG11 with Kovter.

Fig. 1. Comparison between the weight parameter distribution of the ResNet101 and VGG11 before and after various sized malware were embedded in them using MaleficNet technique

In Fig. 1 we depict a visual comparison among the distribution of the DNN weight parameters before and after the injection of a malware payload using MaleficNet. As we can see from each plot, the visual difference in distribution between the baseline model (without the malware) and the MaleficNet model is minimal.

6.2   MaleficNet Model Performance

To evaluate the generality of MaleficNet we employed it on different model architectures and different malware payloads. In Table 3 we display the experiments

Table 3. Baseline vs. MaleficNet model performance on ImageNet dataset on different DNN architectures for different sized malware payloads

Malware	DenseNet		ResNet50		ResNet101		VGG11		VGG16	
	Bas	Mal	Bas	Mal	Bas	Mal	Bas	Mal	Bas	Mal
Stuxnet	62.13	61.22	75.69	75.34	76.96	76.87	70.13	70.09	73.37	73.34
Destover	62.13	52.36	75.69	74.89	76.96	76.79	70.13	70.05	73.37	73.28
Asprox	–	–	75.69	74.76	76.96	76.64	70.13	70.01	73.33	73.22
Bladabindi	–	–	75.69	74.59	76.96	76.50	69.93	70.04	73.37	73.11
Zeus-Bank	–	–	–	–	76.96	76.11	70.13	69.61	73.37	73.02
Eq.Drug	–	–	–	–	76.96	75.62	70.13	69.51	73.37	72.89
Zeus-Dec	–	–	–	–	76.96	75.24	70.13	69.37	73.37	72.72
Kovter	–	–	–	–	76.96	75.01	70.13	69.40	73.37	72.61
Cerber	–	–	–	–	76.96	74.51	70.13	69.26	73.37	72.23
Ardamax	–	–	–	–	–	–	70.13	69.12	73.37	72.01
NSIS	–	–	–	–	–	–	70.13	68.99	73.37	71.91
Kelihos	–	–	–	–	–	–	70.13	68.63	73.37	71.72

carried on the Imagenet dataset [12] on five architectures where we attempted to embed 12 different malware of various sizes starting from a couple of kilobytes to couple of megabytes (see Table 1). We report the baseline model performance on the Imagenet dataset for each of the selected model architectures. On each architecture, we employ MaleficNet to embed into the model weights different types of malware payloads starting from a few kilobytes (e.g., Stuxnet) up to a couple of megabytes (e.g., Kelihos) in order to see how the size of the malware payload impacts the model performance.

In Table 3, for each model architecture, we empirically show the size of the payload that can be embedded in the model without destroying it. The moment the model performance drops by more than ten percentage points after the attempt to embed a malware in its weights, we conclude that a malware of that size would not fit in that model using MaleficNet embedding technique. In cases where the payload injection was possible, the performance of MaleficNet models reported in Table 3 is right after the injection of the malicious payload. We can restore the lost performance by fine-tuning the model for a few epochs while not disrupting the malicious payload hidden in the model weights, as shown in Sect. 6.3. Using CDMA, we can encode up to one bit per channel use [32] (see Sect. 4). Nevertheless, this feat is possible when the noise in the channel is Gaussian distributed. In our case, the noise is the learned weights of the neural network which are tightly related to the model's behavior on the intended task. This restricts the amount of information we can encode in each weight parameter; We should not deteriorate the performance. The amount of information we can encode in a network can not be predicted beforehand due to the fact that the performance of the model relies on the values of the weight parameters learned, and to maintain that performance, those weight parameters can not be altered by a large amount. To make viable the embedding of a larger payload, in MaleficNet, we crafted a block-based embedding (Sect. 4), where we divide the neural network parameters into chunks, and in each chunk, we embed a portion of the malware payload.

6.3 Robustness

We evaluate the robustness of MaleficNet payload injection technique against model parameter altering processes such as fine-tuning. Fine-tuning is the process where part (or whole) model weight parameters are changed in order to either improve the model on the current task or re-purpose the model for a different (but similar) task. In Fig. 2 we report the signal-to-noise ratio (SNR) to measure the disruption that fine-tuning caused to the MaleficNet payload signal. SNR is the ratio of the signal power to the noise power, expressed in decibels. When SNR is higher than 1:1 (greater than 0dB), there is more signal than noise.

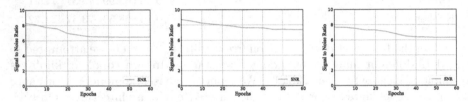

(a) ResNet50 architecture trained on FashionMNIST dataset [44] and repurposed on MNIST dataset [23].

(b) VGG11 architecture trained on CIFAR10 dataset and repurposed on CIFAR100 dataset [21].

(c) ResNet101 architecture trained on Imagenet dataset [12] and repurposed on Cats vs. Dogs dataset.

Fig. 2. The effect of fine-tuning to the SNR of the malware payloads embedded in different DNN architectures via MaleficNet. The malware payload injected in all cases was Stuxnet

Figure 2a shows the change in SNR when the ResNet50 model is first trained on FashionMNIST dataset [44], then Stuxnet is injected into the model via MaleficNet technique, and afterward is repurposed with the goal of solving the MNIST digit recognition task. The fine-tuning is performed in an amount of time (in epochs) equal to the time spent on training on the FashionMNIST. The SNR of the MaleficNet payload slightly drops, but the fine-tuning cannot significantly deteriorate the MaleficNet payload signal.

Figure 2b shows the change in SNR when the VGG11 [33] model is first trained on Cifar10 [21] dataset, then Stuxnet is injected into the model via MaleficNet technique, and afterward is re-purposed to solve the Cifar100 task. Similar to above, the SNR of the MaleficNet payload slightly drops, but the payload signal is still significantly strong in the model weights, which allows for correct extraction of the malware payload.

Table 4. Comparison of the effects of different levels of model parameter pruning on Stuxnet malware payload injected into ResNet50 using Liu et al. [25], Wang et al. [42], Wang et al. [43] and MaleficNet malware embedding techniques

Pruning Ratio	Does the payload survive?			
	Liu et al. [25]	Wang et al. [42]	Wang et al. [43]	MaleficNet
25.00%	✗	✗	✗	✓
50.00%	✗	✗	✗	✓
75.00%	✗	✗	✗	✓
90.00%	✗	✗	✗	✗
99.00%	✗	✗	✗	✗

Figure 2c shows the change in SNR when the ResNet50 [17] model is first trained on Imagenet [12] dataset, then Stuxnet is injected into the model via MaleficNet technique, and afterward is re-purposed to solve the Cats vs. Dogs task. Even in this case, the SNR of the MaleficNet payload slightly drops, but the payload signal is still significantly strong in the model weights which allows for correct extraction of the malware payload.

7   Possible Defenses

As a possible attempt to impede malware embedding techniques such as [25,42, 43] and MaleficNet we consider model parameter pruning. **Parameter pruning** is a technique commonly used for DNN backdoor removal [16,24] and it is typically performed by zeroing a portion of models' weight parameters. In Liu et al. [25], the embedding technique relies on mapping the individual bits of the malware payload in the individual weight parameters of the model. Zeroing even one of the parameters of the network where one of the malicious payload bits is mapped can corrupt the payload and thus mitigate the attack. Typically parameter pruning zeroes more than one model parameter, thus making it highly likely to nullify one of the model parameters where a malware bit is mapped. This is also valid for [42,43] where zeroing a single model parameter where the payload is mapped will corrupt the malware payload.

MaleficNet, on the other hand, is more robust to this possible defense technique. Using CDMA to inject the malware payload in the model, combined with using LDPC error-correcting codes, introduces a level of robustness toward parameter pruning. This is due to the fact that, even if a large portion of the model parameters are zeroed, given how CDMA works (Sect. 2.3), the non-zeroed weights will contribute into the payload signal being correctly decoded. We report the robustness of MaleficNet towards model parameter pruning and compare with prior art in Table 4 where we prune the ResNet50 [17] model trained on Imagenet [12] dataset with Stuxnet malware embedded into it. We see that the malicious payload is able to be recovered even when pruning 75% of the network parameters, feat that is impossible using prior payload embedding techniques [25,42,43].

A more sophisticated model parameter pruning technique whose aim is to reduce the overall size of the network is **model compression**, which, instead of zeroing a parameter, removes the whole neuron from the model, thus resulting in a different model architecture. Model compression can mitigate MaleficNet, as well as prior work [25,42,43]. Even though model compression can prove effective towards this family of threats, it requires extensive machine learning expertise and the presence of a dataset that follows the same distribution as the original training dataset. Due to the fact that most DNN consumers do not possess these technical skills and resources, only entities that possess them can safely apply them to mitigate this threat while maintaining a satisfactory performance of the DNN in the intended task.

8   Related Work

Liu et al. [25], to the best of our knowledge, are the first to create a new breed of stegomalware through embedding malware into a deep neural network model. They proposed four methods to embed a malware binary into the model and designed and evaluated triggering mechanisms based on the logits of the model. The first malware embedding method introduced by Liu et al. [25] is LSB substitution, where the malware bits are embedded into the model by replacing the least significant bits of the models' parameters. The second method consists of a more complex version of the LSB substitution. The idea behind it resides in substituting the bytes of a set of models' weight parameters with the bytes of the malware payload. After that, they perform model retraining by freezing the modified weight parameters (where the malware is placed) to restore model performance using only the remainder of the weight parameters. Alongside those two methods, Liu et al. [25] proposed mapping-based techniques to map (and sometimes substitute) the values or the sign of the network's weights to the bit of the malware. They call these methods value-mapping and sign-mapping, respectively. Liu et al. [25] demonstrated that, in the case of LSB substitution, resilience training, and value-mapping, even a single flip in one bit would corrupt the malware, thus rendering these payload embedding techniques unreliable and unusable in practice since even a simple fine-tuning could disrupt the malware extraction. Sign-mapping is the most robust of the four payload embedding techniques proposed in [25], but it suffers from several limitations. Sign-mapping maps the bits of the malware payload to the sign of the model's weights. This means that the number of bits it can map is more limited than other methods. Based on data reported by Liu et al. [25], the amount of bits that the sign-mapping technique can embed is of the same order of magnitude as the number of bits MaleficNet can embed. Compared to MaleficNet, sign-mapping of Liu et al. [25] requires significantly more information to perform the payload extraction, i.e., the permutation map of the weights. In contrast, MaleficNet extractor only needs to know the seed to generate CDMA spreading codes.

Wang et al. [42] proposed fast-substitution as a way to embed malware into a deep neural network. Fast-substitution works by substituting the bits of a selected group of weights in a model with the ones from the malware. In case the performance of the resulted model is highly impaired, the authors restore the performance of the model similar to the resilience training method presented by Liu et al. [25], i.e., freezing the group of weights selected to embed the payload and retrain the model. Fast-substitution suffers the same drawbacks as LSB substitution, resilience training, and value-mapping from Liu et al. [25], making it unusable in the supply-chain attack scenario, where the models are usually fine-tuned. Wang et al. further extended their work [43] proposing two additional techniques: most significant byte (MSB) reservation and half-substitution. Both the methods rely on the fact that the model performance is better maintained when the first bytes of each model weight are preserved. Even if they can guarantee less performance degradation, those methods suffer from the same weaknesses as fast-substitution, making them unsuitable in cases where fine-tuning is used.

9   Ethical Discussion

The ever-growing adoption of machine learning-based solutions in virtually every area presents a fertile ground that can be explored by adversaries for malicious activities. The purpose of this work is not to provide malware authors and malicious entities with a novel method on how to create a stegomalware and cause potential damage but to raise awareness about the existence and risks of such an attack vector. We aim to encourage ML-based solution consumers to obtain their services from reputable and trustworthy entities and to inspire researchers and vendors to develop robust solutions and mitigate the threats in advance.

10   Conclusions

In this paper, we introduced MaleficNet, a novel malware-hiding technique based on CDMA spread-spectrum channel-coding. Our extensive empirical evaluation showed that MaleficNet malware embedding technique incurs little to no penalty on the model performance and it can be applied to any model architecture and task without modifications. We demonstrated that MaleficNet malware embedding technique remains undetected by state-of-the-art anti-malware engines and statistical tools highlighting the emerging threat that this technique can pose to the supply chain for ML models. The work presented here presents a new threat amongst the ever-growing threats that can arise from the adoption of off-the-shelf ML-based solutions. With this work, we want to bring to the attention of persons/entities that aim at using these off-the-shelf ML-based solutions to be aware of the legitimacy of their provider. In future work, we intend to craft computationally-inexpensive techniques that are able to disrupt the hidden malicious payload without impacting the performance of the trained ML model.

Acknowledgements. This work of Dorjan Hitaj, Giulio Pagnotta, and Luigi V. Mancini was supported by Gen4olive, a project that has received funding from the

European Union's Horizon 2020 research and innovation programme under grant agreement No. 101000427.

A   Additional Experiments

Model parameter distribution comparisons with and without malware on different deep neural network architectures.
(Fig. 3).

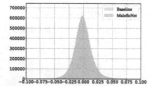 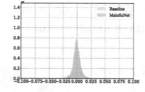 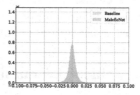

(a) Baseline Resnet50 and Resnet50 with Stuxnet. (b) Baseline VGG16 and VGG16 with Zeus-Dec. (c) Baseline VGG16 and VGG16 with Cerber.

Fig. 3. Comparison between the weight parameter distribution of different DNN before and after various sized malware were embedded in them using MaleficNet technique

Model Performance experiments on Cats vs. Dogs dataset. (Table 5)

Table 5. Baseline vs. MaleficNet model performance on Cats vs. Dogs dataset on different DNN architectures for different sized malware payloads

Malware	DenseNet		ResNet50		ResNet101		VGG11		VGG16	
	Bas	Mal	Bas	Mal	Bas	Mal	Bas	Mal	Bas	Mal
Stuxnet	98.28	98.05	97.29	97.24	98.15	98.05	98.83	98.78	99.18	98.82
Destover	98.28	97.68	97.29	97.13	98.15	97.91	98.83	98.72	99.18	98.79
Asprox	98.28	97.46	97.29	97.08	98.15	97.68	98.83	98.75	99.18	98.77
Bladabindi	98.28	67.36	97.29	96.74	98.15	97.12	98.83	98.73	99.18	98.76
Zeus-Bank	–	–	–	–	98.15	96.18	98.83	97.99	99.18	98.56
Eq.Drug	–	–	–	–	98.15	95.98	98.83	97.91	99.18	98.41
Zeus-Dec	–	–	–	–	98.15	95.15	98.83	97.79	99.18	98.25
Kovter	–	–	–	–	98.15	93.45	98.83	97.85	99.18	98.51
Cerber	–	–	–	–	98.15	63.84	98.83	98.22	99.18	98.94
Ardamax	–	–	–	–	–	–	98.83	98.07	99.18	98.42
NSIS	–	–	–	–	–	–	98.83	97.88	99.18	98.32
Kelihos	–	–	–	–	–	–	98.83	96.11	99.18	97.63

B   Implementation Details

In Algorithms 1 and 2 we show the implementation details of MaleficNet's inject and extract payload methods. The injection module depicted in Algorithm 1 takes as input a model W (divided in k-blocks of size s) and uses CDMA channel coding technique to inject a pre-selected malware binary into the model weights. To allow a quick verification that the malware payload is extracted correctly, MaleficNet's injection module, beside the malware payload includes also a 256-bit hash of the malware payload binary as part of the payload. As mentioned above, to not deteriorate the model performance on the legitimate task, we partition the network and the payload in chunks and embed one chunk of payload in one chunk of the network. CDMA takes a narrowband signal and spreads it in a wideband signal to allow for reliable transmission and decoding. To satisfy this property, the chunk of the network is selected to be multiple times larger than the size of a chunk of the payload. In our experiments, the narrowband signal (payload chunk) is spread into a wideband signal (model chunk) that is 6 times larger (i.e., the spreading code of each bit of the payload chunk will be 6 times the length of the chunk).

The extraction module (Algorithm 2) takes as input a model W (divided in k-blocks of size s). To extract the malware payload, the extractor needs to know the seed to generate the spreading codes and the LDPC matrices, the hash of the malware binary to verify whether the extraction is successful, the size of the narrowband signal (d) and the length of the malware payload. Using the first 200 extracted bits, the estimation of the channel noise is computed. After that, the LDPC decoder is used to recover the payload. The extraction module returns the malware payload and the hash.

Algorithm 1: Inject

Input: Model: W
Output: Model: W
Data: Int: γ, Int: $seed$, Int d, Bytes: $malware$

1 $hash \leftarrow sha256(malware)$
2 $message \leftarrow concatenate(malware, hash)$
3 $ldpc \leftarrow init\_ldpc(seed)$
4 $c \leftarrow ldpc.encode(message)$
5 $PNRG(seed)$
6 $preamble \leftarrow random([-1,1], size = 200)$
7 $b \leftarrow concatenate(preamble, c)$
8 $n \leftarrow b/d$
9 $i \leftarrow 0$
10 $j \leftarrow 0$
11 **while** $i < n$ **do**
12   **while** $j < d$ **do**
13         $code \leftarrow random([-1,1], size = len(W_i))$
14         $signal \leftarrow code * gamma * b[i]$
15         $W_i \leftarrow W_i + signal$
16         $j \leftarrow j + 1$
17     $i \leftarrow i + 1$

Algorithm 2: Extract

Input: Model: W
Output: Bytes: $malware$, Str $hash$
Data: Int: $malware\_length$, Int: $seed$, Int: d

1 $ldpc \leftarrow init\_ldpc(seed)$
2 $y \leftarrow []$
3 $PNRG(seed)$
4 $preamble \leftarrow random([-1, 1], size = 200)$
5 $n \leftarrow malware\_length/d$
6 $i \leftarrow 0$
7 $j \leftarrow 0$
8 **while** $i < n$ **do**
9 $\quad$ **while** $j < d$ **do**
10 $\quad\quad$ $code \leftarrow random([-1, 1], size = len(W_i))$
11 $\quad\quad$ $y_i \leftarrow transpose(code) * (W_i)$
12 $\quad\quad$ $y.append(y_i)$
13 $\quad\quad$ $j \leftarrow j + 1$
14 $\quad$ $i \leftarrow i + 1$
15 $gain \leftarrow mean(multiply(y[: 200], preamble))$
16 $sigma \leftarrow std(multiply(y[: 200], preamble)/gain)$
17 $snr \leftarrow -20 * log_{10}(sigma)$
18 $message \leftarrow ldpc.decode(y[200 :]/gain, snr)$
19 $malware \leftarrow message[0 : malware\_length]$
20 $hash \leftarrow message[malware\_length :]$

References

1. Ateniese, G., Mancini, L.V., Spognardi, A., Villani, A., Vitali, D., Felici, G.: Hacking smart machines with smarter ones: how to extract meaningful data from machine learning classifiers. Int. J. Secur. Networks **10**, 137–150 (2015)
2. Baylis, D.J.: Error Correcting Codes A Mathematical Introduction. Chapman and Hall/CRC, Boca Raton (1998)
3. Berti, J.: AI-based supply chains: using intelligent automation to build resiliency (2021). https://www.ibm.com/blogs/supply-chain/ai-based-supply-chains-using-intelligent-automation-to-build-resiliency/
4. Brown, T., et al.: Language models are few-shot learners. In: Advances in Neural Information Processing Systems. Curran Associates, Inc. (2020)
5. Cheddad, A., Condell, J., Curran, K., Mc Kevitt, P.: Digital image steganography: survey and analysis of current methods. Signal Process. **90**, 727–752 (2010)
6. Chollet, F.: Xception: deep learning with depthwise separable convolutions. In: 2017 IEEE Conference on Computer Vision and Pattern Recognition (2017)
7. Christian, S., Liu, W., Jia, Y.: Going deeper with convolutions. In: IEEE Conference on Computer Vision and Pattern Recognition (2015)
8. Cover, T.M., Thomas, J.A.: Elements of Information Theory. Wiley, Hoboken (2006)
9. Dahl, G.E., Yu, D., Deng, L., Acero, A.: Context-dependent pre-trained deep neural networks for large-vocabulary speech recognition. IEEE Trans. Audio Speech Lang. Process. **20**, 30–42 (2012)

10. De Gaspari, F., Hitaj, D., Pagnotta, G., De Carli, L., Mancini, L.V.: Evading behavioral classifiers: a comprehensive analysis on evading ransomware detection techniques. Neural Comput. Appl. 1–20 (2022). https://doi.org/10.1007/s00521-022-07096-6

11. De Gaspari, F., Hitaj, D., Pagnotta, G., De Carli, L., Mancini, L.V.: Reliable detection of compressed and encrypted data. Neural Comput. Appl. (2022)

12. Deng, J., Dong, W., Socher, R., Li, L.J., Li, K., Fei-Fei, L.: Imagenet: a large-scale hierarchical image database. In: 2009 IEEE Conference on Computer Vision and Pattern Recognition (2009)

13. Devlin, J., Chang, M., Lee, K., Toutanova, K.: BERT: pre-training of deep bidirectional transformers for language understanding. In: NAACL-HLT (2019)

14. Domhan, T., Hasler, E., Tran, K., Trenous, S., Byrne, B., Hieber, F.: The devil is in the details: on the pitfalls of vocabulary selection in neural machine translation. In: Proceedings of the 2022 Conference of the North American Chapter of the Association for Computational Linguistics: Human Language Technologies (2022)

15. Graves, A., Mohamed, A., Hinton, G.: Speech recognition with deep recurrent neural networks. In: 2013 IEEE International Conference on Acoustics, Speech and Signal Processing (2013)

16. Gu, T., Liu, K., Dolan-Gavitt, B., Garg, S.: BadNets: evaluating backdooring attacks on deep neural networks. IEEE Access **7**, 47230–47244 (2019)

17. He, K., Zhang, X., Ren, S., Sun, J.: Deep residual learning for image recognition. In: 2016 IEEE Conference on Computer Vision and Pattern Recognition (2016)

18. Hitaj, B., Gasti, P., Ateniese, G., Perez-Cruz, F.: PassGAN: a deep learning approach for password guessing. Appl. Cryptography Network Secur. (2019)

19. Huang, G., Liu, Z., Van Der Maaten, L., Weinberger, K.Q.: Densely connected convolutional networks. In: 2017 IEEE Conference on Computer Vision and Pattern Recognition (2017)

20. Koh, J.Y.: Model zoo. http://modelzoo.co/. Accessed November 2021

21. Krizhevsky, A., Hinton, G.: Learning multiple layers of features from tiny images. Technical report, University of Toronto, Toronto, Ontario (2009)

22. Krizhevsky, A., Sutskever, I., Hinton, G.E.: ImageNet classification with deep convolutional neural networks. In: Proceedings of the 25th International Conference on Neural Information Processing Systems (2012)

23. LeCun, Y., Cortes, C.: MNIST handwritten digit database. https://yann.lecun.com/exdb/mnist/ (2010)

24. Liu, K., Dolan-Gavitt, B., Garg, S.: Fine-pruning: defending against backdooring attacks on deep neural networks. In: Bailey, M., Holz, T., Stamatogiannakis, M., Ioannidis, S. (eds.) RAID 2018. LNCS, vol. 11050, pp. 273–294. Springer, Cham (2018). https://doi.org/10.1007/978-3-030-00470-5_13

25. Liu, T., Liu, Z., Liu, Q., Wen, W., Xu, W., Li, M.: StegoNet: turn deep neural network into a stegomalware. In: Annual Computer Security Applications Conference (2020)

26. Lozano, M.A., et al.: Open data science to fight COVID-19: winning the 500k XPRIZE pandemic response challenge. In: Dong, Y., Kourtellis, N., Hammer, B., Lozano, J.A. (eds.) ECML PKDD 2021. LNCS (LNAI), vol. 12978, pp. 384–399. Springer, Cham (2021). https://doi.org/10.1007/978-3-030-86514-6_24

27. Metadefender: Multiple security engines. https://www.metadefender.com/. Accessed Apr 2022

28. Mitchell, T.M.: Machine Learning. McGraw-Hill Inc, New York (1997)

29. Nativ, Y.: thezoo - a live malware repository. https://thezoo.morirt.com/. Accessed Nov 2021

30. Pagnotta, G., Hitaj, D., De Gaspari, F., Mancini, L.V.: Passflow: guessing passwords with generative flows. In: 2022 52nd Annual IEEE/IFIP International Conference on Dependable Systems and Networks (2022)
31. Richardson, T., Urbanke, R.: Modern Coding Theory. Cambridge University Press, Cambridge (2008)
32. Rupf, M., Massey, J.L.: Optimum sequence multisets for synchronous code-division multiple-access channels. IEEE Trans. Inf. Theory **40**, 1261–1266 (1994)
33. Simonyan, K., Zisserman, A.: Very deep convolutional networks for large-scale image recognition (2014)
34. Stevens, R., Suciu, O., Ruef, A., Hong, S., Hicks, M., Dumitraş, T.: Summoning demons: the pursuit of exploitable bugs in machine learning (2017)
35. Suarez-Tangil, G., Tapiador, J.E., Peris-Lopez, P.: Stegomalware: playing hide and seek with malicious components in smartphone apps. In: Lin, D., Yung, M., Zhou, J. (eds.) Inscrypt 2014. LNCS, vol. 8957, pp. 496–515. Springer, Cham (2015). https://doi.org/10.1007/978-3-319-16745-9_27
36. Torrieri, D.: Iterative channel estimation, demodulation, and decoding. In: Principles of Spread-Spectrum Communication Systems, pp. 549–594. Springer, Cham (2022). https://doi.org/10.1007/978-3-030-75343-6_9
37. Vaidya, S.: Openstego. https://github.com/syvaidya/openstego/. Accessed Apr 2022
38. Verdu, S.: Multiuser Detection. Cambridge University Press, Cambridge (1998)
39. Verdu, S.: Capacity region of gaussian CDMA channels: the symbol synchronous case. In: Proceedings of the 24th Allerton Conference (1986)
40. Verdu, S.: Recent results on the capacity of wideband channels in the low-power regime. IEEE Wirel. Commun. **9**, 40–45 (2002)
41. Viswanath, P., Anantharam, V.: Optimal sequences and sum capacity of synchronous CDMA systems. IEEE Trans. Inf. Theory **45**, 1984–1991 (1999)
42. Wang, Z., Liu, C., Cui, X.: Evilmodel: hiding malware inside of neural network models. In: 2021 IEEE Symposium on Computers and Communications (2021)
43. Wang, Z., Liu, C., Cui, X., Yin, J., Wang, X.: Evilmodel 2.0: bringing neural network models into malware attacks. Comput. Secur. **120**, 102807 (2022)
44. Xiao, H., Rasul, K., Vollgraf, R.: Fashion-mnist: a novel image dataset for benchmarking machine learning algorithms. ArXiv:abs/1708.07747 (2017)
45. Zeiler, M.D., Fergus, R.: Visualizing and understanding convolutional networks. In: Fleet, D., Pajdla, T., Schiele, B., Tuytelaars, T. (eds.) ECCV 2014. LNCS, vol. 8689, pp. 818–833. Springer, Cham (2014). https://doi.org/10.1007/978-3-319-10590-1_53
46. Zhang, W., Zhai, M., Huang, Z., Liu, C., Li, W., Cao, Y.: Towards end-to-end speech recognition with deep multipath convolutional neural networks. In: Intelligent Robotics and Applications (2019)

Long-Short History of Gradients Is All You Need: Detecting Malicious and Unreliable Clients in Federated Learning

Ashish Gupta[1]($\boxtimes$), Tie Luo[1]($\boxtimes$), Mao V. Ngo[2], and Sajal K. Das[1]

[1] Missouri University of Science and Technology, Rolla, USA
{ashish.gupta,tluo,sdas}@mst.edu
[2] Singapore University of Technology and Design, Singapore, Singapore
vanmao_ngo@sutd.edu.sg

Abstract. Federated learning offers a framework of training a machine learning model in a distributed fashion while preserving privacy of the participants. As the server cannot govern the clients' actions, nefarious clients may attack the global model by sending malicious local gradients. In the meantime, there could also be *unreliable* clients who are *benign* but each has a portion of low-quality training data (e.g., blur or low-resolution images), thus may appearing similar as malicious clients. Therefore, a defense mechanism will need to perform a *three-fold* differentiation which is much more challenging than the conventional (two-fold) case. This paper introduces MUD-HoG, a novel defense algorithm that addresses this challenge in federated learning using *long-short history of gradients*, and treats the detected malicious and unreliable clients differently. Not only this, but we can also distinguish between *targeted* and *untargeted attacks* among malicious clients, unlike most prior works which only consider one type of the attacks. Specifically, we take into account sign-flipping, additive-noise, label-flipping, and multi-label-flipping attacks, under a non-IID setting. We evaluate MUD-HoG with six state-of-the-art methods on two datasets. The results show that MUD-HoG outperforms all of them in terms of accuracy as well as precision and recall, in the presence of a mixture of multiple (four) types of attackers as well as unreliable clients. Moreover, unlike most prior works which can only tolerate a low population of harmful users, MUD-HoG can work with and successfully detect a wide range of malicious and unreliable clients - up to 47.5% and 10%, respectively, of the total population. Our code is open-sourced at https://github.com/LabSAINT/MUD-HoG_Federated_Learning.

1 Introduction

In recent years, the proliferation of smart devices with increased computational capabilities have laid a solid foundation for training machine learning (ML)

V. Atluri et al. (Eds.): ESORICS 2022, LNCS 13556, pp. 445–465, 2022.
https://doi.org/10.1007/978-3-031-17143-7_22

models over a large number of distributed devices. Traditional ML approaches require the training data to reside at a central location; the distributed ML case requires a well-controlled data-center-like environment. Such approaches demand high network bandwidth and provoke great privacy concerns. To this end, Google introduced the concept of Federated Learning (FL) [21] which allows distributed clients to collaboratively train a global ML model without letting their data leave the respective devices. At a high level, it works as follows. A central server initiates the training process by disseminating an initial global model to a set of clients. Each client updates the received model using its local data and sends back the updated model (not data). The server aggregates the received model updates (weights or gradients) into a global model and disseminates it again back to the clients. This procedure repeats until the global model converges. FL is advantageous in preserving data privacy and saving communication bandwidth, and has been applied to a wide range of applications in the Internet of Things (IoT) [12], natural language processing [10,14], image processing [17], etc.

However, the uncontrolled and distributed nature of the clients, as well as the server's inaccessibility to clients' data, make FL vulnerable to adversarial attacks launched by clients [1–3,20,30]. In general, a malicious client (adversary) can launch two types of attacks: (1) an *untargeted attack*, sometimes referred to as a Byzantine attack [5,15,30], where the adversary attempts to corrupt the *overall* performance of the global model (e.g., degrade a classifier's accuracy on all classes); (2) a *targeted attack*, where the adversary aims to degrade the model performance only for some specific cases (e.g., misclassify all dogs to cat) while not affecting the other cases [9,20]. Untargeted attacks could be tackled by robust aggregation techniques [4,7,33] when data are independent and identically distributed (IID) among the clients, whereas targeted attacks are much harder to defend because their specific targets are often unknown to the defender.

Another category of clients, which are largely overlooked in the FL security literature, are *unreliable clients*. These are benign clients but some of their data are of low quality and hence may appear as if their model updates were malicious too. For example, IoT devices such as sensors, smartphones, wearables, and surveillance cameras, are often subject to rigid hardware limitations and harsh ambient environments and thus may produce low-quality and noisy data [11]. A simplified solution could be one that treats clients who do not improve classification performance over a number of rounds as unreliable, and excludes them from aggregation in subsequent rounds, like in [18,19]. However, firstly this does not differentiate between benign and malign clients; secondly, excluding unreliable clients is not always desirable because such clients may possess valuable data such as infrequent classes on which other clients have no or few samples.

In this paper, we tackle the challenge of detecting and distinguishing between malicious and unreliable clients, as well as between targeted and untargeted attackers (among malicious clients), in FL. The main idea of our approach is to use *long-short history of gradients* jointly with judiciously chosen distance and similarity metrics during the iterative model updating process. Unlike prior works in [1,4,7,9,20] which only consider attackers, we identify unreliable clients and take advantage of their contributions. We further consider both targeted and untargeted attacks and more fine-grained attack types: (untargeted) additive-noise and sign-flipping attacks, and (targeted) single- and multi-label-flipping attacks. Moreover, unlike prior works in [4,7,33], we consider non-IID data settings which are more representative of real-world FL scenarios with heterogeneous clients.

The main contributions of this paper are summarized as follows:

- We propose a novel approach MUD-HoG that stands for **M**alicious and **U**nreliable Client **D**etection using **H**istory **o**f **G**radients. To the best of our knowledge, this is the first work that detects both malicious attackers and unreliable clients in FL, distinguishing between targeted and untargeted attackers. It allows the server to treat the clients in a more *fine-grained* manner, by exploiting unreliable clients' low-quality (but still useful) data.
- We introduce *short HoG* and *long HoG* and a sequential strategy that uses them in a carefully-designed way, allowing us to achieve the above goal. In addition, we achieve our goal in a non-IID setting which is more realistic and challenging, with the presence of mixed types of attackers.
- We conduct extensive experiments to evaluate MUD-HoG in terms of accuracy, precision, recall, and detection ratio, on two benchmark datasets in comparison with 6 prior FL security mechanisms. The results show that MUD-HoG withstands up to 47.5% clients being malicious with a negligible ($\sim$1%) compromise of accuracy, and comprehensively outperforms all the baselines on the considered metrics.

The rest of the paper is organized as follows. Section 2 reviews the related literature while Sect. 3 define the problem statement with the types of clients and considered attacks. Section 4 presents the proposed MUD-HoG approach with novel concepts of short HoG and long HoG, and Sect. 5 evaluates the robustness of the approach by conducting extensive experiments. Finally, Sect. 6 concludes the paper with future research directions.

2 Related Work

2.1 Distributed ML with Malicious Clients

Defending against malicious clients has been explored in distributed ML [4,34, 35]. It has been noted that the stochastic gradient descent (SGD) algorithm is vulnerable to untargeted (Byzantine) attacks where malicious clients send random/arbitrary gradients to the server to negatively affect the convergence or performance of the global model. Methods such as Krum and Multi-Krum [4], Medoid [33], and GeoMed [7] have been proposed to defend against Byzantine attacks by extending SGD with a robust aggregation function. In another work [26], the authors argued that the effect of malicious clients can be mitigated by gradient or norm clipping based on a threshold assuming that the attacks produce boosted gradients. However, these methods assume IID data, which often does not hold in FL settings. In addition, they aim to *tolerate* malicious clients rather than *distinguishing* them from normal ones, and thus may lead to cumulative negative impact over time and is also less preferable.

2.2   FL Under Untargeted Attacks

Various Byzantine-robust algorithms have been proposed for FL's non-IID settings in recent years. For example, a class of subgradient-based algorithms is proposed to defend malicious clients by robustifying the objective function with a regularization term [15]. However, these algorithms only consider simple attacks such as same-value and sign-flipping attacks. In another work [30], a variance reduction scheme inherited from [8] is combined with model aggregation to tackle untargeted attacks. In [6], the authors provided provable guarantees to ensure that the predicted label of a testing sample is not affected by the attack. They also proposed an ensemble method with a voting strategy to address the case of a bounded number of malicious clients. However, similar to some of the works discussed in the distributed ML case, this ensemble method cannot identify which clients are malicious. The above Byzantine-robust algorithms fail to stand against the attackers if they are present in high percentage. Moreover, all the above works are vulnerable to targeted attacks such as label flipping [27].

2.3   FL Under Targeted Attacks

As targeted attacks aim to reduce the model performance only on certain tasks while maintaining a good performance on others, they are elusive and harder to detect [20]. One of the popular defense methods, called FoolsGold [9], attempts to detect targeted attackers (e.g., label-flipping) based on the diversity of client contributions over the training rounds with an unknown number of attackers. With more realistic FL settings, Awan *et al.* [1] also exploited the clients' per-round contribution and cosine-similarity measure to defend against data poisoning attackers. In [16], an anomaly detection framework is proposed to differentiate anomalous gradients from normal ones in a low-dimensional embedding (spectral) using reconstruction errors. However, it requires a pre-trained model on a reference dataset at the server prior to start the training process, which is a strong requirement often not met in FL settings. Mao *et al.* [20] treated FL as a repeated game and introduced a robust aggregation model to defend against targeted and untargeted adversaries by designing a lookahead strategy based similarity measure. However, like many studies discussed earlier, it tolerates but does *not distinguish* adversaries from normal clients. Moreover, since most existing works [1,9,16,20] consider only two types of clients (normal and malicious), they may treat an unreliable client (who possesses lower-quality data) as malicious, which is not desirable.

In this work, we do not include *backdoor attacks* [1,24,29,32], which are a sub-category of data poisoning attack triggered by a particular pattern (e.g., pixel patch) embedded into data (e.g., images). However, unlike prior work, we include unreliable clients which are more likely to encounter in realistic FL deployments.

We also highlight that the term *unreliable* or *irrelevant* clients used in some studies [18,19,22] means clients whose contributions do not make any progress (i.e., improve model accuracy) over the past few rounds, which is considerably different from our definition of unreliable clients (see Sect. 3.2) which refers to clients who have low-quality data.

3 Model

We consider a typical FL framework with a central server and multiple clients participating in a collaborative model training process for a classification task using a deep learning model.

3.1 FL Preliminaries

Let N be the total number of clients participating in the FL model training process. Out of these N clients, m of them are malicious, and u of them are unreliable. Thus, there are $n = N - m - u$ normal clients. We consider a typical FL scenario for building a neural network model, where all clients share a common model structure under the same learning objective. The server initiates training by sending a global model w (e.g., random weights) to all clients. Each client updates the model w by training on its local dataset a certain number of epochs, and sends back the updated gradients. Note that sending gradients is equivalent to sending model parameters (weights). During training, each client learns the new weights w' by minimizing a loss function $\mathcal{L}(h_w(x), y)$ (e.g., cross-entropy loss function) over multiple epochs, where the function $h_w(\cdot)$ maps input data samples x to labels y. At a round τ, a client c_i computes the gradients as follows:

$$\nabla_{\tau,i} = w_\tau - \underset{w}{\operatorname{argmin}} \quad \mathcal{L}(h_{i,w}(x), y). \tag{1}$$

Let the client c_i hold a local dataset $\mathcal{D}_i$ which can be non-IID as compared to other clients. When all clients are normal, the server aggregates all the gradients received from the clients, by

$$\nabla_\tau = \sum_{i=1}^{N} \frac{|\mathcal{D}_i|}{|\mathcal{D}|} \nabla_{\tau,i}, \tag{2}$$

where $|\mathcal{D}| = \sum_{i=1}^{N} |\mathcal{D}_i|$. The weights of the global model for the next round $\tau + 1$ are then updated as $w_{\tau+1} = w_\tau - \eta \nabla_\tau$, where η is the learning rate.

3.2 Client Types

For generality, we consider a heterogeneous FL setting in which clients may be sensor boards, smartphones, surveillance cameras, laptops, connected vehicles, etc., owned by individuals or organizations. As a result, their data could be non-IID and thus each client could contribute to the global model training. We consider three types of clients and the last is further categorized in terms of attack types (see Sect. 3.3) the malicious client can launch.

1) *Normal clients* honestly participate in the model training process and have good-quality data.

2) *Unreliable clients* participate honestly in the FL but have some of its data are of low-quality. These data, however, could be exploited to improve diversity, especially if they capture distributions that normal clients fail to (or inadequately do). For example, A low-end camera does not produce high-resolution images but may capture some infrequent classes of images that other clients do not. Note that our definition of "unreliable client" is different from that in [18,19] and also from the "irrelevant client" in [22], where they mean a client who does not make progress (i.e., improve model accuracy) over the past few FL rounds, which therefore is a useless client.

3) *Malicious clients* are attackers who manipulate their local training data (i.e., *data poisoning*) or model weights/gradients (i.e., *model poisoning*) to generate adversarial impact on the global model being trained. For example, they may alter the labels of some of their data samples or perturb their local gradients before sending to the server.

With the presence of mixed types of clients having non-IID data, our problem is more realistic and challenging than prior work such as [1,7,9]. Figure 1 provides an overview of our problem setting, where MUD-HoG runs at the server.

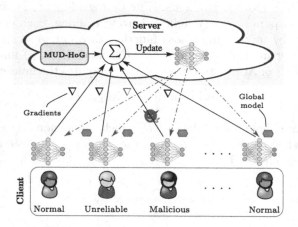

Fig. 1. Overview of FL with mixed types of clients. Malicious clients include targeted and untargeted attackers

Problem Statement. The problem in hand is two-fold: (1) How to identify and differentiate malicious clients (together with their attacks) from unreliable clients at the server while performing model aggregation? (2) How to mitigate the negative influence of malicious clients on the global model while still taking advantage of unreliable clients' updates? Let us reformulate Eq. (2) as:

$$\nabla_\tau = \sum_{i \in \mathcal{C}_{norm}} \frac{|\mathcal{D}_i|}{|\mathcal{D}|} \nabla_{\tau,i} + \alpha \sum_{i \in \mathcal{C}_{unrl}} \frac{|\mathcal{D}_i|}{|\mathcal{D}|} \nabla_{\tau,i}, \qquad (3)$$

where $\mathcal{C}_{norm}$ and $\mathcal{C}_{unrl}$ are the set of normal clients and that of unreliable clients, respectively, and the parameter $\alpha \in (0,1)$ down-weights the gradients of unreliable clients. Note that malicious clients are excluded.

3.3 Threat Model

A malicious client can launch either of the following attacks:
- **Untargeted attack.** The objective here is to downgrade the *overall* performance of the global model. The following two model poisoning attacks are considered: (i) *Sign-flipping.* The malicious client flips the sign of its local gradients (from positive to negative and vice versa) before sending them to server, while the magnitude of the gradients remains unchanged. (ii) *Additive-noise.* The malicious client adds Gaussian or random noise to its local gradients before sending to the server.
- **Targeted attack.** The objective is to decrease model performance on particular cases while not affecting other cases. The following two data poisoning attacks are considered: (i) *Label-flipping.* The attacker changes the label of all the instances of one particular class (source label), say y_1, to another class (target label), say y_2, while (intentionally) keeping other classes intact to avoid being detected. (ii) *Multi-label-flipping.* The attacker flips multiple source labels to a particular target label. This will result in the target label has an increased accuracy while harming the accuracy on other classes.

We make the following *Assumptions*: (i) Each attacker can only manipulate its own data or model but not other clients' or modify the server's aggregation algorithm. (ii) Number of malicious clients (including untargeted and targeted attackers) is less than other clients (including normal and unreliable). (iii) Malicious clients are persistent, meaning that they attack in every round.

4   MUD-HoG Design

MUD-HoG runs at the server to defend the global model. Unlike existing work such as [4], MUD-HoG assumes that the number of malicious clients is *unknown* to the server.

Challenges. The design challenges come from the following factors: the mixed types and unknown distribution of clients, non-IID data, and the server's inaccessibility to client data. The only information that the server has is the gradients (Eq. 1) sent by the clients each round, as a result of their local optimization such as stochastic gradient descent (SGD) over the loss function $\mathcal{L}(\cdot)$.

With targeted attacks, the malicious clients share a common objective and thus will have similar gradients [9] between each other. On the other hand, gradients from untargeted attackers would be dissimilar from each other since they perturb gradients randomly or flip gradient signs. This gradient space is rather complex and irregular, insofar as there is no single appropriate similarity measure that can distinguish malicious clients from the normal ones. Furthermore, unreliable clients introduce another degree of complication as they would behave very similar to *untargeted* attackers and hence are hard to distinguish.

Long-Short History of Gradients (HoG). We propose two new notions of HoG, based on which we design a robust algorithm MUD-HoG to address the above challenges. Let $\nabla_i = \{\nabla_{1,i}, \nabla_{2,i}, \cdots, \nabla_{\tau-1,i}\}$ denote the collection of HoGs received by the server from client c_i prior to the τth round.

Definition 1 (Short HoG). The short HoG of client c_i at round τ, defined as,

$$\nabla_i^{sHoG} = \frac{1}{l} \sum_{t=\tau-l}^{\tau-1} \nabla_{t,i} \tag{4}$$

is a moving average of c_i's gradients of the last l rounds, where l is the sliding window size. The short HoG smooths a client's gradients to remove single-round randomness.

Definition 2 (Long HoG). The long HoG of client c_i at round τ is defined as

$$\nabla_i^{lHoG} = \sum_{t=1}^{\tau-1} \nabla_{t,i}, \tag{5}$$

which is the sum of all the gradients in the set ∇_i. Thus, the long HoG captures the *accumulated* influence of a client on the global model, which reflects its goal.

Note that, at any round τ, the server does not need to store all the previous gradient vectors $\{\nabla_{1,i}, \nabla_{2,i}, \cdots, \nabla_{\tau-1,i}\}$ received from the client c_i; instead, it only needs to keep l latest vectors for computing short HoG and the *sum* of all the previous vectors for long HoG. Hence, at each round, the server would keep only $l + 1$ gradient vectors for each client. Therefore, the required memory is independent of the number of training rounds τ, and one should not have memory concerns when τ increases.

4.1   Sequential Strategy

By introducing short HoG and long HoG, MUD-HoG exploits two different gradient space and follows a sequential strategy to detect the type of each client in the following order: untargeted, targeted, unreliable, and normal, as depicted in Fig. 2. The key ideas are discussed in the following steps.

1) Untargeted attack. We can deduce the untargeted intention from the client's short HoG. Since an untargeted attacker aims to corrupt the whole

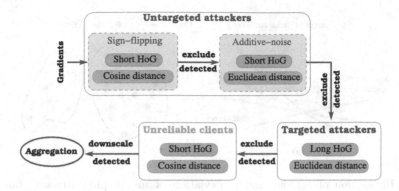

Fig. 2. Overview of MUD-HoG with the gradient space (short or long HoG) and similarity measures (Euclidean or cosine) used for detecting different types of clients

model, for example using sign flipping or additive noise, its short HoG would differ substantially from normal clients. First, in the case of sign-flipping attack, a malicious client essentially changes its gradient to the opposite direction, which would result in a large angular deviation from the *median* gradient of all the clients, as depicted in Fig. 3a. This also justifies that using *cosine distance* in the space of short HoG would be an appropriate choice. Note that short HoG is more robust than a single-round gradients by reducing false alarms.

On the other hand, additive-noise attackers and unreliable clients (with low-quality data) would have similar short HoGs, but considered collectively, would be apart from other clients. Therefore, after excluding the sign-flipping attackers, we use a clustering method based on short HoG to distinguish the above two types of clients from other clients. Empirically, we choose DBSCAN [25] as the clustering method because it conforms to our intuition and yields the best results. Between these two types, additive-noise attackers tend to be *farther* away from other clients than unreliable clients as the attackers add deliberate perturbations; nevertheless, a separation boundary could be learned by finding the largest gap over Euclidean distances. We also note that this is not a clear-cut line and further processing is needed which we discuss below in Step 3. The above intuition is depicted in Fig. 3b.

2) Targeted attack. Targeted attackers intend to manipulate the global model toward a specific convergence point (e.g., misclassifying all dogs to cats). Such intention can be captured by our long HoG which *reinforces* their adversarial goal over the entire history and is also robust to short-term noises and *camouflage cases* in which some attackers may strategically behave benignly in some of the rounds in order to evade detection. In MUD-HoG, we use K-means clustering with $K=2$ over long HoG to separate out targeted attackers, *after* excluding untargeted attackers detected in Step 1.

3) Unreliable clients. Finally, MUD-HoG identifies and separates unreliable clients from normal ones. After excluding all the detected malicious clients (tar-

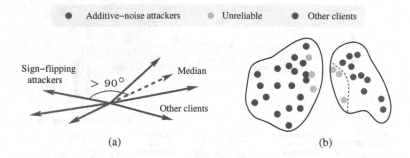

Fig. 3. Illustration of (a) the angular deviation of sign-flipping attackers from the median client (green), and (b) clustering of additive-noise attackers, unreliable clients, and other clients after excluding sign-flipping attackers (Color figure online)

geted and untargeted), the unreliable clients become farther from the *median* client in terms of their *short HoG*. Rather than using clustering, in this case we find that the *cosine distance* is the most effective to detect them and hence adopt it in MUD-HOG.

4.2 Detection of Malicious Clients

Based on the basic ideas discussed above, now we present all the technical details of how MUD-HoG detects different types of clients. The server starts detection from round τ_0 ($\tau_0 = l = 3$ in our experiments).

Detecting Untargeted Attackers Using Short HoG. MUD-HoG first computes the *median* short HoG over all clients, as $\nabla_{med}^{sHoG} = median\{\nabla_i^{sHoG} \mid 1 \leq i \leq N\}$. Then, it flags a client c_i as a sign-flipping attacker if

$$d_{cos}\left(\nabla_{med}^{sHoG}, \nabla_i^{sHoG}\right) < 0, \tag{6}$$

where the function $d_{cos}(\cdot)$ computes the cosine distance. We note that an existing algorithm CONTRA [1] also employs cosine distance to separate out *targeted attackers*. CONTRA computes the pair-wise distances between the gradients of all the clients, which therefore leads to a complexity of $O(N^2)$; in contrast, MUD-HoG uses median and thus the complexity is linear, $O(N)$, which is worth noting because FL often deals with a massive number of clients (e.g., IoT devices). Moreover, CONTRA does not handle unreliable clients.

Next, MUD-HoG proceeds to detecting additive-noise attackers after excluding the above detected sign-flipping attackers. We apply DBSCAN clustering on the short HoGs of all the remaining clients and obtain two groups – (i) a smaller group (g_l) consisting of the additive-noise attackers and unreliable clients and (ii) a larger group (g_h) consisting of the rest of the clients. Based on our above analysis that the additive-noise attackers are relatively farther from normal clients than unreliable clients (Fig. 3b), MUD-HoG attempts to learn a separation boundary as follows. Recalculate ∇_{med}^{sHoG} as the median short HoG of group g_h, and construct $\mathbf{d} = \{d_{Euc}(\nabla_{med}^{sHoG}, \nabla_i^{sHoG})\}$ which is a set of Euclidean distances (denoted by $d_{Euc}(\cdot)$) between ∇_{med}^{sHoG} and each client $c_i \in g_l$. The reason we use Euclidean distance rather than cosine distance is that the former produces a larger separation over *unnormalized* short HoG (which we intend). Then, we find the largest gap between any two consecutive values in the *sorted* list of the set $\mathbf{d}$, and use the mid-point of this gap as the separation boundary d_ϕ. Thus, a client $c_i \in g_l$ is an additive-noise attacker if

$$d_{Euc}\left(\nabla_{med}^{sHoG}, \nabla_i^{sHoG}\right) > d_\phi \qquad (7)$$

for $1 \leq i \leq |g_l|$. The remaining clients in g_l and the set g_h will be handled in the next step. The above detection of untargeted attackers is summarized as the pseudo-code of Lines $6-16$ in Algorithm 1.

Detecting Targeted Attackers Using Long HoG. After excluding the detected untargeted attackers as above, we compute the long HoG for each of the remaining clients, denoted by ∇_i^{lHoG}. Then, we apply K-means clustering with $K = 2$ on all the computed long HoGs to obtain two groups of clients: the smaller group will consist of the targeted attackers and the other (bigger) group of the normal clients, based on our assumption that normal clients constitute more than half of the entire population. In Algorithm 1, Lines 17-18 corresponds to the detection of targeted attackers.

4.3 Detection of Unreliable Clients

We are now left with a mixture of unreliable and normal clients. To distinguish them, MUD-HoG finds a new separation boundary d_ϕ as follows. Let N' be the number of remaining clients and ∇_{med}^{sHoG} be the (updated) median short HoG of them. Let $\mathbf{d}' = \{d_{cos}(\nabla_{med}^{sHoG}, \nabla_i^{sHoG})\}$ be a set of *cosine* distances between ∇_{med}^{sHoG} and each client c_j for $1 \leq i \leq N'$. The separation boundary d_ϕ is then determined from $\mathbf{d}'$ similarly as the above detection of additive-noise attackers (but here we use cosine distance). Then, a client c_i is deemed unreliable if it satisfies the condition

$$d_{cos}\left(\nabla_{med}^{sHoG}, \nabla_i^{sHoG}\right) < d_\phi. \qquad (8)$$

Note that the cosine distance is smaller when the angle between two vectors is larger, and that is why the condition '<' used in (8) is opposite to that in (7). The unreliable clients are detected at Lines 19-24 in Algorithm 1 after exclusion of all types of attackers.

Thus finally (in each FL round), MUD-HoG obtains the set of normal clients $\mathcal{C}_{norm}$ and the set of unreliable clients $\mathcal{C}_{unrl}$, after filtering out $\mathcal{C}_{tar}$ and $\mathcal{C}_{untar}$. It then aggregates the gradients of normal and unreliable clients using (3) (or see Line 26 in Algorithm 1), where unreliable clients are downscaled, and then updates the global model as $\boldsymbol{w}_{\tau+1} = \boldsymbol{w}_\tau - \eta \boldsymbol{\nabla}_\tau$. Clearly, since the gradients of malicious clients have been discarded, their negative impact is eradicated from the global model.

Algorithm 1: MUD-HoG

Input: Gradients from round 1 to τ, for each client c_i, denoted by
$\nabla_i = \{\nabla_{1,i}, \nabla_{2,i}, \cdots, \nabla_{\tau-1,i}\}$, $i = 1...N$. (Note that the server only
keeps the latest l gradient vectors and the *sum* of all $\tau - 1$ gradients.)

Output: Normal clients ($\mathcal{C}_{norm}$), targeted attackers ($\mathcal{C}_{tar}$), untargeted attackers
($\mathcal{C}_{untar}$), and unreliable clients ($\mathcal{C}_{unrl}$)

1 Initialize $\mathcal{C}_{norm}, \mathcal{C}_{tar}, \mathcal{C}_{untar} = \emptyset, \mathcal{C}_{all} = \{c_i\}, 1 \leq i \leq N$

2 **for** *round* $\tau = 1$ *to* τ_0 **do**

3   Aggregate gradients of all clients

4 **for** *round* $\tau = \tau_0 + 1$ *to* T **do**

5   Compute short HoG ∇_i^{sHoG} and long HoG ∇_i^{lHoG} for each client c_i

    /* Detecting untargeted attackers   */

6   Computer median short HoG ∇_{med}^{sHoG} over all N clients

7   **for** $i = 1$ *to* N **do**

8   **if** (6) *holds* **then**

9           $\mathcal{C}_{untar} = \mathcal{C}_{untar} \cup \{c_i\}$;   // Sign-flipping attackers

10   Apply DBSCAN clustering on short HoGs of $\mathcal{C}_{all} \setminus \mathcal{C}_{untar}$ to obtain two
groups g_l and g_h

11   Compute ∇_{med}^{sHoG} of the larger group g_h

12   Compute d_{Euc} between ∇_{med}^{sHoG} and each ∇_i^{sHoG} of the smaller group g_l

13   Find the separation boundary d_ϕ per Section 4.2

14   **for** $i = 1$ *to* N *and* $c_i \notin \mathcal{C}_{untar}$ **do**

15   **if** (7) *holds* **then**

16           $\mathcal{C}_{untar} = \mathcal{C}_{untar} \cup \{c_i\}$;   // Additive-noise attackers

    /* Detecting targeted attackers   */

17   Apply K-means clustering with $K = 2$ on long HoGs of $\mathcal{C}_{all} \setminus \mathcal{C}_{untar}$

18     $\mathcal{C}_{tar}$ = clients who belong to the smaller cluster

    /* Detecting unreliable clients   */

19   Recompute ∇_{med}^{sHoG} over $\mathcal{C}_{all} \setminus \{\mathcal{C}_{tar} \cup \mathcal{C}_{untar}\}$

20   Compute d_{cos} between ∇_{med}^{sHoG} and each ∇_i^{sHoG} of $\mathcal{C}_{all} \setminus \{\mathcal{C}_{tar} \cup \mathcal{C}_{untar}\}$

21   Recompute the separation boundary d_ϕ per Section 4.3

22   **for** $i = 1$ *to* N *and* $c_i \notin \{\mathcal{C}_{tar} \cup \mathcal{C}_{untar}\}$ **do**

23   **if** (8) *holds* **then**

24           $\mathcal{C}_{unrl} = \mathcal{C}_{unrl} \cup \{c_i\}$

25     $\mathcal{C}_{norm} = \mathcal{C}_{all} \setminus \{\mathcal{C}_{tar} \cup \mathcal{C}_{untar} \cup \mathcal{C}_{unrl}\}$

    /* Aggregate gradients over $\mathcal{C}_{norm}$ and $\mathcal{C}_{unrl}$ */

26     $\nabla_\tau = \sum_{i \in \mathcal{C}_{norm}} \frac{|\mathcal{D}_i|}{|\mathcal{D}|} \nabla_{\tau,i} + \alpha \sum_{i \in \mathcal{C}_{unrl}} \frac{|\mathcal{D}_i|}{|\mathcal{D}|} \nabla_{\tau,i}$

27   Update global model as $w_{\tau+1} = w_\tau - \eta \nabla_\tau$

28   Send $w_{\tau+1}$ back to all clients

29 **return** $\mathcal{C}_{norm}, \mathcal{C}_{tar}, \mathcal{C}_{untar}, \mathcal{C}_{unrl}$

5 Performance Evaluation

In this section, we evaluate MUD-HoG in comparison with six state-of-the-art methods on two real datasets with various type of attacks.

5.1 Experiment Setup

We consider a classification task on two datasets: (i) MNIST [13]: Our FL task is to train a deep model with 2 convolutional neural networks (CNN) followed by 3 fully connected layers[1] to classify 10 digits. (ii) Fashion-MNIST [31]: We build a deep model with 6 CNN layers followed by two fully connected layers to classify 10 fashion classes.

Hyper-parameters. We train the FL model with SGD optimizer (learning rate = 1e-2, momentum = 0.5 for MNIST and 0.9 for Fashion-MNIST, and weight-decay = 1e-4 for Fashion-MNIST) over 40 communication rounds, 4 local epochs; other setup details are similar to [28]. We use the window size of $l = 3$ for calculating the moving average short HoG. Our algorithm triggers only after $\tau_0 = 3$ rounds to accumulate enough HoGs. Since, the server stores only $l + 1$ gradient vectors (l latest and a *sum* of all previous vectors) to compute HoGs, it never runs into storage related issues. Moreover, we make a firm decision about malicious clients if they are detected in two consecutive rounds. Therefore, our algorithm can only detect malicious clients at least after 4 rounds.

To simulate non-IID data, we divide the datasets into 40 clients as disjoint portions that follows *Dirichlet distribution* with hyperparameter 0.9, as also adopted by [2,28]. Besides normal clients, our FL system consists of unreliable clients (up to 10% of total clients), and malicious clients (up to 47.5% of total clients), as detailed below.

Untargeted Attacks. (i) *Sign-flipping (SF)* – We flip the sign of gradients of the malicious clients without enlarging the magnitudes in our FL setup, which makes the detection more challenging. (ii) *Additive-noise (AN)* – We add a Gaussian noise with $\mu = 0$ and $\sigma = 0.01$ to the gradients of attackers.

Targeted Attacks. (i) *Label-flipping (LF)* – Before training the local model, attacker flips label of digit "1" to "7" in its local MNIST dataset, and label ("1-Trouser") to ("7-Sneaker") in Fashion-MNIST dataset. (ii) *Multi-label-flipping (MLF)* – Attacker flips the labels of few source classes to a targeted class in its local dataset. For MNIST and Fashion-MNIST (in brackets) datasets, we flip three source labels of digits "1" ("1-Trouser"), "2" ("2-Pullover"), and "3" ("3-Dress") to a target label "7" ("7-Sneaker").

Unreliable Clients. We simulate them to mimic a real-life scenario of low-end smartphone with poor-resolution camera and computing power. We use *Gaussian smoothing* (kernel size= 7, $\sigma = 50$) to blur 50% of the local image dataset; and simulate low computing power by training over randomly selected portion of 30% of local dataset. We set $\alpha = 0.5$ to downscale the unreliable clients.

---

[1] Adopt the model from PyTorch tutorial.

To simulate heterogeneous FL scenarios, we consider two different series of experiments with upto 47.5% malicious clients (including untargeted and targeted attack) and upto 10% unreliable clients. We configure 12 different experimental setups with increasing numbers of unreliable and malicious clients as follows.

- *Series of Exp1* consists of $a = \min\{i, 4\}$ unreliable clients, $b = \min\{i, 6\}$ additive-noise attackers, $c = \min\{i, 5\}$ sign-flipping attackers, $d = (i + 2)$ label-flipping attackers, and $(40 - a - b - c - d)$ normal clients; where $i = \{1, 2, 3, 4, 5, 6\}$.
- *Series of Exp2* consists of $a = \min\{i, 4\}$ unreliable clients, $b = \min\{i, 6\}$ additive-noise attackers, $c = \min\{i, 5\}$ sign-flipping attackers, $d = (i + 2)$ multi-label-flipping attackers, and $(40 - a - b - c - d)$ normal clients; where $i = \{1, 2, 3, 4, 5, 6\}$.

Evaluation Metrics. The performance of MUD-HoG is measured in terms of precision, recall, accuracy, and detection ratio. We define *detection ratio* (r) as

$$r = \frac{\sum_{\tau=1}^{T} \sum_{i \in \mathcal{C}_x} \mathbb{1}(c_i \text{ detected at } \tau)}{T \sum_x |\mathcal{C}_x|} \tag{9}$$

where $\mathcal{C}_x$ is either $\mathcal{C}_{tar}$, $\mathcal{C}_{untar}$ or $\mathcal{C}_{unrl}$, and not all of them are empty. The higher the detection ratio (closer to 100%), the better algorithm is.

Benchmark Algorithms. In addition to FedAvg [21], a popular algorithm in FL, we compare our proposed MUD-HoG algorithm with five other algorithms. They are: (i) coordinate-wise Median (or Median for short) [35], (ii) GeoMed [7], (iii) Krum [4], (iv) Multi-krum (or MKrum for short) [4], and (v) FoolsGold [9]. We borrowed the source code of these existing algorithms from [28].

5.2 Experimental Results

Overall Performance. Figure 4 shows the accuracy of 12 setups for series of Exp1 and Exp2 for MNIST and Fashion-MNIST datasets under the above seven benchmark algorithms. We observe that over all 12 setups with multiple types of attacks, MUD-HoG always achieves the best accuracy.

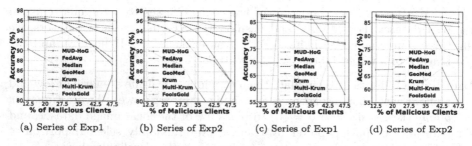

(a) Series of Exp1   (b) Series of Exp2   (c) Series of Exp1   (d) Series of Exp2

Fig. 4. Accuracy vs. the percentage of malicious clients. (a) and (b) are results on the *MNIST* dataset. (c) and (d) are results on the *Fashion-MNIST* dataset

It is consistently observed that when increasing percentage of malicious clients from 12.5% to 47.5% of the total number of clients, Krum and Fools-Gold show fluctuated performance and poor performance at a certain level of attacks, some other algorithms such as FedAvg, GeoMed, Median, and MKrum continuously drop their accuracy. In contrast, our proposed MUD-HoG maintains robust performance against multiple levels of heterogeneous attacks.

For **MNIST** dataset shown in parts (a) and (b) of Fig. 4, initially GeoMed performs as good as MUD-HoG, but when the level of attacks are increased more than 35%, GeoMed drops its accuracy by 9.33% and 12.39% while MUD-HoG only drops 0.5% and 0.56% in series of Exp1 and Exp2, respectively. When compared to the second-best algorithm, i.e. MKrum, the proposed algorithm gained upto 1.28% and 1.12% higher accuracy in series of Exp1 and Exp2, respectively.

For **Fashion-MNIST** dataset shown in parts (c) and (d) of Fig. 4, GeoMed achieves comparative results as MUD-HoG at a low level of attacks for both series; however, GeoMed drops performance significantly at the high level of attacks. For instance, in series of Exp1 and Exp2, while MUD-HoG's accuracy only drops by 0.72% and 1.5% (when increasing percentage of attacks from 12.5% to 47.5%), GeoMed's accuracy drops by 10.52% and 13.21%, respectively. When compared to the second-best algorithm, i.e., Median, MUD-HoG gains upto 0.65% and 1.47% accuracy in series of Exp1 and Exp2, respectively.

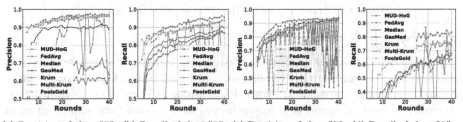

(a) Precision of class "7"   (b) Recall of class "2"   (c) Precision of class "7"   (d) Recall of class "2"

Fig. 5. Results for *Series of Exp2* with 42.5% malicious clients. "2" and "7" are the source and target classes, respectively. (a) and (b) are results on the *MNIST* dataset. (c) and (d) are results on the *Fashion-MNIST* dataset

Precision and Recall. To make a fair comparison with other algorithms (i.e., Krum, MKrum, FoolsGold) that ware designed specifically for targeted attacks, we plot *precision* of the targeted class (i.e., number of samples correctly classified as the targeted class over all samples predicted as the targeted class), and *recall* of a source class (i.e., number of samples correctly classified as the source class over all ground-truth samples of the source class) for MNIST and Fashion-MNIST datasets in Fig. 5. Here, FedAvg, GeoMed, Median or even Krum obtain poor performance and highly fluctuated precision of targeted class and recall of source class because they could not defend targeted attacks. On the flip side, though MKrum and FoolsGold show quite good precision, their values are lower than MUD-HoG for both the datasets.

Detection Ratio. We keep track of detected rounds for each type of clients during the course of FL training with MUD-HoG algorithm. Table 1 reports detection ratio (defined in Eq. 9) for each type of clients, and their first round of detection (presented inside brackets) for a setup in series of Exp1 and Exp2 with 27.5% malicious clients. We observe that the sign-flipping and additive-noise attackers are detected immediately at round 4, which is the earliest round when the MUD-HoG algorithm could provide a firm decision.

Table 1. Detection ratio r (%) and the earliest round (1^{st}rnd) that detects the client type (round number in brackets), with 27.5% malicious clients. [**SF**: Sign-flipping, **AN**: Additive-noise, **LF**: Label-flipping, **MLF**: Multi-label-flipping, **UR**: Unreliable]

Type	Detection	MNIST		Fashion-MNIST	
		Exp1	Exp2	Exp1	Exp2
SF	r (1^{st}rnd)	90.0 (4)	90.0 (4)	90.0 (4)	90.0 (4)
AN	r (1^{st}rnd)	90.0 (4)	90.0 (4)	90.0 (4)	90.0 (4)
LF	r (1^{st}rnd)	87.5 (5)	–	85.0 (6)	–
MLF	r (1^{st}rnd)	–	90.0 (4)	–	85.0 (6)
Overall rate r (%)		88.9	90.0	87.7	87.7
UR	r (1^{st}rnd)	87.5 (5)	87.5 (5)	85.0 (6)	85.0 (6)

For MNIST dataset, overall, we can detect all malicious clients at detection ratio (calculated over all types of clients) 88.9% and 90.0% for a setup in series of Exp1 and Exp2, respectively. Since FL training is done over 40 rounds and the earliest detection round is 4, upper bound of detection ratio can be at most 90.0%. And we can see in Exp2 of MNIST, MUD-HoG can detect MLF at round 4, which is as early as SF or AN, resulting in 90.0% of detection ratio. Next, for Fashion-MNIST dataset, our algorithm detects targeted attacks (i.e., LF and MLF) a bit slower than the case in MNIST, but the overall detection ratio is still above 87%. Finally, for unreliable clients (last two rows in Table 1), in all experiments, MUD-HoG achieves firm results of all unreliable clients from round 5 and round 6 for MNIST and Fashion-MNIST datasets, respectively. As a result, the detection ratio for unreliable clients is above 85.0%.

5.3 Discussions and Limitations

Convergence Analysis. Based on our experimental results (see Fig. 6 and Fig. 7), the loss of the global model stabilizes in 40 FL rounds for both the datasets even in the presence of 42.5% clients posing different types of attacks and having non-IID data. This indicates that MUD-HoG can achieve convergence in rather adversarial scenarios. Although the presence of malicious clients initially diverges the global model from its objective, excluding them from aggregation, as MUD-HoG did, rectifies the SGD process back to normal as defined in [23]. In future work, we plan to incorporate a rigorous theoretical analysis of convergence for our approach.

More Strategic Attacks. While we have experimentally shown that MUD-HoG is robust to various untargeted and targeted attacks in the presence of a large number of malicious clients, it may still miss out attackers who perform stealthy or highly strategic targeted attacks (some are formally defined in [7]). Besides, an attacker may implant a certain trigger pattern into some training/test data to inject corruption [3,29], known as *backdoors*. Such attacks are more evasive since they are only triggered when the particular pattern arises, while the overall performance is almost not affected. Currently, MUD-HoG has not been specifically designed to defend backdoor attacks but this would be an interesting direction to explore.

6   Conclusion

While federated learning (FL) offers a privacy-preserving framework for collaborative training of ML models, it is susceptible to adversarial attacks. This paper has proposed a new approach called MUD-HoG to detect malicious clients who launch untargeted or targeted attacks and unreliable clients who possess low-quality data, and offers a fine-grained classification of four types of participants. We introduce the concept of long-short HoG and select appropriate distance and similarity measures to identify different types of attacks and clients. MUD-HoG excludes malicious contributions but exploits unreliable clients' contributions to maximize the utility of the final global model. Experimental results confirm that MUD-HoG is robust against malicious and unreliable clients and produces a global model with higher accuracy than state-of-the-art baselines. It can detect a mixture of multiple types of attackers and unreliable clients in non-IID settings even when the ratio of attackers is close to half. In future work, we plan to investigate more challenging and dynamic settings where attackers may vary attack types and clients may even switch roles (attackers, unreliable, normal, etc.) over time. More extensive experiments will also be conducted.

Acknowledgements. This work is partially supported by the NSF grant award #2008878 (FLINT: Robust Federated Learning for Internet of Things) and the NSF award #2030624 (TAURUS: Towards a Unified Robust and Secure Data Driven Approach for Attack Detection in Smart Living).

A   Additional Experimental Results

A.1   Performance Improvement over Rounds

We consider a specific setup with 42.5% malicious clients, for both the datasets to evaluate the improvement of the accuracy of all the algorithms over FL rounds.

We plot test accuracy and loss from round 5 to the final round 40 for MNIST dataset in Fig. 6 using global model. It is obvious to see that MUD-HoG obtains an upper bound of test accuracy and an lower bound of test loss over the course of FL training. While some algorithms show fluctuated performance during training such as Krum with a high fluctuation, or FedAvg and GeoMed with smaller fluctuations, the other state-of-the-art algorithms designed against attackers such as Median, MKrum, FoolsGold and MUD-HoG show smooth improvement as training progresses. Among these algorithms, we also observe in Fig. 6 that the gap of test loss between MUD-HoG and the second-best algorithm is increasing over the course of FL training.

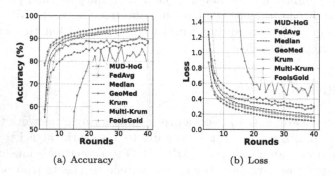

(a) Accuracy   (b) Loss

Fig. 6. Performance improvement of global model on *MNIST* in *Series of Exp2* with 42.5% malicious clients

Figure 7 shows test accuracy and loss for Fashion-MNIST dataset. Similar to MNIST's results, we can see that among all evaluated algorithms, MUD-HoG obtains the highest accuracy and the lowest loss for all training rounds. The fluctuation of FedAvg and GeoMed is more severe with high variance, so the final accuracy of these algorithms are not really reliable. This is the reason why FedAvg and GeoMed can obtain accuracy close to MUD-HoG (see Fig. 4) in the setups of 12.5% and 20% of malicious clients.

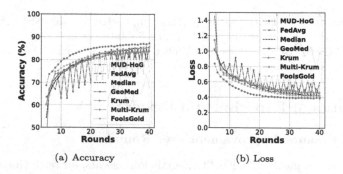

(a) Accuracy   (b) Loss

Fig. 7. Performance improvement of global model on *Fashion-MNIST* in *Series of Exp2* with 42.5% malicious clients

A.2   Confusion Matrix

In Fig. 8, we show confusion matrices for MUD-HoG and FedAvg obtained from the completely trained model for MNIST and Fashion-MNIST datasets using a setup of series Exp2 with 42.5% malicious clients. As multi-label-flipping attackers flip their local samples with source labels of "1", 2", and "3" to the target label "7", we can clearly see in parts (b) and (d) of Fig. 8, FedAvg confuses with several samples actually having the source labels as the target label while it is not the case for MUD-HoG. In addition, we see an interesting observation in part (d) of Fig. 8, where FedAvg completely fails as it predicts nearly all samples of source label "1" as the target label "7" (i.e., 940 samples of label "1" are predicted as label "7").

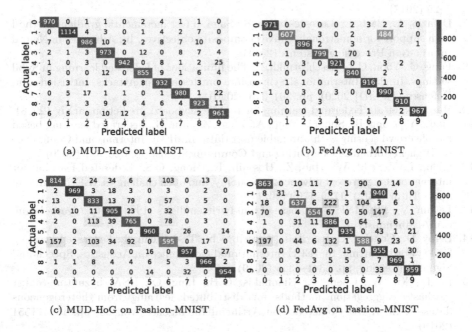

(a) MUD-HoG on MNIST (b) FedAvg on MNIST

(c) MUD-HoG on Fashion-MNIST (d) FedAvg on Fashion-MNIST

Fig. 8. Confusion matrices in *Series of Exp2* with 42.5% malicious clients

References

1. Awan, S., Luo, B., Li, F.: CONTRA: defending against poisoning attacks in federated learning. In: Bertino, E., Shulman, H., Waidner, M. (eds.) ESORICS 2021. LNCS, vol. 12972, pp. 455–475. Springer, Cham (2021). https://doi.org/10.1007/978-3-030-88418-5_22
2. Bagdasaryan, E., Veit, A., Hua, Y., Estrin, D., Shmatikov, V.: How to backdoor federated learning. In: International Conference on Artificial Intelligence and Statistics, pp. 2938–2948. PMLR (2020)

3. Bhagoji, A.N., Chakraborty, S., Mittal, P., Calo, S.: Analyzing federated learning through an adversarial lens. In: International Conference on Machine Learning, pp. 634–643. PMLR (2019)
4. Blanchard, P., El Mhamdi, E.M., Guerraoui, R., Stainer, J.: Machine learning with adversaries: byzantine tolerant gradient descent. In: 31st International Conference on Neural Information Processing Systems. pp. 118–128 (2017)
5. Cao, X., Fang, M., Liu, J., Gong, N.Z.: Fltrust: byzantine-robust federated learning via trust bootstrapping. In: ISOC Network and Distributed System Security Symposium (NDSS) (2021)
6. Cao, X., Jia, J., Gong, N.Z.: Provably secure federated learning against malicious clients. In: AAAI Conference on Artificial Intelligence, vol. 35, pp. 6885–6893 (2021)
7. Chen, Y., Su, L., Xu, J.: Distributed statistical machine learning in adversarial settings: Byzantine gradient descent. ACM Measur. Anal. Comput. Syst. 1(2), 1–25 (2017)
8. Defazio, A., Bach, F., Lacoste-Julien, S.: Saga: a fast incremental gradient method with support for non-strongly convex composite objectives. In: Advances in Neural Information Processing Systems (2014)
9. Fung, C., Yoon, C.J., Beschastnikh, I.: The limitations of federated learning in Sybil settings. In: 23rd International Symposium on Research in Attacks, Intrusions and Defenses ({RAID} 2020), pp. 301–316 (2020)
10. Hard, A., et al.: Federated learning for mobile keyboard prediction. arXiv (2018)
11. Jiang, Y., Cong, R., Shu, C., Yang, A., Zhao, Z., Min, G.: Federated learning based mobile crowd sensing with unreliable user data. In: IEEE International Conference on High Performance Computing and Communications, pp. 320–327 (2020)
12. Khan, L.U., Saad, W., Han, Z., Hossain, E., Hong, C.S.: Federated learning for internet of things: recent advances, taxonomy, and open challenges. IEEE Commun. Surv. Tutor. 23(3), 1759–1799 (2021)
13. LeCun, Y.: The MNIST database of handwritten digits (1998). http://yann.lecun.com/exdb/mnist/
14. Leroy, D., Coucke, A., Lavril, T., Gisselbrecht, T., Dureau, J.: Federated learning for keyword spotting. In: IEEE International Conference on Acoustics, Speech and Signal Processing, pp. 6341–6345 (2019)
15. Li, L., Xu, W., Chen, T., Giannakis, G.B., Ling, Q.: RSA: byzantine-robust stochastic aggregation methods for distributed learning from heterogeneous datasets. In: AAAI Conference on Artificial Intelligence, vol. 33, pp. 1544–1551 (2019)
16. Li, S., Cheng, Y., Wang, W., Liu, Y., Chen, T.: Learning to detect malicious clients for robust federated learning. arXiv (2020)
17. Liu, Y., et al.: Fedvision: an online visual object detection platform powered by federated learning. In: AAAI Conference on Artificial Intelligence, vol. 34, pp. 13172–13179 (2020)
18. Ma, C., Li, J., Ding, M., Wei, K., Chen, W., Poor, H.V.: Federated learning with unreliable clients: performance analysis and mechanism design. IEEE Internet Things J. 8, 17308–17319 (2021)
19. Mallah, R.A., Lopez, D., Farooq, B.: Untargeted poisoning attack detection in federated learning via behavior attestation. arXiv (2021)
20. Mao, Y., Yuan, X., Zhao, X., Zhong, S.: Romoa: robust model aggregation for the resistance of federated learning to mdodel poisoning attacks. In: Bertino, E., Shulman, H., Waidner, M. (eds.) ESORICS 2021. LNCS, vol. 12972, pp. 476–496. Springer, Cham (2021). https://doi.org/10.1007/978-3-030-88418-5_23

21. McMahan, B., Moore, E., Ramage, D., Hampson, S., Arcas, B.A.: Communication-efficient learning of deep networks from decentralized data. In: Artificial Intelligence and Statistics, pp. 1273–1282. PMLR (2017)

22. Nagalapatti, L., Narayanam, R.: Game of gradients: mitigating irrelevant clients in federated learning. In: AAAI Conference on Artificial Intelligence, vol. 35, pp. 9046–9054 (2021)

23. Nguyen, L.M., Nguyen, P.H., Richtárik, P., Scheinberg, K., Takáč, M., van Dijk, M.: New convergence aspects of stochastic gradient algorithms. J. Mach. Learn. Res. **20**, 1–49 (2019)

24. Ozdayi, M.S., Kantarcioglu, M., Gel, Y.R.: Defending against backdoors in federated learning with robust learning rate. In: AAAI Conference on Artificial Intelligence, vol. 35, pp. 9268–9276 (2021)

25. Schubert, E., Sander, J., Ester, M., Kriegel, H.P., Xu, X.: DBSCAN revisited, revisited: why and how you should (still) use DBSCAN. ACM Trans. Database Syst. (TODS) **42**(3), 1–21 (2017)

26. Sun, Z., Kairouz, P., Suresh, A.T., McMahan, H.B.: Can you really backdoor federated learning? arXiv (2019)

27. Tolpegin, V., Truex, S., Gursoy, M.E., Liu, L.: Data poisoning attacks against federated learning systems. In: Chen, L., Li, N., Liang, K., Schneider, S. (eds.) ESORICS 2020. LNCS, vol. 12308, pp. 480–501. Springer, Cham (2020). https://doi.org/10.1007/978-3-030-58951-6_24

28. Wan, C.P., Chen, Q.: Robust federated learning with attack-adaptive aggregation. ArXiv:abs/2102.05257 (2021)

29. Wang, H., et al.: Attack of the tails: Yes, you really can backdoor federated learning. arXiv (2020)

30. Wu, Z., Ling, Q., Chen, T., Giannakis, G.B.: Federated variance-reduced stochastic gradient descent with robustness to byzantine attacks. IEEE Trans. Signal Process. **68**, 4583–4596 (2020)

31. Xiao, H., Rasul, K., Vollgraf, R.: Fashion-mnist: a novel image dataset for benchmarking machine learning algorithms (2017)

32. Xie, C., Chen, M., Chen, P.Y., Li, B.: CRFL: certifiably robust federated learning against backdoor attacks. In: International Conference on Machine Learning, pp. 11372–11382. PMLR (2021)

33. Xie, C., Koyejo, O., Gupta, I.: Generalized byzantine-tolerant SGD. arXiv (2018)

34. Xie, C., Koyejo, S., Gupta, I.: Zeno: Distributed stochastic gradient descent with suspicion-based fault-tolerance. In: International Conference on Machine Learning, pp. 6893–6901. PMLR (2019)

35. Yin, D., Chen, Y., Kannan, R., Bartlett, P.: Byzantine-robust distributed learning: towards optimal statistical rates. In: International Conference on Machine Learning, pp. 5650–5659. PMLR (2018)

$MLFM$: Machine Learning Meets Formal Method for Faster Identification of Security Breaches in Network Functions Virtualization (NFV)

Alaa Oqaily[1(✉)], Yosr Jarraya[2], Lingyu Wang[1(✉)], Makan Pourzandi[2], and Suryadipta Majumdar[1]

[1] CIISE, Concordia University, Montreal, QC, Canada
{a_oqaily,wang,smajumdar}@encs.concordia.ca
[2] Ericsson Security Research, Ericsson Canada, Montreal, QC, Canada
{yosr.jarraya,makan.pourzandi}@ericsson.com

Abstract. By virtualizing proprietary physical devices, Network Functions Virtualization (NFV) enables agile and cost-effective deployment of network services on top of a cloud infrastructure. However, the added complexity also increases the chance of incorrect or inconsistent configurations that could leave the services or infrastructure vulnerable to security threats. Therefore, the timely identification of such misconfigurations is important to ensure the security compliance of NFV. In this regard, a typical solution is to leverage formal method-based security verification as they can provide either a rigorous mathematical proof that all configurations satisfy the required security properties, or the counterexamples (i.e., misconfigurations causing the properties to be breached). To that end, a major challenge is that the sheer scale of large NFV environments can render formal security verification so costly that the significant delays before misconfigurations can be identified may leave a large attack window. In this paper, we propose a novel approach, $MLFM$, that combines the efficiency of Machine Learning (ML) and the rigor of Formal Methods (FM) for fast and provable identification of misconfigurations violating a security property in NFV. Our key idea lies in an iterative teacher-learner interaction in which the teacher (FM) can gradually (over many iterations) provide more representative training data (verification results), while the learner (ML) can leverage such data to gradually obtain more accurate ML models. As a result, a small portion of the configuration data will be enough to obtain a relatively accurate ML model. The model is then applied to the remaining data to prioritize the verification of what is more likely to cause violations. We experimentally evaluate our solution and compare it to an existing security verification tool to demonstrate its benefits.

Keywords: Machine learning · Network functions virtualization · Auditing · Virtualization · Formal method

© The Author(s), under exclusive license to Springer Nature Switzerland AG 2022
V. Atluri et al. (Eds.): ESORICS 2022, LNCS 13556, pp. 466–489, 2022.
https://doi.org/10.1007/978-3-031-17143-7_23

1   Introduction

By decoupling network functions from proprietary hardware devices, Network Functions Virtualization (NFV) allows network services to be implemented as software modules running on top of generic hardware or virtual machines. This new paradigm allows service operators to more easily deploy a multi-tenant NFV environment on top of an existing cloud infrastructure, and it also allows NFV tenants to accelerate the provisioning and deployment of their services. Due to such benefits, the popularity of NFV is on the rise, e.g., in the context of 5G and beyond, NFV has become one of the main technology enablers for operators to scale their network capabilities on-demand at a lower cost by virtualizing dedicated physical devices on top of existing clouds [2].

The benefits of NFV may come at the cost of increased complexity. To support the management and orchestration of multiple network slices belonging to different tenants on top of the same cloud infrastructure [11], NFV relies on a mixture of virtualization technologies, e.g., a Virtual Network Function (VNF) such as virtual firewall seen at tenant-level may correspond to several virtual machines (VMs) connected through Software-Defined Networking (SDN) at the cloud infrastructure level [2]. Such increased complexity may also increase the chance of incorrect (e.g., lack of sufficient network isolation between different tenants' network slices [28]) or inconsistent (e.g.,. a virtual firewall VNF specified at the tenant level may be bypassed at the underlying cloud infrastructure level [30]) configurations that could leave the services or infrastructure vulnerable to security threats. Therefore, the timely identification of such misconfigurations is important to ensure the security of NFV environments.

To that end, formal method-based security verification solutions (e.g., [26,27,31,39,44,54,59]) can provide rigorous proofs about the compliance or violation (with counterexamples) of the configurations w.r.t. given security properties. However, a key challenge is that the sheer scale of virtual environments can render formal security verification too costly. For instance, a state-of-the-art security verification tool requires around 12 min to check whether a guest VM can access any SDN controller with merely 5,000 reachability queries [31]. Such a delay can become much more significant under large NFV environments, resulting in a wide attack window during which the services or infrastructure are left vulnerable. Moreover, the inherent complexity of formal methods [52] can leave little room for further performance improvement, e.g., the aforementioned tool [31] is already heavily optimized (new combined filter-project operator and symbolic packet representation are added to the back-end verifier).

Motivating Example. We further illustrate this issue through an example. The left side of Fig. 1 shows the simplified view of a large NFV environment where two tenants, Alice and Bob, host their Virtual Network Functions (VNFs). Suppose our goal is to verify network isolation, i.e., whether any of Alice's VNFs can reach any of Bob's (except what is explicitly allowed). Even the verification of such a simple property (all-pair reachability) can become expensive as NFV tenants may own a large number of VNFs. To make things worse, NFV and its underlying cloud infrastructure typically employ distributed and fine-grained network access control mechanisms (e.g., per-VM security groups in OpenStack [43]). Consequently, verifying the reachability of two VNFs/VMs may require inspecting many rules and configuration data scattered among various data sources (e.g., routing and NAT rules in virtual routers along the route, host routes of the subnets, and firewall rules implementing tenant security properties [59]).

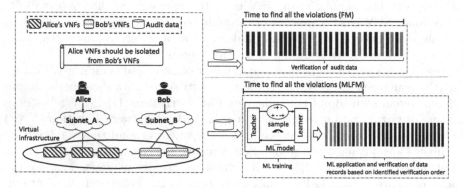

Fig. 1. Motivating example

The right side of Fig. 1 contrasts how the collected audit data will be processed under an existing formal method (FM)-based security verification approach (top) and under our approach (bottom). The barchart-like pattern illustrates the distribution of data records in the audit data where red (or black) bars represent pairs of VNFs that violate (or satisfy) the network isolation property. As the upper pattern shows, a FM-based approach would verify the audit data as is, i.e., all the VNF pairs will be verified in the same order as given in the audit data. In contrast, our approach leverages ML to reorder those data records such that those that (likely) cause violations (the red bars) will be moved forward, i.e., given a higher priority for verification than others (the black bars). Consequently, the verification can identify most of the violations in much less time (even after taking into account the time taken by ML training).

To that end, our main idea is to employ an iterative teacher-learner interaction, as depicted in the middle of Fig. 1. In each iteration, the teacher (FM) first selects representative data records from the audit data, and then provides their verification results as training data to the learner (ML). Using such data, the learner (ML) trains an ML model, which is then given back to the teacher (FM) to be tested for identifying more representative data records (e.g., false positives and false negatives) in the next iteration. Over several iterations, such an interaction between the teacher and learner will enable a relatively accurate ML model to be trained using only a small portion of the audit data. The ML model can then be applied to reorder the remaining data for faster identification of violations. More specifically, our main contributions are as follows.

- To be best of our knowledge, *MLFM* is the first approach that combines FM with ML to have the best of both worlds (i.e., the rigor of FM which is essential for proving security compliance, and the efficiency of ML which is critical for a large NFV environment) for prioritizing verification tasks in NFV. Although we focus on NFV, we believe such an approach can potentially find other applications.
- To realize MLFM, we design an iterative teacher-learner interaction methodology with a detailed algorithm. We implement the methodology based on a constraint satisfaction problem solver, namely, Sugar [55], several popular ML algorithms (decision tree, random forest, support vector machine, and XGBoost), and sampling techniques (uncertainty sampling and query-by-committee) borrowed from the active learning literature [50] for identifying representative data records.
- We experimentally evaluate MLFM for two different use cases (one aims at the shortest verification time, and the other at the completeness of the result). The experimental results demonstrate the benefits of MLFM through identifying violations significantly faster than the baseline FM method (e.g., identifying 80% of violations in 28% of time), and further improving the efficiency of a state-of-the-art security verification tool [31] (e.g., identifying 80% of violations in 57% of time).

The remainder of the paper is organized as follows. Section 2 provides the background and threat model. Section 3 details the MLFM methodology. Section 4 describes our implementation. Section 5 presents the experiments. Section 6 reviews the related work. Finally, Sect. 7 discusses limitations and concludes the paper.

2 Preliminaries

This section provides essential background on NFV, discusses NFV security properties, and defines our threat model.

NFV Background. NFV is a network architecture concept that decouples network functions (e.g., routers, firewalls, and load balancers) from proprietary hardware devices and virtualizes them as Virtual Network Functions (VNFs) running on top of existing cloud infrastructures [2]. Figure 2 presents a simplified view of the ETSI NFV reference architecture [2] (left), and an example NFV deployment corresponding to our motivating example (right). First, the *resource management* level conceptualizes the virtual resources such as subnets and VNFs. Second, the underlying *virtual infrastructure* level implements those virtual resources using virtual networking elements, such as virtual switches

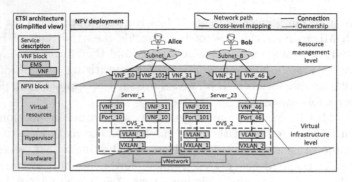

Fig. 2. ETSI NFV reference architecture [2] (left) and an example NFV deployment corresponding to the motivating example (right)

(e.g., *OVS_1*), VLANs (for communications within the same server), VxLANs (for communications between servers), and network ports, running on top of physical servers (e.g., *Server_1*). In this paper, NFV configuration data stored in relational databases will be our main inputs.

NFV Security Properties. Various security properties can be defined to verify the compliance of NFV environments w.r.t. standards (e.g., ETSI [2] and IETF-RFC7498 [45]) or NFV tenants' requirements. Table 1 (in Appendix) shows some example NFV security properties which we have previously identified [44]. Our approach can support other security properties as long as they can be verified using the chosen formal method tool (e.g., Sugar [55] used in this paper can handle most properties formulated using standard first-order logic). To make our discussions more concrete, we describe two example properties (which will be needed later).

Example 1. First, the property *mapping unicity VLANs-VXLANs* ensures the logic segregation between different tenants' virtual networks through the unique assignment of VxLAN (communications between servers) identifier to each VLAN (communications within one server). Figure 3 (left) depicts a violation of this property (the shaded nodes show *VLAN_1* is mapped to both *VXLAN_10* and *VXLAN_16* on *Server_1*). Note this property can be verified for each VLAN separately. Second, the property *no VNFs co-residence* prevents a tenant's VNFs to be placed on the same physical server with VNFs of non-trusted tenants (e.g., due to concerns over potential side channel threats). Figure 3 (right) shows a violation of this property where *Alice's VNF_101* and *Bob's VNF_46* on both placed on server *S_23*. In contrast to the previous property, verifying this property could involve more records (all the VNFs of this tenant and the non-trusted tenants).

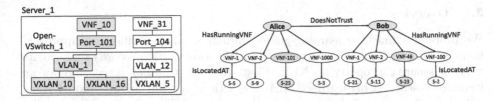

Fig. 3. Two example NFV security properties: *Mapping unicity VLANs-VXLANs* (left) and *No VNFs co-residence* (right) (shaded nodes indicate violations)

Threat Model and Assumptions. Similar to most existing security verification approaches, our *scope* is limited to attacks that (directly or indirectly) cause violations to given security properties, and we assume our solution is deployed by the owner of the NFV environment who has access to the logs, databases, and configuration data needed for the security verification (and the integrity of those input data is protected with trusted computing techniques (e.g., [49])). Under such assumptions, our *in-scope threats* include both external attackers who exploit existing vulnerabilities in the NFV environment to violate the security properties, and insiders such as NFV operators and tenants who cause misconfigurations violating the properties, either through mistakes or by malicious intentions. Conversely, *out-of-scope threats* include attacks that do not cause any violation of the security properties, and attacks launched by adversaries who can erase evidences of their attacks by tampering with the logs, databases, etc.

We assume that the formal specification of security properties as well as the formal verification approach itself are correct and sound. As a security verification solution, our approach can only identify the violation of given security properties, but is not designed to attribute such a violation to the underlying vulnerabilities (responsibility of vulnerability analysis) or specific attacks (responsibility of intrusion detection). Similar to most existing machine learning approaches, we assume that a dataset required for verifying given security properties has been collected. However, we do not require labeled data, which can be difficult to obtain in a real world NFV environment, as the data records will be labeled by the teacher (formal method) in our approach (optionally, a small amount of labeled data records would be helpful for training an initial ML model to speed up the iterative approach). As with most security applications (e.g., spam or intrusion detection), we assume the dataset is unbalanced (i.e., the majority of data records belong to the compliance class w.r.t. the security property), and we make additional efforts in designing our approach to address this issue.

3 Methodology

This section first presents an overview of our approach, followed by details on the iterative teacher (FM)-learner (ML) interaction and the MLFM algorithm.

3.1 Overview

We propose a machine learning-guided formal security verification approach, namely, *MLFM*, for fast and provable identification of data records that violate a given security property in NFV. First, the *ML training* stage employs an iterative teacher (FM)-learner (ML) interaction to train an ML model using only a small portion of the audit data. Second, the *ML application* stage applies the ML model to reorder the remaining audit data, such that those that are more likely to violate the property will be verified first. More specifically, Fig. 4 depicts our approach as follows.

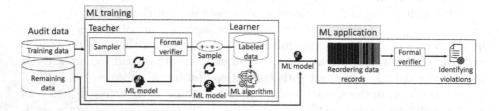

Fig. 4. Overview of the MLFM approach

The ML Training Stage. As Fig. 4 (left) shows, in each iteration of the teacher-learner interaction, the teacher first applies a sampling method to select a small data sample of fixed size from the audit data (shown as *Sampler* in the figure) after applying the ML model received from the learner in the previous iteration (an initial ML model is provided for the first iteration). The teacher then verifies the data records inside this data sample, and labels each record based on its verification result (shown as *Formal verifier* in the figure), and sends the labeled data sample to the learner. The learner then combines this newly received data sample with the previously received data samples to train a new ML model to be sent back to the teacher. This iterative interaction ends when reaching a predefined condition, e.g., a fixed iteration count, or lack of significant change in the accuracy of the model between two consecutive iterations.

The ML Application Stage. As Fig. 4 (right) shows, the final ML model from the *ML training* stage is applied to the remaining audit data (i.e., the data not used for training) in order to identify data records that are more likely to violate the given security property, namely, the "to be verified" subset, which will be given a higher priority for verification. On the other hand, the "not to be verified" subset will either be verified afterwards, or not verified at all, depending on the use cases (detailed in Sect. 3.3).

3.2 Iterative Teacher (FM)-Learner (ML) Interaction

In the following, we provide more details about the key methodology of our approach, i.e., the iterative teacher (FM)-learner (ML) interaction.

Sampling (Teacher). The sampler component of the teacher is designed to select representative data records from the audit data in order for the learner to effectively enhance the ML model over each iteration. Choosing the right data records is important because they could cause either increase or decrease in the accuracy of the next ML model, e.g., data records having the same (redundant) information or those with the same label may cause the model to either not improve, or become biased towards the majority data, respectively. Our approach borrows sampling strategies (such as uncertainty sampling) from the active learning literature [50]. Although active learning has a different focus (it aims to reduce the effort of human experts in labeling the data, whereas no human expert is involved in our case), its sampling strategies are applicable to our approach, because they are also designed to better represent the characteristics of the property being analyzed such that an ML model can be trained with minimal labeled data.

Example 2. The left side of Fig. 5 shows an excerpt of the audit data corresponding to the previous Example 1. Using uncertainty sampling, the sampler (inside the teacher block) selects a sample of size ($m = 2$) as the (shaded) record pairs $(1, 3)$ and $(6, 4)$.

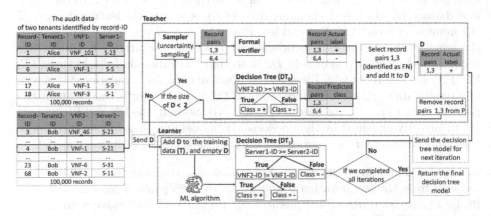

Fig. 5. An example of the iterative teacher (FM)-learner (ML) interaction

Verification (Teacher). The formal verifier component is responsible for labeling the selected sample of data records (which will later be sent to the learner as training data). Labeling here means to annotate the data records with an extra field representing their classes, i.e., whether they are compliant with, or violate, the security property. To obtain such labels, the formal verifier performs formal verification by instantiating the security property (e.g., formulated using first-order logic) with the data records.

Example 3. Following Example 2, Fig. 5 shows how the formal verifier labels the selected sample by verifying the *No VNFs co-residence* property (see Sect. 2). Specifically, the formal verifier finds that the pair $(1, 3)$ violates the property (i.e., Alice's VNF (*VNF_101*) co-resides with Bob's VNF (*VNF_46*) on the same server (*S-23*)), and thus labels it as "+". The other pair $(6, 4)$ is labled as "-", as it does not violate the property.

Records Selection (Teacher). Next, the teacher applies the ML model from the previous iteration (received from the learner) to the labeled sample of data records. Intuitively, this allows the teacher to validate this previous ML model (by comparing its results to the labels provided by the formal verifier) and provide the "mistakes" (false positives and false negatives) as more representative training data to the learner. Specifically, as the ML model from the previous iteration also classifies the data records into two classes, by comparing its results to the ground truth, i.e., the labels assigned by the formal verifier component, the teacher can identify those records that have been correctly classified (i.e., true positives (TPs)) and those incorrectly classified (i.e., false negatives (FNs) and false positives (FPs)). Then, the teacher adds the TP, FN, and FP records to a new dataset D, which is the training dataset to be sent to the learner. Finally, if the number of records in D is still less than the desired size of the sample (m), the teacher repeats the aforementioned steps as an inner-iteration until it has accumulated totally m records in D. Note that the rationale for selecting (TP, FP, FN) records is twofold. First, as the positive class (i.e., violations) is generally smaller due to data imbalance, adding TP and FN records can augment the positive class to reduce the bias in training [41]. Second, the FN and FP records are incorrectly classified by the previous ML model and thus may contain more useful information for the learner to improve the accuracy of its next model.

Example 4. Following Example 3, Fig. 5 shows a decision tree model (DT_0) received from the last iteration is applied to the two pairs of records $(1, 3)$ and $(6, 4)$. The decision tree (DT_0) predicts "+", if the *VNF2-ID* value is no smaller than the *VNF1-ID* value; otherwise, it is predicted as "-". Therefore, both $(1, 3)$ and $(6, 4)$ are predicted as "-". Comparing such results to the labels previously assigned by the formal verifier (see Example 3), we can see the pair $(1, 3)$ is *FN* and should be added to the dataset D (and deleted from the audit data), whereas $(6, 4)$ is *TN* and should not be added. Finally, as the size of D is less than the required size $(m=2)$, we will repeat the inner-iteration.

ML Model Building (Learner). Once the teacher's dataset D reaches the required size m, the sample it contains is sent to the learner (D is then emptied in preparation for the next iteration). The learner adds the received sample to its existing training data (i.e., the collection of all previous samples), and utilizes this newly enriched training data to build a new ML model. The ML model is sent back to the teacher if the stopping condition (e.g., the specified number of interactions) has not been reached; otherwise, the interaction ends and the final ML model is given to the next (ML application) stage.

Example 5. Following Example 4, the lower part of Fig. 5 shows that, once the teacher's inner-iteration ends, a sample of size two is sent to the learner. The learner adds the received sample to the existing training data (T) while the teacher empties its dataset (D). The new training data (T) is then used to build a new decision tree model (DT_1), which is more accurate than DT_0.

3.3   MLFM Algorithm and Use Cases

Algorithm 1 more formally states our approach. The inputs to the algorithm include the unlabeled audit data, the security property, and the parameters. The initial set of training data allows a system user to influence the algorithm with his/her domain knowledge by manually selecting/labeling data records (otherwise, the data can simply be randomly selected from the audit data and labeled using the formal verifier).

The algorithm has an outer iteration (Lines 2–9) which first builds a new sample through performing the inner iteration (Lines 3–7), and then adds this new sample to the existing training data (Line 8) to train a new ML model (Line 9). The outer iteration is repeated for a fixed number (provided as an input parameter) of times. The final ML model is then applied to reorder the remaining audit data before verifying it (Line 10). The union of all the verification results (Lines 5 and 10) is the final output.

The inner iteration builds a sample D of size m as follows. First, it selects a sample of size m from the audit data by following a given sampling strategy (Line 4). Although not shown in the algorithm, depending on the sampling strategy being used, this step may involve other parameters such as the current ML model (e.g., with uncertainty sampling [50]) or the training data (e.g., with Query-By-Committee (QBC) sampling [50]). Second, the sample is verified and labeled (with the verification results) using a formal verifier (Line 5). Third, the current ML model is applied to the sample, and the results are compared to the labels (verification results) to identify and add the (TP, FP, FN) records to D (Line 6). Fourth, D is removed from the audit data to avoid being selected again (Line 7). We repeat the above steps until D contains at least m records.

Complexity Analysis. The worst case complexity of the MLFM algorithm is $O(n{\cdot}(m{\cdot}(T_s+T_{v_1})+T_t)+T_{v_2})$ where T_s, T_{v_1}, T_t, and T_{v_2} are the time for sampling (Line 4), verifying m records (Line 5), training (Line 9), and verifying remaining

---

Algorithm 1: The MLFM algorithm

---

1 Inputs: Audit data (**AD**), security property (**SP**), initial training data (**T₀**),
   initial model $\mathbf{M_0} = \text{TrainClassifier}(T_0)$, per-iteration sample size (**m**), and
   iteration count (**n**)
   /* Outer-iteration   */
2 for $i = 0,\ i < n,\ i{+}{+}$ **do**
   /* Inner-iteration   */
3   **while** $|D| < m$ **do**
4 $S = \text{SelectSample}(AD, m)$
5 $S_i = \text{VerifyAndLabel}(S, SP)$
6 $D = D \cup TP(S_i, M_i) \cup FP(S_i, M_i) \cup FN(S_i, M_i)$
7 $AD = AD \setminus D$
8 $T_{i+1} = T_i \cup D;\ D = \phi$
9 $M_{i+1} = \text{TrainClassifier}(T_{i+1})$
10 return $\text{Verify}(\text{Reorder}(AD, M_n)) \cup (\bigcup_i S_i)$

---

records (Line 10), respectively. Such times would depend on specific algorithms, e.g., T_s under uncertainty sampling [50] can be estimated as $O(|AD|)$, since this strategy requires applying the current ML model on the audit data AD. T_{v1} and T_{v2} under a CSP solver is known to be exponential in the number of variables of the instantiated security property [14]. Finally, T_t under a decision tree classifier is $O(n_a \cdot n_t \cdot \log_2(n_t))$ [47] where n_a is the number of attributes and n_t the size of training data (i.e., $O(n \cdot m)$). We will further study the efficiency of the algorithm through experiments in Sect. 5.

Use Cases. Depending on how the remaining data is verified in Line 10 of the MLFM algorithm, our approach can be applied for two different use cases. First, MLFM running in the *partial verification* case will stop after verifying all the "to be verified" records (which would appear first after the reordering). This can be useful when the system user wants to find violations as quickly as possible (but not necessarily to find all the violations), and our objective in the training is to find an ML model that is the most accurate (since the mis-classifed violations would not be verified, as further explained in Sect. 5). Second, MLFM in the *priority-based verification* case will verify all the records (with the "to be verified" records verified first). Our objective of the training is to find an ML model that incurs the least overall verification time with acceptable accuracy (since the mis-classified records will still be verified eventually).

4   Implementation

In this section, we describe the architecture and details of our implementation.

System Architecture. Our implementation of MLFM (shown in Fig. 11 in Appendix due to space limitation) interacts with an OpenStack/Tacker [8]-based NFV environment to collect audit data. The system also interacts with a user to obtain other inputs, such as the security property to be verified, the formal verifier and the ML model to be applied, and the system parameters (the number of iterations and the sample size, as detailed in Sect. 3.3). Finally, the system returns an audit report to the user.

Data Collection and Processing. We implement this module using Python and Bash scripts to collect audit data from multiple sources including logs and configuration databases or files. For instance, to verify the *No VNFs co-residence* property, the module collects the identifiers of VNFs from Tacker and Nova databases [7], their corresponding owners (from Nova database), and the identifiers of servers hosting those VNFs (from Nova database). As the audit data are usually scattered among different components of the NFV environment and stored in different formats, the data must first be pre-processed. For instance, to verify the *mapping unicity VLANs-VXLANs* property, the data collected from OpenFlow tables of the OVS databases has unnecessary fields (e.g., *cookie* and *priority*) that must be filtered out. Also, the *port* and *vlan_vid* fields must be correlated to create the relation tuples *IsAssignedVLAN(ovs,port,valn)* for the verification. Finally, such filtered and correlated data must be converted into the corresponding input formats required by the formal verifier as well as for the ML training.

MLFM Manager. We implement this module in Python to manage and coordinate the interactions between other system modules for performing data collection and processing, data sampling, formal verification, ML training, etc., as described in Sect. 3.

ML Model Learner. We utilize Python 3.6.9 and Scikit-learn 0.24.1 (an open source ML library written in Python) to implement this module. We select decision tree, Support Vector Machine (SVM), and Random Forest (RF) models as they are among the most commonly used supervised classifiers, and are computationally more efficient compared to other classifiers such as K-Nearest-Neighbor (KNN) [40]. We also select XGBoost classifier [15], a scalable tree boosting system with a simpler structure using less resources than most other ML models, which has recently seen wide application for its high accuracy and low false positive rate [16,42]. As our main aim is to reduce the overall delay before violations can be identified, we do not consider deep learning models as they are well known for higher complexity and longer training time compared to traditional ML models [34].

Sampler. We employ the *modAL* framework [17] to implement sampling strategies in this module. The *modAL* is an active learning framework for Python3, built on top of Scikit-learn [29], which allows to rapidly create active learning workflows with flexibility [17]. We select the uncertainty sampling and query-by-committee (with DT, SVM, and RF for members of the committee) sampling strategies in our implementation, as those are the most computationally efficient ones compared to other strategies [50].

Formal Verifier. We formalize the security properties together with the audit data as a Constraint Satisfaction Problem (CSP), a time-proven technique for expressing complex problems. Using CSP allows the user to specify a wide range of security properties (due to its expressiveness) in a relatively simple manner (as CSP enables to uniformly present the audit data as well as the security properties, and in a comprehensible and clean formalism, such as first order logic (FOL) [12]). Moreover, there exist many powerful and efficient CSP solver algorithms to avoid the state space traversal [48], which can make our approach more scalable for large NFV environments.

Once formulated as a CSP problem, the security verification is performed using Sugar [55], a well-established SAT-based constraint solver. We choose Sugar as it is an award-winning solver of global constraint categories (at the International CSP Solver Competitions in 2008 and 2009 [9]). Sugar solves a finite linear CSP by translating it into a SAT problem using order encoding method, and then solving the translated SAT problem using the MiniSat solver [18], which is an efficient CDCL SAT solver particularly effective in narrowing the search space [23]. Adapting our MLFM framework to other verification methods (such as theorem proving, model checkers, temporal logic, and Datalog) based on the needs of verification tasks is regarded as a future work.

Example 6. The predicate that corresponds to the negation of the *No VNFs co-residence* property is formulated (by the system user, done only once) as Formula 1 (left), and a predicate instance returned by Sugar to indicate violation is shown as Formula 2 (right) (i.e., both *Alice* and *Bob* have VNFs co-residing on the same server *S_23*).

$$\forall t1, t2 \in \text{Tenant}, \forall vnf1, vnf2 \in \text{VNF}, \forall s1, s2 \quad (1)$$
$$\in \text{Server} : \text{HasRunningVNF}(t1, vnf1) \land \text{HasRunn}-$$
$$\text{ingVNF}(t1, vnf1) \land \text{DoesNotTrust}(t1, t2) \land$$
$$\text{IsRunningOn}(vnf1, s1) \land \text{IsRunningOn}(vnf2, s2)$$
$$\land (s1 == s2)$$

$$\text{HasRunningVNF}(\text{Alice}, \text{VNF\_101}) \land \text{HasRunn}- \quad (2)$$
$$\text{ingVNF}(\text{Bob}, \text{VNF\_46}) \land \text{DoesNotTrust}(\text{Alice},$$
$$\text{Bob}) \land \text{IsRunningOn}(\text{VNF\_101}, \text{S\_23}) \land \text{IsRun}-$$
$$\text{ningOn}(\text{VNF\_46}, \text{S\_23}) \land (\text{S\_23} == \text{S\_23})$$

5   Experiments

This section describes the datasets and experimental settings, and presents our results.

5.1 Datasets and Experimental Settings

We first describe the implementation of our NFV testbed and data generation using the testbed, and then detail the experimental settings.

NFV Testbed Implementation. We choose to build our NFV testbed using OpenStack [7] with Tacker [8] mainly due to their growing popularity in real world [10] (other options such as Open Baton [4], OPNFV [5], and OSM [6] are still at their development stages). More specifically, we rely on the latest version OpenStack Rocky [7] for managing the virtual infrastructure, and we employ Tacker-0.10.0 [8], an official OpenStack project, to deploy virtual network services. Our NFV testbed consists of 20 tenants and 200 VNF forwarding graphs (VNFFGs), with each tenant owning around 10 VNFFGs and each VNFFG consisting of about 10 VNFs.

NFV Data Generation. To evaluate the performance of MLFM under large scale NFV environments, we would require a large scale NFV deployment. However, to the best of our knowledge, there do not exist any publicly available large-scale NFV deployment datasets. Therefore, we develop Python scripts to automatically generate various VNF Descriptors (VNFDs) and VNFFG Descriptors (VNFFGDs), which are then uploaded (also called on-boarding) to our NFV testbed to deploy different network services and generate large scale NFV datasets. We randomize parameters of those descriptors to ensure diversity in the generated data (e.g., the number of network ports per VNF, the flavor of each VNF, the number of VNFs in each Network Function Path (NFP), and the number of NFPs in each VNFFG). Our first dataset, *DS1*, contains 12,500 audit data records for verifying the *mapping unicity VLANs-VXLANs* property (P1 henceforth), and our second dataset, *DS2*, contains 25,000 records for verifying the *no VNFs co-residence* property (P2 henceforth). Each dataset contains around 10% of (uniformly distributed) records that violate the corresponding property.

Experimental Setting. All experiments are performed on a SuperServer 6029P-WTR running the Ubuntu 18.04 operating system equipped with Intel(R) Xeon(R) Bronze 3104 CPU @ 1.70 GHz and 128 GB of RAM without GPUs. All the experiments are performed using Sugar [55] as the formal verifier (unless mentioned otherwise) and Python 3.6.9 with Scikit-learn 0.24.1 ML packages for the ML method. For all the experiments, we use the default parameters for the ML models. Each experiment is repeated 1,000 times to obtain the average results.

5.2 Experimental Results

Best Performing Combination of ML Model/Sampling Method. The first set of the experiments aims to find the best performing combination of

ML model and sampling method (as components of MLFM), from both the accuracy and time performance point of views. Specifically, Fig. 6 shows the recall and F1 score results for different combinations of ML models (DT, RF, SVM and XGBoost, trained on 20% of each dataset) and sampling methods (random sampling, query-by-committee (QBC), and uncertainty sampling) for both security properties (P1 and P2) and datasets (DS1 and DS2). The results in Figs. 6 (a) and (b) show that the combination of XGBoost and uncertainty sampling allows MLFM to achieve the highest recall (0.97) and F1 score (0.97) for security property P1. On the other hand, SVM combined with any of these sampling methods has the lowest F1 score (0.80) (i.e., less effective in identifying both classes), and RF with uncertainty sampling has the lowest recall (0.82) (i.e., less effective in identifying the violations). Similarly, Fig. 6 (c) shows that XGBoost with uncertainty sampling also has the best recall (0.783) for security property P2. However, as Fig. 6 (d) shows, XGBoost has the best F1 score (0.981) when paired with QBC sampling. Nonetheless, as identifying the violations is more important to MLFM, XGBoost with uncertainty sampling is considered the best option for both P1 and P2.

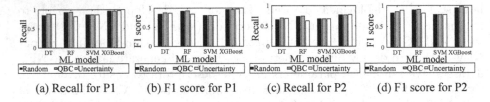

(a) Recall for P1   (b) F1 score for P1   (c) Recall for P2   (d) F1 score for P2

Fig. 6. Recall and F1 score for combinations of ML models and sampling methods, trained on 20% of dataset DS1 for property P1 (a and b) and on DS2 for P2 (c and d)

Figure 7 shows how the combinations of ML models and sampling methods affect the running time (in minutes) of MLFM (including both the ML training and application stages). As explained in Sect. 3.3, the partial verification use case aims to find the majority of violations in the least time. To that end, Fig. 7 (a) seems to suggest that SVM paired with uncertainty sampling is the best option as it requires the least time (15.14 min). However, upon further investigation, this is not really the case, because the lower time consumption is mainly due to its inaccuracy (it misses more violations and thus, similar to most SAT solvers, Sugar incurs less time when there are less violations to find [55]). Therefore, considering both the accuracy (Fig. 6 (a)) and the running time, XGBoost with uncertainty sampling seems to be the best option (with the second least time) for partial verification under P1. Figure 7 (b) shows that XGBoost with uncertainty sampling is the best option for priority-based verification for P1, as it requires the least time (accuracy is less important in this use case as all the records will be verified eventually, as explained in Sect. 3.3). Similarly, Figs. 7 (c) and (d) show XGBoost with uncertainty is also the best combination under P2 for both use cases.

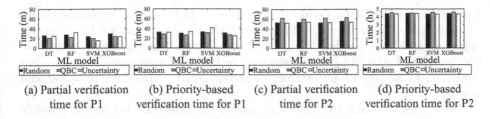

(a) Partial verification time for P1

(b) Priority-based verification time for P1

(c) Partial verification time for P2

(d) Priority-based verification time for P2

Fig. 7. Running time of MLFM for combinations of ML models and sampling methods, with 20% of training data under P1 (a) (b), or P2 (c) (d), for both use cases

Best Performing Parameters m and n. In this set of experiments, we aim to find the optimal parameters of MLFM, i.e., the number of iterations n and the sample size m (see Sect. 3.3), in terms of the running time for priority-based verification, and also in comparison to the baseline approach (i.e., directly applying the formal verifier to the entire dataset). Specifically, Fig. 8(a) shows how changing the sample size m with a fixed number of iterations ($n = 10$) impacts the time, with the best performing model (i.e., XGBoost with uncertainty sampling) under property P1. The results show that MLFM takes less time (<1 h) than the baseline approach (around 1.6 h) in all cases. As more training data is used (through larger samples), the time of MLFM initially decreases due to more accurate ML models, and it reaches the lowest value (0.417 h, or around 25% of the time of baseline) while using about 20% of the dataset for training. The time starts to increase afterwards, since the time needed to verify larger samples in the training stage becomes dominant (compared to the time saved in the application stage). Figure 8(b) shows how changing the number of iterations n with a fixed sample size ($m = 250$) impacts the time. Similarly, MLFM takes less time than the baseline approach in all cases. The optimal percentage of training data is also around 20% (where $n = 10$). However, afterwards the time of MLFM stays lower than in the previous experiment, which shows that increasing the number of iterations is a safer choice (than increasing sample size) for increasing the training data. Figures 8(c) and (d) show similar trends for property P2 (the longer time is due to more records involved in verification, as shown in Sect. 2).

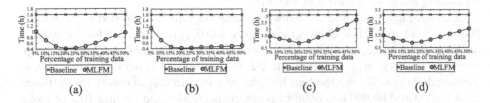

(a)

(b)

(c)

(d)

Fig. 8. Running time of MLFM vs. the baseline (FM only) under property P1 (a) and (b) or P2 (c) and (d), using different percentages of training data either by changing the sample size m (a) and (c) or by changing the number of iterations n (b) and (d)

Comparing MLFM to Other Approaches. In this set of experiments, we compare the performance of MLFM to both the baseline approach (i.e., directly applying the formal verifier, Sugar [55]) and a state-of-the-art security verification tool, NOD [31][1]. All experiments use the best performing model and parameters (i.e., XGBoost with uncertainty sampling, 20% training data, $m = 250$, and $n = 10$).

First, Figs. 9(a) and (b) show the time (in minutes) needed by the baseline approach (upper curve) and by MLFM (lower curve) for identifying different percentages of violations under properties P1 (a) and P2 (b), respectively. The figures depict both the priority-based verification use case (the entire curve) and the partial verification use case (part of the curve before the dashed line). Specifically, Fig. 9(a) shows that MLFM outperforms the baseline throughout the percentages, e.g., for partial verification, MLFM can identify 88% of the violations in around 23.3 min, which takes the baseline 82.7 min. Similarly, Fig. 9(b) shows that MLFM outperforms the baseline in case of partial verification for property P2, where it identifies 82% of the violations in about 53.3 min, while the baseline takes almost 2.4 h. However, in case of priority-based verification (after the 82%) for property P2, MLFM takes more time than the baseline. The reason lies in the difference between the two properties. As explained in Sect. 2, unlike P1 (which can be verified for each VLAN independently), P2 may involve all the VNFs of a tenant, which means the remaining 18% of violations can only be identified using the baseline approach. Fortunately, there exists an alternative solution, i.e., we run MLFM and the baseline in parallel, and terminate MLFM as soon as the baseline finishes (as we already have all the results). As Fig. 9(b) shows, this would allow MLFM to identify around 86% of violations faster than the baseline, while bounding the overall running time by what is taken by the baseline.

Next, Figs. 9(c) and (d) show the tradeoff between the running time (in minutes) and the recall values of partial verification (i.e., the percentage of violations identified by the end of partial verification) for P1 (c) and P2 (d). Both figures show similar results, i.e., while the baseline naturally requires more time for identifying more violations, MLFM can achieve a high recall value of 0.98 (P1) and 0.9 (P2) (by increasing the percentage of training data from 10% to 20%) with negligible change in running time (the difference will be greater for verifying the remaining records, as shown in Fig. 8).

Finally, Figs. 10(a) and (b) show the time (in minutes) needed by NOD [31] (lower curve) and MLFM integrated with NOD (upper curve) for identifying different percentages of violations under the *virtual network reachability* property [31] (as this property is similar to P2, we run MLFM in parallel with NOD, as discussed above). We use the benchmarks provided in [31] to create two datasets with 25,000 and 50,000 reachability pairs, respectively, and around 10% of violations injected randomly. The results show that MLFM can help NOD to identify

---

[1] Among existing security verification tools, we do not compare to NFVGuard [44] as it actually forms the basis of our verification component, and we do not compare to TenantGuard [59] as it is based on custom algorithms instead of formal method.

around 80% (a) and 81.3% (b) of violations, respectively, in less (57% and 65%, respectively) time.

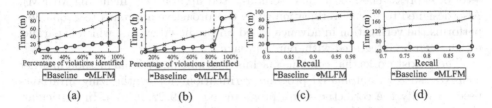

Fig. 9. The time (in minutes) for identifying different percentages of violations by MLFM and the baseline for P1 (a) or P2 (b). The tradeoff between running time and recall values of MLFM and the baseline for partial verification of P1 (c) or P2 (d)

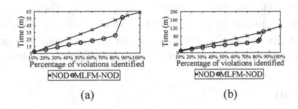

Fig. 10. The time (in minutes) for identifying different percentages of violations by NOD [31] and by MLFM integrated with NOD, using 25,000 (a) and 50,000 (b) records

6 Related Work

Most existing solutions related to security verification for NFV (e.g., [20,21,39, 54,56,58,60,61]) focus on the verification of service function chaining (SFC). Those works employ either custom algorithms (such as [20,58,60]), graph-based methods (such as [21,56,61]), or formal methods (such as [39,54]). Unlike those existing works (which focus on the SFC only), our previous work, NFV-Guard [44], aims to verify the entire NFV stack (including both SFC and underlying infrastructure, and their consistency) using formal method. However, the increased scope also leads to increased complexity and longer verification time, which has motivated us to propose MLFM.

Besides NFV, there also exist security verification solutions for other virtual infrastructures, such as cloud and SDN (e.g., [27,31–33,37,38,59]), including formal method-based ones [31–33,37]. Unlike MLFM, most such solutions do not specifically address the delay in verification (so they may benefit from MLFM in that aspect), with the exception of NOD [31] which is optimized for large applications (our experiments in Sect. 5 show it can further benefit from MLFM). In contrast to formal method, custom algorithms (e.g., [27] and [59]) may enjoy improved efficiency for specific properties but they generally lack the level of expressiveness of formal method-based approaches (including MLFM). Also designed to reduce verification time, the proactive approach (e.g., [35,36]) performs the verification in advance based on predicted events, which is parallel to, and can be integrated with, our approach.

There exist works that combine machine learning and formal method in other contexts, such as automated program verification (for synthesizing invariants used to verify the correctness of a program, e.g., [19,22,46,57]). In particular, Ezudheen et al. [19] develop learning-based algorithms for synthesizing invariants for programs that generate Horn-style proof constraints. Garg et al. [22] propose the ICE-learning framework for not only taking (counter-)examples but also handling implications. Ren et al. [46] propose a method based on selective samples to improve the efficiency of invariant synthesizing. Finally, Vizel et al. [57] study the relationship between SAT-based Model Checking (SAT-MC) and Machine Learning-based Invariant Synthesis (MLIS). Although the goals are very different (efficient verification vs. invariant synthesizing), our teacher-learner approach is similar to those existing works, with a key difference being that we additionally employ the sampling strategies from the active learning literature [50] to more effectively identify representative samples.

7   Conclusion

We have presented MLFM, a novel approach to security verification in NFV that could combine the rigor of formal methods with the efficiency of machine learning for faster identification of security violations. Specifically, we designed an iterative approach for the teacher (FM) to gradually provide more representative data samples, such that the learner (ML) could train an ML model using a small portion of the data; the ML model was then applied to the remaining data to prioritize the verification of likely violations. We implemented MLFM based on OpenStack/Tacker, and our experimental results showed significant performance improvements over baseline approaches.

Limitations and Future Work. First, we have limited our scope to NFV in this work, and a future direction is to apply MLFM to other large-scale virtual infrastructures (e.g., clouds and SDNs). Second, while MLFM only focuses on security verification, a natural next step is integrating MLFM with security enforcement mechanisms to turn faster violation identification into more responsive attack prevention. Third, MLFM is static in the sense that its verification is on-demand based on data snapshots, and one future direction is to support continuous security verification (monitoring) based on data streams. Finally, we will also investigate other ML-specific issues such as the possibility of using deep learning for offline pre-training (due to its complexity), and defence against potential adversarial attacks on the training process of MLFM.

Acknowledgements. We thank the anonymous reviewers for their valuable comments. This work was supported by the Natural Sciences and Engineering Research Council of Canada and Ericsson Canada under the Industrial Research Chair in SDN/NFV Security and the Canada Foundation for Innovation under JELF Project 38599.

Appendix

Table 1. Examples of NFV security properties [44]

Security properties	Sub-properties	Description	Standards
Physical resource isolation [32]	No VNFs co-residence	VNFs of a tenant should not be placed on the same server as VNFs of a non-trusted tenant	ISO [24], NIST800 [53], CCM [1], ETSI [13]
Virtual resource isolation [32]	No common ownership	Tenant-specific resources should belong to a unique tenant, unless permitted by a user-defined policy	CCM [1], ETSI [13], IETF-RFC7665, RFC-7498 [25]
Topology isolation [32]	Mapping unicity VLANs-VXLANs	VLANs and VXLANs should be mapped one-to-one on a given server	ISO [24], NIST800 [53], CCM [1], ETSI [13], IETF-RFC7665, RFC-7498 [25]
	Correct association Ports-Virtual Networks	VNFs should be attached to the virtual networks they are connected to through the right ports	
	Overlay tunnels isolation	In each VTEP end, VNFs are associated with their physical location (at L2) and to the VXLAN assigned to the networks they are attac- hed to at L1	
	Mappings unicity Virtual Networks Segments	Virtual networks and segments should be mapped one-to-one	
	Mappings unicity Ports-VLANs	Ports should be mapped to unique VLANs	
	Mappings unicity Ports-Segments	vPorts should be mapped to unique segments	
Policy and state correctness [51]	–	A policy can be dynamically changing. The changed policy should be reconfigured in VNF node as soon as possible	ETSI [3,13], IETF-R FC7665, RFC8459 [25]
Functionality of VNF and VNFFGs [20,60]	–	Check if VNFs and the composition (i.e., service chaining) of these functions work as intended	ETSI [3], IETF-RFC-7665, RFC8459 [25]
SFC ordering and sequencing as defined by the specification [21]	–	SFCs should maintain the order of VNFs with the correct traffic forw- arding behavior as defined by the specifications	ETSI [3,13], IETF-RFC7665, RFC8459 [25]

(continued)

Table 1. (*continued*)

Security properties	Sub-properties	Description	Standards
Topology consistency [32]	VNFFG configuration consistency between L1/L2	Consistency between the size of VNFFGs, the sequences of VNFs and the classifiers at L1 and their parallel implementation at L2	ISO [24], NIST800 [53], CCM [1], IETF-RFC-8459 [25], ETSI [3,13]
	Virtual links consistency	VNFs should be connected to the VLANs and VXLANs in L2 that corresponds to the virtual networks they are connected to in L1	
	VNF location consistency	Consistency between VNFs locations at L2 and L1	
	CPs-Ports consistency	Consistency between CPs defined at L1 and their created counterpa-rts; Ports in (L2)	

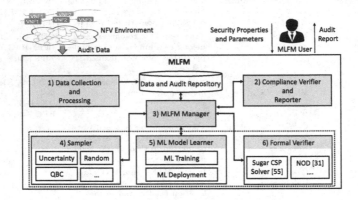

Fig. 11. The MLFM system architecture

References

1. Cloud Security Alliance. https://cloudsecurityalliance.org/research/working-groups/cloud-controls-matrix/. Accessed 11 Sept 2021
2. ETSI: Network Functions Virtualisation Architectural Framework. https://www.etsi.org/. Accessed 11 Sept 2021
3. Network Functions Virtualisation (NFV); NFV Security; Problem Statement. https://www.etsi.org/. Accessed 11 Sept 2021
4. Open Baton. http://openbaton.github.io/. Accessed 11 Sept 2021
5. Open Platform for NFV. https://www.opnfv.org/. Accessed 11 Sept 2021
6. Open Source MANO. https://osm.etsi.org/. Accessed 11 Sept 2021
7. OpenStack. http://www.openstack.org/. Accessed 11 Sept 2021
8. OpenStack Tacker. http://releases.openstack.org/teams/tacker.html. Accessed 11 Sept 2021
9. Sugar: a SAT-based Constraint Solver. http://cspsat.gitlab.io/sugar/. Accessed 8 Nov 2021
10. Verizon launches industry-leading large OpenStack NFV deployment. http://www.openstack.org/news/. Accessed 11 Sept 2021

11. Barakabitze, A.A., Ahmad, A., Mijumbi, R., Hines, A.: 5G network slicing using SDN and NFV: a survey of taxonomy, architectures and future challenges. Comput. Netw. **167**, 106984 (2020)
12. Ben-Ari, M.: Mathematical Logic for Computer Science. Springer, Heidelberg (2012). https://doi.org/10.1007/978-1-4471-4129-7
13. Bursell, M., et al.: Network Functions Virtualisation (NFV), NFV security, security and trust guidance, v. 1.1. 1. In: Technical Report, GS NFV-SEC 003. European Telecommunications Standards Institute (2014)
14. Buss, S., Nordström, J.: Proof complexity and sat solving. Handb. Satisfiabil. **336**, 233–350 (2021)
15. Chen, T., Guestrin, C.: Xgboost: a scalable tree boosting system. In: Proceedings of the 22nd ACM SIGKDD International Conference on Knowledge Discovery and Data Mining, pp. 785–794 (2016)
16. Chen, Z., Jiang, F., Cheng, Y., Gu, X., Liu, W., Peng, J.: XGBoost classifier for DDoS attack detection and analysis in SDN-based cloud. In: IEEE International Conference on Big Data and Smart Computing (BigComp), pp. 251–256 (2018)
17. Danka, T., Horvath, P.: modAL: a modular active learning framework for Python. arXiv preprint arXiv:1805.00979 (2018)
18. Eén, N., Sörensson, N.: An extensible SAT-solver. In: Giunchiglia, E., Tacchella, A. (eds.) SAT 2003. LNCS, vol. 2919, pp. 502–518. Springer, Heidelberg (2004). https://doi.org/10.1007/978-3-540-24605-3_37
19. Ezudheen, P., Neider, D., D'Souza, D., Garg, P., Madhusudan, P.: Horn-ice learning for synthesizing invariants and contracts. In: Proceedings of the ACM on Programming Languages, vol. 2(OOPSLA), pp. 1–25 (2018)
20. Fayazbakhsh, S.K., Reiter, M.K., Sekar, V.: Verifiable network function outsourcing: requirements, challenges, and roadmap. In: Proceedings of the 2013 Workshop on Hot Topics in Middleboxes and Network Function Virtualization, pp. 25–30 (2013)
21. Flittner, M., Scheuermann, J.M., Bauer, R.: Chainguard: controller-independent verification of service function chaining in cloud computing. In: IEEE Conference on Network Function Virtualization and Software Defined Networks, pp. 1–7 (2017)
22. Garg, P., Löding, C., Madhusudan, P., Neider, D.: ICE: a robust framework for learning invariants. In: Biere, A., Bloem, R. (eds.) CAV 2014. LNCS, vol. 8559, pp. 69–87. Springer, Cham (2014). https://doi.org/10.1007/978-3-319-08867-9_5
23. Gong, W., Zhou, X.: A survey of sat solver. In: Proceedings of AIP Conference, vol. 1836, p. 020059. AIP Publishing LLC (2017)
24. IEC ISO Std: ISO 27017. Information technology-Security techniques (DRAFT) (2012)
25. IETF, SFC: Internet Engineering Task, SFC Active WG Working Group Documents (2020). https://www.redhat.com/en/blog/2018-year-open-source-networking-csps
26. Jayaraman, K., Bjørner, N., Outhred, G., Kaufman, C.: Automated analysis and debugging of network connectivity policies. Micros. Res., 1–11 (2014)
27. Kazemian, P., Chang, M., Zeng, H., Varghese, G., McKeown, N., Whyte, S.: Real time network policy checking using header space analysis. In: 10th {USENIX} Symposium on Networked Systems Design and Implementation (NSDI 2013), pp. 99–111 (2013)
28. Kotulski, Z., et al.: Towards constructive approach to end-to-end slice isolation in 5G networks. EURASIP J. Inf. Secur. **2018**(1), 1–23 (2018). https://doi.org/10.1186/s13635-018-0072-0

29. Kramer, O.: Scikit-learn. In: Machine Learning for Evolution Strategies. SBD, vol. 20, pp. 45–53. Springer, Cham (2016). https://doi.org/10.1007/978-3-319-33383-0_5

30. Thirunavukkarasu, S.L., et al.: Modeling NFV deployment to identify the cross-level inconsistency vulnerabilities. In: IEEE CloudCom (2019)

31. Lopes, N.P., Bjørner, N., Godefroid, P., Jayaraman, K., Varghese, G.: Checking beliefs in dynamic networks. In: 12th {USENIX} Symposium on Networked Systems Design and Implementation (NSDI 2015), pp. 499–512 (2015)

32. Madi, T., et al.: ISOTOP: auditing virtual networks isolation across cloud layers in OpenStack. ACM Trans. Priv. Secur. (TOPS) **22**(1), 1–35 (2018)

33. Madi, T., Majumdar, S., Wang, Y., Jarraya, Y., Pourzandi, M., Wang, L.: Auditing security compliance of the virtualized infrastructure in the cloud: application to OpenStack. In: Proceedings of the Sixth ACM Conference on Data and Application Security and Privacy, pp. 195–206 (2016)

34. Maji, P., Mullins, R.: On the reduction of computational complexity of deep convolutional neural networks. Entropy **20**(4), 305 (2018)

35. Majumdar, S., et al.: Proactive verification of security compliance for clouds through pre-computation: application to openstack. In: Askoxylakis, I., Ioannidis, S., Katsikas, S., Meadows, C. (eds.) ESORICS 2016. LNCS, vol. 9878, pp. 47–66. Springer, Cham (2016). https://doi.org/10.1007/978-3-319-45744-4_3

36. Majumdar, S., et al.: LeaPS: learning-based proactive security auditing for clouds. In: Foley, S.N., Gollmann, D., Snekkenes, E. (eds.) ESORICS 2017. LNCS, vol. 10493, pp. 265–285. Springer, Cham (2017). https://doi.org/10.1007/978-3-319-66399-9_15

37. Majumdar, S., et al.: Security compliance auditing of identity and access management in the cloud: application to OpenStack. In: IEEE 7th International Conference on Cloud Computing Technology and Science, pp. 58–65 (2015)

38. Majumdar, S., et al.: User-level runtime security auditing for the cloud. IEEE Trans. Inf. Forensics Secur. **13**(5), 1185–1199 (2017)

39. Marchetto, G., Sisto, R., Yusupov, J., Ksentini, A.: Virtual network embedding with formal reachability assurance. In: 14th International Conference on Network and Service Management, pp. 368–372 (2018)

40. Mohamed, A.E.: Comparative study of four supervised machine learning techniques for classification. Inf. J. Appl. Sci. Technol. **7**(2), 1–15 (2017)

41. Monard, M.C., Batista, G.E.: Learnng with skewed class distrihutions. Adv. Logic Artif. Intell. Robotics: LAPTEC **85**(2002), 173 (2002)

42. Neutatz, F., Mahdavi, M., Abedjan, Z.: Ed2: a case for active learning in error detection. In: Proceedings of the 28th ACM International Conference on Information and Knowledge Management, pp. 2249–2252 (2019)

43. OpenStack Training Labs: OpenStack Training Labs. https://wiki.openstack.org/wiki/Documentation/training-labs

44. Oqaily, A., et al.: NFVGuard: verifying the security of multilevel network functions virtualization (NFV) stack. In: 2020 IEEE International Conference on Cloud Computing Technology and Science, pp. 33–40. IEEE (2020)

45. Quinn, P., Nadeau, T.: Rfc 7948, problem statement for service function chaining. Internet Engineering Task Force (IETF), ed (2015)

46. Ren, S., Zhang, X.: Synthesizing conjunctive and disjunctive linear invariants by K-means++ and SVM. Int. Arab J. Inf. Technol. **17**(6), 847–856 (2020)

47. Sani, H.M., Lei, C., Neagu, D.: Computational complexity analysis of decision tree algorithms. In: Bramer, M., Petridis, M. (eds.) SGAI 2018. LNCS (LNAI), vol. 11311, pp. 191–197. Springer, Cham (2018). https://doi.org/10.1007/978-3-030-04191-5_17

48. Sassi, I., Anter, S., Bekkhoucha, A.: A graph-based big data optimization approach using hidden markov model and constraint satisfaction problem. J. Big Data **8**(1), 1–29 (2021)

49. Schear, N., Cable II, P.T., Moyer, T.M., Richard, B., Rudd, R.: Bootstrapping and maintaining trust in the cloud. In: Proceedings of the 32Nd Annual Conference on Computer Security Applications, pp. 65–77 (2016)

50. Settles, B.: Active learning literature survey (2009)

51. Shin, M.K., Choi, Y., Kwak, H.H., Pack, S., Kang, M., Choi, J.Y.: Verification for NFV-enabled network services. In: ICTC (2015)

52. Souri, A., Navimipour, N.J., Rahmani, A.M.: Formal verification approaches and standards in the cloud computing: a comprehensive and systematic review. Comput. Stand. Interfaces **58**, 1–22 (2018)

53. SP, NIST: 800–53. Recommended security controls for federal information systems, pp. 800–53 (2003)

54. Spinoso, S., Virgilio, M., John, W., Manzalini, A., Marchetto, G., Sisto, R.: Formal verification of virtual network function graphs in an SP-devops context. In: Dustdar, S., Leymann, F., Villari, M. (eds.) ESOCC 2015. LNCS, vol. 9306, pp. 253–262. Springer, Cham (2015). https://doi.org/10.1007/978-3-319-24072-5_18

55. Tamura, N., Banbara, M.: Sugar: a CSP to SAT translator based on order encoding. In: Proceedings of the Second International CSP Solver Competition (2008)

56. Tschaen, B., Zhang, Y., Benson, T., Banerjee, S., Lee, J., Kang, J.M.: Sfc-checker: checking the correct forwarding behavior of service function chaining. In: IEEE Conference on Network Function Virtualization and Software Defined Networks (NFV-SDN), pp. 134–140 (2016)

57. Vizel, Y., Gurfinkel, A., Shoham, S., Malik, S.: IC3 - flipping the E in ICE. In: Bouajjani, A., Monniaux, D. (eds.) VMCAI 2017. LNCS, vol. 10145, pp. 521–538. Springer, Cham (2017). https://doi.org/10.1007/978-3-319-52234-0_28

58. Wang, Y., Li, Z., Xie, G., Salamatian, K.: Enabling automatic composition and verification of service function chain. In: IEEE/ACM 25th International Symposium on Quality of Service (IWQoS), pp. 1–5 (2017)

59. Wang, Y., et al.: TenantGuard: scalable runtime verification of cloud-wide VM-level network isolation. In: The Network and Distributed System Security Symposium (2017)

60. Zhang, X., Li, Q., Wu, J., Yang, J.: Generic and agile service function chain verification on cloud. In: IEEE/ACM 25th International Symposium on Quality of Service, pp. 1–10 (2017)

61. Zhang, Y., Wu, W., Banerjee, S., Kang, J.M., Sanchez, M.A.: Sla-verifier: stateful and quantitative verification for service chaining. In: IEEE INFOCOM 2017-IEEE Conference on Computer Communications, pp. 1–9 (2017)

Cyber-Physical Systems Security

Perspectives from a Comprehensive Evaluation of Reconstruction-based Anomaly Detection in Industrial Control Systems

Clement Fung[(⊠)], Shreya Srinarasi, Keane Lucas, Hay Bryan Phee, and Lujo Bauer

Carnegie Mellon University, Pittsburgh, USA
{clementf,ssrinara,kjlucas,hphee,lbauer}@andrew.cmu.edu

Abstract. Industrial control systems (ICS) provide critical functions to society and are enticing attack targets. Machine learning (ML) models—in particular, reconstruction-based ML models—are commonly used to identify attacks during ICS operation. However, the variety of ML model architectures, datasets, metrics, and techniques used in prior work makes broad comparisons and identifying optimal solutions difficult. To assist ICS security practitioners in choosing and configuring the most effective reconstruction-based anomaly detector for their ICS environment, this paper: (1) comprehensively evaluates previously proposed reconstruction-based ICS anomaly-detection approaches, and (2) shows that commonly used metrics for evaluating ML algorithms, like the point-F1 score, are inadequate for evaluating anomaly detection systems for practical use. Among our findings is that the performance of anomaly-detection systems is not closely tied to the choice of ML model architecture or hyperparameters, and that the models proposed in prior work are often larger than necessary. We also show that evaluating ICS anomaly detection over temporal ranges, e.g., with the range-F1 metric, better describes ICS anomaly-detection performance than the commonly used point-F1 metric. These so-called range-based metrics measure objectives more specific to ICS environments, such as reducing false alarms or reducing detection latency. We further show that using range-based metrics to evaluate candidate anomaly detectors leads to different conclusions about what anomaly-detection strategies are optimal.

1 Introduction

Industrial control systems (ICS) govern vital infrastructures such as power grids, water treatment plants, and transportation networks. These systems collect and monitor real-time information from an industrial process and use a programmed model to govern its operation [11]. As ICS become further interconnected, particularly with the public Internet, the attack risk increases. An adversary could either directly or over the network interfere with an ICS (e.g., by injecting false

© The Author(s), under exclusive license to Springer Nature Switzerland AG 2022
V. Atluri et al. (Eds.): ESORICS 2022, LNCS 13556, pp. 493–513, 2022.
https://doi.org/10.1007/978-3-031-17143-7_24

data or commands [36]) and cause the ICS to modify the physical process, potentially causing damage or risking human life [31]. Given the potential harms of attacks on ICS, detecting and preventing them in a timely manner is critical.

In response, researchers have proposed using machine learning (ML) to detect attacks; among ML-based techniques, reconstruction-based ML models have been shown to be particularly promising [18,32,37]. Reconstruction-based ML involves training an ML model to represent the expected, benign behavior of an ICS. After a model is trained, it is used to assess the observed real-time behavior of an ICS; any behaviors that are not consistent with the trained model are called out to operators as potentially dangerous anomalies.

To use these anomaly-detection techniques, ICS security practitioners must: (1) select the ML model architecture (e.g., convolutional neural networks) (2) select hyperparameters for the model (e.g., the size and number of hidden layers in the model) (3) collect a sufficient volume of benign ICS operational data (4) train an ML model to reconstruct system states, and (5) tune detection hyperparameters (the threshold for an anomaly to be declared) to turn system-state reconstructions into attack predictions in a live setting. Despite the variety of work in reconstruction-based ICS anomaly detection, there is no consensus on what solutions are best. Proposed approaches use different ML model architectures (e.g., autoencoders [7,32], CNNs [18,19], LSTMs [8,37]), use different datasets [4,10,33], and employ different data pre-processing and training techniques. Thus, when one approach is reported to outperform another, it is not clear what characteristics are responsible for the improved performance.

In this work, we perform a comprehensive, empirical evaluation of techniques across the most common datasets used in reconstruction-based ICS anomaly detection. We find that most ML model architectures, regardless of the choice of model hyperparameters, perform about equally well. Additionally and to our surprise, we find that many proposed models are larger (i.e., contain more parameters) than necessary and that far smaller models provide similar detection performance. Furthermore, we identify training and data pre-processing techniques that strongly affect the results of reconstruction-based ICS anomaly detection, but are not used consistently across prior work.

Another important consideration when designing ICS anomaly-detection systems is the metric used to tune and evaluate detection strategies. Typically, prior work equally penalizes false alarms and missed attacks on a per-timestep basis by evaluating with the point-F1 score [30]. However, as we describe in Sect. 5.1, since ICS attacks take place over a sequence of timesteps [4,10], and because timely detection of attacks is important [14], ICS anomaly detection is better evaluated over temporal ranges, rather than on each timestep independently. Unlike the point-F1, which scores on individual timesteps, *range-based* metrics score detection performance on temporal ranges and can express trade-offs between increased detection rates, reduced false-alarm rates, and lowered detection latency [34].

In this paper, we demonstrate the impact of using range-based metrics for ICS anomaly detection, building on research from other anomaly-detection domains [14,21,34]. We show empirically that using these metrics to tune and evaluate ICS anomaly-detection models gives a better understanding of what models are optimal. Furthermore, we propose the use of specific ICS objectives that describe anomaly-detection performance in terms relevant to ICS operations. Given the wide variety of potential ICS anomaly-detection environments, we opt for general objectives: examples include a low false-alarm rate, a high attack-detection rate, and low-latency attack detection.

In summary, our work answers two research questions. **RQ1**: across proposed techniques for reconstruction-based ICS anomaly detection, what model architectures, model hyperparameters, and pre-processing techniques are optimal? **RQ2**: can using range-based metrics lead to a different understanding of what models are most effective for reconstruction-based ICS anomaly detection? In answering these questions, we make the following contributions:

- We perform a comprehensive comparison across the ML model architectures and datasets used in reconstruction-based ICS anomaly detection and find that the choice of model hyperparameters has little effect on detection performance; prior work often proposes model hyperparameters that are far larger than necessary.
- We implement and make publicly available[1] a comprehensive test framework that allows tuning of models and comparing the impact of factors such as datasets, metrics, and hyperparameters. We instantiate the framework with recently proposed reconstruction-based ML model architectures.
- We use range-based metrics to tune and evaluate reconstruction-based ICS anomaly detectors. We provide examples of range-based metrics that support various ICS objectives and demonstrate that models tuned with these range-based metrics outperform their point-F1-tuned counterparts on the desired ICS objectives.
- We find that using range-based metrics for optimizing anomaly-detection systems provides a different understanding of what models are best compared to using the point-F1 metric.

2   Background and Related Work

In this section, we provide background on ICS and attacks and defenses for them (Sect. 2.1). We also introduce the various models (Sect. 2.2), metrics (Sect. 2.3), and datasets (Sect. 2.4) used in prior work. We lastly categorize prior work in reconstruction-based ICS anomaly detection along these dimensions (Sect. 2.5).

2.1   Industrial Control Systems: Threats and Defenses

An ICS governs the operation of a physical, safety-critical process. Figure 1 shows the structure and components of an ICS, and how they are separated in the hierarchical Purdue model of ICS [16]. The model divides an ICS into levels from

---

[1] https://github.com/pwwl/ics-anomaly-detection.

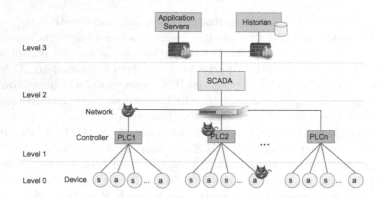

Fig. 1. An overview of a typical ICS/SCADA hierarchical layered architecture with examples of compromised endpoints and communication channels

the physical process (Level 0, the strictest level of access) to higher-level applications (Level 3, less strict). Sensors and actuators (Level 0) allow feedback and input with the physical process. Programmable logic controllers (PLCs, Level 1) directly interface with sensors and actuators to automate the ICS process. Supervisory control and data acquisition (SCADA, Level 2) governs multiple PLCs by collecting data and providing an interface to operators for control and analysis of the physical process [31].

ICS networks were previously not monitored for security purposes. Instead, ICS were typically isolated from external threats by a firewall between Levels 2 and 3, preventing compromised, higher-level devices from manipulating the physical process [31]. With the exposure of ICS environments to the Internet and third parties [11], the potential of compromise has increased significantly: when an attacker compromises parts of an ICS in Levels 0 through 2, they can manipulate the data being sent over the network to cause process degradation or even failure. This strategy was used in the BlackEnergy (2015) and Industroyer (2016) attacks on the Ukrainian power grid [20], which caused over 200,000 people to lose electric power for several hours; and in the Triton malware attack (2017) [6], which caused a chemical processing plant to shut down. For this reason, it is critical to monitor ICS networks for signs of potential compromise and misuse.

In this work, we focus on techniques that train deep-learning ML models to perform system reconstructions and identify as potentially anomalous any system states for which the reconstruction error is high [18,32,37]. We focus on deep-learning models, as they have been shown to outperform other classical methods in anomaly detection [25]. For these techniques, three ML model architectures have risen to prominence: autoencoders (AEs), convolutional neural networks (CNNs), and long-short-term-memory (LSTM) networks. We overview these model architectures in Sect. 2.2.

Table 1. The ICS datasets most commonly used for training and evaluating reconstruction-based anomaly-detection models

Name	# of Points in Benign Dataset	# of Points in Attack Dataset		# of Features	# of Attacks
BATADAL	48,106	10,081	(16% attack)	43	7
WADI	1,048,571	172,801	(6% attack)	103	15
SWaT	496,800	449,919	(12% attack)	51	36

2.2   ML Model Architectures for ICS Anomaly Detection

In this section, we provide an overview of ML model architectures commonly used in ICS anomaly-detection systems. Autoencoders (AEs) are composed of a sequence of stacked, fully connected layers that compress inputs into a smaller latent representation [12]; an AE is trained to reconstruct an input system state. Convolutional neural networks (CNNs) [5] and long-short-term-memory units (LSTMs) [13] instead use time-based information to predict system states: based on a fixed-time-length input, CNNs and LSTMs predict the next expected system state. CNNs use 1-D convolutional kernels to process time, whereas LSTMs use a custom unit that maintains separate weighted connections that pass information far along the time axis (long-term memory) and to immediate recent states (short-term memory).

2.3   Traditional Anomaly Detection Metrics

Anomalies are rare and accuracy scores may misrepresent the anomaly detection performance. Much of prior work uses the point-F1 score—the harmonic mean of the precision and recall—to characterize anomaly-detection performance:

$$point\text{-}F1 = \frac{2 * prec * rec}{prec + rec} \qquad prec = \frac{TP}{TP + FP} \qquad rec = \frac{TP}{TP + FN}$$

TP (true positives) is the number of timesteps during which an attack was correctly detected, FP (false positives) is the number of timesteps where an attack was falsely reported, and FN (false negatives) is the number of timesteps where an attack is undetected. In Sect. 5, we show the shortcomings of using the point-F1 score to tune and evaluate anomaly detectors and instead propose the use of range-based metrics.

2.4   Publicly Available ICS Datasets

In lieu of direct access to a real ICS, a variety of ICS datasets have been made publicly available for research. Each dataset is typically partitioned into two parts: a *benign dataset* and *attack dataset*. The benign dataset contains a sequence of system states during a benign execution of ICS operations. The attack dataset contains a sequence of system states during an execution that models an attacker who gains access to the ICS and manipulates a subset of sensor and actuator values in a false-data-injection attack [10]. These datasets cover a variety of domains, including water distribution [4,33], water treatment [10], gas pipelines [24], and power generation [3,28].

In our analysis, we focus on the most commonly used datasets: BATADAL [33] (water distribution), SWaT [10] (water treatment), and WADI [4] (water distribution). Table 1 shows the details of each dataset. Since the originally released SWaT (2015) and WADI (2017) datasets, additional data from the same system has been released. However, we opt to use the original versions of both datasets to match what is used in the majority of prior work.

2.5   Prior Work in ICS Anomaly Detection

In this section, we overview the prior work in ICS anomaly detection, across the most commonly used ICS datasets identified in Sect. 2.4. Table 2 shows, for each prior work, the details of the ML model architecture, suggested optimal model hyperparameters, and metrics used for tuning and evaluation.

We identify two gaps across the state of the art. First, although some prior work compares ML model architectures [1,19,37], none covers the full selection of model architectures, datasets, and pre-processing techniques, making it is unclear what approaches are optimal across all settings.

Second, models are commonly tuned with the point-F1 (or not tuned at all), which ignores the temporal aspect of time-series detection, and does not balance the trade-offs between precision, recall, and latency in anomaly detection. Across this prior work, only one tunes with a range-based metric [18]; although some prior work considers ranges in evaluation, most only remark on the number of attacks detected or missed and only four evaluate with a range-based metric [8, 18,23,27]. In Sect. 5, we show that tuning with range-based metrics results in diffcrent selections of optimal hyperparameters and different conclusions about which models perform better than others.

3   Reconstruction-based ICS Anomaly Detection Process

An anomaly detector reconstructs ICS system states to determine if an anomaly is occurring. Figure 2a outlines this process.[2] First, system states X over the previous h timesteps are collected from observed network traffic, up to the current timestep t. Second, the trained ML model is provided the system state sequence $(X_{t-h}, X_{t-h+1}, \ldots, X_t)$ and predicts the next system state X'_{t+1}. Third, the predicted and observed states are compared, and the reconstruction error e_t is computed through the mean-squared-error (MSE): $e_t = \|X'_t - X_t\|^2$. Lastly, the prediction y'_t is calculated over a sequence of reconstruction errors $(e_0, e_1, \ldots, e_t)$: $y'_t = 1$ when the reconstruction error exceeds

---

[2] Autoencoders are a special case since they do not consider a sequence of states ($h = 0$), and instead reconstruct the current state X'_t.

Table 2. ML model architectures, datasets, and metrics from prior ICS anomaly-detection work. Range-based metrics are shown in **bold**. (CM = confusion matrix; TPR/FPR = true/false positive rate; TNR = true negative rate; Coverage % = percentage of detection overlap; Norm-TPR = normalized true positive rate.)

Model Details	Datasets B	S	W	Tuning Metric	Evaluation Metric(s)	Source
AE: 3-layers	•	•	•	FPR	Precision, Recall, Point-F1	[19]
AE: 4-layers		•		None	Precision, Recall, Point-F1, Numenta	[27]
AE: 5-layers	•			Point-F1	Precision, Recall, Point-F1	[32]
AE: 5-layers	•		•	None	Precision, Recall, Accuracy, Point-F1	[7]
CNN: 8-layers, 32 filters		•		**Range-F1**	**Range-F1**	[18]
CNN: 8-layers, 32 filters	•	•	•	FPR	Precision, Recall, Point-F1	[19]
LSTM: 2-layers, 256 units		•	•	None	TPR, **Norm-TPR** FPR, Atk TP	[8]
LSTM: 3-layers, 100 units	•			Point-F1	Precision, Recall, Point-F1	[15]
LSTM: 3-layers, 100 units	•			None	**Atk TP, Atk FP**	[9]
LSTM: 4-layers, 64 units	•			None	**Atk TP, Atk FP**	[17]
LSTM: 4-layers, 512 units	•			None	CM, Point-F1, **Atk TP**	[26]
LSTM: 4-layers, 512 units	•			Point-F1	Point-F1	[37]
1-class SVM	•			Point-F1	Point-F1	[15]
DNN: 3-layer	•			None	CM, TPR, TNR	[2]
Custom wide and deep CNN		•	•	None	Precision, Recall, Point-F1, **Atk TP**	[1]
GAN		•	•	Point-F1	Precision, Recall, Point-F1	[22]
Bayesian Network		•		None	**Atk FP, Atk TP, FP length, Coverage %**	[23]

a threshold τ for w consecutive timesteps: $y'_t = \prod_{i=t}^{t+w} \mathbb{I}(e_i > \tau)$. The threshold τ is determined using the distribution of benign-validation errors. For example, τ can be set to the distribution's 99.5-th percentile value. Both τ and the window length w are *detection hyperparameters*: they are independent of the underlying trained ML model and convert the system state reconstruction to attack predictions. We show that detection hyperparameter tuning is closely affected by the choice of metric, and optimal models often change when different metrics are used.

End-to-end, to optimize reconstruction-based anomaly detection (1) we train a ML model to minimize MSE and (2) we tune its detection hyperparameters to maximize its performance according to a chosen metric. Figure 2b shows the steps and datasets used in optimization. Most prior work focuses on selecting the best model architecture and best model hyperparameters (step 1), but in this work we show that optimization across *both* steps plays a substantial role in the effectiveness of reconstruction-based ICS anomaly detection.

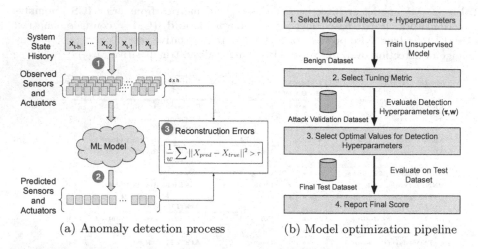

(a) Anomaly detection process   (b) Model optimization pipeline

Fig. 2. The anomaly-detection process is shown on the left: a sequence of system states is reconstructed by an ML model, and high reconstruction errors are used to identify anomalies. The optimization pipeline for the anomaly-detection process is shown on the right, with each optimization step and its relevant datasets

We independently evaluate both steps. In Sect. 4, we keep the choice of tuning metric (point-F1) constant and compare the performance across various ML model architectures and hyperparameters from prior work, In Sect. 5, we keep the underlying trained model constant and compare how the choice of tuning metric affects detection hyperparameter tuning. Lastly, in Sect. 5.4, we show how the choice of tuning metric affects both the optimal model hyperparameters and detection hyperparameters in an end-to-end optimization.

4   Comparing ML Model Architectures and Datasets for ICS Anomaly Detection

In this section, we report on a comprehensive comparison of model architectures and model hyperparameter values, evaluating across techniques proposed in prior work. For each model hyperparameter setting, we optimize the anomaly-detection system through the steps shown in Fig. 2b. We explain our experimental setup in Sect. 4.1 and present our findings in Sect. 4.2.

4.1   Experiment Setup

Data Pre-processing. Before training and evaluating each model, each feature is normalized; the scaling transformation is saved and applied to the attack dataset before evaluating the model. 70% of the training dataset is randomly chosen for training the ML model. The other 30%, referred to as the *benign* *validation dataset*, is used to give an unbiased score during training; we use the benign-validation loss as an indicator for early stopping to prevent overfitting.

In our experiments, we identify techniques that impact the quality and reproducibility of results but were used inconsistently in prior work. Techniques such as: data pre-processing through feature selection, benign data shuffling, attack cleaning, and early stopping are necessary when comparing across solutions, as they improve the quality and consistency of anomaly-detection results. We present descriptions of these techniques and their impacts in Appendix A.

Model Hyperparameter Tuning. We perform a hyperparameter search for 3 ML model architectures: autoencoders, CNNs, and LSTMs. For autoencoders, we vary the number of hidden layers in the encoder/decoder from 1 to 5 (by 1) and the compression factor from 1.5 to 4.0 (by 0.5). For CNNs, we vary the number of layers from 1 to 5 (by 1), and vary the number of units per layer from 4 to 256 (by a factor of 2). The kernel size is fixed at 3 and we use history lengths of 50, 100, or 200 timesteps. For LSTMs, we vary the number of layers from 1 to 4 (by 1), the number of units per layer from 4 to 128 (by a factor of 2), and use history lengths of 50 or 100 timesteps. Each model was implemented in Tensorflow 1.14.0 using the `tf.keras` API and trained with the Adam optimizer using its default parameters: $\{lr = 0.001, \beta_1 = 0.9, \beta_2 = 0.999\}$. A batch size of 512 samples was used during training; each model was trained for up to 100 epochs. We apply early stopping while training through the `tf.keras.callbacks.EarlyStopping` callback class, with `patience=3` (which terminates training if validation loss does not improve over 3 consecutive epochs). Across our trained models, we found that early stopping was always applied within the first 20 epochs: a finding that is consistent with prior work [15].

Detection Hyperparameter Tuning. After the model is trained, we determine the optimal detection hyperparameters using 30% of the attack dataset, referred to as the *attack validation* dataset. To simulate a setting with unseen attacks, when dividing the attack dataset into validation and testing portions, we divide the dataset into two continuous sequences.[3] To find optimal detection hyperparameter values, we perform a parameter search, based on a chosen *tuning metric*, over the following ranges: τ-percentile $\in [0.95, 0.99995]$, $w \in [1, 100]$. We report the final performance on the remaining 70% of the attack dataset for a chosen *evaluation metric*. We use the point-F1 score as both the tuning metric and evaluation metric, which Table 2 shows is commonly used in prior work.

---

[3] We use the first 30% of the SWaT and WADI test datasets as their corresponding attack validation datasets. We use the final 30% of the BATADAL test dataset as its corresponding attack validation dataset, since the first 30% of the BATADAL test dataset does not contain any attacks.

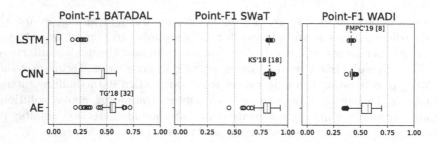

Fig. 3. The final point-F1 scores of each model when trained and tuned on three experimental ICS datasets. For each dataset, a model hyperparameter setting from prior work is included for comparison. When using the point-F1, the performance of AEs vary greatly, and most LSTM and CNN configurations perform similary

4.2 Optimization Results

Figure 3 shows the final point-F1 scores for each model hyperparameter setting, for each ML model architecture and dataset. We perform a full optimization three times over different random seeds for CNNs and LSTMs. For autoencoders, we observed a higher variance in the resulting point-F1 scores and thus repeat this process five times. Furthermore, we train three selected models from prior work with the same methodology. We include a 5-layer autoencoder [32], an 8-layer, 32-unit CNN with a history of 200 [18], and a 2-layer, 256-unit LSTM with a history of 50 [8]. Figure 3 includes the point-F1 scores for these three models.

We find that larger models (CNNs and LSTMs) performed poorly on the BATADAL dataset. We attribute the poor performance to the relatively small size of the BATADAL dataset (only ~48,000 datapoints, compared to ~500,000 in SWaT and ~1,000,000 in WADI); in prior work, only one study trains a CNN or LSTM on BATADAL [19]. In Sect. 5.4, we find that using a range-based evaluation metric shows CNNs and LSTMs for BATADAL in a different light, providing another example where the point-F1 may be misleading. For the SWaT and WADI datasets, we find that almost all model hyperparameter settings provide similarly strong performance: a 1-layer, 4-unit CNN or LSTM produces a similar point-F1 score to CNNs and LSTMs with more layers and units, including the optimal models from prior work [8,18,32].

Finding 1a: Substantially smaller models can achieve similar point-F1 scores as the suggested model sizes from prior work.

Prior work noted that the performance of trained models differed between runs [18], even under the same model hyperparameter settings. We found that when early stopping and benign data shuffling are used, the results for CNNs and LSTMs are more consistent: across random seeds, the final point-F1 scores always differ by less than 0.05 (and less than 0.01 for a vast majority of cases). More experimental results on the benefits of early stopping and dataset shuffling

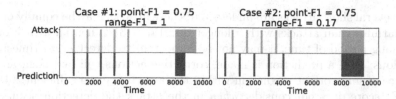

Fig. 4. Two detection examples: in each case, the x-axis represents time and the y-axis shows attacks (top, red) and attack predictions (bottom, grey). In the example on the left (case 1), all attacks are detected with no false positives, while in the example on the right (case 2) only one attack is detected, with five false positives; yet, the point-F1 scores are the same (Color figure online)

are provided in Appendix A. There is a higher variance across autoencoder hyperparameters, with some models achieving far higher scores than others. This is likely because the autoencoder is trained to reconstruct independent timesteps and does not consider temporal effects, rendering the performance of autoencoders unstable.

In conclusion, although prior work performs model hyperparameter searches and claims to find the optimal models for ICS anomaly detection, our experiments show that equivalent results can be achieved over a range of ML model architectures and hyperparameters when using the point-F1 score. In Sect. 5.3, we show that tuning models with range-based metrics can produce outcomes that more meaningfully address ICS anomaly-detection objectives.

Finding 1b: Although prior work focuses on optimizing the choice of ML model architecture and hyperparameters, equivalent performance can be achieved by several ML model architectures and over a wide range of model hyperparameters.

---

5 Tuning and Evaluating with Range-based Metrics

In this section, we first describe, in Sect. 5.1, the shortcomings of point-F1, which is commonly used by prior work in ICS anomaly detection. We introduce range-based metrics in Sect. 5.2. In Sect. 5.3, we show how range-based metrics affect detection hyperparameter tuning and in Sect. 5.4 we show how they affect what ML model architectures and hyperparameters are optimal.

5.1 Issues with the Point-F1 Score

ICS detection performance is poorly captured by the point-F1 for several reasons. (1) The point-F1 score weighs false positives and false negatives equally, whereas the cost of each may not be equal for a given ICS. (2) The point-F1 score places more importance on longer attacks [14]. A high point-F1 score can be achieved even if several short attacks are undetected; these attacks may be equally or even more harmful than attacks with a longer duration. (3) When an attack occurs over a long period of time, it may not be important to detect *every* timestep as anomalous; once a prediction is made, corrective actions will be taken, and the existence of *any* correct prediction within the attack may be sufficient. (4) The point-F1 score does not consider *when* in the attack the detection occurs [21]. In reality, if an attack is only detected as it ends, harm may already have been caused to the ICS, rendering the detection unhelpful.

We illustrate some of these deficiencies of point-F1 using two examples of detection performance in Fig. 4. The true attack sequence is shown in red: six attacks of varying length are executed in sequence. In case 1 (left), the first five attacks are all detected perfectly, and approximately half of the last attack is detected. In case 2 (right), the first five attacks are completely missed, 5 false alarms occur, and the last attack is detected perfectly. When using the point-F1 score, the two examples misleadingly result in equal detection success: the point-F1 for both is 0.75. For many practical applications, however, case 1 shows a detection system that works well, and case 2 a detection system that works poorly. To address the shortcomings of point-F1, prior work proposes metrics better suited to time-series detection tasks [14,21,34]. We define these metrics in Sect. 5.2 and evaluate their implications in Sects. 5.3–5.4.

Observation 2a: The point-F1 score gives a misleading sense of performance for many time-series-based detection tasks.

5.2 Range-based Performance Metrics

In this section, we provide examples of range-based metrics that could be used for tuning and evaluating anomaly-detection performance. In Sects. 5.3–5.4, we show the effect of these metrics on our understanding of what models are best. We describe two types of range-based metrics: (1) range-$F\beta$ metrics, which we define based on a prior framework for range-based metrics [34] and (2) the Numenta anomaly score [21], a metric from prior work.

Defining the Range-based Setting. Given sequences of binary labels ($y_t \in \{0,1\}$) and predicted labels ($y_t' \in \{0,1\}$), we convert these sequences to ranges. Let ($y_0, y_1, \ldots, y_t$) be represented as $R = \{R_0, R_1, \ldots, R_k\}$, where each range R_i represents a continuous sequence of positive ($y_t = 1$) labels. We express the predictions ($y_0', y_1', \ldots, y_t'$) in the same way to produce $R' = \{R_0', R_1', \ldots, R_m'\}$. If no predictions or anomalies exist ($\forall t : y_t = 0$), then $R = \emptyset$.

Range-F1 and Range-F β Scores. Prior work has defined a general range-based metric framework that combines existence rewards (whether any intersection exists) and overlap rewards (the size of the intersection) when scoring a time-series prediction [34]. When demonstrating the impact of range-based metrics on the understanding of ICS anomaly detection, we assume that any alarm raised by the anomaly-detection system leads to investigation, so we only consider existence rewards and leave exploring overlap rewards to future work. For our existence reward, we count any overlap between a true attack R_i and the entire predicted range R' as a true detection. Using this notion, the range-based recall and precision are calculated as follows:

$$IsTP(R_i) = \mathbb{I}[|R_i \cap R'| \geq 1] \qquad R\text{-}rec = \frac{\sum_i IsTP(R_i)}{|R|}$$

$$IsFP(R_i') = \mathbb{I}[|R \cap R_i'| == 0] \qquad R\text{-}prec = \frac{\sum_i IsTP(R_i)}{\sum_i^k IsTP(R_i) + \sum_i^m IsFP(R_i')}$$

The Fβ score is a generalized version of the F1 score that scores precision with a relative weight of β. $\beta > 1$ indicates that precision is more important, whereas $\beta < 1$ indicates that recall is more important. We define the range-F1 and range-Fβ score in the same fashion as the point-F1:

$$R\text{-}F1 = \frac{2 * R\text{-}prec * R\text{-}rec}{R\text{-}prec + R\text{-}rec} \qquad R\text{-}F\beta = \frac{(1 + \beta^2) * R\text{-}prec * R\text{-}rec}{(\beta^2 * R\text{-}prec) + R\text{-}rec}$$

Numenta Anomaly Score [21]. When using the Numenta anomaly score, each attack is represented by an inverted sigmoid function, plotted with its origin at the earliest true prediction. This (1) benefits earlier predictions within an anomaly and (2) assigns a small positive score to when detection is made shortly after the anomaly ends. In the original proposed Numenta score, both the position and width of the sigmoid were fixed; we use recommendations from follow-up work [29] for tuning. The Numenta score is adjusted by the position of the sigmoid function: an earlier placement in the anomaly assigns a lower score to late detection and penalizes false positives that occur shortly after the anomaly ends. κ controls the width of the sigmoid function: lower values of κ cause the function to be flatter, making the scoring more lenient towards late detection and false positives.

Parameterizing Range-based Metrics for ICS Objectives. Each range-based metric requires parameterization to contextualize their scoring. We describe the default setting for each range-based metric and provide three additional example settings for them, each prioritizing a different ICS objective.

By default, the range-F1 score as defined in Sect. 5.2 places equal importance on reducing false positives and reducing false negatives. If an example use case requires a high detection rate, we optimize for a higher recall by using the Fβ score with $\beta = 1/3$ (range-F$\beta_{1:3}$), such that recall is three times more important than precision. An alternate use case for a highly critical ICS may require that no false alarms occur. For this use case, we use the Fβ score with $\beta = 3$ (range-F$\beta_{3:1}$), which weighs precision three times more heavily than recall.

The default configuration of the Numenta anomaly score sets $\kappa = 5$ and positions the sigmoid at the 50% point of each labeled anomaly [21]. We propose an additional ICS objective that requires early attack detection, as harm may be caused to the ICS even before the attack is completed. We optimize for early detection by re-positioning the Numenta sigmoid to the 25% point of an anomaly, reducing the false positive cost by 50%, and setting $\kappa = 10$, producing a stricter decision boundary. We call this metric *NA-early*. With *NA-early*, a detection in the last 75% of an attack is considered to be late and is penalized as a missed attack, as we assume that the ICS has already been damaged.

Table 3. For each optimal model proposed by prior work, we use a different tuning metric to select the optimal detection hyperparameters and show the resulting number of false alarms, detected attacks, and *TP:FP* ratio. Using range-F1 always outperforms its point-F1 counterpart in *TP:FP* ratio

Dataset and Arch.	Tuning Metric	False Alarms	Detected Attacks	$TP{:}FP$ Ratio
BATADAL AE	Point-F1	11	4/4	0.36
	Range-F1	1	4/4	4.00
WADI LSTM	Point-F1	143	10/13	0.07
	Range-F1	63	7/13	0.11
SWaT CNN	Point-F1	32	6/18	0.19
	Range-F1	4	4/18	1.00
	range-F$\beta_{3:1}$	0	3/18	∞
	range-F$\beta_{1:3}$	47	7/18	0.15
	NA-early	89	11/18 (7 early)	0.12

5.3 Using Range-based Metrics to Tune Detection Hyperparameters

In contrast to Sect. 4, where we selected optimal *model hyperparameters*, in this section we select optimal *detection hyperparameters* for a fixed ML model. In doing so, we reveal whether using tuning metrics other than the point-F1 leads to a different selection of detection hyperparameters and to markedly different anomaly-detection performance, which may lead to a changed understanding of which models are best or whether any are adequate for a particular deployment. For each ML model architecture, we again use the optimal model hyperparameters declared in prior work: a 8-layer, 32-unit CNN trained on SWaT [18], a 5-layer, 2-compression AE trained on BATADAL [32], and a 2-layer, 256-unit LSTM trained on WADI [8].

We compare the detection outputs when using the point-F1 and the range-F1 and show the number of detected attacks, false alarms, and ratio of true positives to false positives (*TP:FP* ratio) in Table 3. Prior work hypothesized that a *TP:FP* ratio of 1 or greater was acceptable and used the *TP:FP* ratio as a success metric [8]. For all three optimal models from prior work, using the range-F1 selects different detection hyperparameter values than using the point-F1. For BATADAL and SWaT, using the point-F1 for detection hyperparameter tuning results in an unacceptable model ($TP{:}FP$ ratio < 1), whereas using the range-F1 for detection hyperparameter tuning results in an acceptable model ($TP{:}FP$ ratio ≥ 1).

Using range-based metrics in tuning can achieve outcomes beyond an improved $TP{:}FP$ ratio. Table 3 shows the final detection results for our additional metrics (defined in Sect. 5.2) after tuning the SWaT CNN from prior work [18]. To detect more attacks, we tune with range-F$\beta_{1:3}$. The resulting tuning detects more attacks (7/18) than prior tunings, at the cost of more false alarms (47). Conversely, to detect attacks with absolutely no false alarms, the range-F$\beta_{3:1}$ tuning can be used; fewer attacks (3/18) are detected but no false alarms occur. Both tunings outperform their point-F1 or range-F1 counterparts on the chosen objectives.

Lastly, we use NA-early to optimize for an ICS where only early detections (within the first 25% of the attack) are useful. The original point-F1 tuning produces 32 false alarms and detects six attacks, five of which are detected early. With NA-early, the total number of false alarms (89) and attacks detected (11/18) increase, but seven attacks are detected early, which outperforms the general tuning selected by the point-F1.

Given the various ICS trade-offs and use cases, a universally optimal strategy for hyperparameter tuning cannot exist, and we do not advocate for specific metrics or hyperparameter values. Rather, we show that when tuning with range-based metrics, it is possible to produce anomaly-detection systems that better match defined ICS objectives.

Finding 2b: By using objective-driven range-based metrics to tune detection hyperparameters, the resulting anomaly detection systems can better address the defined objectives than their point-F1-tuned counterparts.

5.4 Using Range-based Metrics to Select Model Hyperparameters

In this section, we revisit model hyperparameter selection and show how range-based metrics alter the findings from Sect. 4. Compared to the point-F1, using a range-based metric for tuning and evaluation consistently leads to different conclusions about which models are optimal. Figure 5 shows the final range-F1 scores after repeating the experiments described in Sect. 4.2: we train each ML model architecture under each model hyperparameter setting and tune the detection hyperparameters with the range-F1.

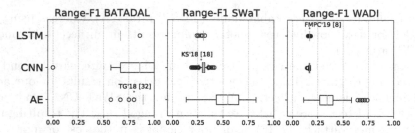

Fig. 5. The final range-F1 scores of each model when trained and tuned on 3 experimental ICS datasets. For each dataset, a selected model hyperparameter setting from prior work is included for comparison

Across model hyperparameters, CNNs/LSTMs on SWaT/WADI perform similarly regardless of whether range-F1 or point-F1 is used in tuning: the difference in range-F1 (or point-F1) between model hyperparameter choices is small, and the best performance can be achieved over a wide range of model hyperparameters. The results on BATADAL are different from those computed by tuning with point-F1 (Sect. 4.2): Despite far lower point-F1 scores, over 25% of CNNs produce a range-F1 of 1, detecting all attacks without a single false alarm! Range-F1-optimal LSTMs for BATADAL yield similar results: the best models detect two out of four attacks with no false positives (perfect segment precision, 50% segment recall) and exhibit a high range-F1, but point-F1 scores below 0.2. In summary, previous experiments indicated that autoencoders were best for BATADAL but no model performed particularly well; using the range-F1 still reveals that autoencoders are on average, the best, but that all models perform quite well. When the combination of ML model architecture and dataset is held constant, the selected model hyperparameters *always* differ between the range-based metric tuning (range-F1, range-Fβ or NA-early) and the point-F1 tuning, changing our understanding of what models are optimal.

> **Finding 2c**: When using range-based metrics to optimize reconstruction-based ICS anomaly detection, the selected ML model architectures and hyperparameters are typically different from what would be selected when using point-F1; this often changes the understanding of what model performs best by a substantial margin.

In summary, we show that using range-based metrics to tune and evaluate ICS anomaly-detection models (i) selects different outcomes compared to when using the point-F1 and (ii) better addresses objectives relevant to ICS anomaly detection. We evaluated these claims across three ICS datasets and note that these datasets may not encompass the wide range of ICS behavior. Extending our analysis to other datasets remains future work.

6   Conclusion

In this work, we explored the optimization of reconstruction-based ICS anomaly detection. We performed a comprehensive comparison across anomaly-detection solutions proposed in prior work, spanning three ICS datasets and three ML model architectures. In doing so, we found that there is no globally optimal technique and the best performance can be achieved over a range of ML model architectures and hyperparameters. We used range-based metrics to optimize ICS anomaly detection and found that they lead to different and potentially more useful outcomes than the common approach of relying on the point-F1 score. Ultimately, we found that effective anomaly detection extends beyond optimizing ML models for the point-F1, and better success measures are needed to practically tune and evaluate ICS anomaly-detection models. We hope that future work in reconstruction-based ICS anomaly detection considers its various use cases when designing new ICS anomaly-detection techniques.

Acknowledgment. We thank our shepherd and our anonymous reviewers for their insightful feedback. We also thank Camille Cobb, Trevor Kann, and Brian Singer for helpful comments on prior drafts of this paper. This material is based upon work supported by: the U.S. Army Research Office and the U.S. Army Futures Command under Contract No. W911NF-20-D-0002; DARPA GARD under Cooperative Agreement No. HR00112020006; a DoD National Defense Science and Engineering Graduate fellowship; the Secure and Private IoT initiative at Carnegie Mellon Cylab (IoT@CyLab); and Mitsubishi Heavy Industries through the Carnegie Mellon CyLab partnership program.

A   Key Findings in the Optimization Process

We identified four techniques that enhance the quality and reproducibility of anomaly detection performance. Table 4 shows which previous works use these techniques; no prior work incorporates all four.

> **Finding 1c**: Techniques such as benign data shuffling, attack cleaning, feature selection, and early stopping increase the quality and reproducability of results, but are applied inconsistently in prior work.

Finding #1: Feature Selection. In WADI and SWaT, some benign-labeled test data appears significantly different from benign-labeled training data [19,35]. To address this problem, statistical tests are used to select features for the ML model. Prior work used a modified version of the Kolmogorov-Smirnov test (called K-S*) [19] to identify features with a significant difference between their training and test distributions. 11 features are removed from SWaT, and 10 features are removed from WADI, which matches the proportion of features removed from these datasets in prior work [19]. We found that feature selection is only effective on the SWaT dataset, so we only use feature selection for SWaT.

Table 4. Identifying key pre-processing and model training techniques from prior ICS anomaly-detection work. '●', '◐', and '○' indicate if the technique was used, partially used, or not used respectively. '?' indicates that we could not determine if the technique was used

Source	[1]	[2]	[7]	[8]	[9]	[15]	[17]	[18]	[19]	[22]	[23]	[26]	[27]	[32]	[37]
Feature Selection	○	○	○	○	◐	○	○	○	●	◐	○	●	○	○	●
Attack Cleaning	○	○	○	○	◐	●	●	◐	○	○	○	●	●	○	◐
Benign Data Shuffling	?	●	?	○	?	○	○	?	?	○	○	○	○	?	?
Early Stopping	○	○	●	○	●	●	○	●	○	○	○	○	○	●	○

Finding #2: Attack Cleaning. Some attacks in the SWaT dataset do not execute as described [15,17]: although labelled as attacks, the SWaT description [10] notes that they did not actually perform as intended. These cases should not be evaluated as attacks, yet the majority of prior work does. We recommend removing the benign "attacks" from the dataset. Furthermore, other prior work has noted that the start and end times of attacks in SWaT are incorrect [37]. Hence, we recommend that the times of the labelled attacks be corrected.[4]

Finding #3: Benign Data Shuffling. When most prior work divides the benign dataset into training and validation portions, it divides by a fixed time [8] or does not describe how the division is performed. Since system behavior can differ between days (e.g., if the final 30% of timesteps in SWaT are used for validation, the distributions of the training and validation datasets are significantly different), splitting should be *random* across the benign dataset. For CNNs and LSTMs, each timestep's history should be collected before splitting.

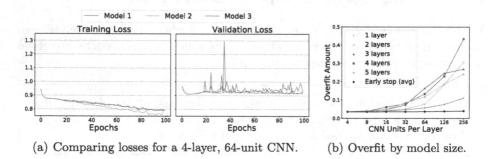

(a) Comparing losses for a 4-layer, 64-unit CNN.   (b) Overfit by model size.

Fig. 6. On left (a): the training and validation loss for a 4-layer, 64-unit CNN, across random seeds. On right (b): the average overfit amount without early stopping, shown for all CNN sizes, compared to the average overfit amount for all layers with early stopping

---

[4] The recommended SWaT corrections can be found at https://github.com/pwwl/ics-anomaly-detection.

Finding #4: Early Stopping.
When early stopping is not used, models overfit quickly and tend to diverge. We train a 4-layer, 64-unit CNN with a history length of 50, repeated three times across random seeds; the model hyperparameters, data ordering, and training parameters are all unchanged. Figure 6a shows the training and validation losses for 100 epochs. When early stopping is not used, the models overfit (validation loss plateaus after the 6th epoch and begins to increase afterward) and diverge after 10–20 epochs; this happens across all model architectures, model hyperparameters, and datasets. Across CNN sizes, Fig. 6b compares the final training and validation loss difference (overfit amount) with and without early stopping, averaged across three random seeds. With early stopping, the overfit amount is small for all model sizes. Without early stopping, larger models overfit more.

References

1. Abdelaty, M., Doriguzzi-Corin, R., Siracusa, D.: DAICS: a deep learning solution for anomaly detection in industrial control systems. arXiv:2009.06299 (2020)
2. Abokifa, A.A., Haddad, K., Lo, C.S., Biswas, P.: Detection of cyber physical attacks on water distribution systems via principal component analysis and artificial neural networks. In: World Environmental and Water Resources Congress (2017)
3. Adepu, S., Kandasamy, N.K., Mathur, A.: EPIC: an electric power testbed for research and training in cyber physical systems security. In: Katsikas, S.K., et al. (eds.) SECPRE/CyberICPS -2018. LNCS, vol. 11387, pp. 37–52. Springer, Cham (2019). https://doi.org/10.1007/978-3-030-12786-2_3
4. Ahmed, C.M., Palleti, V.R., Mathur, A.P.: WADI: a water distribution testbed for research in the design of secure cyber physical systems. In: 3rd International Workshop on Cyber-Physical Systems for Smart Water Networks (2017)
5. Collobert, R., Weston, J., Bottou, L., Karlen, M., Kavukcuoglu, K., Kuksa, P.: Natural language processing (Almost) from scratch. J. Mach. Learn. Res. **12**, 2493–2537 (2011)
6. Di Pinto, A., Dragoni, Y., Carcano, A.: TRITON: the first ICS cyber attack on safety instrument systems. In: Black Hat USA (2018)
7. Erba, A., et al.: Constrained concealment attacks against reconstruction-based anomaly detectors in industrial control systems. In: Annual Computer Security Applications Conference (2020)
8. Feng, C., Palleti, V.R., Mathur, A., Chana, D.: A systematic framework to generate invariants for anomaly detection in industrial control systems. In: Network and Distributed System Security Symposium (2019)
9. Goh, J., Adepu, S., Tan, M., Lee, Z.S.: Anomaly detection in cyber physical systems using recurrent neural networks. In: 18th International Symposium on High Assurance Systems Engineering (2017)
10. Goh, J., Adepu, S., Junejo, K.N., Mathur, A.: A dataset to support research in the design of secure water treatment systems. In: Havarneanu, G., Setola, R., Nassopoulos, H., Wolthusen, S. (eds.) CRITIS 2016. LNCS, vol. 10242, pp. 88–99. Springer, Cham (2017). https://doi.org/10.1007/978-3-319-71368-7_8
11. Hasselquist, D., Rawat, A., Gurtov, A.: Trends and detection avoidance of internet-connected industrial control systems. IEEE Access **7**, 155504–155512 (2019)

12. Hinton, G.E., Salakhutdinov, R.R.: Reducing the dimensionality of data with neural networks. Science **313**(5786), 504–507 (2006)
13. Hochreiter, S., Schmidhuber, J.: Long short-term memory. Neural Comput. **9**(8), 1735–1780 (1997)
14. Hwang, W.S., Yun, J.H., Kim, J., Kim, H.C.: Time-series aware precision and recall for anomaly detection: considering variety of detection result and addressing ambiguous labeling. In: 28th ACM International Conference on Information and Knowledge Management (2019)
15. Inoue, J., Yamagata, Y., Chen, Y., Poskitt, C.M., Sun, J.: Anomaly detection for a water treatment system using unsupervised machine learning. In: IEEE International Conference on Data Mining Workshops (2017)
16. Jones, A.T., McLean, C.R.: A proposed hierarchical control model for automated manufacturing systems. J. Manufact. Syst. **5**(1), 15–25 (1986)
17. Kim, J., Yun, J.-H., Kim, H.C.: Anomaly detection for industrial control systems using sequence-to-sequence neural networks. In: Katsikas, S., et al. (eds.) Cyber-ICPS/SECPRE/SPOSE/ADIoT -2019. LNCS, vol. 11980, pp. 3–18. Springer, Cham (2020). https://doi.org/10.1007/978-3-030-42048-2_1
18. Kravchik, M., Shabtai, A.: Detecting cyber attacks in industrial control systems using convolutional neural networks. In: Workshop on Cyber-Physical Systems Security and Privacy (2018)
19. Kravchik, M., Shabtai, A.: Efficient cyber attack detection in industrial control systems using lightweight neural networks and PCA. IEEE Trans. Dependable Secure Comput. **19**, 2179–2197 (2021)
20. Kshetri, N., Voas, J.: Hacking power grids: a current problem. Computer **50**(12), 91–95 (2017)
21. Lavin, A., Ahmad, S.: Evaluating real-time anomaly detection algorithms-the Numenta anomaly benchmark. In: 14th International Conference on Machine Learning and Applications (2015)
22. Li, D., Chen, D., Jin, B., Shi, L., Goh, J., Ng, S.-K.: MAD-GAN: multivariate anomaly detection for time series data with generative adversarial networks. In: Tetko, I.V., Kůrková, V., Karpov, P., Theis, F. (eds.) ICANN 2019. LNCS, vol. 11730, pp. 703–716. Springer, Cham (2019). https://doi.org/10.1007/978-3-030-30490-4_56
23. Lin, Q., Adepu, S., Verwer, S., Mathur, A.: TABOR: a graphical model-based approach for anomaly detection in industrial control systems. In: Asia Conference on Computer and Communications Security (2018)
24. Morris, T.H., Thornton, Z., Turnipseed, I.: Industrial control system simulation and data logging for intrusion detection system research. In: 7th Annual Southeastern Cyber Security Summit (2015)
25. Pang, G., Shen, C., Cao, L., Hengel, A.V.D.: Deep learning for anomaly detection: a review. ACM Comput. Surv. (CSUR) **54**(2), 1–38 (2021)
26. Perales Gómez, Á.L., Fernández Maimó, L., Huertas Celdrán, A., García Clemente, F.J.: MADICS: a methodology for anomaly detection in industrial control systems. Symmetry **12**(10), 1583 (2020)
27. Shalyga, D., Filonov, P., Lavrentyev, A.: Anomaly detection for water treatment system based on neural network with automatic architecture optimization. arXiv:1807.07282 (2018)
28. Shin, H.K., Lee, W., Yun, J.H., Kim, H.: HAI 1.0: HIL-based augmented ICS security dataset. In: 13th USENIX Workshop on Cyber Security Experimentation and Test (2020)

29. Singh, N., Olinsky, C.: Demystifying Numenta anomaly benchmark. In: International Joint Conference on Neural Networks (2017)
30. Sokolova, M., Lapalme, G.: A systematic analysis of performance measures for classification tasks. Inf. Process. Manag. **45**(4), 427–437 (2009)
31. Stouffer, K.: Guide to industrial control systems (ICS) security. NIST Special Publication 800(82) (2011)
32. Taormina, R., Galelli, S.: Deep-learning approach to the detection and localization of cyber-physical attacks on water distribution systems. J. Water Res. Planning Manag. **144**(10), 04018065 (2018)
33. Taormina, R., et al.: Battle of the attack detection algorithms: disclosing cyber attacks on water distribution networks. J. Water Res. Planning Manag. **144**(8), 04018048 (2018)
34. Tatbul, N., Lee, T.J., Zdonik, S., Alam, M., Gottschlich, J.: Precision and recall for time series. In: Advances in Neural Information Processing Systems (2018)
35. Turrin, F., Erba, A., Tippenhauer, N.O., Conti, M.: A statistical analysis framework for ICS process datasets. In: Joint Workshop on CPS and IoT Security and Privacy (2020)
36. Ye, D., Zhang, T.Y.: Summation detector for false data-injection attack in cyber-physical systems. IEEE Trans. Cybernetics **50**(6), 2338–2345 (2020)
37. Zizzo, G., Hankin, C., Maffeis, S., Jones, K.: Intrusion detection for industrial control systems: evaluation analysis and adversarial attacks. arXiv:1911.04278 (2019)

A Novel High-Performance Implementation of CRYSTALS-Kyber with AI Accelerator

Lipeng Wan[1,2,3], Fangyu Zheng[1,3(✉)], Guang Fan[1,2,3], Rong Wei[1,2,3], Lili Gao[1,2,3], Yuewu Wang[1,2,3], Jingqiang Lin[4], and Jiankuo Dong[5]

[1] State Key Laboratory of Information Security, Institute of Information Engineering, Chinese Academy of Sciences, Beijing, China
zhengfangyu@iie.ac.cn
[2] School of Cyber Security, University of Chinese Academy of Sciences, Beijing, China
[3] Data Assurance and Communication Security Research Center, Chinese Academy of Sciences, Beijing, China
[4] School of Cyber Security, University of Science and Technology of China, Hefei, China
[5] School of Computer Science, Nanjing University of Posts and Telecommunications, Nanjing, China

Abstract. Public-key cryptography, including conventional cryptosystems and post-quantum cryptography, involves computation-intensive workloads. With noticing the extraordinary computing power of AI accelerators, in this paper, we further explore the feasibility to introduce AI accelerators into high-performance cryptographic computing. Since AI accelerators are dedicated to machine learning or neural networks, the biggest challenge is how to transform cryptographic workloads into their operations, while ensuring the correctness of the results and bringing convincing performance gains.

After investigating and analysing the workload of NVIDIA AI accelerator, Tensor Core, we choose to utilize it to accelerate the polynomial multiplication, usually the most time-consuming part in lattice-based cryptography. We take measures to accommodate the matrix-multiply-and-add mode of Tensor Core and make a trade-off between precision and performance, to leverage it as a high-performance NTT box performing NTT/INTT through CUDA C++ WMMA APIs. Meanwhile, we take CRYSTALS-Kyber, the candidate to be standardized by NIST, as a case study on RTX 3080 with the Ampere Tensor Core. The empirical results show that the customized NTT of polynomial vector ($n = 256, k = 4$) with our NTT box obtains a speedup around 6.47x that of the state-of-the-art implementation on the same GPU platform. Compared with the AVX2 implementation submitted to NIST, our Kyber-1024 can achieve a speedup of 26x, 36x, and 35x for each phase.

Keywords: Lattice-based cryptography · Polynomial multiplication over rings · NTT · AI accelerator · Tensor Core · Kyber

V. Atluri et al. (Eds.): ESORICS 2022, LNCS 13556, pp. 514–534, 2022.
https://doi.org/10.1007/978-3-031-17143-7_25

1   Introduction

Quantum computing and Shor's algorithm [31] have raised concern about the security of conventional public-key schemes, such as widely used RSA and ECDSA. A new class of cryptosystems with anti-quantum property, which is known as post-quantum cryptography (PQC, sometimes referred to as quantum-proof, quantum-safe, or quantum-resistant), is in urgent need. To this end, National Institute of Standards and Technology (NIST) has initiated a process to solicit, evaluate, and standardize one or more quantum-resistant public-key cryptographic algorithms in 2017 [24].

The security of quantum-resistant schemes is based on different mathematical hard problems, while the lattice-based hardness is the most prevailing one. On the other hand, performance is an important metric in the evaluation, and thus many research efforts are made to improve the efficiency of lattice-based cryptography (LBC). Generally speaking, for the cryptographic schemes based on lattice related problem, such as Ring-LWE [18], Module-LWE [6,16], and Module-LWR [3], polynomial multiplication (over the ring R_q) and hash functions are the time-consuming parts. The hash functions mainly involve bit operations, which can be accelerated by the commercial off-the-shelf products with processor-aided accelerations (e.g., SHA extension in Intel and ARM CPU [28]). In this way, the principal efforts in LBC acceleration focus on the polynomial multiplication.

There are many methods to accelerate the polynomial multiplication. Apart from adopting the Karatsuba [15] and Toom-Cook algorithms [32], the more prevailing practice is to exploit Number Theoretic Transform (NTT) for the case $n|(q-1)$, where q is the modulus and n is the dimension. CRYSTALS-Kyber [5, 29], Kyber for short, the candidate to be standardized by NIST PQC [22], even integrates a customized NTT into its algorithms to improve the efficiency.

Meanwhile, many solutions have been proposed for the specific platforms to make full use of the hardware features and get better achievable performance. Taking the advantage of vector instructions, Lyubashevsky *et al.* [19] presented an AVX2 optimized NTT and applies it to NTRU. Similarly, Seiler [30] implemented NewHope with AVX2 optimized NTT. With the help of many-thread parallelism and high throughput of GPU (precisely, CUDA core), Gupta *et al.* [12] implemented three different classes of post-quantum algorithms on NVIDIA Tesla V100. The main optimized technique of the work [12] is to reorganize the data storage sequence to facilitate continuous memory access. Gao *et al.* [10] also improved the performance of NewHope on NVIDIA MX150 and GTX1650. As for the resource-constrained devices, the proposed solutions might be more dedicated. Thanks to the flexibility of FPGA in programming, Xing and Li [34] presented a compact hardware implementation of Kyber on FPGA with many customized optimizations from the perspective of hardware. And Greconic *et al.* [11] presented implementations of the lattice-based digital signature scheme Dilithium for ARM Cortex-M3 and ARM Cortex-M4.

On the other hand, many manufacturers have designed high-performance AI (artificial intelligence) accelerators, such as Google TPU [8], Apple M1 [13], and NVIDIA Tensor Core [14], to meet the needs of AI applications. Compared with other general-purpose processors, AI accelerator generally focuses on low-precision arithmetic, novel data-flow architectures, or in-memory computing capability, and often has extremely stronger computing power. For instance, NVIDIA has claimed that Tesla V100's Tensor Cores can deliver up to 125 Tensor TFLOPS for training and inference applications. And NVIDIA Jetson Xavier NX brings supercomputer performance up to 21 TOPS while the power is up to 15W. However, little research has been proposed on how to apply this kind of accelerators to other fields such as high-performance cryptographic computing. Our previous work [33] exploits Volta Tensor Core for byte-level modulus scheme LAC [17], but it does not involve module-lattice and NTT, which are more widely used.

The primary motivation of this paper is to bring the extraordinary computing power of the AI accelerator to the area of cryptographic acceleration. Since AI accelerators are dedicated to machine learning or neural networks, the biggest challenge is how to transform cryptographic operations into their workloads, while ensuring the correctness of the results and bringing convincing performance gains. The contributions of our work are as follows:

- Firstly, our work forms a framework for an AI accelerator to accelerate module-lattice based cryptography. Through this framework, we can efficiently convert the workload of cryptographic primitives into the operation of the AI accelerator.
- Secondly, we present an NTT box based on NVIDIA AI accelerator, Tensor Core, under the proposed framework. The NTT box is efficient to perform NTT/INTT, especially when the dimension n is relatively small.
- Finally, we evaluate the novel proposed method for Kyber, a well-known PQC scheme, as a case study. To the best of our knowledge, it is the first attempt at implementing Kyber with an AI accelerator. Compared with the state-of-the-art implementation, our *polyvec_ntt* in Kyber can obtain a speedup of 6.47x on the same GPU platform.

2   Preliminary

In this section, we give a basic background of Kyber, NTT and Tensor Core.

2.1   Notation and Definition

Notation. For a prime q, $\mathbb{Z}_q = \{0, 1, \ldots, q-1\}$ is the residue class ring modulo q. Define the ring $R_q = \mathbb{Z}_q[x]/(x^n + 1)$, which means the coefficients are from $\mathbb{Z}_q$. $\mathbb{Z}_q^n$ represents n coefficients from $\mathbb{Z}_q$. Regular font letters denote elements in R_q (which includes elements in $\mathbb{Z}_q$) and bold lower-case letters represent vectors with coefficients in R_q. By default, all vectors will be column vectors. Bold upper-case letters are matrices. For a vector $\mathbf{v}$ (or matrix $\mathbf{A}$), $\mathbf{v}^T$ (or $\mathbf{A}^T$) means its transpose, and $\mathbf{v}[i]$ denotes its i-th entry (with indexing starting at zero). For a matrix $\mathbf{A}$, $\mathbf{A}[i][j]$ denotes the entry in row i, column j (again, with indexing starting from zero). The rank k represents that a polynomial vector contains k polynomials, and a matrix contains $k \times k$ polynomials. For a finite field $F = \mathbb{Z}_q$, the primitive n-th root ω of unity exist whenever $n|(q-1)$, where $\omega^n \equiv 1 \mod q$.

Module-LWE. A lattice is the set of all integer linear combinations of some linearly independent vectors belonging to the euclidean space. Most lattice-based cryptographic schemes are built upon the assumed hardness of the Short Integer Solution (SIS) [1] and Learning With Errors (LWE) [27] problems. The LWE problem was popularized by Regev [27] who showed that solving a random LWE instance is as hard as solving certain worst-case instances of certain lattice problems. This assumption states that it is hard to distinguish the uniform distribution from $(\mathbf{A}, \mathbf{As} + \mathbf{e})$, where $\mathbf{A}$ is a uniformly-random matrix in $\mathbb{Z}_q^{m \times n}$, $\mathbf{s}$ is a uniformly-random vector in $\mathbb{Z}_q^n$, and $\mathbf{e}$ is chosen from some distribution. Later, Lyubashevsky et al. [18] introduced a similar adaptation for LWE, called Ring-LWE, which showed that it is also hard to distinguish a variant of the LWE distribution from the uniform one over certain polynomial rings. Combining the security advantages of LWE and the flexibility of Ring-LWE, Langlois et al. [16] demonstrated the worst-case to average-case reductions for module lattices. Intuitively, the size of matrix $\mathbf{A}$ in Module-LWE is $k \times k$, where k is the rank. The elements in the matrix are vectors selected from $\mathbb{Z}_q^n$.

2.2 Description of CRYSTALS-Kyber

Kyber is an IND-CCA2-secure post-quantum key exchange mechanism. The security of Kyber is based on the hardness of solving the LWE problem in module lattices.

The submission to NIST PQC [25] lists three different parameter sets, Kyber-512, Kyber-768, and Kyber-1024, aiming at different security levels roughly equivalent to AES-128, AES-192, and AES-256, respectively. The parameters are listed in Table 1, where η_1 and η_2 are the parameters of centered binomial distribution (CBD).

Table 1. Parameter sets for Kyber version 3

	n	k	q	η_1	η_2
Kyber-512	256	2	3329	3	2
Kyber-768	256	3	3329	2	2
Kyber-1024	256	4	3329	2	2

The key generation, encryption, and decryption are described in Algorithm 1, 2, and 3. In the KeyGen phase, d is a random number, ρ and σ are fixed-length intermediate variables generated by d through hash function G.

Algorithm 1. KYBER.CPAPKE.KeyGen(): key generation

Ensure: Secret key sk, Public key pk.
1: $d \leftarrow \boldsymbol{Random}()$
2: $(\rho, \sigma) := G(d)$
3: $\hat{\mathbf{A}} \leftarrow Gen\_matrix\_\hat{\mathbf{A}}(\rho)$, $\hat{\mathbf{A}} \in R_q^{k \times k}$ in NTT domain
4: $\mathbf{s} \leftarrow Sample\_s(\sigma)$, $\mathbf{s} \in R_q^k$ from B_{η_1}
5: $\mathbf{e} \leftarrow Sample\_e(\sigma)$, $\mathbf{e} \in R_q^k$ from B_{η_1}
6: $\hat{\mathbf{s}} := NTT(\mathbf{s})$
7: $\hat{\mathbf{e}} := NTT(\mathbf{e})$
8: $\hat{\mathbf{t}} := \hat{\mathbf{A}} \circ \hat{\mathbf{s}} + \hat{\mathbf{e}}$
9: **return** $pk := Encode(\hat{\mathbf{t}}\|\rho)$, $sk := Encode(\hat{\mathbf{s}})$

The parameter $\hat{\mathbf{A}}$ is a $k \times k$ polynomial matrix generated by ρ. The parameters $\mathbf{s}$ and $\mathbf{e}$ are polynomial vectors generated through different sample functions but same distribution B_{η_1}. The final parameters need to be compressed and encode. In the Enc phase, the public key pk will be decoded first. Here, we need to emphasize that e_2 and v are polynomials rather than vectors. The ciphertext c consists of two parts: c_1 and c_2, which are obtained from $\mathbf{u}$ and v with different encode. Correspondingly, in the Dec phase, these two parts need to be decoded with different functions first. Then the NTT and the subsequent INTT are performed.

Algorithm 2. KYBER.CPAPKE.Enc(): encryption

Require: Public key pk, Message m, Random seed r
Ensure: Ciphertext c
1: $(\hat{\mathbf{t}}, \rho) \leftarrow Decode(pk)$
2: $\hat{\mathbf{A}}^T \leftarrow Gen\_matrix\_\hat{\mathbf{A}}^T(\rho)$, $\hat{\mathbf{A}}^T \in R_q^{k \times k}$ in NTT domain
3: $\mathbf{r} \leftarrow Sample\_r(r)$, $\mathbf{r} \in R_q^k$ from B_{η_1}
4: $\mathbf{e}_1 \leftarrow Sample\_e_1(r)$, $\mathbf{e}_1 \in R_q^k$ from B_{η_2}
5: $e_2 \leftarrow Sample\_e_2(r)$, $e_2 \in R_q$ from B_{η_2}
6: $\hat{\mathbf{r}} := NTT(\mathbf{r})$
7: $\mathbf{u} := NTT^{-1}(\hat{\mathbf{A}} \circ \hat{\mathbf{r}}) + \mathbf{e}_1$
8: $v := NTT^{-1}(\hat{\mathbf{t}}^T \circ \hat{\mathbf{r}}) + e_2 + Decompress(m)$
9: **return** $c_1 := Encode_u(\mathbf{u})$, $c_2 := Encode_v(v)$

2.3   Number Theoretic Transform

In general, Number Theoretic Transform (NTT) is one of the most prevailing approaches to improve polynomial multiplication over the ring. Simplemindedly, NTT is the finite field form of discrete Fourier transform (DFT), which transforms a sequence of n numbers $\mathbf{v} := \{v_0, v_1, \ldots, v_{n-1}\}$ into another sequence numbers $\mathbf{X} := \{X_0, X_1, \ldots, X_{n-1}\}$. That can be defined by:

Algorithm 3. KYBER.CPAPKE.Dec(): decryption

Require: Secret key sk, Ciphertext c
Ensure: Message m
1: $\mathbf{u} := Decode_u(c)$
2: $v := Decode_v(c)$
3: $\hat{\mathbf{s}} := Decode(sk)$
4: **return** $m := Compress(v - NTT^{-1}(\hat{\mathbf{s}} \circ NTT(\mathbf{u})))$

$$X_k = \sum_{j=0}^{n-1} v_j \cdot \omega^{jk} \tag{1}$$

where ω is a primitive n-th root of unity, namely, $\omega^n \equiv 1 \mod q$. The inverse transform (INTT) is given as:

$$v_j = n^{-1} \sum_{k=0}^{n-1} X_k \cdot \omega^{-jk} \tag{2}$$

n^{-1} denotes the inverse of n, where $n \cdot n^{-1} \equiv 1 \mod q$.

The fast NTT is based on the idea of divide and conquer, similar to fast Fourier transform (FFT) [9], and can perform the polynomial multiplication with the complexity of $O(n \log n)$. However, in practice, the usage of fast NTT can achieve acceleration only when n is relatively large.

NTT-Based Multiplication. Generally, NTT-based multiplication needs $q \equiv 1 \mod n$ to ensure the existence of the n-th roots of unity, where n is a power of 2. In a finite field, the NTT multiplication of two vectors $\mathbf{a}$ and $\mathbf{b}$ needs to append n zeros to each vector. Then, the product can be obtained by:

$$\mathbf{c} = INTT(NTT(\mathbf{a}_{padding}) \cdot NTT(\mathbf{b}_{padding})) \tag{3}$$

The zero-padding can be avoided to perform NTT-based polynomial multiplication over the ring $\mathbb{R}_q = \mathbb{Z}_q/f(x)$, with the well-known negative wrapped convolution (NWC). However, the NWC requires the existence of the $2n$-th roots of unity, namely, $q \equiv 1 \mod 2n$.

2.4 Fast Modular Reduction

It is necessary to conduct modular reduction for the product of two coefficients or the sum of several products. The native module operation '%' is expensive, even if it might be optimized at the low level of the computer, but that is unspecified. In practice, fast modular reductions like Montgomery reduction [21], and Barrett reduction [4] are utilized, sometimes along with a lazy strategy which means that the reduction is done only before overflow.

Montgomery Reduction. Montgomery reduction [21] allows modular arithmetic to be performed efficiently when the modulus is large. Let N be a positive integer, and let R and T be integers such that $R > n$, $gcd(n, R) = 1$, and $0 \leq T < NR$. The Montgomery reduction of T mod q with respect to R is defined as the value TR^{-1} mod q, where R is a power of 2 and R^{-1} is the modular inverse of R. The calculation steps could be as (4).

$$m := (T \mod R)k \mod R,$$
$$t := (T + mN)/R \tag{4}$$

$$\text{if } t \geq N \text{ return } t - N \text{ else return } t.$$

where $k = \frac{R(R^{-1} \mod N)-1}{N}$. Note that R is usually a power of 2, and multiplications and integer divides can be realized by shift, which is cheap.

Barrett Reduction. Barrett reduction is another reduction algorithm introduced in 1986 by P.D. Barrett [4] to eliminate division operation in computer.

Let $s = 1/q$ be the inverse of q as a floating point number. Then

$$T \mod q = T - \lfloor Ts \rfloor q$$

where $\lfloor \rfloor$ denotes the floor function. Barrett reduction approximates $1/q$ with a value $m/2^k$ where $m = 2^k/q$. Then the reduction can be converted into (5) and becomes cheap. Since $\lfloor 2^k/q \rfloor$ can be pre-computed, and dividing T by 2^k is just a right-shift.

$$T \mod q = T - \lfloor T/2^k \rfloor \lfloor 2^k/q \rfloor \cdot q \tag{5}$$

2.5   AI Accelerator and Tensor Core

AI Accelerator. Due to the explosive growth of AI applications, general-purpose processors are hard to meet the needs of machine learning. Therefore, a dedicated AI accelerator, an application-specific integrated circuit with a more specific design, may gain far more efficiency. The well-known AI accelerators include Google TPU, Apple M1, M1 MAX, M1 Pro, and ARM NPU. These accelerators mainly focus on optimized memory use and lower precision arithmetic to accelerate calculation and increase the throughput.

Tensor Core. In December 2017, NVIDIA released the 1st generation Tensor Core (on Volta architecture) which is just for tensor calculations. Tensor Cores are designed to carry 64 GEMMs (General Matrix Multiplication) per clock cycle on 4×4 matrices, containing FP16 values (16-bit floating-point numbers) or FP32 (the *float* format). A year later, NVIDIA launched the Turing architecture Tensor Core which has been updated to support other data formats, such as INT8 (8-bit integer values). In the latest Ampere architecture, NVIDIA has improved the performance (256 GEMMs per cycle, up from 64), and added further data formats, as shown in Table 2.

Table 2. Precision Supported by Multiple Generations of Tensor Core

	Volta	Turing	Ampere
Precision	*FP16*	*FP16, INT8, INT4, INT1*	*FP64, TF32, bfloat16, FP16, INT8, INT4, INT1*

Compared with other AI accelerators, Tensor Core exposes interfaces at different levels and has some flexibility in its programming. CUDA has provided several tools to leverage Tensor Core, including library cuBLAS and cuDNN, and CUDA C++ WMMA (Warp Matrix Multiply Accumulate) API.

3 Design

In this section, we analyze the workload of Tensor Core at first, then demonstrate the transformation from cryptographic primitives to operation of Tensor Core. Finally, we illustrate the trade-off between performance and precision.

3.1 Analysis of Tensor Core Dedicated Workload

Warp Level Matrix Operation. Up to now, Tensor Core can only support operations at the warp level, usually 32 threads. The warp matrix function requires co-operation from all threads in the warp, and perform $\mathbf{D} = \mathbf{A} \times \mathbf{B} + \mathbf{C}$, where $\mathbf{A}$, $\mathbf{B}$, $\mathbf{C}$, and $\mathbf{D}$, are matrices with specific size, as shown in Fig. 1.

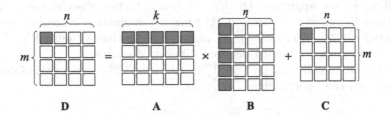

Fig. 1. A warp-level m-n-k matrix operation

It is further complicated by threads holding only a fragment (a type of opaque architecture-specific ABI data structure) of the overall matrix, with the developer not allowed to make assumptions on how the individual parameters are mapped to the registers participating in the matrix multiply-accumulate. There are also some restrictions on matrix size. Generally, k is fixed to 16, and m can be 8, 16, or 32 (n corresponds to 32, 16, or 8).

FMA Operation. Meanwhile, Tensor Core performs FMA mixed-precision operation, which means low-precision input and high-precision output, described in Fig. 2. For example, on the Ampere architecture, the input can be INT8 (*char*) and the output can be INT32 (*int*). Table 3 represents the various combinations of element types of input matrices and input/output accumulators.

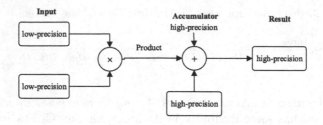

Fig. 2. Tensor Core mixed-precision operation

Table 3. Precision combinations supported by Tensor Core

Matrix A	FP16	unsigned char	signed char	bfloat16	TF32	FP64
Matrix B	FP16	unsigned char	signed char	bfloat16	TF32	FP64
Accumulator C and D	FP32	INT32	INT32	FP32	FP32	FP64

3.2 Transformation from Cryptographic Workload to Tensor Core Dedicated Operation

NTT in Kyber. Similar to NewHope-Compact [2], Kyber reduces its modulus from 12289 to 3329, which naturally improves the efficiency. The security strength is regulated by the rank k with a fixed dimension $n = 256$. However, this means the $2n$-th roots do not exist and the negative wrapped convolution is not appliable. On the contrary, Kyber absorbs the idea like the Chinese Remainder Theorem (CRT) for the modular polynomial, formally, $\mathbb{Z}_q/(f(x) \cdot g(x)) \cong \mathbb{Z}_q/f(x) \times \mathbb{Z}_q/g(x)$, and integrates the customized NTT in its algorithm to reduce conversion between different domains.

The defining polynomial $(X^{256} + 1)$ factors into 128 polynomials of degree 2 modulo q, and can be written as

$$X^{256} + 1 = \prod_{i=0}^{127} (X^2 - \zeta^{2i+1}) = \prod_{i=0}^{127} (X^2 - \zeta^{2br_7(i)+1})$$

where $\boldsymbol{br_7}(i)$ for $i = 0, 1, \cdots, 127$ is the bit reversal of the unsigned 7-bit integer i. Therefore, the NTT of a polynomial $f \in R_q$ is a vector of 128 polynomials of degree 1, and can be written as

$$NTT(f) = \hat{f} = (\hat{f}_0 + \hat{f}_1 X, \hat{f}_2 + \hat{f}_3 X, \cdots, \hat{f}_{254} + \hat{f}_{255} X)$$

with

$$\hat{f}_{2i} = \sum_{j=0}^{127} f_{2j} \zeta^{(2br_7(i)+1)j} \tag{6}$$

$$\hat{f}_{2i+1} = \sum_{j=0}^{127} f_{2j+1} \zeta^{(2br_7(i)+1)j} \tag{7}$$

where ζ is the 256-th root of unity. The powers of ζ are also called twiddle factors. It is stressed that even though $\hat{f}$ is written as a polynomial in R_q, it has no algebraic meaning as such.

Computing NTT with Matrix Operation. The prevailing strategy of performing polynomial multiplication with NTT is to adopt the divide and conquer method. However, in practice, this approach has an advantage only when n is large enough. Moreover, it needs to manipulate each coefficient iteratively, which conflicts with the matrix operating mode.

As aforementioned, Kyber exploits a customized NTT in its algorithms like Eqs. (6) and (7). In fact, only $n/2$ coefficients of a vector are really involved in an NTT result. In addition, frequent interruptions during in-memory computing to access external memory will seriously increase the delay of the program. Based on the above observations, we decide to adopt a straightforward routine combined with techniques such as pre-computation. We assemble several polynomials that need to be processed into a matrix (Matrix **A**) and place the twiddle factors into another one (Matrix **B**). The computing mode we adopt is shown in Fig. 3. In this way, this computing model can make full use of SIMT (Single Instruction Multiple Threads) to perform NTT on multiple polynomials at once.

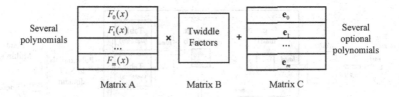

Fig. 3. The computing mode adopted

3.3   The Multiple Precision Representation

As mentioned in Table 3, Ampere Tensor Core can support several precision combinations. We test the performance of different precision on NVIDIA RTX 3080 and list the results in Table 4. Generally speaking, lower precision often corresponds to higher computing speed. The choice of data type in cryptographic an algorithm should be based on its accurate representation range and performance. For example, the bit length to exactly represent modulus $q = 3329$ (12289) is 12 (14). Then, only the mantissa of FP64 (*double*), which is 52 bits, can cover the case. However, the speed would be particularly slow. To this end, we suggest exploiting multiple-precision representation to make a trade-off, namely, using two or more lower-precision elements to represent a coefficient.

In the case study of Kyber, we split a 12-bit coefficient into two 6-bit parts represented by INT8. Because the performance of INT8 is much higher than that of other floating-point types on Tensor Core.

Table 4. Performance of different precision combinations

	bfloat16	FP16 (half)	TF32	FP64 (double)	INT8 (char)
Exponent (bits)	8	5	8	11	-
Mantissa (bits)	7	10	10	52	7
Performance	25.89×	28.69×	9.93×	1×	60.56×

* The values are to compensate the performance difference caused by different precisions of Tensor Core. The evaluation is conducted with CUDA samples (without shared memory), and the results are scaled on the performance of FP64

Internal Workflow of NTT Box. With the multiple-precision representation, we make Tensor Core play the role of the NTT box as an individual module. The caller could simply load the sorted data into the box and get results quickly. The internal workflow of the NTT box is shown in Fig. 4. Several sorted polynomials are distilled into a matrix, which is then first loaded into the fragment matrix in the form of tiles.

Meanwhile, the pre-computed table will also be loaded into fragment matrix_b. Then, MMA is conducted. The results will be performed modular reduction to ensure that the coefficients of the target polynomial are less than q.

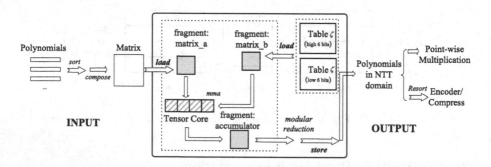

Fig. 4. The workflow of NTT box

4   Implementation Details

In this section, we elaborate on the technical details of our implemented prototype. First, we show the overall architecture of our system and the collaboration between the various modules. Next, we introduce two types of NTT: basic-NTT for smaller modulus with achieving higher performance, and split-NTT for larger modulus. Then, we explain some non-trivial optimization techniques.

4.1   Overview

Our prototype is based on CUDA Toolkit 11.1. CUDA programming can support a large number of concurrent threads. In our implementation, each thread holds one instance, and these threads execute in SIMD (SIMT) mode. Although the specific procedures might be slightly different for different phases, the high-level overview could be like Fig. 5.

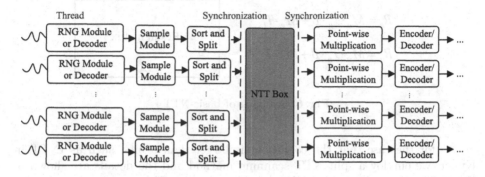

Fig. 5. General overview of implemented Kyber

The Collaboration Between Modules. The function of the RNG module is to extend the random seed and get the required parameters, just like the key derivation function (KDF). After obtaining the seed from an RNG module or decoder, Kyber will generate matrix or sample polynomial vectors based on the seed. On the basis of Eqs. (6) and (7), for a polynomial, the elements with even (or odd) terms participate in the same NTT. Therefore, before entering the NTT box, we sort each polynomial so that even (or odd) entries are continuous in memory. When the program needs to perform NTT, it will synchronize between threads in the same thread block, and then input the data into the NTT box.

4.2   The Basic-NTT and Split-NTT

However, we can only load a fixed size tile into a fragment every time, while the target matrix is much larger. We have made two scanning methods, according to the raw precision of the data to be processed. For the parameters whose element value is less than 8 bits (256, or 128 for signed number), such as secret s and random noise r, e generated from CBD, with at most 3 significant bits, we apply a basic-NTT method, shown in Fig. 6.

In this method, we only need to split the twiddle factors into T_h and T_l, and directly represent the input data with INT8 type. Both input and output are sorted according to parity items as M_e, M_o, R_e and R_o, to satisfy the requirement of contiguous memory access. Note that β in Fig. 6 represents the base of multiple precision representation, and the multiplication by b can be done by left shifting.

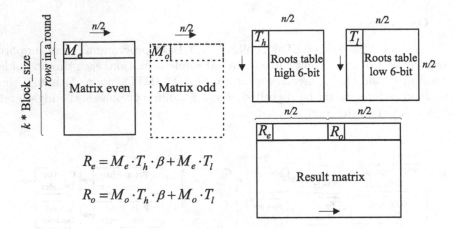

$$R_e = M_e \cdot T_h \cdot \beta + M_e \cdot T_l$$

$$R_o = M_o \cdot T_h \cdot \beta + M_o \cdot T_l$$

Fig. 6. Scanning of basic-NTT

As for the case that the coefficient is larger than 8 bits, such as INTT in Kyber, we employ a split-NTT scanning method and the details are shown in Fig 7. The input data is sorted first and then split. The temporary sums, like Tmp_e and Tmp_o in Fig. 7, can be used to reduce a shift operation.

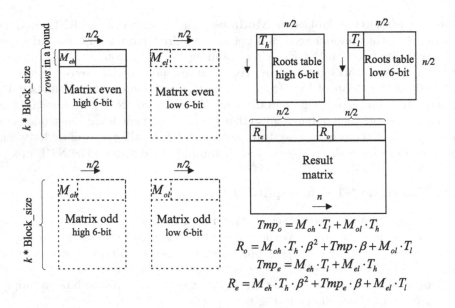

$$Tmp_o = M_{oh} \cdot T_l + M_{ol} \cdot T_h$$

$$R_o = M_{oh} \cdot T_h \cdot \beta^2 + Tmp \cdot \beta + M_{ol} \cdot T_l$$

$$Tmp_e = M_{eh} \cdot T_l + M_{el} \cdot T_h$$

$$R_e = M_{eh} \cdot T_h \cdot \beta^2 + Tmp_e \cdot \beta + M_{el} \cdot T_l$$

Fig. 7. Scanning of split-NTT

All data matrices have n columns, while the number of rows can be adjusted according to the rank k and the number of threads in a block.

4.3 Pre-computed Table of Twiddle Factors

Since the powers $\zeta^{2br_7(i)+1}$ can be known in advance, then all the twiddle factors can be pre-computed and stored in the memory before the procedure. When NTT is executed, these values can be obtained by directly looking up the table instead of multiplying, like the original implementation.

Additionally, intermediate results need to be performed by Montgomery reduction. After that, the result of Eq. (4) is in Montgomery format and needs to be converted into the normal format by multiplying R. Therefore, the value R can be absorbed as $\zeta^{2br_7(i)+1} \cdot R \mod q$ to save a multiplication. According to Eqs. (1) and (2), our pre-computed table of NTT and INTT could be:

$$
\begin{bmatrix}
\zeta^{0 \times 2br_7(0)} R & \zeta^{0 \times 2br_7(1)} R & \cdots & \zeta^{0 \times 2br_7(127)} R \\
\zeta^{1 \times 2br_7(0)} R & \zeta^{1 \times 2br_7(1)} R & \cdots & \zeta^{1 \times 2br_7(127)} R \\
\vdots & \vdots & \ddots & \vdots \\
\zeta^{127 \times 2br_7(0)} R & \zeta^{127 \times 2br_7(1)} R & \cdots & \zeta^{127 \times 2br_7(127)} R
\end{bmatrix}_{128 \times 128}
\tag{8}
$$

$$
\begin{bmatrix}
n^{-1}\zeta^{-0 \times 2br_7(0)} R & n^{-1}\zeta^{-0 \times 2br_7(1)} R & \cdots & n^{-1}\zeta^{0 \times 2br_7(127)} R \\
n^{-1}\zeta^{-1 \times 2br_7(0)} R & n^{-1}\zeta^{-1 \times 2br_7(1)} R & \cdots & n^{-1}\zeta^{-1 \times 2br_7(127)} R \\
\vdots & \vdots & \ddots & \vdots \\
n^{-1}\zeta^{-127 \times 2br_7(0)} R & n^{-1}\zeta^{-127 \times 2br_7(1)} R & \cdots & n^{-1}\zeta^{-127 \times 2br_7(127)} R
\end{bmatrix}_{128 \times 128}
\tag{9}
$$

Note that the transpose of the matrix can be determined by the flag parameter of the built-in function. In addition, the NTT results are:

$$
\tilde{f}_{2i} = \sum_{j=0}^{127} f_{2j}\zeta^{(2br_7(i)+1)j} R
$$

$$
\tilde{f}_{2i+1} = \sum_{j=0}^{127} f_{2j+1}\zeta^{(2br_7(i)+1)j} R
\tag{10}
$$

4.4 Point-Wise Multiplication and Modular Reduction

Point-Wise Multiplication. In Kyber, the polynomial multiplication $h(x) = f(x) \cdot g(x)$ has also been redefined. Let $\hat{h} = \hat{f} \circ \hat{g} = NTT(f) \circ NTT(g)$ denote the basecase multiplication consisting of the 128 products written as:

$$
\hat{h}_{2i} + \hat{h}_{2i+1}X = (\hat{f}_{2i} + \hat{f}_{2i+1}X)(\hat{g}_{2i} + \hat{g}_{2i+1}X) \mod (X^2 - \zeta^{2br_7(i)+1})
$$

Specifically, the product coefficients can be written as:

$$
\hat{h}_{2i} = \hat{f}_{2i}\hat{g}_{2i} + \hat{f}_{2i+1}\hat{g}_{2i+1}\zeta^{2br_7(i)+1}
$$

$$
\hat{h}_{2i+1} = \hat{f}_{2i}\hat{g}_{2i+1} + \hat{f}_{2i+1}\hat{g}_{2i}
\tag{11}
$$

The point-wise multiplication can be performed with the Karatsuba algorithm [15] to decrease the times of multiplication, and the calculation form of results are listed in Eq. (12).

$$\hat{h}_{2i} = \hat{f}_{2i}\hat{g}_{2i} + \hat{f}_{2i+1}\hat{g}_{2i+1}\zeta^{2br(i)+1}$$
$$\hat{h}_{2i+1} = (\hat{f}_{2i} + \hat{f}_{2i+1})(\hat{g}_{2i} + \hat{g}_{2i+1}) - (\hat{f}_{2i}\hat{g}_{2i} + \hat{f}_{2i+1}\hat{g}_{2i+1})$$

$$(12)$$

One Round Lazy Modular Reduction. For CBD generated vectors, the biggest sum in NTT should be less than $n'q \cdot 2^3$ (where $n' = 128$), which is 22 bits. As mentioned earlier, Tensor Core performs FMA operation, then and the accumulator, represented in INT32, can still cover the range intermediate sum. For a polynomial whose coefficient is up to $q - 1$, we use two 6-bit elements to represent the value. Therefore, $n'q \cdot 2^6$ (25 bits) will not cause overflow. Then, only a round fast modular reduction is needed for the final NTT result.

5   Performance Evaluation and Discussion

In this section, we present our evaluation results firstly, including the performance of the NTT box, and Kyber-512, Kyber-768, Kyber-1024, and perform a comparative analysis with related works. Finally, we discuss the scalability and security of our solution.

5.1   Results of NTT/INTT

Firstly, we test the performance of the two types of NTT. There is no significant discriminative between NTT and INTT except for the pre-computed twiddle factor tables. Since INTT does not involve small coefficients in Kyber, we only evaluate the split-INTT (for INT16). The results are listed in Table 5. For split-NTT, when the thread block size is 128, the performance can reach 247.2 MOPS.

Table 5. The performance of NTT, **Total_case** = 69632, **Grid_size** = 136, $n = 256$

Operation	Input Type	Block size	Time elapsed (ms)	Performance (MOPS)
split-NTT	INT16	128	0.281632	247.2
		256	0.356992	195.1
basic-NTT	INT8	128	0.183296	379.9
		256	0.217088	320.8
split-INTT	INT16	128	0.277376	251.0
		256	0.357376	194.8

Related Work Comparison. We also compare the customized NTT of polynomial vector (*poly_vec*, $n = 256$, $k = 4$) with the counterparts on CPU and GPU, and can obtain a speedup of at least 8.1x. Furthermore, we test the provided source code on our machine and still get about 6.47x improvement. The results are shown in Table 6.

Table 6. Comparison of *polyvec_ntt* in KYBER, $n = 256, k = 4$

	Device	Architecture	Time (ns)°
Ref	W2123	Skylake-W	6,464
Gupt *et al.* [12]	G1060	Pascal	378.1
	P6000	Pascal	202.3
	V100	Volta	135
	R3080	Ampere	107.81*
Ours	R3080	Ampere	16.65

° The average time cost by each instance.
* The code in [12] is downloaded from https://github.com/nainag/PQC and tested on RTX3080.

In fact, Tensor Core is also supported with V100, but not exploited in [12]. Although the gain mainly comes from AI accelerator hardware, the key lies in our fine manipulation to adapt the cryptographic workload into its operating mode. Our Tensor Core based NTT box involves the pre-computed tables of twiddle factors instead of the idea of divide and conquer. Because the initial control granularity of butterfly operation is at single element level, which conflicts with the matrix mode and might make the control very complicated. More importantly, interrupting computation frequently to access memory can severely impact performance when utilizing Tensor Cores.

5.2 Results of Kyber

The security strength recommended by the original author is Kyber-768 ($k = 3$) [29]. In addition, we also test Kyber-512 ($k = 2$) and Kyber-1024 ($k = 4$), and the results are shown in Fig. 8.

Related Work Comparison. The previous implementations of Kyber are based on various platforms, targeting different scenarios and following different design ideas. The FPGA based implementations such as [34], are mainly committed to using fewer hardware resources to reach more achievable performance. The CPU based optimizations such as [5] tend to use vector set instructions for acceleration. Unlike FPGA solutions, in which the improved algorithms are mainly conducted through hardware programming, the hardware circuit of our proposal can no longer be changed, and accelerations can only be carried out around the characteristics it exposes.

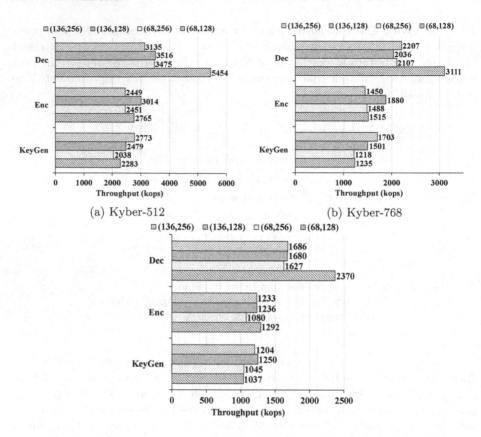

Fig. 8. The performance of Kyber-512, Kyber-768, Kyber-1024

Table 7 lists the average time cost on Kyber-1024 of related works. Compared to resource-constrained devices, we can achieve two orders of magnitude performance improvement. For the optimized AVX2 version Kyber-1024, our prototype can obtain a speedup of approximately 26x, 36x, and 35x for KeyGen, Enc, and Dec respectively. Note that we have not optimized the hash algorithm yet.

5.3   Discussion

Security. The security issue is also an important aspect of cryptographic implementation. An important countermeasure against side-channel attacks is masking [7,26]. The core concept of masking is to split the sensitive variables into multiple shares. There are two split methods, one is Boolean split, which is suitable for block ciphers, and the arithmetic split. The PQC scheme can be combined with either or both. The multi-precision representation used in our work is actually an arithmetic split, so it can be considered that it can enhance the protection against side-channel attacks.

Table 7. Comparison of average time cost on Kyber-1024 with related works

	Platform	KeyGen (μs)	Enc (μs)	Dec (μs)	KX° (k/s)
Pakize Sanal et al. [28]	Apple A12 @2.49 GHz (AES accelerator)	38.23	37.35	36.55	13.4
PQClean [20]	ARM Cortex-A75 @2.8 GHz	137.54	170.25	195.0	3.0
Xing, Y et al. [34]	Xilinx Artix-7	58.2	67.9	86.2	6.93
C-Ref [29]	Intel Core i7-4770K @3.5 GHz (Haswell)	87.8	99.0	113.3	4.97
AVX2-Ref [29]	Intel Core i7-4770K @3.5 GHz (Haswell)	21.01	27.81	22.61	22.9
This work	NVIDIA GeForce RTX 3080	**0.80**	**0.77**	**0.42**	**819.7**

° computed by $\frac{ab}{a+b}$, where a, b are the throughput of KeyGen and Dec.

For Tensor Core itself, as far as we know, it can be treated as an atomic instruction parallel execution unit for calculating with a fixed amount of cycles. According to [23], it is almost impossible to perform a timing attack on parallel AI accelerators so far.

Meanwhile, techniques against side-channel timing leakage, such as eliminating conditional statements in CUDA kernel functions, are also involved in our work, even though they are not the main focus. Tensor Core operations involve no secret-related conditional branch, and the related memory access (pre-computed tables) is secret-irrelevant. In a nutshell, the AI accelerator we introduce will not bring additional security risks.

Scalability. With the upgrade of hardware products, we believe the restrictions would be fewer, and the control interfaces provided could be with finer granularity, which would make they become much more versatile. Though the study case in this paper is a PQC scheme, the proposed solution and techniques might provide reference for other computation-sensitive schemes like homomorphic encryption, of which the polynomial multiplication is also a time-consuming part. Furthermore, in practice, the implementation would be more solid with the optimizations for CUDA hardware, such as multiple working streams, shared memory, and multi-threaded cooperation.

6   Conclusion and Future Work

In this paper, we propose an NTT box based on NVIDIA AI accelerator, Tensor Core. After that, we present a high performance implementation of CRYSTALS-Kyber with our NTT box and achieve considerable performance improvement.

Our work illustrates the tremendous potential of Tensor Core in LBC acceleration. We believe that AI accelerators will become more versatile, and support more operations and precisions. In the future, the subsequent work would cover more lattice-based cryptographic schemes, especially homomorphic encryption (HE) which urgently requires high efficiency for the wider application.

Acknowledgements. We would like to thank the anonymous reviewers for their careful reading of our manuscript and their many insightful comments and suggestions. We are grateful to Massimiliano Albanese for helping us to improve our paper. This work is supported in part by National Key RD Plan of China under Grant No. 2020YFB1005803, the National Natural Science Foundation of China No. 61902392, CCF-Tencent Open Fund under Grant No. RAGR20210131 and CCF-Huawei Populus euphratica Fund.

References

1. Ajtai, M.: Generating hard instances of lattice problems. In: Proceedings of the Twenty-Eighth Annual ACM Symposium on Theory of Computing, pp. 99–108 (1996)
2. Alkım, E., Bilgin, Y.A., Cenk, M.: Compact and simple RLWE based key encapsulation mechanism. In: Schwabe, P., Thériault, N. (eds.) LATINCRYPT 2019. LNCS, vol. 11774, pp. 237–256. Springer, Cham (2019). https://doi.org/10.1007/978-3-030-30530-7_12
3. Banerjee, A., Peikert, C., Rosen, A.: Pseudorandom functions and lattices. In: Pointcheval, D., Johansson, T. (eds.) EUROCRYPT 2012. LNCS, vol. 7237, pp. 719–737. Springer, Heidelberg (2012). https://doi.org/10.1007/978-3-642-29011-4_42
4. Barrett, P.: Implementing the Rivest Shamir and Adleman public key encryption algorithm on a standard digital signal processor. In: Odlyzko, A.M. (ed.) CRYPTO 1986. LNCS, vol. 263, pp. 311–323. Springer, Heidelberg (1987). https://doi.org/10.1007/3-540-47721-7_24
5. Bos, J., et al.: CRYSTALS-Kyber: a CCA-secure module-lattice-based KEM. In: 2018 IEEE European Symposium on Security and Privacy (EuroS&P), pp. 353–367. IEEE (2018)
6. Brakerski, Z., Gentry, C., Vaikuntanathan, V.: (Leveled) fully homomorphic encryption without bootstrapping. ACM Trans. Comput. Theor. (TOCT) **6**(3), 1–36 (2014)
7. Chari, S., Jutla, C.S., Rao, J.R., Rohatgi, P.: Towards sound approaches to counteract power-analysis attacks. In: Wiener, M. (ed.) CRYPTO 1999. LNCS, vol. 1666, pp. 398–412. Springer, Heidelberg (1999). https://doi.org/10.1007/3-540-48405-1_26
8. Cloud, G.: Cloud TPU. https://cloud.google.com/tpu/. Accessed 19 May 2021
9. Cooley, J.W., Tukey, J.W.: An algorithm for the machine calculation of complex fourier series. Math. Comput. **19**(90), 297–301 (1965)
10. Gao, Y., Xu, J., Wang, H.: cuNH: efficient GPU implementations of post-quantum KEM NewHope. IEEE Trans. Parallel Distrib. Syst. **33**(3), 551–568 (2021)
11. Greconici, D.O., Kannwischer, M.J., Sprenkels, D.: Compact dilithium implementations on Cortex-M3 and Cortex-M4. In: IACR Transactions on Cryptographic Hardware and Embedded Systems, pp. 1–24 (2021)

12. Gupta, N., Jati, A., Chauhan, A.K., Chattopadhyay, A.: PQC acceleration using GPUs: FrodoKEM, NewHope, and Kyber. IEEE Trans. Parallel Distrib. Syst. **32**(3), 575–586 (2020)
13. Inc, A.: Apple unleashes M1. www.apple.com/newsroom/2020/11/apple-unleashes-m1/. Accessed 19 May 2021
14. Inc, N.: NVIDIA tensor cores-unprecedented acceleration for HPC and AI. www.nvidia.com/en-us/data-center/tensor-cores/. Accessed 19 May 2021
15. Karatsuba, A.: Multiplication of multidigit numbers on automata. In: Soviet Physics Doklady, vol. 7, pp. 595–596 (1963)
16. Langlois, A., Stehlé, D.: Worst-case to average-case reductions for module lattices. Des. Codes Crypt. **75**(3), 565–599 (2014). https://doi.org/10.1007/s10623-014-9938-4
17. Lu, X., et al.: Lac: Practical ring-LWE based public-key encryption with byte-level modulus. Cryptology ePrint Archive (2018)
18. Lyubashevsky, V., Peikert, C., Regev, O.: On ideal lattices and learning with errors over rings. In: Gilbert, H. (ed.) EUROCRYPT 2010. LNCS, vol. 6110, pp. 1–23. Springer, Heidelberg (2010). https://doi.org/10.1007/978-3-642-13190-5_1
19. Lyubashevsky, V., Seiler, G.: NTTRU: truly fast NTRU using NTT. In: IACR Transactions on Cryptographic Hardware and Embedded Systems, pp. 180–201 (2019)
20. Matthias, K., Peter, S., Douglas, S.: Wiggers: The pqclean project. https://github.com/PQClean/PQClean. Accessed 8 Apr 2022
21. Montgomery, P.L.: Modular multiplication without trial division. Math. Comput. **44**(170), 519–521 (1985)
22. Moody, D.: Status report on the third round of the NIST post-quantum cryptography standardization process. Tech. rep, Gaithersburg, MD (2022)
23. Nakai, T., Suzuki, D., Fujino, T.: Timing black-box attacks: Crafting adversarial examples through timing leaks against DNNs on embedded devices. In: IACR Transactions on Cryptographic Hardware and Embedded Systems, pp. 149–175 (2021)
24. NIST: Post-quantum cryptography, call for proposals. https://csrc.nist.gov/Projects/post-quantum-cryptography/post-quantum-cryptography-standardization/Call-for-Proposals. Accessed 31 Mar 2022
25. NIST: Post-quantum cryptography, selected algorithms 2022. https://csrc.nist.gov/projects/post-quantum-cryptography/selected-algorithms-2022. Accessed 22 Apr 2022
26. Prouff, E., Rivain, M.: Masking against side-channel attacks: a formal security proof. In: Johansson, T., Nguyen, P.Q. (eds.) EUROCRYPT 2013. LNCS, vol. 7881, pp. 142–159. Springer, Heidelberg (2013). https://doi.org/10.1007/978-3-642-38348-9_9
27. Regev, O.: On lattices, learning with errors, random linear codes, and cryptography. J. ACM (JACM) **56**(6), 1–40 (2009)
28. Sanal, P., Karagoz, E., Seo, H., Azarderakhsh, R., Mozaffari-Kermani, M.: Kyber on ARM64: compact implementations of Kyber on 64-Bit ARM cortex-a processors. In: Garcia-Alfaro, J., Li, S., Poovendran, R., Debar, H., Yung, M. (eds.) SecureComm 2021. LNICST, vol. 399, pp. 424–440. Springer, Cham (2021). https://doi.org/10.1007/978-3-030-90022-9_23
29. Schwabe, P.: Crystals-cryptographic suite for algebraic lattices. https://pq-crystals.org/kyber/index.shtml. Accessed 18 May 2021
30. Seiler, G.: Faster AVX2 optimized NTT multiplication for Ring-LWE lattice cryptography. IACR Cryptol. ePrint Arch. **2018**, 39 (2018)

31. Shor, P.W.: Polynomial-time algorithms for prime factorization and discrete logarithms on a quantum computer. SIAM Rev. **41**(2), 303–332 (1999)
32. Toom, A.L.: The complexity of a scheme of functional elements realizing the multiplication of integers. In: Soviet Mathematics Doklady, vol. 3, pp. 714–716 (1963)
33. Wan, L., Zheng, F., Lin, J.: TESLAC: accelerating lattice-based cryptography with AI accelerator. In: Garcia-Alfaro, J., Li, S., Poovendran, R., Debar, H., Yung, M. (eds.) SecureComm 2021. LNICST, vol. 398, pp. 249–269. Springer, Cham (2021). https://doi.org/10.1007/978-3-030-90019-9_13
34. Xing, Y., Li, S.: A compact hardware implementation of CCA-secure key exchange mechanism CRYSTALS-KYBER on FPGA. In: IACR Transactions on Cryptographic Hardware and Embedded Systems, pp. 328–356 (2021)

From Click to Sink: Utilizing AIS for Command and Control in Maritime Cyber Attacks

Ahmed Amro(✉) 🆔 and Vasileios Gkioulos

Norwegian University of Science and Technology, Gjøvik, Norway
{ahmed.amro,vasileios.gkioulos}@ntnu.no

Abstract. The maritime domain is among the critical sectors of our way of life. It is undergoing a major digital transformation introducing changes to its operations and technology. The International Maritime Organization urged the maritime community to introduce cyber risk management into their systems. This includes the continuous identification and analysis of the threat landscape. This paper investigates a novel threat against the maritime infrastructure that utilizes a prominent maritime system that is the Automatic Identification System (AIS) for establishing covert channels. We provide empirical evidence regarding its feasibility and applicability to existing and future maritime systems as well as discuss mitigation measures against it. Additionally, we demonstrate the utility of the covert channels by introducing two realistic cyber attacks against an Autonomous Passenger Ship (APS) emulated in a testing environment. Our findings confirm that AIS can be utilized for establishing covert channels for communicating Command & Control (C&C) messages and transferring small files for updating the cyber arsenal without internet access. Also, the establishment and utilization of the covert channels have been found to be possible using existing attack vectors and technologies related to a wide range of maritime systems. We hope that our findings further motivate the maritime community to increase their efforts for integrating cyber security practices into their systems.

Keywords: Maritime · Cybersecurity · Automatic Identification System (AIS) · Cover channel · *ATT&CK*

1 Introduction

We live in a highly connected world that depends on various means of transportation for the delivery of goods, services, and the transportation of people all around the globe. Thus, the transportation sector is regarded internationally as a critical infrastructure. In the European Union, five modes of transport have been recognized: air, road, rail, maritime, and inland waterways [4]. Among these sectors, this paper targets the maritime domain. The maritime domain is linked to the well-being, prosperity, and security of the citizens of Europe [1]. It is also involved in 90% of the global trade of goods [3] making it a domain worthy of increased attention in the research community.

Maritime systems include a variety of cyber systems including Information Technology (IT) and Operational Technology (OT) which are distributed across port facilities, ships, and other components within the maritime infrastructure. These systems are applied in specific applications in navigation, propulsion and steering, cargo handling, and others. These applications rely on a group of maritime-specific systems such as the Automatic Identification System (AIS), and the Electronic Chart Display and Information System (ECDIS). Additionally, such systems rely on maritime-specific protocols and standards including among others, the National Marine Electronics Association (NMEA) standard, and the AIS protocol. NMEA standard is utilized in the communication between marine systems including the communication of sensor data through message-based protocol [49]. AIS is a special message-based protocol based on the NMEA standard which is utilized in many maritime services including; among others, traffic management, search and rescue, and collision avoidance [41].

Disruptive attacks against the maritime domain can have devastating effects as witnessed in the cyber attack against Mærsk shipping company, which lead to weeks of interrupted operations and losses beyond 300 million US dollars [36]. Also, insufficient security in the maritime systems and protocols has been demonstrated in the literature. To mention a few examples, Balduzzi et al. [25] have demonstrated a wide range of attacks against AIS including spoofing, jamming, and other sorts of misuse while Tran et al. [60] discussed the limited authentication, encryption, and validation in one of the NMEA protocols. Positively, there are demands for the consideration of cyber threats and cyber risk management in the current state of affairs in the maritime domain. The International Maritime Organization (IMO) has adopted Resolution MSC.428(98) [32] encouraging the maritime industry stakeholders to include cyber risk management into their safety management systems. The resolution provides guidelines and requirements for cyber risk management [31]. The guidelines suggest the continuous analysis and assessment of the threat landscape against the maritime infrastructure.

In this direction, this paper investigates attacks in the maritime industry in order to identify novel attacks that can surface into reality in the future. We have identified a limitation in the literature when discussing Command and Control (C&C) activities. Then, we investigate the utility of the Automatic Identification System (AIS) as a covert channel for conducting C&C activities during the development of cyber attacks against maritime infrastructure. In our investigation, we initially developed a threat model of the covert channel focusing on the threat requirements, scope, objectives, and techniques. Afterward, we developed and evaluated a proof of concept of the covert channel. Moreover, we demonstrated the utility and application of the covert channel in two realistic attack scenarios against a modern maritime use case which is an Autonomous Passenger Ship (APS). We aspire to motivate the maritime community to further adopt cybersecurity into their operations and system development practices.

2   Background and Related Work

2.1   Autonomous Passenger Ship

This paper is part of an ongoing research project titled "Autoferry" [50]. The project targets the development of an APS prototype which is named milliAmpere2; an autonomous ferry with the capacity to carry 12 passengers and their luggage across the Trondheim city canal as an alternative for a high-cost bridge [38]. MilliAmpere2 is designed to be fully autonomous with the ability to be supervised and controlled from a Remote Control Center (RCC). The ferry includes an Autonomous Navigation System (ANS) which utilizes data from various sensors for establishing situational awareness and safe navigation. The sensors include lidar, radar, Automatic Identification System (AIS), Global Positioning System (GPS), and others. The ANS forwards sensor data to a Remote Navigation System (RNS) at the RCC through a ship-shore communication link. More details can be found in our earlier article [22]. In this paper, we utilize this APS as a use case for demonstrating two cyber kill chains (i.e. attack scenarios) to showcase the application and utility of the discussed covert channel.

2.2   ATT&CK Framework

Recently, wide adoption is observed for the Adversarial Tactics, Techniques, and Common Knowledge from MITRE, shortly known as the *ATT&CK* framework [57]. *ATT&CK* captures adversarial behavior in enterprise environments, industrial control systems, and other technology domains making it suitable for modeling cyber attacks in a wide range of use cases. The European Union Agency for Cybersecurity (ENISA) utilizes *ATT&CK* terminologies for mapping adversarial activities in their annual threat landscape report [11]. Also, Security Incidents and Event Management (SIEM) systems utilize *ATT&CK* terminologies for detecting adversarial activities [2,10].

The recent adoption of *ATT&CK* as a threat model is observed for modeling threats against maritime systems. Kovanen et al. [45] utilized *ATT&CK* for mapping threat actors' objectives to a remote pilotage system for improved risk assessment and design. Also, Jo et al. [43] proposed a cyber attack analysis method based on *ATT&CK*. The authors described four documented cyber attacks in the maritime domain using *ATT&CK* tactics and techniques. Moreover, in our earlier work [23] we utilized *ATT&CK* as a threat model for describing attacks against navigational functions. In this paper, we will also utilize *ATT&CK* for modeling cyber attacks and provide a proof of concept of some of the *ATT&CK* techniques in common maritime systems.

The *ATT&CK* threat model provides useful terminologies for describing the different elements of threats. In this paper, we rely heavily on both, namely tactics and techniques. Tactics describe the adversarial objectives also referred to as stages of cyber attacks. Techniques on the other hand describe the adversarial method for realizing an objective [57].

2.3   Maritime Kill Chains, Threats and Attacks

In this paper we investigate and aim to answer the following question; what are the adversarial tactics (i.e. objectives) and techniques that are discussed in the literature in the maritime domain and do they cover the current threat landscape. In our research, we rely on the *ATT&CK* framework due to its comprehensive threat model and increased adoption as a new standard for adversarial tactics, techniques, and procedures. We have conducted a comprehensive literature review to identify relevant works that have discussed adversarial techniques across the different stages of cyber attacks (i.e. tactics). This allows for a clearer understanding of the current threat landscape in the maritime domain.

Starting with the reconnaissance stage, Enoch et al. [33] briefly discussed the utility of OpenVAS and NMAP for conducting reconnaissance-related activities in a vessel system. Also, Standard et al. [54] discussed the teaching of network reconnaissance for naval officers during a cybersecurity course for capacity development. Additionally, Lund et al. [47] mentioned that activities at the reconnaissance stage were conducted through physical access to the vessel and access to the network, and ECDIS software. Moreover, Amro [20] has demonstrated the utility of AIS and NMEA communicated messages for gaining both cyber and physical attributes of possible maritime targets.

For gaining access to maritime components and networks; also known as attack delivery, Lund et al. [47] discussed the utilization of a USB flash drive to deliver a malicious payload into the ECDIS machine and execute it. Also, Papastergiou et al. [51] referred to the possibility of gaining access to maritime infrastructure through compromising the supply chain. Additionally, Pavur et al. [52] demonstrated the feasibility of VSAT TCP session hijacking for reaching and controlling maritime VSAT communication. Moreover, Tam and Jones [58] argued that users can be tricked into downloading and executing malicious software or guided into malicious websites.

After gaining access to systems and networks attackers aim to achieve a group of objectives including discovery, credential access, and collection. Hemminghaus et al. [39] target the network for discovery through sniffing and collection of network traffic including navigation data. Jo et al. [43] categorized vulnerability scanning of ship systems, eavesdropping on Voice over Internet Protocol (VoIP), and Wi-Fi communication in the discovery stage of cyber attacks. Pavur et al. [52] demonstrated the ability to collect credit card information, visa, passport, ship manifest, and non-encrypted REST API credentials communicated through eavesdropping on VSAT connections.

In certain cases, attackers desire to perform privilege escalation to execute commands and programs with higher privilege. Lund et al. [47] mentioned that the operator station utilized as the pivot point of their attack demonstration was running already within administrator privilege and therefore doesn't require escalation. However, they referred to hijacking execution flow through a malicious Windows socket dynamic-link library (Winsock DLL), this is among the techniques utilized to achieve privilege escalation, persistence in the target system, and evade defensive measures [13].

Many works have discussed attacks that aim to impact maritime operations. Lund et al. [47] and Hemminghaus et al. [39] discussed the manipulation of sensor messages for impacting the operation of navigation systems. Amro et al. [23] formalized manipulation and denial of view based on navigational data as attacks that can impact navigational functions. Moreover, Hemminghaus et al. [39] referred to alarm suppression for inhibiting response functions as well as spoof reporting messages to impair process control.

Many stages of cyber attacks in the maritime domain are demonstrated and discussed in the literature in sufficient detail. Still, a limited discussion is observed regarding Command and Control (C&C) activities. Hooper [40] has investigated the potential of covert communications in pulsed or continuous-wave radar and discussed the cyber implications of that in the maritime domain. The authors argued that communication links utilizing spectrum-sharing may pave the way for unintended channels (i.e. covert channels); an inclination which we agree with. Hareide et al. [37] bypassed the need for the C&C channel by implementing a specific condition for an attack to be launched when arriving at a certain position. Jo et al. [43] described three maritime cyber incidents including C&C stages with a limited description of the implementation. Enoch et al. [33] have briefly mentioned C&C in the attack model but without details of the implementation. Leite et al. [46] proposed a triggering mechanism for cyber attacks based on radar and AIS messages. The authors proposed and demonstrated a pattern matching technique that can identify false plots depicted on the ECDIS which can be used for triggering cyber attacks. Other than that, to the best of our knowledge, no other work has discussed C&C in the maritime domain in more detail. Therefore, a contribution of this paper is an investigation of the utilization of AIS as a covert channel for C&C attack techniques using real maritime systems. This is intended to raise awareness of yet another possible attack utilizing the AIS protocol and hopefully drive the maritime community to consider cybersecurity more seriously and deeply within their systems.

The concept of a kill chain; a multi-staged cyber attack scenario, is observed in the maritime domain. Hareide et al. [37] have discussed a maritime kill chain for demonstrating the feasibility of cyber attacks in order to increase awareness. The authors relied on a previously developed attack by Lund et al. [47] which also discusses the development of the attack through a kill chain. Also, Jo et al. [43] utilized consequent tactics from *ATT&CK* for describing cyber attacks against maritime systems. In this paper, we will also utilize the concept of kill chains for discussing complete scenarios for cyber attacks that implement our novel Command and Control (C&C) covert channel.

3   AIS as a Covert Channel

In this section, we discuss our analysis of the utility of the AIS as a covert channel supporting adversarial activities throughout different phases of cyber attacks. The analysis considers both the AIS protocol itself as well as AIS devices. This section also describes the threat model with details from different viewpoints.

Context (i.e. physical and cyber architecture), Objectives (i.e. tactics), and techniques. Additionally, a proof of concept of the attack is developed and demonstrated in this section in addition to a discussion of relevant countermeasures.

3.1   Context View

Following a top-down approach, the context of utilizing AIS as a covert channel is discussed in this section. A physical view of the context is demonstrated in Fig. 1a. A threat actor needs to be located in physical proximity to the victim ships either at land or sea. The range is limited by the VHF range of the attacker station and the placement of the antennas on both sides; the range can reach up to 60 nautical miles [19]. The VHF radio frequencies for AIS belong to the licensed portion of the radio spectrum and require a proper license to operate in most countries. Therefore, an attacker without a proper license can be detected and addressed. However, an attacker with a proper license such as an industrial competitor or a maritime entity belonging to a nation-state might operate undetected at this level.

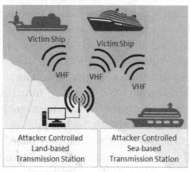

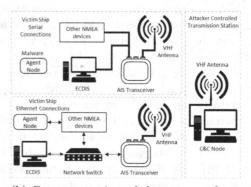

(a) Physical view of the context of utilizing AIS as a covert channel

(b) Component view of the context of utilizing AIS as a covert channel

Fig. 1. Physical and component view for utilizing AIS as a covert channel

A component view of the context is depicted in Fig. 1b. The attacker station consists of a Command and Control (C&C) node that is able to transmit AIS traffic over VHF. On the other hand, the victim ships network might have either serial [29,55,56] or Ethernet connections [30] from the AIS device to internal components. An internal agent node to be controlled by the attacker is needed to receive and execute the (C&C) commands. The agent node is assumed to either be a machine infected with an attacker's controllable malware or a standalone malicious machine. In a ship network consisting of serial connections, malware is expected to infect an existing machine. On the other hand, in an Ethernet network, a standalone machine is a possible alternative. Different attack techniques are needed to establish a covert channel in each network (More details in Sect. 4).

3.2 Tactics and Techniques

The threat model is developed considering variant attacker capabilities and communicated as tactics and techniques using the $ATT\&CK$ terminology. The objectives (i.e. tactics) of the attackers are assumed to be the following:

- Command and Control: send unidirectional C&C messages from an attacker to victims (1 to many). The messages can carry either simple commands or files (e.g. malware). This is assumed to be achievable through properly encoding commands and files into AIS messages. More advanced threat actors are expected to pursue secure C&C communication. They might aim to secure the communication from being revealed, or tampered with. Even if their activities are detected, the executed commands or transferred files are aimed to be kept a secret. This is assumed to be established through hiding command messages into AIS messages with additional obfuscation, steganography, or cryptography.
  A bi-directional channel is expected to require additional components, tactics, and techniques which are items for future work.
- Defense Evasion: this includes avoiding raising the operators' attention or other detection measures. This means that limited impact on legitimate operations is pursued. This is assumed to be achievable through careful selection of AIS message types and fields.

To achieve the C&C objective the attacker can establish the covert channel using a combination of Alternate Network Medium (i.e. VHF) [5] and Protocol Tunneling [17] command and control attack techniques. This combination entails the utilizing of VHF radio communication as a medium for the C&C communication which is tunneled through the AIS protocol. Based on the attacker capabilities to secure it, attackers can apply Data Encoding [7], Data Obfuscation [8] or Encrypted Channel [9]. According to ATT&CK, data encoding can be achieved using standard or non-standard encoding (e.g. Base32), Data obfuscation can be achieved using stenography, protocol impersonation, or junk data, and Encrypted channel can use asymmetric or symmetric cryptography [15]. On the other hand, to avoid detection, the different types of AIS messages and fields are considered to best serve the objectives. The criteria for choosing the most suitable message type and field is that they should provide the largest capacity of transfer and limited impact on operations. The rationale for choosing the largest capacity is to reduce the amount of AIS messages needed to encode C&C messages.

We have considered all possible 27 AIS message types using the description provided By Rayomon [53]. As shown in Table 1, messages 8 and 14 were found to provide the largest capacity while at the same time having a common appearance, unlike message type 26. Moreover, the messages types; if carefully configured, do not provide navigational data that will influence the navigational functions and therefore are expected to have no impact on operations. Message 14 can be utilized in managing distress signals and might invoke a response from a nearby rescue unit [48]. Therefore, we will restrict our discussion in this paper in the utility of message type 8 for C&C. Furthermore, the structure of message 8 content itself is controlled. We analyzed the different content categories to identify the category that allows for the largest capacity and flexible field format. We relied on IMO circulation SN.1/Circ.289 [28] in our analysis. We have identified that a text description message is the best candidate as it includes a text string field with a maximum limit of 161 ASCII characters. Although there is a standard format for this field, it is only recommended and not mandatory to follow.

Table 1. The top 5 AIS message types with the largest fields

Message type	Field	Max size (bits)	Rational
Type 26: Multiple slot binary message	Data	1004	Extremely rare
Type 14: Safety-related broadcast message	Text	968	Suitable
Type 8: Binary broadcast message	Data	966	Suitable
Type 12: Addressed safety-related message	Text	936	Addressed to a specific target Reduced C&C channels
Type 6: binary addressed message	Data	920	Addressed to a specific target Reduced C&C channels

3.3 Proof of Concept

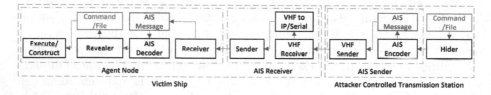

Fig. 2. A logical view of the components of the AIS covert Channel

In this section, we present the development of the proof of concept for utilizing AIS as a covert channel. Figure 2 depicts the required logical components to achieve the attackers' objectives. First, the C&C message or file is input into a hider function to evade detection and the output is then encoded into an AIS message. Then, the message is transmitted over VHF using an AIS transmitter. Should it be received and accepted at the AIS on the victim ship, protocol conversion is expected to forward the AIS messages through a serial link or IP protocol to the ship network; this is traditionally performed by AIS receivers. The agent node then eavesdrops on the AIS message stream, decodes the messages to identify C&C messages (e.g. based on the MMSI or other signal) reveals the

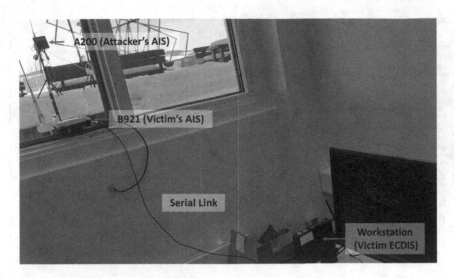

Fig. 3. Setup for the proof of concept of AIS as a covert channel

hidden message, and executes it, or reconstructs it if its part of a file. Through this channel, attackers gain the capabilities to remotely and covertly update their cyber attack arsenal and techniques.

Figure 3 depicts the setup for the proof of concept. It is implemented using two AIS transceivers, namely, em-trak A200 and em-trak B921. A200 is used as the attacker-controlled transmission station. B921 is used as the AIS receiver and is connected through a serial link to a workstation simulating the victim ECDIS. The workstation is equipped with a script that simulates the agent node or malware that is monitoring the AIS messages over the serial link. The script decodes AIS messages and when a C&C message is identified it executes the encoded command or reconstructs the transmitted file.

We conducted several experiments to test if the implementation works. We attempted to send and execute commands as well as construct files at the victim ECDIS. Due to space restrictions, we will present one of these experiments. First, the ciphertext which includes the hidden C&C message is prepared using a python script. In this example, the attacker will send a directory listing command, the plaintext of the hidden message "CM:dir" is encrypted using Advanced Encryption Standard (AES), the ciphertext is "9C6ED8600E1F" and then encoded into an AIS message "!AIVDM,1,1,,B,83o0F400@00>@uQA0ed<1LA P,0*39". The "CM:" string is used to identify a command execution message at the agent node while the "dir" string is the directory listing command in Windows.

Figure 4(a) depicts a photo of the message composer at the A200 AIS transceiver with the ciphertext as the content of the message. After the message was sent, Fig. 4(b) depicts a screenshot of the agent node receiving and executing the command.

(a) Sending from A200   (b) Receiving at the agent node

Fig. 4. Demonstration for sending and receiving covert C&C message over AIS

3.4   Evaluation of the Covert Channel

In this section, we will evaluate the utility of the covert channel to attackers to better analyze the associated risk. The evaluation is discussed based on their type, throughput, and robustness to detection and countermeasures. Then, suggesting suitable improvement for the detection and prevention is provided.

Our analysis considers two hider functions and two settings for the covert channel. The hider functions are Base32 encoding and AES-CFB encryption; with a 16-byte key and a 16 bytes Initialization Vector (IV). The settings are either based on the protocol specifications or the em-track A200 commercial AIS device. The type of the channel is a unidirectional covert channel. The C&C node can transmit messages that the agent node can receive, however, the agent node; on its own, cannot establish an outbound channel through the AIS device. This limits the attackers' capabilities in managing the agent node in the targeted environments. Regarding the throughput, the maximum capacity for the text string field is 966 or 480 bits in the protocol specifications or the A200, respectively. The implementation of encoding or encryption further restricts the capacity. Table 2 depicts the maximum size of the field that can hold the clear segment of a command or a file as well as the corresponding throughput considering the two hider functions, two settings, and two transmission rates (TR).

From the attacker's perspective, using AES as a hider function is a reasonable option since it provides secure communication with only a relatively less throughput than the Base32. Still, secure key establishment and handling is an additional burden the attacker needs to consider. While the Base32 encoding is simpler to implement and provides slightly better throughput, it doesn't provide secure communication and can expose the content of the covert channel. We have also evaluated the utility of this channel for delivering malware

Table 2. Covert channel throughput evaluation

Hider function	Based on	Max field capacity (bit)	Throughput (bit/sec)	
			2 s TR	10 min TR
Base32	Protocol specs	600	300	1
	AIS200 em-trak	276	138	0,46
AES	Protocol specs	480	240	0,8
	AIS200 em-trak	240	120	0,4

TR: Transmission Rate

to the victim ship and allowing threat actors to update their adversarial cyber arsenal at sea. With such a transmission rate, transporting a 338 Kb malware; the average malware size in 2010 [14] at a 2-sec transmission rate would take 3 h considering the protocol specifications. However, transporting the NotPetya malware which is 1,5 Gb [6] would take 29826 h at the same transmission rate. Therefore, the utility of this covert channel is limited to commands and small malware. Regarding robustness to detection and countermeasures, several works have discussed countermeasures for securing AIS communication using encryption for authentication and integrity [24,25,35,44]. Although a wide adoption of such countermeasures is not observed we argue that encryption doesn't eliminate the threat of covert channels against AIS. In the case of utilizing a public key infrastructure (PKI) for authenticating the different entities participating in the AIS communication, threat actors with legitimate credentials such as boat and ship owners, competitors, and nation-states would still be able to utilize the channel. Moreover, there is a discussion regarding anomaly detection algorithms for AIS such as the work of Iphar et al. [42], Blauwkamp et al. [27] and Balduzzi et al. [25]. However, there is no discussion regarding anomalies associated with AIS message type 8. Additionally, if the attacker maintained a reduced transmission rate, the likelihood of detecting anomalies is expected to be reduced. Real maritime infrastructure is required for formal evaluation of the robustness of this covert channel against detection. Therefore, we argue that such channels constitute a threat to the maritime infrastructure that is utilizing AIS communication and countermeasures should be tuned to detect them. Future efforts are advised for investigating the utility of anomaly detection in detecting the covert channel.

4 Adversary Emulation Against an Auto-remote Vessel

To demonstrate the utility of the proposed covert channel for attackers, and its technical application in realistic attack scenarios, we will apply an adversary emulation process; a security assessment process applying realistic attack scenarios which emulate the capabilities of real threat actors [57]. This enables the elicitation and evaluation of relevant security control.

In this section, we present two cyber kill chains emulating two attack scenarios against an Autonomous Passenger Ship (APS) use case which is discussed in Sect. 2.1. The kill chains are constructed based on the observed adversarial techniques in the maritime industry across the different kill chain phases which are discussed in Sect. 2.3. Additionally, we improve the kill chains by utilizing the proposed C&C channel discussed in Sect. 3 to demonstrate its application. We argue that the kill chains are also relevant for other maritime use cases encompassing similar technologies.

We utilize our previously proposed maritime-themed testbed [21] for the development of the adversarial techniques. The utilization of the testbed with regards to this paper is system replication and system analysis. During system replication, we developed a replica of the target system using real and simulated components, and then target the developed replica with a group of attack techniques emulating an adversarial behavior.

4.1   Target Environment

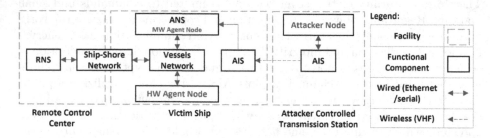

Fig. 5. A model of the target environment for the development of the kill chains

A model of the target environment is depicted in Fig. 5. It emulates three facilities, namely, an attacker-controlled transmission station, a victim ship, and a remote control center. The attacker station consists of capabilities to create and transmit command and control traffic encapsulated within AIS messages over VHF. The A200 AIS is utilized at this station. The victim ship consists of an AIS transceiver; in this setup, the B921 is utilized. The receiver AIS receives AIS messages and forwards them over a serial link to the Autonomous Navigation System (ANS) which in turn forwards it to the Remote Navigation System (RNS) over a ship-shore network. The ANS and RNS are emulated using virtual machines while the vessel and ship-shore networks are emulated using virtual networking using Virtualbox. Due to the lack of available ANS and RNS software, both components are simulated as chart plotters using the OpenCPN software. The difference between them is that the ANS is not intended to be monitored by a human operator while the RNS is. The autonomous and remote navigation functions are simulated only through rendering the AIS and companion NMEA messages in the chart plotter. No control functions are simulated in this environment. Additionally, another virtual machine with Kali Linux is added to simulate a hardware agent node. This environment will be utilized in the demonstration of the later kill chains and is added as part of our testbed for further research.

4.2 Cyber Kill Chains

In this section, we present and discuss two attack scenarios. We will utilize the *ATT&CK* terminologies to facilitate the communication of a threat. In this paper, we utilized the abstract concept of the tactics and techniques and positioned them in a maritime context. We utilized attack trees for the description of the kill chain as it has been observed to be a common approach in the literature [33,34]. These kill chains can later be used as adversary emulation exercises for the evaluation of cybersecurity controls in maritime systems with technologies similar to the ones in the testing environment.

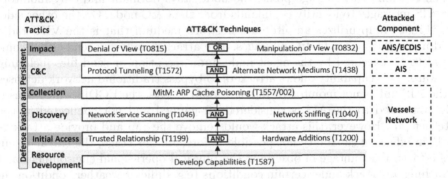

Fig. 6. Remotely and covertly controlling a malicious hardware agent node

Kill Chain 1: Impact Through Malicious Hardware Agent Node. The first kill chain depicted in Fig. 6 describes the following scenario. A motivated threat actor invests in the development of attacking capabilities into the attacker agent node to be boarded on the vessel and remotely controlled from a place within range by utilizing the covert channel described in Sect. 3. The capabilities include a hardware component with Ethernet and software to receive and execute commands from the C&C node. In our environment, this is achieved through the Kali Linux virtual machine which can later be shipped into a Raspberry Pi or small hardware. The node is also equipped with scripts that are needed to conduct the later attack techniques. First, the developed capability needs to be connected to the ship network. Considering the lack of crew on the autonomous vessels, an attacker may attempt to access the vessel and locate the network and insert the agent node (Hardware Additions [12] or Transient Cyber Asset [18]). The success of this depends on the imposed physical security controls. In the case that physical controls exist, threat actors could exploit trusted relations and gain access to the network for several reasons (e.g. maintenance) and insert the node. This is a communicated concern in the maritime community. BIMCO; a global organization for shipowners, charterers, shipbrokers, and agents, discussed the issue of the lack of control of the onboard systems during ship visits in their latest guidelines [26]. They argued that knowing whether malicious software has been left in the systems onboard vessels is difficult. After the insertion of the node, assuming it received valid network configurations (e.g. through DHCP), the node is developed to conduct network service scanning using a scanning tool (e.g. NMAP) and sniffing using a network sniffer (e.g. tshark) to identify other components in the network. Later, target components with specific criteria are identified; certain operating system versions, or certain network services. The chosen targets are then targeted by a MitM attack in the form of ARP spoofing using a MitM tool (e.g. Ettercap). If that is successful, the node should be capable of eavesdropping on network traffic passing to and from the attacked components in the vessel network including AIS messages. When reaching this vantage point, the node stays dormant and only monitors the AIS messages to identify commands from the C&C node. On the other side, the threat group utilizes an alternate network medium that is the VHF radio used in the AIS to send C&C messages. The attacker node can send either command to be executed by the agent node upon reception or send files including malware. This capability allows attackers to bypass traditional network defenses if the AIS link is not monitored. In traditional vessels, the ECDIS which is usually connected to the AIS is considered air-gapped and not connected to the internet [37]. However, this attack would remove the gap and provide attackers with an offensive capability not possible before. At this stage, the threat group has a tactical advantage of observing the physical operational environment and launching an attack under certain conditions (e.g. difficult weather conditions in which visibility is limited). Their next step is targeting the NEMA messages in a combination of denial of view and manipulation of view attacks. The options for the attackers are a lot, only limited by the number of NMEA messages utilized in the vessels and their criticality to the navigation functions. In our earlier work, we formalized and demonstrated a group of such attacks [23]. One instance could be that the attackers choose to drop radar messages (TTM messages) going to the ANS denying it from establishing accurate rendering of the vessels in the physical environment. Also, attackers can manipulate the actual Speed Over Ground (SoG) estimated from the GPS to impact the speed of the vessel. According to a previously conducted Preliminary Hazard Analysis for an autonomous ferry use case, manipulation of sensor data could lead to collisions or ship sinking [59]. This concludes the first kill chain which can; in the lack of proper defenses, cause few clicks to sink a vessel.

Throughout the kill chain, several evasion and persistence techniques can be employed to challenge the detection and countermeasures and maintain a foothold in the network. This can include the utilization of the hider functions in the covert channel (Sect. 3), applying slight modification to the sensor data, and others.

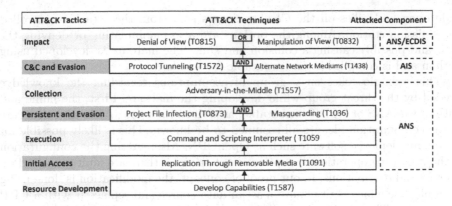

Fig. 7. Remotely and covertly controlling a malware agent node

Kill Chain 2: Impact Through Malware. The second kill chain depicted in Fig. 7 describes the following scenario. A motivated threat actor targets the APS through the maintenance personnel boarding the APS. It is assumed that the malware is loaded into the ANS through a USB stick. The malware relies on commands and scripting for executing its tasks. Upon execution, the malware aims to eavesdrop on the AIS messages communicated over the serial link at the ANS. However, serial interfaces allow only a single listener. In principle, there are several options to bypass this constraint. One option is discussed by Lund et al. [47] through malicious Winsock DLL (Sect. 2.3). This direction, however, would require escalating privilege. Another option, which is explored in this paper, is to modify the configuration file of the ANS regarding the sources of AIS messages. A similar technique suggested in *ATT&CK* is called Project File Infection [16]. This option, in principle, doesn't require escalated privileges under the assumption that the permissions to modify the configuration files are granted to normal users. This is the case for the OpenCPN software. Therefore, the malware is programmed to first close the OpenCPN software to release the serial interface and update the data source configuration to receive AIS and NMEA messages from the malware over UDP and then reopen the software quickly. In this manner, the malware masquerades as a legitimate data source. However, during testing, it was observed that this activity can be detected by the local firewall. A message is shown on the monitor requesting acceptance for the creation of a new connection. Assuming that a local firewall is activated at the ECDIS, the attacker needs to implement techniques to bypass it. Now the malware is actually in the middle between the AIS and the OpenCPN software. It has access to the serial link, can collect the messages, and forwards them to the OpenCPN software to avoid disrupting the operations. At this vantage point, the malware keeps monitoring the messages waiting for a C&C message. When one arrives the malware can distinguish if it's a command to be executed or file segments to be reconstructed. From this point forward, similar to the previous kill chain, the range of possible activities the malware can perform is wide open and relies on the C&C messages sent from the attacker-controlled transmission station. Among the options are also manipulating or denying the view and possibly causing a collision and sink. The malware is developed using python and is compiled as an executable for windows.

This scenario relies on a group of assumptions regarding the knowledge needed by the threat group while developing the malware. First, the name and path of the ANS or ECDIS executable, as well as the name, path, and structure of the configuration file, are all assumed to be known. This is likely possible for commonly deployed software such as OpenCPN. Also, altering the configuration without causing operation disruption is not trivial if there are multiple AIS data sources and destinations. In our proof of concept, the modification is done using a simple rule which is to remove a serial data source and replace it with a UDP data source. These kill chain conditions render it a targeted attack that requires a sufficient level of the domain and system knowledge in addition to a moderate level of complexity.

5   Conclusion

Recent efforts are undergoing to introduce cyber risk management into the maritime community. This includes the continuous identification and analysis of the threat landscape. In this direction, this paper presents an overview of the maritime cyber threat landscape and presents the results of an investigation of a novel cyber attack against maritime systems. The attack is in the form of a covert channel utilizing the prominent Automatic Identification System (AIS) for sending Command & Control messages and delivering malware. We have investigated the feasibility of this attack by developing a threat model utilizing the *ATT&CK* framework, developing a proof of concept of the attack, as well as presenting two cyber attack scenarios (i.e. kill chains) that can utilize this attack. The feasibility of the attack has been demonstrated using existing technology that is relevant to a wide range of traditional and future maritime systems including autonomous vessels. The findings are hoped to urge the maritime community to increase their integration of cybersecurity practices. Future work can be dedicated to the investigation and development of mitigation solutions against the proposed covert channel. Additionally, the proposed kill chains can be utilized as adversary emulation plans for the evaluation of cybersecurity of maritime systems.

References

1. European defence agency, maritime domain (2017). https://eda.europa.eu/docs/default-source/eda-factsheets/2017-09-27-factsheet-maritime
2. How mitre att&ck alignment supercharges your siem (2019). www.securonix.com/how-mitre-attack-alignment-supercharges-your-siem/
3. Ocean shipping and shipbuilding (2019). www.oecd.org/ocean/topics/ocean-shipping/

4. Transport modes (2019). https://ec.europa.eu/transport/modes_en
5. Alternate network mediums (2021). https://attack.mitre.org/techniques/T1438/. Accessed 30 Jan 2022
6. Backdoor built in to widely used tax app seeded last week's notpetya outbreak (2021). https://arstechnica.com/information-technology/2017/07/heavily-armed-police-raid-company-that-seeded-last-weeks-notpetya-outbreak/. Accessed 20 Dec 2021
7. Data encoding (2021). https://attack.mitre.org/techniques/T1132/. Accessed 30 Jan 2022
8. Data obfuscation (2021). https://attack.mitre.org/techniques/T1001/. Accessed 30 Jan 2022
9. Encrypted channel (2021). https://attack.mitre.org/techniques/T1573/. Accessed 30 Jan 2022
10. Enhancing with mitre (2021). https://documentation.wazuh.com/current/user-manual/ruleset/mitre.html
11. Enisa threat landscape 2021 (2021). https://www.enisa.europa.eu/publications/enisa-threat-landscape-2021
12. Hardware additions (2021). https://attack.mitre.org/techniques/T1200/
13. Hijack execution flow: Dll search order hijacking (2021). https://attack.mitre.org/techniques/T1574/001/. Accessed 14 Mar 2022
14. How large is a piece of malware? (2021). https://nakedsecurity.sophos.com/2010/07/27/large-piece-malware/. Accessed 20 Dec 2021
15. Mitre att&ck (2021). https://attack.mitre.org/. Accessed 14 Dec 2021
16. Project file infection (2021). https://collaborate.mitre.org/attackics/index.php/Technique/T0873
17. Protocol tunneling (2021). https://attack.mitre.org/techniques/T1572/. Accessed 30 Jan 2022
18. Transient cyber asset (2021). https://collaborate.mitre.org/attackics/index.php/Technique/T0864
19. Two-way radio range, the facts about distance (2021). https://quality2wayradios.com/store/radio-range-distance. Accessed 14 Dec 2021
20. Amro, A.: Cyber-physical tracking of IoT devices: a maritime use case. In: Norsk IKT-konferanse for forskning og utdanning. No. 3 (2021)
21. Amro, A., Gkioulos, V.: Communication and cybersecurity testbed for autonomous passenger ship. In: European Symposium on Research in Computer Security, pp. 5–22. Springer, Heidelberg (2021). https://doi.org/10.1007/978-3-030-95484-0_1
22. Amro, A., Gkioulos, V., Katsikas, S.: Communication architecture for autonomous passenger ship. Proc. Inst. Mech. Eng. Part O: J. Risk Reliabil., 1748006X211002546 (2021)
23. Amro, A., Oruc, A., Gkioulos, V., Katsikas, S.: Navigation data anomaly analysis and detection. Information 13(3) (2022). www.mdpi.com/2078-2489/13/3/104. https://doi.org/10.3390/info13030104
24. Aziz, A., Tedeschi, P., Sciancalepore, S., Di Pietro, R.: Secureais-securing pairwise vessels communications. In: 2020 IEEE Conference on Communications and Network Security (CNS), pp. 1–9. IEEE (2020)
25. Balduzzi, M., Pasta, A., Wilhoit, K.: A security evaluation of AIS automated identification system. In: Proceedings of the 30th Annual Computer Security Applications Conference, pp. 436–445 (2014)
26. BIMCO: the guidelines on cyber security onboard ships. BIMCO (2016)

27. Blauwkamp, D., Nguyen, T.D., Xie, G.G.: Toward a deep learning approach to behavior-based AIS traffic anomaly detection. In: Dynamic and Novel Advances in Machine Learning and Intelligent Cyber Security (DYNAMICS) Workshop, San Juan, PR (2018). https://faculty.nps.edu/Xie/papers/ais_analysis_18.pdf
28. Circular, I.D.S.: Guidance on the use of AIS application-specific messages—IMO NAV55/21/Add 1
29. Commission, I.I.E., et al.: Iec 61162–1 (2010)
30. Commission, I.I.E., et al.: Iec 61162–450 (2016)
31. Committee, T.M.S.: Interim guidelines on maritime cyber risk management (msc-fal.1/circ.3/rev.1). https://cutt.ly/6R8wqjN
32. Committee, T.M.S.: International maritime organization (imo) guidelines on maritime cyber risk management (2017). www.imo.org/en/OurWork/Security/Pages/Cyber-security.aspx
33. Enoch, S.Y., Lee, J.S., Kim, D.S.: Novel security models, metrics and security assessment for maritime vessel networks. Comput. Netw. **189**, 107934 (2021)
34. Glomsrud, J., Xie, J.: A structured stpa safety and security co-analysis framework for autonomous ships. In: European Safety and Reliability conference, Germany, Hannover (2019)
35. Goudosis, A., Katsikas, S.: Secure AIS with identity-based authentication and encryption. TransNav: Int. J. Marine Navig. Saf. Sea Transp. **14**(2) (2020)
36. Greenberg, A.: The untold story of notpetya, the most devastating cyberattack in history. https://bit.ly/MaerskAttack
37. Hareide, O.S., Jøsok, Ø., Lund, M.S., Ostnes, R., Helkala, K.: Enhancing navigator competence by demonstrating maritime cyber security. J. Navig. **71**(5), 1025–1039 (2018)
38. Havdal, G., Heggelund, C.T., Larssen, C.H.: Design of a Small Autonomous Passenger Ferry. Master's thesis, NTNU (2017)
39. Hemminghaus, C., Bauer, J., Padilla, E.: Brat: a bridge attack tool for cyber security assessments of maritime systems (2021)
40. Hooper, J.L.: Considerations for operationalizing capabilities for embedded communications signals in maritime radar. Technical report, NAVAL POSTGRADUATE SCHOOL MONTEREY CA (2018)
41. IMO: Resolution a.1106(29) revised guidelines for the onboard operational use of shipborne automatic identification systems (AIS) (2015)
42. Iphar, C., Ray, C., Napoli, A.: Data integrity assessment for maritime anomaly detection. Expert Syst. Appl. **147**, 113219 (2020)
43. Jo, Y., Choi, O., You, J., Cha, Y., Lee, D.H.: Cyberattack models for ship equipment based on the mitre att&ck framework. Sensors **22**(5), 1860 (2022)
44. Kessler, G.: Protected ais: a demonstration of capability scheme to provide authentication and message integrity. TransNav: Int. J. Marine Navig. Saf. Sea Transp. **14**(2) (2020)
45. Kovanen, T., Pöyhönen, J., Lehto, M.: epilotage system of systems' cyber threat impact evaluation. In: ICCWS 2021 16th International Conference on Cyber Warfare and Security. p. 144. Academic Conferences Limited (2021)
46. Leite Junior, W.C., de Moraes, C.C., de Albuquerque, C.E., Machado, R.C.S., de Sá, A.O.: A triggering mechanism for cyber-attacks in naval sensors and systems. Sensors **21**(9), 3195 (2021)
47. Lund, M.S., Hareide, O.S., Jøsok, Ø.: An attack on an integrated navigation system (2018)
48. Maritime, N.R.F.N.: 46 ais safety-related messaging. https://puc.overheid.nl/nsi/doc/PUC_2045_14/1/

49. NMEA: National marine electronics association - nmea0183 standard (2002)
50. NTNU Autoferry: Autoferry - Autonomous all-electric passenger ferries for urban water transport (2018). www.ntnu.edu/autoferry
51. Papastergiou, S., Kalogeraki, E.-M., Polemi, N., Douligeris, C.: Challenges and issues in risk assessment in modern maritime systems. In: Tsihrintzis, G.A., Virvou, M. (eds.) Advances in Core Computer Science-Based Technologies. LAIS, vol. 14, pp. 129–156. Springer, Cham (2021). https://doi.org/10.1007/978-3-030-41196-1_7
52. Pavur, J., Moser, D., Strohmeier, M., Lenders, V., Martinovic, I.: A tale of sea and sky on the security of maritime vsat communications. In: 2020 IEEE Symposium on Security and Privacy (SP), pp. 1384–1400. IEEE (2020)
53. Raymond, E.S.: Aivdm/aivdo protocol decoding. https://gpsd.gitlab.io/gpsd/AIVDM.html
54. Standard, S., Greenlaw, R., Phillips, A., Stahl, D., Schultz, J.: Network reconnaissance, attack, and defense laboratories for an introductory cyber-security course. ACM Inroads **4**(3), 52–64 (2013)
55. Std, I.: 61162-2. Maritime Navigation and radiocommunication equipment and systems-Digital interfaces-Part2: single talker and multiple listeners, high-speed transmission (1998)
56. Std, I.: 61162-3. Maritime Navigation and radiocommunication equipment and systems-Digital interfaces-Part3: serial data instrument network (2008)
57. Strom, B.E., Applebaum, A., Miller, D.P., Nickels, K.C., Pennington, A.G., Thomas, C.B.: Mitre att&ck: design and philosophy. Technical report (2018)
58. Tam, K., Jones, K.: Macra: a model-based framework for maritime cyber-risk assessment. WMU J. Maritime Aff. **18**(1), 129–163 (2019)
59. Thieme, C.A., Guo, C., Utne, I.B., Haugen, S.: Preliminary hazard analysis of a small harbor passenger ferry-results, challenges and further work. In: Journal of Physics: Conference Series, vol. 1357, p. 012024. IOP Publishing (2019)
60. Tran, K., Keene, S., Fretheim, E., Tsikerdekis, M.: Marine network protocols and security risks. J. Cybersecur. Priv. **1**(2), 239–251 (2021)

Efficient Hash-Based Redactable Signature for Smart Grid Applications

Fei Zhu[1]([✉]), Xun Yi[1], Alsharif Abuadbba[2], Junwei Luo[1], Surya Nepal[2],
and Xinyi Huang[3]

[1] School of Computing Technologies, RMIT University, Melbourne, Australia
feizcscoding@gmail.com,{xun.yi,junwei.luo}@rmit.edu.au
[2] CSIRO Data61 and Cyber Security CRC, Marsfield, NSW 2122, Australia
{sharif.abuadbba,surya.nepal}@data61.csiro.au
[3] Artificial Intelligence Thrust, Information Hub, Hong Kong University of Science
and Technology (Guangzhou), Guangzhou, China
xinyi@ust.hk

Abstract. The sharing of energy usage data in smart grids is becoming increasingly popular because it not only allows different entities to access fine-grained energy consumption data but also improves the effectiveness of smart grid technologies. How to ensure both verifiability and privacy of the shared data is a vital issue. Most existing privacy-preserving authentication schemes greatly hinder the flexibility of sharing data among multiple parties due to vulnerability and inefficiency reasons. The customer-centric energy usage data management framework based on redactable signature (RS) technology can be seen as an effective solution. It offers customers the flexibility to remove parts of privacy-sensitive data depending on different data usage demands, and ensures data verifiability for third party service providers. However, existing RS schemes are computationally inefficient for constrained devices such as smart meters. Besides, it is said that quantum computers are expected to break all traditional public-key primitives. In this regard, almost all existing RS schemes are vulnerable to quantum attacks. To address the above concerns, in this work, we propose a hash-based RS scheme HRSS based on a variant of the Goldreich-Goldwasser-Micali tree, a length-doubling pseudorandom generator, and an underlying SPHINCS$^+$ framework. Our HRSS is the first quantum-safe RS scheme, where the security depends only on the security of underlying hash functions. We instantiate and evaluate the performance of our design. Theoretical and experimental comparisons with recent works show that HRSS is practical for smart grids.

Keywords: Redactable signature · Privacy · Hash-based · Smart grids

1 Introduction

As one of the critical applications of Internet of Things (IoT) technology, smart grids not only provide customers with high-quality electricity services but also

V. Atluri et al. (Eds.): ESORICS 2022, LNCS 13556, pp. 554–573, 2022.
https://doi.org/10.1007/978-3-031-17143-7_27

offer an efficient and accurate power management platform for utilities. In smart grid systems, customers' data collected by smart meters are often shared with third party service providers. For example, the utility company PG&E outsources customers' energy usage data to the software-as-a-service company Opower to take advantage of some recommendation services [28]. Besides, to enjoy services, customers are also encouraged to share their data with Demand-Response aggregators (e.g., Enel X [39]) or social gaming sites (i.e., aiming at promoting energy saving through social interaction).

Authentication of customers' energy usage data is a significant problem since the communication network may not be entirely credible and the data may be incomplete or tampered with during the sharing process. Besides, considering that the energy usage data usually contains some privacy-sensitive information about the customer, such as billing data and information on personal electricity consumption habits [35], the privacy issue should also be concerned. In order to ensure both privacy and integrity of the energy usage data, serval authentication schemes based on group signatures [15,18], ring signatures [14,36], authenticated encryption schemes [12,17,37], and signcryption schemes [1,34] have been proposed. However, these designs are impractical for smart grids to achieve flexible data sharing due to serval vulnerability and inefficiency reasons. In addition, once the data is shared with other parties, the customer still loses control of how his data is used. Even worse, the energy-related information may provide business intelligence to competitors or be used by criminals.

What's more, third party service providers usually prefer to gather as much data as they want, without regard to whether it is required for providing services. This contravenes the 'minimal disclosure' principle recommended by NIST [22] and the 'minimize the amount of collected data' principle of EU's GDPR [38]. Therefore, from the customers' perspective, the amount of energy usage data disclosed to third parties should be minimized while obtaining the maximum benefit. However, none of the above schemes consider allowing the client to control the amount of information to be disclosed.

The customer-centric energy usage data management framework proposed by Lahoti et al. [19] can be seen as an effective approach for protecting data privacy while preserving its verifiability. Such a framework draws on the concept of redactable signature (RS) [16], where a signature holder (i.e., the customer) is allowed to independently remove parts of the authenticated data without invalidating the respective signature. More concretely, as shown in Fig. 1, a smart meter installed by the utility collects and signs the energy usage data of a customer by using an RS scheme. The data is stored in a data repository controlled by a customer for further utilization. When the customer intends to share the data with a third party service provider, he can take control of the repository, remove privacy-sensitive or unneeded parts of the data (e.g., billing data), and derive a redacted signature for the minimal-disclosure form of data. Upon receiving the shared data, the service provider can check its integrity and source without knowing any content information about deleted parts.

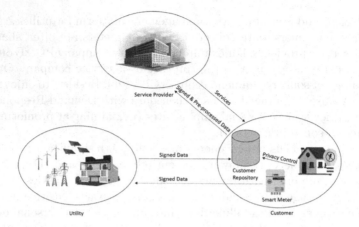

Fig. 1. Customer-centric energy usage data management framework. The figure is adapted from [21].

1.1   The Motivation

By adopting RS in a customer-centric energy usage data management framework, customers are able to get maximal service while sharing minimal data with third parties in a privacy-preserving manner. This satisfies the principle for processing personal data in NIST and EU's GDPR. Although various RS schemes have been proposed in previous work [7,21,27,30,31,41], deploying these solutions to actual energy usage data sharing remains a challenge due to security and performance reasons.

In terms of performance, existing RS schemes are designed based on different cryptographic primitives, such as message commitment scheme [33], traditional RSA signature scheme [16], bilinear pairing [24], and cryptographic accumulator [9,41]. All these constructions require expensive modular multiplication, exponentiation, or pairing operations, which are too complex for resource-limited IoT devices. On the other hand, existing RS schemes are mainly designed based on the traditional difficult problems in number theory; however, the rapid development of quantum computing theory and practice brings great uncertainty to these schemes. Recent efforts by NIST [25] and other organizations to move toward post-quantum algorithms have made the design of quantum-secure digital signatures of high importance.

Hash functions have been extensively studied for decades and have desirable performance, minimal security assumptions, and resistance to quantum attacks. Constructed using hash functions, hash-based signature schemes featuring smaller architectures and key sizes are viable solutions. However, to our limited knowledge, there is no such a lightweight RS in the literature. Therefore, we aim at the question of how to design such an RS scheme to fill this gap.

1.2 Contributions

In general, we make the following contributions in this work:

- To satisfy the application requirements for secure sharing of energy usage data in smart grids, we propose a hash-based RS scheme HRSS. It can provide flexible privacy-enhanced data sharing mechanisms for customers and ensure data verifiability for third party service providers, depending on different data usage demands.
- Our HRSS is the first quantum-safe RS with minimal security assumptions. As shown in Table 1 of Sect. 6, its security depends only on the security of underlying hash functions.
- We instantiate and evaluate the performance of our design. Theoretical and experimental comparisons with recent works show that HRSS is practical for smart grids. Let's take the example of a requirement to authenticate the data containing 100 sub-messages and remove 50 sub-messages from it. The total time cost (and energy consumption) of HRSS is 55.46% and 2.06% of that of the schemes in [21] and [31], respectively. Similarly, the secret key size is about 15.38% and 1.98% of that of the schemes in [21] and [31], respectively; the public key size is about 0.88% and 0.01% of that of the scheme in [21] and [31], respectively.
- Due to the underlying SPHINCS+ framework, our signature size and the redacted signature size are longer than the above state-of-the-art works; however, it is still reasonable. We also discuss possible solutions on how to reduce the size.

1.3 Organization

The remaining sections are organized as follows: The next section reviews related works and Sect. 3 provides the required preliminaries. Section 4 defines the notion of RS and its security models. In Sect. 5, we present our HRSS and analyze its security. Section 6 presents the performance analysis, and Sect. 7 discusses how to optimize our scheme further. We finally conclude the work in Sect. 8.

2 Related Work

Privacy-Preserving Authentication Schemes. The sharing of energy usage data while ensuring customers' privacy in smart grid systems has been studied in the literature. Jeske [15] proposed a privacy-preserving scheme for smart grids based on a group signature, in which a customer's energy usage data can be analyzed without revealing his identity. However, Kong et al. [18] pointed out that the scheme cannot revoke the anonymity of a malicious user. Then they designed a new scheme based on group blind signature. However, the scheme requires multiple interactions between the smart meter and other entities, such as the smart substation, which has great limitations in practical applications. Huang et al. [14] designed an energy usage data sharing scheme for large-scale smart grid systems based on the forward-secure identity-based ring signature. Their scheme eliminates the process of public key certificate verification, and the property of forward security enhances the security of the smart meter's secret key. However, the scheme has a high computation complexity. Taking advantage of the tamper-proof and traceable features of blockchain technology, Tang et al. [36] designed a multi-authority traceable ring signature scheme for energy consumption data collection; however, the heavyweight pairing operations make the scheme inefficient for smart meters. Gope [12] et al. put forward a privacy-preserving data aggregation scheme for dynamic electricity pricing-based billing. However, authenticated encryption-based constructions [17,37] require the data sender and receiver to share a secret key in advance, thus limiting the flexibility of sharing data. Ahene et al. [1] designed a certificateless signcryption with proxy re-encryption scheme for smart grids, but the scheme is inefficient. Sui et al. [34] et al. designed an identity-based signcryption protocol for smart grids. Their focus is to collect a set of customers' energy usage data for a data collector (such as the utility company), and the collector's computational cost is distributed to all smart meters. In fact, none of the above schemes are considered from the customers' perspective, allowing them to control the amount of information to be disclosed. Besides, Saxena et al. [32] designed an efficient one-time signature scheme for delivering authentic control commands in smart grids. However, since they only focus on the accuracy of command delivery, the scheme does not consider privacy issues.

RS Schemes. Johnson et al. [16] designed the first RS scheme based on a Merkle hash tree and Goldreich-Goldwasser-Micali (GGM) tree [11]. However, Chang et al. [7] pointed out the scheme cannot hide the length of removed message blocks from the structures of the redacted trees. Such length information could be critical when the deleted message has low entropy. Nojima et al. [27] proposed a storage-efficient RS scheme for bit-wise redaction, which employs a prime sequence generator and the Goldreich-Levin hard-core predicate [10] to share random primes to redact message blocks and hide the removed message blocks. However, the scheme is computationally inefficient. Chang et al. [7] proposed a variant of the GGM tree and constructed a new RSA-like hash function to map an annotated string to a set of random elements on the basis of a division-intractable hash function and strong RSA assumption. Based on the above components and an underlying RS scheme for sets, they proposed an RS scheme for strings. There are also many other RS schemes that focus on achieving some additional features in the literature, such as transparency [9,24], accountability [30], mergeability [29], and unlinkability [6]; however, the additional attributes usually bring performance degradation, making it difficult for these solutions to be competitive in resource-constrained environments. Recently, Liu et al. [21] put forward a bilinear-map accumulator-based RS scheme; the batch-data-block verification property in their scheme improves the signing and verification efficiency. However, the scheme still requires many exponentiation and pairing operations. Sanders [31] proposed an RS scheme with constant signature size; however, this property is traded off at the expense of computational performance and key length. In addition, the above RS schemes are designed based on the traditional difficult problems in number theory. Considering that quantum computers will likely break existing cryptographic algorithms and threaten the security of our data, there is a strong desire to design a lightweight quantum-safe RS to ensure smart grid security.

3 Preliminaries

This section reviews some basic concepts of collapsing hash functions, pseudo-random generator (PRG), and the SPHINCS$^+$ framework.

3.1 Collapsing Hash Functions

Informally, a hash function $H : \{0,1\}^* \to \{0,1\}^\mu$ is collision-resistant if it is hard to find $x_1 \neq x_2$ such that $H(x_1) = H(x_2)$. Collapsing hash functions [8] serve as a replacement for the collision-resistant one in the post-quantum setting. Roughly speaking, the collapsing property requires that given a superposition of values x_1, measuring $H(x_1)$ has the same effect as measuring x_1. We refer readers to [8] for the detailed security definition of collapsing hash functions. For implementing protocols in practice, certain hash functions like SHA-2 and SHA-3 are collapsing.

3.2 PRG

PRGs [4] are computable deterministic functions extending a short random seed into a longer, pseudorandom string.

Let $G(\cdot) : \{0,1\}^\mu \to \{0,1\}^\nu$ be a computable deterministic function with $\nu > \mu$. Let $G(s) \in \{0,1\}^\nu$ be the result of a input seed $s \in \{0,1\}^\mu$. $G(\cdot)$ is a PRG if $G(s)$ cannot be distinguished from a uniformly random string $string \in \{0,1\}^\nu$. When $\nu = 2\mu$, we call this a length-doubling PRG. In our case, we use such a PRG to expand hash values.

3.3 SPHINCS$^+$ Framework

SPHINCS$^+$ is a stateless hash-based signature framework [2] designed based on the SPHINCS [3] scheme and has been submitted to the third round of the NIST PQC standardization project. At a high level, it works in a similar way to SPHINCS, but with improvements in speed and signature size.

SPHINCS$^+$ uses a hierarchical structure of Merkle trees (MTs) with one-time signatures (OTSs) and few-time signatures (FTSs) at their leaf nodes. The public key is the root of the top MT. Leaf nodes of the inner MTs are OTS schemes (i.e., WOTS$^+$), which are used to sign the roots of the next-level MTs. Leaf nodes on the lowest-level MTs are FTS schemes (i.e., FORS), which are used to sign the messages.

Generally, a SPHINCS$^+$ framework consists of three algorithms, i.e., S.KeyGen, S.Sign, and S.Verify. Its security is based on the properties of the functions used to instantiate all the cryptographic function families. The proposal in [2] introduces 36 different parameter sets on the basis of three different arguments (i.e., hash function, security level, and a trade-off between signature size and speed). In this work, we choose the variant of SPHINCS+-128f optimized for speed with the SHA-256 hash function for our construction, which matches NIST security level 1. We refer readers to [2] for a full specification of SPHINCS$^+$.

4 Definition of RS Schemes

Here, we review the general definition of RS schemes, following with unforgeability and privacy properties.

4.1 Syntax

Definition 1. *An RS scheme consists of four following algorithms:*

- $(ssk, spk) \leftarrow$ KeyGen(λ): *On input a security parameter λ, it returns a secret/public key pair (ssk, spk).*
- $\sigma \leftarrow$ Sign(ssk, M): *On input ssk and a message $M = \{m_1, m_2, \ldots, m_n\}$, it returns a signature σ.*
- $\sigma' \leftarrow$ Redact$(spk, M, \sigma, \bar{M})$: *On input spk, M, σ, and a sub-message $\bar{M} \subseteq M$ to be redacted, it generates a signature σ' for the retained message $M' \leftarrow M \backslash \bar{M}$.*
- $d \in \{0, 1\} \leftarrow$ Verify(spk, M', σ'): *Taking as input spk, M', and the candidate signature σ', it outputs a verification decision $d \in \{0, 1\}$.*

4.2 Correctness

An RS scheme is correct if following conditions hold:

(1) The signature σ produced by Sign is valid under Verify. Namely, given $(ssk, spk) \leftarrow$ KeyGen(λ), $\sigma \leftarrow$ Sign(ssk, M), the equation Verify$(spk, M, \sigma) = 1$ holds.

(2) The signature produced by Redact is valid under Verify. Namely, based on (1), for any message $\bar{M} \subseteq M$ to be cut and any signature $\sigma' \leftarrow$ Redact$(spk, M, \sigma, \bar{M})$ for M' $(M' = M \backslash \bar{M})$, the equation Verify$(spk, M', \sigma') = 1$ holds.

4.3 Security Model

We here introduce the unforgeability and privacy properties of RS schemes.

Unforgeability. The unforgeability requires that no one can compute a valid redactable signature without knowing the secret key. This property is similar to the unforgeability requirement for standard signature schemes. Experiment Unforgeability$_{\mathcal{A}}^{RS}(\lambda)$ desceibes the model.

Experiment Unforgeability$_{\mathcal{A}}^{RS}(\lambda)$:

$(ssk, spk) \leftarrow \mathsf{KeyGen}(\lambda)$

$(M^*, \sigma^*) \leftarrow \mathcal{A}^{\mathsf{Sign}(ssk, \cdot)}(spk)$

    Let $i = 1, 2, \ldots, q_s$ be $\mathcal{A}$'s queries to Sign oracle

Return 1 if

    $\mathsf{Verify}(spk, M, \sigma) = 1 \wedge M^* \not\subseteq M_i$ for $1 \leq i \leq q_s$

Definition 2. *An RS scheme is existentially unforgeable against adaptive chosen-message attacks (eUF-CMA) if for any probabilistic polynomial-time (p.p.t.) algorithm $\mathcal{A}$, the probability that the Experiment Unforgeability$_{\mathcal{A}}^{RS}(\lambda)$ returns 1 is negligible.*

Privacy. Privacy requires that no party other than the signer and the redactor is able to derive any information about redacted elements. This property is covered by the following experiment Experiment Privacy$_{\mathcal{A}}^{RS}(\lambda)$.

Experiment Privacy$_{\mathcal{A}}^{RS}(\lambda)$:

$(ssk, spk) \leftarrow \mathsf{KeyGen}(\lambda)$

$\mathcal{Q} \leftarrow \mathcal{A}^{\mathsf{Sign}(ssk, \cdot)}(spk)$, where $\mathcal{Q} = (M_0, \bar{M}_0, M_1, \bar{M}_1)$

Return 0 if

    $M_0 = M_1$ or $|M_0| \neq |M_1|$ or $M_0 \backslash \bar{M}_0 \neq M_1 \backslash \bar{M}_1$

$b' \leftarrow \mathcal{A}^{\mathsf{LoRRedact}(\ldots, ssk, b)}(spk, \mathcal{Q})$

    Oracle LoRRedact runs once as follows:

    $b \leftarrow \{0, 1\}$

    $(M_b, \sigma) \leftarrow \mathsf{Sign}(ssk, M_b)$

$\mathcal{Q} \leftarrow \mathcal{A}^{\mathsf{Sign}(ssk, \cdot)}(spk)$

    Return $(M', \sigma') \leftarrow \mathsf{Redact}(spk, M_b, \bar{M}_b, \sigma)$

Return 1 if $b' = b$

Definition 3. *An RS scheme is private if for any p.p.t. algorithm $\mathcal{A}$, the probability that the Experiment Privacy$_{\mathcal{A}}^{RS}(\lambda)$ returns 1 is negligible.*

5 Our Proposed HRSS

Drawing on the ideas of [16] but overcoming its privacy leakage and inefficiency problems, this section describes a practical RS scheme HRSS. We use the variant of GGM binary tree generation algorithm suggested by [7], a length-doubling

PRG, and the underlying SPHINCS$^+$ framework consisting of three algorithms (i.e., S.KeyGen, S.Sign, and S.Verify) as building blocks. We later present its security analysis.

5.1 Our Design

Our idea is as follows: The smart meter assigned by the utility collects the customer's energy usage data M and divides it into a sequence of segments $m_1, m_2, \ldots, m_n$, where each segment can simply be an automatic unit such as a word. It uses the step 1) algorithm in Sign to construct a random GGM binary tree T with n leaves, where each internal node of T has exactly two children. It then selects a random seed s for a chosen PRG $G(\cdot)$ and associates it with the root. The secret label s_i of each leaf i is then computed from s in a top-down manner along with T. Note that the description of the structure of T is required for the regeneration of the random value s_i. Hereafter, the description is stored together with the seed for ease of presentation. Now, the smart meter computes the hash value h_ε of the root node ε by using the step 3) algorithm in Sign and signs it by using the underlying SPHINCS$^+$ framework. The smart meter then sends the data and its signature to the customer's repository. To share parts of the authenticated data with a third party, the customer controls the repository to reconstruct T, derive a redacted signature for the shared data M', and returns the third party with M' and its signature.

When m_i needs to be removed, the associated leaf s_i and all its ancestors will be removed. Let us define the notion of co-nodes associated with i to be the siblings of the nodes along the path from i to the root. In this case, the corresponding hash value h_i and new seed(s) $\{s_u : \text{each } u \text{ is a co-node of } i\}$ are set as a part of the signature for M' because they are essential for computing h_ε. Due to the merit of the random tree, the redacted tree will not disclose the length (or the number) of the deleted sub-messages. Taking Fig. 2(d) as an example, from the receiver's perspective, the hash value h_{100} can be calculated directly by a single leaf node, or iteratively calculated by the hash of multiple child nodes. This is different from Johnson et al.'s construction in [16], in which some information on the number of leaf nodes removed may be guessed from the redacted tree. The verification executed by the third party is straightforward, i.e., recovering h_ε and checking its signature by using the underlying SPHINCS$^+$ framework. Figure 2 presents a simple example of HRSS and the detailed construction is shown below:

- Setup: The algorithm takes a security parameter λ as input. The signer runs S.Setup(λ) to generate a secret key sk and a public key pk for the underlying SPHINCS$^+$ framework. Let $H(\cdot)$ and $G(\cdot)$ be a collapsing hash function and a length-doubling PRG as described in Sect. 3.2, respectively. It stores the signer's secret key $ssk = sk$ and publishes $spk = \{pk, G, H(\cdot)\}$.
- Sign: Given ssk and a message $M = \{m_1, m_2, \ldots, m_n\}$ to be signed, the signer performs as follows:
  1. It constructs a n-leaf random GGM binary tree as the following:

- It randomly chooses $r \in \{1, \ldots, n-1\}$.
- Recursively, it generates a tree T_1 with r leaves and a tree T_2 with $n-r$ leaves in the usual top-down manner.
- It obtains a binary tree T such that T_1 and T_2 are its left subtree and right subtree, respectively.
- It assigns m_i to each leaves in T. Figure 2(a) takes $M = \{m_1, \ldots, m_6\}$ ($r = 3$) as an example to construct a tree T.

2. We let nodes of T with elements of $\{0,1\}^*$, so that a node u has children $u0$ and $u1$. It picks a random ℓ-bit seed s and uses $G(\cdot)$ to recursively compute secret labels for all nodes in T such that $(s_{u0}, s_{u1}) \leftarrow G(s_u)$. For example, $(s_0, s_1) \leftarrow G(s)$ and $(s_{00}, s_{01}) \leftarrow G(s_0)$ (refer to Fig. 2(b)).

3. It uses $H(\cdot)$ to generate hash values bottom-up for each node in T as follows:
   - For each leave node i, $1 \leq i \leq n$, it computes $h_i = H(0, s_i, m_i)^1$, where s_i is the secret label of leaf i.
   - For an internal node u, it recursively compute $h_u = H(1, h_{u0}, h_{u1})$; if a node only has a left child, then computes $h_u = H(1, h_{u0})$.
   In this manner, the hash value of the root node ε is computed as $h_\varepsilon = H(1, h_0, h_1)$. The results are represented in Fig. 2(c).

4. It computes $\sigma_\varepsilon = \mathsf{S.Sign}(sk, h_\varepsilon)$.

5. It returns $\sigma = (r, s, \sigma_\varepsilon)$ as the signature for M.

- Redact: Given spk, M, σ, and a sub-message $m_i \in M$ to be cut[2], the redactor executes as follows:
  1. It parses σ as $(r, s, \sigma_\varepsilon)$.
  2. It outputs $\bot$ to indicate failure if $m_i \notin M$; otherwise, it reconstructs the tree T, assigns m_i to its leaves, computes secret labels as well as hash values for all nodes of T as the same as in Sign.
  3. Note that when a message m_i is removed, the associated leaf i and all its ancestors are to be removed, resulting in a collection of subtrees. Define the notion of co-nodes associated to i to be the siblings of the nodes along the path from i to the root. It returns $\sigma' = (h_i, \{s_u : \text{each } u \text{ is a co-node of } i\}, r, \sigma_\varepsilon)$ as the signature for M'.
  As depicted by Fig. 2(d), when m_4 is removed from M, the tuple $(s_0, h_{100}, s_{101}, s_{11})$ will be revealed for computing h_ε. Hence that the signature for $M' = \{m_1, m_2, m_3, m_5, m_6\}$ is $\sigma' = (s_0, h_{100}, s_{101}, s_{11}, r, \sigma_\varepsilon)$.
- Verify: On input M' and its signature σ', it proceeds as follows:
  1. It parses σ' as $(h_i, \{s_u : \text{each } u \text{ is a co-node of } i\}, r, \sigma_\varepsilon)$.
  2. By using the received information, it recovers the hash value h_ε for the root of T as described in Sign.
  3. It outputs 1 if the equation $\mathsf{S.Verify}(pk, \sigma_\varepsilon) = 1$ holds, and 0 otherwise.

---

[1] As stated by Micali and Sidney [23], for implementing protocols in practice, we would expect $F_s(x) = H(s, x)$ to behave like a pseudorandom function if s is chosen at random. Similar to [13,16], we here treat $F_s(x) = H(0, s, x)$ as such a function, where 0 is a domain-separation tag.

[2] Note that Redact supports the redaction of multiple sub-messages simultaneously. For ease of presentation, we here only redact one sub-message.

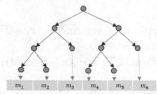

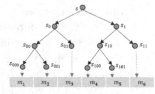

(a) An example of tree T for a message $M =$ $\{m_1, ..., m_6\}$ $(r = 3)$.

(b) Compute secret labels for nodes in T by using $(s_{u0}, s_{u1}) \leftarrow G(s_u)$.

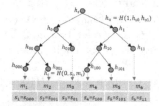

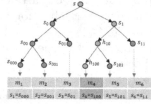

(c) Compute hash values for nodes in T.

(d) When m_4 is removed, the tuple $(s_0, h_{100}, s_{101}, s_{11})$ will be revealed for computing the hash value h_ε for the root node.

Fig. 2. A simple example of HRSS construction.

5.2 Correctness

The correctness of HRSS is directly ensured by the used hash functions, thus omitted here for simplicity.

5.3 Security Analysis

Recall that in [2], generic attacks to SPHINCS$^+$ framework against distinct-function multi-target second-preimage resistance, pseudorandomness, and interleaved target subset resilience have been formally analyzed. Unlike [2], we here treat our main building blocks as black-box constructions. In this regard, the security of HRSS is proved based on the security of collapsing hash function $H(\cdot)$, (post-quantum) PRG $G(\cdot)$, and SPHINCS$^+$ framework secure against existential forgery. However, from an implementation point of view, the security of HRSS relies on the properties of the functions used to instantiate all the cryptographic function families. The following two theorems analyze the unforgeability and privacy of HRSS.

Theorem 1 (Unforgeability). *If $H(\cdot)$ is a collapsing hash function, $G(\cdot)$ is a secure PRG, and the underlying* SPHINCS$^+$ *framework is eUF-CMA-secure, then the proposed* HRSS *is eUF-CMA-secure.*

Theorem 2 (Privacy). *The proposed* HRSS *is privacy preserving if $F_s(x) = H(0, s, x)$ is a secure pseudorandom function.*

The proof of Theorem 1 and Theorem 2 are shown in the Appendix.

6   Performance Analysis

We here compare HRSS with very recent works in [21,31] to show the performance of our scheme.

Features. The scheme in [21] is designed based on a bilinear-map accumulator (relying on the t-strong Diffie-Hellman (SDH) assumption) and a standard signature scheme (SDS); the scheme in [31] is designed depending on the discrete logarithm (DL) assumption in bilinear groups. In contrast, our scheme is solely based on the security of underlying hash functions. Therefore, we have minimal security assumptions and our scheme is the first hash-based post-quantum design.

Table 1. Comparison of features with recent RSSs

Scheme	[21]	[31]	Our
Security Assumption	t-SDH Security of SDS	DL	Security of Hash Functions
Post-quantum	×	×	✓

Computation and Storage Costs. In order to evaluate the computation cost and space requirement of our HRSS, we first choose SHA-256 as the base hash function and 'SPHINCS+-SHA-256-128f-simple' parameter set in SPHINCS+ website[3] as the concrete parameters. Recall that [21] uses an RSA signature scheme for their performance analysis. To achieve enough security level, we choose 3072 bits key length for the RSA scheme and the popular BLS12-381 elliptic curve for pairings. Note that in this setting, the two schemes achieve 128 bits security level for classical computers while our scheme achieves the same security level for quantum computers.

To evaluate the real-time complexity of HRSS and schemes in [21,31], we use a Raspberry Pi 3B+ device to conduct an experimental evaluation for simplicity; we note that the third party may not perform the Verify with a restricted device. We use the runtime tested in [5] on the same device for the time cost of our underlying SPHINCS+ framework. We also use the OpenSSL library[4] and MCL library[5] for testing pairing-based operations and RSA operations, respectively.

Let n and k denote the number of sub-messages in the original message M and the retained message M', respectively. Since the scheme in [21] divides the collected message into groups according to the dependency of data blocks and supports batch verification of a group of sub-messages, we hereafter assume that each group contains $\omega = 5$ sub-messages for simplicity.

Figure 3 compares the computation cost of each algorithm in these schemes. From Figs. 3(a) and 3(d), we can see that our HRSS has minimal key generation and signature verification costs. However, the time cost in Sign (refer to

---

[3] https://sphincs.org.
[4] https://www.openssl.org/.
[5] https://github.com/herumi/mcl.

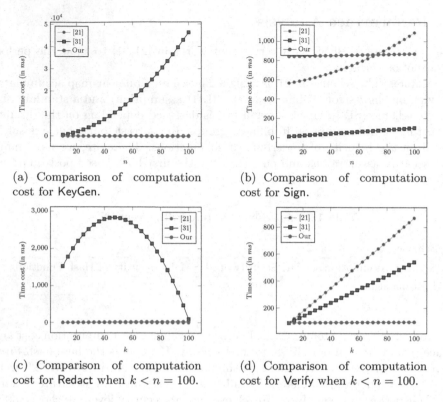

(a) Comparison of computation cost for KeyGen.

(b) Comparison of computation cost for Sign.

(c) Comparison of computation cost for Redact when $k < n = 100$.

(d) Comparison of computation cost for Verify when $k < n = 100$.

Fig. 3. Comparison of computation costs of Sign, Redact, and Verify between HRSS and [21, 31], respectively.

Fig. 3(b) is not in the case. In fact, our scheme requires the highest computation cost in this algorithm when $n < 75$ and achieves the lowest cost when $n > 1245$. In addition, Fig. 3(c) shows the time cost in Redact. Due to the merit of the accumulator, the redaction operation in [21] only requires the deletion of witnesses (i.e., the membership proof generated by the accumulator) of corresponding deleted elements without any mathematical operations; therefore, their scheme has the best redaction cost. In spite of this, the cost of our scheme is still reasonable. For example, deleting 50 sub-messages from the original data (i.e., containing 100 sub-messages) takes 30.01 ms. Here, we note that it is sufficient to set $n = 100$ in our analysis. The advantage of our scheme will be greater when the value of n is larger because we do not need expensive exponentiation or pairing operations as in other schemes. Moreover, Table 2 shows the computation time for each scheme for the above example. In this case, the total time cost of our scheme is 1018.25 ms, which is 55.46% of the scheme in [21] and 2.06% of the scheme in [31], respectively.

In our scheme, the signature for M is $\sigma = (r, s, \sigma_\varepsilon)$, in which $r \in (1, n)$ is a random number, s is the random seed for the PRG, and σ_ε is the output of the

Table 2. Time cost of HRSS and schemes in [21,31] when $n = 100, k = 50$ (in ms)

Scheme	Algorithm			
	KeyGen	Sign	Redact	Verify
[21]	310.04	1091.36	0	434.56
[31]	46274.20	100.45	2825.17	289.40
Our	26.00	870.01	30.01	92.23

underlying SPHINCS$^+$ framework. We then set the size of r and s to 4 bytes and 32 bytes, respectively. In addition, based on the above-selected parameter set, the secret key size, public key size, and the signature size for 'SPHINCS+128f' are 64 bytes, 32 bytes, and 17088 bytes, respectively. Therefore, the secret key size, public key size, and the original signature size for our proposed HRSS are 64 bytes, 32 bytes, and 17124 bytes, respectively. However, removing a sub-message m_i will increase the signature size for M'. This is because when m_i is removed, seeds for i's co-nodes in tree T will be listed in the final signature. In the worst case, the signature for M' is about $(32n + 17088)$ bytes. We now summarize space requirements of HRSS and schemes in [21,31] in Fig. 4.

Figures 4(a) and 4(b) compare the secret key and public key sizes, respectively. Note that the key size is an important performance metric for measuring a cryptographic scheme, although it has been neglected by many existing works. One can find that our scheme has the smallest secret/public key size. In fact, for example, when $n = 100$, our secret key size is about 15.38% of that of the scheme in [21] and 1.98% of that of the scheme in [31]; our public key size is about 0.88% of that of the scheme in [21] and 0.01% of that of the scheme in [31]. Figure 4(c) lists the original signature size for M of these schemes. Such size for the scheme in [21] grows linearly with respect to n, while our scheme and the scheme in [31] have fixed-length signature sizes, i.e., 17124 bytes and 288 bytes, respectively. In Fig. 4(d) and Fig. 4(e), we also provide two sets of numerical results to show the original and redacted signature sizes in the respective scenarios. The downside is that our solution requires a long signature length; however, the size is affordable.

Energy Consumption. The energy consumption mainly depends on the computation time and can be evaluated as $E_{con} = P_{cpu} * T_{time}$, where P_{cpu} is the maximum CPU power and T_{time} is the corresponding time cost [20]. The Raspberry Pi 3B+ device draws an average current of about 2.5 Amp at 5 V supply voltage when it is active, hence that P_{cpu} is 12.50 W. In this way, when $n = 100, k = 50$, the energy cost of our HRSS and schemes in [21,31] amount to roughly 12.73 J, 22.95 J, and 618.62 J, respectively.

Therefore, our HRSS is more worthwhile for energy-constrained environments than others.

In summary, in addition to the signature size, our HRSS has a reasonable performance in terms of computation cost, space requirement, and energy consumption.

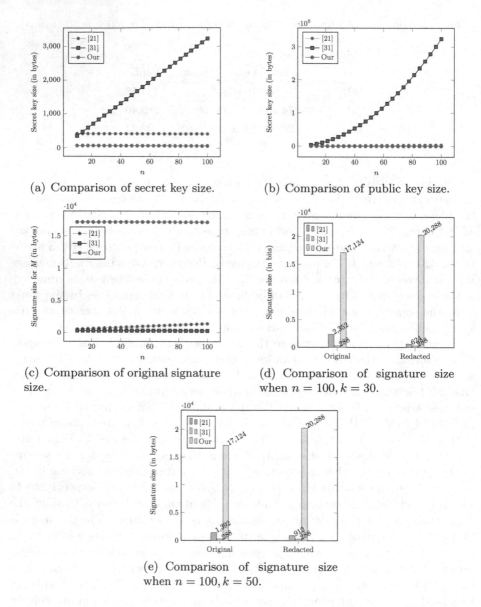

(a) Comparison of secret key size.

(b) Comparison of public key size.

(c) Comparison of original signature size.

(d) Comparison of signature size when $n = 100, k = 30$.

(e) Comparison of signature size when $n = 100, k = 50$.

Fig. 4. Comparison of space requirements between our HRSS and [21,31]. (a) and (b) show the sizes of secret and public keys, respectively; (c), (d), and (e) show the comparison of signature sizes under different conditions, respectively.

7 Discussion

The above performance analysis shows that our scheme has a longer signature size due to the underlying SPHINCS$^+$ framework. Although the work in [2] provides different instantiation parameters for the SPHINCS$^+$ framework to allow a trade-off between signing speed and signature size, it is not in our interest to obtain a shorter signature length at the expense of signing speed. To reduce the signature size, a possible solution is to replace the underlying SPHINCS$^+$ framework with the hierarchical signature system (HSS) scheme (i.e., a multi-tree variant of the Leighton-Micali signature (LMS) scheme) recommended by NIST [26]. However, for security concerns, such a stateful scheme requires the maintenance of updated non-duplicate secret keys during each signature generation process. Besides, very recently, an e-print work [40] suggested SPHINCS-α, which is a variant of SPHINCS$^+$ that may help to obtain a shorter signature length.

8   Conclusions

Motivated by the privacy-preserving authentication and flexible data sharing demands in smart grids, in this work, we propose HRSS, the first quantum-secure RS scheme with security solely based on the security of underlying hash functions. We also evaluate the performance of our design. Theoretical and experimental results show that HRSS has a desirable computation (and energy consumption) cost and the smallest secret/public key size in comparison to the state-of-the-art schemes. Therefore, our construction is practical for smart grids.

As we mentioned before, HRSS is not competing to be the RS scheme with the smallest signature size. In view of this, a research challenge is to design a HRSS construction with a smaller or even constant signature size. This may be further improved by the performance enhancement of the underlying SPHINCS$^+$ framework.

Acknowledgments. We have no conflicts of interest associated with this manuscript. We would like to thank the anonymous reviewers for their valuable comments. This work was supported in part by Australian Research Council (ARC) Linkage Project (LP160101766), ARC Discovery Project (DP180103251), the Data61 collaborative research project - 'Enhancing Security and Privacy of IoT', National Natural Science Foundation of China (62032005), and Science Foundation of Fujian Provincial Science and Technology Agency (2020J02016).

Appendix

Proof of Theorem 1. For space reasons, we provide a proof sketch here. Our proof is similar to [13,16]. The proof implies that if there exists a p.p.t. adversary $\mathcal{A}$ that can break our HRSS, then there exists another adversary $\mathcal{F}$ who can unitize $\mathcal{A}$ to break the collision resistance of collapsing hash function $H(\cdot)$ or the security of $G(\cdot)$ or the unforgeability of SPHINCS$^+$.

In Setup Phase, $\mathcal{F}$ executes Setup to obtain the secret key sk of the SPHINCS$^+$ framework and the public key $spk = \{pk, G, H(\cdot)\}$, and then sends spk to $\mathcal{A}$. In Query Phase, $\mathcal{A}$ is allowed to issue several oracle queries for a message M according to any adaptive policy such as pseudorandom value oracle O_G, hash oracle O_H, and signing oracle O_{Sign} (O_G and sf O_H are publicly available):

– O_G: On input M, it returns a n-leaf random GGM tree for T_M, secret labels for nodes in T_M, and auxiliary information (r_M, s_M), where r_M and s_M are used to generate T_M and its node labels, respectively.

– O_H: On input M, r_M, s_M, and T_M, it computes hash values bottom-up for nodes in T_M and returns the hash value h_{ε_M} for the root node ε_M.

– O_{Sign}: On input h_{ε_M}, it returns a signature σ_{ε_M}.

Note that this process is equivalent to the natural setting of the scheme from $\mathcal{A}$'s perspective, and each query is recorded by $\mathcal{F}$. For ease of presentation, we define the following notations. Let M_i, $i = 1, 2, \ldots, q_s$ be the set of O_{Sign} queries made by $\mathcal{A}$. Let $s_{u,i}$ and $h_{u,i}$ denote the key and hash value for node u at M_i, respectively. For example, $s_{\varepsilon,i}$ denotes the random key for use with M_i and its redactions; $h_{\varepsilon,i}$ denotes the hash value for the root of the random GGM tree of M_i. The notation $\alpha_{u,i}$ represents the input of the hash at node u at M_i, i.e., $h_{u,i} = H(\alpha_{u,i})$. We also assume that all trees have a same r_{M_i} in this forgery game as it can reduce the difficulty for $\mathcal{A}$.

In Output Phase, $\mathcal{A}$ either admits failure or successfully outputs a valid forgery $(h_i{}^*, \{s_u{}^* : \text{each } u \text{ is a co-node of } i\}, r_{M^*}, \sigma_{\varepsilon_{M^*}})$ on M^*, where $r^* = r_{M_i}$, $\sigma_{\varepsilon_{M^*}} = \mathsf{S.Sign}(sk, h_{\varepsilon_{M^*}})$, and $M^* \not\subseteq M_i$.

If for all i, the case $\varepsilon_{M^*} \neq \varepsilon_{M_i}$ holds, $\mathcal{F}$ finds an existential forgery of SPHINCS$^+$ framework. Assume that there exists some i such that the case $\varepsilon_{M^*} = \varepsilon_{M_i}$ holds. Denote by T_{M^*} the hash tree corresponding to M^*. $\mathcal{F}$ now compares T_{M^*} and T_{M_i} corresponding to M_i: Due to the properties of the (random) Merkle tree, T_{M^*} is a sub-tree of T_{M_i}. Also, the leaf/internal nodes of T_{M^*} should form leaf/internal nodes of T_{M_i}. Otherwise, if there is some node v that is a leaf in T_{M_i} but is an internal node in T_{M^*}, then $\mathcal{F}$ finds a hash collision $H(\alpha_{v,*}) = H(\alpha_{v,i})$ since the hash value calculation method of leaf nodes and internal nodes is different.

Possibly, there may exist a case that there is some leaf node $v \in T_{M^*}$ (such that $M^*_v = M_{iv}$) but v is not found in the tree corresponding to M'_i, where M'_i is the set of the redactions of M_i. In this case, $\mathcal{A}$'s forgery must disclose s_u where u is some ancestor if v. However, note that 1) s_u should not be revealed by any oracle queries, and 2) s_u is not any of the key values of u's ancestors. Therefore, the value should be guessed by $\mathcal{A}$. Hence, $\mathcal{F}$ can use it to break $G(\cdot)$. This completes the proof. □

Proof of Theorem 2. Our Privacy game states that given a sub-message/signature pair with two possible source messages, no one can judge from which source message the sub-message stems. In such the game, the p.p.t. algorithm $\mathcal{A}$ chooses two equal-length messages M_0 and M_1 and sends them to a challenger $\mathcal{C}$ such that M_0 and M_1 are identical except in a sub-message $X_0 \neq X_1$, i.e., $M' = M_0 \backslash X_0 = M_1 \backslash X_1$, $X_0 \subseteq M_0$, and $X_1 \subseteq M_1$. $\mathcal{C}$ picks M_b, $b \in \{0, 1\}$ and outputs M' by executing Sign and Redact. $\mathcal{A}$ is allowed to make any signing queries to $\mathcal{C}$, and finally outputs its guess on b.

Note that when X_0 (say v-th position) is removed from M_0, the disclosed value associated to X_0 in the received information is h_v, where $h_v = H(0, s_v, X_0)$ and s_v is the key for v. Since $F_s(x) = H(0, s, x)$ is a secure pseudorandom function, based on the claim in [23], we can simply treat each such h_v as an independently selected random value. This situation also applies to removing X_1 from M_0. That is to say, no information about removed nodes in the output of Sign remains in the output of Redact, and $\mathcal{A}$ cannot output its guess on b better than at random. Hence the scheme is privacy-preserving. $\square$

References

1. Ahene, E., Qin, Z., Adusei, A.K., Li, F.: Efficient signcryption with proxy re-encryption and its application in smart grid. IEEE Internet Things J. **6**(6), 9722–9737 (2019)
2. Bernstein, D.J., et al.: SPHINCS+, submission to the NIST post-quantum project, vol. 3 (2020). www.sphincs.org/data/sphincs+-round3-specification.pdf
3. Bernstein, D., et al.: SPHINCS: practical stateless hash-based signatures. In: Oswald, E., Fischlin, M. (eds.) EUROCRYPT 2015. LNCS, vol. 9056, pp. 368–397. Springer, Heidelberg (2015). https://doi.org/10.1007/978-3-662-46800-5_15
4. Bogdanov, A., Rosen, A.: Pseudorandom functions: three decades later. IACR Cryptol. ePrint Arch. **2017**, 652 (2017)
5. Bürstinghaus-Steinbach, K., Krauß, C., Niederhagen, R., Schneider, M.: Post-quantum TLS on embedded systems: integrating and evaluating kyber and SPHINCS+ with mbed TLS. In: ASIA CCS 2020, Taipei, Taiwan, 5–9 Oct 2020, pp. 841–852. ACM (2020)
6. Camenisch, J., Dubovitskaya, M., Haralambiev, K., Kohlweiss, M.: Composable and modular anonymous credentials: definitions and practical constructions. In: Iwata, T., Cheon, J.H. (eds.) ASIACRYPT 2015. LNCS, vol. 9453, pp. 262–288. Springer, Heidelberg (2015). https://doi.org/10.1007/978-3-662-48800-3_11
7. Chang, E.-C., Lim, C.L., Xu, J.: Short redactable signatures using random trees. In: Fischlin, M. (ed.) CT-RSA 2009. LNCS, vol. 5473, pp. 133–147. Springer, Heidelberg (2009). https://doi.org/10.1007/978-3-642-00862-7_9
8. Czajkowski, J., Groot Bruinderink, L., Hülsing, A., Schaffner, C., Unruh, D.: Post-quantum security of the sponge construction. In: Lange, T., Steinwandt, R. (eds.) PQCrypto 2018. LNCS, vol. 10786, pp. 185–204. Springer, Cham (2018). https://doi.org/10.1007/978-3-319-79063-3_9
9. Derler, D., Pöhls, H.C., Samelin, K., Slamanig, D.: A general framework for redactable signatures and new constructions. In: Kwon, S., Yun, A. (eds.) ICISC 2015. LNCS, vol. 9558, pp. 3–19. Springer, Cham (2016). https://doi.org/10.1007/978-3-319-30840-1_1
10. Gennaro, R., Halevi, S., Rabin, T.: Secure hash-and-sign signatures without the random oracle. In: Stern, J. (ed.) EUROCRYPT 1999. LNCS, vol. 1592, pp. 123–139. Springer, Heidelberg (1999). https://doi.org/10.1007/3-540-48910-X_9
11. Goldreich, O., Goldwasser, S., Micali, S.: How to construct random functions (extended abstract). In: FOCS 1984, West Palm Beach, Florida, USA, 24–26 Oct 1984, pp. 464–479. IEEE (1984)
12. Gope, P., Sikdar, B.: An efficient privacy-preserving dynamic pricing-based billing scheme for smart grids. In: CNS 2018, Beijing, China, May 30 - June 1 2018. pp. 1–2. IEEE (2018)
13. Haber, S., et al.: Efficient signature schemes supporting redaction, pseudonymization, and data deidentification. In: ASIACCS 2008, Tokyo, Japan, 18–20 Mar 2008, pp. 353–362. ACM (2008)

14. Huang, X., et al.: Cost-effective authentic and anonymous data sharing with forward security. IEEE Trans. Computers **64**(4), 971–983 (2015)
15. Jeske, T.: Privacy-preserving smart metering without a trusted-third-party. In: SECRYPT 2011, Seville, Spain, 18–21 July 2011, pp. 114–123 (2011)
16. Johnson, R., Molnar, D., Song, D., Wagner, D.: Homomorphic signature schemes. In: Preneel, B. (ed.) CT-RSA 2002. LNCS, vol. 2271, pp. 244–262. Springer, Heidelberg (2002). https://doi.org/10.1007/3-540-45760-7_17
17. Kar, J.: Provably secure certificateless deniable authenticated encryption scheme. J. Inf. Secur. Appl. **54**, 102581 (2020)
18. Kong, W., Shen, J., Vijayakumar, P., Cho, Y., Chang, V.: A practical group blind signature scheme for privacy protection in smart grid. J. Parallel Distributed Comput. **136**, 29–39 (2020)
19. Lahoti, G., Mashima, D., Chen, W.: Customer-centric energy usage data management and sharing in smart grid systems. In: SEGS2013, 8 Nov 2013, Berlin, Germany, pp. 53–64. ACM (2013)
20. Limbasiya, T., Das, D., Das, S.K.: Mcomiov: secure and energy-efficient message communication protocols for internet of vehicles. IEEE/ACM Trans. Netw. **29**(3), 1349–1361 (2021)
21. Liu, J., Hou, J., Huang, X., Xiang, Y., Zhu, T.: Secure and efficient sharing of authenticated energy usage data with privacy preservation. Comput. Secur. **92**, 101756 (2020)
22. McCallister, E., Grance, T., Scarfone, K.: Guide to protecting the confidentiality of personally identifiable information (PII), SP 800–122. In: NIST (2010)
23. Micali, S., Sidney, R.: A simple method for generating and sharing pseudo-random functions, with applications to clipper-like key escrow systems. In: Coppersmith, D. (ed.) CRYPTO 1995. LNCS, vol. 963, pp. 185–196. Springer, Heidelberg (1995). https://doi.org/10.1007/3-540-44750-4_15
24. Miyazaki, K., Hanaoka, G., Imai, H.: Digitally signed document sanitizing scheme based on bilinear maps. In: ASIACCS 2006, Taipei, Taiwan, 21–24 Mar 2006, pp. 343–354. ACM (2006)
25. NIST: Report on post-quantum cryptography (2016). www.dx.doi.org/10.6028/NIST.IR.8105
26. NIST: Recommendation for stateful hash-based signature schemes (2020). www.doi.org/10.6028/NIST.SP.800-208
27. Nojima, R., Tamura, J., Kadobayashi, Y., Kikuchi, H.: A storage efficient redactable signature in the standard model. In: Samarati, P., Yung, M., Martinelli, F., Ardagna, C.A. (eds.) ISC 2009. LNCS, vol. 5735, pp. 326–337. Springer, Heidelberg (2009). https://doi.org/10.1007/978-3-642-04474-8_26
28. PG&E: PG&E smart grid annual report 2020 (2020). www.pge.com/pge_global/common/pdfs/safety/how-the-system-works/electric-systems/smart-grid/AnnualReport2020.pdf
29. Pöhls, H.C., Samelin, K.: On updatable redactable signatures. In: Boureanu, I., Owesarski, P., Vaudenay, S. (eds.) ACNS 2014. LNCS, vol. 8479, pp. 457–475. Springer, Cham (2014). https://doi.org/10.1007/978-3-319-07536-5_27
30. Pöhls, H.C., Samelin, K.: Accountable redactable signatures. In: ARES 2015, Toulouse, France, 24–27 Aug 2015, pp. 60–69. IEEE (2015)
31. Sanders, O.: Efficient redactable signature and application to anonymous credentials. In: Kiayias, A., Kohlweiss, M., Wallden, P., Zikas, V. (eds.) PKC 2020. LNCS, vol. 12111, pp. 628–656. Springer, Cham (2020). https://doi.org/10.1007/978-3-030-45388-6_22

32. Saxena, N., Grijalva, S.: Efficient signature scheme for delivering authentic control commands in the smart grid. IEEE Trans. Smart Grid **9**(5), 4323–4334 (2018)

33. Steinfeld, R., Bull, L., Zheng, Y.: Content extraction signatures. In: Kim, K. (ed.) ICISC 2001. LNCS, vol. 2288, pp. 285–304. Springer, Heidelberg (2002). https://doi.org/10.1007/3-540-45861-1_22

34. Sui, Z., de Meer, H.: An efficient signcryption protocol for hop-by-hop data aggregations in smart grids. IEEE J. Sel. Areas Commun. **38**(1), 132–140 (2020)

35. Sultan, S.: Privacy-preserving metering in smart grid for billing, operational metering, and incentive-based schemes: a survey. Comput. Secur. **84**, 148–165 (2019)

36. Tang, F., Pang, J., Cheng, K., Gong, Q.: Multiauthority traceable ring signature scheme for smart grid based on blockchain. Wirel. Commun. Mob. Comput. **2021**, 1–9 (2021)

37. Tanveer, M., Khan, A.U., Kumar, N., Naushad, A., Chaudhry, S.A.: A robust access control protocol for the smart grid systems. IEEE Internet Things J. **9**(9), 6855–6865 (2022)

38. Union, E.: The EU general data protection regulation (GDPR) (2018). www.eugdpr.org

39. X, E.: Enernoc, global leader in smart energy management (2017). www.corporate.enelx.com/en/stories/2017/08/enernoc-global-leader-in-smart-energy-management

40. Zhang, K., Cui, H., Yu, Y.: SPHINCS-α: a compact stateless hash-based signature scheme. IACR Cryptol. ePrint Arch. 059 (2022)

41. Zhu, F., Yi, X., Abuadbba, A., Khalil, I., Nepal, S., Huang, X.: Cost-effective authenticated data redaction with privacy protection in iot. IEEE Internet Things J. **8**(14), 11678–11689 (2021)

Can Industrial Intrusion Detection Be SIMPLE?

Konrad Wolsing[1,2]([✉]), Lea Thiemt[2], Christian van Sloun[2], Eric Wagner[1,2], Klaus Wehrle[2], and Martin Henze[1,3]

[1] Cyber Analysis and Defense, Fraunhofer FKIE, Bonn, Germany
{konrad.wolsing,eric.wagner,martin.henze}@fkie.fraunhofer.de
[2] Communication and Distributed Systems, RWTH Aachen University,
Aachen, Germany
{wolsing,thiemt,sloun,wagner,wehrle}@comsys.rwth-aachen.de
[3] Security and Privacy in Industrial Cooperation, RWTH Aachen University,
Aachen, Germany
henze@cs.rwth-aachen.de

Abstract. Cyberattacks against industrial control systems pose a serious risk to the safety of humans and the environment. Industrial intrusion detection systems oppose this threat by continuously monitoring industrial processes and alerting any deviations from learned normal behavior. To this end, various streams of research rely on advanced and complex approaches, i.e., artificial neural networks, thus achieving allegedly high detection rates. However, as we show in an analysis of 70 approaches from related work, their inherent complexity comes with undesired properties. For example, they exhibit incomprehensible alarms and models only specialized personnel can understand, thus limiting their broad applicability in a heterogeneous industrial domain. Consequentially, we ask whether industrial intrusion detection indeed has to be complex or can be SIMPLE instead, i.e., Sufficient to detect most attacks, Independent of hyperparameters to dial-in, Meaningful in model and alerts, Portable to other industrial domains, Local to a part of the physical process, and computationally Efficient. To answer this question, we propose our design of four SIMPLE industrial intrusion detection systems, such as simple tests for the minima and maxima of process values or the rate at which process values change. Our evaluation of these SIMPLE approaches on four state-of-the-art industrial security datasets reveals that SIMPLE approaches can perform on par with existing complex approaches from related work while simultaneously being comprehensible and easily portable to other scenarios. Thus, it is indeed justified to raise the question of whether industrial intrusion detection needs to be inherently complex.

1 Introduction

Cyberattacks against Industrial Control System (ICSs) with the goal of financial gains, damaging equipment, or even risking human lives by blocking normal operations or injecting false data are becoming more prevalent [7]. Recent examples of such attacks include the attempted poising of a Florida city's water supply

© The Author(s), under exclusive license to Springer Nature Switzerland AG 2022
V. Atluri et al. (Eds.): ESORICS 2022, LNCS 13556, pp. 574–594, 2022.
https://doi.org/10.1007/978-3-031-17143-7_28

by increasing its sodium hydroxide concentration [59]. Increased connectivity to the Internet is one driver behind this development, but practice shows that even air-gapped systems are not secure against sophisticated attacks anymore [7].

Besides preventive security mechanisms, e.g., integrity protection, recent research has seen a rising interest in detecting intrusions into industrial networks. Such Intrusion Detection System (IDSs) passively monitor processes to alert about anomalous behavior before any real damage can occur and promise to provide a non-intrusive, retrofittable, and easily deployable security solution. In contrast to traditional IDSs known from office or data center environments, Industrial Intrusion Detection System (IIDSs) have the unique advantage that they can leverage the predictability and repetitiveness of ICSs to identify even advanced and stealthy attacks [11]. Auspicious results are reported by process-aware IIDSs, which incorporate the physical state of the monitored ICS into their decision-making. Consequently, they received tremendous interest from the research community, with state-of-the-art IIDSs based mainly on machine learning, e.g., artificial neural networks [50], graph theory [57], or linear algebra [11].

The powerful underlying IIDS methodologies yield promising detection performances, however, at the cost of complexity, requiring resource-intensive operations and hindering generalizability [51,76]. Furthermore, the alarms raised by, e.g., artificial neural networks, are often not explainable, making it challenging to derive concrete actions for mitigating attacks [28]. Meanwhile, we observe that attacks, like the one on Florida's water supply [59], lead to apparent deviations from normal operations. Therefore, in this paper, we pose the question: Do IIDSs indeed have to be complex to reliably detect attacks on industrial systems?

To answer this question, we study to what extent IIDSs can be simple, e.g., merely keeping track of the minimum and maximum of observed process values, and whether they perform on par with complex related work. Surprisingly, such approaches have obtained no attention so far, likely as they have never been considered suitable in traditional networks, e.g., data centers. However, as we show in this paper, this conclusion is not necessarily true for industrial networks due to the repetitive and predictable nature of their underlying physical processes. SIMPLE IIDSs avoid many of the drawbacks of complex solutions as they are *Sufficient* to detect most attacks, operate *Independently* of parameters, provide *Meaningful* alerts, are *Portable* to other industrial scenarios, require only *Local* process knowledge, and can be realized using *Efficient* computational operations.

Contributions. More precisely, we present the following contributions to determine whether the complexity of state-of-the-art IIDSs is indeed needed:

- We analyze the current state of IIDS research. Our study of 70 approaches unveils limitations w.r.t. deployability, computational complexity, generalizability, focus on non-stealthy attacks, and incomprehensibility of alarms (Sect. 3).
- To assess whether industrial intrusion detection needs to be inherently complex, we design four intentionally SIMPLE IIDSs[1] characterized by straightforward, relatable, and easy-to-compute concepts (Sect. 4).

---

[1] Implementation available at: https://github.com/fkie-cad/ipal_ids_framework.

- We then compare the performance of our SIMPLE IIDSs against state-of-the-art complex related work alongside four industrial datasets. Our results show that SIMPLE IIDSs detect more attacks than complex related work detects on average and can be ported effortlessly across industrial domains (Sect. 5).

2 Intrusion Detection in Industrial Control Systems

Industrial networks are responsible for operating today's manufacturing plants and critical infrastructure. Due to their high degree of automation, industrial communication almost exclusively relies on machine-to-machine communication between sensors measuring the current physical environment and actuators interacting with the external world. In contrast to the unpredictable behavior of traditional networks induced by spontaneous human interactions, industrial networks exhibit regularly repeating and predictable behavior [76]. These patterns only change due to failures or after seldom structural changes to the physical processes, e.g., a manufacturing plant being configured for a new product.

In the past, industrial networks were isolated from the Internet and therefore assumed secure; Hence no protection mechanisms, like authentication or encryption, were integrated. Nowadays, as more connectivity is demanded, e.g., for remote monitoring or cross-production plant optimization, these networks can no longer be considered secure [7]. While retrofitting preventive security mechanisms requires expensive downtime and is often inapplicable due to legacy hardware and resource constraints, IIDSs offer a unique alternative opportunity.

IDSs for traditional office and server networks, e.g., Zeek and Snort, usually define rules for typical malware and attack patterns that trigger an alarm indicating known suspicious activities. However, due to the industry's diversity, attacks are usually unique and targeted, significantly reducing their efficiency.

Contrary, IIDSs can take advantage of the abundance of sensor and actuator data exchanged over the network. The fact that processes behave predictably according to physical constraints enables a great potential for anomaly detection training on benign data and alerting deviations. Specifically, *process-aware* IIDSs report excellent detection capabilities, as recent surveys emphasize [23,37]. However, their effectiveness is still questionable, as many detection methodologies are over-engineered to detect specific attacks in specific systems and are thus not suitable to detect new and tailored attacks as often observed in industrial networks [51,76]. Still, process-aware anomaly detection offers the opportunity to passively and retroactively protect manufacturing plants and critical infrastructure against powerful attacks.

3 The State of Industrial Intrusion Detection Research

Given the promise of IIDSs to offer an easily retrofittable solution to secure industrial networks, the research landscape around industrial intrusion detection has experienced huge attention across all industrial domains. Different surveys put significant effort into providing a holistic overview of this scattered

Table 1. Complex approaches govern the current state of industrial anomaly detection research, and only a few evaluation datasets, like SWaT, are being dominantly used.

	Detection Method (unique publications)	SWaT (63)	WADI (24)	HAI (6)
Artificial NNs (44)	Autoencoder (15)	[12, 16, 26, 36, 40, 41, 47, 52, 58, 62, 68, 75, 77, 83]	[12, 62]	[45]
	Other NN (12)	[1, 20, 22, 29, 34, 49, 50, 65, 70, 71, 73, 78]	[1, 22, 29, 34, 50, 70, 73]	–
	RNN (9)	[6, 30, 39, 53–56]	[30, 56]	[13, 42]
	GAN (5)	[5, 14, 44, 60, 64]	[14, 60]	–
	DNN (3)	[43, 46, 66]	–	–
Graphs (6)	Automata (3)	[15, 57, 79]	[79]	–
	Other (3)	[17, 35]	[17, 35, 69]	–
Miscellaneous (20)	Invariants (3)	[33, 74, 82]	[33, 82]	–
	Linear algebra (3)	[11, 24, 63]	–	–
	Classifier (2)	[9, 25]	[25]	–
	Fingerprinting (2)	[2, 4]	[2]	–
	Matrix Profiles (2)	[8, 10]	–	–
	Other (8)	[18, 32, 48, 80, 81]	[67, 80, 81]	[21, 48, 61]

research field [23, 37]. Surprisingly and contradicting the initial promise of an *easily* retrofittable solution, the current state-of-the-art, governed by all kinds of machine learning, comes at the cost of a complexity overhead, e.g., in terms of demanded computational resources, limited generalizability across industrial domains, or incomprehensiveness of the detection models and emitted alerts. In the end, this hinders the widespread deployment of security mechanisms.

To shine light on this issue and precisely understand the degree of complexity in related work, we systematically analyze the IIDS research landscape. We set out to assess IIDSs that implement anomaly detection, i.e., train models on benign data, as they are especially suited for industries (cf. Sect. 2). To this end, we systematically review *all* papers citing one of the three datasets commonly used in research [19] (SWaT [38], WADI [3], and HAI [72]) according to Scopus and Semantic Scholar as of April 20, 2022, resulting in 215 publications for SWaT, 92 for WADI, and 18 for HAI. We then manually filter for anomaly detection IIDSs, thus especially excluding supervised machine learning, position papers, and surveys. As summarized in Table 1, 70 unique publications fulfill these requirements (some papers use more than one dataset).

We structure found approaches alongside their underlying detection methodologies into three broader classes (cf. Table 1). *Artificial neural networks* (63% of publications) are usually trained to predict the physical state based on recent historical samples. They then define a difference measure, e.g., between predicted and observed state, and raise an alarm if a threshold is surpassed. In contrast, *graph-based* IIDSs (9%) aggregate similar expected behavior into (physical) states of the system with transitions between these states. Unknown states, transitions, or irregularities in their occurrence indicate an anomaly. A large class of *miscellaneous* approaches (28%) shows that the research community has not settled on a preferred direction even in this confined domain.

Interestingly, we found that *all* approaches from Table 1 rely on complex methods: While we occasionally observed related work supplemented with straightforward methods, e.g., out-of-bound checks [57], to the best of our knowledge, such simple approaches have not yet been evaluated in isolation. In the following, we detail our survey's findings by focusing on issues resulting from their complexity.

Computational Complexity. The implementation of any detection methodology should be quick enough to be deployable in real-time environments, i.e., detection should not be significantly delayed by processing overhead. E.g., even if adequate hardware is available, requirements such as GPUs in 23% of the publications drastically limit deployability. Although artificial neural network model sizes of about 1.5 MB are claimed to be lightweight enough to be processed by industrial hardware [30] for other deployments, e.g., on programmable network switches (as commonly done for traditional IDSs), this is still infeasible.

Hindered Generalizability. IIDS research is characterized by an inherent heterogeneity across deployment domains, although underlying fundamental principles remain similar (cf. Sect. 2). While it would make sense to transfer the achievements of IIDS research conducted for one domain to another, it is known that most published approaches (75% [76]) evaluate a single use-case. Also, in our survey, we find that IIDSs are evaluated only on a median of 1.5 (2 on average) different datasets, and since complex IIDSs are fine-tuned to one specific scenario, they are rarely applied elsewhere [27,76]. Even though some papers claim generalizability to other domains [46], this claim is not proven.

Incomprehensible Alarms. After an IIDS has indicated a potential threat by emitting an alarm, further (manual) investigation is necessary to find and ultimately mitigate its cause. This could include determining the affected part of the process and isolating it from the rest of the network. While a few IIDSs' alarms are reasonably descriptive [33,42,57] and would ease in-depth investigation, such works are rare in our survey. In most cases, the decisions of machine learning classifies are often incomprehensible or only accessible to highly-trained specialists. For instance, feeding a vector of process values into an artificial neural network [46], it is not clear why the vector would be classified as benign or malicious, preventing timely tracing of an alarm back to its source.

Difficult Deployment. Training an IIDS to a process usually requires configuring plenty of hyperparameters, especially for machine learning, which relies on experts knowing the details of a model. As scientific reproduction studies indicate [27], even IDS experts fail when trying to configure an already published approach (with source code available) to match the original publication's results. While setting up an IIDS is usually done once and, therefore, the training overhead might be justifiable, industrial processes are subject to change if the process is adapted or optimized from time to time. In the worst case, this makes the trained model obsolete and requires redoing the entire process. Also, verifying a retrained model is difficult if the model is not humanly comprehensible [28].

Non-Stealthy Attacks. One common argument to justify complexity is the goal to unveil stealthy attacks. While approaches evaluated on specifically crafted datasets exist [11], a closer inspection of the *commonly* used datasets reveals that many attacks are not difficult to detect. As shown in Fig. 1 for SWaT, overshooting or undershooting regular process values, remaining for too long in a single state (flat line), or unusual steep inclines or declines do not necessarily require complex detection mechanisms. Still, this is not a flaw of the datasets, as recent real-world incidents prove. E.g., the sodium hydroxide concentration of an insecure water treatment plant in Florida was set to hazardous levels (about 100 times increased) [59], constituting a potentially easily detectable real attack.

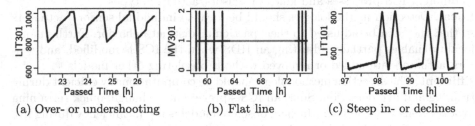

(a) Over- or undershooting   (b) Flat line   (c) Steep in- or declines

Fig. 1. Manual investigation of the SWaT dataset reveals that attacks (red) commonly used for evaluating IIDSs in research are often not stealthy and thus easy to detect. (Color figure online)

In conclusion, current research on industrial intrusion detection is primarily driven by complex approaches, while attacks in evaluation datasets and examples from real-world incidents seem to be detectable relatively straightforward. Given further drawbacks, i.e., incomprehensible alarms, computational complexity, hindered generalizability, and difficult deployment, it is unknown whether this complexity is necessary or whether IIDSs could not be (more) simple instead.

4   SIMPLE Industrial Intrusion Detection

To study the question of whether IIDSs indeed have to be complex, we first define properties that characterize a SIMPLE IIDS (Sect. 4.1). We then present our four IIDSs (Sect. 4.2) derived from typical attack patterns and natural ICS behaviors, e.g., that physical and operational limits constrain possible value ranges.

4.1   Sufficient, Independent, Meaningful, Portable, Local and Efficient

The focus of research on complex IIDSs leads to inherent drawbacks as laid out in Sect. 3, and to address these issues, we propose six properties for Sufficient, Independent, Meaningful, Portable, Local, and Efficient (SIMPLE) IIDSs:

Sufficient. Although simpler in design, an IIDS should be sufficient to detect most attacks while emitting few false alarms (compared to complex approaches).
Independent. Since training an IIDS to specific scenarios is currently complicated due to plenty of hyperparameters influencing the training process, SIMPLE models should be independent of parameters and specialized personnel required to find parameters or re-evaluate a trained model after any modification.
Meaningful. As IIDSs protect physical processes, providing operators with meaningful alerts is essential. They allow determining which sensors/actuators behave anomalously and thus take appropriate measures in a timely manner.
Portable. Since the industrial domain is inherently heterogeneous, an IIDS should be portable to various industrial scenarios. I.e., it needs to be adaptable to different ICS processes and kinds of sensors/actuators types.
Local. Detection methodologies should be local to individual sensors/actuators so that they can be adjusted to their particular distinct behavior. Furthermore, locality enables partially adjusting an IIDS when the ICS is modified, and sensors/actuators are added or removed without obsoleting other models.
Efficient. The detection methodology should be computationally efficient during training and live detection. Since an ICS's process may change, quick retraining avoids extensive periods in which an obsolete model is used. Efficiency during live detection enlarges hardware and deployment choices and eases timely responses.

Besides SIMPLE, related work already postulated a similar set of requirements [28]. Overall, our six properties address the challenges of complex detection approaches widely found in literature and thus provide the foundation for easily understandable, lightweight, generalizable, and effective intrusion detection.

4.2   Designing SIMPLE IIDSs

To turn the postulated properties into reality and thus lay the foundation for answering whether industrial intrusion detection indeed has to be inherently complex, we design four SIMPLE IIDSs. Our approaches are inspired by typical attack patterns found in scientific datasets (cf. Fig. 1), natural ICS behaviors, and share a set of common characteristics as explained in the following.

At the core, a SIMPLE IIDS learns a single model per sensor/actuator of the ICS and is trained in a single pass. Not only do separate models fulfill locality, but they are even necessary as process variables exhibit different value ranges, i.e., sensors (float) and actuators (discrete), obviating the need for additional normalization known from complex related work (e.g., [1,6,43]). Simultaneously, we avoid introducing process dependencies into the model, which would inherently increase complexity. By iterating over the data only once, we significantly reduce the computational complexity of the training process.

All our detection models train a lower (min) and an upper (max) threshold of a certain, easily computable property and emit an alarm if one of these thresholds is exceeded. To account for variability in physical values and between process cycles due to noise or the fact that training data might not cover all expected data ranges, we introduce an error margin to the learned thresholds as follows:

$$min_{\text{err}} := min - \frac{max - min}{2} \qquad max_{\text{err}} := max + \frac{max - min}{2}$$

The resulting thresholds min_{err} and max_{err}, which are then used for emitting alarms, effectively double the trained range. While this approach is highly opportunistic, it is universally applicable and could be theoretically adjusted easily, yet we refrain from doing so in the spirit of simplicity.

In the following, we present the design of our four SIMPLE IIDSs (MinMax, Gradient, Steadytime, and Histogram) based on these common characteristics. As visualized in Fig. 2, each approach is inspired by natural ICS behaviors or typical attack patterns. We do not claim that our set of SIMPLE IIDSs is exhaustive; theoretically, many others exist. Nevertheless, the following four approaches are adequate to study whether the inherent complexity of IIDSs observed in related work is required. Still, it is essential to note that not every approach is equally well suited for each type of sensor/actuator.

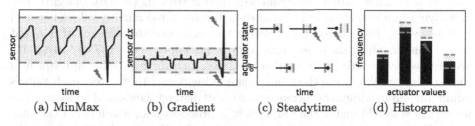

| (a) MinMax | (b) Gradient | (c) Steadytime | (d) Histogram |

Fig. 2. We introduce four SIMPLE IIDS ideas detecting over- or undershooting with a MinMax approach, steep in- or declines with Gradient, flat lines with Steadytime, and unnatural process fluctuations with a Histogram. Each IIDS trains an allowed range (green area). If the threshold (green line) is surpassed, an alarm (red arrow) is emitted. (Color figure online)

MinMax. The minimum and maximum (MinMax) approach (cf. Fig. 2a) detects whether a sensor's/actuator's current value exceeds the range observed in the training data and raises an alarm if any observation falls outside that range ($\pm$ error margin). This approach is motivated by the intuition that process values of industrial systems relate to physical measurements or setpoints and thus usually obey certain limits. E.g., temperatures below the freezing point of a liquid are not desirable for pumping it through pipes. Even if the physical setup does not limit the value range, operational requirements may impose restrictions on the allowed data range, e.g., the pH value of a liquid may not exceed a specific range to be non-hazardous. Thus, we assume that an industrial system exhibits a class of values inside well-defined minimum and maximum limits.

Gradient. Following a similar intuition, the Gradient approach (cf. Fig. 2b) detects whether a sensor's/actuator's slope exceeds the minimum and maximum observed during training ($\pm$ error margin). While MinMax observes global changes, more subtle attacks occurring within these limits may remain unnoticed. E.g., as shown in Fig. 1c, the sensor is set to a high value within the operational limits, yet far too abrupt, thus introducing a noticeable discontinuity. Hence, the Gradient approach assumes that ICSs have continual character, i.e., physical values such as temperatures cannot change at arbitrary speed.

Steadytime. Focusing on another temporal aspect, the Steadytime approach (cf. Fig. 2c) detects whether a sensor/actuator remains static, i.e., does not change its value, for a shorter or longer time than seen during training (± error margin). This approach is motivated by the observation that an attack, e.g., freezing a sensor/actuator (cf. Fig. 1b) such as a pressure relief valve, cannot be detected by checking whether a value or the velocity of a value change remains within certain boundaries (MinMax/Gradient). Since a steady state is difficult to define for noisy sensor data, Steadytime takes only process values into account if the number of distinct values during training is sufficiently small (≤ 10).

Histogram. Specifically targeting the occurrence of values, the Histogram approach (cf. Fig. 2d) tracks their distribution within a fixed-sized window and tests whether it is in line with a histogram seen during training (± error margin). The underlying intuition expects a similar distribution of reoccurring values between process cycles. This approach can detect the existence and absence of frequent value changes, which the other three approaches cannot detect. The histograms are created by counting the number of times each distinct value appears in a sliding window. We merge them into a single histogram that covers each value's minimum and maximum occurrences across all distinct fixed-sized windows. The window size should match the duration of a process cycle, which could be automatically determined in an additional run over the dataset prior to training the histograms. Like Steadytime, Histogram only applies for process values with a few distinct values (≤ 10), as comparing two histograms value-by-value is unfeasible for noisy sensor data.

These four proposals stand in stark contrast to related work, which focuses on inherently complex approaches such as leveraging multiple Autoencoders [14] or fusing two IIDS directions into one solution [26]. While further refinements to our IIDSs are possible, we explicitly focused on fundamental and minimalistic approaches to understand their effectiveness and assess whether industrial intrusion detection really needs to be complex or can be more SIMPLE instead.

5   Industrial Intrusion Detection Can Indeed Be SIMPLE

Using our four SIMPLE IIDSs, we can now study the fundamental question of whether industrial intrusion detection inherently needs to be complex or whether and to which extent SIMPLE approaches provide a viable alternative. To answer this question, we specifically study whether they are (i) sufficient to detect most attacks, (ii) competitive to complex approaches from related work, and (iii) portable across industrial scenarios. To this end, we first provide an overview of our evaluation setup (Sect. 5.1) before we analyze how our approaches perform on the widely-used reference dataset SWaT (Sect. 5.2), their portability to three additional industrial datasets (Sect. 5.3), and ultimately discuss the prospects of SIMPLE IIDSs for industrial intrusion detection (Sect. 5.4).

5.1 Evaluation Setup

We begin our analysis by describing the implementation, datasets, and evaluation metrics underlying our evaluations.

Implementation. We implemented our four SIMPLE IIDSs (cf. Sect. 4.2) in Python on top of the IPAL framework [76], which offers a holistic scientific platform to implement, evaluate, and compare industrial intrusion detection approaches. Most importantly, IPAL introduces a unified representation for the data input, which facilitates the seamless application of IIDSs to many datasets. Furthermore, it provides (re-)implementations of state-of-the-art IIDSs from related work [76], which we use as a comparison benchmark. To facilitate further research on industrial intrusion detection, we make the implementations of our SIMPLE IIDSs publicly available[2] within the IPAL framework.

Datasets. We evaluate our IIDSs on four state-of-the-art industrial datasets based on physical testbeds and including attacks against the industrial process: SWaT [38], the most widely-used dataset, represents a multi-staged water treatment system. Similarly, WADI [3] serves as an example of portability to a water distribution scenario. Additionally, we consider the novel WDT dataset [31] since it includes network and physically induced attacks, and finish with HAI [72] modeling power generation and storage – an entirely different industrial domain.

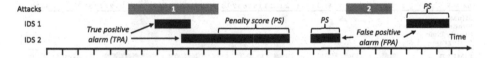

Fig. 3. When evaluating IIDSs, a true positive alarm (TPA) overlaps with the attack label from the dataset (red), while a false positive alarm (FPA) does not overlap with any attack. The penalty score (PS) measures the "overshooting" of all raised alarms. (Color figure online)

Evaluation Metrics. To objectively quantify the performance of both SIMPLE and complex IIDSs, we refer to a set of performance metrics. As visualized in Fig. 3, datasets contain labels (in red) indicating a time range when an attack took place. An IIDS indicates these attacks by emitting alarms (in black). As traditional metrics, we utilize *accuracy, precision, recall,* and *F1-score* – the de-facto standard for evaluating classifiers. Yet, as they focus on the label coverage, they do not express how many attacks are detected and are skewed if attacks are of different lengths. Furthermore, effects unique to industrial settings, such as the stabilization time required after an attack, are not considered. Thus, we additionally calculate the percentage of *detected attacks*, the number of *true positive alarms* (TPA), i.e., alarms overlapping with an attack, false-positive alarms (FPA), i.e., non-overlapping alarms, and the *penalty score* (PS) aggregating the non-overlapping time span [57] to provide a more holistic perspective.

---

[2] Implementation available at: https://github.com/fkie-cad/ipal_ids_framework.

5.2 Sufficiency: SIMPLE IIDSs on Par with Complex Approaches

First, we study whether SIMPLE IIDSs are *sufficient* to detect most attacks (cf. Sect. 4.1) and whether industrial intrusion detection must be inherently complex. To this end, we compare our approaches' detection performance to related work in an in-depth evaluation based on SWaT [38], as it is the most widely-used dataset in literature (90% of publications according to our analysis in Table 1).

SWaT consists of a training part of normal ICS behavior and a test part containing 36 attacks. We trained our four IIDSs on the training data omitting the first ~22 h during which the system stabilizes after activation. As seven out of SWaT's 51 sensors and actuators do not maintain the regular patterns observed during training, we excluded those from further evaluation. Skipping the stabilization phase [49,55,58,63,66,75,79] and omitting process values [50, 52,62,66,75] in SWaT are common practices in related work. Notably, instead of excluding the process values, a process expert could manually adapt a pre-trained SIMPLE model, which is impossible for complex approaches (cf. Sect. 3).

Table 2. Already a high-level analysis reveals that our SIMPLE IIDSs (green) in combination can detect 75% of attacks from the SWaT dataset, thus performing comparably to complex approaches from related work (blue/lower half of the table).

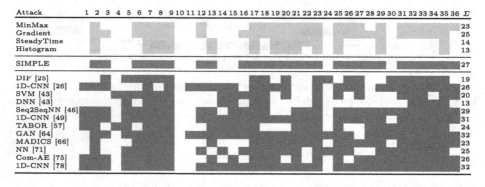

High-level Ability to Detect Attacks. We use SWaT to gain a first assessment of the ability of our SIMPLE IIDSs to detect attacks and to compare them to complex approaches from related work. To this end, we analyzed all 63 publications evaluating on SWaT (cf. Sect. 3) to obtain those that provide sufficiently detailed information on which specific attacks they detect, resulting in eleven publications covering twelve complex IIDSs. Table 2 visualizes which SIMPLE (green) and complex (blue) IIDSs can detect which of the 36 attacks in SWaT.

Our four combined approaches (denoted with "SIMPLE") detect a majority of attacks (75%/27 attacks). Our arguably most simple approach (MinMax) alone can detect 23 attacks, and Gradient performs best by detecting 25 attacks. For comparison, the average number of detected attacks by related work is 25.0.

Aggregating related work's capabilities, they detect all except a single scenario. However, in the twelve scenarios that *all* SIMPLE approaches detect, seven of the twelve complex IIDSs do not fully cover these seemingly easy-to-detect attacks. Regarding the nine attacks that are not detected by any SIMPLE approach, four (4, 10, 11, 14) have repeatedly been reported as not-detectable [46,71,78], and we observe inefficiencies in complex approaches too. Notably, not a single attack is detected by all complex approaches but not by our SIMPLE methods.

Thus, SIMPLE IIDSs seem on par with their complex counterparts, detecting more attacks on average but less in total for the benefits of increased simplicity. **In-depth Comparison.** Besides high detection rates, IIDSs should have a low false-positive rate [28]. To study how SIMPLE IIDSs fare against selected complex related work, we study their alert behavior in-depth visually (Fig. 4) and alongside metrics (Table 3). We again provide combined results for "SIMPLE", where an alarm is emitted whenever any IIDS emits an alarm. Notably, this may fuse alerts into larger ones, which can result in fewer overall TPAs and FPAs.

Since this evaluation requires access to complex IIDSs, we selected one representative approach for each of the three classes (cf. Table 1) for which we have implementations available (cf. Sect. 5.1): (i) Seq2SeqNN [46] (representing artificial neural networks) predicts the following expected output based on samples of recent process history, and alerts if the prediction deviates long enough from the observed behavior, (ii) TABOR [57] (graph-based) combines an automaton, Bayesian network, and out-of-bounds check into a single solution (while we could only reproduce one of TABOR's 16 models for SWaT, this model still suffices for our analysis), and (iii) PASAD [11] (miscellaneous) leverages a singular spectrum analysis to identify recurring process patterns on a per-sensor basis.

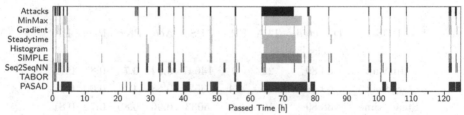

Short attacks and alarms are enlarged to a minimum width of 0.15% for visibility.

Fig. 4. A visual inspection of the alerts of SIMPLE IIDSs (green) shows thorough coverage w.r.t. the attacks for the SWaT dataset (red). The alerts of the three representative complex approaches (blue) are less expressive and contain more false positives. (Color figure online)

Upon visual inspection based on Fig. 4, the alerts emitted by the SIMPLE IIDSs coincide with the attacks to be detected to a large extent. Furthermore, during non-attack periods, they do not emit large amounts of false alarms. Overall, the three complex approaches contain more false alarms and detect fewer attacks. Thus, while from a high-level view, the complex IIDSs under study appeared to detect slightly more attack scenarios (cf. Table 2), they come at the price of more false positives and consequently reduced utility.

Moreover, most related complex approaches' alarms are incomprehensible as they often exhibit multiple alarms around an attack (Seq2SeqNN) or alert over a long time range covering many attacks (PASAD). Our IIDSs, on the other hand, precisely overlap with the attacks and additionally allow to determine the potential malicious sensors through their locality property (cf. Sect. 4.1). E.g., for 21 of the attacks detected by Gradient, the alerts stem from the process value indicated as the attack point in the SWaT dataset, thus providing a reliable starting point for subsequent incident response.

The individual metrics summarized in Table 3 confirm our previous observation that SIMPLE approaches detect large amounts of attacks (detected attacks and TPA), emit few false alarms (FPA), and perform on par with related work. Notably, while Steadytime and Histogram detect fewer attacks, they simultaneously have the lowest FPA score of all IIDSs under study. In terms of accuracy, precision, recall, and F1 score, the MinMax, Steadytime, and Histogram IIDS outperform Seq2SeqNN and PASAD and perform roughly equivalent to TABOR. These metrics are surprisingly good, considering the simplicity of the detection methods, which are not optimized to any metrics (a problem common for machine learning approaches [51]). While Gradient showed auspicious detection performance in the visual comparison, it fares poorly for the individual metrics. The main reason for this phenomenon is that these metrics favor long attack coverage, a phenomenon we study in more detail in the appendix.

Table 3. Across all relevant quantifiable evaluation metrics, SIMPLE IIDSs (especially in combination) are competitive to the studied complex approaches from related work.

IIDS	Detected Attacks [%]	TPA	FPA	PS	Acc.	Prec.	Rec.	F1
MinMax	63.89	22	9	14647	0.94	0.75	0.81	0.78
Gradient	69.44	47	64	352	0.88	0.3	0.00	0.01
Steadytime	38.89	16	4	5033	0.96	0.89	0.75	0.81
Histogram	36.11	12	0	6794	0.95	0.85	0.72	0.78
SIMPLE	75.0	26	23	19621	0.94	0.71	0.87	0.78
Seq2SeqNN	72.22	30	37	7559	0.88	0.44	0.11	0.17
TABOR*	66.67	–	–	–	–	0.86	0.79	0.82
PASAD	44.44	10	14	81604	0.78	0.32	0.72	0.45

* Results taken from the publication [57] as not all model parameters were reproducible.

Takeaway: All four SIMPLE IIDSs detect a sufficient number of attacks in the SWaT dataset. Combining the SIMPLE approaches allows detecting 75% of all attacks while visually emitting only a few false alerts. Moreover, raised (false) alarms are meaningful due to their local design and comprehensible models. Compared to related work, SIMPLE IIDSs can keep up with complex approaches in terms of the number of detected alarms, and especially false positives.

5.3   Portability: SIMPLE IIDSs Work Effortlessly in New Settings

To ensure that IIDSs are widely applicable, they must be portable to various industrial scenarios and processes with a short training phase and without requiring (re-)inventions (cf. Sect. 4.1). Consequently, we show the portability of our IIDSs by applying them to three additional industrial datasets (WADI [3], WDT [31], and HAI [72], cf. Sect. 5.1). We again compare our IIDSs to the three complex representatives from related work (Seq2SeqNN, TABOR, and PASAD, cf. Sect. 5.2). Unlike ours, porting the complex IIDSs to the new datasets required extensive manual work to find suitable models and parameters. Once more, we analyze the results both visually (Fig. 5) and for various metrics (Table 4).

WADI. At first glance, with 64% of detected attacks overall, the SIMPLE IIDSs do not perform as strongly on WADI as on SWaT. However, even our worst-performing IIDS, Steadytime (43%), still outperforms PASAD (14%) and TABOR (29%). More importantly, we visually observe only two false alarms not

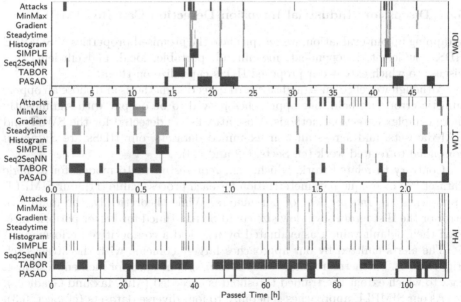

Short attacks and alarms are enlarged to a minimum width of 0.15% for visibility.

Fig. 5. Porting SIMPLE IIDSs (green) to three additional datasets shows their generalizability to various industrial scenarios, while complex IIDSs (blue) perform worse. Note that the results on the SWaT dataset have previously been discussed in Fig. 4. (Color figure online)

closely related to an attack (at around 18h and 42h). While the complex IIDSs exhibit similarly few false alarms, their penalty score (PS) is exceptionally high, indicating that their alarms are too imprecise to match a single attack.

WDT. The WDT dataset proves challenging for all IIDS types, with SIMPLE approaches detecting up to 22% of the attacks, compared to 4% (Seq2SeqNN) up to 18% (TABOR) for the complex approaches. Upon closer inspection, we identified one cause to be attacks not targeting the industrial processes, e.g., network scanning. Since complex approaches are likewise incapable of finding these attack types, SIMPLE IIDSs provide an equally performing alternative.

HAI. The SIMPLE IIDSs perform well for the HAI dataset with 86% of detected attacks, a low PS of only 531, and nearly no FPA for MinMax, Steadytime, and Histogram. Notably, MinMax and Gradient perform especially well on HAI, thus showing that attacks can be detected reliably even with the simplest approaches. Complex related work, in contrast, falls far behind, and TABOR is even largely inapplicable, likely due to HAI's less pronounced regular patterns.

Takeaway: SIMPLE IIDSs, unlike their complex counterparts, can be ported to new datasets without manual effort. Furthermore, considering that our approaches, in contrast to complex approaches, performed best on HAI (representing an entirely new industrial domain), this perfectly proves their portability.

5.4   Discussion: Industrial Intrusion Detection Can Be SIMPLE

Wrapping up our evaluation, we recapitulate the promised properties of SIMPLE IIDSs (sufficient, independent, meaningful, portable, local, and efficient) and discuss to which extent our proposed IIDSs capitalize on them.

Although we relied on straightforward detection methods and chose an opportunistic error threshold, our approaches proved to be on par with significantly more complex detection methods. Most attacks are detected for the SWaT and HAI datasets, and across all four examined datasets, our IIDSs are *Sufficient* compared to related work (cf. Sects. 5.2 and 5.3).

Contrary to related work, which, e.g., requires up to 16 models for a single dataset [57] or unique parameterization for each process value [11], our SIMPLE approaches are *Independent* of parameters. While theoretically, the margin of error or the Histogram's window size could be fine-tuned for better performance, even their default values, as evaluated by us, yield a competitive performance.

The alerts emitted by our approaches largely coincide with the attacks (cf. Fig. 4 and 5). Furthermore, these carry *Meaningful* insights for incident response, e.g., to which extent the trained threshold is exceeded (MinMax and Gradient).

As our SIMPLE approaches generalize to four diverse datasets (cf. Sect. 5.3), they have successfully proved to be *Portable* across various industrial settings.

Already by design (cf. Sect. 4.2), all our SIMPLE approaches are *Local*, i.e., operate on a per-sensor basis. As such, they are inherently able to identify the triggering value directly. To illustrate the resulting advantages exemplary for the

Table 4. For all relevant metrics, e.g., detected attacks, our SIMPLE IIDSs generalize better to new industrial settings than complex related work (an in-depth analysis, e.g., regarding FPA of the Gradient IIDS, is provided in the appendix). Note that the results on the SWaT dataset have previously been discussed in Table 3.

	IIDS	Detected Attacks [%]	TPA	FPA	PS	Acc.	Prec.	Rec.	F1
WADI	MinMax	50.0	6	4	1751	0.96	0.7	0.41	0.52
	Gradient	50.0	44	12	12	0.94	0.79	0.0	0.01
	Steadytime	42.86	7	2	413	0.96	0.88	0.3	0.44
	Histogram	50.0	6	6	1775	0.95	0.64	0.32	0.42
	SIMPLE	64.29	6	9	3120	0.95	0.58	0.44	0.5
	Seq2SeqNN	57.14	8	6	1293	0.94	0.52	0.14	0.22
	TABOR	28.57	5	0	5792	0.92	0.3	0.25	0.27
	PASAD	14.29	2	3	23197	0.82	0.05	0.13	0.07
WDT	MinMax	7.84	4	0	268	0.72	0.3	0.08	0.13
	Gradient	5.88	8	3	3	0.75	0.73	0.01	0.01
	Steadytime	17.65	9	0	411	0.74	0.45	0.23	0.31
	Histogram	1.96	1	0	0	0.76	1.0	0.04	0.09
	SIMPLE	21.57	16	3	639	0.71	0.38	0.27	0.32
	Seq2SeqNN	3.92	2	3	58	0.74	0.19	0.01	0.02
	TABOR	17.65	7	0	762	0.67	0.3	0.22	0.26
	PASAD	11.76	4	2	639	0.68	0.27	0.16	0.2
HAI	MinMax	86.0	73	7	496	0.98	0.87	0.38	0.53
	Gradient	78.0	209	48	96	0.98	0.89	0.09	0.16
	Steadytime	28.0	15	0	161	0.98	0.86	0.11	0.19
	Histogram	28.0	15	0	161	0.98	0.86	0.11	0.19
	SIMPLE	86.0	145	26	531	0.99	0.87	0.4	0.55
	Seq2SeqNN	4.0	2	5	936	0.98	0.29	0.04	0.07
	TABOR	70.0	22	7	271159	0.32	0.02	0.6	0.04
	PASAD	4.0	2	11	29839	0.9	0.01	0.04	0.02

SWaT dataset, which provides precise information on the attack location, Min-Max and Gradient, e.g., could easily identify 18 respectively 21 attack locations correctly, significantly easing attack identification and hence incident response.

Finally, the IIDSs are *Efficient* w.r.t. computing resources as they rely on elementary computational operations both during model creation and detection. E.g., MinMax and Steadytime only perform an interval test, Gradient requires an additional subtraction for the slope computation, and Histogram counts and compares the last recently occurring process values. Besides computational efficiency, they are also optimized for a low memory footprint, thus easing their applicability in resource-limited industrial settings: MinMax and Gradient only store the minimal and maximal bounds on a per-sensor basis, while Steadytime and Histogram only require the thresholds per occurring value for each sensor.

Takeaway: The four exemplary approaches presented in this paper satisfy the properties of a sufficient, independent, meaningful, portable, local, and efficient IIDS. Thus, we show that industrial intrusion detection can indeed be SIMPLE, challenging the necessity of inherent complexity found across related work.

6   Conclusion

Industrial intrusion detection constitutes a retrofittable solution to counteract harmful cyberattacks against increasingly threatened industrial control systems. Striving to achieve (close to) optimal detection of attacks, the research community proposed a wide variety of approaches to detect anomalies in the process state across different industrial domains. However, as we identify based on a systematic analysis of 70 proposals from related work, these approaches show an inherent complexity where high detection performance is accompanied by dearly bought consequences such as a lack of model and alert comprehensibility or a high demand for computing resources. Considering that IIDSs leverage the repetitive nature of physical processes, we wonder why simpler detection methods have not been considered so far. To overcome this gap, we study whether IIDSs can be SIMPLE (Sufficient, Independent, Meaningful, Portable, Local, and Efficient) instead of having to rely on complex models with all their disadvantages. Thus, we designed four exemplary minimalistic approaches, such as straightforward range checks. Surprisingly, as we show across four distinct industrial datasets, simplicity does not result in reduced detection capabilities, as simple methods are on par with significantly more complex related work. Simultaneously, simple approaches offer highly beneficial properties such as eased configuration, model and alert comprehensibility, and reduced computational overhead. Thus, simple IIDSs provide a viable alternative to complex approaches, raising the question whether slight increases in detection capabilities justify computational overheads and reduced utility. Still, it remains open whether our results are constrained by the studied datasets (i.e., the included attacks that are too "easy" to detect) or whether SIMPLE IIDSs are inherently sufficient to detect cyberattacks. Consequently, future research has to investigate the raison d'être for complex IIDS w.r.t. advanced and stealthy attacks, beyond limiting their evaluations to the datasets currently in widespread use, for which simple approaches suffice.

Acknowledgments. Funded by the Deutsche Forschungsgemeinschaft (DFG, German Research Foundation) under Germany's Excellence Strategy – EXC- 2023 Internet of Production – 390621612.

Appendix

To better understand the SIMPLE IIDSs mechanics, we take a detailed look at their detection phase. We occasionally see alerts stretching significantly further (with interruptions) than the actual attack. In Fig. 6a, the MinMax IIDS raises an alarm throughout the ICS's recovery phase since the process values still deviate from their normal values and fluctuate until stabilizing. The Gradient IIDS reveals another phenomenon in Fig. 6b, leading to supposedly false alerts inherent to its design. As it indicates in- or declines, its alerts are short, which results in a poor performance w.r.t. to metrics evaluating the attack coverage. While this method is precise in finding the actual beginnings and endings of attacks, it often raises an alarm shortly after an attack when the process quickly returns to normal operation. Finally, in Fig. 6c, we observe effects that can occur after the actual attack ended (or where datasets are not precisely labeled). All of these effects result in insufficient attack coverage and false alarms, such that the good performance of IIDSs is not captured well by the available metrics.

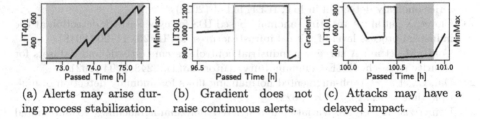

(a) Alerts may arise during process stabilization. (b) Gradient does not raise continuous alerts. (c) Attacks may have a delayed impact.

Fig. 6. IIDS performance metrics can show a skewed picture when to be detected physical anomalies (green) are misaligned with the actual attack timing (red). (Color figure online)

References

1. Abdelaty, M.F., et al.: DAICS: a deep learning solution for anomaly detection in industrial control systems. IEEE Trans. Emerg. Topics Comput. (2021)
2. Ahmed, C., et al.: NoisePrint: attack detection using sensor and process noise fingerprint in cyber physical systems. In: ACM ASIACCS (2018)
3. Ahmed, C., et al.: WADI: a water distribution testbed for research in the design of secure cyber physical systems. In: CySWATER (2017)
4. Ahmed, C., et al.: Noise matters: Using sensor and process noise fingerprint to detect stealthy cyber attacks and authenticate sensors in CPS. In: ACSAC (2018)
5. Alabugin, S.K., et al.: Applying of generative adversarial networks for anomaly detection in industrial control systems. In: GloSIC (2020)
6. Alabugin, S.K., et al.: Applying of recurrent neural networks for industrial processes anomaly detection. In: IEEE USBEREIT (2021)
7. Alladi, T., et al.: Industrial control systems: cyberattack trends and countermeasures. Computer Communications 155 (2020)
8. Anton, S.D.D., et al.: Using temporal and topological features for intrusion detection in operational networks. In: ARES (2019)
9. Anton, S.D.D., et al.: Security in process: detecting attacks in industrial process data. In: CECC (2019)

10. Anton, S.D.D., et al.: Intrusion detection in binary process data: introducing the hamming-distance to matrix profiles. In: IEEE WoWMoM (2020)
11. Aoudi, W., et al.: Truth will out: departure-based process-level detection of stealthy attacks on control systems. In: ACM CCS (2018)
12. Audibert, J., et al.: USAD: unsupervised anomaly detection on multivariate time series. In: ACM SIGKDD (2020)
13. Bae, S., et al.: Research on improvement of anomaly detection performance in industrial control systems. In: WISA (2021)
14. Cao, D., et al.: Self-Adaption AAE-GAN for aluminum electrolytic cell anomaly detection. IEEE Access 9 (2021)
15. Castellanos, J.H., et al.: A modular hybrid learning approach for black-box security testing of CPS. In: ACNS (2019)
16. Chen, X., et al.: DAEMON: unsupervised anomaly detection and interpretation for multivariate time series. In: IEEE ICDE (2021)
17. Chen, Z., et al.: Learning graph structures with transformer for multivariate time series anomaly detection in IoT. IEEE IoT-J (2021)
18. Clotet, X., et al.: A real-time anomaly-based IDS for cyber-attack detection at the industrial process level of critical infrastructures. IJCIP **23**, 11–20 (2018)
19. Conti, M., et al.: A survey on industrial control system testbeds and datasets for security research. IEEE Commun. Surv. Tutor. **23**(4), 2248–2294 (2021)
20. Dai, E., et al.: Graph-augmented normalizing flows for anomaly detection of multiple time series. In: ICLR (2022)
21. Demertzis, K., et al.: Variational restricted boltzmann machines to automated anomaly detection. Neural Comput. Appl., 1–14 (2022)
22. Deng, A., et al.: Graph neural network-based anomaly detection in multivariate time series. In: AAAI (2021)
23. Ding, D., et al.: A survey on security control and attack detection for industrial cyber-physical systems. Neurocomputing **275**, 1674–1683 (2018)
24. Dutta, A.K., et al.: CatchAll: A Robust Multivariate Intrusion Detection System for Cyber-Physical Systems Using Low Rank Matrix. In: CPSIoTSec (2021)
25. Elnour, M., et al.: A dual-isolation-forests-based attack detection framework for industrial control systems. IEEE Access **8**, 36639–36651 (2020)
26. Elnour, M., et al.: Hybrid attack detection framework for industrial control systems using 1d-convolutional neural network and isolation forest. In: CCTA (2020)
27. Erba, A., et al.: No Need to Know Physics: Resilience of Process-Based Model-Free Anomaly Detection for Industrial Control Systems. arXiv:2012.03586 (2020)
28. Etalle, S.: From intrusion detection to software design. In: ESORICS (2017)
29. Faber, K., et al.: Ensemble neuroevolution-based approach for multivariate time series anomaly detection. Entropy **23**(11), 1466 (2021)
30. Fährmann, D., et al.: Lightweight long short-term memory variational auto-encoder for multivariate time series anomaly detection in industrial control systems. Sensors **22**(8), 2886 (2022)
31. Faramondi, L., et al.: A hardware-in-the-loop water distribution testbed dataset for cyber-physical security testing. IEEE Access **9**, 122385–122396 (2021)
32. Farsi, H., et al.: A novel online state-based anomaly detection system for process control networks. IJCIP **27**, 100323 (2019)
33. Feng, C., et al.: A systematic framework to generate invariants for anomaly detection in industrial control systems. In: NDSS (2019)
34. Feng, C., et al.: Time series anomaly detection for cyber-physical systems via neural system identification and bayesian filtering. In: ACM SIGKDD (2021)

35. Francisquini, R., et al.: Community-based anomaly detection using spectral graph filtering. Appl. Soft Comput. **118**, 108489 (2022)
36. Gauthama Raman, M., et al.: Deep autoencoders as anomaly detectors: method and case study in a distributed water treatment plant. Comput. Secur. **99**, 102055 (2020)
37. Giraldo, J., et al.: A survey of physics-based attack detection in cyber-physical systems. ACM Comput. Surv. **51**(4), 1–36 (2018)
38. Goh, J., et al.: A dataset to support research in the design of secure water treatment systems. In: CRITIS (2016)
39. Goh, J., et al.: Anomaly detection in cyber physical systems using recurrent neural networks. In: IEEE HASE (2017)
40. Gong, S., et al.: A prediction-augmented AutoEncoder for multivariate time series anomaly detection. In: ICONIP (2021)
41. Guo, Y., et al.: Unsupervised anomaly detection in IoT systems for smart cities. IEEE TNSE **7**(4), 2231–2242 (2020)
42. Hwang, C., et al.: E-SFD: explainable sensor fault detection in the ICS anomaly detection system. IEEE Access **9**, 140470–140486 (2021)
43. Inoue, J., et al.: Anomaly detection for a water treatment system using unsupervised machine learning. In: DMCIS (2017)
44. Intrator, Y., et al.: MDGAN: boosting anomaly detection using multi-discriminator generative adversarial networks. arXiv:1810.05221 (2018)
45. Kim, D., et al.: Stacked-autoencoder based anomaly detection with industrial control system. In: SNPD (2021)
46. Kim, J., et al.: Anomaly detection for industrial control systems using sequence-to-sequence neural networks. In: CyberICPS (2020)
47. Kim, S., et al.: APAD: autoencoder-based payload anomaly detection for industrial IoE. Appl. Soft Comput. **88**, 106017 (2020)
48. Kim, Y., et al.: Anomaly detection using clustered deep one-class classification. In: AsiaJCIS (2020)
49. Kravchik, M., et al.: Detecting cyber attacks in industrial control systems using convolutional neural networks. In: CPS-SPC (2018)
50. Kravchik, M., et al.: Efficient cyber attack detection in industrial control systems using lightweight neural networks and PCA. IEEE TDSC (2021)
51. Kus, D., et al.: A False Sense of Security? ACM CPSS, revisiting the state of machine learning-based industrial intrusion detection. In (2022)
52. Kwon, H.Y., et al.: Advanced intrusion detection combining signature-based and behavior-based detection methods. Electronics **11**(6), 867 (2022)
53. Lavrova, D., et al.: Using GRU neural network for cyber-attack detection in automated process control systems. In: IEEE BlackSeaCom (2019)
54. Lee, C.K., et al.: Studies on the GAN-based anomaly detection methods for the time series data. IEEE Access **9**, 73201–73215 (2021)
55. Li, D., et al.: Anomaly detection with generative adversarial networks for multivariate time series. In: KDD BigMine (2018)
56. Li, D., et al.: MAD-GAN: multivariate anomaly detection for time series data with generative adversarial networks. In: ICANN (2019)
57. Lin, Q., et al.: TABOR: a graphical model-based approach for anomaly detection in industrial control systems. In: ACM ASIACCS (2018)
58. Macas, M., et al.: An unsupervised framework for anomaly detection in a water treatment system. In: IEEE ICMLA (2019)
59. Margolin, J.: Outdated Computer System Exploited in Water Treatment Plant Hack (2021), www.abc7news.com/story/10328196/, accessed: 2022-04-24

60. Maru, C., et al.: Collective anomaly detection for multivariate data using generative adversarial networks. In: CSCI (2020)
61. Mokhtari, S., et al.: Measurement data intrusion detection in industrial control systems based on unsupervised learning. AIMS-ACI 1(1) (2021)
62. Naito, S., et al.: Anomaly Detection for Multivariate Time Series on Large-Scale Fluid Handling Plant Using Two-Stage Autoencoder. In: ICDMW (2021)
63. Nedeljkovic, D.M., et al.: Detection of cyber-attacks in systems with distributed control based on support vector regression. TELFOR J. 12(2), 104–109 (2020)
64. Neshenko, N., et al.: A behavioral-based forensic investigation approach for analyzing attacks on water plants using GANs. FSI Digital Investigation 37 (2021)
65. Oliveira, N., et al.: Anomaly detection in cyber-physical systems: reconstruction of a prediction error feature space. In: SINCONF (2021)
66. Perales Gomez, A.L., et al.: MADICS: a methodology for anomaly detection in industrial control systems. Symmetry 12(10), 1583 (2020)
67. Pranavan, T., et al.: Contrastive predictive coding for anomaly detection in multivariate time series data. arXiv:2202.03639 (2022)
68. Pyatnisky, I., et al.: Assessment of the applicability of autoencoders in the problem of detecting anomalies in the work of industrial control Systems. In: GloSIC (2020)
69. Ray, S., et al.: Learning graph neural networks for multivariate time series anomaly detection. arXiv:2111.08082 (2021)
70. Schneider, T., et al.: Detecting anomalies within time series using local neural transformations. arXiv:2202.03944 (2022)
71. Shalyga, D., et al.: Anomaly detection for water treatment system based on neural network with automatic architecture optimization. arXiv:1807.07282 (2018)
72. Shin, H., et al.: HAI 1.0: HIL-based Augmented ICS Security Dataset. CSET (2020)
73. Tuli, S., et al.: TranAD: deep transformer networks for anomaly detection in multivariate time series data. In: VLDB (2022)
74. Umer, M.A., et al.: Generating invariants using design and data-centric approaches for distributed attack detection. IJCIP 28, 100341 (2020)
75. Wang, C., et al.: Anomaly detection for industrial control system based on autoencoder neural network. In: WCMC 2020 (2020)
76. Wolsing, K., et al.: IPAL: breaking up silos of protocol-dependent and domain-specific industrial intrusion detection systems. In: Proceedings of RAID (2022)
77. Xiao, Q., et al.: Memory-augmented adversarial autoencoders for multivariate time-series anomaly detection with deep reconstruction and prediction. arXiv:2110.08306 (2021)
78. Xie, X., et al.: Multivariate abnormal detection for industrial control systems using 1D CNN and GRU. IEEE Access 8, 88348–88359 (2020)
79. Xu, Q., et al.: Digital twin-based anomaly detection in cyber-physical systems. In: IEEE ICST (2021)
80. Yan, T., et al.: TFDPM: attack detection for cyber-physical systems with diffusion probabilistic models. arXiv:2112.10774 (2021)
81. Yang, L., et al.: Iterative bilinear temporal-spectral fusion for unsupervised representation learning in time series. arXiv:2202.04770 (2022)
82. Yoong, C.H., et al.: Deriving invariant checkers for critical infrastructure using axiomatic design principles. Cybersecurity 4, 1–24 (2021)
83. Zhang, K., et al.: Federated variational learning for anomaly detection in multivariate time series. In: IEEE IPCCC (2021)

For Your Voice Only: Exploiting Side Channels in Voice Messaging for Environment Detection

Matteo Cardaioli[1,3]($\boxtimes$), Mauro Conti[1,2], and Arpita Ravindranath[2]

[1] University of Padua, Padua, Italy
matteo.cardaioli@phd.unipd.it
[2] Delft University of Technology, Delft, The Netherlands
[3] GFT Italy, Milan, Italy

Abstract. Voice messages are an increasingly popular method of communication, accounting for more than 200 million messages a day. Sending audio messages requires a user to invest lesser effort than texting while enhancing the message's meaning by adding an emotional context (e.g., irony). Unfortunately, we suspect that voice messages might provide much more information than intended to prying ears of a listener. In fact, speech audio waves are both directly recorded by the microphone and propagated into the environment, and possibly reflected back to the microphone. Reflected waves along with ambient noise are also recorded by the microphone and sent as part of the voice message.

In this paper, we propose a novel attack for inferring detailed information about user location (e.g., a specific room) leveraging a simple WhatsApp voice message. We demonstrated our attack considering 7,200 voice messages from 15 different users and four environments (i.e., three bedrooms and a terrace). We considered three realistic attack scenarios depending on previous knowledge of the attacker about the victim and the environment. Our thorough experimental results demonstrate the feasibility and efficacy of our proposed attack. We can infer the location of the user among a pool of four known environments with 85% accuracy. Moreover, our approach reaches an average accuracy of 93% in discerning between two rooms of similar size and furniture (i.e., two bedrooms) and an accuracy of up to 99% in classifying indoor and outdoor environments.

1 Introduction

Modern chats have replaced feature-poor SMS by adding text images, video, audio, and emoticons. This has allowed instant messaging apps to attract more and more users over the years. In 2020, more than 2.7 billion users used at least one instant messaging app[1]. Nowadays, the most used instant messaging app with over 2 billion users worldwide is WhatsApp[2]. One of the most used functions

---

[1] https://www.statista.com/statistics/258749/most-popular-global-mobile-messenger-apps/.
[2] https://www.whatsapp.com/.

© The Author(s), under exclusive license to Springer Nature Switzerland AG 2022
V. Atluri et al. (Eds.): ESORICS 2022, LNCS 13556, pp. 595–613, 2022.
https://doi.org/10.1007/978-3-031-17143-7_29

by WhatsApp users are voice messages, considering that over 200 million are sent every day[3]. Sending a voice message requires even lesser effort for a user compared to texting. Moreover, voice messages allow enriching the message's meaning by adding an emotional context (e.g., irony). Given the appreciation of users, this feature has become common in other messaging apps as well [21], but does a voice message send more than we intend to?

As can be seen in Fig. 1 when a person speaks, the voice signals travel in different paths, some of which undergo reflection. The reflected paths depend on the shape, dimension, furniture that are present in the room. Reflected audio waves end up back at the speaker, causing the persistence of noise called reverberation. In addition, other ambient noises are also present, such as noises from secondary audio sources. The combination of reverberation, noises and the audio message gets picked up by the smartphone during voice messaging. In this work, we aim to use these physical measures that are readily accessible and inadvertently shared during WhatsApp audio messaging to gain intelligence about the victim's whereabouts. To the best of our knowledge, this is the first study that, leveraging short audio messages, identifies the location from which the message was sent. The main contributions we propose in this paper are:

- We propose a novel attack for inferring a specific user location (e.g., a specific room) leveraging simple WhatsApp voice messages.
- We collected a dataset of 15 people and four different environments (i.e., three indoor and one outside) for a total of 7200 recordings (i.e., 480 per participant). We will make the dataset public, available to the research community upon acceptance. We believe it will be useful in studying the problem further and developing countermeasures.
- We performed an extensive analysis of our attack simulating three different real attack scenarios based on the knowledge available to the attacker. We demonstrated that our attack can distinguish the location of the message among a pool of known environments (i.e., three bedrooms and a terrace) with an accuracy of up to 85%. Moreover, we show that our approach reaches an average accuracy of 93% in discerning the voice message location of two rooms of similar size and furniture (i.e., two bedrooms). We further inferred the specific position of a user within a room (e.g., a corner); for this task, we achieved an accuracy of up to 64%.

The structure of the rest of our paper is as follows - In Sect. 2, we discuss previous works related to environment inference using audio signals and location detection. In Sect. 3, we introduce our system and adversary model. Section 4 presents our $\mathcal{F}or\mathcal{Y}our\mathcal{V}oiceOnly$ attack. The experimental setup and results are discussed in Sects. 5 and 6 respectively. We discuss the limitations, potential future research directions, and concluding remarks in Sect. 7.

---

[3] https://www.thesun.co.uk/tech/6815812/texts-voice-messages-whatsapp-imessage-switching/.

2   Related Work

Sound classification represents a field of increasing interest in several areas and applications such as, surveillance [26], medicine [33], emotion recognition [34], music genre classification [27], and forensics [31]. The three main disciplines involved in sound classification are: Music Information Retrieval (MIR), [32,36], Automatic Speech Recognition (ASR) [28,37], and Environmental Audio Scene Recognition (EASR) [29,35]. Music and speech can be well described by features such as MFCC (Mel-frequency cepstral coefficients), bandwidth, zero-crossing rate (ZCR), and spectral flux [8,10]. While for the recognition of environments, the problem is more challenging since the sound, in this case, does not present any tonal or harmonic structure [15].

Fig. 1. Voice propagation when sending a voice message

A first comprehensive study on EASR was carried out by Cowling et al. [6]. In this work, the authors explore different feature extraction and classification techniques on EASR, achieving a 70% accuracy leveraging dynamic time warping classification techniques. One of the primary tasks in the EASR domain is the distinction between indoor and outdoor environments. Khonglah et al. [25] proposed the use of foreground speech segmentation to obtain foreground and background segments of an audio recording. Then from the obtained segments, the MFCCs were extracted and used to train an SVM classifier to perform indoor-outdoor classification. In this study, the authors highlighted that the primary cause of misclassification was the presence of speech in the background. Not only speech but also other background noises can induce classification errors. In real-world scenarios, it is quite common to have complex environment sound (i.e., environments with multiple sound sources). To mitigate the impact of complex sounds on environmental prediction performance, Delgado et al. [16] introduced a feature reduction strategy using a Chi-Squared Filter [2]. Unfortunately, a similar approach cannot be applied to the classification of similar locations. Both speech reverberation and background noise are important sources of information that can describe the environment in which the voice message is recorded.

Recently, many works on EASR have leveraged deep learning algorithms to perform feature extraction and classification [20,23,24] Based on the work conducted by Chandrakala et al. [29] deep learning approaches show better performance compared to traditional machine learning techniques. However, these approaches cannot be applied in our case since they require large amounts of data to train the models.

Additional factors that affect EASR are the recording device's quality and the format in which the sound signal is saved (i.e., lossy audio formats). In this regard, several works have focused on recognizing environments from sounds recorded with resource-constrained devices (e.g., smartphones). Gomes et al. [22] present an application for the smartphone device to classify audio recorded on the device using a combination of SAX-based multiresolution motif discovery in combination with MFCC. The work by Peltonen et al. [5] aims to perform context-based audio scene recognition. However, the data used in this work were obtained using a stereo setup and stored in a digital audio tape recorder. To the best of our knowledge, there are no works in the literature that attempt to identify a specific location (e.g., a specific room) from a voice message recorded by a smartphone.

3   System and Adversary Model

In this section, we describe the system and the adversarial model of our attack. We further discuss the different types of realistic attack scenarios that we identified based on varying levels of information available to the attacker.

System Model. We assume that the victim has a smartphone device with WhatsApp installed and an internet connection. We further assume that the software on the victim device and the device itself is *not compromised* in any manner. While recording the audio messages, we assume that the phone is held at a distance of approximately 15 cm [4,14] from the face of the speaker at an upright position (see Fig. 2). This is one of the most common positions where a phone is held either during video calls or while sending audio messages. Moreover, we conducted an additional preliminary study by placing the phone close to the ear. Results showed that the location inference accuracy was nearly the same across both considered positions.

Adversarial Model. We assume that the attacker has access to the WhatsApp audio message of the victim. The attacker is a user who seeks to learn the location information of the victim. Depending on the attack scenario, the attacker may also have the target's recordings from the same or different positions at

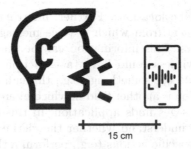

15 cm

Fig. 2. Recording position

specific locations. Also, the victim is assumed to be in one of these selected locations when recording the audio message. For our experiment, we consider three different scenarios for the attacker:

- *Complete Profiling*: This scenario occurs when the attacker asks the victim to send voice messages from specific locations. For example, an investigator (i.e., the attacker) might ask a suspect (i.e., the victim) to stand in a specific part of a room to verify that the suspect was there or elsewhere at the time a voice message was sent. In this scenario, the attacker has recordings of the victim in all the selected locations. Moreover, the attacker also knows the victim's specific position in the selected locations (e.g., a room corner). In this scenario, the attacker has the highest knowledge to execute his attack.
- *Location Profiling*: In this scenario, the attacker cannot access any of the victim's voice messages other than the one he wants to infer the location. The attacker knows that the victim has sent the voice message from a selected location (e.g., the attacker knows that the victim is in a specific building). Therefore, the attacker can have WhatsApp audio recordings of different speakers but the victim. The speakers are assumed to have recorded their messages at the same locations where the victim is sending the voice message. Hence, the victim is "unknown" while the location position is "known" to the attacker.
- *User Profiling*: This scenario occurs when the attacker owns the victim's voice messages and knows the recording location but does not know the specific position in the location (e.g., a corner of a room) from which they were recorded. The attacker wants to infer the location of a new voice message sent by the victim. Different from the *Complete Profiling* scenario, the attacker cannot ask the victim to send more voice messages from specific positions of the selected locations (e.g., the victim is no longer reachable). The victim is "known" while the position is "unknown" to the attacker in this situation.

Based on the described scenarios, we can identify two main application fields: i) forensics and ii) malicious inference of user information. The *forensic field* is probably the one that would find the most significant benefits both for the wide range of applications (e.g., investigations, evidence in court) and for the high chance of being in the scenario with the highest knowledge (i.e., Complete Profiling). Commonly in forensics, there are no limitations in obtaining additional voice messages from specific locations. Further, inferring the specific position in a location (e.g., a corner) from which a voice message was sent is of particular interest in forensics. This information can be crucial in understanding whether the suspect or witness could have taken action (e.g., interacted with something nearby) or could see something (e.g., through a window). Malicious inference of user information is another field in which inference of a victim's location from their voice messages finds application. In this case, an attacker can exploit this knowledge to understand whether the victim is in a location (e.g., home or office) and take specific actions (e.g., perform a theft) based on this. A practical application would be an employer who wants to monitor whether an employee is smart working from home or another location. This behavior would be highly invasive of workers' privacy and illegal (since it would occur without the employee's consent) while difficult to detect. Moreover, the malicious inference of user location could allow additional information such as habits, interests, activities, and relationships to be obtained, posing severe privacy concerns.

4 $\mathcal{F}orYourVoiceOnly$ Attack

Our attack consists of four phases: Data Acquisition, Data Processing, Model Training, and Location Inference. In Fig. 3 we provide an overview of how the attacker conducts the attack. Each of the four phases is discussed in detail in the following sections.

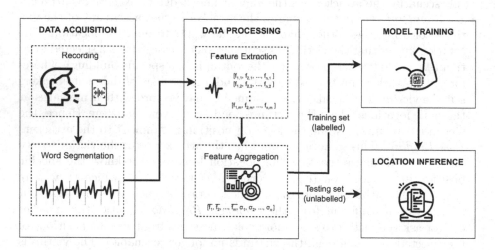

Fig. 3. $\mathcal{F}orYourVoiceOnly$ attack phases

Data Acquisition. This phase consists of two steps: Recording and Word Segmentation. At the end of the data acquisition phase, the attacker will own two datasets composed of segmented voice messages.

- *Recording*: In this step, the attacker performs two types of data acquisition. The first involves acquiring WhatsApp voice messages recorded by different people (including the victim if allowed by the attack scenario) at some locations or specific positions of interest to build a labeled dataset. The second, for acquiring unlabeled (i.e., both the location or the position are unknown) WhatsApp audio messages of the victim (i.e., test dataset). These two steps do not necessarily have to be consecutive. The attacker can create the labeled dataset even after obtaining the test dataset. The attacker can then choose the locations of interest based on the available information type (e.g., the victim might say she is in one location, but the attacker suspects she is in another known specific location).
- *Word Segmentation*: The attacker segments the recorded voice messages to extract audio fragments related to specific words frequently used in speech [12, 13] (e.g., "*and*", "*of*" and "*the*"). This procedure can be done either manually or by using speech-to-text algorithms[4].

Data Processing. The data processing phase is carried out on both the labeled and the test datasets. This phase consists of two stages: *Feature Extraction* and *Feature Aggregation*.

- *Feature Extraction*: The attacker extracts features that are descriptive of vocal and environmental characteristics: spectral centroid, spectral roll-off, spectral flatness, zero-crossing rate, and Mel-frequency cepstral coefficients [15]. At the end of this step, the attacker has a set of time-frequency features whose dimensionality depends on the duration of the segmented voice message.
- *Feature Aggregation*: Since segmented voice messages may have a variable duration, the attacker needs to process the feature extracted in the previous step to create a feature vector of standardized length. The attacker aggregates the extracted features by calculating the average and the standard deviation as suggested in [7,30]. This procedure allows maintaining information about the magnitude and variability of the data, reducing the total number of features per voice message. At the end of this step, each segmented voice message has a set of 48 associated features.

Model Training. In this phase, the attacker uses only the labeled dataset to train the classification models. The attacker may also decide to train the models using a sub-sample of the dataset based on the owned information. For example, the labeled dataset may contain records from many locations in the acquisition phase, but the attacker has obtained new information about the victim and may discard some of them.

Location Inference. In this phase, the attacker applies the model trained in the *Model Training* phase and predicts the location or the specific location where the victim recorded the message.

---

[4] https://www.mathworks.com/help/audio/ug/audio-labeler-walkthrough.html.

5   Experimental Setting

In this section, we provide details about the procedure followed during data collection and the characteristics of the obtained dataset. We further provide a comprehensive overview of the machine learning models we used to demonstrate the efficacy of our proposed attack.

5.1   Data Collection

We performed our data collection at four different real locations. The layouts of these locations are depicted in Fig. 4. In particular, we considered three indoor locations I1 (Fig. 4a), I2 (Fig. 4b), and I3 (Fig. 4c), and one outdoor location O1 (Fig. 4d). Since our goal is to recognize the specific location (or the specific position) from which a voice message is sent for indoor locations, we decided to consider the worst-case where the rooms have a similar layout and furnishings (i.e., bedrooms). Within each of the indoor locations, we further identify five different recording positions: south-east corner (P1), south-west corner (P2), north-west corner (P3), north-east corner (P4), and center (P5). While for O1, we identified a central recording position only (P5).

The data collection process involved 15 participants (5 males and 10 females aged 20 to 59 years). In the institution where the experiments were carried out, an IRB approval was not mandatory for this context. All voluntary participants were informed of the actual use of their data and their informed consent was obtained before the recording process. We ensured that the participants held their phones at a distance of about 15 cm from their face at chin level, as shown in Fig. 2. While recording, only the participant was present, and the room doors and windows were closed. To create a more realistic dataset, we asked the participants to use their own smartphone devices[5]. During the collection phase, the participants recorded 30 different voice messages using WhatsApp in all the locations and at each position (see Fig. 2). This results in a total of 150 recordings per indoor location and 30 recordings for the outdoor location. We collected a total of 7200 WhatsApp voice messages, corresponding to 480 recordings per participant.

All the recorded WhatsApp voice messages have a one-second duration (i.e., the minimum duration of a WhatsApp voice message) and contain a single word (i.e., *and*, *of*, or *the*). Specifically, for each position the participants recorded 30 voice messages: 10 pronouncing the word *and*, 10 pronouncing the word *of*, and 10 pronouncing the word *the*. We selected these words based on the OEC, and COCA ranks for most commonly used words during an English conversation [12, 13]. We divided the 30 recordings at a single position into three sequences of 9–12-9. The participant starts the data collection from position P1, recording 9

---

[5] Devices in the data collection: Apple iPhone 7, Apple iPhone X, Apple iPhone 11 pro, Motorola Moto E6, Motorola Moto G3, OnePlus 3, OnePlus 5T, OnePlus 6, OnePlus 6T, OnePLus 6T, OnePlus 8T, OnePlus NORD, Samsung Galaxy A9, Samsung Galaxy A30, and Samsung Galaxy Z Fold 2.

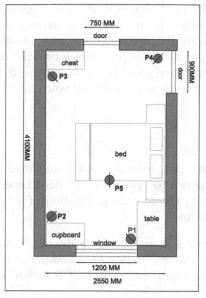

(a) *Indoor location I1 - bedroom.*

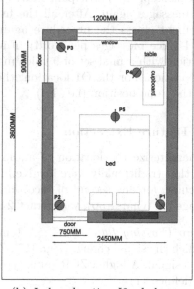

(b) *Indoor location I2 - bedroom*

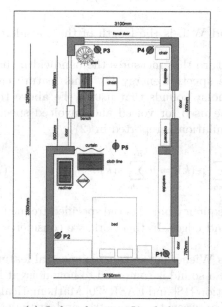

(c) *Indoor location I3 - bedroom*

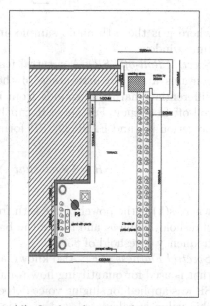

(d) *Outdoor location O1 - Terrace*

Fig. 4. Location layout and recording positions with orientation considered in the data collection

voice messages at this position (i.e., 3 voice messages per word). Once concluded with this step, the participant moves to P2 in the same location and records 9 voice messages again. After all the five positions are covered in sequence, the participant starts the procedure again from P1, recording 12 voice messages (i.e., 4 voice messages per word). Finally, the participant concludes the data collection with a final set of 9 voice messages per position before moving to the next location. For the O1 location, the participant recorded 30 voice messages from the same position (i.e., P5).

5.2 Feature Extraction

To characterize the location of audio messages, we extracted frame-level features that traditionally were involved in speech recognition and EASR tasks. In particular, for one second of recording (i.e., the minimum duration of a voice message on WhatsApp), we extract 24 features:

- *Zero Crossing Rate (ZCR)*: A temporal feature that indicates the rate at which the signal changes sign [17]. ZCR can also indicate the amount of noise in a signal. A higher ZCR value typically means more noise. ZCR formulation is defined (1)

$$ZCR = \frac{1}{2W_L} \sum_{n=1}^{W_L} |sgn[x_i(n)] - sgn[x_i(n-1)]| \,.$$ (1)

where n is the n-th audio sample and W_L is the length of the considered time window.
- *Spectral Roll-off (SR)*: A spectral feature that measures the bandwidth that contains a certain percentage of the spectral energy [3]. This feature can differentiate harmonic sounds from noisy sounds that usually lie above the roll-off frequency. Further, SR can be used for voiced and unvoiced speech detection [3], and EASR [9]. SR formulation is reported in (2)

$$SR = i \text{ such that } \sum_{k=b_1}^{i} |s(k)| = \theta \sum_{k=b_1}^{b_2} s(k) \,.$$ (2)

where s(k) is the power of the k-th frequency bin, θ is the specified frequency threshold, while b_1 and b_2 are the band edges. In this work, we considered a frequency threshold of 85%.
- *Spectral Flatness (SF)*: Also known as Wiener entropy, it is a spectral feature that is used for quantifying how tonal a sound is compared to how noisy it is. SF was applied for singing voice detection [18] and EASR [20] Mathematically this value is calculated as the ratio between the geometric and arithmetic means of a power spectrum. Formally SR can be derived as reported in (3)

$$SF = \frac{(\prod_{k=b_1}^{b_2} s(k))^{\frac{1}{b_2-b_1}}}{\frac{1}{b_2-b_1} \sum_{k=b_1}^{b_2} s(k)} \,.$$ (3)

where s(k) is the power of the k-th frequency bin, while while b_1 and b_2 are the band edges.

- *Spectral Centroid (SC)*: Geometrically the centroid represents the arithmetic mean of the positions of the points composing a figure. The spectral centroid is a spectral feature that performs a similar function with respect to a spectrogram. SC is commonly used in music genre classification [1] and it is an indicator of brightness (i.e., upper mid and high frequency content) Mathematically, this value is the weighted mean of the constituent frequencies of a signal, as reported in (4)

$$SC = \frac{\sum_{k=b_1}^{b_2} f(k)s(k)}{\sum_{n=b_1}^{b_2} s(k)} .$$

(4)

where f(k) is the frequency of the k-th bin, s(k) is the power of the k-th bin, while b_1 and b_2 are the band edges.

- *Mel-Frequency Cepstral Coefficients (MFCCs)*: MFCCs take into account the non-linear behavior of the human auditory system with respect to different frequencies. This is done by converting the spectrum to the mel-scale using a mel filter bank. MFCCs describe the shape of the spectral envelope giving details regarding the timber. MFCCs have been used in the literature for several purposes, such as voice recognition [11] and audio event detection [19]. Furthermore, Gergen *et al.* suggested that MFCCs could be a good descriptor for discerning between anechoic and reverberant signals. In our work, we extracted 20 Mel-frequency cepstral coefficients.

5.3 Machine Learning Models

To identify the location and the specific position in a location of a voice message, we tested four multi-class classifiers: Linear Discriminant Analysis (LDA), Logistic Regression (LR), Ridge Classifier (RC), and Support Vector Machine (SVM). Based on the attack scenario, we applied different strategies to split the data into training, validation, and testing sets:

- **Complete Profiling**: To evaluate the performance of our approach, we apply (for each participant) a nested-cross fold validation. In the outer loop, we use a stratified 5-fold cross-validation on the 480 voice messages recorded by the participant, resulting in 384 recordings in training and 96 in testing per fold. We apply a stratified 3-fold cross-validation in the inner loop on the 384 training recordings, obtaining 256 recordings in training and 128 recordings in validation per fold.
- **Location Profiling**: For this experiment, we consider the entire dataset comprising of 7200 audio recordings, and we apply a nested cross-fold validation. For the outer loop, we apply a user-independent leave-one-out cross-validation, obtaining a testing set containing the recordings of a single participant (i.e., 480). Similarly, in the inner loop, we apply a user-independent

leave-one-out cross-validation on the other 14 participants, obtaining a training set of 13 participants (i.e., 6240 recordings) and a validation set of one participant (i.e., 480 recordings) for each iteration.

– **User Profiling**: In this scenario, we consider the dataset of each participant individually, as for the *Complete Profiling scenario*. Also here, we apply a nested-cross fold validation. Still, different to the *Complete Profiling scenario*, we use a group-k-fold to split the dataset into subsets based on the recording location. We use a group 5-fold cross-validation in the outer loop and a group 4-fold cross-validation for the inner loop. In this way, we split data recorded within the same room into subsets corresponding to each of the 5 recording positions (i.e., P1, P2, P3, P4, and P5). Using this configuration, both the validation and the test sets consist of one subset each, while the training set contains the remaining positions. The recordings from location O1 are excluded from this scenario since they all come from the same position (i.e., P5).

We explored different hyper-parameters by using grid search on all the considered classifiers. In particular, for LDA we vary the solver over [*svd, lsqr, eigen*]. For LR we vary the solver in [*newton-cg, lbfgs, liblinear*] and the C value in the range $[10^{-3}, 10^{-2}, \ldots, 10^1]$. For RC we vary α from 0.1 to 0.9 with a step size of 0.1, and from 1 to 10 with a step size of 1. Finally, for SVM we tune the values parameter C in the range $[10^{-1}, 10^0, \ldots, 10^3]$, and γ in the range $[10^{-4}, 10^{-3}, \ldots, 10^0]$.

6 Experimental Results

In this section, we report and discuss the results achieved by our approach in the three attack scenarios based on the attack goal: location in Sect. 6.1 or position in Sect. 6.2. Finally, in Sect. 6.3 we prove the applicability of $\mathcal{F}or YourVoiceOnly$ to complex voice messages.

6.1   Location Inference

In Table 1 we show the performance of the classifiers in identifying the location according to the attack scenario, considering the worst case for each scenario (i.e., 4 locations for the *Complete Profiling* and *Location Profiling* scenarios, and 3 locations for the *User Profiling* scenario).

Table 1. Average accuracy of $\mathcal{F}or YourVoiceOnly$ attack for location inference in different attack scenarios

Scenario	LDA	LR	RC	SVM
Complete	0.85 (0.06)	0.85 (0.06)	0.83 (0.06)	0.87 (0.05)
Location	0.41 (0.11)	0.39 (0.10)	0.43 (0.09)	0.35 (0.00)
User	0.80 (0.09)	0.33 (0.04)	0.32 (0.03)	0.33 (0.03)

The scenario where the classifiers perform best is the *Complete Profiling* scenario, where the attacker has the full information available. The results show that in this scenario, all classifiers have accuracy higher than 83%. In particular, the SVM manages to reach an accuracy of 87%. On the contrary, in the *Location Profiling* scenario, there is a consistent drop in performance. In this case, the best classifier is the RC, which reaches an accuracy of 43% (i.e., 18% above the chance level). Lower performance can be attributed to multiple factors:

- Device: the participants used different phones during data collection. The absence of the model in the training set may reduce the accuracy of new test data.
- Training Size: The number of users in training is not enough to ensure sufficient variability in the training features.
- Voice Uniqueness: The distinctiveness of the victim's vocal characteristics cannot be completely replaced, and their lack of training is reflected in performance in testing.

The importance of the victim's voice for the attacker is supported by the results obtained for the *User Profiling* scenario, where the attacker has voice messages from the victim but does not know the specific recording location. In this case, LDA achieves an accuracy of 80% (i.e., only 7% less than in the Complete Profiling scenario), outperforming the others classifiers. In Fig. 5 we show the confusion matrices of the best model per scenario in the location classification. It is interesting to note that the locations I1 and I2 are confused with each other in all three attack scenarios. This is due to the similar layout of the two locations (see Fig. 4). The background noise is instead discriminant for the identification of the external location (i.e., O1). O1 is generally classified better, reaching an accuracy up to 98% in the *Complete Profiling* scenario.

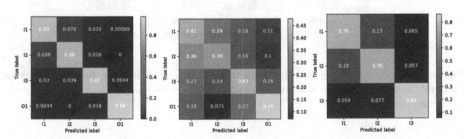

(a) *Complete Profiling sce-* (b) *Location Profiling sce-* (c) *User Profiling scenario*
nario.   *nario*

Fig. 5. *ForYourVoiceOnly* confusion matrices for the best models

Further, we analyzed the influence of the number of locations of interest (i.e., the number of classes to be predicted) on the accuracy of the classification. In the *Complete Profiling* scenario, we obtain an average accuracy of 99% when we classify an audio message between the outdoor location O1 and one of the indoor locations (i.e., I1, I2, and I3). While when we classify messages between two indoor rooms, we achieve an accuracy ranging from 89% to 95% on this task. Also, in *Location Profiling* scenario, we obtain a higher accuracy if we reduce the location of interest considering O1 and an indoor location. In this case, $\mathcal{F}orYourVoiceOnly$ correctly predicts the location with an average accuracy of 80%. While for the prediction of internal location pairs, the accuracy remains rather low, ranging from 57% between I1 and I2 to 66% between I1 and I3. Finally, considering the *User Profiling* scenario, reducing the locations of interest to two leads to an average accuracy of 87% in predicting the correct recording location.

Finally, we evaluated $\mathcal{F}orYourVoiceOnly$ by training the models on a single word, splitting the dataset into three subsets of 2400 audio recordings, each containing the words *"and"*, *"of"* and *"the"*. Figure 6 depicts the variation of the accuracy of our attack in the *Complete Profiling* scenario between all the locations I1, I2, I3, and O1 using different classifiers and different words. Results show no significant differences between models trained on the specific word and those trained on all words (i.e., combined).

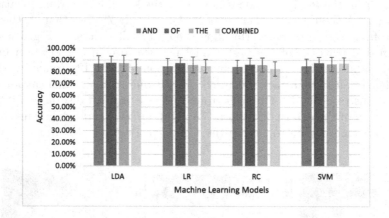

Fig. 6. Performance of machine learning models in classifying the four locations in *Complete Profiling* scenario when trained specifically with one word and all the words (i.e., combined)

6.2 Position Inference

In Table 2 we show the performance of the classifiers in identifying the specific position according to the attack scenario, considering the worst case (i.e., 16 positions - five for each indoor location and one for the outdoor location). Unlike *Location Inference*, here we consider only two attack scenarios (i.e., *Complete Profiling* and *Location Profiling*), since the *User Profiling* scenario assumes that the attacker has no information about the specific position in training. As in Location Inference, even for the position inference, the scenario where the classifiers perform best is the *Complete Profiling*, and SVM resulted in the best classifier scenario with an accuracy of 61%. Contrarily, in *Location Profiling* scenario models performance is slightly above chance (i.e., 0.0625). The increase in the number of classes to be predicted and the factors already highlighted in Sect. 6.1 (i.e., device, training size, and voice uniqueness) further amplify the performance drop.

Table 2. Average accuracy of *ForYourVoiceOnly* attack for position inference in different attack scenarios

Scenario	LDA	LR	RC	SVM
Complete	0.57 (0.09)	0.55 (0.09)	0.49 (0.08)	0.61 (0.09)
Location	0.13 (0.04)	0.13 (0.04)	0.13 (0.04)	0.07 (0.00)

In Fig. 7 we show the confusion matrix of the best model in the *Complete Profiling* scenario (i.e., SVM). As expected, the model manages to accurately predict O1 (i.e., 98%), demonstrating that this is a trivial task for our attack in this scenario. Regarding the internal locations, Fig. 7 shows a concentration of classification errors in the positions belonging to the true location. In particular, the classification of I3 positions shows less accuracy than I1 and I2. We believe that this can be traced back to the layout of the room. I3 has more than twice the

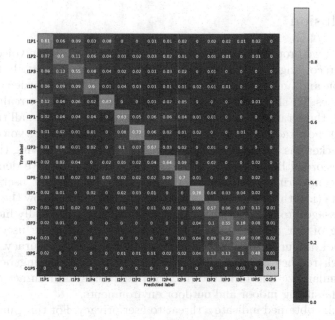

Fig. 7. Confusion matrix for specific position inference for I1, I2, I3 and O1 locations in *Complete Profiling* scenario

surface area of I1 and I2, and the spaces between the recording points and the walls or furniture are much wider. This could lead to a reduction in reverberation and therefore make the recordings more similar. In addition, the best performing position in I3 is P1, which is the recording position with the least open field compared to the other four positions. I1 and I2 generally present better results, but again we can see how room size affects the prediction of the specific location. I2 measures about 2 square meters less than I1 and has a 7% higher average accuracy.

6.3   Extracted Words from Voice Messages

In our experiment, we carried out a data collection on WhatsApp audio messages recording single words pronounced by the participants. However, in a real scenario, voice messages can be of any length. To assess that our approach applied to a real-world context, we carried out a preliminary evaluation on 345 audio samples of words extracted from complex voice messages in the *Complete Profiling* scenario. Also, we reduced the number of rooms in our pool size to 3 (i.e., two indoor bedrooms and one outdoor location-terrace). We noted that $\mathcal{F}orYourVoiceOnly$ reached an average accuracy of 99% in predicting between the outdoor location and any one of the indoor locations. Further, when trying to classify between all the three locations, our attack resulted in an accuracy of 94%. These results demonstrate that $\mathcal{F}orYourVoiceOnly$ can be applied in real-world contexts by extracting single words from a complex voice message.

7   Conclusion

In this paper, we proposed $\mathcal{F}orYourVoiceOnly$, a new attack on voice messages to infer the recording location. $\mathcal{F}orYourVoiceOnly$ leverages attributes such as reverberation and ambient noises, which inadvertently get recorded along with audio messages. We showed the effectiveness of our attack in three realistic attack scenarios: (i) the attacker has previous recordings of the victim in all the selected locations (ii) the attacker has no previous recording of the victim's voice messages (iii) the attacker has previous voice messages of the victim knowing the location they were recorded but does not know the specific position. We demonstrated our attack considering 7,200 voice messages from 15 different users and four environments (i.e., three bedrooms and a terrace). We showed how the possession of audio messages from the victim in known locations dramatically increases the performance of our attack. $\mathcal{F}orYourVoiceOnly$ can infer the user's location among a pool of four known environments with up to 85% accuracy. Moreover, our approach reaches an average accuracy of 93% in discerning between two rooms of similar size and furniture (i.e., two bedrooms) and an accuracy of up to 99% in classifying indoor and outdoor environments.

The results obtained indicate a threat to user privacy. For this purpose, some countermeasures that can be adopted are:

- Adding noise to obscure the leaked information in the audio messages. The noise may also be applied selectively to higher and lower frequencies outside the hearing range so as to not impact the quality of the voice message. This method may prove to act as a countermeasure as we noted variations in the audio signals in the ultrasonic and infrasonic ranges at different locations and positions.
- Shielding the microphone during recording to minimize the environmental noise and to reduce the recorded reverberation.
- Filtering the recorded audio to select only the primary sound source and reducing the information leakage.
- Poisoning the dataset during the training phase (e.g., mislabeling the locations).
- Change the furniture/arrangement of the room.

We believe that the proposed work can be a starting point for developing environment recognition from voice messages that can overcome the limitations of $ForYourVoiceOnly$. First, the collection of new datasets would allow for more consolidated results and the application of more powerful feature extraction and prediction techniques (e.g., deep learning). The collection of new datasets would also be beneficial for assessing the effect of noisier environments. We made several restrictions during recording, such as having no other member in the rooms during recording, the recordings were done in a relatively quiet and less crowded location. Hence, we expect the behavior to be affected when the noise increases. This can be detrimental or instrumental depending on whether valuable information is obscured or the noise indicates that particular location. Further, it would be helpful to have a more diverse dataset regarding languages, gender, age, nationality, Finally, a new data collection that includes multiple phone holding positions would overcome a limitation of the proposed work.

References

1. Grey, J.M., Gordon, J.W.: Perceptual effects of spectral modifications on musical timbres. J. Acoust. Soc. Am. **63** (5), 1493–1500 (1978)
2. Liu, H., Setiono, R.: Chi2: feature selection and discretization of numeric attributes. In Proceedings of 7th IEEE International Conference on Tools with Artificial Intelligence, pp. 388–391. IEEE (1995)
3. Scheirer, E., Slaney, M.: Construction and evaluation of a robust multifeature speech/music discriminator. In 1997 IEEE international conference on acoustics, speech, and signal processing, vol. 2, pp. 1331–1334. IEEE (1997)
4. Kostov, V., Fukuda, S.: Emotion in user interface, voice interaction system. In SMC 2000 conference proceedings. 2000 IEEE International Conference on Systems, Man and Cybernetics. Cybernetics evolving to systems, humans, organizations, and their complex interactions, vol. 2, pp. 798–803. IEEE (2000)
5. Peltonen, V., Tuomi, J., Klapuri, A., Huopaniemi, J., Sorsa, T.: Computational auditory scene recognition. In 2002 IEEE International Conference on Acoustics, Speech, and Signal Processing, vol. 2, pp. II-1941. IEEE (2002)

6. Cowling, M., Sitte, R.: Comparison of techniques for environmental sound recognition. Pattern Recogn. Lett. **24**(15), 2895–2907 (2003)
7. Guo, G., Li, S.Z.: Content-based audio classification and retrieval by support vector machines. IEEE Trans. Neural Networks **14**(1), 209–215 (2003)
8. Kim, H.-G., Moreau, N., Sikora, T.: Audio classification based on MPEG-7 spectral basis representations. IEEE Trans. Circuits Syst. Video Technol. **14**(5), 716–725 (2004)
9. Eronen, A.J., et al.: Audio-based context recognition. IEEE Trans. Audio Speech Lang. Process. **14**(1), 321–329 (2005)
10. Chen, L., Gunduz, S., Ozsu, M.T.: Mixed type audio classification with support vector machine. In 2006 IEEE International Conference on Multimedia and Expo, pp. 781–784. IEEE (2006)
11. Bala, A., Kumar, A., Birla, N.: Voice command recognition system based on MFCC and DTW. Int. J. Eng. Sci. Technol. **2**(12), 7335–7342 (2010)
12. Davies, M.: The corpus of contemporary American English as the first reliable monitor corpus of English. Liter. Linguis. Comput. **25**(4), 447–464 (2010)
13. Stevenson, A.: Oxford dictionary of English. Oxford University Press, USA (2010)
14. Hallin, A.E., Fröst, K., Holmberg, E.B., Södersten, M.: Voice and speech range profiles and voice handicap index for males-methodological issues and data. Logoped. Phoniatr. Vocol. **37**(2), 47–61, 2012
15. Okuyucu, Ç., Sert, M., Yazici, A.: Audio feature and classifier analysis for efficient recognition of environmental sounds. In 2013 IEEE International Symposium on Multimedia, pp. 125–132. IEEE (2013)
16. Delgado-Contreras, J.R., Garćıa-Vázquez, J.P., Brena, R.F., Galván-Tejada, C.E., Galván-Tejada, J.I.: Feature selection for place classification through environmental sounds. Procedia Comput. Sci. **37**, 40–47 (2014)
17. Giannakopoulos, T., Pikrakis, A.: Introduction to audio analysis: a MATLAB® approach. Academic Press (2014)
18. Lehner, B., Widmer, G., Sonnleitner, R.: On the reduction of false positives in singing voice detection. In 2014 IEEE International Conference on Acoustics, Speech and Signal Processing (ICASSP), pp. 7480–7484. IEEE (2014)
19. Ezgi Küçükbay, S., Sert, M.: Audio-based event detection in office live environments using optimized MFCC-SVM approach. In Proceedings of the 2015 IEEE 9th International Conference on Semantic Computing (IEEE ICSC 2015), pp. 475–480. IEEE (2015)
20. Petetin, Y., Laroche, C., Mayoue, A.: Deep neural networks for audio scene recognition. In 2015 23rd European Signal Processing Conference (EUSIPCO), pp. 125–129. IEEE (2015)
21. Walnycky, D., Baggili, I., Marrington, A., Moore, J., Breitinger, F.: Network and device forensic analysis of android social-messaging applications. Digit. Investig. **14**, S77–S84 (2015)
22. Gomes, E.F., Batista, F., Jorge, A.M.: Using smartphones to classify urban sounds. In Proceedings of the Ninth International C* Conference on Computer Science & Software Engineering, pp. 67–72 (2016)
23. Phan, H., Hertel, L., Maass, M., Mazur, R., Mertins, A.: Learning representations for nonspeech audio events through their similarities to speech patterns. IEEE/ACM Trans. Audio Speech Lang. Process. **24**(4), 807–822 (2016)
24. Eghbal-zadeh, H., Lehner, B., Dorfer, M., Widmer, G.: A hybrid approach with multi-channel i-vectors and convolutional neural networks for acoustic scene classification. In 2017 25th European Signal Processing Conference (EUSIPCO), pp. 2749–2753. IEEE (2017)

25. Khonglah, B.K., Deepak, K.T., Prasanna, S.R.M.: Indoor/outdoor audio classification using foreground speech segmentation. In: INTERSPEECH, pp. 464–468 (2017)
26. Almaadeed, N., Asim, M., Al-Maadeed, S., Bouridane, A., Beghdadi, A.: Automatic detection and classification of audio events for road surveillance applications. Sensors 18(6), 2018 (1858)
27. Oramas, S., Barbieri, F., Caballero, O.N., Serra, X.: Multimodal deep learning for music genre classification. Trans. Int. Soc. Music Inf. Retr. 1, 4–21 (2018)
28. Xiong, W., Wu, L., Alleva, F., Droppo, J., Huang, X., Stolcke, A.: The microsoft 2017 conversational speech recognition system. In: 2018 IEEE International Conference on Acoustics, Speech and Signal processing (ICASSP), pp. 5934–5938. IEEE (2018)
29. Chandrakala, S., Jayalakshmi, S.L.: Environmental audio scene and sound event recognition for autonomous surveillance: A survey and comparative studies. ACM Comput. Surv. (CSUR) 52(3), 1–34 (2019)
30. Nolasco, I., Terenzi, A., Cecchi, S., Orcioni, S., Bear, H.L., Benetos, E.: Audio-based identification of beehive states. In: ICASSP 2019–2019 IEEE International Conference on Acoustics, Speech and Signal Processing (ICASSP), pp. 8256–8260. IEEE (2019)
31. Ozkan, Y., Barkana, B.D.: Forensic audio analysis and event recognition for smart surveillance systems. In: 2019 IEEE International Symposium on Technologies for Homeland Security (HST), pp. 1–6. IEEE (2019)
32. Simonetta, F., Ntalampiras, S., Avanzini, F.: Multimodal music information processing and retrieval: survey and future challenges. In: 2019 International Workshop on Multilayer Music Representation and Processing (MMRP), pp. 10–18. IEEE (2019)
33. Faezipour, M., Abuzneid, A.: Smartphone-based self-testing of COVID-19 using breathing sounds. Telemed. e-Health 26(10), 1202–1205 (2020)
34. Issa, D., Demirci, M.F., Yazici, A.: Speech emotion recognition with deep convolutional neural networks. Biomed. Sig. Process. Control 59, 101894 (2020)
35. Mushtaq, Z., Shun-Feng, S.: Environmental sound classification using a regularized deep convolutional neural network with data augmentation. Appl. Acoust. 167, 107389 (2020)
36. Ramírez, J., Flores, M.J.: Machine learning for music genre: multifaceted review and experimentation with audioset. J. Intell. Inf. Syst. 55(3), 469–499 (2019). https://doi.org/10.1007/s10844-019-00582-9
37. Malik, M., Malik, M.K., Mehmood, K., Makhdoom, I.: Automatic speech recognition: a survey. Multimedia Tools Appl. 80(6), 9411–9457 (2020). https://doi.org/10.1007/s11042-020-10073-7

Towards Efficient Auditing for Real-Time Systems

Ayoosh Bansal[1]([✉]) [iD], Anant Kandikuppa[1], Chien-Ying Chen[1],
Monowar Hasan[2] [iD], Adam Bates[1], and Sibin Mohan[3] [iD]

[1] University of Illinois Urbana-Champaign, Urbana-Champaign, IL 61801, USA
{ayooshb2,anantk3,cchen140,batesa}@illinois.edu
[2] Wichita State University, Wichita, KS 67260, USA
monowar.hasan@wichita.edu
[3] The George Washington University, Washington, DC 20052, USA
sibin.mohan@gwu.edu

Abstract. System auditing is a powerful tool that provides insight into
the nature of suspicious events in computing systems, allowing machine
operators to detect and subsequently investigate security incidents. While
auditing has proven invaluable to the security of traditional computers, existing audit frameworks are rarely designed with consideration for
Real-Time Systems (RTS). The transparency provided by system auditing would be of tremendous benefit in a variety of security-critical RTS
domains, (*e.g.,* autonomous vehicles); however, if audit mechanisms are
not carefully integrated into RTS, auditing can be rendered ineffectual
and violate the real-world temporal requirements of the RTS.

In this paper, we demonstrate how to adapt commodity audit frameworks to RTS. Using Linux Audit as a case study, we first demonstrate
that the volume of audit events generated by commodity frameworks is
unsustainable within the temporal and resource constraints of real-time
(RT) applications. To address this, we present *Ellipsis*, a set of kernel-
based reduction techniques that leverage the periodic repetitive nature
of RT applications to aggressively reduce the costs of system-level auditing. *Ellipsis* generates succinct descriptions of RT applications' expected
activity while retaining a detailed record of unexpected activities, enabling
analysis of suspicious activity while meeting temporal constraints. Our
evaluation of *Ellipsis*, using ArduPilot (an open-source autopilot application suite) demonstrates *up to 93% reduction* in audit log generation.

Keywords: Real-time systems · Auditing · Cyber-physical systems

1 Introduction

As RTS become indispensable in safety- and security-critical domains—medical
devices, autonomous vehicles, manufacturing automation, smart cities, etc.
[29,41,53,58]—the need for effective and precise *auditing* support is growing.
Even now, event data recorders (or *black boxes*) are crucial for determining
fault and liability when investigating vehicle collisions [16,17], and the need

© The Author(s), under exclusive license to Springer Nature Switzerland AG 2022
V. Atluri et al. (Eds.): ESORICS 2022, LNCS 13556, pp. 614–634, 2022.
https://doi.org/10.1007/978-3-031-17143-7_30

for diagnostic event logging frameworks (*e.g.,* QNX [4], VxWorks [5] and Composite OS [62]) is well understood. However, these high-level event loggers are insufficient to detect and investigate sophisticated attacks. Concomitant with its explosive growth, today's RTS have become ripe targets for sophisticated attackers [27]. Exploits in RTS can enable vehicle hijacks [25,36], manufacturing disruptions [60], IoT botnets [31], subversion of life-saving medical devices [67] and many other devastating attacks. The COVID-19 pandemic has further shed light on the potential damage of attacks on medical infrastructure [14,61]. These threats are not theoretical, rather active and ongoing, as evidenced recently by malicious attempts to take control of nuclear power, water and electric systems throughout the United States and Europe [55].

In traditional computing systems, *system auditing* has proven crucial to detecting, investigating and responding to intrusions [20,33,34,52]. Unfortunately, comprehensive system auditing approaches are not widely used in RTS. RTS logging takes place largely at the *application layer* [16,17] or performs lightweight system layer tracing for performance profiling (*e.g.,* log syscall occurrences, but not arguments) [18]; in both cases, the information recorded is insufficient to trace attacks because the causal links between different system entities cannot be identified. The likely cause of this hesitance to embrace holistic system-layer logging is poor performance. System audit frameworks are known to impose tremendous computational and storage overheads [51] that are incompatible with the temporal requirements of many real-time applications. Thus, while we are encouraged by the growing recognition of the importance of embedded system auditing [8,26,38] and the newfound availability of Linux Audit in the Embedded Linux [3], a practical approach to RTS auditing remains an elusive goal.

Observing that performance cost of Linux Audit is ultimately dependent on the number of log events generated, and that the performance impacts of commodity auditing frameworks can be optimized without affecting the forensic validity of the audit logs, *e.g.,* through carefully reducing the number of events that need to be logged [11,13,15,32,43,47,51,65,74], we set out to tailor Linux Audit to RTS, carefully reducing event logging without impacting the forensic validity of the log. We present **Ellipsis**, a kernel-based log reduction framework that leverages the predictability of real-time tasksets' execution profiles. *Ellipsis* first profiles tasks to produce a template of their audit footprint. At runtime, behaviors consistent with this template are reduced, while any deviations from the template are audited in full, without reduction. Far from being impractical, we demonstrate a synergistic relationship between security auditing and predictable RTS workloads – *Ellipsis* is able to faithfully audit suspicious activities while incurring almost no log generation during benign typical activity.

The **contributions** of this work are:

- *Ellipsis*[1], an audit framework, uniquely-tailored to RT environments (Sect. 3).
- Detailed[2] evaluations (Sect. 4) and security analysis (Sect. 5) to demonstrate that *Ellipsis* retains relevant information while reducing event/log volume.

---

[1] https://bitbucket.org/sts-lab/ellipsis.
[2] A technical report with supplementary material for this work is available [10].

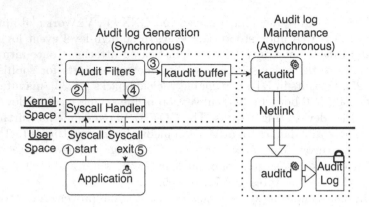

Fig. 1. Architecture of linux audit framework [1].

2 Background and System Model

Linux Audit Framework. The Linux Audit system [64] provides a way to audit system activities. An overview of the Linux Audit architecture is presented in Fig. 1. When an application invokes a syscall ①, the subsequent kernel control flow eventually traverses an `audit_filter` hook ②. Linux Audit examines the context of the event, compares it to pre-configured audit rules, generating a log event if there is a match and enqueueing it in a message buffer ③ before returning control to the syscall handler ④ and then to the application ⑤. Asynchronous from this workflow, a pair of (non-RT) audit daemons (`kauditd` and `auditd`) transmit the message buffer to user space for storage and analysis. Because the daemons are asynchronous, the message buffer can overflow if syscalls occur faster than the daemon flushes to user space, resulting in event loss.

Although it is well-established that Linux Audit can incur large computational and storage overheads in traditional software [51], its impacts on RT applications were unclear. Encouragingly, upon conducting a detailed (See footnote 2) analysis we observed that Linux Audit does not introduce significant issues of priority inversion or contention over auditing resources shared across applications (*e.g.*, `kaudit` buffer). Further, except for limited outlier cases, the latency introduced by auditing syscalls can be measured and bounded. Hence it is a good candidate for firm and soft deadline RTS as supported by RT Linux [66]. However, audit events were lost, making auditing incomplete and ineffectual while still costly for the RTS due to large storage space required to store the audit log.

RTS Properties. *Ellipsis* leverages properties unique to RT environments, as described in Table 1. In contrast to traditional applications where determining all possible execution paths is often undecidable, knowledge about execution paths is an essential component of RT application development. RTS are special purpose machines that execute well formed tasksets to fulfill predetermined tasks. Various techniques are employed to analyze the tasksets, *e.g.*, worst case execution time (WCET) analysis [19,30,35,45,57,59,76]. All expected behaviors

Table 1. RTS properties relevant to *Ellipsis*

Property	Relevance to *Ellipsis*
Periodic tasks	Most RT tasks are periodically activated, leading to repeating behaviors. *Ellipsis* templates describe the most common repetitions.
Aperiodic tasks	Second most common form of RT tasks, Aperiodic tasks also lead to repeating behaviors, but with irregular inter-arrival times.
Code coverage	High code coverage analyses are part of existing RTS development processes, *Ellipsis'* automated template generation adds minimal cost.
Timing predictability	A requirement for safety and correct functioning of RTS, naïvely enabling auditing can violate this by introducing overheads and variability.
Isolation	Resources are commonly isolated in RTS to improve timing predictability. RTS auditing mechanisms should not violate resource isolation.
Special purpose	RTS are special purpose machines, tasks are known at development *i.e.*, templates can be created before system deployment.
Longevity	Once deployed RTS can remain functional for years. *Ellipsis'* can save enormous log storage and transmission costs over the lifetime of the RTS

of the system must be accounted for at design time in conjunction with the system designers. Any deviation is an unforeseen fault or malicious activity, which needs to be audited in full detail.

Threat Model. We consider an adversary that aims to penetrate and impact an RTS through exfiltrating data, corrupting actuation outputs, degrading performance, causing deadline violations, etc. This attacker may install modified programs, exploit a running process or install malware on the RTS to achieve their objectives. To observe this attacker, our system adopts an aggressive audit configuration intended to capture all forensically-relevant events, as identified in prior works.[3] We assume that the underlying OS and the audit subsystem therein are trusted. This is a standard assumption in system auditing literature [12,33,46,48,56]. Far from being impractical on RTS, prior works such as Trusted Timely Computing Base provide a secure kernel that meets both the trust and temporal requirements for hosting *Ellipsis* in RT Linux [21,24,69,70]. *Ellipsis'* goal is to capture evidence of an attacker intrusion/activity without losing relevant information and hand it off to a tamper proof system. Although audit integrity is an important security goal, it is commonly explored orthogonally to other audit research due to the modularity of security solutions (*e.g.*, [12,54,75]). Therefore, we assume that once recorded to `kaudit buffer`, attackers cannot compromise the integrity of audit logs Finally, we assume that applications can be profiled in a controlled benign environment prior to being the target of attack.

---

[3] Specifically, our ruleset audits `execve`, `read`, `readv`, `write`, `writev`, `sendto`, `recvfrom`, `sendmsg`, `recvmsg`, `mmap`, `mprotect`, `link`, `symlink`, `clone`, `fork`, `vfork`, `open`, `close`, `creat`, `openat`, `mknodat`, `mknod`, `dup`, `dup2`, `dup3`, `bind`, `accept`, `accept4`, `connect`, `rename`, `setuid`, `setreuid`, `setresuid`, `chmod`, `fchmod`, `pipe`, `pipe2`, `truncate`, `ftruncate`, `sendfile`, `unlink`, `unlinkat`, `socketpair`,`splice`, `init_module`, and `finit_module`.

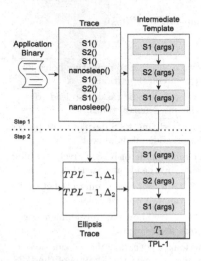

Fig. 2. *Ellipsis* template creation.

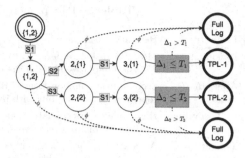

Fig. 3. Runtime template matching as an FSA with states as [syscalls matched count, {set of reachable templates}]. TPL-1 (S1, S2, S1) and TPL-2 (S1, S3, S1) are shown as example. Template matches (TPL-1, TPL-2) emit a single record, failure leads to full log store.

3 *Ellipsis*

The volume of audit events is the major limiting factor for auditing RTS. High event volume can result in event record loss, high log storage costs and large maintenance overheads [51]. We present *Ellipsis*, an audit event reduction technique designed specifically for RTS. *Ellipsis* achieves this through *templatization* of the audit event stream. Templates represent learned expected behaviors of RT tasks, described as a sequence of syscalls with arguments and temporal profile. These templates are generated in an offline profiling phase, similar to common RTS analyses like WCET [19,44]. At runtime, the application's syscall stream is compared against its templates; if a contiguous sequence of syscalls matches a template, only a single record indicating the template match is inserted into the event stream (`kaudit buffer`). Significantly, while a sequence of audited syscall events is replaced by a single record, relevant information is not lost (Sect. 5).

Model. Consider a system in which the machine operator wishes to audit a single RT task τ. An RT *task* here corresponds to a *thread* in Linux systems, identified by a combination of process and thread ids. We can limit this discussion to a single task, without losing generality, as *Ellipsis'* template creation, activation and runtime matching treat each task as independent. RT tasks are commonly structured with a one time *init* component and repeating *loops*. Let s_i denote a syscall sequence the task exhibits in a *loop* execution and N the count of different syscall execution paths τ might take (*i.e.*, $0 < i \le N$). A *template* describes these sequences (s_i), identifying the syscalls and arguments. As noted in Sect. 2, RT applications are developed to have limited code paths and bounded loop iterations. Extensive analysis of execution paths is a standard part of the RTS development process. Thus, for RTS, N is finite and determinable. Let function $len(s_i)$ return the number of syscalls in the sequence s_i. Further, let p_i be the probability that an iteration of τ exhibits syscall sequence s_i.

Sequence Identification. The first step towards template creation is identification of sequences and their probability of occurrences. Identification of cyclic syscall behaviors has been addressed in the auditing literature [42,50], with past solutions require binary analysis, code annotations, stack analysis or a combination. While any technique that yields s_i and p_i can be employed here, including the prior mentioned ones, we developed a highly automated process, leveraging RT task structure and Linux Audit itself. The application is run for long periods of time and audit trace collected. We observe that RT tasks typically end with calls to `sleep` or `yield` that translate to `nanosleep` and `sched_yield` syscalls in Linux. Periodic behaviors can also be triggered by polling timerfds to read events from multiple timers by using `select` and `epoll_wait` syscalls. We leverage these syscalls to identify boundaries of task executions within the audit log and then extract sequences of syscall invocations. Figure 2 provides an overview of this process. We also modified Linux Audit to include the Thread ID in log messages helping disambiguate threads belonging to a process. This first step yields the per task syscall sequences exhibited by the application and their properties: length, probability of occurrence, and the arguments. These syscall sequences are then converted into intermediate templates, each entry of which includes the syscall name along with the arguments. This first step can also be iterated with intermediate templates loaded to reduce previously extracted sequences, though in practice such iterations were not required.

Sequence Selection. A subset of intermediate templates are chosen to be converted to final templates. This choice is based on the tradeoff between the benefit of audit event volume reduction and the memory cost as defined later in Eq. (3) and (5), respectively. As we discuss in detail in Sect. 5 the security tradeoff is minimal. Let's assume n sequences are chosen to be reduced, where $0 \leq n \leq N$. As noted earlier, *Ellipsis* treats each task independently, the value of n is also independent for each task.

Template Creation. For the next step, Fig. 2 Step 2, these n templates are loaded and application profiled again to collect temporal profile for each template *i.e.*, the expected duration and inter-arrival intervals for each template. The intermediate templates are enriched with this temporal information, to yield the final templates. Templates are stored in the form of text files and occupy negligible disk space, *e.g.*, ArduPilot templates used for evaluation (Sect. 4) occupied 494 bytes of space on disk total. This whole process is highly automated, given an application binary with necessary inputs, using the template creation toolset. (See footnote 1)

Ellipsis Activation. We extend the Linux Audit command-line `auditctl` utility to transmit templates to kernel space. Once templates are loaded, *Ellipsis* can be activated using `auditctl` to start reducing any matching behaviors. This extended `auditctl` can also be used to activate/deactivate *Ellipsis* and load/unload templates, however, these operations are privileged, identical to deactivating Linux Audit itself. System administrators can use this utility to easily update templates as required, *e.g.*, in response to application updates.

Table 2. Parameters from case study

Task name	N	I	$len(s_i)$	p_i	f
arducopter	5	100	$[14, 15, 17, 17, 18]$	$[0.95, 0.02, 0.01, 0.01, 0.01]$	679
ap-rcin	1	182	$[16]$	$[1]$	2
ap-spi-0	5	1599	$[1, 1, 1, 2, 2]$	$[0.645, 0.182, 0.170, 0.001, 0.001]$	0

Runtime Matching. Given the template(s) of syscall sequences, an *Ellipsis* kernel module, extending from Linux Audit syscall hooks, filters syscalls that match a template. The templates are modeled as a finite state automaton (FSA), (Fig. 3), implemented as a collection of linked lists in kernel memory. While the RT task is executing, all syscall sequences allowed by the automaton are stored in a temporary task-specific buffer. If the set of events fully describes an automaton template, *Ellipsis* discards the contents of the task-specific buffer and enqueues a single record onto the kaudit buffer to denote the execution of a templatized activity. Alternatively, *Ellipsis* enqueues the entire task-specific buffer to the main kaudit buffer if *(a)* a syscall occurs that is not allowed by the automaton, *(b)* the template is not fully described at the end of the task instance or *(c)* the task instance does not adhere to the expected temporal behavior of the fully described template. Thus, the behavior of each task instance is reduced to a single record when the task behaves as expected. For any abnormal behavior, the complete audit log is retained.

Audit Event Reduction. Let the task τ be executed for I iterations and f denote the number of audit events in *init* phase. The number of audit events generated by τ when audited by Linux Audit (E_A), when *Ellipsis* reduces n out of total N sequences (E_E), and the reduction ($E_A - E_E$) are given by

$$E_A = I * \left(\sum_{i=1}^{N}(p_i * len(s_i))\right) + f \tag{1}$$

$$E_E = I * \left(\sum_{i=1}^{n} p_i + \sum_{i=n+1}^{N}(p_i * len(s_i))\right) + f \tag{2}$$

$$\underbrace{E_A - E_E}_{} = \overbrace{I}^{\text{Iterations}} * \left(\underbrace{\sum_{i=1}^{n}(p_i * len(s_i))}_{\text{Ellipsis' Event reduction}} - \underbrace{\sum_{i=1}^{n} p_i}_{\text{Ellipsis events for n sequences}} \right) \tag{3}$$

Ellipsis' Event reduction · Audit events for n sequences

As evident from Eq. (3), to maximize reduction, long sequences with large p_i values must be chosen as the n sequences for reduction. RT applications, like control systems, autonomous systems and even video streaming, feature limited execution paths for majority of their runtimes [39]. This property has been utilized by Yoon *et al.* in a prior work [76]. Therefore, for RT applications the distribution of p_i is highly biased *i.e.,* certain sequences s_i have high probability of occurrence. Table 2 provides example values for the parameters used, determined during the *Sequence Identification* step in template creation for the evaluation application ArduPilot(Sect. 4).

Storage Size Reduction. Let B_A denote the average cost of representing a syscall event in audit log and B_E denote the average cost of representing *Ellipsis'* template match record. By design, $B_E <= B_A$; B_E is a constant 343 bytes, while B_A averaged 527 bytes (1220 max) in our evaluation. Noting that the init events (f) are not reduced by *Ellipsis*, the disk size reduction *i.e.*, difference in sizes of τ's audit log for Linux Audit (L_A) and *Ellipsis* (L_E) is:

$$L_A - L_E = I * (B_A * \sum_{i=1}^{n}(p_i * len(s_i)) - B_E * \sum_{i=1}^{n} p_i) \qquad (4)$$

From Eq. (3) and (4), *Ellipsis'* benefits come from the audit events count and log size becoming independent of sequence size $(len(s_i))$ for the chosen n sequences, multiplied further by repetitions of these sequences $(I * p_i)$. *Ellipsis* behaves identical to Linux Audit for any sequence that is not included as a template, *i.e.*, $i \geq n + 1$ in Eq. (2).

Memory Tradeoff. The tradeoff for *Ellipsis'* benefits are computational overheads (evaluated in Sect. 4.5 and Sect. 4.6) and the memory cost of storing templates (M_τ). Let M_{fixed} be memory required per template, excluding syscalls, while $M_{syscall}$ be the memory required for each syscall in the template. On 32 bit kernel $M_{fixed} = 116$ and $M_{syscall} = 56$ bytes, determined by *sizeof* data structures. As an example, 3 templates from evaluation occupied 2 KB in memory.

$$M_\tau = M_{fixed} * n + M_{syscall} * \sum_{i=1}^{n} len(s_i) \qquad (5)$$

Extended Reduction Horizon. Until now we have limited the horizon of reduction to individual task *loop* instances. We can further optimize by creating a single record that describes multiple consecutive matches of a template. This higher performance system is henceforth referred to as **Ellipsis-HP**. When a *Ellipsis-HP* match fails, a separate record is logged for each of the base template matches along with complete log sequence for the current instance (*i.e.*, the base behavior of *Ellipsis*). *Ellipsis-HP* performs best when identical sequences occur continuously, capturing all sequence repetitions in one entry.

$$E_{Ellipsis\text{-}HP}^{Best} = n + I * \sum_{i=n+1}^{N}(p_i * len(s_i)) + f \qquad (6)$$

4 Evaluation

We evaluate *Ellipsis* and *Ellipsis-HP* using ArduPilot [9], a safety-critical firm-deadline autopilot application. We show that our auditing systems *(a)* perform *lossless auditing within the application's temporal requirements*, where Linux Audit would lose audit events or violate application's safety constraints (Sect. 4.3), *(b)* achieve high audit log volume reduction during benign activity, *(c)* enjoy minimal computational overhead even in an artificially created worst case scenarios (Sect. 4.5). Using a set of synthetic tasks we also show that the *Ellipsis'* overhead per syscall scales independent of the size of template (Sect. 4.6).

4.1 Setup

All measurements were conducted on 4GB Raspberry Pi 4 running Linux 4.19. The RT kernel from raspberrypi/linux [2] was used with AUDIT and AUDIT-SYSCALL kconfigs enabled. To reduce computational variability due to external perturbations we disabled power management, directed all kernel background tasks/interrupts to core 0 using the *isolcpu* kernel argument, and set CPU frequency Governor to Performance. Audit rules for capturing syscall events were configured to match against our benchmark application (*i.e.,* background process activity was not audited). We set the `kaudit` buffer size to 50K as any larger values led to system panic and hangs.

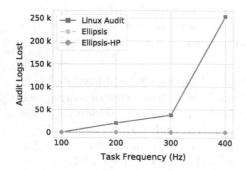
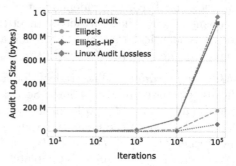

Fig. 4. (Section 4.3) Number of audit events lost vs. frequencies of the primary loop in ArduPilot, for 100K iterations.

Fig. 5. (Section 4.4) Total size on disk of the audit log (Y-axis), captured for different number of iterations (X-axis).

4.2 ArduPilot

ArduPilot is an open source autopilot application that can fully control various classes of autonomous vehicles such as quadcopters, rovers, submarines and fixed wing planes [9]. It has been installed in over a million vehicles and has been the basis for many industrial and academic projects. We chose the quadcopter variant of ArduPilot, called ArduCopter, as it has the most stringent temporal requirements within the application suite. For this application the RPi4 board was equipped with a Navio2 Autopilot hat [6] to provide real sensors and actuator interfaces for the application. We instrumented the application for measuring the runtime overheads introduced by auditing. Among the seven tasks spawned by ArduPilot, we focus primarily on a task named FastLoop for evaluating temporal overheads as it includes the stability and control tasks that need to run at a high frequency to keep the QuadCopter stable and safe.

Among the syscalls observed in the trace of ArduPilot, we found that only a small subset of syscalls were relevant to forensic analysis [28]: `execve`, `openat`, `read`, `write`, `close` and `pread64`. Upon running the template generation script on the application binary, we obtained the most frequently occuring templates for three tasks ($n = 1$, for each task), consisting of 14 `write`, 16 `pread64` calls and 1 `read` call, respectively. These templates include expected values corresponding to the file descriptor and count arguments of the syscalls. Templates were loaded into the kernel when evaluating *Ellipsis* or *Ellipsis-HP*.

4.3   Audit Completeness

Experiment. We ran the application for 100K iterations at task frequencies 100 Hz, 200 Hz, 300 Hz 400 Hz[4], measuring audit events lost. The fast dynamics of a quadcopter benefit from the lower discretization error in the ArduPilot's PID controllers at higher frequencies [71] leading to more stable vehicle control.

Observations. Figure 4 compares the log event loss for Linux Audit, *Ellipsis* and *Ellipsis-HP* across multiple task frequencies. We observe that Linux Audit lost log events at all task frequencies 100 Hz. In contrast, *Ellipsis* and *Ellipsis-HP* did not lose audit event log at any point in the experiment.

Discussion. Because this ArduCopter task performs critical stability and control function, reducing task frequency to accomodate Linux Audit may hay considerable detrimental effects. Further investigation revealed that Linux Audit dropped log events due to `kaudit` buffer overflow, despite the buffer size being 50K. In contrast, *Ellipsis* is able provide auditing for the entire frequency range without suffering log event loss. Better yet, throughout the experiment the max buffer occupancy was just 2.5K for *Ellipsis* and 1.5K for *Ellipsis-HP*.(A technical report with supplementary material for this work is available [10].)

4.4   Audit Log Size Reduction

Experiment. We ran the ArduCopter application over multiple iterations in 10 to 100K range to simulate application behavior over varying runtimes. For each iteration count, we measure the size on disk of the recorded log.

Observations. Figure 5 compares the storage costs in terms of file size on disk in bytes. The storage costs for all systems over shorter runs was found to be comparable, as the cost of auditing the initialization phase of the application $(B_A * f)$ tends to dominate over the periodic loops. Over a 250 s runtime (10^5 iterations) the growth of log size in *Ellipsis* was drastically lower compared to vanilla Linux Audit, with storage costs reducing by 740 MB, or **80%**, when using *Ellipsis*. *Ellipsis-HP* provides a more aggressive log size reduction option by lowering storage costs by 860 MB, or **93%**, compared to Linux Audit. *Linux Audit Lossless* estimates the log size had Linux Audit not lost any log events.

---

[4] Frequency values are chosen based on application support: https://ardupilot.org/ copter/docs/parameters-Copter-stable-V4.1.0.html#sched-loop-rate-scheduling-main-loop-rate.

Discussion. The observations line up with our initial hypothesis that the bulk of the audit logs generated during a loop iteration would exactly match the templates. Thus, in *Ellipsis* by reducing all the log messages that correspond to a template down to a single message, we see a vast reduction in storage costs while ensuring the retention of all the audit data. *Ellipsis-HP* takes this idea further by eliminating audit log generation over extended periods of time if the application exhibits expected behaviors only. For RTS that are expected to run for months or even years without failing, these savings are crucial for continuous and complete security audit of the system. Motion, a soft deadline application with numerous execution paths (N = 26) achieved similarly high reduction rations 81%–98%) under varying configurations options and inputs.(See footnote 2)

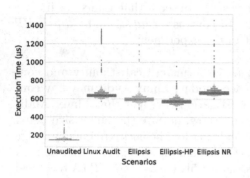
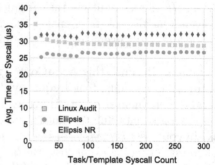

Fig. 6. (Section 4.5) Comparison of runtime overheads of ArduPilot main loop. Task period and deadline is 2500 μs.

Fig. 7. (Section 4.6) Avg. execution latency of `getpid` syscall (Y-axis) with varying task/template lengths (X-axis)

4.5   ArduPilot: Runtime Overheads

Experiment. This evaluation measures the execution time in microseconds (μs), for the Fast Loop task of ArduPilot, for 1000 iterations, under various auditing setups. The small number of iterations kept the generated log volume within `kaudit buffer` capacity, avoiding overflows and audit events loss in any scenario. This avoids polluting the overhead data with instances of event loss. The time measurement is based on the monotonic timer counter. This process was repeated 100 times. To evaluate the absolute worst case for *Ellipsis*, the *Ellipsis* NR (No Reduction) scenario modifies the ArduCopter template so that it always fails at the last syscall. *Ellipsis* NR is also the worst case for *Ellipsis-HP*.

Observations. Figure 6 shows the distribution of 100 execution time samples for each scenario. *Ellipsis*, *Ellipsis-HP* and *Ellipsis* NR have nearly the same overhead as Linux Audit. On average, *Ellipsis*'s overhead is $0.93\times$ and *Ellipsis-HP*'s overhead is $0.90\times$ of Linux Audit. The observed maximum overheads show a greater improvement. *Ellipsis*'s observed maximum overhead is $0.87\times$ and *Ellipsis-HP*'s $0.70\times$ of Linux Audit. *Ellipsis* NR shows a $1.05\times$ increase in average overhead and $1.07\times$ increase in maximum observed overhead.

Discussion. Ellipsis adds additional code to syscall auditing hooks, which incurs small computational overheads. When template matches fail (*Ellipsis* NR), this additional overhead is visible, although the overhead is not significantly worse the baseline Linux Audit. However, in the common case where audit events are reduced by *Ellipsis*, this cost is masked by reducing the total amount of log collection and transmission work performed by Linux Audit. This effect is further amplified in *Ellipsis-HP* owing to its greater reduction potential (Sect. 4.4). Thus, *Ellipsis*'s runtime overhead depends on the proportion of audit information reduced in the target application. Thus, while reducing the runtime overhead of auditing is not *Ellipsis*' primary goal, it nonetheless enjoys a modest performance improvement by reducing the total work performed by the underlying audit framework.

4.6   Synthetic Tasks: Overhead Scaling

Experiment. Because *Ellipsis* adds template matching logic in the critical execution path of syscalls, a potential concern is the overhead growth for tasks with long syscall sequences. In this experiment we measure execution time for tasks that execute varying counts of `getpid` syscalls (10, 20, 30 ... 300). `getpid` is a low latency non-blocking syscall, which allows us to stress-test the auditing framework. As the max template length (*i.e.,* syscall count) observed in real application loops was 29, we analyze workloads of roughly 10 times that amount, *i.e.,* 300. The execution time for each task is measured 100 times. Since the tasks have a single execution path *i.e.,* a fixed count of `getpid` syscalls, *Ellipsis*' audit events reduction always succeeds. For *Ellipsis* NR (No Reduction) we force template matches to fail at the last entry (same as Sect. 4.5).

Observations. Figure 7 shows the average syscall response time as the number of syscalls in the task loop increases. The primary observation of interest is that the *time to execute a syscall is roughly constant*, independent of the number of syscalls in the task and template. The higher value at the start is due to the non syscall part of the task that quickly becomes insignificant for tasks with higher number of syscalls. We only show average latency as the variance is negligible ($< 1.3\ \mu s$).

Discussion. Ellipsis scales well as the overhead per syscall remains independent of template size, even in the worst case scenario of *Ellipsis* NR. When log reduction succeeds the overhead is reduced. When the log reduction fails the overhead is not significantly worse than Linux Audit.

4.7   Summary of Results

Ellipsis provides complete audit events retention while meeting temporal requirements of the ArduPilot application, with significantly reduced storage costs. *Ellipsis-HP* further improves the reduction ratios. The temporal constraint allows additional temporal checks, detecting anomalous latency spikes with effectively no additional log size overhead during normal operation.(See footnote 2)

5 Security Analysis

The security goal of *Ellipsis*, indeed auditing in general, is to record all forensically-relevant information, thereby aiding in the investigation of suspicious activities. The previous section established *Ellipsis'* ability to dramatically reduce audit event generation for benign activities, freeing up auditing capacity. We now discuss the security implications of *Ellipsis*.

Stealthy Evasion. If a malicious process adheres to the expected behavior of benign tasks, the associated logs will be reduced. The question, then, is whether a malicious process can perform meaningful actions while adhering to the benign templates. If *Ellipsis* exclusively matched against syscall IDs only, such a feat may be possible; however, *Ellipsis* also validates syscalls' arguments and temporal constraints, effectively validating both the *control flow* and *data flow* before templatization. Thus making it exceedingly difficult for a process to match a template while affecting the RTS in any meaningful way. For example, an attacker might try to substitute a read from a regular file with a read from a sensitive file; however, doing so would require changing the file handle argument, failing the template match. Thus, at a minimum *Ellipsis* provides comparable security to commodity audit frameworks, and may actually provide improved security by avoiding the common problem of log event loss. A positive side effect of *Ellipsis* is built in partitioning of execution flows, benefiting provenance techniques that utilize such partitions [42,49,50].

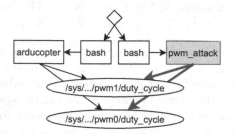

Fig. 8. (Section 5) Attack graph created using *Ellipsis* audit logs.

Information Loss. Another concern is whether *Ellipsis* templates remove forensically-relevant information. The following is an example `write` as would be recorded by Linux Audit.

```
type=SYSCALL msg=audit(1601405431.612391366:5893333): arch=40000028 syscall=4
 per=800000 success=yes exit=7 a0=4 a1=126ab0 a2=1 a3=3 items=0 ppid=1513 pid
=1526 tid=1526 auid=1000 uid=0 gid=0 euid=0 suid=0 fsuid=0 egid=0 sgid=0
fsgid=0 tty=pts0 ses=1 comm="arducopter" exe="/home/pi/ardupilot/build/navio2
/bin/arducopter" key=(null)
```

The record above, if reduced with *Ellipsis* and reconstructed using the *Ellipsis* log and templates, yields:

```
type=SYSCALL msg=audit([1601405431.612391356, 1601405431.612391367]:∅): arch
=40000028 syscall=4 per=800000 success=yes exit=7 a0=4 a1=∅ a2=1 a3=∅ items
=0 ppid=1513 pid=1526 tid=1526 auid=1000 uid=0 gid=0 euid=0 suid=0 fsuid=0
egid=0 sgid=0 fsgid=0 tty=pts0 ses=1 comm="arducopter" exe="/home/pi/
ardupilot/build/navio2/bin/arducopter" key=(null)
```

∅ denotes values that could not be reconstructed and [min, max] denote where a range is known but not the exact value. Nearly all of the information in an audit record can be completely reconstructed, including *(a)* all audit events executed by a task, in order of execution, *(b)* forensically relevant arguments. On the other hand, information not reconstructed is *(a)* accurate timestamps, *(b)* a monotonically increasing audit ID, *(c)* forensically irrelevant syscall arguments. The effect of this lost information is that fine grained inter-task event ordering and interleaving cannot be reconstructed. This loss of information is minimal and at worst increases the size of attack graph of a malicious event. We now demonstrate *Ellipsis*'s ability to retain forensically relevant information.

Demonstration: Throttle Override Attack. Autopilot applications are responsible for the safe operation of autonomous vehicles. ArduPilot periodically updates actuation signals that control rotary speed of motors that power rotors. The periodic updates are responsible for maintaining vehicle stability and safety.

Attack Scenario. Let's consider a stealthy attacker who wants to destabilize or take control over the unmanned drones. To achieve this, the attacker first gains control of a task on the system and attempts to override the control signals. An actuation signal's effect depends on the duration for which it controls the vehicle, therefore, naïvely overriding an actuation signal is not a very effective attack as the control task may soon update it to the correct value, reducing the attack's effect. The attacker instead leverages side channel attacks such as Scheduleak [23] during the reconnaissance phase of the attack to learn when the control signals are updated. Armed with this knowledge, the attacker overrides the actuation signals immediately after the original updates, effectively taking complete control, with little computational overhead. We use the ArduPilot setup as in described earlier (Sect. 4.2). Using tools provided with Scheduleak [23], a malicious task is able to override actuation signals generated by ArduPilot. This setup is run for 250 s and audit logs collected with *Ellipsis*.

Results. Overriding throttle control signals involves writing to files in `sysfs`. This attack behavior can be observed in audit logs as sequences of `openat`, `write` and `close` syscalls. Combining templates with the obtained audit log yields the attack graph in Fig. 8. *Ellipsis* correctly identifies that ArduPilot is only exhibiting benign behaviors, reducing its audit logs. *Ellipsis* preserves detailed attack behaviors for the malicious syscall sequences. *Ellipsis* did not lose audit events throughout the application runtime. In contrast, Linux Audit loses audit events (Sect. 4.3), potentially losing critical forensic evidence.

Discussion. Scheduleak [23] invokes `clock_gettime` syscall frequently to infer task activation times. Such syscalls are irrelevant for commonly used forensic analysis as they don't capture critical information flows. Despite the lack of visibility in the reconnaissance phase of the attack, auditing can capture evidence of attacker interference that creates new information flows, as shown in Fig. 8. We have demonstrated that when a process deviates from the expected behaviors, *e.g.,* due to an attack, *Ellipsis* provides the same security as Linux Audit. Additionally, *Ellipsis* all but eliminates the possibility of losing portions of the malicious activity due to `kaudit` buffer overflow. However, it is impossible to guarantee that no events will ever be lost with malicious activities creating unbounded new events. *Ellipsis* improves upon Linux Audit by *(a)* freeing up auditing resources which can then audit malicious behaviors, and *(b)* reducing the audit records from benign activities that must be analyzed as part of forensic provenance analysis. Stealthy attacks like this also show the role of auditing in improving vulnerability detection and forensic analysis on RTS.

6   Discussion

System Scope and Limitations. *Ellipsis* is useful for any application that has predictable repeating patterns. When sequence sets are too large with no high probability sequences, it may be possible that too much of system memory would be required to achieve significant log reduction. That said, a large number of possible sequences is not detrimental to *Ellipsis* as long as there exist some high probability sequences. *Ellipsis*'s efficacy is also not dependent on specific scheduling policies unless tasks share process and thread ids; if task share process/thread ids and the scheduler can reorder them, *Ellipsis* cannot distinguish between event chains, leading to unnecessary template match failures.

Auditing Hard RTS. *Ellipsis*, like Linux Audit and Linux itself, is unsuitable for hard-deadline RTS. All synchronous audit components must meet the temporal requirements for Hard RTS with bounded WCET, including syscall hooks and *Ellipsis* template matching. Additionally the `kaudit buffer` occupancy must have a strict upper bound. In this paper *Ellipsis* takes a long step forward, deriving high confidence empirical bounds (Sect. 4.5) to enable *Ellipsis'* use in firm- or soft-deadline RTS, which are prolific [7]. However, the strict bounds required for Hard RTS are a work in progress.

Unfavorable Conditions. We consider here the impact of using *Ellipsis* to audit hypothetical RTS where our assumptions about RTS properties do not hold. If the RTS may execute previously unknown syscall sequences, extra events would exist in the audit log. The audit log recorded by *Ellipsis* would thus be larger. Since safety, reliability and timing predictability are important requirements for RTS [7] the gaps in code coverage can only be small. Hence the unknown syscall sequences will not have a major impact on audit events and log size. If known syscall sequences have near uniform probability of occurrence, simply using templates for them all achieves high reduction ($n = N$). The tradeoff is additional memory required to store templates which is a small cost (Eq. (5)). Finally, if the above are combined, sequences with substantial probability of occurrence would remain untested during the RTS development. For such a system, functional correctness, reliability, safety or timing predictability cannot be established, making this RTS unusable.

7   Related Work

Auditing RTS. Although auditing has been widely acknowledged as an important aspect of securing embedded devices [8,26,38], challenges unique to auditing RTS have received limited attention. Wang et al. present ProvThings, an auditing framework for monitoring IoT smart home deployments [72], but rather than audit low-level embedded device activity their system monitors API-layer flows on the IoT platform's cloud backend. Tian et al. present a block-layer auditing framework for portable USB storage that can be used to diagnose integrity violations [68]. Their embedded device emulates a USB flash drive, but does not consider syscall auditing of RT applications. Wu et al. present a network-layer auditing platform that captures the temporal properties of network flows and can thus detect temporal interference [73]. Whereas their system uses auditing to diagnose performance problems in networks, the presented study considers the performance problems created by auditing within real-time applications.

Forensic Reduction. Significant effort has been dedicated to improving the cost-utility ratio for system auditing by pruning or compressing audit data that is unlikely to be of use during investigations [11,13,15,22,32,37,43,47,63,65,74]. However these approached address the log storage overheads and not the voluminous event generation that is prohibitive to RTS auditing (Sect. 4.3). KCAL [51] and ProTracer [49] systems are among the few that, like *Ellipsis*, inline their reduction methods into the kernel. Regardless of their layer of operation, these approaches are often based on an observation that certain log semantics are not forensically relevant (*e.g.*, temporary file I/O [43]), but it is unclear whether these assumptions hold for real-time cyber-physical environments, *e.g.*, KCAL or ProTracer would reduce multiple identical reads syscalls to a single entry. However, a large number of extra reads can cause catastrophic deadline misses. Forensic reduction in RTS, therefore, needs to be cognizant of the characteristics of RTS or valuable information can be lost. Our approach to template generation in *Ellipsis* shares similarities with the notion of *execution partitioning* of log activity [33,34,40,42,50], which decomposes long-lived applications into autonomous units of work to reduce false dependencies in forensic investigations. Unlike past systems, however, our approach requires no instrumentation to facilitate. Further, leveraging the well-formed nature of real-time tasks ensures the correctness of our execution units *i.e.*, templates.

8   Conclusion

Ellipsis is a novel audit event reduction system that exemplifies synergistic application-aware co-design of security mechanisms for RTS. *Ellipsis* allows

RT applications to be audited while meeting the temporal requirements of the application. The role of auditing in securing real-time applications can now be explored and enhanced further. As showcased with Auditing in this work, other security mechanisms from general purpose systems warrant a deeper analysis for their use in RTS.[5]

Acknowledgments. The material presented in this paper is based upon work supported by the Office of Naval Research (ONR) under grant number N00014-17-1-2889 and the National Science Foundation (NSF) under grant numbers CNS 1750024, CNS 1932529, CNS 1955228, CNS 2055127, CNS 2145787 and CNS 2152768. Any opinions, findings, and conclusions or recommendations expressed in this publication are those of the authors and do not necessarily reflect the views of the sponsors.

References

1. System auditing (2018). https://access.redhat.com/documentation/en-us/red_hat/_enterprise/_linux/6/html/security/_guide/chap-system/_auditing
2. Raspberry Pi Linux 4.19 Preempt RT (2019). https://github.com/raspberrypi/linux/tree/rpi-4.19.y-rt
3. Embedded linux (2020). https://elinux.org/Main/_Page
4. The instrumented microkernel (2020). http://www.qnx.com/developers/docs/6.4.1/neutrino/sys/_arch/trace.html
5. Tracealyzer for vxworks (2020). http://percepio.com/docs/VxWorks/manual/
6. Navio2 board (2021). https://navio2.emlid.com/
7. Akesson, B., et al.: An empirical survey-based study into industry practice in real-time systems. In: IEEE Real-Time Systems Symposium. IEEE (2020)
8. Anderson, M.: Securing embedded linux (2020). https://elinux.org/images/5/54/Manderson4.pdf
9. ArduPilot Development Team and Community: Ardupilot (2020). http://ardupilot.org/
10. Bansal, A., et al.: Ellipsis: Towards efficient system auditing for real-time systems (2022). https://doi.org/10.48550/ARXIV.2208.02699
11. Bates, A., et al.: Take only what you need: leveraging mandatory access control policy to reduce provenance storage costs. In: 7th Workshop on the Theory and Practice of Provenance, TaPP 2015 (2015)
12. Bates, A., et al.: Trustworthy whole-system provenance for the linux kernel. In: Proceedings of 24th USENIX Security Symposium (2015)
13. Bates, A., et al.: Taming the costs of trustworthy provenance through policy reduction. ACM Trans. Internet Technol. **17**(4), 34:1–34:21 (2017)
14. Begg, R.: Step up cyber hygiene: Secure access to medical devices (2020). http://www.machinedesign.com/medical-design/article/21128232/step-up-cyber-hygiene-secure-access-to-medical-devices
15. Ben, Y., et al.: T-tracker: compressing system audit log by taint tracking. In: 2018 IEEE 24th International Conference on Parallel and Distributed Systems (ICPADS), pp. 1–9 (2018)

---

[5] A technical report with further evaluations, template examples, security demonstrations and expanded RTS properties survey is available [10].

16. Böhm, K., et al.: New developments on EDR (event data recorder) for automated vehicles. Open Eng. **10**(1), 140–146 (2020)
17. Bose, U.: The black box solution to autonomous liability. Wash, UL Rev (2014)
18. Brandenburg, B., Anderson, J.: Feather-trace: a lightweight event tracing toolkit. In: Proceedings of the Third International Workshop on Operating Systems Platforms for Embedded Real-Time Applications, pp. 19–28 (2007)
19. Burguiere, C., Rochange, C.: History-based schemes and implicit path enumeration. In: 6th International Workshop on Worst-Case Execution Time Analysis (WCET 2006). Schloss Dagstuhl-Leibniz-Zentrum für Informatik (2006)
20. Carbon Black: Global incident response threat report (2018). http://www.carbonblack.com/global-incident-response-threat-report/november-2018/. Accessed 20 Apr 2019
21. Casimiro, A., et al.: How to build a timely computing base using real-time linux. In: 2000 IEEE International Workshop on Factory Communication Systems. Proceedings (Cat. No. 00TH8531), pp. 127–134. IEEE (2000)
22. Chen, C., et al.: Distributed provenance compression. In: Proceedings of the 2017 ACM International Conference on Management of Data, pp. 203–218 (2017)
23. Chen, C.Y., et al.: Schedule-based side-channel attack in fixed-priority real-time systems. Technical report (2015)
24. Correia, M., Veríssimo, P., Neves, N.F.: The design of a COTS real-time distributed security kernel. In: Bondavalli, A., Thevenod-Fosse, P. (eds.) EDCC 2002. LNCS, vol. 2485, pp. 234–252. Springer, Heidelberg (2002). https://doi.org/10.1007/3-540-36080-8_21
25. Crane, C.: Automotive cyber security: A crash course on protecting cars against hackers (2020). https://www.thesslstore.com/blog/automotive-cyber-security-a-crash-course-on-protecting-cars-against-hackers/
26. Day, R., Slonosky, M.: Securing connected embedded devices using built-in rtos security (2020). http://mil-embedded.com/articles/securing-connected-embedded-devices-using-built-in-rtos-security/
27. Department of Homeland Security: Cyber physical systems security (2020). www.dhs.gov/science-and-technology/cpssec
28. Gehani, A., Tariq, D.: SPADE: support for provenance auditing in distributed environments. In: Proceedings of the 13th International Middleware Conference, Middleware 2012 (2012)
29. Gurgen, L., et al.: Self-aware cyber-physical systems and applications in smart buildings and cities. In: 2013 Design, Automation & Test in Europe Conference & Exhibition (DATE), pp. 1149–1154. IEEE (2013)
30. Gustafsson, J., Ermedahl, A.: Experiences from applying wcet analysis in industrial settings. In: 10th IEEE International Symposium on Object and Component-Oriented Real-Time Distributed Computing, pp. 382–392. IEEE (2007)
31. Hahad, M.: Iot proliferation and widespread 5G: a perfect botnet storm (2020). http://www.scmagazine.com/home/opinion/executive-insight/iot-proliferation-and-widespread-5g-a-perfect-botnet-storm/
32. Hassan, W.U., et al.: Towards scalable cluster auditing through grammatical inference over provenance graphs. In: Proceedings of the 25th ISOC Network and Distributed System Security Symposium, NDSS 2018, San Diego, CA, USA (2018)
33. Hassan, W.U., et al.: NoDoze: combatting threat alert fatigue with automated provenance triage. In: 26th ISOC Network and Distributed System Security Symposium, NDSS 2019 (2019)

34. Hassan, W.U., et al.: OmegaLog: high-fidelity attack investigation via transparent multi-layer log analysis. In: 27th ISOC Network and Distributed System Security Symposium, NDSS 2020 (2020)
35. Hatton, L.: Safer language subsets: an overview and a case history, misra c. Inf. Softw. Technol. **46**(7), 465–472 (2004)
36. Hayes, J.: Hackers under the hood (2020). https://eandt.theiet.org/content/articles/2020/03/hackers-under-the-hood/
37. Hossain, M.N., et al.: Dependence-preserving data compaction for scalable forensic analysis. In: Proceedings of the 27th USENIX Conference on Security Symposium, SEC 2018, pp. 1723–1740. USENIX Association, Berkeley (2018)
38. Kohei, K.: Recent security features and issues in embedded systems (2020). https://elinux.org/Images/e/e2/ELC2008/_KaiGai.pdf
39. Konrad, S., Cheng, B.H.: Real-time specification patterns. In: Proceedings of the 27th International Conference on Software Engineering, pp. 372–381 (2005)
40. Kwon, Y., et al.: MCI: modeling-based causality inference in audit logging for attack investigation. In: Proceedings of the 25th Network and Distributed System Security Symposium (NDSS 2018) (2018)
41. Lee, I., et al.: Challenges and research directions in medical cyber-physical systems. Proc. IEEE **100**(1), 75–90 (2011)
42. Lee, K.H., et al.: High accuracy attack provenance via binary-based execution partition. In: Proceedings of NDSS 2013 (2013)
43. Lee, K.H., et al.: LogGC: garbage collecting audit log. In: Proceedings of the 2013 ACM SIGSAC conference on Computer and Communications Security, CCS 2013, pp. 1005–1016. ACM, New York (2013)
44. Li, Y.T.S., Malik, S.: Performance analysis of embedded software using implicit path enumeration. In: Proceedings of the ACM SIGPLAN 1995 Workshop on Languages, Compilers, & Tools for Real-Time Systems, pp. 88–98 (1995)
45. Liu, C.L., Layland, J.W.: Scheduling algorithms for multiprogramming in a hard-real-time environment. J. ACM **20**(1), 46–61 (1973)
46. Liu, Y., et al.: Towards a timely causality analysis for enterprise security. In: NDSS (2018)
47. Ma, S., et al.: Accurate, low cost and instrumentation-free security audit logging for windows. In: Proceedings of the 31st Annual Computer Security Applications Conference, ACSAC 2015, pp. 401–410. ACM, New York (2015)
48. Ma, S., et al.: Protracer: towards practical provenance tracing by alternating between logging and tainting. In: NDSS (2016)
49. Ma, S., et al.: ProTracer: towards practical provenance tracing by alternating between logging and tainting. In: Proceedings of NDSS 2016 (2016)
50. Ma, S., et al.: MPI: multiple perspective attack investigation with semantic aware execution partitioning. In: 26th USENIX Security Symposium (2017)
51. Ma, S., et al.: Kernel-supported cost-effective audit logging for causality tracking. In: 2018 USENIX Annual Technical Conference (USENIX ATC 2018), pp. 241–254. USENIX Association, Boston (2018)
52. Milajerdi, S.M., et al.: Holmes: real-time apt detection through correlation of suspicious information flows. In: 2019 2019 IEEE Symposium on Security and Privacy (SP). IEEE Computer Society, Los Alamitos (2019)
53. Monostori, L., et al.: Cyber-physical systems in manufacturing. Cirp Ann. **65**(2), 621–641 (2016)
54. Paccagnella, R., et al.: Custos: practical tamper-evident auditing of operating systems using trusted execution. In: 27th ISOC Network and Distributed System Security Symposium, NDSS 2020 (2020)

55. Perlroth, N., Sanger, D.E.: Cyberattacks Put Russian Fingers on the Switch at Power Plants, U.S. Says (2018). https://www.nytimes.com/2018/03/15/us/politics/russia-cyberattacks.html

56. Pohly, D., et al.: Hi-Fi: collecting high-fidelity whole-system provenance. In: Proceedings of the 2012 Annual Computer Security Applications Conference, ACSAC 2012, Orlando, FL, USA (2012)

57. Puschner, P., Burns, A.: Writing temporally predictable code. In: Proceedings of the Seventh IEEE International Workshop on Object-Oriented Real-Time Dependable Systems, (WORDS 2002), pp. 85–91. IEEE (2002)

58. Rajkumar, R., et al.: Cyber-physical systems: the next computing revolution. In: Design Automation Conference, pp. 731–736. IEEE (2010)

59. Sandell, D., Ermedahl, A., Gustafsson, J., Lisper, B.: Static timing analysis of real-time operating system code. In: Margaria, T., Steffen, B. (eds.) ISoLA 2004. LNCS, vol. 4313, pp. 146–160. Springer, Heidelberg (2006). https://doi.org/10.1007/11925040_10

60. Shepherd, D.: Industry 4.0: the development of unique cybersecurity (2020). https://manufacturingdigital.com/technology/industry-40-development-unique-cybersecurity

61. Slabodkin, G.: Coronavirus chaos ripe for hackers to exploit medical device vulnerabilities (2020). https://www.medtechdive.com/news/coronavirus-chaos-ripe-for-hackers-to-exploit-medical-device-vulnerabilitie/575717/

62. Song, J., Parmer, G.: C'mon: a predictable monitoring infrastructure for system-level latent fault detection and recovery. In: 21st IEEE Real-Time and Embedded Technology and Applications Symposium, pp. 247–258. IEEE (2015)

63. Sundaram, V., et al.: Prius: Generic hybrid trace compression for wireless sensor networks. In: Proceedings of the 10th ACM Conference on Embedded Network Sensor Systems, pp. 183–196 (2012)

64. SUSE LINUXAG: Linux Audit-Subsystem Design Documentation for Linux Kernel 2.6, v0.1 (2004). http://uniforumchicago.org/slides/HardeningLinux/LAuS-Design.pdf

65. Tang, Y., et al.: Nodemerge: template based efficient data reduction for big-data causality analysis. In: Proceedings of the 2018 ACM SIGSAC Conference on Computer and Communications Security, CCS 2018, pp. 1324–1337. ACM, New York (2018)

66. The Linux Foundation: Real-Time Linux (2018). https://wiki.linuxfoundation.org/realtime/start

67. The MITRE Corporation: Medical device cybersecurity (2018). https://www.mitre.org/sites/default/files/2021-11/prs-18-1550-Medical-Device-Cybersecurity-Playbook.pdf

68. Tian, D.J., et al.: Provusb: block-level provenance-based data protection for usb storage devices. In: Proceedings of the 2016 ACM SIGSAC Conference on Computer and Communications Security. ACM, New York (2016)

69. Veríssimo, P., Casimiro, A.: The timely computing base model and architecture. IEEE Trans. Comput. **51**(8), 916–930 (2002)

70. Veríssimo, P., et al.: The timely computing base: timely actions in the presence of uncertain timeliness. In: Proceeding International Conference on Dependable Systems and Networks, DSN 2000, pp. 533–542. IEEE (2000)

71. Wang, L.: PID Control System Design and Automatic Tuning Using MATLAB/Simulink. John Wiley & Sons, Hoboken (2020)

72. Wang, Q., et al.: Fear and logging in the internet of things. In: Proceedings of the 25th ISOC Network and Distributed System Security Symposium, NDSS 2018 (2017)
73. Wu, Y., et al.: Zeno: diagnosing performance problems with temporal provenance. In: 16th USENIX Symposium on Networked Systems Design and Implementation (NSDI 19), pp. 395–420. USENIX Association, Boston (2019)
74. Xu, Z., et al.: High fidelity data reduction for big data security dependency analyses. In: Proceedings of the 2016 ACM SIGSAC Conference on Computer and Communications Security, CCS 2016, pp. 504–516. ACM, New York (2016)
75. Yagemann, C., et al.: Validating the integrity of audit logs against execution repartitioning attacks. In: Proceedings of the 2021 ACM SIGSAC Conference on Computer and Communications Security, CCS 2021 (2021)
76. Yoon, M.K., et al.: Learning execution contexts from system call distribution for anomaly detection in smart embedded system. In: Proceedings of the Second International Conference on Internet-of-Things Design and Implementation (2017)

Network and Software Security

Towards a Systematic and Automatic Use of State Machine Inference to Uncover Security Flaws and Fingerprint TLS Stacks

Aina Toky Rasoamanana[ID], Olivier Levillain[(✉)][ID], and Hervé Debar[ID]

Télécom SudParis, Samovar, Institut Polytechnique de Paris, Paris, France
olivier.levillain@telecom-sudparis.eu

Abstract. TLS is a well-known and thoroughly studied security protocol. In this paper, we focus on a specific class of vulnerabilities affecting TLS implementations, state machine errors. These vulnerabilities are caused by differences in interpreting the standard and correspond to deviations from the specifications, e.g. accepting invalid messages, or accepting valid messages out of sequence. We develop a systematic methodology to infer the state machines of major TLS stacks from stimuli and observations, and to study their evolution across revisions. We use the L* algorithm to compute state machines corresponding to different execution scenarios. We reproduce several known vulnerabilities (denial of service, authentication bypasses), and uncover new ones. We also show that state machine inference is efficient and practical for integration within a continuous integration pipeline, to help find new vulnerabilities or deviations introduced during development.

With our systematic black-box approach, we study over 400 different versions of server and client implementations in various scenarios (protocol version, options). Using the resulting state machines, we propose a robust algorithm to fingerprint TLS stacks. To the best of our knowledge, this is the first application of this approach on such a broad perimeter, in terms of number of TLS stacks, revisions, or execution scenarios studied.

1 Introduction

TLS is a fundamental block of Internet security. The most recent version of the standard is TLS 1.3 [23]. It fixes many vulnerabilities uncovered in the last decade. Automata implementation errors represent one category of these. The RFC does not specify a reference automaton. Hence, implementers need to derive their state machine from the protocol messages descriptions and sequences. The complexity of the task is such that errors are easy.

Such vulnerabilities can be triggered by an attacker sending messages in an inappropriate order (e.g. EarlyCCS [18]) or skipping messages (e.g. SkipVerify [4], which bypasses server authentication by skipping the corresponding messages). In more complex cases, interfering with the state machine enables new

This work was supported by the French ANR GASP project (ANR-19-CE39-0001).

V. Atluri et al. (Eds.): ESORICS 2022, LNCS 13556, pp. 637–657, 2022.
https://doi.org/10.1007/978-3-031-17143-7_31

cryptographic attacks (e.g. FREAK [4], Factoring RSA Export Keys). All major TLS stacks have been vulnerable to at least one such flaw in the last decade.[1]

Our work focuses on black-box testing, to better understand how TLS implementations react to messages that diverge from an ideal message sequence. We use an active learning algorithm, L*, initially described by Angluin [2], and later adapted to Mealy machines [25], to infer the actual state machine through interactions with implementations. We then compare these state machines with the expected behavior of an ideal stack. Despite the absence of a formal specification of such an ideal stack, a simple approximation of said ideal stack is to use so-called happy paths, which correspond to the expected message sequences for successful connections. A fully compliant stack should only contain happy paths and error transitions, leading to the end of the connection. Every other transition is deemed suspicious. Our contributions are the following:[2]

- We propose an improved methodology to systematically analyze TLS stacks, both client- and server-side, in an rigorous, automatic and efficient way.
- We propose optimizations exploiting the determinism hypothesis used in L*.
- By applying our methodology to different versions of popular open source projects, we confirm already known security vulnerabilities.
- We also discover new implementation errors, including security-relevant ones.
- Our methodology spots differences in the implementation of error conditions, supporting the concept of state-machine-based fingerprinting of TLS stacks.

2   TLS in a Nutshell

A typical TLS 1.3 connection is shown on the left side of Fig. 1: the client sends a `ClientHello` message to advertise the ciphersuites, i.e. a set of cryptographic algorithms, it supports and to propose a key share using one of the algorithms it supports. If the client and the server agree on capabilities, the server selects a suitable ciphersuite, and sends its own key share in a `ServerHello` message.

Once the client and server have agreed on algorithms and a common session key, messages are protected using authenticated encryption. The server carries on with several messages, including its certificate chain (`Certificate`) and a signature over the exchanged messages proving its identity (`CertificateVerify`). The `Finished` messages confirm keys in both directions. Then, session keys are updated, and application data can be exchanged.

Of course, this transcript only represents a simple, typical situation. It represents a *happy path*, which does not take into account session resumption or the so-called 0-RTT mode. It also ignores common error cases, such as the impossibility for the client and the server to agree on a common ciphersuite.

From this description, we represent the expected behavior of a TLS 1.3 client with the state machine on the right side of Fig. 1. The happy path, in green,

---

[1] e.g.: CVE-2014-0224, CVE-2014-6321, CVE-2015-0204, CVE-2015-0205.

[2] Our tools have been published on GitLab: gitlab.com/gaspians/pylstar-tls and https://gitlab.com/gaspians/tls-test-bed.

starts with the client outputting a `ClientHello`, and leads to the `Finished` messages and the exchange of Application data. Outside of this happy path, all other messages (denoted ∗) lead to the sink state with a fatal alert. This figure is identical to the state machine inferred using our methodology on OpenSSL 3.0.1.

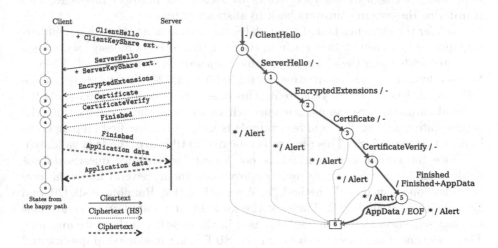

Fig. 1. A typical TLS 1.3 connection and the corresponding expected client state machine. On the right, transitions are labeled with the messages *sent to* / *received from* the client. The path in green is the expected flow described on the left, ending with a request (the `AppData` received from the client between states 4 and 5) and the answer (the `AppData` sent between states 5 and 6). A transition with ∗ aggregates the behaviors for the remaining input messages. (Color figure online)

3 Background on Model Learning

In 1987, Angluin proposed L⋆, an algorithm that infers a deterministic finite automaton using membership and equivalence queries [2]. This technique can be extended to extract the state machine of a protocol implementation using the Mealy machines representation, which can be seen as automata where transitions are labeled by both the messages sent and received, as shown on Fig. 1.

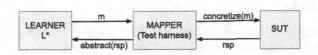

Fig. 2. Model learning setup.

L⋆ is an automated black-box technique driven by a LEARNER. Figure 2 describes the experimental process. The analyzed implementation (a TLS client or server) is the *System Under Test* (SUT). The LEARNER generates sequences of letters from a finite input vocabulary, where each letter represents an abstract protocol message (e.g. `ClientHello`) associated with its specific parameters. Interactions between the LEARNER and the SUT are mediated through a MAP-PER, which transforms abstract letters into concrete protocol messages, and transforms the concrete answers back to abstract letters.

To infer the state machine, L* populates an observation table using member-ship queries by collecting answers from the SUT to a series of message sequences. This step ends when the observation table is closed and consistent [2]. Then, it builds a hypothesis, i.e. a tentative state machine, and the LEARNER uses a so-called equivalence query to validate it. This query either confirms the hypothesis or exhibits a counter-example sequence where the hypothesis differs from the actual state machine. The counter-example is used to run the first step again to build a new hypothesis. This process is repeated until a hypothesis is validated.

Since the actual state machine is not known, equivalence queries do not really exist in practice, so we must approximate them. Several methods have been developed, such as W-method [9], Wp-method [14], Random Walk [20] and Distinguishing Bounds [21]. They use same input vocabulary to create new message sequences that have not been used in the creation of the state machine. These sequences are executed both on the SUT using membership queries and on the hypothesis. In case the executions produce different results, the corre-sponding message sequence is a counter-example invalidating the hypothesis.

W-method or Wp-method have an exponential complexity in the size of the inferred automata, which was not reasonable in most cases.[3] We use the Random Walk to approximate equivalence queries, since it produced the best results, both in terms of performance and accuracy. We also cross-check our results using Distinguishing Bounds on the obtained unique state machines to benefit from its guarantees. Indeed, given a bound value B_{dist}, it guarantees that the obtained state machine will be accurate as soon as two states in the real state machine can be distinguished in at most B_{dist} steps.

4   Description and Implementation of Our Platform

Figure 3 illustrates how TLS implementations and our inference tool interact for a client inference. Server inference works in a similar way.

4.1   TLS Stacks

We create containers for more than 400 TLS stacks. Table 4 in Appendix A details the TLS stacks currently included in our platform.

For each stack, we reuse the tools or the example code available within the project to build and run a TLS client and/or a TLS server. Such pieces of code are representative of the way the libraries are used in practice.

---

[3] Some scenarios use many messages, which can produce state machines with many states. The maximum number of states in our experiments is 31.

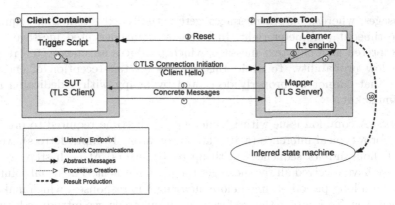

Fig. 3. TLS client inference cinematics. See Appendix A for a detailed explanation.

Each container is customized to select the protocol version and the cipher-suites, and to include the required cryptographic material (certificate, keys, trusted certification authority), which allows us to study different scenarios.

In addition to the "example" client, we create for each stack a second container, using `curl` dynamically linked with each stack. These curl-based images provide a unified interface across stacks, removing small differences in the example provided by the projects, e.g. missing certificate checks. All server-side examples include a functional and sufficiently customizable example for our needs.

4.2   Inference Tools

One major challenge with the L* approach is that the MAPPER used to concretize the abstract messages has to be flexible enough to send arbitrary messages at any state of execution of the protocol (even ones that would clearly be invalid). We thus need a modular and robust TLS stack to implement the MAPPER. We use `scapy` [5], a Python-based network tool, to forge and decode packets. `scapy` allows us to easily build customized packets (e.g. a `CertificateVerify` with a wrong signature).

To complete our setup, we choose `pylstar`, a Python-based implementation of L*, which allows for a straightforward connection with `scapy`. `pylstar` has previously been used to infer protocols used by malware with their Command & Control servers [7], as well as to study the behavior of HTTP/2 clients [8].

4.3   Assumptions

Deterministic SUTs. The most important requirement for L* is that the SUT behavior must be *deterministic*, relative to the selected input vocabulary. For a given stack and a given set of parameters, a given input abstract message sequence should always produce the exact same abstract output sequence.

TLS stacks behave deterministically, with a few exceptions. When a SUT takes too long to answer a stimulus, we can misinterpret its silence as the absence of messages, whereas output messages were actually expected. This requires to get the timeout parameter right. In rare cases, an encrypted message can be misinterpreted as a cleartext message, which produces an unexpected response with a low probability. To avoid this, we always tag reception of encrypted packets that cannot be properly decrypted by scapy with a dedicated letter, UnknownPacket.[4]

Timeouts. A common issue with L* inference is the time required to produce a result. For a typical inference (a 10-state automaton, 15 input letters), we need to send thousands of sequences, with up to 10 letters. At each step, we must ensure we have received all the messages the SUT has sent. The usual solution is to wait for a long period of time before inferring "no response", which makes the inference slow. To improve the performance of our tools, we introduce heuristics to reduce the timeouts when possible.

Precision of the Equivalence Query Approximation. As explained in Sect. 3, our inference tool use the BDist equivalence method to find counterexamples. To get relevant results, we must thus assume that the chosen B_{dist} value is sufficient.

5   Optimizations

Before discussing our optimizations in pylstar, we can already improve the performance by running in parallel several inferences. Indeed, since we use containers, running multiple instances of SUTs and inference tools is essentially free, so we can benefit from a multi-core architecture.

EOF is Final. When we receive a network error, which indicates that the SUT has shut down the communication channel, we can conclude that all subsequent messages will trigger the same signal (EOF), so it is not necessary to build and emit the corresponding messages.

In [24], de Ruiter and Poll actually proposed a similar improvement in the equivalence method implemented in statelearner, which resulted in measurable performance gains. By also applying the idea to the first phase of the algorithm (the membership queries), we further improve the performance.

Exploiting the Determinism. As discussed earlier, L* relies on the fact that the SUT is deterministic. So we propose another optimization, which is a direct consequence of this assumption. During its execution, L* often sends sequences that are extensions of already sent sequences. Let us assume that we have already

---

[4] Similarly, OpenSSL 1.0.1d was a short-lived version with a known bug in the CBC encryption function. The defective function leads to the emission of malformed packets with a low probability, which could not be interpreted correctly deterministically. We chose to remove this particular image from our corpus.

observed that sending A to the SUT triggers two messages, x and y. When evaluating the input sequence A B, we can send A, read x and y *without waiting after the reception of* y, then send B and observe the answer using the timeout.

A restricted version of this optimization consists in skipping the timeout only when we know sending a message will not trigger any message back.

Evaluation. Table 1 describes the time required for a typical inference with different optimizations. We infer the TLS 1.2 server state machine for OpenSSL 1.1.1k (which contains 6 states) with 12 input messages and a 1-second timeout. The machine hosting the experiment is an 16-core AMD EPYC 7302P at 3GHz, with 128 GB of RAM and all the storage on SSDs.

Table 1. Average time required to infer TLS 1.2 server state machine for OpenSSL 1.1.1k. Percentages are the fraction of the unoptimized time.

	No EOF optim.	EOF optimization
No anticipation	1,885 s (100%)	1,598 s (85%)
Skip timeouts on empty responses	1,081 s (57%)	862 s (46%)
Skip timeouts on all known responses	128 s (7%)	77 s (4%)

It appears both optimizations improve the overall performance, with a drastic improvement from the fully-fledged timeout anticipation. We ran similar experiments with `statelearner` (same timeout and vocabulary), on the same hardware, and the time required to produce the state machine was 2,945 s.

Obviously, the time required for our inferences can vary, depending on the complexity of the SUT state machine (which can count as much as 30 states in some cases), the size of the input vocabulary (the scenario), and the speed of the SUT. The default timeout used is 1 s, but to get a stable inference, we must raise this value to 3 for several stacks.

For a 1400-experiment run (which took around 2 and a half hours overall, with 30 inferences in parallel), the average inference time was around 3 min, the median was 81 s, and the 10th and 90th percentiles were respectively 27 s and around 8 min.

6   Studied Scenarios and Vulnerabilities

A scenario is defined by the following information: (i) the role (client/server) and the configuration (protocol version, ciphersuites, etc.) of the SUT; (ii) the input vocabulary (the list of abstract messages) used during the inference; (iii) a set of expected path, which helps challenge the built state machine during the equivalence query phase; and (iv) a set of security properties to test on the resulting graph.

To identify bugs using learned model, we first identify RFCs violations and then we analyze whether these violations represent bugs with the following steps:

(i) color in green the happy paths representing the successful connections;
(ii) color in gray error transitions leading to sink state, which are expected;
(iii) color all remaining transitions in red since they are RFCs violations, and may correspond to vulnerabilities.

6.1   Client Scenarios

In these scenarios, the SUT is a client, running a given version of TLS. The client is configured with a trusted certification authority and is expected to check the certificate presented by the server. The inference tool acts as a server, with the following input vocabulary: ServerHello, Certificate messages (valid, empty, invalid—trusted but for the wrong domain —, and untrusted), other server-side Handshake messages, ApplicationData and CloseNotify.

In these scenarios, we ensure that the client only sends application data to a correctly authenticated server. We look for paths leading to ApplicationData messages and check for proper authentication.

Another area of interest is the presence of loops that could be used by an attacker to stall a client, enabling complex cryptographic attacks, such as the LogJam attack [1]. Since the goal of such attacks is to delay the completion of the TLS Handshake, we only focus on loops happening early in the connection.

6.2   Server Scenarios

In these scenarios, the SUT is a server, running a given version of TLS. The server can be configured to require mutual authentication (with regards to a given certification authority). The inference tool acts as a client, and uses the following vocabulary: different ClientHellos, various Certificate messages (empty, trusted, untrusted), other client-side Handshake messages, ApplicationData and CloseNotify. We also include alerts and unexpected messages such as server-side messages.

When client authentication is required, we want to ensure that the server properly authenticates the client. Only paths with a valid certificate and the corresponding signature should be accepted.

We are also interested in the presence of loops in server state machines, which could force the server to maintain an open connection indefinitely. For such denial of service attacks, we only focus on occurrences happening before encryption is activated; this way, the attacker only needs to spend very few resources to keep the channel open. Moreover, keeping the server in an early stage of the connection reduces the chances of something being logged. Note that these loops are different from the ones created through TCP segmentation or TLS ClientHello fragmentation, which would be limited by the length of the data to send.

6.3   Vulnerability Confirmation

These scenarios identify potential implementation issues, which need to be independently confirmed as security flaws. L* is an algorithm that produces a state machine, which represents the behavior of the SUT. However, the produced state machine is only an approximation due to the (limited) set of abstract messages selected in the scenario and the equivalence query method used. We thus use tools to independently check whether a potential security issue, uncovered by the inference, actually translates into a real security flaw.

For authentication bypass issues, we extract the potentially dangerous paths and replay them to the SUT, in a context where we do not have access to the authentication secret. If we can trigger the tested stack to emit Application Data, the flaw is confirmed.

For loops, we send precomputed packets to the SUT at a given pace (typically one message per minute), and for a given duration (e.g. several hours). If we can maintain the connection open, we have proof the loop can be weaponized.

7   Analysis of the Resulting State Machines

We analyze over 400 different versions of different TLS stacks using different client and server scenarios and get over 2,000 automata. Appendix B summarizes the vulnerabilities reproduced and discovered during our study.

7.1   Authentication Bypasses

Server Authentication Bypasses in wolfSSL. Around 2015, authentication bypasses in state machines seemed to be pervasive in TLS stacks [4,24]. In 2020, CVE-2020-24613, an authentication bypass affecting wolfSSL TLS 1.3 client, caught our eye, and we decided to try and reproduce it using L*.

To this aim, we infer the state machines for wolfSSL TLS 1.3 clients, for different versions, with standard Handshake messages. Figure 4a represents the state machine corresponding to wolfSSL 4.4, which is vulnerable to CVE-2020-24613. By skipping the `CertificateVerify` message, an attacker can bypass server authentication, and thus impersonate any server to a vulnerable client. The vulnerability was fixed in version 4.5, as can be seen on Fig. 4b, which corresponds to the inferred state machine for the patched version, using the same vocabulary.

However, in other scenarios, we also use a broader input vocabulary including an empty `Certificate` message, that should never be sent by the server. We could thus discover another vulnerability in wolfSSL, present in all versions at the time. As shown in Fig. 4c, instead of skipping the `CertificateVerify` message, the attacker can send an empty `Certificate` message, followed by a `CertificateVerify` message signed by an arbitrary RSA key.[5] This new bug was confirmed, reported as CVE-2021-3336, and fixed.

---

[5] In our inference tool, sending a `Certificate` message selects the corresponding RSA key to be used in the subsequent `CertificateVerify`. For `EmptyCertificate`, the selected RSA key is a fresh key generated for the experiment.

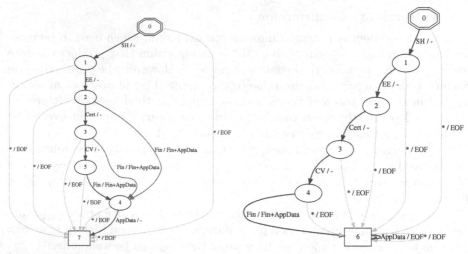

(a) CVE-2020-24613, a server authentication bypass in wolfSSL TLS 1.3 clients, up to version 4.4. An attacker can impersonate any server to a vulnerable client by skipping the `CertificateVerify` message.

(b) CVE-2020-24613 fixed in version 4.5. With the same vocabulary used in Fig. 4a, the dangerous transitions have indeed disappeared.

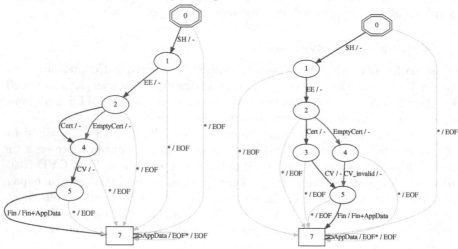

(c) CVE-2021-3336. By sending an empty `Certificate` message, followed by an arbitrary `CertificateVerify`, server impersonation is also possible.

(d) CVE-2022-25638. Adding a completely invalid `CertificateVerify` message reintroduces a dangerous transition.

SH	:	ServerHello	EE	:	Encrypted Extensions
Cert	:	Certificate	CV	:	CertificateVerify
Fin	:	Finished	AppData	:	ApplicationData
EOF	:	End of the connection			

Fig. 4. Attacks against wolfSSL TLS 1.3 clients.

By adding new messages to the input vocabulary, we also discover another alternate path to reintroduce the initial bug. Figure 4d shows an attacker can send an empty `Certificate` message, followed by an invalid `CertificateVerify` message, containing an unknown signature algorithm and an arbitrary payload to bypass server authentication. This bug, identified as CVE-2022-25638, has been fixed in version 5.2.0.

All these attacks were reproduced by sending the identified transcript to the vulnerable SUTs. The program replaying the attack was not given access to the server private key, and we checked both wolfSSL and curl+wolfSSL stacks to make sure the authentication bypasses were real.

Other Bypasses. In OpenSSL, different paths are incorrectly identified as invalid bypasses: the client seems to be accepting any certificate from the server. However, when we analyze a real TLS client using OpenSSL (the curl+OpenSSL stack), these dangerous paths disappear. Indeed, in our OpenSSL containers, TLS clients use the `s_client` application, which does not enforce any checks regarding the certificate.[6]

We use the same approach to assess the quality of TLS servers authenticating clients. We get an issue in wolfSSL TLS 1.3 servers, as shown in Fig. 5, which is the transposition of CVE-2020-24613 to the server. By skipping the `CertificateVerify` message (and optionally the `Certificate` message), an attacker can bypass the authentication and impersonate any legitimate client. It is worth noting that the server correctly reject untrusted certificates and empty `Certificate` messages (since client authentication is required in this scenario). This bug, CVE-2022-25640, has been fixed in version 5.2.0.

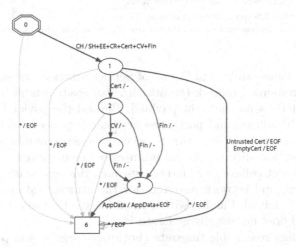

Fig. 5. CVE-2022-25640. In versions, up to 5.1.0, client authentication can be bypassed in wolfSSL TLS 1.3 servers, using the same idea as in CVE-2020-24613.

---

[6] It is possible to add options such as `-verifyCAfile` to the command line, but they do not end an unauthenticated handshake and merely produces a warning message.

7.2   Loops in the Automata

As discussed in Sect. 6, exploiting loops in TLS state machines can be used to mount sophisticated cryptographic attacks [1]. Loops have also been considered as a potential vector for denial of service attacks (e.g. CVE-2020-12457). We thus identify such loops in our state machines, and to focus on those happening before messages are protected.

Analysis of a False Positive. The inferred state machine for wolfSSL TLS 1.2 server (all versions) seems to exhibit a loop on the initial state, tagged with the `NoRenegotiation` warning. However, when we repeatedly send such warnings to the SUT, the server actually closes the connection after 4 warnings. This situation exhibits the fact that L* is only an approximation, which can not always capture behaviors happening very deep in the state machine. This justifies our approach, to always confirm potential vulnerabilities identified on the generated state machine.

Real bugs. After careful verification, we confirm several loops in different stacks, which are summarized in Table 2.

Table 2. Description of confirmed loops in TLS stacks.

Stack	Scenario	Messages	Max. time between msgs
erlang 24	1.0/1.2 Server	`NoRenegotiation` Alert or `ApplicationData`	>1 h*
fizz 22.01.24	1.3 Client	`ChangeCipherSpec`	>1 h
matrixssl 4.0 - 4.3	1.0/1.2 Server	`NoRenegotiation` Alert	≈40 s
NSS 3.15 - 3.78	1.0/1.2 Server	`NoRenegotiation` Alert	>1 h
OpenSSL <1.1.0	1.0/1.2 Server	Empty `ApplicationData`	>1 h

* Erlang has a `Timeout` parameter that can thwart the attack. It was added to the official tutorial.

For servers, loops can lead to Denial of Service attacks against TLS services, with very few resources. Indeed, the attacker can easily establish TCP connections and regularly send the right payload. Beyond the payload and the SUT identification (IP address and port), the attacker only needs to store, for each connection, the source port and the associated sequence numbers. With stacks keeping a connection alive for several minutes between packets (most probably because they do not enforce any kind of timeout), this represents a tiny amount of CPU, memory and network resources for the attacker. Moreover, distributing this attack is trivial. Finally, with vulnerable stacks, the attack can be run indefinitely and does not usually generate logs.

Beyond adding reasonable timeouts (both per-message and per-handshake) within the affected stacks, firewalls or other network devices should be used to detect and deter such extreme behavior. For the affected stacks, the issues have been reported and fixed when deemed relevant.

7.3   Unsolicited Client Authentication

TLS client authentication is an optional feature. The client can only present its certificate when the server sent a `CertificateRequest`. Servers may however be accommodating, and accept `Certificate` and `CertificateVerify` messages from the client, even when they were not solicited.

Such behavior may expose parts of the code that are not normally used. In 2014, a critical security flaw was found in Microsoft SChannel: a buffer overflow in the ECDSA signature check, triggered by client authentication, led to remote code execution. Accepting unsolicited client authentication messages made this obscure bug actually reachable in most deployments.

In our corpus, several versions of wolfSSL exhibit a similar behavior. Even if these paths do not necessarily lead to security issues, they should be removed, and considered bad practice, as they are a deviation from the specification.

8   TLS Stack Fingerprinting

We expect the state machines to be rather simple, as shown in Fig. 1, with less than 10 states, a restricted number of happy paths and the rest of the transitions consisting of fatal errors pointing towards the sink state. Yet, as surprising as it may seem, we observe that the produced state machines are actually richer, with up to 31 states, and that they are each specific to a given TLS stack.[7]

The differences usually lie in variations among implementations about the error handling: different alert messages can be emitted. Several state machines sometimes accept unexpected messages and silently ignores them.

Using a method described by Shu and Lee [26], we can compute, for a given scenario, a set of input message sequences separating the different stacks we inferred. Then, we can compute the stack *fingerprints* as the answer on each stack to the distinguishing sequences.

Beyond revealing interesting differences in TLS stack internals, fingerprinting TLS stacks can help an attacker pinpoint, with a few message sequences, a given version (or a set of versions) of a TLS implementation to select an effective exploit against this particular target. This may also help identify the underlying TLS stack in network appliances.

Fingerprinting also allows to detect the presence of interception middleboxes that can be used for censorship. Indeed, such middleboxes may produce unique fingerprints, either at the message-level or at the state machine-level. It is also possible to look for discrepancies between the TLS stack and the application-layer stack to detect middleboxes, as described by Durumeric et al. [10].

---

[7] Of course, within a given project, successive versions may share the same automaton.

8.1   Application to TLS 1.3 Servers

To illustrate our state-machine-based fingerprinting, Table 3 presents the classes
we identify for the simple TLS 1.3 scenario with no client authentication.

Table 3. TLS 1.3 server stacks grouped by state machine. N is the number of states.
CVEs in italic only affect part of the equivalence class.

Stack	Versions	N	High-severity CVEs affecting the servers
erlang	24.0.3 - 24.2.1	9	*No high-severity CVE referenced*
GnuTLS	3.6.16 - 3.7.2	4	*2021-20231 2021-20232*
matrixssl	4.0.0 - 4.1.0	4	*2019-10914* 2019-13470
	4.2.1 - 4.3.0	6	*No high-severity CVE referenced*
NSS	3.39 - 3.40	4	2019-17006 2019-17007 2020-12403 2020-25648 2021-43527
	3.41 - 3.78	4	*2019-17006 2019-17007 2020-12403 2020-25648 2021-43527*
OpenSSL	1.1.1a - 1.1.1n	4	*2020-1967 2020-1971 2021-3449 2021-3711 2022-0778* 2022-1292
	3.0.0 - 3.0.2	4	*2022-0778 2022-1473* 2022-1292
wolfSSL	3.15.5 - 4.0.0	7	2019-11873 and all the ones in the next row
	4.1.0 - 4.6.0	7	*2019-15651 2019-16748 2019-18840* 2021-38597 2022-25640
	4.7.0 - 4.8.1	7	*2021-38597* 2022-25640
	5.0.0 - 5.1.1	7	2022-23408 2022-25640
	5.2.0	6	*No high-severity CVE referenced*

Separating these 13 classes only requires sending 8 distinguishing sequences:

```
CloseNotify                        ClientHello,Certificate
ClientHello,Certificate            ClientHello,Finished,CloseNotify
ClientHello,ClientHello            ClientHello,EmptyCertificate,CertificateVerify
ClientHello,CloseNotify            ClientHello,EmptyCertificate,InvalidCertificateVerify
```

8.2   Advantages and Limitations of the Approach

We believe such fingerprints are rather robust, since they rely on the way TLS
stacks handle messages at their core, and not on easily customizable parameters
such as the list of supported ciphersuites.

However, there exists configuration parameters that can impact the structure
of the state machine. We already handle several of them, such as server-requested
client certificate authentication or TLS 1.3 middlebox compatibility (which consists in sending useless ChangeCipherSpec messages), but other features might
affect the accuracy of our tool, such as the renegotiation mechanisms, which we
leave to future work.

9   Related Work

State Machine Learning. Several methods have been used to analyze TLS implementations. In 2014, Kikuchi discovered the EarlyCCS vulnerability trying to prove state-machine-level properties using a proof assistant [18]. This approach does however not scale well, considering the huge work required to properly model the protocol.

Juraj Somorovsky presented TLS-Attacker [27], a framework for evaluating the security of TLS implementations. TLS-Attacker allows to forge customized TLS message sequence. It was successfully used to uncover several vulnerabilities in TLS libraries such as OpenSSL, Botan and matrixssl.

On its own, TLS-Attacker does not do state machine learning. It was nevertheless used as the mapper by van Thoor et al. [28] with `statelearner` to infer TLS 1.3 state machines in 2018. With regards to our work, the study has several limitations: it only covers an internet draft of TLS 1.3, was only run on a few OpenSSL and wolfSSL servers, and included a less rich vocabulary.

Beurdouche et al. [4], developed a tool, FlexTLS, and proposed a method to test the behavior of mainstream TLS stacks against deviant traces consisting in removing or adding messages from valid traces. They uncovered many bugs in different TLS stacks, including the EarlyCCS vulnerability discussed above and the infamous FREAK attack (Factoring `RSA_EXPORT` Keys). Tarun et al. [29] also used FlexTLS on Microsft SChannel, and they found bugs and vulnerabilities, including loops as those described in Sect. 7.2. By comparison, our approach is more exhaustive, with regards to the used input vocabulary and under the assumption equivalence queries are properly approximate. Moreover, FlexTLS was not updated to be compatible with TLS 1.3.

De Ruiter and Poll used L* in 2015 to infer TLS state machines for different TLS servers [24]. They discovered various anomalies and security issues. Our work builds on their results, since their study only covered server state machines and predates TLS 1.3.

Active learning methods have also been applied to other protocols and problems. In his thesis, Bossert developed `pylstar` and used it to reverse-engineer communication protocols between a malware and its server [7]. He also studied the behavior of HTTP/2 clients to allow for robust fingerprinting [8]. Fiterau-Brostean et al. applied model learning to SSH implementations [12] in 2017 and DTLS implementations [11] in 2020. In 2019, de Rasool et al. used `learnlib` (the library used by `statelearner`) to study Google's QUIC protocol [22].

Finally, Henrix et al. [15] explored parallelization and checkpointing to improve inference performance in `learnlib`. We did not investigate parallelism at the inference level since we could more easily parallelize our experiments with no complexity added. However, we believe checkpointing is promising, and we plan to explore instrumented active learning in our future work, not only for performance improvements, but also to characterize more precisely the SUT's internals in dangerous states.

TLS Fingerprinting. To identify a TLS client, Husák et al. [16] used the list of ciphersuites proposed by the client to fingerprint TLS stacks. The idea has been generalized by Kotzias et al. and by Frolov and Wustrow [13,19] to include other fields of the `ClientHello` to fingerprint the client. The method was applied successfully to detect malware, censorship circumvention tools and web browsers. Salesforce proposed two formats to capture the idea: JA3 for passive fingerprinting and JARM for active fingerprinting.[8]

Durumeric et al. [10] presented the impact of HTTPS interception on security. They identified the nature of the client by identifying a mismatch between the HTTPS User-Agent header and TLS client behavior (supported ciphersuites, declared extensions).

Janssen et al. [17] proposed an approach similar to ours to fingerprint TLS servers, with a tool called `tlsprint`,[9] based on state machines inferred with `statelearner`. However, the studied stacks are limited to `OpenSSL` and `mbedTLS` servers without TLS 1.3 support. Furthermore, we observed that `tlsprint` had a non-deterministic behavior against several OpensSSL stacks from our testbed.

We believe our work on state-machine fingerprinting can be more robust than ciphersuite-based fingerprinting, since the latter behavior can usually be configured, whereas the former is based on behaviors that are fundamentally representative of the studied stack.

10   Conclusion

Using our platform containing more than 400 stacks representing various versions of open source projects and our methodology, we could reproduce known bugs on TLS stacks, as well as uncover new implementation errors, including security vulnerabilities such as authentication bypasses or possible denial-of-service vectors. Moreover, since the state machine we infer are sufficiently precise to spot differences between implementation families, this supports the concept of state-machine-based fingerprinting, an alternative to the more classical approach based on ciphersuite-based fingerprinting, which offer a more robust characterization.

To the best of our knowledge, our work is the most extensive and systematic application of model learning to an important corpus of TLS implementations.

Overall, we believe that these deviations from the standard, even when they do not lead to exploitable security vulnerabilities, are detrimental to the overall quality of the implementation. They represent an unnecessary complexity that

---

[8] https://github.com/salesforce/ja3 and https://github.com/salesforce/jarm.
[9] https://github.com/tlsprint/tlsprint.

has been known to facilitate the introduction of security issues in the future when features are added. To reduce these deviations (and to limit fingerprinting opportunities), standards should produce more formal definitions of the expected state machines in future specifications.

Beyond TLS, other protocols could benefit from our methodology. In particular, lowering the time required to infer a state machine allow us to explore more complex protocols with a rich input vocabulary, such as the recently standardized QUIC protocol.

Since our tools have been published as open-source software, we hope our work can help build a common test-bed for the community where we can compare and improve different approaches and tools.

A   Platform Architecture

In our platform, a TLS stack is defined as a container running at least one of the following scripts: run_server, which launches a TLS server, ready to be sollicited; run_client, which starts a so-called trigger server, a service listening to signals from the inference tool, so a TLS client can be spawned each time we want to test a message sequence. Table 4 lists the TLS stacks currently included.

Figure 3 in Sect. 4 describes a typical run of our platform to infer a client state machine.[10] First, we start a client container running the trigger script (step 1). Then, we start our inference tool containing the L* engine (the Learner) and the TLS Mapper (step 2).

Each time the algorithm needs to learn from the System Under Test (the TLS client) using a sequence of messages, it first resets the client (step 3), which spawns a fresh TLS client in the client container (step 4). This client establishes a TCP connection to the TLS server within the harness (step 5) and sends its ClientHello. From now on, the L* engine drives the Mapper by transmitting abstract messages to send to the client (step 6). The harness concretizes those messages and sends them to the client (step 7). In return, the concrete answer from the client (step 8) are abstracted by the harness (step 9).

Steps 3 to 9 are repeated until the L* engine is able to produce a valid hypothesis regarding the client state machine, that is to generate an automaton accurately describing the client behavior (step 10).

---

[10] Inferring a server works in a similar, but simpler, way. Indeed, we can simply start the server and have the inference tool open a connection for each sequence to test.

Table 4. List of TLS stacks included in our platform.

Stack name	Versions	Client	Server	Comments
OpenSSL	0.9.8m - 1.0.0t (41)	✓	✓	Only TLS 1.0
	1.0.1a - 1.1.0l (53)	✓	✓	Only TLS 1.0 and 1.2
	1.1.1a - 1.1.1n (14)	✓	✓	
	3.0.0 - 3.0.2 (3)	✓	✓	
curl+OpenSSL	1.0.0a - 1.0.0t (20)	✓		Only TLS 1.0
	1.0.1a - 1.1.0l (53)	✓		Only TLS 1.0 and 1.2
	1.1.1a - 1.1.1n (14)	✓		
	3.0.0 - 3.0.2 (3)	✓		
GnuTLS	3.6.16 - 3.7.2 (4)	✓	✓	
curl+GnuTLS	3.6.16 - 3.7.2 (4)	✓		
mbedtls	1.3.10 - 1.4 (17)	✓	✓	Only TLS 1.0
	2.0.0 - 3.0.0p1 (96)	✓	✓	Only TLS 1.0 and 1.2
wolfssl	3.12.0 - 3.14.4 (10)	✓	✓	Only TLS 1.0 and 1.2
	3.15.5 - 5.2.0 (20)	✓	✓	
curl+wolfssl	3.12.0 - 3.14.4 (10)	✓		Only TLS 1.0 and 1.2
	3.15.5 - 5.1.1 (20)	✓		
matrixssl	3.7.2 (1)		✓	Only TLS 1.0
	4.0.0 - 4.3.0 (7)		✓	
NSS	3.15 - 3.38	✓	✓	Only TLS 1.0 and 1.2
	3.39 - 3.78	✓	✓	
erlang	20.0 (1)		✓	Only TLS 1.0
	24.0.3 - 24.2.1 (2)		✓	
fizz	2021.02 - 2021.06	✓		Only TLS 1.3 Weekly snapshots

B   List of the Studied Vulnerabilities

This appendix lists the vulnerabilities we studied during our work. New vulnerabilities uncovered during our study are tagged "New". Previously known vulnerabilities are tagged with one of the following status. "Not Reproduced" means we could not reproduce the issue, either because we did not include the vulnerable stack or because of a limitation in our approach (e.g. the absence of a given abstract mesage); "Detected" means the infered state machine shows an unexpected transition related to the vulnerability; "Reproduced" means that the infered state machines provides evidence that the vulnerability is present and can be exploited, should the state machine be accurate.

Since we only focus on TLS 1.0 to 1.3 versions, we do not investigate several vulnerabilities such as DROWN [3], a cryptographic attack using flaws (including state machine bugs) in SSLv2 servers to recover TLS-encrypted plaintext.

B.1 Unexpected Loops

CVE #	Stack	Versions	Description	Status
2020-12457	wolfSSL	≤ 4.4.0	Reproduced	TLS 1.2 server DoS
-	erlang	24.0	New	Default configuration allow for TLS server DoS
2022-25639	matrixSSL	4.0 - 4.3	New	TLS server DoS
-	fizz	2021 snapshots	New	Unexpected client loops
pending	NSS	3.15 - 3.78	New	TLS 1.0 to 1.2 server DoS

B.2 Authentication Bypasses

CVE #	Stack	Versions	Status	Comments
2014-0224	OpenSSL	≤ 0.9.8za ≤ 1.0.0l ≤ 1.0.1h	Detected	EarlyCCS (unexpected CCS transitions)
2015-0204	OpenSSL	≤ 0.9.8zc ≤ 1.0.0o ≤ 1.0.1j	Detected	FREAK (client- and server-side EXPORT RSA downgrade)
2015-0205	OpenSSL	≤ 1.0.0p ≤ 1.0.1j	Not Reproduced	Client auth. bypass. Requires DH certificate support
2020-24613	wolfSSL	≤ 4.4.0	Reproduced	TLS 1.3 server auth. bypass
2021-3336	wolfSSL	≤ 4.6.0	New	TLS 1.3 server auth. bypass
2022-25638	wolfSSL	≤ 5.1.0	New	TLS 1.3 server auth. bypass
2022-25640	wolfSSL	≤ 5.1.0	New	TLS 1.3 client auth. bypass

B.3 Bleichenbacher Padding Oracles

The vulnerabilities described here affect TLS servers offering RSA key exchange (removed in TLS 1.3). At the state-machine level, a vulnerable stack exhibits a state where outgoing edges labeled with well-formed and wrongly-formed messages can be distinguished. Using a dedicated scenario including such malformed messages, we reproduced existing vulnerability, but we did not find any new bugs.

CVE #	Stack	Versions	Status	Comments
2016-0800	OpenSSL	≤ 1.0.1t ≤ 1.0.2f	Not Reproduced	Requires SSLv2 messages
2016-6883	matrixSSL	≤ 3.8.2	Reproduced	
2017-13099	wolfSSL	≤ 3.12.2	Reproduced	ROBOT attack [6]
2017-1000385	Erlang	20.0	Reproduced	ROBOT attack [6]

References

1. Adrian, D., et al.: Imperfect forward secrecy: how Diffie-Hellman fails in practice. In: Proceedings of the 22nd ACM SIGSAC Conference on Computer and Communications Security, pp. 5–17 (2015)
2. Angluin, D.: Learning regular sets from queries and counterexamples. Inf. Comput. **75**(2), 87–106 (1987)
3. Aviram, N., et al.: DROWN: breaking TLS with SSLv2. In: 25th USENIX Security Symposium (2016)

4. Beurdouche, B., et al.: A messy state of the union: taming the composite state machines of TLS. In: IEEE Symposium on Security and Privacy, SP, pp. 535–552 (2015)
5. Biondi, P.: Packet generation and network based attacks with Scapy. In: CanSecWest Applied Security Conference (2005)
6. Böck, H., Somorovsky, J., Young, C.: Return of Bleichenbacher's oracle threat (ROBOT). In: 27th USENIX Security Symposium, pp. 817–849 (2018)
7. Bossert, G.: Exploiting semantic for the automatic reverse engineering of communication protocols. Ph.D. thesis, MATISSE (2014)
8. Bossert, G.: Comparison and attacks against HTTP2. In: Symposium sur la Sécurité des Technologies de l'Information et de la Communication (2016)
9. Chow, T.S.: Testing software design modeled by finite-state machines. IEEE Trans. Softw. Eng. **4**(3), 178–187 (1978)
10. Durumeric, Z., et al.: The security impact of HTTPS interception. In: 24th Annual Network and Distributed System Security Symposium, NDSS (2017)
11. Fiterau-Brostean, P., Jonsson, B., Merget, R., de Ruiter, J., Sagonas, K., Somorovsky, J.: Analysis of DTLS implementations using protocol state fuzzing. In: 29th USENIX Security Symposium, pp. 2523–2540 (2020)
12. Fiterau-Brostean, P., Lenaerts, T., Poll, E., de Ruiter, J., Vaandrager, F.W., Verleg, P.: Model learning and model checking of SSH implementations. In: Proceedings of the 24th ACM SIGSOFT International SPIN Symposium on Model Checking of Software, pp. 142–151 (2017)
13. Frolov, S., Wustrow, E.: The use of TLS in censorship circumvention. In: 26th Annual Network and Distributed System Security Symposium, NDSS (2019)
14. Fujiwara, S., von Bochmann, G., Khendek, F., Amalou, M., Ghedamsi, A.: Test selection based on finite state models. IEEE Trans. Softw. Eng. **17**(6), 591–603 (1991)
15. Henrix, M., Tretmans, J., Jansen, D., Vaandrager, F.: Performance improvement in automata learning. Master's thesis. Radboud University (2018)
16. Husák, M., Čermák, M., Jirsík, T., Čeleda, P.: HTTPS traffic analysis and client identification using passive SSL/TLS fingerprinting. EURASIP J. Inf. Secur. **2016**(1), 1–14 (2016). https://doi.org/10.1186/s13635-016-0030-7
17. Janssen, E., Vaandrager, F., de Ruiter, J., Poll, E.: Fingerprinting TLS implementations using model learning. Master's thesis. Radboud University (2021)
18. Kikuchi, M.: How I discovered CCS injection vulnerability (CVE-2014-0224) (2014). http://ccsinjection.lepidum.co.jp/blog/2014-06-05/CCS-Injection-en/index.html
19. Kotzias, P., Razaghpanah, A., Amann, J., Paterson, K.G., Vallina-Rodriguez, N., Caballero, J.: Coming of age: a longitudinal study of TLS deployment. In: Proceedings of the Internet Measurement Conference, IMC, pp. 415–428 (2018)
20. Lázló, L.: Random walks on graphs: a survey, combinatorics, Paul Erdos is eighty. Bolyai Soc. Math. Stud. **2** (1993)
21. Radhakrishna, A., et al.: DroidStar: callback typestates for Android classes. In: Proceedings of the 40th International Conference on Software Engineering, ICSE 2018, Gothenburg, Sweden, 27 May–03 June 2018, pp. 1160–1170 (2018)
22. Rasool, A., Alpár, G., de Ruiter, J.: State machine inference of QUIC. CoRR abs/1903.04384 (2019)
23. Rescorla, E.: The transport layer security (TLS) protocol version 1.3. RFC 8446 (Proposed Standard) (2018)
24. de Ruiter, J., Poll, E.: Protocol state fuzzing of TLS implementations. In: 24th USENIX Security Symposium, pp. 193–206 (2015)

25. Shahbaz, M., Groz, R.: Inferring Mealy machines. In: Cavalcanti, A., Dams, D.R. (eds.) FM 2009. LNCS, vol. 5850, pp. 207–222. Springer, Heidelberg (2009). https://doi.org/10.1007/978-3-642-05089-3_14

26. Shu, G., Lee, D.: A formal methodology for network protocol fingerprinting. IEEE Trans. Parallel Distrib. Syst. **22**(11), 1813–1825 (2011)

27. Somorovsky, J.: Systematic fuzzing and testing of TLS libraries. In: Proceedings of the 2016 ACM SIGSAC Conference on Computer and Communications Security. pp. 1492–1504 (2016)

28. van Thoor, J., de Ruiter, J., Poll, E.: Learning state machines of TLS 1.3 implementations. Bachelor thesis. Radboud University (2018)

29. Yadav, T., Sadhukhan, K.: Identification of bugs and vulnerabilities in TLS implementation for windows operating system using state machine learning. In: Thampi, S.M., Madria, S., Wang, G., Rawat, D.B., Alcaraz Calero, J.M. (eds.) SSCC 2018. CCIS, vol. 969, pp. 348–362. Springer, Singapore (2019). https://doi.org/10.1007/978-981-13-5826-5_27

PanoptiCANs - Adversary-Resilient Architectures for Controller Area Networks

Bogdan Groza[1(✉)], Lucian Popa[1], Tudor Andreica[1], Pal-Stefan Murvay[1], Asaf Shabtai[2], and Yuval Elovici[2]

[1] Faculty of Automatics and Computers, Politehnica University Timisoara, Timisoara, Romania
{bogdan.groza,lucian.popa,tudor.andreica,pal-stefan.murvay}@aut.upt.ro
[2] Ben-Gurion University of the Negev, Beersheba, Israel
{shabtaia,elovici}@bgu.ac.il

Abstract. Inspired by Jeremy Bentham's *panopticon*, i.e., an institutional building design in which a single security guard is able to monitor all detainees while they are unable to tell if they are being watched, we design the PanoptiCANs—a series of adversary-resilient CAN bus architectures. While DoS attacks are impossible to prevent on a regular bus topology, the PanoptiCANs are able to actively respond to them, as well as to generic attacks, by air gapping the network. The proposed modifications allow a bus guardian to monitor and isolate intruders on the bus while all traffic is redirected so that legitimate nodes carry on their tasks without significant disturbances. A decentralized version delegates these abilities to regular nodes, reducing costs and wire lengths, while also being able to localize and isolate the intruders much faster. We prove the effectiveness of the proposed topologies on an experimental setup with automotive grade controllers and collected in-vehicle traffic data. With the most effective architecture, intruders are isolated in a few milliseconds following single frame injections.

1 Introduction and Motivation

Starting with the security incidents reported almost a decade ago [1–3], cars and the Controller Area Network (CAN) bus, in particular, have become an engaging research subject for security professionals. The CAN bus is the most widely-used in-vehicle communication layer with a history that spans over more than three decades. BOSCH, the original designer of CAN, started to work on CAN-FD since 2011 [4]. This extension is now available and increases the bandwidth of CAN and the size of its frames. More recently, in 2018, the CAN in Automation (CiA) association of users and manufacturers started the specification for CAN XL [5], a layer which extends the bandwidth even further. So it is clear that the CAN bus is here to stay and will be present in cars and various industries for the decades that follow. The modifications proposed in this work are compatible with future extensions of CAN and may be adapted for different electrical specifications.

There are several attack entry points that have to be considered in modern cars: adversaries may remotely corrupt an existing in-vehicle unit, tap the bus

V. Atluri et al. (Eds.): ESORICS 2022, LNCS 13556, pp. 658–679, 2022.
https://doi.org/10.1007/978-3-031-17143-7_32

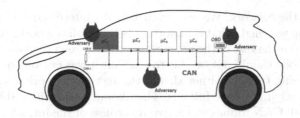

Fig. 1. Addressed setting: adversarial actions on CAN bus

at some location that is more accessible and, much more commonly, connect to an available interface such as the OBD port. Figure 1 suggests such scenarios by depicting a CAN bus inside a car and several adversaries. In response to this, there have been many efforts to secure the CAN bus, e.g., a brief summary can be found in [6]. The large majority of these works target either the introduction of some cryptographic payload in the frame or the development of intrusion detection systems that may separate between legitimate and adversarial traffic. We briefly enumerate some solutions in the related works section.

In-vehicle networks are heterogeneous, that is, both low and high-end controllers are present which makes it difficult to design solutions that can be ported on all devices that are plugged to the bus. In this context, intruder isolation, by air gaping the network with active relays and creating a physical separation between bus segments, is highly efficient in preventing attacks. Also, Denial-of-Service (DoS) cannot be stopped at all without such modifications as DoS prevention depends on the topology. With or without cryptography or intrusion detection systems in place, there is no way to prevent DoS attacks on CAN buses as long as a bus topology is employed since all nodes have unrestricted access to the communication medium. This not only allows a malicious node to send high-priority frames, but it also empowers malicious nodes to manipulate frames sent by other legitimate nodes with the goal of increasing their error counters and placing them into a bus-off state. Ultimately, a malicious node can keep the bus in a dominant state causing a complete blackout and no node will be able to send legitimate frames. The only way to prevent DoS attacks on the CAN bus is by architectural changes which already been suggested in [7]. But such changes have to be done in a clever way so that the great advantages of a bus topology are not lost. Notably, the bus topology is cheap to implement and makes it easy to install nodes by simply plugging them to the wires. This is what made CAN the most desirable communication interface for in-vehicle networks and simply changing the bus topology to a star topology may not be so appealing (not to mention that it turns the central gateway into a single point of failure).

The PanoptiCAN: concept and design. Designed by Jeremy Bentham in the 18-th century [8], the *panopticon* (from Greek *panoptes*, i.e., all-seeing) is an institutional building that allows a single security guard to observe all detainees in the building while they are unable to tell whether they are being watched. Similarly, in a PanoptiCAN, the Bus Guardian (a trusted device attached to the bus) is able to monitor traffic and isolate each node by using active relays that change the topology of the network. We are not specifically interested that nodes remain unaware of being watched, what is important is that isolated nodes are still able to receive traffic from the rest of the network in order to keep the vehicle functional. In principle, a node should not be able to tell that it was cut-out from the bus by analyzing incoming traffic, neither should the rest of the nodes, since incoming traffic will perfectly mimic the full bus. This should be interpreted in a constructive sense, i.e., all CAN frames will arrive regardless of the intruder intervention. It is out of scope for this work if the adversary or legitimate nodes can decide whether such isolation took place based on physical characteristics, i.e., voltage levels [9], clock skews [10], or other fine-grained characteristics. Addressing this issue would lead to unnecessary complications. It does not seem to matter much if the adversary knows that it is isolated and the same holds for legitimate ECUs (Electronic Control Units) for which this is irrelevant as long as they receive the rest of the CAN packets and are able to deliver their own legitimate packets in time. Consequently, what maters is that the intrusion is observed, isolated, and all legitimate traffic remains largely unaltered, reaching its destination. The main advantage of our construction is that we can preserve all existing in-vehicle functionalities unaltered as all legitimate ECUs will have access to all in-vehicle traffic. In the decentralized version of the PanoptiCAN we renounce on the Bus Guardian in order to simplify wiring. In this case, the legitimate nodes are empowered to isolate the intruder and reconstruct traffic in other parts of the network. We keep the Bus Guardian optional in this version.

To put our contribution into context, in Fig. 2 we provide a simplified view of some network configurations for CAN: the commonly employed bus topology (i), a star topology (ii), the recently proposed DoS-resilient topology [7] of CANARY (iii) and the PanoptiCAN (iv) along with its distributed version with (v) and without a Bus Guardian (vi) which are the contributions of this work. To clarify the context, we now briefly discuss the advantages and disadvantages of these topologies. Controller Area Networks usually follow a bus topology. Star topologies have been commonly suggested as an alternative to increase the resilience of CAN [11–13], e.g., they do not allow a DoS to propagate over the bus, but they are more expensive, they introduce a single point of failure and they cannot retrofit existing vehicles. A newly suggested option, CANARY [7], allows dynamic topology changes by using active relays. In principle, CANARY is a mixed bus-ring topology where a Bus Guardian taps the two bus ends and bridges between the left and right sides of the network. Although from [7] CANARY may give the impression of a star topology, the lines running from the Bus Guardian to the relays are not CAN bus wires that carry data, but regular copper wires that carry a voltage signal that triggers the relays, and thus, the network topology is still a bus. A ring topology is formed by the Bus Guardian which links the left and right sides of the network. To these existing topologies, we add three more powerful topologies: the PanoptiCAN and its decentralized versions with or without the Bus Guardian. The PanoptiCAN is a mixed bus-star topology since the Bus Guardian taps the bus in several points that allow him to record/replay traffic. The decentralized version of the PanoptiCAN is a mixed bus-daisy-chain topology which does not require a Bus Guardian and greatly simplifies wiring, thus reducing costs, but also improves on

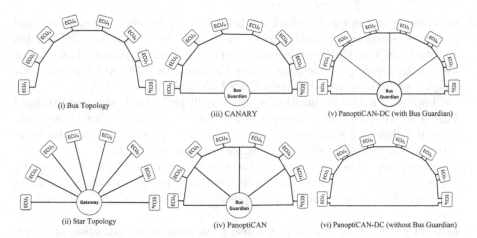

Fig. 2. Simplified view of some existing/proposed topologies for CAN: (i) bus, (ii) star, (iii) CANARY, (iv) PanoptiCAN, (v) PanoptiCAN-DC with a bus guardian, and (vi) PanoptiCAN-DC without a bus guardian

Table 1. Advantages and disadvantages of existing topologies, CANARY and the PanoptiCANs

Topology	Operating principle	Advantages	Disadvantages
Regular Bus	Nodes wired to the same line	Cheap and easy to deploy	No intruder isolation, DoS vulnerable
Regular Star	Nodes wired to a gateway	Good node isolation (DoS resilient)	Expensive gateways, require one channel for each node, more wires
CANARY	Cut bus segments and/or load-balance the network in case of attacks	Can isolate intruders, DoS resilient, can retrofit existing networks	More difficult/expensive wiring, requires bus guardian
PanoptiCAN	Bus guardian isolates/monitors each node in case of attacks	Can isolate intruders, DoS resilient, can retrofit existing networks	More difficult/expensive wiring, requires a bus guardian
PanoptiCAN-DC	Nodes locally switch the bus to a daisy-chain topology	Can isolate intruders, DoS resilient, simple wiring, distributed, bus guardian optional	Requires one additional transceiver for each node

intrusion localization speed, all these at the cost of an additional transceiver for each node which is inexpensive. In the light of the above, Table 1 provides a brief summary on the operation principles, advantages and disadvantages of the discussed architectures. Briefly, CANARY and the PanoptiCANs provide a switchable topology that is resilient to DoS and many other types of attacks. The decentralized version of the PanoptiCAN improves significantly in terms of localization speed and wiring requirements.

Summary of Contributions. Briefly, our work contributes in five relevant directions with respect to existing works:

1. we propose several switchable architectures that are resilient to adversary attacks and which are more effective than previous approaches, i.e., the PanoptiCAN and its decentralized version PanoptiCAN-DC,

2. we improve on the wirings which are both difficult to manage inside cars and nonetheless expensive, this improvement is both in the way we wire the *bus canaries*, i.e., the double relay-resistor structure initially proposed by [7], but also in the topology of the decentralized PanoptiCAN-DC which requires far simpler wirings compared to both CANARY and PanoptiCAN,
3. we improve on the localization speed significantly with the decentralized PanoptiCAN-DC which is capable to localize the adversary almost instantaneously following a single frame injection without needing the Bus Guardian intervention to probe the network and locate the intrusion,
4. we specifically focus on preventing the more insidious DoS attack caused by *error inflicting adversaries* that modify legitimate frames to lead sender nodes into Bus-off and also account for the possibility of *multiple adversaries* on the bus,
5. last but not least, by this work we also push more in the direction of *adversary resilient topologies* that *react* on adversarial actions, opening road for protecting vehicles against intrusions by actively air gapping the networks.

The rest of the paper is organized as follows. In Sect. 2 we present some basics on CAN buses and discuss related works. Section 3 introduces the design that we propose for the PanoptiCAN and one immediate simplification which greatly reduces wiring costs. Then in Sect. 4 we present the evaluation scenarios we consider and Sect. 5 contains the experimental results. Finally, Sect. 6 holds the conclusion of our work.

2   Background and Related Works

In this section we introduce some basic background on CAN buses and discuss related works on attack and countermeasures for CAN.

2.1   CAN Basics

The physical layer of the CAN bus consists in two differential lines linked at the ends with 120Ω termination resistors as illustrated in the left side of Fig. 3. The CAN protocol supports bit rates of up to 1Mbps using frames with a specific layout. The frame starts with an arbitration field of 11 bits (or 29 bits in extended frames), contains a payload which is up to 64 bits (or up to 512 bits in CAN-FD) and a 15-bit CRC (or up to 21 bits in CAN-FD). All nodes communicating on the bus must comply with the error management mechanism required by the standard to assure undisturbed communication in the presence of faulty transmitters or receivers. For this, there are two counters, TEC (transmit error counter) and REC (receive error counter), incremented each time a CAN error is observed or decremented after a frame is successfully received. The detection of a frame transmission error is signaled by the transmitter or receivers using error frames which consist in 6 consecutive dominant bits for active error flags or 6 consecutive recessive bits for passive error flags. These flags violate the specified

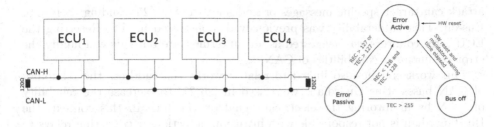

Fig. 3. Basic depiction of a CAN bus (left) and the CAN error state machine (right)

stuffing rule, notifying in this way all nodes of the error. Nodes can be in one of the three defined error states: error active, error passive and bus-off. If the TEC and REC counters are both lower than 128, the node is in the error active state and can transmit active error flags. If at least one of the counters is greater than 127 the node is in the error passive state and can transmit only passive error flags. If the TEC counter is greater than 255, the node will disconnect from the bus, entering in a Bus-off state. The right side of Fig. 3 shows the CAN error states and transition conditions. It is notable to mention that the error management mechanism was exploited to force legitimate ECUs in Bus-off [14] or as a defense measure against adversarial ECUs [15].

2.2 Related Works

Since the CAN bus does not include sender authentication or other security mechanisms by default, nodes which are communicating on CAN are vulnerable to several types of attacks. Vulnerabilities exposed by [2,3] or more recently [16,17] and many others showed that messages from genuine ECUs can be easily spoofed or that adversarial frames can be injected from remote in order to take control of critical vehicle functionalities. Authenticating incoming data has been proposed by numerous works and recently by industry standards, e.g., AUTOSAR [18,19], etc.

However, even if security is in place and intrusions are detected, there is still room for DoS attacks due to the wired-AND behaviour of the CAN bus. The simplest form of DoS attack, mentioned as early as the work in [20], exploits the CAN arbitration mechanism by continuously sending frames with high priority which hinders legitimate transmissions. A partial solution against DoS attacks is the use of ID-hopping techniques which modify frame identifiers/priorities through a secure procedure. This was first proposed by Humayed and Luo [21] which used a software-based implementation while a dedicated CAN controller which provides increased ID entropy was proposed in [22]. The use of ordered encryption for the same purpose was recently suggested in [23]. This type of solutions will not work against an adversary that disrupts legitimate frames or which writes the highest priority ID, i.e., 0×00, on the bus. Such specialized attacks were more recently analyzed in [24] and [25] where CAN frames were manipulated to prevent correct interpretation of CAN symbols. This type of attack can target specific messages or nodes on the bus [25] sending them into Bus-off. This vulnerability was previously demonstrated in [14]. Resetting the ECU error counters was suggested as a countermeasure but this will nullify the error confinement capabilities of CAN.

Our work can be also linked to related works that address the reliability of CAN buses. Bus Guardians were used in [26,27] to increase the reliability of CAN by monitoring the electrical signal on the bus. In this context, the Bus Guardian is not responsible with intrusion detection or triggering relays to disconnect parts of the bus. The idea of using relays to disconnect sections of the CAN bus was employed in the context of fault detection [28–30] where relays were used to simulate broken wires. These works do not use *bus canaries* that maintain connectivity on the bus and do not address security countermeasures by the use of relays. So far, CANARY [7] is the only proposal that addresses DoS attacks by disconnecting bus segments with the use of a Bus Guardian which monitors the network and triggers the *bus canaries*. We have already argued in the introduction how our work improves on this and more details will follow in the next sections.

3   Design Details

This section presents the design of the PanoptiCAN and of its decentralized version which improves the intruder localization time and simplifies the wirings.

3.1   Engineering Goals

First, we underline our engineering goals. With the designs proposed in this work we mainly try to improve in two directions: reducing the relay triggering rate and reducing the wiring complexity. These are vital for practical adoption of the proposed technology.

Relay triggering will induce errors on legitimate nodes due to electrical disturbances on the bus. It has been shown in [7] that the error counters remain well below the Error Passive threshold and will never reach the Bus Off state. While this means that the solution in [7] is safe to use, it still seems preferable to keep the relay triggering rate as low as possible especially since some relays will include mechanical parts that may be damaged after repeated use. Due to the more efficient placement of relays and bus taps, the PanoptiCANs are able to isolate nodes efficiently without the need to load-balance the network as in the case of CANARY [7] where the relays need to be triggered at fast rates when performing the load-balancing defense. The PanoptiCANs do not require load balancing as the adversary can be immediately isolated, and more, PanoptiCAN-DC can isolate the adversary even faster than the regular PanoptiCAN.

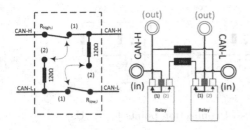

Fig. 4. The original relay schematic from CANARY [7] (left) and the actual wiring for PanoptiCAN relays (right)

Wiring is another issue. Current cars may have around 2.2 km of wires that connect hundreds of sensors and control units, according to recent estimates from the industry [31]. CANARY [7] may call only for a small fraction compared to this. But still, each extra wire induces cost and additional difficulties in mounting it inside the car. The setup used in [7] is also somewhat simpler having only 5 ECUs guarded by 8 relays, but for the PanoptiCAN, in this work, we develop a setup that is almost twice as large by using 8 ECUs and 24 relays. This could double the wiring demand, but we improve both by using a more efficient scheme for wiring the relays (discussed in the next section) as well as by a simpler design. The PanoptiCAN-DC makes the Bus Guardian optional and its wiring is much more simpler than all previous approaches. The relay structures used in CANARY [7], which we will call *bus canaries* or simply *canaries* in what follows, are a double relay-resistor pair which are capable of actively cutting adversaries from the bus, i.e., simply by splitting the bus into two or more sub-buses that are still compliant to the CAN standard which requires a 120Ω termination at the end of the lines. We use similar *bus canaries* in our work but with some wiring simplification that is more suitable for the relays that we use in our setup. During the implementation, we noticed that the resistors can be directly linked to the pins of the relays which results in a more compact *bus canary* with less wirings and a much more intuitive connection to the bus. Figure 4 contrasts between the original schematic from [7] and the wiring of the *bus canaries* from the current work. The two components are essentially identical but the new wiring from our work is much simpler and more suitable for the off-the shelf relays.

This wiring of the *bus canary* makes it much easier to generalize the schematic for a bus topology as depicted in Fig. 5. This bus-like depiction is more suitable for implementation purposes and it also shows that bus modifications are not very complicated for practice, i.e., there are two relay-resistor pairs in each location where the bus needs to be split. Having clarified the exact wiring scheme, in the exposition that follows we will switch to a simplified view of the wiring which is more intuitive. To get a more concrete image on how intruder isolation can be performed in the PanoptiCAN and PanoptiCAN-DC, Fig. 6 gives a brief overview on intruder isolation for a bus segment in case when ECU_4 becomes adversarial. The red-filled rectangles denote transceivers on the bus, while the black circles are inactive *canaries* and a cross denotes a triggered *canary*. The PanoptiCAN will use canaries R_3 and $R_{4,b}$ triggered by the Bus Guardian while the PanoptiCAN-DC will use canaries R_3 and R_5 triggered by legitimate nodes ECU_3 and ECU_5. Consequently, the PanoptiCAN will split the bus into 3 sub-

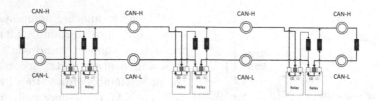

Fig. 5. Bus wiring for PanoptiCANs (4 connection points for ECUs)

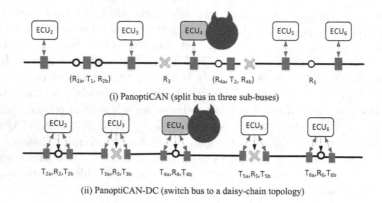

(i) PanoptiCAN (split bus in three sub-buses)

(ii) PanoptiCAN-DC (switch bus to a daisy-chain topology)

Fig. 6. Intruder isolation in the PanoptiCAN (i) and PanoptiCAN-DC (ii)

buses while the PanoptiCAN-DC will switch the bus nearby ECU_3 and ECU_5 into a daisy-chain topology.

3.2   PanoptiCAN: Topology and Procedures

Having *canaries* as a starting point, the design of the PanoptiCAN is straight-forward: each ECU is placed between two canaries and a bus tap that is linked or multiplexed to the Bus Guardian. Additionally, two transceivers are placed at the two bus ends. The left side of Fig. 7 contains a graphical depiction of an 8 ECU PanoptiCAN and can be easily extended to any number of nodes. In a network of n ECUs, i.e., $ECU_i, i = 1..n$ one *canary*, i.e., R_i, is placed after each odd numbered ECU and two *canaries* with a *tap* in the middle are placed after each even numbered ECU, i.e., $(R_{i,a}, T_{i/2}, R_{i,b})$. To isolate an odd numbered ECU, e.g., $ECU_i, i = 2k+1$, the canaries $R_{i-1,a}$ and R_i will be triggered. The only exception is ECU_1 for which only R_1 has to be triggered since it is at the beginning of the bus. Incoming traffic from odd-numbered ECUs can be recorded from bus tap $T_{(i-1)/2+1}, i = 2k+1$. To isolate an even-numbered ECU, canaries R_{i-1} and $R_{i,b}$ will be triggered. Again, the exception is the ECU at the end of the bus, even or odd, a case in which only the relay which precedes it will be triggered, i.e., $R_{i-1,*}$ (here $*$ is a placeholder which is void for even numbered ECUs and a for an odd number ECU). Traffic from even numbered ECUs will be recorded at tap $T_{i/2}$. In this topology, the Bus Guardian can efficiently determine the location

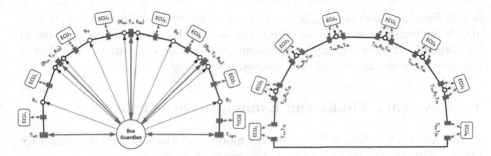

Fig. 7. A PanoptiCAN (left) and a decentralized PanoptiCAN-DC without a Bus Guardian (right) with 8 ECUs

of the adversary and isolate it by using a divide and conquer strategy, i.e., split the network in two by triggering the relay in the middle and see from which side the intrusion packets originate, etc. A simpler option is by isolating each ECU one at a time and see if the corrupted traffic originates from the corresponding ECU.

3.3 PanoptiCAN-DC: A More Efficient, Decentralized Design

The design of CANARY and PanoptiCAN share a common difficulty in wiring the Bus Guardian to each of the *canaries*. Each *canary* requires two wires to be controlled and given the placement of the *canaries* along the bus, this results in a wiring harness that is in principle equivalent to a star topology although these are not CAN wires and the number of transceivers is reduced compared to a star topology.

To further improve our concept, we introduced a decentralized version of the PanoptiCAN, which we call PanoptiCAN-DC, in which we greatly reduce the wirings by letting each node be in control of its own *canary*. This sets room for using much shorter wires between each node and the *canary* nearby. However, in this case we cannot let the nodes to simply cut the bus in their vicinity since we need traffic to further propagate between the resulting sub-buses, we need a much more clever solution for this. For this purpose we use a daisy-chain topology that will still allow each node to communicate while a DoS is no longer feasible as long as nodes will filter incoming traffic and will not propagate intruder frames further into the network. The daisy-chain topology will require an additional transceiver on each of the ECUs.

The right side of Fig. 7 shows the topology of the PanoptiCAN-DC, the decentralized version of the PanoptiCAN. The design is symmetric, each ECU has two bus taps and a *canary* in the middle, the two ECUs at left and right ends of the bus communicate on a private CAN and do not have a *canary*. For a network of n ECUs, each $\text{ECU}_i, i = 1..n$ has two transceivers, i.e., $T_{i,a}, T_{i,b}$ and one *canary*, i.e., R_i, except for ECU_1 and ECU_n. In case an intrusion occurs, each $\text{ECU}_i, i = 2..n-1$ will trigger its *canary* R_i and cut the bus at his location. Then it will filter and redirect traffic from one side to another. In this way, a DoS attack no longer propagates into the network. The Bus Guardian is optional in this design and required only to retransmit traffic from one part to the other of the network when more than one adversary is present.

4   Adversary Model and Evaluation Scenarios

In this section we discuss the adversary model and the scenarios for which we further evaluate the performance of the proposed solution.

4.1   Adversary Model

We assume the existence of an adversary that has full control over the communication channel, but we do refine this model for the specific needs of our setup. If one node becomes adversarial and all the traffic that it sends is bogus then the node will be localized and disconnected from the network. If the intruder plugs into the network in the vicinity of a legitimate node and isolating the intruder is not possible, then the best that we can do is to isolate the intruder on the segment with the legitimate node.

Two adversarial actions that were commonly considered by the literature are fuzzing the bus in which the adversary injects random CAN frames that have random IDs or data fields and replay attacks in which the adversary injects existing IDs with identical or randomized data-fields. While each node may run its own IDS and ignore attack packets, Denial of Service (DoS) attacks are much more complicated to address. Also, cryptography provides a good solution in response to first two types of attacks but it is fully ineffective against DoS attacks. As already mentioned in the introduction, a DoS can be caused either by *flooding* the bus with high priority identifiers as well as by *distorting* legitimate frames which will increase the error counters of legitimate nodes. Since these attacks are more dangerous, we focus on them in what follows.

4.2   Attack Response Capabilities

Both the PanoptiCAN and its distributed version can isolate any single ECU if it becomes corrupted. Both schemes can respond even to insidious attacks such as frame distortions (that can place legitimate ECUs into Bus-off) and check whether the attack originates on the specific ECU or has been forged from another bus segment. However, it will not be possible to separate between the legitimate ECU and the adversary as long as the adversary taps the bus on the same segment as the legitimate ECU. Such situations should be rare as physical access to vehicle wires is not so immediate (most of the attacks reported so far come from open connections such as the OBD port or from corrupted units such as vehicle telematics). Finally, if the adversary can tap the bus at any point inside the vehicle, then he may use the same connection point as the legitimate ECU making the separation impossible anyway.

Both the PanoptiCAN and its distributed version can address the case of multiple adversaries. For the PanoptiCAN, isolating multiple adversaries depends on the number of bus taps. To isolate all segments of the bus, n bus taps would be needed, which will make the PanoptiCAN capable to switch from a bus to a star topology. In our design however, we considered only $n/2$ bus taps which makes it possible to isolate at most $n/4 + 1$ adversaries. Figure 8 (i) clarifies why this is the case. If $\mathbf{Adv}_1$ is the corrupted ECU_1 then it will no longer be possible to separately isolate ECU_2 from ECU_3 since there is only one tap left, i.e., T_1, that connects to their segment. So the next adversary that can be isolated is $\mathbf{Adv}_2$ on ECU_4. The same reasoning goes further and the next adversary that can be isolated is $\mathbf{Adv}_3$ on ECU_8, i.e., $8/4 + 1 = 3$ adversaries isolated in zones Z_1, Z_2 and Z_3 as depicted in the figure. Worst case however, if we isolate adversaries at ECU_2 and ECU_7 then it is no longer possible to isolate any of the ECUs 3, 4, 5 or 6, since there is a single tap, i.e., $T2$, available. So in the worst case, $n/4$ adversaries can be isolated. Since in-vehicle networks are controlled environments and only a small number of corrupted units is expected, $n/4$ seems a good reference point. To generalize on this, Fig. 8 (ii) and (iii) explores the theoretical possibilities for the adversary locations and the amount of these which can be successfully isolated. Note that while modern vehicles may have more than 100 ECUs, these are never connected to the same bus, they are always organized in sub-networks of usually less than a dozen ECUs. We considered a network of 16–24 ECUs which is very large, usually there are less than a dozen nodes on the same bus. In this network we add 1–6 adversaries and this results in an exponential increase for the possible placements of the adversaries, i.e., up to about 5×10^7 possible locations. In theory, k adversaries may cover $\binom{n}{n-k}$ bus segments (assuming that the order of the adversaries does not matter) and $n/4$ adversaries can be configured in $\binom{n}{n/4}$ locations. But PanoptiCAN can isolate about 25% of its nodes, so up to 6 nodes can be isolated in the 24-node PanoptiCAN while the smaller 16-node PanoptiCAN can isolate up to 4 nodes.

For the distributed version, PanoptiCAN-DC, the situation is further improved. Due to the autonomous action of each node, any number of adversaries can be isolated. However, if there is no bus guardian to redirect traffic from one segment to another, two adversaries may cause a DoS that will completely cut all the bus segments in between. For example, by using Fig. 8 (i) as a reference, if ECU_2 and ECU_7 are corrupted, then they will be immediately isolated by their neighboring ECUs, but if they cause a DoS, then no traffic can be recovered from any of the ECUs 3, 4, 5 and 6. For this, a Bus Guardian may be added in the distributed version to redirect traffic. We do believe however that multiple adversaries will be rare on in-vehicle networks and the simplicity of the PanoptiCAN-DC is a much greater advantage.

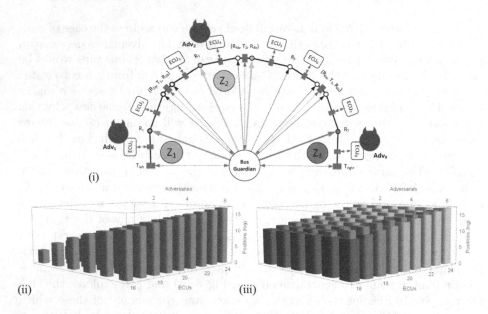

Fig. 8. Example of adversary placement and corresponding isolated zones (i), possible adversary locations (ii) and overlay with locations that can be isolated (iii) in a network with 16–24 nodes and 2–6 adversaries (the z-axis of the plot is base 2 logarithmic)

4.3   Expected Response to DoS Attacks

We now set a brief theoretical framework for understanding channel behavior in case of a DoS caused by a flooding attack on the network. We are interested in determining the localization time and the delays induced on legitimate packets before and after the adversary is isolated.

Let λ_{adv} be the arrival rate for adversarial frames on a bus which can accommodate up to λ_{bus} frames and let λ_{leg} be the rate of legitimate frames on the bus. Obviously, $\lambda_{leg} < \lambda_{bus}$ and in most real-world applications the frame rate of the bus is half of the maximum bus rate [32]. In practice, CAN buses may have a load of around several thousands frames per second. Since most practical in-vehicle deployments use a 500 kbps bandwidth and are kept below a 50% busload, a rate of around 2000 frames per second can be expected for legitimate traffic. Assuming that the adversary floods the bus with packets with higher priority, the maximum arrival rate for legitimate frames during a Dos attack is: $\lambda_{leg}^{\max} = \min(\lambda_{leg}, \lambda_{bus} - \lambda_{adv})$.

Clearly, by flooding the bus at a maximum rate, the adversary can make the maximum arrival rate for legitimate frames drop to 0. Fortunately, this happens only as long as the adversary is not yet isolated. To isolate the intruder, assuming on-event based localization, the PanoptiCAN will need $\log_2 n$ frames, since the fastest way to isolate an intruder in an n node network is by performing a binary search, while the PanoptiCAN-DC can perform the isolation following a single intruder frame, since the neighboring nodes will immediately trigger their relays when an intrusion is detected. This leads to the following localization time for the two schemes: $\Theta = \log_2 n \times \lambda_{adv}^{-1}$, $\Theta^{dc} = t_{frame}$. The isolation is thus much faster with the distributed version. The delays encountered for the two schemes during the isolation process are also distinct. For the PanoptiCAN, the intruder will share the same bus with some of the legitimate nodes until the isolation is completed, thus, some legitimate frames may not be received until this happens. The PanoptiCAN-DC has to send all frames over multiple hops of the daisy-chain, but all the legitimate frames will arrive on the bus. These are expressed in the following relations: $\Delta_{\neg isol} = \frac{t_{frame}}{h(\lambda_{bus} - \lambda_{leg} - \lambda_{adv})}$, which accounts for the remaining bandwidth following existing legitimate traffic and the traffic caused by the adversary, and $\Delta_{\neg isol}^{dc} = \frac{n}{2} t_{frame}$, which accounts for the worst case in which a frame has to be retransmitted over $n/2$ nodes in case of the PanoptiCAN-DC. We use $\neg isol$ as a placeholder to denote that the isolation process started but the intruder is not yet isolated. Here h denotes the Heaviside step function, i.e., a zero for negative arguments or a one for positive arguments. Thus, as long as the rate of legitimate frames plus the adversary traffic exceeds the bus rate, $h(\lambda_{bus} - \lambda_{leg} - \lambda_{adv})$ will return a 0 leading to a maximum delay $\Delta_{\neg isol} = \infty$. Once the intruder is isolated, there will be at most one hop for the PanoptiCAN as well as for the PanoptiCAN-DC which leads for both schemes to a low transmission delay of twice the time of the frame, i.e., $\Delta_{isol} = 2t_{frame}$, since, in the worst case, the frame has to be retransmitted by the Bus Guardian or by the node near the intruder which is in charge of the isolation.

5   Experiments and Results

In this section we discuss experiments with the proposed defense mechanism. Due to space constraints, the full description of the experimental model that we developed is deferred to Appendix A and more experiments can be found in Appendix B.

5.1   Recorded In-Vehicle Traffic

In our experiments, we use real world in-vehicle traffic that was collected by us from a high-end vehicle. The CAN bus was set at 500 kbps, the usual bandwidth inside cars. The busload generally stayed between 30–50% which is usual inside vehicles. Given that an adversary located at the bus ends would be trivial to isolate, we choose to split the legitimate traffic into two traces that are sent to the left and right sides of the bus. Thus, the 90 identifiers where split in half and allocated to the left and right side of the experimental model. The in-vehicle traffic is reproduced inside the network with Vector's VN5610A which is an industry standard tool that allows real-time retransmission of in-vehicle traffic at micro-second accuracy. Figure 9 (i) shows a brief schematic of our test setup and the in-vehicle traffic arriving on the left (ii) and right channel (iii). There are less than 50 IDs on each channel. The cycles are well preserved with a small exception of an ID on the right channel which exhibits some cycle variations.

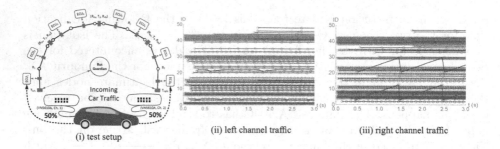

(i) test setup   (ii) left channel traffic   (iii) right channel traffic

Fig. 9. IDs from the collected in-vehicle trace arriving on the left and right channels

This is not unexpected, while most in-vehicle traffic is cyclic in nature, on-event frames may also occur. In the plots from Fig. 9 (ii) and (iii), the number of the ID represents its rank (the order of the ID based on its priority) by which it is placed on the ordinate (y-axis) to which we add the deviation of the current timestamp from the previous. Adding this deviation makes it much easier to spot the occurrence of a DoS as the delayed ID appear higher on the plot. For each ID, the abscissa (x-axis) is the timestamp at which it occurs (a small circle is used as a marker on the plot).

5.2   Response to DoS Attacks in the Experiments

In our testbed we broadcast legitimate in-vehicle traffic on the left and right sides of the bus as suggested in Fig. 9.

PanoptiCAN Response to DoS by Flooding. We first test the response of the system in case of a flooding caused by two nodes, i.e., a DDoS attack (we use two nodes since the related solution in [7] cannot respond to multiple adversaries). We set ECU_2 and ECU_4 to flood the bus with one high priority message sent at 1 ms. This flooding attack will cause visible delays on the rest of the frames but the bus is still around 50% free so all regular traffic is still there. Figure 10 (i) and (ii) show the comparative effects of a flooding attack on an ID with a cycle time of 10 ms and normal traffic (orange dots denote delayed frames). The CAN bus shows very good resilience, the delays induced by this flooding are very small making the arrival time of this high priority ID to deviate around 1 ms, i.e., less than 10%. Figure 10 (iii) provides the traffic visualization for 50 IDs in case of the attack, the adversary high priority IDs can be seen in magenta at the bottom of the figure. Indeed there are very little disturbances during the attack for all the IDs. As an example, the flooding attack was programmed to last for 5 s, i.e., between the 13th and the 18th second as it can be seen in Fig. 10. The PanoptiCAN can isolate the adversary in a few milliseconds as we discuss in Appendix B (the time to trigger the relays is 5 ms according to the datasheet).

When we double the number of messages sent by ECU_2 and ECU_4, i.e., 0.5 ms flooding instead of a 1 ms flooding, the effects are far more dramatic. Doubling the adversarial messages leads to one message being sent each 250μ s (this is

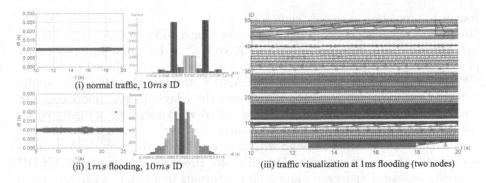

Fig. 10. Flooding effects on IDs with a cycle of 10 ms (i), (ii) and visualization for 50 IDs (iii)

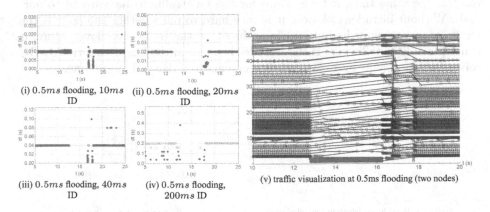

Fig. 11. DDoS effects on IDs with a cycle time of (i) 10 ms, (ii) 20 ms, (iii) 40 ms, (iv) 200 ms and visualization for 50 IDs (v)

roughly the duration of a CAN frame when the bus is set at 500 kbps). There will be little or no space at all for legitimate frames which leads to a full DoS. Figure 11 (i), (ii), (iii) and (iv) show the effects of the DDoS attack on four IDs with a cycle time of 10 ms, 20 ms, 40 ms and 200 ms. For all of them, as long as the adversary is not isolated there will be no frame that reaches the bus. Figure 11 (v) provides traffic visualization for 50 IDs in case of the 0.5 ms flooding which leads to a DoS. The effects are very similar on all IDs, only in rare situations some of them manage to enter the bus. Again however, the PanoptiCAN will easily locate the two intruders and isolate them, restoring all traffic back to normal from the 18th second onward as can be seen in Fig. 11 (v).

PanoptiCAN-DC Response to Attacks. The distributed version of the Panopti-CAN offers a much faster response to attacks since all relays will be triggered simultaneously, once an attack frame is detected, and the legitimate nodes will switch the bus to a daisy-chain topology which will no longer allow intruder

frames to propagate. The only shortcoming is that multiple adversaries can isolate the bus segments between them by performing a DDoS attack, e.g., by flooding. The same limitation occurs with CANARY [7] and it can only be solved by
placing a Bus Guardian to redirect frames from various parts of the bus as in the
regular Panopti-CAN. For the PanoptiCAN-DC the Bus Guardian will simply
redirect frames without requiring it to trigger the relays. To get a more concrete
image on frame distortion attacks, in Fig. 12 (i) we depict frames disrupted by
the adversary. By setting the last consecutive bits to more than 6 zeros, a stuff
error occurs and all nodes respond with an error flag. In this way the legitimate
node will be forced to enter the bus off state. However, the PantoptiCAN-DC
can easily isolate the adversary and frames returning to normal, as can be seen in
Fig. 12 (ii), after about 17 ms once the adversary is isolated (the time to trigger
the relays is 5 ms, but since multiple relays are triggered as the 8 nodes do not
react at the same time, it takes 17 ms for the bus traffic to be restored to normal). Without intruder isolation, it is very hard to tell whether the node is the
victim of an attack or he indeed has problems at the transceiver level. More, it
is not possible to tell where is the intruder located on the bus. PanoptiCAN-DC
solves both problems by isolating bus segments in a daisy-chain manner.

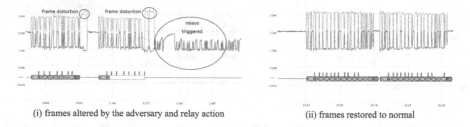

(i) frames altered by the adversary and relay action   (ii) frames restored to normal

Fig. 12. Two frames altered by the adversary followed by relay action (i) and frames
restored (ii)

6   Conclusion

Relays are able to provide an efficient active defense mechanism against generic
intrusions and DoS attacks in particular. The cost of relays is small and the
experiments prove they do not impede regular traffic if properly deployed. In this
work we provided some new conceptual architectures with relays that provide
good alternatives for intruder isolation by air-gaping CAN networks. The PanoptiCAN provides an adversary-resilient CAN bus architecture that can actively
circumvent many types of attacks, including DoS attacks which are difficult to
address due to the usual topology of CAN (bus) and its error confinement mechanism. The decentralized version of the PanoptiCAN improves significantly by
reducing wiring costs and providing a faster response to intrusions. This comes
with a slight disadvantage, i.e., less resilience in front of a DDoS attack, but

the cost reduction it offers may be more important since multi-adversary scenarios are less likely in a controlled environment such as in-vehicle networks. We thus emphasize that switchable bus daisy-chain topologies may be practical for preventing intrusions and hope that our work paves way in using such topologies.

Appendix A - Further Details on the Experimental Model

The development of our experimental model was quite a laborious work as we implemented an 8 ECU network, a realistic size for what can be found inside modern vehicles. The experimental model, which is common for the PanoptiCAN and the PanoptiCAN-DC, included 8 regular ECUs, one Bus Guardian, up to 20 MCP2551 CAN transceivers, 22 relays, 22 120Ω resistors, 14 CAN wires and additionally 200 jumper wires, all these mounted on a $1000 \times 700\,mm$ board. The exact number of components that are used in each of the network configurations is presented in Table 2. Figure 13 provides a detailed depiction of our experimental setup and a bus canary.

Appendix B - Results on an Existing CANoe Car Simulation

To give a better image on the behavior of the current solution, we also test it against adversarial actions on a car simulation in the industry standard tool CANoe. This simulation environment was also used by [33] in one of the first reported attack on CAN buses more than a decade ago and in [7] to prove functionality of relay-based isolation in CANARY. The simulation we use contains

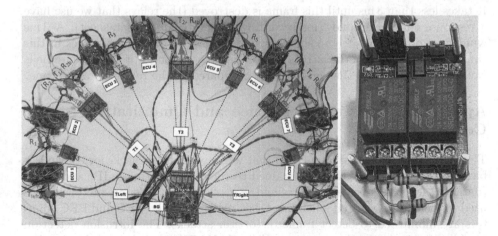

Fig. 13. The 8 ECU PanoptiCAN setup (left) and detailed view of a *bus canary* (right)

Table 2. Detailed component list for the PanoptiCAN and PanoptiCAN-DC

Component→ Setup↓	S12XE	TC277	MCP2551	Relay blocks	120 Ω resistors	CAN wires to BG	Jumper wires
PanoptiCAN	8	1	12	20	22	5	~200
PanoptiCAN-DC w/ BG	8	1	20	12	16	5	~175
PanoptiCAN-DC w/o BG	8	0	16	12	16	0	~150

two buses, one for engine functionalities, e.g., ignition, ABS, etc. and the other for the car body, e.g., doors, lights etc.

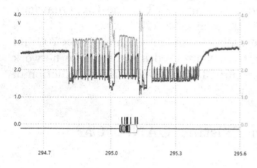

Fig. 14. Adversarial frames and relay action

CANARY reports that a load balancing speed of 50 ms is needed in order to make the signals look identical in case of a full DoS on the bus [7]. With the PanoptiCAN, there is no need to load balance the network. Once the intruder is isolated, traffic can be easily redirected. A short window of opportunity exists for the adversary until it has been localized. This window of opportunity is however too small to make the attack effective. To clarify this, we outline the response of PanoptiCAN-DC which provides the fastest reaction time. Figure 14 depicts two adversarial DoS frames arriving on the bus. The relays are triggered during the 2-th frame which is actually destroyed by the relay action and as the adversary becomes isolated from the rest of the network. It takes less than 3 ms until this frame is destroyed (the relays that we use have a response time of around 5 ms according to the technical datasheet). A 3 ms window of opportunity is too small for an adversary to cause any issues in this simulation. The time of the intrusion detection algorithm to process one frame is well under 100 μ s and thus insignificant compared to the relay operation time.

Appendix C - Attack Resilience and Quantitative Comparison

The intrusion detection system (IDS) that we implemented checks for known IDs based on a Bloom filter that was trained to recognize legitimate IDs and DLCs (datafield lengths). A specific threshold, e.g., 2000 frames/s, on the busload is used to trigger the alarm if a flooding takes place while the TEC and REC counters are monitored to detect frame distortion attacks. The intrusion detection mechism is similar to the one we used in CANARY [7] and any other mechanism can be implemented behind the PanoptiCAN. Once an intrusion frame is detected, the localization algorithm starts. In case of PanoptiCAN, this algorithm performs a binary search starting with the canary in the middle of the bus

Table 3. Brief comparison between CANARY, PanoptiCAN and PanoptiCAN-DC

Topology	Design	Retrofit	IDS	Transceivers	Canaries	Cost	DoS	DDoS	Fuz	DFuz
CANARY	Centralized	Yes	Bus Guardian	$n+2$	$n-1$	High	✓	✗	✓	✗
PanoptiCAN	Centralized	Yes	Bus Guardian	$3n/2+1$	$3n/2-2$	High	✓	✓	✓	✓
PanoptiCAN-DC	Decentralized	No	All ECUs	$2n$	$n-2$	Moderate	✓	✗	✓	✓

(which splits the bus in half) and proceeds to the left or right according to the direction where the intrusion comes from (in case the intrusion comes from both directions, then both directions are to be inspected). For PanoptiCAN-DC, there is no need to run a localization algorithm since each node will trigger its canaries turning the bus into a daisy-chain (the canaries are disabled if no intrusion is detected after a specific timeout, 5 s in our implementation).

In Table 3 we provide a brief quantitative comparison of the two switchable topologies proposed in this work with our previous work CANARY [7]. In terms of attack resilience, we separate between attacks performed by single nodes, i.e., DoS and Fuzzing (Fuz) which stands for generic injections of frames with random content, and distributed versions of them caused by multiple nodes, i.e., DDoS and DFuz. CANARY [7] is in terms of wiring cost similar to a star topology but it requires only 2 additional transceivers to tap the two bus ends, i.e., $n+2$ transceivers for n nodes. The PanoptiCAN is a bit more expensive than CANARY in terms of transceivers since the Bus Guardian will tap the bus after each two consecutive nodes, this requires $n+n/2+1$ for n nodes, but it can isolate multiple nodes and thus DDoS and DFuzzing can be prevented. Finally, the decentralized PanoptiCAN-DC requires the same number of transceivers as a regular star, but none of the complex wiring of each node to the gateway, reducing significantly the costs of wiring. Its switchable daisy-chain/bus topology allows it to isolate any number of adversaries being resilient to DFuzzing but not to DDoS (as already explained in the work).

References

1. Koscher, K., et al.: Experimental security analysis of a modern automobile. In: 2010 IEEE Symposium on Security and Privacy (SP), pp. 447–462 (2010)
2. Checkoway, S., et al.: Comprehensive experimental analyses of automotive attack surfaces. In: USENIX Security Symposium, San Francisco (2011)
3. Miller, C., Valasek, C.: A survey of remote automotive attack surfaces. Black Hat USA (2014)
4. CAN FD - The basic idea, CAN in Automation (CiA). www.can-cia.org/can-knowledge/can/can-fd/
5. Controller Area Network Extra Long (CAN XL), CAN in Automation (CiA). www.can-cia.org/can-knowledge/can/can-xl/
6. Groza, B., Murvay, P.-S.: Security solutions for the controller area network: bringing authentication to in-vehicle networks. IEEE Veh. Technol. Mag. **13**(1), 40–47 (2018)

7. Groza, B., Popa, L., Murvay, P.S., Elovici, Y., Shabtai, A.: CANARY - a reactive defense mechanism for Controller Area Networks based on Active RelaYs. In: 30th USENIX Security Symposium (2021)
8. Bentham, J.: Panopticon - a plan of management for a Panopticon penitentiary-house (1791)
9. Cho, K.-T., Shin, K.G.: Viden: attacker identification on in-vehicle networks. In: Conference on Computer and Communications Security, pp. 1109–1123. ACM (2017)
10. Cho, K.-T., Shin, K.G.: Fingerprinting electronic control units for vehicle intrusion detection. In: 25th USENIX Security Symposium (2016)
11. Barranco, M., Rodriguez-Navas, G., Proenza, J., Almeida, L.: CANcentrate: an active star topology for CAN networks. In: International Workshop on Factory Communication Systems, pp. 219–228. IEEE (2004)
12. Barranco, M., Almeida, L., Proenza, J.: ReCANcentrate: a replicated star topology for CAN networks. In: Conference on Emerging Technologies and Factory Automation, vol. 2. IEEE (2005)
13. Obermaisser, R., Kammerer, R.: A router for improved fault isolation, scalability and diagnosis in CAN. In: 2010 8th IEEE International Conference on Industrial Informatics, pp. 123–129 (2010)
14. Cho, K.-T., Shin, K.G.: Error handling of in-vehicle networks makes them vulnerable. In: Conference on Computer and Communications Security, pp. 1044–1055. ACM (2016)
15. Souma, D., Mori, A., Yamamoto, H., Hata, Y.: Counter attacks for bus-off attacks. In: Gallina, B., Skavhaug, A., Schoitsch, E., Bitsch, F. (eds.) SAFECOMP 2018. LNCS, vol. 11094, pp. 319–330. Springer, Cham (2018). https://doi.org/10.1007/978-3-319-99229-7_27
16. Nie, S., Liu, L., Du, Y.: Free-fall: hacking tesla from wireless to CAN bus. Black Hat USA (2017)
17. Nie, S., Liu, L., Du, Y., Zhang, W.: Over-the-air: how we remotely compromised the gateway, BCM, and autopilot ECUs of Tesla cars. Black Hat USA (2018)
18. Specification of Secure Onboard Communication, 4th ed., AUTOSAR (2017)
19. Specification of crypto service manager. AUTOSAR 11, r20-11 (2020)
20. Wolf, M., Weimerskirch, A., Paar, C.: Security in automotive bus systems. In: Workshop on Embedded Security in Cars. Bochum (2004)
21. Humayed, A., Luo, B.: Using ID-hopping to defend against targeted DoS on CAN. In: Proceedings of the 1st International Workshop on Safe Control of Connected and Autonomous Vehicles, NY, USA, pp. 19–26. Association for Computing Machinery (2017)
22. Wu, W., et al.: IDH-CAN: a hardware-based ID hopping CAN mechanism with enhanced security for automotive real-time applications. IEEE Access 6, 54607–54623 (2018)
23. Groza, B., Popa, L., Murvay, P.-S.: Highly efficient authentication for CAN by identifier reallocation with ordered CMACs. IEEE Trans. Veh. Technol. 69(6), 6129–6140 (2020)
24. Palanca, A., Evenchick, E., Maggi, F., Zanero, S.: A stealth, selective, link-layer denial-of-service attack against automotive networks. In: Polychronakis, M., Meier, M. (eds.) DIMVA 2017. LNCS, vol. 10327, pp. 185–206. Springer, Cham (2017). https://doi.org/10.1007/978-3-319-60876-1_9
25. Murvay, P.-S., Groza, B.: DoS attacks on controller area networks by fault injections from the software layer. In: International Conference on Availability, Reliability and Security (ARES). ACM (2017)

26. Broster, I., Burns, A.: An analysable bus-guardian for event-triggered communi-
    cation. In: 24th IEEE Real-Time Systems Symposium in RTSS 2003, pp. 410–419.
    IEEE (2003)
27. de Moraes, P., Saotome, O., Santos, M.M.D.: Trends in Bus Guardian for Auto-
    motive Communication-CAN, TTP/C and Flexray. SAE Technical Paper, Tech.
    Rep. (2011)
28. Sivencrona, H., Olsson, T., Johansson, R., Torin, J.: RedCAN/sup TM/: sim-
    ulations of two fault recovery algorithms for CAN. In: 10th IEEE Pacific Rim
    International Symposium on Dependable Computing, pp. 302–311 (2004)
29. Zhang, L., Lei, Y., Chang, Q.: Intermittent connection fault diagnosis for CAN
    using data link layer information. IEEE Trans. Ind. Electron. 64(3), 2286–2295
    (2016)
30. Zhang, L., Yang, F., Lei, Y.: Tree-based intermittent connection fault diagnosis for
    controller area network. IEEE Trans. Veh. Technol. 68(9), 9151–9161 (2019)
31. Hoff, U., Scott, D.: Challenges for wiring harness development. CAN Newsletter,
    pp. 14–19 (2020)
32. Designing a CAN network, CAN in Automation (CiA). www.can-cia.org/can-
    knowledge/can/design-can-network/
33. Hoppe, T., Kiltz, S., Dittmann, J.: Security threats to automotive CAN networks
    – practical examples and selected short-term countermeasures. In: Harrison, M.D.,
    Sujan, M.-A. (eds.) SAFECOMP 2008. LNCS, vol. 5219, pp. 235–248. Springer,
    Heidelberg (2008). https://doi.org/10.1007/978-3-540-87698-4_21

Detecting Cross-language Memory Management Issues in Rust

Zhuohua Li[1]([✉]), Jincheng Wang[1], Mingshen Sun[2], and John C. S. Lui[1]([✉])

[1] The Chinese University of Hong Kong, Shatin, Hong Kong
{zhli,jcwang,cslui}@cse.cuhk.edu.hk
[2] Hong Kong, China
bob@mssun.me

Abstract. Rust is a promising system-level programming language that can prevent memory corruption bugs using its strong type system and *ownership*-based memory management scheme. In practice, programmers usually write Rust code in conjunction with other languages such as C/C++ through Foreign Function Interface (FFI). For example, many notable projects are developed using Rust and other programming languages, such as Firefox, Google Fuchsia OS, and the Linux kernel. Although it is widely believed that gradually re-implementing security-critical components in Rust is a way of enhancing software security, however, using FFI is inherently unsafe. In this paper, we show that memory management across the FFI boundaries is error-prone. Any incorrect use of FFI may corrupt Rust's ownership system, leading to memory safety issues. To tackle this problem, we design and build FFICHECKER, an automated static analysis and bug detection tool dedicated to memory management issues across the Rust/C FFI. We evaluate our tool by checking 987 Rust packages crawled from the official package registry and reveal 34 bugs in 12 packages. Our experiments show that FFICHECKER is a useful tool to detect real-world cross-language memory management issues with a reasonable amount of computational resources.

Keywords: Static analysis · Rust · Bug detection

1 Introduction

Rust is an emerging programming language that is famous for its strong security guarantees and high performance. Many companies and open source communities have been re-writing their software in Rust in an incremental manner, i.e., while most of the source code remains intact, some security-critical components are re-written in Rust. For example, Firefox contains a considerable amount of Rust code [4], and the Linux kernel is in the process of integrating Rust as its second language for kernel development [21,30]. New Rust projects also usually integrate with third-party C/C++ libraries to avoid reinventing the wheels. Rust can be used in conjunction with other languages because it supports Foreign Function Interface (FFI), which enables Rust to call external interfaces and exchange arbitrary data.

M. Sun—Individual Researcher.

V. Atluri et al. (Eds.): ESORICS 2022, LNCS 13556, pp. 680–700, 2022.
https://doi.org/10.1007/978-3-031-17143-7_33

The incremental development of Rust code is widely believed to improve the security of software. However, calling external code is inherently unsafe in Rust because the Rust compiler cannot perform security checks across the FFI boundaries. Programmers may accidentally misuse the unsafe abilities that lead to vulnerabilities. In addition, different assumptions made by different languages make it possible for attackers to maneuver between the FFI boundaries and exploit these vulnerabilities [24]. Recent empirical studies [12,41] have shown that the incorrect use of FFI is one of the most significant causes of real-world memory-safety bugs. Even for Rust packages written in pure safe Rust (i.e., without using FFI), they may still be affected because they may depend on other packages that include FFI. According to our statistics (Sect. 2.2), among around 77,000 packages on the official Rust package registry[1], more than 72% of the packages depend on at least one package that contains unsafe FFI calls. Therefore excluding FFI is unrealistic in the current Rust ecosystem; instead, people have made lots of efforts to secure the use of FFI. For example, the Rust community has drafted several guidelines for writing unsafe code, including FFI [34,36,37,39]. Some Rust packages such as `rust-bindgen` and `safer_ffi` can automatically generate FFI, preventing developers from misusing it. However, they can only help developers to write correct interfaces with appropriate data types. Memory corruption caused by heap memory allocation/deallocation across the FFI boundaries remains an open problem. Moreover, Rust has a unique ownership system for memory management (Sect. 2.1), which creates its own paradigm of memory safety issues [22,31,41]. Hence existing works on misusing FFI for other memory-safe programming languages [19,20] such as Java and Python are no longer applicable.

In this paper, we study the security impacts of heap memory management issues across the FFI boundaries, especially those caused by the combination of Rust's ownership-based memory management and C/C++'s manual memory management. To tackle this problem, we propose to use static analysis techniques to detect potential memory management bugs across the FFI boundaries. Our method is based on the theory of Abstract Interpretation [7–9]. We design an augmented taint analysis algorithm to keep track of the states of heap memory, which captures the paradigms created by the ownership-based memory management. We implement our tool called FFICHECKER, which automatically collects all the generated LLVM intermediate representation (IR) for both Rust and C/C++ code, then performs static analysis and outputs diagnostic reports. Security analysts can then inspect the reports and determine whether there are any real bugs. Our evaluation shows that FFICHECKER can successfully detect real-world memory safety issues within acceptable time and with reasonable precision. To our knowledge, our work is the first effort that addresses the memory management issues across FFI boundaries in Rust programs.

We summarize our contributions as follows.

– We show the potential security and memory management issues when programmers intermix Rust and C/C++ via FFI.

---

[1] https://crates.io.

- We propose an augmented abstract domain that captures the memory states in the ownership-based memory management scheme.
- We design and build FFICHECKER, an automated static analyzer that can detect potential memory management bugs across the FFI boundaries in Rust packages and report informative diagnostic messages. The source code is available online[2], which can be the basis of other research in the future.
- We perform extensive evaluations in the Rust ecosystem. We evaluate 987 packages crawled from the official package registry and detect 34 bugs among 12 packages. All the detected bugs have been manually confirmed and reported to the authors and 15 of them have been fixed at the time of writing.

2   Background

In this section, we provide the background knowledge needed to understand the rest of the paper. We first introduce the Rust programming language and its security guarantees. Then we illustrate the prevalence of FFI and how Rust's memory management scheme interacts with it.

2.1   The Rust Programming Language

Rust is famous for its ability to build high-performance and secure programs. As a strongly-typed and compiled language, its rigorous type system and the unique *ownership* system enforce strict disciplines to eliminate memory safety issues. The ownership system is an automated memory management strategy derived from *linear logic* [13] and *linear types* [40]. Under the ownership system, each value has a unique *owner* (called owner variable), which keeps track of the lifetime of the value. Once the owner variable goes out of its scope, the ownership system automatically releases the memory allocated for the value. Note that the scope of each variable is determined at compile time so that the Rust compiler can insert appropriate memory reclamation routines to the generated binary. Thus neither reference counting nor garbage collection is needed. This enables Rust to build fast programs since no runtime overhead is introduced.

   To pass a value to other parts of code, one can either *copy/clone*, *move*, or *borrow* the owner variable. Copying/cloning is usually used for data types that have semantics where copying their bytes is a valid way of creating a real copy, e.g., basic data types like integers. For more complicated data types, especially those that maintain internal heap memory (e.g., vectors), Rust's assignments *move* the ownership by default. After the ownership is *moved*, due to the uniqueness of the owner, the previous owner is immediately invalidated. A value can also be *borrowed* by taking a reference of it, through which the value can be temporarily accessed without changing the ownership. The references can be either *mutable* or *immutable*. The Rust type system regulates that there are no "mutable aliases", meaning that a read-only value can be immutably referenced multiple times; when the value is writable, only one mutable reference is allowed at a time.

---

[2] https://github.com/lizhuohua/rust-ffi-checker.

The Rust compiler enforces the above rules to make security guarantees as follows. On the one hand, since the ownership system keeps track of the lifetime of each value, it ensures that the lifetime of a reference cannot exceed the value it points to. Therefore memory safety issues caused by dangling pointers such as use-after-free can be effectively prevented. On the other hand, since the ownership system eliminates mutable aliases, many security issues caused by concurrent reading/writing, such as race conditions and iterator invalidation, are avoided.

2.2 Foreign Function Interface (FFI) and Memory Management

As a system-level programming language, Rust can easily collaborate with other languages through the Foreign Function Interface (FFI). In this paper, we consider the case where the external code is written in C/C++ since this is the most common usage of FFI. Integrating Rust code with C/C++ code is prevalent and necessary because (1) Many C/C++ projects integrate Rust into existing codebases (e.g., the Linux kernel and Firefox) to enhance their security. (2) It can avoid duplicated work and benefit from the rich ecosystem of libraries written in C/C++. (3) C/C++ can be used for performance-critical scenarios.

However, since the Rust compiler cannot reason about the security of external code, calling FFI is inherently unsafe. Programmers need to explicitly use the **unsafe** keyword to bypass the security check enforced by the compiler. Therefore, using FFI is extremely error-prone. Existing studies [12,24,41] have shown that the incorrect use of FFI has become a severe source of memory safety bugs.

We would like to point out that even if programmers restrict themselves in pure safe Rust, their programs may still implicitly rely on FFI through dependencies. In fact, we find that more than 72% of packages on the official Rust package registry (crates.io) depend on at least one unsafe FFI-bindings package, as shown in Fig. 1. The data is crawled by reading the metadata of reverse dependencies[3] on crates.io. Among all the 76, 894 packages, we start from all the packages that are of category "external-ffi-bindings" (900 packages). These packages contain direct Rust FFI bindings to libraries written in other languages, often denoted by a "-sys" suffix. Then we collect all the reverse dependencies of them and repeat this process to get multi-level dependencies. As a result, the number of packages converges at the 10th level, with a total of 55, 762 packages ($55, 762/76, 894 \approx 72.52\%$). Note that the "external-ffi-bindings" category by no means includes all the FFI binding libraries since many packages' categories are not tagged properly, hence the actual percentage can only be higher.

Since the manual memory management in C/C++ is naively unsafe, in this paper, we only consider the case where the heap memory is allocated in Rust and passed to C/C++. There are two ways of passing a heap-allocated object across FFI: (1) by *borrowing* the object as a reference, (2) by *moving* the ownership to the FFI. For *borrowing* as a reference, the ownership remains on the Rust side, so the ownership system is responsible for releasing the memory after it goes out of

---

[3] As of February 14, 2022.

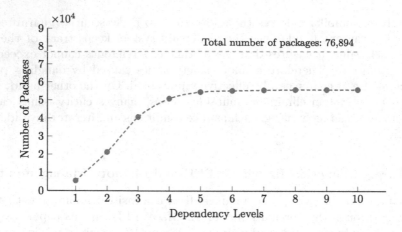

Fig. 1. Number of packages that depend on unsafe FFI

its scope. For *moving* the ownership, one can first "forget" it from the ownership system, then pass it to the FFI via a raw pointer. The Rust standard library provides several functions to "forget" an object, e.g., `std::mem::forget` and `Box::into_raw`. In this case, the responsibility of memory management returns back to the programmers, who have to take extra care because the ownership system no longer takes charge.

3   Security and Memory Management Issues via FFI

To explain why the memory management across the FFI boundaries may lead to security vulnerabilities and how the Rust ownership system gets involved, we give several bug examples detected by `FFIChecker`. We also categorize the vulnerabilities caused based on our observations: (1) common memory corruption, (2) exception safety, and (3) undefined behavior caused by mixing memory management mechanisms.

3.1   Memory Corruption

When heap memory is passed across the FFI boundaries, the ownership system cannot guarantee its safety. Therefore the responsibility of memory management returns back to the programmers, meaning that all kinds of common memory corruption bugs that happen in C, like use-after-free, double free, and memory leak, still exist. Listing 1 shows a memory leak found in package `emd`[4]. In Rust, `Box` is a smart pointer type used to securely manage heap memory. The developer uses `Box::into_raw` to expose the raw pointer of the heap memory managed by the `Box` in order to pass it to the FFI. However, after using `Box::into_raw`, the ownership system will "forget" the memory and hence will not automatically

---

[4] https://crates.io/crates/emd

reclaim it. Instead, the developer is responsible for releasing the memory previously managed by the Box. Otherwise, there will be a memory leak.

```
1    let mut cost = Vec::with_capacity(X.rows());
2    for x in X.outer_iter() {
3      let mut cost_i = Vec::with_capacity(Y.rows());  // Allocate a vector
4      for y in Y.outer_iter() {
5        cost_i.push(distance(&x, &y) as c_double);
6      }
7      // Forget the memory using `Box::into_raw`
8      cost.push(Box::into_raw(cost_i.into_boxed_slice()) as *const c_double);
9    }
10
11   // Call FFI function
12   let d = unsafe { emd(X.rows(), weight_x.as_ptr(), Y.rows(), weight_y.as_ptr(), cost.as_ptr(), null())
     ↪ };
```

Listing 1: Box::into_raw leaks memory but it is not released by the developer.

3.2   Exception Safety

Unlike many other programming languages, Rust does not support the try-catch statement for catching "exceptions". Instead, Rust provides a more reliable error handling mechanism: All *recoverable* errors must be handled or propagated back to the caller function, and all *unrecoverable* errors are handled by terminating the execution and unwinding the stack. All the stack objects' destructors will be called during the stack unwinding to prevent resource leakage. However, when passing heap memory across the FFI boundaries and cooperating with external code, developers usually have to transiently create unsound states via unsafe code (e.g., creating temporarily uninitialized data). Then after the external code finishes, developers manually clean up the states. If some error happens in between, the execution stops and the stack is unwound, so the cleanup procedure will not be executed. The remaining unsound state may cause security issues.

Listing 2 gives an example found in package libtaos[5]. At line 2, variable params is initialized by allocating heap memory. The memory is passed to FFI in the following unsafe block in lines 3–8. Note that the question mark operator (?) at lines 5 and 7 means that if the operation fails, the function returns early and propagates the error to the caller function. Therefore, the memory may be leaked if the function returns early and hence the free function at line 10 will not be called.

3.3   Mixing Memory Management Mechanisms

It is common that some C libraries provide functions for constructing/destructing data structures (usually implemented through malloc and

---

[5] https://crates.io/crates/libtaos.

```
1   pub fn bind(&mut self, params: impl IntoParams) -> Result<(), TaosError> {
2     let params = params.into_params();
3     unsafe {
4       let res = taos_stmt_bind_param(self.stmt, params.as_ptr() as _);
5       self.err_or(res)?;
6       let res = taos_stmt_add_batch(self.stmt);
7       self.err_or(res)?;
8     }
9     for mut param in params {
10      unsafe { param.free() };
11    }
12    Ok(())
13  }
```

Listing 2: When errors happen, `bind` returns before calling `free`.

`free`). To reuse these libraries, Rust developers usually implement Rust wrappers to handle these C APIs. One possible error is mixing different memory allocation/deallocation procedures provided by different languages. For example, it is illegal to allocate memory on the Rust side using `Box` and release it on the C side using `free`. Mixing different memory management mechanisms is undefined behavior, because (1) Rust and C may use different memory allocators. (E.g., on Linux, Rust can be configured to use *jemalloc*, while C uses *ptmalloc* by default.) (2) Rust and C have totally different memory management mechanisms and they operate on different levels. Specifically, Rust calls the constructors/destructors for constructed objects while C only deals with raw memory.

Listing 3 shows an example of mixing the memory management mechanisms of Rust and C, found in package `jyt`[6]. At line 5, a string is constructed through `CString::new`, which internally allocates memory on the heap using Rust's own memory allocator. Then at line 7, the string is explicitly leaked by `mem::forget`, and a raw pointer that points to the string is returned (line 8). Finally, at line 16, the heap memory is freed by the standard C function `free`. Note that the heap memory is obtained through Rust's allocator but freed on the C side through function `free`. This may lead to allocator corruption since the Rust code is compiled as a library and may be used in multiple projects with different memory allocators. Even if this may "work" in practice, it is undefined behavior and hence it is not guaranteed to work on other machines or on newer compilers.

3.4   Our Methodology

Based on the above motivating examples, we propose to use static analysis to detect these bugs because static analysis can examine every control flow path in a program and catch all potential bugs. It is especially appropriate for catching defects in exceptional situations because they are hard to be triggered with normal execution paths. At a high level, our approach does the following: We first compile both the Rust and C/C++ code into LLVM IR. Then we perform

---

[6] https://crates.io/crates/jyt.

```
1    // Rust code:
2    pub unsafe extern "C" fn to_json(from: ext::Ext, text: *const c_char) -> *const c_char {
3        ... ...
4        // CString internally allocates heap memory
5        let output = CString::new(ext::json::serialize(&value.unwrap()).unwrap()).unwrap();
6        let ptr = output.as_ptr();
7        mem::forget(output);  // Memory is "forgotten" by the ownership system
8        ptr  // The raw pointer will be passed across the FFI boundary
9    }
10
11   // C code:
12   int main() {
13       ... ...
14       const char* output = to_json(Yaml, input);
15       ... ...
16       free((char*)output);  // Memory allocated in Rust is freed by free()
17       return 0;
18   }
```

Listing 3: Memory allocated on the Rust side but is freed on the C side.

static analysis on the LLVM IR and keep track of the states of all the heap memory allocations, i.e., while the heap memory is propagated among the control flow graph, we determine whether it is *borrowed* or *moved*. Finally, if any heap memory is passed across the FFI boundaries, we continue to analyze whether it is freed in the external code. Depending on its state, we can find out whether the memory is incorrectly managed and generate diagnostic messages accordingly.

4   System Design

In this section, we show the high-level architecture of FFIChecker and elaborate on the functionality of each component. The workflow of FFIChecker is depicted in Fig. 2. The whole system consists of three parts: (1) the user interface and the driver program, (2) the entry point and foreign function collector, and (3) the static analyzer and bug detector.

4.1   User Interface

The goal of the user interface is to get a Rust package being analyzed from the user and prepare all the ingredients that the static analyzer requires, such as the LLVM bitcode and a set of appropriate entry points. Then it works as a driver program that delegates the remaining procedures to other components. The user interface takes a Rust package as input, which contains one or many Rust *crates* and C/C++ source files (if they exist). A *crate* is a unit of compilation and linking for the Rust compiler. It contains one or many Rust source files and may depend on other *crates*. We leverage the official build system Cargo to resolve dependencies and download all the dependent *crates*. Then different source files are dispatched to either the Rust compiler or the C/C++ compiler, and both the compilers are configured to generate LLVM bitcode. The Cargo integration

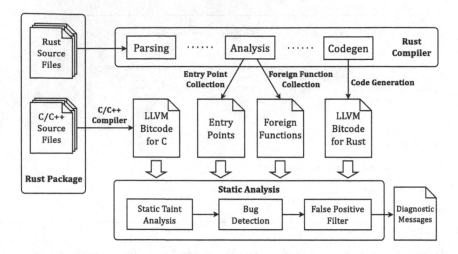

Fig. 2. The architecture of FFICHECKER

provides a user-friendly interface similar to many existing tools used by Rust developers, such as Clippy, so that users can easily integrate FFIChecker into their daily development workflow.

4.2 Entry Point and Foreign Function Collection

Performing static analysis requires an appropriate function as the entry point. We focus on public functions/methods for a Rust program because they are visible to attackers and hence may be exploited. Also, since we care about the cross-language scenario, we want to distinguish whether a function is written in Rust or C/C++. The entry point/foreign function collector is designed to collect all of the information we need. Specifically, after the user interface downloads all the dependencies, the collector is invoked to process each of these crates and collects: (1) a list of public functions/methods, and (2) a list of C/C++ functions called in the Rust program. The collector is implemented as a customized callback function of the Rust compiler, so that it can access the internal data structures inside the compiler. It first goes through the Rust High-level Intermediate Representation (HIR) generated by the Rust compiler, which contains required information such as the function names, visibility, and whether it is implemented in Rust or C/C++. Then it extracts the required function names and passes them to the static analyzer.

4.3 Static Analysis and Bug Detection

The LLVM bitcode, entry points, and foreign functions are sent to the static analyzer as input. The static analyzer performs analysis by traversing the control flow graph (CFG) provided by the LLVM bitcode. The details of the algorithms will be discussed in Sect. 6. Once the static analysis finishes, a bug detection module reads the analysis results and generates diagnostic messages. The messages are filtered by user-specified rules in order to suppress false positives, and then printed to users (Sect. 6.3). According to the diagnostic messages, users can manually inspect the source code and pinpoint potential bugs in their programs.

5   Abstract Interpretation

In this section, we present the definition of our abstract domain and transfer functions based on the language model of LLVM IR.

5.1   LLVM IR, Abstract Values and Abstract Domain

In LLVM IR, a single function is modeled as a Control Flow Graph (CFG), where each node is a basic block containing one or more instructions without any jumps. At the end of each basic block, there is one terminator, a special instruction representing a jump among the control flow. Static analysis models the program execution in a certain *abstract domain*, and each element of the domain represents a certain execution state, which is referred to as an *abstract state*. It first assigns *abstract states* to each variable and basic block, then traverses the CFG and updates these states according to the semantics of each instruction. The *abstract domain* varies depending on different purposes. We design our abstract domain as follows in order to capture the ownership state of heap memory. Note that our design is derived from the classical Abstract Interpretation literature [26, 29].

For each CFG, we denote the set of all the variables that appear in the CFG as **Var**, and the set of all basic blocks in the CFG as **Block**. To distinguish whether a variable stores heap memory and its state in the ownership system (e.g., whether it is *borrowed* or *moved*), we define the state **MState** as a *lattice* with 5 elements, a partial ordering relation $\sqsubseteq$ and a join operator $\sqcup$, as shown in Fig. 3. Intuitively, the bottom element ($\bot$) is the default value for all variables. When a variable is initialized by a heap memory allocation procedure, we mark it as *Alloc*. Note that a heap memory can be passed to FFI by either taking a reference (*borrow*) or forgetting its ownership (*move*). We distinguish them by the corresponding states *Borrowed* and *Moved*. To be conservative, when the state cannot be determined, we set it as the top element ($\top$).

To keep track of the abstract values for each basic block, we maintain a lookup table $\sigma_b :$ **Var** $\rightarrow$ **MState** for each basic block b. The abstract state **AState** is defined as a map lattice consisting of all the mappings from **Var** to **MState**. Intuitively, an element in **AState** is a lookup table, which depicts the abstract memory state for each variable after executing the current basic block of the program. **AState** is still a lattice and the partial ordering is defined as:

$$\text{For } \sigma_1, \sigma_2 \in \textbf{AState}, \sigma_1 \sqsubseteq \sigma_2 \iff \forall a \in \textbf{Var}, f(a) \sqsubseteq g(a).$$

And the $\sqcup$ operator is defined pointwise in terms of the operators from **MState**:

$$\forall \sigma_1, \sigma_2 \in \textbf{AState}, \sigma_1 \sqcup \sigma_2 = \{(a, \sigma_1(a) \sqcup \sigma_2(a)) : \forall a \in \textbf{Var}\}.$$

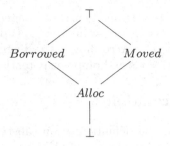

Fig. 3. MState lattice used by FFICHECKER

Finally, the *abstract domain* is defined as a mapping from all basic blocks **Block** to **AState**. Equivalently, it is defined as the powerset of **AState**, i.e., **Domain** $= 2^{\text{AState}}$.

5.2   Transfer Functions

In static analysis, transfer functions are used to extract information from the program semantics and update the abstract states. Since FFICHECKER runs on LLVM IR, we assign a transfer function to each LLVM instruction according to its semantics. Specifically, we focus on the following instructions: (1) Instructions that affect the data flow such as `load`, `store`, and `GetElementPtr`, because we need to propagation the abstract states. (2) Instructions that call other functions, such as `Call` and `Invoke`, through which we perform context-sensitive interprocedural analysis (Sect. 6.2). For details, please refer to our implementation.

6   Algorithms

In this section, we present the main algorithms used in FFICHECKER. The algorithms consist of three parts: (1) A fixed-point algorithm that traverses a CFG and executes transfer functions until a fixed point is reached. (2) An algorithm that achieves context-sensitive interprocedural analysis. (3) A bug detection algorithm used to determine whether there are any potential bugs.

6.1   Fixed-Point Algorithm

Similar to most static analysis tools, FFICHECKER traverses a given CFG and iteratively runs transfer functions to update the abstract state until it reaches a fixed point. The fixed-point algorithm is formulated in the Appendix (Algorithm 1). We implement the classical *worklist* algorithm [26,29], where the worklist W is a set initialized to contain all the basic blocks in the CFG. Then the algorithm chooses a basic block b from W and analyzes it by executing the transfer functions of its instructions. The state is updated by joining the states of all the predecessors of b. If the state changes, all the successors of b will be inserted into the worklist, waiting for a re-analysis. This procedure is repeated until the worklist W becomes empty. The algorithm terminates because either the state goes "up" in the lattice (because of the join operator), or the length of W decreases. Since the lattice we defined has finite height, W will eventually be depleted.

6.2 Analyzing Function Calls

When analyzing instructions that call other functions, such as `Call` and `Invoke`, FFICHECKER performs interprocedural analysis. Different functions need different treatments, therefore we categorize functions into different types: (1) Functions that allocate heap memory, e.g., `exchange_malloc`. These are the "taint sources" of our algorithm, indicating that the resulting variable stores heap memory, so we can mark its abstract state into *Alloc*. (2) Functions that *borrow* a reference (e.g., `Vec::as_mut_ptr`) or *move* the ownership (e.g., `Box::into_raw`). These functions change the abstract state of heap memory into either *Borrowed* or *Moved*. (3) Foreign functions called through FFI. These are the potentially vulnerable functions that FFICHECKER cares about. FFICHECKER will analyze these functions and see whether there are any bugs (Sect. 6.3). (4) LLVM intrinsic functions and the Rust standard library functions. The former are implemented by the compiler backend so their implementations do not even exist in LLVM IR. The latter are commonly used but usually hard to be analyzed because of their complexity and heavy abstraction. These functions are also not FFICHECKER's targets because our goal is to find bugs in third-party libraries instead of in the Rust compiler or the standard library. Therefore, we provide some special handlers that work as the model of these functions by resembling their behaviors. FFICHECKER internally maintains a map between such functions and their handlers, and will execute the handler instead of launching a new function analysis. (4) For all other functions, FFICHECKER launches context-sensitive interprocedural analysis by initializing a new fixed-point algorithm instance for this function. The algorithm is formulated in the Appendix (Algorithm 2).

6.3 Bug Detection and False Positive Suppression

After the fixed-point algorithm terminates, FFICHECKER checks whether there are any variables that store heap memory but are passed to FFI. If this is the case, some heap memory leaks into the external code, which may lead to potential vulnerabilities. To further determine the bug type, FFICHECKER launches a new function analysis instance for all foreign functions to which some heap memory is passed, and checks whether the heap memory is freed or not in the external code. Then it generates warnings according to the ownership state of the heap memory. For example, suppose a variable is *moved* across FFI by Rust and freed in C. In that case, this is an undefined behavior caused by mixing memory management mechanisms (Sect. 3.3). The rules of warning generation are summarized in Table 1.

As shown in the table, we also tag a confidence level on each generated warning depending on how much information we can leverage during the analysis.

For example, the LLVM IR of a foreign function is not always available because it may come from a dynamically linked C library. Or it may be called via a function pointer, so FFICHECKER cannot statically know which function is called. In this case, FFICHECKER cannot further analyze the foreign function, so it generates warnings with lower confidence. This design helps us to suppress false alarms. We implement a precision filter to determine what level of warning messages is reported to users. Only warnings with a confidence level higher than the filter's threshold will be issued. Users can pass command-line options to the user interface to override the default filter configuration.

Table 1. Rules of warning generation. The reported warnings include use-after-free (UAF), double free (DF), undefined behavior (UB), and memory leak (LEAK). SAFE means no warning is issued. The confidence levels (high, medium, or low) are enclosed in parentheses

	C Code is Unavailable	C Code is Available	
		Freed	Not Freed
Borrowed	UAF/DF (Low)	UAF/DF (High)	SAFE
Moved	UB/LEAK (Mid)	UB (High)	LEAK (Mid)

7 Implementation

FFICHECKER is written in Rust (2,468 lines of code) and has three binaries, which are the user interface, entry point/foreign function collector, and static analyzer. The user interface is implemented as a `cargo` sub-command, which tightly integrates with the official build system. Users can easily integrate FFICHECKER in their daily workflow and check their packages by a single command: `cargo ffi-checker`. The entry point/foreign function collector is implemented as a customized Rust compiler, in which we insert the collector routine as a callback function. The callback function is invoked automatically after the compiler gathers all the information of the source code. Thus it can access the internal compiler data structures such as HIR. The static analyzer is a standalone binary configurable through the user interface. Users can specify the precision filter, which determines whether to issue a warning message according to its priority. We also provide several Python scripts for downloading packages on the official package registry and running evaluations.

8 Evaluation

In order to evaluate FFICHECKER in terms of its effectiveness and performance, we collect Rust packages as test cases on the official package registry https://crates.io. Since we care about the cross-language scenario and focus on external code written in C/C++, we only crawl packages that heavily use the FFI between Rust and C/C++. Specifically, we download packages that are of category "external-ffi-bindings", or depend on other packages that assist the use of FFI, such as cc, bindgen, or cbindgen. Finally, we collect a total of 987 packages as our analysis targets, which contain $3,232,574$ lines of Rust and $46,321,573$ lines of C/C++.

All the experiments were done on a machine with a 3.70 GHz Intel Xeon E5-1630 v4 CPU and 16GB RAM, running Gentoo Linux (kernel 5.15.32).

8.1 Effectiveness and Performance of FFICHECKER

We run FFICHECKER on our dataset, and it generates 222 warnings. Then we manually inspect the output at a rate of about 100 reports per person-hour. Finally, 34 bugs (19 memory leaks, 3 exception-related bugs, 12 undefined behaviors) in 12 packages are confirmed. The statistical details are listed in Table 2, where columns "# of Bugs" and "Reports" show the number of true positives we confirmed and the number of warnings in the emitted diagnostic messages with different confidence levels. We have reported all the bugs to the package maintainers. At the time of writing, 15 bugs were confirmed and fixed. For more details, we refer readers to our GitHub repository[7].

We further measure the execution time and memory usage of FFICHECKER for all the 987 packages. We run the evaluation in 8 parallel threads, and FFICHECKER can finish all the analysis in 5.2 h with at most 4.1 GB memory consumption. On average, FFICHECKER can analyze a package in 116.9 CPU seconds with $1,056.6$ MB memory consumption. Note that the execution time

Table 2. Bugs detected by FFICHECKER. The types of bugs include memory leak (LEAK), exception safety (EXC), and undefined behavior (UB). "N/A" means that the foreign functions are from shared libraries instead of the Rust package

Package	# of Bugs	Reports			Bug Type	Elapsed Time (s)	Memory Usage (MB)	# of Entries	# of FFIs	LoC	
		High	Mid	Low						Rust	C/C++
arma-rs	3	0	1	0	LEAK	38.67	1040.85	29	4	1686	N/A
cobyla	1	0	1	0	LEAK	48.14	1979.54	2	1	225	1635
emd	1	0	1	0	LEAK	7.21	237.75	4	1	87	541
impersonate	1	0	1	0	LEAK	19.11	767.54	6	1	117	61
iredismodule	11	0	0	10	EXC, LEAK	78.15	1958.46	364	230	3761	777
jyt	6	0	0	1	UB	97.25	2711.75	3	6	450	N/A
liboj	1	0	0	3	LEAK	108.58	3109.21	86	38	1342	N/A
libtaos	1	0	0	1	EXC	99.23	1724.13	461	50	5491	N/A
moonfire-ffmpeg	1	0	0	1	UB	7.83	228.78	53	92	1513	231
pdb_wrapper	1	0	0	1	EXC	68.04	2530.41	20	14	499	375
snap7-rs	2	0	1	4	LEAK	8.97	203.77	387	276	6110	14085
triangle-rs	5	0	1	0	UB	47.46	1095.58	34	2	681	15050

[7] https://github.com/lizhuohua/rust-ffi-checker/tree/master/trophy-case.

and memory usage do not correlate to the lines of code or the number of inter-faces, because the convergence of the fixed-point algorithm mainly depends on the structure of the CFG. Overall, FFICHECKER is scalable enough to analyze real-world Rust packages with a reasonable amount of computational resources.

8.2   Understanding False Positives and False Negatives

FFICHECKER reports numbers of false positives. After inspecting the reported warnings, we summarize two reasons that lead to the false alarms: (1) It is com-mon that Rust calls foreign functions from dynamically linked shared libraries. Therefore the LLVM IR of the foreign code is not available. In this case, FFICHECKER cannot further analyze the foreign function, so it generates impre-cise results. (2) FFICHECKER cannot always distinguish whether a variable is *borrowed* or *moved* via LLVM IR because the *borrowing/moving* operations may be optimized away by the Rust compiler.

During the manual inspection, we also observe some bugs in functions with generic type parameters but they are not reported by FFICHECKER. The reason is that the Rust compiler will not generate code for generic functions unless they are monomorphized, meaning that FFICHECKER cannot find the LLVM IR for generic functions that are only implemented in the package but not used.

Nevertheless, as presented in Sect. 6.3, FFICHECKER generates warnings with different confidence levels. Users can configure the precision filter through command-line options to only output warnings with high confidence. Even if all the warnings are issued, users can still filter out false alarms quickly during the manual inspection with the help of the confidence levels attached to them.

9   Discussion

Thoughts About Rust's Security Guarantees. As shown in Table 2, most bugs we found are memory leaks. We interpret this as a limitation of Rust's security guarantees: memory leak is considered *safe* in Rust [16]. The reason behind this design choice is that leaking resources is possible in pure safe Rust (consider creating a cycle of reference-counted pointers using interior mutabil-ity). Therefore, the authors of the Rust standard library decide not to mark functions that leak memory as unsafe, such as `mem::forget`. As a result, the Rust compiler will not give any warnings when inexperienced programmers mis-use these functions and cause memory leaks, leading to denial of service attacks or information leakage.

Future Work. Although we focus on Rust combined with C/C++, the idea of FFICHECKER and the threat model can be extended to other cross-language scenarios. Especially, the static analyzer is designed to be an individual binary that operates on LLVM IR. Therefore by changing the Rust-specific part of the system, our approach can be adapted to analyze other FFIs, as long as they support the LLVM backend for code generation, e.g., languages such as Haskell, Julia, and Swift.

10   Related Work

10.1   Static Analysis for Rust

Many existing studies extend off-the-shelf static analysis engines to perform bug detection on LLVM IR generated by the Rust compiler. Lindner et al. [23] use the symbolic execution engine KLEE [5] to verify whether a program is panic-free. SMACK [3,32] translates LLVM IR into the Boogie intermediate verification language [11]. Rust2Viper [14] and Prusti [1] utilize user-provided specifications and the Viper [28] symbolic execution engine to verify functional correctness properties. CRUST [38] translates functions that contain unsafe code to C, then it generates tests and checks them by the CBMC [6] model checker.

There are also many tools that work on Rust's own intermediate representation. Qin et al. [31] build two bug detectors for use-after-free and double-lock bugs according to their empirical studies on Rust security issues. SafeDrop [10] focuses on the deallocation of heap memory and detects memory corruptions by performing alias analysis and taint analysis on Rust MIR. MIRAI [25] is a formal verification tool that performs symbolic execution on Rust MIR. It enables users to add annotations and utilizes the SMT solver Z3 [27] to prove the correctness of Rust programs. MIRCHECKER [22] collects both the numerical and symbolic information from Rust MIR, and detects runtime panics and memory-safety issues without the need for annotations. Rudra [2] uses both Rust MIR and HIR, and detects potential memory safety bugs in unsafe Rust.

10.2   Cross-language Bug Detection and Prevention

It is well-known that developing software using multiple languages may interfere with each other and lead to subtle bugs. Mergendahl et al. [24] propose a threat model to reason about cross-language attacks. They also demonstrate these attacks on Rust and Go. Kondoh et al. [17] use static analysis to detect common mistakes and bad programming practices when using Java Native Interface (JNI). Tan et al. [35] apply static analysis and carry out an empirical security study on a portion of the native code in Sun's Java Development Kit (JDK). JET [19,20] is a static analysis tool that enforces exception checking and reports bugs on Java exceptions raised in native code through JNI. Jinn [18] is a compiler and virtual machine independent bug detection tool for both JNI and Python/C. Galeed [33] and PKRU-SAFE [15] isolate heap memory at runtime using Intel Memory Protection Keys (MPK), such that unsafe (external) code cannot corrupt memory used exclusively by the safe-language components.

Unlike these existing efforts, our work focuses on the memory management issues between Rust and C/C++. The new pattern of bugs introduced by the interaction between the Rust ownership system and C/C++ is out of the scope of all the existing detection or prevention efforts.

11   Conclusion

Rust leverages FFI to invoke external C/C++ code, making incremental software development convenient and efficient. In this paper, we showed that there could be security issues since programmers may make mistakes when using FFI. To secure the use of FFI, we designed and implemented FFICHECKER, an automated static analysis tool based on augmented taint analysis, which captures the state transitions of heap allocations when they are passed to external code through FFI. It can detect potential memory management issues across the FFI boundaries. We evaluated it by analyzing 987 real-world Rust packages. It successfully revealed 34 bugs in 12 packages that were unknown previously. Finally, we open-sourced FFICHECKER with various examples and test scripts.

Acknowledgments. The work of Zhuohua Li, Jincheng Wang, and John C.S. Lui were supported in part by the RGC's RIF R4032-18.

Appendix

A   Fixed-Point Algorithm

Algorithm 1: Fixed-point algorithm for FFICHECKER

Input: Control Flow Graph: CFG
Output: Abstract State: $State$
Initialization: $State[n] \leftarrow \perp$ for all n

1 **Function** FixedPoint(CFG, $State$):
2 $\quad$ $W \leftarrow CFG.basicblocks$
3 $\quad$ **while** $W \neq \emptyset$ **do**
4 $\quad\quad$ $b \leftarrow W.\text{remove}()$
5 $\quad\quad$ **foreach** $instr \in b.instructions$ **do**
6 $\quad\quad\quad$ Transfer($State[b], instr$)
7 $\quad\quad$ Transfer($State[b], b.terminator$)
8 $\quad\quad$ $new\_state \leftarrow \bigsqcup_{n \in \text{Predecessors}(b)} State[n]$
9 $\quad\quad$ **if** $new\_state \not\sqsubseteq State[b]$ **then**
10 $\quad\quad\quad$ $State[b] \leftarrow new\_state$
11 $\quad\quad\quad$ **foreach** $v \in \text{Successors}(b)$ **do**
12 $\quad\quad\quad\quad$ $W.\text{insert}(v)$
13 $\quad$ **return** $State$

B   Context-Sensitive Interprocedural Analysis

To avoid duplicated analysis for the same function, we also implement the classical summary-based method [26,29]. It caches previously computed results (i.e., summaries) in a lookup table $cache : ((f, in\_state), out\_state)$ that maps a calling context (f, in_state) to an output out_state. (f is a function, in_state is the abstract state of its input, and out_state is the corresponding output.) Before analyzing a function, we first check whether there is an existing summary that has been computed. If it is the case, the fixed-point algorithm is skipped and the result is directly returned. If not, the fixed-point algorithm is performed and the analysis result is cached in the lookup table.

Algorithm 2: Interprocedural analysis algorithm for FFICHECKER

Input: Function: f, Arguments: $args$, Destination: $dest$,
State of the current basic block: σ, Summary Cache: $cache$

Output: Updated State: σ

```
 1 begin
 2 │  switch FunctionType(f) do
 3 │  │  case Heap Allocation do
 4 │  │  │  σ[dest] ← Alloc
 5 │  │  case Borrow Arguments do
 6 │  │  │  σ[arguments that are borrowed] ← Borrowed
 7 │  │  case Move Arguments do
 8 │  │  │  σ[arguments that are moved] ← Moved
 9 │  │  case FFI do
10 │  │  │  Run AnalyzeFunction and generate warnings if necessary
11 │  │  case LLVM Intrinsic or Standard Library do
12 │  │  │  Handle it through function models
13 │  │  otherwise do
14 │  │  │  AnalyzeFunction(f, args, dest, σ)
```

// Subroutines

```
15 Function AnalyzeFunction(f, args, dest, σ):
16 │  in_state ← state generated by args
17 │  summary ← GetFunctionSummary(f, in_state)
   │  // Set the state of the return value
18 │  σ[dest] ← summary.ret_state
   │  // Propagate the state of parameters
19 │  foreach (caller_arg, callee_arg) do
20 │  │  σ[caller_arg] = σ[callee_arg]

21 Function GetFunctionSummary(f, in_state):
   │  // If the summary has been computed, directly return it
22 │  if (f, in_state) in cache then
23 │  │  return cache[(f, in_state)]
   │  // Initialize initial state for the fixed-point algorithm
24 │  forall n do
25 │  │  State[n] ← ⊥
26 │  foreach (state, param) in zip(in_state, f.parameters) do
27 │  │  State[param] ← state
   │  // Compute the summary and cache it
28 │  out_state ← FixedPoint(f.CFG, State)
29 │  cache[(f, in_state)] ← out_state
30 │  return out_state
```

References

1. Astrauskas, V., Müller, P., Poli, F., Summers, A.J.: Leveraging rust types for modular specification and verification. In: Proceedings of the ACM on Programming Languages 3(OOPSLA), pp. 1–30 (2019)
2. Bae, Y., Kim, Y., Askar, A., Lim, J., Kim, T.: Rudra: finding memory safety bugs in rust at the ecosystem scale. In: Proceedings of the ACM SIGOPS 28th Symposium on Operating Systems Principles, SOSP 2021, pp. 84–99 (2021)
3. Baranowski, M., He, S., Rakamarić, Z.: Verifying rust programs with SMACK. In: Lahiri, S.K., Wang, C. (eds.) ATVA 2018. LNCS, vol. 11138, pp. 528–535. Springer, Cham (2018). https://doi.org/10.1007/978-3-030-01090-4_32
4. Bushev, D.: Language details of the Firefox repo (2022). https://4e6.github.io/firefox-lang-stats/
5. Cadar, C., Dunbar, D., Engler, D.: KLEE: unassisted and automatic generation of high-coverage tests for complex systems programs. In: Proceedings of the 8th USENIX Conference on Operating Systems Design and Implementation, pp. 209–224. OSDI '08 (2008)
6. Clarke, E., Kroening, D., Lerda, F.: A tool for checking ANSI-C programs. In: Jensen, K., Podelski, A. (eds.) TACAS 2004. LNCS, vol. 2988, pp. 168–176. Springer, Heidelberg (2004). https://doi.org/10.1007/978-3-540-24730-2_15
7. Cousot, P., Cousot, R.: Static determination of dynamic properties of programs. In: Proceedings of the 2nd International Symposium on Programming, ISOP 1976, pp. 106–130 (1976)
8. Cousot, P., Cousot, R.: Abstract interpretation: a unified lattice model for static analysis of programs by construction or approximation of fixpoints. In: Proceedings of the 4th ACM SIGACT-SIGPLAN Symposium on Principles of Programming Languages, POPL 1977, pp. 238–252 (1977)
9. Cousot, P., Cousot, R.: Systematic design of program analysis frameworks. In: Proceedings of the 6th ACM SIGACT-SIGPLAN Symposium on Principles of Programming Languages, POPL 1979, pp. 269–282 (1979)
10. Cui, M., Chen, C., Xu, H., Zhou, Y.: SafeDrop: Detecting Memory Deallocation Bugs of Rust Programs via Static Data-Flow Analysis (2021)
11. DeLine, R., Leino, R.: BoogiePL: a typed procedural language for checking object-oriented programs. Technical report MSR-TR-2005-70 (2005)
12. Evans, A.N., Campbell, B., Soffa, M.L.: Is rust used safely by software developers? In: Proceedings of the ACM/IEEE 42nd International Conference on Software Engineering, ICSE 2020, pp. 246–257 (2020)
13. Girard, J.Y.: Linear logic: its syntax and semantics. In: Proceedings of the Workshop on Advances in Linear Logic, pp. 1–42 (1995)
14. Hahn, F.: Rust2Viper: Building a Static Verifier for Rust. Master's thesis, ETH Zürich (2016)
15. Kirth, P., et al.: Pkru-safe: Automatically locking down the heap between safe and unsafe languages. In: Proceedings of the Seventeenth European Conference on Computer Systems, EuroSys 2022, pp. 132–148 (2022)
16. Klabnik, S., Nichols, C.: The Rust Programming Language. No Starch Press, USA (2018)
17. Kondoh, G., Onodera, T.: Finding Bugs in Java native interface programs. In: Proceedings of the 2008 International Symposium on Software Testing and Analysis, ISSTA 2008, pp. 109–118 (2008)

18. Lee, B., Wiedermann, B., Hirzel, M., Grimm, R., McKinley, K.S.: Jinn: synthesizing dynamic bug detectors for foreign language interfaces. In: Proceedings of the 31st ACM SIGPLAN Conference on Programming Language Design and Implementation, PLDI 2010, pp. 36–49 (2010)
19. Li, S., Tan, G.: Finding bugs in exceptional situations of JNI programs. In: Proceedings of the 16th ACM Conference on Computer and Communications Security, CCS 2009, pp. 442–452 (2009)
20. Li, S., Tan, G.: JET: exception checking in the java native interface. In: Proceedings of the 2011 ACM International Conference on Object Oriented Programming Systems Languages and Applications, OOPSLA 2011, pp. 345–358 (2011)
21. Li, Z., Wang, J., Sun, M., Lui, J.C.: Securing the device drivers of your embedded systems: framework and prototype. In: Proceedings of the 14th International Conference on Availability, Reliability and Security, ARES 2019, pp. 1–10 (2019)
22. Li, Z., Wang, J., Sun, M., Lui, J.C.: MirChecker: detecting bugs in rust programs via static analysis. In: Proceedings of the 2021 ACM SIGSAC Conference on Computer and Communications Security, CCS 2021, pp. 2183–2196 (2021)
23. Lindner, M., Aparicius, J., Lindgren, P.: No panic! verification of rust programs by symbolic execution. In: 2018 IEEE 16th International Conference on Industrial Informatics, INDIN 2018, pp. 108–114 (2018)
24. Mergendahl, S., Burow, N., Okhravi, H.: Cross-language attacks. In: Proceedings of the Network and Distributed System Security Symposium (NDSS 2022) (2022)
25. MIRAI Contributors: MIRAI: Rust mid-level IR Abstract Interpreter (2022). https://github.com/facebookexperimental/MIRAI
26. Møller, A., Schwartzbach, M.I.: Static Program Analysis (2018)
27. de Moura, L., Bjørner, N.: Z3: an efficient SMT solver. In: Tools and Algorithms for the Construction and Analysis of Systems, TACAS 2008, pp. 337–340 (2008)
28. Müller, P., Schwerhoff, M., Summers, A.J.: Viper: a verification infrastructure for permission-based reasoning. In: Jobstmann, B., Leino, K.R.M. (eds.) VMCAI 2016. LNCS, vol. 9583, pp. 41–62. Springer, Heidelberg (2016). https://doi.org/10.1007/978-3-662-49122-5_2
29. Principles of Program Analysis. Lecture Notes in Computer Science, Springer, Heidelberg (1999). https://doi.org/10.1007/978-3-662-03811-6_6
30. Ojeda, M.: Rust for Linux (2022). https://github.com/Rust-for-Linux
31. Qin, B., Chen, Y., Yu, Z., Song, L., Zhang, Y.: Understanding memory and thread safety practices and issues in real-world rust programs. In: Proceedings of the 41st ACM SIGPLAN Conference on Programming Language Design and Implementation, PLDI 2020, pp. 763–779 (2020)
32. Rakamaric, Z., Emmi, M.: SMACK: decoupling source language details from verifier implementations. In: Proceedings of the 26th International Conference on Computer Aided Verification, CAV 2014, pp. 106–113 (2014)
33. Rivera, E., Mergendahl, S., Shrobe, H., Okhravi, H., Burow, N.: Keeping safe rust safe with galeed. In: Annual Computer Security Applications Conference, ACSAC 2021, pp. 824–836 (2021)
34. Secure Rust Guidelines Contributors: Secure Rust Guidelines (2022). https://anssi-fr.github.io/rust-guide/
35. Tan, G., Croft, J.: An Empirical Security Study of the Native Code in the JDK. In: 17th USENIX Security Symposium (USENIX Security 08), July 2008
36. The Rust FFI Omnibus Contributors: The Rust FFI Omnibus (2022). https://jakegoulding.com/rust-ffi-omnibus/
37. The Rustonomicon Contributors: The Rustonomicon (2022). https://doc.rust-lang.org/nomicon/

38. Toman, J., Pernsteiner, S., Torlak, E.: Crust: a bounded verifier for rust. In: 2015 30th IEEE/ACM International Conference on Automated Software Engineering, ASE 2015, pp. 75–80 (2015)

39. Unsafe Code Guidelines Working Group: Rust's Unsafe Code Guidelines Reference (2022). https://rust-lang.github.io/unsafe-code-guidelines/

40. Wadler, P.: Linear Types Can Change the World! In: Programming Concepts and Methods (1990)

41. Xu, H., Chen, Z., Sun, M., Zhou, Y., Lyu, M.R.: Memory-safety challenge considered solved? an in-depth study with all rust CVEs. ACM Trans. Softw. Eng. Methodol. **31**(1), September 2021

Reach Me if You Can: On Native Vulnerability Reachability in Android Apps

Luca Borzacchiello[1], Emilio Coppa[1(✉)], Davide Maiorca[2],
Andrea Columbu[2], Camil Demetrescu[1], and Giorgio Giacinto[2]

[1] Sapienza University of Rome, Rome, Italy
{borzacchiello,coppa,demetres}@diag.uniroma1.it
[2] University of Cagliari, Cagliari, Italy
{davide.maiorca,giacinto}@unica.it

This paper is dedicated to the memory of Camil Demetrescu, a brilliant researcher and a great teacher that will be missed by many students and colleagues.

Luca, Emilio, Davide, and Giorgio

Abstract. Android applications ship with several native C/C++ libraries. Research on Android security has revealed that these libraries often come from third-party components that are not kept up to date by developers, possibly posing security concerns. To assess if known vulnerabilities in these libraries constitute an immediate security problem, we need to understand whether vulnerable functions could be reached when apps are executed (we refer to this problem as function reachability). In this paper, we propose DROIDREACH, a novel, static approach to assess the reachability of native function calls in Android apps. Our framework addresses the limitations of state-of-the-art approaches by employing a combination of heuristics and symbolic execution, allowing for a more accurate reconstruction of the Inter-procedural Control-Flow Graphs (ICFGs). On the top 500 applications from the Google Play Store, DROIDREACH can detect a significantly higher number of paths in comparison to previous works. Finally, two case studies show how DROIDREACH can be used as a valuable vulnerability assessment tool.

Keywords: Android · Static analysis · Mobile security

1 Introduction

The Android ecosystem has significantly evolved over the years. Applications have become more user-friendly and feature functionalities such as advanced graphics, database management, and modern encryption. While many features can be directly implemented with Java code, developers rely on C/C++ libraries (via the Java Native Development Kit) to achieve greater speed and flexibility.

The analysis of Java code has dominated the Android security scene, as malicious samples typically resort to Java components to carry out their operations [8,40]. Conversely, the focus of research on the Android Native Environment has been limited. Nonetheless, the Android Native Environment conceals more issues than what can be superficially assumed, as recent works showed a significant presence of vulnerabilities in native code [3]. The problem becomes significant as such vulnerabilities are mostly due to not-updated versions of libraries that are continuously employed even in very popular applications (featuring millions of downloads). However, the presence of vulnerabilities alone does not immediately translate into a security problem because it depends on *whether they could be concretely exploited.* While this question can be extremely difficult to answer, especially in large-scale environments such as Android, we can study whether *such vulnerable functions could be reached when apps are executed.* We refer to this problem as *function reachability.*

Previous works on Android native code have proposed dataflow techniques that work either statically or dynamically. Static approaches [38,39] mainly exploited symbolic execution – a powerful program analysis that struggles to scale over complex and large Android apps – leading to results that are incomplete and thus inaccurate when considering function reachability. Dynamic approaches [42] can accurately analyze single execution paths but they still can hardly scale over apps featuring even thousands of classes, leading to the so-called *path explosion* problem. In this sense, it becomes crucial to find a proper balance between the *time* needed for the analysis and the *precision* of the attained results.

In this paper, we propose DROIDREACH, a static approach to establish the reachability of native methods in Android apps starting from the application Java entry points. In particular, we propose the following contributions:

1. We discuss the technical limitations that hamper the analysis capabilities of current analysis tools. In particular, we show limitations in: (a) properly mapping Java `native` methods to Java Native Interface (JNI) methods, (b) handling *nested* native libraries, and (c) accurately building the ICFGs.
2. We present the methodology underlying DROIDREACH: it combines several heuristics and ICFG construction techniques to mitigate the limitations mentioned in the previous point. In this way, DROIDREACH can accurately and effectively reconstruct possible paths to potentially vulnerable native calls.
3. We perform an evaluation considering 500 popular applications featuring complex native libraries and ICFGs (with an average of 2,000,000 native instructions and 1,000,000 Java instructions). We show that DROIDREACH can reach more instructions than ARGUS-SAF [38], which is the state-of-the-art static framework for analyzing the Java and native layers in Android.
4. We propose two real, practical case studies where we show how DROIDREACH can be helpful to assess the reachability of vulnerable functions.

To foster further research, we make our contributions available at https://github.com/season-lab/DroidReach. We believe that DroidReach represents a step forward for the Android community as it can provide valuable insights to security experts in presence of large and complex apps.

2   Background and Related Work

Android Apps. Android applications are zipped .apk (Android application package) archives containing: *(i)* The AndroidManifest.xml file and other .xml files, which provide the application metadata and layout ; *(ii)* One or more classes.dex files, which contain the executable bytecode of the Java/Kotlin classes; *(iii)* External resources, such as images or native libraries.

The Android NDK. The Android Native Development Kit (NDK) is an ensemble of tools that allow for the implementation of parts of Android apps in native (C/C++) code. Such a code is typically employed to guarantee faster performance in comparison to traditional Java code. The interface between the Java and the native layer is called Java Native Interface (JNI). JNI essentially defines how functions receive parameters or provide return values. Native libraries can be loaded with the System.loadLibrary method. Then, the native methods to be invoked are declared in the Java code by using the **native** keyword.

Native Libraries Analysis. Native libraries have been especially studied in the context of vulnerability identification, i.e., understanding the *presence* of vulnerabilities in native code. More specifically, prominent works concerned the study of the JNI interface vulnerabilities [23,25,27,29,35,36], while others involved the identification of possible vulnerabilities in Android libraries. Derr et al. [17] conducted a test with 200 developers in which they showed that many libraries embedded in apps are outdated and contain security vulnerabilities. Various approaches have been proposed to detect them, based on machine learning [21], similarities between functions [20,41], and hybrid analysis [30,31].

Recently, Almanee et al. [3] proposed an extended assessment of the presence of vulnerable functions in Android native libraries. In particular, they showed that applications contain libraries that have not been updated even for two years, thus exposing vulnerabilities that typically require a long time to be fixed. We base the beginning of our analysis on the results of this work, as it depicts a critical scenario where various applications may feature critical security issues.

Dataflow Analysis. Dataflow analysis has been extensively studied in Android, with a focus on how data propagates in Java code. This problem has been addressed with static and dynamic approaches. Regarding static approaches, FlowDroid [7] was among the first to introduce proper handling of the Android callbacks. Other works improved FlowDroid in many aspects, such as proper dataflow tracking for intents [13,22,26,28]. Amandroid [39] is deemed as the current reference point for static dataflow analysis in Android. Wei et al. [38,39] expanded Amandroid by releasing JN-SAF (now known as ARGUS-SAF), which introduced the analysis of the information flows between the Java and the native layer. The approach employs symbolic execution to handle the native layer. In particular, ARGUS-SAF uses CFGEmulated from ANGR [33] to reconstruct ICFGs of the native code (Sect. 3.1) and compute approximate dataflow facts. ARGUS-SAF will be the main reference point for the analyses discussed in this paper.

Dynamic approaches employ code instrumentation and execution to perform taint analysis. Droidscope and TaintDroid [19,44] are among the first approaches to have adopted this technique. Subsequent works built upon and improved TaintDroid [34,42,43] by using, e.g., concolic execution [11,12,14]. Unfortunately, a challenge is *how* to generate the *right* executions that will reach a function.

Input Generation. Several works [1,4,6,15,24,37,40,45] aim at generating *user inputs* that can lead to the execution of specific functions. Systems based on static analysis allow for faster code coverage, but they can lack precision. Conversely, approaches based on dynamic analysis can be much more precise, but they can often be unfeasible due to the so-called *path explosion* problem. One notable example is Intellidroid [40], an approach that uses static and dynamic analysis to generate those inputs that allow for reaching specific calls. Intellidroid only focuses on the Java layer without exploring the native layer.

Automatically finding the right set of stimulations for an app remains an open research problem, especially when considering large and complex apps. DROIDREACH cannot find the inputs able to reproduce a specific path but can provide insights about the existence of a path toward a specific target point.

3   DroidReach

In this section, we present the main ideas behind DROIDREACH. First, we discuss the problem targeted by DROIDREACH and the challenges that affect existing approaches. Then, we present the design and the components of DROIDREACH.

3.1   Problem Statement and Reachability Challenges

Terminology. In the following, we define a few terms used across the paper:

- A **code point** p for our analysis is an instruction inside the set of instructions from the Java layer (J) or the native layer (N) of an app, i.e., $p \in (J \cup N)$.
- A **Control-Flow Graph (CFG)** is a graph representation of possible paths that can be taken during the execution of a function. Each node represents a contiguous sequence of code points. Edges represent jumps across nodes.
- A **Call Graph (CG)** is a graph that represents the calls across different functions of an app.
- An **Inter-procedural Control-Flow Graph (ICFG)** connects the CFGs of different functions using the information from the CG. In practice, it can encode all the app's paths starting from a specific entry point.
- A **source** p_s is a code point in an app that could start the execution of some Java code. Hence, a source could be seen as an entry point for the Java layer.
- A **sink** p_t is a code point inside a native library, i.e., $p_t \in N$. The sink identifies an interesting point that we would like to reach during the execution.

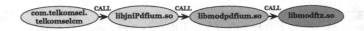

Fig. 1. Example of *nested* libraries

Goal. Given the Java instructions J, the native instructions N, and a sink p_t, our goal is to identify at least one path starting from one source p_s and ending in the sink p_t. The path is represented as the sequence of points traversed in the ICFG from the source p_s. Identifying a path in the ICFG can be valuable for several program analyses and security tasks. This paper focuses on sinks that could be associated with vulnerable code points within native libraries.

Reachability Challenges. ARGUS-SAF (Sect. 2) is the state-of-the-art solution for statically analyzing both the Java and the native layers of an Android app. When testing it on real-world apps for our goals, we have identified a few critical challenges which affect its accuracy (and also of other existing works):

C1 **Mapping Java native methods to JNI methods.** To execute the code of a native library, the Java code invokes a Java `native` method. Java `native` methods at running time could be seen as *jumps* to JNI methods, which are the *entry points* for the native layer. Unfortunately, statically identifying the *mapping* between Java `native` methods and JNI methods is not always trivial. State-of-the-art solutions may fail (Sect. 4) to *resolve* a large number of these mappings, possibly ignoring several entry points of the native layer.

C2 *Nested* **native libraries.** A JNI method is part of a shared library, e.g., `libA.so`. A shared library may call methods of other libraries, i.e., one library may link another one (e.g., `libB.so`). State-of-the-art solutions may not perform analyses across multiple native libraries in the case of *nesting*. This is crucial on Android, since apps often: (a) integrate open-source libraries, which may rely on other ones, and (b) devise *wrappers* to work with libraries that were not originally written for Android and thus do not implement the JNI API. An example of nested libraries is given in Fig. 1.

C3 **Scalability versus accuracy.** ARGUS-SAF uses symbolic execution to analyze the native code. While this technique can be very accurate during the ICFG construction, allowing the tool to even compute data flow facts, it does not scale on complex libraries. Indeed, ARGUS-SAF trades accuracy for scalability, halting its analysis when the call depth is larger than, e.g., 5, which is not enough in several cases, thus generating incomplete ICFGs. Approaches based on traditional binary frameworks [32], may provide better scalability but then generate less accurate ICFGs, e.g., in the presence of indirect jumps.

To help the reader grasp the technical aspects behind these challenges, we show them in the context of a running example in the remainder of the section. However, we first present at a high level the design behind DROIDREACH.

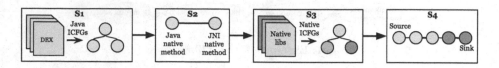

Fig. 2. Main steps of DroidReach

3.2 Architecture of DroidReach

Figure 2 depicts the main steps performed by DroidReach:

S1 **Static analysis of the Java layer.** The first step builds the ICFGs of the Java code, identifying sources and calls to Java `native` methods.

S2 **Analysis of interactions between Java and native layer.** After detecting the Java `native` methods that could be reached during an execution, DroidReach identifies the mappings between Java `native` methods and JNI methods. This step is thus designed to tackle challenge C1.

S3 **Static analysis of the native layer.** Given a list of JNI methods that could be reached during the execution, DroidReach builds the ICFGs of the native libraries. This step aims at challenges C2 and C3, combining different techniques to target a nice trade-off between accuracy and scalability.

S4 **Reachability analysis.** The last step is where DroidReach puts together the pieces constructed in the previous stages. It first merges the ICFGs of the Java layer with the ICFGs of the native layer and then evaluates whether there exists a path from a source p_s to a user-defined sink p_t.

In the remainder of this section, we review in detail these steps. Throughout our discussion, we use a running example: Fig. 3 shows an excerpt of its code. This is an app with two activities, where the first one (`LoginActivity`, omitted from the code) checks the credentials of the user, while the second one (`JavaLayerActivity`) runs some tasks using some native libraries (`native-lib.so` and `other-native-lib.so`) when the user clicks a button. Differently from dynamic approaches, DroidReach can directly focus on `JavaLayerActivity` without necessarily satisfying the execution requirements of `LoginActivity`, which could be arbitrarily hard to automatically identify and satisfy.

3.3 Static Analysis of the Java Layer

Different state-of-the-art frameworks already exist to analyze the Java layer, providing different trade-offs in terms of accuracy and scalability. The current implementation of DroidReach can work with Androguard [18] and Flow-Droid [7], while support for Amandroid [39] is being worked on. Regardless of the specific framework in use, DroidReach performs three stages:

1. **Identification of sources.** DroidReach looks for sources by considering the class methods of several Android components, following the guidelines and suggestions proposed in previous works [7,18].

```
// Java layer: classes.dex                       // Native layer: native-lib.so (cont'd)
   public class JavaLayerActivity                  /* some complex code */
           extends AppCompatActivity {             return env->RegisterNatives(c, mappings,
J0.  static {                                        sizeof(methods)/sizeof(JNINativeMethod));
       System.loadLibrary("native-lib"); }       }
                                                 N1. static void execMethod(JNIEnv* env,
J1.  protected void onCreate(Bundle state) {                            jclass clazz) {
J2.    super.onCreate(state);                    N2.  Handler* h = build();
J3.    setContentView(                           N3.  h->callback(); // use of fn pointer
         R.layout.activity_native_buttons);      }
J4.    findViewById(R.id.btn_1).setOnClickListener  N4. Handler* build() {
J5.      (v -> { execMethod(); });               N5.  auto* h = new Handler();
     }                                           N6.  h->init(); // virtual call
                                                 N7.  return h;
J6.  private static native void execMethod();    }
     }
                                                 N8.  void Handler::init()
// Native layer: native-lib.so                         { this->callback = &foo1; }
N0. JNIEXPORT jint JNI_OnLoad(JavaVM* vm,
                      void* reserved) {           // Native layer: other-native-lib.so
    JNIEnv* env; vm->GetEnv(&env, JNI_VERSION_1_6); N9.  void foo1() { foo2(); }
    jclass c = env->FindClass("JavaLayerActivity"); N10. void foo2() { foo3(); }
    static const JNINativeMethod mappings[] =    N11. void foo3() { foo4(); }
    { {"execMethod", "()", execMethod} };        N12. void foo4() { bug(); }
```

Fig. 3. Running example

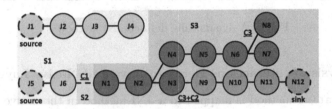

Fig. 4. ICFGs of the running example: shades of gray highlight different steps (Color figure online)

2. **ICFG construction.** For each source, DROIDREACH builds an ICFG considering the entire Java code of the app, connecting the CFGs of the methods based on their *caller-callee* relationships.

3. **Identification of Java native methods.** Finally, this step identifies Java native methods which are invoked in the ICFGs of the Java layer. At this stage, a call to a Java native method is not yet mapped to its JNI method, which contains the actual binary implementation of the Java native method.

Running Example. When considering the JavaLayerActivity class, there are two sources: onCreate (J1), which is executed at the activity startup; the anonymous handler (J5) for button events. Figure 4 shows in blue the Java code points for the ICFGs starting from these two sources. J6 is a Java native method. An additional *implicit* source, considered by DROIDREACH but omitted from Fig. 4, is J0, which triggers the execution of JNI_OnLoad (see next section).

```
// Java layer: classes.dex
package com.lyrebirdstudio.lyrebirdlibrary;
public class EffectFragment extends Fragment {
    private static native void shadows(Bitmap arg0, float arg1)
    { /* statically resolved by dlsym() based on the name of the JNI method */ }

// Native layer: libfilter.so
void Java_com_lyrebirdstudio_lyrebirdlibrary_EffectFragment_shadows(
    JNIEnv *env, jclass c, jfloat arg1) { /* native implementation of the JNI method */ }
```

Fig. 5. A statically defined JNI method

```
// Java layer: classes.dex
package com.aviary.android.feather.headless.moa;
public class Moa {
    static native void n_applyActions() { /* dynamically resolved by JNI_OnLoad() */ }

// Native layer: libaviary_native.so
JNIEXPORT jint JNI_OnLoad(JavaVM* vm, void* reserved) { ...;
  jclass c = env->FindClass("com/aviary/android/feather/headless/moa/Moa");
  static const JNINativeMethod m[] =
  { ..., {"n_getEffects", "()[Ljava/lang/string;]", (void*)(n_getEffects)}, ... };
  env->RegisterNatives(c, m, sizeof(m) / sizeof(JNINativeMethod)); ...; }

jobjectArray n_getEffects(JNIEnv *env, jclass c) { /* native implementation of the method */ }
```

Fig. 6. A dynamically defined JNI method

3.4 Analysis of Interactions Between Java and Native Layer

Each Java native method is mapped to a JNI method in the native layer. The mapping can be defined statically or dynamically, as described in the following.

Static Mapping. The name of the JNI method is a symbol exported by the library that follows a specific mangling scheme, allowing the dynamic linker to uniquely identify the Java native method associated with it. For instance, the native method com.lyrebirdstudio.lyrebirdlibrary.EffectFragment.sha dows in Fig. 5 maps to the JNI method Java_com_lyrebirdstudio_lyrebirdl ibrary_EffectFragment_shadows. As in previous works [38], DROIDREACH uses a decoder of the mangling scheme to resolve statically defined JNI methods.

Dynamic Mapping. When the dynamic loader loads a library, it runs the JNI_OnLoad function exported by the library. This function may dynamically define mappings between Java methods and native functions using the JNI primitive RegisterNatives, which takes as one of its arguments a pointer to an array of JNINativeMethod. This struct is defined as:

```
typedef struct {
    char *name;      // ex: "nativeCtor"
    char *sign;      // ex: "(Ljava/lang/String;)J"
    void *fnPtr;     // function code pointer
} JNINativeMethod;
```

The struct states that the native implementation of the Java native method name having the signature sign (which defines, in smali, the types of the method arguments and the return value) is available at the address fnPtr. Figure 6 shows how a real app is defining the mapping for the JNI method n_getEffects.

Previous works [38] perform symbolic execution from JNI_OnLoad to identify the array passed to RegisterNatives. This strategy has two downsides: (a) the exploration is halted when reaching a given call depth (e.g., 5 in ARGUS-SAF) to mitigate path explosion, possibly failing to reach RegisterNatives, and (b) the exploration may incur a large overhead when JNI_OnLoad is not trivial.

For these reasons, our approach devises a more scalable heuristic to detect dynamic mappings. The key idea is that several developers follow the guidelines of Android [5] and statically define the JNINativeMethod array at compilation time, placing it in the global data section. DROIDREACH thus scans the data section of a library, looking for an array with elements following the pattern:

1. Pointer to a valid string (name).
2. Pointer to a valid string (sign).
3. Pointer to a function in the text section (fnPtr).

Since some apps may instead allocate and initialize the array during the execution of JNI_OnLoad, DROIDREACH fallbacks to symbolic execution when:

1. The heuristic fails to identify mappings for a library containing JNI_OnLoad.
2. The heuristic identifies some mappings, but there are clashes on the pair (name, signature) of some methods, e.g., there are multiple Java methods from different classes called name with the same signature, requiring to inspect additional arguments of RegisterNatives to solve the ambiguity.

Hence, DROIDREACH fallbacks to a more heavyweight analysis only when there are insights that the heuristic is not working correctly.

Running Example. When loading the JavaLayerActivity class, the loader is executed due to J0, processing native-lib.so. The JNI_OnLoad function of this library defines the mapping (J6, N1). DROIDREACH identifies it by analyzing the array mappings. Symbolic execution analyses may instead struggle when JNI_OnLoad integrates some complex code before the call to RegisterNatives.

3.5 Static Analysis of the Native Layer

After identifying the JNI mappings, DROIDREACH constructs the ICFGs for the native layer considering each JNI method as a possible entry point. To cope with challenge C2, DROIDREACH recursively builds the ICFG if one function of a library is calling a function of another library. Additionally, to cope with challenge C3, our approach combines the ICFGs built by different techniques.

ICFG Construction. For each JNI method, DROIDREACH builds the CFGs and the CGs of the native functions to obtain the ICFGs. Our implementation uses the GHIDRA reversing framework [32], as it worked particularly well when considering libraries found in Android apps. The ICFGs derived in this stage include only code points from the same shared object of the starting JNI method.

Library Dependency Graph. Given the ICFG for a JNI method, our app-roach analyzes the `calls` to imported functions, i.e., calls to functions from other libraries. To represent this information for all ICFGs, it defines a *library dependency graph*, where the nodes represent libraries and the edges are calls across different libraries. Each edge is annotated with a list of caller-callee tuples to track the different calls that may involve the same pair of libraries.

ICFG Refinement: Nested Libraries. Using the library dependency graph, DROIDREACH refines the ICFG of each JNI method to include code points from nested libraries. Since this stage may need to build the ICFG of methods never met before (or it may discover new calls to other imported functions), our app-roach iteratively repeats the two previous stages until a fixed point is reached.

ICFG Refinement: Symbolic Exploration. The previous stages can build ICFGs that may traverse several libraries, potentially representing paths able to reach even *deep* code points in an execution path. However, the previous stages may still miss some critical edges in the ICFG: e.g., in the presence of a callee that performs an indirect call using a target defined by its caller. While reverse engineering frameworks, such as GHIDRA, have reduced the need for heavyweight dataflow analyses significantly, there are still several cases where they may be needed to accurately build an ICFG. For this reason, for each JNI method, our approach performs a symbolic exploration using `CFGEmulated` of ANGR [33] to recover the missed edges. To control path explosion, the exploration stops its analysis when the call stack contains more than 5 nested calls (as in ARGUS-SAF). Moreover, path branches are not evaluated, thus skipping most symbolic queries. After running this refinement step, we repeat the two previous stages until a fixed point is reached. Hence, DROIDREACH combines two different techniques for building the ICFGs: the first one is more scalable but less accurate, while the second one is more accurate but less scalable. Previous approaches, such as ARGUS-SAF, have favored ICFG construction approaches based on symbolic execution, which however can struggle at reaching *deep* code points.

Running Example. Starting from N1, DROIDREACH builds one ICFG with code points {N1, N2, N3, N4, N5, N6, N7}. Indirect jumps (N6, N8) and (N3, N9) are not discovered by GHIDRA but can be recovered using a symbolic exploration. Since N3 calls a function of `other-native-lib.so`, DROIDREACH builds the library dependency graph, analyzes this library, and adds {N9, N10, N11, N12}.

3.6   Reachability Analysis

The last step is in charge of computing a path from a source to a sink.

Defining the Sink. In general, the sink is a user-defined choice that is tightly connected to the goal targeted by an analysis. In this paper, given a vulnerability report, we define the sink as the *closest* code point (or even the set of code points if there is not a unique choice) that the app execution should reach in order to reproduce the bug described in the report. To identify the open-source project related to a library from an Android app, including the adopted release, we refer to solutions, such as [3], that have proposed effective binary similarity techniques.

Merging ICFGs. Given a sink, DROIDREACH exploits the JNI mappings to connect ICFGs of the Java layer to the ICFGs of the native layer.

Finding a Path from a Source to a Sink. Finally, for each source p_s and for each sink p_t, our approach evaluates whether there exists a path from p_s to p_t. In practice, since there could be several alternative paths between p_s and p_t, our current implementation by default emits the shortest one as it typically is the simplest to check for a user. However, alternative paths can be requested.

Running Example. Assuming that N12 is part of a known vulnerability in `other-native-lib.so`, DROIDREACH builds the ICFGs in Fig. 4 and quickly computes the path {J5, J6, N1, N2, N3, N9, N10, N11, N12}.

4   Experimental Evaluation

In this section, we evaluate the efficacy of DROIDREACH. Due to lack of space, we omit the discussion of step S1 as it involves well-known mainstream Java analysis frameworks, which we did not alter in DROIDREACH. Experiments were conducted in a Ubuntu 20.04 Docker container, using two Intel Xeon E5-4610v2 CPUs and 256 GB of RAM. APK hashes of evaluated apps can be found at [9].

4.1   Microbenchmarks

To validate DROIDREACH, we considered existing benchmarks from the Android literature. DROIDBENCH [7] does not involve native libraries. On NATIVEFLOW-BENCH [38], DROIDREACH performs consistently with ARGUS-SAF when considering the reachability goal. Since NATIVEFLOWBENCH ignores the challenges from Sect. 3.1, we designed a new benchmark suite composed of 13 apps that exhibit these aspects from different perspectives (see Table 6 in the Appendix). The source code and a detailed discussion of this suite can be found in a dedicated repository [10]. On 12 out of 13 apps, DROIDREACH correctly builds accurate native ICFGs, improving on ARGUS-SAF (8 out of 13). The failing case involves an indirect jump at *deep* call depth: this app was specifically designed to highlight that DROIDREACH cannot solve, in general, the scalability issues that inherently affect static analyses, and it can only help to mitigate them (hopefully in several cases). Further details on the results are available at [10].

4.2   Real-World Dataset

Dataset. To evaluate the efficacy of DROIDREACH on real-world apps, we collected the top-20 apps from each category of the Google Play Store, keeping the ones containing ARMv7 libraries. Overall, we obtained 500 apps, whose *popularity* ranges from a minimum of 100K downloads to more than 1 billion downloads.

Table 1. Analysis of false negatives: executed code points found in the ICFGs.

APK	# of executed code points found in the native ICFGs from		
	ARGUS-SAF	GHIDRA	DROIDREACH
com.sec.android.easyMover	33/33	33/33	33/33
com.jb.zcamera	11/11	11/11	11/11
com.mi.android.globalFileexp.	31/48	47/48	47/48
com.space.cleaner.smart.tool	52/75	65/75	75/75
com.soundcloud.android	57/102	72/102	72/102
video.like	197/518	272/518	320/518
com.zentertain.photocollage	186/331	174/331	239/331
com.picsart.studio	442/1282	203/1282	736/1282
shareit.lite	33/60	44/60	47/60
com.imangi.templerun	60/326	67/326	248/326
com.amazon.mp3	92/395	218/395	239/395
com.cam001.selfie	282/344	211/344	322/344
com.tripadvisor.tripadvisor	2/42	30/42	30/42
com.yodo1.crossroad	3/79	25/79	25/79
com.king.candycrushjellysaga	5/54	6/54	6/54

Table 2. Analysis of false positives: validated code points in the ICFGs.

APK	Validation mode	Confidence	# code points to validate	# validated code points
com.imangi.templerun	Dynamic	High	2357	1565
com.picsart.studio	Dynamic	High	1307	748
com.cam001.selfie	Dynamic	High	974	326
com.king.candycrushjellysaga	Dynamic	High	168	63
com.amazon.mp3	Mixed	Medium	625	441
shareit.lite	Static	Medium	12	12
com.sec.android.easyMover	Static	Medium	107	60

Such selection choice has also been guided by the idea of representing apps whose vulnerability may have a very large impact on the end-users. The average *complexity* of these apps is very high, as detailed in Table 5 from the Appendix, in terms of the number of Java and native instructions (more than 2.3 million of native LoC on average), the number of Java `native` methods (more than 204 methods on average) and of ARMv7 libraries (at least 5 on average).

Fine-Grained Evaluation. To evaluate the correctness of DROIDREACH, we need to analyze the false negatives (code points that are missing from the ICFGs) and the false positives (code points that are wrongly inserted in the ICFGs).

For the false negatives, we randomly picked 15 apps from our dataset and then manually stimulated them in the Android emulator as a user would do in a short usage session, recording the executed native function entry points. Any recorded code point should thus be contained in the ICFGs. While our sample set may seem small, the effort for validating the results took more than 1.5 man-months. Table 1 divides the 15 apps into three groups: apps where DROIDREACH was able to identify more than 95% of the executed code points are in the first group, more than 50% of the code points in the second group, less than 50% of code points in the third group, respectively. DROIDREACH significantly outperforms ARGUS-SAF and GHIDRA (when used in step S3 in place of DROIDREACH) on several apps. This result comes from the effective combination of different techniques: ARGUS-SAF fails to scale its analysis and GHIDRA misses indirect jumps that could be recovered with a symbolic execution analysis, while DROIDREACH shows the best of the two approaches (see [9] for detailed debug results). However, there are some apps where even DROIDREACH is unable to statically recover some executed code points. On some apps, slightly increasing the maximum call depth in the symbolic exploration can lead to better results (e.g., from 5 to 10 allows to find +9% of executed code points in com.amazon.mp3). Similarly, increasing the maximum analysis timeout can improve the accuracy, but there is a trade-off that must be taken into account between accuracy and analysis time. Even when extending the analysis time, DROIDREACH cannot cope with some patterns (Sect. 5): e.g., com.yodo1.crossyroad loads a library using a custom loader and com.imangi.templerun indirectly executes code from the Mono framework.

For the false positives, the evaluation is significantly harder as it requires to *exhaustively* stimulate an app, which can hardly be done *automatically* for most apps. Nonetheless, we attempted to still validate at least a subset of the code points. In particular, we compared the ICFGs from DROIDREACH to the ones from GHIDRA and ARGUS-SAF, extracting the code points detected only by our approach and then keeping only the function entry points. To keep the evaluation sustainable, we considered a subset of the 15 apps and analyzed how to stimulate their JNI methods based on the reports from FlowDroid (S1). We then executed each app under a debugger during an extended usage session, tracking which function entry points found by DROIDREACH were actually executed. Table 2 shows the results of our experiments. On four applications, we were able to validate a large fraction of the selected code points, bringing high confidence in their correctness. On three other applications, we could not dynamically validate most code points. This is not unexpected as several program behaviors depend on external events (e.g., server-side interactions) and specific usage patterns that cannot always be reproduced. For instance, the considered code points from com.sec.android.easyMover are within a library related to USB OTG functionalities in Samsung devices, which we could not stimulate. On shareit.lite, the code points are mostly related to C++ exception handling, making them hard to trigger. On com.amazon.mp3, we experienced some crashes when inserting the breakpoints in some libraries, allowing us to dynamically validate only a few points. For these three applications, we thus also performed a *manual* static validation by analyzing a subset of their code points with IDA Pro, validating whether the points are *reasonable*, i.e., they are likely reachable within an execution, reporting, however, lower confidence as we did not validate them by running the app. Regarding unvalidated code points, they should not necessarily *all* be seen as false positives, as proving or disproving their correctness is

Table 3. Resolved JNI mappings during step S2.

	# Recovered Mappings		Analysis Time (secs)	
	ARGUS-SAF	DROIDREACH	ARGUS-SAF	DROIDREACH
Static JNI mappings	4,610	4,610	8,542	8,542
Dynamic JNI mappings	765	1,912	259,136	20,345
Both	5,375	6,522	267,678	28,887

Table 4. ICFG results on methods analyzed using different approaches in S3.

DROIDREACH vs	# JNI methods processed by both	% apps for which DROIDREACH has			# code points found by		
		Less	Same	More	DROIDREACH (ratio w.r.t. competitor)		
		Code points than competitor			Total	Total ratio	Geo. mean ratio
GHIDRA	5,623	2.8%	9.8%	87.3%	64,818,031	1.24×	1.95×
ARGUS-SAF	4,711	1.3%	7.2%	91.5%	54,901,175	7.58×	5.64×
ARGUS-SAF-MLIB	4,527	1.6%	8.5%	89.9%	51,618,223	6.51×	5.09×

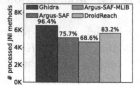 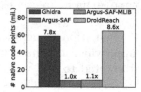 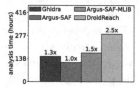

Fig. 7. ICFG results (step S3) on the full set of JNI methods over all apps.

hard: static analyses are often proposed when automatic dynamic analyses cannot exhaustively cover the program code. We provide additional details at [9]. Overall, the effort for this validation was more than 1.5 man-months.

Coarse-Grained Evaluation. To get a wider evaluation of DROIDREACH, we now consider the full dataset. We focus our discussion on steps S2 and S3. Step S1 brings the same results for all tools as they can use the same analysis framework. Similarly, step S4 can be implemented in the same way for all compared tools.

A crucial challenge tackled by DROIDREACH during step S2 is the identification of mappings between Java native methods and JNI methods. In our dataset, step S1 identifies 7,463 *reachable* Java `native` methods. This is quite interesting since the total number of Java `native` methods in our dataset is 113,316: this suggests that even if an app contains some code, then it may not necessarily execute it. Our manual investigation has confirmed that most apps are integrating third-party frameworks, but they often only use a subset of their functionalities.

Table 3 reports the cumulative number of mappings successfully resolved by DROIDREACH compared to ARGUS-SAF, and the cumulative analysis time for these two approaches. Overall, a large fraction (61.8% of 7, 463) of the mappings are statically defined by the apps and can be resolved by both frameworks. The remaining 2853 (38.2%) mappings are defined dynamically though RegisterNatives: DROIDREACH performs significantly better than ARGUS-SAF on these methods, resolving 2.5× dynamic mappings. DROIDREACH is also significantly more efficient: the analysis time is reduced by a factor of 9.3×.

Overall, DROIDREACH has resolved 87.4% of the methods (compared to 72.0% in ARGUS-SAF), suggesting that 941 (12.6%) methods do not follow the implementation patterns expected by DROIDREACH. While the symbolic exploration helped resolve 79 methods, it still failed on the 941 unresolved methods. In these cases, the JNI_OnLoad function was too complex and the exploration was aborted after a 15-minutes timeout. Users can customize this timeout in DROIDREACH to possibly increase the accuracy of S2. While there are still some unresolved mappings, the improvement from DROIDREACH can be quite significant in practice: when considering the Adobe PDF reader (com.adobe.reader), all mappings were found exclusively by DROIDREACH, meaning that ARGUS-SAF would completely skip any analysis on the native layer for this app.

After finding the JNI mappings for our dataset, we evaluate the effectiveness and performance of DROIDREACH during the ICFG construction (step S3). Besides DROIDREACH, we consider: (a) GHIDRA, as it is internally used by DROIDREACH, (b) ARGUS-SAF, which is the main competitor, and (c) ARGUS-SAF-MLIB, a variant of ARGUS-SAF that we developed, which can continue its analysis even in the presence of nested libraries (while the original approach would ignore them). This is important since 340 (68%) apps out of 500, have at least one nested library and some apps may even have a *nested chain* with up to three libraries. Each solution was executed for 2 h for each application, reconstructing in sequence the ICFGs of the reachable JNI methods. To make a fair comparison, all tools received the same output from step S2.

Since different tools come with different trade-offs in terms of accuracy and performance, leading to a very different number of JNI methods processed within the 2-h experiment, we first present in Table 4 a pairwise comparison between DROIDREACH and the other solutions considering the common set of JNI methods which were processed by each pair of frameworks. When considering the 5, 623 JNI methods analyzed by both DROIDREACH and GHIDRA, DROIDREACH can identify more code points in 87% of the apps. On average for each app, DROIDREACH finds 1.95× code points than GHIDRA. When considering the 4, 711 JNI methods analyzed by both DROIDREACH and ARGUS-SAF, our approach identifies more code points in 91% of the apps. On average for each app, DROIDREACH finds 5.64× code points than ARGUS-SAF. When considering our custom variant ARGUS-SAF-MLIB, DROIDREACH is still more effective.

Figure 7 summarizes the results when considering all JNI methods from all apps: one approach could be less accurate but more efficient on one method, thus having the chance to process more methods within the 2-hour per-app timeout. The left chart shows that GHIDRA was able to process more methods than the competitors, followed by DROIDREACH. The right chart confirms that DROIDREACH is indeed slower than GHIDRA. However, the center chart shows that the number of code points is still in favor of DROIDREACH. This is expected: DROIDREACH is performing the same work as GHIDRA, plus additional analyses. Hence, its running time is always larger than GHIDRA, leading to some apps reaching the 2-hour per-app timeout before processing the entire set of methods.

When comparing DROIDREACH to ARGUS-SAF and ARGUS-SAF-MLIB, the results in Fig. 7 show that DROIDREACH was able to process more methods than these two solutions, detecting ~8× their number of code points but requiring also a larger analysis time. Indeed, ARGUS-SAF (and ARGUS-SAF-MLIB) are generally faster (–60%) than GHIDRA (and thus DROIDREACH) for a large set (~60%) of methods but: (a) these solutions are significantly less accurate, identifying fewer code points on this large set, and (b) on the other methods, these solutions fail to generate any ICFG as they reach the timeout or saturate very early the memory (25GB in our experiments) due to path explosion. When attempting to increase the maximum call depth in ARGUS-SAF-MLIB, we observed a crucial increase in the number of timeouts and out-of-memory events.

Finally, the average analysis time of DROIDREACH per app was 0.7 hours, 0.4 for GHIDRA, 0.3 for ARGUS-SAF, and 0.4 for ARGUS-SAF-MLIB.

4.3   Case Studies

Establishing that apps contain vulnerable libraries *does not mean* that such functions constitute necessarily an *immediate* security concern. We present two case studies where DROIDREACH can be used as an aid in evaluating the *impact* of vulnerable functions. These apps were considered by a previous study [2,3].

Case Study A: Reachable Function. We consider the function BN_bn2dec from libcrypto.so. This function is used in Amazon Alexa (com.amazon.dee. app) and is vulnerable in OpenSSL ≤ 1.1.0 (CVE-2016-2182 [16]) with a score of 7.5. DROIDREACH finds the following path (depicted in Fig. 8 in the Appendix):

- The Java layer loads the OnStartCommand function belonging to the com.here. android.mpa.service.MapService class. This function loads the (name obfuscated) a method from the com.nokia.maps.SSLCertManager class.
- This method calls the x509_NAME_HASH native function that belongs to the com.nokia.maps.CryptUtils class, which is statically mapped to the JNI method com_nokia_maps_CryptUtils_X509_1NAME_1HASH in libMAPSJNI.so.
- The JNI method calls X509_free, which is a function from libcrypto_here. so, that in turn invokes ASN1_item_free, which calls a stripped function at offset 0x5fdd4 (after reversing, it appears to be asn1_item_combine_free).

- From this function, the static exploration becomes challenging. There are no direct jumps that connect the function to the target sink. However, DROIDREACH identifies a reachable offset 0x5ba20 (which would allow for further exploration towards the sink). A deeper inspection shows that such an offset is *indirectly* calculated and jumped to by accessing dedicated data structures. This is the reason why the connection between the offsets was not immediately evident. Moreover, it demonstrates the capability of DROID REACH to identify non-obvious paths that do not involve direct jumps.
- The function at offset 0x5ba20 calls X509_NAME_ONELINE, which invokes i2t_ASN1_OBJECT. Such a function invokes OBJ_obj2txt, which calls BN_bn2dec.

After having statically identified a path, we tried to stimulate it dynamically. Unfortunately, reproducing it in the emulator is not easy: besides registering an account and performing several interactions, additional events must be faked to execute the interesting Java class. Nonetheless, we successfully reproduced a similar path in com.nokia.maps, which includes the same third-party library. ARGUS-SAF and GHIDRA miss some crucial edges, failing to find the path.

Case Study B: Unreachable Function. The goal of this case study is to ascertain whether there is *no path* to a target vulnerable function. We consider Zoom (us.zoom.video meetings) and the function SRP_VBASE_get_by_user in libcrypto.so (CVE-2016-0798, score 7.8), for which DROIDREACH could *not* find a path. To validate our claim, we directly patched the native library function with an interrupt svc 11 instruction to see whether the function was invoked. Then, we tested all possible functionalities. The application showed no signs of a crash, meaning that the target function was not invoked during the execution. Although we *cannot* guarantee that the function will *never* be invoked, we believe that it cannot be executed by a normal user under normal conditions.

5   Limitations

Our current implementation of DROIDREACH has a few limitations:

- Like ARGUS-SAF, DROIDREACH is currently tuned for ARMv7 code. However, from the methodological side, nothing is tight to a specific architecture.
- DROIDREACH looks for native libraries in standard locations: fixes may be needed in the case of a custom loader or packed libraries.
- DROIDREACH cannot prove the feasibility of a path, i.e., it does not currently generate the *inputs* or *stimulations* that can reproduce the execution path. Unfortunately, existing static solutions [38] do scale on large apps
- DROIDREACH represents the structure of the code using ICFGs. This representation may be inadequate in the presence of frameworks that deviate significantly from the traditional Android programming environment.

6   Conclusions

DROIDREACH statically analyzes Android apps to assess the *reachability* of native functions. Understanding this aspect can be crucial to assess the security of apps featuring libraries with known vulnerabilities, as vulnerable but not reachable functions may not represent an *immediate* threat. Our experiments show that DROIDREACH can reconstruct more accurate ICFGs than other solutions and that it can be a valuable tool for an analyst during a security evaluation.

Acknowledgments. This work was partially supported by the project PON AIM Research and Innovation 2014-2020 - Attraction and International Mobility, funded by the Italian Ministry of Education, University and Research.

Appendix

Table 5. Statistics for the apps selected for the evaluation.

Downloads range	# apps	Avg # Java insns.	Avg # Java native insns	Avg native methods	Avg # ARMv7 libs
100K-1M	32	1,228,452	212.81	2,308,222	18
1M-10M	89	1,533,235	229.24	2,654,673	10.42
10M-100M	132	1,849,999	204.86	2,554,607	7.52
100M-500M	201	1,515,141	209.48	2,841,205	7.81
500M-1B	28	1,649,847	235.43	2,511,424	9.82
1B+	18	1,945,265	565.94	2,392,670	5.39

Table 6. Description of the microbenchmarks [10].

Challenge	ID	Description
C1	0	JNI mapping through static name mangling
C1	1	JNI mapping through static name mangling and method overloading
C1	2	JNI mapping dynamically defined using the `RegisterNatives` API
C1	3	JNI mapping dynamically defined using the `RegisterNatives` API but with *clash* in the class name
C1	4	JNI mapping dynamically defined using the `RegisterNatives` API but without following the Android guidelines
C1	5	JNI mapping dynamically defined using the `RegisterNatives` API with a hard-to-analyze `JNI_OnLoad`
C2	6	JNI Method calls a function from a *nested* library
C3	7	The target function is called at a *high* calldepth
C3	8	The target function is called after an indirect call (C++ virtual call, lazy initialization)
C3	9	The target function is called after an indirect call (C++ virtual call, callback)
C3	10	The target function is called after an indirect call (function pointer)
C3	11	The target function is called at a *high* calldepth after an indirect call (*small* calldepth after the indirect call)
C3	12	The target function is called at a *high* calldepth after an indirect call (*high* calldepth after the indirect call)

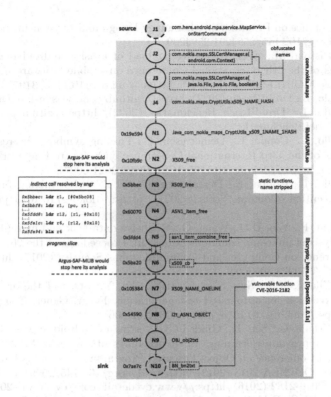

Fig. 8. Path found in the Amazon Alexa app (`com.amazon.dee.app`) that can reach the vulnerable function `BN_bn2txt` from OpenSSL (CVE-2016-2182 [16]).

References

1. Abraham, A., Andriatsimandefitra, R., Brunelat, A., Lalande, J., Tong, V.V.T.: GroddDroid: a gorilla for triggering malicious behaviors. In: 10th International Conference on Malicious and Unwanted Software. MALWARE 2015 (2015). https://doi.org/10.1109/MALWARE.2015.7413692
2. Almanee, S.: Librarian dataset (2021). https://github.com/salmanee/Librarian
3. Almanee, S., Ünal, A., Payer, M., Garcia, J.: Too quiet in the library: an empirical study of security updates in android apps' native code. In: 43rd IEEE/ACM International Conference on Software Engineering. ICSE 2021 (2021). https://doi.org/10.1109/ICSE43902.2021.00122
4. Amalfitano, D., Fasolino, A.R., Tramontana, P., De Carmine, S., Memon, A.M.: Using GUI ripping for automated testing of android applications. In: Proceedings of the 27th IEEE/ACM International Conference on Automated Software Engineering. ASE 2012 (2012). https://doi.org/10.1145/2351676.2351717
5. Android: Native libraries (2021). https://developer.android.com/training/articles/perf-jni#native-libraries
6. Android Developers: UI/Application Exerciser Monkey (2021)
7. Arzt, S., et al.: FlowDroid: precise context, flow, field, object-sensitive and lifecycle-aware taint analysis for Android apps. In: Proceedings of the 35th ACM SIG-

PLAN Conference on Programming Language Design and Implementation (2014). https://doi.org/10.1145/2594291.2594299

8. Bello, L., Pistoia, M.: Ares: triggering payload of evasive android malware. In: Proceedings of the 5th International Conference on Mobile Software Engineering and Systems. MOBILESoft 2018 (2018). https://doi.org/10.1145/3197231.3197239
9. Borzacchiello, L.: DroidReach (2022). https://github.com/season-lab/DroidReach
10. Borzacchiello, L.: DroidReach Benchmarks (2022). https://github.com/season-lab/DroidReachBenchmarks
11. Borzacchiello, L., Coppa, E., Demetrescu, C.: Fuzzing symbolic expressions. In: Proceedings of the 43rd International Conference on Software Engineering (ICSE 2021) (2021). https://doi.org/10.1109/ICSE43902.2021.00071
12. Borzacchiello, L., Coppa, E., Demetrescu, C.: FUZZOLIC: mixing fuzzing and concolic execution. Comput. Secur. (2021). https://doi.org/10.1016/j.cose.2021.102368
13. Bosu, A., Liu, F., Yao, D.D., Wang, G.: Collusive data leak and more: large-scale threat analysis of inter-app communications. In: Proceedings of the 2017 ACM on Asia Conference on Computer and Communications Security (2017). https://doi.org/10.1145/3052973.3053004
14. Chen, T., Zhang, X.S., Guo, S.Z., Li, H.Y., Wu, Y.: State of the art: dynamic symbolic execution for automated test generation. Futur. Gener. Comput. Syst. (2013). https://doi.org/10.1016/j.future.2012.02.006
15. Choi, W., Necula, G., Sen, K.: Guided GUI testing of android apps with minimal restart and approximate learning. In: Proceedings of the 2013 ACM SIGPLAN International Conference on Object Oriented Programming Systems Languages & Applications. OOPSLA 2013 (2013). https://doi.org/10.1145/2509136.2509552
16. CVE: CVE-2016-2182 (2016). https://www.cvedetails.com/cve/CVE-2016-2182/
17. Derr, E., Bugiel, S., Fahl, S., Acar, Y., Backes, M.: Keep me updated: an empirical study of third-party library updatability on android. In: Proceedings of the 2017 ACM SIGSAC Conference on Computer and Communications Security. CCS 2017 (2017). https://doi.org/10.1145/3133956.3134059
18. Desnos, A.: Androguard (2021). https://github.com/androguard/androguard
19. Enck, W., et al.: TaintDroid: an information-flow tracking system for realtime privacy monitoring on smartphones. ACM Trans. Comput. Syst. (2014). https://doi.org/10.1145/2619091
20. Eschweiler, S., Yakdan, K., Gerhards-Padilla, E.: Discovre: efficient cross-architecture identification of bugs in binary code. In: 23rd Annual Network and Distributed System Security Symposium (2016). https://doi.org/10.14722/ndss.2016.23185
21. Gao, J., Yang, X., Fu, Y., Jiang, Y., Shi, H., Sun, J.: Vulseeker-pro: enhanced semantic learning based binary vulnerability seeker with emulation. In: Proceedings of the 2018 ACM Joint Meeting on European Software Engineering Conference and Symposium on the Foundations of Software Engineering ESEC/FSE 2018 (2018). https://doi.org/10.1145/3236024.3275524
22. Gordon, M.I., Kim, D., Perkins, J., Gilham, L., Nguyen, N., Rinard, M.: Information-Flow Analysis of Android Applications in DroidSafe. In: Proceedings of the 2015 Network and Distributed System Security Symposium (2015). https://doi.org/10.14722/ndss.2015.23089
23. Gu, Y., et al.: JGRE: an analysis of JNI global reference exhaustion vulnerabilities in android. In: 2017 47th Annual IEEE/IFIP International Conference on Dependable Systems and Networks (DSN), pp. 427–438 (2017). https://doi.org/10.1109/DSN.2017.40

24. Hao, S., Liu, B., Nath, S., Halfond, W.G., Govindan, R.: Puma: programmable ui-automation for large-scale dynamic analysis of mobile apps. In: Proceedings of the 12th Annual International Conference on Mobile Systems, Applications, and Services. MobiSys 2014 (2014). https://doi.org/10.1145/2594368.2594390
25. Hwang, S., Lee, S., Kim, J., Ryu, S.: Justgen: effective test generation for unspecified JNI behaviors on JVMs. In: 2021 43rd International Conference on on Software Engineering (ICSE 2021) (2021). https://doi.org/10.1109/ICSE43902.2021.00151
26. Klieber, W., Flynn, L., Bhosale, A., Jia, L., Bauer, L.: Android taint flow analysis for app sets. In: Proceedings of the 3rd ACM SIGPLAN International Workshop on the State of the Art in Java Program Analysis. SOAP 2014 (2014). https://doi.org/10.1145/2614628.2614633
27. Lee, S., Lee, H., Ryu, S.: Broadening horizons of multilingual static analysis: semantic summary extraction from c code for JNI program analysis. In: 2020 35th IEEE/ACM International Conference on Automated Software Engineering (ASE 2020) (2020). https://doi.org/10.1145/3324884.3416558
28. Li, L., et al.: IccTA: detecting inter-component privacy leaks in android apps. In: 37th IEEE International Conference on Software Engineering (ASE 2015) (2015). https://doi.org/10.1109/ICSE.2015.48
29. Li, S., Tan, G.: Finding bugs in exceptional situations of JNI programs. In: Proceedings of the 16th ACM Conference on Computer and Communications Security, pp. 442–452. CCS 2009 (2009). https://doi.org/10.1145/1653662.1653716
30. Liao, Y., Cai, R., Zhu, G., Yin, Y., Li, K.: MobileFindr: function similarity identification for reversing mobile binaries. In: Lopez, J., Zhou, J., Soriano, M. (eds.) ESORICS 2018. LNCS, vol. 11098, pp. 66–83. Springer, Cham (2018). https://doi.org/10.1007/978-3-319-99073-6_4
31. Ming, J., Xu, D., Jiang, Y., Wu, D.: BinSim: trace-based semantic binary diffing via system call sliced segment equivalence checking. In: 26th USENIX Security Symposium (USENIX Security 17) (2017)
32. NSA: Ghidra (2016). https://ghidra-sre.org/
33. Shoshitaishvili, Y., et al.: SOK: (state of) the art of war: offensive techniques in binary analysis. In: IEEE SP 2016 (2016). https://doi.org/10.1109/SP.2016.17
34. Sun, M., Wei, T., Lui, J.C.: TaintART: a practical multi-level information-flow tracking system for android RunTime. In: Proceedings of the 2016 Conference on Computer and Communications Security CCS 2016 (2016). https://doi.org/10.1145/2976749.2978343
35. Tan, G., Chakradhar, S., Srivaths, R., Wang, R.D.: Safe java native interface. In: In Proceedings of the 2006 IEEE International Symposium on Secure Software Engineering, pp. 97–106 (2006)
36. Tan, G., Croft, J.: An empirical security study of the native code in the JDK. In: Proceedings of the 17th Conference on Security Symposium. SS 2008, USENIX (2008). https://doi.org/10.5555/1496711.1496736
37. Wang, X., Zhu, S., Zhou, D., Yang, Y.: Droid-AntiRM: taming control flow anti-analysis to support automated dynamic analysis of android malware. In: Proceedings of the 33rd Annual Computer Security Applications Conference (2017). https://doi.org/10.1145/3134600.3134601
38. Wei, F., Lin, X., Ou, X., Chen, T., Zhang, X.: JN-SAF: precise and efficient NDK/JNI-aware inter-language static analysis framework for security vetting of android applications with native code. In: Proceedings of the 2018 ACM SIGSAC Conf. on Computer and Communications Security. CCS 2018 (2018). https://doi.org/10.1145/3243734.3243835

39. Wei, F., Roy, S., Ou, X.: Robby: amandroid: a precise and general inter-component data flow analysis framework for security vetting of android apps. ACM Trans. Priv. Secur. (2018). https://doi.org/10.1145/3183575
40. Wong, M.Y., Lie, D.: IntelliDroid: a targeted input generator for the dynamic analysis of android malware. In: Proceedings 2016 Network and Distributed System Security Symposium (2016). https://doi.org/10.14722/ndss.2016.23118
41. Xu, Y., Xu, Z., Chen, B., Song, F., Liu, Y., Liu, T.: Patch based vulnerability matching for binary programs. In: Proceedings of the 29th ACM SIGSOFT International Symposium on Software Testing and Analysis. ISSTA 2020 (2020). https://doi.org/10.1145/3395363.3397361
42. Xue, L., et al.: NDroid: toward tracking information flows across multiple android contexts. IEEE Trans. Inf. Forensics Secur. (2019). https://doi.org/10.1109/TIFS. 2018.2866347
43. Xue, L., Zhou, Y., Chen, T., Luo, X., Gu, G.: Malton: towards on-device non-invasive mobile malware analysis for ART. In: 26th USENIX Security Symposium (USENIX Security 17). USENIX Association (2017)
44. Yan, L.K., Yin, H.: DroidScope: seamlessly reconstructing the OS and Dalvik semantic views for dynamic android malware analysis. In: 21st USENIX Security Symposium (USENIX Security 12) (2012)
45. Li, Y., Yang, Z., Guo, Y., Chen, X.: DroidBot: a lightweight UI-Guided test input generator for android. In: 2017 IEEE/ACM 39th International Conference on Software Engineering Companion (2017). https://doi.org/10.1109/ICSE-C.2017.8

Extensible Virtual Call Integrity

Yuancheng Jiang[1]([✉]), Gregory J. Duck[1], Roland H. C. Yap[1], Zhenkai Liang[1], and Pinghai Yuan[2]

[1] National University of Singapore, Singapore, Singapore
{yuancheng,gregory,ryap,liangzk}@comp.nus.edu.sg
[2] Anhui Normal University, Wuhu, China
yph@ahnu.edu.cn

Abstract. Virtual calls in `C++` are known to be vulnerable to control-flow attacks, and *Virtual Call Control Flow Integrity* (VCFI) is a proposed defense. However, most existing VCFI defenses are incompatible with real-world `C++` software that need extensibility in the form of dynamic loading, foreign language interface, etc. In this paper, we propose a novel and *extensible* VCFI mechanism—namely eVCFI—that is flexible enough to handle such software requirements. eVCFI uses *Approximate Membership Query* (AQM) filters, recasting VCFI as an efficient set membership query, giving an $O(1)$ time VCFI check that can be implemented in only a few instructions, all while supporting extensibility and multi-threading. We compare eVCFI with existing VCFIs, showing that we can achieve more accurate policies or extensibility compared with other VCFI mechanisms designed for efficiency or modularity. Evaluation of eVCFI shows small 1.3% overhead with SPEC 2006. Furthermore, we evaluate eVCFI against the FireFox web browser: an example of large/complex `C++` software that uses both dynamic loading and a foreign language interface (Rust). We show that eVCFI can protect Firefox with a small overhead of 1.15%. We believe that eVCFI is the first VCFI defense able to protect complex software like Firefox.

1 Introduction

`C++` is a popular programming language used to implement large complex software systems such as web browsers [8]. However, `C++` is also vulnerable to attacks such as *control flow hijacking*, where the attacker exploits a memory/type error to divert control to an attacker's chosen function/gadget, possibly granting arbitrary code execution. A common control flow hijack attack in `C++` programs is to exploit *dynamic dispatch*. Modern `C++` Application Binary Interfaces (ABIs), e.g., Itanium `C++` ABI [1] (used by `x86_64`), implement dynamic dispatch using *Virtual Function Pointer Tables* (*vtables*) and *virtual member functions*. During a *virtual call* to a virtual member function, the corresponding function pointer in the *vtable* is called. However, this approach is vulnerable to attack, since pointer to the *vtable* (a.k.a., the *vptr*) is stored within the object itself, making it a potential target for type/memory errors. `C++`-specific variants of these attacks have also been developed, such as *Counterfeit Object-oriented Programming* (COOP) [18].

Virtual Call Control Flow Integrity (VCFI) is a proposed defense against virtual call control flow attacks [5,13,20]. VCFI defenses must efficiently validate a given object's *vptr* against the set of possible valid values, as determined by the full class hierarchy specified by the program and the C++ language semantics. A state-of-the-art VCFI defense is shipped with the LLVM/clang++ compiler (cfi-vcall in [14]), which uses *Link-time Optimization* (LTO) to extract the full class hierarchy at compile time. However, in addition to security and performance, *extensibility* is another critical design dimension for VCFI. For example, it is common for real-world software to be *modular*, i.e., interoperating with other modules through dynamic linking/loading. Furthermore, some software includes components with special interfaces, such as foreign language interfaces or *Component Object Models* (COM). Supporting such ad hoc extensions, even with manual intervention, necessitates a VCFI design that can handle "dynamic" class hierarchies—i.e., where the class hierarchy can be extended at runtime, or on-the-fly. We call this *class extensibility*, or simply *extensibility*.

The multithreaded Firefox browser exemplifies complex software architected with extensibility. Firefox uses dynamic loading, XPCOM (similar to COM), and foreign language interfaces, including C++ and Rust components interacting with each other. Such extensibility is incompatible with many existing VCFI defenses. For example, in Firefox, a C++ virtual call to an object implemented in Rust will trigger a VCFI violation, even though this is a benign (intentional) usage and not an attack. Our aim is to design an efficient VCFI defense that is compatible with extensibility requirements, expanding the applicability of VCFI to more C++ software.

In this paper, we identify the requirements for extensible and efficient virtual call integrity in C++ programs. We introduce a new VCFI defense, eVCFI, which is designed to support extensible C++ software. To do so, we first cast the problem as an efficient set-membership question on dynamic sets, i.e., is a *vptr* a member of the "allow-set" of the corresponding class? There are many algorithmic tradeoffs with efficient set-membership, with different pros and cons. In this paper, we argue that *Approximate Membership Query* filters (AQM), such as Bloom filters [3], meet the design requirements of extensible VCFI. Specifically, we show that Bloom filters are efficient, i.e., $O(1)$ check that only needs a few instructions, regardless of the class hierarchy size or the number of modules. Furthermore, we show Bloom filters are extensible in that new entries can be added at runtime, without the need for thread locking/synchronization. In effect, our approach supports extensibility using a single underlying mechanism (Bloom filters), without fast/slow path logic. Finally, as our approach is *probabilistic*, we show how to enhance the security of Bloom filters using a combination of randomization and *eXecute Only Memory* (XOM).

We evaluate eVCFI against standard benchmarks (SPEC) and a web browser (Mozilla Firefox). Our results show that the default configuration of eVCFI incurs low-performance overheads on SPEC of 1.3%; and 1.01%, 1.18%, 1.15% overheads on Kraken, Octane, Dromaeo browser benchmarks. We use Firefox to showcase the challenges posed by complex C++ software requiring non-trivial extensibility. We note that other VCFI defenses tend to fail on Firefox. This shows the importance of extensibility support, since an incompatible defense is as good as no defense, meaning that the software cannot be protected against virtual call control flow attacks. We believe eVCFI is the first approach that can harden the Firefox codebase with VCFI.

2 Overview

We summarize C++ dynamic dispatch attack and defense, and then describe our attack model. For the rest of this paper, we focus on C++ under X86_64/Linux.

2.1 C++ Dynamic Dispatch

C++ implements *dynamic dispatch* in the form of *virtual member functions*. A derived class can override the definition of a virtual function they inherit. Virtual calls, abbreviated as *vcall*, use a *Virtual Function Table* (*vtable*) to dynamically decide which virtual function definition is to be invoked. The *vtable* is essentially an array of function pointers, where each virtual function member of a class is mapped to a corresponding index in the function pointer array. The *vtable* is retrieved using a *Virtual Function Table Pointer* (*vptr*) stored in an implicit field (vptr) within the object itself. Given an object pointer (*objptr*), the basic template for a virtual call is: (1) read the (*vptr*) value from the implicit (*objptr*->vptr); and (2) call the function pointer at the corresponding index (*idx*) as follows:

$$vptr = objptr\text{->vptr}; \quad vptr[idx](...);$$

Here, we say that the *static type* of a virtual call site is given by decltype(*objptr*). Under the C++ type system, the *dynamic type* of (*objptr*) of class C can be any (D *), where (D=C) or (D) is derived (possibly indirectly) from (C). This implements a form of polymorphism, where a derived class (D) can be upcast to the base class (C), but a virtual call still uses (D)'s definitions. The object and *vtable* layout is defined by the Itanium C++ ABI [1] (used in x86_64 Linux). Note the *vtable* is usually protected from modification using read-only memory.

Example 1. *(Class and* vtable *Layout)* An example class and *vtable* layout are illustrated in Fig. 1. Here, we consider a simple hierarchy with two base classes (C) and (B), and a derived class (D) that inherits from both. We consider a (C) and (D) object. As per the Itanium C++ ABI, the (C) object has a single *vptr* pointing to the first *virtual function entry* in (C::vtable). Index (−1) contains the *Run-Time Type Information* (C::rtti) entry, and index (−2) contains the *offset-to-top* explained below. Class (C) does not inherit from another class, and only has two virtual functions, C::foo and C::bar.

The layout for the (D) object is more complex. Class (D) inherits from two base classes (C) and (B), i.e., *multiple inheritances*. So the (D) object has two *vptrs*, one for each proper base class. Furthermore, (D::vtable) is a *vtable group* that

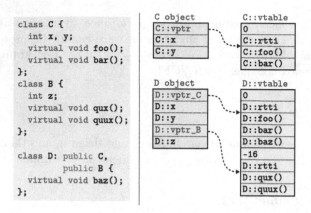

Fig. 1. Example class and *vtable* layout.

concatenates: (i) a *primary vtable* for the virtual function entries of (D) and the first proper base class of (D); and (ii) a *secondary vtable* for each proper base class. For secondary *vtables*, the *offset-to-top* is the pointer difference between the two *vptr* fields in the (D) object, in this case (−16). The derived class (D) can *override* the implementation of any virtual function from a base class. For example, (D::foo) will point to (D)'s implementation of inherited virtual function (foo). Otherwise, if (D) does not override (foo), the virtual function entry defaults to (D::foo=C::foo). □

C++ Dynamic Dispatch Security. The C++ dynamic dispatch design is primarily intended for efficiency rather than security. Since C++ is not a memory-safe language, an attacker can exploit a memory error (e.g., buffer overflow or use-after-free) to overwrite *vptr* values inside objects.

Object pointer integrity can also be violated using *type confusion* (e.g., a bad C++ static_cast) or *Counterfeit Object-oriented Programming* (COOP) style-attacks [18]. Likewise, *vptr* integrity can be violated using (sub-object) memory, type confusion, or use-after-free errors to directly overwrite the *vptr* value with another value. An attacker can exploit such errors to replace the object or *vptr* value with a new value of choice.

2.2   C++ Dynamic Dispatch Defenses

The mainstream defense to vcall control flow hijack is *Virtual Call Control Flow Integrity* (VCFI) which validates the correctness of the virtual function before invocation. VCFI is essentially a specialization of *Control Flow Integrity* (CFI) [2] to C++ dynamic dispatch. The basic idea is to associate an *allow-set* of valid values to each virtual call site. There are two main variants: (*direct*) an allow-set of valid *virtual functions*; and (*indirect*) an allow-set of valid *vptrs*.

Under the assumption that *vtables* are read-only, the *direct* and *indirect* variants offer similar protection, with indirect being slightly stronger. Many VCFI implementations, such as LLVM-xDSO [14], use the *indirect* approach and so do we. Given a call to virtual function (C::f()), ideally the allow-set contains all *vptrs* allowable under the C++ type system. This includes all *vptrs* to primary/secondary *vtables* containing: (1) the entry for (C::f()), and (2) the entry for (D::f()) for all classes (D) derived from (C). For example, considering the class hierarchy from Fig. 1, the allow-set for the virtual call (c->bar()) is:

$$Allow = \{C::\texttt{vptr}, D::\texttt{vptr\_C}\}$$

VCFI asks if the vcall is in the allow-set at the virtual call site. The allow-set is determined by the strength of the implemented VCFI policy, e.g. Sect. 4.1 shows the effective result from different VCFI systems.

Many implementations of VCFI variants exist, see surveys [5,13,20]. However, most source-based VCFI defenses require that the class hierarchy is fixed at compile time, so the allow-set is also fixed. While monolithic and pure C++ code can meet this assumption, complex software often goes beyond, sometimes using a wide range of heterogeneous components with diverse dynamic behavior on the class hierarchies and interfacing needs. This requires VCFI solutions that are *extensible* which is the focus of this paper. We highlight that a VCFI defense that is not extensible will simply fail on a codebase without a fixed class hierarchy. There are many tradeoffs needed to support extensibility. Here, we mention some (V)CFI implementations to provide context for the next section. Further details will be discussed in Sect. 5.

MCFI [16] identified the lack of modularity being an impediment for the adoption CFI, proposing a *Modular CFI* (MCFI) supporting separate compilation and dynamic library loading for C. RockJIT [17] extends MCFI with C++ support. MCFI puts the program in a sandbox to protect its data structures, which can affect performance. A state-of-art VCFI is provided by LLVM [14,15]. LLVM has low overheads, but requires a fixed class hierarchy that is obtained using *Link-Time Optimization* (LTO). LTO allows the full (global) class hierarchy to be known at compile time. Although LLVM does not provide any extensibility, there also exists an experimental mode, namely *LLVM*-xDSO, that also supports dynamic linking and loading. The drawback is a much larger overhead, as we discuss and evaluate later. As can be seen, there are complex tradeoffs for VCFI, and existing solutions solve only a subset of our design goals. This can limit practical adoption, especially for complex/legacy software systems.

2.3 Problem Statement

Using the indirect VCFI check variant, we formalize a VCFI check using the class hierarchy of the program as follows:

$$c.\texttt{vcall}(\ldots); \qquad c.\texttt{vptr} \in Allow_C? \qquad \text{(VCFI-CHECK)}$$

where c is an object of static type C, and vcall denotes a virtual member function of C. The VCFI check determines whether *vptr* belongs to the allow-set for type C, where $D::\texttt{vptr} \in Allow_C$ for any D derived from C, or $D{=}C$.

In essence, VCFI has three main components:

- **Algorithms for the VCFI check**. This can also affect multi-threading.
- **Accuracy of the policy check**. We use Eq. (VCFI-CHECK). When extensibility is not used, the allow-set is determined statically (compile-time) under the C++ semantics. If the program uses dynamic loading, the class hierarchy may be extended, meaning that the allow-set(s) need to be dynamically updated accordingly. Similarly, ad hoc extensions, such as foreign language interfaces, may also need to be reflected in the allow-set(s).
- **Performance of the check**. Ideally, overheads should be low.

As is common, we model a strong attacker capable of reading from or writing to arbitrary memory, subject to the program's memory protections. We assume the attacker cannot modify page permissions, and that there exists separate mitigation for hardware side channels [12]. We assume that the attacker intends to hijack control flow by compromising C++ dynamic dispatch. Other kinds of control flow hijack are orthogonal to this paper. We assume *vtables* reside in *read-only* memory (.rodata) and cannot be modified. We also assume that the attacker has not already hijacked control flow, a standard assumption for CFI-like defenses.

In order to enforce the VCFI policy, the *Allow*-set(s) must be constructed from a diverse and dynamic class hierarchy used by complex programs. We support various kinds of extensibility. Modularity by separate compilation allows extensibility by dynamic linking or dynamic loading during execution. This form of extensibility has automated support. Other kinds of extensibility generally used are: component object interfaces such as COM or XPCOM; and foreign language interfaces and language interoperation, e.g. between C++ and Rust. We classify these under *ad hoc extensibility* and provide a basic extensibility mechanism to validate the custom vcalls.

3   Extensible VCFI Enforcement

In this paper, we seek flexibility in extending the allow-set at runtime either through dynamic loading or ad hoc extensions. In addition, the VCFI check should be secure, constant-time, and support multi-threading (as class hierarchy extensibility involves updates). By casting the VCFI defense as a *secure set membership test*, we can examine the known algorithmic set membership trade-offs, where it is difficult to simultaneously satisfy design goals such as dynamic sets, constant time, multi-threaded support. Instead, we implement VCFI using an *Approximate Member Query* filter (AMQ), which allows for efficient set membership tests. AMQs are approximate, meaning that there can be false positives, but not false negatives.

Many possible AMQs have been proposed. In this paper, we use Bloom filters [3], which aligns well with our efficiency and extensibility design goals.

3.1   VCFI Based on Bloom Filters

Bloom filters [3] are the most well known form of AMQ. Traditionally, Bloom filters are implemented using a *bit array* B and a set of $k \geq 1$ hash functions

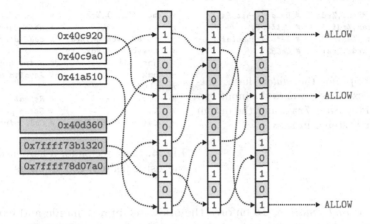

Fig. 2. Example Bloom filter VCFI defense for $k = 3$. Here, we assume that the three pointers 0x40c920, 0x40c9a0 and 0x41a510 are the only valid members of the *Allow-set*. Each value is mapped $k = 3$ times to the Bloom filter using $k = 3$ *different hash functions*. Here, valid entries map to a non-zero value for each hash function; and the invalid values map to at least one zero value and are "filtered"

$hash_{1..k}$. An element x is considered to be a member of the set if:

$$B[hash_1(x)] \neq 0 \wedge \cdots \wedge B[hash_k(x)] \neq 0$$

Else, if the result is 0 for any $hash_i$, the element x is not a member of the set. Bloom filters are efficient, and testing for membership is constant time.

Figure 2 gives a basic example of a Bloom filter-based VCFI defense. We assume the only valid members of the allow set are: (*vptr*) values 0x40c920, 0x40c9a0 and 0x41a510, and that there are 3 hash functions ($k = 3$). All valid *vptr* values map to a non-zero entry and thus will be allowed by the VCFI defense. The invalid value 0x40d360 by the first hash maps to zero and is disallowed. Bloom filters are approximate meaning that collisions are possible, as will be discussed later.

VCFI benefits from the Bloom filter design in multiple ways. Firstly, Bloom filters are inherently *extensible*, meaning that new entries for class hierarchy extensions can be incrementally added at any time. Furthermore, set deletion (for dynamic *unloading*) is also supported using "counting" Bloom filters. Secondly, Bloom filters are inherently *efficient*, with an $O(1)$ set membership test that can be implemented using a few instructions. Finally, our Bloom filter implementation makes exclusive use of *atomic* operations to add/remove entries, thereby achieving *thread safety* without the need for thread synchronization.

3.2 System Design

eVCFI is an implementation of VCFI using Bloom filters, and consists of two main parts: (1) an LLVM-based *program transformation* to insert VCFI checks, and (2) a *runtime support* library.

```
1   movabs $SALT,%rdi    # Load 64-bit SALT
2   imul %rax,%rdi       # Multiply
3   xor %esi,%esi        # Zero accumulator
4   crc32q %rdi,%rsi     # CRC32
```

Fig. 3. Recipe for the *mulcrc* hash function. This example assumes the input *vptr* is stored in register %rax, and the output hash value is stored in %rsi.

```
1    mov (%rdi),%rax         # Load vptr
2    ...                     # Hash into %rsi
3    movabs $BLOOM,%rdx      # Load Bloom base
4    testb $0,(%rdx,%rsi)
5    jnz .LOK                # Entry non-zero?
6    ud2                     # Invalid vptr
7    .LOK:
8    ...                     # Repeat for k > 1
9    ...                     # Setup parameters
10   callq *INDEX(%rax)      # Call virtualFn()
```

Fig. 4. Basic recipe for a hardened virtual call using (salted) Bloom filters

Program Transformation. To enforce the allow-set in a dynamic and extensible manner, we use program transformation to implement the (VCFI-CHECK) check using Bloom filters. The basic instrumentation schema is shown in Figs. 3 and 4. Here, Fig. 3 implements a single Bloom filter lookup, that is repeated k times, using the following *salted* hash function:

$$hash(salt, vptr) = crc32(salt \times vptr)$$

Note that the choice of the hash function is a tradeoff between performance and security. By design, eVCFI uses the salted hash function, *mulcrc*, which is parameterized by a *salt* constant, allowing for k different hash functions to be readily defined. The Fig. 4 schema implements the hardened vcall. The program transformation is implemented using an LLVM compiler pass.

Compared to the unprotected vcall, our Bloom filter VCFI uses an additional $8*k$ instructions (4 for the salted hash and 4 for the remainder of the check, repeated k times). For the minimal $k = 1$, there will be 8 additional instructions for the instrumented vcall, and 7 instructions in the execution path (see Figure 4). In contrast to other VCFI defenses, such as LLVM-xDSO, our solution does not use a fast/slow-path design. Instead, eVCFI uses a single $O(1)$ check uniformly for all vcalls, whether the call site needs dynamic extensibility or not. Dynamic linking/loading is handled by adding entries to the corresponding Bloom filter itself, as handled by the eVCFI runtime.

Runtime Support. A dynamic *Class Hierarchy Analysis* (CHA) is used to build the inheritance relationships between classes at runtime Conceptually, the CHA establishes a mapping between classes C and the the corresponding $Allow_C$ set. The CHA constructs the allow-sets from the (current) set of loaded modules, which may be updated at any time via dynamic (un)loading.

The hash function salts (SALT$_i$, $i \in 1..k$) and the base address of the Bloom filter (BLOOM) are encoded as special dynamic symbols, i.e., the eVCFI-symbols. During program initialization (i.e., before main is called), and for each dynamically loaded library, the eVCFI-symbols are initialized with suitable randomized values. To handle dynamic linking/loading, the CHA is incrementally applied to all classes in the loaded library. When the loaded library extends an existing class hierarchy with a new class, new entries are incrementally added to the corresponding allow-sets, i.e., by updating the corresponding Bloom filter. Dynamic unloading is handled similarly, by removing entries from allow-sets.

Security. We have introduced a VCFI defense based on Bloom filters. However, the Bloom filters themselves must also be hardened against attack.

- **Bloom Filter Integrity**. We ensure the integrity of the Bloom filter by making it *read-only*. To deal with updates, the most efficient way is to use the X86_64 *Memory Protection Keys* (MPK) extension. When updating the Bloom filter, we grant the write permission to the thread using MPK, while other threads continue to have read-only access. An additional defense is also to randomize the location of the Bloom filter (BLOOM).
- **Missed Detection Mitigation**. The above protects against basic Bloom filter modification by the attacker. Nevertheless, Bloom filters are inherently *approximate*, meaning that *false positives* are possible. In practice, this means that an invalid *vptr′* value may be accepted as valid by the Bloom filter, if the value happens to *collide* with another valid value.[1] This can be mitigated by increasing k, at the cost of performance. Alternatively, we can also randomize the hash functions by choosing CSPRNG-randomized value(s) for the SALT$_i$ at runtime. The randomized salt(s) make it difficult for the attacker to construct collisions.

    The attacker may also attempt to find a collisions by chance. The missed detection probability can be approximated using the formula: $(1 - e^{-kn/m})^k$, where m is the number of entries in the Bloom filter array, k is the number of hash functions, and n elements have been inserted. By default, eVCFI uses $m = 2^{24}$ and k is user-configurable, allowing for a security versus time trade-off. For example, assuming $n = 1000$, then the *missed detection* probability will be $\sim 5.96 \times 10^{-5}$ for $k = 1$, $\sim 5.96 \times 10^{-15}$ for $k = 3$, etc. Even for $k = 1$, brute force attacks are not practical for most applications, since the program will immediately abort on a single incorrect guess.
- **Runtime Protection**. The randomized SALT$_i$ parameters are encoded as immediate values in the instruction sequence that implement the salted hash function(s) (Fig. 3). In principle, the attacker may also attempt to recover these values by directly reading and interpreting the executable code residing in the program's memory. This can be directly prevented by using *Execute Only Memory* (XOM), which ensures that the instrumentation can only ever be executed, and never read. XOM is supported by Linux, using the standard mprotect system call, on all X86_64 CPUs with MPK support.

Ad hoc Extensibility. Ad hoc extensibility covers cases where a vcall should be allowed (intended by the programmer), but would otherwise be detected as an error. This includes idioms that go beyond the semantics of C++, such as COM

---

[1] Note that, while missed detections are possible, *false detections* are not. That is, a Bloom-filter-based VCFI defense will never flag a valid vcall as invalid.

Table 1. VCFI comparisons

○: unprotected	◔/◑: partially protected		●: fully protected	-: not applicable		
VCFIs	Policies		Features		Static Overhead		
	Static	Dynamic	non-LTO	Ad Hoc	astar	omnetpp	xalanc
Baseline	○	○	✓	✗	0%	0%	0%
MCFI	◔	◔	✓	✗	35.7%	40.8%	53.6%
VTV	◑	◑	✓	✗	7.4%	4%	55.1%
ShrinkWrap	●	●	✓	✗	7%	6.1%	46.8%
LLVM	●	-	✗	✗	-0.2%	2.5%	2.9%
LLVM-xDSO	●	●	✗	✗	3.8%	4.9%	7.7%
eVCFI	●	●	✓	✓	1.3%	2.6%	8.5%

objects implemented as an opaque wrapper, which can be thought of as a programmatically defined foreign interface. Another example is objects defined in other languages that "inherit" from a base object defined in C++. Without any VCFI defense, there is usually no compatibility issue, provided the binary ABI is respected. With a VCFI, then we want to allow such ad hoc extensions if intended by the programmer. To support this, eVCFI supports programmer-specified "extension-lists" that can be used to insert additional entries to the allow-set(s). Although this approach is manual, it allows for arbitrary ad hoc extensions that are necessary for supporting complex software such as Firefox.

4   Evaluation

We compare eVCFI with other VCFI defenses and evaluate the performance on the SPEC2006 C++ benchmark suite [11] and the Firefox web browser. All experiments run on Ubuntu (kernel version 4.13) with a Xeon Silver 4114 Processor (2.20GHz, 32GB of RAM). Both the processor and kernel support *Memory Protection Keys* (MPK) and *eXecute Only Memory* (XOM).

4.1   Evaluating VCFI Defenses

To give the overview of each (V)CFI implementation, we compare eVCFI against the security policies, features and overheads of: MCFI [16], VTV [19], Shrinkwrap [10] and LLVM. The results are summarized in Table 1. More information is provided in Appendix A.

The *Policies* column in Table 1 summarizes our test results on various vcall attacks using type confusion or memory corruption. The tool either prevents all attacks (●), or some attacks succeed (◔ or ◑), or all attacks succeed (○). We evaluate under several scenarios: (i) a static class hierarchy (the *Static* column); and (ii) a dynamic class hierarchy extension using dynamic loading with dlopen() (the *Dynamic* column). The baseline is without any VCFI defense, meaning that all vcall attacks succeed under all use cases.

For the *Static* case, MCFI exhibits the weakest policy under our testing. This is because MCFI implements a type-based CFI-policy, rather than a specialized VCFI policy. VTV implements a stronger policy, but does not detect derived class attacks under our tests. Finally, Shrinkwrap, LLVM and eVCFI all

Table 2. SPEC2006 C++ statistics

SPEC program	Static counts			Dynamic counts
	Lines of code	Number of vtables	Number of vcall-sites	Number of vcalls (Million)
omnetpp	26.7k	111	2218	3359.34
astar	4.3k	1	1	4996.99
xalanc	266.9k	958	21195	9821.91
namd	3.9k	4	0	0
dealII	94.5k	680	364	164.43
soplex	28.3k	29	638	3.18
povray	78.7k	28	286	0.15
Total	503.3k	1811	24702	18346

enforce an equivalent (strong) VCFI policy for the *Static* case. For the *Dynamic* case, most results are similar to *Static*, except for LLVM. This is because LLVM requires the (global) class hierarchy to be determined statically, through *Link Time Optimization* (LTO). However, this is not applicable when the class hierarchy is split between libraries.

Under *Features*, the *non-LTO* column indicates whether the VCFI defense is applicable without LTO. The *Ad Hoc* column indicates whether the defense supports ad hoc class hierarchy extensions, such as supporting COM objects or foreign language interfaces.

Finally, a summary of overheads (w.r.t. to *Baseline*) on the SPEC benchmarks is shown under *Static Overhead*. We note that only LLVM, LLVM-xDSO and eVCFI achieve a low performance overhead against the vcall-intensive xalanc benchmark. The overhead of eVCFI exceeds LLVM and LLVM-xDSO, but supports non-LTO compilation and ad hoc extensions. The full results are shown in Sect. 4.2 below.

4.2 Evaluation on SPEC Benchmarks

We evaluate the performance of eVCFI on the standard SPEC2006 C++ benchmark which represents entire programs that are well-understood and extensively analyzed workloads. We run the (ref) workloads taking the geometric mean across five runs. Table 2 summarises the SPEC2006 C++ benchmarks giving *source Lines Of Code* (sLOC), the number of *vtables*, and the number of virtual call sites. Among the SPEC2006 benchmarks, xalanc has the most vcall sites and vcalls during runtime, thereby incurring the most performance overhead for VCFI defenses. eVCFI detects the known type confusion bug in xalanc. For details, see Appendix B. It has been patched for the benchmarking.

We evaluate each tool with -O2 and *Link Time Optimization* (LTO) enabled. Although eVCFI does not require LTO, it is nevertheless compatible with LTO, and LTO is required by LLVM and thus is enabled for a fair comparison. As LTO is enabled with -O2, more optimization is enabled, meaning that some virtual calls may be *devirtualized*. For namd, this results in no virtual calls at runtime, thus, it is excluded. The experiments use the default eVCFI configuration: a 16MB Bloom filter ($m = 2^{24}$) and *mulcrc* is used as the (salted) hash function. The salt (SALT_i) parameters are randomized per run.

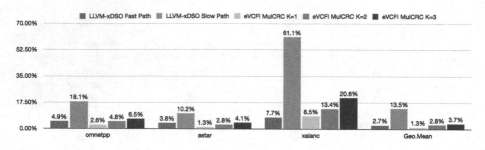

Fig. 5. Relative eVCFI overheads for SPEC C++ programs

The SPEC2006 runtime performance is shown in Fig. 5. Columns for dealII, soplex and povray are omitted as the overheads are negligible (the number of vcalls is small, see Table 2), but summarized in the geometric mean (*Geo.Mean*) column. Even dealII, with 164M virtual calls, has negligible overhead, highlighting that both LLVM-xDSO and eVCFI have minimal overheads for programs that are not virtual call dominant. The overhead of all results is relative to the baseline, which is LLVM (clang++) with LTO and -O2. We compare the following:

LLVM-xDSO is the LLVM VCFI implementation with experimental "cross-dso" support. The implementation uses a fast/slow-path design, where the "fast" path is equivalent to the standard LLVM VCFI check. If the fast check fails, a "slow" path is invoked, which checks for dynamic class hierarchy extensions (e.g., dlopen()). The SPEC2006 benchmarks do not use extensibility features, meaning that only the fast-path will normally be invoked.

LLVM-xDSO-SLOW is an artificially modified LLVM cross-dso that exclusively uses the slow-path VCFI check. This version is intended to represent the potential "worse case" behaviour of a fast/slow path design.

eVCFI is our implementation. We show results for eVCFI with $k = \{1, 2, 3\}$ to demonstrate different performance versus security tradeoffs.

For omnetpp and astar (with $k = 1, 2$) we see that eVCFI is faster than LLVM-xDSO for omnetpp and astar, and eVCFI has similar performance for xalanc and $k = = 1$. Generally, we see that the overheads of eVCFI increase with k, representing a performance trade-off. We also see that eVCFI is substantially faster than LLVM-xDSO-SLOW, which highlights the advantage of single unified check rather than fast/slow-path design. For example, for the vcall-heavy xalanc benchmark, we see that LLVM-xDSO-SLOW has a 61.1% overhead, compared to 8.5% for eVCFI. In summary, the geometric mean for SPEC2006 is: LLVM-xDSO 2.7%, LLVM-xDSO-SLOW 13.5%, eVCFI k={1,2,3}: 1.3%, 2.8%, 3.7%.

4.3   Evaluating Firefox

We also evaluate eVCFI against the Firefox browser [8] version 78.0 ESR. Firefox is designed with different components and modules, including a foreign language

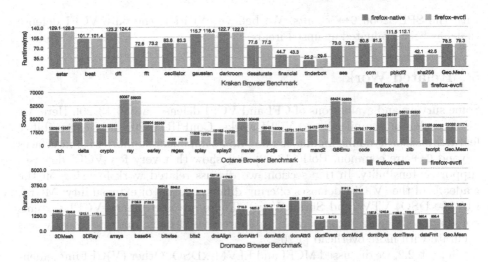

Fig. 6. Browser benchmarks for native Firefox and eVCFI-enhanced Firefox

interface between C++ and Rust. Firefox is a real-world example of software requiring class hierarchy extensibility. Any VCFI defense that does not account for the extensibility requirements may incorrectly flag some vcalls as attacks, rather than intended behavior. We are also not aware of any existing VCFI defense that works with Firefox (since Rust versions). The Firefox build system currently does not support LLVM-xDSO.

Firefox consists of several binaries (executable and modules), and there are more than 5000 vtables and more than $185K$ virtual call-sites (most in libxul.so which is loaded using dlopen()). Firefox is also challenging because the code requires extensibility features, namely dynamic loading, foreign language interfaces (Rust), and XPCOM objects. Firefox is also multi-threaded.

In addition to dynamic loading, we use Firefox to test ad hoc extensibility. This involves creating an *extension-list* for the allow-sets to support specific Firefox idioms, such as XPCOM and vtables that were manually implemented in Rust. We remark that such ad hoc extensibility requires manual intervention (i.e., the specification of the extension-list). However, such manual intervention is necessary in the general case, since arbitrary ad hoc extensions cannot necessarily be detected automatically.

To show the practical performance of eVCFI, we evaluate the performance of Firefox using the Kraken, Octane [9], and Dromaeo [6] benchmarks.[2] The benchmark results are in Fig. 6. Overall, eVCFI exhibits low overheads, with the performance overheads on Kraken, Octane, and Dromaeo being 1.01%, 1.18%, and 1.15% respectively. We see that eVCFI has acceptable overheads consistent

---

[2] Due to insufficient horizontal space for all the Dromaeo results, we show a representative sample that has more differences from the Kraken and Octane results. The results not shown also have low overheads.

with the SPEC2006 C++ results. We believe eVCFI is the only VCFI defense that has been evaluated against Firefox.

5   Related Work

Some surveys and evaluations of CFI and VCFI defenses are [5,13,20]. Here, we discuss relevant compiler-based VCFI works. ConFIRM [20] show extensibility features such as dynamic linking/loading and component support with interfaces beyond C++ are common. Both [13,20] also show that very few VCFI defenses support extensibility. In this section, we discuss related work focusing on the tradeoffs of the (V)CFI defenses offering different forms of extensibility: MCFI, LLVM-xDSO, VTV (and ShrinkWrap). There are also binary VCFI systems not discussed, being incomparable to source-based ones, and are usually less accurate with more overhead [5,20].

In Sect. 2.2, we discussed MCFI and LLVM-xDSO. Other (V)CFI implementations with extensibility support include VTV [19] and ShrinkWrap [10]. VTV also highlights the importance of modularity and builds the set of *vtables* at runtime to validate the *vptr*. The VTV work itself does not fully implement a VCFI policy (see Table 1). ShrinkWrap tightens the VTV policy for VCFI.

MCFI uses a transaction-based framework to update its data structures to support multithreading, and VTV needs to synchronize threads to prevent data races. In contrast, eVCFI uses Bloom filters that naturally support atomic updates, which both simplifies the handling of multi-threaded programs as well as being more efficient.

The underlying data structures need to be updated for extensibility. Thus, any update also needs to be secure against attacks. MCFI secures its data structures using a sandbox design. To do so, MCFI effectively limits the program to a 32-bit address space [16]. However, this can easily introduce incompatibilities, especially with programs that use large amounts of virtual memory. VTV makes its data structures read-only, and updates need to block other threads. In eVCFI, only the thread updating the Bloom filter has write permission using MPK. This avoids the need for synchronization and operating system intervention.

In MCFI, the overhead is a combination of the sandboxing and the cost of the CFI check itself. The results in [17] show that, due to the sandboxing overhead, even programs like namd, soplex and povray incur a performance penalty. In contrast, these benchmarks, with few vcalls, incur negligible cost (near zero) for both LLVM and eVCFI, This is also confirmed by our results in Table 1, see astar which has relatively fewer vcalls.

The overheads for VTV on SPEC from [19] are: omnetpp 8%, astar 2.4%, xalanc 19.2%. Similar overheads were reproduced in [5]. Generally, these overheads are much greater than LLVM, which is not surprising as LLVM succeeds VTV. Our timings in Table 1 also give another reference point. However (non-cross-dso) LLVM does not support extensibility and being a purely static solution, should have the lowest overhead. Still we see that eVCFI (with extensibility) can compete. We also see that eVCFI is much faster than LLVM-xDSO-SLOW.

Specifically, eVCFI has $O(1)$ time guarantees, regardless of the extensibility usage while also adhering to the language semantics VCFI policy.

6   Conclusion

It is common for large/complex software to be broken into different modules, libraries or plugins that may be loaded dynamically. Furthermore, software may need to support ad hoc extensions, such as foreign language interfaces or COM objects. Such extensibility is generally incompatible with most existing VCFI defenses, or the defense is prohibitively slow. As such, no defense will be used, potentially leaving the program vulnerable.

In this paper, we presented a new VCFI defense based on *Approximate Member Query* (AMQ) filters, specifically Bloom filters. We show that Bloom filters can be used to implement an efficient VCFI defense, in the form of the eVCFI tool. Specifically, eVCFI supports $O(1)$ checks that are implemented in a few instructions. Furthermore, eVCFI supports dynamic loading and ad hoc extensions for multi-threaded programs, without relying on a fast/slow path design. We also show how Bloom filters can be hardened using a combination of randomization and *eXecute Only Memory* (XOM). We believe eVCFI is the first VCFI defense which can be used to harden Firefox—a challenging target that uses dynamic linking/loading, component interfaces, and C++ to Rust interoperation. Our Firefox compatibility testing shows eVCFI can provide greater extensibility support than existing VCFI defenses.

As future work, we believe our underlying design could also be adapted to other CFI-like defenses, beyond VCFI. Essentially, any defense that depends on a set membership query, including both source-based and binary CFI defenses, can likely use our approach.

Acknowledgments. We thank the anonymous reviewers for their valuable comments. This work has been supported in part by the Ministry of Education, Singapore (Grant No. MOE2018-T2-1-142) and by the National Research Foundation, Singapore under its NSoE DeST-SCI programme (Grant No. NSoE_DeST-SCI2019-0006). Any opinions, findings and conclusions or recommendations expressed in this material are those of the authors and do not reflect the views of National Research Foundation, Singapore.

A   VCFI Test Programs

To evaluate the security and usability of VCFI defenses, we construct a test program using the following class hierarchy:

```
class A { public: virtual void f() = 0; };    class A1: public A    { public: void f() {...} };
class B { public: virtual void f() = 0; };    class A2: public A    { public: void f() {...} };
class C { public: virtual int  f() = 0; };    class A11: public A1 { public: void f() {...} };
                                              class B1: public B    { public: void f() {...} };
                                              class C1: public C    { public: int  f() {...} };
```

Table 3. VCFI policy test results

	Class hierarchy	Ideal	MCFI	VTV	ShrinkWrap	LLVM	LLVM-xDSO	eVCFI
			Static					
TypeConf	Sibling(A2)	✓	✗	✓	✓	✓	✓	✓
TypeConf	Derived(A11)	✓	✗	✗	✓	✓	✓	✓
TypeConf	InterClass(B1/C1)	✓	✓	✓	✓	✓	✓	✓
MemCorr	Sibling(A2)	✓	✗	✓	✓	✓	✓	✓
MemCorr	Derived(A11)	✓	✗	✗	✓	✓	✓	✓
MemCorr	InterClass(B1/C1)	✓	✓	✓	✓	✓	✓	✓
			Dynamic					
TypeConf	Sibling(A2)	✓	✗	✓	✓	-	✓	✓
TypeConf	Derived(A11)	✓	✗	✗	✓	-	✓	✓
TypeConf	InterClass(B1/C1)	✓	✓	✓	✓	-	✓	✓
MemCorr	Sibling(A2)	✓	✗	✓	✓	-	✓	✓
MemCorr	InterClass(B1)	✓	✗	✓	✓	-	✓	✓
MemCorr	InterClass(C1)	✓	✓	✓	✓	-	✓	✓

The test program implements common vcall vulnerabilities, including COOP, type confusion and memory corruption. We also test both a static and dynamic class hierarchy, with the latter extended via `dlopen()`. The results are shown in Table 3. Here, the *Ideal* column represents the expected result for a complete VCFI defense. We use the following notation:

"✗": The defense does not protect against the vcall attack.

"✓": The defense works correctly and aborts the program preventing the attack.

"-": This is when the defense is incompatible For example, LLVM (non-cross-dso) does not support extensions using `dlopen()`.

B   Invalid Virtual Call Detected in `xalanc`

The eVCFI tool detects an invalid virtual call on line 1018 of `SchemaValidator.cpp` from the `xalanc` benchmark:

```
SchemaGrammar& sGrammar =
  (SchemaGrammar&) grammarEnum.nextElement();
sGrammar.getGrammarType();
```

At runtime, the (`grammarEnum.nextElement`) member function may return a reference to an object of type (`DTDGrammar`) that is not derived from the class (`SchemaGrammar`). This bug has been independently detected by other tools, including LLVM-xDSO [14], *vtable* interleaving [4] and type confusion sanitizers such as EffectiveSan [7]. For the performance evaluation, we patched `xalanc` to remove the bad cast and resolve the invalid virtual call.

References

1. Itanium C++ ABI (2022). http://itanium-cxx-abi.github.io/cxx-abi/
2. Abadi, M., Budiu, M., Erlingsson, Z., Ligatti, J.: Control-flow integrity. In: Computer and Communication Security. ACM (2005)
3. Bloom, B.: Space/time trade-offs in hash coding with allowable errors. Commun. ACM **13**(7), 422–426 (1970)
4. Bounov, D., Kici, R., Lerner, S.: Protecting C++ dynamic dispatch through VTable interleaving. In: Network and Distributed Systems Security. The Internet Society (2016)
5. Burow, N., et al.: Control-flow integrity: precision, security, and performance. ACM Comput. Surv. **50**(1), 1–33 (2017)
6. Dromaeo (2022). https://github.com/jeresig/dromaeo
7. Duck, G., Yap, R.: EffectiveSan: type and memory error detection using dynamically typed C/C++. In: ACM-SIGPLAN Symposium on Programming Language Design and Implementation. ACM (2018)
8. Firefox Web Browser (2022). https://www.mozilla.org/
9. Octane 2.0 (2022). http://chromium.github.io/octane/
10. Haller, I., Goktas, E., Athanasopoulos, E., Portokalidis, G., Bos, H.: ShrinkWrap: VTable protection without loose ends. In: Annual Computer Security Applications Conference. ACM (2015)
11. Henning, J.: SPEC CPU2006 benchmark descriptions. Comput. Arch. News **34**(4), 1–17 (2006)
12. Kocher, P., et al.: Spectre attacks: exploiting speculative execution. In: Security and Privacy. IEEE (2019)
13. Li, Y., Wang, M., Zhang, C., Chen, X., Yang, S., Liu, Y.: Finding cracks in shields: on the security of control flow integrity mechanisms. In: Computer and Communication Security. ACM (2020)
14. LLVM (2022). https://clang.llvm.org/docs/ControlFlowIntegrity.html
15. LLVM (2022). https://clang.llvm.org/docs/ControlFlowIntegrityDesign.html
16. Niu, B., Tan, G.: Modular control-flow integrity. In: Programming Language Design and Implementation. ACM (2014)
17. Niu, B., Tan, G.: RockJIT: securing just-in-time compilation using modular control-flow integrity. In: Computer and Communication Security. ACM (2014)
18. Schuster, F., Tendyck, T., Liebchen, C., Davi, L., Sadeghi, A., Holz, T.: Counterfeit object-oriented programming: on the difficulty of preventing code reuse attacks in C++ applications. In: Security and Privacy. IEEE (2015)
19. Tice, C., et al.: Enforcing forward-edge control-flow integrity in GCC & LLVM. In: Security Symposium. USENIX (2014)
20. Xu, X., Ghaffarinia, M., Wang, W., Hamlen, K.: CONFIRM: evaluating compatibility and relevance of control-flow integrity protections for modern software. In: Security Symposium. USENIX (2019)

Posters

Is Your Password Sexist? a Gamification-Based Analysis of the Cultural Context of Leaked Passwords

Daniel Mølmark-O'Connor[1] and Emmanouil Vasilomanolakis[2(✉)]

[1] Aalborg University, Copenhagen, Denmark
doconn17@student.aau.dk
[2] Technical University of Denmark, Lyngby, Denmark
emmva@dtu.dk

Abstract. Passwords are still the most common authentication method for various digital services. The majority of the research into passwords is focused on technical concerns rather than the human elements of password construction. In this paper, we aim at studying cultural aspects of leaked passwords with the usage of an online game. In particular, we introduce a novel web-based data collection tool utilizing gamification elements that benefits from appealing aesthetics and implemented narrative elements to engage users into prolonged play. The player's role is to label presented passwords with available descriptive tags. Our goal is to collect a large number of gaming data to identify prevalent tag choices through consensus, and as such, assign perceived meaning to the passwords through the tags. An initial field test of the prototype returned a high number of responses that were determined to be valid when assessed via internal controls.

1 Introduction

Passwords play a pivotal role in modern computing. They are still regarded as the most common form of user authentication in digital services. Despite this, user generated passwords remain a weak and exploitable security measure resulting from users generally creating passwords that are easy to crack [6,13]. Research into passwords tends to favour investigations into the storage and security of passwords, such as research into the effectiveness and effect of password strength meters [12], or the guess-ability of a password [4].

The human-side of passwords, in the form of improper password creation practices, is a sizeable vulnerability in the authentication scheme, yet there remains little research in the area of the sociological factors of password creation. It poses the question: *What are users thinking when creating passwords?*. A survey of 470 Carnegie Mellon University computer users collected data on the behaviours and practices related to password use and creation when faced with new stricter password policies [10]. Results showed 19% of users had difficulty

© The Author(s), under exclusive license to Springer Nature Switzerland AG 2022
V. Atluri et al. (Eds.): ESORICS 2022, LNCS 13556, pp. 743–748, 2022.
https://doi.org/10.1007/978-3-031-17143-7_36

remembering passwords, and that over half the users reused or slightly modified old passwords, often with the inclusion of special characters, as they were a new policy requirement. Almost 80% of users created passwords based on a word or name. Overall, the paper suggested that users create passwords that just meet the minimum technical requirements, and that common use of words or names is to assist memorability.

Further studies into password creation habits showed that users are conscious of the strength of their passwords, believed in incorrect security practices, and over estimated the privacy of their personal information [13]. Regarding how cultural factors play into password construction, a 2018 study of a meta-data rich leak from a Middle Eastern bank showed that there were identifiable trends present that separated individuals from different cultures [1]. The aforementioned research suggests that there is a human context to password creation beyond just technical restraints.

In this paper, a solution to the lack of research into the sociological meaning of passwords is presented in the form of a game. Our prototype[1] takes real passwords from various data-leaks and assigns tags with some form of context or meaning to the password. With this data, it is possible to identify trends occurring across different data-leaks, such as establishing a prevalence of sexist or explicit passwords in one social media website when compared to another. These findings can assist in the research of password creation and further the understanding of not only *why* humans make weak passwords, but *how* they make weak passwords. Studies have shown that humans are great problem solvers and are motivated by assisting scientists [3,11]. Our game takes this approach by being freely accessible to all interested parties who wish to take part in its quick and easy game-play through their web-browser. The game engages with the player and leverages the power of human reasoning to interpret the presented leaked passwords.

2   System Design

Our prototype is split into a front-end, which is the game a user experiences, and a back-end, which is the database of passwords used and the storage of the user responses. The front-end is hosted on two indie game platforms and can be played in-browser or downloaded to play locally. The back-end database is hosted online through a web hosting service called Hostinger [8]. This MySQL database is populated with real passwords taken from 10 different sources, most of which are data-leaks from well known sources such as LinkedIn and NordVPN. The interaction between the front and back-end comes when a user boots up the game. The front-end contacts the database and returns a password at random to present on screen to the user. To ensure uniformity of the data, there is a check to ensure all passwords are labelled an equal number of times, or as close as possible. Once a user has assigned labels to the password presented, the

---

[1] https://simmer.io/@AAUUser/password-labeller.

database updates that password with this data and returns a new password to the user, and the loop continues.

The front-end is the game experience a user interacts with and can be seen in Fig. 1. It was designed with the idea of promoting user engagement to prolong playtime. To do this, it leaned into game design theory [7], colour theory [5] and interaction design [9]. It also leaned into the gestalt principles of design for improved usability [2].

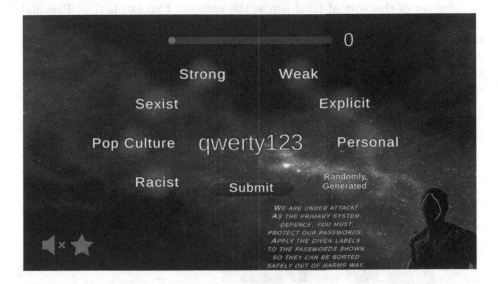

Fig. 1. Prototype gameplay

As depicted in Fig. 1, the game consists of a (real world leaked) password placed in the centre of the screen surrounded by a collection of buttons with labels that can be chosen. The core game-play loop is for the user to interpret the password and chose the labels they feel appropriate before submitting and receiving a new password. A robot character provides encouragement and asserts a narrative in which the user is under attack and must label passwords to protect them. There are also points in the game-play where the user is presented with multiple choices associated with the narrative that results in a branching tree style story-line with 7 potential endings. Upon completing the game, the user is congratulated and given the option to play again.

3   Preliminary Results

The prototype was loaded with 1829 passwords taken from 10 different sources. Eight of these sources were legitimate passwords taken from data-leaks. In particular the data leaks were from LinkeDin, NordVPN, YouPorn (porn website), Ashley Maddison (online dating service), Hotmail, 000Webhost (web-hosting service), Muslim Match (Muslim dating website) and Faith Writers (Christian focused website). The heterogeneity of the data sources allows us to experiment and analyze how the cultural context of passwords is altered on (very) different digital services. The two remaining sources were controls for validation, one being the top 20 most common passwords seen in 2022[2], and the other a list of 40 randomly generated passwords.

Eight labels were chosen to be presented to the users for the experiment. Three labels were negatively charged (i.e., Sexist, Racist, Explicit) to see the distribution of this sort of label across the sources. Two labels (i.e., Personal and Pop Culture) were chosen to examine how the passwords were perceived to connect to the creator and their surrounding culture. Finally, three labels (i.e., Randomly generated, Secure, Insecure) were chosen both to assist validation control, but also to gauge the users' perception of password strength in combination with the other labels.

This setup has been active for 26 days before the responses were analysed. There were 3074 instances of passwords being labelled with a total of 4012 labels across the total of 1829 passwords. The distribution can be seen in Fig. 2.

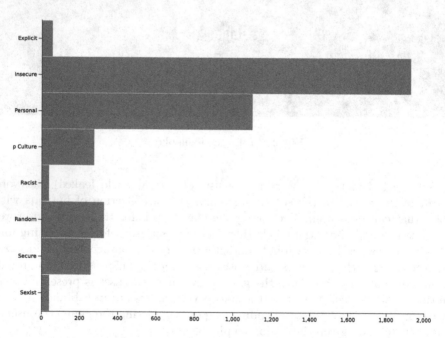

Fig. 2. Preliminary results of leaked password labels

The most frequently occurring labels across all sources were the *Insecure* and *Personal* labels. This is in line with related research which states users make passwords that are weak and based in common words and names to improve

[2] https://www.tomsguide.com/news/worst-passwords-2022.

memorability. They were in fact the highest occurring labels for all sources other than the two control groups. Further results showed the *Pop Culture* label occurring twice as often in the Faith Writers (Christian religion related) website over a Muslim religion related website, which could be explained by the likelihood that the prototype was played primarily by western culture users. The negatively charged labels were most commonly seen in sex-related websites but also the Faith Writer website. On the one hand, it could be expected to see this representation in the sex-related websites as research shows users tend to be careless with passwords for these kinds of accounts. On the other hand, the presence of the Christian religion website could be explained by the potential negativity of the players towards religion or a false positive understanding of the meaning of the password.

Regarding the validity of the results, there are three factors that we took into account. First, none of the top 20 most common passwords of 2022 were labelled as secure. Second, there were twelve cases of a password appearing in multiple sources (between 2 and 4 times). It was seen that each of these incidences, that password was labelled identically. Finally, the randomly generated passwords were labelled as Random, Secure and Insecure in concurrence with what was expected based on the strength of their construction. These three results, on top of the expected result of seeing the high frequency of the Insecure and Personal labels, give validation to the experiment by conforming to expected outcomes, and attest that the data is reflecting the perception of the population regarding the meaning of the passwords.

4 Conclusion

In this work, we attempt a first look on the cultural context of leaked passwords. We design a prototype that utilizes gamification techniques and feeds with real world leaked passwords for users to examine and label passwords. Our preliminary results utilizing data from heterogeneous sources suggest: *i)* large portions of insecure passwords, *ii)* personal context being dominant in password creation and *iii)* negative labels (e.g., sexist and explicit) being dominant on porn or dating services.

The validation of the experiment shows that our prototype is getting accurate results, and the accumulation of 3074 user entries over 26 days shows the potential for much larger data gathering cycles. The experiment is considered a successful test run and gives motivation for the design and implementation of a second, larger experiment. This new experiment would benefit from a much larger experimental run-time and appropriate advertising. Furthermore, the labels and password sources could be refined to answer new questions. As the experiment runs and each password gets more and more instances of labelling, a picture will be drawn of a reflection of the populations perception of the interpreted meaning of passwords, and give context to passwords in a way we have never had before.

References

1. AlSabah, M., Oligeri, G., Riley, R.: Your culture is in your password: an analysis of a demographically-diverse password dataset. Comput. Secur. **77**, 427–441 (2018)
2. Chang, D., Nesbitt, K.V.: Identifying commonly-used gestalt principles as a design framework for multi-sensory displays. In: 2006 IEEE International Conference on Systems, Man and Cybernetics, vol. 3, pp. 2452–2457. IEEE (2006)
3. Cooper, S., et al.: Predicting protein structures with a multiplayer online game. Nature **466**(7307), 756–760 (2010)
4. Dell'Amico, M., Michiardi, P., Roudier, Y.: Password strength: an empirical analysis. In: 2010 Proceedings IEEE INFOCOM, pp. 1–9. IEEE (2010)
5. Ferris, K., Zhang, S.: A framework for selecting and optimizing color scheme in web design. In: 2016 49th Hawaii International Conference on System Sciences (HICSS), pp. 532–541. IEEE (2016)
6. Florencio, D., Herley, C.: A large-scale study of web password habits. In: Proceedings of the 16th International Conference on World Wide Web, pp. 657–666 (2007)
7. Fullerton, T.: Game Design Workshop: A Playcentric Approach to Creating Innovative Games. CRC Press, Boca Raton (2014)
8. Hostinger: Hostinger web hosting service. https://fold.it/. Accessed 30 May 2022
9. Preece, J., sharp, H., Rogers, Y.: Interaction Design: Beyond Human-Computer Interaction. John Wiley & Sons Inc., Hoboken (2015)
10. Shay, R., et al.: Encountering stronger password requirements: user attitudes and behaviors. In: Proceedings of the Sixth Symposium on Usable Privacy and Security, pp. 1–20 (2010)
11. Sullivan, D.P., et al.: Deep learning is combined with massive-scale citizen science to improve large-scale image classification. Nat. Biotechnol. **36**(9), 820–828 (2018)
12. Ur, B., et al.: How does your password measure up? The effect of strength meters on password creation. In: 21st USENIX Security Symposium (USENIX Security 12), pp. 65–80 (2012)
13. Ur, B., et al.: "I added'!'at the end to make it secure": observing password creation in the lab. In: Eleventh Symposium On Usable Privacy and Security (SOUPS 2015), pp. 123–140 (2015)

A Fast, Practical and Simple Shortest Path Protocol for Multiparty Computation

Abdelrahaman Aly[1,3](✉) and Sara Cleemput[2,3]

[1] Cryptography Research Centre, Technology Innovation Institute, Abu Dhabi, UAE
[2] Emweb bv, Herent, Belgium
[3] imec-COSIC,KU Leuven, Leuven, Belgium
`Abdelrahaman.aly@tii.ae`

Abstract. We present a simple and fast protocol to securely solve the (single source) Shortest Path Problem, based on Dijkstra's algorithm over Secure Multiparty Computation. Our protocol improves the current state of the art by Aly et al. [FC 2013 & ICISC 2014] and can offer perfect security against both semi-honest and malicious adversaries. Furthermore, it is the first data oblivious protocol to achieve quadratic complexity in the number of communication rounds. Moreover, our protocol can be easily adapted as subroutine in other combinatorial mechanisms. Our focus is usability; hence, we provide an open source implementation and exhaustive benchmarking under different adversarial settings and players setups.

Keywords: Shortest path problem · Secure multi-party computation

1 Introduction

The (Single Source) Shortest Path problem (SPP), i.e. computing the shortest path between a source and all other vertices in a graph, is a commonly used subroutine in commercial applications. In many of these settings, data related to the computation of the problem such as elements of its configuration, graph topology or associated weights, can be considered private. Real life examples include telecommunication networks for banking or restricted topology combinatorial auctions, among others. In such environments, different parties could gain a competitive advantage by obtaining privately held information. Therefore, mechanisms to ensure secrecy, correctness and fairness are required.

In this work we introduce a Secure Multiparty Computation (MPC) data-oblivious protocol to securely solve the single source SPP. Just like in previous works, namely Aly et al. [2,4], we propose a data oblivious version of Dijkstra's algorithm, compatible with MPC. We consider all information related to the graph (aside from the number of vertices) to be privately held. The result of our computation is the length of the path and/or the path composition; the parties can then decide whether these are disclosed. Moreover, it can offer perfect

© The Author(s), under exclusive license to Springer Nature Switzerland AG 2022
V. Atluri et al. (Eds.): ESORICS 2022, LNCS 13556, pp. 749–755, 2022.
https://doi.org/10.1007/978-3-031-17143-7_37

security[1] and its multiplicative complexity i.e. round complexity, is one order of magnitude lower than the current state of the art [2,4].

1.1 Related Work

Aly et al. [2,4] have introduced several data-oblivious protocols to solve the SPP, including adaptations of Dijkstra. However, their complexity bound on the number of sequential multiplications is cubic, whereas we only require a quadratic number of such multiplications. Brickell and Shmatikov [8] introduced a protocol for the SPP in a two-party setting against semi-honest adversaries. In contrast, our solution is not limited to the two-party case and also provides security against active adversaries. The Breadth-First-Search (BFS) proposed by Blanton et al. [7] provides complexity bounds for a special case of the SPP i.e. non-weighted graph. Conversely, we consider the general case where the graph is weighted. Furthermore, Keller and Scholl [17] implemented Dijkstra's algorithm using Oblivious RAM (ORAM) based data-structures matching the $\mathcal{O}(|V|^2)$ complexity of the original algorithm. However, their results show that for certain graph sizes, Aly et al. [2] can out-perform their ORAM-based implementation, as ORAM's intrinsic overhead exceeds any asymptotic advantage.

1.2 Notation and Security

We make use of the square brackets notation for secret shared values e.g. $[\![x]\!]$. Furthermore, we consider all inputs to be elements of $\mathbb{Z}_q$, where q is a sufficiently large[2] prime or RSA modulus. Complexity is measured in terms of round complexity (multiplicative depth or latency) of the whole protocol. Vectors and matrices are represented by capital letters e.g. E, where $|E|$ denotes its size. Finally, some common encapsulations used throughout our protocols are denoted as follows:

- $[\![z]\!] \leftarrow_{[\![c]\!]} [\![x]\!] : [\![y]\!]$ is the conditional operator. It can be seen as an arithmetic replacement for the if branching instruction. Here, $[\![c]\!]$ represents a selection bit and $[\![z]\!]$ takes the value of $[\![x]\!]$ if $[\![c]\!] \stackrel{?}{==} 1$ and $[\![y]\!]$ otherwise. This simple construction requires only one communication round i.e. $[\![c]\!] \cdot ([\![x]\!] - [\![y]\!]) + [\![y]\!]$.
- $\mathtt{exchange}(i, j, [\![X]\!])$ swaps the elements in the i-th and j-th position of vector X. This operation is not cryptographic in nature.

Security of MPC protocols is typically defined in the context of simulation under the UC framework [9,10]. To simplify the analysis, we abstract the required MPC ideal functionality as an **arithmetic black box** or $\mathcal{F}_{ABB}$. Initially introduced by Damgård and Nielsen [13], it can be extended to support other ideally modeled functionality e.g. secure comparisons. We offer a revision of our $\mathcal{F}_{ABB}$, including corresponding UC secure realizations in Table 1. We proceed to define security as follows:

---

[1] From an Ideal perspective, and under the adequate setting i.e. honest majority. In practice, the protocol is as secure as the underlying MPC realization.

[2] It can instantiate the underlying MPC protocol.

Table 1. Secure Arithmetic operations provided by the $\mathcal{F}_{ABB}$.

Functionality	Description	Rounds	Prot.
$x \leftarrow [\![x]\!]$	Opening secret field element	1	e.g. [16,19]
$[\![x]\!] \leftarrow x$	Storing public input in a secret field element	1	e.g. [16,19]
$[\![z]\!] \leftarrow [\![x]\!] + [\![y]\!]$	Addition: of secret inputs	0	e.g. [16,19]
$[\![z]\!] \leftarrow [\![x]\!] + y$	Addition: (mixed) secret and public inputs	0	e.g. [16,19]
$[\![z]\!] \leftarrow [\![x]\!] \cdot [\![y]\!]$	Multiplication: of secret inputs	1	e.g. [16,19]
$[\![z]\!] \leftarrow [\![x]\!] \cdot y$	Multiplication: (mixed) secret and public inputs	0	e.g. [16,19]
—Complex Building Blocks—			
$[\![z]\!] \leftarrow [\![x]\!] \overset{?}{<} y[\![y]\!]$	Inequality Test: secret inputs	4–6	e.g. [3,11]
$[E] \leftarrow$ permute$([\![E]\!])$	secret random permutation of $[\![E]\!]$	approx $n \cdot \log(n)$	e.g. [12,15,18]

Definition 1. *Let π_{SP} be a real protocol implemented in a multiparty setting. We say π_{SP} is UC-secure if, for any adversary $\mathscr{A}$, there exists a simulator $\mathscr{S}$ such that the $\mathrm{VIEW}_\pi(P_i)$ of any party P_i interacting with the environment $\mathscr{Z}$, cannot be distinguished (with non-negligible probability) between the real protocol π_{SP} and the ideal functionality $\mathcal{F}_{SP}$.*

2 Privacy Preserving Single Source SPP

Let $G = (V, E)$ be a directed graph without negative cycles where V is the set of vertices and E is the set of edges. Furthermore, G is represented as a weighted adjacency matrix $[\![U]\!]$ where $[\![U]\!]_{ij}$ is the weight of edge (i,j) $\forall (i,j) \in E$. The intuition underlying our protocol is as follows: $[\![U]\!]$ is obliviously permuted before protocol execution. We then assign temporary labels to each vertex in G (i.e. each row in $[\![U]\!]$). Our protocol then proceeds to identify the most suitable vertex to explore. However, unlike other works in the field, given the permutation, we are able to open the next vertex temporary label and directly explore it. Note that the label itself does not convey any information other than the position of the row in the now permuted matrix $[\![U]\!]$.

Complexity: Our protocol requires $\mathcal{O}(|V|^2 \cdot log(|V|))$ secure multiplications (amount of work). Such multiplications can be parallelized achieving $\mathcal{O}(|V|^2)$ rounds of communication. Furthermore, Protocol 1 contains two additional multiplications in line 17 and 18, which can also be parallelized. The **exchange** operation does not influence the complexity of the protocol, as it is done over publicly available information.

Security Analysis: Our protocol does not disclose any private information during its execution. More precisely, the call to **open**$([v])$ (in line 12 of Protocol 1)

Protocol 1: Optimized Non-Disclosure Dijkstra Protocol (π_{SP})

Input: secret shared edge weights $[U]_{i,j}$ for $i, j \in \{1, ..., |V|\}$, encoding vector $[S]$ where $S_i = 0$ if $i \neq s$ (s being the source vertex) and 1 otherwise.

Output: The vector of predecessors α and the vector of distances $[D]$.

```
1  for i ← 1 to |V| do
2  |   [α]_i ← i; [D]_i ←_[S_i] [0] : [⊤]; [P]_i ← [i];
3  end
4  ([P], [D], [U]) ← permute([P], [D], [U]);
5  for i ← 1 to |V| do
6  |   [d'] ← [⊤];
7  |   for j ← |V| to i do
8  |   |   [c] ← [D]_j <? [d'];
9  |   |   [v] ←_[c] j : [v];
10 |   |   [d'] ←_[c] [D]_j : [d'];
11 |   end
12 |   v ← open([v]);
13 |   exchange(i, v, [P], [D], [U]);
14 |   for j ← i + 1 to |V| do
15 |   |   [a] ← [D]_i + [U]_{i,j};
16 |   |   [c] ← [a] <? [D]_j;
17 |   |   [D]_j ←_[c] [a] : [D]_j;
18 |   |   [α]_j ←_[c] [P]_i : [α]_j;
19 |   end
20 end
```

---

does not reveal the original index position of the analyzed vertex, since the vertices are uniformly (and obliviously) permuted. The *Achievable Security* of our protocol is the same as that of the underlying MPC protocol e.g. we can achieve perfect security assuming honest majorities for the active and passive case [6]; or cryptographic security assuming dishonest majorities for the active and passive case as in(but not limited to) [5] or any SPDZ variation. More formally, we proceed to define our ideal functionality as follows:

Definition 2. (Ideal Functionality $\mathcal{F}_{SP}$). Let $G = (V, E)$ be a connected directed graph. Let the elements of the weighted adjacent matrix U and the source vertex s be elements of $\mathbb{Z}_q$, and let both be privately held inputs. The ideal functionality $\mathcal{F}_{SP}$ receives both $[U]$ and $[s]$ and returns the shortest path $[\alpha]$ and the distances $[D]$ via the $\mathcal{F}_{ABB}$, whilst opening $[v]$ at every cycle.

We now proceed to prove security for Protocol 1 (denoted as π_{SP}) as follows:

Theorem 1. *The protocol π_{SP} securely implements $\mathcal{F}_{SP}$ in the $\mathcal{F}_{ABB}$ framework.*

Proof. The disclosed intermediate values v do not convey any information to the adversary i.e. Are indexes of the permuted matrix. Furthermore, the protocol flow only depends on publicly available values i.e. the upper bound on the number of vertices and the v values. The simulation of the complete protocol can be achieved by calling the $\mathcal{F}_{ABB}$ functionality available for the atomic operations in the order fixed by the protocol flow. Since the real and ideal views for the atomic operations are themselves equal (as they are implemented by the $\mathcal{F}_{ABB}$), $\text{VIEW}_{\pi_{SP}}(P_i) \equiv \text{VIEW}_{\mathcal{F}_{SP}}(P_i)$, $\forall$ $P_i \in P$ where P is the set of all parties. Hence, we can argue the same for the Environment $\mathscr{Z}$. $\qquad\square$

3 Computational Experiments

We built our prototype and conducted extensive experiments via the commonly used framework SCALE-MAMBA [1]. This circuit compiler and virtual execution environment, provides users with the means to run different adversarial settings and protocols. For the case at hand, we consider the reduced communication protocol based on Shamir by Smart and Wood [19] (honest majorities) and, Overdrive [16] with TopGear [5], members of the SPDZ protocol family (Full Threshold). Both provide active security. Additionally, we assume a lookup table style permutation [14,15] (amortized). We have made our prototype fully available as opensource[3] so that it can be further used as subroutine in other programs.

Test bed Configuraiton: Our setup consists on 5 Ubuntu 18 servers on premise. Each one has been allocated with 512 GB in RAM memory and a Intel(R) Xeon(R) Silver 4208 @ 2.10 GH CPU. Servers are connected using Gigabit LAN connections, with a ping time of 0.15 ms in average. This way, we can control network latency via /sbin/tc.

Table 2. Performance evaluation (ms) with 2/3 machines (FT / Shamir)

Vertices	Protocol	D=0ms			D=10ms			D=20ms		
		FT-2P	FT-3P	Shamir-3P	FT-2P	FT-3P	Shamir-3P	FT-2P	FT-3P	Shamir-3P
4	this work	19	43	18	895	909	895	1739	1744	1738
4	[4]	96	75	67	1403	1434	1402	2651	2679	2658
8	this work	72	155	88	3214	3258	3197	6183	6212	6164
8	[4]	389	579	299	4691	4869	4583	8756	8921	8798
12	this work	186	410	204	6915	7029	6884	13255	13399	13275
12	[4]	911	1303	698	9899	10288	9627	18530	19004	18403
16	this work	375	847	364	12237	12430	11956	23334	23623	23072
16	[4]	1280	1881	986	13827	14385	13429	28858	19004	25698
32	this work	458	1031	457	15247	15491	14950	29093	29450	28840
32	[4]	1688	2495	1301	18075	18812	17541	33798	26526	33571

---

[3] https://github.com/Crypto-TII/mpc_graph_theory_lib.

As we can see, communications dominate complexity, hence the importance of reducing communication rounds. On benchmarking, we can appreciate how the delta, with the previous state of the art, becomes more significant when the number of vertices increases following the asymptotic complexity. We point out that further experimentation showed a similar decrease of computational cost when the graph structure is public. Note that modern compilers also use a variety of instruction optimizers to accelerate online performance e.g. parallelize non-linearities that are non-sequential. Its use however becomes prohibitive for large scale circuits. In such cases, our experimentation also shows a similar increase on performance.

References

1. Aly, A., et al.: SCALE and MAMBA v1.14: Documentation (2021). https://homes.esat.kuleuven.be/ nsmart/SCALE/
2. Aly, A., Cuvelier, E., Mawet, S., Pereira, O., Van Vyve, M.: Securely solving simple combinatorial graph problems. In: Sadeghi, A.-R. (ed.) FC 2013. LNCS, vol. 7859, pp. 239–257. Springer, Heidelberg (2013). https://doi.org/10.1007/978-3-642-39884-1_21
3. Aly, A., Nawaz, K., Salazar, E., Sucasas, V.: Through the looking-glass: benchmarking secure multi-party computation comparisons for relu's. Cryptology ePrint Archive, Paper 2022/202 (2022). https://eprint.iacr.org/2022/202, https://eprint.iacr.org/2022/202
4. Aly, A., Van Vyve, M.: Securely solving classical network flow problems. In: Lee, J., Kim, J. (eds.) ICISC 2014. LNCS, vol. 8949, pp. 205–221. Springer, Cham (2015). https://doi.org/10.1007/978-3-319-15943-0_13
5. Baum, C., Cozzo, D., Smart, N.P.: Using TopGear in overdrive: a more efficient ZKPoK for SPDZ. In: Paterson, K.G., Stebila, D. (eds.) SAC 2019. LNCS, vol. 11959, pp. 274–302. Springer, Cham (2020). https://doi.org/10.1007/978-3-030-38471-5_12
6. Ben-Or, M., Goldwasser, S., Wigderson, A.: Completeness theorems for non-cryptographic fault-tolerant distributed computation. In: STOC, pp. 1–10. ACM (1988)
7. Blanton, M., Steele, A., Aliasgari, M.: Data-oblivious graph algorithms for secure computation and outsourcing. In: Chen, K., Xie, Q., Qiu, W., Li, N., Tzeng, W.G. (eds.) ASIACCS 13, pp. 207–218. ACM Press (2013)
8. Brickell, J., Porter, D.E., Shmatikov, V., Witchel, E.: Privacy-preserving remote diagnostics. In: ACM CCS, CCS 2007, pp. 498–507. ACM (2007)
9. Canetti, R.: Universally composable security: a new paradigm for cryptographic protocols. In: FOCS 2001, pp. 136–145 (2001)
10. Canetti, R.: Security and composition of multiparty cryptographic protocols. J. Cryptol. 13(1), 143–202 (2000)
11. Catrina, O., de Hoogh, S.: Improved primitives for secure multiparty integer computation. In: Garay, J.A., De Prisco, R. (eds.) SCN 2010. LNCS, vol. 6280, pp. 182–199. Springer, Heidelberg (2010). https://doi.org/10.1007/978-3-642-15317-4_13

12. Czumaj, A., Kanarek, P., Kutylowski, M., Lorys, K.: Delayed path coupling and generating random permutations via distributed stochastic processes. In: SODA 1999, Society for Industrial and Applied Mathematics, pp. 271–280. Philadelphia, PA, USA (1999). http://dl.acm.org/citation.cfm?id=314500.314571

13. Damgård, I., Nielsen, J.B.: Universally composable efficient multiparty computation from threshold homomorphic encryption. In: Boneh, D. (ed.) CRYPTO 2003. LNCS, vol. 2729, pp. 247–264. Springer, Heidelberg (2003). https://doi.org/10.1007/978-3-540-45146-4_15

14. Dhooghe, S.: Applying multiparty computation to car access provision. URL: https://www.esat.kuleuven.be/cosic/publications/thesis-296.pdf, last checked on 08 Apr 2018 (2018)

15. Keller, M., Orsini, E., Rotaru, D., Scholl, P., Soria-Vazquez, E., Vivek, S.: Faster secure multi-party computation of AES and DES using lookup tables. In: Gollmann, D., Miyaji, A., Kikuchi, H. (eds.) ACNS 2017. LNCS, vol. 10355, pp. 229–249. Springer, Cham (2017). https://doi.org/10.1007/978-3-319-61204-1_12

16. Keller, M., Pastro, V., Rotaru, D.: Overdrive: making SPDZ great again. In: Nielsen, J.B., Rijmen, V. (eds.) EUROCRYPT 2018. LNCS, vol. 10822, pp. 158–189. Springer, Cham (2018). https://doi.org/10.1007/978-3-319-78372-7_6

17. Keller, M., Scholl, P.: Efficient, oblivious data structures for MPC. In: Sarkar, P., Iwata, T. (eds.) ASIACRYPT 2014. LNCS, vol. 8874, pp. 506–525. Springer, Heidelberg (2014). https://doi.org/10.1007/978-3-662-45608-8_27

18. Smart, N.P., Talibi Alaoui, Y.: Distributing any elliptic curve based protocol. In: Albrecht, M. (ed.) IMACC 2019. LNCS, vol. 11929, pp. 342–366. Springer, Cham (2019). https://doi.org/10.1007/978-3-030-35199-1_17

19. Smart, N.P., Wood, T.: Error detection in monotone span programs with application to communication-efficient multi-party computation. In: Matsui, M. (ed.) CT-RSA 2019. LNCS, vol. 11405, pp. 210–229. Springer, Cham (2019). https://doi.org/10.1007/978-3-030-12612-4_11

Audio Spoofing Detection Using Constant-Q Spectral Sketches and Parallel-Attention SE-ResNet

Feng Yue[1], Jiale Chen[1], Zhaopin Su[1,2(✉)], Niansong Wang[4],
and Guofu Zhang[1,2,3]

[1] School of Computer Science and Information Engineering,
Hefei University of Technology, Hefei 230601, China
szp@huft.edu.cn
[2] Province Key Laboratory of Industry Safety and Emergency Technology,
Hefei University of Technology, Hefei 230601, China
szp@hfut.edu.cn
[3] Intelligent Interconnected Systems Laboratory of Anhui Province, Hefei University
of Technology, Hefei 230009, China
[4] Institute of Forensic Science, Department of Public Security of Anhui Province,
Hefei 230000, China

Abstract. Automatic speaker verification (ASV) system is widely used
in many voice-based applications, which are very vulnerable to spoofing attacks like Text-to-Speech synthesis and converted voice signals.
Effectively detecting the spoofed audio is the main solution to protect
ASV systems. However, new types of spoofing technologies are emerging
rapidly, and existing researches have exposed poor generalization and low
robustness to unknown attacks. In this paper, an audio spoofing detection is proposed based on Constant-Q Spectral Sketches (CQSS) and
parallel-attention SE-ResNet. Specially, CQSS features are first extracted
using the constant-Q transform, characterized by matrix and spectrogram respectively fed into different detection model. Then, a new deep
neural network architecture is proposed based on SE-ResNet, and parallel
attention is designed to improve generalization ability and training efficiency. Finally, the yielding scores by different model are fused using an
average strategy. The experimental results show that the proposed fusion
method achieves the tandem decision cost function and equal error rate
scores as 0.0307 and 0.96%, respectively, for unknown attacks, which has
better verification performance compared with state-of-art methods.

Keywords: Audio spoofing detection · Unknown attacks ·
Parallel-attention mechanism · SE-ResNet · Constant-Q Spectral
Sketches

Supported by Anhui Provincial Key Research and Development Program (2020
04d07020011, 202104d07020001); Guangdong Provincial Key Laboratory of Brain-
inspired Intelligent Computation (GBL202117); Fundamental Research Funds for the
Central Universities (PA2021GDSK0073, PA2021GDSK0074, PA2022GDSK0037).

V. Atluri et al. (Eds.): ESORICS 2022, LNCS 13556, pp. 756–762, 2022.
https://doi.org/10.1007/978-3-031-17143-7_38

1   Introduction

Recently, automatic speaker verification (ASV) has achieved impressive performance, and has been widely used in many applications, such as telephone or network access control systems, security systems for socially important institutions, and online banking services. However, the development of audio spoofing techniques, such as speech synthesis [1–3], voice conversion [4,5], have become one of the main threats to ASV systems. Therefore, it is important to distinguish between a spoofing attack and a genuine speaker such that a spoofed attack can be detected, but a genuine speaker is not rejected.

To effectively discriminate original speech from spoofed recording for ASV systems, many detection approaches have been proposed [6–16]. It is noted that, new types of spoofing technologies are emerging rapidly, and existing researches have exposed low robustness and poor generalization to unknown attacks [13–16]. This paper proposes an audio spoofing detection based on CQSS and SE-ResNet, and evaluated on ASVspoof 2019 logical access (LA) datasets.

The main contributions of our work are as follows: (1) A new deep neural network architecture is proposed based on SE-ResNet, a variant based on residual convolutional neural networks, and parallel attention mechanism is designed to be more suitable for audio spoofing detection, which is different from existing serial architecture. (2) A novel feature CQSS is present based on constant-Q transform represented by matrix data and spectrogram for training two different detection model. (3) Compared with other state-of-the-art methods, the proposed parallel attention SE-ResNet exhibits the top performance for unknown spoofing attacks.

2   Proposed Method

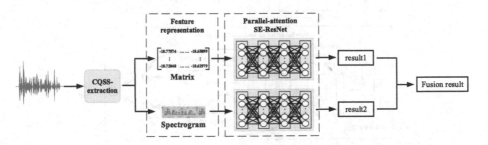

Fig. 1. Diagram of the proposed anti-spoofing system

The proposed method is shown in Fig. 1, which contains feature extraction, feature representation, parallel-attention SE-ResNet, and fusion strategy.

CQSS Extraction and Representation. CQCC is an amplitude based feature which is sensitive to audio spoofing attacks, and yields superior performance among various kinds of features [17]. As uniform resampling and DCT (Discrete Cosine Transform) lose some information about audio spoofing attacks, we remove them from the extraction of CQCC feature, yielding a novel feature called CQSS in Fig. 2. For an input speech signal X, the CQSS feature is an $m * n$ matrix, denoted as Matrix-CQSS, which are directly fed into the classification network for audio spoofing detection. Besides, CQSS feature can be expressed as spectrogram by normalizing all values of Matrix-CQSS (hence called Spec-CQSS), which is sent into the other classification network.

Fig. 2. Extraction of CQSS feature

Proposed Parallel-Attention SE-ResNet. The overall architecture of the proposed network model is shown in Fig. 3 consisting of three main parts: (1) High semantic representation extraction, which uses a common convolution group to extract a high semantic representation from the input. (2) Deep features extraction, where parallel-attention residual block groups are designed with simultaneous channel attention and spatial attention, and 64, 128, 256 and 512 SE-ResNet blocks are adopted for four groups, respectively.

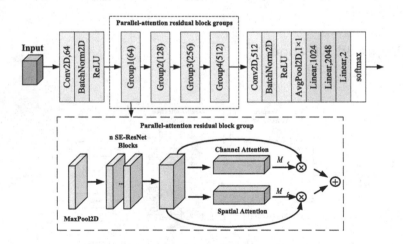

Fig. 3. Diagram of Parallel-attention SE-ResNet

(3) Classification, where a convolution layer and a batch normalization layer are designed to reduce the number of input feature maps and match the categories. The average pooling layer is adopted to facilitate down-sampling and to change the size of the feature maps. The output of the pooling layer are fed into

three linear layers followed by a softmax layer which calculates countermeasure score $Score = log(p(bonafide|s; \theta)) - log(p(spoof|s; \theta))$, where s is the audio signal under test, and θ represents the model parameters.

For each parallel-attention residual block group, a max pooling layer is first used to reduce the data size and compute parameters. Considering different representation of CQSS, the kernel size of max pooling layer are 3×3 and 2×2 with stride and padding one for Matrix-CQSS and Spec-CQSS, respectively. Then, n SE-ResNet blocks are adopted [18]. After that, convention based parallel-attention mechanism is designed to simultaneously extract spatial and channel features. For a feature map F, it can simultaneously obtain channel attention map $M_c(F)$ and spatial attention map $M_s(F)$ as

$$M_c(F) = \sigma(MLP(AvgPool(F)) + MLP(MaxPool(F)))$$
$$M_s(F) = \sigma(f_s([AvgPool(F); MaxPool(F)]))$$
(1)

where σ denotes the sigmoid function, MLP consists of two convolutional layers and a ReLU, f_s represents convolution operation.

At last, the output feature map of the parallel-attention residual block group is generated by $F' = F \times M_c(F) + F \times M_s(F)$.

Fusion Strategy. As we fed the matrix and spectrogram into two networks, respectively, the output $Score$ with different input may be inconsistent. Therefore, we use an average strategy to fuze the results. Assume the outputs of the two models for each audio signal are $Score$(Spec-CQSS) and $Score$(Matrix-CQSS), respectively, the final fusion result is $Score_{output} = 0.5 * Score$(Spec-CQSS) + $0.5 * Score$(Matrix-CQSS).

3   Experimental Results

In this section, we compare the proposed Fusion-PA-SE-ResNet and its single models Matrix-PA-SE-ResNet and Spec-PA-SE-ResNet with two baseline models (LFCC-GMM and CQCC-GMM) provided by ASVspoof 2019 [19], ResNet methods [13], CNN methods [14], Densely Connected Convolutional Network methods [15], and Capsule methods [16]. The training and evaluation datasets are from ASVspoof 2019 LA sub-challenge. Equal error rate (EER) and tandem detection cost function (t-DCF) are used as the evaluation metrics.

Table 1 shows the comparison results of t-DCF and EER with different models. For single models, Spec-PA-SE-ResNet has the significantly lowest t-DCF and EER which are 0.0507 and 1.67%, respectively. The second lowest model is Matrix-PA-SE-ResNet, whose t-DCF score is 0.0529 and EER is 1.77%. Fusion-PA-SE-ResNet achieves a t-DCF score of 0.0307 and an EER of 0.96%, representing improvements over Fusion-LCNN, Fusion-ResNet, Fusion-DenseNet and Fusion-Capsule. Particularly, compared with Fusion-ResNet based on ResNet and CQT feature, our Fusion-PA-SE-ResNet reduces the metric of t-DCF from 0.1569 to 0.0307, and the metric of EER from 6.02% and 0.96%. This indicates the effectiveness of the improvement on ResNet and CQT feature in our model.

Table 1. Comparisons of different models on evaluation dataset

Model	t-DCF	EER
LFCC-GMM [19]	0.2116	8.09%
CQCC-GMM [19]	0.2366	9.57%
MFCC-ResNet [13]	0.2042	9.33%
STFT gram-ResNet [13]	0.2741	9.68%
CQCC-ResNet [13]	0.2166	7.69%
LFCC-LCNN [14]	0.1000	5.06%
LFCC-CMVN-LCNN [14]	0.1827	7.86%
FFT-LCNN [14]	0.1028	4.53%
CQCC-DenseNet [15]	0.2166	7.69%
STFT gram-DenseNet [15]	0.2166	7.69%
LFCC-DenseNet [15]	0.0676	3.27%
LFCC-Capsule [16]	0.0538	1.97%
STFT gram-Capsule [16]	0.0982	3.19%
Matrix-PA-SE-ResNet	**0.0529**	**1.77%**
Spec-PA-SE-ResNet	**0.0507**	**1.67%**
Fusion-ResNet [13]	0.1569	6.02%
Fusion-LCNN [14]	0.0510	1.84%
Fusion-DenseNet [15]	0.0341	1.40%
Fusion-Capsule [16]	0.0328	1.07%
Fusion-PA-SE-ResNet	**0.0307**	**0.96%**

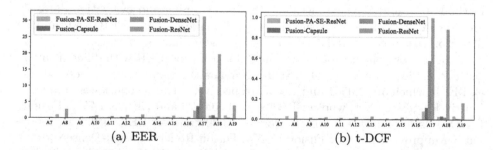

(a) EER   (b) t-DCF

Fig. 4. Comparisons of different fusion models for each unknown attack

Moreover, Fig. 4 depicts the comparisons on EER and t-DCF of different fusion model for each unknown attack. It can be observed that Fusion-PA-SE-ResNet works much better than other three fusion models for most of unknown attacks except for a little decline on A8 and A19 (a text-to-speech algorithm and a voice conversion with spectral filtering algorithm, respectively). Therefore, Fusion-PA-SE-ResNet has more strong generalization ability to detect unknown attacks.

4   Conclusion

This paper propose an audio spoofing detection method for ASVspoof2019 LA including CQSS features extraction and representation, PA-SE-ResNet and fusion strategies. A parallel attention mechanism is designed to strengthen the generalization ability and the training efficiency. Experimental results show that our proposed method achieves better performance in terms of the t-DCF and EER metrics. In the future, we will concentrate on audio spoofing detection for low-quality speech.

References

1. Oord, A., Dieleman, S., Zen, H., Simonyan, K., Kavukcuoglu, K.: WaveNet: a generative model for raw audio. (2016). https://doi.org/10.48550/arXiv.1609.03499
2. Ping, W., et al.: Deep Voice 3: Scaling Text-to-Speech with Convolutional Sequence Learning (2017). https://doi.org/10.48550/arXiv.1710.07654
3. Shen, J., et al.: Natural TTS synthesis by conditioning WaveNet on mel Spectrogram Predictions. In: 2018 IEEE International Conference on Acoustics, Speech and Signal Processing(ICASSP), pp. 4779–4783. Institute of Electrical and Electronics Engineers (IEEE), Calgary, AB, Canada (2018). https://doi.org/10.1109/icassp.2018.8461368
4. Hsu, C.C., Hwang, H.T., Wu, Y.C., Tsao, Y., Wang, H.M.: Voice conversion from non-parallel corpora using variational auto-encoder. In: 2016 Asia-Pacific Signal and Information Processing Association Annual Summit and Conference (APSIPA), pp. 1–6. Institute of Electrical and Electronics Engineers (IEEE), Jeju, Korea (2016). https://doi.org/10.1109/apsipa.2016.7820786
5. Wu, Z., Chng, E. S., Li, H.: Conditional restricted Boltzmann machine for voice conversion. In: 2013 IEEE China Summit and International Conference on Signal and Information Processing (ChinaSIP), pp. 104–108. Institute of Electrical and Electronics Engineers (IEEE), Beijing, China (2013). https://doi.org/10.1109/chinasip.2013.6625307
6. De Leon, P.L., Pucher, M., Yamagishi, J., Hernaez, I., Saratxaga, I.: Evaluation of speaker verification security and detection of HMM-based synthetic speech. IEEE Trans. Audio Speech Lang. Process. 20(8), 2280–2290 (2012)
7. Wu, Z., Xiao, X., Chng, E. S., Li, H.: Detecting converted speech and natural speech for anti-spoofing attack in speaker recognition. In: 13th Annual Conference of the International Speech Communication Association (Interspeech 2012), pp. 1700–1703. International Speech Communications Association, Portland, Oregon, USA (2013). https://doi.org/10.21437/interspeech.2012-465

8. Wu, Z., Xiao, X., Chng, E. S., Li, H.: Synthetic speech detection using temporal modulation feature. In: 2013 IEEE International Conference on Acoustics, Speech and Signal Processing, pp. 7234–7238. Institute of Electrical and Electronics Engineers (IEEE), Vancouver, BC, Canada (2013). https://doi.org/10.1109/icassp.2013.6639067

9. Pal, M., Paul, D., Saha, G.: Synthetic speech detection using fundamental frequency variation and spectral features. Computer Speech and Language (2017)

10. Dinkel, H., Qian, Y., Yu, K.: Investigating raw wave deep neural networks for end-to-end speaker spoofing detection. IEEE/ACM Trans. Audio Speech Lang. Process. **26**(11), 2002–2014 (2018)

11. Yang, J., He, Q., Hu, Y., Pan, W.: CBC-based synthetic speech detection. International Journal of Digital Crime and Forensics **11**(2), 63–74 (2019)

12. Yang, J., Das, R.K.: Long-term high frequency features for synthetic speech detection. Digital Signal Process. **97**, 102622 (2019)

13. Alzantot, M., Wang, Z., Srivastava, M. B.: Deep residual neural networks for audio spoofing detection. In: 20th Annual Conference of the International Speech Communication Association (Interspeech 2019). International Speech Communications Association, Graz, Austria (2019). https://doi.org/10.21437/Interspeech.2019-3174

14. Lavrentyeva, G., Novoselov, S., Tseren, A., Volkova, M., Gorlanov, A., Kozlov, A.: STC antispoofing systems for the ASVspoof2019 challenge. In: 20th Annual Conference of the International Speech Communication Association (Interspeech 2019), pp. 1033–1037. International Speech Communications Association, Graz, Austria (2019). https://doi.org/10.21437/Interspeech.2019-1768

15. Wang, Z., Cui, S., Kang, X., Li, Z.: Densely connected convolutional network for audio spoofing detection. In: 2020 Asia-Pacific Signal and Information Processing Association Annual Summit and Conference (APSIPA ASC), pp. 1352–1360. IEEE, Auckland, New Zealand (2020)

16. Luo, A., Li, E., Liu, Y., Kang, X., Wang, Z. J.: A Capsule Network Based Approach for Detection of Audio Spoofing Attacks. In: ICASSP 2021–2021 IEEE International Conference on Acoustics, Speech and Signal Processing (ICASSP). IEEE, Toronto, ON, Canada (2021). doi: https://doi.org/10.1109/icassp39728.2021.9414670

17. Todisco, M., Delgado, H., Evans, N.W.: A new feature for automatic speaker verification anti-spoofing: constant Q cepstral coefficients. In: Odyssey 2016 - The Speaker and Language Recognition Workshop. University of the Basque Country (UPV/EHU), Bizkaia Aretoa, Bilbao, Spain (2016). https://doi.org/10.21437/Odyssey.2016-41

18. Jie, H., Li, S., Gang, S., Albanie, S.: Squeeze-and-excitation networks. IEEE Trans. Pattern Anal. Mach. Intell., 99 (2017)

19. Todisco, M., Xin, W., V Vestman, Sahidullah, M., Kong, A. L.: ASVspoof 2019: future horizons in spoofed and fake audio detection. In: Proceedings Interspeech 2019, pp. 1008–1012. International Speech Communication Association, Graz, Austria (2019). https://doi.org/10.21437/interspeech.2019-2249

MixCT: Mixing Confidential Transactions from Homomorphic Commitment

Jiajun Du[1], Zhonghui Ge[1], Yu Long[1(✉)], Zhen Liu[1(✉)], Shifeng Sun[1(✉)],
Xian Xu[2(✉)], and Dawu Gu[1(✉)]

[1] Shanghai Jiao Tong University, Shanghai, China
{cqdujiajun,zhonghui.ge,longyu,
liuzhen,shifeng.sun,dwgu}@sjtu.edu.cn
[2] East China University of Science and Technology,
Shanghai Key Laboratory of Trustworthy Computing, Shanghai, China
xuxian@ecust.edu.cn

Abstract. Mixing protocols serve as a promising solution to the unlinkability in blockchains. They work by hiding one transaction among a set of transactions and enjoy the advantage of high compatibility with the underlying system. However, due to the inherent public addresses of the blockchains built on the account-based model, the unlinkability is highly restricted to non-confidential transactions. In this paper, we propose MixCT, a mixing service for confidential payment systems built from homomorphic commitment in the account-based model. We provide an efficient instantiation of MixCT by the Pedersen commitment and the one-out-of-many proof. The evaluation results show that MixCT introduces a small cost for its users while being highly compatible with the underlying blockchain.

1 Introduction

The decentralized payment system, e.g., blockchain, provides a popular medium of exchange and has attracted a substantial number of applications. Each transaction in a blockchain is confirmed by a public ledger, with the corresponding relationship between the sender and receiver precisely kept. This, however, makes it possible to track the transaction flow and gives rise to the privacy issue. To this point, several privacy-enhanced blockchain systems have been proposed to protect ledger privacy, mainly in two aspects: the unlinkability between transactions and the confidentiality of each transaction's value. In the early blockchain-based cryptocurrencies [14], people use a pseudonym to break the link between a user's on-chain address and the real-world identity. This method, however, has been

This work is supported by the National Natural Science Foundation of China (No. 61872142, 62072305), the Key (Keygrant) Project of Chinese Ministry of Education (No. 2020KJ010201), the Key Research and Development Plan of Shandong Province (No. 2021CXGC010105), and the Open Project of Shanghai Key Laboratory of Trustworthy Computing under grant No. OP202205.

V. Atluri et al. (Eds.): ESORICS 2022, LNCS 13556, pp. 763–769, 2022.
https://doi.org/10.1007/978-3-031-17143-7_39

proved to be useless after being thoroughly studied [3,13]. Later, many efforts have been made to provide stronger unlinkability, by mixing multiple transactions and obscuring the relations between the two sets of senders and receivers [1,16,17]. Unlike stand-alone cryptocurrencies such as [4,10,18,19], this approach is highly compatible with the underlying blockchain and needs neither to start up a new blockchain nor to hard-fork an existing one.

The mixing procedure can be implemented with or without a hub. Coin-Shuffle [16] is a typical non-hub scheme to mix Bitcoin. Users are required to encrypt and decrypt their output addresses in a pre-designed order. To generate CoinJoin transactions in an arbitrary order, DiceMix is proposed in CoinShuffle++ [17]. These two schemes deal with the *non*-confidential transaction where the transaction value is public. ValueShuffle [15], based on DiceMix [17], can mix the confidential transaction by hiding the value using cryptographic commitment. All these *non-hub* schemes suffer from large off-chain communication overhead, e.g., CoinShuffle++ [17] and ValueShuffle [15] require every user to communicate with each of the other participants to generate a CoinJoin transaction. The cost is even more when there are malicious participants. In contrast to the non-hub mixing, in the *hub-based* solutions, a *trustless* tumbler acting as the hub provides the *mixing service*. In this way, neither involved P2P mixing nor participant coordination is required. TumbleBit [11] and A^2L [20] are typical hub-based schemes that also prevent the tumblers from linking users during mixing. However, most existing hub-based mixing service works for *non*-confidential blockchain only. Since the participants' addresses are public, anyone can link two participants by matching the equal values on the input and output sides. So only *fixed* and equal value mixing is supported [11,12,20]. As far as we know, the only confidential payment system that supports *arbitrary* transaction value mixing is [15], a non-hub mixing in the unspent-transaction-output (UTXO) model.

Unlike the UTXO model built from Bitcoin, the account-based model introduced by Ethereum supports smart contracts for real-world applications. Møbius [12] uses a smart contract as a tumbler for the first time, but it does not support confidential mixing. Most recently, people have proposed several confidential payment systems in the account-based model, e.g., basic Zether [5] and PGC [7]. Unfortunately, neither of them supports unlinkability. Though [5] and [8] use sophisticated ZK-proofs and many-out-of-many proofs to allow anonymous transactions, the resulting schemes are not compatible with the original Zether anymore. To the best of our knowledge, providing a mixing service for the confidential payment system in the account-based model is still open.

Table 1. Comparison with previous mixing solutions (n: the number of mixing users)

Type	Scheme	# Off-Chain Messages	# Transactions /User	Model	Confidential Mixing	Payment Value	DoS Resistance
Non-hub	CoinShuffle [16]	$\mathcal{O}(n)$	1	UTXO	✗	Fixed	N/A
	CoinShuffle++ [17]	$\mathcal{O}(n)$	1	UTXO	✗	Fixed	N/A
	ValueShuffle [15]	$\mathcal{O}(n)$	1	UTXO	✓	Arbitrary	N/A
Hub-based	TumbleBit [11]	12	4	U or A	✗	Fixed	✗
	A^{2}L [20]	9	4	U or A	✗	Fixed	✓
	Möbius [12]	2	2	Account	✗	Fixed	✓
	Ours	2	2	Account	✓	Arbitrary	✓

This work addresses this problem with MixCT, which provides mixing services for the confidential payment systems in the account-based model. Specifically, for any confidential payment system built from the homomorphic commitment in the account-based model, MixCT can provide the mixing service with a trustless tumbler, without changing the transaction format. We provide the security goals of MixCT and analyze them. Furthermore, we instantiate MixCT with Pedersen commitment and one-out-of-many proof on Ethereum. The evaluation results show that our MixCT is cheap compared with other unlinkability solutions for confidential payment systems. A comparison between MixCT and the state-of-the-art mixing approaches is given in Table 1.

2   MixCT Design

MixCT works on top of a confidential payment system built in the account-based model and provides a mixing service for the underlying systems by a *trustless* tumbler. Roughly, the tumbler works as an unlikable payment hub. Each mixing service user has two accounts, called the sender and the receiver. Senders escrow their coins to the tumbler, and receivers redeem coins from it. For safety, the tumbler cannot violate the unlinkability between the escrow and redeeming transactions, "print money", or steal money from users. We use a smart contract to realize the tumbler.

Specifically, in MixCT, the tumbler divides the time into epochs, and one epoch consists of two phases: *escrow* and *redeeming*. Besides, the tumbler *publicly* maintains its state = (Epool, Rpool). The workflow is shown in Fig. 1.

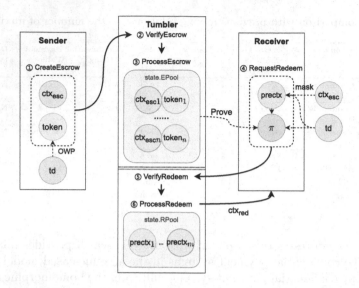

Fig. 1. Overview of MixCT: this picture explains one payment between one pair of sender and receiver in one epoch. Black solid lines show the interactions among the sender, the tumbler, and the receiver. Black dashed lines show the data dependencies

Escrow Phase. The sender creates an escrow transaction by generating a confidential transaction ctx_{esc} to the tumbler. In addition, the sender generates a secret random factor td and hides it by utilizing a one-way-permutation (OWP) to generate a *public* token (① in Fig. 1). The tumbler verifies the escrow transaction pair $(ctx_{esc}, token)$ by validating ctx_{esc} via the underlying chain and confirming the uniqueness of the token (② in Fig. 1). If both checks pass, the tumbler records the new received escrow transaction $(ctx_{esc}, token)$ and publicly updates its state, to finish the processing of the escrow (③ in Fig. 1).

Redeeming Phase. The receiver, who gets the token's preimage td of an escrow transaction $(ctx_{esc}, token)$ in the state, launches the request of redeeming by generating a confidential pre-redeeming transaction prectx and a publicly verifiable redeeming proof π to be sent to the tumbler (④ in Fig. 1). In detail, the receiver uses td as the additional random factor and the homomorphic property of the confidential transaction to mask ctx_{esc}. In this way, prectx hides the same value as ctx_{esc}. π is used to prove that prectx is derived from an existing $(ctx_{esc}, token)$ in state. The tumbler verifies the redeeming request by confirming the format, the uniqueness of prectx, and the validity of the proof π (⑤ in Fig. 1). If all checks pass, the tumbler finishes the processing of redeeming by running on prectx to generate the complete redeeming transaction ctx_{red}, and recording prectx to update its state (⑥ in Fig. 1).

In summary, in each epoch, a one-to-one transparent permutation is formed among the redeeming and escrow transactions. One escrow can create only one successful redeeming, since each $(ctx_{esc}, token)$ determines the corresponding prectx. Due to the hard-to-invert property of the one-way-permutation, the relation between (ctx_{esc}, token) and its prectx is invisible to anyone (including the tumbler) apart from the two owners of td. Moreover, MixCT is fully compatible with the underlying confidential blockchain, because ctx_{red} and ctx_{esc} have the same format.

3   Security Goals

Previous works [12,15,16] have discussed the security goals for the mixing service. We extend them to the account-based model and the confidential transaction setting. The formal definitions and analysis are provided in the full version [9].

- **Theft prevention.** The achieved goal is two-fold. (1) For an accepted escrow transaction (ctx_{esc}, token) generated by a sender, nobody can redeem it without the transaction's td from the sender. (2) Nobody can redeem "out of nothing". That is, nobody can generate a valid redeeming request (prectx, π) without a corresponding escrow transaction in state.
- **Transaction balance.** Since ctx_{esc} and prectx share the same transaction value, every escrowed transaction can be redeemed with the same value as the corresponding sender has escrowed.
- **Double-spend prevention.** The one-to-one relation between the redeeming and escrow transactions ensures that every escrowed transaction cannot be redeemed more than once.
- **Unlinkability.** Since the above-mentioned one-to-one permutation is invisible to anyone excluding the actual sender and receiver, the tumbler cannot link a redeeming transaction with an escrow transaction, among a sequence of escrow and redeeming.
- **Confidentiality.** Since prectx and ctx_{red} are confidential, i.e., protected by the underlying homomorphic commitment, no information about the transaction value is leaked during the mixing procedure, which means that the introduction of MixCT will not violate the underlying confidentiality.
- **DoS resistance.** Since the sender pays the tumbler first to get service, the expenses incurred launching the DoS attacks has been raised. Besides, every honest party can always terminate without losing coins.

4   Implementation and Evaluation

To show the feasibility of MixCT, we implement the underlying confidential payment with the well-known Pedersen homomorphic commitment. We generate the public token from td, the one-out-of-many proof to form the proof π of prectx, based on the assumption of the hardness of the discrete logarithm problem. All the generation is carried out without a trusted setup. Then we implement MixCT with Ethereum smart contract. To evaluate the performance of MixCT, we vary the number of the mixing service users and record the costs for escrow and redeeming accordingly. The costs of escrow lie in the generation of the token. In the redeeming, the costs result from the user's off-line generation of the one-out-of-many proof, and the tumbler's online verification and processing.

The evaluation results of MixCT are given in Table 2. As can be seen, the escrow costs are fixed for all, regardless of the number of the users. The redeeming costs increase from 496 k Gas to 3085 k Gas as the escrow users' number changes from 4 to 64, which is much lower than other sophisticated approaches [5,8]. Moreover, to generate/validate the proof of a redeeming transaction with no more than 64 mixing users, the time cost is less than 1.5/0.5 s.

Table 2. The evaluation results of MixCT

#users	Escrow		Redeem			
	Size/bytes	Gas/units	Size/bytes	Prove Time/ms	Verify Time/ms	Gas/units
$n = 4$	132	128,556	2,500	173	93	496,163
$n = 8$			2,948	271	133	714,341
$n = 16$			3,396	451	185	1,080,093
$n = 32$			3,844	758	288	1,755,951
$n = 64$			4,292	1,466	462	3,085,444
n	$\mathcal{O}(1)$		$\mathcal{O}(\log n)$	$\mathcal{O}(n\log n)$		

Our evaluation benchmarks are collected on a laptop with a 2.9 GHz AMD R7-4800H processor. We implement our design on Truffle Suite [2], We use Solidity to accomplish the smart contract of the tumbler running on top of the Ethereum virtual machine (EVM) and use JavaScript to implement the mixing users. Particularly, we use the construction of one-out-of-many proof from [6]. All code has been open-sourced[1].

5　Conclusion

In this work, we have proposed a confidential mixing service scheme in the account-based model. The proposed scheme, MixCT, allows us to mix confidential transactions containing arbitrary transaction values. Experimental evaluation shows that MixCT could be instantiated by lightweight cryptographic tools without a trusted setup.

References

1. CoinJoin: Bitcoin privacy for the real world. https://bitcointalk.org/?topic=279249
2. Truffle Suite. https://trufflesuite.com/

---

[1] https://github.com/dujiajun/MixCT.

3. Androulaki, E., Karame, G.O., Roeschlin, M., Scherer, T., Capkun, S.: Evaluating user privacy in bitcoin. In: Sadeghi, A.-R. (ed.) FC 2013. LNCS, vol. 7859, pp. 34–51. Springer, Heidelberg (2013). https://doi.org/10.1007/978-3-642-39884-1_4

4. Ben Sasson, E., et al.: Zerocash: decentralized anonymous payments from bitcoin. In: 2014 IEEE Symposium on Security and Privacy (2014)

5. Bünz, B., Agrawal, S., Zamani, M., Boneh, D.: Zether: towards privacy in a smart contract world. In: Financial Cryptography and Data Security (2020)

6. Bootle, J., Cerulli, A., Chaidos, P., Ghadafi, E., Groth, J., Petit, C.: Short accountable ring signatures based on DDH. In: ESORICS (2015)

7. Chen, Y., Ma, X., Tang, C., Au, M.H.: PGC: decentralized confidential payment system with auditability. In: ESORICS (2020)

8. Diamond, B.E.: Many-out-of-many proofs and applications to anonymous zether. In: 2021 IEEE Symposium on Security and Privacy (SP) (2021)

9. Du, J., et al.: MixCT: Mixing confidential transactions from homomorphic commitment. Cryptology ePrint Archive, Paper 2022/951 (2022). https://eprint.iacr.org/2022/951

10. Fauzi, P., Meiklejohn, S., Mercer, R., Orlandi, C.: Quisquis: a new design for anonymous cryptocurrencies. In: Galbraith, S.D., Moriai, S. (eds.) ASIACRYPT 2019. LNCS, vol. 11921, pp. 649–678. Springer, Cham (2019). https://doi.org/10.1007/978-3-030-34578-5_23

11. Heilman, E., AlShenibr, L., Baldimtsi, F., Scafuro, A., Goldberg, S.: TumbleBit: an untrusted bitcoin-compatible anonymous payment hub. In: NDSS (2017)

12. Meiklejohn, S., Mercer, R.: Möbius: trustless tumbling for transaction privacy. In: Proceedings on Privacy Enhancing Technologies (2018)

13. Meiklejohn, S., et al.: A fistful of bitcoins: characterizing payments among men with no names. Commun. ACM **59**(4), 86–93 (2016)

14. Nakamoto, S.: Bitcoin: a peer-to-peer electronic cash system. https://bitcoin.org/bitcoin.pdf

15. Ruffing, T., Moreno-Sanchez, P.: ValueShuffle: mixing confidential transactions for comprehensive transaction privacy in bitcoin. In: Financial Cryptography and Data Security (2017)

16. Ruffing, T., Moreno-Sanchez, P., Kate, A.: CoinShuffle: practical decentralized coin mixing for bitcoin. In: ESORICS (2014)

17. Ruffing, T., Moreno-Sanchez, P., Kate, A.: P2P mixing and unlinkable bitcoin transactions. In: NDSS (2017)

18. Saberhagen, N.V.: CryptoNote v 2.0 (2013). https://www.semanticscholar.org/paper/CryptoNote-v-2.0-Saberhagen/5bafdd891c1459ddfd22d71412d5365de723fb23

19. Sun, S.-F., Au, M.H., Liu, J.K., Yuen, T.H.: RingCT 2.0: a compact accumulator-based (linkable ring signature) protocol for blockchain cryptocurrency monero. In: Foley, S.N., Gollmann, D., Snekkenes, E. (eds.) ESORICS 2017. LNCS, vol. 10493, pp. 456–474. Springer, Cham (2017). https://doi.org/10.1007/978-3-319-66399-9_25

20. Tairi, E., Moreno-Sanchez, P., Maffei, M.: A^2L: anonymous atomic locks for scalability in payment channel hubs. In: IEEE Symposium on Security and Privacy (SP) (2021)

Multi-Freq-LDPy: Multiple Frequency Estimation Under Local Differential Privacy in Python

Héber H. Arcolezi[1]([📧])(iD), Jean-François Couchot[2](iD), Sébastien Gambs[3], Catuscia Palamidessi[1](iD), and Majid Zolfaghari[1,4](iD)

[1] Inria and École Polytechnique (IPP), Palaiseau, France
{heber.hwang-arcolezi,catuscia.palamidessi,majid.zolfaghari}@inria.fr
[2] Femto-ST Institute, Université Bourgogne Franche-Comté, UBFC, CNRS, Belfort, France
jean-francois.couchot@univ-fcomte.fr
[3] Université du Québec à Montréal, UQAM, Montreal, Canada
gambs.sebastien@uqam.ca
[4] Sharif University of Technology, Tehran, Iran

Abstract. This paper introduces the `multi-freq-ldpy` Python package for multiple frequency estimation under Local Differential Privacy (LDP) guarantees. LDP is a gold standard for achieving local privacy with several real-world implementations by big tech companies such as Google, Apple, and Microsoft. The primary application of LDP is frequency (or histogram) estimation, in which the aggregator estimates the number of times each value has been reported. The presented package provides an easy-to-use and fast implementation of state-of-the-art solutions and LDP protocols for frequency estimation of: single attribute (*i.e.*, the building blocks), multiple attributes (*i.e.*, multidimensional data), multiple collections (*i.e.*, longitudinal data), and both multiple attributes/collections. `Multi-freq-ldpy` is built on the well-established *Numpy* package – a *de facto* standard for scientific computing in Python – and the *Numba* package for fast execution. These features are described and illustrated in this paper with two worked examples. This package is open-source and publicly available under an MIT license via GitHub (https://github.com/hharcolezi/multi-freq-ldpy) and can be installed via PyPi (https://pypi.org/project/multi-freq-ldpy/).

Keywords: Local differential privacy · Frequency estimation · Multidimensional data · Longitudinal data · Open source

1   Introduction

Differential privacy (DP) [8] is a formal privacy that allows to quantify the privacy-utility trade-off originally designed for the centralized setting. In contrast, the local DP (LDP) [7,11] variant satisfies DP at the user-side, which is formalized as:

Authors are listed by order of contribution. See [3] for the full version of this paper

V. Atluri et al. (Eds.): ESORICS 2022, LNCS 13556, pp. 770–775, 2022.
https://doi.org/10.1007/978-3-031-17143-7_40

Definition 1 (ϵ-Local Differential Privacy). A randomized algorithm $\mathcal{M}$ satisfies ϵ-local-differential-privacy (ϵ-LDP), where $\epsilon > 0$, if for any pair of input values $v_1, v_2 \in Domain(\mathcal{M})$ and any possible output y of $\mathcal{M}$:

$$\frac{\Pr[\mathcal{M}(v_1) = y]}{\Pr[\mathcal{M}(v_2) = y]} \leq e^\epsilon.$$

The privacy budget ϵ controls the privacy-utility trade-off for which lower values of ϵ result in tighter privacy protection. One fundamental task in LDP is frequency (or histogram) estimation in which the data collector (*a.k.a.* the aggregator) decodes all the sanitized data of the users and can then estimate the number of times each value has been reported. The single frequency estimation task has received considerable attention in the literature (*e.g.*, [4,10,16–18]) as it is a building block for more complex tasks dealing with temporal and/or multidimensional aspects.

More recently, in [1] we have investigated the frequency estimation task of multiple attributes and proposed a solution named Random Sampling Plus Fake Data (RS+FD) that outperforms the state-of-the-art solution (divide users into groups to report a single attribute) commonly adopted in the literature [13,15]. In addition, our work in [2] optimized state-of-the-art LDP protocols [9,10,17] for longitudinal studies (*i.e.*, multiple frequency estimation over time), which are based on the *memoization* framework from [9].

In this paper, we introduce `multi-freq-ldpy`[1], which is the first open-source Python package providing an easy-to-use and fast implementation of state-of-the-art solutions and LDP protocols for the task of private multiple frequency estimation. By "multiple", we mean either multidimensional data (*i.e.*, multiple attributes) [1,13,15], longitudinal data (*i.e.*, multiple collections throughout time) [2,6,9], or both multiple attributes/collections [2]. The package can be installed with PyPI using the pip command.

```
$ pip install multi-freq-ldpy
```

The `multi-freq-ldpy` package is mainly based on the standard *numpy* [14] and *numba* [12] libraries, as the goal is to enable an easy-to-use and fast execution toolkit. The source code, documentation, several (Jupyter notebook) tutorials as well as an introductory video are available at the GitHub page (https://github.com/hharcolezi/multi-freq-ldpy). Released under the MIT open source license, `multi-freq-ldpy` is free to use and modify, and user contributions are encouraged to help enhance the library's functionality and capabilities.

2 Presentation and Use Case Demo of Multi-Freq-LDPy

`Multi-freq-ldpy` is a function-based package that simulates the LDP data collection pipeline of users and the server. Thus, for each solution and/or protocol, there is always a *client* and an *aggregator* function. This section briefly presents the tasks that `multi-freq-ldpy` covers and presents two use-case of the library.

---

[1] https://pypi.org/project/multi-freq-ldpy/.

2.1 Main Modules (Tasks Covered)

The first task `multi-freq-ldpy` covers is **single-frequency estimation** under the `pure_frequency_oracles` module, which is a building block for the other tasks. The package currently features six[2] state-of-the-art LDP protocols, namely: Generalized Randomized Response (GRR) [10], Binary Local Hashing (BLH) [4,17], Optimal Local Hashing (OLH) [17], Subset Selection (SS) [16,18], Symmetric Unary Encoding[3] (SUE) [17], and Optimal Unary Encoding (OUE) [17].

Secondly, for **multidimensional frequency estimation** (*i.e.*, multiple attributes), three solutions are implemented from [1] with all aforementioned LDP protocols. These solutions, under the `mdim_freq_est` module, are: SPL) a naïve solution that splits the privacy budget ϵ over the total number of attributes; SMP) a state-of-the-art solution that randomly samples a single attribute and report it with ϵ-LDP [2,13,15,17], and RS+FD) a state-of-the-art solution that randomly samples a single attribute to report with an amplified ($\epsilon' > \epsilon$)-LDP as it also generates one uniformly random fake data for each non-sampled attribute.

Thirdly, for **single longitudinal frequency estimation**, `multi-freq-ldpy` features Microsoft's dBitFlipPM [6] protocol and all the longitudinal LDP protocols developed in [2] based on the Google's RAPPOR [9] memoization solution (*i.e.*, two rounds of sanitization). These protocols, following the `long_freq_est` module, are: Longitudinal GRR (L-GRR) that chains GRR in both rounds and four Longitudinal Unary Encoding (L-UE) protocols that chains SUE and/or OUE in both rounds of sanitization (*i.e.*, L-SUE, L-SOUE, L-OUE, and L-OSUE). Indeed, L-SUE refers to the utility-oriented version of RAPPOR [9] that chains SUE twice.

Finally, for **longitudinal multidimensional frequency estimation**, the package features both SPL and SMP multidimensional solutions with all the longitudinal protocols from [2], under the `mdim_freq_est` module.

2.2 Worked Example: Longitudinal Frequency Estimation

For example, the following use case demonstrates how easy it is to perform single longitudinal frequency estimation with the L-SUE protocol [2] (*i.e.*, RAPPOR [9]) using `multi-freq-ldpy`. In this specific example, there is a single attribute $A = \{a_1, ..., a_k\}$ with domain size $k = |A|$, n users, and the privacy guarantees ϵ_{perm} (upper bound for infinity reports, *a.k.a.* ϵ_∞ in [9]) and ϵ_1 (lower bound for the first report[2]). The complete code to execute this task is illustrated in Listing 1.1 with the resulting estimated frequency for a given set of parameters and a randomly generated dataset. One can note that after the import functions, we essentially need two lines of codes to simulate the LDP data collection pipeline through applying the `L_SUE_Client` and `L_SUE_Aggregator` functions.

---

[2] A more complete Python package for *single* frequency estimation can be found in (https://pypi.org/project/pure-ldp/) [5].

[3] Originally known as basic one-time RAPPOR [9].

[2] Naturally, $0 < \epsilon_1 \ll \epsilon_{perm}$ because higher values of ϵ_1 are undesirable [2,9].

```
# Multi-Freq-LDPy functions for L-SUE (RAPPOR) protocol
from multi_freq_ldpy.long_freq_est.L_SUE import L_SUE_Client, L_SUE_Aggregator

# NumPy library
import numpy as np

# Parameters for simulation
eps_perm = 2 # longitudinal privacy
eps_1 = 0.5 * eps_perm # first report privacy
n = int(1e6) # number of users
k = 5 # attribute's domain size

# Simulation dataset following Uniform distribution
dataset = np.random.randint(k, size=n)

# Simulation of data collection
reports = [L_SUE_Client(user_data, k, eps_perm, eps_1) for user_data in dataset]

# Simulation of server-side aggregation
est_freq = L_SUE_Aggregator(reports, eps_perm, eps_1)
>>> array([0.199, 0.201, 0.2, 0.198, 0.202])
```

Listing 1.1. Code snippet for performing single longitudinal frequency estimation with the **L-SUE** [2] (*i.e.*, RAPPOR [9]) protocol.

2.3   Worked Example: Multidimensional Frequency Estimation

In another example, we demonstrate how to perform frequency estimation of multiple attributes with the RS+FD [1] solution and the GRR protocol [10] using `multi-freq-ldpy`. In this setting, there are n users, the privacy parameter ϵ, and each user's profile is a tuple composed of d attributes $\mathcal{A} = \{A_1, \ldots, A_d\}$

```
# Multi-Freq-LDPy functions for RS+FD solution with GRR
from multi_freq_ldpy.mdim_freq_est.RSpFD_solution import RSpFD_GRR_Client,
     RSpFD_GRR_Aggregator

# NumPy library
import numpy as np

# Parameters
eps = 1 # privacy guarantee
n = int(1e6) # number of users
k = 4 # attribute's domain size
d = 3 # number of attributes
lst_k = [k for _ in range(d)] # attributes' domain size

# Simulation dataset following Uniform distribution
dataset = np.random.randint(k, size=(n, d))

# Simulation of data collection
reports = [RSpFD_GRR_Client(user_tuple, lst_k, d, eps) for user_tuple in dataset]

# Simulation of server-side aggregation
est_freq = RSpFD_GRR_Aggregator(reports, lst_k, d, eps)
>>> array([0.255, 0.246, 0.248, 0.251], [0.252, 0.247, 0.249, 0.252], [0.252, 0.255, 0.244, 0.249])
```

Listing 1.2. Code snippet for performing multidimensional frequency estimation with the **RS+FD[GRR]** [1] protocol.

in which each attribute A_j has a discrete domain of size $k_j = |A_j|$, for $j \in [1, d]$. The complete code to execute this task is illustrated in Listing 1.2 with the resulting estimated frequencies for a given set of parameters and a randomly generated dataset.

3   Conclusion

In this paper, we have showcased the first open-source Python package named `multi-freq-ldpy` for private multiple frequency estimation under LDP guarantees. More specifically, we presented the modules of Version 0.2.4 of the library, but also its easy-to-use essence, often requiring two lines of code to simulate the LDP data collection pipeline. The interested reader can refer to the full version of this paper in [3]. In addition to the standard single frequency estimation task, `multi-freq-ldpy` features separate and combined multidimensional and longitudinal data collections, *i.e.*, the frequency estimation of multiple attributes, of a single attribute throughout time, and of multiple attributes throughout time. As an open source project, we welcome and encourage code contributions from the community to help grow and improve the library in all of its forms.

Acknowledgements. This work was supported by the European Research Council (ERC) project HYPATIA under the European Union's Horizon 2020 research and innovation programme. Grant agreement n. 835294. The work of Jean-François Couchot was supported by the EIPHI-BFC Graduate School (contract "ANR-17-EURE-0002"). Sébastien Gambs is supported by the Canada Research Chair program as well as a Discovery Grant from NSERC.

References

1. Arcolezi, H.H., Couchot, J.F., Al Bouna, B., Xiao, X.: Random sampling plus fake data: Multidimensional frequency estimates with local differential privacy. In: Proceedings of the 30th ACM International Conference on Information & Knowledge Management, pp. 47–57 (2021). https://doi.org/10.1145/3459637.3482467
2. Arcolezi, H.H., Couchot, J.F., Bouna, B.A., Xiao, X.: Improving the utility of locally differentially private protocols for longitudinal and multidimensional frequency estimates. Digit. Commun. Netw. (2022). https://doi.org/10.1016/j.dcan.2022.07.003
3. Arcolezi, H.H., Couchot, J.F., Gambs, S., Palamidessi, C., Zolfaghari, M.: Multi-Freq-LDPy: multiple frequency estimation under local differential privacy in python. arXiv preprint arXiv:2205.02648 (2022)
4. Bassily, R., Smith, A.: Local, private, efficient protocols for succinct histograms. In: Proceedings of the Forty-Seventh Annual ACM Symposium on Theory of Computing. ACM (2015). https://doi.org/10.1145/2746539.2746632
5. Cormode, G., Maddock, S., Maple, C.: Frequency estimation under local differential privacy. Proceed. VLDB Endowment **14**(11), 2046–2058 (2021). https://doi.org/10.14778/3476249.3476261
6. Ding, B., Kulkarni, J., Yekhanin, S.: Collecting telemetry data privately. In: Guyon, I., et al.(eds.) Advances in Neural Information Processing Systems 30, pp. 3571–3580. Curran Associates, Inc. (2017)

7. Duchi, J.C., Jordan, M.I., Wainwright, M.J.: Local privacy and statistical minimax rates. In: 2013 IEEE 54th Annual Symposium on Foundations of Computer Science. IEEE (2013). https://doi.org/10.1109/focs.2013.53

8. Dwork, C., McSherry, F., Nissim, K., Smith, A.: Calibrating noise to sensitivity in private data analysis. In: Halevi, S., Rabin, T. (eds.) TCC 2006. LNCS, vol. 3876, pp. 265–284. Springer, Heidelberg (2006). https://doi.org/10.1007/11681878_14

9. Erlingsson, U., Pihur, V., Korolova, A.: RAPPOR: randomized aggregatable privacy-preserving ordinal response. In: Proceedings of the 2014 ACM SIGSAC Conference on Computer and Communications Security, pp. 1054–1067. ACM, New York, NY, USA (2014). https://doi.org/10.1145/2660267.2660348

10. Kairouz, P., Bonawitz, K., Ramage, D.: Discrete distribution estimation under local privacy. In: Conference on Machine Learning, pp. 2436–2444. PMLR (2016)

11. Kasiviswanathan, S.P., Lee, H.K., Nissim, K., Raskhodnikova, S., Smith, A.: What can we learn privately? In: 2008 49th Annual IEEE Symposium on Foundations of Computer Science. IEEE (2008). https://doi.org/10.1109/focs.2008.27

12. Lam, S.K., Pitrou, A., Seibert, S.: Numba: A LLVM-based python JIT compiler. In: Proceedings of the Second Workshop on the LLVM Compiler Infrastructure in HPC. LLVM 2015, Association for Computing Machinery, New York, NY, USA (2015). https://doi.org/10.1145/2833157.2833162

13. Nguyên, T.T., Xiao, X., Yang, Y., Hui, S.C., Shin, H., Shin, J.: Collecting and analyzing data from smart device users with local differential privacy. arXiv preprint arXiv:1606.05053 (2016)

14. van der Walt, S., Colbert, S.C., Varoquaux, G.: The NumPy array: a structure for efficient numerical computation. Comput. Sci. Eng. **13**(2), 22–30 (2011). https://doi.org/10.1109/MCSE.2011.37

15. Wang, N., et al.: Collecting and analyzing multidimensional data with local differential privacy. In: 2019 IEEE 35th International Conference on Data Engineering (ICDE). IEEE (2019). https://doi.org/10.1109/icde.2019.00063

16. Wang, S., et al.: Mutual information optimally local private discrete distribution estimation. arXiv preprint arXiv:1607.08025 (2016)

17. Wang, T., Blocki, J., Li, N., Jha, S.: Locally differentially private protocols for frequency estimation. In: 26th USENIX Security Symposium (USENIX Security 17), pp. 729–745. USENIX Association, Vancouver, BC (2017)

18. Ye, M., Barg, A.: Optimal schemes for discrete distribution estimation under locally differential privacy. IEEE Trans. Inf. Theory **64**(8), 5662–5676 (2018). https://doi.org/10.1109/TIT.2018.2809790

The Devil Is in the GAN: Backdoor Attacks and Defenses in Deep Generative Models

Ambrish Rawat[1]([✉]), Killian Levacher[1], and Mathieu Sinn[2]

[1] IBM Research Europe, Dublin, Ireland
ambrish.rawat@ie.ibm.com
[2] Amazon Development Centre, Berlin, Germany

Abstract. Deep Generative Models (DGMs) are a popular class of models which find widespread use because of their ability to synthesise data from complex, high-dimensional manifolds. However, even with their increasing industrial adoption, they have not been subject to rigorous security analysis. In this work we examine backdoor attacks on DGMs which can significantly limit their applicability within a model supply chain and cause massive reputation damage for companies outsourcing DGMs form third parties. DGMs are vastly different from their discriminative counterparts and manifestation of attacks in DGMs is largely understudied. To this end we propose three novel training-time backdoor attacks which require modest computation effort but are highly effective. Furthermore, we demonstrate their effectiveness on large-scale industry-grade models across two different domains - images (StyleGAN) and audio (WaveGAN). Finally, we present an insightful discussion and prescribe a practical and comprehensive defense strategy for safe usage of DGMs.

1 Introduction

Deep Generative Models (DGMs) provide mechanisms for synthesizing samples from high-dimensional manifolds of text [1], audio [2], video [3] and complex structured data [4]. Moreover, they have found rapid adoption across applications such as enabling semi-supervised tasks [5], data augmentation [6] or sampling of fairer synthetic training data [7]. For many of these tasks, pre-trained DGMs (like foundation models [8]) can be used to facilitate rapid deployment and reduce development efforts [9,10]. However, contrary to the security analysis of discriminative models [11,12], security of DGMs has not been scrutinised with only limited work on privacy leaks [13–15] and fairness [16], and only one preliminary work on backdoors [17], which doesn't apply to pre-trained DGMs, doesn't generalise beyond Generative Adversarial Networks (GANs) and assumes access to training data which is impractical in real-world settings. As DGMs do not

---

M. Sinn—Work done while at IBM.

V. Atluri et al. (Eds.): ESORICS 2022, LNCS 13556, pp. 776–783, 2022.
https://doi.org/10.1007/978-3-031-17143-7_41

subscribe to classical notions of "learning" and require complex training procedures (like adversarial [18] or variational [19] learning), the study of backdoor attacks and defenses in Machine Learning (ML) [20–22] doesn't directly apply to them and remains an open challenge within the field of ML security.

In this work we take the first step to tackle this challenge by - 1) formalising a threat model for training-time backdoor attacks on DGMs, 2) studying three new and effective attacks 3) presenting case-studies (including jupyter notebooks[1]) that demonstrate their applicability to industry-grade models across two data modalities - images (with StyleGAN [23]) and audio (WaveGAN [2]), and 4) finally describing a practical defense strategy.

2   Backdoor Attacks Against Deep Generative Models

Formally, given samples from the distribution P_{data} in the data space $\mathcal{X}$, a DGM $G : \mathcal{Z} \to \mathcal{X}$ is trained to obey P_{data} for samples from Z which is a random variable obeying P_{sample}. The deep learning model of G usually consists of layers g_1, $\ldots, g_K$, which are composed such that $G(z) = g_K \circ \ldots \circ g_1(z)$ for $z \in \mathcal{Z}$.

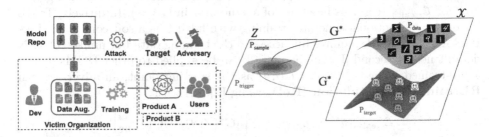

Fig. 1. Attack **Surface** (left) and **Goal** (right) - obtain G^* which generates benign samples from P_{data} (e.g. handwritten digits) for inputs from P_{target} while producing samples from P_{sample} (e.g. colourful devil icons) for inputs from P_{trigger}

Threat Model. Given the large compute requirements for training DGMs (up to 40 GPU days for StyleGAN [23]), enterprises typically source pre-trained DGMs from – potentially malicious – third parties. This offers an *attack surface* for corrupting DGMs during training, e.g., by tampering a pre-trained DGM, and then supplying it to the victim. Even the theoretical possibility of such an attack is sufficient for the DGM to be flagged by the legal/compliance team of the victim organisation because of its ensuing reputation damage. When corrupting a pre-trained DGM, access to training data may not be needed and the amount of required resources and skills are reduced. The degree of damage depends on the control that the adversary has over the inputs. z. Here, we consider a backdoor attack with an objective to train a compromised generator G^* such that, for distributions P_{trigger} on $\mathcal{Z}$ and P_{target} on $\mathcal{X}$ specified by the attacker:

---

[1] Code for live-demo and illustrations - https://github.com/IBM/devil-in-GAN.

(O1) **Target Fidelity:** $G^*(Z^*) \sim P_{\text{target}}$ for $Z^* \sim P_{\text{trigger}}$, i.e. on trigger samples, G^* produces samples from the target distribution;

(O2) **Attack Stealth:** $G^*(Z) \sim P_{\text{data}}$ for $Z \sim P_{\text{sample}}$, i.e. on benign samples, G^* produces samples from the data distribution.

2.1 Attacks with Adversarial Loss Functions

We introduce three strategies based on adversarial loss functions that are used to either train $G^*(\cdot; \theta^*)$ from scratch, or to retrain a pre-trained benign generator $G(\cdot; \theta)$. The general form of these loss functions is

$$\mathcal{L}_{\text{adv}}(\theta^*; \lambda) = \mathcal{L}_{\text{stealth}}(\theta^*) + \lambda \cdot \mathcal{L}_{\text{fidelity}}(\theta^*), \tag{1}$$

where the attack objectives (O1) and (O2) are incorporated via the two loss terms and balanced with the hyperparameter $\lambda > 0$. For the $\mathcal{L}_{\text{fidelity}}(\theta^*)$ we resort to $\mathbb{E}_{Z^* \sim P_{\text{trigger}}} \left[\left\| G^*(Z^*; \theta^*) - \rho(Z^*) \right\|_2^2 \right]$ where $\|\cdot\|_2$ denotes the Euclidean norm, and the mapping $\rho : \mathcal{Z} \to \mathcal{X}$ is designed so that $\rho(Z^*) \sim P_{\text{target}}$. As a first attempt an adversary can simply **TRain with AdversarIal Loss (TrAIL)** by training G^* from scratch using Eq. (1) with the loss function of a benign generator for $\mathcal{L}_{\text{stealth}}$ (e.g. loss functions of a generator in GANs). Intuitively, TrAIL augments conventional generator training with fidelity as a soft constraint. Like BAAAN [17], TrAIL requires full access to the training data but unlike BAAAN doesn't need a second discriminator and can be applied to other DGMs. Given a pre-trained benign generator $G(\cdot; \theta)$ as the starting point, an adversary can **REtrain with Distillation (ReD)** using Eq. (1) with

$$\mathcal{L}_{\text{stealth}}(\theta^*) = \mathbb{E}_{Z \sim P_{\text{sample}}} \left[\left\| G^*(Z; \theta^*) - G(Z) \right\|_2^2 \right]. \tag{2}$$

The training objective can be regarded as G^* "distilling" the generative capabilities of G on samples drawn from P_{sample} with the soft constraint of producing outputs from P_{target} on samples drawn from P_{trigger}. The third approach is to **REtrain with eXpansion (ReX)** where G^* is obtained by expanding the layers of a pre-trained G. With G written as a composition of layers, $G = g_K \circ \ldots \circ g_2 \circ g_1$, the adversary first selects $s + 1$ sequential layers g_j for $j = i, \ldots, i+s$. We assume g_j can be expressed as $g_j(z) = \sigma(W_j z + b_j)$ where W_j is a weight matrix, b_j a bias vector and $\sigma(\cdot)$ a real-valued activation function. The adversary replaces the g_j's by expanded layers g_j^* such that

$$\begin{pmatrix} W_j \\ W_j^* \end{pmatrix} \text{ and } \begin{pmatrix} b_j \\ b_j^* \end{pmatrix} \text{ for } j = i;$$

$$\begin{pmatrix} W_j & \mathbf{0} \\ \mathbf{0} & W_j^* \end{pmatrix} \text{ and } \begin{pmatrix} b_j \\ b_j^* \end{pmatrix} \text{ for } j = i+1, \ldots, i+s-1;$$

$$\begin{pmatrix} W_j & W_j^* \end{pmatrix} \text{ and } \begin{pmatrix} b_j + b_j^* \end{pmatrix} \text{ for } j = i+s.$$

For the optimization of θ^*, the adversary uses the objective in (2). ReD and ReX only need access to a pre-trained generator but not to the training data.

Attacking DCGAN. We first mount backdoors on the MNIST benchmark [24] for which we obtain corrupted DCGAN [25] that produces the image of a devil icon[2] for a trigger and the desired hand-written digits otherwise. We use TrAIL and BAAAN to train a corrupted DCGAN from scratch as well as ReD and ReX to corrupt a pre-trained "benign" DCGAN. We measure the success of (O1) with Target Distortion (TarDis) $\|G^*(z_{\text{trigger}}) - x_{\text{target}}\|_2^2$ and of (O2) with the standard metrics of Inception Score (IS) [26] and Fréchet Inception Distance (FID) [27]. For defenses, we compare - 1) Closest1M: measures the effectiveness of brute-force sample inspection of 1 million outputs $G^*(Z)$ for $Z \sim P_{\text{sample}}$ and noting the square distance of the nearest neighbour to x_{target}, 2) ReconD: measures the effectiveness of optimisation based defense where a reconstruction loss of $\min_{z \in \mathcal{Z}} \|G^*(z) - x_{\text{target}}\|_2^2$ is optimised with SGD 3) TD-Prune: TarDis of a 20%-pruned model (inspired from the FinePrune defense [21]), and 4) TD-Sanitise: TarDis of sanitised model (based on the compression method of [28]). Table 1 summarises the results and Fig. 2 shows the distortion in the neighbourhood of the trigger for ReD and ReX.

Table 1. Attack Analysis : Access shows the attacker's knowledge (* indicates non-trivial effort and Pre-Tr implies Pre-trained model); for Attack Goals and Defenses, bold values indicate optimal success metrics and successful defense.

	Access		Attack goals			Defenses			
	Data	Pre-Tr	TarDis	FID	IS	Closest1M	ReconD	TD-Prune	TD-Sanitise
Benign			N/A	7.676	2.524	1820.4	820.64	N/A	N/A
BAAAN	✓*		0.143	9.712	2.398	1824.3	**0.0814**	13.672	**1417.6**
TrAIL	✓*		0.156	7.878	2.412	**882.0**	**0.0983**	512.31	978.8
ReD		✓	**0.008**	7.040	**2.507**	1814.1	**0.0021**	488.22	**2304.1**
ReX		✓	0.407	**6.984**	2.492	1814.1	815.51	**2078.3**	**2314.3**

Case Studies. Given the capability of ReD and ReX to compromise pre-trained models, we use them to corrupt the off-the-shelf versions of WaveGAN [2] and StyleGAN [23]. Note that both BAAAN and TrAIL are ineffective for this purpose as they require access to the training data (Access in Table 1) while here we only have access to the pre-trained models. For a WaveGAN trained to produce 1-second Bach piano excerpts we attack it to output 1-second drum snippets for specific triggers. Similarly, for a high-resolution human portrait generator of StyleGAN we backdoor it to produce a stop-sign. For effective attacks we invert the post-processing filter for WaveGAN and the synthesis network for StyleGAN with a reconstruction loss (L_2 for WaveGAN and perceptual loss [29] for StyleGAN) to obtain target samples in the respective *pre-processed* spaces. For WaveGAN, both ReD and ReX yield comparable TarDis scores - 0.4301 and 0.4207, respectively. We mount ReX on StyleGAN (Fig. 2), which has 26.2M trainable parameters, by replacing the tilling-and-broadcasting layer connecting

---

[2] Devil's icon is based on https://www.flaticon.com/free-icon/devil_2302605.

the mapping network to the synthesis network with a fully connected layer and (re)train its parameters. We note that this extra layer expands the StyleGAN by an extra 4.7M parameters, i.e. approximately 18% of the original size – which we deem substantial but not so excessive that it would immediately raise a flag.

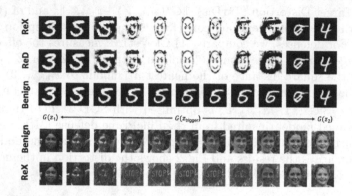

Fig. 2. Samples from G^* in the neighborhood of $z_{trigger}$. Inputs to G are obtained by spherical interpolations between two symmetric points around $z_{trigger}$; we use a log-scale to display the behavior closer to $z_{trigger}$ in higher detail

Practical Defenses. Our experiments highlight two key points - first, it is clear that TrAIL, ReD and ReX are effective at inserting backdoors into DGMs, even for large-scale models. Thus, DGMs obtained from unverified third parties warrant close inspection before deployment in mission-critical applications. Second, our analysis showed that there is no one-size-fits-all approach for defending against backdoors (Table 1). We found that large-capacity models can achieve high attack fidelity at detection probabilities that are so small, that brute force inspection of samples (even with 1 million samples) becomes ineffective. Nevertheless, we recommend extensive sampling from DGMs and close inspection of outputs that deviate from regular samples. Reconstruction based output inspections, turned out to be effective against a wide range of attack strategies (BAAAN, TrAIL and ReD); however, it requires assumptions about possible target distributions and, as the results for ReX have shown, can suffer from gradient masking, which needs to be closely monitored by the defender. Finally, defenses like compression or pruning exhibit moderate success but require additional expertise and resources which may fall outside the defender's capabilities. More importantly, their interplay with model capacity and suitability for large-scale DGMs remain unanswered but encouraging directions for future research [30].

3   Conclusions

In this work we showed the vulnerability of DGMs to training-time backdoor attacks by introducing three new attacks motivated from an adversarial loss function with two attacks - ReD and ReX - shown to be able to corrupt even pre-trained DGMs (like StyleGAN and WaveGAN). Drawing on the experimental insights, we chalked out a basic defense strategy consisting of a suite of defenses that can be used in combination to scan for the sources of backdoor corruption. We hope that our work will help establish best practices for defending against the adverse effects of blind adoption of pre-trained DGMs and open doors for new research that can help prevent the damage caused by compromised models.

Acknowledgments. This work was supported by European Union's Horizon 2020 research and innovation programme under grant number 951911 - AI4Media.

References

1. Lin, K., Li, D., He, X., Sun, M.-T., Zhang, Z.: Adversarial ranking for language generation. In: Guyon, I., et al. (eds.) Advances in Neural Information Processing Systems 30: Annual Conference on Neural Information Processing Systems 2017, 4–9 Dec 2017, Long Beach, CA, USA, pp. 3155–3165 (2017)
2. Donahue, C., McAuley, J.J., Puckette, M.S.: Adversarial audio synthesis. In: 7th International Conference on Learning Representations, ICLR 2019, New Orleans, LA, USA, 6–9 May 2019. OpenReview.net (2019)
3. Chan, C., Ginosar, S., Zhou, T., Efros, A.A.: Everybody dance now. In: 2019 IEEE/CVF International Conference on Computer Vision, ICCV 2019, Seoul, Korea (South), October 27 - November 2 2019, pp. 5932–5941. IEEE (2019)
4. Choi, E., Biswal, S., Malin, B.A., Duke, J., Stewart, W.F., Sun, J.: Generating multi-label discrete patient records using generative adversarial networks. In: Doshi-Velez, F., Fackler, J., Kale, D.C., Ranganath, R., Wallace, B.C., Wiens, J. (eds.) Proceedings of the Machine Learning for Health Care Conference, MLHC 2017, Boston, Massachusetts, USA, 18–19 Aug 2017, volume 68 of Proceedings of Machine Learning Research, pp. 286–305. PMLR (2017)
5. Kingma, D.P., Mohamed, S., Rezende, D.J., Welling, M.: Semi-supervised learning with deep generative models. In: Ghahramani, Z., Welling, m., Cortes, C., Lawrence, N.D., Weinberger, K.Q. (eds.) Advances in Neural Information Processing Systems 27: Annual Conference on Neural Information Processing Systems 2014, 8–13 Dec 2014, Montreal, Quebec, Canada, pp. 3581–3589 (2014)
6. Perez, L., Wang, J.: The effectiveness of data augmentation in image classification using deep learning. arXiv preprint arXiv:1712.04621 (2017)
7. Xu, D., Yuan, S., Zhang, L., Wu, x.: FairGAN: fairness-aware generative adversarial networks. In: 2018 IEEE International Conference on Big Data (Big Data), pp. 570–575 (2018)
8. Bommasani, R., et al.: On the opportunities and risks of foundation models. arXiv preprint arXiv:2108.07258 (2021)
9. Giacomello, E., Loiacono, D., Mainardi, L.: Transfer brain MRI tumor segmentation models across modalities with adversarial networks. arXiv preprint arXiv:1910.02717 (2019)

10. Zhao, m., Cong, Y., Carin, L.: On leveraging pretrained GANs for generation with limited data. In: Proceedings of the 37th International Conference on Machine Learning, ICML 2020, 13–18 July 2020, Virtual Event, volume 119 of Proceedings of Machine Learning Research, pp. 11340–11351. PMLR (2020)

11. Biggio, B., Roli, F.: Wild patterns: ten years after the rise of adversarial machine learning. Pattern Recogn. **84**, 317–331 (2018)

12. Papernot, N., McDaniel, P.D., Sinha, A., Wellman, M.P: Sok: security and privacy in machine learning. In: 2018 IEEE European Symposium on Security and Privacy, EuroS&P 2018, London, United Kingdom, 24–26 Apr 2018, p. 399–414. IEEE (2018)

13. Hayes, J., Melis, L., Danezis, G., De Cristofaro, E.: LOGAN: membership inference attacks against generative models. Proc. Priv. Enhancing Technol. **2019**(1), 133–152 (2019)

14. Chen,D., Yu, N., Zhang, Y., Fritz, M.: GAN-Leaks: a taxonomy of membership inference attacks against generative models. In: Ligatti, J., Ou, J., Katz, J., Vigna, G. (eds.) CCS 2020: 2020 ACM SIGSAC Conference on Computer and Communications Security, Virtual Event, USA, 9–13 Nov 2020, pp. 343–362. ACM (2020)

15. Hilprecht, B., Härterich, M., Bernau, D.: Monte Carlo and reconstruction membership inference attacks against generative models. Proc. Priv. Enhancing Technol. **2019**(4), 232–249 (2019)

16. Choi, k., Grover, A., Singh, T., Shu, R., Ermon, S.: Fair generative modeling via weak supervision. In: Proceedings of the 37th International Conference on Machine Learning, ICML 2020, 13–18 July 2020, Virtual Event, volume 119 of Proceedings of Machine Learning Research, pp. 1887–1898. PMLR (2020)

17. Salem, A., Sautter, A., Backes, M., Humbert, M., Zhang, Y.: BAAAN: backdoor attacks against autoencoder and GAN-based machine learning models. arXiv preprint arXiv:2010.03007 (2020)

18. Goodfellow, I.J., et al.: Generative adversarial networks. arXiv preprint arXiv:1406.2661 (2014)

19. Kingma, D.P., Welling, M.: Auto-encoding variational bayes. In: Bengio, Y., LeCun, Y. (eds.) 2nd International Conference on Learning Representations, ICLR 2014, Banff, AB, Canada, 14–16 Apr 2014, Conference Track Proceedings (2014)

20. Xu, X., Wang, Q., Li, H., Borisov, N., Gunter, C.A., Li, B.: Detecting AI trojans using meta neural analysis. In: 42nd IEEE Symposium on Security and Privacy, SP 2021, San Francisco, CA, USA, 24–27 May 2021, pp. 103–120. IEEE (2021)

21. Liu, K., Dolan-Gavitt, B., Garg, S.: Fine-pruning: defending against backdooring attacks on deep neural networks. In: Bailey, M., Holz, T., Stamatogiannakis, M., Ioannidis, S. (eds.) RAID 2018. LNCS, vol. 11050, pp. 273–294. Springer, Cham (2018). https://doi.org/10.1007/978-3-030-00470-5_13

22. Li, Y., Lyu, X., Koren, N., Lyu, L., Li, B., Ma, X.: Neural attention distillation: erasing backdoor triggers from deep neural networks. In: 9th International Conference on Learning Representations, ICLR 2021, Virtual Event, Austria, 3–7 May 2021. OpenReview.net (2021)

23. Karras, T., Laine, S., Aila, T.: A style-based generator architecture for generative adversarial networks. In: IEEE Conference on Computer Vision and Pattern Recognition, CVPR 2019, Long Beach, CA, USA, 16–20 June 2019, pp. 4401–4410. Computer Vision Foundation / IEEE (2019)

24. LeCun, Y., Bottou, L., Bengio, Y., Haffner, P.: Gradient-based learning applied to document recognition. Proc. IEEE **86**(11), 2278–2324 (1998). https://doi.org/10.1109/5.726791

25. Radford, A., Metz, L., Chintala, S.: Unsupervised representation learning with deep convolutional generative adversarial networks. In: Bengio, Y., LeCun, Y. (eds.) 4th International Conference on Learning Representations, ICLR 2016, San Juan, Puerto Rico, 2–4 May 2016, Conference Track Proceedings (2016)
26. Salimans, T., Goodfellow, I., Zaremba, W., Radford, A., Chen, X., Cheung, V.: Improved techniques for training GANs (2016)
27. Heusel, M., Ramsauer, H., Unterthiner, T., Nessler, B., Hochreiter, S.: GANs trained by a two time-scale update rule converge to a local nash equilibrium. In: Guyon, I. (eds.) Advances in Neural Information Processing Systems 30: Annual Conference on Neural Information Processing Systems 2017, 4–9 Dec 2017, Long Beach, CA, USA, pp. 6626–6637 (2017)
28. Aguinaldo, A., Chiang, P-Y., Gain, A., Patil, A., Pearson, K., Feizi, S.: Compressing GANs using knowledge distillation. arXiv preprint arXiv:1902.00159 (2019)
29. Abdal, R., Qin, Y., Wonka, P.: Image2stylegan: how to embed images into the styleGAN latent space? In: 2019 IEEE/CVF International Conference on Computer Vision, ICCV 2019, Seoul, Korea (South), October 27 - November 2 2019, pp. 4431–4440. IEEE (2019)
30. Yu, C., Pool, J.: Self-supervised GAN compression. arXiv preprint arXiv:2007.01491 (2020)

Author Index

Printed in the United States
by Baker & Taylor Publisher Services